VISUAL BASIC® 2005
How to Program
THIRD EDITION

Deitel® Ser

How To Program Series

Advanced Java™ 2 Platform How to Program

C How to Program, 4/E

C++ How to Program, 5/E – Including Cyber Classroom

e-Business and e-Commerce How to Program

Internet and World Wide Web How to Program, 3/E

Java™ How to Program, 6/E – Including Cyber Classroom

Small C++ How to Program, 5/E – Including Cyber Classroom

Small Java™ How to Program, 6/E – Including Cyber Classroom

Perl How to Program

Python How to Program

Visual Basic® 2005 How to Program, 3/E

Visual C++® .NET How to Program

Visual C#® 2005 How to Program, 2/E

Wireless Internet & Mobile Business How to Program

XML How to Program

ies Page

Simply Series

Simply C++: An Application-Driven
Tutorial Approach

Simply C#: An Application-Driven
Tutorial Approach

Simply Java™ Programming: An
Application-Driven Tutorial
Approach

Simply Visual Basic® .NET: An
Application Driven Tutorial
Approach (Visual Studio .NET
2002 Edition)

Simply Visual Basic® .NET: An
Application Driven Tutorial
Approach (Visual Studio .NET
2003 Edition)

Also Available

SafariX Web Books
www.SafariX.com

To follow the Deitel publishing program, please register at:

www.deitel.com/newsletter/subscribe.html

for the free *DEITEL® BUZZ ONLINE* e-mail newsletter.

To communicate with the authors, send e-mail to:

deitel@deitel.com

For information on corporate on-site seminars offered by Deitel & Associates, Inc.
worldwide, visit:

www.deitel.com or write to deitel@deitel.com

For continuing updates on Prentice Hall/Deitel publications visit:

www.deitel.com,
www.prenhall.com/deitel or
www.InformIT.com/deitel

Library of Congress Cataloging-in-Publication Data
On file

Vice President and Editorial Director, ECS: *Marcia J. Horton*
Associate Editor: *Jennifer Cappello*
Assistant Editor: *Carole Snyder*
Executive Managing Editor: *Vince O'Brien*
Managing Editor: *Bob Engelhardt*
Production Editors: *Donna M. Crilly, Marta Samsel*
Director of Creative Services: *Paul Belfanti*
A/V Production Editor: *Xiaohong Zhu*
Art Studio: *Artworks, York, PA*
Creative Director: *Juan López*
Art Director: *Kristine Carney*
Cover Design: *Abbey S. Deitel, Harvey M. Deitel, Francesco Santalucia, Kristine Carney*
Interior Design: *Harvey M. Deitel, Kristine Carney*
Manufacturing Manager: *Alexis Heydt-Long*
Manufacturing Buyer: *Lisa McDowell*
Executive Marketing Manager: *Robin O'Brien*

© 2006 by Pearson Education, Inc.
Upper Saddle River, New Jersey 07458

10 9 8 7 6 5 4 3 2 1

ISBN 0-13-186900-0

Pearson Education Ltd., *London*
Pearson Education Australia Pty. Ltd., *Sydney*
Pearson Education Singapore, Pte. Ltd.
Pearson Education North Asia Ltd., *Hong Kong*
Pearson Education Canada, Inc., *Toronto*
Pearson Educación de Mexico, S.A. de C.V.
Pearson Education–Japan, *Tokyo*
Pearson Education Malaysia, Pte. Ltd.
Pearson Education, Inc., *Upper Saddle River, New Jersey*

VISUAL BASIC® 2005
HOW TO PROGRAM
THIRD EDITION

H. M. Deitel
Deitel & Associates, Inc.

P. J. Deitel
Deitel & Associates, Inc.

PEARSON
Prentice
Hall

Upper Saddle River, New Jersey 07458

Trademarks

To my wife Michelle and my daughter Jessica:
*   You are the joys of my life.*
Paul

To Barbara:
*   I love you.*
Harvey

Contents

17 Graphics and Multimedia · 785

18 Files and Streams · 850

22 Web Services

Preface

"Live in fragments no longer, only connect."
—Edgar Morgan Foster

Welcome to the world of Windows, Internet and Web programming with Visual Basic, Visual Studio 2005 and the .NET 2.0 platform! This book presents leading-edge computing technologies for computer science students, software developers and IT professionals.

At Deitel & Associates, we write computer science textbooks for college students and professional books for software developers. We also teach this material in industry seminars at organizations worldwide.

This book was a joy to create. To start, we put the previous edition under the microscope:

- We audited our Visual Basic presentation against the most recent Microsoft Visual Basic Language Specification, which can be found at www.microsoft.com/downloads/details.aspx?FamilyID=6d50d709-eaa4-44d7-8af3-e14280403e6e&DisplayLang=en.

- All of the chapters have been significantly updated and upgraded.

- We changed to an early classes and objects pedagogy. Now readers build reusable classes starting with a very friendly treatment in Chapter 4.

- We updated our object-oriented presentation to use the latest version of the *UML (Unified Modeling Language)—UML™ 2.0*—the industry-standard graphical language for modeling object-oriented systems.

- We added an optional OOD/UML automated teller machine (ATM) case study in Chapters 1, 3–9 and 11. The case study includes a complete Visual Basic code implementation of the ATM in Appendix J.

- We added several multi-section, object-oriented programming case studies.

- We incorporated key new features of Microsoft's latest release of Visual Basic—Visual Basic 2005—and added discussions on generics, .NET remoting and debugging.

- We significantly enhanced our treatment of XML, ADO.NET, ASP.NET and Web services.

All of this has been carefully scrutinized by a substantial team of academics, .NET industry developers and members of the Microsoft Visual Basic development team.

We believe that this book and its support materials have everything instructors and students need for an informative, interesting, challenging and entertaining Visual Basic educational experience. In this Preface, we overview various conventions used in the book, such as syntax coloring the code examples and code highlighting. We also discuss the book's comprehensive suite of ancillary materials that help instructors maximize their students' learning experience, including the Prentice Hall *Instructor's Resource Center*, Power-Point® Slide lecture notes, companion Web site, SafariX (Pearson Education's WebBook publications) and more.

Visual Basic 2005 How to Program, 3/e presents 220 complete, working Visual Basic programs and depicts their inputs and outputs in actual screen shots of running programs. This is our signature "live-code" approach—we present concepts in the context of complete working programs.

As you read this book, if you have questions, send an e-mail to deitel@deitel.com; we will respond promptly. For updates on this book and the status of Visual Basic software, and for the latest news on all Deitel publications and services, visit www.deitel.com regularly and be sure to sign up for the free *Deitel® Buzz Online* e-mail newsletter at www.deitel.com/newsletter/subscribe.html.

Before You Begin

Downloading Microsoft Visual Basic 2005 Express Edition Software

On November 7, 2005 Microsoft released its Visual Studio 2005 development tools, including the Visual Basic 2005 Express Edition. Per Microsoft's Web site, Microsoft Express Editions are "lightweight, easy-to-use and easy-to-learn tools for the hobbyist, novice and student developer." According to the Microsoft Express Editions FAQ page (msdn.microsoft.com/vstudio/express/support/faq/), "Effective April 19th, 2006, all Visual Studio 2005 Express Editions are free permanently. SQL Server 2005 Express Edition has always been and will continue to be a free download."

You may use this software to compile and execute the example programs in the book. You can download Visual Basic 2005 Express Edition at:

> msdn.microsoft.com/vstudio/express/vb/

When you install this software, you should install the help documentation and SQL Server 2005 Express. Microsoft provides a dedicated forum for help using the Express Edition:

> forums.microsoft.com/msdn/ShowForum.aspx?ForumID=24

Visual Basic 2005 How to Program, 3/e Code Examples

The book's source code is available for download at www.deitel.com/books/vbhtp3. Once you download the complete examples.zip file, use a ZIP file tool such as WinZip (available from www.winzip.com) to extract the files to the C:\ folder on your computer. This will create an examples folder that contains subfolders for each chapter (e.g., ch01, ch02, etc.)

Additional Software Downloads

For the examples in Chapter 17, Graphics and Multimedia, we use Microsoft Agent. If students use the examples in a lab environment, more than likely this software will have to be installed as part of the lab setup. Microsoft Agent can be downloaded from:

> www.microsoft.com/msagent/downloads/default.asp

For Chapter 20, you will need SQL Server 2005 Express Edition, which is available at

```
msdn.microsoft.com/vstudio/express/sql/
```

Note that you do not need to download this separately if you choose to install it as part of the Visual Basic 2005 Express installation.

For Chapters 21 and 22, you will need Visual Web Developer 2005 Express Edition, which is available at

```
msdn.microsoft.com/vstudio/express/vwd/
```

Like Visual Basic 2005 Express, the other express editions are free for download until November 6, 2006, after which Microsoft may charge a fee for these tools. For these two chapters, you may also want to install the IIS Web server to test the examples. For more information about installing IIS, please visit

```
www.microsoft.com/resources/documentation/windows/xp/all/proddocs/
en-us/iiiisin2.mspx?mfr=true
```

If you prefer not to install IIS, you can use the built-in test server in Visual Web Developer 2005 Express to test the examples in Chapters 21 and 22.

We provide updates on the status of the software used in this book at www.deitel.com and in our free e-mail newsletter www.deitel.com/newsletter/subscribe.html.

Features in *Visual Basic 2005 How to Program, 3/e*

This new edition contains many new and enhanced features.

Updated for Visual Studio 2005, Visual Basic 2005 and .NET 2.0

We updated the entire text to reflect Microsoft's latest release of Visual Basic 2005. New items include:

- Screenshots updated to the Visual Studio 2005 IDE.

- Property accessors with different access modifiers.

- Viewing exception data with the Exception Assistant (a new feature of the Visual Studio 2005 Debugger).

- Using drag-and-drop techniques to create data-bound windows forms in ADO.NET 2.0.

- Using the IDE's **Data Sources** window to create application-wide data connections.

- Using a `BindingSource` to simplify the process of binding controls to an underlying data source in ADO.NET 2.0.

- Using a `BindingNavigator` to enable simple navigation, insertion, deletion and editing of database data on a Windows Form.

- Using the **Master Page Designer** to create a common look and feel for ASP.NET Web pages.

- Using Visual Studio 2005 smart tag menus to perform common programming tasks when new controls are dragged onto a Windows Form or ASP.NET Web page.

- Using Visual Web Developer's built-in Web server to test ASP.NET 2.0 applications and Web services.

- Using an `XmlDataSource` to bind XML data sources to a control.

- Using a `SqlDataSource` to bind a SQL Server database to a control or set of controls.

- Using an `ObjectDataSource` to bind a control to an object that serves as a data source.

- Using the ASP.NET 2.0 "login" and "create new user" controls to personalize access to Web applications.

- Using generics and generic collections to create general models of methods and classes that can be declared once, but used with many types of data.

- Using generic collections from the `Systems.Collections.Generic` namespace.

New Interior Design
Working with the creative services team at Prentice Hall, we redesigned the interior styles for our *How to Program Series* books. In response to reader requests, we now place the key terms and the index's page reference for each defining occurrence in bold blue text for easier reference. We emphasize on-screen components in the **bold Helvetica** font (e.g., the **File** menu) and emphasize Visual Basic program text in the `Lucida` font (for example, `int x = 5`).

Syntax Coloring
We syntax color all the Visual Basic code, similar to the way most Visual Basic integrated-development environments and code editors syntax color code. This greatly improves code readability—an especially important goal, given that this book contains 16,400+ lines of code. Our syntax-coloring conventions are as follows:

```
comments appear in green
keywords appear in dark blue
errors and ASP.NET delimiters appear in red
constants and literal values appear in light blue
all other code appears in plain, black
```

Code Highlighting
Extensive code highlighting makes it easy for readers to spot each program's featured code segments—we place gray rectangles around the key code.

Early Classes and Objects Approach
We still introduce basic object-technology concepts and terminology in Chapter 1. In the previous edition, we developed custom classes in Chapter 9, but in this edition, we start doing that in the completely new Chapter 4. Chapters 5–8 have been carefully rewritten with a very friendly "early classes and objects approach."

Carefully Tuned Treatment of Object-Oriented Programming in Chapters 9–11
We performed a high-precision upgrade of *Visual Basic 2005 How to Program, 3/e*. This edition is clearer and more accessible—especially if you are new to object-oriented programming (OOP). We completely rewrote the OOP chapters, integrating an employee payroll class hierarchy case study and motivating interfaces with an accounts payable hierarchy.

Case Studies

We include many case studies, some spanning multiple sections and chapters:

- The GradeBook class in Chapters 4, 5, 6 and 8.
- The optional, OOD/UML ATM system in the Software Engineering sections of Chapters 1, 3–9 and 11.
- The Time class in several sections of Chapter 9.
- The Employee payroll application in Chapters 10 and 11.
- The GuestBook ASP.NET application in Chapter 21.
- The secure book database ASP.NET application in Chapter 21.
- The airline reservation Web service in Chapter 22.

Integrated GradeBook Case Study

To reinforce our early classes presentation, we present an integrated case study using classes and objects in Chapters 4–6 and 8. We incrementally build a GradeBook class that represents an instructor's grade book and performs various calculations based on a set of student grades—finding the average, finding the maximum and minimum, and printing a bar chart. Our goal is to familiarize you with the important concepts of objects and classes through a real-world example of a substantial class. We develop this class from the ground up, constructing methods from control statements and carefully developed algorithms, and adding instance variables and arrays as needed to enhance the functionality of the class.

The Unified Modeling Language (UML)—Using the UML 2.0 to Develop an Object-Oriented Design of an ATM

The Unified Modeling Language™ (UML™) has become the preferred graphical modeling language for designing object-oriented systems. All the UML diagrams in the book comply with the UML 2.0 specification. We use UML class diagrams to visually represent classes and their inheritance relationships, and we use UML activity diagrams to demonstrate the flow of control in each of Visual Basic's control statements.

This *Third Edition* includes a new, optional (but highly recommended) case study on object-oriented design using the UML. The case study was reviewed by a distinguished team of OOD/UML academic and industry professionals, including leaders in the field from Rational (the creators of the UML and now a division of IBM) and the Object Management Group (responsible for maintaining and evolving the UML). In the case study, we design and fully implement the software for a simple automated teller machine (ATM). The Software Engineering Case Study sections at the ends of Chapters 1, 3–9 and 11 present a carefully paced introduction to object-oriented design using the UML. We introduce a concise, simplified subset of the UML 2.0, then guide the reader through a first design experience intended for the novice object-oriented designer/programmer. The case study is not an exercise; rather, it is an end-to-end learning experience that concludes with a detailed walkthrough of the complete Visual Basic code. The Software Engineering Case Study sections help readers develop an object-oriented design to complement the object-oriented programming concepts they begin learning in Chapter 1 and implementing in Chapter 4. In the first of these sections at the end of Chapter 1, we introduce basic OOD concepts and terminology. In the optional Software Engineering Case Study sections at the ends of Chapters 3–6, we consider more substantial issues, as we undertake a challenging problem with the techniques of OOD. We analyze a typical requirements document that specifies the system to be built, determine the classes needed to implement that system, determine the attributes the classes need to have, determine the behaviors the classes need to exhibit and specify how the classes must interact with one another to meet the system requirements. In Appendix J, we include a complete Visual Basic implementation of the object-oriented system that we design in the earlier chapters. We employ a carefully developed, incremental object-oriented design process to produce a UML model for our ATM system. From this design, we produce a substantial working Visual Basic implementation using key programming notions, including classes, objects, encapsulation, visibility, composition, inheritance and polymorphism.

Web Forms, Web Controls and ASP.NET 2.0

The .NET platform enables developers to create robust, scalable Web-based applications. Microsoft's .NET server-side technology, Active Server Pages (ASP), allows programmers to build Web documents that respond to client requests. To enable interactive Web pages, server-side programs process information users input into HTML forms. ASP .NET provides enhanced visual programming capabilities, similar to those used in building Windows forms for desktop programs. Programmers can create Web pages visually, by dragging and dropping Web controls onto Web forms. Chapter 21, ASP.NET, Web Forms and Web Controls, introduces these powerful technologies.

Web Services and ASP.NET 2.0

Microsoft's .NET strategy embraces the Internet and Web as integral to software development and deployment. Web services technology enables information sharing, e-commerce and other interactions using standard Internet protocols and technologies, such as Hypertext Transfer Protocol (HTTP), Extensible Markup Language (XML) and Simple Object Access Protocol (SOAP). Web services enable programmers to package application functionality in a manner that turns the Web into a library of reusable software components. In Chapter 22, we present a Web service that allows users to manipulate huge integers— integers too large to be represented with Visual Basic's built-in data types. In this example, a user enters two huge integers and presses buttons to invoke Web services that add, subtract and compare the two integers. We also present a blackjack Web service and a database-driven airline reservation system.

Object-Oriented Programming

Object-oriented programming is the most widely employed technique for developing robust, reusable software. This text offers a rich treatment of Visual Basic's object-oriented programming features. Chapter 4 introduces how to create classes and objects. These concepts are extended in Chapter 9. Chapter 10 discusses how to create powerful new classes quickly by using inheritance to "absorb" the capabilities of existing classes. Chapter 11 familiarizes the reader with the crucial concepts of polymorphism, abstract classes, concrete classes and interfaces, which facilitate powerful manipulations among objects belonging to an inheritance hierarchy.

XML

Use of the Extensible Markup Language (XML) is exploding in the software-development industry and in the e-business community, and is pervasive throughout the .NET platform.

Because XML is a platform-independent technology for describing data and for creating markup languages, XML's data portability integrates well with Visual Basic-based portable applications and services. Chapter 19 introduces XML, XML markup and the technologies, such as DTDs and Schema, which are used to validate XML documents' contents. We also explain how to manipulate XML documents programmatically using the Document Object Model (DOM™) and how to transform XML documents into other types of documents via Extensible Stylesheet Language Transformation (XSLT) technology.

ADO.NET 2.0

Databases store vast amounts of information that individuals and organizations must access to conduct business. As an evolution of Microsoft's ActiveX Data Objects (ADO) technology, ADO.NET represents a new approach for building applications that interact with databases. ADO.NET uses XML and an enhanced object model to provide developers with the tools they need to access and manipulate databases for large-scale, extensible, mission-critical multi-tier applications. Chapter 20 introduces the capabilities of ADO.NET and the Structured Query Language (SQL) to manipulate databases.

Visual Studio 2005 Debugger

In Appendix C, we explain how to use key debugger features, such as setting "breakpoints" and "watches," stepping into and out of methods, and examining the method call stack.

Teaching Approach

Visual Basic 2005 How to Program, 3/e contains a rich collection of examples that have been tested on Windows XP. The book concentrates on the principles of good software engineering and stresses program clarity. We avoid arcane terminology and syntax specifications in favor of teaching by example. We are educators who teach leading-edge topics in industry classrooms worldwide. Dr. Harvey M. Deitel has 22 years of college teaching experience and 17 years of industry teaching experience. Paul Deitel has 14 years of industry teaching experience. The Deitels have taught courses at all levels to government, industry, military and academic clients of Deitel & Associates.

Learning Visual Basic via the Live-Code Approach

Visual Basic 2005 How to Program, 3/e is loaded with live-code examples—each new concept is presented in the context of a complete working Visual Basic application that is immediately followed by one or more sample executions showing the program's inputs and outputs. This style exemplifies the way we teach and write about programming. We call this method of teaching and writing the "live-code" approach.

World Wide Web Access

All of the source-code examples for *Visual Basic 2005 How to Program, 3/e,* (and for our other publications) are available for download from:

```
www.deitel.com/books/vbhtp3
www.prenhall.com/deitel
```

Site registration is quick and easy. Download all the examples, then run each program as you read the corresponding text discussions. Making changes to the examples and immediately seeing the effects of those changes is a great way to enhance your Visual Basic learning experience.

Objectives

Each chapter begins with a statement of objectives. This lets students know what to expect and gives them an opportunity, after reading the chapter, to determine if they have met these objectives.

Quotations

The learning objectives are followed by quotations. Some are humorous, philosophical or offer interesting insights. We hope that you will enjoy relating the quotations to the chapter material. Many of the quotations are worth a second look after reading the chapter.

Outline

The chapter outline helps students approach the material in a top-down fashion, so they can anticipate what is to come, and set a comfortable and effective learning pace.

16,452 Lines of Code in 220 Example Programs (with Program Outputs)

Our live-code programs range in size from just a few lines of code to substantial examples containing hundreds of lines of code (e.g., our ATM system implementation contains 597 lines of code). Each program is followed by screenshots of the outputs produced when the program is run, so you can confirm that the programs run as expected. Our programs demonstrate the diverse features of Visual Basic. The code is syntax colored, with Visual Basic keywords, comments and other program text emphasized with variations of bold, italic and gray text. This makes reading the code easier, especially in the larger programs.

822 Illustrations/Figures

An abundance of charts, tables, line drawings, programs and program outputs is included. We model the flow of control in control statements with UML activity diagrams. UML class diagrams model the fields, constructors and methods of classes. We use additional types of UML diagrams throughout our optional OOD/UML ATM case study.

378 Programming Tips

We include programming tips to help students focus on important aspects of program development. We highlight these tips in the form of *Good Programming Practices*, *Common Programming Errors*, *Error-Prevention Tips*, *Look-and-Feel Observations*, *Performance Tips*, *Portability Tips* and *Software Engineering Observations*. These tips and practices represent the best we have gleaned from a combined six decades of programming and teaching experience. One of our students—a mathematics major—told us that she feels this approach is like the highlighting of axioms, theorems and corollaries in mathematics books; it provides a basis on which to build good software.

 Good Programming Practices

Good Programming Practices *call attention to techniques that will help you produce programs that are clearer, more understandable and more maintainable.*

Common Programming Errors

Students learning a language tend to make certain kinds of errors frequently. Pointing out these Common Programming Errors *reduces the likelihood that readers will make the same mistakes.*

Error-Prevention Tips

When we first designed this tip type, we thought the tips would contain suggestions for exposing bugs and removing them from programs. In fact, many of the tips describe aspects of Visual Basic that prevent bugs from getting into programs in the first place, thus simplifying the testing and debugging processes.

Look-and-Feel Observations

We provide Look-and-Feel Observations *to highlight graphical-user-interface conventions. These observations help you design attractive, user-friendly graphical user interfaces that conform to industry norms.*

Performance Tips

Students like to "turbo charge" their programs. We include Performance Tips *that highlight opportunities for improving program performance—making programs run faster or minimizing the amount of memory that they occupy.*

Portability Tips

We include Portability Tips *to help you write portable code and to explain how Visual Basic achieves its high degree of portability.*

Software Engineering Observations

The object-oriented programming paradigm necessitates a complete rethinking of the way we build software systems. Visual Basic is an effective language for achieving good software engineering. The Software Engineering Observations *highlight architectural and design issues that affect the construction of software systems, especially large-scale systems.*

Wrap-Up Section

Each chapter ends with a brief "wrap-up" section that recaps the chapter content and transitions to the next chapter.

Summary Bullets

Each chapter ends with additional pedagogical devices. We present a thorough, bullet-list-style summary of the chapter, section by section. This helps the students review and reinforce key concepts.

Terminology

We include an alphabetized list of the important terms defined in each chapter—again, for further reinforcement. Each term also appears in the index, and the defining occurrence of each term is highlighted in the index with a bold, blue page number so the student can locate the definitions of terms quickly.

Self-Review Exercises and Answers
Extensive self-review exercises and answers are included for self-study. This gives you a chance to build confidence with the material and prepare for the regular exercises. We encourage students to do all the self-review exercises and check their answers.

Exercises
Each chapter concludes with a set of exercises, including simple recall of important terminology and concepts; writing individual Visual Basic statements; writing small portions of Visual Basic methods and classes; writing complete Visual Basic methods, classes and applications and writing major term projects. The large number of exercises across a wide variety of areas enables instructors to tailor their courses to the unique needs of their classes and to vary course assignments each semester. Instructors can use these exercises to form homework assignments, short quizzes and/or major examinations. The solutions for the vast majority of the exercises are included in the Prentice Hall *Instructor's Resource Center*, which is *available only to instructors* through their Prentice Hall representatives. [**NOTE: Please do not write to us requesting access to the Prentice Hall *Instructor's Resource Center*. Access is limited strictly to college instructors teaching from the book. Instructors may obtain access only through their Prentice Hall representatives.**]

Approximately 5700 Index Entries
We have included an extensive index which is especially useful to developers who use the book as a reference.

"Double Indexing" of Visual Basic Live-Code Examples
Visual Basic 2005 How to Program, 3/e has 220 live-code examples, which we have double indexed. For every source-code program in the book, we indexed the figure caption both alphabetically and as a subindex item under "Examples." This makes it easier to find examples using particular features.

A Tour of the Optional Case Study on Object-Oriented Design with the UML

In this section we tour the book's optional case study on object-oriented design with the UML. This tour previews the contents of the Software Engineering Case Study sections (in Chapters 1, 3–9, 11 and Appendix J). After completing this case study, you will be thoroughly familiar with an object-oriented design and implementation for a significant Visual Basic application.

The design presented in the ATM case study was developed at Deitel & Associates, Inc. and scrutinized by academic and industry professionals. Our primary goal was to create a simple design that would be clear to OOD and UML novices, while still demonstrating key OOD concepts and the related UML modeling techniques.

Section 1.17—(Only Required Section of the Case Study) Software Engineering Case Study: Introduction to Object Technology and the UML—introduces the object-oriented design case study with the UML. The section presents basic concepts and terminology of object technology, including classes, objects, encapsulation, inheritance and polymorphism. We discuss the history of the UML. This is the only required section of the case study.

Section 3.10—(Optional) Software Engineering Case Study: Examining the ATM Requirements Document—discusses a *requirements document* that specifies the requirements for a system that we will design and implement—the software for a simple automated teller machine (ATM). We investigate the structure and behavior of object-oriented systems in general. We discuss how the UML will facilitate the design process in subsequent Software Engineering Case Study sections by providing several additional types of diagrams to model our system. We include a list of URLs and book references on object-oriented design with the UML. We discuss the interaction between the ATM system and its user. Specifically, we investigate the scenarios that may occur between the user and the system itself—these are called *use cases*. We model these interactions, using UML *use case diagrams*.

Section 4.19—(Optional) Software Engineering Case Study: Identifying the Classes in the ATM Requirements Documents—begins to design the ATM system. We identify its classes by extracting the nouns and noun phrases from the requirements document. We arrange these classes into a UML class diagram that describes the class structure of our simulation. The class diagram also describes relationships, known as *associations*, among classes.

Section 5.16—(Optional) Software Engineering Case Study: Identifying Class Attributes in the ATM System—focuses on the attributes of the classes discussed in Section 3.10. A class contains both *attributes* (data) and *operations* (behaviors). As we see in later sections, changes in an object's attributes often affect the object's behavior. To determine the attributes for the classes in our case study, we extract the adjectives describing the nouns and noun phrases (which defined our classes) from the requirements document, then place the attributes in the class diagram we created in Section 3.10.

Section 6.11—(Optional) Software Engineering Case Study: Identifying Objects' States and Activities in the ATM System—discusses how an object, at any given time, occupies a specific condition called a *state*. A *state transition* occurs when the object receives a message to change state. The UML provides the *state machine diagram*, which identifies the set of possible states that an object may occupy and models that object's state transitions. An object also has an *activity*—the work it performs in its lifetime. The UML provides the *activity diagram*—a flowchart that models an object's activity. In this section, we use both types of diagrams to begin modeling specific behavioral aspects of our ATM system, such as how the ATM carries out a withdrawal transaction and how the ATM responds when the user is authenticated.

Section 7.20—(Optional) Software Engineering Case Study: Identifying Class Operations in the ATM System—identifies the operations, or services, of our classes. We extract from the requirements document the verbs and verb phrases that specify the operations for each class. We then modify the class diagram of Section 3.10 to include each operation with its associated class. At this point in the case study, we will have gathered all information possible from the requirements document. As future chapters introduce such topics as inheritance, we will modify our classes and diagrams.

Section 8.17—(Optional) Software Engineering Case Study: Collaboration Among Objects in the ATM System—provides a "rough sketch" of the model for our ATM system. In this section, we see how it works. We investigate the behavior of the simulation by discussing *collaborations*—messages that objects send to each other to communicate. The class operations that we discovered in Section 6.10 turn out to be the collaborations among the objects in our system. We determine the collaborations, then collect them into a *communication diagram*—the UML diagram for modeling collaborations. This diagram reveals which objects collaborate and when. We present a communication diagram of the collaborations among objects to perform an ATM balance inquiry. We then present the UML *sequence diagram* for modeling interactions in a system. This diagram emphasizes the chronological ordering of messages. A sequence diagram models how objects in the system interact to carry out withdrawal and deposit transactions.

Section 9.14—(Optional) Software Engineering Case Study: Starting to Program the Classes of the ATM System—takes a break from designing the behavior of our system. We begin the implementation process to emphasize the material discussed in Chapter 8. Using the UML class diagram of Section 3.10 and the attributes and operations discussed in Section 4.11 and Section 6.10, we show how to implement a class in Visual Basic from a design. We do not implement all classes—because we have not completed the design process. Working from our UML diagrams, we create code for the Withdrawal class.

Section 11.8—(Optional) Software Engineering Case Study: Incorporating Inheritance and Polymorphism into the ATM System—continues our discussion of object-oriented programming. We consider inheritance—classes sharing common characteristics may inherit attributes and operations from a "base" class. In this section, we investigate how our ATM system can benefit from using inheritance. We document our discoveries in a class diagram that models inheritance relationships—the UML refers to these relationships as *generalizations*. We modify the class diagram of Section 3.10 by using inheritance to group classes with similar characteristics. This section concludes the design of the model portion of our simulation. We implement this model in Visual Basic in Appendix J.

Appendix J—ATM Case Study Code—The majority of the case study involves designing the model (i.e., the data and logic) of the ATM system. In this appendix, we fully implement that model in Visual Basic, using all the UML diagrams we created. We apply the concepts of object-oriented design with the UML and object-oriented programming in Visual Basic that you learned in the chapters. By the end of this appendix, you will have completed the design and implementation of a real-world system, and should feel confident tackling larger systems, such as those that professional software engineers build.

Appendix K—UML 2: Additional Diagrams Types—Overviews the UML 2 diagram types not discussed the OOD/UML Case Study.

Teaching Resources for *Visual Basic 2005 How to Program, 3/e*

Visual Basic 2005 How to Program, 3/e, has extensive instructor resources. The Prentice Hall *Instructor's Resource Center* contains the *Solutions Manual* with solutions to the vast majority of the end-of-chapter exercises, a *Test Item File* of multiple-choice questions (approximately two per book section) and PowerPoint® slides containing all the code and figures in the text, plus bulleted items that summarize the key points in the text. Instructors can customize the slides. If you are not already a registered faculty member, contact your Prentice Hall representative or visit vig.prenhall.com/replocator/.

DEITEL® Buzz Online Free E-mail Newsletter

Our free e-mail newsletter, the *Deitel® Buzz Online,* includes commentary on industry trends and developments, links to free articles and resources from our published books and upcoming publications, product-release schedules, errata, challenges, anecdotes, information on our corporate instructor-led training courses and more. It's also a good way for you to keep posted about issues related to *Visual Basic 2005 How to Program, 3/e.* To subscribe, visit

www.deitel.com/newsletter/subscribe.html

What's New at Deitel

Free Content Initiative. We are pleased to bring you guest articles and free tutorials selected from our current and forthcoming publications as part of our Free Content Initiative. In each issue of our *Deitel® Buzz Online* newsletter, we announce the latest additions to our free content library. Let us know what topics you'd like to see and let us know if you'd like to submit guest articles!

www.deitel.com/articles/

Resource Centers and the Deitel Internet Business Initiative. We have created many resource centers (at www.deitel.com) on such topics as Visual Basic, .NET, C#, C++, Java, AJAX, Ruby, PHP, Perl, Python, MySQL, RSS, XML, Web Services, Windows Vista, Google Analytics, Google Base, Google Video, the Internet Business Initiative, Mash-Ups, Ning, Podcasting, Computer Games, Game Programming, Attention Economy, Affiliate Programs, Sudoku, Web 2.0 and Skype, with many more coming.

www.deitel.com/resourcecenters.html

These resource centers enhance the reader's learning experience. We announce new resource centers in each issue of the *Deitel® Buzz Online* as well.

Acknowledgments

It is a great pleasure to acknowledge the efforts of many people whose names may not appear on the cover, but whose hard work, cooperation, friendship and understanding were crucial to the production of the book. Many people at Deitel & Associates, Inc. devoted long hours to this project.

- Andrew B. Goldberg is a Computer Science graduate of Amherst College. Andrew co-authored the updates to Chapters 19–22. He co-designed and co-authored the new, optional OOD/UML ATM case study. He also co-authored Appendices J and K.

- Su Zhang holds B.Sc. and a M.Sc. degrees in Computer Science from McGill University. Su contributed to Chapters 26 and 27 as well as Appendix J.

- Cheryl Yaeger graduated from Boston University with a bachelor's degree in Computer Science. Cheryl co-authored the updates to Chapters 3–14.

- Barbara Deitel, Chief Financial Officer at Deitel & Associates, Inc. applied copy-edits to the book.

- Abbey Deitel, President of Deitel & Associates, Inc., and an Industrial Management graduate of Carnegie Mellon University, co-authored Chapter 1.

- Christi Kelsey, a graduate of Purdue University with a degree in business and a minor in information systems, co-authored Chapter 2, the Preface and Appendix C. She also worked closely with the production team at Prentice Hall coordinating virtually every aspect of the production of the book.

We would also like to thank three participants of our Honors Internship and Co-op programs who contributed to this publication—Nick Santos, a Computer Science major at Dartmouth College; Jeffrey Peng, a Computer Science major at Cornell University and William Chen, a Computer Science major at Cornell University.

We are fortunate to have worked on this project with the talented and dedicated team of publishing professionals at Prentice Hall. We especially appreciate the extraordinary efforts of Marcia Horton, Editorial Director of Prentice Hall's Engineering and Computer Science Division. Jennifer Cappello and Dolores Mars did an extraordinary job recruiting the review team for this book and managing the review process. Francesco Santalucia and Kristine Carney did a wonderful job designing the book's cover. Vince O'Brien, Bob Engelhardt, Donna Crilly and Marta Samsel did a marvelous job managing the production of the book.

We'd like to give special thanks to Paul Vick, (Architect, Visual Basic) and author of the *Microsoft Visual Basic Language Specification, Version 8.0*, and Janie Schwark, Senior Business Manager, Division of Developer Marketing, both of Microsoft for their special effort in working with us on this project.

We wish to acknowledge the efforts of our reviewers. Adhering to a tight time schedule, they scrutinized the text and the programs, providing countless suggestions for improving the accuracy and completeness of the presentation.

Microsoft Reviewers
Corneliu Barsan, Microsoft
Dharmesh Chauhan, Microsoft
John Chen, Microsoft
Eric Gruber, Microsoft
Manish Jayaswal, Microsoft
Cameron McColl, Microsoft
Alexandre Moura, Microsoft
Baiju Nair, Microsoft
Cat Rambo, Microsoft
Thom Robbins, Microsoft
Chris Smith, Microsoft Compiler UI Team
Craig Vick, Microsoft

Industry Reviewers
Harlan Brewer, SES Consulting
Kunal Cheda, Computer Enterprises, Inc. U.S
James Huddleston, Independent Consultant
Terrell Hull, Independent Consultant
Amit Kalani, TechContent Corporation
Tysen Leckie, Edge Technologies
John Mueller, DataCon Services

Academic Reviewers
Karen Arlien, Bismarck State College
Robert Benavides, Collin County CC
Rekha Bhowmik, Winston-Salem State University
Chadi Boudiab, Georgia Perimeter College

Brian Larson, Modesto Junior College
Gavin Osborne, Saskatchewan Institute of Applied Science and Technology
Warren Wiltsie, Fairleigh Dickinson University

UML Case Study Reviewers
Scott Ambler, Ambysoft, Inc.
Rekha Bhowmik, Winston-Salem State University
Chadi Boudiab, Georgia Perimeter College
Brian Cook, Zurich North America
Sergio Davalos, University of Washington-Tacoma
Sujay Ghuge, Verizon IT
Manu Gupta, Patni Computer Systems
Terrell Hull, Independent Consultant
James Huddleston, Independent Consultant
Jeff Jones, Route Match Software
John Mueller, DataCon Services
Davyd Norris, Rational/IBM
Gavin Osborne, Saskatchewan Institute

Visual C# 2005 How to Program, 2/e was written in parallel with this book and many of the comments from the C# review team proved valuable to us in completing this book, so we wanted to acknowledge their contributions:

Microsoft Reviewers
George Bullock, Program Manager at Microsoft, `Microsoft.com` Community Team
Dharmesh Chauhan, Microsoft
Shon Katzenberger, Microsoft
Matteo Taveggia, Microsoft
Matt Tavis, Microsoft

Industry Reviewers
Alex Bondarev, Investor's Bank and Trust
Peter Bromberg, Senior Architect Merrill Lynch and C# MVP
Vijay Cinnakonda, TrueCommerce, Inc.
Jay Cook, Alcon Laboratories
Jeff Cowan, Magenic, Inc.
Ken Cox, Independent Consultant, Writer and Developer and ASP.NET MVP
Stochio Goutsev, Independent Consultant, writer and developer and C# MVP
James Huddleston, Independent Consultant
Rex Jaeschke, Independent Consultant and Editor of the *C# Standard ECMA-334, 2005*, produced by committee Ecma TC39/TG2.
Saurabh Nandu, AksTech Solutions Pvt. Ltd.
Simon North, Quintiq BV
Mike O'Brien, State of California Employment Development Department
José Antonio González Seco, Andalucia's Parliament

Devan Shepard, XMaLpha Technologies
Pavel Tsekov, Caesar BSC
John Varghese, UBS
Stacey Yasenka, Software Developer at Hyland Software and C# MVP

Academic Reviewers
Rekha Bhowmik, California Lutheran University
Ayad Boudiab, Georgia Perimiter College
Harlan Brewer, SES Consulting
Sam Gill, San Francisco State University
Gavin Osborne, Saskatchewan Institute of Applied Science and Technology
Catherine Wyman, DeVry-Phoenix

And thanks to the many other members of the Microsoft team who answered our questions throughout this process:

Anders Hejlsburg, Technical Fellow (C#)
Brad Abrams, Lead Program Manager (.NET Framework)
Jim Miller, Software Architect (.NET Framework)
Joe Duffy, Program Manager (.NET Framework)
Joe Stegman, Lead Program Manager (Windows Forms)
Kit George, Program Manager (.NET Framework)
Luca Bolognese, Lead Program Manager (C#)
Luke Hoban, Program Manager (C#)
Mads Torgersen, Program Manager (C#)
Peter Hallam, Software Design Engineer (C#)
Scott Nonnenberg, Program Manager (C#)
Shamez Rajan, Program Manager (Visual Basic)

Well, there you have it! Visual Basic is a powerful programming language that will help you write programs quickly and effectively. Visual Basic scales nicely into the realm of enterprise systems development to help organizations build their business-critical and mission-critical information systems. As you read the book, we would sincerely appreciate your comments, criticisms, corrections and suggestions for improvement. Please address all correspondence to:

deitel@deitel.com

We will respond promptly, and we will post corrections and clarifications on our Web site:

www.deitel.com

We hope you enjoy reading *Visual Basic 2005 How to Program, Third Edition* as much as we enjoyed writing it!

Paul J. Deitel
Dr. Harvey M. Deitel

About the Authors

Paul J. Deitel, CEO and Chief Technical Officer of Deitel & Associates, Inc., is a graduate of the MIT's Sloan School of Management, where he studied Information Technology. Through Deitel & Associates, Inc., he has delivered Java, C and C++ courses to industry clients, including IBM, Sun Microsystems, Dell, Lucent Technologies, Fidelity, NASA at the Kennedy Space Center, the National Severe Storm Laboratory, White Sands Missile Range, Rogue Wave Software, Boeing, Stratus, Cambridge Technology Partners, Open Environment Corporation, One Wave, Hyperion Software, Adra Systems, Entergy, CableData Systems, Nortel Networks and many more. Paul is one of the world's most experienced Java trainers, having taught about 100 professional Java courses. He has also lectured on C++ and Java for the Boston Chapter of the Association for Computing Machinery. He and his father, Dr. Harvey M. Deitel, are the world's best-selling programming language textbook authors.

Dr. Harvey M. Deitel, Chairman and Chief Strategy Officer of Deitel & Associates, Inc., has 45 years of academic and industry experience in the computer field. Dr. Deitel earned B.S. and M.S. degrees from the Massachusetts Institute of Technology and a Ph.D. from Boston University. He has 20 years of college teaching experience, including earning tenure and serving as the Chairman of the Computer Science Department at Boston College before founding Deitel & Associates, Inc., with his son, Paul J. Deitel. He and Paul are the co-authors of several dozen books and multimedia packages and they are writing many more. With translations published in Japanese, German, Russian, Spanish, Traditional Chinese, Simplified Chinese, Korean, French, Polish, Italian, Portuguese, Greek, Urdu and Turkish, the Deitels' texts have earned international recognition. Dr. Deitel has delivered hundreds of professional seminars to major corporations, academic institutions, government organizations and the military.

About Deitel & Associates, Inc.

Deitel & Associates, Inc., is an internationally recognized corporate training and content-creation organization specializing in computer programming languages, Internet and World Wide Web software technology, object technology education and Internet business development. The company provides instructor-led courses on major programming languages and platforms, such as Java, Advanced Java, C, C++, C#, Visual C++, Visual Basic, XML, Perl, Python, object technology, and Internet and World Wide Web programming. The founders of Deitel & Associates, Inc., are Dr. Harvey M. Deitel and Paul J. Deitel. The company's clients include many of the world's largest computer companies, government agencies, branches of the military and business organizations. Through its 30-year publishing partnership with Prentice Hall, Deitel & Associates, Inc. publishes leading-edge programming textbooks, professional books, interactive multimedia *Cyber Classrooms*, *Complete Training Courses*, Web-based training courses and e-content for popular course management systems such as WebCT, Blackboard and Pearson's CourseCompass. Deitel & Associates, Inc., and the authors can be reached via e-mail at:

deitel@deitel.com

To learn more about Deitel & Associates, Inc., its publications and its worldwide *DIVE INTO*® Series Corporate Training curriculum, see the last few pages of this book or visit:

www.deitel.com

and subscribe to the free *Deitel*® *Buzz Online* e-mail newsletter at:

www.deitel.com/newsletter/subscribe.html

Individuals wishing to purchase Deitel books, Cyber Classrooms, Complete Training Courses and Web-based training courses can do so through:

www.deitel.com/books/index.html

Bulk orders by corporations, the government, the military and academic institutions should be placed directly with Prentice Hall.

Introduction to Computers, the Internet and Visual Basic

OBJECTIVES

In this chapter you will learn:

- Basic hardware and software concepts.

- The different types of programming languages.

- Which programming languages are most widely used.

- The history of the Visual Basic programming language.

- Some basics of object technology.

- The history of the UML—the industry-standard object-oriented system modeling language.

- The history of the Internet and the World Wide Web.

- The motivation behind and an overview of Microsoft's .NET initiative, which involves the Internet in developing and using software systems.

- To test-drive a Visual Basic 2005 application that enables you to draw on the screen.

1.1 Introduction

Welcome to Visual Basic 2005! We have worked hard to provide you with accurate and complete information regarding this powerful computer programming language which, from this point forward, we shall refer to simply as Visual Basic. Visual Basic is appropriate for technically oriented people with little or no programming experience, and for experienced programmers to use in building substantial information systems. *Visual Basic 2005 How to Program, Third Edition*, is an effective learning tool for each of these audiences. We hope that working with this text will be an informative, challenging and entertaining learning experience for you.

How can one book appeal to both novices and skilled programmers? The core of this book emphasizes achieving program clarity through the proven techniques of object-oriented programming (OOP) and event-driven programming. Nonprogrammers learn basic skills that underlie good programming; experienced developers receive a rigorous explanation of the language and may improve their programming styles. Perhaps most important, the book presents hundreds of complete, working Visual Basic programs and depicts their inputs and outputs. We call this the live-code approach. All of the book's examples may be downloaded from www.deitel.com/books/vbhtp3/index.html and www.prenhall.com/deitel.

Computer use is increasing in almost every field of endeavor. Computing costs have been decreasing dramatically due to rapid developments in both hardware and software technologies. Computers that might have filled large rooms and cost millions of dollars a few decades ago can now be inscribed on silicon chips smaller than a fingernail, costing a few dollars each. Fortunately, silicon is one of the most abundant materials on earth—it's an ingredient in common sand. Silicon chip technology has made computing so economical that about a billion general-purpose computers are in use worldwide, helping people in business, industry and government, and in their personal lives.

We hope that you will enjoy learning with *Visual Basic 2005 How to Program, Third Edition*. You are embarking on a challenging and rewarding path. As you proceed, if you have any questions, please send e-mail to

    deitel@deitel.com

To keep current with Visual Basic developments at Deitel & Associates and to receive updates to this textbook, please register for our free e-mail newsletter, the *Deitel® Buzz Online,* at

    www.deitel.com/newsletter/subscribe.html

1.2 What Is a Computer?

A computer is a device capable of performing computations and making logical decisions at speeds millions, billions and even trillions of times faster than human beings can. For example, many of today's personal computers can perform a billion additions per second. A person operating a desk calculator could spend an entire lifetime performing calculations and still not complete as many calculations as even today's more modest personal computers can perform in one second. (Points to ponder: How would you know whether the person added the numbers correctly? How would you know whether the computer added the numbers correctly?) The most powerful computers are called supercomputers; some of these are already performing trillions of additions per second!

Computers process data under the control of sets of instructions called computer programs. These programs guide computers through orderly sets of actions that are specified by people known as computer programmers.

A computer consists of various devices referred to as hardware (e.g., the keyboard, screen, mouse, hard drive, memory, DVDs and processing units). The programs that run on a computer are referred to as software (e.g., word processing programs, e-mail, games, etc.). Hardware costs have been declining dramatically in recent years, to the point that personal computers have become a commodity. Historically, however, software development costs have risen steadily as programmers develop ever more powerful and complex applications without being able to significantly improve the software development process. In this book, you will learn object-oriented programming—a technology that is dramatically reducing software development costs.

1.3 Computer Organization

Regardless of differences in physical appearance, virtually every computer may be envisioned as being divided into six logical units or sections:

1. **Input unit.** This is the "receiving" section of the computer. It obtains information (data and computer programs) from **input devices** (e.g., keyboards and mouse devices) and places this information at the disposal of the other units so that it can be processed. Information also can be entered in many other ways, including by speaking to your computer, scanning images and having your computer receive information from a network, such as the Internet.

2. **Output unit.** This is the "shipping" section of the computer. It takes information that the computer has processed and places it on various **output devices** to make the information available for use outside the computer. Most information output from computers today is displayed on screens, printed on paper or used to control other devices. Computers also can output their information to networks, such as the Internet.

3. **Memory unit.** This is the rapid-access, relatively low-capacity "warehouse" section of the computer. The memory unit retains information entered through the input unit so that it will be immediately available for processing when needed. The memory unit also retains processed information until it can be placed on output devices by the output unit. Information in the memory unit is typically lost when the computer's power is turned off. The memory unit is often called either **memory** or **primary memory**. (Historically, this unit has been called "core memory," but that term is fading from use today.)

4. **Arithmetic and logic unit (ALU).** This is the "manufacturing" section of the computer. It is responsible for performing calculations, such as addition, subtraction, multiplication and division. It contains the decision mechanisms that allow the computer, for example, to compare two items from the memory unit to determine whether they are equal.

5. **Central processing unit (CPU).** This is the "administrative" section of the computer. It coordinates and supervises the operation of the other sections. The CPU tells the input unit when information should be read into the memory unit, tells the ALU when information from the memory unit should be used in calculations and tells the output unit when to send information from the memory unit to certain output devices. Many of today's computers have multiple CPUs and thus can perform many operations simultaneously—such computers are called **multiprocessors**.

6. **Secondary storage unit.** This is the long-term, high-capacity "warehousing" section of the computer. Programs or data not actively being used by the other units normally are placed on secondary storage devices, such as your hard drive, until they are again needed, possibly hours, days, months or even years later. Information in secondary storage takes much longer to access than information in primary memory, but the cost per unit of secondary storage is much less than that of primary memory. Other secondary storage devices include CDs and DVDs, which can hold up to hundreds of millions of characters and billions of characters, respectively.

1.4 **Early Operating Systems**

Computers of the 1950s could perform only one job or task at a time. This is often called single-user batch processing. The computer runs one program at a time while processing data in groups or batches. In these early systems, users generally submitted their jobs to a computer center on decks of punched cards and often had to wait hours or even days before printouts were returned to their desks. Computers were very large (often filling entire rooms) and expensive (often costing millions of dollars). Personal computers did not exist; people did not have computers at their desks and in their homes.

Software systems called operating systems were developed to make using computers more convenient. Early operating systems smoothed and speeded up the transition between jobs, increasing the amount of work, or throughput, computers could process.

As computers became more powerful, it became evident that single-user batch processing was inefficient, because so much time was spent waiting for slow input/output devices to complete their tasks. It was thought that many jobs or tasks could share the resources of the computer to achieve better utilization. This is achieved by multiprogramming—the simultaneous operation of many jobs that are competing to share the computer's resources. With early multiprogramming operating systems, users still submitted jobs on decks of punched cards and waited hours or days for results.

In the 1960s, several groups in industry and the universities pioneered timesharing operating systems. Timesharing is a special case of multiprogramming in which users access the computer through terminals, typically devices with keyboards and screens. Dozens or even hundreds of users share the computer at once. The computer actually does not run the users' jobs simultaneously. Rather, it runs a small portion of one user's job, then moves on to service the next user, perhaps providing service to each user several times per second. Thus, the users' programs *appear* to be running simultaneously. An advantage of timesharing is that user requests receive almost immediate responses.

1.5 **Personal Computing, Distributed Computing and Client/Server Computing**

In the early years of computing, computer systems were too large and too expensive for individuals to own. In the 1970s, silicon chip technology appeared, making it possible for computers to be much smaller and so economical that individuals and small organizations could own these machines. In 1977, Apple Computer—creator of today's popular Macintosh personal computers and iPod digital music players—popularized personal computing. In 1981, IBM, the world's largest computer vendor, introduced the IBM Personal Computer, legitimizing personal computing in business, industry and government organizations.

These computers were "stand-alone" units—people transported disks back and forth between computers to share information (creating what was often called "sneakernet"). Although early personal computers were not powerful enough to timeshare several users, these machines could be linked together in computer networks, sometimes over telephone lines and sometimes in local area networks (LANs) within an organization. This led to the phenomenon of distributed computing, in which an organization's computing, instead of being performed only at some central computer installation, is distributed over networks to the geographically dispersed sites where the organization's work is performed. Personal computers were powerful enough to handle the computing requirements of individual users as well as the basic communications tasks of passing information between computers electronically.

Today's personal computers are as powerful as the million-dollar machines of just a few decades ago; complete personal computer systems often sell for as little as $500–1000. The most powerful desktop machines provide individual users with enormous capabilities. Information is shared easily across computer networks, where computers called **file servers** offer a common data store that may be used by **client** computers distributed throughout the network, hence the term **client/server computing**. In Chapters 19–22 you'll learn how to build Internet- and Web-based applications; we'll talk about Web servers (computers that distribute content over the Web) and Web clients (computers that request and receive the content offered up by Web servers).

1.6 Hardware Trends

Every year, people generally expect to pay at least a little more for most products and services. The opposite has been the case in the computer and communications fields, especially with regard to the costs of hardware supporting these technologies. For many decades, hardware costs have fallen rapidly, if not precipitously. Every year or two, the capacities of computers have approximately doubled without any increase in price. This often is called **Moore's Law**, named after the person who first identified and explained the trend, Gordon Moore, co-founder of Intel—the company that manufactures the vast majority of the processors in today's personal computers. Moore's Law is especially true in relation to the amount of memory that computers have for programs, the amount of secondary storage (such as disk storage) they have to hold programs and data over longer periods of time, and their processor speeds—the speeds at which computers execute their programs (i.e., do their work). Similar growth has occurred in the communications field, in which costs have plummeted as enormous demand for communications bandwidth has attracted intense competition. We know of no other fields in which technology improves so quickly and costs fall so rapidly. Such phenomenal improvement in the computing and communications fields is truly fostering the so-called Information Revolution.

When computer use exploded in the 1960s and 1970s, many people discussed the dramatic improvements in human productivity that computing and communications would cause, but these improvements did not materialize. Organizations were spending vast sums of money on these technologies, but without realizing the expected productivity gains. The invention of microprocessor chip technology and its wide deployment in the late 1970s and 1980s laid the groundwork for the productivity improvements that individuals and businesses have achieved in recent years.

1.7 Microsoft's Windows® Operating System

Microsoft Corporation became the dominant software company in the 1980s and 1990s. In 1981, Microsoft released the first version of its DOS operating system for the IBM Personal Computer (DOS is an acronym for "Disk Operating System"). In the mid-1980s, Microsoft developed the **Windows operating system**, a graphical user interface built on top of DOS. Microsoft released Windows 3.0 in 1990; this new version featured a user-friendly interface and rich functionality. The Windows operating system became incredibly popular after the 1993 release of Windows 3.1, whose successors, Windows 95 and

Windows 98, virtually cornered the desktop operating systems market by the late 1990s. These operating systems, which borrowed from many concepts (such as icons, menus and windows) popularized by early Apple Macintosh operating systems, enabled users to navigate multiple applications simultaneously. Microsoft entered the corporate operating systems market with the 1993 release of Windows NT®. Windows XP, which is based on the Windows NT operating system, was released in 2001 and combines Microsoft's corporate and consumer operating system lines. Windows is by far the world's most widely used operating system.

The biggest competitor to the Windows operating system is Linux. The name Linux derives from Linus, after Linus Torvalds, who developed Linux, and UNIX—the operating system upon which Linux is based; UNIX was developed at Bell Laboratories and was written in the C programming language. Linux is a free, open-source operating system, unlike Windows, which is proprietary (owned and controlled by Microsoft). The source code for Linux is freely available to users, and they can modify it to fit their needs.

1.8 Machine Languages, Assembly Languages and High-Level Languages

Programmers write instructions in various programming languages, some directly understandable by computers and others requiring intermediate translation steps. Hundreds of computer languages are in use today. These may be divided into three general types:

1. Machine languages
2. Assembly languages
3. High-level languages

Machine Languages

Any computer can directly understand only its own machine language—the "natural language" of a computer that is defined by its hardware design. Machine languages generally consist of strings of numbers (ultimately reduced to 1s and 0s) that instruct computers to perform their most elementary operations one at a time. Machine languages are machine dependent (i.e., any given machine language can be used on only one type of computer). Such languages are cumbersome for humans, as illustrated by the following section of an early machine-language program that adds overtime pay to base pay and stores the result in gross pay:

```
+1300042774
+1400593419
+1200274027
```

Assembly Languages

Machine-language programming was simply too slow and tedious for most programmers. Instead of using the strings of numbers that computers could directly understand, programmers began using English like abbreviations to represent the elementary machine operations. These abbreviations formed the basis of assembly languages. Translator programs called assemblers were developed to convert early assembly-language programs to machine language at computer speeds. The following section of an assembly-language program also adds overtime pay to base pay and stores the result in gross pay:

```
load     basepay
add      overpay
store    grosspay
```

Although such code is clearer to humans, it is incomprehensible to computers until translated to machine language.

High-Level Languages

Computer usage increased rapidly with the advent of assembly languages, but programmers still had to use many instructions to accomplish even the simplest tasks. To speed the programming process, high-level languages were developed in which single statements could be written to accomplish substantial tasks. Translator programs called compilers convert high-level language programs into machine language. High-level languages allow programmers to write instructions that look almost like everyday English and contain commonly used mathematical notations. A payroll program written in a high-level language might contain a statement such as

```
grossPay = basePay + overTimePay
```

From the programmer's standpoint, obviously, high-level languages are preferable to machine and assembly language. Microsoft's Visual Studio languages (e.g., Visual Basic, Visual C# and Visual C++) and other languages, such as C, C++ and Java are among the most widely used high-level programming languages. Figure 1.1 compares machine, assembly and high-level languages.

The process of compiling a high-level language program into machine language can take a considerable amount of computer time. Interpreter programs were developed to execute high-level language programs directly, although much more slowly. Interpreters are popular in program development environments in which new features are being added and errors corrected. Once a program is fully developed, a compiled version can be produced to run most efficiently. Interpreters are also popular with so-called scripting languages on the Web. We'll study the development of Web-based applications in Chapters 19–22.

1.9 Visual Basic

Visual Basic evolved from BASIC (Beginner's All-Purpose Symbolic Instruction Code), developed in the mid-1960s by Professors John Kemeny and Thomas Kurtz of Dartmouth College as a language for writing simple programs. BASIC's primary purpose was to familiarize novices with programming techniques.

The widespread use of BASIC on various types of computers (sometimes called hardware platforms) led to many enhancements to the language. When Bill Gates founded Microsoft Corporation, he implemented BASIC on several early personal computers. With the development of the Microsoft Windows graphical user interface (GUI) in the late 1980s and the early 1990s, the natural evolution of BASIC was Visual Basic, introduced by Microsoft in 1991. Visual Basic makes the development of Windows applications convenient.

Until the first version of Visual Basic appeared in 1991, developing Microsoft Windows-based applications was a difficult and cumbersome process. Although Visual Basic is derived from the BASIC programming language, it is a distinctly different language that

	Sample code	Translator	From the programmer's perspective	From the computer's perspective
Machine language	+1300042774 +1400593419 +1200274027	None	Slow, tedious, error prone	Natural lanuage of a computer; the only language the computer can understand directly
Assembly language	LOAD BASEPAY ADD OVERPAY STORE GROSSPAY	Assembler	English-like abbreviations, easier to understand	Assemblers convert assembly language into machine language so the computer can understand
High-level language	grossPay = basePay + overTimePay	Compiler	Instructions resemble everyday English; single statements accomplish substantial tasks	Compilers convert high-level languages into machine language so the computer can understand

Fig. 1.1 | Comparing machine, assembly and high-level languages.

offers such powerful features as graphical user interfaces, event handling, object-oriented programming, and exception handling. Visual Basic is an event-driven language (i.e., the programs respond to user-initiated events such as mouse clicks and keystrokes), and is a visual programming language in which programs are created using an **Integrated Development Environment (IDE)**. With the IDE, a programmer can write, run, test and debug Visual Basic programs conveniently, thereby reducing the time it takes to produce a working program to a fraction of what it would take without using the IDE. **Debugging** is the process of fixing errors in an application.

The advancement of programming tools and consumer-electronic devices created many challenges. Integrating software components from diverse languages proved difficult. Developers also discovered they needed Web-based applications that could be accessed and used via the Internet. As programmable devices, such as personal digital assistants (PDAs) and cell phones, grew in popularity in the late 1990s, the need for these components to interact with others via the Internet rose dramatically. As a result of the popularity of mobile electronic devices, software developers realized that their clientele was no longer restricted to desktop users. Developers recognized the need for software accessible to anyone from almost any type of device.

To address these needs, Microsoft announced the introduction of its **.NET** (pronounced "dot-net") strategy in 2000. The .NET platform is one over which Web-based applications can be distributed to a variety of devices (such as PDAs and cell phones) and to desktop computers. The .NET platform enables programs created in different programming languages to communicate easily with each other.

Visual Basic offers powerful object-oriented programming capabilities, including a substantial library of components, allowing programmers to develop applications even faster. Also, Visual Basic applications can interact via the Internet, using industry standards such as XML, which we discuss in Chapter 19, and the XML-based Simple Object Access Protocol (SOAP), which we discuss in Chapter 22, Web Services.

1.10 C, C++, Java and Visual C#

C

The C programming language was implemented by Dennis Ritchie at Bell Laboratories in 1973. C first gained widespread recognition as the development language of the UNIX operating system. C is a hardware-independent language, and, with careful design, it is possible to write C programs that are portable to most computers.

C++

C++ was developed by Bjarne Stroustrup in the early 1980s at Bell Laboratories. C++ provides a number of features that "spruce up" the C language, but, more important, it provides capabilities for **object-oriented programming (OOP)**. Many of today's major operating systems are written in C or C++. At a time when the demand for new and more powerful software is soaring, the ability to build software quickly, correctly and economically remains an elusive goal. This problem can be addressed in part through the use of **objects,** or reusable software **components** that model items in the real world (we will discuss object technology in Section 1.17). A modular, object-oriented approach to design and implementation can make software development groups much more productive than is possible using earlier programming techniques. Furthermore, object-oriented programs are often easier to understand, correct and modify.

Java

Microprocessors are having a profound impact in intelligent consumer electronic devices. Recognizing this, Sun Microsystems in 1991 funded an internal corporate research project that resulted in the development of a C++-based language. When a group of Sun people visited a local coffee shop, the name Java was suggested and it stuck. As the World Wide Web exploded in popularity in 1993, Sun saw the possibility of using Java to add **dynamic content** (e.g., interactivity, animations and the like) to Web pages. Sun formally announced the language in 1995. This generated immediate interest in the business community because of the commercial potential of the Web. Java is now used to develop large-scale enterprise applications, to enhance the functionality of Web servers (the computers that provide the content we see in our Web browsers), to provide applications for consumer devices (such as cell phones, pagers and personal digital assistants) and for many other purposes. Visual Basic is similar in capability to Java. Current versions of C++, such as Microsoft's Visual C++ and Borland's C++Builder, also have similar capabilities.

Visual C#

In 2000, Microsoft announced the C# (pronounced "C-Sharp") programming language—created specifically for the .NET platform (which is discussed in Section 1.14).

C# has roots in C, C++ and Java, adapting the best features of each. Like Visual Basic, C# is object oriented and contains a powerful class library of prebuilt components, enabling programmers to develop applications quickly—Visual Basic and C# share the Framework Class Library (FCL); the FCL is discussed in Section 1.14. Both languages have similar capabilities to Java and are appropriate for demanding application development tasks, especially for building today's popular Web-based applications.

1.11 Other High-Level Languages

Although hundreds of high-level languages have been developed, only a few have achieved broad acceptance other than those we've discussed.

Fortran

IBM Corporation developed Fortran (FORmula TRANslator) in the mid-1950s to create scientific and engineering applications that require complex mathematical computations. Fortran is still widely used.

COBOL

COBOL (COmmon Business Oriented Language) was developed in 1959 by a group of computer manufacturers in conjunction with government and industrial computer users. COBOL is used primarily for commercial applications that require the precise and efficient manipulation of large amounts of data. Much of today's business software is still programmed in COBOL.

Pascal

During the 1960s, many large software-development efforts encountered severe difficulties. People began to realize that software development was a far more complex activity than they had imagined. Research activity resulted in the evolution of structured programming—a disciplined approach to the creation of programs that are clear, demonstrably correct and easy to modify. One of the results of this research was the development of the Pascal programming language by Professor Nicklaus Wirth in 1971. Pascal, named after the mathematician and philosopher Blaise Pascal, was designed for teaching structured programming in academic environments and rapidly became the preferred introductory programming language in most colleges. Unfortunately, the language lacked many features needed to make it useful in commercial, industrial and government applications. By contrast, C, which also arose from research on structured programming, did not have the limitations of Pascal, and programmers quickly adopted it.

Ada

The Ada programming language was developed under the sponsorship of the United States Department of Defense (DOD) through the early 1980s. DOD wanted a single language that would meet its needs. The language was named after Lady Ada Lovelace, daughter of the poet Lord Byron. Lady Lovelace is generally credited with writing the world's first computer program, in the early 1800s (for the Analytical Engine mechanical computing device designed by Charles Babbage). An important capability of Ada is multitasking, which allows programmers to specify that many activities are to occur in parallel. As we will see in Chapter 15, Visual Basic offers a similar capability, called multithreading.

1.12 The Internet and the World Wide Web

The Internet—a global network of computers—was initiated almost four decades ago with funding supplied by the U.S. Department of Defense. Originally designed to connect the main computer systems of about a dozen universities and research organizations, its chief benefit proved early on to be the capability for quick and easy communication via what came to be known as electronic mail (e-mail). This is true even on today's Internet, with e-mail, instant messaging and file transfer facilitating communications among hundreds of millions of people worldwide. The Internet has exploded into one of the world's premier communication mechanisms and continues to grow rapidly.

The World Wide Web allows computer users to locate and view multimedia-based documents on almost any subject over the Internet. Even though the Internet was developed decades ago, the introduction of the Web was a relatively recent event. In 1989, Tim Berners-Lee of CERN (the European Organization for Nuclear Research) began to develop a technology for sharing information via hyperlinked text documents. Berners-Lee called his invention the HyperText Markup Language (HTML). He also wrote communication protocols to form the backbone of his new information system, which he referred to as the World Wide Web.

In the past, most computer applications ran on computers that were not connected to one another, whereas today's applications can be written to communicate among the world's computers. The Internet mixes computing and communications technologies. It makes our work easier. It makes information instantly and conveniently accessible worldwide. It enables individuals and small businesses to get worldwide exposure. It is changing the way business is done. People can search for the best prices on virtually any product or service. Special-interest communities can stay in touch with one another. Researchers can be made instantly aware of the latest breakthroughs. The Internet and the World Wide Web are surely among humankind's most profound creations. In Chapters 19–23, you will learn how to build Internet- and Web-based applications.

In 1994, Tim Berners-Lee founded an organization, called the World Wide Web Consortium (W3C), that is devoted to developing nonproprietary, interoperable technologies for the World Wide Web. One of the W3C's primary goals is to make the Web universally accessible—regardless of disabilities, language or culture.

The W3C (www.w3.org) is also a standardization organization. Web technologies standardized by the W3C are called Recommendations. Current W3C Recommendations include the Extensible Markup Language (XML). We introduce XML in Section 1.13 and present it in detail in Chapter 19, Extensible Markup Language (XML). It is the key technology underlying the next version of the Word Wide Web, sometimes called the "semantic Web." It is also one of the key technologies that underlies Web services, which we discuss in Chapter 22.

1.13 Extensible Markup Language (XML)

As the popularity of the Web exploded, HTML's limitations became apparent. HTML's lack of extensibility (the ability to change or add features) frustrated developers, and its ambiguous definition allowed erroneous HTML to proliferate. The need for a standardized, fully extensible and structurally strict language was apparent. As a result, XML was developed by the W3C.

Data independence, the separation of content from its presentation, is the essential characteristic of XML. Because XML documents describe data, any application conceivably can process them. Software developers are integrating XML into their applications to improve Web functionality and interoperability.

XML is not limited to Web applications. For example, it is increasingly being employed in databases—the structure of an XML document enables it to be integrated easily with database applications. As applications become more Web enabled, it is likely that XML will become the universal technology for data representation. All applications employing XML would be able to communicate with one another, provided that they could understand their respective XML markup schemes, or vocabularies.

The Simple Object Access Protocol (SOAP) is a technology for the transmission of objects (marked up as XML) over the Internet. Microsoft's .NET technologies (discussed in the next two sections) use XML and SOAP to mark up and transfer data over the Internet. XML and SOAP are at the core of .NET—they allow software components to interoperate (i.e., communicate easily with one another). Since SOAP's foundations are in XML and HTTP (Hypertext Transfer Protocol—the key communication protocol of the Web), it is supported on most types of computer systems. We discuss XML in Chapter 19, Extensible Markup Language (XML) and SOAP in Chapter 22, Web Services.

1.14 Microsoft's .NET

In 2000, Microsoft announced its .NET initiative (www.microsoft.com/net), a new vision for embracing the Internet and the Web in the development and use of software. One key aspect of .NET is its independence from a specific language or platform. Rather than being forced to use a single programming language, developers can create a .NET application in any .NET-compatible language. Programmers can contribute to the same software project, writing code in the .NET languages (such as Microsoft's Visual Basic, Visual C++, Visual C# and many others) in which they are most competent. Part of the initiative includes Microsoft's ASP.NET technology, which allows programmers to create applications for the Web. We discuss ASP.NET in Chapter 21, ASP.NET, Web Forms and Web Controls. We use ASP.NET technology in Chapter 22 to build applications that use Web Services.

The .NET architecture can exist on multiple platforms, not just Microsoft Windows–based systems, further extending the portability of .NET programs. One example is Mono (www.mono-project.com/Main_Page), an open-source project by Novell. Another is DotGNU Portable .NET (www.dotgnu.org).

A key component of the .NET architecture is Web services, which are reusable application software components that can be used over the Internet. Clients and other applications can use Web services as reusable building blocks. One example of a Web service is Dollar Rent a Car's reservation system.[1] An airline partner wanted to enable customers to make rental-car reservations from the airline's Web site. To do so, the airline needed to access Dollar's reservation system. In response, Dollar created a Web service that allowed the airline to access Dollar's database and make reservations. Web services enable computers at the two companies to communicate over the Web, even though the airline uses UNIX systems and Dollar uses Microsoft Windows. Dollar could have created a one-time solution for that particular airline, but then would not have been able to reuse such a cus-

---

1.   www.microsoft.com/resources/casestudies/CaseStudy.asp?CaseStudyID=11626

tomized system. Dollar's Web service enables many airlines, hotels and travel companies to use its reservation system without creating a custom program for each relationship.

The .NET strategy extends the concept of software reuse to the Internet, allowing programmers and companies to concentrate on their specialties without having to implement every component of every application. Instead, companies can buy Web services and devote their resources to developing their own products. For example, a single application using Web services from various companies could manage bill payments, tax refunds, loans and investments. An online merchant could buy Web services for credit-card payments, user authentication, network security and inventory databases to create an e-commerce Web site.

1.15 The .NET Framework and the Common Language Runtime

The Microsoft .NET Framework is at the heart of the .NET strategy. This framework manages and executes applications and Web services, contains a class library (called the .NET Framework Class Library, or FCL), enforces security and provides many other programming capabilities. The details of the .NET Framework are found in the Common Language Infrastructure (CLI), which contains information about the storage of data types (i.e., data that has predefined characteristics such as a date, percentage or currency amount), objects and so on. The CLI has been standardized by Ecma International (originally known as the European Computer Manufacturers Association), making it easier to create the .NET Framework for other platforms. This is like publishing the blueprints of the framework—anyone can build it by following the specifications.

The Common Language Runtime (CLR) is another central part of the .NET Framework—it executes .NET programs. Programs are compiled into machine-specific instructions in two steps. First, the program is compiled into Microsoft Intermediate Language (MSIL), which defines instructions for the CLR. Code converted into MSIL from other languages and sources can be woven together by the CLR. The MSIL for an application's components is placed into the application's executable file. When the application executes, another compiler (known as the just-in-time compiler or JIT compiler) in the CLR translates the MSIL in the executable file into machine-language code (for a particular platform), then the machine-language code executes on that platform.

If the .NET Framework exists (and is installed) for a platform, that platform can run any .NET program. The ability of a program to run (without modification) across multiple platforms is known as platform independence. Code written once can be used on another type of computer without modification, saving both time and money. In addition, software can target a wider audience—previously, companies had to decide whether converting their programs to different platforms (sometimes called porting) was worth the cost. With .NET, porting programs is no longer an issue (at least once .NET itself has been made available on the platforms).

The .NET Framework also provides a high level of language interoperability. Programs written in different languages are all compiled into MSIL—the different parts can be combined to create a single unified program. MSIL allows the .NET Framework to be language independent, because .NET programs are not tied to a particular programming language. Any language that can be compiled into MSIL is called a .NET-compliant language. Figure 1.2 lists many of the programming languages that are available for the .NET platform (msdn.microsoft.com/netframework/technologyinfo/overview/default.aspx).

.NET programming languages	
APL	Mondrian
Visual C#	Oberon
COBOL	Oz
Component Pascal	Pascal
Curriculum	Perl
Eiffel	Python
Forth	RPG
Fortran	Scheme
Haskell	Smalltalk
Java	Standard ML
JScript	Visual Basic
Mercury	Visual C++

Fig. 1.2 | .NET languages.

The .NET Framework Class Library (FCL) can be used by any .NET language. The FCL contains a variety of reusable components, saving programmers the trouble of creating new components. This book explains how to develop .NET software with Visual Basic.

1.16 Test-Driving a Visual Basic Application

In this section, you will "test-drive" a Visual Basic application that enables you to draw on the screen using the mouse. You will run and interact with the working application. You will build a similar application in Chapter 13, Graphical User Interface Concepts: Part 1.

The **Drawing** application allows you to draw with different brush sizes and colors. The elements and functionality you see in this application are typical of what you will learn to program in this text. We use fonts to distinguish between IDE features (such as menu names and menu items) and other elements that appear in the IDE. Our convention is to emphasize IDE features (such as the **File** menu) in a bold **sans-serif Helvetica** font and to emphasize other elements, such as file names (e.g., Form1.vb), in a sans-serif Lucida font. The following steps show you how to test-drive the application.

1. *Checking your setup.* Confirm that you have installed Visual Basic 2005 Express or Visual Studio 2005 as discussed in the *Preface*.

2. *Locating the application directory.* Open Windows Explorer and navigate to the C:\examples\Ch01\Drawing directory.

3. *Running the* **Drawing** *application.* Now that you are in the correct directory, double click the file name Drawing.exe to run the application (Fig. 1.3).

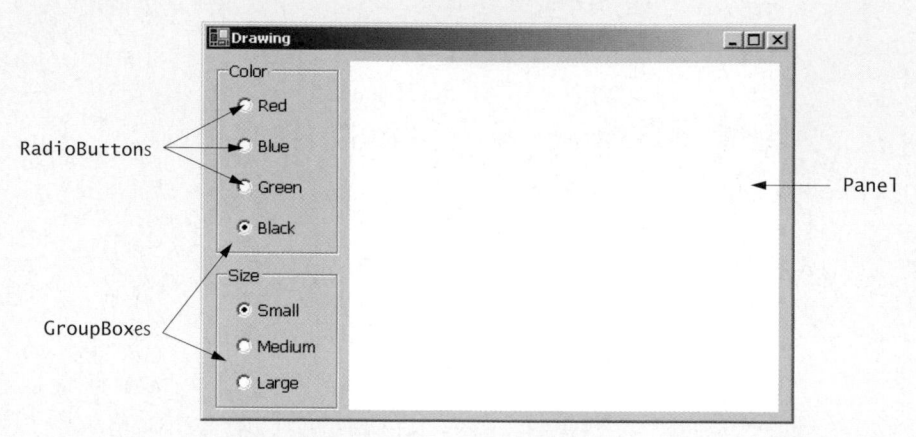

Fig. 1.3 | Visual Basic **Drawing** application.

In Fig. 1.3, several graphical elements—called controls—are labeled. The controls include two GroupBoxes (in this case, **Color** and **Size**), seven RadioButtons and a Panel (these controls will be discussed in depth later in the text). The **Drawing** application allows you to draw with a red, blue, green or black brush of small, medium or large size. You will explore these options in this test-drive.

You can use existing controls—which are objects—to get powerful applications running in Visual Basic much faster than if you had to write all of the code yourself. In this text, you will learn how to use many preexisting controls, and how to write your own program code to customize your applications.

The brush's properties, selected in the RadioButtons (the small circles where you select an option by clicking the mouse) labeled **Black** and **Small**, are default settings, which are the initial settings you see when you first run the application. Programmers include default settings to provide reasonable choices which the application will use if the user chooses not to change the settings. You will now choose your own settings.

4. *Changing the brush color.* Click the RadioButton labelled **Red** to change the color of the brush. Hold the mouse button down with the mouse pointer positioned anywhere on the white Panel, then drag the mouse to draw with the brush. Draw flower petals as shown in Fig. 1.4. Then click the RadioButton labeled **Green** to change the color of the brush again.

5. *Changing the brush size.* Click the RadioButton labeled **Large** to change the size of the brush. Draw grass and a flower stem as shown in Fig. 1.5.

6. *Finishing the drawing.* Click the RadioButton labeled **Blue**. Then click the RadioButton labeled **Medium**. Draw raindrops as shown in Fig. 1.6 to complete the drawing.

7. *Closing the application.* Click the close box, ▼ to close your running application.

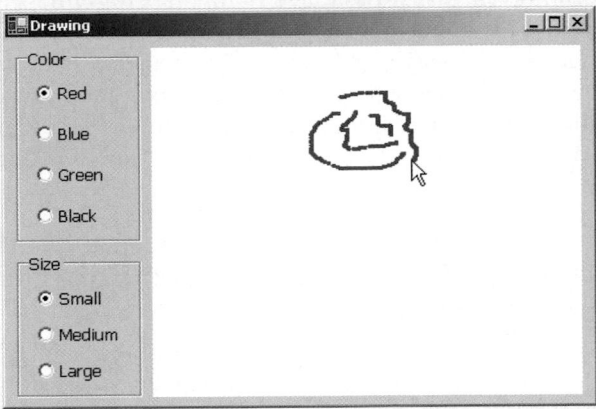

Fig. 1.4 | Drawing with a new brush color.

Fig. 1.5 | Drawing with a new brush size.

Fig. 1.6 | Finishing the drawing.

Additional Applications in **Visual Basic 2005 How to Program, 3/e**

Figure 1.7 lists a few of the hundreds of applications in the examples and exercises in this text. We encourage you to practice running some of them. The examples folder for Chapter 1 contains all of the files required to run each application listed in Fig. 1.7. Simply double click the file names for any application you would like to run. [*Note:* The Garage.exe application assumes that the user inputs a value from 0 to 24.]

1.17 (Only Required Section of the Case Study) Software Engineering Case Study: Introduction to Object Technology and the UML

Now we begin our early introduction to object orientation, a natural way of thinking about the world and writing computer programs. Chapters 1, 3–9 and 11 each end with a brief Software Engineering Case Study section in which we present a carefully paced introduction to object orientation. Our goal here is to help you develop an object-oriented way of thinking and to introduce you to the Unified Modeling Language™ (UML™)—a graphical language that allows people who design object-oriented software systems to use an industry-standard notation to represent them.

In this, the only required section of the case study (because it contains foundational information for all readers), we introduce basic object-oriented concepts and terminology. The optional case study sections in Chapters 3–9 and 11, and in Appendix J present an object-oriented design and implementation of the software for a simple automated teller machine (ATM) system. The Software Engineering Case Study sections at the ends of Chapters 3–8

- analyze a typical requirements document that describes a software system (the ATM) to be built
- determine the objects required to implement that system
- determine the attributes the objects will have
- determine the behaviors these objects will exhibit
- specify how the objects will interact with one another to meet the system requirements

Application name	File to execute
Parking Fees	Garage.exe
Tic Tac Toe	TicTacToe.exe
Drawing Stars	DrawStars.exe
Drawing Shapes	DrawShapes.exe
Drawing Polygons	DrawPolygons.exe

Fig. 1.7 | Examples of Visual Basic applications found in this book.

The Software Engineering Case Study sections at the ends of Chapters 9 and 11 modify and enhance the design presented in Chapters 3–8. Appendix J contains a complete, working Visual Basic implementation of the object-oriented ATM system.

Although our case study is a scaled-down version of an industry-level problem, we nevertheless cover many common industry practices. You will experience a solid introduction to object-oriented design with the UML. Also, you will sharpen your code-reading skills by touring a complete, straightforward and well-documented Visual Basic implementation of the ATM.

Basic Object Technology Concepts

We begin our introduction to object orientation with some key terminology. Everywhere you look in the real world you see objects—people, animals, plants, cars, planes, buildings, computers and so on. Humans think in terms of objects. Telephones, houses, traffic lights, microwave ovens and water coolers are just a few more objects we see around us every day.

We sometimes divide objects into two categories: animate and inanimate. Animate objects are "alive" in some sense—they move around and do things. Inanimate objects do not move on their own. Objects of both types, however, have some things in common. They all have attributes (e.g., size, shape, color and weight), and they all exhibit behaviors (e.g., a ball rolls, bounces, inflates and deflates; a baby cries, sleeps, crawls, walks and blinks; a car accelerates, brakes and turns; a towel absorbs water). We will study the kinds of attributes and behaviors that software objects have.

Humans learn about objects by studying their attributes and observing their behaviors. Different objects can have similar attributes and can exhibit similar behaviors. Comparisons can be made, for example, between babies and adults and between humans and chimpanzees.

Object-oriented design (OOD) models software in terms similar to those that people use to describe real-world objects. It takes advantage of class relationships, where objects of a certain class, such as a class of vehicles, have the same characteristics—cars, trucks, little red wagons and roller skates have much in common. OOD takes advantage of inheritance relationships, where new classes of objects are derived by absorbing characteristics of existing classes and adding unique characteristics of their own. An object of class "convertible" certainly has the characteristics of the more general class "automobile," but more specifically, the roof goes up and down.

Object-oriented design provides a natural and intuitive way to view the software design process—namely, modeling objects by their attributes, behaviors and interrelationships, just as we describe real-world objects. OOD also models communication between objects. Just as people send messages to one another (e.g., a sergeant commands a soldier to stand at attention), objects also communicate via messages. A bank account object may receive a message to decrease its balance by a certain amount because the customer has withdrawn that amount of money.

OOD encapsulates (i.e., wraps) attributes and operations (behaviors) into objects—an object's attributes and operations are intimately tied together. Objects have the property of information hiding. This means that objects may know how to communicate with one another across well-defined interfaces, but normally they are not allowed to know how other objects are implemented—implementation details are hidden within the objects themselves. You can drive a car effectively, for instance, without knowing the details of how engines, transmissions, brakes and exhaust systems work internally—as long as you know how to use the accelerator pedal, the brake pedal, the steering wheel and so on. Information hiding, as you will see, is crucial to good software engineering.

Languages like Visual Basic are **object oriented**. Programming in such a language is called **object-oriented programming (OOP)**, and it allows computer programmers to conveniently implement an object-oriented design as a working software system. Languages like C, on the other hand, are **procedural**, so programming tends to be **action oriented**. In C, the unit of programming is the **function**. In Visual Basic, the unit of programming is the **class** from which objects are eventually **instantiated** (an OOP term for "created"). Visual Basic classes contain **methods** (Visual Basic's equivalent of C's functions) that implement operations, and data that implements attributes.

Classes, Fields and Methods

Visual Basic programmers concentrate on creating their own **user-defined types** called **classes**. Each class contains data as well as the set of methods that manipulate that data and provide services to **clients** (i.e., other classes that use the class). The data components of a class are called attributes or **fields**. For example, a bank account class might include an account number and a balance. The operation components of a class are called methods. For example, a bank account class might include methods to make a deposit (increase the balance), make a withdrawal (decrease the balance) and inquire what the current balance is. Programmers use built-in types and user-defined types as the "building blocks" for constructing new user-defined types (classes). The **nouns in a system specification** help the Visual Basic programmer determine the set of classes from which objects are created that work together to implement the system.

Classes are to objects as blueprints are to houses—a class is a "plan" for building objects of the class. Just as we can build many houses from one blueprint, we can instantiate (create) many objects from one class. You cannot cook meals in the kitchen of a blueprint, but you can cook meals in the kitchen of a house. You cannot sleep in the bedroom of a blueprint, but you can sleep in the bedroom of a house.

Classes can have relationships with other classes. For example, in an object-oriented design of a bank, the "bank teller" class needs to relate to other classes, such as the "customer" class, the "cash drawer" class, the "safe" class, and so on. These relationships are called **associations**.

Packaging software as classes makes it possible for future software systems to **reuse** the classes. Groups of related classes often are packaged as reusable **components**. Just as realtors often say that the three most important factors affecting the price of real estate are "location, location and location," people in the software development community often say that the three most important factors affecting the future of software development are "reuse, reuse and reuse."

Software Engineering Observation 1.1

Reuse of existing classes when building new classes and programs saves time, money and effort. Reuse also helps programmers build more reliable and effective systems, because existing classes and components often have gone through extensive testing, debugging and performance tuning.

Indeed, with object technology, you can build much of the new software you will need by combining existing classes, just as automobile manufacturers combine interchangeable parts. Each new class you create will have the potential to become a valuable software asset that you and other programmers can reuse to speed and enhance the quality of future software development efforts.

Introduction to Object-Oriented Analysis and Design (OOAD)

Soon you will be writing programs in Visual Basic. How will you create the code for your programs? Perhaps, like many beginning programmers, you will simply turn on your computer and start typing. This approach may work for small programs (like the ones we present in the early chapters of the book), but what if you were asked to create a software system to control thousands of automated teller machines for a major bank? Or what if you were asked to work on a team of 1,000 software developers building the next generation of the U.S. air traffic control system? For projects so large and complex, you could not simply sit down and start writing programs.

To create the best solutions, you should follow a detailed process for analyzing your project's requirements (i.e., determining *what* your system is supposed to do) and developing a design that satisfies them (i.e., deciding *how* your system should do it). Ideally, you would go through this process and carefully review the design (and have your design reviewed by other software professionals) before writing any code. If this process involves analyzing and designing your system from an object-oriented point of view, it is called object-oriented analysis and design (OOAD). Experienced programmers know that proper analysis and design can save many hours by helping avoid an ill-planned system development approach that has to be abandoned partway through its implementation, possibly wasting considerable time, money and effort.

OOAD is the generic term for the process of analyzing a problem and developing an approach for solving it. Small problems like the ones discussed in the first few chapters of this book, do not require an exhaustive OOAD process. It may be sufficient, before you begin writing Visual Basic code, to write pseudocode—an informal text-based means of expressing program logic. Pseudocode is not actually a programming language, but we can use it as a kind of outline to guide us as we write our code. We introduce pseudocode in Chapter 5.

As problems and the groups of people solving them increase in size, OOAD quickly becomes more appropriate than pseudocode. Ideally, a group should agree on a strictly defined process for solving its problem and a uniform way of communicating the results of that process to one another. Although many different OOAD processes exist, a single graphical language for communicating the results of *any* OOAD process has come into wide use. This language, known as the Unified Modeling Language (UML), was developed in the mid-1990s under the initial direction of three software methodologists: Grady Booch, James Rumbaugh and Ivar Jacobson.

History of the UML

In the 1980s, increasing numbers of organizations began using OOP to build their applications, and a need developed for a standard object-oriented analysis and design (OOAD) process. Many methodologists—including Grady Booch, James Rumbaugh and Ivar Jacobson—individually produced and promoted separate processes to satisfy this need. Each process had its own notation, or "language" (in the form of graphical diagrams), to convey the results of analysis (i.e., determining *what* a proposed system is supposed to do) and design (i.e., determining *how* a proposed system should be implemented to do what it is supposed to do).

By the early 1990s, different organizations were using their own unique processes and notations. At the same time, these organizations also wanted to use software tools that would support their particular processes. Software vendors found it difficult to provide tools for so many processes. A standard notation and standard process were needed.

In 1994, James Rumbaugh joined Grady Booch at Rational Software Corporation (now a division of IBM), and the two began working to unify their popular processes. They soon were joined by Ivar Jacobson. In 1996, the group released early versions of the UML to the software engineering community and requested feedback. Around the same time, an organization known as the Object Management Group™ (OMG™) invited submissions for a common modeling language. The OMG (www.omg.org) is a nonprofit organization that promotes the standardization of object-oriented technologies by issuing guidelines and specifications, such as the UML. Several corporations—among them HP, IBM, Microsoft, Oracle and Rational Software—had already recognized the need for a common modeling language. In response to the OMG's request for proposals, these companies formed the UML Partners—the consortium that developed the UML version 1.1 and submitted it to the OMG. The OMG accepted the proposal and, in 1997, assumed responsibility for the continuing maintenance and revision of the UML. We present the recently adopted UML 2 terminology and notation throughout this book.

What is the UML?

The **Unified Modeling Language** (UML) is the most widely used graphical representation scheme for modeling object-oriented systems. It has indeed unified the various popular notational schemes. Those who design systems use the language (in the form of diagrams, many of which we discuss throughout our ATM case study and other portions of the book) to model their systems.

An attractive feature of the UML is its flexibility. The UML is **extensible** (i.e., capable of being enhanced with new features) and is independent of any particular OOAD process. UML modelers are free to use various processes in designing systems, but all developers can now express their designs with one standard set of graphical notations.

The UML is a feature-rich graphical language. In our subsequent (and optional) Software Engineering Case Study sections on developing the software for an automated teller machine (ATM), we present a simple, concise subset of these features. We then use this subset to guide you through a first design experience with the UML. We sincerely hope you enjoy working through it.

Internet and Web UML Resources

For more information about the UML, refer to the following Web sites. For additional UML sites, please refer to the Internet and Web resources listed at the end of Section 3.10.

www.uml.org

This UML resource site from the Object Management Group (OMG) provides specification documents for the UML and other object-oriented technologies.

www.ibm.com/software/rational/uml

This is the UML resource page for IBM Rational—the successor to the Rational Software Corporation (the company that created the UML).

www.uml.org/#Links-Tutorials

The Object Management Group's list of recommended UML tutorials.

bdn.borland.com/article/0,1410,31863,00.html

A short tutorial on the UML from the Borland Developer Network.

Recommended Readings

The following books provide information about object-oriented design with the UML.

- Arlow, J., and I. Neustadt. *UML and the Unified Process: Practical Object-Oriented Analysis and Design, Second Edition.* London: Addison-Wesley, 2005.
- Fowler, M. *UML Distilled, Third Edition: A Brief Guide to the Standard Object Modeling Language.* Boston: Addison-Wesley, 2004.
- Rumbaugh, J., I. Jacobson and G. Booch. *The Unified Modeling Language User Guide, Second Edition.* Reading, MA: Addison-Wesley, 2005.

For additional books on the UML, please refer to the recommended readings listed at the end of Section 3.10, or visit www.amazon.com, www.bn.com and www.informIT.com. IBM Rational provides a recommended reading list for UML books at www.ibm.com/software/rational/info/technical/books.jsp.

Section 1.17 Self-Review Exercises

1.1   List three examples of real-world objects that we did not mention. For each object, list several attributes and behaviors.

1.2   Pseudocode is _____.
   a) another term for OOAD
   b) a programming language used to display UML diagrams
   c) an informal means of expressing program logic
   d) a graphical representation scheme for modeling object-oriented systems

1.3   The UML is used primarily to _____.
   a) test object-oriented systems
   b) design object-oriented systems
   c) implement object-oriented systems
   d) Both a and b

Answers to Section 1.17 Self-Review Exercises

1.1   [*Note:* Answers may vary.] a) A television's attributes include the size of the screen, the number of colors it can display, and its current channel and volume. A television turns on and off, changes channels, displays video and plays sounds. b) A coffee maker's attributes include the maximum volume of water it can hold, the time required to brew a pot of coffee and the temperature of the heating plate under the coffee pot. A coffee maker turns on and off, brews coffee and heats coffee. c) A turtle's attributes include its age, the size of its shell and its weight. A turtle crawls, retreats into its shell, emerges from its shell and eats vegetation.

1.2   c.

1.3   b.

1.18 **Wrap-Up**

This chapter introduced basic hardware and software concepts and basic object technology concepts, including classes, objects, attributes and behaviors. We discussed the different types of programming languages and which languages are most widely used. We presented a brief history of operating systems, including Microsoft's Windows. We discussed the history of the Internet and the Web. We presented the history of Visual Basic programming and Microsoft's .NET initiative, which allows you to program Internet and Web-based applications using Visual Basic (and other languages). You learned the steps for executing a Visual Basic application. You test-drove a sample Visual Basic application similar to the types of applications you will learn to program in this book. You learned about the history and purpose of the UML—the industry-standard graphical language for modeling software systems. We launched our early objects and classes presentation with the first of our Software Engineering Case Study sections (and the only one which is required). The remaining (all optional) sections of the case study use object-oriented design and the UML to design the software for our simplified automated teller machine system. We present the complete Visual Basic code implementation of the ATM system in Appendix J.

In the next chapter, you will use the Visual Studio IDE (Integrated Development Environment) to create your first Visual Basic application using the techniques of visual programming. You will also learn about Visual Studio's help features.

1.19 Web Resources

Deitel & Associates Web Sites

www.deitel.com/books/vbhtp3/index.html
The Deitel & Associates site for *Visual Basic 2005 How to Program, Third Edition* includes links to the book's examples and other resources.

www.deitel.com
Please check this site for updates, corrections and additional resources for all Deitel publications.

www.deitel.com/newsletter/subscribe.html
Please visit this site to subscribe to the free *Deitel® Buzz Online* e-mail newsletter to follow the Deitel & Associates publishing program and to receive updates on Visual Basic 2005 and this book.

www.prenhall.com/deitel
Prentice Hall's site for Deitel publications. Includes detailed product information, sample chapters and *Companion Web Sites* containing book- and chapter-specific resources for students and instructors.

Microsoft Web Sites

msdn.microsoft.com/vbasic/default.aspx
The Microsoft Visual Basic Developer Center site includes product information, downloads, tutorials, chat groups and more. Includes case studies on companies using Visual Basic in their businesses.

msdn.microsoft.com/vstudio/default.aspx
Visit this site to learn more about Microsoft's Visual Studio products and resources.

www.gotdotnet.com/
This is the site for the Microsoft .NET Framework Community. It includes message boards, a resource center, sample programs and more.

www.thespoke.net
Students can chat, post their code, rate other students' code, create hubs and post questions at this site.

Resources

www.w3.org
The World Wide Web Consortium (W3C) develops technologies for the Internet and the Web. This site includes links to W3C technologies, news and frequently asked questions (FAQs).

www.startvbdotnet.com/
Intended for novices, this site includes tutorials and links to numerous Visual Basic resources.

`www.vbexplorer.com/VBExplorer/VBExplorer.asp`
Includes tutorials, downloads, tips, downloads, games and more.

`www.devx.com/vb/`
This Visual Basic developers' Web site include links to articles, downloads, demos and code.

`www.error-bank.com/`
The Error Bank is a collection of .NET errors, exceptions and solutions.

`www.vbdotnetforums.com/`
This site allows you to chat with other Visual Basic developers, including the Visual Basic team at Microsoft.

UML Resources

`www.uml.org`
This UML resource page from the Object Management Group (OMG) provides specification documents for the UML and other object-oriented technologies.

`www.ibm.com/software/rational/uml`
This is the UML resource page for IBM Rational—the successor to the Rational Software Corporation (the company that created the UML).

Visual Basic Games

`www.homestead.com/vbgames6/game.html`
Check out Visual Basic games or post your own at this site.

`www.vbexplorer.com/VBExplorer/vb_game_downloads.asp`
Download Visual Basic games and graphics from this site.

`www.codetoad.com/visual_basic/games/`
This programmers' resource site includes links to several Visual Basic games.

Summary

Section 1.1 Introduction
- Computers that might have filled large rooms and cost millions of dollars a few decades ago can now be inscribed on silicon chips smaller than a fingernail, costing a few dollars each.
- Silicon chip technology has made computing so economical that about a billion general-purpose computers are in use worldwide, helping people in business, industry and government, and in their personal lives.

Section 1.2 What Is a Computer?
- Computers process data under the control of sets of instructions called computer programs. These programs guide the computer through sets of actions specified by computer programmers.
- A computer consists of various devices referred to as hardware (e.g., the keyboard, screen, disks, memory and processing units).
- The computer programs that run on a computer are referred to as software.
- A computer is a device capable of performing computations and making logical decisions at speeds millions, billions and even trillions of times faster than humans can.

Section 1.3 Computer Organization

- The input unit is the "receiving" section of the computer. It obtains information from input devices and places it at the disposal of the other units for processing.

- The output unit is the "shipping" section of the computer. It takes information processed by the computer and places it on output devices to make it available for use outside the computer.

- The memory unit is the rapid-access, relatively low-capacity "warehouse" section of the computer. It retains information that has been entered through the input unit, making it immediately available for processing when needed, and retains information that has already been processed until it can be placed on output devices by the output unit.

- The arithmetic and logic unit (ALU) is the "manufacturing" section of the computer. It is responsible for performing calculations and making decisions.

- The central processing unit (CPU) is the "administrative" section of the computer. It coordinates and supervises the operation of the other sections.

- The secondary storage unit is the long-term, high-capacity "warehousing" section of the computer. Programs or data not being used by the other units are normally placed on secondary storage devices (e.g., disks) until they are needed, possibly hours, days, months or even years later.

Section 1.4 Early Operating Systems

- Software systems called operating systems were developed to help make using computers more convenient.

- Multiprogramming involves the simultaneous operation of many jobs that are competing to share the computer's resources.

Section 1.5 Personal Computing, Distributed Computing and Client/Server Computing

- With distributed computing, an organization's computing is distributed over networks to the sites where the work of the organization is performed.

- The most powerful desktop machines provide individual users with enormous capabilities. Information is shared easily across computer networks, where computers called file servers offer a common data store that may be used by client computers distributed throughout the network, hence the term client/server computing.

Section 1.6 Hardware Trends

- Every year or two, the capacities of computers approximately double while their prices remain relatively constant. This often is called Moore's Law, named after the person who first observed the trend—Gordon Moore, co-founder of Intel.

- The invention of microprocessor chip technology and its wide deployment in the late 1970s and 1980s laid the groundwork for the productivity improvements that individuals and businesses have achieved in recent years.

Section 1.7 Microsoft's Windows® Operating System

- In the mid-1980s, Microsoft developed the Windows operating system, a graphical user interface built on top of the DOS operating system.

- The Windows operating system became incredibly popular after the 1993 release of Windows 3.1, whose successors, Windows 95 and Windows 98, virtually cornered the desktop operating systems market by the late 1990s.

- These operating systems, which borrowed many concepts (such as icons, menus and windows) popularized by early Apple Macintosh operating systems, enabled users to navigate multiple applications simultaneously.

- Windows XP, which is based on the Windows NT operating system, was released in 2001 and combines Microsoft's corporate and consumer operating system lines. Windows is by far the most widely used operating system.

- The biggest competitor to the Windows operating system is Linux. Linux is a free, open-source operating system.

Section 1.8 Machine Languages, Assembly Languages and High-Level Languages

- Any computer can directly understand only its own machine language. Machine languages generally consist of strings of numbers (ultimately reduced to 1s and 0s) that instruct computers to perform their most elementary operations one at a time.

- English-like abbreviations form the basis of assembly languages. Translator programs called assemblers convert assembly-language programs to machine language.

- Compilers translate high-level language programs into machine-language programs. High-level languages (like Visual Basic) contain English words and conventional mathematical notations.

- Interpreter programs execute high-level language programs directly, although much more slowly. Once a program is fully developed, a compiled version can be produced to run efficiently.

Section 1.9 Visual Basic

- Visual Basic offers powerful features including graphical user interfaces, event handling, object-oriented programming and exception handling.

- Visual Basic is an event-driven language (i.e., the programs respond to user-initiated events such as mouse clicks and keystrokes) and a visual programming language in which programs are created using an Integrated Development Environment (IDE).

- With the IDE, a programmer can write, run, test and debug Visual Basic programs conveniently, thereby reducing the time it takes to produce a working program to a fraction of what it would have taken without using the IDE.

- The .NET framework is one over which Web-based applications can be distributed to a variety of devices (such as PDAs and cell phones) and to desktop computers.

- The .NET framework allows programs created in different programming languages to communicate easily with each other.

- Visual Basic offers enhanced object orientation, including a powerful library of components, allowing programmers to develop applications even more quickly.

- Visual Basic also enables enhanced language interoperability—software components implemented in different programming languages can interact as never before.

- Visual Basic applications can interact via the Internet, using industry standards such as XML and the Simple Object Access Protocol (SOAP)

Section 1.10 C, C++, Java and Visual C#

- The C programming language was implemented by Dennis Ritchie at Bell Laboratories in 1973. C first gained widespread recognition as a development language of the UNIX operating system.

- C++ was developed by Bjarne Stroustrup in the early 1980s at Bell Laboratories. C++ provides a number of features that "spruce up" the C language, but, more important, it provides capabilities for object-oriented programming (OOP).

- Objects are reusable software components that model items in the real world. A modular, object-oriented approach to design and implementation can make software development groups much more productive than is possible using only earlier programming techniques, such as structured programming. Object-oriented programs are often easier to understand, correct and modify.

- Java is now used to develop large-scale enterprise applications, to enhance the functionality of Web servers, to provide applications for consumer devices and for many other purposes.

- Visual C# was created by Microsoft specifically for the .NET platform. Like Visual Basic, Visual C# is object-oriented and contains a powerful class library of prebuilt components (i.e., the Framework Class Library), enabling programmers to develop applications quickly.

Section 1.11 Other High-Level Languages

- Fortran (FORmula TRANslator) was developed by IBM Corporation in the mid-1950s for scientific and engineering applications that require complex mathematical computations.

- Pascal, named after the mathematician and philosopher Blaise Pascal, was designed for teaching structured programming in academic environments.

- COBOL (COmmon Business Oriented Language) was developed in the late 1950s. COBOL is used primarily for commercial applications that require precise and efficient data manipulation.

- Ada was developed under the sponsorship of the United States Department of Defense (DOD) through the early 1980s. An important capability of Ada is multitasking, which allows programmers to specify that many activities are to occur in parallel. The language was named after Lady Ada Lovelace, daughter of the poet Lord Byron. She is generally credited with writing the world's first computer program, in the early 1800s.

Section 1.12 The Internet and the World Wide Web

- The Internet—a global network of computers—was initiated almost four decades ago with funding supplied by the U.S. Department of Defense. Originally designed to connect the main computer systems of about a dozen universities and research organizations, the Internet today is accessible by hundreds of millions of computers worldwide.

- The World Wide Web allows computer users to locate and view multimedia-based documents on almost any subject over the Internet.

- In 1989, Tim Berners-Lee of CERN (the European Organization for Nuclear Research) began to develop a technology for sharing information via hyperlinked text documents. Berners-Lee called his invention the HyperText Markup Language (HTML).

- The World Wide Web Consortium (W3C) is devoted to developing nonproprietary, interoperable technologies for the World Wide Web. One of the W3C's primary goals is to make the Web universally accessible—regardless of disabilities, language or culture.

Section 1.13 Extensible Markup Language (XML)

- XML is a standardized, fully extensible and structurally strict language for describing data.

- Data independence, the separation of content from its presentation, is the essential characteristic of XML. Because XML documents describe data, any conceivable application can process them.

- The Simple Object Access Protocol (SOAP) is a technology for the transmission of objects (marked up as XML) over the Internet.

- Microsoft's .NET uses XML and SOAP to mark up and transfer data over the Internet. XML and SOAP are at the core of .NET—they allow software components to interoperate (i.e., communicate easily with one another).

Section 1.14 Microsoft's .NET

- In 2000, Microsoft announced its .NET initiative, a new vision for embracing the Internet and the Web in the development and use of software. One key aspect of .NET is its independence from a specific language or platform. Rather than being forced to use a single programming language, developers can create a .NET application in any .NET-compatible language.

- Microsoft's ASP.NET technology allows programmers to create applications for the Web.

- A key component of the .NET architecture is Web services, which are reusable application components that can be used over the Internet. Clients and other applications can use these Web services as reusable building blocks.

- The .NET strategy extends the concept of software reuse to the Internet, allowing programmers and companies to concentrate on their specialties without having to implement every component of every application. Instead, companies can buy Web services and devote their resources to developing their own products.

Section 1.15 The .NET Framework and the Common Language Runtime

- Microsoft's .NET Framework manages and executes applications and Web services, contains a class library called the Framework Class Library (FCL), enforces security and provides many other programming capabilities.

- The details of the .NET Framework are found in the Common Language Infrastructure (CLI), which contains information about the storage of data types, objects and so on.

- The Common Language Runtime (CLR) executes .NET programs.

- Programs are compiled into machine-specific instructions in two steps. First, the program is compiled into Microsoft Intermediate Language (MSIL), which defines instructions for the CLR.

- The Microsoft Intermediate Language (MSIL) defines instructions for the CLR.

- When an application executes, another compiler (known as the just-in-time compiler or JIT compiler) in the CLR translates the MSIL in the executable file into machine-language code (for a particular platform), then the machine-language code executes on that platform. This second compilation phase is known as just-in-time compilation.

- The Framework Class Library (FCL) can be used by any .NET language. It contains reusable components, saving programmers the trouble of creating new components.

Section 1.16 Test-Driving a Visual Basic Application

- You can use existing controls—which are objects—to get powerful applications running in Visual Basic much faster than if you had to write all of the code yourself.

- The default settings for controls are the initial settings you see when you first run the application. Programmers include default settings to provide reasonable choices which the application will use if the user chooses not to change the settings.

Section 1.17 (Only Required Section of the Case Study) Software Engineering Case Study: Introduction to Object Technology and the UML

- The Unified Modeling Language (UML) is a graphical language that allows people who build systems to represent their object-oriented designs in a common notation.

- Object-oriented design (OOD) models software components in terms of real-world objects. It takes advantage of class relationships, where objects of a certain class have the same characteristics. It also takes advantage of inheritance relationships, where newly created classes of objects are derived by absorbing characteristics of existing classes and adding unique characteristics of their own. OOD encapsulates data (attributes) and functions (behavior) into objects—the data and functions of an object are intimately tied together.

- Objects have the property of information hiding—objects of one class are normally not allowed to know how objects of other classes are implemented.

- Object-oriented programming (OOP) allows programmers to implement object-oriented designs as working systems.

- Visual Basic programmers concentrate on creating their own user-defined types called classes. Each class contains data as well as the set of methods that manipulate that data and provide services to clients (i.e., other classes or methods that use the class).

- The data components of a class are called attributes or fields. The operation components of a class are called methods.

- Classes can have relationships with other classes. These relationships are called associations.

- Packaging software as classes makes it possible for future software systems to reuse the classes. Groups of related classes are often packaged as reusable components.

- An instance of a class is called an object.

- With object technology, programmers can build much of the software they will need by combining standardized, interchangeable parts called classes.

- The process of analyzing and designing a system from an object-oriented point of view is called object-oriented analysis and design (OOAD).

Terminology

action
action oriented
Ada programming language
"administrative" section of the computer
arithmetic and logic unit (ALU)
ASP.NET
assembler
assembly language
association
attribute of a class
batch processing
behavior of an object
C programming language
C# programming language
C++ programming language
central processing unit (CPU)
class
class library
client of a class
client/server computing
COBOL programming language
Common Language Infrastructure (CLI)
Common Language Runtime (CLR)
compiler
component
computer
computer program
computer programmer
control
data
data independence

debugging
design
distributed computing
dynamic content
e-mail (electronic mail)
encapsulate
extensible
field of a class
file server
Fortran programming language
Framework Class Library (FCL)
function
hardware
hardware platform
high-level language
HTML (HyperText Markup Language)
HTTP (Hypertext Transfer Protocol)
information hiding
inheritance
input device
input unit
instantiate an object of a class
Integrated Development Environment (IDE)
interface
Internet
interpreter
Java programming language
job
just-in-time (JIT) compiler
language independence
language interoperability in .NET

live-code approach
local area network (LAN)
logical unit
machine dependent
machine language
"manufacturing" section of the computer
member function
memory
memory unit
method
Microsoft .NET
Microsoft Intermediate Language (MSIL)
Moore's Law
multiprocessor
multiprogramming
multitasking
multithreading
.NET Framework
.NET initiative
.NET-compliant language
nouns in a system specification
object
object oriented
object-oriented analysis and design (OOAD)
object-oriented design (OOD)
object-oriented programming (OOP)
operating system
operation of a class
output device
output unit
Pascal programming language
personal computer

personal computing
platform independence
portability
primary memory
procedural programming
"receiving" section of the computer
requirements
reusable software component
secondary storage unit
"shipping" section of the computer
SOAP (Simple Object Access Protocol)
software
software reuse
structured programming
supercomputer
task
throughput
timesharing
translation
translator program
UML (Unified Modeling Language)
user-defined type
Visual Basic programming language
Visual C# programming language
visual programming
W3C (World Wide Web Consortium)
Web service
Windows operating system
World Wide Web (WWW)
XML (Extensible Markup Language)
XML vocabulary

Self-Review Exercises

1.1   Fill in the blanks in each of the following statements:

a) Computers can directly understand only their native _____ language, which is composed only of 1s and 0s.

b) Computers process data under the control of sets of instructions called computer _____.

c) The _____ is the long-term, high-capacity "warehousing" section of the computer.

d) The three types of languages discussed in the chapter are machine languages, _____ and _____.

e) Programs that translate high-level language programs into machine language are called _____.

f) Visual Studio is a(n) _____ (IDE) in which Visual Basic programs are developed.

g) C is widely known as the development language of the _____ operating system.

h) Microsoft's _____ provides a large programming library for the .NET languages.

    i) The Department of Defense developed the Ada language with a capability called _____, which allows programmers to specify activities that can proceed in parallel. Visual Basic offers a similar capability called multithreading.

    j) Web services use _____ and _____ to mark up and send information over the Internet, respectively.

1.2 State whether each of the following is *true* or *false*. If *false*, explain why.

    a) The UML is used primarily to implement object-oriented systems.

    b) Visual Basic is an object-oriented language.

    c) To use a control in Visual Basic, you must write all of the code. This process can be time consuming.

    d) Visual Basic is the only language available for programming .NET applications.

    e) Procedural programming models the world more naturally than object-oriented programming.

    f) Computers can directly understand high-level languages.

    g) MSIL is the common intermediate format to which all .NET programs compile, regardless of their original .NET language.

    h) The .NET Framework is portable to non-Windows platforms.

    i) Compiled programs run faster than their corresponding interpreted programs.

    j) Multiprogramming involves the simultaneous operation of many jobs that are competing to share the computer's resources.

Answers to Self-Review Exercises

1.4 a) machine. b) programs. c) secondary storage unit. d) assembly languages, high-level languages. e) compilers. f) Integrated Development Environment. g) UNIX. h) Framework Class Library (FCL). i) multitasking. j) XML, SOAP.

1.5 a) False. The UML is used primarily to design object-oriented systems. b) True. c) False. Visual Basic allows you to use existing controls to get powerful applications running faster than if you had to write all of the code yourself. d) False. Visual Basic is one of many .NET languages (others are Visual C# and Visual C++). e) False. Object-oriented programming (because it focuses on *things*) is a more natural way to model the world than procedural programming. f) False. Computers can directly understand only their own machine languages. g) True. h) True. i) True. j) True.

Exercises

1.3 Categorize each of the following items as either hardware or software:

    a) CPU.

    b) Compiler.

    c) Input unit.

    d) A word-processor program.

    e) A Visual Basic program.

1.4 Translator programs, such as assemblers and compilers, convert programs from one language (referred to as the source language) to another language (referred to as the target language). Determine which of the following statements are *true* and which are *false*:

    a) A compiler translates high-level language programs into target-language programs.

    b) An assembler translates source language programs into machine language programs.

    c) A compiler converts source-language programs into target-language programs.

    d) High-level languages are generally machine dependent.

    e) A machine-language program requires translation before it can be run on a computer.

    f) The Visual Basic compiler translates high-level language programs into SMIL.

1.5   What are the basic requirements of a .NET language? What is needed to run a .NET program on a new type of computer (machine)?

1.6   Expand each of the following acronyms:
   a) W3C.
   b) XML.
   c) SOAP.
   d) OOP.
   e) CLR.
   f) CLI.
   g) FCL.
   h) MSIL.
   i) UML.
   j) OMG.
   k) IDE.

1.7   What are the key benefits of the .NET Framework and the CLR? What are the drawbacks?

1.8   List three examples of real-world objects that we did not mention. For each object, list several attributes and behaviors.

1.9   What are the advantages to using object-oriented techniques?

1.10   You are probably wearing on your wrist one of the world's most common types of objects—a watch. Discuss how each of the following terms and concepts applies to the notion of a watch: object, attributes and behaviors.

1.11   What was the key reason that Visual Basic was developed as a special version of the BASIC programming language?

1.12   What is the key accomplishment of the UML?

1.13   What did the chief benefit of the early Internet prove to be?

1.14   What is the key capability of the Web?

1.15   What is the key vision of Microsoft's .NET initiative?

1.16   How does the FCL facilitate the development of .NET applications?

1.17   What are Web services and why are they so crucial to Microsoft's .NET strategy?

1.18   What is the key advantage of standardizing .NET's CLI (Common Language Infrastructure) with Ecma?

1.19   Why is programming in an object-oriented language such as Visual Basic more "natural" than programming in a procedural programming language such as C?

1.20   Despite the obvious benefits of reuse made possible by OOP, what do many organizations report as the key benefit of OOP?

1.21   Why is Visual Basic said to be an event-driven language?

1.22   Why is XML so crucial to the development of future software systems?

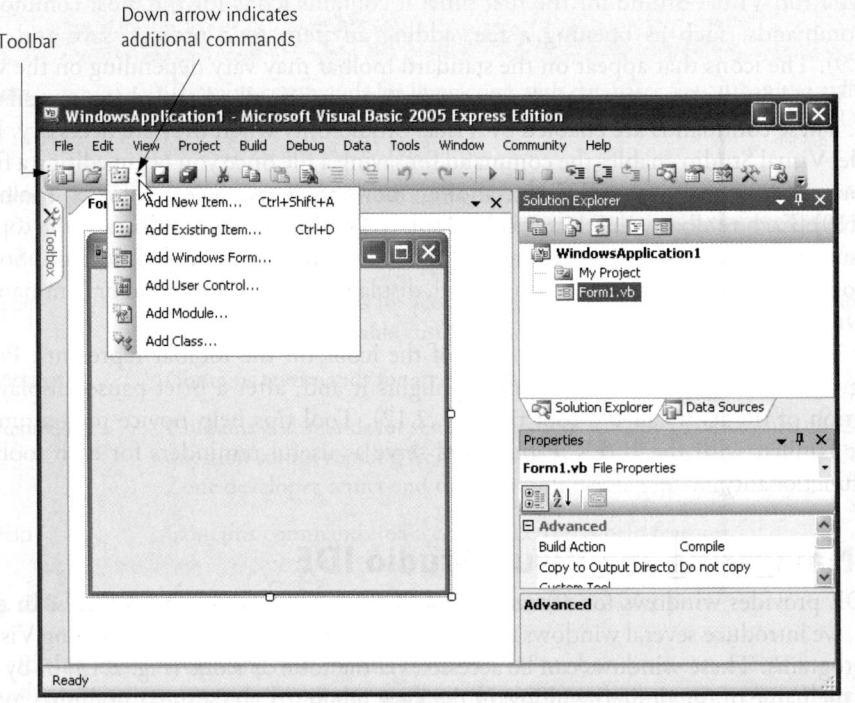

Fig. 2.11 | IDE toolbar icon showing additional command.

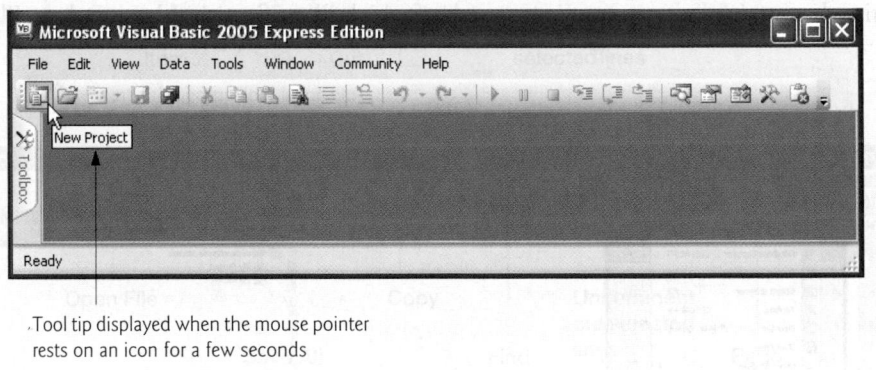

Fig. 2.12 | Tool tip demonstration.

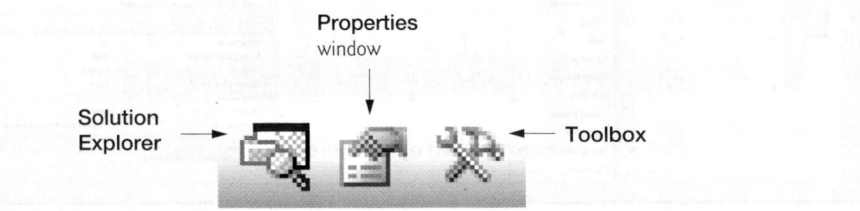

Fig. 2.13 | Toolbar icons for three Visual Studio windows.

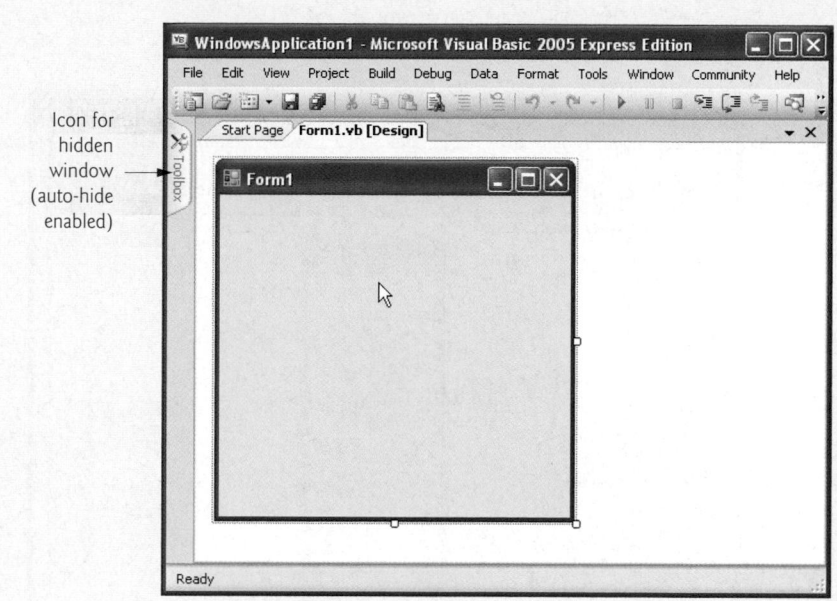

Icon for hidden window (auto-hide enabled)

Fig. 2.14 | Auto-hide feature demonstration.

the mouse pointer over one of these icons displays that window (Fig. 2.15). The window is hidden again when the mouse pointer is moved outside the window's area. To "pin down" a window (i.e., to disable auto-hide and keep the window open), click the pin icon. When auto-hide is enabled, the pin icon is horizontal (Fig. 2.15); when a window is "pinned down," the pin icon is vertical (Fig. 2.16).

The next few sections overview three of the main windows used in Visual Studio—the **Solution Explorer**, the **Properties** window and the **Toolbox**. These windows show information about the project and include tools that help you build your programs.

2.4.1 Solution Explorer

The **Solution Explorer** window (Fig. 2.17) provides access to all of the files in a solution. If the **Solution Explorer** window is not shown in the IDE, you can display it by clicking the Solution Explorer icon in the IDE (Fig. 2.13), by selecting **View > Solution Explorer** or by typing *<Ctrl> <Alt> L*. When Visual Studio is first run, the **Solution Explorer** is empty; there are no files to display. Once you open a new or existing solution, the **Solution Explorer** displays the contents of the solution.

The solution's **startup project** is the project that runs when the program executes. If you have multiple projects in a given solution, you can specify the startup project by right-clicking the project name in the **Solution Explorer** window, then selecting the **Set as StartUp Project**. For our single-project solution, the startup project is the only project (in this case, **WindowsApplication1**) and the project name appears in bold text in the **Solution Explorer** window. We discuss only single-project solutions in this text. For programmers using Visual Studio for the first time, the **Solution Explorer** window lists only the **My Project** and **Form1.vb** files (Fig. 2.17). The **Solution Explorer** window includes a toolbar that contains several icons.

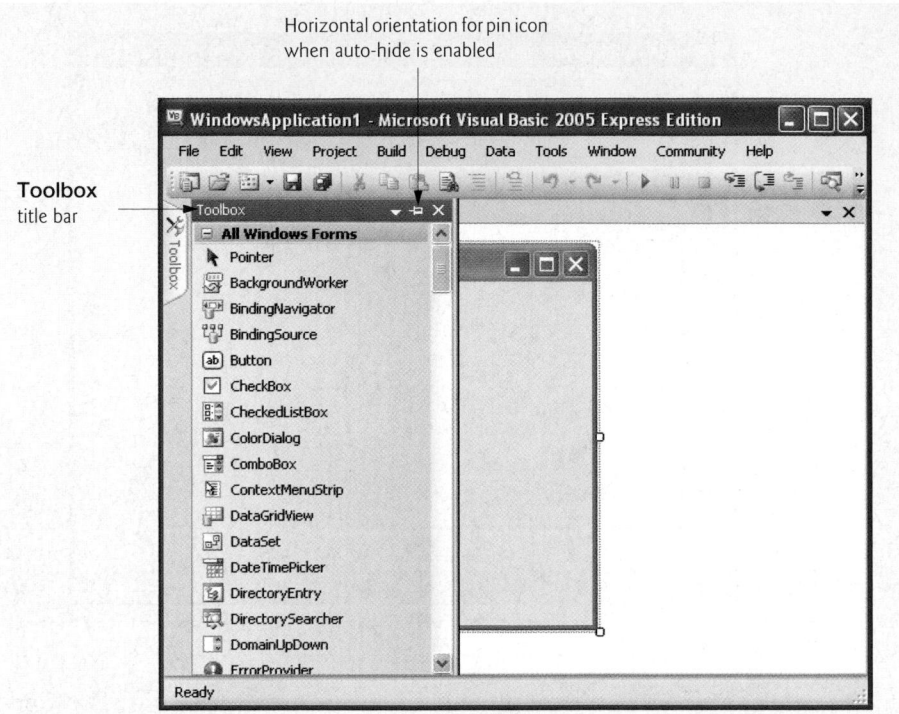

Fig. 2.15 | Displaying a hidden window when auto-hide is enabled.

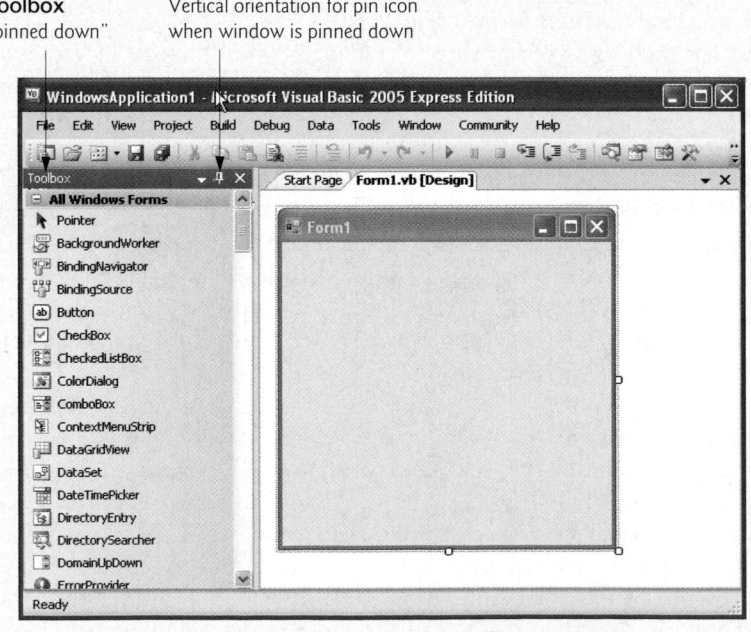

Fig. 2.16 | Disabling auto-hide ("pinning down" a window).

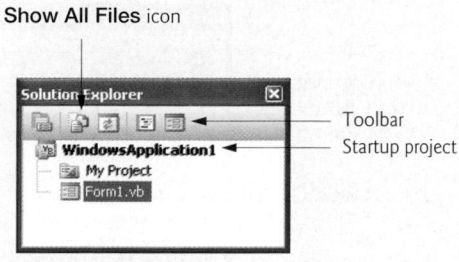

Fig. 2.17 | **Solution Explorer** with an open project.

The Visual Basic file that corresponds to the form shown in Fig. 2.4 is named Form1.vb (selected in Fig. 2.17). Visual Basic files use the .vb filename extension, which is short for "Visual Basic."

By default, the IDE displays only files that you may need to edit—other files generated by the IDE are hidden. When clicked, the Show All Files icon (Fig. 2.17) displays all the files in the solution, including those generated by the IDE (Fig. 2.18). The plus and minus boxes that appear can be clicked to expand and collapse the project tree, respectively. Click the plus box to the left of **My Project** to display items grouped under the heading to the right of the plus box (Fig. 2.19); click the minus box to collapse the tree from its expanded state (Fig. 2.20). Other Visual Studio windows also use this plus-box/minus-box convention.

2.4.2 Toolbox

The **Toolbox** contains icons representing controls used to customize forms (Fig. 2.21). Using visual programming, programmers can "drag and drop" controls onto the form, which is faster and simpler than building them by writing GUI code (we discuss writing this type of code in Chapter 5, Control Statements: Part 1). Just as you do not need to know how to build an engine to drive a car, you do not need to know how to build controls to use them. Reusing pre-existing controls saves time and money when you develop programs. You will use the **Toolbox** when you create your first program later in the chapter.

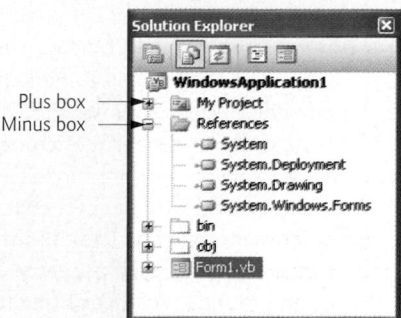

Fig. 2.18 | **Solution Explorer** showing plus boxes and minus boxes for expanding and collapsing the tree to reveal or hide project files.

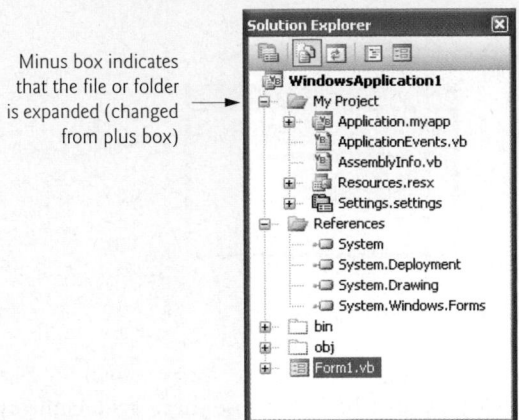

Minus box indicates that the file or folder is expanded (changed from plus box)

Fig. 2.19 | **Solution Explorer** expanding the **My Project** file after clicking its plus box.

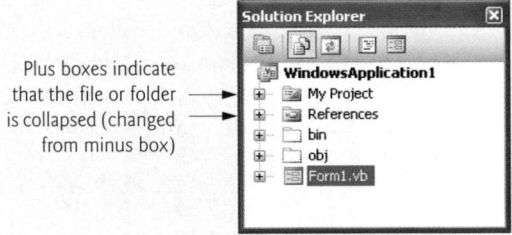

Plus boxes indicate that the file or folder is collapsed (changed from minus box)

Fig. 2.20 | **Solution Explorer** collapsing all files after clicking any minus boxes.

The **Toolbox** groups the prebuilt controls into categories—**All Windows Forms, Common Controls, Containers, Menus & Toolbars, Data, Components, Printing, Dialogs** and **General** are listed in Fig. 2.21. Again, note the use of plus and minus boxes which can expand or collapse a group of controls. We discuss many of the **Toolbox**'s controls and their functionality throughout the book.

2.4.3 Properties Window

To display the **Properties** window if it is not visible, select **View > Properties Window**, click the **Properties** window icon shown in Fig. 2.13, or press the *F4* key. The Properties window displays the properties for the currently selected Form (Fig. 2.22), control or file in design view. Properties specify information about the form or control, such as its size, color and position. Each form or control has its own set of properties; a property's description is displayed at the bottom of the **Properties** window whenever that property is selected.

Figure 2.22 shows Form1's **Properties** window. The left column lists the form's properties; the right column displays the current value of each property. You can sort the properties either alphabetically (by clicking the Alphabetical icon) or categorically (by clicking the Categorized icon). The properties can be sorted alphabetically from A–Z or Z–A; sorting by category groups the properties according to their use (i.e., **Appearance, Behavior, Design**, etc.). Depending on the size of the **Properties** window, some of the properties may

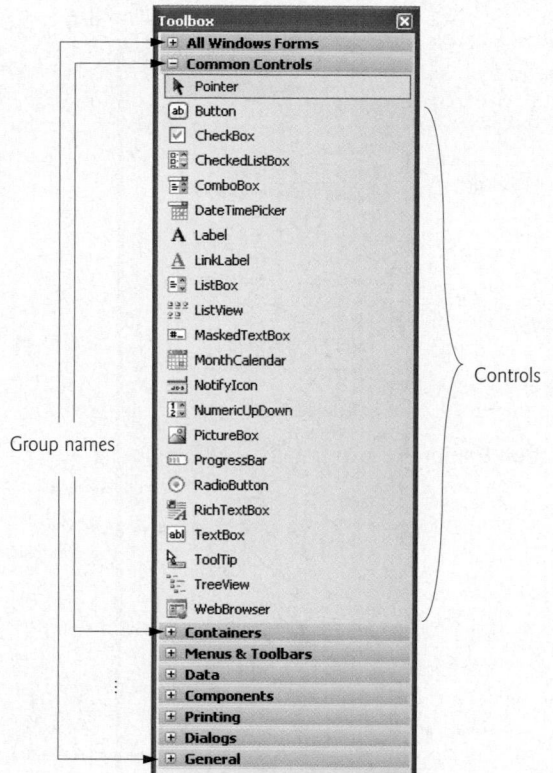

Fig. 2.21 | **Toolbox** window displaying controls for the **Common Controls** group.

be hidden from view on the screen. Users can scroll through the list of properties by dragging the scrollbox up or down inside the scrollbar, or by clicking the arrows at the top and bottom of the scrollbar. We show how to set individual properties later in this chapter.

The **Properties** window is crucial to visual programming; it allows you to modify a control's properties visually, without writing code. You can see which properties are available for modification and, in many cases, can learn the range of acceptable values for a given property. The **Properties** window displays a brief description of the selected property, helping you understand its purpose. A property can be set quickly using this window and no code needs to be written.

At the top of the **Properties** window is the component selection drop-down list, which allows you to select the form or control whose properties you wish to display in the **Properties** window (Fig. 2.22). Using the component selection drop-down list is an alternative way to display a form's or control's properties without selecting the actual form or control in the GUI.

2.5 Using Help

Visual Studio provides extensive help features. The Help menu commands are summarized in Fig. 2.23.

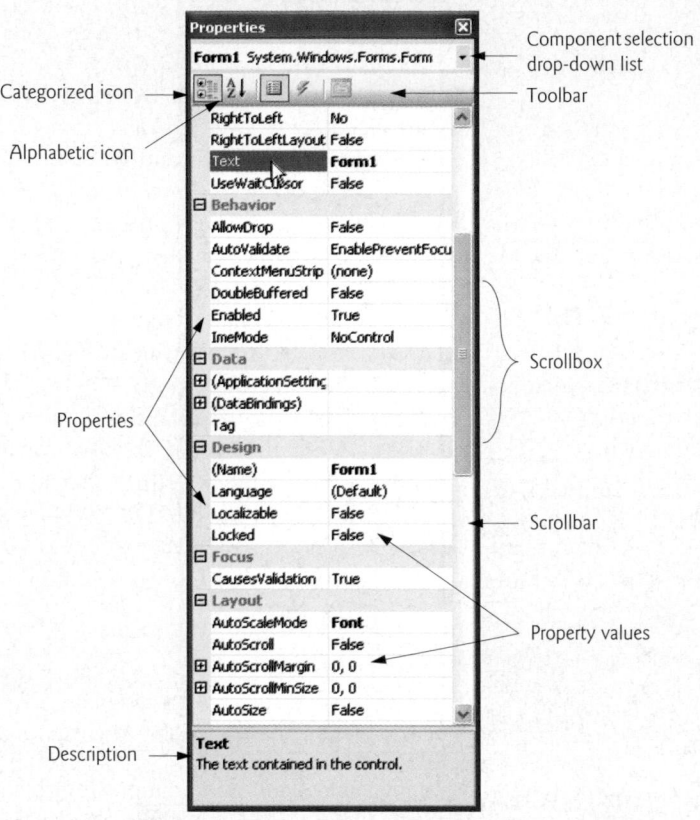

Fig. 2.22 | **Properties** window.

Command	Description
How Do I?	Contains links to relevant topics, including how to upgrade programs and learn more about Web services, architecture and design, files and I/O, data, debugging and more.
Search	Finds help articles based on search keywords.
Index	Displays an alphabetized list of topics you can browse.
Contents	Displays a categorized table of contents in which help articles are organized by topic.

Fig. 2.23 | **Help** menu commands.

Dynamic help (Fig. 2.24) is an excellent way to get information quickly about the IDE and its features. It provides a list of articles pertaining to the "current content" (i.e., the items around the location of the mouse cursor). To open the **Dynamic Help** window, select **Help > Dynamic Help**. Then, when you click a word or component (such as a form or a control), links to relevant help articles appear in the **Dynamic Help** window. The window lists help topics, code samples and "Getting Started" information. There is also a toolbar that provides access to the **How Do I?**, **Search**, **Index** and **Contents** help features.

Visual Studio also provides **context-sensitive help**, which is similar to dynamic help, except that it immediately displays a relevant help article rather than presenting a list of articles. To use context-sensitive help, click an item, such as the form, and press the *F1* key. Figure 2.25 displays help articles related to a form.

The **Help** options can be set in the **Options** dialog (accessed by selecting **Tools > Options...**). To display all the settings that you can modify (including the settings for the **Help** options), make sure that the **Show all settings** checkbox in the lower-left corner of the dialog is checked (Fig. 2.26). To change whether the **Help** is displayed in the IDE window or in a separate window, select **Help** on the left, then locate the **Show Help Using:** drop-down list on the right. Depending on your preference, selecting **External Help Viewer** displays a relevant help article in a separate window outside the IDE (some programmers like to view Web pages separately from the project on which they are working in the IDE); selecting **Integrated Help Viewer** displays a help article as a tabbed window inside the IDE.

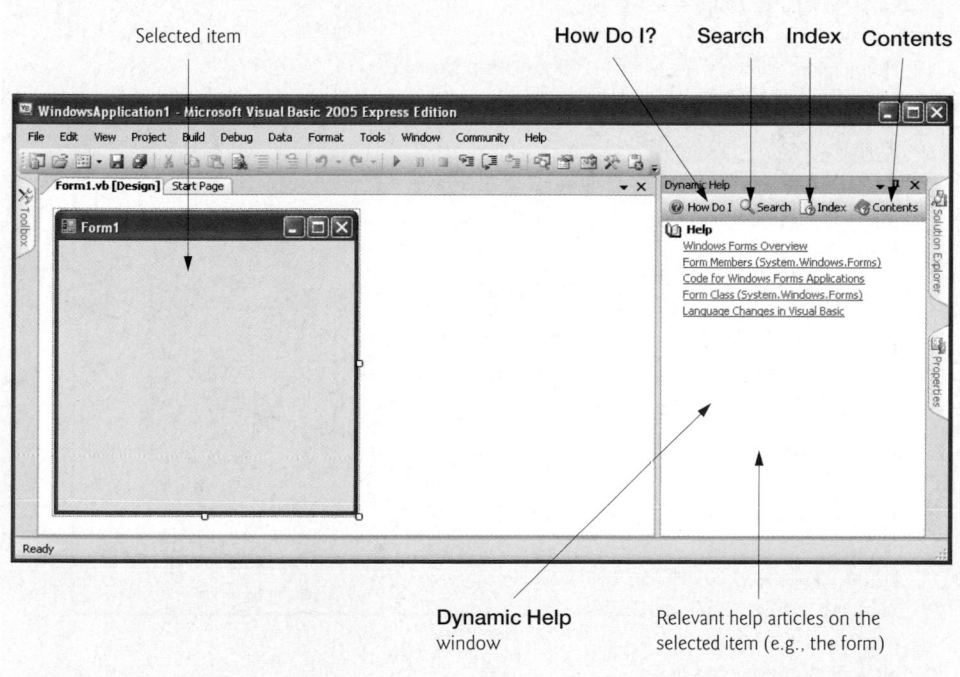

Fig. 2.24 | **Dynamic Help** window.

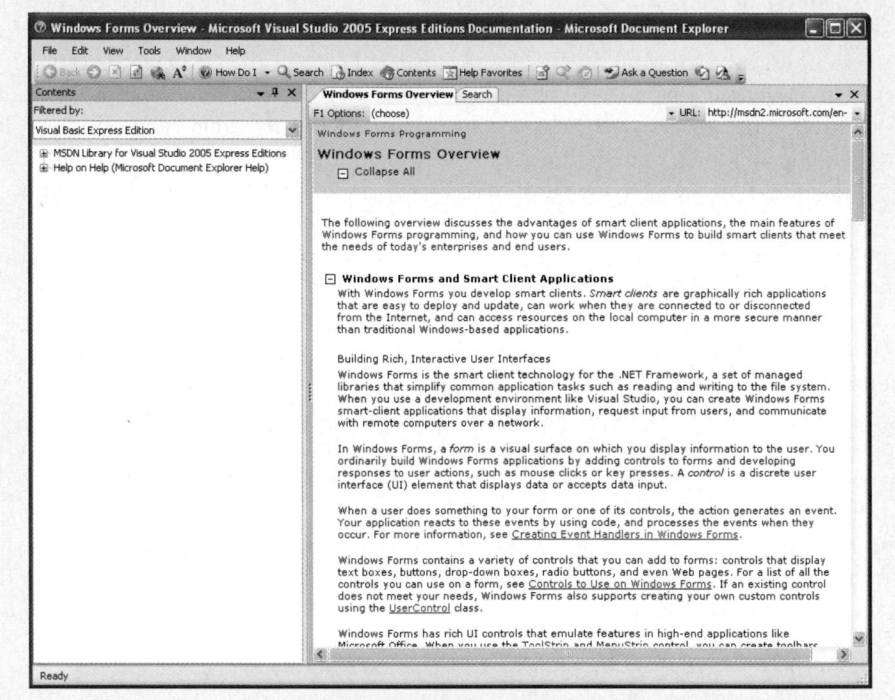

Fig. 2.25 | Using context-sensitive help.

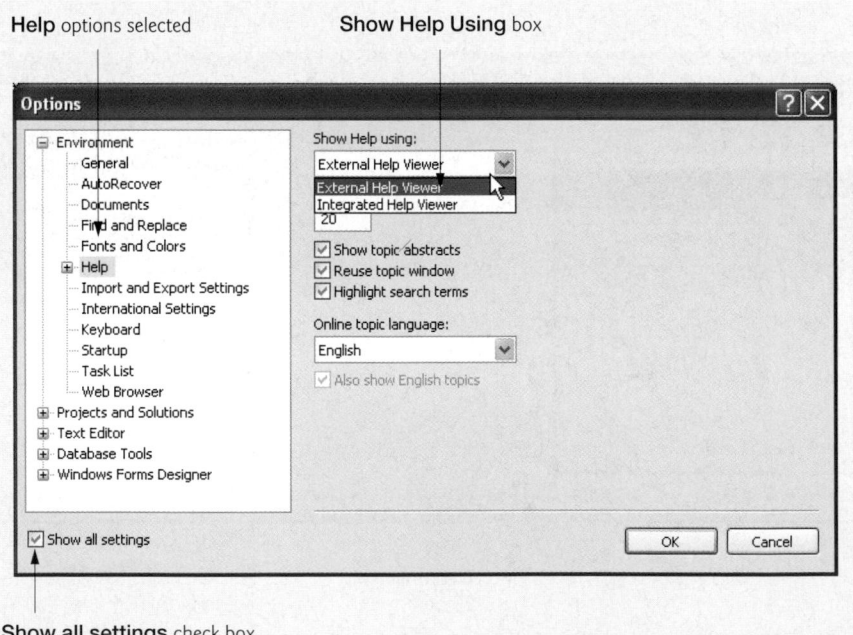

Fig. 2.26 | **Options** dialog displaying **Help** settings.

2.6 Using Visual Programming to Create a Simple Program that Displays Text and an Image

In this section, we create a program that displays the text "Welcome to Visual Basic!" and an image of the Deitel & Associates bug mascot. The program consists of a single form that uses a Label and a PictureBox. Figure 2.27 shows the result of the program as it executes. The program and the bug image are available with this chapter's examples. You can download the examples from www.deitel.com/books/vbhtp3/index.html. Please read the Before You Begin section of the *Preface* to ensure that you install the examples correctly on your computer.

To create the program whose output is shown in Fig. 2.27, you will not write a single line of program code. Instead, you will use the techniques of visual programming. Visual Studio processes programmer actions (such as mouse clicking, dragging and dropping) to generate program code. Chapter 3 begins our discussion of writing program code. Throughout the book, you produce increasingly substantial and powerful programs that usually include a combination of code written by you and code generated by Visual Studio. The generated code can be difficult for novices to understand—fortunately programmers rarely need to look at this code.

Visual programming is useful for building GUI-intensive programs that require a significant amount of user interaction. Visual programming cannot be used to create programs that do not have GUIs—you must write such code directly.

To create, run and terminate this first program, perform the following steps:

1. *Create the new project.* If a project is already open, close it by selecting **File > Close Solution**. A dialog asking whether to save the current project might appear. Click **Save** to save any changes. To create a new Windows application for the program, select **File > New Project...** to display the **New Project** dialog (Fig. 2.28). From the template options, select **Windows Application**. Name the project **ASimpleProgram** and click **OK**. [*Note:* File names must conform to certain rules. For example, file

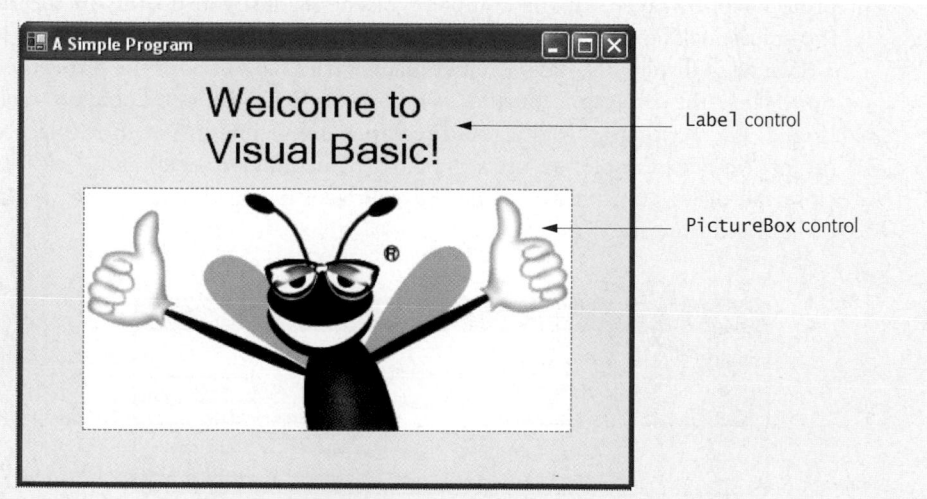

Fig. 2.27 | Simple program executing.

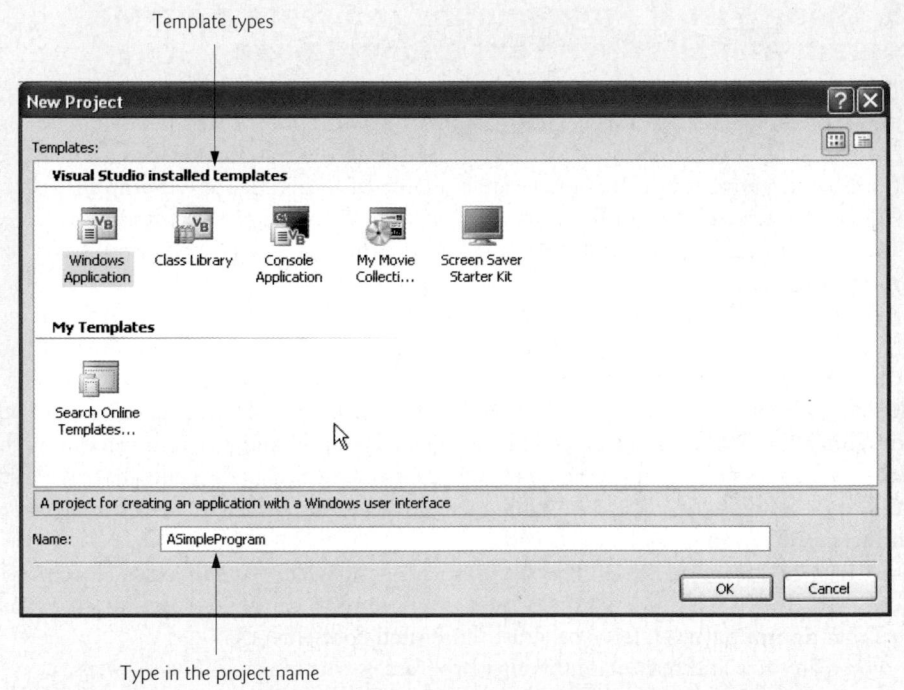

Fig. 2.28 | **New Project** dialog.

names cannot contain symbols (e.g., ?, :, *, <, >, # and %) or Unicode® control characters (Unicode is a special character set described in Appendix E). Also, file names cannot be system reserved names, such as "CON", "PRN", "AUX" and "COM1" or "." and "..", and cannot be longer than 256 characters in length.] We mentioned earlier in this chapter that you must set the directory in which the project will be saved. In the complete Visual Studio, you do this in the **New Project** dialog. To specify the directory in Visual Basic 2005 Express, select **File > Save All** to display the **Save Project** dialog (Fig. 2.29). To set the project location, click the **Browse...** button, which opens the **Project Location** dialog (Fig. 2.30). Navigate through the directories, select one in which to place the project (in our example, we use a directory named **My Projects**) and click **OK** to close the dialog. Click **Save** in the **Save Project** dialog (Fig. 2.29) to save the project and close the dialog.

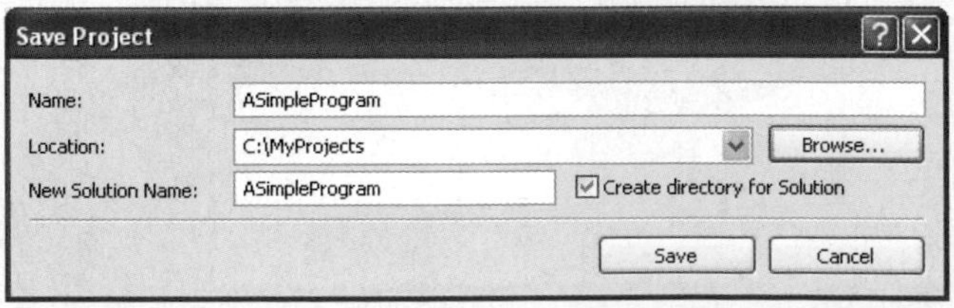

Fig. 2.29 | **Save Project** dialog.

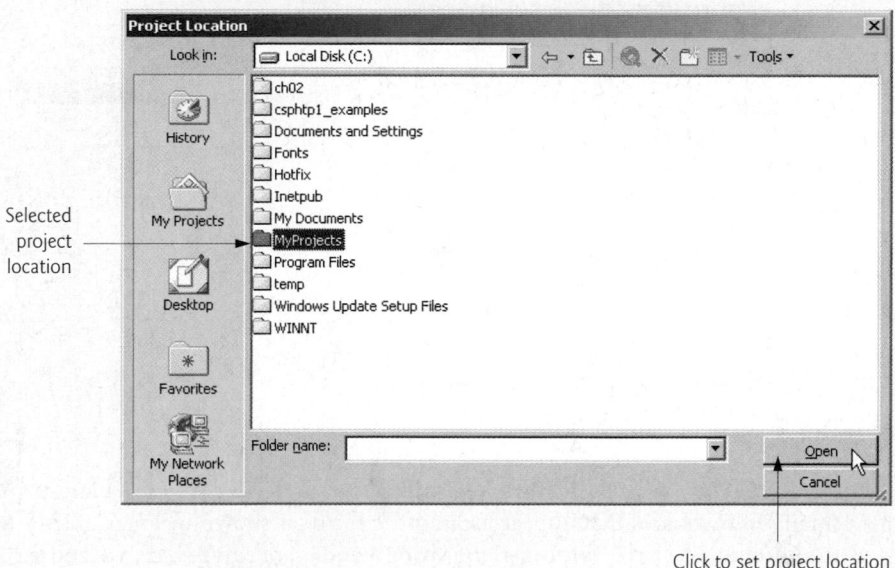

Selected
project
location

Click to set project location

Fig. 2.30 | Setting the project location in the **Project Location** dialog.

When you first begin working in the IDE, it is in **design mode** (i.e., the program is being designed and is not executing). While the IDE is in design mode, programmers have access to all the environment windows (e.g., **Toolbox, Properties**), menus and toolbars, as you will see shortly.

2. *Set the text in the form's title bar.* The text in the form's title bar is determined by the form's **Text property** (Fig. 2.31). If the **Properties** window is not open, click the properties icon in the toolbar or select **View > Properties Window**. Click anywhere in the form to display the form's properties in the **Properties** window. Click in the textbox to the right of the Text property box and type "A Simple Program," as in Fig. 2.31. Press the *Enter* key (*Return* key) when finished; the form's title bar is updated immediately (Fig. 2.32).

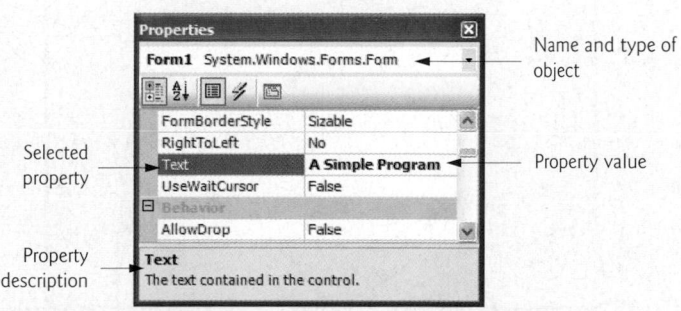

Name and type of
object

Selected
property

Property value

Property
description

Fig. 2.31 | Setting the form's Text property in the **Properties** window.

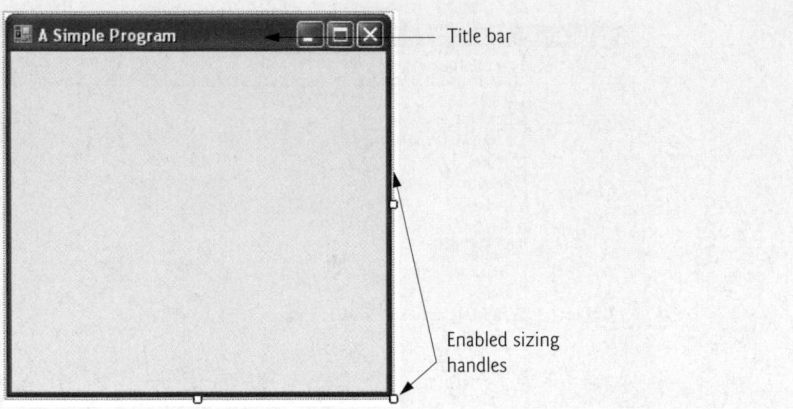

Fig. 2.32 | Form with enabled sizing handles.

3. *Resize the form.* Click and drag one of the form's **enabled sizing handles** (the small white squares that appear around the form, as shown in Fig. 2.32). Using the mouse, select the bottom-right sizing handle and drag it down and to the right to make the form larger (Fig. 2.33).

4. *Change the form's background color.* The **BackColor property** specifies a form's or control's background color. Clicking BackColor in the **Properties** window causes a down-arrow button to appear next to the value of the property (Fig. 2.34). When clicked, the down-arrow button displays a set of other options, which vary depending on the property. In this case, the arrow displays tabs for **Custom**, **Web** and **System** (the default). Click the **Custom tab** to display the **palette** (a grid of colors). Select the box that represents light blue. Once you select the color, the palette closes and the form's background color changes to light blue (Fig. 2.35).

Fig. 2.33 | Resized form.

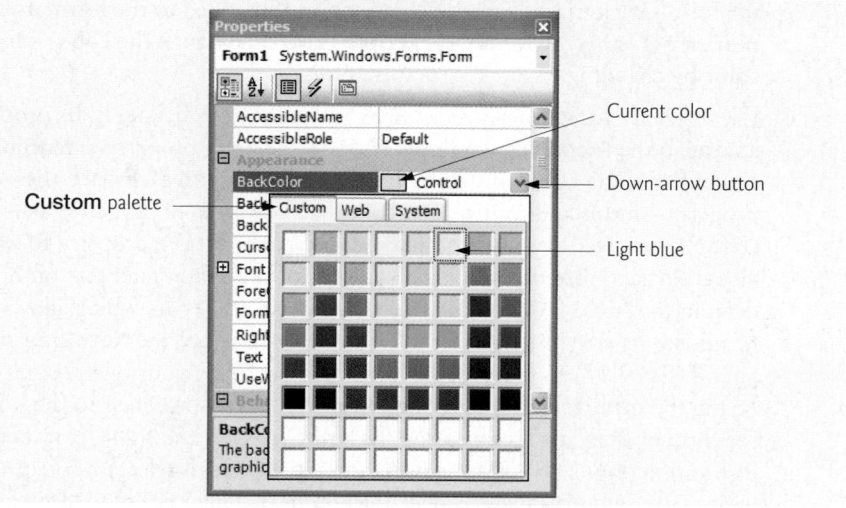

Fig. 2.34 | Changing the form's `BackColor` property.

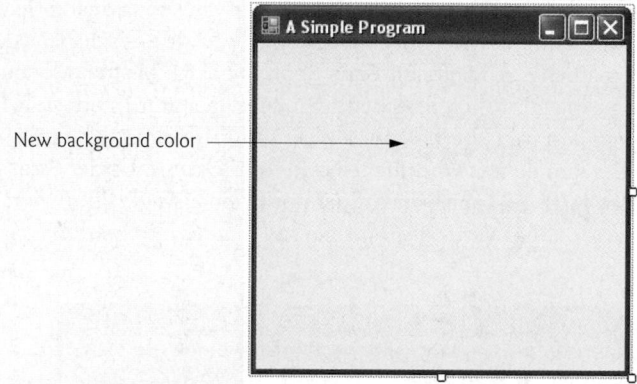

Fig. 2.35 | Form with new `BackColor` property applied.

5. *Add a Label control to the Form.* If the **Toolbox** is not already open, select **View > Toolbox** to display the set of controls you will use for creating your programs. For the type of program we are creating in this chapter, the typical controls we use will be located in either the **All Windows Forms** category of the **Toolbox** or the **Common Controls** group. If either group name is collapsed, expand it by clicking the plus sign (the **All Windows Forms** and **Common Controls** groups are shown in Fig. 2.21). Next, double click the `Label` control in the **Toolbox**. This action causes a label to appear in the upper-left corner of the form (Fig. 2.36). [*Note:* If the `Form` is behind the **Toolbox**, you may need to close the **Toolbox** to see the `Label`.] Although double clicking any **Toolbox** control places the control on the form, you also can "drag" controls from the **Toolbox** to the form (you may prefer dragging the control because you can position it wherever you want). Our `Label` displays the text **Label1** by default. Note that our `Label`'s background color is the same as

the form's background color. When a control is added to the form, its `BackColor` property is set to the form's `BackColor`. You can change the `Label`'s background color by changing its `BackColor` property.

6. *Customize the Label's appearance.* Select the `Label` by clicking it. Its properties now appear in the **Properties** window. The `Label`'s `Text` property determines the text (if any) that the `Label` displays. The form and `Label` each have their own `Text` property—forms and controls can have the same types of properties (such as `Back-Color`, `Text`, etc.) without conflict. Set the `Label`'s `Text` property to **Welcome to Visual Basic!**. Note that the `Label` resizes to fit all the typed text on one line. By default, the `AutoSize property` of the `Label` is set to `True`, which allows the `Label` to update its size to fit all of the text if necessary. Set the `AutoSize` property to `False` (Fig. 2.37) so that you can resize the `Label` on your own. Resize the `Label` (using the sizing handles) so that the text fits. Move the `Label` to the top center of the form by dragging it or by using the keyboard's left and right arrow keys to adjust its position (Fig. 2.38). Alternatively, when the `Label` is selected, you can center the `Label` control horizontally by selecting **Format > Center In Form > Horizontally**.

7. *Set the Label's font size.* To change the font type and appearance of the `Label`'s text, select the value of the **Font property**, which causes an **ellipsis button** (⬚) to appear next to the value (Fig. 2.39). When the ellipsis button is clicked, a dialog that provides additional values—in this case, the **Font dialog** (Fig. 2.40)—is displayed. You can select the font name (e.g., **Microsoft Sans Serif, MingLiU, Mistral, Modern No. 20**—the font options may be different depending on your system), font style (**Regular, Italic, Bold**, etc.) and font size (**16, 18, 20**, etc.) in this dialog. The text in the **Sample** area provides sample text with the selected font settings. Under **Size**, select **24** points and click **OK**. If the `Label`'s text does not fit on a single line, it wraps to the next line. Resize the `Label` vertically if it's not large enough to hold the text.

Label control ———

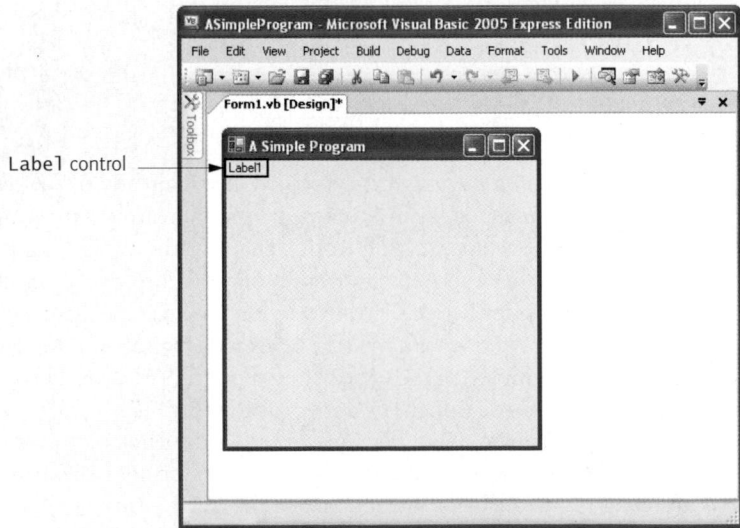

Fig. 2.36 | Adding a `Label` to the form.

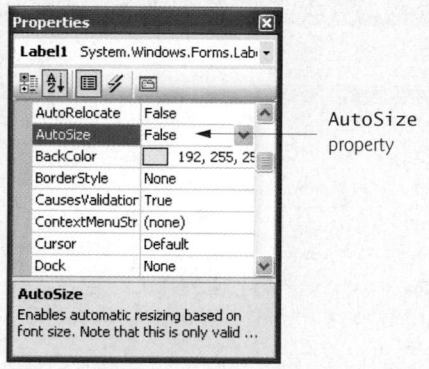

Fig. 2.37 | Changing the Label's AutoSize property to False.

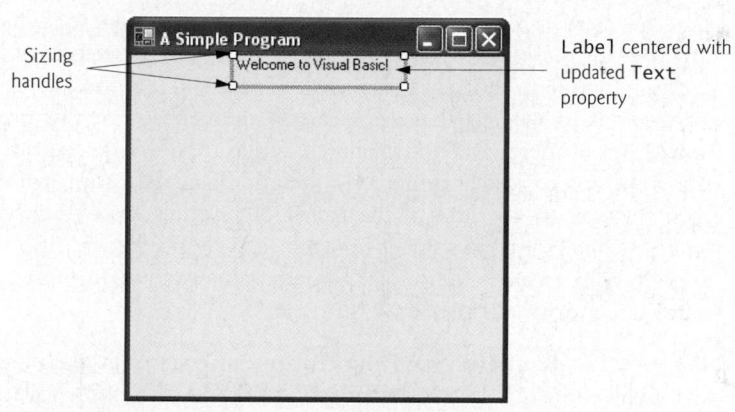

Fig. 2.38 | GUI after the form and Label have been customized.

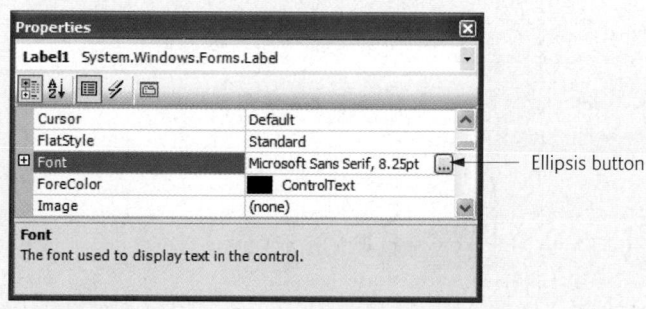

Fig. 2.39 | **Properties** window displaying the Label's properties.

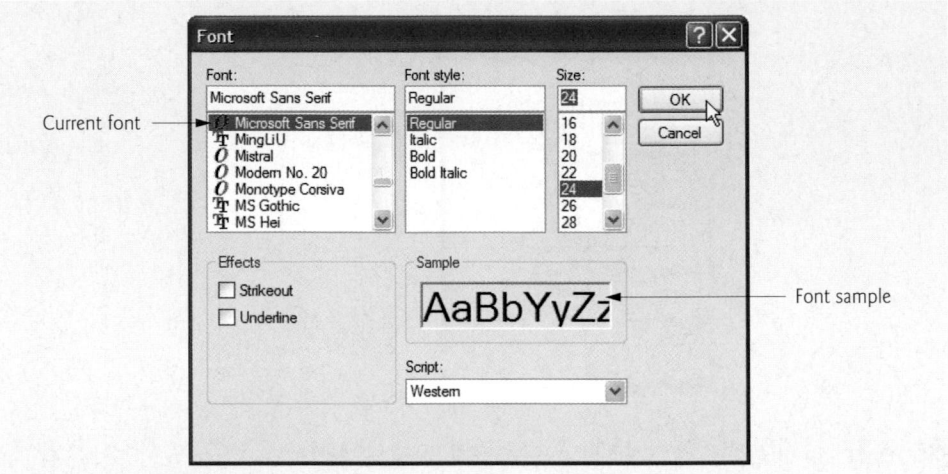

Current font

Font sample

Fig. 2.40 | **Font** dialog for selecting fonts, styles and sizes.

8. *Align the Label's text.* Select the Label's **TextAlign** property, which determines how the text is aligned within the Label. A three-by-three grid of buttons representing alignment choices is displayed (Fig. 2.41). The position of each button corresponds to where the text appears in the Label. For this program, set the TextAlign property to MiddleCenter in the three-by-three grid; this selection causes the text to appear centered in the middle of the Label, with equal spacing from the text to all sides of the Label. The other TextAlign values, such as TopLeft, TopRight, and BottomCenter, can be used to position the text anywhere within a Label. Certain alignment values may require that you resize the Label larger or smaller to better fit the text.

9. *Add a PictureBox to the form.* The PictureBox control displays images. The process involved in this step is similar to that of *Step 5*, in which we added a Label to the form. Locate the PictureBox in the **Toolbox** (Fig. 2.21) and double click it to add it to the form. When the PictureBox appears, move it underneath the Label, either by dragging it or by using the arrow keys (Fig. 2.42).

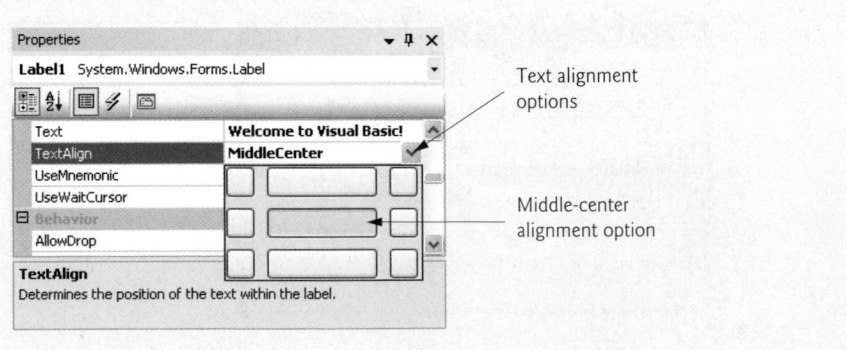

Text alignment options

Middle-center alignment option

Fig. 2.41 | Centering the Label's text.

Fig. 2.42 | Inserting and aligning a `PictureBox`.

10. *Insert an image.* Click the `PictureBox` to display its properties in the **Properties** window (Fig. 2.43). Locate the `Image property`, which displays a preview of the image, if one exists. No picture has been assigned, so the value of the `Image` property displays **(none)**. Click the ellipsis button to display the **Select Resource** dialog (Fig. 2.44). This dialog is used to import files, such as images, to any program. Click the **Import...** button to browse for an image to insert. In our case, the picture is `bug.png`. In the dialog that appears, locate the image file, select it and click **OK**. The image is previewed in the **Select Resource** dialog (Fig. 2.45). Click **OK** to place the image in your program. Supported image formats include PNG (Portable Network Graphics), GIF (Graphic Interchange Format), JPEG (Joint Photographic Experts Group) and BMP (Windows bitmap). Creating a new image requires image-editing software, such as Jasc® Paint Shop Pro™ (www.jasc.com), Adobe® Photoshop™ Elements (www.adobe.com) or Microsoft Paint (provided with Windows). To size the image to the `PictureBox`, change the `SizeMode property` to `StretchImage` (Fig. 2.46), which scales the image to the size of the `PictureBox`. Resize the `PictureBox`, making it larger (Fig. 2.47).

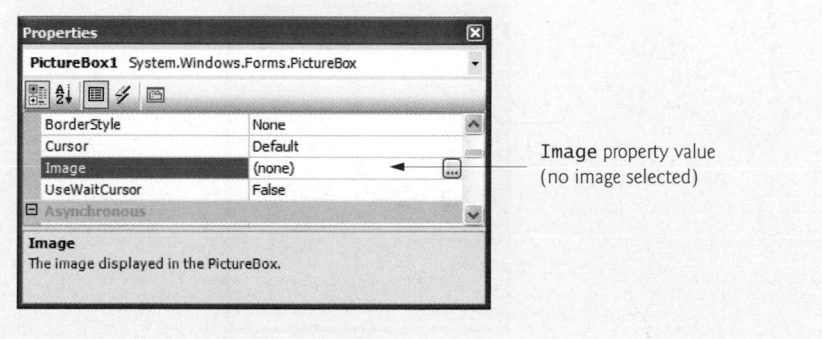

Fig. 2.43 | `Image` property of the `PictureBox`.

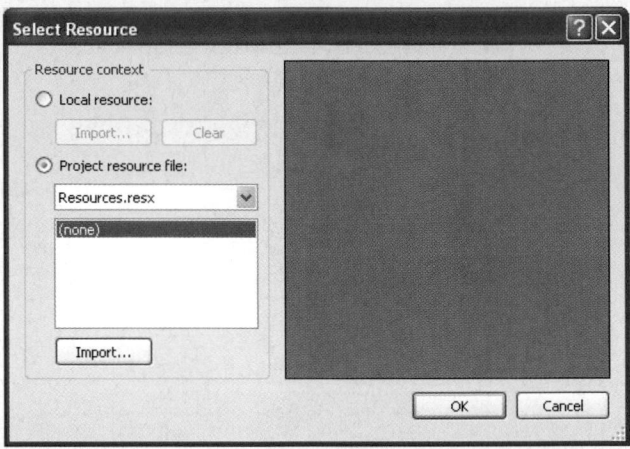

Fig. 2.44 | **Select Resource** dialog to select an image for the PictureBox.

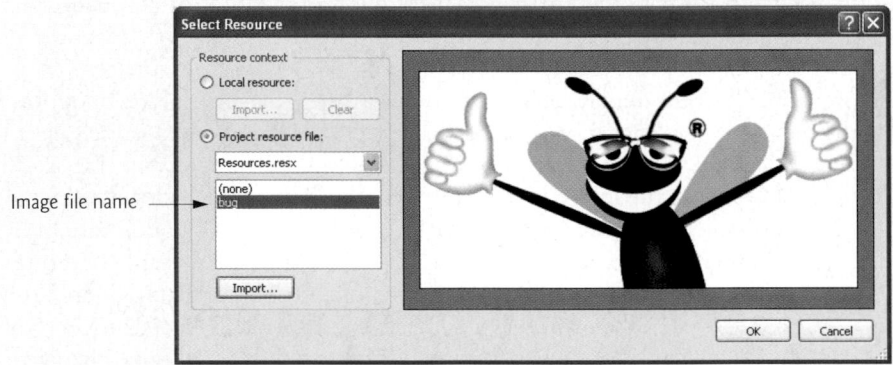

Image file name

Fig. 2.45 | **Select Resource** dialog displaying a preview of selected image.

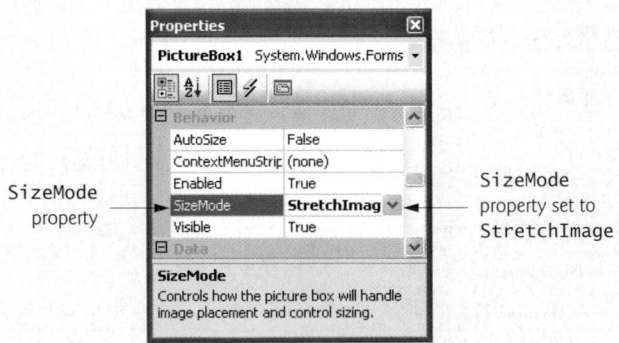

SizeMode property

SizeMode property set to StretchImage

Fig. 2.46 | Scaling an image to the size of the PictureBox.

Fig. 2.47 | `PictureBox` displaying an image.

11. *Save the project.* Select **File > Save All** to save the entire solution. The solution file contains the name and location of its project, and the project file contains the names and locations of all the files in the project.

12. *Run the project.* Recall that up to this point we have been working in the IDE design mode (i.e., the program being created is not executing). In **run mode**, the program is executing, and you can interact with only a few IDE features—features that are not available are disabled (grayed out). The text **Form1.vb [Design]*** in the project tab (Fig. 2.48) means that we are designing the form visually rather

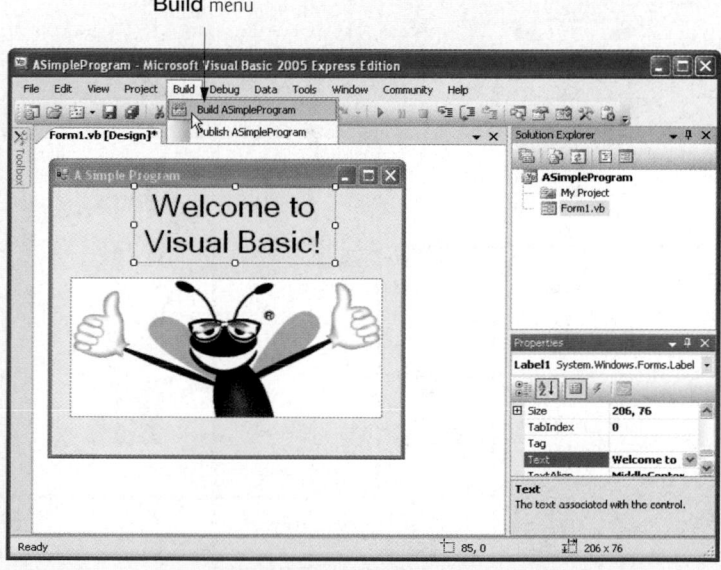

Fig. 2.48 | Building a solution.

than programmatically. If we had been writing code, the tab would have contained only the text **Form1.vb**. The * at the end of the text in the tab indicates that the file has been changed and should be saved. To run the program you must first build the solution. Select **Build > Build ASimpleProgram** to compile the project (Fig. 2.48). Once you build the solution (the IDE will display "**Build succeeded**" in the lower-left corner—also known as the status bar), select **Debug > Start Debugging** to execute the program (or you can select the *F5* key). Figure 2.49 shows the IDE in run mode (indicated by the title bar text **A Simple Program (Running) – Microsoft Visual Basic 2005 Express Edition**). Note that many toolbar icons and menus are disabled since they cannot be used while the program is running. The running program will appear in a separate window outside the IDE as shown in the lower-right portion of Fig. 2.49.

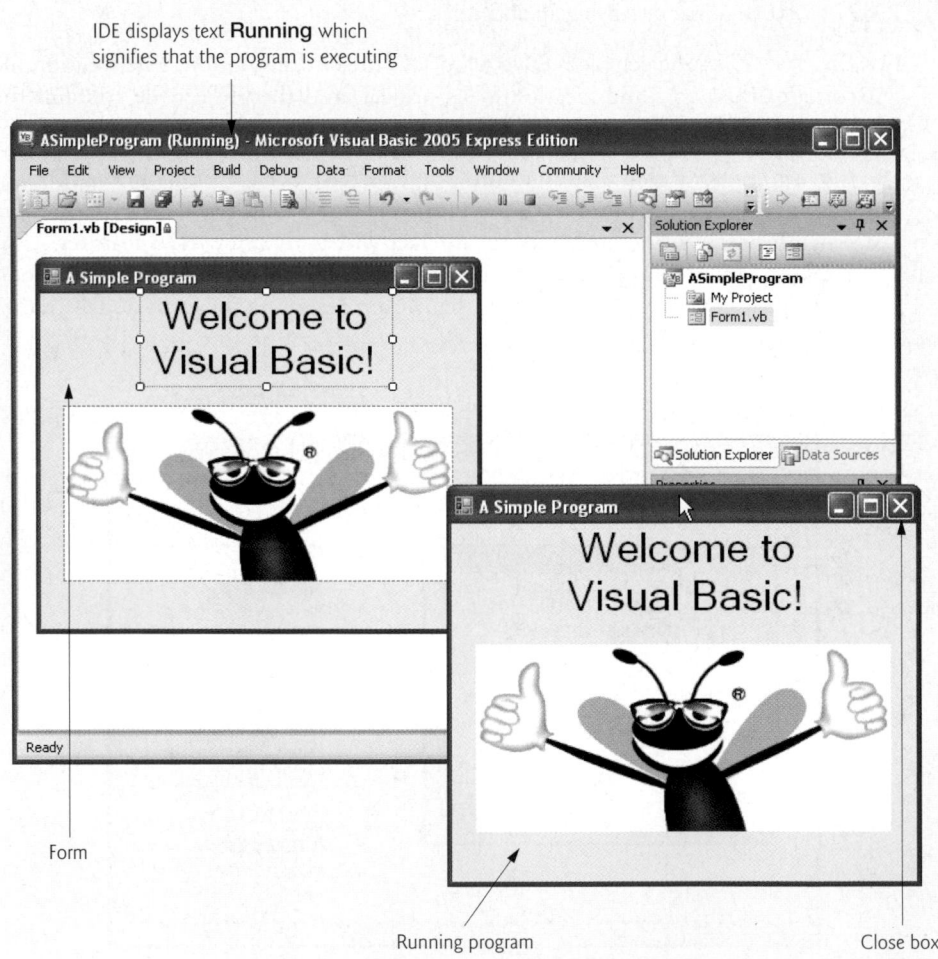

Fig. 2.49 | IDE in run mode, with the running program in the foreground.

13. *Terminate execution.* Click the running program's close box (the **X** in the top-right corner of the running program's window). This action stops the program's execution and returns the IDE to design mode.

2.7 Wrap-Up

In this chapter, we introduced key features of the Visual Studio Integrated Development Environment (IDE). You used the technique of visual programming to create a working Visual Basic program without writing a single line of code. Visual Basic programming is a mixture of the two styles—visual programming allows you to develop GUIs easily and avoid tedious GUI programming; conventional programming (which we introduce in Chapter 3) allows to specify the behavior of your programs.

You created a Visual Basic Windows application with one form. You worked with the **Solution Explorer**, **Toolbox** and **Properties** windows, which are essential to developing Visual Basic programs. The **Solution Explorer** window allows you to manage your solution's files visually. The **Toolbox** window contains a rich collection of controls for creating GUIs. The **Properties** window allows you to set the attributes of a form and controls.

You explored Visual Studio's help features, including the **Dynamic Help** window and the **Help** menu. The **Dynamic Help** window displays links related to the item that you select with the mouse. You also learned how to set **Help** options to display help resources internally or externally in a Web browser. We also demonstrated context-sensitive help.

You used visual programming to design the GUI portions of a program quickly and easily, by dragging and dropping controls (a `Label` and a `PictureBox`) onto a form or by double clicking controls in the **Toolbox**.

In creating the **ASimpleProgram** program, you used the **Properties** window to set the `Text` and `BackColor` properties of the form. You learned that `Label` controls display text and that `PictureBox`es display images. You displayed text in a `Label` and added an image to a `PictureBox`. You also worked with the `AutoSize`, `TextAlign` and `SizeMode` properties of a `Label`.

In the next chapter, we discuss "nonvisual," or "conventional," programming—you will create your first programs that contain Visual Basic code that you write, instead of having Visual Studio write the code. You will study console applications (programs that display only text and do not have a GUI). You will also learn memory concepts, arithmetic, decision making and how to use a dialog to display a message.

2.8 Web Resources

`msdn.microsoft.com/vstudio`
Microsoft's Visual Studio site provides news, documentation, downloads and other resources.

`msdn.microsoft.com/vbasic/default.aspx`
This site provides information on the newest release of Visual Basic, including downloads, community information and resources.

`www.worldofdotnet.net`
This site offers Visual Studio news and links to newsgroups and other resources.

`www.vbi.org`
This site contains articles, reviews of books and software, documentation, downloads, links and searchable information on Visual Basic listed by subject.

www.devx.com/vb

This site has a dedicated zone for Visual Basic developers; it contains articles, opinions, newsgroups, code, tips and other resources discussing Visual Basic 2005.

www.visualbasicforum.com

This forum provides Visual Basic developers the opportunity to post their thoughts to the Visual Basic community, including opinions on new features, issues encountered, resource links and more.

Summary

2.1 Introduction

- Visual Studio is Microsoft's Integrated Development Environment (IDE) for creating, running and debugging programs written in a variety of .NET programming languages.

- Creating simple programs by dragging and dropping predefined building blocks into place is called visual programming.

2.2 Overview of the Visual Studio 2005 IDE

- The **Start Page** contains a list of links to resources either within the Visual Studio 2005 IDE or on the Internet.

- A project is a group of related files, such as the Visual Basic code and any images that might make up a program.

- The Visual Studio 2005 IDE organizes programs into projects and solutions; a solution may contain one or more projects.

- Dialogs are windows that facilitate user-computer communication.

- Visual Studio provides templates for the project types available for users to create, including Windows applications and console applications.

- The **Form** represents the main window of the Windows application that you are creating.

- Collectively, the form and controls constitute the program's graphical user interface (GUI), which is the visual part of the program with which the user interacts.

2.3 Menu Bar and Toolbar

- Commands for managing the IDE and for developing, maintaining and executing programs are contained in the menus, which are located on the menu bar.

- Menus contain groups of commands (menu items) that, when selected, cause the IDE to perform actions (e.g., open a window, save a file, print a file and execute a program).

- Tool tips help you become familiar with the IDE's features.

2.4 Navigating the Visual Studio 2005 IDE

- The **Solution Explorer** window lists all the files in the solution.

- The **Toolbox** contains controls for customizing forms.

- By using visual programming, you can place predefined controls onto the form instead of writing the code yourself.

- Moving the mouse pointer over a hidden window's icon opens that window. When the mouse pointer leaves the area of the window, the window is hidden. This feature is known as auto-hide. To "pin down" a window (i.e., to disable auto-hide), click the pin icon.

- The **Properties** window displays the properties for a form or control (in design mode). Properties are information about a form or control, such as size, color and position. The **Properties** window allows you to modify controls visually, without writing code.

- Each control has its own set of properties. The left column of the **Properties** window shows the properties of the control; the right column displays property values. This window's toolbar contains options for organizing properties either alphabetically when the **Alphabetic** icon is clicked or categorically (e.g., **Appearance**, **Behavior**, **Design**) when the **Categorized** icon is clicked.

2.5 Using Help

- The **Help** menu contains a variety of options: The **How Do I?** menu provides specific resources to help users accomplish a given task, such as converting programs from Visual Basic 6, participating in community discussions, and so on. The **Contents** menu displays a categorized table of contents; the **Index** menu displays an alphabetical index that the programmer can browse; the **Search** menu allows programmers to find particular help articles, by entering search keywords.

- **Dynamic Help** provides a list of articles based on the current content (i.e., the items in the vicinity of the mouse pointer).

- Context-sensitive help is similar to dynamic help, except that it immediately brings up a relevant help article instead of a list of articles. To use context-sensitive help, click an item and press the *F1* key.

2.6 Using Visual Programming to Create a Simple Program Displaying Text and an Image

- Visual Basic programming usually involves a combination of writing a portion of the program code and having the Visual Studio generate the remaining code.

- The text that appears at the top of the form (the title bar) is specified in the form's `Text` property.

- To resize the form, click and drag one of the form's enabled sizing handles (the small squares around the form). Enabled sizing handles appear as white boxes.

- The `BackColor` property specifies the background color of a form. The form's background color is the default background color for any controls added to the form.

- Double clicking any **Toolbox** control icon places a control of that type on the form. Alternatively, you can drag and drop controls from the **Toolbox** to the form.

- The `Label`'s `Text` property determines the text (if any) that the `Label` displays. The form and `Label` each have their own `Text` property.

- A property's ellipsis button, when clicked, displays a dialog containing additional options.

- In the **Font** dialog, you can select the font for a form's or `Label`'s text.

- The `TextAlign` property determines how the text is aligned within a `Label`'s boundaries.

- The `PictureBox` control displays images. The `Image` property specifies the image to displayed.

- Select **File > Save All** to save the entire solution.

- A program that is in design mode is not executing.

- In run mode, the program is executing; you can interact with only a few IDE features.

- When designing a program visually, the name of the Visual Basic file appears in the project tab, followed by **[Design]**.

- Terminate execution by clicking the close box.

Terminology

active tab

Alphabetical icon

application

auto-hide

`AutoSize` property of `TextBox`

`BackColor` property of `Form`

background color
BMP (Windows bitmap)
Categorized icon
clicking with the mouse
close a project
collapse a tree
component selection
context-sensitive help
customize a form
Data menu
debug a program
Debug menu
design mode
dialog
double clicking
down arrow
dragging
dynamic help
Dynamic Help window
Edit menu
ellipsis button
expand a tree
external help
F1 help key
File menu
Font property of Label
font size
font style
Font window
form
Format menu
form's background color
form's title bar
GIF (Graphics Interchange Format)
graphical user interface (GUI)
Graphics Interchange Format (GIF)
GUI (graphical user interface)
Help menu
icon
IDE (Integrated Development Environment)
Integrated Development Environment (IDE)
Image property of PictureBox
input
internal help
Joint Photographic Experts Group (JPEG)
JPEG (Joint Photographic Experts Group)
Label
menu

menu bar in Visual Studio
menu item
Microsoft Developers Network (MSDN)
Microsoft Visual Basic 2005 Express Edition
mouse pointer
MSDN (Microsoft Developers Network)
New Project dialog
opening a project
output
palette
PictureBox
pin a window
PNG (Portable Network Graphics)
Portable Network Graphics (PNG)
project
Project Location dialog
Project menu
Properties window
property of a form or control
run mode
Save Project dialog
Select Resource dialog
Show All Files icon
selecting an item with the mouse
SizeMode property of PictureBox
sizing handle
solution
Solution Explorer in Visual Studio
Start Page
startup project
StretchImage value
tabbed window
Text property
TextAlign property of Label
title bar
tool tip
toolbar
toolbar icon
Toolbox
Tools menu
.vb file extension
View menu
visual programming
Visual Basic 2005 Express Edition
Visual Studio
Windows application
Windows menu

Self-Review Exercises

2.1 Fill in the blanks in each of the following statements:

a) The technique of _____ allows programmers to create GUIs without writing any code.

b) A(n) _____ is a group of one or more projects that collectively form a Visual Basic program.

c) The _____ feature hides a window when the mouse pointer is moved outside the window's area.

d) A(n) _____ appears when the mouse pointer hovers over an icon.

e) The _____ window allows programmers to browse solution files.

f) A plus box indicates that the tree in the **Solution Explorer** can _____.

g) The properties in the **Properties** window's can be sorted _____ or _____.

h) A form's _____ property specifies the text displayed in the form's title bar.

i) The _____ allows programmers to add controls to the form in a visual manner.

j) Using _____ displays relevant help articles, based on the current context.

k) The _____ property specifies how text is aligned within a Label's boundaries.

2.2 State whether each of the following is *true* or *false*. If *false*, explain why.

a) The title bar displays the IDE's mode.

b) The **X** box toggles auto-hide.

c) The toolbar icons represent various menu commands.

d) The toolbar contains icons that represent controls.

e) Both forms and Labels have a title bar.

f) Control properties can be modified only by writing code.

g) PictureBoxes typically display images.

h) Visual Basic files use the file extension .bas.

i) A form's background color is set using the BackColor property.

Answers to Self-Review Exercises

2.1 a) visual programming. b) solution. c) auto-hide. d) tool tip. e) **Solution Explorer**. f) expand. g) alphabetically, categorically. h) Text. i) **Toolbox**. j) **Dynamic Help**. k) TextAlign.

2.2 a) True. b) False. The pin icon toggles auto-hide. The **X** box closes a window. c) True. d) False. The **Toolbox** contains icons that represent controls. e) False. Forms have a title bar but Labels do not (although they do have Label text). f) False. Control properties can be modified using the **Properties** window. g) True. h) False. Visual Basic files use the file extension .vb. i) True.

Exercises

2.3 Fill in the blanks in each of the following statements:

a) When an ellipses button is clicked, a(n) _____ is displayed.

b) To save every file in a solution, select _____.

c) Using _____ help immediately displays a relevant help article. It can be accessed using the _____ key.

d) "GUI" is an acronym for _____.

2.4 State whether each of the following is *true* or *false*. If *false*, explain why.

a) A control can be added to a form by double clicking its control icon in the **Toolbox**.

b) The form, Label and PictureBox have identical properties.

c) If your machine is connected to the Internet, you can browse the Internet from the Visual Studio 2005 IDE.

    d) Visual Basic programmers usually create complex programs without writing any code.

    e) Sizing handles are visible during execution.

2.5   Some features that appear throughout Visual Studio perform similar actions in different contexts. Explain and give examples of how the plus and minus boxes, ellipsis buttons, down-arrow buttons and tool tips act in this manner. Why do you think the Visual Studio 2005 IDE was designed this way?

2.6   Fill in the blanks in each of the following statements:

    a) The _____ property specifies which image a `PictureBox` displays.

    b) The _____ menu contains commands for arranging and displaying windows.

    c) The _____ property determines a form's or control's background color.

2.7   Briefly describe each of the following terms:

    a) toolbar

    b) menu bar

    c) **Toolbox**

    d) control

    e) form

    f) solution

[*Note:* In the following exercises, you are asked to create GUIs using controls that we have not yet discussed in this book. The exercises will give you practice with visual programming only—the programs will not perform any actions. You will be placing controls from the **Toolbox** on a form to familiarize yourself with what each control looks like. We have provided step-by-step instructions for you. If you follow these, you should be able to replicate the screen images we provide.]

2.8   *(Notepad GUI)* Create the GUI for the notepad as shown in Fig. 2.50.

    a) *Manipulating the Form's properties.* Change the `Text` property of the `Form` to My Notepad.

    b) *Adding a MenuStrip to the Form.* After inserting the `MenuStrip`, add items by clicking the **Type Here** section, typing a menu name (e.g., **File**, **Edit**, **View** and **About**) and then pressing *Enter*.

    c) *Adding a RichTextBox to the Form.* Change the `Size` property to 267, 220 or use the sizing handles. Change the `Text` property to "Enter Text Here." Finally, set the `Location` property to 13, 34.

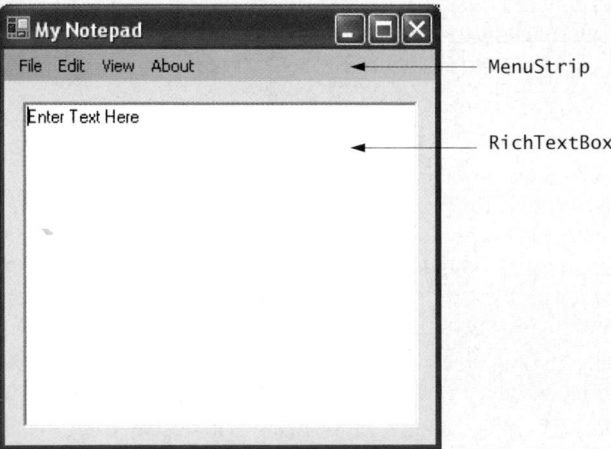

Fig. 2.50 | Notepad GUI.

2.9 *(Calendar and Appointments GUI)* Create the GUI for the calendar as shown in Fig. 2.51.

a) *Manipulating the Form's properties.* Change the Text property of the Form to My Scheduler. Set the Form's Size property to 332, 470.

b) *Adding Labels to the Form.* Add two Labels to the Form. Both should be of equal size (178, 21) and should be centered in the Form horizontally, as shown. Set the Label's Text properties to match the figure as shown, using 12-point font size. Also set the BackColor property to Yellow.

c) *Adding a MonthCalendar control to the Form.* Add this control to the Form and center it horizontally in the appropriate place between the two Labels.

d) *Adding a RichTextBox control to the Form.* Add a RichTextBox control to the Form and center it below the second Label. Resize the RichTextBox accordingly.

2.10 *(Calculator GUI)* Create the GUI for the calculator as shown in Fig. 2.52.

a) *Manipulating the Form's properties.* Change the Size property of the Form to 272, 192. Change the Text property of the Form to Calculator. Change the Font property to Tahoma.

b) *Adding a TextBox to the Form.* Set the TextBox's Text property in the **Properties** window to 0. Change the Size property to 240, 21. Set the TextAlign property to Right; this right aligns text displayed in the TextBox. Finally, set the TextBox's Location property to 8, 16.

c) *Adding the first Panel to the Form.* Panel controls are used to group other controls. Change the Panel's BorderStyle property to Fixed3D to make the inside of the Panel appear recessed. Change the Size property to 88, 112. Finally, set the Location property to 8, 48. This Panel contains the calculator's numeric keys.

d) *Adding the second Panel to the Form.* Change the Panel's BorderStyle property to Fixed3D. Change the Size property to 72, 112. Finally, set the Location property to 112, 48. This Panel contains the calculator's operator keys.

e) *Adding the third (and last) Panel to the Form.* Change the Panel's BorderStyle property to Fixed3D. Change the Size property to 48, 72. Finally, set the Location property to 200, 48. This Panel contains the calculator's **C** (clear) and **C/A** (clear all) keys.

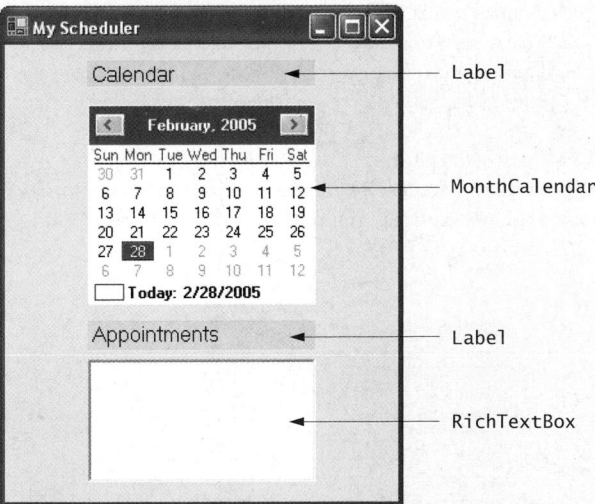

Fig. 2.51 | Calendar and appointments GUI.

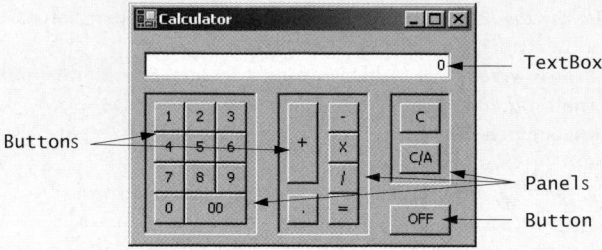

Fig. 2.52 | Calculator GUI.

f) *Adding Buttons to the Form.* There are 20 Buttons on the calculator. Add a Button to the Panel by dragging and dropping it on the Panel. Change the Text property of each Button to the calculator key it represents. The value you enter in the Text property will appear on the face of the Button. Finally, resize the Buttons, using their Size properties. Each Button labeled 0–9, x, /, -, = and . should have a size of 24, 24. The 00 and OFF Buttons have size 48, 24. The + Button is sized 24, 64. The C (clear) and C/A (clear all) Buttons are sized 32, 24.

2.11   *(Alarm Clock GUI)* Create the GUI for the alarm clock as shown in Fig. 2.53.

a) *Manipulating the Form's properties.* Change the Size property of the Form to 256, 176. Change the Text property of the Form to Alarm Clock. Change the Font property to Tahoma.

b) *Adding Buttons to the Form.* Add six Buttons to the Form. Change the Text property of each Button to the appropriate text. Change the Size properties of the **Hour**, **Minute** and **Second** Buttons to 56, 23. The **ON** and **OFF** Buttons get size 40, 23. The **Timer** Button gets size 48, 32. Align the Buttons as shown.

c) *Adding a Label to the Form.* Add a Label to the Form. Change the Text property to SNOOZE. Set its Size to 248, 23. Set the Label's TextAlign property to MiddleCenter. Finally, to draw a border around the edge of the **Snooze** Label, change the BorderStyle property of the **Snooze** Label to FixedSingle.

d) *Adding a GroupBox to the Form.* GroupBoxes are like Panels, except that GroupBoxes can display a title. Change the Text property to AM/PM, and set the Size property to 72, 72. To place the GroupBox in the correct location on the Form, set the Location property to 104, 38.

e) *Adding **AM/PM** RadioButtons to the GroupBox.* Change the Text property of one RadioButton to AM and the other to PM. Then place the RadioButtons as shown by setting the Location of the **AM** RadioButton to 16, 16 and that of the **PM** RadioButton to 16, 40. Set their Size properties to 48, 24.

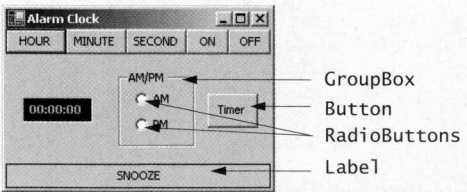

Fig. 2.53 | Alarm clock GUI.

f) *Adding the time* Label *to the Form.* Add a Label to the Form and change its Text property to 00:00:00. Change the BorderStyle property to Fixed3D and the BackColor to Black. Set the Size property to 64, 23. Use the Font property to make the time bold. Change the ForeColor to Silver (located in the **Web** tab) to make the time stand out against the black background. Set TextAlign to MiddleCenter to center the text in the Label. Position the Label as shown.

2.12   *(Radio GUI)* Create the GUI for the radio as shown in Fig. 2.54. [*Note:* All colors used in this exercises are from the **Web** palette and the image can be found in the examples folder for Chapter 2.]

a) *Manipulating the Form's properties.* Change the Form's Text property to Radio and the Size to 576, 240. Change the Font property to Tahoma. Set BackColor to PeachPuff.

b) *Adding the* **Pre-set** *Stations GroupBox and Buttons.* Set the GroupBox's Size to 232, 64, its Text to Pre-set Stations, its ForeColor to Black and its BackColor to RosyBrown. Change its Font to bold. Finally, set its Location to 24, 16. Add six Buttons to the GroupBox. Set each BackColor to PeachPuff and each Size to 24, 23. Change the Buttons' Text properties to 1, 2, 3, 4, 5, 6, respectively.

c) *Adding the* **Speakers** *GroupBox and CheckBoxes.* Set the GroupBox's Size to 160, 72, its Text to Speakers and its ForeColor to Black. Set its Location to 280, 16. Add two CheckBoxes to the Form. Set each CheckBox's Size to 56, 24. Set the Text properties for the CheckBoxes to Rear and Front.

d) *Adding the* **Power On/Off** *Button.* Add a Button to the Form. Set its Text to Power On/Off, its BackColor to RosyBrown, its ForeColor to Black and its Size to 72, 64. Change its Font style to Bold.

e) *Adding the* **Volume Control** *GroupBox, the* **Mute** *CheckBox and the* **Volume** *TrackBar.* Add a GroupBox to the Form. Set its Text to Volume Control, its BackColor to RosyBrown, its ForeColor to Black and its Size to 200, 80. Set its Font style to Bold. Add a CheckBox to the GroupBox. Set its Text to Mute and its Size to 56, 24. Add a TrackBar to the GroupBox.

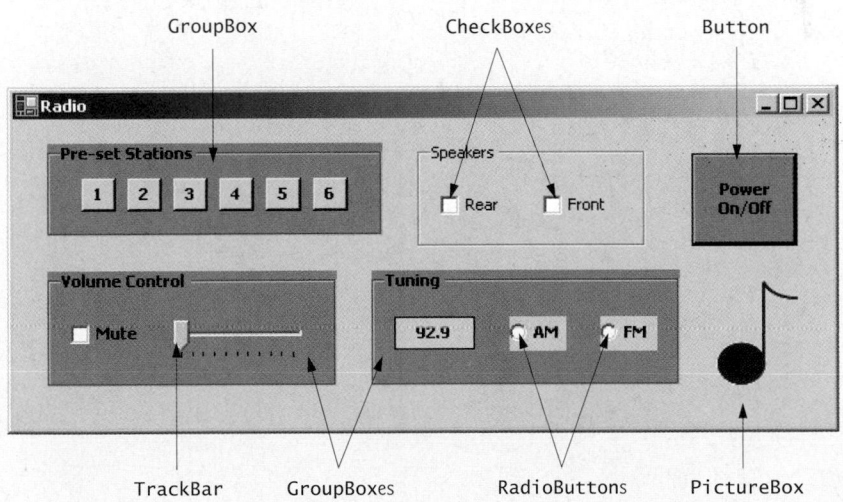

Fig. 2.54 | Radio GUI.

f) *Adding the* **Tuning** *GroupBox, the radio station* Label *and the* **AM/FM** *RadioButtons.* Add a GroupBox to the Form. Set its Text to Tuning, its ForeColor to Black and its BackColor to RosyBrown. Set its Font style to Bold and its Size to 216, 80. Add a Label to the Form. Set its BackColor to PeachPuff, its ForeColor to Black, its BorderStyle to FixedSingle, its Font style to Bold, its TextAlign to MiddleCenter and its Size to 56, 23. Set its Text to 92.9. Place the Label as shown in the figure. Add two RadioButtons to the GroupBox. Change the BackColor to PeachPuff and change the Size to 40,24. Set the Text of one to AM and the other's to FM.

g) *Adding the image.* Add a PictureBox to the Form. Set its BackColor to Transparent, its SizeMode to StretchImage and its Size to 56, 72. Set the Image property to Music-Note.gif (located in the examples folder for Chapter 2).

Introduction to Visual Basic Programming

Comment is free, but facts are sacred.

—C. P. Scott

When faced with a decision, I always ask, "What would be the most fun?"

—Peggy Walker

Equality, in a social sense, may be divided into that of condition and that of rights.

—James Fenimore Cooper

OBJECTIVES

In this chapter, you will learn:

- To write simple Visual Basic programs using code rather than visual programming.
- To write statements that input data from the keyboard and output data to the screen.
- To declare and use data of various types.
- To store and retrieve data from memory.
- To use arithmetic operators to perform calculations.
- To use the precedence of arithmetic operators to determine the order in which operators are applied.
- To write decision-making statements.
- To use equality and relational operators to compare operands.
- To use message dialogs to display messages.

3.1 Introduction

In this chapter, we introduce Visual Basic programming with program code and present examples to demonstrate how your programs can display messages and obtain information from the user at the keyboard for processing. The first two programs simply display text on the screen. The next obtains two numbers from the user, calculates their sum and displays the result. The accompanying discussion shows you how to perform various arithmetic calculations and save their results for later use. The fourth example demonstrates decision-making fundamentals by showing you how to compare two numbers in various ways, then display messages based on the comparison results. The final example demonstrates how to display text in a special window known as a message dialog.

We introduce console applications—that is, applications that do not have a graphical user interface. There are several types of Visual Basic projects (you have already seen Windows applications in Chapter 2); the console application is one of the simplest types. When a console application is executed in Visual Basic 2005 Express, its text output appears in the Console window. A console application can also be executed outside the IDE in a Windows Command Prompt. Programs can input and output information in a variety of ways. For example, in Chapter 2, we created a simple graphical user interface (GUI) for a Windows application, using visual programming techniques. We will briefly return to Windows applications in Chapter 5, Control Statements: Part 1 and Chapter 6, Control Statements: Part 2, respectively. These chapters provide a more detailed introduction to program development in Visual Basic. We discuss Windows applications in detail in Chapter 13, Graphical User Interface Concepts: Part 1 and Chapter 14, Graphical User Interface Concepts: Part 2.

3.2 Displaying a Line of Text

We begin by considering a simple program (Fig. 3.1) that displays a line of text. When this program runs, its output appears in a Command Prompt window. We show such output

```
 1   ' Fig. 3.1: Welcome1.vb
 2   ' Simple Visual Basic program.
 3
 4   Module FirstWelcome
 5
 6      Sub Main()
 7
 8         Console.WriteLine("Welcome to Visual Basic!")
 9
10      End Sub ' Main
11
12   End Module ' FirstWelcome
```

```
Welcome to Visual Basic!
```

Fig. 3.1 | Simple Visual Basic program.

in a blue box following the program listing. You will see exactly what a Command Prompt window looks like later in this section, when we guide you step-by-step through the process of creating a console application.

Analyzing the Program

This program illustrates several important Visual Basic features. For your convenience, all program listings in this text include line numbers—these are not part of the Visual Basic language. The line numbers help us refer to specific parts of a program. We will soon show how to display line numbers in program files. Each program is followed by one or more windows showing the program's execution output.

Line 1 of Fig. 3.1 begins with a single-quote character (') which indicates that the remainder of the line is a comment. Programmers insert comments in programs to improve the readability of the code—you can write anything you want in a comment. Comments can be placed either on their own lines (we call these "full-line comments") or at the end of a line of Visual Basic code (we call these "end-of-line comments"). The Visual Basic compiler ignores comments—they do not cause the computer to perform any actions when you run a program. The comment in line 1 simply indicates the figure number (Fig. 3.1) and the file name (Welcome1.vb) in which we stored this program. The comment in line 2 provides a brief description of the program. By convention, we begin every program in this manner (you can, of course, say anything you want in a comment).

Visual Basic console applications consist of pieces called modules, which are logical groupings of methods that simplify program organization. Lines 4–12 define our first module. These lines collectively are called a module declaration. We discuss the method in lines 6–10 momentarily—methods perform tasks and can return information when the tasks are completed. Every console application in Visual Basic consists of at least one module and one method in that module. In Chapter 7, Methods: A Deeper Look, we discuss methods in detail.

The word `Module` (line 4) is an example of a keyword. Keywords are words reserved for use by Visual Basic. A complete list of Visual Basic keywords is presented in Fig. 3.2. We discuss many of Visual Basic's keywords throughout this book. Visual Basic has a larger set of keywords than most other programming languages.

Visual Basic keywords

AddHandler	AddressOf	Alias	And
AndAlso	Ansi	As	Assembly
Auto	Boolean	ByRef	Byte
ByVal	Call	Case	Catch
CBool	CByte	CChar	CDate
CDbl	CDec	Char	CInt
Class	CLng	CObj	Const
Continue	CSByte	CShort	CSng
CStr	CType	CUInt	CULng
CUShort	Date	Decimal	Declare
Default	Delegate	Dim	DirectCast
Do	Double	Each	Else
ElseIf	End	Enum	Erase
Error	Event	Exit	False
Finally	For	Friend	Function
Get	GetType	Global	GoTo
Handles	If	Implements	Imports
In	Inherits	Integer	Interface
Is	IsNot	Lib	Like
Long	Loop	Me	Mod
Module	MustInherit	MustOverride	MyBase
MyClass	Namespace	Narrowing	New
Next	Not	Nothing	NotInheritable
NotOverridable	Object	Of	On
Operator	Option	Optional	Or
OrElse	Overloads	Overridable	Overrides
ParamArray	Partial	Preserve	Private
Property	Protected	Public	RaiseEvent
ReadOnly	ReDim	REM	RemoveHandler
Resume	Return	SByte	Select
Set	Shadows	Shared	Short
Single	Static	Step	Stop
String	Structure	Sub	SyncLock
Then	Throw	To	True
Try	TryCast	TypeOf	UInteger
ULong	Unicode	Until	UShort

Fig. 3.2 | Keywords in Visual Basic. (Part 1 of 2.)

Visual Basic keywords			
Using	When	While	Widening
With	WithEvents	WriteOnly	Xor

The following are retained as keywords, although they are no longer supported in Visual Basic 2005

EndIf	GoSub	Let	Variant	Wend

Fig. 3.2 | Keywords in Visual Basic. (Part 2 of 2.)

The name of the `Module`—`FirstWelcome` in line 4—is known as an identifier, which is a series of characters consisting of letters, digits and underscores (`_`). Identifiers cannot begin with a digit and cannot contain spaces. Examples of valid identifiers are `value1`, `FirstWelcome`, `xy_coordinate`, `_total` and `grossPay`. The name `7Welcome` is not a valid identifier because it begins with a digit, and the name `input field` is not a valid identifier because it contains a space.

Common Programming Error 3.1

Identifiers cannot be keywords, so it is an error, for example, to choose any of the words in Fig. 3.2 as a `Module` name. The Visual Basic compiler helps you locate such errors in your programs. Though keywords cannot be used as identifiers, they can be used in strings and comments.

Visual Basic keywords and identifiers are not case sensitive. This means that uppercase and lowercase letters are considered to be identical, which causes `firstwelcome` and `FirstWelcome` to be interpreted as the same identifier. Although keywords appear to be case sensitive, they are not. Visual Basic Express applies its "preferred" case (i.e., the casing used in Fig. 3.2) to each letter of a keyword, so when you type `module` and press the *Enter* key, Visual Basic changes the lowercase `m` to uppercase, as in `Module`, even though `module` would be perfectly correct.

Lines 3, 5, 7, 9 and 11 (Fig. 3.1) are blank lines. Blank lines, space characters and tab characters are used throughout a program to make it easier to read. Collectively, these are called whitespace characters. We use lots of blank lines in our early programs. We'll use fewer later in the book as you become more comfortable reading Visual Basic programs.

Good Programming Practice 3.1

Use whitespace to enhance program readability.

Line 6 is present in all Visual Basic console applications. These begin executing at `Main`, which is known as the entry point of the program. The keyword `Sub` that appears before `Main` indicates that `Main` is a method.

Note that lines 6–10 are indented three spaces relative to lines 4 and 12. Indentation improves program readability. We refer to spacing conventions that enhance program clarity as *Good Programming Practices*. We show how to set the indent size in Visual Basic Express shortly.

The keyword **Sub** (line 6) begins the body of the method declaration (the code that will be executed as part of our program). The keywords **End Sub** (line 10) close the method declaration's body. The keyword `Sub` is short for "subroutine"—an early term for method.

Note that the line of code (line 8) in the method body is indented three additional spaces to the right relative to lines 6 and 10. This emphasizes that line 8 is part of the `Main` method's body. We do this throughout the text to enhance readability. Again, the indentation is whitespace and is ignored by the compiler.

Good Programming Practice 3.2

Indent the entire body of each method declaration one additional "level" of indentation. This emphasizes the structure of the method, improving its readability. In this text, one level of indentation is set to three spaces—this keeps the code readable yet concise.

Using `Console.WriteLine` to Display Text

Line 8 in Fig. 3.1 does the "real work" of the program, displaying the phrase `Welcome to Visual Basic!` on the screen. Line 8 instructs the computer to perform an action—namely, to print (i.e., display on the screen) the series of characters contained between the double quotation marks. Characters and the surrounding double quotes are called strings, which also are called character strings or string literals.

The entire line, including `Console.WriteLine` and its string in the parentheses, is called a statement. When this statement executes, it displays (or prints) the message `Welcome to Visual Basic!` in the **Console** window (Fig. 3.1).

Note that `Console.WriteLine` contains two identifiers (i.e., `Console` and `WriteLine`) separated by the dot separator (`.`). The identifier to the right of the dot separator is the method name, and the identifier to the left of the dot separator is the class name to which the method belongs. Classes organize groups of related methods and data; methods perform tasks and can return information when the tasks are completed. For instance, the `Console` class contains methods, such as `WriteLine`, that communicate with users via the **Console** window. The statement in line 8 is known as a method call because it "calls" a method (i.e., method `WriteLine` of class `Console`) to ask the method to perform its task. Sometimes a method receives values, known as arguments, from its caller—it uses these arguments while performing its task. In Fig. 3.1, the string in parentheses in line 8 is the argument to method `WriteLine`. We discuss methods and classes in detail in Chapter 9.

When method `WriteLine` completes its task, it positions the output cursor (the location where the next output character will be displayed) at the beginning of the next line in the **Console** window. This behavior is similar to what happens when you press the *Enter* key when typing in a text editor window—the cursor is repositioned at the beginning of the next line. Program execution terminates when the program encounters the keywords `End Sub` in line 10. The `Module` is a package that contains the program's methods; the methods contain the statements that perform the actions of the program.

3.3 Creating Your First Console Application in Visual Basic Express

Now that we have presented our first console application (Fig. 3.1), we provide a step-by-step explanation of how to create and run it using Visual Basic 2005 Express.

Creating the Console Application

Select **File > New Project...** to display the **New Project** dialog (Fig. 3.3). Click **Console Application** to ensure that it is selected in the section labeled **Visual Studio installed templates**.

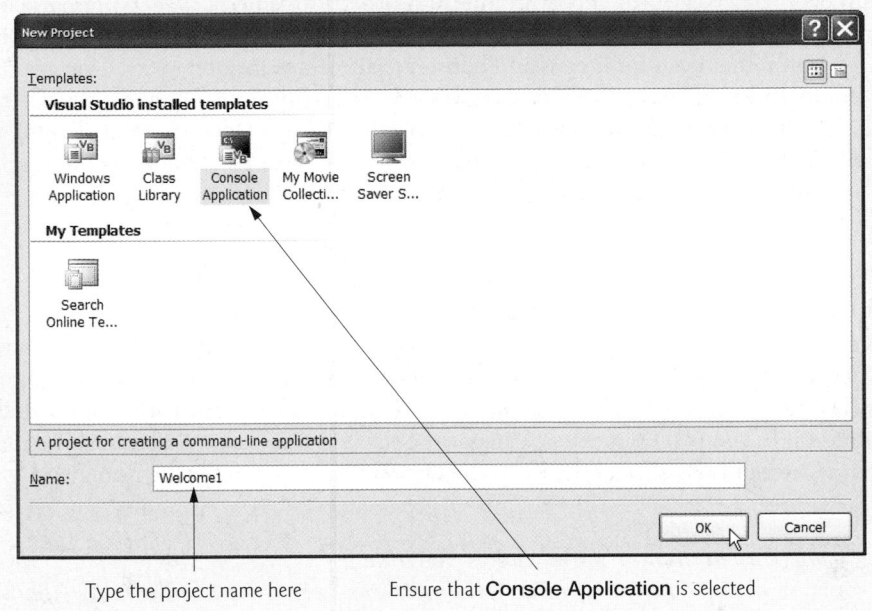

Type the project name here   Ensure that **Console Application** is selected

Fig. 3.3 | Creating a **Console Application** with the **New Project** dialog.

In the dialog's **Name** field, type `Welcome1`. Click **OK** to create the project. The IDE now contains the open console application, as shown in Fig. 3.4. Note that the editor window contains four lines of Visual Basic code provided by the IDE. The code coloring scheme used by the IDE is called syntax-color highlighting and helps you visually differentiate

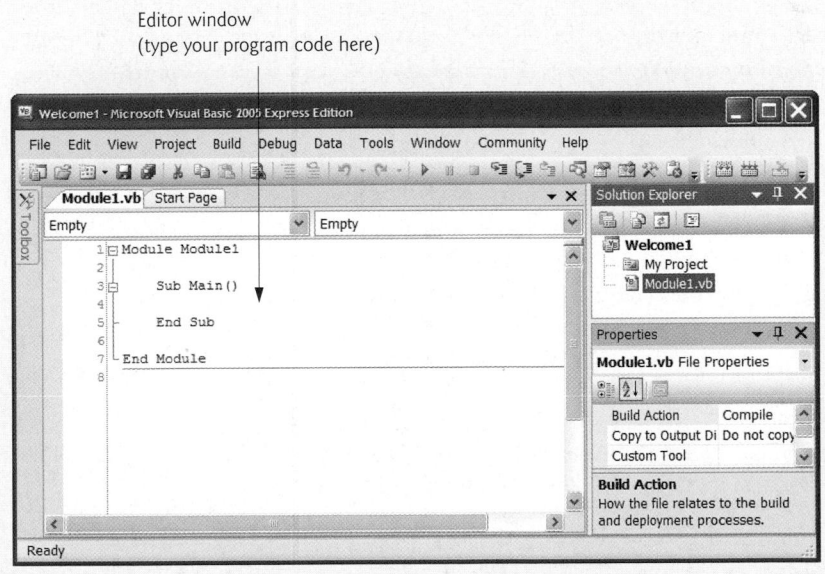

Fig. 3.4 | IDE with an open console application.

program elements. Keywords appear in blue and other text is black. When present, comments are colored green. In this book, we color our code similarly—blue for keywords, green for comments, cyan for literals and constants and black for other text. One example of a literal is the string passed to `Console.WriteLine` in line 8 of Fig. 3.1. You can customize the colors shown in the code editor by selecting **Tools > Options...** and clicking the **Show all settings** checkbox. Then click the plus sign, +, next to **Environment** and select **Fonts and Colors**. Here you can change the colors for various code elements.

Modifying the Editor Settings to Display Line Numbers
Visual Basic 2005 Express provides many ways to personalize your coding experience. In this step, we specify how to change the settings so that your code matches that of this book. To have the IDE display line numbers, select **Tools > Options....** In the dialog that appears (Fig. 3.5), ensure that the **Show all settings** check box in the lower left corner of the dialog is unchecked. In the **Text Editor Basic** category of the left pane, select **Editor**. On the right, check the **Line Numbers** check box. Keep the **Options** dialog open for the next step.

Setting Code Indentation to Three Spaces per Indent
In the **Options** dialog that you opened in the previous step, enter **3** for both the **Tab Size** and **Indent Size** fields (Fig. 3.5). Any new code you add will now use three spaces for each level of indentation. Click **OK** to save your settings, close the dialog and return to the editor window. Note that lines 3 and 5 (Fig. 3.4) are still indented four spaces because this code was created before we changed the indentation settings. Go to line 3 and move the code back one space to conform to our new convention, then move the cursor to the next line of code. After you do this, line 5 updates its indentation to match that of line 3. As you create applications in this book, Visual Basic Express will often update code to conform to various code conventions and the latest settings specified in Visual Basic Express.

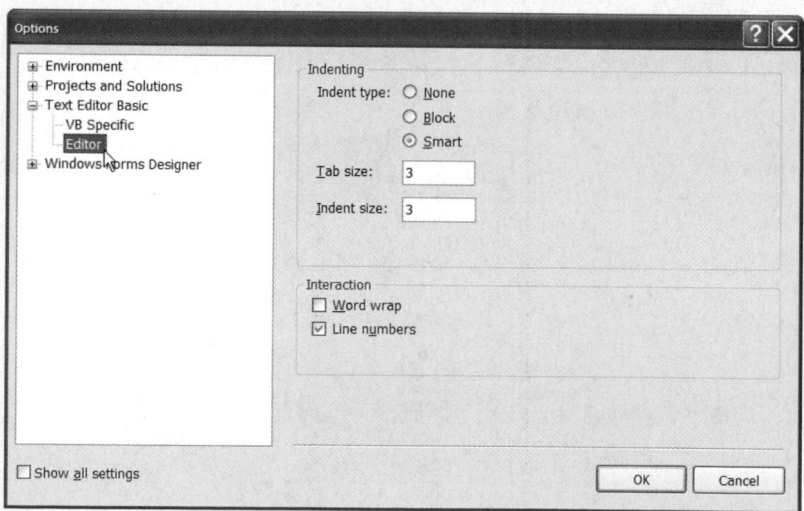

Fig. 3.5 | Modifying the IDE settings.

Changing the Name of the Program File

For programs in this book, we change the name of the program file (i.e., `Module1.vb`) to a more descriptive name for each application we develop. To rename the file, click `Module1.vb` in the **Solution Explorer** window. This displays the program file's properties in the **Properties** window (Fig. 3.6). Change the **File Name** property to `Welcome1.vb`.

Changing the Name of the Module

Changing the name of the program file does not affect the module name in the program code. Module names must be modified in the editor window. Do so by replacing the identifier `Module1` in the code with `FirstWelcome`.

Setting the Startup Object

Each Visual Basic project has a **startup object** that specifies where the application begins executing. Now that we have modified the name of the module where `Main` resides, we need to update the application's startup object as well. In the **Solution Explorer** window, double click the **My Project** item (near the top of Fig. 3.6). A page appears (Fig. 3.7) where you can set several properties of your application. Select **FirstWelcome** (our new module name) from the **Startup object** drop-down list.

Writing Code

Click the **Welcome1.vb** tab in the IDE to view the editor window. In the editor window (Fig. 3.4), add the comments from lines 1 and 2 of Fig. 3.1. Then type the code contained in line 8 of Fig. 3.1 between the lines `Sub Main()` and `End Sub`. After you type the class name and the dot separator (i.e., `Console.`), a window containing a scrollbar is displayed (Fig. 3.8). This IDE feature, called *IntelliSense*, lists a class's **members**, which include method names. Note that tabs (**All** and **Common**) are provided so that you can view either

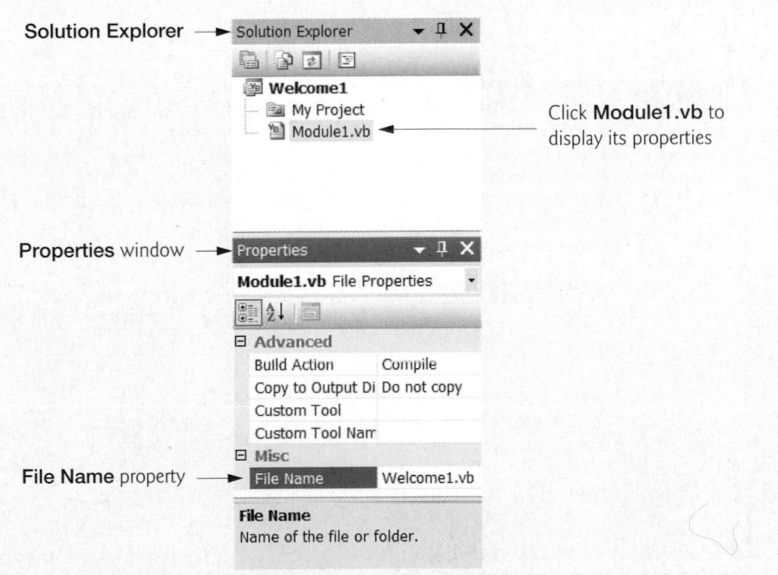

Fig. 3.6 | Renaming the program file in the **Properties** window.

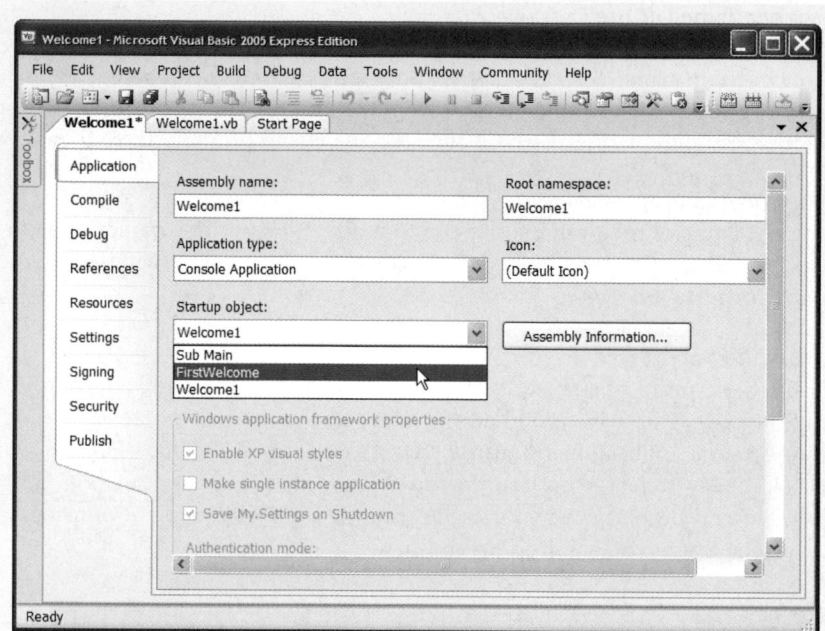

Fig. 3.7 | Setting the startup object.

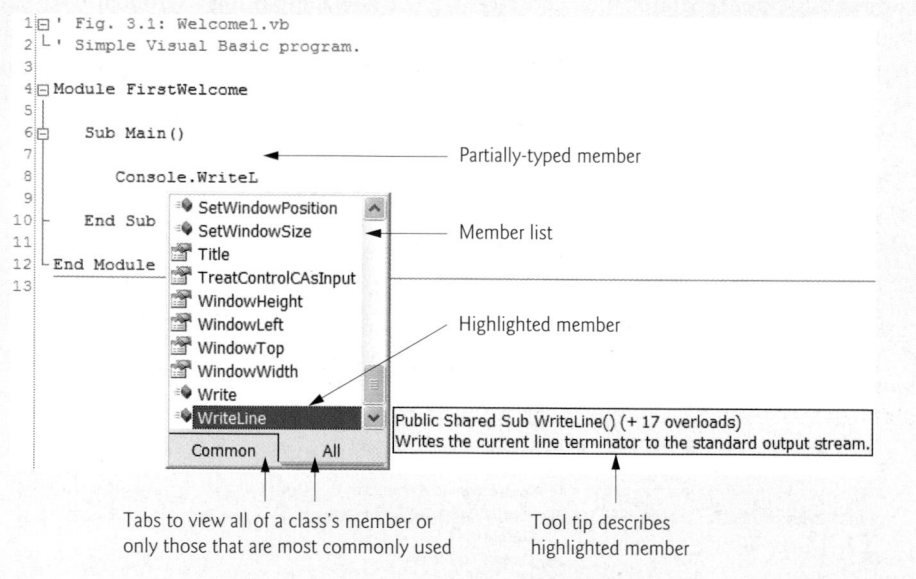

Fig. 3.8 | *IntelliSense* feature of Visual Basic Express.

all available class members or only those that are commonly used. As you type characters, Visual Basic Express highlights the first member that matches all the characters typed, then displays a tool tip containing a description of that member. You can either type the complete member name (e.g., WriteLine), double click the member name in the member list or press the *Tab* key to complete the name. Once the complete name is provided, the *IntelliSense* window closes. When you type the open parenthesis character, (, after Console.WriteLine, the *Parameter Info* window is displayed (Fig. 3.9). This window contains information about the method's parameters. As you will learn in Chapter 7, there can be several versions of a method—that is, a class or module can define several methods that have the same name as long as they have different numbers and/or types of parameters. These methods all perform similar tasks. The *Parameter Info* window indicates how many versions of the selected method are available and provides up and down arrows for scrolling through the different versions. For example, there are 18 versions of the Write-Line method—we use one of these 18 versions in our program. The *Parameter Info* window is one of the many features provided by the IDE that help you develop programs. In the next several chapters, you will learn more about the information displayed in these windows. The *Parameter Info* window is especially helpful when a programmer wants to see the different ways in which a method can be used. From the code in Fig. 3.1, we already know that we intend to display a string with WriteLine, so you can simply close the *Parameter Info* window by pressing the *Esc* key. Finish entering line 8, as well as the comments in lines 10 and 12 of Fig. 3.1.

Saving the Program

Select **File > Save All** to display the **Save Project** dialog (Fig. 3.10). In the **Location** text box, specify the directory where you want to save this project. We choose to save the project in the MyProjects directory on the C: drive. Select the **Create directory for Solution** check box, and click **Save**.

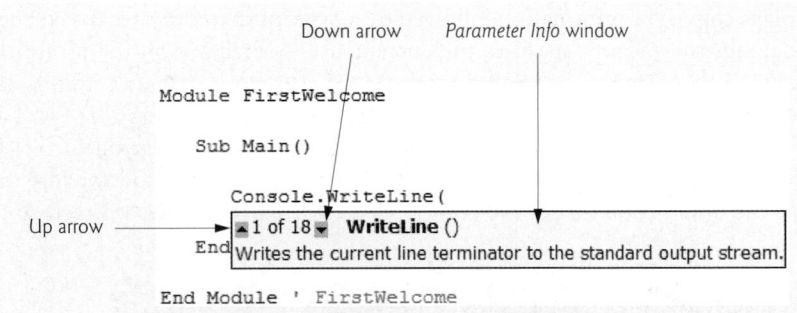

Fig. 3.9 | *Parameter Info* window.

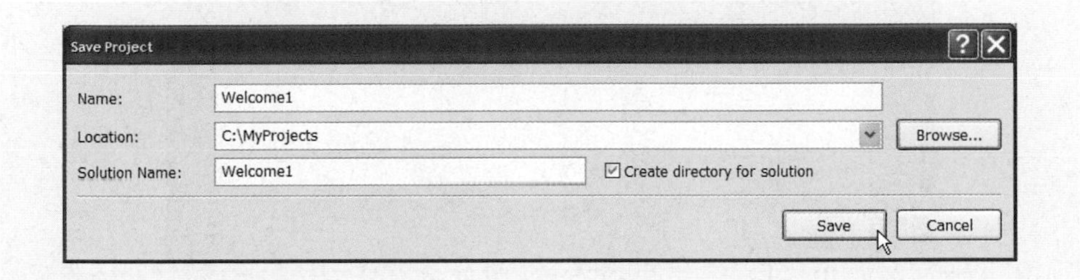

Fig. 3.10 | **Save Project** dialog.

Compiling and Running the Program

You are now ready to compile and execute your program. To compile the program, select **Build > Build Welcome1**. This creates a new file (named Welcome1.exe, in the project's directory structure) that contains the Microsoft Intermediate Language (MSIL) code for the program. The .exe file extension indicates that the file is executable.

To execute this console application (i.e., Welcome1.exe), select **Debug > Start Debugging**, which invokes the Main method. The statement in line 8 of Main displays Welcome to Visual Basic!, however, the window disappears immediately. Figure 3.11 shows the results of the program's execution. To enable the window to remain on the screen so you can view the results, you can use the **Debug** menu's **Start Without Debugging** option. This option is not in the menu by default, so you must add it. To do so, select **Tools > Customize....** In the **Commands** tab of the dialog that appears, select **Debug** from the **Categories** pane, then locate **Start Without Debugging** in the **Commands** pane. Drag the **Start Without Debugging** option over the **Debug** menu in the IDE (which will open the menu), then position the mouse just below the **Start / Continue** option and release the mouse button. Click **Close** to dismiss the **Customize** dialog. You can now execute the program using the select **Debug > Start Without Debugging** option. The window showing the results will remain on the screen until you press a key or click the window's close box. Leave the application open in Visual Basic Express, as we will go back to it later in this section.

Running the Program from the Command Prompt

As we mentioned at the beginning of this chapter, you can execute applications outside the IDE in a **Command Prompt**. This is useful when you simply want to run an application rather than open it for modification. To open the **Command Prompt**, click the Windows **Start** button, then select **All Programs > Accessories > Command Prompt**. The window (Fig. 3.12) displays copyright information followed by a prompt that indicates the current directory. By default, the prompt specifies the current user's directory on the local machine (in our case, C:\Documents and Settings\deitel). On your machine, the folder name deitel will be replaced with your username. A flashing cursor appears at the end of the prompt to indicate that the **Command Prompt** window is waiting for you to type a command. Enter the command cd (which stands for "change directory") followed by the directory where the application's .exe file is located (i.e., the bin\Release directory of

Fig. 3.11 | Executing the program shown in Fig. 3.1.

Default prompt displays when
Command Prompt is opened

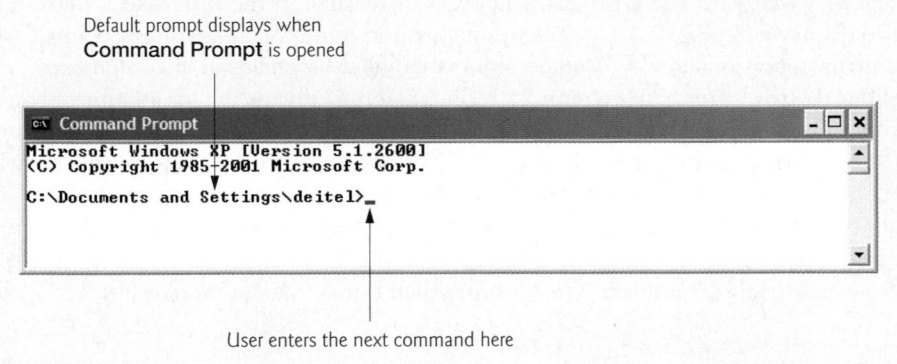

User enters the next command here

Fig. 3.12 | Executing the program shown in Fig. 3.1 from a **Command Prompt**.

your application). For example, the command cd C:\MyProjects\Welcome1\Welcome1\bin\Release (Fig. 3.13) changes the current directory to the Welcome1 application's bin\Release directory. The next prompt displays the new directory followed by the flashing cursor. After changing to the proper directory, you can run the compiled application by entering the name of the .exe file (i.e., Welcome1.exe). The application will run to completion, then the prompt will display again, awaiting the next command. To close the **Command Prompt**, type exit and press *Enter*. [*Note:* Many environments show **Command Prompt** windows with black backgrounds and white text. We adjusted these settings in our environment to make our screen captures more readable.]

Syntax Errors, Error Messages and the **Error List** *Window*

Go back to the application in Visual Basic Express. When you type a line of code and press the *Enter* key, the IDE responds either by applying syntax-color highlighting or by generating a syntax error, which indicates a violation of Visual Basic's rules for creating correct programs (i.e., one or more statements are not written correctly). Syntax errors occur for various reasons, such as missing parentheses and misspelled keywords. When a syntax error occurs, the IDE underlines the error in blue and provides a description of the error in the

Updated prompt showing   Type this to change to the
the new current directory   application's directory

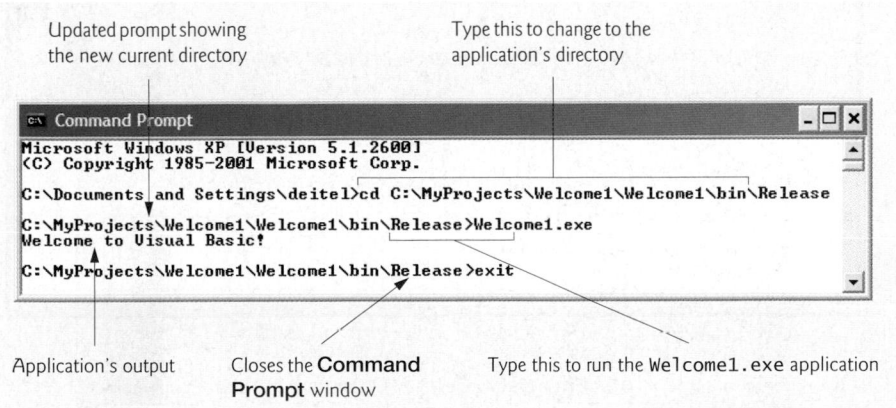

Application's output   Closes the **Command**   Type this to run the Welcome1.exe application
                           Prompt window

Fig. 3.13 | Executing the program shown in Fig. 3.1 from a **Command Prompt**.

Error List window. If the **Error List** window is not visible in the IDE, select **View > Error List** to display it. In Fig. 3.14, we intentionally omitted the first parenthesis in line 8. The first error contains the text "**Method arguments must be enclosed in parentheses.**" and specifies that the error is in column 25 of line 8. This informs the programmer that one or more parentheses are missing in line 8. The second error—"**End of statement expected.**"—specifies that this error is in column 50 of line 8. This error message appears when the compiler thinks that the line contains a complete statement, followed by the beginning of another statement. Visual Basic allows only one statement per line. Although we are attempting to include only one statement in line 8, the missing parenthesis causes the compiler to incorrectly assume that there is more than one statement on that line.

Error-Prevention Tip 3.1

*One syntax error can lead to multiple entries in the **Error List** window. Each error that you address could eliminate several subsequent error messages when you recompile your program. So, when you see a particular error you know how to fix, correct it and recompile—this may make the other errors disappear.*

3.4 Displaying a Single Line of Text with Multiple Statements

The message Welcome to Visual Basic! can be displayed using multiple statements. Figure 3.15 uses two method calls to produce the same output as the program in Fig. 3.1.

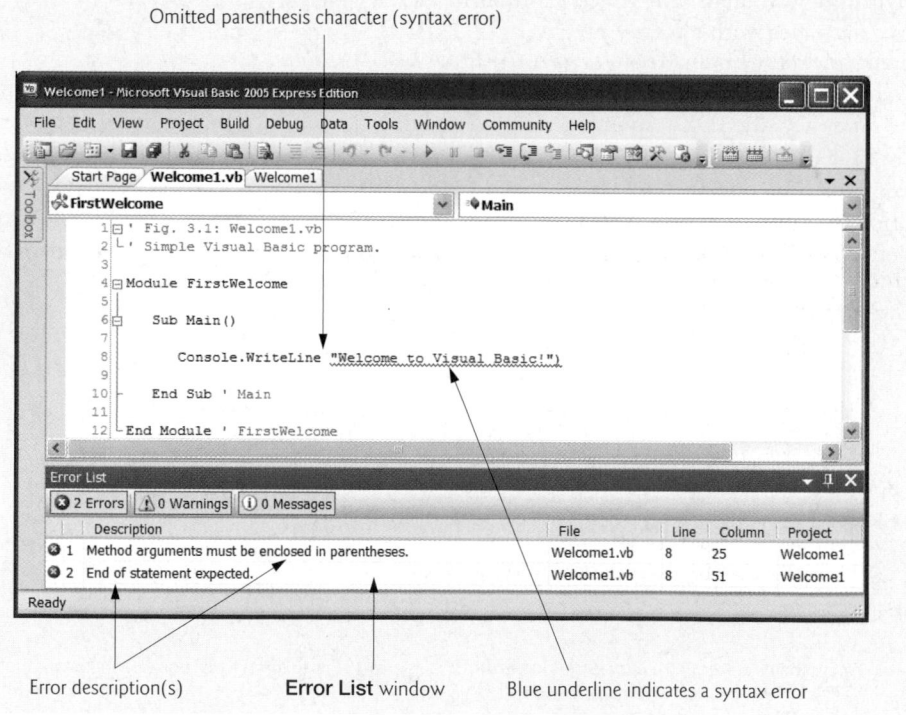

Fig. 3.14 | Syntax error indicated by the IDE.

```
1    ' Fig. 3.15: Welcome2.vb
2    ' Displaying a line of text with multiple statements.
3
4    Module SecondWelcome
5
6       Sub Main()
7
8          Console.Write("Welcome to ")
9          Console.WriteLine("Visual Basic!")
10
11       End Sub ' Main
12
13   End Module ' SecondWelcome
```

```
Welcome to Visual Basic!
```

Fig. 3.15 | Displaying a line of text with multiple statements.

Lines 8–9 of Fig. 3.15 display only one line of text in the **Console** window. The first statement calls Console method **Write** to display a string. Unlike WriteLine, Write does not position the output cursor at the beginning of the next line in the **Console** window after displaying its string. Instead, the next character displayed in the **Console** window appears immediately to the right of the last character displayed with Write. Thus, when line 9 executes, the first character displayed ("V") appears immediately after the last character displayed with Write (i.e., the space character after the word "to" in line 8). Each Write or WriteLine outputs its characters at the exact location where the previous Write's or WriteLine's output ended.

3.5 Adding Integers

Our next program (Fig. 3.16) inputs two integers (whole numbers) entered at the keyboard by a user, computes the sum of these integers and displays the result. As the user enters each integer and presses the *Enter* key, the integer is read into the program and added to the total.

```
1    ' Fig. 3.16: Addition.vb
2    ' Addition program.
3
4    Module Addition
5
6       Sub Main()
7
8          ' variables used in the addition calculation
9          Dim number1 As Integer
10         Dim number2 As Integer
11         Dim total As Integer
12
```

Fig. 3.16 | Addition program that adds two integers entered by the user. (Part 1 of 2.)

```
13          ' prompt for and read the first number from the user
14          Console.Write("Please enter the first integer: ")
15          number1 = Console.ReadLine()
16
17          ' prompt for and read the second number from the user
18          Console.Write("Please enter the second integer: ")
19          number2 = Console.ReadLine()
20
21          total = number1 + number2 ' add the numbers
22
23          Console.WriteLine("The sum is " & total) ' display the sum
24
25      End Sub ' Main
26
27   End Module ' Addition
```

```
Please enter the first integer: 45
Please enter the second integer: 72
The sum is 117
```

Fig. 3.16 | Addition program that adds two integers entered by the user. (Part 2 of 2.)

Lines 9–11 are **declarations,** which begin with keyword `Dim` (a contraction of the word "dimension"). The words `number1`, `number2` and `total` are the names of variables—locations in the computer's memory where values can be stored for use by a program. All variables must be declared before they can be used in a program. The declarations in lines 9–11 specify that the variables `number1`, `number2` and `total` are data of type `Integer`; that is, these variables store **integer** values (i.e., whole numbers such as 919, −11, 0 and 138624). Types already defined in Visual Basic, such as `Integer`, are known as **primitive types**. Primitive type names are keywords. The 15 primitive types are listed in Fig. 3.17 and discussed further in Chapter 7. Recall that keywords cannot be used as identifiers.

A variable name can be any valid identifier. Variables of the same type can be declared in separate statements or they can be declared in one statement with each variable in the declaration separated by a comma. The latter format uses a **comma-separated list** of variable names.

Primitive Types		
Boolean	Byte	Char
Date	Decimal	Double
Integer	Long	SByte
Short	Single	String
UInteger	ULong	UShort

Fig. 3.17 | Primitive types in Visual Basic.

Good Programming Practice 3.3

Choosing meaningful variable names helps a program to be "self-documenting" (i.e., the program can be understood by others without the use of documentation manuals or excessive comments).

Good Programming Practice 3.4

A common convention (and the one used in this book) is to have the first word in a variable-name identifier begin with a lowercase letter. Every word in the name after the first word should begin with a uppercase letter. For example, identifier firstNumber has a capital N beginning its second word, Number. We use a similar convention for module names, except that the first letter of the first word is also capitalized. Although identifiers are not case sensitive, using these conventions helps make your programs more readable. In this book, we use widely adopted Visual Basic naming conventions.

Good Programming Practice 3.5

Declaring each variable on a separate line allows for easy insertion of an end-of-line comment next to each declaration. We will follow this convention.

Line 14 prompts the user to enter the first of two integers that will be summed. Line 15 obtains the value entered by the user and assigns it to variable number1. The statement in line 14 is called a **prompt**, because it directs the user to take a specific action. The method **ReadLine** (line 15) causes the program to pause and wait for user input. After entering the integer via the keyboard, the user presses the *Enter* key to send the integer to the program.

Once the user has entered a number and pressed *Enter*, the number is assigned to variable number1 (line 15) by an **assignment**, =. The statement is read as, "number1 *gets* the value returned by method ReadLine of the Console class." We call the entire statement an **assignment statement** because it assigns a value to a variable. Lines 18–19 prompt the user to enter a second integer and assign the entered value to number2.

Good Programming Practice 3.6

Place spaces on either side of a binary operator to make the operator stand out and improve the readability of the statement.

Technically, the user can send any character to the program as input. For this program, if the user types a non-integer value, such as "hello," a **run-time error** (an error that has its effect at execution time) occurs (Fig. 3.18). Chapter 12, Exception Handling, discusses how to handle such errors to make programs more robust—that is, able to handle run-time errors and continue executing.

The assignment statement in line 21 (Fig. 3.16) calculates the sum of the Integer variables number1 and number2 and assigns the result to variable total. The statement is read as, "total *gets* the value of number1 + number2." Most calculations are performed in assignment statements.

Line 23 displays the total of the two values. The argument to method WriteLine

```
"The sum is " & total
```

uses the **string concatenation operator**, **&**, to combine the string literal "The sum is " and the value of the variable total (the Integer variable containing the sum calculated in line

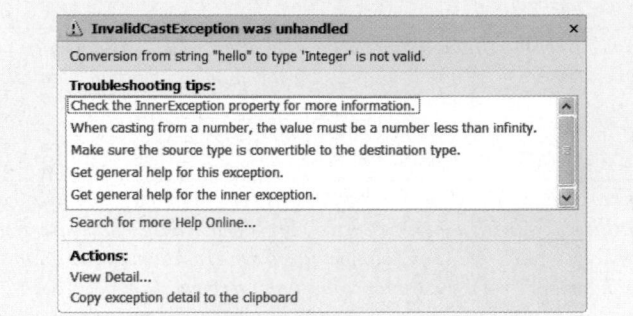

Fig. 3.18 | Dialog displaying a run-time error.

21). The string concatenation operator is called a **binary operator**, because it has two operands—"The sum is" and total. The string concatenation operator is used to combine two strings (i.e., to join them together). This operation results in a new, longer string. If an operand given to the string concatenation operator is a number (e.g., an integer), the program automatically creates a string representation of the number.

When reading or writing a program, you may find it difficult to match End Sub statements with their method declarations. For this reason, you may want to include an end-of-line comment after End Sub (indicating which method is ending), as we do in line 25. This practice is especially helpful when modules contain multiple methods. Although, for now, our modules contain only one method, we place the comment after End Sub as a *Good Programming Practice*.

Good Programming Practice 3.7

Follow a method's End Sub with an end-of-line comment containing the name of the method that the End Sub terminates.

3.6 Memory Concepts

Variable names, such as number1, number2 and total, correspond to locations in the computer's memory. Every variable has a **name**, **type**, **size** and **value**. In the addition program of Fig. 3.16, when the statement (line 15)

```
number1 = Console.ReadLine()
```

executes, the data input by the user in the **Console** window is placed into a memory location to which the name number1 has been assigned by the compiler. Suppose the user enters the characters 45 and presses *Enter*. This input is returned by ReadLine and assigned to number1. The program places the Integer value 45 into location number1, as shown in Fig. 3.19.

Whenever a value is placed in a memory location, this value replaces the value previously stored in that location. The previous value is destroyed (lost).

Suppose that the user then enters the characters 72 and presses *Enter*. Line 19

```
number2 = Console.ReadLine()
```

places the Integer value 72 into location number2, and memory appears, as shown in Fig. 3.20.

Fig. 3.19 | Memory location showing name and value of variable `number1`.

Once the program has obtained values for `number1` and `number2`, it adds these values and places their total into variable `total`. The statement (line 21)

```
total = number1 + number2
```

performs the addition and replaces (i.e., destroys) `total`'s previous value. After `total` is calculated, memory appears, as shown in Fig. 3.21. Note that the values of `number1` and `number2` appear exactly as they did before they were used in the calculation of `total`. Although these values were used when the computer performed the calculation, they were not destroyed. As this illustrates, when a value is read from a memory location, the process is nondestructive.

3.7 Arithmetic

Most programs perform arithmetic calculations. The arithmetic operators are summarized in Fig. 3.22. Note the use of various special symbols not used in algebra. For example, the asterisk (*) indicates multiplication, and the keyword `Mod` represents the `Mod` operator (also known as the modulus or modulo operator), which will be discussed shortly. Most of the arithmetic operators in Fig. 3.22 are binary operators, because each operates on two operands. For example, the expression `sum + value` contains the binary operator + and the two operands `sum` and `value`. Visual Basic also provides unary operators that take only one operand. For example, unary versions of plus (+) and minus (–) are provided, so that programmers can write expressions such as +9 and –19.

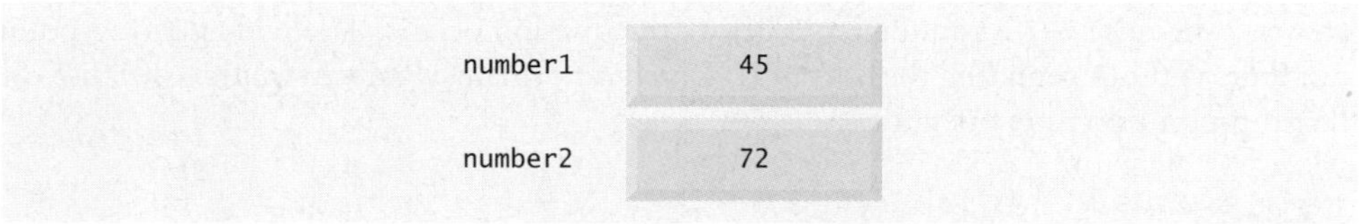

number1	45
number2	72

Fig. 3.20 | Memory locations after values for variables `number1` and `number2` have been input.

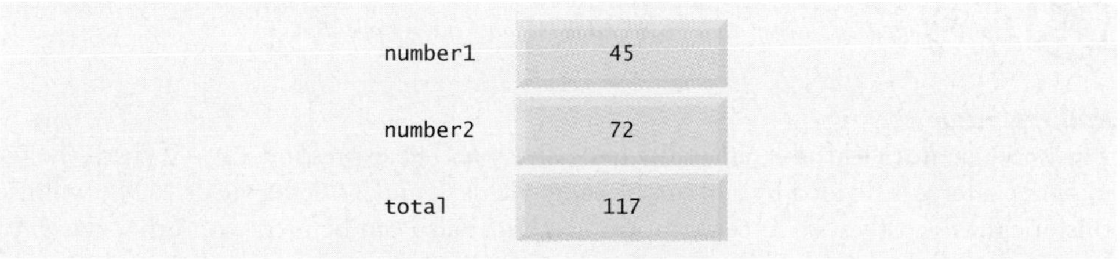

number1	45
number2	72
total	117

Fig. 3.21 | Memory locations after an addition operation.

Visual Basic operation	Arithmetic operator	Algebraic expression	Visual Basic expression
Addition	+	$f + 7$	f + 7
Subtraction	–	$p - c$	p - c
Multiplication	*	bm	b * m
Division (floating point)	/	x / y or $\frac{x}{y}$ or $x \div y$	x / y
Division (integer)	\	none	v \ u
Modulus	Mod	$r \bmod s$	r Mod s
Exponentiation	^	q^p	q ^ p
Unary minus	–	$-e$	-e
Unary plus	+	$+g$	+g

Fig. 3.22 | Arithmetic operators.

Division Operators

Visual Basic has separate operators for **integer division** (the backslash, \) and **floating-point division** (the forward slash, /). Integer division takes two Integer operands and yields an Integer result; for example, the expression 7 \ 4 evaluates to 1, and the expression 17 \ 5 evaluates to 3. Any fractional part in an Integer division result simply is truncated (i.e., discarded)—no rounding occurs. When **floating-point numbers** (i.e., numbers that contain a decimal point, such as 2.3456 and –845.7840) are used with the integer division operator, the numbers are first rounded to the nearest whole number, then divided. This means that, although 7.1 \ 4 evaluates to 1 as expected, the statement 7.7 \ 4 evaluates to 2, because 7.7 is rounded to 8 before the division occurs. To divide floating-point numbers without rounding the operands (which is normally what you want to do), use the floating-point division operator.

Common Programming Error 3.2

Using the integer division operator (\) when the floating-point division operator (/) is expected (i.e., when one or both of the operands is a floating-point value) can lead to incorrect results.

Error-Prevention Tip 3.2

Ensure that each integer division operator has only integer operands.

Mod Operator

The Mod operator yields the remainder after division. The expression x Mod y yields the remainder after x is divided by y. Thus, 7 Mod 4 yields 3, and 17 Mod 5 yields 2. We will use this operator mostly with Integer operands, but it also can be used with other types. In later chapters, we consider interesting applications of the Mod operator, such as determining whether one number is a multiple of another.

Arithmetic Expressions in Straight-Line Form

Arithmetic expressions in Visual Basic must be entered into the computer in straight-line form. Thus, expressions such as "a divided by b" must be written as a / b so that all constants, variables and operators appear in a straight line. The algebraic notation

$$\frac{a}{b}$$

is generally not acceptable to compilers, although some special-purpose software packages do exist that support more natural notation for complex mathematical expressions.

Parentheses for Grouping Subexpressions

Parentheses are used in Visual Basic expressions in the same manner as in algebraic expressions. For example, to multiply a times the quantity b + c, we write a * (b + c).

Rules of Operator Precedence

Visual Basic applies the operators in arithmetic expressions in a precise sequence determined by the following rules of operator precedence, which are similar to those followed in algebra:

1. Exponentiation is applied first. If an expression contains several exponentiation operations, they are applied from left to right.

2. Unary plus and minus, + and - (also called sign operations), are applied next. If an expression contains several sign operations, they are applied from left to right. Sign operations + and - are said to have the same level of precedence.

3. Multiplication and floating-point division operations are applied next. If an expression contains several multiplication and floating-point division operations, they are applied from left to right. Multiplication and floating-point division have the same level of precedence.

4. Integer division is applied next. If an expression contains several Integer division operations, they are applied from left to right.

5. Modulus operations are applied next. If an expression contains several modulus operations, they are applied from left to right.

6. Addition and subtraction operations are applied last. If an expression contains several addition and subtraction operations, they are applied from left to right. Addition and subtraction have the same level of precedence.

Operators in expressions contained within a pair of parentheses are evaluated before those that are outside a pair of parentheses. Parentheses can be used to group expressions and change the order of evaluation to occur *in any sequence desired by the programmer*. With nested parentheses, the operators contained in the innermost pair of parentheses are applied first.

The rules of operator precedence enable Visual Basic to apply operators in expressions in the correct order. When we say operators are applied from left to right, we are referring to the associativity of the operators. All binary operators in Visual Basic associate from left to right. If there are multiple operators, each with the same precedence, the order in which the operators are applied is determined by the operators' associativity. Figure 3.23 summarizes the rules of operator precedence. This table will be expanded as we introduce addi-

Operator(s)	Operation	Order of evaluation (precedence)
^	Exponentiation	Evaluated first. If there are several such operators, they are evaluated from left to right.
+, −	Sign operations	Evaluated second. If there are several such operators, they are evaluated from left to right.
*, /	Multiplication and Division	Evaluated third. If there are several such operators, they are evaluated from left to right.
\	Integer division	Evaluated fourth. If there are several such operators, they are evaluated from left to right.
Mod	Modulus	Evaluated fifth. If there are several such operators, they are evaluated from left to right.
+, −	Addition and Subtraction	Evaluated sixth. If there are several such operators, they are evaluated from left to right.

Fig. 3.23 | Precedence of arithmetic operators.

tional operators in subsequent chapters. Appendix A contains a complete operator-precedence chart.

Notice, before the table, that we take note of nested parentheses. Not all expressions with several pairs of parentheses contain nested parentheses. For example, although the expression

a * (b + c) + c * (d + e)

contains multiple sets of parentheses, none of the parentheses are nested. Rather, these sets are said to be "on the same level."

Sample Algebraic and Visual Basic Expressions

Now consider several expressions in light of the rules of operator precedence. Each example lists an algebraic expression and its Visual Basic equivalent. The following is an example of an arithmetic mean (average) of five terms:

Algebra: $\quad m = \dfrac{a + b + c + d + e}{5}$

Visual Basic: m = (a + b + c + d + e) / 5

The parentheses are required, because floating-point division has higher precedence than addition. The entire quantity (a + b + c + d + e) is to be divided by 5. If the parentheses are erroneously omitted, we obtain a + b + c + d + e / 5, which evaluates as

$a + b + c + d + \dfrac{e}{5}$

The following is the equation of a straight line:

Algebra: $\quad y = mx + b$

Visual Basic: y = m * x + b

No parentheses are required. The multiplication is applied first, because multiplication has a higher precedence than addition.

The following example contains modulus (Mod), multiplication, division, addition and subtraction operations (we use the text "mod" to represent modulus in algebra):

Algebra: $z = pr \bmod q + w/x - y$

Visual Basic: z = p * r Mod q + w / x - y

The circled numbers under the statement indicate the order in which Visual Basic applies the operators. The multiplication and division operators are evaluated first in left-to-right order (i.e., they associate from left to right). The Mod operator is evaluated next. The addition and subtraction operators are applied next, from left to right.

Evaluation of a Second-Degree Polynomial

To develop a better understanding of the rules of operator precedence, consider how the second-degree polynomial $y = ax^2 + bx + c$ is evaluated:

y = a * x ^ 2 + b * x + c

The circled numbers under the statement indicate the order in which Visual Basic applies the operators. In Visual Basic, x^2 is represented as x ^ 2.

Now, suppose that a, b, c and x in the preceding expression are initialized as follows: a = 2, b = 3, c = 7 and x = 5. Figure 3.24 illustrates the order in which the operators are applied.

As in algebra, it is acceptable to place unnecessary parentheses in an expression to make the expression clearer—these are called redundant parentheses. For example, many people might parenthesize the preceding assignment statement for clarity as

y = (a * x ^ 2) + (b * x) + c

Good Programming Practice 3.8

Redundant parentheses can make complex expressions easier to read.

Error-Prevention Tip 3.3

When you are uncertain about the order of evaluation in a complex expression, use parentheses to force the order, as you would do in an algebraic expression. Doing so can help avoid subtle bugs.

3.8 Decision Making: Equality and Relational Operators

This section introduces Visual Basic's If...Then statement, which allows a program to make a decision based on the truth or falsity of some expression. The expression in an If...Then statement is called a condition. If the condition is met (i.e., the condition is

Step 1.   y = 2 * 5 ^ 2 + 3 * 5 + 7   (Exponentiation first)

           5 ^ 2 is 25

Step 2.   y = 2 * 25 + 3 * 5 + 7   (Leftmost multiplication)

           2 * 25 is 50

Step 3.   y = 50 + 3 * 5 + 7   (Multiplication before addition)

           3 * 5 is 15

Step 4.   y = 50 + 15 + 7   (Leftmost addition)

           50 + 15 is 65

Step 5.   y = 65 + 7   (Last addition)

           65 + 7 is 72

Step 6.   y = 72   (Last operation—place 72 in y)

Fig. 3.24 | Order in which a second-degree polynomial is evaluated.

true), the statement in the If...Then statement's body executes. If the condition is not met (i.e., the condition is false), the body statement is not executed. Conditions in If...Then statements can be formed by using the **equality operators** and **relational operators** (also called **comparison operators**), which are summarized in Fig. 3.25. The relational and equality operators all have the same level of precedence and associate from left to right.

Standard algebraic equality operator or relational operator	Visual Basic equality or relational operator	Example of Visual Basic condition	Meaning of Visual Basic condition
Equality operators			
=	=	x = y	x is equal to y
≠	<>	x <> y	x is not equal to y
Relational operators			
>	>	x > y	x is greater than y
<	<	x < y	x is less than y
≥	>=	x >= y	x is greater than or equal to y
≤	<=	x <= y	x is less than or equal to y

Fig. 3.25 | Equality and relational operators.

Common Programming Error 3.3

It is a syntax error to reverse the symbols in the operators <>, >= and <= (as in ><, =>, =<).

The next example uses six If...Then statements to compare two numbers entered into a program by the user. If the condition in any of these statements is true, the output statement associated with that If...Then executes. The user enters these values, which are stored in variables number1 and number2, respectively. The comparisons are performed, and the results of the comparison are displayed in the **Console** window. The program and outputs are shown in Fig. 3.26.

```vb
1   ' Fig. 3.26: Comparison.vb
2   ' Using equality and relational operators.
3
4   Module Comparison
5
6      Sub Main()
7
8         ' declare Integer variables for user input
9         Dim number1 As Integer
10        Dim number2 As Integer
11
12        ' read first number from user
13        Console.Write("Please enter first integer: ")
14        number1 = Console.ReadLine()
15
16        ' read second number from user
17        Console.Write("Please enter second integer: ")
18        number2 = Console.ReadLine()
19
20        If number1 = number2 Then ' number1 is equal to number2
21           Console.WriteLine(number1 & " = " & number2)
22        End If
23
24        If number1 <> number2 Then ' number1 is not equal to number2
25           Console.WriteLine(number1 & " <> " & number2)
26        End If
27
28        If number1 < number2 Then ' number1 is less than number2
29           Console.WriteLine(number1 & " < " & number2)
30        End If
31
32        If number1 > number2 Then ' number1 is greater than number2
33           Console.WriteLine(number1 & " > " & number2)
34        End If
35
36        ' number1 is less than or equal to number2
37        If number1 <= number2 Then
38           Console.WriteLine(number1 & " <= " & number2)
39        End If
40
```

Fig. 3.26 | Performing comparisons with equality and relational operators. (Part 1 of 2.)

```
41          ' number1 is greater than or equal to number2
42          If number1 >= number2 Then
43              Console.WriteLine(number1 & " >= " & number2)
44          End If
45
46      End Sub ' Main
47
48  End Module ' Comparison
```

```
Please enter first integer: 1000
Please enter second integer: 2000
1000 <> 2000
1000 < 2000
1000 <= 2000
```

```
Please enter first integer: 515
Please enter second integer: 49
515 <> 49
515 > 49
515 >= 49
```

```
Please enter first integer: 333
Please enter second integer: 333
333 = 333
333 <= 333
333 >= 333
```

Fig. 3.26 | Performing comparisons with equality and relational operators. (Part 2 of 2.)

Lines 9–10 declare the variables that are used in method Main. The comment that precedes the declarations indicates the purpose of the variables in the program. Lines 14 and 18 retrieve inputs from the user and assign the values to Integer variables number1 and number2, respectively.

The If...Then statement in lines 20–22 compares the values of the variables number1 and number2 for equality. If the values are equal, the statement in line 21 outputs a string indicating that the two numbers are equal. Note that assignment and the equality operator both use the = symbol. When a condition is expected (such as after the If keyword in an If...Else statement), the = is used as an equality operator.

If number1 contains the value 333 and number2 contains the value 333, the expression in line 21 evaluates as follows: number1 is converted to a string and concatenated with the string " = ", then number2 is converted to a string and concatenated with the resulting string from the first concatenation. At this point, the string "333 = 333" is displayed by WriteLine. As the program proceeds through the remaining If...Then statements (lines 24–44), additional strings are output by the WriteLine statements. For example, when given the value 333 for number1 and number2, the conditions in lines 37 and 42 also are true. Thus, the output displayed (in the third output of Fig. 3.26) is:

```
333 = 333
333 <= 333
333 >= 333
```

Notice the indentation of the body statements within the If...Then statements throughout the program. Such indentation enhances program readability.

 Good Programming Practice 3.9

Indent the statement in the body of an If...Then statement to emphasize the body statement and enhance program readability.

The table in Fig. 3.27 shows the precedence of the operators introduced in this chapter. The operators are displayed from top to bottom in decreasing order of precedence.

3.9 Using a Message Dialog to Display a Message

The programs discussed thus far display output in the **Console** window. Visual Basic programs often use message dialogs to display output. Message dialogs are windows that display messages to the user. Visual Basic provides class **MessageBox** for creating message dialogs. We use a message dialog in Fig. 3.28 to display the square root of 2. For this program to compile and execute, you must perform several steps discussed later in this section. Be sure to read the entire section as you create this example.

Note that in the output for Fig. 3.28, the square root of 2 is displayed with many digits to the right of the decimal point. In many applications, you won't need such precise output. In the next chapter, we demonstrate how to display only a few digits to the right of the decimal point.

Operators	Type
^	exponentiation
+ -	sign operations (unary)
* /	multiplication and floating-point division
\	Integer division
Mod	modulus
+ -	addition and subtraction (binary)
= <> < <= > >=	equality and relational

Fig. 3.27 | Precedence of the operators introduced in this chapter.

```
1  ' Fig. 3.28: SquareRoot.vb
2  ' Displaying the square root of 2 in a dialog.
3
4  Imports System.Windows.Forms ' Namespace containing class MessageBox
5
6  Module SquareRoot
```

Fig. 3.28 | Displaying text in a message dialog. (Part 1 of 2.)

```
7
8      Sub Main()
9
10         Dim root As Double = Math.Sqrt(2) ' calculate the square root of 2
11
12         ' display the results in a message dialog
13         MessageBox.Show("The square root of 2 is " & root, _
14            "The Square Root of 2")
15
16      End Sub ' Main
17
18   End Module ' SquareRoot
```

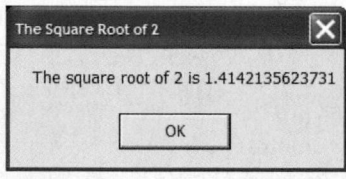

Fig. 3.28 | Displaying text in a message dialog. (Part 2 of 2.)

Displaying a MessageBox

Figure 3.28 presents a program that creates a simple GUI (i.e., the message dialog). The .NET Framework Class Library (FCL) contains a rich collection of classes that can be used to construct GUIs. FCL classes are grouped by functionality into namespaces, which make it easier for programmers to find the classes needed to perform particular tasks. Line 4 is an Imports statement indicating that we are using the features provided by the namespace System.Windows.Forms, which contains windows-related classes (i.e., forms and dialogs). We will discuss this namespace in more detail after we discuss the code in this example.

Line 10 calls the Sqrt method of the Math class to compute the square root of 2. The value returned is a floating-point number, so we declare the variable root as type Double. Variables of type Double can store floating-point numbers. We declare and initialize root in a single statement.

Note the use of spacing in lines 13–14 of Fig. 3.28. To improve readability, long statements may be split over several lines using the line-continuation character, _ . Line 13 uses the line-continuation character to indicate that line 14 is a continuation of the preceding line. A single statement can contain as many line-continuation characters as necessary. At least one whitespace character must precede each line-continuation character.

Common Programming Error 3.4

Splitting a statement over several lines without including the line-continuation character is a syntax error.

Common Programming Error 3.5

Failure to precede the line-continuation character (_) with at least one whitespace character is a syntax error.

Common Programming Error 3.6

Placing anything, including comments, on the same line after a line-continuation character is a syntax error.

Common Programming Error 3.7

Splitting a statement in the middle of an identifier or string is a syntax error.

Good Programming Practice 3.10

If a single statement must be split across lines, choose breaking points that make sense, such as after a comma in a comma-separated list or after an operator in a lengthy expression. If a statement is split across two or more lines, indent all subsequent lines with one level of indentation.

Lines 13–14 (Fig. 3.28) call method Show of class MessageBox. This method takes a comma-separated argument list. The first argument is the string that is displayed in the message dialog. The second argument is the string that is displayed in the message dialog's title bar.

Good Programming Practice 3.11

Place a space after each comma in a method's argument list to make method calls more readable.

Analyzing the MessageBox

When executed, lines 13–14 (Fig. 3.28) display the message dialog shown in Fig. 3.29. The message dialog includes an **OK** button that allows the user to dismiss (i.e., close) the message dialog by clicking the button. After you dismiss the message dialog, the program reaches the end of Main and terminates. You can also dismiss the message dialog by clicking the dialog's close box—the button with an **X** in the dialog's upper-right corner. You will see various dialogs throughout this book, some with more buttons than the **OK** button and the close box. In Chapter 13, you will learn how to determine which button was pressed and have your application respond accordingly. For instance, you can have one action occur when the user clicks the **OK** button and a different action occur when the user clicks the close box. By default, these buttons simply dismiss the dialog.

If you create this example and enter the code in Fig. 3.28, you will notice that line 13 gives you the error **Name 'MessageBox' is not declared**. Some classes provided by Visual Basic (such as MessageBox) must be added to the project before they can be used in a program. These compiled classes are located in a file, called an assembly, that has a **.dll**

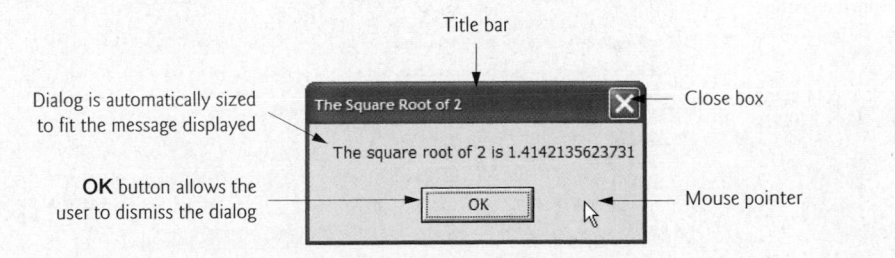

Fig. 3.29 | Message dialog displayed by calling MessageBox.Show.

(dynamic link library) file extension. Information about the assembly our program must reference so that it can use class `MessageBox` can be found in the Visual Basic Express documentation—also called the **MSDN (Microsoft Developer Network) Documentation**. To locate this information, select **Help > Index**. This displays the Visual Basic Express documentation in a separate window that contains an **Index** dialog (Fig. 3.30).

Type the class name `MessageBox` in the **Look for:** box, and select the appropriate filter, which narrows the search to a subset of the documentation—we selected **Visual Basic Express** in Fig. 3.30. You should select whichever edition of Visual Basic you are using. Next, click the **about MessageBox class** link (Fig. 3.30) to display documentation for the `MessageBox` class (Fig. 3.31). The documentation lists the assembly that contains the class. Class `MessageBox` is located in assembly **System.Windows.Forms.dll**. Note that the file name is listed in Fig. 3.31 using lowercase letters. Uppercase and lowercase letters can be used interchangeably, because file names are not case sensitive.

Adding a Reference to an Assembly

We must add a reference to this assembly if we wish to use class `MessageBox` in our program. Visual Basic 2005 Express provides a simple process for adding a reference. To see

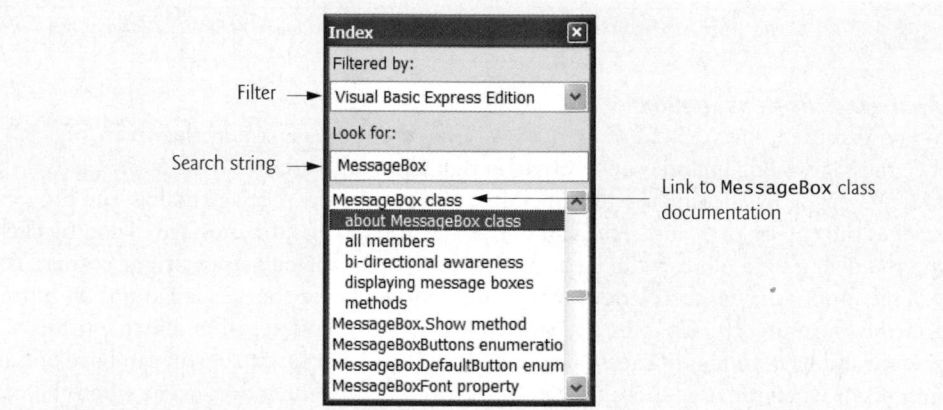

Fig. 3.30 | Obtaining documentation for a class by using the **Index** dialog.

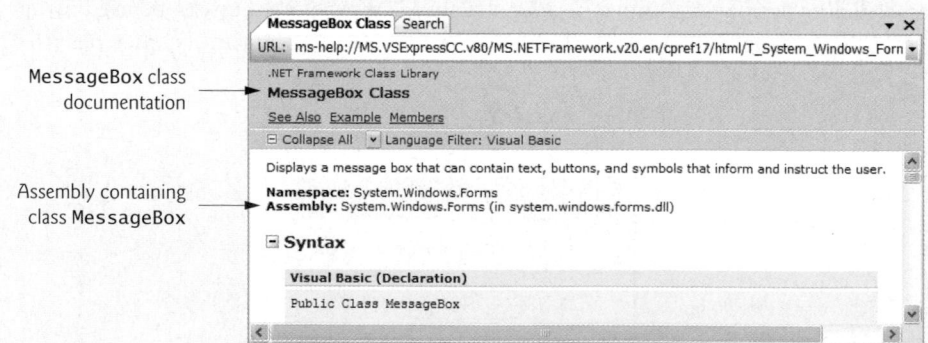

Fig. 3.31 | Documentation for the `MessageBox` class.

which assemblies are currently referenced in a project, you need to view the project's **References** folder. To do this, click the **Show All Files** button of the **Solution Explorer** (Fig. 3.32), which displays any of the project's files that are normally hidden by the IDE. If you expand the **References** folder (i.e., click the + to the left of the folder name), you will see that **System.Windows.Forms** is not listed. It *is* listed in Fig. 3.33(c)—we will discuss this figure shortly.

To add a reference to an existing project, select **Project > Add Reference...** to display the **Add Reference** dialog (Fig. 3.33(a)). Scroll through the list of DLLs in the **.NET** tab and click `System.Windows.Forms.dll` to add it to the **References** folder, then click **OK**. Note that **System.Windows.Forms** was not originally listed in the **References** folder (Fig. 3.33(b)), but after we add the reference using the **Add Reference** dialog, it *is* listed (Fig. 3.33(c)).

Common Programming Error 3.8

Including a namespace with the Imports *statement without adding a reference to the proper assembly results in a compilation error.*

Now that the assembly `System.Windows.Forms.dll` is referenced, we can use the classes that are part of the assembly. The namespace that includes class `MessageBox`, `System.Windows.Forms`, also is specified with the Imports statement in line 4 of our code (Fig. 3.28). The Imports statement is not added to the program by Visual Basic 2005 Express; you must add this line to your code.

We did not have to add references to any of our previous programs because Visual Basic 2005 Express adds references to some assemblies when the project is created. The references added depend on the project type that you select in the **New Project** dialog. In addition, some assemblies do not need to be referenced. For example, class `Console` is located in the assembly `mscorlib.dll`, but we did not need to reference this assembly explicitly to use it.

GUI Components and the System.Windows.Forms Namespace

The `System.Windows.Forms` namespace contains many classes that help Visual Basic programmers define graphical user interfaces (GUIs) for their applications. GUI components (such as `Button`s) facilitate both data entry by the user and presenting data outputs to the user. For example, Fig. 3.34 is an Internet Explorer window with a menu bar containing various menus, such as **File**, **Edit** and **View**. Below the menu bar is a tool bar that consists of buttons. Each button, when clicked, executes a task. Beneath the tool bar is a combo box in which the user can type the location of a Web site to visit. To the left of this combo

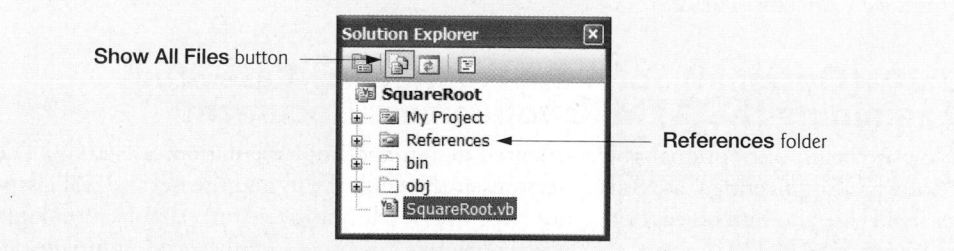

Fig. 3.32 | Viewing a project's references.

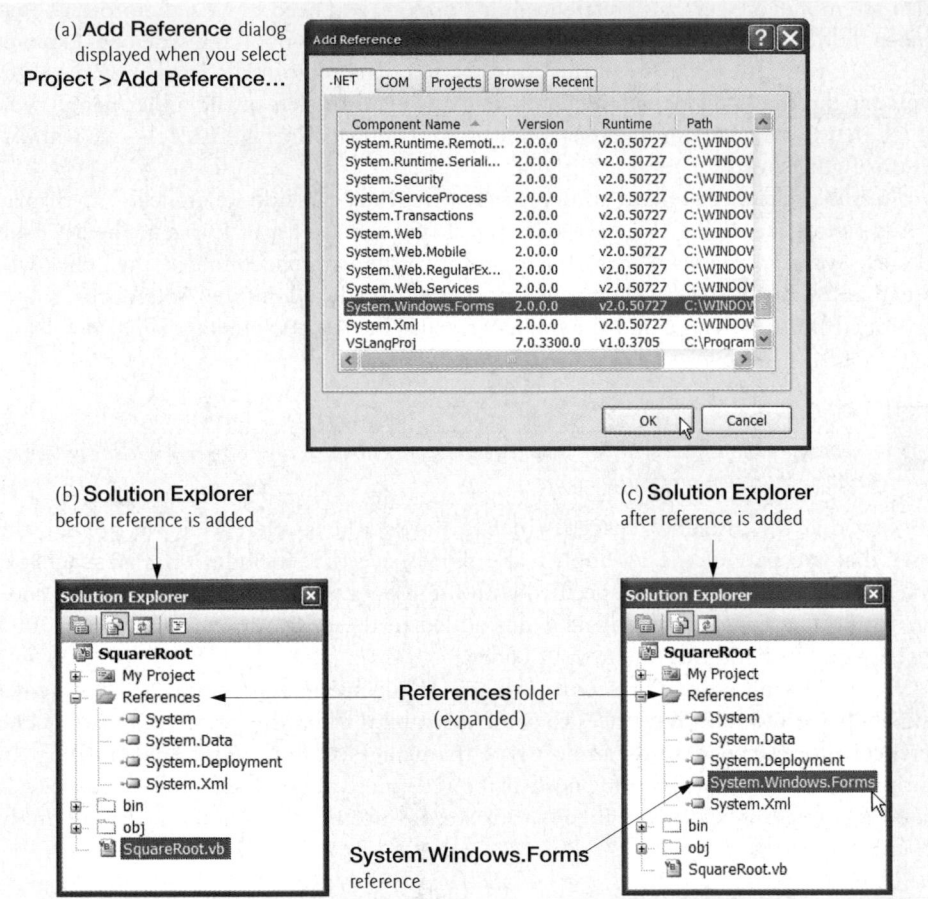

(a) Add Reference dialog displayed when you select **Project > Add Reference...**

(b) Solution Explorer before reference is added

(c) Solution Explorer after reference is added

References folder (expanded)

System.Windows.Forms reference

Fig. 3.33 | Adding an assembly reference to a project in the Visual Basic 2005 Express IDE.

box is a label that indicates the purpose of the text box (in this case, **Address**). The menus, buttons, text boxes and labels are part of Internet Explorer's GUI. They enable users to interact effectively with the Internet Explorer program. Visual Basic provides classes for creating the GUI components shown here. Other classes that create GUI components are described throughout this book (beginning in the next chapter), and covered in detail in Chapter 13, Graphical User Interface Concepts: Part 1 and Chapter 14, Graphical User Interface Concepts: Part 2.

3.10 (Optional) Software Engineering Case Study: Examining the ATM Requirements Document

Now we begin our optional object-oriented design and implementation case study. The "Software Engineering Case Study" sections at the ends of this and the next several chapters will ease you into object orientation. We will develop software for a simple automated teller machine (ATM) system, providing you with a concise, carefully paced, complete design and implementation experience. In Chapters 4–9 and 11, we will perform the various

Label   Button (displaying an icon)   Menu (e.g., **Help**)   Combo box   Menu bar   Tool bar

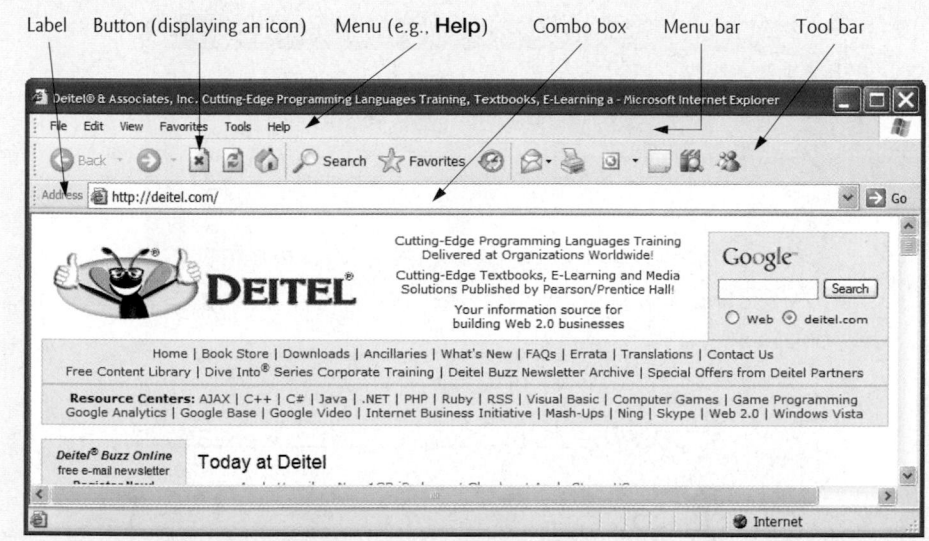

Fig. 3.34 | Internet Explorer window with GUI components.

steps of an object-oriented design (OOD) process using the UML, while relating these steps to the object-oriented concepts discussed in the chapters. Appendix J implements the ATM using Visual Basic object-oriented programming (OOP) techniques. We present the complete case study solution. This is not an exercise; rather, it is an end-to-end learning experience that concludes with a detailed walkthrough of the complete Visual Basic code that implements our design. It will begin to acquaint you with the kinds of substantial problems encountered in industry, and their potential solutions.

We begin our design process by presenting a requirements document that specifies the ATM system's purpose and *what* it must do. Throughout the case study, we refer to the requirements document to determine precisely what functionality the system must provide.

Requirements Document
A small local bank intends to install a new automated teller machine (ATM) to allow users (i.e., bank customers) to perform basic financial transactions (Fig. 3.35). For simplicity, each user can have only one account at the bank. ATM users should be able to view their account balance, withdraw cash (i.e., take money out of an account) and deposit funds (i.e., place money into an account).

The user interface of the automated teller machine contains the following hardware components:

- a screen that displays messages to the user;
- a keypad that receives numeric input from the user;
- a cash dispenser that dispenses cash to the user; and
- a deposit slot that receives deposit envelopes from the user.

The cash dispenser begins each day loaded with 500 $20 bills. [*Note:* Certain elements of the ATM described here simplify various aspects of a real ATM. For example, commercial

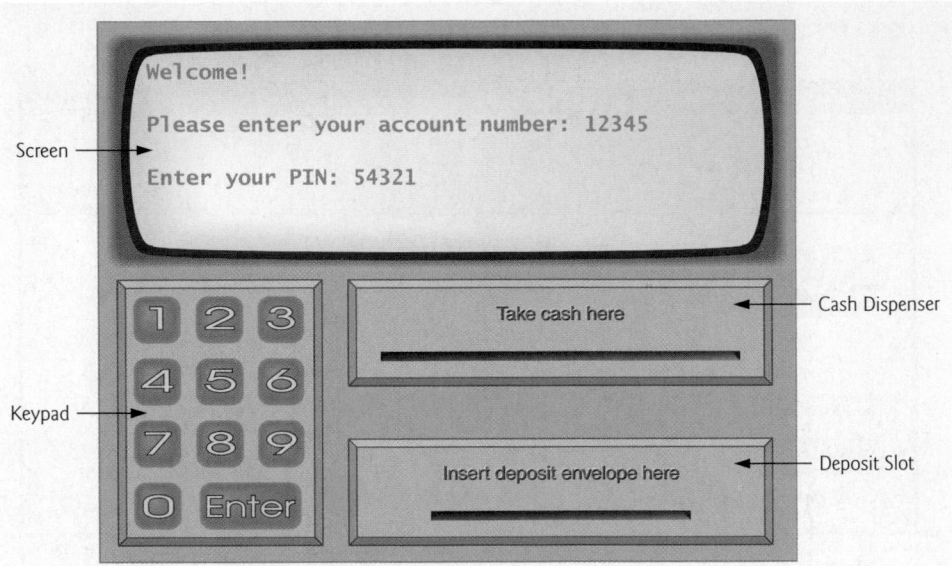

Fig. 3.35 | Automated teller machine user interface.

ATMs typically contain a device that reads a user's account number from an ATM card, whereas our ATM asks the user to type an account number on the keypad (which you will simulate with your personal computer's keypad). Also, commercial ATMs usually print a paper receipt at the end of a session, but all output from this ATM appears on the screen.]

The bank wants you to develop software to perform the financial transactions initiated by bank customers through the ATM. The bank will integrate the software with the ATM's hardware at a later time. The software should simulate the functionality of the hardware devices (e.g., cash dispenser, deposit slot) in software components, but it need not concern itself with how these devices perform their duties. The ATM hardware has not been developed yet, so instead of writing your software to run on the ATM, you should develop a first version of the software to run on a personal computer. This version should use the computer's monitor to simulate the ATM's screen, and the computer's keyboard to simulate the ATM's keypad.

An ATM session consists of authenticating a user (i.e., proving the user's identity) based on an account number and personal identification number (PIN), followed by creating and executing financial transactions. To authenticate a user and perform transactions, the ATM must interact with the bank's account information database. [*Note:* A database is an organized collection of data stored on a computer.] For each bank account, the database stores an account number, a PIN and a balance indicating the amount of money in the account. [*Note:* The bank plans to build only one ATM, so we do not need to worry about multiple ATMs accessing the database at the same time. Furthermore, we assume that the bank does not make any changes to the information in the database while a user is accessing the ATM other than those initiated bt this ATM session itself. Also, any business system like an ATM faces reasonably complicated security issues that go well beyond the scope of this book—we make the simplifying assumption that the bank trusts the ATM to access and manipulate the information in the database without significant security measures.]

Upon approaching the ATM, the user should experience the following sequence of events (see Fig. 3.35):

1. The screen displays a welcome message and prompts the user to enter an account number.

2. The user enters a five-digit account number, using the keypad.

3. For authentication purposes, the screen prompts the user to enter the PIN (personal identification number) associated with the specified account number.

4. The user enters a five-digit PIN, using the keypad.

5. If the user enters a valid account number and the correct PIN for that account, the screen displays the main menu (Fig. 3.36). If the user enters an invalid account number or an incorrect PIN, the screen displays an appropriate message, then the ATM returns to *Step 1* to restart the authentication process.

After the ATM authenticates the user, the main menu (Fig. 3.36) displays a numbered option for each of the three types of transactions—balance inquiry (option 1), withdrawal (option 2) and deposit (option 3). The main menu also displays an option that allows the user to exit the system (option 4). The user then chooses either to perform a transaction (by entering 1, 2 or 3) or to exit the system (by entering 4). If the user enters an invalid option, the screen displays an error message, then redisplays the main menu.

If the user enters 1 to make a balance inquiry, the screen displays the user's account balance. To do so, the ATM must retrieve the balance from the bank's database.

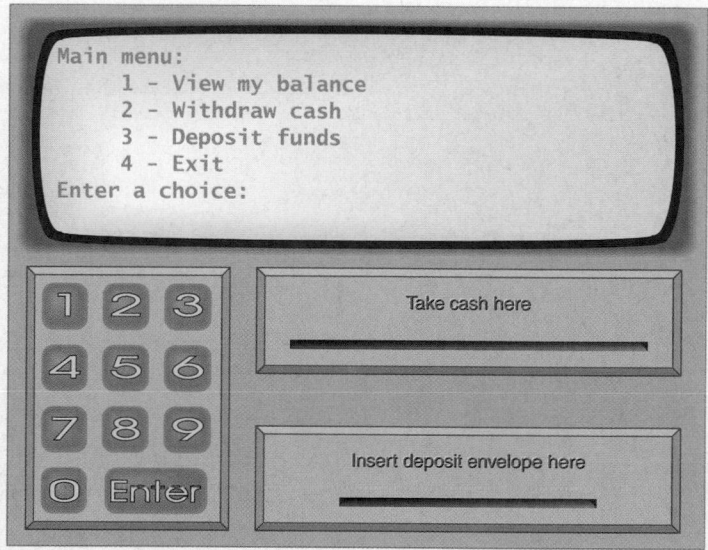

Fig. 3.36 | ATM main menu.

The following actions occur when the user enters 2 to make a withdrawal:

1. The screen displays a menu (shown in Fig. 3.37) containing standard withdrawal amounts: $20 (option 1), $40 (option 2), $60 (option 3), $100 (option 4) and $200 (option 5). Option 6 allows the user to cancel the transaction.

2. The user enters a menu selection (1–6) using the keypad.

3. If the withdrawal amount chosen is greater than the user's account balance, the screen displays a message stating this and telling the user to choose a smaller amount. The ATM then returns to *Step 1*. If the withdrawal amount chosen is less than or equal to the user's account balance (i.e., an acceptable withdrawal amount), the ATM proceeds to *Step 4*. If the user chooses to cancel the transaction (option 6), the ATM displays the main menu (Fig. 3.36) and waits for user input.

4. If the cash dispenser contains enough cash to satisfy the request, the ATM proceeds to *Step 5*. Otherwise, the screen displays a message indicating the problem and telling the user to choose a smaller withdrawal amount. The ATM then returns to *Step 1*.

5. The ATM debits (reduces) the user's account balance in the bank's database by the withdrawal amount.

6. The cash dispenser dispenses the desired amount of money to the user.

7. The screen displays a message reminding the user to take the money.

The following actions occur when the user enters 3 (from the main menu) to make a deposit:

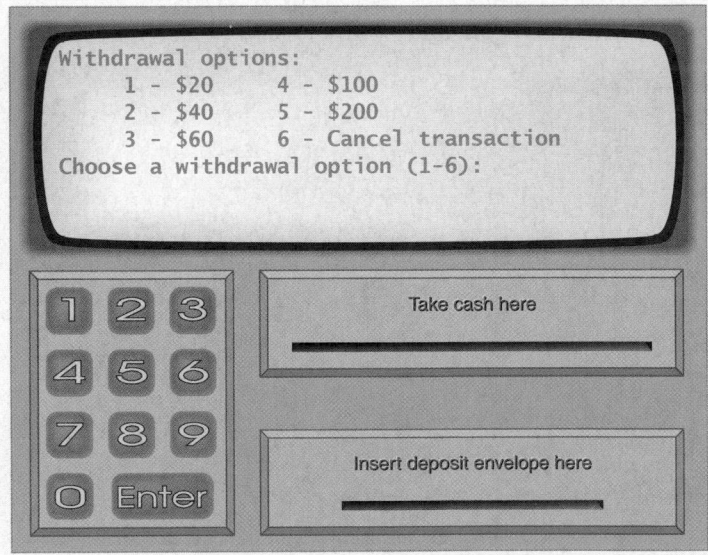

Fig. 3.37 | ATM withdrawal menu.

1. The screen prompts the user to enter a deposit amount or to type 0 (zero) to cancel the transaction.

2. The user enters a deposit amount or 0, using the keypad. [*Note:* The keypad does not contain a decimal point or a dollar sign, so the user cannot type a dollar amount (e.g., $147.25). Instead, the user must enter a deposit amount as a number of cents (e.g., 14725). The ATM then divides this number by 100 to obtain a number representing a dollar amount (e.g., $14725 \div 100 = 147.25$).]

3. If the user specifies a deposit amount, the ATM proceeds to *Step 4*. If the user cancels the transaction (by entering 0), the ATM displays the main menu (Fig. 3.36) and waits for user input.

4. The screen displays a message telling the user to insert a deposit envelope into the deposit slot.

5. If the deposit slot receives a deposit envelope within two minutes, the ATM credits (i.e., increases) the user's account balance in the bank's database by the deposit amount. [*Note:* This money is not immediately available for withdrawal. The bank first must verify the amount of cash in the deposit envelope, and any checks in the envelope must clear (i.e., money must be transferred from the check writer's account to the check recipient's account). When either of these events occurs, the bank appropriately updates the user's balance stored in database. This occurs independently of the ATM system.] If the deposit slot does not receive a deposit envelope within two minutes, the screen displays a message that the system has canceled the transaction due to inactivity. The ATM then displays the main menu and waits for user input.

After the system successfully executes a transaction, the system should redisplay the main menu (Fig. 3.36) so that the user can perform additional transactions. If the user chooses to exit the system (by entering option 4), the screen should display a thank you message, then display the welcome message for the next user.

Analyzing the ATM System

The preceding statement presented a simplified requirements document. Typically, such a document is the result of a detailed process of **requirements gathering** that might include interviews with potential users of the system and specialists in fields related to the system. For example, a systems analyst who is hired to prepare a requirements document for banking software (e.g., the ATM system described here) might interview people who have used ATMs and financial experts to gain a better understanding of *what* the software must do. The analyst would use the information gathered to compile a list of **system requirements** to guide systems designers.

The process of requirements gathering is a key task of the first stage of the software life cycle. The **software life cycle** specifies the stages through which software evolves from the time it is conceived to the time at which it is retired from use. These stages typically include analysis, design, implementation, testing, debugging, deployment, maintenance and retirement. Several software life cycle models exist, each with its own preferences and specifications for when and how often software engineers should perform the various stages. **Waterfall models** perform each stage once in succession, whereas **iterative models** may repeat one or more stages several times throughout a product's life cycle.

The analysis stage of the software life cycle focuses on precisely defining the problem to be solved. When designing any system, one must certainly *solve the problem right*, but of equal importance, one must *solve the right problem*. Systems analysts collect the requirements that indicate the specific problem to solve. Our requirements document describes our simple ATM system in sufficient detail that you do not need to go through an extensive analysis stage—it has been done for you.

To capture what a proposed system should do, developers often employ a technique known as **use case modeling**. This process identifies the **use cases** of the system, each of which represents a different capability that the system provides to its clients. For example, ATMs typically have several use cases, such as "View Account Balance," "Withdraw Cash," "Deposit Funds," "Transfer Funds Between Accounts" and "Buy Postage Stamps." The simplified ATM system we build in this case study requires only the first three use cases.

Each use case describes a typical scenario in which the user uses the system. You have already read descriptions of the ATM system's use cases in the requirements document. The lists of steps required to perform each type of transaction (i.e., balance inquiry, withdrawal and deposit) actually described the three use cases of our ATM—"View Account Balance," "Withdraw Cash" and "Deposit Funds."

Use Case Diagrams

We create a **use case diagram** to model the interactions between a system's clients (in this case study, bank customers) and the system. The goal is to show the kinds of interactions users have with a system without providing the details—these are shown in other UML diagrams (which we present throughout the case study). Use case diagrams are often accompanied by informal text that describes the use cases in more detail—like the text that appears in the requirements document. Use case diagrams are produced during the analysis stage of the software life cycle. In larger systems, use case diagrams are simple but indispensable tools that help system designers focus on satisfying the users' needs.

Figure 3.38 shows the use case diagram for our ATM system. The stick figure represents an **actor**, which defines the roles that an external entity—such as a person or another system—plays when interacting with the system. For our automated teller machine, the actor is a User who can view an account balance, withdraw cash and deposit funds using

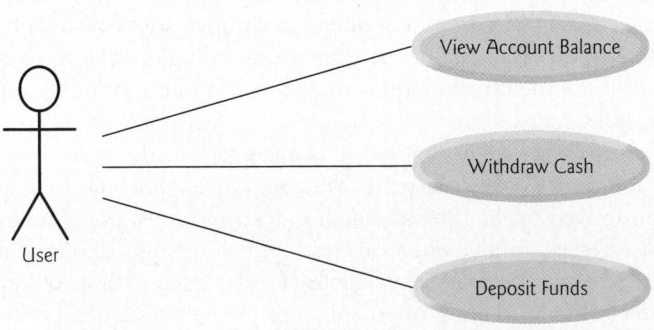

Fig. 3.38 | Use case diagram for the ATM system from the user's perspective.

the ATM. The User is not an actual person, but instead comprises the roles that a real person—when playing the part of a User—can play while interacting with the ATM. Note that a use case diagram can include multiple actors. For example, the use case diagram for a real bank's ATM system might also include an actor named Administrator who refills the cash dispenser each day.

We identify the actor in our system by examining the requirements document, which states, "ATM users should be able to view their account balance, withdraw cash and deposit funds." The actor in each of the three use cases is simply the User who interacts with the ATM. An external entity—a real person—plays the part of the User to perform financial transactions. Figure 3.38 shows one actor, whose name, User, appears below the actor in the diagram. The UML models each use case as an oval connected to an actor with a solid line.

Systems designers must analyze the requirements document or a set of use cases, and design the system before programmers implement it in a particular programming language. During the analysis stage, systems designers focus on understanding the requirements document to produce a high-level specification that describes *what* the system is supposed to do. The output of the design stage—a design specification—should specify *how* the system should be constructed to satisfy these requirements. In the next several "Software Engineering Case Study" sections, we perform the steps of a simple object-oriented design (OOD) process on the ATM system to produce a design specification containing a collection of UML diagrams and supporting text. Recall that the UML can be used with any OOD process. Many such processes exist, the best known of which is the Rational Unified Process™ (RUP) developed by Rational Software Corporation (now a division of IBM). RUP is a rich process for designing "industrial strength" applications. For this case study, we employ a simplified design process.

Designing the ATM System

We now begin the design stage of our ATM system. A system is a set of components that interact to solve a problem. For example, to perform the ATM system's designated tasks, our ATM system has a user interface (Fig. 3.35), contains software that executes financial transactions and interacts with a database of bank account information. System structure describes the system's objects and their interrelationships. System behavior describes how the system changes as its objects interact with one another. Every system has both structure and behavior—designers must specify both. There are several distinct types of system structures and behaviors. For example, the interactions among objects in the system differ from those between the user and the system, yet both constitute a portion of the system behavior.

The UML 2 specifies 13 diagram types for documenting system models. Each diagram type models a distinct characteristic of a system's structure or behavior—six diagram types relate to system structure; the remaining seven relate to system behavior. We list here only the six types of diagrams used in our case study—one of these (class diagrams) models system structure—the remaining five model system behavior. We overview the remaining seven UML diagram types in Appendix K, UML 2: Additional Diagram Types:

1. Use case diagrams, such as the one in Fig. 3.38, model the interactions between a system and its external entities (actors) in terms of use cases (system capabilities, such as "View Account Balance," "Withdraw Cash" and "Deposit Funds").

2. **Class diagrams**, which you will study in Section 4.9, model the classes, or "building blocks," used in a system. Each noun or "thing" described in the requirements document is a candidate to be a class in the system (e.g., "account," "keypad"). Class diagrams help us specify the structural relationships between parts of the system. For example, the ATM system class diagram will, among other things, specify that the ATM is physically composed of a screen, a keypad, a cash dispenser and a deposit slot.

3. **State machine diagrams**, which you will study in Section 6.11, model the ways in which an object changes state. An object's **state** is indicated by the values of all the object's attributes at a given time. When an object changes state, that object may subsequently behave differently in the system. For example, after validating a user's PIN, the ATM transitions from the "user not authenticated" state to the "user authenticated" state, at which point the ATM allows the user to perform financial transactions (i.e., view account balance, withdraw cash, deposit funds).

4. **Activity diagrams**, which you will also study in Section 6.11, model an object's activity—the object's workflow (sequence of events) during program execution. An activity diagram models the actions the object performs and specifies the order in which it performs these actions. For example, an activity diagram shows that the ATM must obtain the balance of the user's account (from the bank's account information database) before the screen can display the balance to the user.

5. **Communication diagrams** (called **collaboration diagrams** in earlier versions of the UML) model the interactions among objects in a system, with an emphasis on *what* interactions occur. You will learn in Section 8.17 that these diagrams show which objects must interact to perform an ATM transaction. For example, the ATM must communicate with the bank's account information database to retrieve an account balance.

6. **Sequence diagrams** also model the interactions among the objects in a system, but unlike communication diagrams, they emphasize *when* interactions occur. You will learn in Section 8.17 that these diagrams help show the order in which interactions occur in executing a financial transaction. For example, the screen prompts the user to enter a withdrawal amount before cash is dispensed.

In Section 4.9, we continue designing our ATM system by identifying the classes from the requirements document. We accomplish this by extracting key nouns and noun phrases from the requirements document. Using these classes, we develop our first draft of the class diagram that models the structure of our ATM system.

Internet and Web Resources

The following URLs provide information on object-oriented design with the UML.

www-306.ibm.com/software/rational/uml/

Lists frequently asked questions about the UML, provided by IBM Rational.

www.agilemodeling.com/essays/umlDiagrams.htm

Provides in-depth descriptions and tutorials on each of the 13 UML 2 diagram types.

www.borland.com/us/products/together/index.html

Provides a free 30-day license to download a trial version of Borland® Together® Control-Center™—a software development tool that supports the UML.

`www-306.ibm.com/software/rational/offerings/design.html`
Provides information about IBM Rational software available for designing systems. Provides downloads of 30-day trial versions of several products, such as IBM Rational Rose® XDE (e Xtended Development Environment) Developer.

`www.embarcadero.com/products/describe/index.html`
Provides a 15-day trial license for the Embarcadero Technologies® UML modeling tool Describe.™

`www.ilogix.com/rhapsody/rhapsody.cfm`
Provides a free 30-day license to download a trial version of I-Logix Rhapsody®—a UML 2-based model-driven development environment.

`argouml.tigris.org`
Contains information and downloads for ArgoUML, a free open-source UML tool.

`www.objectsbydesign.com/books/booklist.html`
Lists books on the UML and object-oriented design.

`www.objectsbydesign.com/tools/umltools_byCompany.html`
Lists software tools that use the UML, such as IBM Rational Rose, Embarcadero Describe, Sparx Systems Enterprise Architect, I-Logix Rhapsody and Gentleware Poseidon for UML.

`www.ootips.org/ood-principles.html`
Provides answers to the question, "What makes a good object-oriented design?"

`www.cetus-links.org/oo_uml.html`
Introduces the UML and provides links to numerous UML resources.

Recommended Readings

The following books provide information on object-oriented design with the UML.

Ambler, S. *The Elements of the UML 2.0 Style*. New York: Cambridge University Press, 2005.

Booch, G. *Object-Oriented Analysis and Design with Applications*, Third Edition. Boston: Addison-Wesley, 2004.

Eriksson, H., et al. *UML 2 Toolkit*. Hoboken, N.J.: John Wiley & Sons, 2003.

Kruchten, P. *The Rational Unified Process: An Introduction*. Boston: Addison-Wesley, 2004.

Larman, C. *Applying UML and Patterns: An Introduction to Object-Oriented Analysis and Design*, Second Edition. Upper Saddle River, NJ: Prentice Hall, 2002.

Roques, P. *UML in Practice: The Art of Modeling Software Systems Demonstrated Through Worked Examples and Solutions*. Hoboken, N.J.: John Wiley & Sons, 2004.

Rosenberg, D., and K. Scott. *Applying Use Case Driven Object Modeling with UML: An Annotated e-Commerce Example*. Reading, MA: Addison-Wesley, 2001.

Rumbaugh, J., I. Jacobson and G. Booch. *The Complete UML Training Course*. Upper Saddle River, NJ: Prentice Hall, 2000.

Rumbaugh, J., I. Jacobson and G. Booch. *The Unified Modeling Language Reference Manual*. Reading, MA: Addison-Wesley, 1999.

Rumbaugh, J., I. Jacobson and G. Booch. *The Unified Software Development Process*. Reading, MA: Addison-Wesley, 1999.

Software Engineering Case Study Self-Review Exercises

3.1   Suppose we enabled a user of our ATM system to transfer money between two bank accounts. Modify the use case diagram of Fig. 3.38 to reflect this change.

3.2 _____ model the interactions among objects in a system with an emphasis on *when* these interactions occur.
  a) Class diagrams
  b) Sequence diagrams
  c) Communication diagrams
  d) Activity diagrams

3.3 Which of the following choices lists stages of a typical software life cycle in sequential order?
  a) design, analysis, implementation, testing
  b) design, analysis, testing, implementation
  c) analysis, design, testing, implementation
  d) analysis, design, implementation, testing

Answers to Software Engineering Case Study Self-Review Exercises

3.1 Figure 3.39 contains a use case diagram for a modified version of our ATM system that also allows users to transfer money between accounts.

3.2 b.

3.3 d.

3.11 Wrap-Up

You learned many features of Visual Basic in this chapter, including displaying data on the screen, inputting data from the keyboard and declaring variables of primitive types `Integer` and `Double`. You used the `WriteLine`, `Write` and `ReadLine` methods of class `Console` to build simple interactive programs that input and output text. We explained how variables are stored in, and retrieved from, memory. You learned how to use arithmetic operators to perform calculations, and the order in which Visual Basic applies these operators (i.e., the rules of operator precedence). We demonstrated how Visual Basic's `If...Then` statement allows a program to perform actions based on a condition. You learned how to create conditions using the equality and relational operators. We demonstrated several features of Visual Basic 2005 Express, including creating console applications, modifying the IDE's settings and adding references to assemblies.

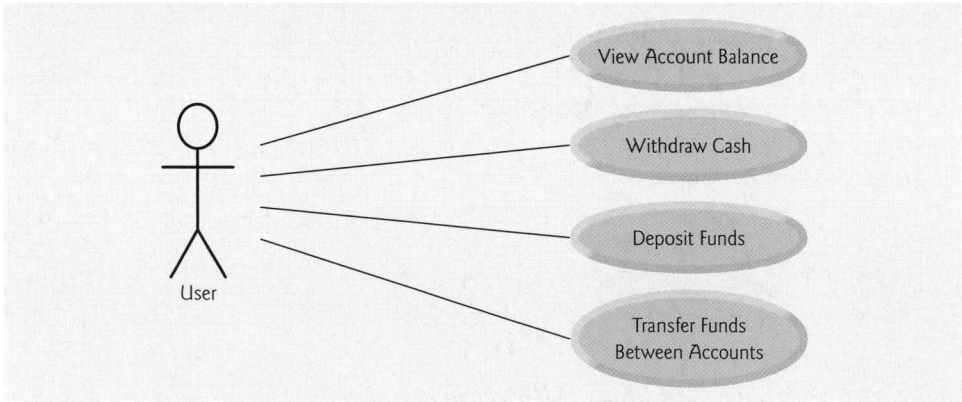

Fig. 3.39 | Use case diagram for a modified version of our ATM system that also allows users to transfer money between accounts.

In the next chapter, we re-introduce Visual Basic Windows applications that provide graphical user interfaces. The chapter begins our discussion of **structured programming**. We demonstrate creating applications using pseudocode, an informal language that helps programmers develop programs. We study how to specify and vary the order in which statements are executed—this is called **flow of control**. You will learn how to use control statements to select between alternative actions based on the truth or falsity of a condition, or to perform actions repeatedly based on a condition. You will see several case studies that demonstrate the types of repetition that can occur in Visual Basic programs.

3.12 Web Resources

www.developer.com/net/vb

The Visual Basic section of developer.com provides Visual Basic articles, including many for novice Visual Basic programmers.

www.devx.com/dotnet

This site contains information about the .NET platform, with topics ranging from Visual Basic to ASP.NET. The site includes links to articles, books and current news.

www.vbcity.com

The vbCity site lists numerous links to articles, books and tutorials on Visual Basic. You can submit code and have it rated by other developers. The site also polls visitors on many Visual Basic topics and provides access to archives, which include code listings and news.

www.cyber-matrix.com/vb.htm

This site links to Visual Basic tutorials, books, tips and tricks, programming tools, magazines, news groups and more.

searchvb.techtarget.com

This site offers a search engine designed specifically to discover Visual Basic Web sites.

www.aewnet.com/root/dotnet/vbnet

The site links to demos, articles, tutorials and other Visual Basic sites. There is also a message board where programmers can start discussions on various topics.

Summary

Section 3.1 Introduction

- A console application is an application that does not have a graphical user interface.

Section 3.2 Displaying a Line of Text

- The single-quote character ('), when placed outside a string, indicates that the remainder of the line of code is a comment.

- Inserting comments in your programs improves the readability of your code. Comments are ignored by the Visual Basic compiler; they do not cause the computer to perform any actions when the program is run.

- Visual Basic console applications consist of pieces called modules, which are logical groupings of methods that simplify program organization.

- Methods perform tasks and can return information when the tasks are completed. Every console application in Visual Basic consists of at least one module declaration and one method.

- Keywords are words that are reserved for use by Visual Basic; programmers must choose other names as identifiers.

- The name of a module is an identifier. An identifier is a series of characters, consisting of letters, digits and underscores (_), that does not begin with a digit and does not contain spaces.

- Visual Basic keywords and identifiers are not case sensitive—uppercase and lowercase letters are considered to be identical. Thus, firstwelcome and FirstWelcome are the same identifier.

- Blank lines, tabs and space characters are often used to make programs easier to read. Collectively, blank lines, tabs and space characters are known as whitespace.

- Console applications begin executing at method Main, which is known as the entry point of the program.

- Keyword Sub begins the body of a method declaration. Keywords End Sub close the method declaration's body.

- Characters delimited by double quotation marks are called strings, character strings or string literals.

- Methods perform tasks and return data when the tasks are completed. Groups of related methods are organized into classes or modules.

- The dot separator (.) selects a member of a particular class.

- The Console class contains methods, such as WriteLine, that communicate with users via the **Console** window.

Section 3.3 Creating Your First Console Application in Visual Basic Express

- Syntax-color highlighting helps programmers visually differentiate program elements. In Visual Basic 2005 Express, keywords are blue, text is black and comments are green. You can customize the colors shown in the code editor.

- After the programmer types a class name and the dot separator, the *IntelliSense* feature lists the class's members, which include method names.

- The *Parameter Info* window displays information about a method's arguments when you type the opening left parenthesis after the method's name. This window is one of the many features provided by the IDE to aid program development.

- The .exe file extension denotes that a file is executable.

Section 3.4 Displaying a Single Line of Text with Multiple Statements

- Unlike WriteLine, Write does not position the output cursor to the beginning of the next line in the **Console** window after displaying its string.

Section 3.5 Adding Integers

- The ReadLine method causes the program to pause and wait for user input. Once the user presses the *Enter* key, the input is returned to the program and execution resumes.

- A syntax error indicates a violation of Visual Basic's rules for creating correct programs (i.e., one or more statements are not written correctly).

- Variables are locations in the computer's memory where values can be stored for use by a program. Every variable has a name, type, size and value.

- All variables must be declared before they can be used in a program.

- Declarations begin with keyword Dim and allow you to specify the name and type of a variable.

- Types already defined in Visual Basic, such as Integer, are known as primitive types.

- Primitive type names are keywords.

- Variables of type Integer store integer values (i.e., whole numbers such as 919, –11 and 0).

- A run-time error is an error that affects the program during execution (unlike a syntax error, which affects the program when it is compiled).
- The symbol = is used to assign a value to a variable.

Section 3.6 Memory Concepts
- Whenever a value is placed in a memory location, it replaces the value previously stored in that location. The previous value is destroyed.
- When a value is read from a memory location, the process is nondestructive, meaning that the value in memory is not changed.

Section 3.7 Arithmetic
- Binary operators operate on two operands; unary operators operate on one operand.
- Visual Basic has separate operators for Integer division (the backslash, \) and floating-point division (the forward slash, /). Integer division yields an Integer result. Any fractional part in Integer division is truncated (i.e., discarded).
- The Mod operator yields the remainder after division.
- Arithmetic expressions in Visual Basic must be written in straight-line form to enter programs into a computer.
- Parentheses are used in Visual Basic expressions in the same manner as in algebraic expressions.
- Visual Basic applies the operators in arithmetic expressions in a precise sequence, which is determined by the rules of operator precedence.
- If an expression contains multiple operators with the same precedence, the order in which the operators are applied is determined by the associativity of the operators. In Visual Basic, all binary operators associate from left to right.
- As in algebra, you can place redundant parentheses in an expression to make it easier to read.

Section 3.8 Decision Making: Equality and Relational Operators
- Visual Basic's If...Then statement allows a program to make a decision based on the truth or falsity of a condition. If the condition is true, the statement in the body of the If...Then statement executes. If the condition is false, the body statement does not execute.
- Conditions in If...Then statements can be formed by using the equality operators and relational operators. Equality operators and relational operators are also called comparison operators.
- All relational and equality operators have the same level of precedence and associate from left to right.

Section 3.9 Using a Message Dialog to Display a Message
- Message dialogs are windows that display messages to the user. Visual Basic provides the class MessageBox for creating message dialogs.
- The .NET Framework Class Library organizes groups of related classes into namespaces.
- The System.Windows.Forms namespace contains windows-related classes (i.e., forms and dialogs) that help Visual Basic programmers define graphical user interfaces (GUIs) for their applications.
- GUI components facilitate data entry by the user and formatting and presenting data outputs to the user.
- An Imports statement indicates that a program uses the features provided by a specific namespace, such as System.Windows.Forms.

- To improve readability, long statements may be split over several lines with the line-continuation character (_). Although a single statement can contain as many line-continuation characters as necessary, at least one whitespace character must precede each line-continuation character.

- Assemblies that contain compiled classes for reuse in applications are located in files with a .dll (dynamic link library) extension.

Terminology

action
Add Reference dialog
addition operator (+)
argument to a method
arithmetic operator
assembly
assignment (=)
assignment statement
associativity of operators
binary operator
body of a method
case sensitive
character string
class
class name
close a dialog
Command Prompt
comment
comparison operator
condition
console application
Console class
Console window
declaration
dialog
Dim keyword
dismiss (hide) a dialog
.dll file extension
dot separator (.)
Double primitive type
double quotes ("") to delineate a string
dynamic link library (.dll)
end-of-line comment
End Module keywords
End Sub keywords
entry point of a program
equality operator (=)
Error List window
.exe file extension
executable file (.exe)
exponentiation operator (^)
false condition

File Name property of a file in the **Solution Explorer**
filter
floating-point division operator (/)
floating-point number
flow of control
full-line comment
greater than operator (>)
greater than or equal to operator (>=)
GUI component
identifier
If...Then selection statement
implicit conversion
Imports statement
inequality operator (<>)
integer division operator (\)
Integer primitive type
integer value
IntelliSense
keyword
less than operator (<)
less than or equal to operator (<=)
line-continuation character (_)
location in the computer's memory
Main method
Math class
member of a class
MessageBox class
method
method call
method name
Mod (modulus, modulo) operator
Module keyword
module
MSDN Documentation
multiplication operator (*)
namespace
nested parentheses
operand
operator precedence
output cursor
Parameter Info window

precedence
primitive type
prompt
ReadLine method of class Console
redundant parentheses
relational operators (<, >, <=, >=)
rules of operator precedence
run-time error
Show method of class MessageBox
sign operations (+ and -)
single-line comment
single-quote character (')
Sqrt method of class Math
startup object
statement
straight-line form
string concatenation operator (&)
string literal

structured programming
Sub keyword
subtraction operator (-)
syntax error
syntax-color highlighting
System.Windows.Forms namespace
true condition
unary minus operator (-)
unary operator
unary plus operator (+)
variable
variable name
variable size
variable type
variable value
whitespace character
Write method of class Console
WriteLine method of class Console

Self-Review Exercises

3.1   Fill in the blanks in each of the following statements:

a) Keyword _____ begins the body of a module, and keywords _____ end the body of a module.

b) The _____ symbol begins a comment.

c) _____, _____ and _____ collectively are known as whitespace.

d) Class _____ contains methods for displaying dialogs.

e) _____ are words reserved for use by Visual Basic.

f) Visual Basic console applications begin execution at method _____.

g) Methods _____ and _____ of class Console display information in the **Console** window.

h) Keyword _____ begins the method body, and keywords _____ end the method body.

i) A Visual Basic program uses a(n) _____ statement to indicate that a namespace is being used.

j) When a value is placed in a memory location, this value _____ the previous value in that location.

k) The indication that operators are applied from left to right refers to the _____ of the operators.

l) Visual Basic's If...Then statement allows a program to make a decision based on the _____ or _____ of a condition.

m) Types such as Integer are often called _____ types.

n) A variable is a location in the computer's _____ where a value can be stored for use by a program.

o) The expression to the _____ of an assignment (=) is always evaluated first before the assignment occurs.

p) Expressions in Visual Basic must be written in _____ form to facilitate entering programs into the computer.

3.2   State whether each of the following is *true* or *false*. If *false*, explain why.

a) Comments cause the computer to print the text after the ' on the screen when the program executes.

b) All variables must be declared before they can be used in a Visual Basic program.
c) Visual Basic considers the variable names `number` and `NuMbEr` to be different.
d) The arithmetic operators `*`, `/`, `+` and `-` all have the same level of precedence.
e) A string of characters contained between double quotation marks is called a phrase or phrase literal.
f) Method `Display` of class `MessageBox` displays a message dialog.
g) Integer division yields an `Integer` result.

Answers to Self-Review Exercises

3.1   a) `Module`, `End Module`. b) single quotation mark, `'`. c) Blank lines, space characters, tab characters. d) `MessageBox`. e) Keywords. f) `Main`. g) `Write`, `WriteLine`. h) `Sub`, `End Sub`. i) `Imports`. j) replaces. k) associativity. l) truth, falsity. m) primitive. n) memory. o) right. p) straight-line.

3.2   a) False. Comments do not cause any action to be performed when the program executes. They are used to document programs and improve their readability. b) True. c) False. Visual Basic identifiers are not case sensitive, so these variable names are identical. d) False. The operators `*` and `/` are on the same level of precedence, and the operators `+` and `-` are on a lower level of precedence. e) False. A string of characters is called a string or string literal. f) False. Method `Show` of class `MessageBox` displays a message dialog. g) True.

Exercises

[*Note:* For the exercises in this chapter, assume that outputs are to be displayed in a Command Prompt window unless otherwise directed. For instance, you may be asked to display your output in a message dialog.]

3.3   Write Visual Basic statements that accomplish each of the following tasks:
a) Display the message `"Hello"` using class `MessageBox`.
b) Assign the product of variables `number` and `userData` to variable `result`.
c) State that a program performs a sample payroll calculation (i.e., use text that helps to document a program).

3.4   What displays in the message dialog when each of the following statements is performed? Assume that the value of `x` is 2 and the value of `y` is 3.
a) `MessageBox.Show(x, "x")`
b) `MessageBox.Show((x + x), "(x + x)")`
c) `MessageBox.Show("x + y")`

3.5   Given $z = 8e^5 - n$, which of the following are correct statements for this equation?
a) `z = 8 * e ^ 5 - n`
b) `z = ( 8 * e ) ^ 5 - n`
c) `z = 8 * ( e ^ 5 ) - n`
d) `z = 8 * e ^ ( 5 - n )`

3.6   Indicate the order of evaluation of the operators in each of the following Visual Basic statements, and show the value of `x` after each statement is performed.
a) `x = 7 + 3 * 3 \ 2 - 1`
b) `x = 2 Mod 2 + 2 * 2 - 2 / 2`
c) `x = ( 3 * 9 * ( 3 + ( 9 * 3 / ( 3 ) ) ) )`

3.7   Write a program that displays the numbers 1 to 4 on the same line, with each pair of adjacent numbers separated by one space. Write the program using the following:
a) Use one `Write` statement.
b) Use four `Write` statements.

3.8   Write a program that prompts the user for two integers, obtains them from the user and prints their sum, product, difference and integer quotient.

3.9   Write a program that inputs from the user the radius of a circle and displays the circle's diameter, circumference and area. Use the following formulas (*r* is the radius): *diameter = 2r, circumference = 2πr, area = πr²*. Use *3.14159* for π.

3.10   Write a program that displays a box, an oval, an arrow and a diamond using asterisks (*) as follows:

```
*********        ***           *             *
*       *      *     *       ***           *   *
*       *     *       *     *****          *     *
*       *     *       *       *          *       *
*       *     *       *       *         *         *
*       *     *       *       *          *       *
*       *     *       *       *           *     *
*       *      *     *        *            *   *
*********        ***          *              *
```

3.11   What does the following group of statements print?

```
Console.Write("*        * ")
Console.WriteLine(" *****")
Console.WriteLine("*      *   *    *")
Console.Write(" *    *    **")
Console.WriteLine("***")
Console.WriteLine(" * *     *     *")
Console.Write("   ")
Console.WriteLine("*        *****")
```

3.12   Write a program that reads two integers and determines and prints whether the first is a multiple of the second. For example, if the user inputs 15 and 3, the first number is a multiple of the second. If the user inputs 2 and 4, the first number is not a multiple of the second. [*Hint:* Use the Mod operator.]

3.13   Write a program that inputs one number consisting of five digits from the user, separates the number into its individual digits and prints the digits separated from one another by three spaces each. For example, if the user types in the number 42339, the program should display:

```
4   2   3   3   9
```

[*Hint:* This exercise is possible with the techniques discussed in this chapter. You will need to use both the integer division and modulus operations to "pick off" each digit.]

3.14   Using only the programming techniques discussed in this chapter, write a program that calculates the squares and cubes of the numbers from 0 to 5 and displays the resulting values in table format as follows:

```
number  square  cube
0       0       0
1       1       1
2       4       8
3       9       27
4       16      64
5       25      125
```

This program does not require any input from the user.

3.15   Write an application that reads five integers and determines and prints the largest and the smallest integers in the group. Use only the programming techniques you learned in this chapter.

3.16   Write a program that reads a first name and a last name from the user as two separate inputs and concatenates the first name and last name, separating them by a space. Display the concatenated name in a message dialog. To do this exercise, you will need to store user input in variables of type `String`, a primitive type used to represent string data. You can create variables of type `String` just as you created variables of types `Integer` and `Double`, except using the keyword `String`:

```
Dim firstName As String
Dim lastName As String
```

Variables `firstName` and `lastName` can now be used to store user input, display text in a message dialog, and perform other tasks. You will learn more about type `String` in the next chapter.

3.17   Write a program that inputs five numbers and determines and prints the number of negative numbers input, the number of positive numbers input and the number of zeros input. Do not count zero as either a positive or negative number. Display your output in a message dialog.

4

Introduction to Classes and Objects

OBJECTIVES

In this chapter, you will learn:

- What classes, objects, methods, instance variables and properties are.
- How to declare a class and use it to create an object.
- How to implement a class's behaviors as methods.
- How to implement a class's attributes as instance variables and properties.
- How to call an object's methods to make them perform their tasks.
- The differences between instance variables of a class and local variables of a method.
- How to use a constructor to ensure that an object's attributes are initialized when the object is created.
- The differences between value types and reference types.
- How to use properties to ensure that only valid data is placed in attributes.

4.1 Introduction

We introduced the basic terminology and concepts of object-oriented programming in Section 1.17. In Chapter 3, you began to use those concepts to create simple applications that displayed messages to the user, obtained information from the user, performed calculations and made decisions. One common feature of every application in Chapter 3 was that all the statements that performed tasks were located in method Main, in a module. Many of the applications you develop in this book will consist of one or more classes, each containing one or more methods. These classes will then be used in the module that contains Main. If you become part of a development team in industry, you may work on applications that contain hundreds, or even thousands, of classes. In this chapter, we present a simple framework for organizing object-oriented applications in Visual Basic.

First, we motivate the notion of classes with a real-world example. Then we present five complete working applications to demonstrate creating and using your own classes. These examples begin our integrated case study on developing a grade-book class that instructors can use to maintain student test scores. This case study is enhanced over the next several chapters, culminating with the version presented in Chapter 8, Arrays.

4.2 Classes, Objects, Methods and Instance Variables

We will begin with a simple analogy to help you understand classes and their contents. Suppose you want to drive a car and make it go faster by pressing down on its accelerator pedal. What must happen before you can do this? Well, before you can drive a car, someone has to design the car. A car typically begins as engineering drawings, similar to the blueprints used to design a house. These engineering drawings include the design for an accelerator pedal to make the car go faster. The pedal "hides" the complex mechanisms that actually make the car go faster, just as the brake pedal "hides" the mechanisms that slow the car and the steering wheel "hides" the mechanisms that turn the car. This enables people with little or no knowledge of how engines work to easily drive a car.

Unfortunately, you cannot drive a car's engineering drawings. Before you can drive a car, the car must be built from the engineering drawings that describe it. A completed car has an actual accelerator pedal to make it go faster, but even that is not enough—the car will not accelerate on its own, so the driver must press the accelerator pedal.

Now let's use our car example to introduce the key programming concepts of this section. Performing a task in a program requires a method. The method describes the mechanisms that actually perform its tasks. The method hides these mechanisms from its user, just as the accelerator pedal of a car hides from the driver the complex mechanisms that make the car go faster. In Visual Basic, we begin by creating a program unit called a class to house a method, just as a car's engineering drawings house the design of an accelerator pedal. In a class, you provide one or more methods that are designed to perform the class's tasks. For example, a class that represents a bank account might contain many methods, including one to deposit money in the account, another to withdraw money from the account and a third to inquire what the current balance is.

Just as you cannot drive an engineering drawing of a car, you cannot "drive" a class. Just as someone has to build a car from its engineering drawings before you can actually drive it, you must build an object of a class before you can get a program to perform the tasks the class describes how to do. That is one reason Visual Basic is known as an object-oriented programming language.

When you drive a car, pressing its gas pedal sends a message to the car to perform a task—that is, to go faster. Similarly, you send messages to an object—each message is known as a method call and tells one of an object's methods to perform its task.

Thus far, we have used the car analogy to introduce classes, objects and methods. In addition to the capabilities a car provides, it also has many attributes, such as its color, the number of doors, the amount of gas in its tank, its current speed and its odometer reading (i.e., its total miles driven since it was built). Like the car's capabilities, its attributes are represented as part of a car's design in its engineering diagrams. As you drive a car, these attributes are always associated with the car. For example, each car knows how much gas is in its own gas tank, but not how much is in the tanks of other cars. Similarly, an object has attributes that are carried with it as it's used in a program. These attributes are specified in the object's class. For example, a bank account object has a balance attribute that represents the amount of money in the account. Each bank account object knows the balance in the account it represents, but not the balances of the other accounts in the bank. Attributes are specified by the class's instance variables.

This chapter presents five simple examples that demonstrate the concepts introduced in the context of the car analogy. The examples incrementally build a GradeBook class:

1. The first example presents a GradeBook class with one method that simply displays a welcome message when it is called. We show how to create an object of the class and call the method so that it displays the welcome message.

2. The second example modifies the first by allowing the method to receive a course name as an argument and display the name as part of the welcome message.

3. The third example shows how to store the course name in a GradeBook object. We show how to use the convenient notation of "properties" to set the course name in the object and obtain the course name from the object.

4. The fourth example demonstrates how the data in a GradeBook object can be initialized when the object is created—the initialization is performed by the class's constructor (a special type of method with the name New).

5. The last example enhances class GradeBook by introducing data validation, which ensures that data in an object adheres to a particular format or is in a proper value range. For example, a Date object should accept month values only in the range 1–12. In our GradeBook example, the property that sets the course name for a GradeBook object ensures that the course name is 25 or fewer characters. If not, the property uses only the first 25 characters of the course name and displays a warning message. Restrictions like this are common in information systems that have to display data in fixed-size boxes in a form on the screen.

The GradeBook examples in this chapter do not process or store grades. We begin processing grades with the version of class GradeBook in Chapter 5, Control Statements: Part 1, and we store grades in the version of GradeBook in Chapter 8, Arrays.

4.3 Declaring a Class with a Method and Instantiating an Object of a Class

We begin with an example that consists of class GradeBook (Fig. 4.1) and module GradeBookTest (Fig. 4.2). Class GradeBook (declared in file GradeBook.vb) displays a message on the screen (Fig. 4.2) welcoming the instructor to the grade-book application. Module GradeBookTest (declared in file GradeBookTest.vb) contains the Main method that instantiates (creates) and uses an object of class GradeBook. The class and module are placed in separate files for clarity, but it is possible to place them in the same file.

Adding a Class to a Visual Basic Project

For each example in this chapter, you will add a class to your console application. To do this, right click the project name in the **Solution Explorer** and select **Add > Class...** from the menu that appears. In the **Add New Item** dialog that appears, enter the name of your new file, in this case GradeBook.vb. A new file will be added to your project with an empty GradeBook class. Add the code from Fig. 4.1 to this file—we will discuss this code shortly.

Class *GradeBook*

The GradeBook class declaration (Fig. 4.1) contains a DisplayMessage method (lines 5–7) that displays a message on the screen. Recall that a class is like a blueprint—we need to make an object of class GradeBook and call its method to get line 6 to execute and display its message. We do this in the Main method in Fig. 4.2.

The class declaration begins at line 3. The keyword Public is an access modifier. For now, we will simply declare every class Public. Every class declaration contains keyword

```
1  ' Fig. 4.1: GradeBook.vb
2  ' Class declaration with one method.
3  Public Class GradeBook
4     ' display a welcome message to the GradeBook user
5     Public Sub DisplayMessage()
6        Console.WriteLine("Welcome to the Grade Book!")
7     End Sub ' DisplayMessage
8  End Class ' GradeBook
```

Fig. 4.1 | Class declaration with one method.

`Class` followed immediately by the class's name. Every class's body ends with the keywords `End Class`, as in line 8 of class `GradeBook`.

Method *DisplayMessage*

Class `GradeBook` has one method—`DisplayMessage` (lines 5–7). The method declaration begins with keyword `Public` to indicate that the method is "available to the public"—that is, it can be called from outside the class declaration's body by methods of other classes or modules (these other classes and modules are called clients of the class). Keyword `Sub` indicates that this method will perform a task but will not return (i.e., give back) any information to its calling method when it completes its task. You have already used methods that return information—for example, in Chapter 3 you used `Console` method `ReadLine` to input an integer typed by the user at the keyboard. When `ReadLine` inputs a value, it returns that value for use in the program.

The name of the method, `DisplayMessage`, follows keyword `Sub`. By convention, method names begin with an uppercase letter and all subsequent words in the name begin with a capital letter (recall that Visual Basic is not case sensitive). The parentheses after the method name are used to indicate any parameters—additional information that is required by the method to perform its task (we discuss parameters in more detail in Section 4.4). An empty set of parentheses, as in line 5, indicates that this method does not require any additional information and does not need any parameters. We refer to the part of the method in line 5 as the method header. Like `Main`, method `DisplayMessage` ends with keywords `End Sub`.

The body of a method contains statements that perform the method's task. In this case, the method contains one statement (line 6) that displays the message `"Welcome to the Grade Book!"` in the **Console** window. After this statement executes, the method has completed its task.

Note that the `DisplayMessage` method declaration is similar to the declaration of `Main`. We discuss methods in depth in Chapter 7, Methods: A Deeper Look.

In Chapter 3, each module we declared had one method named `Main`. Class `GradeBook`, likewise, has one method. Recall that `Main` is a special method that is required to begin the execution of every application. `Main` is called automatically by the runtime when you execute an application. Most methods do not get called automatically. As you will soon see, you must call method `DisplayMessage` to tell it to perform its task.

Using Class *GradeBook*

We will now use class `GradeBook` in an application. A Visual Basic project that contains only class `GradeBook` is not an application that can be executed because `GradeBook` does not contain `Main`. If you try to compile such a project, you will get the error message:

```
'Sub Main' was not found in 'GradeBook.GradeBookTest'.
```

This was not a problem in Chapter 3, because every application you created contained a `Main` method. To fix this problem for the `GradeBook`, either we must declare a separate class or module that contains `Main`, or we must place `Main` in class `GradeBook`. We use a separate module (`GradeBookTest` in this example) containing `Main` to test each new class we create in this chapter.

Module GradeBookTest

The GradeBookTest module declaration (Fig. 4.2; lines 3–12) contains the Main method (lines 5–11) that controls our application's execution. The module contains only a Main method, which is typical of many modules that begin an application's execution.

Lines 5–11 declare method Main. In this application, we would like to call class GradeBook's DisplayMessage method to display the welcome message in the **Console** window. Typically, you cannot call a method that belongs to another class until you create an object of that class. We begin by declaring variable gradeBook (line 7). Note that the variable's type is GradeBook—the class we declared in Fig. 4.1. Each new class you create becomes a new type in Visual Basic that can be used to declare variables and create objects. Programmers can declare new class types as needed; this is one reason why Visual Basic is known as an extensible language.

Variable gradeBook is initialized with the result of the object creation expression New GradeBook() (Fig. 4.2; line 7). Operator New creates a new object of the class specified to the right of the New keyword (i.e., GradeBook). The class name is followed by a set of parentheses. As you will learn in Section 4.7, those parentheses in combination with a class name represent a call to a constructor, a special type of method that is used only when an object is created to initialize the object's data. In that section you will see that arguments can be placed in the parentheses to specify initial values for the object's data. In this example, we simply leave the parentheses empty. When there are no arguments to be placed in the parentheses, Visual Basic allows for the parentheses to be omitted, as in the next example. Although Visual Basic is not case sensitive, it does allow us to create objects (e.g., gradeBook) with the "same" name as their class (e.g. GradeBook)—we do this throughout the book.

We can now use object gradeBook to call method DisplayMessage. Line 10 calls DisplayMessage (declared in lines 5–7 of Fig. 4.1) using variable gradeBook followed by a dot separator (.), the method name DisplayMessage and an empty set of parentheses. This call causes the DisplayMessage method to perform its task. This method call differs from the method calls in Chapter 3 that displayed information in the **Console** window— each of those method calls provided arguments that specified the data to display. At the

```
 1    ' Fig. 4.2: GradeBookTest.vb
 2    ' Create a GradeBook object and call its DisplayMessage method.
 3    Module GradeBookTest
 4       ' Main begins program execution
 5       Sub Main()
 6          ' initialize gradeBook to refer to a new GradeBook object
 7          Dim gradeBook As New GradeBook()
 8
 9          ' call gradeBook's DisplayMessage method
10          gradeBook.DisplayMessage()
11       End Sub ' Main
12    End Module ' GradeBookTest
```

```
Welcome to the Grade Book!
```

Fig. 4.2 | Creating an object of class GradeBook and calling its DisplayMessage method.

beginning of line 10, "gradeBook." indicates that Main should use the object of class GradeBook that was created in line 7. The empty parentheses in line 5 of Fig. 4.1 indicate that method DisplayMessage has no parameters—that is, DisplayMessage does not require additional information to perform its task. For this reason, the method call (line 10 of Fig. 4.2) specifies an empty set of parentheses after the method name to indicate that no arguments are being passed to method DisplayMessage. When method Display-Message completes its task, Main continues executing at line 11, which is the end of method Main, so the program terminates.

UML Class Diagram for Class *GradeBook*

Figure 4.3 presents a UML class diagram for class GradeBook of Fig. 4.1. Recall from Section 1.17 that the UML is a graphical language that programmers use to represent their object-oriented systems in a standardized manner. In the UML, each class is modeled in a class diagram as a rectangle with three compartments. The top compartment contains the name of the class centered horizontally in boldface type. The middle compartment contains the class's **attributes**, which correspond to instance variables in Visual Basic. In Fig. 4.3, the middle compartment is empty because the version of class GradeBook in Fig. 4.1 does not have any attributes. The bottom compartment contains the class's **operations**, which correspond to methods in Visual Basic. The UML models an operation by listing its name followed by a set of parentheses. Class GradeBook has one method, DisplayMessage, so the bottom compartment of Fig. 4.3 lists the operation with this name. Method DisplayMessage does not require additional information to perform its tasks, so the parentheses following DisplayMessage in the class diagram are empty, just as they were in the method's declaration in line 5 of Fig. 4.1. The plus sign (+) in front of the operation name indicates that DisplayMessage is a public operation in the UML (because it is a Public method in Visual Basic). We will often use UML class diagrams to summarize a class's attributes and operations.

4.4 Declaring a Method with a Parameter

In our car analogy in Section 4.2, we discussed the fact that pressing a car's gas pedal sends a message to the car to perform a task—make the car go faster. But how fast should the car accelerate? The farther down you press the pedal, the faster the car accelerates. So the message to the car actually includes both the task to perform and additional information that helps the car perform the task. This additional information is known as a parameter (mentioned briefly in Section 4.3)—the value of the parameter helps the car determine how fast to accelerate. Similarly, a method can require one or more parameters that represent additional information it needs to perform its task. A method call supplies values—called ar-

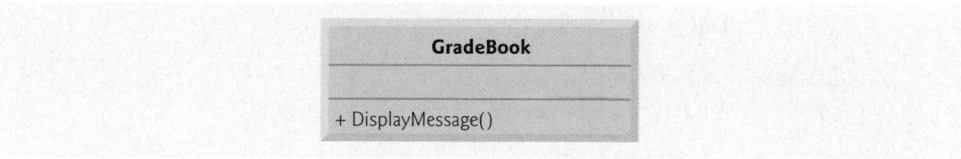

Fig. 4.3 | UML class diagram indicating that class GradeBook has a public DisplayMessage operation.

guments—for each of the method's parameters. For example, the method call to `Console.WriteLine` requires an argument that specifies the data to output in a Command Prompt window. Similarly, to deposit funds into a bank account, a `Deposit` method specifies a parameter that represents the deposit amount. When the `Deposit` method is called, the argument value representing the deposit amount is assigned to the method's parameter. The method then makes a deposit of that amount, increasing the balance in the bank account.

Our next example declares class `GradeBook` (Fig. 4.4) with a `DisplayMessage` method that displays the course name as part of the welcome message. (See the sample execution in Fig. 4.5.) The new `DisplayMessage` method requires a parameter that represents the course name to output (line 5).

Before discussing the new features of class `GradeBook`, let us see how the new class is used from the `Main` method of module `GradeBookTest` (Fig. 4.5). Line 7 initializes variable `gradeBook` to reference a new `GradeBook` object. Note that empty parentheses are

```vb
1   ' Fig. 4.4: GradeBook.vb
2   ' Class declaration with a method that has a parameter.
3   Public Class GradeBook
4      ' display a welcome message to the GradeBook user
5      Public Sub DisplayMessage(ByVal courseName As String)
6         Console.WriteLine( _
7            "Welcome to the grade book for " & vbCrLf & courseName & "!")
8      End Sub ' DisplayMessage
9   End Class ' GradeBook
```

Fig. 4.4 | Class declaration with one method that has a parameter.

```vb
1   ' Fig. 4.5: GradeBookTest.vb
2   ' Create a GradeBook object and call its DisplayMessage method.
3   Module GradeBookTest
4      ' Main begins program execution
5      Sub Main()
6         ' initialize gradeBook to reference a new gradeBook object
7         Dim gradeBook As New GradeBook()
8
9         ' prompt for the course name
10        Console.WriteLine("Please enter the course name:")
11
12        ' read the course name
13        Dim nameOfCourse As String = Console.ReadLine()
14
15        Console.WriteLine() ' output a blank line
16
17        ' call gradeBook's DisplayMessage method
18        ' and pass nameOfCourse as an argument
19        gradeBook.DisplayMessage(nameOfCourse)
20     End Sub ' Main
21  End Module ' GradeBookTest
```

Fig. 4.5 | Creating a GradeBook object and passing a String to its DisplayMessage method. (Part 1 of 2.)

```
Please enter the course name:
CS101 Introduction to Visual Basic Programming

Welcome to the grade book for
CS101 Introduction to Visual Basic Programming!
```

Fig. 4.5 | Creating a GradeBook object and passing a String to its DisplayMessage method. (Part 2 of 2.)

used in the object-creation expression (New GradeBook()), because no arguments need to be passed to create a GradeBook object. Line 10 prompts the user to enter a course name. Line 13 reads the name from the user and assigns it to the nameOfCourse variable, using method ReadLine to perform the input. The user types the course name and presses *Enter* to submit the course name to the program. Variable nameOfCourse is declared as a String (line 13). **String** is the type used for strings in Visual Basic, such as names, addresses, cities, states and product descriptions. Strings can consist of up to 2,147,483,648 (2^{31}) characters.

Line 19 calls gradeBook's DisplayMessage method. The argument nameOfCourse in parentheses is passed to method DisplayMessage so that it can perform its task. The value of variable nameOfCourse in Main (i.e., whatever course name the user types) becomes the value of method DisplayMessage's parameter courseName in line 5 of Fig. 4.4. When you execute this application, you will see that method DisplayMessage outputs a welcome message with the course name you type (Fig. 4.5).

More on Arguments and Parameters
When you declare a method, you must specify in the method's declaration whether the method requires data to perform its task. To do so, you place additional information in the method's **parameter list**, which is located in the parentheses that follow the method name. The parameter list may contain any number of parameters, including none at all. In Fig. 4.4, DisplayMessage's parameter list (line 5) declares that the method requires one parameter. Each parameter must specify a type and an identifier. In this case, the type String and the identifier courseName indicate that method DisplayMessage requires a String parameter named courseName in order to perform its task. At the time the method is called, the argument value in the call (in this case, the value of nameOfCourse in line 19 of Fig. 4.5) is assigned to the corresponding parameter in the method header (in this case, courseName in line 5 of Fig. 4.4). Then the method body uses the parameter courseName to access the value. Lines 6–7 of Fig. 4.4 display parameter courseName's value. The parameter variable's name (Fig. 4.4, line 5) can be the same or different from the argument variable's name (Fig. 4.5, line 19)—there is no conflict if the names are identical, because as we will see in Chapter 7, Methods: A Deeper Look, these names appear in different "scopes."

Note that the parameter declaration in the parameter list looks similar to a variable declaration, but uses keyword **ByVal** instead of Dim. ByVal specifies that the calling program should pass a copy of the value of the argument in the method call to the parameter, which can be used in the method body. Section 7.13 discusses argument-passing options in detail.

A method can specify multiple parameters by separating each from the next with a comma. The number of arguments in a method call must match the number of parameters in the called method's parameter list. Also, the argument types in the method call must be "consistent" with the types of the corresponding parameters in the method's declaration. (As you will learn in subsequent chapters, an argument's type and its corresponding parameter's type are not always required to be identical.) In our example, the method call (line 19 of Fig. 4.5) passes one argument of type String (nameOfCourse is declared as a String in line 13 of Fig. 4.5) and the method declaration specifies one parameter of type String (line 5 in Fig. 4.4), so the type of the argument in the method call is identical to the type of the parameter in the method header.

Updated UML Class Diagram for Class *GradeBook*

The UML class diagram in Fig. 4.6 models class GradeBook of Fig. 4.4. Like Fig. 4.1, this GradeBook class contains public operation DisplayMessage. However, this version of DisplayMessage has a parameter. The UML models a parameter a bit differently from Visual Basic, by listing the parameter name in the parentheses following the operation name, followed by a colon and the parameter type. The UML has several data types that are similar to the Visual Basic types. For example, UML types String and Integer correspond to Visual Basic types String and Integer, respectively. Unfortunately, the UML does not provide types that correspond to every Visual Basic type. For this reason, and to avoid confusion between UML types and Visual Basic types, we use only Visual Basic types in our UML diagrams. Class GradeBook's method DisplayMessage (Fig. 4.4) has a String parameter named courseName, so Fig. 4.6 lists courseName : String between the parentheses following DisplayMessage.

4.5 Instance Variables and Properties

In Chapter 3, we declared all of an application's variables in the Main method. Variables declared in the body of a particular method are known as local variables and can be used only in that method. When a method terminates, the values of its local variables are lost. In contrast, an object's attributes are carried with the object as it is used in a program. Such attributes exist before a method is called on the object, while the method is executing, and after the method completes execution.

Attributes are represented as variables in a class declaration. Such variables are called instance variables and are declared inside a class declaration but outside the bodies of the class's other members, such as methods (and properties, which are discussed later in this section). Each object of a class maintains its own copy of an instance variable—that is, each object (instance) of the class has a separate instance of the variable in memory. [*Note:* In

Fig. 4.6 | UML class diagram indicating that class GradeBook has a DisplayMessage operation with a courseName parameter of type String.

Chapter 9, Classes and Objects: A Deeper Look, we discuss another type of variable called a Shared variable, where all objects of a class share one copy of the variable.] The following example demonstrates a GradeBook class that contains a courseNameValue instance variable to represent a particular GradeBook object's course name.

GradeBook *Class with an Instance Variable and a Property*

The next version of class GradeBook (Fig. 4.7) maintains the course name as instance variable courseNameValue (line 5) so that the course name can be used or modified at any time during an application's execution. The class also contains one method—DisplayMessage (lines 19–24)—and one property—CourseName (line 8–16). Recall from Chapter 2 that properties are used to manipulate an object's attributes. For example, in that chapter, we used a Label's Text property to specify the text to display on the Label. In this example, we use a property in code rather than in the **Properties** window of the IDE. To do this, we first declare a property as a member of the GradeBook class. As you will soon see, the GradeBook's CourseName property can be used to store a course name in a GradeBook (in instance variable courseNameValue) or retrieve the GradeBook's course name (from instance variable courseNameValue). Method DisplayMessage—which now specifies no parameters—still displays a welcome message that includes the course name. However, the method now uses the CourseName property to obtain the course name from instance variable courseNameValue.

```vb
1   ' Fig. 4.7: GradeBook.vb
2   ' GradeBook class that contains instance variable courseNameValue
3   ' and a property to get and set its value.
4   Public Class GradeBook
5      Private courseNameValue As String ' course name for this GradeBook
6
7      ' property CourseName
8      Public Property CourseName() As String
9         Get ' retrieve courseNameValue
10            Return courseNameValue
11         End Get
12
13         Set(ByVal value As String) ' set courseNameValue
14            courseNameValue = value ' store the course name in the object
15         End Set
16      End Property ' CourseName
17
18      ' display a welcome message to the GradeBook user
19      Public Sub DisplayMessage()
20         ' use property CourseName to display the
21         ' name of the course this GradeBook represents
22         Console.WriteLine("Welcome to the grade book for " _
23            & vbCrLf & CourseName & "!")
24      End Sub ' DisplayMessage
25   End Class ' GradeBook
```

Fig. 4.7 | GradeBook class that contains a courseNameValue instance variable and a CourseName property.

A typical instructor teaches more than one course, each with its own course name. Line 5 declares instance variable courseNameValue as a String. Line 5 is a declaration for an instance variable because it is in the body of the class (lines 4–25) but outside the bodies of the class's method (lines 19–24) and property (lines 8–16). Every GradeBook object requires its own copy of instance variable courseNameValue because each object represents a GradeBook for a different course. All the methods and properties of class GradeBook can directly manipulate its instance variable courseNameValue, but it is considered good practice for methods to use properties to manipulate instance variables (as we do in line 23 of method DisplayMessage)—we will see why in Section 4.8, Validating Data with Set Accessors in Properties.

Note that line 23 contains the identifier, vbCrLf, which is not declared explicitly in the program. Identifier vbCrLf is one of several predefined **constants** provided by Visual Basic. Constants contain values that programmers cannot modify. The constant vbCrLf represents a combination of the **carriage return** and **linefeed** characters. Outputting this constant's value causes subsequent text to display at the beginning of the next line. The effect of this constant is similar to calling Console.WriteLine().

Although not demonstrated in this example, Visual Basic also provides the **vbTab** constant, which represents a *Tab* character. Both the vbCrLf and vbTab constants are defined in the Constants module. To view the complete list of constants, select **Help > Index** and type **Constants module** in the **Look for** field. Then select **Constants module** from the index list to view all of Visual Basic's predefined constants.

Access Modifiers *Public and Private*

Most instance variable declarations are preceded with the access modifier Private (as in line 5 of Fig. 4.7). Variables, methods and properties that are declared Private are accessible only to methods and properties of the class in which they are declared. Note that the keyword Dim is replaced by Private in an instance variable declaration.

Declaring instance variables with access modifier Private is known as **information hiding**. When a program creates (instantiates) an object of class GradeBook, variable courseNameValue is encapsulated (hidden) in the object and can be accessed only by methods and properties of the object's class.

Software Engineering Observation 4.1

Precede every instance variable declaration, method declaration and property declaration with an access modifier. In most cases, instance variables should be declared Private, and methods and properties should be declared Public. If these modifiers are omitted, instance variables are Private by default, and methods and properties are Public by default. (We will see in Section 9.2 that it is appropriate to declare certain methods and properties Private if they should be accessed only by other methods and properties of the class.)

Software Engineering Observation 4.2

Declaring the instance variables of a class as Private and the methods of the class as Public facilitates debugging, because problems with data manipulations are localized to the class's methods and properties.

Setting and Getting the Values of *Private* Instance Variables

How can we allow a program to manipulate a class's Private instance variables but ensure that they remain in a valid state? We need to provide controlled ways for programmers to "get" (i.e., retrieve) the value in an instance variable and "set" (i.e., modify) the value in an instance variable. For these purposes, programmers using languages other than Visual Basic normally use methods known as *get* and *set* methods. These methods typically are made `Public`, and provide ways for the client to access or modify `Private` data. Historically, these methods begin with the words "get" and "set"—in our class `GradeBook` for example, if we were to use such methods they might be called `GetCourseNameValue` and `SetCourseNameValue`, respectively. Although it is possible to define methods with these names, Visual Basic properties provide a more elegant solution.

GradeBook *Class with a Property*

The `GradeBook` class's `CourseName` property declaration is located in lines 8–16 of Fig. 4.7. The property begins in line 8 with an access modifier (in this case, `Public`), followed by the keyword **Property**, the property's name—CourseName—and an empty set of parentheses. The keywords `As String` indicate that property `CourseName` represents a `String` (which in this example is the instance variable `courseNameValue`).

Properties contain accessors that handle the details of returning and modifying data. A property declaration can contain a **Get** accessor, a **Set** accessor or both. The `Get` accessor (lines 9–11) enables a client to read the value of `Private` instance variable `courseNameValue`; the `Set` accessor (lines 13–15) enables a client to modify `courseNameValue`.

After defining a property, you can use it like a variable in your code. For example, you can assign a value to a property using an assignment statement. This executes the code in the property's `Set` accessor to set the value of the corresponding instance variable. Similarly, referencing the property to use its value (for example, to display it on the screen) executes the code in the property's `Get` accessor to obtain the corresponding instance variable's value. We will demonstrate how to use properties in a program shortly. When we use properties in our examples, our convention is to append "`Value`" to instance variable names (e.g., `courseNameValue`). Visual Basic is not case sensitive, so we cannot have both an instance variable named `courseName` and a property named `CourseName` in the same class.

Get *and* Set *Accessors*

Let us look more closely at property `CourseName`'s `Get` and `Set` accessors (Fig. 4.7). The `Get` accessor (lines 9–11) begins with the keyword **Get** and ends with the keywords **End Get**. The accessor's body contains a **Return statement**, which consists of the keyword **Return** followed by an expression. The expression's value is returned to the client code that references the property. In this example, the value of `courseNameValue` is returned when the property `CourseName` is referenced. For example, the following statement

```
Dim theCourseName As String = gradeBook.CourseName
```

executes property `CourseName`'s `Get` accessor, which returns the value of instance variable `courseNameValue`. That value is then stored in variable `theCourseName`. Note that property `CourseName` can be used as simply as if it were an instance variable. The property notation allows the client to think of the property as the underlying data. Again, the client cannot directly manipulate instance variable `courseNameValue` because it is `Private`.

The `Set` accessor (lines 13–15) begins with the keyword **Set** and ends with the keywords **End Set**. Following the keyword `Set` in line 13 is a pair of parentheses enclosing the

Set accessor's parameter. When the property CourseName appears in an assignment statement, as in

```
gradeBook.CourseName = "CS100 Introduction to Computers"
```

the text "CS100 Introduction to Computers" is automatically passed to the parameter named value in line 13, and the Set accessor executes. Line 14 then stores value in instance variable courseNameValue. Set accessors do not return any data when they complete their tasks.

When you type the first line of a property declaration in the IDE and press *Enter*, the IDE creates empty Get and Set accessors for you. The parameter for the Set accessor is named value by default, so we use this parameter name in our examples. You can choose a different name if you like.

The statements inside the property's accessors at lines 10 and 14 (Fig. 4.7) each access courseNameValue even though it was declared (as Private) outside the accessors. We can use variable courseNameValue in the methods and properties of class GradeBook because courseNameValue is an instance variable of the class. The order in which methods and properties are declared in a class does not determine when they are called at execution time, so you can declare method DisplayMessage (which uses property CourseName) before you declare property CourseName. Within the property itself, the Get and Set accessors can appear in any order, and either accessor can be omitted. In Chapter 9, we discuss how to omit either a Set or Get accessor to create a "read-only" or "write-only" property, respectively.

Using Property CourseName in Method DisplayMessage
Method DisplayMessage (lines 19–24 of Fig. 4.7) does not receive any parameters. Lines 22–23 output a welcome message that includes the value of instance variable courseNameValue. We do not reference courseNameValue directly. Instead, we access property CourseName (line 23), which automatically executes the property's Get accessor, returning the value of courseNameValue.

GradeBookTest Module That Demonstrates Class GradeBook
Module GradeBookTest (Fig. 4.8) creates a GradeBook object and demonstrates property CourseName. Line 8 creates a GradeBook object that is referenced by variable gradeBook of type GradeBook. Lines 11–12 display the initial course name by referencing the object's CourseName property—this executes the property's Get accessor, which returns the value of courseNameValue. Note that the first line of the output does not contain a course name. Variables have a **default initial value**—a value provided by Visual Basic when the programmer does not specify the variable's initial value. The default value for numeric types like Integer is zero. As we will see in the next section, String is a reference type; the default value for reference types is **Nothing**—a keyword which indicates that a variable does not yet refer to an object. When you display a String variable that contains the value Nothing, no text is displayed on the screen.

Line 15 prompts the user to enter a course name. Local String variable theName (declared in line 18) is initialized with the course name entered by the user, which is returned by the call to Console.ReadLine(). Line 20 assigns theName to the gradeBook object's CourseName property. When a value is assigned to CourseName, the value specified

```
 1    ' Fig. 4.8: GradeBookTest.vb
 2    ' Create and manipulate a GradeBook object.
 3    Module GradeBookTest
 4       ' Main begins program execution
 5       Sub Main()
 6          ' line 8 creates a GradeBook object that is referenced by
 7          ' variable gradeBook of type GradeBook
 8          Dim gradeBook As New GradeBook
 9
10          ' display initial value of property CourseName (invokes Get)
11          Console.WriteLine( _
12             "Initial course name is: " & gradeBook.CourseName & vbCrLf)
13
14          ' prompt for course name
15          Console.WriteLine("Please enter the course name:")
16
17          ' read course name
18          Dim theName As String = Console.ReadLine()
19
20          gradeBook.CourseName = theName ' set the CourseName (invokes Set)
21          Console.WriteLine() ' output a blank line
22
23          ' display welcome message including the course name (invokes Get)
24          gradeBook.DisplayMessage()
25       End Sub ' Main
26    End Module ' GradeBookTest
```

```
Initial course name is:

Please enter the course name:
CS101 Introduction to Visual Basic Programming

Welcome to the grade book for
CS101 Introduction to Visual Basic Programming!
```

Fig. 4.8 | Creating and manipulating a GradeBook object (invoking properties).

(in this case, theName) is assigned to parameter value (line 13 of Fig. 4.7) of CourseName's Set accessor (lines 13–15, Fig. 4.7). Then parameter value is assigned by the Set accessor to instance variable courseNameValue (line 14 of Fig. 4.7). Line 21 (Fig. 4.8) displays a blank line, then line 24 calls gradeBook's DisplayMessage method to display the welcome message containing the course name.

GradeBook's UML Class Diagram with a Property

Figure 4.9 contains an updated UML class diagram for the version of class GradeBook in Fig. 4.7. We model properties in the UML as attributes—the property (in this case, CourseName) is listed as a public attribute—as indicated by the plus (+) sign—preceded by the word "Property" in guillemets (« and »). Using descriptive words in guillemets (called **stereotypes** in the UML) helps distinguish properties from other attributes and operations. The UML indicates the type of the property by placing a colon and a type after the property name. The Get and Set accessors of the property are implied (otherwise, the

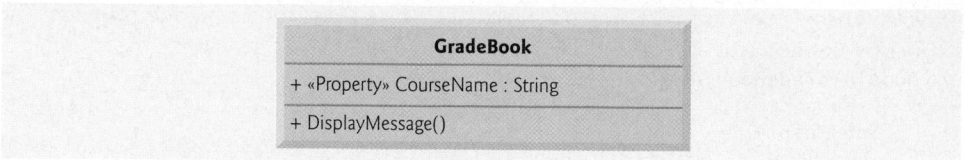

Fig. 4.9 | UML class diagram indicating that class GradeBook has a courseNameValue attribute of type String, one property and one method.

property would be inaccessible), so they are not listed in the UML diagram. In some cases, a property may require only a Get accessor to allow client code to retrieve the property's value. This is known as a "read-only" property. You can indicate this in a class diagram by placing the annotation {ReadOnly} after the property's type.

The diagram shows that class GradeBook also contains one Public method Display-Message, which the class diagram lists this operation in the third compartment. Recall that the plus (+) sign before an operation name indicates that the operation is Public.

When we demonstrated how to declare a property in Visual Basic code, you saw that we typically name a property the same as the instance variable it manipulates, but with a capital first letter (e.g., property CourseName manipulates instance variable courseName). A class diagram helps you design a class, so it is not required to show every implementation detail of the class. Since an instance variable that is manipulated by a property is really an implementation detail of that property, our class diagram does not show the courseName-Value instance variable. A programmer implementing the GradeBook class based on this class diagram would create the instance variable courseNameValue as part of the implementation process (as we did in Fig. 4.7).

In some cases, you may find it necessary to model the Private instance variables of a class, because they are not implementation details of properties. Like properties, instance variables are attributes of a class and are modeled in the middle compartment of a class diagram. The UML represents instance variables as attributes by listing the attribute name, followed by a colon and the attribute type. To indicate that an attribute is private, a class diagram would list a minus sign (–) before the attribute's name. For example, the instance variable courseNameValue in Fig. 4.7 would be modeled as "– courseNameValue : string"

Software Engineering with Properties and *Set* and *Get* Accessors

Using properties as described earlier in this section would seem to violate the notion of Private data. Although providing a property with Get and Set accessors may appear to be the same as making its corresponding instance variable Public, this is not the case. A Public instance variable can be read or written by any method in the program. If an instance variable is Private, the client code can access the instance variable only indirectly through the class's non-Private methods or properties. This allows the class to control the manner in which the data is set or returned. For example, Get and Set accessors can translate between the format of the data used by the client and the format stored in the Private instance variable.

Consider a Clock class that represents the time of day as a Private Integer instance variable timeValue containing the number of seconds since midnight. Suppose the class provides a Time property of type String to manipulate this instance variable. Although Get accessors typically return data exactly as it is stored in an object, they need not expose the data in this "raw" format. When a client refers to a Clock object's Time property, the property's Get accessor could use instance variable timeValue to determine the number of hours, minutes and seconds since midnight, then return the time as a String of the form "HH:MM:SS". Similarly, suppose a Clock object's Time property is assigned a String of the form "HH:MM:SS". Using the String capabilities presented in Section 4.8 and the method Convert.ToInt32 presented in Section 7.10, the Time property's Set accessor could convert this String to an Integer number of seconds and store the result in the Clock object's Private instance variable timeValue. The Time property's Set accessor can also provide data validation capabilities that scrutinize attempts to modify the instance variable's value to ensure that the value it receives represents a valid time (e.g., "12:30:45" is valid but "42:85:70" is not). We demonstrate data validation in Section 4.8. So, although a property's accessors enable clients to manipulate Private data, they carefully control those manipulations and the object's Private data remains safely encapsulated (i.e., hidden) in the object. This is not possible with Public instance variables, which can easily be set by clients to invalid values.

Properties of a class should also be used by the class's own methods to manipulate the class's Private instance variables, even though the methods can directly access the Private instance variables. Accessing an instance variable via a property's accessors—as in the body of method DisplayMessage (Fig. 4.7, line 23)—creates a better, more robust class that is easier to maintain and less likely to malfunction. If we decide to change the representation of instance variable courseNameValue in some way, the declaration of method DisplayMessage will not require modification—only the bodies of property CourseName's Get and Set accessors that directly manipulate the instance variable will need to change. For example, suppose that we want to represent the course name as two separate instance variables—courseNumber (e.g., "CS101") and courseTitle (e.g., "Introduction to Visual Basic Programming"). The DisplayMessage method can still use property CourseName's Get accessor to obtain the full course name to display as part of the welcome message. In this case, the Get accessor would need to build and return a String containing the courseNumber followed by the courseTitle. Method DisplayMessage would continue to display the complete course title "CS101 Introduction to Visual Basic Programming," because it is unaffected by the change to the class's instance variables.

Software Engineering Observation 4.3

Accessing Private data through Set and Get accessors not only protects the instance variables from receiving invalid values, but also hides the internal representation of the instance variables from that class's clients. Thus, if representation of the data changes (often, to reduce the amount of required storage or to improve performance), only the properties' implementations need to change—the clients' implementations need not change as long as the services provided by the properties are preserved.

4.6 Value Types and Reference Types

Data types in Visual Basic are divided into two categories—value types and reference types. A variable of a value type (such as Integer) simply contains a value of that type. For example, Fig. 4.10 shows an Integer variable named count that contains the value 7.

By contrast, a variable of a reference type (sometimes called a reference) contains the memory address where the data referred to by that variable is stored. Such a variable is said

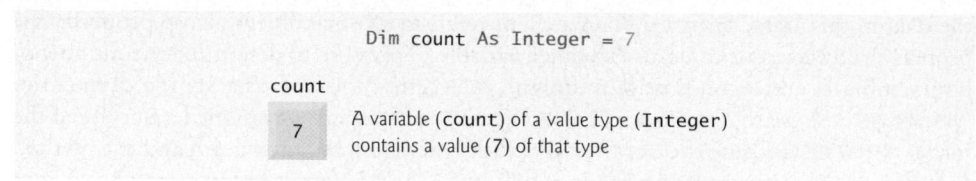

Fig. 4.10 | Value type variable.

to **refer to an object** in the program. Line 8 of Fig. 4.8 creates a GradeBook object, places it in memory and stores the object's memory address in reference variable gradeBook of type GradeBook as shown in Fig. 4.11. Note that the GradeBook object is shown with its courseNameValue instance variable.

Reference type instance variables (such as gradeBook in Fig. 4.11) are initialized by default to the value Nothing. Except for type String, Visual Basic's primitive types are value types—String is a reference type. For this reason, the String variable courseName-Value is shown in Fig. 4.11 with an empty box representing the variable in memory.

A client of an object must use a reference to the object to **invoke** (i.e., call) the object's methods and access the object's properties. In Fig. 4.8, the statements in Main use variable gradeBook, which contains the GradeBook object's reference, to send messages to the GradeBook object. These messages are calls to methods (like DisplayMessage) or references to properties (like CourseName) that enable the program to interact with GradeBook objects. For example, the statement (in line 20)

```
gradeBook.CourseName = theName ' set the CourseName (invokes Set)
```

uses gradeBook to set the course name by assigning a value to property CourseName. This sends a message to the GradeBook object to invoke the CourseName property's Set accessor. The message includes as an argument the value (i.e., the value of theName, namely CS101 Introduction to Visual Basic Programming) that CourseName's Set accessor requires to perform its task. The Set accessor uses this information to set the courseNameValue instance variable. In Section 7.11, we discuss value types and reference types in detail.

4.7 Initializing Objects with Constructors

As mentioned in Section 4.5, when an object of class GradeBook (Fig. 4.7) is created, its instance variable courseNameValue is initialized to Nothing by default. What if you want to provide a course name when you create a GradeBook object? Each class you declare can

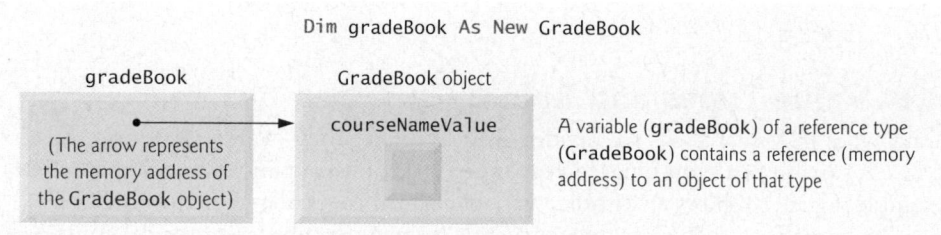

Fig. 4.11 | Reference type variable.

provide a constructor that can be used to initialize an object of the class when the object is created. In fact, Visual Basic requires a constructor call for every object that is created. The New keyword calls the class's constructor to perform the initialization. The constructor call is indicated by the class name followed by parentheses. For example, line 8 of Fig. 4.8 first uses New to create a GradeBook object. The lack of parentheses after "New GradeBook" indicates a call to the class's constructor that takes no arguments. By default, the compiler provides a **default constructor** with no parameters in any class that does not explicitly include a constructor.

When you declare a class, you can provide your own constructor to specify custom initialization for objects of your class. For example, a programmer might want to specify a course name for a GradeBook object when the object is created, as in

```
Dim gradeBook As New GradeBook( _
    "CS101 Introduction to Visual Basic Programming")
```

This passes the argument "CS101 Introduction to Visual Basic Programming" to the GradeBook object's constructor, which uses the argument value to initialize instance variable courseNameValue. The preceding statement requires that the class provide a constructor with a String parameter. Figure 4.12 contains a modified GradeBook class with such a constructor.

```
1   ' Fig. 4.12: GradeBook.vb
2   ' GradeBook class with a constructor to initialize the course name.
3   Public Class GradeBook
4       Private courseNameValue As String ' course name for this GradeBook
5
6       ' constructor initializes course name with String supplied as argument
7       Public Sub New(ByVal name As String)
8          CourseName = name ' initialize courseNameValue via property
9       End Sub ' New
10
11      ' property CourseName
12      Public Property CourseName() As String
13         Get ' retrieve courseNameValue
14            Return courseNameValue
15         End Get
16
17         Set(ByVal value As String) ' set courseNameValue
18            courseNameValue = value ' store the course name in the object
19         End Set
20      End Property ' CourseName
21
22      ' display a welcome message to the GradeBook user
23      Public Sub DisplayMessage()
24         ' use property CourseName to display the
25         ' name of the course this GradeBook represents
26         Console.WriteLine("Welcome to the grade book for " _
27            & vbCrLf & CourseName & "!")
28      End Sub ' DisplayMessage
29   End Class ' GradeBook
```

Fig. 4.12 | GradeBook class with a constructor that receives a course name.

Lines 7–9 declare the constructor for class GradeBook—a constructor must have the name New. As with the other methods we have declared, a constructor specifies in its parameter list the data it requires to perform its task. When you create a new object, this data is placed in the parentheses that follow the class name (as in lines 8–11 of Fig. 4.13). Line 7 (Fig. 4.12) indicates that class GradeBook's constructor has a parameter called name of type String.

Line 8 of the constructor's body assigns name to property CourseName. This causes the Set accessor of property CourseName to execute, which (in line 18) assigns parameter value to instance variable courseNameValue. You might be wondering why we bother using property CourseName—the constructor certainly could perform the assignment courseNameValue = name. In Section 4.8, we will modify the Set accessor of property CourseName to perform validation (in this case, to ensure that the courseNameValue is 25 or fewer characters in length). At that point the benefits of using property CourseName from the constructor will become clear.

Figure 4.13 demonstrates initializing GradeBook objects using this constructor. Lines 8–9 create and initialize a GradeBook object. The constructor of class GradeBook is called with the argument "CS101 Introduction to Visual Basic Programming" to initialize the course name. The object-creation expression in lines 8–9 returns a reference to the new object, which is assigned to variable gradeBook1. Lines 10–11 repeat this process for another GradeBook object, this time passing the argument "CS102 Data Structures in Visual Basic" to initialize the course name for gradeBook2. Lines 14–17 use each object's CourseName property to display the course names and show that they were initialized properly when the objects were created. The output confirms that each GradeBook maintains its own copy of instance variable courseNameValue.

```
1   ' Fig. 4.13: GradeBookTest.vb
2   ' GradeBook constructor used to specify the course name at the
3   ' time each GradeBook object is created.
4   Module GradeBookTest
5      ' Main begins program execution
6      Sub Main()
7         ' create GradeBook object
8         Dim gradeBook1 As New GradeBook( _
9            "CS101 Introduction to Visual Basic Programming")
10        Dim gradeBook2 As New GradeBook( _
11           "CS102 Data Structures in Visual Basic")
12
13        ' display initial value of CourseName for each GradeBook
14        Console.WriteLine( _
15           "gradeBook1 course name is: " & gradeBook1.CourseName)
16        Console.WriteLine( _
17           "gradeBook2 course name is: " & gradeBook2.CourseName)
18     End Sub ' Main
19  End Module ' GradeBookTest
```

```
gradeBook1 course name is: CS101 Introduction to Visual Basic Programming
gradeBook2 course name is: CS102 Data Structures in Visual Basic
```

Fig. 4.13 | Constructor used to initialize GradeBook objects.

Like other methods, constructors also can take arguments. However, an important difference between constructors and methods is that constructor declarations cannot return values (even though, as you know, each constructor does return a reference—to an object of its class type). Normally, constructors are declared Public. If a class does not include a constructor, the class's instance variables are initialized to their default values.

Error-Prevention Tip 4.1

Unless default initialization of your class's instance variables is acceptable, provide a constructor to ensure that these variables are properly initialized with meaningful values when each new object of your class is created.

Adding the Constructor to Class *GradeBook's* UML Class Diagram

The UML class diagram of Fig. 4.14 models the class GradeBook of Fig. 4.12, which has a constructor that has a name parameter of type String. Like operations, the UML models constructors in the third compartment of a class in a class diagram. To distinguish a constructor from a class's operations, the UML places the word "constructor" between guillemets (« and ») before the constructor's name (New). It is customary to list constructors before other operations in the third compartment.

4.8 Validating Data with Set Accessors in Properties

In Section 4.5, we introduced properties whose Set accessors allow clients of a class to modify the value of a Private instance variable. In Fig. 4.7, class GradeBook defines property CourseName's Set accessor to assign the value received in its parameter value to instance variable courseNameValue (line 14). This CourseName property does not ensure that courseNameValue contains valid data. In this section, we enhance our property to include data validation in its Set accessor. Property CourseName (Fig. 4.12) does not ensure that the course name adheres to any particular format or follows any other rules regarding what a "valid" course name is. Suppose that a university can display student transcripts in an online form that can hold course names of only 25 or fewer characters. If the university uses a system containing GradeBook objects to generate the transcripts, we might want class GradeBook to ensure that its courseNameValue never contains more than 25 characters. The program of Figs. 4.15–4.16 enhances class GradeBook's property CourseName to perform this validation (also known as validity checking).

GradeBook *Class Definition*

GradeBook's class definition in Fig. 4.15 contains all the same members as Fig. 4.12. Since the name and type of the property remain unchanged, clients of this class need not be

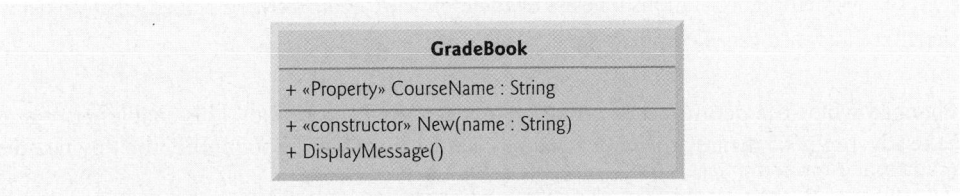

Fig. 4.14 | UML class diagram indicating that class GradeBook has a constructor that has a name parameter of type String.

```vb
1  ' Fig. 4.15: GradeBook.vb
2  ' GradeBook class with a property that performs validation.
3  Public Class GradeBook
4     Private courseNameValue As String ' course name for this GradeBook
5
6     ' constructor initializes CourseName with String supplied as argument
7     Public Sub New(ByVal name As String)
8        CourseName = name ' validate and store course name
9     End Sub ' New
10
11    ' property that gets and sets the course name; the Set accessor
12    ' ensures that the course name has at most 25 characters
13    Public Property CourseName() As String
14       Get ' retrieve courseNameValue
15          Return courseNameValue
16       End Get
17
18       Set(ByVal value As String) ' set courseNameValue
19          If value.Length <= 25 Then ' if value has 25 or fewer characters
20             courseNameValue = value ' store the course name in the object
21          End If
22
23          If value.Length > 25 Then ' if value has more than 25 characters
24             ' set courseNameValue to first 25 characters of value
25             ' start at 0, length of 25
26             courseNameValue = value.Substring(0, 25)
27
28             Console.WriteLine( _
29                "Name """ & value & """ exceeds maximum length (25).")
30             Console.WriteLine( _
31                "Limiting course name to first 25 characters." & vbCrLf)
32          End If
33       End Set
34    End Property ' CourseName
35
36    ' display a welcome message to the GradeBook user
37    Public Sub DisplayMessage()
38       ' this statement uses property CourseName to get the
39       ' name of the course this GradeBook represents
40       Console.WriteLine("Welcome to the grade book for " _
41          & vbCrLf & CourseName & "!")
42    End Sub ' DisplayMessage
43 End Class ' GradeBook
```

Fig. 4.15 | Method declarations for class GradeBook with a CourseName property that validates the length of instance variable courseNameValue.

changed when the definition of property CourseName is modified. This enables clients to take advantage of the improved GradeBook class without having to modify their own code.

Validating the Course Name with GradeBook Property CourseName
The enhancement to class GradeBook is in the definition of CourseName's Set accessor (Fig. 4.15, lines 18–33). The If...Then statement in lines 19–21 determines whether pa-

rameter value contains a valid course name (i.e., a String of 25 or fewer characters). If the course name is valid, line 20 stores it in instance variable courseNameValue. Note the expression value.Length in line 19. Length is a property of class String that returns the number of characters in the String. Parameter value is a String object, so the expression value.Length returns the number of characters in value. If value.Length is less than or equal to 25, value is valid and line 20 executes.

The If...Then statement in lines 23–32 handles the case in which CourseName receives an invalid course name (i.e., a name longer than 25 characters). Even if the String in parameter value is too long, we still want to leave the GradeBook object in a **consistent state**—that is, a state in which the object's instance variable courseNameValue contains a String of 25 or fewer characters. We choose to truncate (i.e., shorten) the specified course name and assign the first 25 characters of value to the courseNameValue instance variable (unfortunately, this could truncate the course name awkwardly). Class String provides method **Substring** that returns a new String object created by copying part of an existing String object. The call in line 26 (i.e., value.Substring(0, 25)) passes two integers (0 and 25) to value's method Substring. These arguments indicate the portion of the string value that Substring should return. The first argument specifies the starting position in the original String from which characters are to be copied—the first character in every string is considered to be at position 0. The second argument specifies the number of characters to copy. Therefore, the call in line 26 returns a 25-character substring of value starting at position 0 (i.e., the first 25 characters in value). For example, if value holds "CS101 Introduction to Visual Basic Programming", Substring returns "CS101 Introduction to Vis". After the call to Substring, line 26 assigns the substring returned by Substring to courseNameValue. In this way, property CourseName ensures that courseNameValue is always assigned a string containing 25 or fewer characters. If the property has to truncate the course name to make it valid, lines 28–31 display a warning message. Note that line 29 displays a string of text that includes double quotes ("). Double quotes are normally used to delimit string literals, so to display double quotes in a string, you use two double quotes in a row.

Testing Class *GradeBook*

Figure 4.16 demonstrates the modified version of class GradeBook featuring validation. Lines 8–9 create a GradeBook object named gradeBook1. Note that the GradeBook constructor (lines 7–9 of Fig. 4.15) references property CourseName to initialize courseNameValue. In previous versions of the class, the benefit of referencing the property CourseName in the constructor was not evident. Now, however, the constructor takes advantage of the validation provided by the Set accessor of the CourseName property. The constructor simply assigns a value to CourseName rather than duplicate the Set accessor's validation code. When line 9 of Fig. 4.16 passes an initial course name of "CS101 Introduction to Visual Basic Programming" to the GradeBook constructor, the constructor passes this value to the Set accessor of CourseName, where the actual initialization occurs. This course name contains more than 25 characters, so the body of the second If...Then statement (lines 23–32 of Fig. 4.15) executes, causing courseNameValue to be initialized to the truncated 25-character course name "CS101 Introduction to Vis" (the truncated part of the String is highlighted in red in line 9 of Fig. 4.16). The output in Fig. 4.16 contains the warning message output by lines 28–31 of Fig. 4.15. Line 10 of Fig. 4.16 creates another Grade-

```vb
1   ' Fig. 4.16: GradeBookTest.vb
2   ' Create and manipulate a GradeBook object; illustrate validation.
3   Module GradeBookTest
4      ' Main begins program execution
5      Sub Main()
6         ' create two GradeBook objects;
7         ' initial course name of gradeBook1 is too long
8         Dim gradeBook1 As New GradeBook( _
9            "CS101 Introduction to Visual Basic Programming")
10        Dim gradeBook2 As New GradeBook("CS102 VB Data Structures")
11
12        ' display each GradeBook's course name (by invoking Get)
13        Console.WriteLine("gradeBook1's initial course name is: " & _
14           gradeBook1.CourseName)
15        Console.WriteLine("gradeBook2's initial course name is: " & _
16           gradeBook2.CourseName)
17        Console.WriteLine() ' display blank line
18
19        ' place in gradeBook1's course name a valid-length String
20        gradeBook1.CourseName = "CS101 VB Programming"
21
22        ' display each GradeBook's course name (by invoking Get)
23        Console.WriteLine( _
24           "gradeBook1's course name is: " & gradeBook1.CourseName)
25        Console.WriteLine( _
26           "gradeBook2's course name is: " & gradeBook2.CourseName)
27     End Sub ' Main
28  End Module ' GradeBookTest
```

```
Name "CS101 Introduction to Visual Basic Programming" exceeds maximum length
(25).
Limiting course name to first 25 characters.

gradeBook1's initial course name is: CS101 Introduction to Vis
gradeBook2's initial course name is: CS102 VB Data Structures

gradeBook1's course name is: CS101 VB Programming
gradeBook2's course name is: CS102 VB Data Structures
```

Fig. 4.16 | Creating and manipulating a GradeBook object in which the course name is limited to 25 characters in length.

Book object called gradeBook2—the valid course name passed to the constructor contains fewer than 25 characters (it contains 24 characters to be exact).

Lines 13–16 of Fig. 4.16 display the truncated course name for gradeBook1 (we highlight this in red in the program output) and the course name for gradeBook2. Line 20 assigns a new value to gradeBook1's CourseName property, to change the course name in the GradeBook object to a shorter name that does not need to be truncated. Then lines 23–26 output the course names for the GradeBook objects again.

A class's Set accessors cannot return values that indicate a failed attempt to assign invalid data to objects of the class. Such return values could be useful to a class's clients for handling errors—clients could then take appropriate actions. Chapter 12 presents exception handling—a mechanism that can be used (among other things) to notify a class's clients of attempts to set objects of that class to inconsistent states. To keep the program of Figs. 4.15–4.16 simple at this early point in the book, the CourseName property's Set accessor in Fig. 4.15 prints an appropriate message on the screen and sets courseName-Value to the first 25 characters of the specified course name.

Set and Get Accessors with Different Access Modifiers

By default, the Get and Set accessors of a property have the same access as the property—in other words, for a Public property, the accessors also are Public. In Visual Basic, it is possible to declare the Get and Set accessors with different access modifiers. In this case, one of the accessors must have the same access as the property and the other must be more restrictive than the property. For example, in a Public property, the Get accessor might be Public and the Set accessor might be Private.

Error-Prevention Tip 4.2

The benefits of data integrity are not automatic simply because instance variables are made Private—the programmer must provide appropriate validity checking and report the errors.

Error-Prevention Tip 4.3

Set accessors that set the values of Private data should verify that the intended new values are proper; if they are not, the Set accessors should place the Private instance variables into an appropriately consistent state.

4.9 (Optional) Software Engineering Case Study: Identifying the Classes in the ATM Requirements Document

Now we begin designing the ATM system that we introduced in Chapter 3. In this section, we identify the classes that are needed to build the ATM system by analyzing the nouns and noun phrases that appear in the requirements document. We introduce UML class diagrams to model the relationships among these classes. This is an important first step in defining the structure of our system.

Identifying the Classes in a System

We begin our OOD process by identifying the classes required to build the ATM system. We will eventually describe these classes using UML class diagrams and implement these classes in Visual Basic. First, we review the requirements document of Section 3.10 and find key nouns and noun phrases to help us identify classes that comprise the ATM system. We may decide that some of the nouns and noun phrases are attributes of other classes in the system. We may also conclude that some of the nouns and noun phrases do not correspond to parts of the system and thus should not be modeled at all. Additional classes may become apparent as we proceed through the design process.

Figure 4.17 lists the nouns and noun phrases in the requirements document. We list them from left to right in the order in which they appear in the requirements document.

We create classes only for the nouns and noun phrases that have significance in the ATM system. We do not need to model "bank" as a class, because the bank is not a part of the ATM system—the bank simply wants us to build the ATM. "User" and "customer"

Nouns and noun phrases in the requirements document		
bank	money / funds	account number
ATM	screen	PIN
user	keypad	bank database
customer	cash dispenser	balance inquiry
transaction	$20 bill / cash	withdrawal
account	deposit slot	deposit
balance	deposit envelope	

Fig. 4.17 | Nouns and noun phrases in the requirements document.

also represent entities outside of the system—they are important because they interact with our ATM system, but we do not need to model them as classes in the ATM system itself. Recall that we modeled an ATM user (i.e., a bank customer) as the actor in the use case diagram of Fig. 3.38.

We do not model "$20 bill" or "deposit envelope" as classes. These are physical objects in the real world, but they are not part of what is being automated. We can adequately represent the presence of $20 bills in the system using an attribute of the class that models the cash dispenser. (We assign attributes to classes in Section 5.16.) For example, the cash dispenser maintains a count of the number of bills it contains. The requirements document does not say anything about what the system should do with deposit envelopes after it receives them. We can assume that simply acknowledging the receipt of an envelope—an operation performed by the class that models the deposit slot—is sufficient to represent the presence of an envelope in the system. (We assign operations to classes in Section 7.20.)

In our simplified ATM system, representing various amounts of "money," including the "balance" of an account, as attributes of other classes seems most appropriate. Likewise, the nouns "account number" and "PIN" represent significant pieces of information in the ATM system. They are important attributes of a bank account. They do not, however, exhibit behaviors. Thus, we can most appropriately model them as attributes of an account class.

Though the requirements document frequently describes a "transaction" in a general sense, we do not model the broad notion of a financial transaction at this time. Instead, we model the three types of transactions (i.e., "balance inquiry," "withdrawal" and "deposit") as individual classes. These classes possess specific attributes needed for executing the transactions they represent. For example, a withdrawal needs to know the amount of money the user wants to withdraw. A balance inquiry, however, does not require any additional data. Furthermore, the three transaction classes exhibit unique behaviors. A withdrawal includes dispensing cash to the user, whereas a deposit involves receiving a deposit envelope from the user. [*Note:* In Section 11.8, we "factor out" common features of all transactions into a general "transaction" class using the object-oriented concepts of abstract classes and inheritance.]

We determine the classes for our system based on the remaining nouns and noun phrases from Fig. 4.17. Each of these refers to one or more of the following:

- ATM
- screen
- keypad
- cash dispenser
- deposit slot
- account
- bank database
- balance inquiry
- withdrawal
- deposit

The elements of this list are likely to be classes we will need to implement our system, although it's too early in our process to claim that this list is complete.

We can now begin modeling the classes in our system based on the list we have created. We capitalize class names in the design process—a UML convention—as we will do when we write the actual Visual Basic code that implements our design. If the name of a class contains more than one word, we run the words together and capitalize each word (e.g., `MultipleWordName`). Using these conventions, we create classes `ATM`, `Screen`, `Keypad`, `CashDispenser`, `DepositSlot`, `Account`, `BankDatabase`, `BalanceInquiry`, `Withdrawal` and `Deposit`. We construct our system using all of these classes as building blocks. Before we begin building the system, however, we must gain a better understanding of how the classes relate to one another.

Modeling Classes

The UML enables us to model, via **class diagrams**, the classes in the ATM system and their interrelationships. Figure 4.18 represents class `ATM`. In the UML, each class is modeled as a rectangle with three compartments. The top compartment contains the name of the class, centered horizontally and appearing in boldface. The middle compartment contains the class's attributes (which we discuss in Section 5.16 and Section 6.11.) The bottom compartment contains the class's operations (which we discuss in Section 7.20). In Fig. 4.18 the middle and bottom compartments are empty, because we have not yet determined the `ATM` class's attributes and operations.

Class diagrams also show the relationships between the classes of the system. Figure 4.19 shows how classes `ATM` and `Withdrawal` relate to one another. For the

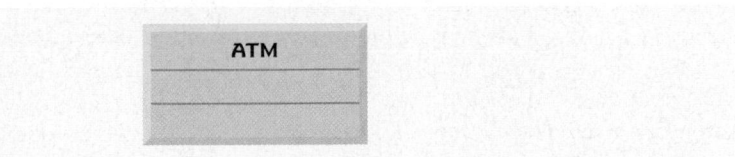

Fig. 4.18 | Representing a class in the UML using a class diagram.

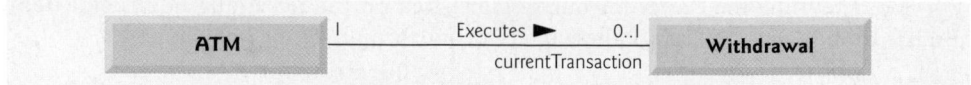

Fig. 4.19 | Class diagram showing an association among classes.

moment, we choose to model only this subset of the ATM classes for simplicity. We present a more complete class diagram later in this section. Notice that the rectangles representing classes in this diagram are not subdivided into compartments. The UML allows the suppression of class attributes and operations in this manner, when appropriate, to create more readable diagrams. Such a diagram is said to be an elided diagram—one in which some information, such as the contents of the second and third compartments, is not modeled. We will place information in these compartments in Section 5.16 and Section 7.20.

In Fig. 4.19, the solid line that connects the two classes represents an association—a relationship between classes. The numbers near each end of the line are multiplicity values, which indicate how many objects of each class participate in the association. In this case, following the line from the ATM to the Withdrawal reveals that, at any given moment, one ATM object participates in an association with either zero or one Withdrawal objects—zero if the current user is not performing a transaction or has requested a different type of transaction, and one if the user has requested a withdrawal. The UML can model many types of multiplicity (Fig. 4.20).

An association can be named. For example, the word Executes above the line connecting classes ATM and Withdrawal in Fig. 4.19 indicates the name of that association. This part of the diagram reads "one object of class ATM executes zero or one objects of class Withdrawal." Note that association names are directional, as indicated by the filled arrowhead—so it would be improper, for example, to read the preceding association from right to left as "zero or one objects of class Withdrawal execute one object of class ATM."

Symbol	Meaning
0	None
1	One
m	An integer value
0..1	Zero or one
m, n	m or n
$m..n$	At least m, but not more than n
*	Any nonnegative integer (zero or more)
0..*	Zero or more (identical to *)
1..*	One or more

Fig. 4.20 | Multiplicity types.

The word `currentTransaction` at the `Withdrawal` end of the association line in Fig. 4.19 is a **role name**, which identifies the role the `Withdrawal` object plays in its relationship with the `ATM` object. A role name adds meaning to an association between classes by identifying the role a class plays in the context of an association. A class can play several roles in the same system. For example, in a college personnel system, a person may play the role of "professor" when relating to students. The same person may take on the role of "colleague" when participating in a relationship with another professor, and "coach" when coaching student athletes. In Fig. 4.19, the role name `currentTransaction` indicates that the `Withdrawal` object participating in the `Executes` association with an object of class `ATM` represents the transaction currently being processed by the ATM. In other contexts, a `Withdrawal` object may take on other roles (e.g., the previous transaction). Notice that we do not specify a role name for the `ATM` end of the `Executes` association. Role names in class diagrams are often omitted when the meaning of an association is clear without them.

In addition to indicating simple relationships, associations can specify more complex relationships, such as objects of one class being composed of objects of other classes. Consider a real-world automated teller machine. What "pieces" does a manufacturer put together to build a working ATM? Our requirements document tells us that the ATM is composed of a screen, a keypad, a cash dispenser and a deposit slot.

In Fig. 4.21, the **solid diamonds** attached to the association lines of class `ATM` indicate that class `ATM` has a **composition** relationship with classes `Screen`, `Keypad`, `CashDispenser` and `DepositSlot`. Composition implies a whole/part relationship. The class that has the composition symbol (the solid diamond) on its end of the association line is the whole (in this case, `ATM`), and the classes on the other end of the association lines are the parts—in this case, classes `Screen`, `Keypad`, `CashDispenser` and `DepositSlot`. The compositions in Fig. 4.21 indicate that an object of class `ATM` is formed from one object of class `Screen`, one object of class `CashDispenser`, one object of class `Keypad` and one object of class `DepositSlot`—the ATM "has a" screen, a keypad, a cash dispenser and a deposit slot. The "has-a" relationship defines composition. (We will see in Section 11.8 that the "is-a" relationship defines inheritance.)

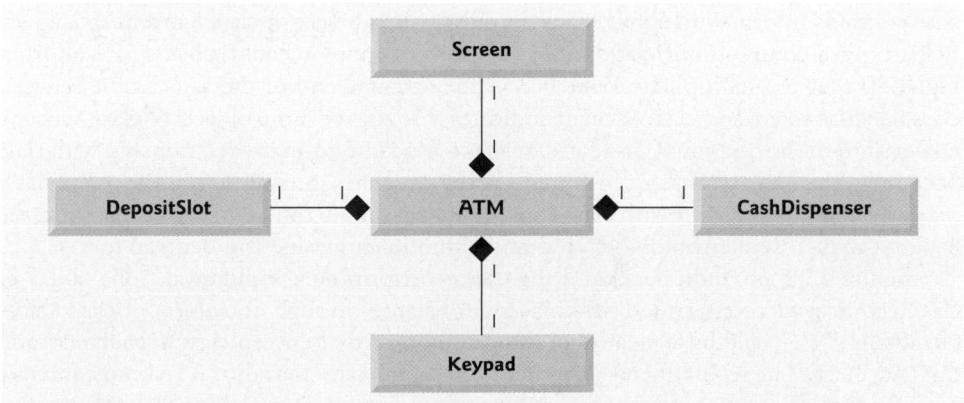

Fig. 4.21 | Class diagram showing composition relationships.

According to the UML specification, composition relationships have the following properties:

1. Only one class in the relationship can represent the whole (i.e., the diamond can be placed on only one end of the association line). For example, either the screen is part of the ATM or the ATM is part of the screen, but the screen and the ATM cannot both represent the whole in the relationship.

2. The parts in the composition relationship exist only as long as the whole, and the whole is responsible for creating and destroying its parts. For example, the act of constructing an ATM includes manufacturing its parts. Furthermore, if the ATM is destroyed, its screen, keypad, cash dispenser and deposit slot are also destroyed.

3. A part may belong to only one whole at a time, although the part may be removed and attached to another whole, which then assumes responsibility for the part.

The solid diamonds in our class diagrams indicate composition relationships that fulfill these three properties. If a "has-a" relationship does not satisfy one or more of these criteria, the UML specifies that hollow diamonds be attached to the ends of association lines to indicate **aggregation**—a weaker form of composition. For example, a personal computer and a computer monitor participate in an aggregation relationship—the computer "has a" monitor, but the two parts can exist independently, and the same monitor can be attached to multiple computers at once, thus violating the second and third properties of composition.

Figure 4.22 shows a class diagram for the ATM system. This diagram models most of the classes that we identified earlier in this section, as well as the associations between them that we can infer from the requirements document. [*Note:* Classes `BalanceInquiry` and `Deposit` participate in associations similar to those of class `Withdrawal`, so we have chosen to omit them from this diagram for simplicity. In Chapter 11, we expand our class diagram to include all the classes in the ATM system.]

Figure 4.22 presents a graphical model of the structure of the ATM system. This class diagram includes classes `BankDatabase` and `Account`, and several associations that were not present in either Fig. 4.19 or Fig. 4.21. The class diagram shows that class `ATM` has a **one-to-one relationship** with class `BankDatabase`—one `ATM` object authenticates users against one `BankDatabase` object. In Fig. 4.22, we also model the fact that the bank's database contains information about many accounts—one object of class `BankDatabase` participates in a composition relationship with zero or more `Account` objects. Recall from Fig. 4.20 that the multiplicity value 0..* at the `Account` end of the association between class `BankDatabase` and class `Account` indicates that zero or more objects of class `Account` take part in the association. Class `BankDatabase` has a **one-to-many relationship** with class `Account`—the `BankDatabase` can contain many `Account`s. Similarly, class `Account` has a **many-to-one relationship** with class `BankDatabase`—there can be many `Account`s in the `BankDatabase`. Recall from Fig. 4.20 that the multiplicity value * is identical to 0..*.

Figure 4.22 also indicates that if the user is performing a withdrawal, "one object of class `Withdrawal` accesses/modifies an account balance through one object of class `BankDatabase`." We could have created an association directly between class `Withdrawal` and class `Account`. The requirements document, however, states that the "ATM must interact with the bank's account information database" to perform transactions. A bank account contains sensitive information, and systems engineers must always consider the security of

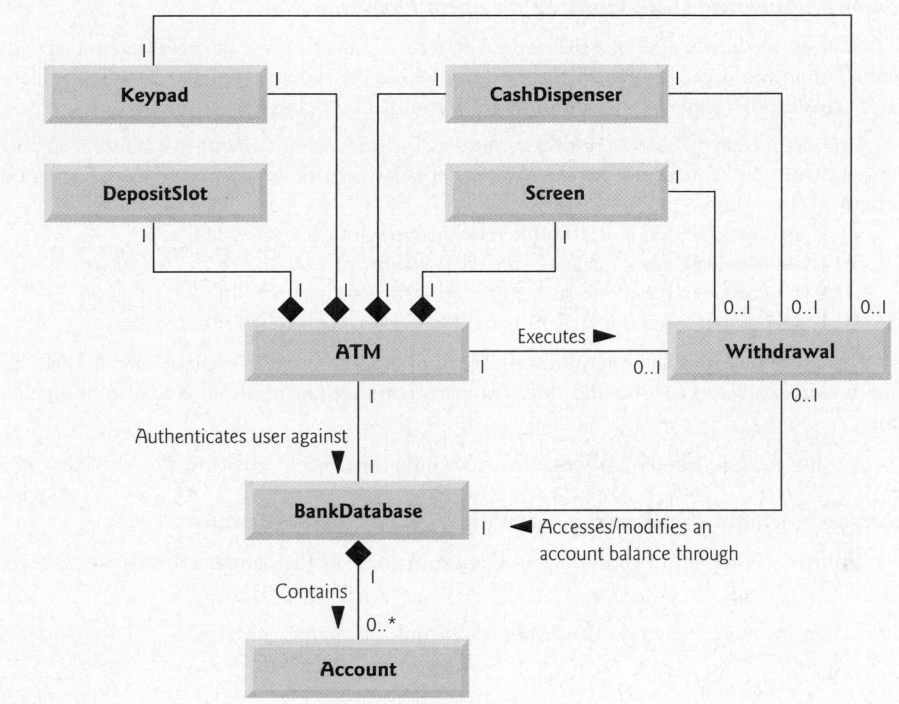

Fig. 4.22 | Class diagram for the ATM system model.

personal data when designing a system. Thus, only the BankDatabase can access and manipulate an account directly. All other parts of the system must interact with the database to retrieve or update account information (e.g., an account balance).

The class diagram in Fig. 4.22 also models associations between class Withdrawal and classes Screen, CashDispenser and Keypad. A withdrawal transaction includes prompting the user to choose a withdrawal amount and receiving numeric input. These actions require the use of the screen and the keypad, respectively. Furthermore, dispensing cash to the user requires access to the cash dispenser.

Classes BalanceInquiry and Deposit, though not shown in Fig. 4.22, take part in several associations with the other classes of the ATM system. Like class Withdrawal, each of these classes associates with classes ATM and BankDatabase. An object of class Balance-Inquiry also associates with an object of class Screen to display the balance of an account to the user. Class Deposit associates with classes Screen, Keypad and DepositSlot. Like withdrawals, deposit transactions require use of the screen and the keypad to display prompts and receive inputs, respectively. To receive a deposit envelope, an object of class Deposit associates with an object of class DepositSlot.

We have identified the classes in our ATM system, although we may discover others as we proceed with the design and implementation. In Section 5.16, we determine the attributes for each of these classes, and in Section 6.11, we use these attributes to examine how the system changes over time. In Section 7.20, we determine the operations of the classes in our system.

Software Engineering Case Study Self-Review Exercises

4.1 Suppose we have a class Car that represents a car. Think of some of the different pieces that a manufacturer would put together to produce a whole car. Create a class diagram (similar to Fig. 4.21) that models some of the composition relationships of class Car.

4.2 Suppose we have a class File that represents an electronic document in a stand-alone, non-networked computer represented by class Computer. What sort of association exists between class Computer and class File?

> a) Class Computer has a one-to-one relationship with class File.
> b) Class Computer has a many-to-one relationship with class File.
> c) Class Computer has a one-to-many relationship with class File.
> d) Class Computer has a many-to-many relationship with class File.

4.3 State whether the following statement is *true* or *false*, and if *false*, explain why: A UML class diagram in which a class's second and third compartments are not modeled is said to be an elided diagram.

4.4 Modify the class diagram of Fig. 4.22 to include class Deposit instead of class Withdrawal.

Answers to Software Engineering Case Study Self-Review Exercises

4.1 Figure 4.23 presents a class diagram that shows some of the composition relationships of a class Car.

4.2 c. In a computer network, this relationship could be many-to-many.

4.3 True.

4.4 Figure 4.24 presents a class diagram for the ATM including class Deposit instead of class Withdrawal (as in Fig. 4.22). Note that class Deposit does not associate with class CashDispenser, but does associate with class DepositSlot.

4.10 Wrap-Up

In this chapter, you learned the basic concepts of classes, objects, methods, instance variables and properties. You learned how to declare instance variables of a class to maintain separate data for each object of the class, and how to declare methods that operate on that data. You learned how to call a method to tell it to perform its task and how to pass infor-

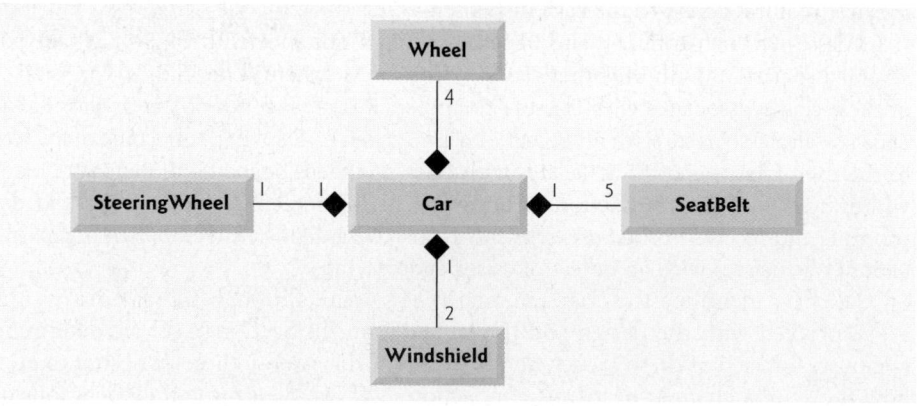

Fig. 4.23 | Class diagram showing some composition relationships of a class Car.

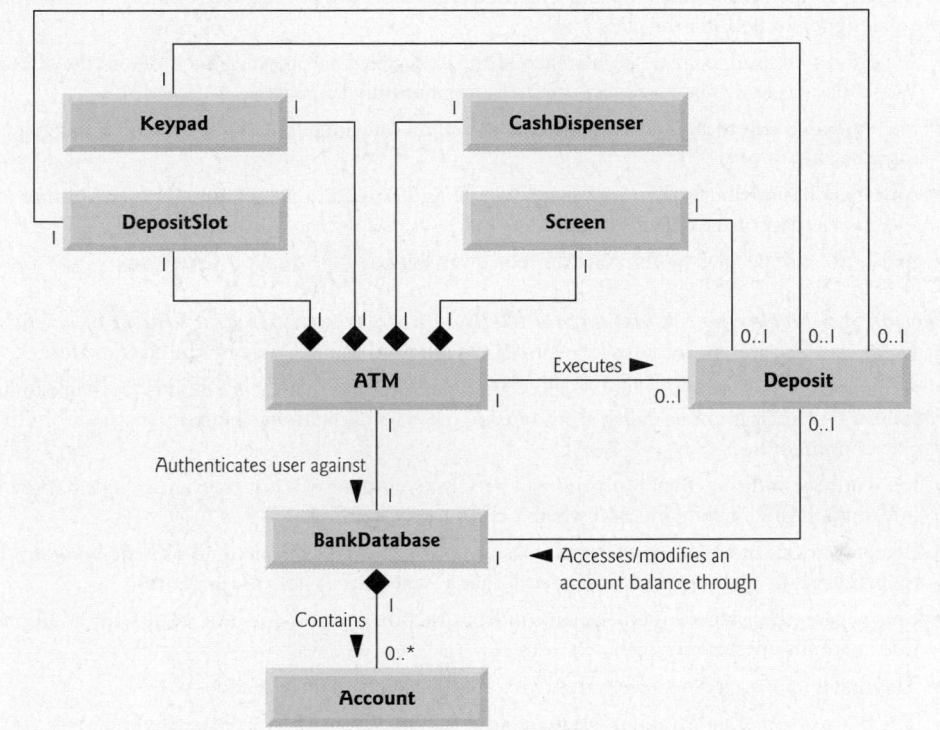

Fig. 4.24 | Class diagram for the ATM system model including class `Deposit`.

mation to methods as arguments. We explained the difference between a local variable of a method and an instance variable of a class. You learned how to use a class's constructor to specify the initial values for an object's instance variables. You saw how UML class diagrams model the constructors, operations, attributes and properties of classes. Finally, we demonstrated how `Set` accessors in properties can be used to validate an object's data and ensure that the object is maintained in a consistent state.

In the next chapter we begin our introduction to control statements, which specify the order in which a program's actions are performed. You will use these statements in your programs to specify more complex sets of tasks. You will learn how to execute code based on the truth or falsity of a condition, and how to indicate that code should be repeated based on a condition.

Summary

Section 4.1 Introduction
- If you become part of a development team in industry, you may work on applications that contain hundreds, or even thousands, of classes. Each class will contain one or more methods.

Section 4.2 Classes, Objects, Methods and Instance Variables
- Performing a task in a program requires a method. The method describes the mechanisms that actually perform its tasks. The method hides from its user the complex tasks that it performs.

- A program unit called a class houses a method. In a class, you provide one or more methods that are designed to perform the class's tasks.

- A class can be used to create an instance of the class called an object. This is one of the reasons Visual Basic is known as an object-oriented programming language.

- Each message sent to an object is known as a method call and tells a method of the object to perform its task.

- An object has attributes that are carried with it as it is used in a program. These attributes are specified as part of the object's class.

- Attributes are specified by the class's instance variables.

Section 4.3 Declaring a Class with a Method and Instantiating an Object of a Class

- Every class declaration contains keyword Class followed immediately by the class's name.

- A method declared with the Public access modifier indicates that the method is "available to the public"—that is, it can be called from outside the class declaration's body by methods of other classes or modules.

- Keyword Sub indicates that a method will perform a task but will not return (i.e., give back) any information to its calling method when it completes its task.

- By convention, method names begin with an uppercase first letter, and all subsequent words in the name begin with a capital letter (recall that Visual Basic is not case sensitive).

- Empty parentheses after a method name indicate that the method does not require any additional information to perform its task.

- The first line of a method is commonly referred to as the method header.

- The body of a method contains a statement or statements that perform the method's task.

- Main is a special method that is always called automatically by the runtime when you execute an application. Most methods do not get called automatically.

- A Visual Basic application must have a method Main in order to execute.

- Typically, you cannot call a method that belongs to another class until you create an object of that class.

- Each new class you create becomes a new type in Visual Basic that can be used to declare variables and create objects. Programmers can declare new class types as needed; this is one reason why Visual Basic is known as an extensible language.

- Object-creation expressions beginning with the New keyword create new objects.

- To call a method of an object, follow the variable name with a dot separator (.), the method name and a set of parentheses containing the method's arguments.

- In the UML, each class is modeled in a class diagram as a rectangle with three compartments. The top compartment contains the name of the class centered horizontally in boldface type. The middle compartment contains the class's attributes, which correspond to instance variables in Visual Basic. The bottom compartment contains the class's operations, which correspond to methods in Visual Basic.

- The UML models operations by listing the operation name followed by a set of parentheses.

Section 4.4 Declaring a Method with a Parameter

- A method can require one or more parameters that represent additional information it needs to perform its task.

- A method call supplies values—called arguments—for each of the method's parameters.

- String is a type used for strings in Visual Basic, such as names, addresses, cities, states and product descriptions.

- When you declare a method, you must specify in the method's declaration whether the method requires data to perform its task.

- A parameter list may contain any number of parameters, including none at all. Empty parentheses following the method name indicate that a method does not require any parameters.

- Each parameter must specify a type and an identifier.

- At the time a method is called, the argument value in the call is assigned to the corresponding parameter in the method header. Then the method body uses the parameter to access the value.

- Parameter declarations in the parameter list use keyword ByVal to specify that the calling program should pass a copy of the value of the argument in the method call to the parameter.

- The number of arguments in a method call must match the number of parameters in the parameter list of the called method's declaration.

- The argument types in the method call must be consistent with the types of the corresponding parameters in the method's declaration.

- The UML models a parameter a bit differently from Visual Basic by listing the parameter name, followed by a colon and the parameter type in the parentheses following the operation name.

Section 4.5 Instance Variables and Properties

- Variables declared in the body of a particular method are known as local variables and can be used only in that method.

- An object has attributes that are carried with it as it is used in a program. Such attributes exist before a method is called on the object and after the method completes execution.

- Attributes are represented as instance variables and are declared inside a class declaration but outside the bodies of the class's other members.

- Each object of a class maintains its own copy of an instance variable—that is, each object of the class has a separate instance of the variable in memory.

- Variables or methods declared with access modifier Private are accessible only to methods and properties of the class in which they are declared.

- Declaring instance variables with access modifier Private is known as information hiding.

- In Visual Basic, properties provide a controlled way for programmers to "get" (i.e., retrieve) the value in an instance variable and "set" (i.e., modify) the value in an instance variable.

- Properties can scrutinize attempts to modify an instance variable's value (known as data validation), thus ensuring that the new value for that instance variable is valid.

- Properties contain accessors that handle the details of modifying and returning data.

- A property declaration can contain a Get accessor, a Set accessor or both. The Get accessor enables a client to read the value of a Private instance variable. The Set accessor enables a client to modify that instance variable's value.

- After defining a property, you can use it the same way as you use a variable.

- Using properties would seem to violate the notion of Private data. However, a Set accessor can provide data-validation capabilities to ensure that the value is set properly; Get and Set accessors can translate between the format of the data used by the client and the format used in the Private instance variable.

- The UML represents instance variables as attributes by listing the attribute name, followed by a colon and the attribute type.

- Public class members are preceded by a plus (+) sign in UML class diagrams.

- Private class members are preceded by a minus (-) sign in UML class diagrams.

- We model properties in the UML as attributes—a property is listed as an attribute with the word "Property" in guillemets (« and »). Using guillemets helps distinguish properties from other attributes and operations. The UML indicates the type of the property by placing a colon and type after the property name.

Section 4.6 Value Types and Reference Types
- Data types in Visual Basic are divided into two categories—value types and reference types.

- A variable of a value type contains data of that type.

- A variable of a reference type (sometimes called a reference) contains the address of a location in memory where an object is stored.

- Reference type instance variables are initialized by default to the value Nothing.

- A client of an object must use a reference to the object to invoke (i.e., call) the object's methods and access the object's properties.

Section 4.7 Initializing Objects with Constructors
- Each class you declare can provide a constructor that can be used to initialize an object of the class when the object is created.

- Keyword New calls the class's constructor to perform the initialization.

- By default, the compiler provides a default constructor with no parameters in any class that does not explicitly include a constructor.

- When you declare a class, you can provide your own constructor to specify custom initialization for objects of your class.

- A constructor must have the name New.

- Constructor declarations cannot return values.

- A class's instance variables are initialized to their default values if no constructor is provided.

- Like operations, the UML models constructors in the third compartment of a class in a class diagram. To distinguish a constructor from a class's operations, the UML places the word "constructor" between guillemets (« and ») before the constructor's name.

Section 4.8 Validating Data with Properties
- Properties can be used to keep an object in a consistent state—that is, a state in which the object's instance variables contain valid data.

- A class's Set accessors cannot return values indicating a failed attempt to assign invalid data to objects of the class. Such return values could be useful to a class's clients for handling errors—clients could then take appropriate actions. Chapter 12 presents exception handling—a mechanism that can be used (among other things) to notify a class's clients of attempts to set objects of that class to inconsistent states.

- In Visual Basic, it is possible to declare the Get and Set accessors of a property with different access modifiers. In this case, one of the accessors must have the same access as the property and the other must be more restrictive than the property. Private is more restrictive than Public.

Terminology

access modifier	attribute in the UML
accessor	ByVal keyword

calling method (caller)
carriage return
class diagram in the UML
Class keyword
client of a class
consistent state of an object
constant
constructor
create an object of a class
data validation
declare a method of a class
default constructor
default value of an instance variable
End Class keywords
End Get keywords
End Set keywords
extensible language
Get accessor of a property
information hiding
instance variable
instantiate an object of a class
invoke a method
Length property of class String
line feed
local variable
message (send to an object)

method call
method header
New keyword
Nothing keyword
object-creation expression
operation in the UML
operation parameter in the UML
parameter
parameter list
Private access modifier
property declaration
Property keyword
Public access modifier
refer to an object
reference
reference type
Return statement
Set accessor of a property
String primitive type
Substring method of class String
validation
validity checking
value type
vbCrLf
vbTab

Self-Review Exercises

4.1   Fill in the blanks in each of the following:
a) A house is to a blueprint as a(n) _____ is to a class.
b) Every class declaration contains keyword _____ followed immediately by the class's name.
c) _____ creates an object of the class specified to the right of it.
d) Each parameter must specify both a(n) _____ and a(n) _____.
e) The number of characters in a String can be determined using class String's _____ property.
f) When each object of a class maintains its own copy of an attribute, the attribute is represented as a(n) _____.
g) Declaring instance variables with access modifier Private is known as _____.
h) Keyword Public is a(n) _____.
i) Keyword _____ indicates that a method will perform a task but will not return any information when it completes its task.
j) The keyword _____ represents a "reference to nothing."
k) String method _____ returns a new String object created by copying part of an existing String object.
l) _____ is a primitive type used for strings in Visual Basic, such as names, addresses, cities, states and product descriptions.
m) In a method header, the parentheses after the method name are used to indicate any _____—additional information that is required by the method to perform its task.

n) Methods of a class are depicted as _____ in UML class diagrams.

o) Properties contain _____ and _____ that handle the details of returning and modifying data, respectively.

p) Types in Visual Basic are divided into two categories—_____ types and _____ types.

4.2 State whether each of the following is *true* or *false*. If *false*, explain why.

a) By convention, method names begin with a lowercase letter and all subsequent words in the name begin with an uppercase letter.

b) A property's Get accessor enables a client to modify the value of the instance variable associated with the property.

c) Empty parentheses following a method name in a method declaration indicate that the method does not require any parameters to perform its task.

d) Variables or methods declared with access modifier Private are accessible only to other members of the class in which they are declared.

e) After defining a property, you can use it the same way you use a method, but with empty parentheses because no arguments are passed to a property.

f) Variables declared in the body of a particular method are known as instance variables and can be used in all methods of the class.

g) A client of an object must use a reference to the object to invoke (i.e., call) the object's methods and access the object's properties.

h) A property declaration must contain both a Get accessor and a Set accessor.

i) Reference type instance variables are initialized by default to Nothing.

j) Any class that contains Main can be used to execute an application.

k) The number of arguments in a method call must match the number of parameters in the method declaration's parameter list.

l) A class's Set accessors can return values indicating failed attempts to assign invalid data to objects of the class.

4.3 What is the difference between a local variable and an instance variable?

4.4 Explain the purpose of a method parameter. What is the difference between a parameter and an argument?

Answers to Self-Review Exercises

4.1 a) object. b) Class. c) New. d) type, name. e) Length. f) instance variable. g) information hiding. h) access modifier. i) Sub. j) Nothing. k) Substring. l) String. m) parameters. n) operations. o) Get accessors and Set accessors. p) value, reference.

4.2 a) False. By convention, method names begin with an uppercase letter and all subsequent words in the name begin with an uppercase letter. b) False. A property's Get accessor enables a client to retrieve the value of the instance variable associated with the property. A property's Set accessor enables a client to modify the value of the instance variable associated with the property. c) True. d) True. e) False. After defining a property, you can use it the same way you use a variable. f) False. Such variables are called local variables and can be used only in the method in which they are declared. g) True. h) False. A property declaration can contain a Get accessor, a Set accessor or both. i) True. j) True. k) True. (You will learn in Chapter 7 that there is an exception to this with so-called optional arguments.) l) False. A class's Set accessors cannot return values indicating failed attempts to assign invalid data to objects of the class. Chapter 12 presents exception handling—a mechanism that can be used (among other things) to notify a class's clients of attempts to set objects of that class to inconsistent states.

4.3   A local variable is declared in the body of a method and can be used only in that method declaration. An instance variable is declared in a class, but not in the body of any of the class's methods or properties. Every object (instance) of a class has a separate copy of the class's instance variables. Also, instance variables are accessible to all methods and properties of the class. (We will see an exception to this in Chapter 9, Classes and Objects: A Deeper Look; instance variables are not accessible to Shared methods of a class.)

4.4   A parameter represents additional information that a method requires to perform its task. Each parameter required by a method is specified in the method's declaration. An argument is the actual value for a method parameter. When a method is called, the argument values are passed to the method so that it can perform its task.

Exercises

4.5   What is the purpose of the New keyword? Explain what happens when this keyword is used in an application.

4.6   What is a default constructor? How are an object's instance variables initialized if a class has only a default constructor?

4.7   Explain the purpose of an instance variable.

4.8   Explain why a class might provide a property for an instance variable.

4.9   *(Modifying Class* GradeBook*)* Modify class GradeBook (Fig. 4.15) as follows:
   a) Include a second String instance variable that represents the name of the course's instructor.
   b) Provide a property to access and modify the instructor's name. This property does not need to provide any validation.
   c) Modify the constructor to specify two parameters—one for the course name and one for the instructor's name.
   d) Modify method DisplayMessage such that it first outputs the welcome message and course name, then outputs "This course is presented by: " followed by the instructor's name.

Use your modified class in a test module that demonstrates the class's new capabilities.

4.10   *(*Account *Class)* Create a class called Account that a bank might use to represent customers' bank accounts. Your class should include one instance variable of type Integer to represent the account balance (in whole dollars). [*Note:* In subsequent chapters, we will use floating-point values to represent dollar amounts with cents.] Your class should provide a constructor that receives an initial balance and uses it to initialize the instance variable. The constructor should validate the initial balance to ensure that it is greater than or equal to 0. The class should provide two methods and a property. Method Credit should add an amount to the current balance. Method Debit should withdraw money from the Account and should ensure that the debit amount does not exceed the Account's balance. If it does, the balance should be left unchanged and the method should print a message indicating "Debit amount exceeded account balance." Property Balance should provide access to the current balance, but no validation is necessary. Create a module that creates two Account objects and tests the methods and property of class Account.

4.11   *(*Invoice *Class)* Create a class called Invoice that a hardware store might use to represent an invoice for an item sold at the store. An Invoice should include four pieces of information as instance variables—a part number (type String), a part description (type String), a quantity of the item being purchased (type Integer) and a price per item (type Integer). Your class should have a constructor that initializes the four instance variables. Provide a property for each instance variable. If the quantity is not positive, it should be set to 0. If the price per item is not positive, it should be set to 0. Use validation in the properties for these instance variables to ensure that they remain positive. In addition, provide a method named `DisplayInvoiceAmount` that calculates and displays the invoice amount (i.e., multiplies the quantity by the price per item). Write a test module named `InvoiceTest` that demonstrates class `Invoice`'s capabilities.

4.12 *(Employee Class)* Create a class called `Employee` that includes three pieces of information as instance variables—a first name (type `String`), a last name (type `String`) and a monthly salary (type `Integer`). Your class should have a constructor that initializes the three instance variables. Provide a property for each instance variable. The property for the monthly salary should ensure that its value remains positive—if an attempt is made to assign a negative value, leave the original value. Write a test module named `EmployeeTest` that demonstrates class `Employee`'s capabilities. Create two Employee objects and display each object's *yearly* salary. Then give each `Employee` a 10% raise and display each `Employee`'s yearly salary again.

4.13 *(DateInformation Class)* Create a class called `DateInformation` that includes three pieces of information as instance variables—a month (type `Integer`), a day (type `Integer`) and a year (type `Integer`). Your class should provide properties that enable a client of the class to `Get` and `Set` the month, day and year values. The `Set` accessors for the month and day should provide simple validation to ensure that the month value is in the range 1–12 and the day value is in the range 1–31. There is no need to validate the year in this example. [*Note:* In Chapter 9, we develop a version of this class with more extensive validation that checks for leap years and day ranges specific to each month (e.g., January—31 days, June—30 days, and February—28 days unless it is a leap year).] If the month value is less than 1 or greater than 12, the `Set` accessor for the month should set the month to 1. Similarly, if the day value is less than 1 or greater than 31, the `Set` accessor for the day should set the day to 1. Your class should have a constructor that initializes the three instance variables and uses the class's properties to set each instance variable's value. This ensures that the month and day are validated. Provide a method `DisplayDate` that displays the month, day and year separated by forward slashes (/). Write a test module named `DateInformationTest` that demonstrates class `DateInformation`'s capabilities.

5

Control Statements: Part 1

Let's all move one place on.
—Lewis Carroll

The wheel is come full circle.
—William Shakespeare, *King Lear*

How many apples fell on Newton's head before he took the hint?
—Robert Frost

All the evolution we know of proceeds from the vague to the definite.
—Charles Sanders Peirce

5.1 Introduction

Before writing a program to solve a problem, it is essential to have a thorough understanding of the problem and a carefully planned approach. When writing a program, it is equally important to recognize the types of building blocks that are available and to employ proven program-construction principles. In this chapter and the next, we present the theory and principles of structured programming with control statements. Control statements are important in building and manipulating objects.

In this chapter, we introduce Visual Basic's If...Then, If...Then...Else, While, Do While...Loop and Do Until...Loop statements, five of the building blocks that allow programmers to specify the logic required for methods to perform their tasks. We devote a portion of this chapter (and Chapters 6 and 8) to further developing the GradeBook class introduced in Chapter 4. In particular, we add a method to the GradeBook class that uses control statements to calculate the average of a set of student grades. Another example demonstrates how to combine control statements by "stacking" and "nesting" to solve a particular problem. You will notice that some examples use classes and a test module to demonstrate a concept, while others use only a module. When it does not make sense to create a reusable class to demonstrate a simple concept, we write the code in the Main method of a module.

Throughout most of this chapter we use console applications to demonstrate new programming techniques. We devote one section to enhancing the Windows application you created in Chapter 2 to include your own Visual Basic code.

5.2 **Algorithms**

Any computing problem can be solved by executing a series of actions in a specific order. A procedure for solving a problem, in terms of

1. the actions to be executed and
2. the order in which these actions are to be executed

is called an algorithm. The following example demonstrates the importance of correctly specifying the order in which the actions are to be executed.

Consider the "rise-and-shine algorithm" followed by one junior executive for getting out of bed and going to work: (1) get out of bed, (2) take off pajamas, (3) take a shower, (4) get dressed, (5) eat breakfast and (6) carpool to work. This routine prepares the executive for a productive day at the office.

However, suppose that the same steps are performed in a slightly different order: (1) get out of bed, (2) take off pajamas, (3) get dressed, (4) take a shower, (5) eat breakfast, (6) carpool to work. In this case, our junior executive shows up for work soaking wet.

Specifying the order in which statements (actions) execute in a program is called program control. This chapter investigates program control using Visual Basic's control statements.

5.3 **Pseudocode**

Pseudocode is an informal language that helps programmers develop algorithms. It is similar to everyday English; it is convenient and user-friendly, but it is not an actual computer programming language. The pseudocode we present is particularly useful for developing algorithms that will be converted to structured portions of Visual Basic programs.

Pseudocode programs are not executed on computers. Rather, they help you "think out" a program before attempting to write it in a programming language, such as Visual Basic. In this chapter, we provide several pseudocode programs.

Software Engineering Observation 5.1

Pseudocode helps you conceptualize a program during the program-design process. The pseudocode program can be converted to Visual Basic at a later point.

The style of pseudocode that we present consists solely of characters, so that programmers can create, share and modify pseudocode programs using text editor programs. You can easily convert a carefully prepared pseudocode program to a corresponding Visual Basic program. Much of this conversion is as simple as replacing pseudocode statements with their Visual Basic equivalents.

Pseudocode normally describes only statements representing the actions that occur after a programmer converts a program from pseudocode to Visual Basic and the program is run on a computer. Such actions might include input, output or calculations. We typically do not include variable declarations such as

```
Dim number As Integer
```

in our pseudocode. However, some programmers choose to list variables and mention their purposes at the beginning of pseudocode algorithms. We show several pseudocode algorithms and explain how you can develop your own.

5.4 **Control Structures**

Normally, statements in a program are executed one after another in the order in which they are written. This is called sequential execution. However, various Visual Basic statements enable you to specify the next statement to be executed as one that is not the next in sequence. A transfer of control occurs when an executed statement does not directly follow the previously executed statement in the program.

During the 1960s, it became clear that the indiscriminate use of transfers of control was causing difficulty for software development groups. A key problem was the GoTo statement, which allows you to specify a transfer of control to one of a wide range of possible destinations in a program. The excessive use of GoTo statements caused programs to become quite unstructured and hard to follow—such disorganized programs were referred to as "spaghetti code." Since then, the notion of structured programming has become almost synonymous with "GoTo elimination."

The research of Bohm and Jacopini demonstrated that all programs containing GoTo statements could be written without them.[1] A challenge of the era was for programmers to shift their styles to "GoTo-less programming." It was not until the 1970s that most programmers started taking structured programming seriously. The results were impressive, with software development groups reporting reduced development times, more frequent on-time delivery of systems and more frequent within-budget completion of software projects. The key to these successes is that structured programs are clearer, easier to debug and modify and more likely to be bug-free in the first place.

Bohm and Jacopini's work demonstrated that all programs could be written in terms of only three control structures—the sequence structure, the selection structure and the repetition structure. The term "control structures" comes from the field of computer science. When we introduce Visual Basic's implementation of control structures, we will refer to them as "control statements."

Sequence Structure in Visual Basic

The sequence structure is built into Visual Basic. Unless directed to act otherwise, the computer executes Visual Basic statements sequentially. The UML activity diagram in Fig. 5.1

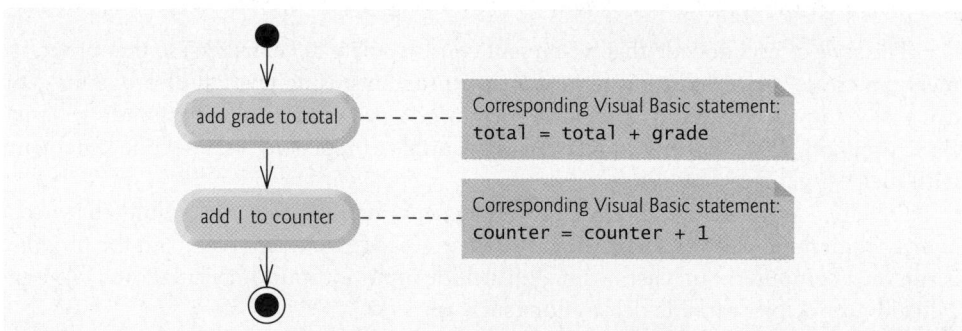

Fig. 5.1 | Sequence-structure activity diagram.

1. C. Bohm and G. Jacopini, "Flow Diagrams, Turing Machines, and Languages with Only Two Formation Rules," *Communications of the ACM*, Vol. 9, No. 5, May 1966, pp. 366–371.

illustrates a typical sequence structure in which two calculations are performed in order. Visual Basic lets us have as many actions as we want in a sequence structure. As we will soon see, anywhere a single action may be placed, we may place several actions in sequence.

The two statements in Fig. 5.1 involve adding a grade to a `total` variable and adding the value 1 to a `counter` variable. Such statements might appear in a program that takes the average of several student grades. To calculate an average, the total of the grades being averaged is divided by the number of grades. A counter variable would be used to keep track of the number of values being averaged. You will see similar statements in the program in Section 5.11.

UML Activity Diagrams

Activity diagrams are part of the UML. An activity diagram models the workflow (also called the activity) of a portion of a software system. A workflow may include a portion of an algorithm, such as the sequence structure in Fig. 5.1. Activity diagrams are composed of special-purpose symbols, such as the action state symbol (a rectangle with its left and right sides replaced with arcs curving outward; there are two of these in Fig. 5.1), the diamond symbol (there are none in this figure) and the small circle symbol; these symbols are connected by transition arrows, which represent the flow of the activity.

Like pseudocode, activity diagrams help programmers develop and represent algorithms. Activity diagrams clearly show how control structures operate.

Consider the sequence-structure activity diagram in Fig. 5.1. It contains two action states that represent actions to perform. Each action state contains an action expression—"add grade to total" or "add 1 to counter"—that specifies a particular action to perform. Other actions might include calculations or input/output operations. The transition arrows represent transitions that indicate the order in which the actions represented by the action states occur—the program that implements the activities illustrated by the activity diagram in Fig. 5.1 first adds `grade` to `total`, then adds 1 to `counter`.

The solid circle symbol located at the top of the activity diagram represents the activity's initial state—the beginning of the workflow before the corresponding program performs the modeled activities. The solid circle surrounded by a hollow circle that appears at the bottom of the activity diagram represents the final state—the end of the workflow after the corresponding program performs its activities.

Figure 5.1 also includes rectangles with the upper-right corners folded over. These are called notes in the UML. Notes are optional explanatory remarks that describe the purpose of symbols in the diagram. Notes can be used in any UML diagram—not just activity diagrams. Figure 5.1 uses UML notes to show the Visual Basic code associated with each action state in the activity diagram. A dotted line connects each note with the element that the note describes. An activity diagram normally does not show the Visual Basic code that implements the activity. We use notes here for this purpose to illustrate how the diagram relates to Visual Basic code. For more information on the UML, visit `www.uml.org`.

Selection Statements in Visual Basic

Visual Basic provides three types of selection statements. The `If...Then` selection statement (which we introduced briefly in Chapter 3 and study in detail in Section 5.5) either performs (selects) an action (or sequence of actions) if a condition is true, or skips the action (or sequence of actions) if the condition is false. The `If...Then...Else` selection statement, which we introduce in Section 5.6, performs an action (or sequence of actions) if a condition is true, and performs a different action (or sequence of actions) if the condition is false. The Select...Case statement, which we introduce in Chapter 6, performs one of many different actions (or sequences of actions), depending on the value of an expression.

The If...Then statement is called a single-selection statement because it selects or ignores a single action (or a sequence of actions). The If...Then...Else statement is called a double-selection statement because it selects between two different actions (or sequences of actions). The Select...Case statement is called a multiple-selection statement because it selects among many different actions or sequences of actions.

Repetition Statements in Visual Basic

Visual Basic provides seven types of repetition statements (also called looping statements or loops) that enable programs to perform statements repeatedly based on the value of a condition. The repetition statements are the While, Do While...Loop, Do...Loop While, Do Until...Loop, Do...Loop Until, For...Next and the For Each...Next statements. (The repetition statements While, Do While...Loop and Do Until...Loop are covered in this chapter; the Do...Loop While, Do...Loop Until, and For...Next statements are covered in Chapter 6, Control Statements: Part 2; and the For Each...Next statement is covered in Chapter 8, Arrays.) The words If, Then, Else, End, Select, Case, While, Do, Until, Loop, For, Next and Each are all Visual Basic keywords (Fig. 3.2).

Summary of Control Statements in Visual Basic

Visual Basic has only three kinds of control structures, which from this point forward we refer to as control statements: the sequence structure, selection statements (three types—If...Then, If...Then...Else and Select...Case) and repetition statements (seven types—While, Do While...Loop, Do...Loop While, Do Until...Loop, Do...Loop Until, For...Next and For Each...Next)—for a total of 11 types of control statements. Every program is formed by combining as many of each type of control statement as is necessary. We can model each control statement as an activity diagram. Each diagram contains one initial state and one final state, which represent the control statement's entry point and exit point, respectively. These single-entry/single-exit control statements make it easy to build programs—the control statements are "attached" to one another by "connecting" the exit point of one control statement to the entry point of the next (which we accomplish simply by following one control statement immediately by another). This is similar to stacking building blocks, so we call it control-statement stacking. Section 5.12 shows an example of control-statement stacking. There is only one other way to connect control statements, and that is through control-statement nesting, where one control statement is placed inside another. We discuss control-statement nesting in Sections 5.13 and 5.14.

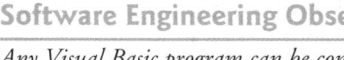 **Software Engineering Observation 5.2**

Any Visual Basic program can be constructed from only 11 different types of control statements (sequence, three types of selection statements and seven types of repetition statements) combined in only two ways (control-statement stacking and control-statement nesting).

5.5 If...Then Selection Statement

In a program, a selection statement chooses among alternative courses of action. For example, suppose that the passing grade on an examination is 60 (out of 100). Then the pseudocode statement

> *If student's grade is greater than or equal to 60 then*
>   *Print "Passed"*

determines whether the condition "student's grade is greater than or equal to 60" is true or false. If the condition is true, then "Passed" is printed, and the next pseudocode statement in order is "performed" (remember that pseudocode is not a real programming language). If the condition is false, the print statement is ignored, and the next pseudocode statement in order is "performed."

The preceding pseudocode *If* statement may be written in Visual Basic as

```
If studentGrade >= 60 Then
    Console.WriteLine("Passed")
End If
```

Note that the Visual Basic code corresponds closely to the pseudocode, demonstrating the usefulness of pseudocode as a program-development tool. The statement in the body of the If...Then statement outputs the string "Passed". Note also that the output statement in this selection statement is indented. Such indentation is optional, but it is recommended because it emphasizes the organization of structured programs.

The Visual Basic compiler ignores white-space characters, such as spaces, tabs and blank lines used for indentation and vertical spacing, unless the whitespace characters are contained in strings. Some whitespace characters are required, however, such as the space between variable names and keywords. Programmers insert extra whitespace characters to enhance program readability.

The preceding If...Then selection statement also could be written on a single line as

```
If studentGrade >= 60 Then Console.WriteLine("Passed")
```

In the multiple-line format, all statements (there can be many) in the body of the If...Then are executed if the condition is true. In the single-line format, only the statement immediately after the Then keyword is executed if the condition is true. Although writing the If...Then selection statement in the latter format saves space, some programmers feel that the organization of the statement is clearer when the multiple-line format is used.

Whereas syntax errors are caught by the compiler, logic errors, such as the error caused when the wrong relational operator is used in the condition of a selection statement, affect the program only at execution time. A fatal logic error causes a program to fail and terminate prematurely. A nonfatal logic error does not terminate a program's execution but causes the program to produce incorrect results.

Figure 5.2 is an activity diagram that illustrates the single-selection If...Then statement. It contains what is perhaps the most important symbol in an activity diagram—the diamond, or decision symbol, which indicates that a decision is to be made. A decision symbol indicates that the workflow will continue along a path determined by the symbol's associated guard conditions, which can be true or false. Each transition arrow emerging from a decision symbol has a guard condition (specified in square brackets above or next to the transition arrow). If a particular guard condition is true, the workflow enters the action state to which that transition arrow points. Exactly one of the guard conditions associated with a decision symbol must be true when a decision is made. In Fig. 5.2, if the grade is greater than or equal to 60, the program prints "Passed" to the screen, then transitions to the final state of this activity. If the grade is less than 60, the program immediately transitions to the final state without displaying a message.

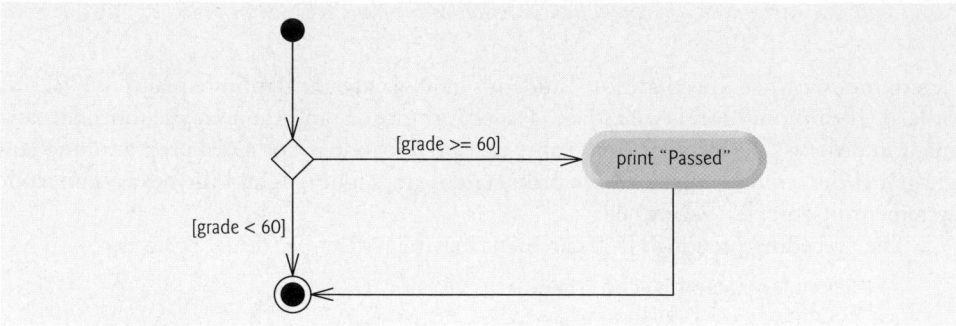

Fig. 5.2 | If...Then single-selection statement activity diagram.

Note that the If...Then statement is a single-entry/single-exit statement (as are all Visual Basic control statements). The activity diagrams for the remaining control statements also contain initial states, transition arrows, action states that indicate actions to perform, decision symbols (with associated guard conditions) that indicate decisions to be made, and final states.

To understand the process of structured programming better, we can envision 11 bins, each containing single-entry/single-exit UML activity diagrams of a different type of the 11 possible control statements. The activity diagrams in each bin are empty—nothing is written in the action states and no guard conditions are written alongside the transition arrows emerging from the decision symbols. Your task is to assemble a program using as many of these UML activity diagrams as the algorithm demands, combining them in only two possible ways (stacking or nesting) and filling in the actions and decisions and guard conditions in a manner appropriate to the algorithm.

5.6 If...Then...Else Selection Statement

As we have explained, the If...Then selection statement performs an indicated action (or sequence of actions) only when the condition evaluates to true; otherwise, the action (or sequence of actions) is skipped. The If...Then...Else selection statement allows you to specify that a different action (or sequence of actions) is to be performed when the condition is true than when the condition is false. For example, the pseudocode statement

> *If student's grade is greater than or equal to 60 then*
> *Print "Passed"*
> *Else*
> *Print "Failed"*

prints "Passed" if the student's grade is greater than or equal to 60, and prints "Failed" if the student's grade is less than 60. In either case, after printing occurs, the next pseudocode statement in sequence is "performed."

The preceding pseudocode *If...Else* statement may be written in Visual Basic as

```
If studentGrade >= 60 Then
    Console.WriteLine("Passed")
Else
    Console.WriteLine("Failed")
End If
```

Note that the body of the Else clause is indented so that it lines up with the body of the If clause.

Good Programming Practice 5.1

Indent both body statements of an If...Then...Else statement to improve readability.

Good Programming Practice 5.2

A standard indentation convention should be applied consistently throughout your programs. It is difficult to read programs that do not use uniform spacing conventions.

Figure 5.3 illustrates the flow of control in the If...Then...Else statement. Once again, note that (besides the initial state, transition arrows and final state) the only other symbols in this activity diagram represent action states and decisions.

Nested If...Then...Else Statements

Nested If...Then...Else statements test for multiple conditions by placing If...Then...Else statements inside other If...Then...Else statements. For example, the following pseudocode statement will print "A" for exam grades greater than or equal to 90, "B" for grades in the range 80–89, "C" for grades in the range 70–79, "D" for grades in the range 60–69 and "F" for all other grades.

> *If student's grade is greater than or equal to 90 then*
>   *Print "A"*
> *Else*
>   *If student's grade is greater than or equal to 80 then*
>   *Print "B"*
>   *Else*
>   *If student's grade is greater than or equal to 70 then*
>   *Print "C"*
>   *Else*
>   *If student's grade is greater than or equal to 60 then*
>   *Print "D"*
>   *Else*
>   *Print "F"*

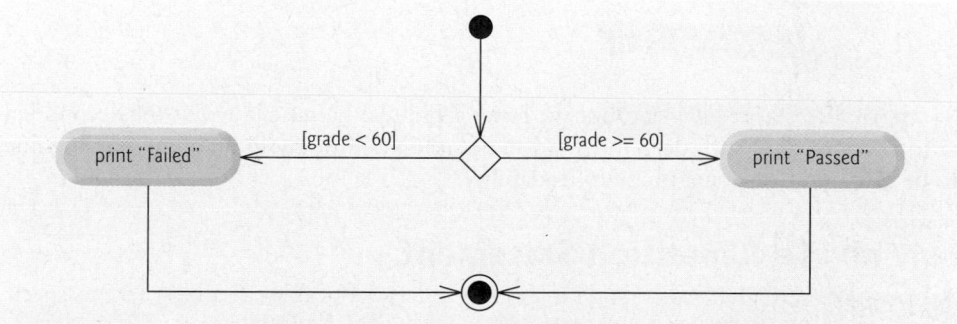

Fig. 5.3 | If...Then...Else double-selection statement activity diagram.

The pseudocode above may be written in Visual Basic as

```
If studentGrade >= 90 Then
    Console.WriteLine("A")
Else
    If studentGrade >= 80 Then
        Console.WriteLine("B")
    Else
        If studentGrade >= 70 Then
            Console.WriteLine("C")
        Else
            If studentGrade >= 60 Then
                Console.WriteLine("D")
            Else
                Console.WriteLine("F")
            End If
        End If
    End If
End If
```

If studentGrade is greater than or equal to 90, the first four conditions are true, but only the Console.WriteLine statement in the body of the first test is executed. After that particular Console.WriteLine executes, the Else part of the "outer" If...Then...Else statement is skipped, and the program proceeds with the next statement after the last End If.

Good Programming Practice 5.3

If there are several levels of indentation, each level should be indented additionally by the same amount of space; this gives programs a neatly structured appearance.

Some Visual Basic programmers prefer to write the preceding If...Then...Else statement using the ElseIf keyword as

```
If grade >= 90 Then
    Console.WriteLine("A")
ElseIf grade >= 80 Then
    Console.WriteLine("B")
ElseIf grade >= 70 Then
    Console.WriteLine("C")
ElseIf grade >= 60 Then
    Console.WriteLine("D")
Else
    Console.WriteLine("F")
End If
```

Both forms are equivalent, but the latter is popular because it avoids the deep indentation of the code. Such deep indentation often leaves little room on a line, forcing lines to be split and decreasing program readability.

5.7 While Repetition Statement

A repetition statement (also called a looping statement or a loop) allows you to specify that an action should be repeated, depending on the value of a condition (called the loop-continuation condition). The pseudocode statements

> *While there are more items on my shopping list*
> *Purchase next item*
> *Cross it off my list*

describe the repetitive actions that occur during a shopping trip. The condition "there are more items on my shopping list" can be true or false. If it is true, then the actions "Purchase next item" and "Cross it off my list" are performed in sequence. These actions execute repeatedly while the condition remains true. The statement(s) contained in the *While* repetition statement constitute the body of the *While*. Eventually, the condition becomes false (when the last item on the shopping list has been purchased and crossed off the list). At this point, the repetition terminates, and the first statement after the repetition statement executes.

As an example of a `While` statement (sometimes more formally referred to as the `While...End While` statement), consider a program designed to find the first power of 3 larger than 100 (Fig. 5.4). In line 5, we take advantage of a Visual Basic feature that allows variable initialization to be incorporated into a declaration. When the `While` statement is entered (line 9), `product` is 3. Variable `product` is repeatedly multiplied by 3 (line 11), taking on the values 3, 9, 27, 81 and 243, successively. When `product` becomes 243, the condition `product <= 100` in the `While` statement becomes false. This terminates the repetition with 243 as `product`'s final value. Execution continues with the next statement after the keywords `End While` in line 12. [*Note:* If a `While` statement's condition is initially false, the body statement(s) are not performed.]

```vb
 1    ' Fig. 5.4: PowersOfThree.vb
 2    ' Demonstration of While statement.
 3    Module PowersOfThree
 4       Sub Main()
 5          Dim product As Integer = 3
 6
 7          ' statement multiplies and displays product
 8          ' while product is less than or equal to 100
 9          While product <= 100
10             Console.Write(product & "   ")
11             product = product * 3 ' compute next power of 3
12          End While
13
14          Console.WriteLine() ' write blank line
15
16          ' print result
17          Console.WriteLine("First power of 3 " & _
18             "larger than 100 is " & product)
19       End Sub ' Main
20    End Module ' PowersOfThree
```

```
3  9  27  81
First power of 3 larger than 100 is 243
```

Fig. 5.4 | `While` repetition statement used to print powers of 3.

The UML activity diagram of Fig. 5.5 illustrates the flow of control that corresponds to the `While` statement shown in Fig. 5.4 (we have omitted the display of `product` each time through the loop at line 10). Once again, the symbols in the diagram (besides the initial state, transition arrows, a final state and three notes) represent an action state and a decision. This diagram also introduces the UML's merge symbol, which joins two flows of activity into one flow of activity. The UML represents both the merge symbol and the decision symbol as diamonds (this can be confusing). In this diagram, the merge symbol joins the transitions from the initial state and the action state, so they both flow into the decision that determines whether the loop should begin (or continue) executing. The decision and merge symbols can be distinguished by the number of "incoming" and "outgoing" transition arrows. A decision symbol has one transition arrow pointing to the diamond and two or more transition arrows pointing out from the diamond to indicate possible transitions from that point. In addition, each transition arrow pointing out of a decision symbol has a guard condition next to it (exactly one of which must be true when a decision is made). A merge symbol has two or more transition arrows pointing to the diamond and only one transition arrow pointing from the diamond, to indicate multiple activity flows merging to continue the activity. Note that, unlike the decision symbol, the merge symbol does not have a counterpart in Visual Basic code. None of the transition arrows associated with a merge symbol have guard conditions.

The activity diagram of Fig. 5.5 clearly shows the repetition of the `While` statement discussed earlier in this section. The transition arrow emerging from the action state connects back to the merge, which transitions back to the decision that is tested each time through the loop until the guard condition `product > 100` becomes true. Then the `While` statement exits (reaches its final state) and control passes to the next statement in sequence in the program.

 Common Programming Error 5.1

Failure to provide the body of a `While` statement with an action that eventually causes the loop-continuation condition to become false is a logic error. Normally, such a repetition statement never terminates, resulting in a logic error called an "infinite loop."

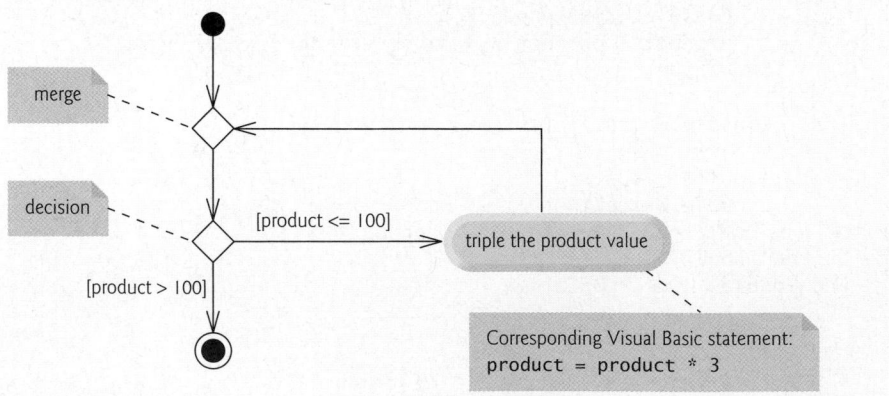

Fig. 5.5 | `While` repetition statement activity diagram.

5.8 Do While...Loop Repetition Statement

The Do While...Loop repetition statement behaves like the While repetition statement. As an example of a Do While...Loop statement, consider another version of the program designed to find the first power of 3 larger than 100 (Fig. 5.6).

When the Do While...Loop statement is entered (line 9), the value of product is 3. The variable product is repeatedly multiplied by 3, taking on the values 3, 9, 27, 81 and 243, successively. When product becomes 243, the condition in the Do While...Loop statement, product <= 100, becomes false. This terminates the repetition, with the final value of product being 243. Program execution continues with the next statement after the Do While...Loop statement. Because the While and Do While...Loop statements behave in the same way, the activity diagram in Fig. 5.5 also illustrates the flow of control of the Do While...Loop repetition statement.

Common Programming Error 5.2

Failure to provide the body of a Do While...Loop statement with an action that eventually causes the loop-continuation condition in the Do While...Loop to become false creates an infinite loop.

5.9 Do Until...Loop Repetition Statement

Unlike the While and Do While...Loop repetition statements, the Do Until...Loop repetition statement tests a condition for falsity for repetition to continue. Statements in the body of a Do Until...Loop are executed repeatedly as long as the condition (known as the loop-termination condition) evaluates to false. The program of Fig. 5.7 find the first power of 3 larger than 100 by using a Do Until...Loop repetition statement.

```vb
1   ' Fig. 5.6: DoWhile.vb
2   ' Demonstration of the Do While...Loop statement.
3   Module DoWhile
4      Sub Main()
5         Dim product As Integer = 3 ' initialize product
6
7         ' statement multiplies and displays the
8         ' product while it is less than or equal to 100
9         Do While product <= 100
10            Console.Write(product & "  ")
11            product = product * 3
12         Loop
13
14         Console.WriteLine() ' write blank line
15
16         ' print result
17         Console.WriteLine("First power of 3 " & _
18            "larger than 100 is " & product)
19      End Sub ' Main
20   End Module ' DoWhile
```

```
3  9  27  81
First power of 3 larger than 100 is 243
```

Fig. 5.6 | Do While...Loop repetition statement demonstration.

```
 1   ' Fig. 5.7: DoUntil.vb
 2   ' Demonstration of the Do Until...Loop statement.
 3   Module DoUntil
 4      Sub Main()
 5         Dim product As Integer = 3
 6
 7         ' find first power of 3 larger than 100
 8         Do Until product > 100
 9            Console.Write(product & "   ")
10            product = product * 3
11         Loop
12
13         Console.WriteLine() ' write blank line
14
15         ' print result
16         Console.WriteLine("First power of 3 " & _
17            "larger than 100 is " & product)
18      End Sub ' Main
19   End Module ' DoUntil
```

```
3  9  27  81
First power of 3 larger than 100 is 243
```

Fig. 5.7 | Do Until...Loop repetition statement demonstration.

Once again, the activity diagram of Fig. 5.5 illustrates the flow of control in the Do Until...Loop repetition statement shown in Fig. 5.7. This time, however, we focus on the leftmost guard condition—product > 100—the loop-termination condition for our control statement. Because we are using a Do Until...Loop statement, the statement's actions (lines 9–10) are performed when the statement's loop-termination condition is false (i.e., product is less than or equal to 100). When the loop-termination condition (product > 100, the leftmost guard condition) is true the statement exits.

Common Programming Error 5.3

Failure to provide the body of a Do Until...Loop statement with an action that eventually causes the loop-termination condition in the Do Until...Loop to become true creates an infinite loop.

5.10 Compound Assignment Operators

Visual Basic provides several **compound assignment operators** for abbreviating assignment statements. For example, the statement

```
value = value + 3
```

can be abbreviated with the **addition assignment operator, +=** as

```
value += 3
```

The += operator adds the value of the right operand to the value of the left operand and stores the result in the left operand's variable. Any statement of the form

variable = variable operator expression

can be written in the form

variable operator= expression

where *operator* is one of the binary operators +, -, *, ^, &, / or \, and *variable* is an *lvalue* ("left value"). An *lvalue* is a variable or property that can appear on the left side of an assignment statement. We will learn how to declare constants in Section 7.16—constants cannot be *lvalues*. Figure 5.8 includes the compound assignment operators, sample expressions using these operators and explanations.

The =, +=, -=, *=, /=, \=, ^= and &= operators are always applied last in an expression. When an assignment statement is evaluated, the expression to the right of the operator is always evaluated first, then the value is assigned to the *lvalue* on the left. Figure 5.9 calculates a power of two using the exponentiation assignment operator. Lines 12 and 16 have the same effect on the variable result. Both statements raise result to the value of variable exponent. Note that the results of these two calculations are identical.

Compound assignment operator	Sample expression	Explanation	Assigns
Assume: c = 4, d = "He"			
+=	c += 7	c = c + 7	11 to c
-=	c -= 3	c = c - 3	1 to c
*=	c *= 4	c = c * 4	16 to c
/=	c /= 2	c = c / 2	2 to c
\=	c \= 3	c = c \ 3	1 to c
^=	c ^= 2	c = c ^ 2	16 to c
&=	d &= "llo"	d = d & "llo"	"Hello" to d

Fig. 5.8 | Compound assignment operators.

```vb
1    ' Fig. 5.9: Assignment.vb
2    ' Using a compound assignment operator to calculate a power of 2.
3    Module Assignment
4       Sub Main()
5          Dim exponent As Integer ' power input by user
6          Dim result As Integer = 2 ' number to raise to a power
7
8          ' prompt user for exponent
9          Console.Write("Enter an integer exponent: ")
10         exponent = Console.ReadLine() ' input exponent
11
12         result ^= exponent ' same as result = result ^ exponent
13         Console.WriteLine("result ^= exponent: " & result)
```

Fig. 5.9 | Exponentiation using a compound assignment operator. (Part 1 of 2.)

```
14
15          result = 2 ' reset result to 2
16          result = result ^ exponent ' same as result ^= exponent
17          Console.WriteLine("result = result ^ exponent: " & result)
18      End Sub ' Main
19  End Module ' Assignment
```

```
Enter an integer exponent: 8
result ^= exponent: 256
result = result ^ exponent: 256
```

Fig. 5.9 | Exponentiation using a compound assignment operator. (Part 2 of 2.)

5.11 Formulating Algorithms: Counter-Controlled Repetition

To illustrate how algorithms are developed, we modify the GradeBook class of Chapter 4 to solve two variations of a problem that averages student grades. Consider the following problem statement:

> A class of 10 students took a quiz. The grades (integers in the range 0 to 100) for this quiz are available to you. Determine the class average on the quiz.

The class average is equal to the sum of the grades divided by the number of students (10). The algorithm for solving this problem on a computer must input each grade, keep track of the total of all grades input, perform the averaging calculation and print the result.

Pseudocode Algorithm with Counter-Controlled Repetition

Let us use pseudocode to list the actions to execute and specify the order of execution. We use **counter-controlled repetition** to input and process the grades one at a time. This technique uses a variable called a **counter** (or **control variable**) to specify the number of times that a set of statements will execute. Counter-controlled repetition also is called **definite repetition** because the number of repetitions is known before the loop begins executing. In this example, repetition terminates when the counter exceeds 10. This section presents a fully developed pseudocode algorithm (Fig. 5.10) and a version of class GradeBook (Fig. 5.11) that implements the algorithm in a method. The section then presents an application (Fig. 5.12) that demonstrates the algorithm in action. In Sections 5.12—5.14, we demonstrate how to use pseudocode to develop algorithms from scratch.

Note the references in the pseudocode algorithm (Fig. 5.10) to a total and a counter. A **total** is a variable used to accumulate the sum of several values. A counter is a variable used to count—in this case, the grade counter records the number of grades input by the user. It is important that variables used as totals and counters have appropriate initial values before they are used. Counters usually are initialized to 1 (but we will see examples where it is appropriate to initialize counters to other values, most commonly zero). Totals generally are initialized to zero. In Visual Basic, numeric variables are initialized to 0 when they are declared, unless another value is assigned to the variable in its declaration.

Good Programming Practice 5.4

Although Visual Basic initializes numeric variables to 0, it is a good practice to initialize certain variables explicitly to avoid confusion and improve program readability.

1	*Set total to zero*
2	*Set grade counter to one*
3	
4	*While grade counter is less than or equal to ten*
5	*Prompt the user to enter the next grade*
6	*Input the next grade*
7	*Add the grade into the total*
8	*Add one to the grade counter*
9	
10	*Set the class average to the total divided by ten*
11	*Print the class average*

Fig. 5.10 | Pseudocode algorithm that uses counter-controlled repetition to solve the class-average problem.

```vb
1  ' Fig. 5.11: GradeBook.vb
2  ' GradeBook class that solves class-average problem using
3  ' counter-controlled repetition.
4  Public Class GradeBook
5     Private courseNameValue As String ' course name for this GradeBook
6
7     ' constructor initializes CourseName with String supplied as argument
8     Public Sub New(ByVal name As String)
9        CourseName = name ' validate and store course name
10    End Sub ' New
11
12    ' property that gets and sets the course name; the Set accessor
13    ' ensures that the course name has at most 25 characters
14    Public Property CourseName() As String
15       Get ' retrieve courseNameValue
16          Return courseNameValue
17       End Get
18
19       Set(ByVal value As String) ' set courseNameValue
20          If value.Length <= 25 Then ' if value has 25 or fewer characters
21             courseNameValue = value ' store the course name in the object
22          Else ' if name has more than 25 characters
23             ' set courseNameValue to first 25 characters of parameter name
24             ' start at 0, length of 25
25             courseNameValue = value.Substring(0, 25)
26
27             Console.WriteLine( _
28                "Course name (" & value & ") exceeds maximum length (25).")
29             Console.WriteLine( _
30                "Limiting course name to first 25 characters." & vbCrLf)
31          End If
32       End Set
33    End Property ' CourseName
34
```

Fig. 5.11 | Counter-controlled repetition: Class-average problem. (Part 1 of 2.)

```vbnet
35         ' display a welcome message to the GradeBook user
36      Public Sub DisplayMessage()
37            ' this statement uses property CourseName to get the
38            ' name of the course this GradeBook represents
39            Console.WriteLine("Welcome to the grade book for " _
40               & vbCrLf & CourseName & "!" & vbCrLf)
41      End Sub ' DisplayMessage
42
43      ' determine class average based on 10 grades entered by user
44      Public Sub DetermineClassAverage()
45         Dim total As Integer ' sum of grades entered by user
46         Dim gradeCounter As Integer ' number of grades input
47         Dim grade As Integer ' grade input by user
48         Dim average As Integer ' average of grades
49
50         ' initialization phase
51         total = 0 ' set total to zero
52         gradeCounter = 1 ' prepare to loop
53
54         ' processing phase
55         While gradeCounter <= 10 ' loop 10 times
56            ' prompt for and input grade from user
57            Console.Write("Enter grade: ") ' prompt for grade
58            grade = Console.ReadLine() ' input the next grade
59            total += grade ' add grade to total
60            gradeCounter += 1 ' add 1 to gradeCounter
61         End While
62
63         ' termination phase
64         average = total \ 10 ' integer division yields integer result
65
66         ' display total and average of grades
67         Console.WriteLine(vbCrLf & "Total of all 10 grades is " & total)
68         Console.WriteLine("Class average is " & average)
69      End Sub ' DetermineClassAverage
70   End Class ' GradeBook
```

Fig. 5.11 | Counter-controlled repetition: Class-average problem. (Part 2 of 2.)

Implementing Counter-Controlled Repetition in Class GradeBook

Class GradeBook (Fig. 5.11) contains a constructor (lines 8–10) that assigns a value to the class's property CourseName. Lines 14–33 and 36–41 declare property CourseName and method DisplayMessage, respectively. Lines 44–69 declare method DetermineClassAverage, which implements the class-averaging algorithm described by the pseudocode in Fig. 5.10.

Lines 45–48 declare local variables total, gradeCounter, grade and average to be of type Integer. In this example, variable total accumulates the sum of the grades entered and gradeCounter counts the number of grades entered. Variable grade stores the most recent grade value entered (line 58).

Note that the declarations (in lines 45–48) appear in the body of method DetermineClassAverage. Recall that variables declared in a method body are local variables and can be used only from their declaration until the end of the method declaration. A local variable's declaration must appear before the variable is used in that method. A local variable cannot be accessed outside the method in which it is declared.

In the versions of class `GradeBook` in this chapter, we simply read and process a set of grades. The averaging calculation is performed in method `DetermineClassAverage` using local variables—we do not preserve any information about student grades in instance variables of the class. In versions of the class in Chapter 8, Arrays, we maintain the grades in memory using an instance variable that refers to a data structure known as an array. This allows a `GradeBook` object to perform various calculations on the same set of grades without requiring the user to enter the grades multiple times.

Good Programming Practice 5.5

Separating declarations from other statements with a blank line improves readability.

The assignments (in lines 51–52) initialize `total` to 0 and `gradeCounter` to 1. Line 55 indicates that the `While` statement should continue looping (also called **iterating**) as long as the value of `gradeCounter` is less than or equal to 10. While this condition remains true, the `While` statement repeatedly executes the statements in its body (lines 57–60).

Line 57 displays the prompt `"Enter grade: "`. Line 58 reads the grade entered by the user and assigns it to the variable `grade`. Then line 59 adds the new `grade` entered by the user into the variable `total` using the += compound assignment operator.

Line 60 adds 1 to `gradeCounter` to indicate that the program has processed another grade and is ready to input the next grade from the user. Incrementing `gradeCounter` eventually causes it to exceed 10. At that point the `While` loop terminates because its condition (line 55) becomes false.

When the loop terminates, line 64 performs the averaging calculation and assigns its result to the variable `average`. Line 67 displays the text `"Total of all 10 grades is "` followed by variable `total`'s value. Line 68 then displays the text `"Class average is "` followed by variable `average`'s value. Method `DetermineClassAverage` returns control to the calling method (i.e., `Main` in `GradeBookTest` of Fig. 5.12) after reaching line 69.

Software Engineering Observation 5.3

Experience has shown that the most difficult part of solving a problem on a computer is developing the algorithm for the solution. Once a correct algorithm has been specified, the process of producing a working Visual Basic program from the algorithm is normally straightforward.

Module *GradeBookTest*

Module `GradeBookTest` (Fig. 5.12) creates an object of class `GradeBook` (Fig. 5.11) and demonstrates its capabilities. Line 7 of Fig. 5.12 creates a new `GradeBook` object and assigns it to variable `gradeBook`. The string in line 7 is passed to the `GradeBook` constructor (lines 8–10 of Fig. 5.11). Line 9 calls `gradeBook`'s `DisplayMessage` method to display a welcome message to the user. Line 10 then calls `gradeBook`'s `DetermineClassAverage` method to allow the user to enter 10 grades, for which the method then calculates and prints the average, performing the algorithm shown in Fig. 5.10.

Notes on Integer Division

The averaging calculation performed by method `DetermineClassAverage` in response to the method call at line 10 in Fig. 5.12 produces an integer result. The program's output

```
 1    ' Fig. 5.12: GradeBookTest.vb
 2    ' Create GradeBook object and invoke its DetermineClassAverage method.
 3    Module GradeBookTest
 4       Sub Main()
 5          ' create GradeBook object gradeBook and
 6          ' pass course name to constructor
 7          Dim gradeBook As New GradeBook("CS101 Introduction to VB")
 8
 9          gradeBook.DisplayMessage() ' display welcome message
10          gradeBook.DetermineClassAverage() ' find average of 10 grades
11       End Sub ' Main
12    End Module ' GradeBookTest
```

```
Welcome to the grade book for
CS101 Introduction to VB!

Enter grade: 65
Enter grade: 78
Enter grade: 89
Enter grade: 67
Enter grade: 87
Enter grade: 98
Enter grade: 93
Enter grade: 85
Enter grade: 82
Enter grade: 100

Total of all 10 grades is 844
Class average is 84
```

Fig. 5.12 | Module GradeBookTest creates an object of class GradeBook (Fig. 5.11) and invokes its DetermineClassAverage method.

indicates that the sum of the grade values in the sample execution is 844, which, when divided by 10, should yield the floating-point number 84.4. However, the result of the calculation total \ 10 (line 64 of Fig. 5.11) is the integer 84, because the integer division operator is used. Recall that the integer division operator takes two integer operands and returns an integer result. We use the floating-point division operator in the next section to determine a floating-point average.

 Common Programming Error 5.4

Assuming that integer division rounds (rather than truncates) can lead to incorrect results. For example, 7 divided by 4, which yields 1.75 in conventional arithmetic, truncates to 1 in integer arithmetic, rather than rounding to 2.

5.12 Formulating Algorithms: Sentinel-Controlled Repetition

Let us generalize Section 5.11's class-average problem. Consider the following problem:

Develop a class-averaging program that processes grades for an arbitrary number of students each time it is run.

In the previous class-average example, the problem statement specified the number of students, so the number of grades (10) was known in advance. In this example, no indication is given of how many grades are to be input. The program must process an arbitrary number of grades. How can it determine when to stop the input of grades? How will it know when to calculate and print the class average?

One way to solve this problem is to use a special value called a sentinel value (also called a signal value, a dummy value or a flag value) to indicate "end of data entry." The user enters grades until all legitimate grades have been entered. The user then types the sentinel value to indicate that no more grades will be entered. Sentinel-controlled repetition is called indefinite repetition because the number of repetitions is not known before the loop begins its execution.

It is crucial to employ a sentinel value that cannot be confused with an acceptable input value. Grades on a quiz are nonnegative integers, so –1 is an acceptable sentinel value for this problem. A run of the class-average program might process a stream of inputs such as 95, 96, 75, 74, 89 and –1. The program would then compute and print the class average for the grades 95, 96, 75, 74 and 89. The sentinel value, –1, should not enter into the averaging calculation.

Common Programming Error 5.5

Choosing a sentinel value that is also a legitimate data value could result in a logic error that would cause a program to produce incorrect results.

Developing the Pseudocode Algorithm with Top-Down, Stepwise Refinement: The Top and the First Refinement

When solving more complex problems, such as the one in this example, the pseudocode representation might not be obvious. For this reason we approach the class-average program with top-down, stepwise refinement, a technique for developing well-structured algorithms. We begin with a pseudocode representation of the top—a single statement that conveys the overall function of the program:

> *Determine the class average for the quiz*

The top is, in effect, a *complete* representation of a program. Unfortunately, the top rarely conveys sufficient detail from which to write a Visual Basic program. Therefore, we conduct the refinement process. This involves dividing the top into a series of smaller tasks that are listed in the order in which they must be performed, resulting in the following first refinement:

> *Initialize variables*
> *Input, sum and count the quiz grades*
> *Calculate and print the class average*

Software Engineering Observation 5.4

Each refinement, including the top, is a complete specification of the algorithm; only the level of detail in each refinement varies.

Software Engineering Observation 5.5

Many algorithms can be divided logically into three phases—an initialization phase that initializes the program variables, a processing phase that inputs data values and adjusts program variables accordingly, and a termination phase that calculates and prints the results.

Proceeding to the Second Refinement

The preceding *Software Engineering Observation* is often all you need for the first refinement in the top-down process. To proceed to the **second refinement**, we commit to specific variables. In this example, we need a running total of the numbers, a count of how many numbers have been processed, a variable to receive the value of each grade as it is input by the user and a variable to hold the calculated average. The pseudocode statement

> *Initialize variables*

can be refined as follows:

> *Initialize total to zero*
> *Initialize grade counter to zero*

Note that only the variables *total* and *counter* need to be initialized before they are used. The variables *average* and *grade* (the program in Fig. 5.14 uses these variables for the calculated average and the user input, respectively) need not be initialized (although, as you know, Visual Basic nevertheless initializes them to the default value zero) because the assignment of their values does not depend on their previous values, as is the case for *total* and *counter*.

The pseudocode statement

> *Input, sum and count the quiz grades*

requires a repetition statement (i.e., a loop) that inputs and processes each grade. We do not know in advance how many grades are to be processed, so we use sentinel-controlled repetition. The user enters legitimate grades one at a time. After the last legitimate grade is typed, the user enters the sentinel value. The program tests for the sentinel value after each grade is input and terminates the loop when the user enters the sentinel value. The second refinement of the preceding pseudocode statement is then

> *Prompt the user to enter the first grade*
> *Input the first grade (possibly the sentinel)*
>
> *While the user has not yet entered the sentinel*
>   *Add this grade into the running total*
>   *Add one to the grade counter*
>   *Prompt the user to enter the next grade*
>   *Input the next grade (possibly the sentinel)*

The pseudocode statement

> *Calculate and print the class average*

can be refined as follows:

> *If the grade counter is not equal to zero then*
>   *Set the average to the total divided by the counter*
>   *Print the class average*
> *Else*
>   *Print "No grades were entered"*

The counter will be zero if the user enters the sentinel value first. We test for the possibility of division by zero—a logic error that, if undetected, would cause the program to fail or produce invalid output. The complete second refinement of the pseudocode algorithm for the class-average problem is shown in Fig. 5.13.

Error-Prevention Tip 5.1

When performing division by an expression whose value could be zero, explicitly test for this case and handle it appropriately in your program. Such handling could be as simple as printing an error message. Sometimes more sophisticated processing is required, such as using the techniques of Chapter 12, Exception Handling.

Good Programming Practice 5.6

Include blank lines in pseudocode algorithms to improve readability. The blank lines separate pseudocode control statements and the algorithms' phases.

The pseudocode algorithm in Fig. 5.13 solves the more general class-averaging problem presented at the beginning of this section. This algorithm was developed after only two levels of refinement—sometimes more levels of refinement are necessary.

Software Engineering Observation 5.6

You terminate the top-down, stepwise refinement process when the pseudocode algorithm is specified in sufficient detail for the pseudocode to be converted to a Visual Basic program.

Implementing Sentinel-Controlled Repetition in Class GradeBook

Figure 5.14 shows the Visual Basic class `GradeBook` containing the method `DetermineClassAverage` that implements the pseudocode algorithm of Fig. 5.13. Although each grade is an integer, the averaging calculation is likely to produce a number with a decimal point—a real number or floating-point number. The type `Integer` cannot represent such a number, so this class uses type `Double` to do so.

```
 1   Initialize total to zero
 2   Initialize grade counter to zero
 3
 4   Prompt the user to enter the first grade
 5   Input the first grade (possibly the sentinel)
 6
 7   While the user has not yet entered the sentinel
 8       Add this grade into the running total
 9       Add one to the grade counter
10       Prompt the user to enter the next grade
11       Input the next grade (possibly the sentinel)
12
13   If the grade counter is not equal to zero then
14       Set the average to the total divided by the counter
15       Print the class average
16   Else
17       Print "No grades were entered"
```

Fig. 5.13 | Class-average problem pseudocode algorithm with sentinel-controlled repetition.

```vb
1  ' Fig. 5.14: GradeBook.vb
2  ' GradeBook class that solves class-average problem using
3  ' sentinel-controlled repetition.
4  Public Class GradeBook
5     Private courseNameValue As String ' course name for this GradeBook
6
7     ' constructor initializes CourseName with String supplied as argument
8     Public Sub New(ByVal name As String)
9        CourseName = name ' validate and store course name
10    End Sub ' New
11
12    ' property that gets and sets the course name; the Set accessor
13    ' ensures that the course name has at most 25 characters
14    Public Property CourseName() As String
15       Get ' retrieve courseNameValue
16          Return courseNameValue
17       End Get
18
19       Set(ByVal value As String) ' set courseNameValue
20          If value.Length <= 25 Then ' if value has 25 or fewer characters
21             courseNameValue = value ' store the course name in the object
22          Else ' if name has more than 25 characters
23             ' set courseNameValue to first 25 characters of parameter name
24             ' start at 0, length of 25
25             courseNameValue = value.Substring(0, 25)
26
27             Console.WriteLine( _
28                "Course name (" & value & ") exceeds maximum length (25).")
29             Console.WriteLine( _
30                "Limiting course name to first 25 characters." & vbCrLf)
31          End If
32       End Set
33    End Property ' CourseName
34
35    ' display a welcome message to the GradeBook user
36    Public Sub DisplayMessage()
37       ' this statement uses property CourseName to get the
38       ' name of the course this GradeBook represents
39       Console.WriteLine("Welcome to the grade book for " _
40          & vbCrLf & CourseName & "!" & vbCrLf)
41    End Sub ' DisplayMessage
42
43    ' determine class average based on 10 grades entered by user
44    Public Sub DetermineClassAverage()
45       Dim total As Integer ' sum of grades entered by user
46       Dim gradeCounter As Integer ' number of grades input
47       Dim grade As Integer ' grade input by user
48       Dim average As Double ' average of all grades
49
50       ' initialization phase
51       total = 0 ' clear total
52       gradeCounter = 0 ' prepare to loop
53
```

Fig. 5.14 | Sentinel-controlled repetition: Class-average problem. (Part 1 of 2.)

```vb
54          ' processing phase
55          ' prompt for input and read grade from user
56          Console.Write("Enter grade or -1 to quit: ")
57          grade = Console.ReadLine()
58
59          ' sentinel-controlled loop where -1 is the sentinel value
60          While grade <> -1
61             total += grade ' add grade to total
62             gradeCounter += 1 ' add 1 to gradeCounter
63
64             ' prompt for and input next grade from user
65             Console.Write("Enter grade or -1 to quit: ") ' prompt
66             grade = Console.ReadLine() ' input next grade
67          End While
68
69          ' termination phase
70          If gradeCounter <> 0 Then ' if user entered at least one grade
71             ' calculate average of all grades entered
72             average = total / gradeCounter
73
74             ' display total and average (with two digits of precision)
75             Console.WriteLine(vbCrLf & "Total of the " & gradeCounter & _
76                " grades entered is " & total)
77             Console.WriteLine("Class average is {0:F}", average)
78          Else ' no grades were entered, so output appropriate message
79             Console.WriteLine("No grades were entered")
80          End If
81       End Sub ' DetermineClassAverage
82    End Class ' GradeBook
```

Fig. 5.14 | Sentinel-controlled repetition: Class-average problem. (Part 2 of 2.)

In this example, we see that control statements may be stacked on top of one another (i.e., placed in sequence) just as a child stacks building blocks. The While statement (lines 60–67) is followed in sequence by an If...Then...Else statement (lines 70–80). Much of the code in this program is identical to the code in Fig. 5.11, so we concentrate on the new features and issues.

Line 48 declares Double variable average. This variable allows us to store the calculated class average as a floating-point number. We discuss floating-point numbers in more detail shortly. Line 52 initializes gradeCounter to 0, because no grades have been entered yet. Remember that this program uses sentinel-controlled repetition to input the grades from the user. To keep an accurate record of the number of grades entered, the program increments gradeCounter only when the user inputs a valid grade value. Recall that Integer variables are initialized to zero by default, so lines 51–52 can be omitted.

Program Logic for Sentinel-Controlled Repetition vs. Counter-Controlled Repetition
Compare the program logic for sentinel-controlled repetition in this application with that for counter-controlled repetition in Fig. 5.11. In counter-controlled repetition, each iteration (repetition) of the While statement (e.g., lines 55–61 of Fig. 5.11) reads a value from the user for the specified number of iterations. In sentinel-controlled repetition, the program reads the first value (lines 56–57 of Fig. 5.14) before reaching the While. This value

determines whether the program's flow of control should enter the body of the `While`. If the condition of the `While` is false, the user entered the sentinel value, so the body of the `While` does not execute (i.e., no grades were entered). If, on the other hand, the condition is true, the body begins execution, and the loop adds the `grade` value to the `total` (line 61). Lines 65–66 in the loop's body input the next value from the user. Next, program control reaches the end of the `While` statement, so execution continues with the test of the `While`'s condition (line 60). The condition uses the most recent `grade` input by the user to determine whether the loop's body should execute again. Note that the value of variable `grade` is always input from the user immediately before the program tests the `While` condition. This allows the program to determine whether the value just input is the sentinel value *before* processing that value (i.e., adding it to the `total`). If the sentinel value is input, the loop terminates, and the program does not add –1 to the `total`.

Good Programming Practice 5.7
In a sentinel-controlled loop, the prompts requesting data entry should explicitly remind the user of the sentinel value.

After the loop terminates, the `If...Then...Else` statement at lines 70–80 executes. The condition at line 70 determines whether any grades were input. If none were input, the `Else` part (lines 78–79) of the `If...Then...Else` statement executes and displays the message `"No grades were entered"` and the method returns control to the calling method.

Floating-Point Numbers and Type *Double*
Although each grade entered is an integer, the averaging calculation is likely to produce a number with a decimal point (i.e., a floating-point number). The type `Integer` cannot represent floating-point numbers, so this program uses data type `Double` to store floating-point numbers.

Visual Basic provides two primitive types for storing floating-point numbers in memory—`Single` and `Double`. The primary difference between them is that `Double` variables can store numbers of larger magnitude and finer detail (i.e., more digits to the right of the decimal point—also known as the number's precision) than `Single` variables.

Floating-Point Number Precision and Memory Requirements
Variables of type `Single` represent single-precision floating-point numbers and have seven significant digits. Variables of type `Double` represent double-precision floating-point numbers. These require twice as much memory as `Single` variables and provide 15 significant digits—approximately double the precision of `Single` variables. For the range of values required by most programs, variables of type `Single` should suffice, but you can use `Double` to play it safe. In some applications, even variables of type `Double` will be inadequate—such applications are beyond the scope of this book. Most programmers represent floating-point numbers with type `Double`. In fact, Visual Basic treats all the floating-point numbers you type in a program's source code (such as 7.33 and 0.0975) as `Double` values by default. Such values in the source code are known as floating-point literals. See Section 7.11 for the ranges of values for `Single`s and `Double`s.

Floating-Point Numbers are Approximations
Although floating-point numbers are not always 100% precise, they have numerous applications. For example, when we speak of a "normal" body temperature of 98.6, we do not

need to be precise to a large number of digits. When we read the temperature on a thermometer as 98.6, it may actually be 98.5999473210643. Calling this number simply 98.6 is fine for most applications involving body temperatures. Due to the imprecise nature of floating-point numbers, type `Double` is preferred over type `Single` because `Double` variables can represent floating-point numbers more accurately. For this reason, we use type `Double` throughout the book.

Floating-point numbers also arise as a result of division. In conventional arithmetic, when we divide 10 by 3, the result is 3.3333333..., with the sequence of 3s repeating infinitely. The computer allocates only a fixed amount of space to hold such a value, so clearly the stored floating-point value can be only an approximation.

 Common Programming Error 5.6

Using floating-point numbers in a manner that assumes they are represented precisely can lead to logic errors.

Implicitly Converting Between Primitive Types

If at least one grade was entered, line 72 of Fig. 5.14 calculates the average of the grades. Recall from Fig. 5.11 that we used the integer division operator to yield an integer result. Since we are now calculating a floating-point value, we use the floating-point division operator. But the operands of the division in line 72 are of type `Integer`. To perform a floating-point calculation with integer values, we must temporarily treat these values as floating-point numbers for use in the calculation.

The floating-point division operator is defined to operate on values of three types—`Single`, `Double` and `Decimal` (you will learn about type `Decimal` in Chapter 6). To ensure that the operator's operands are one of these three types, Visual Basic performs an operation called **implicit conversion** on selected operands. For example, in an expression using the floating-point division operator, if both operands are of type `Integer`, the operands will be **promoted** to `Double` values for use in the expression. In this example, the values of `total` and `gradeCounter` are promoted to type `Double`, then the floating-point division is performed and the result of the calculation is assigned to `average`. You will learn more about the implicit conversion rules in Section 7.9.

Formatting for Floating-Point Numbers

Line 77 outputs the class average. In this example, we decided to display the class average rounded to the nearest hundredth and to output the average with exactly two digits to the right of the decimal point. Note that the call to method `WriteLine` in line 77 uses the string "{0:F}" to indicate that the value of `average` should be displayed in the command prompt as a **fixed-point number**, (i.e., a number with a specified number of places after the decimal point). This is an example of **formatted output**, where a value's data is formatted for display purposes. The numeric value that appears before the colon (in this case, 0) indicates which of `WriteLine`'s arguments will be formatted—0 specifies the first argument that occurs *after* the string is passed to `WriteLine`, namely `average`. Additional values can be inserted into the string to specify other arguments. If we had passed `total` as a third argument to method `WriteLine` and used the string "{1:F}" the value to be formatted would be `total`. The value after the colon (in this case, F) is known as a **format specifier**, which indicates how a value is to be formatted. The format specifier F indicates that a fixed-point number should (by default) be displayed with two decimal places. This can be changed by placing a numeric value after the format specifier. For example, the string "{0:F3}" would display a fixed-point value with three decimal places. Some of the more common format specifiers are summarized in Fig. 5.15. The format specifiers are case insensitive. Also, the format specifiers D and X can be used only with integer values.

Good Programming Practice 5.8

When formatting with two positions to the right of the decimal point, some programmers prefer to use the format specifier F2 for clarity.

The three grades entered during the sample execution of module GradeBookTest (Fig. 5.16) total 257, which yields the average 85.666666…. The format specifier causes the output to be rounded to the specified number of digits. In this program, the average is rounded to the hundredths position and is displayed as 85.67.

Format Code	Description
C	Currency. Precedes the number with $, separates every three digits with commas and sets the number of decimal places to two.
E	Scientific notation. Displays one digit to the left of the decimal and six digits to the right of the decimal, followed by the character E and a three-digit integer representing the exponent of a power of 10. For example, 956.2 is formatted as 9.562000E+002.
F	Fixed point. Sets the number of decimal places to two.
G	General. Visual Basic chooses either E or F for you, depending on which representation generates a shorter string.
D	Decimal integer. Displays an integer as a whole number in standard base-10 format.
N	Number. Separates every three digits with a comma and sets the number of decimal places to two.
X	Hexadecimal integer. Displays the integer in hexadecimal (base-16) notation. We discuss hexadecimal notation in Appendix B.

Fig. 5.15 | Formatting codes for Strings.

```
1    ' Fig. 5.16: GradeBookTest.vb
2    ' Create GradeBook object and invoke its DetermineClassAverage method.
3    Module GradeBookTest
4       Sub Main()
5          ' create GradeBook object gradeBook and
6          ' pass course name to constructor
7          Dim gradeBook As New GradeBook("CS101 Introduction to VB")
```

Fig. 5.16 | GradeBookTest module creates an object of class GradeBook (Fig. 5.14) and invokes its DetermineClassAverage method. (Part I of 2.)

```
 8
 9          gradeBook.DisplayMessage() ' display welcome message
10          gradeBook.DetermineClassAverage() ' find average of grades
11      End Sub ' Main
12   End Module ' GradeBookTest
```

```
Welcome to the grade book for
CS101 Introduction to VB!

Enter grade or -1 to quit: 97
Enter grade or -1 to quit: 88
Enter grade or -1 to quit: 72
Enter grade or -1 to quit: -1

Total of the 3 grades entered is 257
Class average is 85.67
```

Fig. 5.16 | GradeBookTest module creates an object of class GradeBook (Fig. 5.14) and invokes its DetermineClassAverage method. (Part 2 of 2.)

5.13 Formulating Algorithms: Nested Control Statements

For the next example, we once again formulate an algorithm by using pseudocode and top-down, stepwise refinement, and write a corresponding Visual Basic program. We have seen that control statements can be stacked on top of one another (in sequence) just as a child stacks building blocks. In this case study, we examine the only other structured way control statements can be combined, namely, through the nesting of one control statement within another.

Consider the following problem statement:

A college offers a course that prepares students for the state licensing exam for real estate brokers. Last year, 10 of the students who completed this course took the licensing exam. The college wants to know how well its students did on the exam. You have been asked to write a program to summarize the results. You have been given a list of the 10 students. Next to each name is written a "P" if the student passed the exam and an "F" if the student failed the exam.

Your program should analyze the results of the exam as follows:

1. *Input each exam result (i.e., a "P" or an "F"). Display the message "Enter result" on the screen each time the program requests another exam result.*

2. *Count the number of passes and failures.*

3. *Display a summary of the exam results, indicating the number of students who passed and the number who failed.*

4. *If more than eight students passed the exam, print the message "Raise tuition."*

After reading the problem statement carefully, we make the following observations:

1. The program must process exam results for 10 students. A counter-controlled loop can be used because the number of test results is known in advance.

2. Each exam result is a string—either a "P" or an "F." Each time the program reads an exam result, the program must determine whether the input is a "P" or an "F." We test for a "P" in our algorithm. If the input is not a "P," we assume it is an "F." An exercise at the end of the chapter considers the consequences of this assumption. For instance, consider what happens in this program when the user enters a lowercase "p."

3. Two counters store the exam results—one counts the number of students who passed the exam and the other counts the number of students who failed the exam.

4. After the program has processed all the exam results, it must determine whether more than eight students passed the exam.

Let us proceed with top-down, stepwise refinement. We begin with a pseudocode representation of the top:

Analyze exam results and decide if tuition should be raised

Once again, the top is a *complete* representation of the program, but several refinements are likely to be needed before the pseudocode can evolve naturally into a Visual Basic program.

Our first refinement is

Initialize variables
Input the ten exam grades, and count passes and failures
Print a summary of the exam results and decide if tuition should be raised

Here, too, even though we have a complete representation of the entire program, further refinement is necessary. We must commit to specific variables. Counters are needed to record the passes and failures. A counter controls the looping process and a variable stores the user input. The pseudocode statement

Initialize variables

can be refined as follows:

Initialize passes to zero
Initialize failures to zero
Initialize student to one

Only the counters for the number of passes, number of failures and number of students need to be initialized.

The pseudocode statement

Input the 10 exam results, and count passes and failures

requires a loop that successively inputs the result of each exam. We know in advance that there are precisely 10 exam results, so counter-controlled looping is appropriate. Inside the loop (i.e., *nested* within the loop), a double-selection statement will determine whether each exam result is a pass or a failure and will increment the appropriate counter. The refinement of the preceding pseudocode statement is then

> *While student is less than or equal to 10*
> > *Prompt the user to enter the next exam result*
> > *Input the next exam result*
>
> > *If the student passed then*
> > > *Add one to passes*
> > *Else*
> > > *Add one to failures*
>
> > *Add one to student*

Note the use of blank lines to set off the *If…Else* control statement to improve readability. The pseudocode statement

> *Print a summary of the exam results and decide if tuition should be raised*

may be refined as follows:

> *Print the number of passes*
> *Print the number of failures*
>
> *If more than eight students passed then*
> > *Print "Raise tuition"*

Complete Second Refinement of Pseudocode and Conversion to Class `Analysis`

The complete second refinement of the pseudocode appears in Fig. 5.17. Note that blank lines are also used to set off the *While* statement for readability. This pseudocode is now suf-

```
 1   Initialize passes to zero
 2   Initialize failures to zero
 3   Initialize student to one
 4
 5   While student is less than or equal to 10
 6       Prompt the user to enter the next exam result
 7       Input the next exam result
 8
 9       If the student passed then
10           Add one to passes
11       Else
12           Add one to failures
13
14       Add one to student
15
16   Print the number of passes
17   Print the number of failures
18
19   If more than eight students passed then
20       Print "Raise tuition"
```

Fig. 5.17 | Pseudocode for examination-results problem.

ficiently refined for conversion to Visual Basic. The class that implements the pseudocode algorithm is shown in Fig. 5.18, and two sample executions appear in Fig. 5.19.

Lines 7–10 of Fig. 5.18 declare the variables that method ProcessExamResults of class Analysis uses to process the examination results. Several of these declarations use Visual Basic's ability to incorporate variable initialization into declarations (passes is initialized to 0, failures is initialized to 0 and student is initialized to 1). Looping programs may require initialization at the beginning of each repetition—such reinitialization would normally be performed by assignment statements rather than in declarations.

The While statement (lines 13–25) loops 10 times. During each iteration, the loop inputs and processes one exam result. Note that the If...Then...Else statement (lines 18–22) for processing each result is nested in the While statement. If the result is "P", the If...Then...Else statement increments passes; otherwise, it assumes the result is "F" and increments failures. [*Note:* Strings *are* case sensitive—uppercase and lowercase

```
 1    ' Fig. 5.18: Analysis.vb
 2    ' Analysis of examination results.
 3    Public Class Analysis
 4       ' input and analyze exam results
 5       Public Sub ProcessExamResults()
 6          ' initializing variables in declarations
 7          Dim passes As Integer = 0 ' number of passes
 8          Dim failures As Integer = 0 ' number of failures
 9          Dim student As Integer = 1 ' student counter
10          Dim result As String ' one exam result (obtains value from user)
11
12          ' process 10 students using counter-controlled loop
13          While student <= 10
14             Console.Write("Enter result (P = pass, F = fail): ")
15             result = Console.ReadLine()
16
17             ' nested control statement
18             If result = "P" Then
19                passes += 1 ' increment number of passes
20             Else
21                failures += 1 ' increment number of failures
22             End If
23
24             student += 1 ' increment student counter
25          End While
26
27          ' display exam results
28          Console.WriteLine( _
29             "Passed: " & passes & vbCrLf & "Failed: " & failures)
30
31          ' raise tuition if more than 8 students passed
32          If passes > 8 Then
33             Console.WriteLine("Raise tuition")
34          End If
35       End Sub ' ProcessExamResults
36    End Class ' Analysis
```

Fig. 5.18 | Nested control statements: Examination-results problem.

letters are different. Only "P" represents a passing grade. In the exercises, we ask you to enhance the program by processing lowercase inputs such as "p" and "f".] Line 24 increments student before the loop condition is tested again at line 13. After 10 values have been input, the loop terminates and lines 28–29 display the number of passes and the number of failures. The If...Then statement at lines 32–34 determines whether more than eight students passed the exam and, if so, outputs the message "Raise Tuition".

AnalysisTest Module That Demonstrates Class Analysis

Module AnalysisTest (Fig. 5.19) creates an Analysis object (line 5) and invokes the object's ProcessExamResults method (line 6) to process a set of exam results entered by the user. Figure 5.19 shows the input and output from two sample executions of the program. During the first sample execution, the condition at line 32 of method ProcessExamResults in Fig. 5.18 is true—more than eight students passed the exam, so the program outputs a message indicating that the tuition should be raised.

```vb
1   ' Fig. 5.19: AnalysisTest.vb
2   ' Test program for class Analysis.
3   Module AnalysisTest
4      Sub Main()
5         Dim application As New Analysis() ' create Analysis object
6         application.ProcessExamResults() ' call method to process results
7      End Sub ' Main
8   End Module ' AnalysisTest
```

```
Enter result (P = pass, F = fail): P
Enter result (P = pass, F = fail): F
Enter result (P = pass, F = fail): P
Enter result (P = pass, F = fail): P
Enter result (P = pass, F = fail): P
Enter result (P = pass, F = fail): P
Enter result (P = pass, F = fail): P
Enter result (P = pass, F = fail): P
Enter result (P = pass, F = fail): P
Enter result (P = pass, F = fail): P
Passed: 9
Failed: 1
Raise tuition
```

```
Enter result (P = pass, F = fail): P
Enter result (P = pass, F = fail): P
Enter result (P = pass, F = fail): P
Enter result (P = pass, F = fail): F
Enter result (P = pass, F = fail): F
Enter result (P = pass, F = fail): P
Enter result (P = pass, F = fail): P
Enter result (P = pass, F = fail): P
Enter result (P = pass, F = fail): P
Enter result (P = pass, F = fail): P
Passed: 8
Failed: 2
```

Fig. 5.19 | Test program for class Analysis (Fig. 5.18).

5.14 Formulating Algorithms: Nested Repetition Statements

Let us present another complete example. Once again, we formulate the algorithm using pseudocode and top-down, stepwise refinement, then write the corresponding program. We use nested repetition statements to solve the problem.

Consider the following problem statement:

> *Write a program that draws in the command prompt a filled square consisting solely of one type of character, such as the asterisk (*). The side of the square and the character to be used to fill the square should be entered by the user. The length of the side should not exceed 20 characters. If the user enters a value over 20, the message "Side is too large" should be printed.*

Your program should draw the square as follows:

1. Input the side of the square.

2. Validate that the side is less than or equal to 20. [*Note:* It is possible for the user to enter a value less than 1. We explore in the chapter exercises how this can be detected.]

3. Use repetition to draw the square by printing only one fill character at a time.

After reading the problem statement, we make the following observations:

1. The program must draw *side* rows, each containing *side* fill characters, where *side* is the value entered by the user. Counter-controlled repetition should be used.

2. A test must be employed to ensure that the value of *side* is less than or equal to 20. If it is not, the message "Side is too large" should be printed.

3. Four variables should be used—one that represents the length of the side of the square, one that represents (as a String) the fill character to be used, one that represents the row in which the next symbol should appear and one that represents the column in which the next symbol should appear.

Evolving the Pseudocode

Let us proceed with top-down, stepwise refinement. We begin with a pseudocode representation of the top:

> *Draw a square of fill characters*

Once again, it is important to emphasize that the top is a complete representation of the program, but several refinements are likely to be needed before the pseudocode can be easily evolved into a program.

Our first refinement is

> *Prompt for the fill character*
> *Input the fill character*
>
> *Prompt for the side of the square*
> *Input the side of the square*
>
> *Draw the square if its side is less than or equal to 20; otherwise print an error message*

Here, too, even though we have a complete representation of the entire program, further refinement is necessary.

The pseudocode statement

> *Draw the square if its side is less than or equal to 20; otherwise print an error message*

can be refined as

> *If the side of the square is less than or equal to 20 then*
> > *Draw the square*
>
> *Else*
> > *Print "Side is too large"*

which explicitly tests whether *side is less than or equal to 20*. If the condition (i.e., "*side is less than or equal to 20*") is true, the square is drawn. If the condition is false, a message is displayed to the user.

Drawing the Square
The pseudocode statement

> *Draw the square*

can be implemented by using one loop nested inside another. In this example, it is known in advance that there are *side* rows of *side* fill characters each, so counter-controlled repetition is appropriate. One loop controls the row in which each fill character is to be printed. A nested loop prints each fill character (one at a time) for that row. The refinement of the preceding pseudocode statement is

> *Set row to one*
>
> *While row is less than or equal to side*
> > *Set column to one*
> >
> > *While column is less than or equal to side*
> > > *Print the fill character*
> > > *Increment column by one*
> >
> > *Print a line feed/carriage return*
> > *Increment row by one*

The value of *row* is set to one to prepare to display the square's first row. The outer *While* statement loops while *row* is less than or equal to *side*—that is, for each row of the square. Within this *While* statement, *column* is set to one, as we prepare to display the first fill character of the current row. After *column* is set to one, the inner loop executes to completion (i.e., until *column* exceeds *side*). Each iteration of the inner loop prints one fill character (which in line 46 of the class of Fig. 5.21 we follow by a space, to make the output look more like a square). After each row of symbols, a line feed/carriage return is printed to move the cursor to the beginning of the next line, to prepare to print the next row of the square. Variable *row* is incremented by 1. If the outer loop condition allows the body of the loop to be executed again (because *row* is less than or equal to *side*), *column* is reset to 1, and the inner loop executes again, printing another row of fill characters. Variable *row* is incremented by 1. This process is repeated until the value of *row* exceeds *side*, at which point the square of fill characters has been printed.

The complete second refinement appears in Fig. 5.20. Note that blank lines are used to separate the nested control statements for readability.

The pseudocode now is refined sufficiently for conversion to Visual Basic. The Visual Basic class and test program are shown in Fig. 5.21 and Fig. 5.22, respectively.

> **Software Engineering Observation 5.7**
>
> *Many experienced programmers write programs without ever using program-development tools like pseudocode. They feel that their ultimate goal is to solve the problem on a computer and that writing pseudocode merely delays producing final outputs. Although this might work for simple and familiar problems, it can lead to serious errors and delays in large, complex projects.*

```
 1    Prompt for the fill character
 2    Input the fill character
 3
 4    Prompt for the side of the square
 5    Input the side of the square
 6
 7    If the side of the square is less than or equal to 20 then
 8        Set row to one
 9
10        While row is less than or equal to side
11            Set column to one
12
13            While column is less than or equal to side
14                Print the fill character
15                Increment column by one
16
17            Print a line feed/carriage return
18            Increment row by one
19    Else
20        Print "Side is too large"
```

Fig. 5.20 | Second refinement of the pseudocode.

```
 1    ' Fig. 5.21: Box.vb
 2    ' Class can be used to draw a square of a specified length, using
 3    ' a specified fill character.
 4    Public Class Box
 5        Private sideValue As Integer ' length of side of square
 6        Private fillCharacterValue As String ' character used to draw square
 7
 8        ' property provides access to side length of box
 9        Public Property Side() As Integer
10            Get
11                Return sideValue ' return side length
12            End Get
13
```

Fig. 5.21 | Nested repetition statements used to print a square of symbols. (Part 1 of 2.)

```vb
14          Set(ByVal value As Integer)
15              sideValue = value ' modify side length
16          End Set
17      End Property ' Side
18
19      ' property provides access to fill character for drawing box
20      Public Property FillCharacter() As String
21          Get
22              Return fillCharacterValue ' return fill character
23          End Get
24
25          Set(ByVal value As String)
26              fillCharacterValue = value ' modify fill character
27          End Set
28      End Property ' FillCharacter
29
30      ' display box
31      Public Sub Display()
32          Dim row As Integer ' current row
33          Dim column As Integer ' current column
34
35          If Side <= 20 Then ' if true, then print the box
36              row = 1
37
38              ' this While is nested inside the If in lines 35-55
39              While row <= Side ' controls row being printed
40                  column = 1 ' prepare to print first character in the row
41
42                  ' this loop prints one row of the square
43                  ' and is nested inside the While in lines 39-52
44                  While column <= Side
45                      ' print fill character and a space
46                      Console.Write(FillCharacter & " ")
47                      column += 1 ' increment column
48                  End While
49
50                  Console.WriteLine() ' position cursor to next line
51                  row += 1 ' increment row
52              End While
53          Else ' condition (Side <= 20) is false
54              Console.WriteLine("Side too large")
55          End If
56      End Sub ' Display
57  End Class ' Box
```

Fig. 5.21 | Nested repetition statements used to print a square of symbols. (Part 2 of 2.)

```vb
1   ' Fig. 5.22: BoxTest.vb
2   ' Program draws square by creating an object of class Box.
3   Module BoxTest
4       ' Main begins program execution
```

Fig. 5.22 | Using class Box to draw a square. (Part 1 of 2.)

```
5      Sub Main()
6         Dim box As New Box()
7
8         ' obtain fill character and side length from user
9         Console.Write("Enter fill character: ")
10        box.FillCharacter = Console.ReadLine()
11        Console.Write("Enter side length (must be 20 or less): ")
12        box.Side = Console.ReadLine()
13
14        box.Display() ' display box
15     End Sub ' Main
16  End Module ' BoxTest
```

```
Enter fill character: #
Enter side length (must be 20 or less): 8
# # # # # # # #
# # # # # # # #
# # # # # # # #
# # # # # # # #
# # # # # # # #
# # # # # # # #
# # # # # # # #
# # # # # # # #
```

```
Enter fill character: *
Enter side length (must be 20 or less): 5
* * * * *
* * * * *
* * * * *
* * * * *
* * * * *
```

```
Enter fill character: $
Enter side length (must be 20 or less): 37
Side too large
```

Fig. 5.22 | Using class **Box** to draw a square. (Part 2 of 2.)

5.15 Visual Basic Programming in a Windows Application

In Chapter 2, we showed how to create a simple GUI application using visual programming—that is, defining the appearance of an application by dragging and dropping GUI controls onto a Form and setting properties in design mode without writing any program code. The application you created in Chapter 2 (Fig. 2.27) displayed text and an image, but did not perform any other actions. In Chapters 3, 4 and 5 we have focused on console applications, which do not provide a GUI but perform various actions, such as finding the average of several grades and displaying the results as text in the command prompt. Most Visual Basic programmers use a combination of visual programming and conventional programming techniques. In this section, you will see that when you build a GUI, Visual Basic code (which makes use of predefined FCL classes) is generated by the IDE to define that GUI. You will modify a GUI control's property programmatically, causing the text displayed on the Form to change at runtime. You will also learn how to add code to a GUI application to perform an action when the Form is loaded.

Before proceeding, load the project ASimpleProgram from your Chapter 4 examples folder into the IDE. This is the same program as the one you created in Chapter 2. Change the name of the file from Form1.vb to FrmASimpleProgram.vb to enhance clarity. Then double click this file in the **Solution Explorer** to open the file in design mode. Select the Form by clicking it. Notice in the **Properties** window that Visual Basic changed the Form's name to FrmASimpleProgram when you changed the name of the file from Form1.vb to FrmASimpleProgram.vb.

Next, let's change the name of the Form's controls for clarity. To do this, simply select the control, and modify the Name property (listed in the **Properties** window as **(Name)**), entering the new identifier you want to represent the control. Use this technique to change the name of the Label to lblWelcome and the name of the PictureBox to picBug. This enables us to easily identify the Form's controls in the program code.

Good Programming Practice 5.9

The prefixes Frm, lbl and pic allow Forms, Labels and PictureBoxes, respectively, to be identified easily in program code.

Viewing Windows-Generated Code

Let us view the code that defines our Windows application. When you use visual programming to create a program's GUI, the IDE generates the Visual Basic code that defines how the GUI appears. The code that defines the GUI application is stored in two files—one to define the initial appearance of the GUI (e.g., the background color of the Form or the size of a Label), and one to define the behavior of the GUI (i.e., what happens when a Button is clicked or text is entered in a TextBox). Unlike a console application's code, a Windows application's program code is not displayed initially in the editor window. Once you open the file FrmASimpleProgram.vb in design mode, you can view the code by selecting **View > Code**. Figure 5.23 shows the code editor displaying the program code. This is the file that defines your GUI's behavior.

Note that FrmASimpleProgram.vb does not contain a Module. Instead Windows applications use classes. You have used FCL classes, such as Console and MessageBox, and you have created your own classes in Chapters 4 and 5.

The class declared in Fig. 5.23 is called FrmASimpleProgram and is currently empty, as we have not yet defined the application's behavior. Recall that the application's initial GUI appearance is defined in another file. To view that file, go into the **Solution Explorer**

Fig. 5.23 | IDE showing program code for ASimpleProgram.vb.

and click the **Show All Files** button. Then click the plus sign to the left of **FrmASimpleProgram.vb**, and double click **FrmASimpleProgram.Designer.vb**. The file is shown in Fig. 5.24.

This code appears complex (and especially so for this early in the book), but it is created for you by the IDE, and normally you will not edit it. It is important for novice programmers to be aware of the code that the IDE generates, even though much of the code is not explained until Chapters 9–14. This type of code is present in every Windows application. If the IDE did not provide the code, you would have to write it, which would require a considerable amount of time and would be an error-prone process.

Inheriting Predefined Functionality

Keyword `Inherits` (line 3 of Fig. 5.24) indicates that the class `FrmASimpleProgram` inherits existing pieces from another class. The class from which `FrmASimpleProgram` inherits—`System.Windows.Forms.Form`—appears to the right of the `Inherits` keyword. This is the class `Form` preceded by its namespace and a dot separator. The namespace and class name together form the class's **fully-qualified name**. In this inheritance relationship, `Form` is called the **base class**, and `FrmASimpleProgram` is called the **derived class**. This inheritance results in a `FrmASimpleProgram` class definition that has the attributes (data) and behaviors (methods) of class `Form`.

Every Windows application consists of at least one class that inherits from class **Form**. A key benefit of inheriting from class `Form` is that someone else has previously defined everything about "what it means to be a `Form`." The Windows operating system expects every window, including `Form`, to have certain capabilities (attributes and behaviors). However, because class `Form` already provides these capabilities, you do not need to "reinvent the wheel" by defining all those capabilities yourself. In fact, class `Form` has over 200

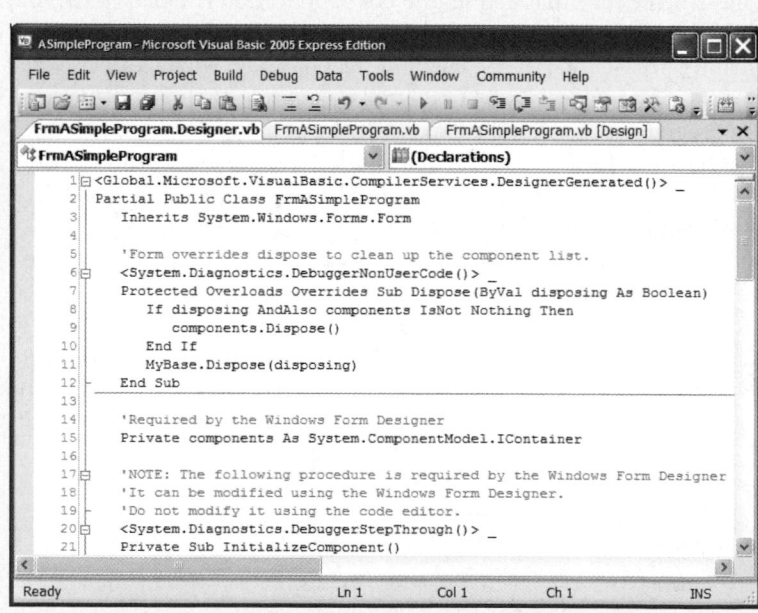

Fig. 5.24 | Windows Form Designer generated code.

methods! The use of `Inherits` to absorb the capabilities of class `Form` enables you to create `Form`s quickly and easily.

When you created this application in Chapter 2, you used the **Properties** window to set properties for the `Form`, `Label` and `PictureBox`. Once a property was set, the `Form` or control was updated immediately. `Form`s and controls contain a set of default values for their properties, which are displayed initially in the **Properties** window when a `Form` or control is selected. These default values provide the initial characteristics of a `Form` or control. When a control (such as a `Label`) is first placed on the `Form`, the IDE adds code to the class's designer file (e.g., `FrmASimpleProgram.Designer.vb`) that creates the control and sets some of the control's property values, such as the name of the control and its location on the `Form`. Figure 5.25 shows the portion of `ASimpleProgram.Designer.vb` that sets the `lblWelcome`'s `Font`, `Location`, `Name`, `Size`, `TabIndex`, `Text` and `TextAlign` properties. These lines specify property values that are set when the `Label` is first placed on the `Form`, or edited by you in the **Properties** window (your line numbers may differ if you have made your own changes to the original application). The control contains many more properties—those not set in the code contain their default values. Recall from Chapter 2 that you explicitly set values for the `Label`'s `Text` and `TextAlign` properties. The values set in the **Properties** window are reflected in this code. Note that the code sets properties of control `lblWelcome`. Had we not updated the name of this control, every instance of the identifier `lblWelcome` would be replaced with its default name, in this case `Label1`.

Modifying Properties in Design View
The values assigned to the properties are based on the values in the **Properties** window. We now demonstrate how the IDE updates the generated code when a control's property is modified. While performing the steps in this section, you must switch between code view and design view. To switch views, select the corresponding tabs—**FrmASimpleProgram.vb** or **FrmASimpleProgram.Designer.vb** for code view (we will specify which file as necessary)

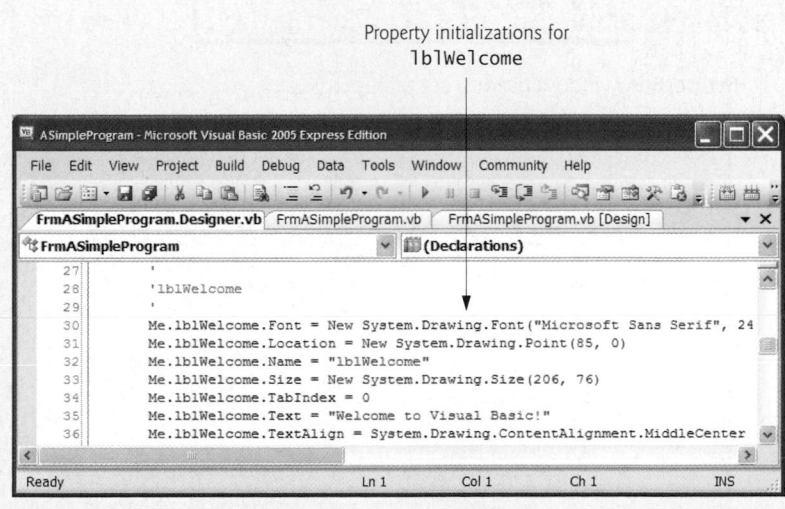

Fig. 5.25 | Property initializations generated by the Windows Form Designer for `lblWelcome`.

and **FrmASimpleProgram.vb [Design]** for design view. Alternatively, you can select **View > Code** (for **FrmASimpleProgram.vb**) or **View > Designer** (for **FrmASimpleProgram.vb [Design]**). Now you will modify the application's code:

1. *Modifying the* Label *control's* Text *property using the* **Properties** *window.* If you have not already done so, switch to design view. Recall that properties can be changed in design view by clicking a Form or control to select the desired property, then modifying it in the **Properties** window. Select the Label (lblWelcome) control and change its Text property to "Deitel and Associates" (Fig. 5.26).

2. *Examining the change in code view.* Switch to code view (ASimpleProgram.Design.vb) and examine the code (Fig. 5.27). Note that the Label's Text property is now assigned the text that you entered in the **Properties** window (line 35). When a property is changed in design mode, the Windows Form Designer updates the appropriate line of code for you in the class to reflect the new value. Once again, note that your code lines may be different.

Modifying Properties Programmatically

Now that you have seen how properties are updated in code in response to changes in the **Properties** window, we show how you can write code to modify a property. You'll also see how to specify code that executes when a GUI application loads.

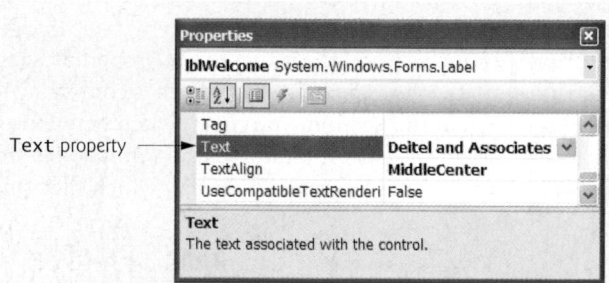

Fig. 5.26 | **Properties** window used to set a property value.

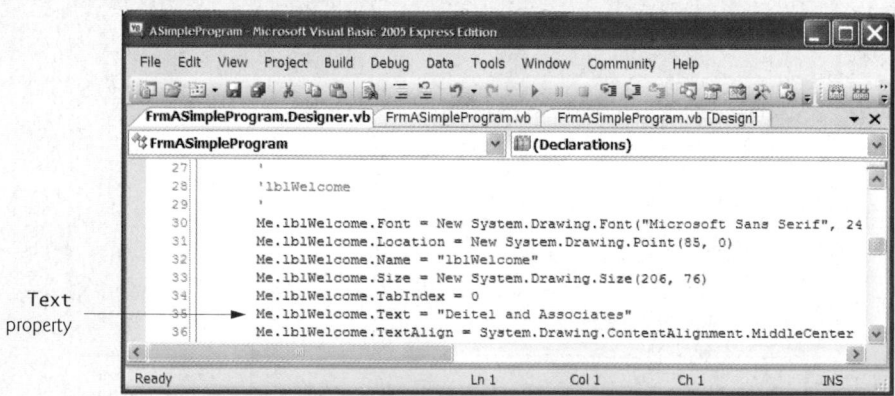

Fig. 5.27 | Windows Form Designer–generated code reflecting new property value.

1. *Adding an event handler to your application.* In the preceding steps, we set properties at design time. Often, however, it is necessary to modify a property while a program is running. For example, to display the result of a calculation, a `Label`'s text can be assigned a `String` containing the result. In the applications we have created so far, such code is located in `Main`. In Windows applications, you can create a method that executes when the `Form` loads into memory during program execution. Like `Main`, this method is invoked when the program is run. Double clicking the `Form` in design view adds a method named `FrmASimpleProgram_Load` to the class (Fig. 5.28). Be sure to double click the background of the `Form`, that is, the portion of the `Form` that is not covered with another control. Note that `FrmASimpleProgram_Load` is not part of the Windows Form Designer–generated code found in `ASimpleProgram.Designer.vb`; rather it is added by the IDE to the `FrmASimpleProgram.vb` file. This is because this method will be used to define the behavior of the application. Method `FrmASimpleProgram_Load` is a type of method known as an event handler. **Event handlers** respond to state changes in the GUI. Such state changes are known as **events**. Most events represent user actions, such as clicking a `Button` or entering text in a `TextBox`. In the event handler created here, the event is the loading of the `Form` when the application begins. When this event is **raised** (i.e., the event occurs), `FrmASimpleProgram_Load` is executed, performing any statements in its body (we will add a statement to this method shortly). Most of a GUI application's functionality is executed based on events. You will see many examples of events and event handling throughout this book.

2. *Changing the `Label`'s `Text` property at runtime.* Add the statement `lblWelcome.Text = "Visual Basic!"` to the body of the method declaration (Fig. 5.29). Note that we use the dot separator to access a property of `lblWelcome`. This is because GUI controls are actually objects, just like the objects you created and used in Chapter 4 and 5.

3. *Examining the results of the `FrmASimpleProgram_Load` method.* Switch back to design view. Note that the text in the `Label` is still "`Deitel and Associates`" and that the **Properties** window still displays the value "`Deitel and Associates`" as the `Label`'s `Text` property value. The code generated by the IDE has not changed either. Instead, the property value is changed in the `FrmASimpleProgram_Load`

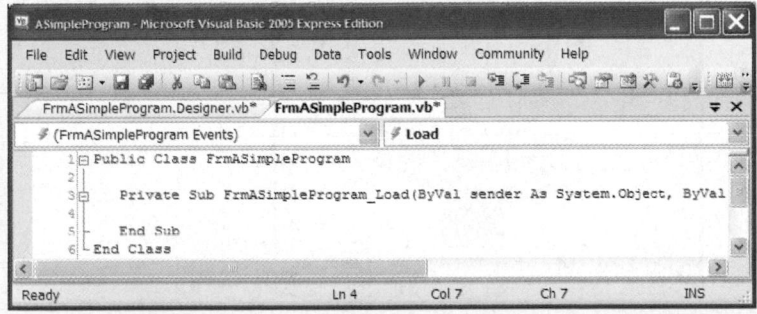

Fig. 5.28 | Method `FrmASimpleProgram_Load` created when `Form` is double clicked.

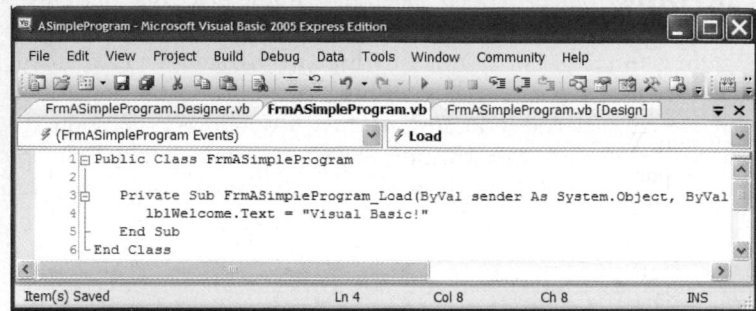

Fig. 5.29 | Method `FrmASimpleProgram_Load` containing program code.

method, causing the property value to be updated at runtime. Select **Build > Build ASimpleProgram** then **Debug > Start** to run the program. Once the Form is displayed, the text in the `Label` reflects the property assignment in `FrmASimpleProgram_Load` (Fig. 5.30).

4. *Terminating program execution.* Click the close button to terminate program execution. Once again, notice that both the `Label` and the `Label`'s `Text` property contain the text "`Deitel and Associates`". Remember that the event handler `FrmASimpleProgram_Load` changes the text to **Visual Basic!** only when the application runs.

This example combined conventional programming and visual programming. We provided a brief overview of the code that the IDE generates for a Windows application, and showed how to add code that performs actions when the application's Form loads. The topics covered in this section provide a basis for the more complex GUI applications that you'll create throughout this book. Our next GUI program appears in Chapter 7, which finds the maximum of three input values. The user enters input into `TextBoxes` then clicks a `Button` to indicate that the application should determine and display the maximum value.

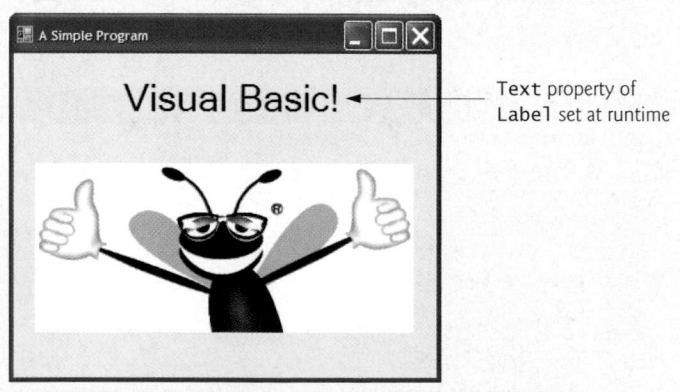

Fig. 5.30 | Changing a property value at runtime.

5.16 (Optional) Software Engineering Case Study: Identifying Class Attributes in the ATM System

In Section 4.9, we began the first stage of an object-oriented design (OOD) for our ATM system—analyzing the requirements document and identifying the classes needed to implement the system. We listed the nouns and noun phrases in the requirements document and identified a separate class for each one that plays a significant role in the ATM system. We then modeled the classes and their relationships in a UML class diagram (Fig. 4.22). Classes have attributes (data) and operations (behaviors). Class attributes are implemented in Visual Basic programs as properties and instance variables (and Shared variables, as we will see in Section 9.10), and class operations are implemented as methods and properties. In this section, we determine many of the attributes needed in the ATM system. In Section 6.11, we examine how these attributes represent an object's state. In Section 7.20, we determine the operations for our classes.

Identifying Attributes

Consider the attributes of some real-world objects: A person's attributes include height, weight and whether the person is left-handed, right-handed or ambidextrous. A radio's attributes include its station setting, its volume setting and its AM or FM setting. A car's attributes include its speedometer and odometer readings, the amount of gas in its tank and what gear it is in. A personal computer's attributes include its manufacturer (e.g., Dell, Gateway, Sun, Apple or HP), type of screen (e.g., LCD or CRT), main memory size and hard disk size.

We can identify many attributes of the classes in our system by looking for descriptive words and phrases in the requirements document. For each one we find that plays a significant role in the ATM system, we create an attribute and assign it to one or more of the classes identified in Section 4.9. We also create attributes to represent any additional data that a class may need as such needs become clear throughout the design process.

Figure 5.31 lists the words or phrases from the requirements document that describe each class. For example, the requirements document describes the steps taken to obtain a "withdrawal amount," so we list "amount" next to class Withdrawal.

Class	Descriptive words and phrases
ATM	user is authenticated
BalanceInquiry	account number
Withdrawal	account number amount
Deposit	account number amount
BankDatabase	[no descriptive words or phrases]

Fig. 5.31 | Descriptive words and phrases from the ATM requirements document. (Part 1 of 2.)

Class	Descriptive words and phrases
Account	account number PIN balance
Screen	[no descriptive words or phrases]
Keypad	[no descriptive words or phrases]
CashDispenser	begins each day loaded with 500 $20 bills
DepositSlot	[no descriptive words or phrases]

Fig. 5.31 | Descriptive words and phrases from the ATM requirements document. (Part 2 of 2.)

Figure 5.31 leads us to create one attribute of class ATM. Class ATM maintains information about the state of the ATM. The phrase "user is authenticated" describes a state of the ATM (we discuss states in detail in Section 6.11), so we include userAuthenticated as a Boolean attribute (i.e., an attribute that has a value of either True or False). This attribute indicates whether the ATM has successfully authenticated the current user—userAuthenticated must be True for the system to allow the user to perform transactions and access account information. This attribute helps ensure the security of the data in the system.

Classes BalanceInquiry, Withdrawal and Deposit share one attribute. Each transaction involves an "account number" that corresponds to the account of the user making the transaction. We assign an integer attribute accountNumber to each transaction class to identify the account to which an object of the class applies.

Descriptive words and phrases in the requirements document also suggest some differences in the attributes required by each transaction class. The requirements document indicates that to withdraw cash or deposit funds, users must enter a specific "amount" of money to be withdrawn or deposited, respectively. Thus, we assign to classes Withdrawal and Deposit an attribute amount to store the value supplied by the user. The amounts of money related to a withdrawal and a deposit are defining characteristics of these transactions that the system requires for them to take place. In Visual Basic, monetary amounts are represented with type Decimal (which you will learn more about in Chapter 6). Note that class BalanceInquiry does not need additional data to perform its task—it requires only an account number to indicate the account whose balance should be retrieved.

Class Account has several attributes. The requirements document states that each bank account has an "account number" and a "PIN," which the system uses for identifying accounts and authenticating users. We assign to class Account two Integer attributes: accountNumber and pin. The requirements document also specifies that an account maintains a "balance" of the amount of money in the account, and that the money the user deposits does not become available for a withdrawal until the bank verifies the amount of cash in the deposit envelope and any checks in the envelope clear. An account must still record the amount of money that a user deposits, however. Therefore, we decide that an account should represent a balance using two attributes of type Decimal—availableBalance and `totalBalance`. Attribute `availableBalance` tracks the amount of money that a user can withdraw from the account. Attribute `totalBalance` refers to the total amount of money that the user has "on deposit" (i.e., the amount of money available, plus the amount of cash deposits waiting to be verified or checks waiting to clear). For example, suppose an ATM user deposits $50.00 in cash into an empty account. The `totalBalance` attribute would increase to $50.00 to record the deposit, but the `availableBalance` would remain at $0 until a bank employee counts the amount of cash in the envelope and confirms that it is correct. [*Note:* We assume that the bank updates the `availableBalance` attribute of the `Account` soon after the ATM transaction occurs, in response to confirming that $50 in cash was found in the deposit envelope. We assume that this update occurs through a transaction that a bank employee performs using some a bank system other than the ATM. Thus, we do not discuss this "external" transaction in our case study.]

Class `CashDispenser` has one attribute. The requirements document states that the cash dispenser "begins each day loaded with 500 $20 bills." The cash dispenser must keep track of the number of bills it contains to determine whether enough cash is on hand to satisfy withdrawal requests. We assign to class `CashDispenser` an integer attribute `billCount`, which is initially set to 500.

For real problems in industry, there is no guarantee that requirements documents will be rich enough and precise enough for the object-oriented systems designer to determine all the attributes or even all the classes. The need for additional classes, attributes and behaviors may become clear as the design process proceeds. As we progress through this case study, we too will continue to add, modify and delete information about the classes in our system.

Modeling Attributes

The class diagram in Fig. 5.32 lists some of the attributes for the classes in our system— the descriptive words and phrases in Fig. 5.31 helped us identify these attributes. For simplicity, Fig. 5.32 does not show the associations among classes—we showed these in Fig. 4.22. Systems designers commonly do this. Recall that in the UML, a class's attributes are placed in the middle compartment of the class's rectangle. We list each attribute's name and type separated by a colon (:), followed in some cases by an equal sign (=) and an initial value.

Consider the `userAuthenticated` attribute of class `ATM`:

```
userAuthenticated : Boolean = False
```

This attribute declaration contains three pieces of information about the attribute. The **attribute name** is `userAuthenticated`. The **attribute type** is `Boolean`. In Visual Basic, an attribute can be represented by a primitive type, such as `Boolean`, `Integer`, `Double` or `Decimal`, or a class type—as discussed in Chapter 4. We have chosen to model only primitive-type attributes in Fig. 5.32—we discuss the reasoning behind this decision shortly. For simplicity, we use Visual Basic primitive type names in our UML diagrams. These type names sometimes differ from those defined in the UML specification.

We can also indicate an initial value for an attribute. Attribute `userAuthenticated` in class `ATM` has an initial value of `False`. This indicates that the system initially does not consider the user to be authenticated. If an attribute has no initial value specified, only its name and type (separated by a colon) are shown. For example, the `accountNumber` attribute of class `BalanceInquiry` is an `Integer`. Here we show no initial value, because

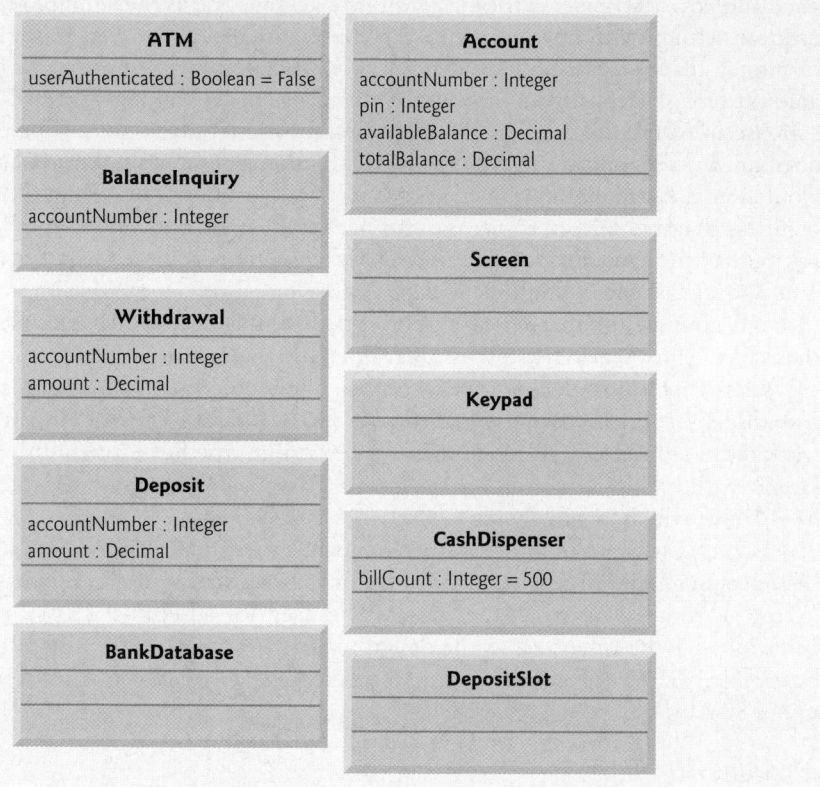

Fig. 5.32 | Classes with attributes.

the value of this attribute is a number that we do not yet know. This number will be determined at execution time based on the account number entered by the current ATM user. Recall that Visual Basic initializes all instance variables to their default values.

Figure 5.32 does not contain attributes for classes Screen, Keypad and DepositSlot. These are important components of our system, for which our design process simply has not yet revealed any attributes.

Software Engineering Observation 5.8

Early in the design process classes often lack attributes (and operations). Such classes should not necessarily be eliminated, however, because attributes (and operations) may become evident in the later phases of design and implementation.

Note that Fig. 5.32 also does not include attributes for class BankDatabase. Recall that in Visual Basic, attributes can be represented by either primitive types or class types. We have chosen to include only primitive-type attributes in Fig. 5.32 (and in similar class diagrams throughout the case study). A class-type attribute is modeled more clearly as an association (in particular, a composition) between the class with the attribute and the attribute's own class. For example, the class diagram in Fig. 4.22 indicates that class Bank-Database participates in a composition relationship with zero or more Account objects. From this composition, we can determine that when we implement the ATM system in

Visual Basic, we will be required to create an attribute of class BankDatabase to hold zero or more Account objects. Similarly, we will assign attributes to class ATM that correspond to its composition relationships with classes Screen, Keypad, CashDispenser and DepositSlot. These composition-based attributes would be redundant if modeled in Fig. 5.32, because the compositions modeled in Fig. 4.22 already convey the fact that the database contains information about zero or more accounts and that an ATM is composed of a screen, keypad, cash dispenser and deposit slot. Software developers typically model these whole/part relationships as composition associations rather than as attributes required to implement the relationships. We show how such composition relationships are implemented in Section 9.7.

The class diagram in Fig. 5.32 provides a solid basis for the structure of our model, but the diagram is not complete. In Section 6.11, we identify the states and activities of the objects in the model, and in Section 7.20 we identify the operations that the objects perform. As we present more of the UML and object-oriented design, we will continue to strengthen the structure of our model.

Software Engineering Case Study Self-Review Exercises

5.1   We typically identify the attributes of the classes in our system by analyzing the _____ in the requirements document.
   a) nouns and noun phrases
   b) descriptive words and phrases
   c) verbs and verb phrases
   d) All of the above.

5.2   Which of the following is not an attribute of an airplane?
   a) length
   b) wingspan
   c) fly
   d) number of seats

5.3   Describe the meaning of the following attribute declaration of class CashDispenser in the class diagram in Fig. 5.32:

```
billCount : Integer = 500
```

Answers to Software Engineering Case Study Self-Review Exercises

5.1   b.

5.2   c. Fly is an operation or behavior of an airplane, not an attribute.

5.3   This declaration indicates that attribute billCount is an Integer with an initial value of 500; billCount keeps track of the number of $20 bills available in the CashDispenser at any given time.

5.17 Wrap-Up

This chapter presented basic problem-solving techniques that programmers use to build programs. We demonstrated how to develop an algorithm (i.e., an approach to solving a problem) in pseudocode, evolving it through several refinements until it is ready to be translated to Visual Basic code that can be executed. This process is called top-down, step-wise refinement.

You learned that only three types of control structures—sequence, selection and repetition—are needed to develop any algorithm. We demonstrated two of Visual Basic's selection statements—the If...Then single-selection statement and the If...Then...Else double-selection statement. The If...Then statement is used to execute a set of one or more statements based on a condition—if the condition is true, the statements execute; if it is false, the statements are skipped. The If...Then...Else double-selection statement is used to execute one set of statements if a condition is true, and another set if the condition is false. We discussed the While and Do While...Loop repetition statements, where a set of statements is executed repeatedly as long as a loop-continuation condition remains true. We discussed the Do Until...Loop repetition statement, where a set of statements is executed repeatedly as long as a loop-termination condition remains false. We used control-statement stacking to compute the average of a set of student grades with counter-controlled repetition and then with sentinel-controlled repetition, and we used control-statement nesting to analyze and make decisions based on a set of exam results, and also to display a square of fill characters. We introduced compound assignment operators, which can be used for abbreviating assignment statements. The chapter concluded with an introduction to adding event handlers to a GUI application. Here, you learned how to modify a GUI application programmatically. In Chapter 6, Control Statements: Part 2, we present additional selection and repetition statements. In the next few chapters, we build Windows applications that interact more with the user.

Summary

Section 5.2 Algorithms

- Computing problems are solved by executing actions in a specific order.

- An algorithm is a procedure for solving a problem in terms of the actions to be executed and the order in which these actions are to be executed.

- Program control refers to the task of ordering a program's statements correctly.

Section 5.3 Pseudocode

- Pseudocode is an informal language that helps programmers develop algorithms and "think out" a program before attempting to write it in a programming language.

- A carefully prepared pseudocode program can be converted easily to a corresponding Visual Basic program.

Section 5.4 Control Structures

- Normally, statements in a program are executed one after another in the order in which they are written. This is called sequential execution.

- Various Visual Basic statements enable you to specify that the next statement to be executed might not be the next one in sequence. This is called a transfer of control.

- Bohm and Jacopini's work demonstrated that all programs could be written in terms of only three control structures—the sequence structure, the selection structure and the repetition structure.

- The sequence structure is built into Visual Basic. Unless directed otherwise, the computer executes Visual Basic statements one after the other in the order in which they are written.

- A UML activity diagram models the workflow (also called the activity) of a software system.

- Activity diagrams are composed of special-purpose symbols, such as action state symbols, diamonds and small circles. These symbols are connected by transition arrows that represent the flow of activity.
- Like pseudocode, activity diagrams help programmers develop and represent algorithms.
- An action state is represented as a rectangle with its left and right sides replaced by arcs curving outward. An action expression appears inside the action state.
- The arrows in an activity diagram represent transitions that indicate the order in which the actions represented by action states occur.
- The solid circle located at the top of an activity diagram represents the initial state—the beginning of the workflow before the program performs the modeled actions.
- The solid circle surrounded by a hollow circle that appears at the bottom of the activity diagram represents the final state—the end of the workflow after the program performs its actions.
- Rectangles with the upper-right corners folded over are called notes in the UML. Notes are optional explanatory remarks that describe the purpose of symbols in the diagram. A dotted line connects each note with the element that it describes.
- The If...Then single-selection statement selects or ignores a single action (or a single group of actions) based on the truth or falsity of a condition.
- The If...Then...Else double-selection statement selects between two different actions (or groups of actions) based on the truth or falsity of a condition.
- A multiple-selection statement selects among many different actions or groups of actions.
- Visual Basic provides seven types of repetition statements (also called looping statements or loops) that enable programs to perform statements repeatedly based on the value of a condition.
- Programs are formed by combining as many of each type of Visual Basic's 11 control statements as is appropriate for the algorithm the program implements.
- Single-entry/single-exit control statements make it easy to build programs.
- In control-statement stacking, the control statements are attached to one another by connecting the exit point of one control statement to the entry point of the next.
- In control-statement nesting, one control statement is placed inside another.
- Algorithms in Visual Basic programs are constructed from only 11 different types of control statements combined in only two ways (control-statement stacking and control-statement nesting).

Section 5.5 *If...Then Selection Statement*
- Syntax errors are caught by the compiler. Logic errors affect the program only at execution time. Fatal logic errors cause a program to fail and terminate prematurely. Nonfatal logic errors do not terminate a program's execution but cause the program to produce incorrect results.
- The diamond or decision symbol in an activity diagram indicates that a decision is to be made. A decision symbol indicates that the workflow will continue along a path determined by the symbol's associated guard conditions, which can be true or false.
- Each transition arrow emerging from a decision symbol has a guard condition (specified in square brackets above or next to the transition arrow). If a particular guard condition is true, the workflow enters the action state to which that transition arrow points.

Section 5.6 *If...Then...Else Selection Statement*
- The If...Then...Else selection statement allows you to specify that a different action (or sequence of actions) is to be performed when the condition is true than when the condition is false.

- Nested If...Then...Else statements test for multiple conditions by placing If...Then...Else statements inside other If...Then...Else statements.

Section 5.7 `While` Repetition Statement

- The UML's merge symbol joins two flows of activity into one flow of activity. The UML represents both the merge symbol and the decision symbol as diamonds.

- The While repetition statement allows you to specify that an action is to be repeated while a specific condition remains true.

- Eventually, the loop-continuation condition in a While statement becomes false. At this point, the repetition terminates, and the first statement after the repetition statement executes.

- Failure to provide the body of a While statement with an action that eventually causes the loop-continuation condition to become false is a logic error. Normally, such a repetition statement never terminates, resulting in an error called an "infinite loop."

Section 5.8 `Do While...Loop` Repetition Statement

- The Do While...Loop repetition statement allows you to specify that an action is to be repeated while a specific condition remains true.

- Eventually, the loop-continuation condition in a Do While...Loop statement becomes false. At this point, the repetition terminates, and the first statement after the repetition statement executes.

- Failure to provide in the body of a Do While...Loop statement an action that eventually causes the loop-continuation condition to become false is a logic error. Normally, such a repetition statement never terminates, resulting in an infinite loop.

Section 5.9 `Do Until...Loop` Repetition Statement

- Statements in the body of a Do Until...Loop are executed repeatedly as long as the loop-termination condition evaluates to false.

- Failure to provide the body of a Do Until...Loop statement with an action that eventually causes the loop-termination condition in the Do Until...Loop to become true creates an infinite loop.

Section 5.10 Compound Assignment Operators

- Visual Basic provides the compound assignment operators +=, -=, *=, /=, \=, ^= and &= for abbreviating assignment statements.

Section 5.11 Formulating Algorithms: Counter-Controlled Repetition

- In counter-controlled repetition, a counter is used to repeat a set of statements a certain number of times. Counter-controlled repetition is also called definite repetition because the number of repetitions is known before the loop begins executing.

- A total is a variable used to calculate the sum of a series of values.

Section 5.12 Formulating Algorithms: Sentinel-Controlled Repetition

- In sentinel-controlled repetition, the number of repetitions is not known before the loop begins executing. Sentinel-controlled repetition uses a sentinel value (also called a signal value, dummy value or flag value) to terminate repetition.

- We approach programming problems with top-down, stepwise refinement, a technique essential to the development of well-structured algorithms.

- The top is a single statement that conveys the overall function of the program. As such, the top is a complete representation of a program.

- Through the process of refinement, we divide the top into a series of smaller tasks that are listed in the order in which they must be performed. Each refinement, including the top, is a complete specification of the algorithm; only the level of detail in each refinement varies.

- Many algorithms can be divided logically into three phases: An initialization phase that initializes the program variables, a processing phase that inputs data values and adjusts program variables such as counts and totals accordingly, and a termination phase that calculates and prints the results.

- You terminate the top-down, stepwise refinement process when the pseudocode algorithm is specified in sufficient detail for the pseudocode to be converted to a Visual Basic program. The implementation of the Visual Basic program is then straightforward.

- Data type `Double` stores double-precision floating-point numbers. Visual Basic also provides data type `Single` for storing single-precision floating-point numbers. Data type `Double` requires more memory to store a floating-point value, but is more accurate than type `Single`. Most programmers use `Double` to represent floating-point numbers.

- A format specifier can be used to indicate how a value is to be formatted for output.

Section 5.13 Formulating Algorithms: Nested Control Statements
- Besides being stacked on top of one another (in sequence), control statements can be combined through the nesting of one control statement within another.

Section 5.14 Formulating Algorithms: Nested Repetition Statements
- Repetition statements can be nested within each other, as well as stacked on top of one another.

Section 5.15 Visual Basic Programming in a Windows Application
- With visual programming, the IDE generates program code that creates the GUI. This code contains instructions for creating the Form and every control on it.

- Using keyword `Inherits` to extend from class `Form` enables programmers to create `Form`s quickly, without reinventing the wheel. Every Windows application consists of at least one class that `Inherits` from class `Form` in the `System.Windows.Forms` namespace.

- Forms and controls contain a set of default values for their properties, which are displayed initially in the **Properties** window when a `Form` or control is selected. These default values provide the initial characteristics a `Form` or control has when it is created.

- When a change, such as changing a property value, is made in design mode, the Windows Form Designer creates code that implements the change.

- Often it is necessary to modify a property while a program is running. In Windows applications, such code is placed in a method that executes when the `Form` is loaded. This method can be created by double clicking the `Form` in design view.

- Event handlers respond to (i.e., perform actions when) a state change occurs in the GUI. This state change is known as an event. Most events represent user actions, such as clicking a `Button` or altering a value.

Terminology

&= string concatenation assignment operator
*= multiplication assignment operator
+= addition assignment operator
/= division assignment operator
-= subtraction assignment operator
\= integer division assignment operator

^= exponentiation assignment operator
action
action expression in the UML
action state in the UML
action state symbol in the UML
activity diagram in the UML

activity of a portion of a software system
algorithm
arrow in the UML
attribute of a class
carriage return
compound assignment operator
constant
control statement
control-statement nesting
control-statement stacking
control structure
counter
counter-controlled loop
counter-controlled repetition
decision symbol in the UML
definite repetition
diamond symbol in the UML
division by zero
Do Until...Loop repetition statement
Do While...Loop repetition statement
dotted line in the UML
double-precision floating-point number
double-selection statement
dummy value
event
event handler
F format specifier
fatal logic error
final state in the UML
first refinement in pseudocode
fixed-point number
flag value
floating-point literal
flow of control
format specifier
formatted output
fully-qualified name
GoTo statement
guard condition in the UML
If...Then...Else double-selection statement
implicit conversion
indefinite repetition
initial state in the UML
initialization phase
iteration
level of refinement
levels of nesting
logic error
loop
loop-continuation condition

loop-termination condition
looping statement
lvalue ("left value")
merge symbol in the UML
multiple-selection statement
Name property of a control
nested control statements
nonfatal logic error
note in the UML
order of actions in an algorithm
precision
procedure for solving a problem
processing phase
program control
program development tool
promote
pseudocode
pseudocode algorithm
pseudocode statement
raise an event
repetition statement
repetition structure
second refinement in pseudocode
selection statement
selection structure
sentinel-controlled repetition
sentinel value
sequence statement
sequence structure
sequential execution
signal value
single-entry/single-exit control statement
single-precision floating-point number
Single primitive type
single-selection statement
small circle symbol in the UML
solid circle symbol in the UML
stacked control statements
stepwise refinement
String primitive type
structured programming
top in pseudocode
top-down, stepwise refinement
total
transfer of control
transition arrow in the UML
transition in the UML
visual programming
While repetition statement

Self-Review Exercises

5.1 Answer each of the following questions.
  a) All programs can be written in terms of three types of control structures: _____, _____ and _____.
  b) The _____ statement executes one action (or sequence of actions) when a condition is true and another action (or sequence of actions) when a condition is false.
  c) Repetition of a set of instructions a specific number of times is called _____ repetition.
  d) When it is not known in advance how many times a set of statements will be repeated, a(n) _____, _____, _____ or _____ value can be used to terminate the repetition.
  e) Specifying the order in which statements are to be executed in a computer program is called program _____.
  f) _____ is an artificial and informal language that helps programmers develop algorithms.
  g) _____ are words reserved by Visual Basic to implement various features, such as the language's control statements.
  h) The _____ selection statement is called a multiple-selection statement because it selects among many different actions (or sequences of actions).

5.2 State whether each of the following is *true* or *false*. If *false*, explain why.
  a) It is difficult to convert pseudocode into a Visual Basic program.
  b) Sequential execution refers to statements in a program that execute one after another.
  c) It is recommended that Visual Basic programmers use the GoTo statement for program control to enhance program clarity.
  d) The If...Then statement is called a single-selection statement.
  e) The sequence structure is not built into Visual Basic.
  f) Pseudocode closely resembles actual Visual Basic code.
  g) The While statement is terminated with the keywords End While.

5.3 Write two different Visual Basic statements that each add 1 to Integer variable number.

5.4 Write a statement or a set of statements to accomplish each of the following:
  a) Sum the odd integers between 1 and 99 using a While statement. Assume that variables sum and count have been declared as Integers.
  b) Sum the squares of the even integers between 1 and 15 using a Do While...Loop repetition statement. Assume that the Integer variables sum and count have been declared and initialized to 0 and 2, respectively.
  c) Print the numbers from 20 to 1 to the command prompt using a Do Until...Loop and Integer counter variable counterIndex. Assume that the variable counterIndex is initialized to 20.
  d) Repeat Exercise 5.4 (c) using a Do While...Loop statement.

5.5 Write a Visual Basic statement to accomplish each of the following tasks:
  a) Declare variables sum and number to be of type Integer.
  b) Assign 1 to variable number.
  c) Assign 0 to variable sum.
  d) Total variables number and sum, and assign the result to variable sum.
  e) Print "The sum is: " followed by the value of variable sum to the command prompt.

5.6 Combine the statements that you wrote in Exercise 5.5 into a program that calculates and prints the sum of the Integers from 1 to 10. Use a While statement to loop through the calculation and increment statements. The loop should terminate when the value of control variable number becomes 11.

5.7   Identify and correct the error(s) in each of the following (you may need to add code):
   a) Assume that value has been initialized to 50. The values from 0 to 50 should be summed.

```
While value >= 0
    sum += value
End While
```

   b) This segment should read an unspecified number of positive values from the user and sum them. Assume that number and total are declared as Integers.

```
total = 0

Do Until number = -1
    Console.Write("Enter a positive value; -1 to terminate: ")
    number = Console.ReadLine()
    total += number
Loop

Console.WriteLine(total)
```

   c) The following code should print the squares of 1 to 10.

```
Dim number As Integer = 1

Do While number < 10
    Console.WriteLine(number ^ 2)
While End
```

   d) This segment should print the values from 888 to 1000. Assume value is declared as an Integer.

```
value = 888

While value <= 1000
    value -= 1
End While
```

5.8   State whether each of the following is *true* or *false*. If the answer is *false*, explain why.
   a) Pseudocode is a structured programming language.
   b) The body of a Do While...Loop is executed only if the loop-continuation test is false.
   c) The body of a While is executed only if the loop-continuation test is false.
   d) The body of a Do Until...Loop is executed only if the loop-termination condition is false.

Answers to Self-Review Exercises

5.1   a) sequence, selection, repetition. b) If...Then...Else. c) counter-controlled or definite. d) sentinel, signal, flag or dummy. e) control. f) pseudocode. g) Keywords. h) Select...Case.

5.2   a) False. Pseudocode normally converts easily into Visual Basic code. b) True. c) False. Most programmers argue that GoTo statements violate structured programming and cause considerable problems. d) True. e) False. The sequence structure is built into Visual Basic—statements execute in the order in which they are written, unless explicitly directed to do otherwise. f) True. g) True.

5.3   number = number + 1
   number += 1

5.4   a) ```
count = 1
sum = 0

While count <= 99
    sum += count
    count += 2
End While
```
        b)  ```
Do While count <= 15
    sum += count ^ 2
    count += 2
Loop
```
        c) ```
Do Until counterIndex < 1
    Console.Write(counterIndex & " ")
    counterIndex -= 1
Loop
```
        d)  ```
Do While counterIndex >= 1
    Console.Write(counterIndex & " ")
    counterIndex -= 1
Loop
```

5.5   a) ```
Dim sum As Integer
Dim number As Integer
```
        b)  `number = 1`
        c)  `sum = 0`
        d)  `sum += number` or `sum = sum + number`
        e)  `Console.WriteLine("The sum is: " & sum)`

5.6

```
 1   ' Ex. 5.6: Calculate.vb
 2   ' Calculates the sum of the integers from 1 to 10.
 3   Module Calculate
 4      Sub Main()
 5         Dim sum As Integer = 0
 6         Dim number As Integer = 1
 7
 8         While number <= 10
 9            sum += number
10            number += 1
11         End While
12
13         Console.WriteLine("The sum is: " & sum)
14      End Sub ' Main
15   End Module ' Calculate
```

```
The sum is: 55
```

5.7   a) Error: Repetition condition may never become false, resulting in an infinite loop.

        ```
While value >= 0
    sum += value
    value -= 1
End While
```
```

b) Error: The sentinel value (-1) is added to `total`, producing an incorrect sum.

```
total = 0
Console.Write("Enter a positive value; -1 to terminate: ")
number = Console.ReadLine()

Do Until number = -1
    total += number
    Console.Write("Enter a positive value; -1 to terminate: ")
    number = Console.ReadLine()
Loop

Console.WriteLine(total)
```

c) Errors: The counter is never incremented, resulting in an infinite loop. The repetition condition uses the wrong relational operator. Keywords `While End` are used instead of keyword `Loop`.

```
Dim number As Integer = 1

Do While number <= 10
    Console.WriteLine(number ^ 2)
    number += 1
Loop
```

d) Error: The values are never printed and are decremented instead of incremented.

```
value = 888

While value <= 1000
    Console.WriteLine(value)
    value += 1
End While
```

5.8 a) False. Pseudocode is not a programming language.
     b) False. The loop condition must evaluate to true for the body to be executed.
     c) False. The loop condition must evaluate to true for the body to be executed.
     d) True.

Exercises

5.9 Drivers are concerned with the mileage obtained by their automobiles. One driver has kept track of several tankfuls of gasoline by recording the miles driven and the gallons used for each tankful. Develop a program that inputs the miles driven and gallons used (both as `Doubles`) for each tankful. The program should calculate and display the miles per gallon obtained for each tankful and print the combined miles per gallon obtained for all tankfuls. All average calculations should produce floating-point results. Use a sentinel value of -1.0 for the miles driven to terminate repetition. Avoid division by zero—if the user enters zero for the number of gallons, inform the user that the input value for gallons must be greater than zero. Be sure to check the total number of gallons for zero as well (when calculating the combined miles per gallon), in case someone enters -1.0 before entering a value for gallons greater than zero. [*Note:* Be careful—the miles per gallon for all tankfuls is not the average of the miles per gallon figures for each tankful.]

5.10 Develop a program that determines whether a department store customer has exceeded the credit limit on a charge account. For each customer, the following facts are available:
     a) Account number
     b) Balance at the beginning of the month

    c) Total of all items charged by this customer this month

    d) Total of all credits applied to this customer's account this month

    e) Allowed credit limit

The program should input the account number as an Integer, but use Doubles for the other variables. The program should calculate the new balance (= *beginning balance + charges − credits*), display the new balance and determine whether it exceeds the customer's credit limit. For customers whose credit limit is exceeded, the program should display the message, "Credit limit exceeded." Use a sentinel value of -1 for the account number to terminate repetition.

5.11 A palindrome is a number or a text phrase that reads the same backwards and forwards. For example, all of the following five-digit Integers are palindromes: 12321, 55555, 45554 and 11611; the five-digit Integers 43235, 64445 and 12322 are not palindromes. Write an application that reads in a five-digit Integer and determines whether it is a palindrome. [*Hint:* Break the number into its separate digits first. Then check whether the first digit equals the fifth digit, and the second digit equals the fourth digit.]

5.12 A company wants to transmit data over the telephone but is concerned that its phones may be tapped. All the data is transmitted as four-digit Integers. The company has asked you to write a program that encrypts its data so that it may be transmitted more securely. Your program should read a four-digit Integer entered by the user and encrypt it as follows: Replace each digit by *(the sum of that digit and 7) modulo 10*. Then swap the first digit with the third, and swap the second digit with the fourth. Print the encrypted Integer. Write a separate program that inputs an encrypted four-digit Integer and decrypts it to form the original number.

5.13 The factorial of a nonnegative Integer *n* (0, 1, 2, ...) is written *n*! (pronounced "*n* factorial") and is defined as follows:

    $n! = n \cdot (n - 1) \cdot (n - 2) \cdot \ldots \cdot 1$ (for values of *n* greater than or equal to 1)

and

    $n! = 1$ (for *n* = 0).

For example, 5! = 5 · 4 · 3 · 2 · 1, which is 120.

    a) Write a program that reads a nonnegative Integer from the user and computes and prints its factorial. To calculate the factorials of large values of *n*, data type Long (a 64-bit integer value) must be used. Type Long is designed to store integer values in a range much larger than that of type Integer. We discuss primitive type Long in more detail in Chapter 6.

    b) Write a program that estimates the value of the mathematical constant *e* by using the first 15 terms of the series:

$$e = 1 + \frac{1}{1!} + \frac{1}{2!} + \frac{1}{3!} + \ldots$$

    c) Write an application that computes the value of e^x by using the first 15 terms of the series:

$$e^x = 1 + \frac{x}{1!} + \frac{x^2}{2!} + \frac{x^3}{3!} + \ldots$$

5.14 Modify the class of Fig. 5.18 to process the four Strings: "P", "p", "F" and "f". If any other String input is encountered, a message should be displayed informing the user of invalid input. Only increment the loop's counter if one of the four previously mentioned Strings is input. Use the program of Fig. 5.19 to test your new program.

5.15 Modify the class of Fig. 5.21 to test whether the value input for the side is less than 1 and, if it is, issue an appropriate error message. [*Hint:* This requires that another If...Then statement be added to the code. In the next chapter we will show you how to solve this problem more elegantly using logical operators.] Use Fig. 5.22 to test your new program.

5.16   Write a program that uses counter-controlled repetition with a `While` statement to print the following table of values: [*Hint:* Use `vbTab` to separate the columns of output.]

N	10*N	100*N	1000*N
1	10	100	1000
2	20	200	2000
3	30	300	3000
4	40	400	4000
5	50	500	5000

5.17   The process of finding the largest value (i.e., the maximum of a group of values) is used frequently in computer applications. For example, a program that determines the winner of a sales contest would input the number of units sold by each salesperson. The salesperson who sells the most units would win the contest. Write a Visual Basic application that inputs a series of 10 integers and determines and displays the largest. Your program should use at least the following three variables:
   a) `counter`: A counter to count to 10 (i.e., to keep track of how many numbers have been input and to determine when all 10 numbers have been processed)
   b) `number`: The current integer input to the program
   c) `largest`: The largest number found so far.

5.18   Write an application that inputs an integer containing only 0s and 1s (i.e., a "binary" integer) and displays its decimal equivalent. [*Hint:* Use the modulus and division operators to pick off the "binary number's" digits one at a time, from right to left. In the decimal number system, the rightmost digit has a positional value of 1 and the next digit to the left has a positional value of 10, then 100, then 1000, and so on. The decimal number 234 can be interpreted as 4 * 1 + 3 * 10 + 2 * 100. In the binary number system, the rightmost digit has a positional value of 1, the next digit to the left has a positional value of 2, then 4, then 8, and so on. The decimal equivalent of binary 1101 is 1 * 1 + 0 * 2 + 1 * 4 + 1 * 8, or 1 + 0 + 4 + 8 or, 13.]

5.19   Write an application that reads three nonzero values entered by the user and determines whether they could represent the sides of a triangle.

Who can control his fate?
—William Shakespeare,
Othello

*The used key is always
bright.*
—Benjamin Franklin

*Not everything that can be
counted counts, and not
every thing that counts can
be counted.*
—Albert Einstein

*Every advantage in the past
is judged in the light of the
final issue.*
—Demosthenes

6

Control
Statements:
Part 2

OBJECTIVES

In this chapter you will learn:

- The essentials of counter-controlled repetition.

- To use the For...Next, Do...Loop While and
  Do...Loop Until repetition statements to execute
  statements in a program repeatedly.

- To perform multiple selection using the Select...Case
  selection statement.

- To use the Exit statement to break out of a repetition
  statement.

- To use the Continue statement to break out of the
  current iteration of a repetition statement.

- To use logical operators to form more complex
  conditions.

6.1 Introduction

Chapter 5 began our introduction to the types of building blocks that are available for problem solving. We used those building blocks to employ proven program-construction techniques. In this chapter, we introduce Visual Basic's remaining control statements. The control statements we study here and in Chapter 5 help us build and manipulate objects. We continue our early emphasis on object-oriented programming, presenting the next version of our GradeBook class.

We demonstrate the For...Next, Select...Case, Do...Loop While and Do...Loop Until control statements. Through a series of short examples using While...End While and For...Next, we explore the essentials of counter-controlled repetition. We create a Grade-Book class that uses a Select...Case multiple-selection statement to count the number of A, B, C, D and F grades in a set of letter grades entered by the user. We introduce the Exit and Continue program control statements. Finally, we discuss the logical operators, which enable you to use more powerful conditional expressions in control statements.

6.2 Essentials of Counter-Controlled Repetition

This section uses the While repetition statement introduced in Chapter 5 to highlight the elements required to perform counter-controlled repetition. Counter-controlled repetition requires

1. the name of a control variable (or loop counter) that is used to determine whether the loop continues to iterate

2. the initial value of the control variable

3. the increment (or decrement) by which the control variable is modified each time through the loop

4. the condition that tests for the final value of the control variable (i.e., whether looping should continue)

The example in Fig. 6.1 uses the four elements of counter-controlled repetition to display the even integers in the range 2–10. The declaration in line 5 *names* the control variable (counter), indicates that it is of type Integer, reserves space for it in memory and sets it to an *initial value* of 2.

Consider the While statement (lines 7–10). Line 8 displays the current value of counter, and line 9 *increments* the control variable by 2 to prepare for the next iteration (repetition) of the loop. The loop-continuation condition in the While statement (line 7) tests whether the value of the control variable is less than or equal to 10—the *final value* for which the condition is true. The body of the While is performed even when the control variable is 10. The loop terminates when the control variable exceeds 10 (i.e., when counter becomes 12, because the loop is incrementing by 2 each time).

6.3 For...Next Repetition Statement

Section 6.2 presented the essentials of counter-controlled repetition with the While statement. Visual Basic also provides the For...Next repetition statement, which specifies the counter-controlled repetition details in a single line of code. To illustrate the power of For...Next, we rewrite the program of Fig. 6.1 using the For...Next statement in Fig. 6.2.

The Main method of the program operates as follows: When the For...Next statement (lines 7–9) begins its execution, the control variable counter is declared as an Integer and initialized to 2, thus addressing the first two elements of counter-controlled repetition— control variable *name* and *initial value*. Next, the implied loop-continuation condition counter <= 10 is tested. The **To keyword** is required in the For...Next statement. The optional **Step keyword** specifies the increment (i.e., the amount that is added to counter each time the For...Next body is executed). If Step and the value following it are omitted, the increment defaults to 1. Programmers typically omit the Step portion for increments of 1. The increment of a For...Next statement could be negative, in which case it is a decrement, and the loop actually counts downwards.

```
1   ' Fig. 6.1: WhileCounter.vb
2   ' Using the While statement to demonstrate counter-controlled repetition.
3   Module WhileCounter
4      Sub Main()
5         Dim counter As Integer = 2 ' name and initialize loop counter
6
7         While counter <= 10 ' test final value of loop counter
8            Console.Write(counter & " ")
9            counter += 2 ' increment counter
10        End While
11
12        Console.WriteLine()
13     End Sub ' Main
14  End Module ' WhileCounter
```

```
2 4 6 8 10
```

Fig. 6.1 | Counter-controlled repetition with the While...End While statement.

```vb
1   ' Fig. 6.2: ForCounter.vb
2   ' Using the For...Next statement for counter-controlled repetition.
3   Module ForCounter
4      Sub Main()
5         ' initialization, repetition condition and
6         ' incrementing are all included in For...Next statement
7         For counter As Integer = 2 To 10 Step 2
8            Console.Write(counter & " ")
9         Next
10
11        Console.WriteLine()
12     End Sub ' Main
13  End Module ' ForCounter
```

```
2 4 6 8 10
```

Fig. 6.2 | Counter-controlled repetition with the For...Next statement.

In this example, the initial value of counter is 2, so the implied condition is satisfied (i.e., true), and the counter's value 2 is output in line 8. The required **Next** keyword marks the end of the For...Next repetition statement. When the Next keyword is reached, variable counter is incremented by the specified value of 2, and the loop begins again with the loop-continuation test.

At this point, the control variable is equal to 4. This value does not exceed the final value, so the program performs the body statement again. This process continues until the counter value of 10 has been printed and the control variable counter is incremented to 12, causing the (implied) loop-continuation test to fail and repetition to terminate. The program continues by performing the first statement after the For...Next statement. (In this case, method Main terminates, because the program reaches the End Sub statement at line 12.)

Good Programming Practice 6.1

Place a blank line before and after each control statement to make it stand out in the program.

Good Programming Practice 6.2

Vertical spacing above and below control statements, as well as indentation of the bodies of control statements, gives programs a two-dimensional appearance that enhances readability.

Error-Prevention Tip 6.1

Use a For...Next loop for counter-controlled repetition. Off-by-one errors (which occur when a loop is executed for one more or one less iteration than is necessary) tend to disappear, because the terminating value is clear.

For...Next *Statement Header Components*

Figure 6.3 takes a closer look at the For...Next statement from Fig. 6.2. The first line of the For...Next statement sometimes is called the **For...Next header**. Note that the For...Next header specifies each of the items needed for counter-controlled repetition with a control variable.

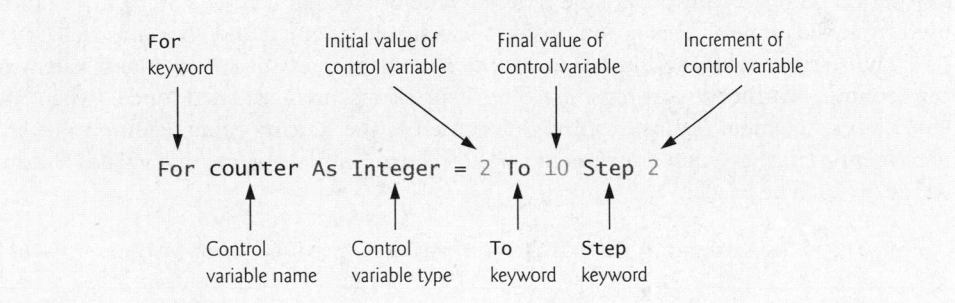

Fig. 6.3 | For...Next header components.

The general form of the For...Next statement is

```
For initialization To finalValue Step increment
    statement
Next
```

where the *initialization* expression initializes the loop's control variable, *finalValue* determines whether the loop should continue executing (if the control variable is less than or equal to *finalValue*) and *increment* specifies the amount the control variable should be incremented each time through the loop. In most cases, the For...Next statement can be represented by an equivalent While statement, as follows:

```
initialization

While variable <= finalValue
    statement
    increment
End While
```

There is an exception to this rule, which we will discuss in Section 6.9.

Note in Fig. 6.3 that the counter variable is both initialized and declared in the For...Next header. The counter variable may be declared before the For...Next statement. For example, the code in Fig. 6.2 could have been written as

```
Dim counter As Integer

For counter = 2 To 10 Step 2
    Console.Write(counter & " ")
Next
```

Although both forms are correct, declaring the control variable in the For...Next header is more clear and concise. The difference between the two forms is that if the *initialization* expression in the For...Next statement header declares the control variable (as we have done in Fig. 6.2), the control variable can be used only in the body of the For...Next statement—it will be unknown outside the For...Next statement. This restricted use of the control variable name is known as the variable's **scope**. The scope of a variable specifies where it can be used in a program. Scope is discussed in detail in Chapter 7, Methods: A

Deeper Look. If the control variable is declared before the For...Next statement, it can be used from the point of declaration, inside the control statement and after it as well.

The starting value, ending value and increment portions of a For...Next statement can contain arithmetic expressions. The expressions are evaluated once (when the For...Next statement begins executing) and used as the starting value, ending value and increment of the For...Next statement's header. For example, assume that value1 = 2 and value2 = 10. The header

```
For j As Integer = value1 To 4 * value1 * value2 Step value2 \ value1
```

is equivalent to the header

```
For j As Integer = 2 To 80 Step 5
```

If the loop-continuation condition is initially false (e.g., if the starting value is greater than the ending value and the increment is positive), the For...Next's body is not performed. Instead, execution proceeds with the first statement after the For...Next statement.

The control variable frequently is printed or used in calculations in the For...Next body, but it does not have to be. It is common to use the control variable exclusively to control repetition and never mention it in the For...Next body.

Common Programming Error 6.1

Counter-controlled loops should not be controlled with floating-point variables. Floating-point values are represented only approximately in the computer's memory; this can lead to imprecise counter values and inaccurate tests for termination.

Error-Prevention Tip 6.2

Although the value of the control variable can be changed in the body of a For...Next loop, avoid doing so, because this practice can lead to subtle errors.

Common Programming Error 6.2

In nested For...Next loops, the use of the same control-variable name in more than one loop is a compilation error.

For Statement UML Activity Diagram

The activity diagram for the For...Next statement is similar to that of the While statement (Fig. 5.5). For example, the activity diagram of the For...Next statement

```
For counter As Integer = 1 To 10
    Console.WriteLine(counter)
Next
```

is shown in Fig. 6.4. This activity diagram makes it clear that the initialization occurs only once and that incrementing occurs *after* each execution of the body statement. Note that (besides an initial state, transition arrows, a merge, a final state and several notes) the diagram contains only action states and a decision.

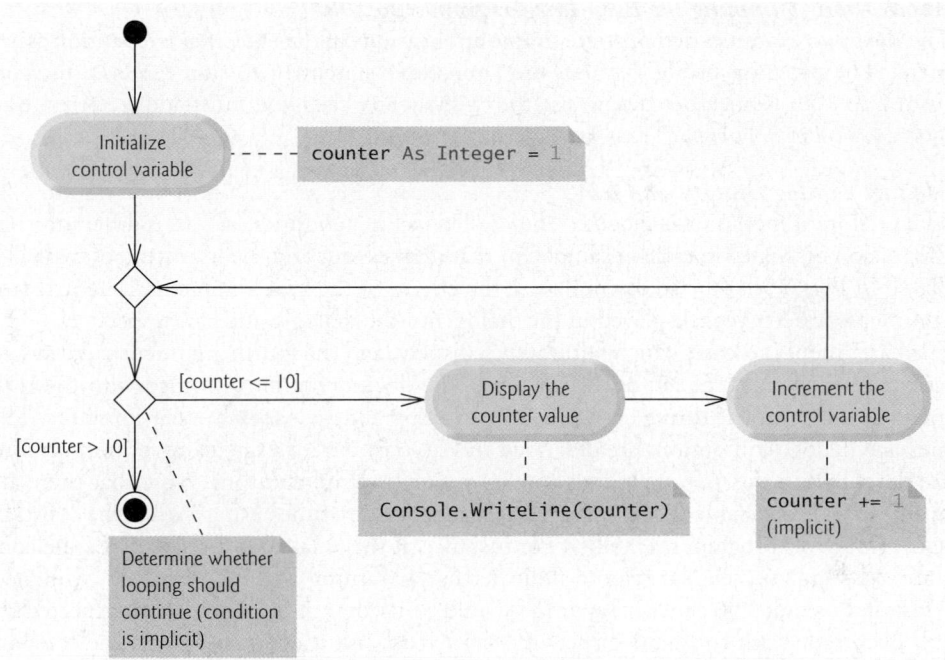

Fig. 6.4 | For...Next repetition statement activity diagram.

6.4 Examples Using the For...Next Statement

The following examples demonstrate different ways of varying the control variable in a For...Next statement. In each case, we write the appropriate For...Next header.

a) Vary the control variable from 1 to 100 in increments of 1.

    For i = 1 To 100 or For i = 1 To 100 Step 1

b) Vary the control variable from 100 to 1 in increments of –1 (decrements of 1).

    For i = 100 To 1 Step –1

c) Vary the control variable from 7 to 77 in increments of 7.

    For i = 7 To 77 Step 7

d) Vary the control variable from 20 to 2 in increments of –2 (decrements of 2).

    For i = 20 To 2 Step –2

e) Vary the control variable over the sequence of the following values: 2, 5, 8, 11, 14, 17, 20.

    For i = 2 To 20 Step 3

f) Vary the control variable over the sequence of the following values: 99, 88, 77, 66, 55, 44, 33, 22, 11, 0.

    For i = 99 To 0 Step –11

Application: Summing the Even Integers from 2 to 100

The next two examples demonstrate simple applications of the For...Next repetition statement. The program in Fig. 6.5 uses the For...Next statement to sum the even integers from 2 to 100. Remember that to use the MessageBox class you must add a reference to System.Windows.Forms.dll, as explained in Section 3.9.

Message Dialog Buttons and Icons

The version of method MessageBox.Show called in Fig. 6.5 (lines 14–16) is different from the version discussed in earlier examples in that it takes four arguments instead of two. The dialog in Fig. 6.5 is labeled to emphasize the effects of the four arguments. The first two arguments are Strings displayed in the dialog and the dialog's title bar, respectively. The third argument indicates which button(s) to display, and the fourth argument indicates an icon that appears to the left of the message. The documentation provided with the IDE includes the complete listing of MessageBoxButtons and MessageBoxIcon constants. The message dialog icon options are described in Fig. 6.6; the message dialog button options are described in Fig. 6.7, including how to display multiple buttons. Note that there are multiple icon constants that display the same icon. Sometimes using a different constant name improves program readability. For instance, it may make more sense to use the constant MessageBoxIcon.Warning to indicate that a warning is being displayed, while the constant MessageBoxIcon.Exclamation would be used to indicate that an unexpected result occurred. Both constants display the same icon, but the names used in the code are clearer based on context.

```vb
 1  ' Fig. 6.5: Sum.vb
 2  ' Using For...Next statement to demonstrate summation.
 3  Imports System.Windows.Forms
 4
 5  Module Sum
 6     Sub Main()
 7        Dim sum As Integer = 0
 8
 9        ' add even numbers from 2 to 100
10        For number As Integer = 2 To 100 Step 2
11           sum += number
12        Next
13
14        MessageBox.Show("The sum is " & sum, _
15           "Sum even integers from 2 to 100", _
16           MessageBoxButtons.OK, MessageBoxIcon.Information)
17     End Sub ' Main
18  End Module ' Sum
```

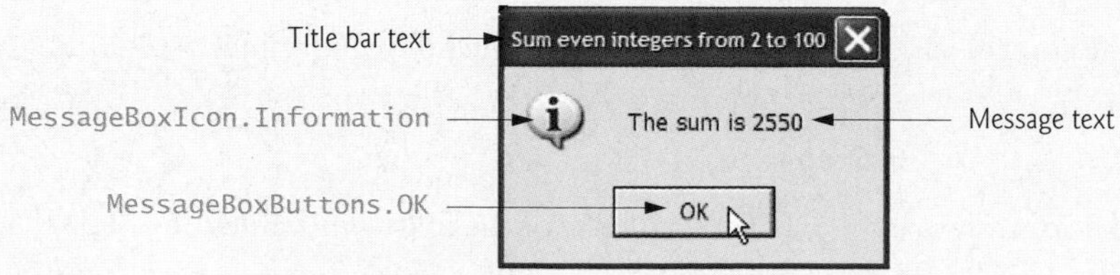

Title bar text — Sum even integers from 2 to 100

MessageBoxIcon.Information — The sum is 2550 — Message text

MessageBoxButtons.OK — OK

Fig. 6.5 | For...Next statement used for summation.

MessageBoxIcon constants	Icon	Description
`MessageBoxIcon.Exclamation` and `MessageBoxIcon.Warning`		Both constants display an icon containing an exclamation point. Typically used to caution the user against potential problems or display information that may be unexpected.
`MessageBoxIcon.Information` and `MessageBoxIcon.Asterisk`		Both constants display an icon containing the letter "i." Typically used to display information about the state of the application.
`MessageBoxIcon.Question`		This constant displays an icon containing a question mark. Typically used to ask the user a question.
`MessageBoxIcon.Error`, `MessageBoxIcon.Stop` and `MessageBoxIcon.Hand`		These constants display an icon containing an ∞ in a red circle. Typically used to alert the user of errors or critical situations.
`MessageBoxIcon.None`		This constant causes no icon to be displayed.

Fig. 6.6 | Message dialog icon constants.

MessageBoxButton constants	Description
`MessageBoxButtons.OK`	**OK** button. Allows the user to acknowledge a message. Included by default.
`MessageBoxButtons.OKCancel`	**OK** and **Cancel** buttons. Allow the user to either continue or cancel an operation.
`MessageBoxButtons.YesNo`	**Yes** and **No** buttons. Allow the user to respond to a question.
`MessageBoxButtons.YesNoCancel`	**Yes**, **No** and **Cancel** buttons. Allow the user to respond to a question or cancel an operation.
`MessageBoxButtons.RetryCancel`	**Retry** and **Cancel** buttons. Allow the user to retry or cancel an operation that has failed.
`MessageBoxButtons.AbortRetryIgnore`	**Abort**, **Retry** and **Ignore** buttons. When one of a series of operations has failed, these buttons allow the user to abort the entire sequence, retry the failed operation or ignore the failed operation and continue.

Fig. 6.7 | Message dialog button constants.

Application: Compound Interest Calculations

The next example computes compound interest using the For…Next statement. Consider the following problem statement:

> *A person invests $1000.00 in a savings account that yields 5% interest. Assuming that all the interest is left on deposit, calculate and print the amount of money in the account at the end of each year over a period of 10 years. To determine these amounts, use the following formula:*
>
> $$a = p \, (1 + r)^n$$
>
> *where*
>
> > *p is the original amount invested (i.e., the principal)*
> > *r is the annual interest rate (e.g., .05 stands for 5%)*
> > *n is the number of years*
> > *a is the amount on deposit at the end of the nth year.*

This problem involves a loop that performs the indicated calculation for each of the 10 years that the money remains on deposit. The solution is shown in Fig. 6.8.

Lines 7–8 declare two Decimal variables. Type Decimal is used for monetary calculations. Line 9 declares rate as type Double. Variable principal is initialized to 1000.00 and rate is initialized to 0.05, (i.e., 5%). Variable output (line 12) will be used to store the output that we will eventually display in a message dialog.

```vb
1    ' Fig. 6.8: Interest.vb
2    ' Calculating compound interest.
3    Imports System.Windows.Forms
4
5    Module Interest
6       Sub Main()
7          Dim amount As Decimal ' dollar amounts on deposit
8          Dim principal As Decimal = 1000.00 ' amount invested
9          Dim rate As Double = 0.05 ' interest rate
10
11         ' amount after each year
12         Dim output As String = "Year" & vbTab & "Amount on deposit" & vbCrLf
13
14         ' calculate amount after each year
15         For year As Integer = 1 To 10
16            amount = principal * (1 + rate) ^ year
17            output &= _
18               (year & vbTab & String.Format("{0:C}", amount) & vbCrLf)
19         Next
20
21         ' display output
22         MessageBox.Show(output, "Compound Interest", _
23            MessageBoxButtons.OK, MessageBoxIcon.Information)
24      End Sub ' Main
25   End Module ' Interest
```

Fig. 6.8 | For…Next statement used to calculate compound interest. (Part 1 of 2.)

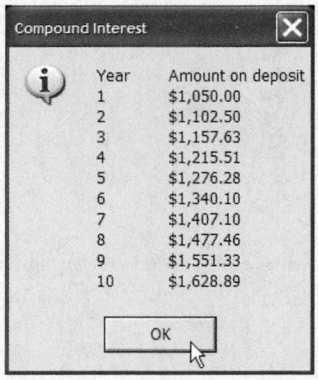

Fig. 6.8 | For...Next statement used to calculate compound interest. (Part 2 of 2.)

The For...Next statement (lines 15–19) iterates 10 times, varying control variable year from 1 to 10 in increments of 1. Line 16 performs the calculation from the problem statement

$$a = p \, (1 + r)^{\,n}$$

where a is the amount, p is the principal, r is the rate and n is the year.

Formatting Currency Output

Lines 17–18 append additional text to the end of String output. The text includes the current year value, a tab character (vbTab) to position to the second column, the result of the method call String.Format("{0:C}", amount) and, finally, a line feed (vbCrLf) to start the next output on the next line. Method **Format** of class String takes a formatted string and the values to be formatted as arguments, and returns the resulting text with the formatting applied. The first argument passed to Format is the format string. In Chapter 5, we used the format string "{0:F}" to print a floating-point number with two digits after the decimal. Line 18 uses the format string "{0:C}". The C (for "currency") format specifier indicates that its corresponding value (amount) should be displayed in monetary format—with a dollar sign to the left and commas in the proper locations. For example, the value 1334.50, when formatted using the C format specifier, will appear as "$1,334.50."

Type *Decimal* vs. Type *Double*

Variables amount and principal are declared as type Decimal. We do this because we are dealing with fractional parts of dollars and need a type that allows precise calculations with monetary amounts—Single and Double, because they only approximate values, do not. Using floating-point types, such as Single or Double, to represent dollar amounts (assuming that dollar amounts are displayed with two digits to the right of the decimal point) can cause errors. For example, two Double dollar amounts stored in the machine could be 14.234 (normally rounded to 14.23) and 18.673 (normally rounded to 18.67). When these amounts are added together, they produce the internal sum 32.907, which normally rounds to 32.91. Thus, the output could appear as

```
   14.23
 + 18.67
 ───────
   32.91
```

but a person adding the individual numbers as displayed would expect the sum to be 32.90. Therefore, it is inappropriate to use `Single` or `Double` for dollar amounts. You have been warned!

Error-Prevention Tip 6.3

Do not use variables of type `Single` or `Double` to perform precise monetary calculations. The imprecision of floating-point numbers can cause errors that result in incorrect monetary values. Use the type `Decimal` for monetary calculations.

Variable `rate`, of type `Double`, is used in the calculation `1 + rate`, which appears as the left operand of the exponentiation operator. In fact, this calculation produces the same result each time through the loop, so performing the calculation in the body of the `For...Next` loop is wasteful.

Performance Tip 6.1

Avoid placing inside a loop the calculation of an expression whose value does not change each time through the loop. Such an expression should be evaluated only once and prior to the loop.

6.5 GradeBook Case Study: `Select...Case` Multiple-Selection Statement

Chapter 5 presented the `If...Then` single-selection statement and the `If...Then...Else` double-selection statement. Occasionally, an algorithm contains a series of decisions that test a variable or expression separately for each value that the variable or expression might assume. The algorithm then takes different actions based on those values. Visual Basic provides the **`Select...Case` multiple-selection statement** to handle such decision making.

***GradeBook* Class with `Select...Case` Statement to Count A, B, C, D and F Grades.**
Figure 6.9 contains an enhanced version of the `GradeBook` class introduced in Chapter 4 and further developed in Chapter 5. The new version not only calculates the average of a set of numeric grades entered by the user, but uses a `Select...Case` statement to determine whether each grade is the equivalent of an A, B, C, D or F and to increment the appropriate grade counter. The class also displays a summary of the number of students who received each grade. An extra counter is used to display the number of students who received a perfect score of 100 on the exam. Figure 6.10 shows a sample execution of the `GradeBookTest` module that uses an object of class `GradeBook` to process a set of grades.

```
 1   ' Fig. 6.9: GradeBook.vb
 2   ' GradeBook class uses Select...Case statement to count letter grades.
 3   Public Class GradeBook
 4      Private courseNameValue As String ' name of course
```

Fig. 6.9 | `GradeBook` class uses `Select...Case` statement to count A, B, C, D and F grades. (Part 1 of 4.)

```vb
 5      Private total As Integer ' sum of grades
 6      Private gradeCounter As Integer ' number of grades entered
 7      Private aCount As Integer ' count of A grades
 8      Private bCount As Integer ' count of B grades
 9      Private cCount As Integer ' count of C grades
10      Private dCount As Integer ' count of D grades
11      Private fCount As Integer ' count of F grades
12      Private perfectScoreCount As Integer ' count of perfect scores
13
14      ' constructor initializes course name;
15      ' Integer instance variables are initialized to 0 by default
16      Public Sub New(ByVal name As String)
17         CourseName = name ' initializes CourseName
18      End Sub ' New
19
20      ' property that gets and sets the course name; the Set accessor
21      ' ensures that the course name has at most 25 characters
22      Public Property CourseName() As String
23         Get ' retrieve courseNameValue
24            Return courseNameValue
25         End Get
26
27         Set(ByVal value As String) ' set courseNameValue
28            If value.Length <= 25 Then ' if value has 25 or fewer characters
29               courseNameValue = value ' store the course name in the object
30            Else ' if name has more than 25 characters
31               ' set courseNameValue to first 25 characters of parameter name
32               ' start at 0, length of 25
33               courseNameValue = value.Substring(0, 25)
34
35               Console.WriteLine( _
36                  "Course name (" & value & ") exceeds maximum length (25).")
37               Console.WriteLine( _
38                  "Limiting course name to first 25 characters." & vbCrLf)
39            End If
40         End Set
41      End Property ' CourseName
42
43      ' display a welcome message to the GradeBook user
44      Public Sub DisplayMessage()
45         Console.WriteLine("Welcome to the grade book for " _
46            & vbCrLf & CourseName & "!" & vbCrLf)
47      End Sub ' DisplayMessage
48
49      ' input arbitrary number of grades from user
50      Public Sub InputGrades()
51         Console.Write( _
52            "Enter the grades in the range 0-100, negative value to quit: ")
53         Dim grade As Integer = Console.ReadLine() ' input grade
54
```

Fig. 6.9 | GradeBook class uses Select...Case statement to count A, B, C, D and F grades. (Part 2 of 4.)

```vb
55          ' loop until user enters a sentinel value
56          While grade >= 0
57              total += grade ' add grade to total
58              gradeCounter += 1 ' increment number of grades
59
60              ' call method to increment appropriate counter
61              IncrementLetterGradeCounter(grade)
62
63              ' input next grade
64              Console.Write("Enter the grades in the range 0-100, " & _
65                  "negative value to quit: ")
66              grade = Console.ReadLine()
67          End While
68      End Sub ' InputGrades
69
70      ' add 1 to appropriate counter for specified grade
71      Private Sub IncrementLetterGradeCounter(ByVal grade As Integer)
72          Select Case grade ' determine which grade was entered
73              Case 100 ' perfect score
74                  perfectScoreCount += 1 ' increment perfectScoreCount
75                  aCount += 1 ' increment aCount
76              Case 90 To 99 ' grade was between 90 and 99
77                  aCount += 1 ' increment aCount
78              Case 80 To 89 ' grade was between 80 and 89
79                  bCount += 1 ' increment bCount
80              Case 70 To 79 ' grade was between 70 and 79
81                  cCount += 1 ' increment cCount
82              Case 60 To 69 ' grade was between 60 and 69
83                  dCount += 1 ' increment dCount
84              Case Else ' grade was less than 60
85                  fCount += 1 ' increment fCount
86          End Select
87      End Sub ' IncrementLetterGradeCounter
88
89      ' display a report based on the grades entered by user
90      Public Sub DisplayGradeReport()
91          Console.WriteLine(vbCrLf & "Grade Report:")
92
93          ' if user entered at least one grade
94          If (gradeCounter > 0) Then
95              ' calculate average of all grades entered
96              Dim average As Double = total / gradeCounter
97
98              ' output summary of results
99              Console.WriteLine("Total of the {0} grades entered is {1}", _
100                 gradeCounter, total)
101             Console.WriteLine("Class average is {0:F2}", average)
102             Console.WriteLine("Number of students who received each grade:")
103             Console.WriteLine("A: " & aCount) ' display number of A grades
104             Console.WriteLine("B: " & bCount) ' display number of B grades
```

Fig. 6.9 | GradeBook class uses Select...Case statement to count A, B, C, D and F grades. (Part 3 of 4.)

```
105            Console.WriteLine("C: " & cCount) ' display number of C grades
106            Console.WriteLine("D: " & dCount) ' display number of D grades
107            Console.WriteLine("F: " & fCount) ' display number of F grades
108            Console.WriteLine(vbCrLf & "Number of students who received " & _
109               "perfect scores: " & perfectScoreCount)
110         Else ' no grades were entered, so output appropriate message
111            Console.WriteLine("No grades were entered")
112         End If
113      End Sub ' DisplayGradeReport
114   End Class ' GradeBook
```

Fig. 6.9 | GradeBook class uses Select...Case statement to count A, B, C, D and F grades. (Part 4 of 4.)

Like earlier versions of the class, class GradeBook (Fig. 6.9) declares instance variable courseNameValue (line 4) and contains property CourseName (lines 22–41) and method DisplayMessage (lines 44–47), which access the course name and display a welcome message to the user, respectively. The class also contains a constructor (lines 16–18) that initializes the course name.

This version of class GradeBook declares instance variables total (line 5) and grade-Counter (line 6), which keep track of the sum of the grades entered by the user and the number of grades entered, respectively. Lines 7–11 declare counter variables for each grade category. Line 12 declares perfectScoreCount, a counter for the number of students who received a perfect score of 100 on the exam. The class maintains total, gradeCounter and the six counters as instance variables so that they can be used or modified in any of the class's methods. Note that the class's constructor (lines 16–18) sets only the course name; the remaining instance variables are Integers and are initialized to 0 by default.

This version of class GradeBook contains three additional methods—InputGrades, IncrementLetterGradeCounter and DisplayGradeReport. Method InputGrades (lines 50–68) reads an arbitrary number of integer grades from the user using sentinel-controlled repetition and updates instance variables total and gradeCounter. The method calls method IncrementLetterGradeCounter (lines 71–87) to update the appropriate letter-grade counter for each grade entered. Note that method IncrementLetterGradeCounter is declared Private—we will discuss why later in the section. Method DisplayGrade-Report (lines 90–113) outputs a report containing the total of all the grades entered, the average of the grades, the number of students who received each letter grade and the number of students who received a perfect score.

Let's examine these methods in more detail. Lines 51–53 in method InputGrades prompt the user to enter a grade, which is assigned to variable grade. In this example, we are using any negative number as a sentinel. The While statement (lines 56–67) executes if there is more data to input (i.e., if the grade is not a sentinel value).

Line 57 adds grade to total. Line 58 increments gradeCounter. The DisplayGrade-Report method uses these variables to compute the average. Line 61 calls method IncrementLetterGradeCounter to increment the appropriate letter-grade counter based on the numeric grade entered. Lines 64–66 prompt the user and input the next grade.

Method IncrementLetterGradeCounter uses a Select...Case statement (lines 72–86) to determine which counter to increment. In this example, we assume that the user enters a valid grade in the range 0–100. A grade in the range 90–100 represents an A, 80–89 represents a B, 70–79 represents a C, 60–69 represents a D and 0–59 represents an F. Line 72

```
Select Case grade
```

begins the Select...Case statement. The expression following the keywords Select Case (in this case, grade) is called the **controlling expression**. The controlling expression is compared sequentially with each Case. If a matching Case is found, the code in the Case executes, then program control proceeds to the first statement after the Select...Case statement (line 87).

Common Programming Error 6.3

Duplicate Case statements are logic errors. At run time, the first matching Case is executed.

The first Case statement (line 73) determines whether the value of grade is equal to 100. If this is true, the statements in lines 74–75 execute, incrementing both aCount (because a grade of 100 is an A) and perfectScoreCount. Note that a Case statement can specify multiple actions—in this case, incrementing both aCount and perfectScore-Count. The next Case statement (line 76) determines whether grade is between 90 and 99 inclusive. In this case, only aCount is incremented (line 77). Keyword To specifies the range; lines 78–83 use this keyword to present a series of similar Cases. Each case increments the appropriate counter.

Common Programming Error 6.4

If the value on the left side of the To keyword in a Case statement is larger than the value on the right side, the Case is ignored during program execution; this is probably a logic error.

If no match occurs between the controlling expression's value and a Case label, the optional **Case Else** (lines 84–85) executes. We use the Case Else in this example to process all controlling-expression values that are less than 60, that is, all failing grades. If no match occurs and the Select...Case does not contain a Case Else, program control simply continues with the first statement after the Select...Case. Case Else commonly is used to deal with invalid input. When employed, the Case Else must be the last Case.

The required **End Select** keywords terminate the Select...Case statement. Note that the body parts of the Select...Case statement are indented to emphasize structure and improve program readability.

Error-Prevention Tip 6.4

Provide a Case Else in Select...Case statements. Cases not handled in a Select...Case statement are ignored unless a Case Else is provided. The inclusion of a Case Else statement can facilitate the processing of exceptional conditions.

Types of **Case** *Statements*

Case statements also can use relational operators to determine whether the controlling expression satisfies a condition. For example

```
Case Is < 0
```

uses keyword **Is** along with the relational operator, <, to test for values less than 0.

Multiple values can be tested in a Case statement where the values are separated by commas, as in

```
Case 0, 5 To 9
```

which tests for the value 0 or values in the range 5–9.

GradeBookTest *Module That Demonstrates Class* GradeBook

Module GradeBookTest (Fig. 6.10) creates a GradeBook object (line 7). Line 9 invokes the object's DisplayMessage method to output a welcome message to the user. Line 10 invokes the object's InputGrades method to read grades from the user and keep track of the sum of all the grades entered and the number of grades. Recall that method InputGrades also calls method IncrementLetterGradeCounter to keep track of the number of students who received each letter grade. Line 11 invokes method DisplayGradeReport of class GradeBook, which outputs a report based on the grades entered (as in the sample execution in Fig. 6.10). Line 94 of class GradeBook (Fig. 6.9) determines whether the user entered at least one grade—this helps us avoid dividing by zero. If so, line 96 calculates the average of the grades. Lines 99–109 then output the totals of all the grades, the class average, the number of students who received each letter grade and the number of students who received a perfect score. If no grades were entered, line 111 outputs an appropriate message.

```
 1   ' Fig. 6.10: GradeBookTest.vb
 2   ' Create GradeBook object, input grades and display grade report.
 3   Module GradeBookTest
 4      Sub Main()
 5         ' create GradeBook object gradeBook1 and
 6         ' pass course name to constructor
 7         Dim gradeBook1 As New GradeBook("CS101 Introduction to VB")
 8
 9         gradeBook1.DisplayMessage() ' display welcome message
10         gradeBook1.InputGrades() ' read grades from user
11         gradeBook1.DisplayGradeReport() ' display report based on grades
12      End Sub ' Main
13   End Module ' GradeBookTest
```

```
Welcome to the grade book for
CS101 Introduction to VB!

Enter a grade in the range 0-100, negative value to quit: 99
Enter a grade in the range 0-100, negative value to quit: 92
Enter a grade in the range 0-100, negative value to quit: 45
Enter a grade in the range 0-100, negative value to quit: 57
Enter a grade in the range 0-100, negative value to quit: 63
Enter a grade in the range 0-100, negative value to quit: 71
Enter a grade in the range 0-100, negative value to quit: 76
Enter a grade in the range 0-100, negative value to quit: 85
Enter a grade in the range 0-100, negative value to quit: 90
Enter a grade in the range 0-100, negative value to quit: 100
Enter a grade in the range 0-100, negative value to quit: -1
```

(continued on next page...)

Fig. 6.10 | GradeBookTest creates a GradeBook object and invokes its methods. (Part 1 of 2.)

```
Grade Report:
Total of the 10 grades entered is 778
Class average is 77.80
Number of students who received each grade:
A: 4
B: 1
C: 2
D: 1
F: 2

Number of students who received a perfect score: 1
```

Fig. 6.10 | `GradeBookTest` creates a `GradeBook` object and invokes its methods. (Part 2 of 2.)

Note that module `GradeBookTest` (Fig. 6.10) does not directly call `GradeBook` method `IncrementLetterGradeCounter` (lines 71–87 of Fig. 6.9). This method is used exclusively by method `InputGrades` of class `GradeBook` to update the appropriate letter-grade counter as each new grade is entered by the user. Method `IncrementLetterGrade-Counter` exists solely to support the operation of class `GradeBook`'s other methods and thus is declared `Private`. Methods declared `Private` can be called only by other members of the class in which the `Private` methods are declared. Such `Private` methods are commonly referred to as **utility methods** or **helper methods**.

Using the `With` Statement

The **`With` statement** allows you to make multiple references to the same object in a concise manner. For example, we can replace lines 9–11 of Fig. 6.10 (which all reference the same object, `gradeBook1`) with

```
With gradeBook1
   .DisplayMessage() ' display welcome message
   .InputGrades() ' read grades from user
   .DisplayGradeReport() ' display report based on grades
End With
```

These lines of code are collectively known as a **`With` statement block**. At the beginning of the block, we specify the object (`gradeBook1`) that we will be using in the block. The `With` statement allows you to access an object's members in the block without having to specify the name of the object before the dot separator, e.g., `.DisplayMessage()` instead of `gradeBook1.DisplayMessage()`.

Select...Case Statement UML Activity Diagram

Figure 6.11 shows the UML activity diagram for the general `Select...Case` statement. Again, note that (besides an initial state, transition arrows, merges, a final state and several notes) the diagram contains only action states and decisions.

In Chapter 11, Object-Oriented Programming: Polymorphism, we present a more elegant method of implementing multiple-selection logic. We use a technique called polymorphism to create programs that are often clearer, more manageable, and easier to extend than programs that use `Select...Case` logic.

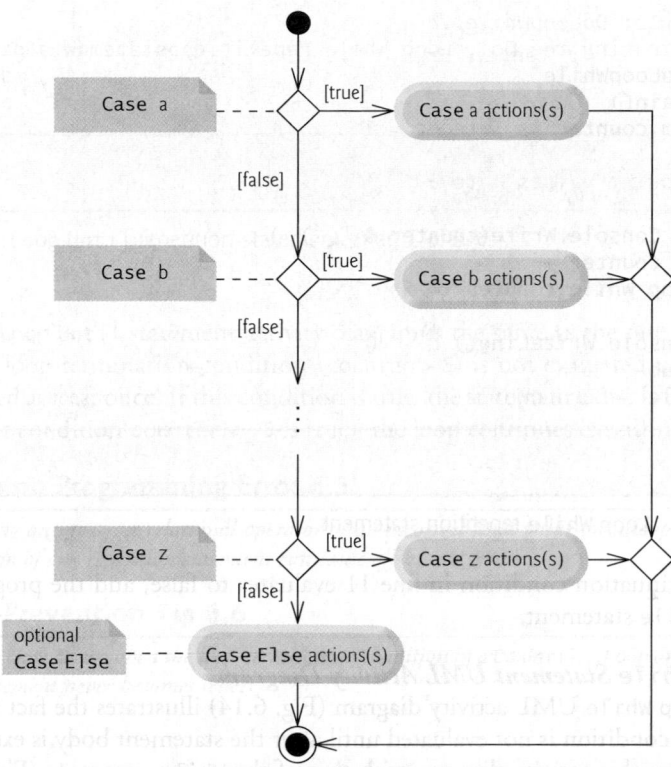

Fig. 6.11 | Select...Case multiple-selection statement UML activity diagram.

6.6 Do...Loop While Repetition Statement

The **Do...Loop While** repetition statement is similar to the **While** statement and **Do While...Loop** statement. In the **While** and **Do While...Loop** statements, the loop-continuation condition is tested at the *beginning* of the loop, before the body of the loop is performed. The **Do...Loop While** statement tests the loop-continuation condition *after* the loop body is performed; therefore, in a **Do...Loop While** statement, the loop body is always executed at least once. When a **Do...Loop While** statement terminates, execution continues with the statement after the **Loop While** clause. The program in Fig. 6.12 uses a **Do...Loop While** statement to output the values 1–5.

Error-Prevention Tip 6.5

Infinite loops occur when the loop-continuation condition in a While, Do While...Loop *or* Do...Loop While *statement never becomes false.*

Lines 8–11 demonstrate the **Do...Loop While** statement. The first time that the statement is encountered, lines 9–10 are executed, displaying the value of counter (at this point, 1) then incrementing counter by 1. Then the condition in line 11 is evaluated. Variable counter is 2, which is less than or equal to 5; because the loop-continuation condition is met, the **Do...Loop While** statement executes again. In the fifth iteration of the statement, line 9 outputs the value 5, and line 10 increments counter to 6. At this point,

The **Exit Select** statement can be used to exit a Select...Case statement. The **Exit Property** statement can be used to exit from a property. We encounter different forms of the Exit statement throughout the book.

6.9 Using the Continue Statement in Repetition Statements

The **Continue** statement skips the remaining statements in the loop body of a repetition statement and causes control to proceed to the next iteration of the loop. Like the Exit statement, Continue comes in many forms. The **Continue Do** statement can be executed in a Do While...Loop, Do...Loop While, Do Until...Loop or Do...Loop Until statement to cause the program to skip the remainder of the current iteration of that repetition statement. Similarly, the **Continue For** statement and **Continue While** statement cause the program to skip the remainder of the current iteration of For...Next and While loops, respectively. Unlike the Exit statement, the Continue statement is used to alter program control only in repetition statements.

When Continue For is encountered in a For...Next statement, execution continues with the statement's increment expression, then the program evaluates the loop-continuation test. When Continue is used in another type of repetition statement, the program evaluates the loop-continuation (or loop-termination) test immediately after the Continue statement executes. If a control variable's increment occurs in the loop after the Continue statement, the increment is skipped.

Figure 6.16 demonstrates the Continue For, Continue Do and Continue While statements in their respective repetition statements. Each repetition statement displays the values 1–4 and 6–10; the value 5 is skipped in each case using an appropriate form of the Continue statement.

```
1    ' Fig. 6.16: ContinueTest.vb
2    ' Using the Continue statement in repetition statements.
3    Module ContinueTest
4       Sub Main()
5          Dim counter As Integer ' loop counter
6
7          ' skipping an iteration of a For...Next statement
8          For counter = 1 To 10
9             If counter = 5 Then
10               Continue For ' skip to next iteration of loop if counter = 5
11            End If
12
13            Console.Write(counter & " ") ' output counter
14         Next
15
16         Console.WriteLine(vbCrLf & _
17            "Skipped printing in For...Next at counter = 5" & vbCrLf)
18         counter = 0 ' reset counter
19
```

Fig. 6.16 | Continue statement in repetition statements. (Part 1 of 2.)

```
20              ' skipping an iteration of a Do Until...Loop statement
21          Do Until counter >= 10
22              counter += 1 ' increment counter
23
24              If counter = 5 Then
25                  Continue Do ' skip to next iteration of loop if counter = 5
26              End If
27
28              Console.Write(counter & " ") ' output counter
29          Loop
30
31          Console.WriteLine(vbCrLf & _
32              "Skipped printing in Do Until...Loop at counter = 5" & vbCrLf)
33          counter = 0 ' reset counter
34
35          ' skipping an iteration of a While statement
36          While counter < 10
37              counter += 1 ' increment counter
38
39              If counter = 5 Then
40                  Continue While ' skip to next iteration of loop if counter = 5
41              End If
42
43              Console.Write(counter & " ") ' output counter
44          End While
45
46          Console.WriteLine( _
47              vbCrLf & "Skipped printing in While at counter = 5")
48      End Sub ' Main
49  End Module ' ContinueTest
```

```
1 2 3 4 6 7 8 9 10
Skipped printing in For...Next at counter = 5

1 2 3 4 6 7 8 9 10
Skipped printing in Do Until...Loop at counter = 5

1 2 3 4 6 7 8 9 10
Skipped printing in While at counter = 5
```

Fig. 6.16 | Continue statement in repetition statements. (Part 2 of 2.)

The header of the For...Next statement (line 8) indicates that the body of the loop is to execute 10 times. During each execution, the If...Then statement (lines 9–11) determines whether the control variable, counter, is equal to 5. If it is not, line 13 displays the current value of counter and the repetition statement continues to iterate. When the value of counter reaches 5, the Continue For statement (line 10) executes, which terminates the current iteration of the loop, causing the display of the current value of counter to be skipped. The control variable is incremented, then the program evaluates the loop-continuation test. The value of counter is now 6, so the For...Next statement continues to loop, eventually printing the values 1–4 and 6–10.

Line 18 sets counter to 0, so that we can loop through the values 1–10 again, this time using a Do Until...Loop statement. Line 21 indicates that the loop is to continue executing until counter is greater than or equal to 10. Line 22 increments counter. The If...Then statement in lines 24–26 tests whether counter is 5. If it is, the Continue Do statement (line 25) executes, causing the display of the variable counter to be skipped. The program then immediately evaluates the loop-termination test (line 21). The value of counter is still 5, which is not greater than or equal to 10, so the loop continues. During the next iteration, the value of counter is incremented to 6, so the loop executes to completion, eventually displaying the values 1–4 and 6–10. We placed the increment at the beginning of the loop (line 22) so that it would not be skipped during the iteration when the Continue statement executes. If we had placed the increment after the If...Then statement, the value of counter would reach 5 and never be incremented in subsequent iterations. The If...Then condition would repeatedly evaluate to true, causing an infinite loop.

Line 33 once again sets counter to 0. The While statement in lines 36–44 executes while counter is less than 10. Once again, the increment appears at the beginning of the loop. When the value of counter is 5, the If...Then statement's condition (line 39) evaluates to true, and the Continue While statement (line 40) executes, terminating the current iteration of the While statement. Note that the While statement also displays only the values 1–4 and 6–10.

The Exit and Continue statements can be used in nested control statements. For instance, Exit For or Continue For can be used in a While statement, as long as the While statement is itself located in a For...Next statement. In such an example, the Exit or Continue statement would be applied to the proper control statement based on the keywords used in the Exit or Continue statement—in this example, the For keyword is used, so the For...Next statement is the control statement whose flow of control will be altered. If there are nested loops of the same type (e.g., a For...Next statement within a For...Next statement), the statement that immediately surrounds the Exit or Continue statement is the one affected.

In Section 6.3, we stated that While could be used in most cases in place of For...Next. The one exception occurs when the increment expression in the While follows a Continue statement. In this case, the increment does not execute before the program evaluates the repetition-continuation condition, so the While does not execute in the same manner as the For...Next.

6.10 **Logical Operators**

So far, we have studied only simple conditions, such as count <= 10, total > 1000 and number <> sentinelValue. Each selection and repetition statement evaluated only one condition with one of the operators >, <, >=, <=, = and <>. To make a decision that relied on the evaluation of multiple conditions, we performed these tests in separate statements or in nested If...Then or If...Then...Else statements.

To handle multiple conditions more efficiently, Visual Basic provides logical operators that can be used to form complex conditions by combining simple ones. The logical operators are And, Or, AndAlso, OrElse, Xor and Not. We consider examples that use each of these operators.

*Logical **And** Operator*

Suppose we wish to ensure that two conditions are *both* true in a program before a certain path of execution is chosen. In such a case, we can use the logical And operator as follows:

```
If gender = "F" And age >= 65 Then
   seniorFemales += 1
End If
```

This If...Then statement contains two simple conditions. The condition gender = "F" determines whether a person is female and the condition age >= 65 determines whether a person is a senior citizen. The two simple conditions are evaluated first, because the precedences of = and >= are both higher than the precedence of And. The If...Then statement then considers the combined condition

```
gender = "F" And age >= 65
```

This condition evaluates to true if and only if *both* simple conditions are true. When this combined condition is true, the seniorFemales count is incremented by 1. However, if either or both of the simple conditions are false, the program skips the increment and proceeds to the statement following the If...Then statement. The readability of the preceding combined condition can be improved by adding redundant (i.e., unnecessary) parentheses:

```
(gender = "F") And (age >= 65)
```

Figure 6.17 illustrates the effect of using the And operator with two expressions. The table lists all four possible combinations of true and false values for *expression1* and *expression2*. Such tables often are called **truth tables**. Visual Basic evaluates to true or false expressions that include relational operators, equality operators and logical operators.

Logical *Or* Operator

Now let us consider the **Or** operator. Suppose we wish to ensure that either *or* both of two conditions are true before we choose a certain path of execution. We use the Or operator as in the following program segment:

```
If (semesterAverage >= 90 Or finalExam >= 90) Then
   Console.WriteLine("Student grade is A")
End If
```

This statement also contains two simple conditions. The condition semesterAverage >= 90 is evaluated to determine whether the student deserves an "A" in the course because of an outstanding performance throughout the semester. The condition finalExam >= 90 is evaluated to determine whether the student deserves an "A" in the course because of an outstanding performance on the final exam. The If...Then statement then considers the combined condition

```
(semesterAverage >= 90 Or finalExam >= 90)
```

expression1	expression2	expression1 And expression2
False	False	False
False	True	False
True	False	False
True	True	True

Fig. 6.17 | Truth table for the logical And operator.

and awards the student an "A" if either or both of the conditions are true. Note that the text "Student grade is A" is *always* printed, unless both of the conditions are false. Figure 6.18 provides a truth table for the Or operator. The And operator has a higher precedence than the Or operator.

Logical AndAlso and OrElse Operators

The **logical AND operator with short-circuit evaluation** (**AndAlso**) and the **logical inclusive OR operator with short-circuit evaluation** (**OrElse**) are similar to the And and Or operators, respectively, with one exception—an expression containing AndAlso or OrElse operators is evaluated only until its truth or falsity is known. For example, evaluation of the expression

```
(gender = "F" AndAlso age >= 65)
```

stops immediately if gender is not equal to "F" (i.e., the entire expression is false); the evaluation of the second expression is irrelevant because the first condition is false. Evaluation of the second condition occurs if and only if gender is equal to "F" (i.e., the entire expression could still be true if the condition age >= 65 is true). This performance feature for the evaluation of AndAlso and OrElse expressions is called **short-circuit evaluation**.

> **Performance Tip 6.2**
>
> *In expressions using operator AndAlso, if the separate conditions are independent of one another, place the condition most likely to be false as the leftmost condition. In expressions using operator OrElse, make the condition most likely to be true the leftmost condition. Each of these suggestions can reduce a program's execution time.*

Normally, the AndAlso and OrElse operators can be used in place of And and Or. An exception to this rule occurs when the right operand of a condition produces a **side effect** such as a modification of a variable's value or a required method call, as in the following program segment:

```
Console.WriteLine("How old are you?")
If (gender = "F" And Console.ReadLine() >= 65) Then
    Console.WriteLine("You are a female senior citizen.")
End If
```

Here, the And operator guarantees that the condition Console.ReadLine() >= 65 is evaluated, so ReadLine is called regardless of whether the overall expression is true or false. If operator AndAlso had been used, the call to Console.ReadLine might not be evaluated. It is better to write this code as two separate statements—a first that stores the result of

expression1	expression2	expression1 Or expression2
False	False	False
False	True	True
True	False	True
True	True	True

Fig. 6.18 | Truth table for the logical Or operator.

`Console.ReadLine()` in a variable, and a second that uses the variable with either the operator `AndAlso` or the operator `And` in the condition.

Error-Prevention Tip 6.8

Avoid expressions with side effects in conditions, because side effects often cause subtle errors.

*Logical **Xor** Operator*

A condition containing the **logical exclusive OR** (`Xor`) operator is true if and only if one of its operands results in a true value and the other results in a false value. If both operands are true or both are false, the entire condition is false. Figure 6.19 presents a truth table for the logical exclusive OR operator (`Xor`). This operator always evaluates both of its operands (i.e., there is no short-circuit evaluation).

*Logical **Not** Operator*

The `Not` (logical negation) operator enables a programmer to "reverse" the meaning of a condition. Unlike the logical operators `And`, `AndAlso`, `Or`, `OrElse` and `Xor`, which each combine two conditions (i.e., these are all binary operators), the logical negation operator is a unary operator, requiring only one operand. The logical negation operator is placed before a condition to choose a path of execution if the original condition (without the logical negation operator) is false. The logical negation operator is demonstrated by the following program segment:

```
If Not (grade = sentinelValue) Then
    Console.WriteLine("The next grade is " & grade)
End If
```

The parentheses around the condition `grade = sentinelValue` are necessary because the logical negation operator (`Not`) has a higher precedence than the equality operator. Figure 6.20 provides a truth table for the logical negation operator.

expression1	expression2	expression1 Xor expression2
False	False	False
False	True	True
True	False	True
True	True	False

Fig. 6.19 | Truth table for the logical exclusive OR (`Xor`) operator.

expression	Not expression
False	True
True	False

Fig. 6.20 | Truth table for operator `Not` (logical negation).

In most cases, you can avoid using logical negation by expressing the condition differently with relational or equality operators. For example, the preceding statement can be written as follows:

```
If grade <> sentinelValue Then
    Console.WriteLine("The next grade is " & grade)
End If
```

This flexibility helps you express conditions more naturally.

Logical Operators Example

The application in Fig. 6.21 demonstrates the use of the logical operators by displaying their truth tables.

```
1   ' Fig. 6.21: LogicalOperators.vb
2   ' Using logical operators.
3   Module LogicalOperators
4      Sub Main()
5         ' display truth table for And
6         Console.WriteLine("And" & vbCrLf & _
7            "False And False: " & (False And False) & vbCrLf & _
8            "False And True: " & (False And True) & vbCrLf & _
9            "True And False: " & (True And False) & vbCrLf & _
10           "True And True: " & (True And True) & vbCrLf)
11
12        ' display truth table for Or
13        Console.WriteLine("Or" & vbCrLf & _
14           "False Or False: " & (False Or False) & vbCrLf & _
15           "False Or True: " & (False Or True) & vbCrLf & _
16           "True Or False: " & (True Or False) & vbCrLf & _
17           "True Or True: " & (True Or True) & vbCrLf)
18
19        ' display truth table for AndAlso
20        Console.WriteLine("AndAlso" & vbCrLf & _
21           "False AndAlso False: " & (False AndAlso False) & vbCrLf & _
22           "False AndAlso True: " & (False AndAlso True) & vbCrLf & _
23           "True AndAlso False: " & (True AndAlso False) & vbCrLf & _
24           "True AndAlso True: " & (True AndAlso True) & vbCrLf)
25
26        ' display truth table for OrElse
27        Console.WriteLine("OrElse" & vbCrLf & _
28           "False OrElse False: " & (False OrElse False) & vbCrLf & _
29           "False OrElse True: " & (False OrElse True) & vbCrLf & _
30           "True OrElse False: " & (True OrElse False) & vbCrLf & _
31           "True OrElse True: " & (True OrElse True) & vbCrLf)
32
33        ' display truth table for Xor
34        Console.WriteLine("Xor" & vbCrLf & _
35           "False Xor False: " & (False Xor False) & vbCrLf & _
36           "False Xor True: " & (False Xor True) & vbCrLf & _
37           "True Xor False: " & (True Xor False) & vbCrLf & _
38           "True Xor True: " & (True Xor True) & vbCrLf)
```

Fig. 6.21 | Logical operator truth tables. (Part 1 of 2.)

```
39
40            ' display truth table for Not
41          Console.WriteLine("Not" & vbCrLf & "Not False: " & _
42              (Not False) & vbCrLf & "Not True: " & (Not True) & vbCrLf)
43       End Sub ' Main
44    End Module ' LogicalOperators
```

```
And
False And False: False
False And True: False
True And False: False
True And True: True

Or
False Or False: False
False Or True: True
True Or False: True
True Or True: True

AndAlso
False AndAlso False: False
False AndAlso True: False
True AndAlso False: False
True AndAlso True: True

OrElse
False OrElse False: False
False OrElse True: True
True OrElse False: True
True OrElse True: True

Xor
False Xor False: False
False Xor True: True
True Xor False: True
True Xor True: False

Not
Not False: True
Not True: False
```

Fig. 6.21 | Logical operator truth tables. (Part 2 of 2.)

Lines 6–10 demonstrate operator And; lines 13–17 demonstrate operator Or. The remainder of method Main demonstrates the AndAlso, OrElse, Xor and Not operators. We use keywords **True** and **False** in the program to specify values of the Boolean type. Note that when a Boolean value is concatenated to a String, Visual Basic concatenates the string "False" or "True" based on the Boolean's value.

Summary of Operator Precedence
The chart in Fig. 6.22 displays the precedence of the operators introduced so far. The operators are shown from top to bottom in decreasing order of precedence.

Operators	Type
^	exponentiation
+ -	unary plus and minus
* /	multiplicative operators
\	integer division
Mod	modulus
+ -	additive operators
&	concatenation
< <= > >= = <>	relational and equality
Not	logical NOT
And AndAlso	logical AND
Or OrElse	logical inclusive OR
Xor	logical exclusive OR
= += -= *= /= \= ^= &=	assignment

Fig. 6.22 | Precedence of the operators discussed so far.

6.11 (Optional) Software Engineering Case Study: Identifying Objects' States and Activities in the ATM System

In Section 5.16, we identified many of the class attributes needed to implement the ATM system and added them to a class diagram (Fig. 5.32). In this section, we show how these attributes represent an object's state. We identify some key states that our objects may occupy and discuss how objects change state in response to various events occurring in the system. We also discuss the workflow, or *activities*, that objects perform in the ATM system. We present the activities of the BalanceInquiry and Withdrawal transaction objects.

State Machine Diagrams

Each object in a system goes through a series of discrete states. An object's current state is indicated by the values of the object's attributes at that time. State machine diagrams model key states of an object and show under what circumstances the object changes state. Unlike the class diagrams presented in earlier case study sections, which focused primarily on the system's structure, state machine diagrams model some of the system's behavior.

Figure 6.23 is a simple state machine diagram that models some of the states of an ATM object. The UML represents each state in a state machine diagram as a rounded rectangle with the name of the state placed inside it. A solid circle with an attached stick arrowhead designates the initial state. Recall that we modeled this state information as the Boolean attribute userAuthenticated in the class diagram of Fig. 5.32. This attribute is initialized to False, or the "User not authenticated" state, according to the state machine diagram.

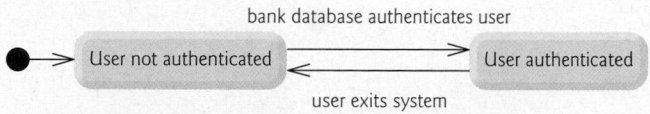

Fig. 6.23 | State machine diagram for some of the states of the ATM object.

The arrows with stick arrowheads indicate **transitions** between states. An object can transition from one state to another in response to various events that occur in the system. The name or description of the event that causes a transition is written near the line that corresponds to the transition. For example, the ATM object changes from the "User not authenticated" state to the "User authenticated" state after the bank database authenticates the user. Recall from the requirements document that the database authenticates a user by comparing the account number and PIN entered by the user with those of the corresponding account in the database. If the database indicates that the user has entered a valid account number and the correct PIN, the ATM object transitions to the "User authenticated" state and changes its userAuthenticated attribute to a value of True. When the user exits the system by choosing the **Exit** option from the main menu, the ATM object returns to the "User not authenticated" state in preparation for the next ATM user.

Software Engineering Observation 6.1

Software designers do not generally create state machine diagrams showing every possible state and state transition for all attributes—there are simply too many of them. State machine diagrams typically show only the most important or complex states and state transitions.

Activity Diagrams

Like a state machine diagram, an activity diagram models aspects of system behavior. Unlike a state machine diagram, an activity diagram models an object's workflow (sequence of events) during program execution. An activity diagram models the actions the object will perform and in what order. Recall that we used UML activity diagrams to illustrate the flow of control for the control statements presented in Chapters 5 and 6.

The activity diagram in Fig. 6.24 models the actions involved in executing a Balance-Inquiry transaction. We assume that a BalanceInquiry object has already been initialized and assigned a valid account number (that of the current user), so the object knows which balance to retrieve. The diagram includes the actions that occur after the user selects a balance inquiry from the main menu and before the ATM returns the user to the main menu—a BalanceInquiry object does not perform or initiate these actions, so we do not model them here. The diagram begins with retrieving the available balance of the user's account from the database. Next, the BalanceInquiry retrieves the total balance of the account. Finally, the transaction displays the balances on the screen.

The UML represents an action in an activity diagram as an action state modeled by a rectangle with its left and right sides replaced by arcs curving outward. Each action state contains an action expression—for example, "get available balance of user's account from database"—that specifies an action to be performed. An arrow with a stick arrowhead connects two action states, indicating the order in which the actions represented by the action states occur. The solid circle (at the top of Fig. 6.24) represents the activity's initial state—the beginning of the workflow before the object performs the modeled actions. In this

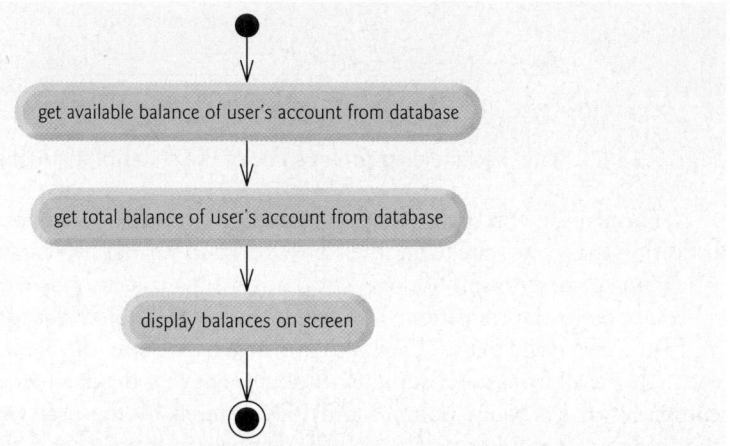

Fig. 6.24 | Activity diagram for a `BalanceInquiry` transaction.

case, the transaction first executes the "get available balance of user's account from database" action expression. Second, the transaction retrieves the total balance. Finally, the transaction displays both balances on the screen. The solid circle enclosed in an open circle (at the bottom of Fig. 6.24) represents the final state—the end of the workflow after the object performs the modeled actions.

Figure 6.25 shows a more complex activity diagram for a `Withdrawal` transaction. We assume that a `Withdrawal` object has been assigned a valid account number. We do not model the user selecting a withdrawal from the main menu or the ATM returning the user to the main menu because these are not actions performed by a `Withdrawal` object. The transaction first displays a menu of standard withdrawal amounts (Fig. 3.37) and an option to cancel the transaction. The transaction then inputs a menu selection from the user. The activity flow now arrives at a decision symbol to determine the next action based on the associated guard conditions. If the user cancels the transaction, the system displays an appropriate message and the cancellation flow reaches a merge symbol (at the bottom of the activity diagram), where this activity flow joins the transaction's other possible activity flows (which we discuss shortly). Note that a merge can have any number of incoming transition arrows, but only one outgoing transition arrow. The decision at the bottom of the diagram determines whether the transaction should repeat from the beginning. When the user has canceled the transaction, the guard condition "cash dispensed or user canceled transaction" is true, so control transitions to the activity's final state.

If the user selects a withdrawal amount from the menu, `amount` (an attribute of class `Withdrawal` originally modeled in Fig. 5.32) is set to the value chosen by the user. The transaction next gets the available balance of the user's account (i.e., the `availableBalance` attribute of the user's `Account` object) from the database. The activity flow then arrives at another decision. If the requested withdrawal amount exceeds the user's available balance, the system displays an error message informing the user of the problem. Control then merges with the other activity flows before reaching the decision at the bottom of the diagram. The guard decision "cash not dispensed and user did not cancel" is true, so the activity flow returns to the top of the diagram, and the transaction prompts the user to input a new amount.

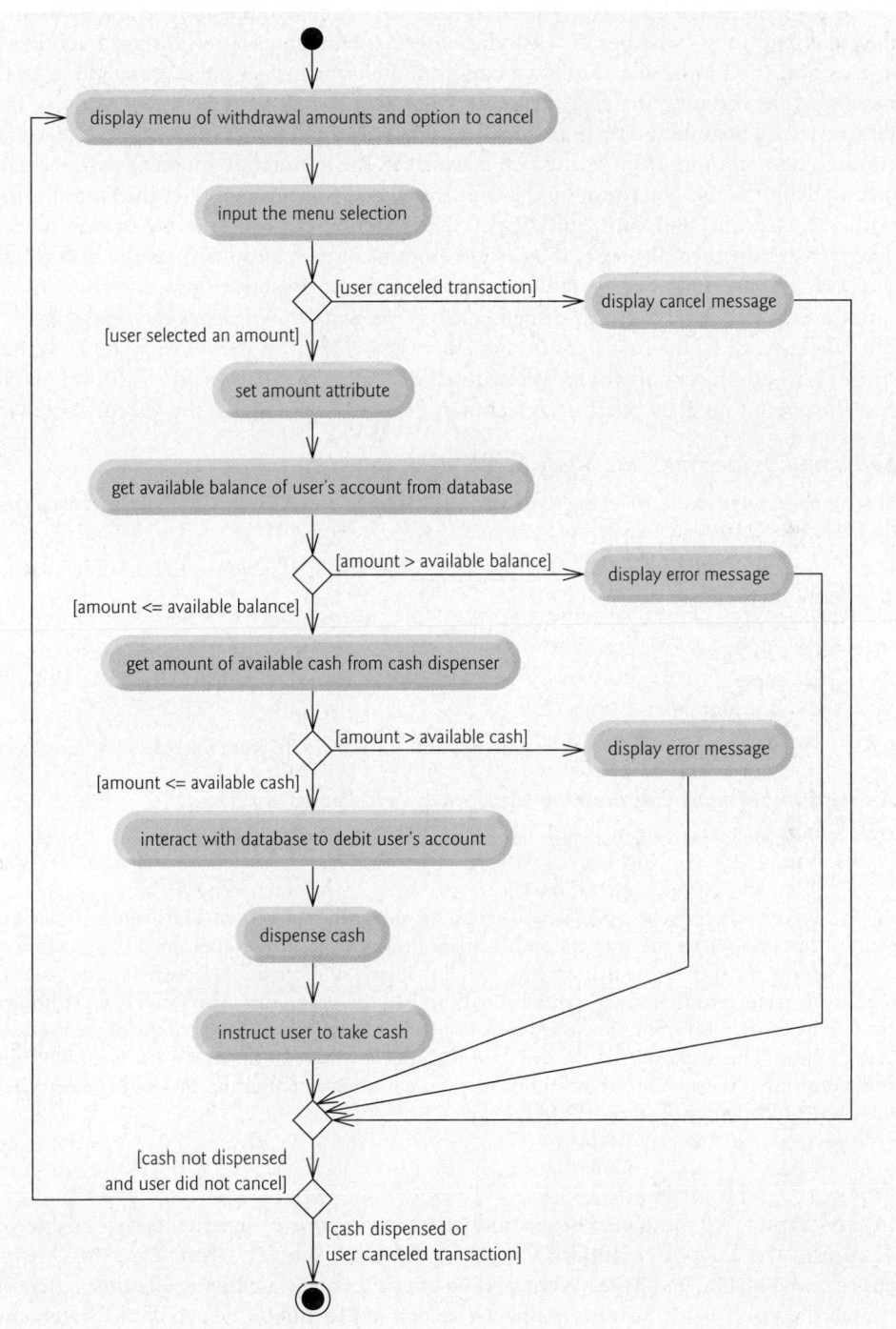

Fig. 6.25 | Activity diagram for a `Withdrawal` transaction.

If the requested withdrawal amount is less than or equal to the user's available balance, the transaction tests whether the cash dispenser has enough cash to satisfy the request. If it does not, the transaction displays an appropriate error message and passes through the merge before reaching the final decision. Cash was not dispensed, so the activity flow returns to the beginning of the activity diagram, and the transaction prompts the user to choose a new amount. If sufficient cash is available, the transaction interacts with the database to debit the user's account by the withdrawal amount (i.e., subtract the amount from both the availableBalance and totalBalance attributes of the user's Account object). The transaction then dispenses the desired amount of cash and instructs the user to take the cash. The main flow of activity next merges with the two error flows and the cancellation flow. In this case, cash was dispensed, so the activity flow reaches the final state.

We have taken the first steps in modeling the behavior of the ATM system and have shown how an object's attributes affect the object's activities. In Section 7.20, we investigate the operations of our classes to create a more complete model of the system's behavior.

Software Engineering Case Study Self-Review Exercises

6.1 State whether the following statement is *true* or *false*, and if *false*, explain why: State machine diagrams model structural aspects of a system.

6.2 An activity diagram models the _____ that an object performs and the order in which it performs them.
   a) actions
   b) attributes
   c) states
   d) state transitions

6.3 Based on the requirements document, create an activity diagram for a deposit transaction.

Answers to Software Engineering Case Study Self-Review Exercises

6.1 False. State machine diagrams model some of the behavior of a system.

6.2 a.

6.3 Figure 6.26 presents an activity diagram for a deposit transaction. The diagram models the actions that occur after the user chooses the deposit option from the main menu and before the ATM returns the user to the main menu. Recall that part of receiving a deposit amount from the user involves converting an integer number of cents to a dollar amount. Also recall that crediting an account by the deposit amount involves increasing only the totalBalance attribute of the user's Account object. The bank updates the availableBalance attribute of the user's Account object only after confirming the amount of cash in the deposit envelope and after the enclosed checks clear—this occurs independently of the ATM system.

6.12 Wrap-Up

In this chapter, we completed our introduction to the control statements that enable you to control the flow of execution. Chapter 5 discussed the If...Then, If...Then...Else, While...End While, Do While...Loop and Do Until...Loop statements. Chapter 6 demonstrated the For...Next, Select...Case, Do...Loop While and Do...Loop Until statements. We have shown that any algorithm can be developed using combinations of the sequence structure (i.e., statements listed in the order in which they are to execute), the three types of selection statements—If...Then, If...Then...Else and Select...Case—and the seven

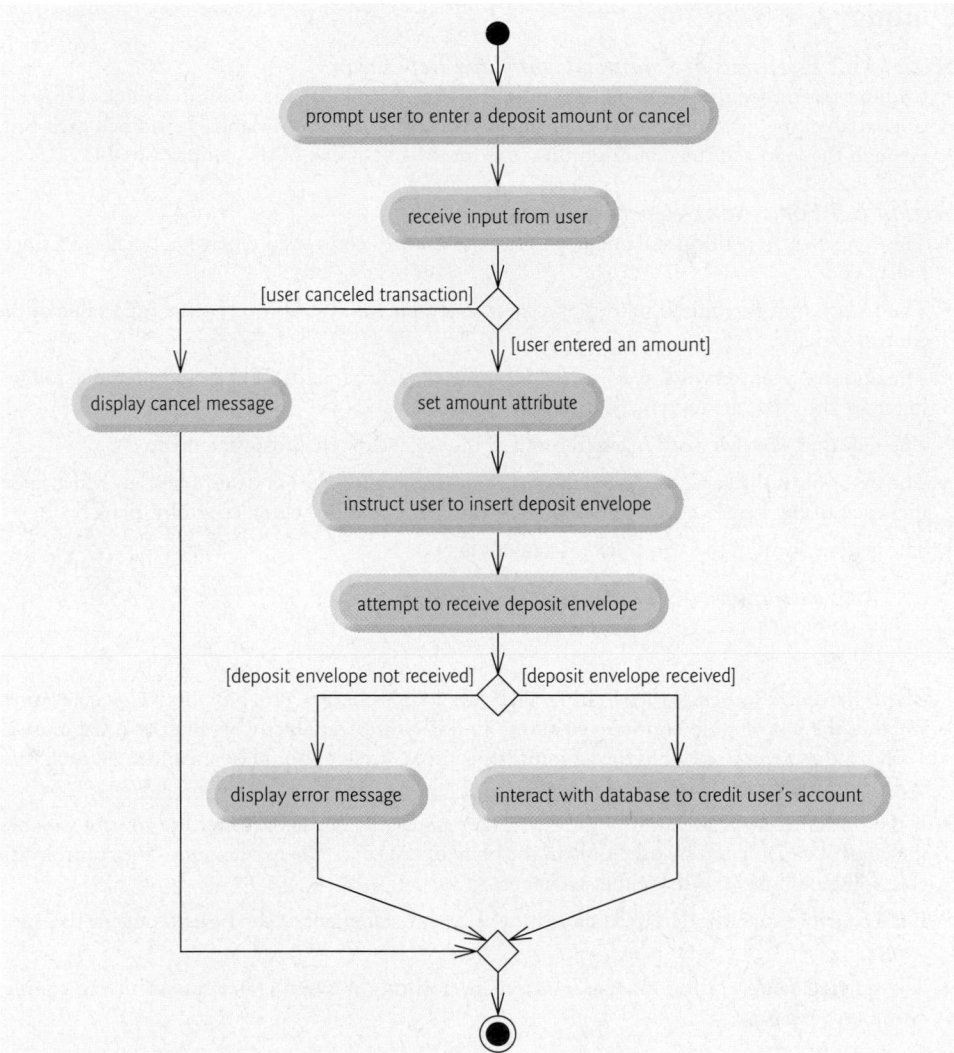

Fig. 6.26 | Activity diagram for a `Deposit` transaction.

types of repetition statements—While...End While, Do While...Loop, Do Until...Loop, Do...Loop While, Do...Loop Until, For...Next and For Each...Next (which we discuss in Chapter 8). In Chapters 5 and 6, we discussed how you can combine these building blocks to utilize proven program-construction and problem-solving techniques. We demonstrated how to alter the flow of program control using the various Exit and Continue statements. We introduced the logical operators, which enable you to use more complex conditional expressions in control statements. In Chapter 7, we examine methods in greater depth. So far you have learned how to create methods in classes, and a Main method in a module. Chapter 7 introduces the different types of methods, including how and when to use each of them. You will learn how to use methods to organize a complex object-oriented program into small, manageable pieces.

Summary

Section 6.2 Essentials of Counter-Controlled Repetition

- Counter-controlled repetition requires the name of a control variable, the initial value of the control variable, the increment (or decrement) by which the control variable is modified each time through the loop and the condition that tests for the final value of the control variable.

Section 6.3 For...Next Repetition Statement

- The For...Next repetition statement specifies the counter-controlled repetition details in a single line of code.

- The To keyword is required in the For...Next statement and is followed by the final value of the control variable.

- The optional Step keyword specifies the increment (or decrement). If Step and the value following it are omitted, the increment defaults to 1.

- The required Next keyword marks the end of the For...Next repetition statement.

- The first line of the For...Next statement sometimes is called the For...Next header, which specifies each of the items needed for counter-controlled repetition with a control variable.

- The general form of the For...Next statement is

  ```
  For initialization To finalValue Step increment
     statement
  Next
  ```

  where the *initialization* expression initializes the loop's control variable, *finalValue* determines whether the loop should continue executing (if the control variable is less than or equal to *finalValue*) and *increment* specifies the amount the control variable should be incremented each time through the loop.

- If the *initialization* expression in the For...Next statement header declares the control variable, the control variable can be used only in the body of the For...Next statement—the control variable will be unknown outside the statement.

- If the control variable is declared before the For...Next statement, it can be used outside the statement.

- The starting value, ending value and increment portions of a For...Next statement can contain arithmetic expressions.

Section 6.4 Examples Using the For...Next Statement

- Method MessageBox.Show can be used to specify a message to be displayed in a message dialog, as well as the icon and button(s) displayed in the dialog.

- The buttons to be displayed in a message dialog are specified using the MessageBoxButtons constants.

- The icon to be displayed in a message dialog is specified using the MessageBoxIcon constants.

- Type Decimal is used for monetary calculations.

- Using floating-point types, such as Single or Double, to represent dollar amounts (assuming that dollar amounts are displayed with two digits to the right of the decimal point) can cause errors.

- Method Format of class String takes a formatted string and the values to be formatted as arguments, and returns the resulting text with the formatting applied.

- The C (for "currency") format specifier indicates that its corresponding value should be displayed in monetary format.

Section 6.5 *Select...Case Multiple-Selection Statement*

- Occasionally, an algorithm contains a series of decisions in which the algorithm tests a variable or expression separately for each value that the variable or expression might assume. The algorithm then takes different actions based on those values. The Select...Case multiple-selection statement handles such decision making.

- The expression following the keywords Select Case is called the controlling expression. The controlling expression is compared sequentially with each Case. If a matching Case is found, the code in the Case executes, then program control proceeds to the first statement after the Select...Case statement.

- A Case statement can use the To keyword to specify a range of values to be compared.

- If no match occurs between the controlling expression's value and a Case label, the optional Case Else executes. Case Else commonly is used to deal with invalid input. When employed, the Case Else must be the last Case.

- The required End Select keywords terminate the Select...Case statement.

- Case statements also can use relational operators to determine whether the controlling expression satisfies a condition. For example

      Case Is < 0

  uses keyword Is along with the relational operator, <, to test for values less than 0.

- Methods declared Private can be called only by other members of the same class. Such Private methods are commonly referred to as utility methods or helper methods because they are used to support the operation of those members.

- The With statement allows you to access an object's members in a block of code without specifying the name of the object before the dot separator. Programmers often employ the With statement when there are many references to an object's members in a relatively small region of code.

Section 6.6 *Do...Loop While Repetition Statement*

- The Do...Loop While statement tests the loop-continuation condition *after* the loop body is performed; therefore, in a Do...Loop While statement, the loop body is always executed at least once.

Section 6.7 *Do...Loop Until Repetition Statement*

- The Do...Loop Until repetition statement is similar to the Do Until...Loop statement, except that the loop-termination condition is tested after the loop body is performed; therefore, the loop body executes at least once.

Section 6.8 *Using the Exit Statement in Repetition Statements*

- The Exit Do statement can be executed in a Do While...Loop, Do...Loop While, Do Until...Loop or Do...Loop Until statement, to cause the program to exit immediately from that repetition statement.

- The Exit For and Exit While statements cause immediate exit from For...Next and While...End While loops, respectively.

Section 6.9 *Using the Continue Statement in Repetition Statements*

- The Continue statement skips the remaining statements in the loop body of a repetition statement and causes control to proceed to the next iteration of the loop.

- The Continue Do statement can be executed in a Do While...Loop, Do...Loop While, Do Until...Loop or Do...Loop Until statement, to cause the program to skip the remainder of the current iteration of that repetition statement.

- The Continue For and Continue While statements cause the program to skip the remainder of the current iteration of For...Next and While...End While loops, respectively.

- Unlike the Exit statement, the Continue statement is used to alter program control only in repetition statements.

- When Continue For is encountered in a For...Next statement, execution continues with the statement's increment expression, then the program evaluates the loop-continuation test. When Continue is used in other repetition statements, the program evaluates the loop-continuation (or loop-termination) test immediately after the Continue statement executes. If a control variable's increment occurs in the loop after the Continue statement, the increment is skipped.

- The Exit and Continue statements can be used in nested control statements. For instance, Exit For or Continue For can be used in a While statement, as long as the While statement is itself located in a For...Next statement.

Section 6.10 Logical Operators

- To handle multiple conditions, Visual Basic provides logical operators that can be used to form complex conditions by combining simple ones.

- The logical And operator can be used to ensure that two conditions are *both* true in a program before a certain path of execution is chosen. The complex condition evaluates to true *if and only if* both of the simple conditions are true.

- The logical Or operator can be used to ensure that either *or* both of two conditions are true before we choose a certain path of execution. The complex condition evaluates to true except when both of the conditions are false.

- The And operator has a higher precedence than the Or operator.

- The operators AndAlso and OrElse are similar to the And and Or operators, with one exception— an expression containing AndAlso or OrElse operators is evaluated only until its truth or falsity is known. Evaluation of the second condition occurs only as necessary to determine the final result of the expression—this performance feature is called short-circuit evaluation.

- Normally, the AndAlso and OrElse operators can be used in place of And and Or. An exception to this rule occurs when the right operand of a condition produces a side effect (such as a modification of a variable's value) or a required method call.

- A condition containing the logical exclusive OR (Xor) operator is true if and only if one of its operands results in a true value and the other results in a false value. If both operands are true or both are false, the entire condition is false.

- The Not operator enables a programmer to "reverse" the meaning of a condition.

Terminology

And operator	Decimal primitive type
AndAlso operator	decrement of a control variable
C format specifier	Do...Loop Until repetition statement
Case Else statement	Do...Loop While repetition statement
Case statement	Exit Do statement
Continue Do statement	Exit For statement
Continue For statement	Exit Property statement
Continue statement	Exit Select statement
Continue While statement	Exit statement
control variable name	Exit While statement
controlling expression of a Select...Case	False keyword

final state

final value of a control variable

For...Next header

For...Next repetition statement

Format method of class String

helper method

increment of a control variable

initial value of a control variable

Is keyword

logical operator

MessageBoxButtons constants

MessageBoxIcon constants

name of a control variable

Not operator

Or operator

OrElse operator

scope

Select...Case multiple-selection statement

short-circuit evaluation

side effect

simple condition

Step keyword

To keyword

True keyword

truth table

utility method

With statement

With statement block

Xor (exclusive OR) operator

Self-Review Exercises

6.1   State whether each of the following is *true* or *false*. If *false*, explain why.

    a) The Case Else is required in the Select...Case selection statement.

    b) The expression x > y And a < b is true if either x > y is true or a < b is true.

    c) An expression containing the Or operator is true if either or both of its operands is true.

    d) The expression x <= y AndAlso y > 4 is true if x is less than or equal to y and y is greater than 4.

    e) Logical operator Or performs short-circuit evaluation.

    f) A While...End While statement with the header

```
While (x > 10 And x < 100)
```

    iterates while 10 < x < 100.

    g) The Exit Do, Exit For and Exit While statements, when executed in a repetition statement, cause immediate exit from the current iteration of the repetition statement.

    h) The Do...Loop While statement tests the loop-continuation condition before the loop body is performed.

    i) The Or operator has a higher precedence than the And operator.

6.2   Fill in the blanks in each of the following statements:

    a) Keyword _____ is optional in a For...Next header when the control variable's increment is one.

    b) Monetary values should be stored in variables of type _____.

    c) A Case that handles all values greater than a specified value must precede the > operator with the _____ keyword.

    d) In a For...Next statement, incrementing occurs _____ the body of the statement is performed.

    e) Placing expressions whose values do not change inside _____ statements can lead to poor performance.

    f) In a Do...Loop While repetition statement, the body of the loop is executed _____.

    g) The expression following the keywords Select Case is called the _____.

6.3   Write a statement or a set of statements to accomplish each of the following:

    a) Sum the odd integers between 1 and 99 using a For...Next statement. Assume that the Integer variables sum and count have been declared.

b) Write a statement that exits a `While` loop.
c) Print the integers from 1 to 20, using a `Do...Loop While` loop and the counter variable x. Assume that the variable x has been declared but not initialized. Print only five integers per line. [*Hint:* Use the calculation x Mod 5. When the value of this is 0, print a carriage return; otherwise, print a tab character. Call `Console.WriteLine` to output the carriage return and call `Console.Write(vbTab)` to output the tab character.]
d) Repeat part c, using a `For...Next` statement.

Answers to Self-Review Exercises

6.1 a) False. The `Case Else` is optional. b) False. Both of the simple conditions must be true for the entire expression to be true. c) True. d) True. e) False. Logical operator `Or` always evaluates both of its operands. f) True. g) False. The `Exit Do`, `Exit For` and `Exit While` statements, when executed in a repetition statement, cause immediate exit from the repetition statement. The `Continue Do`, `Continue For` and `Continue While` statements, when executed in a repetition statement, cause immediate exit from the current iteration of the repetition statement. h) False. The `Do...Loop While` statement tests the loop-continuation condition after the loop body is performed. i) False. The `And` operator has higher precedence than the `Or` operator.

6.2 a) `Step`. b) `Decimal`. c) `Is`. d) after. e) repetition. f) at least once. g) controlling expression.

6.3 a) `sum = 0`

```
For count = 1 To 99 Step 2
    sum += count
Next
```

b) `Exit While`
c) `x = 1`

```
Do
    Console.Write(x)

    If x Mod 5 = 0 Then
        Console.WriteLine()
    Else
        Console.Write(vbTab)
    End If

    x += 1
Loop While x <= 20
```

or

```
x = 1

Do
    If x Mod 5 = 0 Then
        Console.WriteLine(x)
    Else
        Console.Write(x & vbTab)
    End If

    x += 1
Loop While x <= 20
```

```
d) For x = 1 To 20

       Console.Write(x)

       If x Mod 5 = 0 Then
          Console.WriteLine()
       Else
          Console.Write(vbTab)
       End If
    Next
```

or

```
    For x = 1 To 20
       If x Mod 5 = 0 Then
          Console.WriteLine(x)
       Else
          Console.Write(x & vbTab)
       End If
    Next
```

Exercises

6.4 A mail-order house sells five products whose retail prices are as follows: Product 1, $2.98; product 2, $4.50; product 3, $9.98; product 4, $4.49 and product 5, $6.87. Write an application that reads a series of pairs of numbers as follows:

   a) product number;
   b) quantity sold.

Your program should use a Select...Case statement to determine the retail price for each product. It should calculate and display the total retail value of all products sold. Use a sentinel-controlled loop to determine when the program should stop looping and display the final results.

6.5 Modify the compound-interest application of Fig. 6.8 to repeat its steps for interest rates of 5, 6, 7, 8, 9 and 10%. Use a For...Next loop to vary the interest rate. Display a MessageBox for each interest rate value.

6.6 Modify the application in Fig. 6.8 to use only integers to calculate the compound interest. [*Hint:* Treat all monetary amounts as integral numbers of pennies. Then "break" the result into its dollar portion and cents portion by using the division and modulus operators, respectively. Insert a period between the dollar and cents portions.]

6.7 The *factorial* method is used frequently in probability problems. The factorial of a positive integer n (written $n!$ and pronounced "n factorial") is equal to the product of the positive integers from 1 to n. Even for relatively small values of n, the factorial method yields extremely large numbers. For instance, when n is 13, $n!$ is 6227020800—a number too large to be represented with type Integer (a 32-bit integer value). To calculate the factorials of large values of n, type Long (a 64-bit integer value) must be used. Write a program that evaluates the factorials of the integers from 1 to 20 using type Long. Display the results in a two column output table. [*Hint:* Create a Windows application, use Labels as the columns and the vbCrLf constant to line up the rows. Create an event handler as you did in Section 5.15 to append text to the Label's Text properties. To make the output clearer, set each Label's BorderStyle property to Fixed3D.] The first column should display the n values (1–20). The second column should display $n!$.

6.8 Write a program that prints a table of the binary, octal, and hexadecimal equivalents of the decimal numbers in the range 1–256. If you are not familiar with these number systems, read Appendix B, Number Systems, first.

6.9 (*Pythagorean Triples*) Some right triangles have sides that are all integers. A set of three integer values for the sides of a right triangle is called a Pythagorean triple. These three sides must satisfy the relationship that the sum of the squares of the two sides is equal to the square of the hypotenuse. Write a program to find all Pythagorean triples for side1, side2 and hypotenuse, none larger than 30. Use a triple-nested For...Next loop that tries all possibilities. This is an example of "brute force" computing.

6.10 Write a program that displays the following patterns separately, one below the other. Use For...Next loops to generate the patterns. All asterisks (*) should be printed by a single statement of the form Console.Write("*") (this causes the asterisks to print side by side). A statement of the form Console.WriteLine() can be used to position to the next line, and a statement of the form Console.WriteLine(" ") can be used to display spaces for the last two patterns. There should be no other output statements in the program. [*Hint:* The last two patterns require that each line begin with an appropriate number of blanks.] Maximize your use of repetition (with nested For...Next statements) and minimize the number of output statements.

```
(a)                    (b)                    (c)                    (d)
*                      **********             **********                      *
**                     *********              *********                      **
***                    ********               ********                      ***
****                   *******                *******                      ****
*****                  ******                 ******                      *****
******                 *****                  *****                      ******
*******                ****                   ****                      *******
********               ***                    ***                      ********
*********              **                     **                      *********
**********             *                       *                     **********
```

6.11 Modify Exercise 6.10 to combine your code from the four separate triangles of asterisks into a single program that prints all four patterns side by side, making clever use of nested For...Next loops.

6.12 Write a program that prints the following diamond shape. You may use output statements that print a single asterisk (*), a single space or a single carriage return. Maximize your use of repetition (with nested For...Next statements) and minimize the number of output statements.

```
    *
   ***
  *****
 *******
*********
 *******
  *****
   ***
    *
```

6.13 Modify the program you wrote in Exercise 6.12 to read an odd number in the range from 1 to 19 to specify the number of rows in the diamond. Your program should then display a diamond of the appropriate size. Use a Do...Loop Until statement to validate user input.

7

Methods: A Deeper Look

The greatest invention of the nineteenth century was the invention of the method of invention.
—Alfred North Whitehead

Form ever follows function.
—Louis Henri Sullivan

Call me Ishmael.
—Herman Melville, *Moby Dick*

When you call me that, smile!
—Owen Wister

O! call back yesterday, bid time return.
—William Shakespeare

Answer me in one word.
—William Shakespeare

There is a point at which methods devour themselves.
—Frantz Fanon

OBJECTIVES

In this chapter you will learn:

- To construct programs modularly from methods.

- That **Shared** methods are associated with a class rather than a specific instance of the class.

- To use common **Math** methods from the Framework Class Library.

- To create new methods.

- The mechanisms used to pass information between methods.

- Simulation techniques that employ random number generation.

- How the visibility of identifiers is limited to specific regions of programs.

- To write and use recursive methods (methods that call themselves).

7.1 Introduction

Most computer programs that solve real-world problems are much larger than the programs presented in the first few chapters of this book. Experience has shown that the best way to develop and maintain a large program is to construct it from small, simple pieces. This technique is called **divide and conquer**. We introduced methods in Chapter 3. In this chapter, we study methods in greater depth. We emphasize how to declare and use methods to facilitate the design, implementation, operation and maintenance of large programs.

You will see that it is possible for certain methods, called Shared methods, to be called without the need for an object of the class to exist. You will learn how to declare a method with more than one parameter. You will also learn how Visual Basic keeps track of which method is currently executing, how local variables of methods are maintained in memory and how a method knows where to return after it finishes executing.

We will take a brief diversion into simulation techniques with random-number generation and develop a version of the casino dice game called craps that will use most of the programming techniques you have learned to this point in the book. In addition, we will introduce two techniques for declaring constants in your programs.

You will learn that applications can have more than one method of the same name. This technique, called overloading, is used for convenience and clarity when implementing methods that perform similar tasks using different types or numbers of arguments. In certain situations, you can replace a series of overloaded method declarations with a single "generic" method—we study this powerful code reuse capability in Chapter 25, Generics.

7.2 Modules, Classes and Methods

Programs consist of many pieces, including modules and classes. These modules and classes are composed of smaller pieces called methods. You combine new modules and classes with "prepackaged" classes available in the .NET Framework Class Library (FCL) and in various other class libraries. Related classes are typically grouped into namespaces (and compiled into library files) so that they can be imported into programs and reused. You will learn how to package your own classes into class libraries in Section 9.13. The FCL provides a rich collection of classes and methods for performing common mathematical calculations (Chapter 3), error checking (Chapter 12), building sophisticated GUI applications (Chapters 13 and 14), string and character manipulations (Chapter 16), graphics (Chapter 17), input/output operations (Chapter 18), XML processing (Chapter 19), database manipulations (Chapter 20), creating applications for the Web (Chapter 21 and 22) and many other useful operations. This framework makes your job easier, because the methods provide many of the capabilities you need. In earlier chapters, we introduced some FCL classes, such as `Console`, which provides methods for inputting and outputting data and `MessageBox`, used to display message dialogs.

Software Engineering Observation 7.1

When possible, use .NET Framework classes and methods instead of writing new classes and methods. This reduces program development time and can prevent the introduction of errors.

Performance Tip 7.1

.NET Framework Class Library methods are written to perform efficiently.

You can create your own classes and methods to meet the unique requirements of a particular application. Two types of methods exist: **subroutines** and **functions**. We discuss the differences between subroutines and functions shortly. Throughout this book, the term "method" refers to both subroutines and functions unless otherwise noted.

You write methods to define specific tasks that a program may use one or more times during its execution. Although the same method can be executed from multiple points in a program, the actual statements that define the method are written only once.

Let's briefly review some of the basics of methods. A method is invoked (i.e., made to perform its designated task) by a method call. The method call specifies the method name and provides information (as arguments) that the **callee** (i.e, the method being called) requires to do its job. When the method completes its task, it returns control to the caller (i.e., the calling method). In some cases, the method also returns a result to the caller. A common analogy for this is the hierarchical form of management. A boss (the caller) asks a worker (the callee) to perform a task and return (i.e., report) the results when the task is done. The boss does not need to know how the worker performs the designated task. The worker might call other workers—the boss would be unaware of this. This hiding of implementation details promotes good software engineering. Figure 7.1 depicts a Boss method communicating with worker methods Worker1, Worker2 and Worker3 in a hierarchical manner. Note that Worker1 also acts as a "boss" method to Worker4 and Worker5 in this example.

There are several motivations for dividing code into methods. First, the divide-and-conquer approach makes program development more manageable. Another motivation is software reusability—the ability to use existing methods as building blocks for new programs. When proper naming and definition conventions are applied, programs can be created from standardized pieces that accomplish specific tasks, to minimize the need for customized code. A third motivation is to avoid repeating code in a program—when code is packaged as a method, the code can be executed from various points in a program simply by calling the method.

Software Engineering Observation 7.2

To promote reusability, the capabilities of each method should be limited to the performance of a single, well-defined task, and the name of the method should express that task effectively.

Software Engineering Observation 7.3

If you cannot choose a concise method name that expresses the task performed by a method, the method could be attempting to perform too many diverse tasks. Consider dividing such a method into several smaller methods.

7.3 Subroutines: Methods That Do Not Return a Value

The programs presented earlier in the book each contain at least one method declaration that calls FCL methods (such as Console.WriteLine) to accomplish the program's tasks. All of the methods that you have defined so far, such as DisplayMessage in class Grade-Book, are known as subroutines—methods that perform tasks but do not return a value. Functions are methods that do return a value to the calling method. An example of a function that you have seen is Console.ReadLine, which returns to the caller the data entered by the user at the keyboard. We show how to declare functions in Section 7.4.

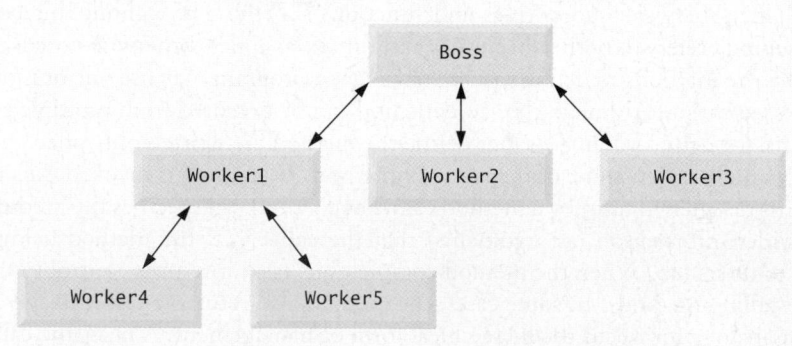

Fig. 7.1 | Hierarchical boss-method/worker-method relationship.

Consider the console application in Fig. 7.2, which uses a subroutine (invoked from the application's Main method) to print a worker's payment information.

The program contains two method declarations. Lines 4–10 define method Main, the subroutine that executes when the console application is loaded. Lines 13–16 define method PrintPay, a subroutine that executes when it is called from method Main.

Main makes four calls (lines 6–9) to subroutine PrintPay, causing PrintPay to execute four times. Although the method arguments in this example are constants, recall that arguments can also be variables or expressions. For example, the statement

```
PrintPay(employeeExtraHours, employeeWage * 1.5)
```

could be used to display payment information for an employee who is being paid time-and-a-half for working overtime—this statement calculates only the overtime portion of the person's pay.

When Main calls PrintPay, the program makes a copy of the value of each argument (e.g., 40 and 10.5 in line 6), and program control transfers to the first line of method PrintPay. Method PrintPay receives the copied values and stores them in the parameters hours and wage. Then PrintPay calculates hours * wage and displays the result, using the currency format (line 15). When the End Sub statement (line 16) is encountered, control is returned to the next statement in the calling method, Main.

The first line of method PrintPay (line 13) shows that PrintPay declares a Double parameter hours and a Decimal parameter wage. These parameters hold the values passed to PrintPay so that they can be accessed within this method. Note that the entire declaration of method PrintPay appears within the body of module Payment.

```
 1   ' Fig. 7.2: Payment.vb
 2   ' Subroutine that prints payment information.
 3   Module Payment
 4      Sub Main()
 5         ' call subroutine PrintPay 4 times
 6         PrintPay(40, 10.5)
 7         PrintPay(38, 21.75)
 8         PrintPay(20, 13)
 9         PrintPay(30, 14)
10      End Sub ' Main
11
12      ' print dollar amount earned in console window
13      Sub PrintPay(ByVal hours As Double, ByVal wage As Decimal)
14         ' pay = hours * wage
15         Console.WriteLine("The payment is {0:C}", hours * wage)
16      End Sub ' PrintPay
17   End Module ' Payment
```

```
The payment is $420.00
The payment is $826.50
The payment is $260.00
The payment is $420.00
```

Fig. 7.2 | Subroutine for printing payment information.

Subroutine Declarations

The format of a subroutine declaration is

```
Sub  method-name(parameter-list)
       declarations and statements
End Sub
```

Subroutines in previous versions of Visual Basic were referred to as **Sub procedures** because of the use of keyword `Sub`. The *parameter-list* is a comma-separated list in which the subroutine declares each parameter variable's type and name. There must be one argument in the method call for each parameter in the method header (we will see an exception to this when we study `Optional` parameters in Section 7.18). The type of each argument must be consistent with its corresponding parameter's type, i.e., Visual Basic must be able to implicitly convert the value of the argument to a value of the parameter's type. For example, a parameter of type `Double` could receive a value of 7.35, 22 or –0.03546, but not `"hello"`, because a `Double` variable cannot contain a `String`. In Section 7.9 we discuss this issue in detail. If a method does not receive any values, the parameter list is empty (i.e., the method name is followed by an empty set of parentheses).

Common Programming Error 7.1

Declaring a variable in the method's body with the same name as a parameter variable in the method header is a compilation error.

Error-Prevention Tip 7.1

Although it is allowable, an argument passed to a method should not have the same name as the corresponding parameter name in the method declaration. This prevents ambiguity that could lead to logic errors.

The declarations and statements in the method declaration form the method body. The method body contains code that performs actions, generally by manipulating or processing the method's parameters. The body of a method declared with `Sub` must be terminated with keywords `End Sub`. The method body is also referred to as a **block**. A block is a group of declarations and executable statements.

Control returns to the next statement in the caller when execution reaches the `End Sub` statement in the called method.

Software Engineering Observation 7.4

Method names tend to be verbs because methods typically perform actions. By convention, method names begin with an uppercase first letter. For example, a method that sends an e-mail message might be named `SendMail`.

Error-Prevention Tip 7.2

Small methods are easier to test, debug and understand than large methods.

Good Programming Practice 7.1

When a parameter is declared without a type, its type is assumed to be `Object`. Explicitly declaring a parameter's type improves program clarity.

7.4 Functions: Methods That Return a Value

Functions (known as **Function** procedures in earlier versions of Visual Basic) are methods that **return a value** to the caller (whereas subroutines do not). The console application in Fig. 7.3 uses the function Square to calculate the squares of the integers from 1–10.

The For...Next statement (lines 8–10) displays the results of squaring the integers from 1–10. Each iteration of the loop calculates and displays the square of control variable counter (line 9).

Function Square is invoked (line 9) with the expression Square(counter). When program control reaches this expression, the program calls Square (lines 14–16). At this point, the program makes a copy of the value of counter (the argument), and program control transfers to the first line of Square. Square receives the copy of counter's value and stores it in the parameter y. Line 15 is a **Return** statement, which terminates execution of the method and returns the result of y $\wedge$ 2 to the calling program. The result is returned to the point in line 9 where Square was invoked. Line 9 displays in the command prompt the value of counter and the value returned by Square. This process is repeated 10 times. Note that returning a value from a function is similar to returning a value from the Get accessor of a property.

```
1   ' Fig. 7.3: SquareInteger.vb
2   ' Function that squares a number.
3   Module SquareInteger
4      Sub Main()
5         Console.WriteLine("Number" & vbTab & "Square")
6
7         ' square integers from 1 to 10
8         For counter As Integer = 1 To 10
9            Console.WriteLine(counter & vbTab & Square(counter))
10        Next
11     End Sub ' Main
12
13     ' function Square is executed when it is explicitly called
14     Function Square(ByVal y As Integer) As Integer
15        Return y ^ 2 ' return square of parameter value
16     End Function ' Square
17  End Module ' SquareInteger
```

```
Number   Square
1        1
2        4
3        9
4        16
5        25
6        36
7        49
8        64
9        81
10       100
```

Fig. 7.3 | Function for squaring an integer.

Function Declarations

The format of a function declaration is

```
Function method-name(parameter-list) As return-type
    declarations and statements
End Function
```

The *method-name*, *parameter-list*, and *declarations and statements* in a function declaration behave like the corresponding elements in a subroutine declaration. In the function header, the *return-type* indicates the type of the result returned from the function to its caller. The statement

```
Return expression
```

can occur anywhere in a function body and returns the value of *expression* to the caller. If necessary, Visual Basic attempts to convert the *expression* to the function's return-type. Functions `Return` exactly one value. When a `Return` statement is executed, control returns immediately to the point at which that function was invoked.

Common Programming Error 7.2

If the expression in a `Return` statement cannot be converted to the function's return-type, a run-time error is generated.

Common Programming Error 7.3

Failure to return a value from a function (e.g., by forgetting to provide a `Return` statement) causes the function to return the default value for the return-type, possibly producing incorrect output.

7.5 Shared Methods and Class Math

As you know, every class provides methods that perform common tasks on objects of the class. For example, to display the grade information in a `GradeBook` object, we defined and called method `DisplayGradeReport` (Section 6.5). Recall that when we call `GradeBook` methods such as `DisplayGradeReport`, we first need to create a `GradeBook` object.

Although most methods of a class execute in response to method calls on specific objects, this is not always the case. Sometimes a method performs a task that does not depend on the contents of an object. Such a method applies to the class in which it is declared and is known as a **Shared** method or a *class method*. It is not uncommon for a class to contain a group of convenient `Shared` methods to perform common tasks. For example, recall that we use method `WriteLine` of class `Console` throughout this book; method `WriteLine` is a `Shared` method.

Methods that are declared in modules are `Shared` by default. To declare a `Shared` method in a class, place the `Shared` modifier before the keyword `Sub` or `Function` in the method's header. To call a `Shared` method, specify the name of the class or module in which the method is declared, followed by the dot (.) separator and the method name, as in

```
ClassName.methodName(arguments)
```

We use various `Math` class `Shared` methods here. Class `Math` provides a collection of methods that enable you to perform common mathematical calculations. For example, you can calculate the square root of `900.0` with the `Shared` method call

```
Math.Sqrt(900.0)
```

which evaluates to and returns 30.0. Method Sqrt takes an argument of type Double and returns a result of type Double. To output the value of the preceding method call in the command prompt, you could write

```
Console.WriteLine(Math.Sqrt(900.0))
```

In this statement, the value that Sqrt returns becomes the argument to method Write-Line. Note that we did not create a Math object before calling method Sqrt. Most Math class methods are Shared and are therefore called by preceding the name of the method with the class name Math and a dot (.) separator.

Software Engineering Observation 7.5

It is not necessary to add an assembly reference to use the Math class methods in a program, because class Math is located in namespace System, which is implicitly added to all .NET applications.

Method arguments may be constants, variables or expressions. If c = 13.0, d = 3.0 and f = 4.0, then the statement

```
Console.WriteLine(Math.Sqrt(c + d * f))
```

calculates and prints the square root of 13.0 + 3.0 * 4.0 = 25.0—namely, 5.0. Figure 7.4 summarizes several Math class methods. In the figure, *x* and *y* are of type Double. Methods Min and Max have overloaded versions for several types. We discuss method overloading in Section 7.17.

Method	Description	Example
Abs(*x*)	returns the absolute value of *x*	Abs(23.7) is 23.7 Abs(0) is 0 Abs(-23.7) is 23.7
Ceiling(*x*)	rounds *x* to the smallest integer not less than *x*	Ceiling(9.2) is 10.0 Ceiling(-9.8) is -9.0
Cos(*x*)	returns the trigonometric cosine of *x* (*x* in radians)	Cos(0.0) is 1.0
Exp(*x*)	returns the exponential e^x	Exp(1.0) is approximately 2.71828182845905 Exp(2.0) is approximately 7.38905609893065
Floor(*x*)	rounds *x* to the largest integer not greater than *x*	Floor(9.2) is 9.0 Floor(-9.8) is -10.0
Log(*x*)	returns the natural logarithm of *x* (base *e*)	Log(2.7182818284590451) is approximately 1.0 Log(7.3890560989306504) is approximately 2.0

Fig. 7.4 | Math class methods. (Part I of 2.)

Method	Description	Example
Max(x, y)	returns the larger value of x and y (also has versions for Single, Integer and Long values)	Max(2.3, 12.7) is 12.7 Max(-2.3, -12.7) is -2.3
Min(x, y)	returns the smaller value of x and y (also has versions for Single, Integer and Long values)	Min(2.3, 12.7) is 2.3 Min(-2.3, -12.7) is -12.7
Pow(x, y)	calculates x raised to the power y (x^y)	Pow(2.0, 7.0) is 128.0 Pow(9.0, .5) is 3.0
Sin(x)	returns the trigonometric sine of x (x in radians)	Sin(0.0) is 0.0
Sqrt(x)	returns the square root of x	Sqrt(9.0) is 3.0 Sqrt(2.0) is 1.4142135623731
Tan(x)	returns the trigonometric tangent of x (x in radians)	Tan(0.0) is 0.0

Fig. 7.4 | Math class methods. (Part 2 of 2.)

Math Class Constants **PI** *and* **E**

Class Math also declares two commonly used mathematical constants: Math.PI and Math.E. The constant Math.PI (3.14159265358979323846) is the ratio of a circle's circumference to its diameter. The constant Math.E (2.7182818284590452354) is the base value for natural logarithms (calculated with Shared Math method Log). These values are declared in class Math with the modifiers Public and Const. Making them Public allows you to use the values in your own classes. Keyword Const declares a constant—a value that cannot be changed after the variable is initialized. Both PI and E are declared Const because their values never change. Constants are implicitly Shared, so they can be accessed via the class name Math and a dot (.) separator, just like class Math's methods. Recall from Section 4.5 that when each object of a class maintains its own copy of an attribute, the variable that represents the attribute is also known as an instance variable—each object (instance) of the class has a separate instance of the variable in memory. There are also variables for which each object of a class does not have a separate instance of the variable. That is the case with Shared variables. When objects of a class containing Shared variables are created, all the objects of that class share one copy of the class's Shared variables. Together the Shared variables and instance variables represent the so-called fields of a class. You will learn more about Shared members in Section 9.10.

7.6 GradeBook Case Study: Declaring Methods with Multiple Parameters

Chapters 3–6 presented classes containing simple methods that had at most one parameter. Methods often need to receive more than one piece of information to perform their tasks. We now consider how to write methods with multiple parameters.

Declaring Method Maximum

The application in Figs. 7.5–7.6 uses a user-declared method called Maximum to determine and return the largest of three Integer values entered by the user. When the application begins execution, class GradeBookTest's Main method (lines 4–11 of Fig. 7.6) creates one object of class GradeBook (line 6) and uses this object to call method InputGrades (line 9). This method is declared in lines 43–57 of class GradeBook (Fig. 7.5). Lines 48–53 prompt the user to enter three Integer values and read them from the user. Line 56 calls method Maximum (declared in lines 60–76) to determine the largest of the three Integer arguments. When method Maximum returns the result to line 56, the program assigns Maximum's return value to instance variable maximumGrade. Then line 10 of Fig. 7.6 calls method DisplayGradeReport, which outputs the maximum value.

Consider method Maximum (lines 60–76). Lines 60–61 indicate that the method returns an Integer value, the method's name is Maximum and the method requires three Integer parameters (x, y and z) to accomplish its task. When a method has more than one parameter, the parameters are specified as a comma-separated list. When Maximum is called in line 56, the parameter x is initialized with the value of the argument grade1, the parameter y is initialized with the value of the argument grade2 and the parameter z is initialized with the value of the argument grade3. There must be one argument in the method call for each parameter (sometimes called a **formal parameter**) in the method declaration. Also, the type of each argument must be consistent with the type of the corresponding parameter.

```vb
1   ' Fig. 7.5: GradeBook.vb
2   ' Definition of class GradeBook that finds the maximum of three grades.
3   Public Class GradeBook
4      Private courseNameValue As String ' name of course
5      Private maximumGrade As Integer ' maximum of three grades
6
7      ' constructor initializes course name
8      Public Sub New(ByVal name As String)
9         CourseName = name ' initializes CourseName
10        maximumGrade = 0 ' this value will be replaced by maximum grade
11     End Sub ' New
12
13     ' property that gets and sets the course name; the Set accessor
14     ' ensures that the course name has at most 25 characters
15     Public Property CourseName() As String
16        Get ' retrieve courseNameValue
17           Return courseNameValue
18        End Get
19
20        Set(ByVal value As String) ' set courseNameValue
21           If value.Length <= 25 Then ' if value has 25 or fewer characters
22              courseNameValue = value ' store the course name in the object
23           Else ' if name has more than 25 characters
24              ' set courseNameValue to first 25 characters of parameter name
25              ' start at 0, length of 25
26              courseNameValue = value.Substring(0, 25)
```

Fig. 7.5 | User-declared method Maximum that has three Integer parameters. (Part 1 of 3.)

```vbnet
27
28              Console.WriteLine( _
29                 "Course name (" & value & ") exceeds maximum length (25).")
30              Console.WriteLine( _
31                 "Limiting course name to first 25 characters." & vbCrLf)
32           End If
33        End Set
34     End Property ' CourseName
35
36     ' display a welcome message to the GradeBook user
37     Public Sub DisplayMessage()
38        Console.WriteLine("Welcome to the grade book for " _
39           & vbCrLf & CourseName & "!" & vbCrLf)
40     End Sub ' DisplayMessage
41
42     ' input three grades from user
43     Public Sub InputGrades()
44        Dim grade1 As Integer ' first grade entered by user
45        Dim grade2 As Integer ' second grade entered by user
46        Dim grade3 As Integer ' third grade entered by user
47
48        Console.Write("Enter the first grade: ")
49        grade1 = Console.ReadLine()
50        Console.Write("Enter the second grade: ")
51        grade2 = Console.ReadLine()
52        Console.Write("Enter the third grade: ")
53        grade3 = Console.ReadLine()
54
55        ' store the maximum in maximumGrade
56        maximumGrade = Maximum(grade1, grade2, grade3)
57     End Sub ' InputGrades
58
59     ' returns the maximum of its three integer parameters
60     Function Maximum(ByVal x As Integer, ByVal y As Integer, _
61        ByVal z As Integer) As Integer
62
63        Dim maximumValue As Integer = x ' assume x is the largest to start
64
65        ' determine whether y is greater than maximumValue
66        If (y > maximumValue) Then
67           maximumValue = y ' make y the new maximumValue
68        End If
69
70        ' determine whether z is greater than maximumValue
71        If (z > maximumValue) Then
72           maximumValue = z ' make z the new maximumValue
73        End If
74
75        Return maximumValue
76     End Function ' Maximum
77
```

Fig. 7.5 | User-declared method Maximum that has three Integer parameters. (Part 2 of 3.)

```
78        ' display a report based on the grades entered by user
79        Public Sub DisplayGradeReport()
80           ' output maximum of grades entered
81           Console.WriteLine("Maximum of grades entered: " & maximumGrade)
82        End Sub ' DisplayGradeReport
83     End Class ' GradeBook
```

Fig. 7.5 | User-declared method `Maximum` that has three `Integer` parameters. (Part 3 of 3.)

```
1     ' Fig. 7.6: GradeBookTest.vb
2     ' Create a GradeBook object, input grades and display grade report.
3     Module GradeBookTest
4        Sub Main()
5           ' create GradeBook object
6           Dim gradeBook1 As New GradeBook("CS101 Introduction to VB")
7
8           gradeBook1.DisplayMessage() ' display welcome message
9           gradeBook1.InputGrades() ' read grades from user
10          gradeBook1.DisplayGradeReport() ' display report based on grades
11       End Sub ' Main
12    End Module ' GradeBookTest
```

```
Welcome to the grade book for
CS101 Introduction to VB!

Enter the first grade: 65
Enter the second grade: 87
Enter the third grade: 45
Maximum of grades entered: 87
```

```
Welcome to the grade book for
CS101 Introduction to VB!

Enter the first grade: 45
Enter the second grade: 65
Enter the third grade: 87
Maximum of grades entered: 87
```

```
Welcome to the grade book for
CS101 Introduction to VB!

Enter the first grade: 87
Enter the second grade: 45
Enter the third grade: 65
Maximum of grades entered: 87
```

Fig. 7.6 | Application to test class `GradeBook`'s `Maximum` method.

To determine the maximum value, we begin with the assumption that parameter x contains the largest value, so line 63 declares local variable maximumValue and initializes it with the value of parameter x. Of course parameter y or z may contain the actual largest value, so we must compare each of these values with maximumValue. The If...Then statement in lines 66–68 determines whether y is greater than maximumValue, and if so, line 67 assigns y to maximumValue. The If...Then statement in lines 71–73 determines whether z is greater than maximumValue, and if so, line 72 assigns z to maximumValue. At this point the largest of the three values resides in maximumValue, so line 75 returns that value to line 56. When program control returns to the point in the program where Maximum was called, Maximum's parameters x, y and z are no longer accessible to the program—we will see why in Section 7.8. Note that methods can return at most one value, but the returned value could be a reference to an object that contains many values.

Note that maximumGrade is an instance variable in class GradeBook. Variables should be declared as instance variables of a class only if they are required for use in more than one method of the class or if the program should save their values between calls to the class's methods.

Implementing Method `Maximum` *by Reusing Method* `Math.Max`

Recall from Fig. 7.4 that class Math has a Max method that can determine the larger of two values. The entire body of our maximum method could also be implemented with two calls to Math.Max, as follows:

```
Return Math.Max(x, Math.Max(y, z))
```

The outer call to Math.Max specifies arguments x and Math.Max(y, z). Before any method is called, all its arguments are evaluated to determine their values. If an argument is a method call, the method call is performed to determine its return value. So, in the preceding statement, Math.Max(y, z) is evaluated first to determine the maximum of y and z. Then the result is passed as the second argument to the other call to Math.Max, which returns the larger of its two arguments. Using Math.Max in this manner is a good example of software reuse—we find the largest of three values by reusing Math.Max, which finds the largest of two values. Note how concise this code is compared to lines 63–75 of Fig. 7.5.

7.7 Notes on Declaring and Using Methods

There are three ways to call a method:

1. Using a method name by itself to call another method of the same class or module—such as Maximum(number1, number2, number3) in line 56 of Fig. 7.5.

2. Using a variable that contains a reference to an object, followed by a dot (.) and the method name to call a method of the referenced object—such as the method call in line 10 of Fig. 7.6, gradeBook1.DisplayGradeReport(), which calls a method of class GradeBook from the Main method of module GradeBookTest.

3. Using the class or module name and a dot (.) to call a Shared method of a class or module (all methods of a module are implicitly Shared). One example of this is Math.Sqrt(900.0) in Section 7.5.

Note that a Shared method can call only other Shared methods of the same class directly (i.e., using the method name by itself) and can manipulate only Shared members in the same class directly. To access the class's non-Shared members, a Shared method must use a reference to an object of the class. Recall that Shared methods relate to the class, whereas non-Shared methods are associated with a specific instance (object) of the class and may manipulate the instance variables of that object. Many objects of a class, each with its own copies of the instance variables, may exist at the same time. Suppose a Shared method were to invoke a non-Shared method directly. How would the method know which object's instance variables to manipulate? What would happen if no objects of the class existed at the time the non-Shared method was invoked? Thus, a Shared method cannot access non-Shared members of the same class directly.

Control can be returned to the statement that calls a method by using the Return statement or by reaching the end of the method (End Sub or End Function). If the method does not return a result but uses a Return statement to return control to the calling method, the Return statement cannot include an expression. If the method does return a result, the statement

> Return *expression*

evaluates the *expression*, then returns the result to the caller.

Common Programming Error 7.4

Declaring a method outside the body of a class or module declaration or inside the body of another method is a syntax error.

Common Programming Error 7.5

Omitting the return-value-type *in a method declaration, if that method is a function, is a syntax error.*

Common Programming Error 7.6

Redeclaring a method parameter as a local variable in the method's body is a compilation error.

Common Programming Error 7.7

Returning a value from a method that is a subroutine is a compilation error.

7.8 **Method Call Stack and Activation Records**

To understand how Visual Basic performs method calls, we first need to consider a data structure (i.e., collection of related data items) known as a stack. You can think of a stack as analogous to a pile of dishes. When a dish is placed on the pile, it is normally placed at the top (referred to as **pushing** the dish onto the stack). Similarly, when a dish is removed from the pile, it is normally removed from the top (referred to as **popping** the dish off the stack). Stacks are known as **last-in, first-out (LIFO) data structures**—the last item pushed (inserted) onto the stack is the first item popped (removed) from the stack.

When a program calls a method, the called method must know how to return to the correct location in its caller, so the return address in the calling method is pushed onto the **method call stack**. If a series of nested method calls occurs (e.g., method A calls method B, and method B calls method C), the successive return addresses are pushed onto the stack in last-in, first-out order so that each method can return to its caller.

The method call stack also contains the memory for the local variables used in each invocation of a method during a program's execution. A method's local variables also include its parameters. This data, stored as a portion of the method call stack, is known as the **activation record** or **stack frame** of the method call. When a method call is made, the activation record for that method call is pushed onto the method call stack. When the method returns to its caller, the activation record for the returning method call is popped off the stack and those local variables are no longer known to the program. If a local variable holding a reference to an object is the only variable in the program with a reference to that object, when the activation record containing that local variable is popped off the stack, the object can no longer be accessed by the program and it will eventually be deleted from memory by the CLR during garbage collection. We discuss garbage collection in Section 9.9.

Of course, the amount of memory in a computer is finite, so only a certain amount of memory can be used to store activation records on the method call stack. If more method calls occur than can have their activation records stored on the method call stack, an error known as a **stack overflow** occurs.

7.9 Implicit Argument Conversions

An important feature of argument passing is **implicit argument conversion**—converting an argument's value to a type that the method expects to receive in its corresponding parameter. Visual Basic supports both widening and narrowing conversions. A **widening conversion** occurs when an argument is converted to a parameter of another type that can hold more data, whereas a **narrowing conversion** occurs when there is potential for data loss during the conversion (i.e., a conversion to a parameter of a type that holds a smaller amount of data). Figure 7.7 lists the widening conversions supported by Visual Basic that occur between primitive types. In addition to the conversions in Fig. 7.7, all primitive type variables can be converted to type `Object` without losing data.

Type	Conversion types
`Boolean`	no possible widening conversions to other primitive types
`Byte`	`UShort`, `Short`, `UInteger`, `Integer`, `ULong`, `Long`, `Decimal`, `Single` or `Double`
`Char`	`String`
`Date`	no possible widening conversions to other primitive types
`Decimal`	`Single` or `Double`
`Double`	no possible widening conversions to other primitive types
`Integer`	`Long`, `Decimal`, `Single` or `Double`
`Long`	`Decimal`, `Single` or `Double`

Fig. 7.7 | Widening conversions between primitive types. (Part 1 of 2.)

Type	Conversion types
SByte	Short, Integer, Long, Decimal, Single or Double
Short	Integer, Long, Decimal, Single or Double
Single	Double
String	no possible widening conversions to other primitive types
UInteger	ULong, Long, Decimal, Single or Double
ULong	Decimal, Single or Double
UShort	UInteger, Integer, ULong, Long, Decimal, Single or Double

Fig. 7.7 | Widening conversions between primitive types. (Part 2 of 2.)

For example, the Math class method Sqrt can be called with an Integer argument, even though the method is defined in class Math with a Double parameter. The statement

```
Console.Write(Math.Sqrt(4))
```

correctly evaluates Math.Sqrt(4) and prints the value 2. Visual Basic implicitly converts the Integer argument 4 to the Double value 4.0 before the argument is passed to Math.Sqrt. In this case, the argument does not precisely correspond to the parameter type in the method declaration, so an implicit widening conversion changes the value to the proper type before the method is called. Visual Basic also performs narrowing conversions on arguments passed to methods. For example, if a Double variable containing the value 4.0 were passed to a method expecting an Integer variable, the value would be converted to 4. Some implicit narrowing conversions can cause runtime errors. In the next section, we discuss measures you can take to avoid such runtime errors. In Chapter 12, Exception Handling, we discuss how to handle the errors caused by failed narrowing conversions.

Common Programming Error 7.8

Converting a primitive-type value to a value of another primitive type may change the value if the conversion is not a widening conversion. For example, converting a floating-point value to an integral value truncates any fractional part of the floating-point value (e.g., 4.7 becomes 4).

Conversions occur not only for values passed as arguments to methods, but also for expressions containing values of two or more types. In such expressions, the values' original types are maintained, while temporary copies of the values are converted for use in the expression. Each value is converted to the "widest" type in the expression (i.e., widening conversions are made until the values are of the same type as the "widest" type). For example, if singleNumber is of type Single and integerNumber is of type Integer, when Visual Basic evaluates the expression

```
singleNumber + integerNumber
```

the value of integerNumber is converted to type Single (the widest type in the expression), then added to singleNumber, producing a Single result.

7.10 Option Strict and Data-Type Conversions

Visual Basic provides several options for controlling the way the compiler handles types. These options can help you eliminate such errors as those caused by narrowing conversions. The first option is **Option Explicit**, which is set to **On** by default—it has been enabled in the programs we created in Chapters 2–6. **Option Explicit** forces you to explicitly declare all variables before they are used in a program. Forcing explicit declarations eliminates various errors. For example, when **Option Explicit** is set to **Off**, the compiler interprets misspelled variable names as new variables and implicitly declares them to be of type **Object**. (Class **Object** is the base type of all types in Visual Basic. We will discuss class **Object** in more detail in Chapter 10.) This creates subtle errors that can be difficult to debug. To set **Option Explicit** to **Off**, double click **My Project** in **Solution Explorer**. This opens a window that allows you to change the properties of the project. In this window, click the **Compile** tab (Fig. 7.8), then select the value **Off** from the **Option Explicit** drop-down list. If **Option Explicit** is **Off**, any undeclared variables are implicitly declared as being of type **Object**. Note that all variables have a type regardless of whether **Option Explicit** is **On**, so Visual Basic is known as a **strongly-typed language**.

A second option, which defaults to **Off**, is **Option Strict**. Visual Basic provides **Option Strict** as a means of increasing program clarity and reducing debugging time. When set to **On**, **Option Strict** causes the compiler to check all conversions and requires you to perform an explicit conversion for all narrowing conversions that could cause data loss (e.g., conversion from **Double** to **Integer**) or program termination (e.g., conversion of a **String**, such as "hello", to type **Integer**). To set **Option Strict** to **On**, double click **My Project** in the **Solution Explorer**—this opens a window that allows you to change the properties of the project. In that window, click the **Compile** tab and select the value **On** in the **Option Strict** drop-down list (Fig. 7.8). An **explicit conversion** is a conversion that uses a cast operator

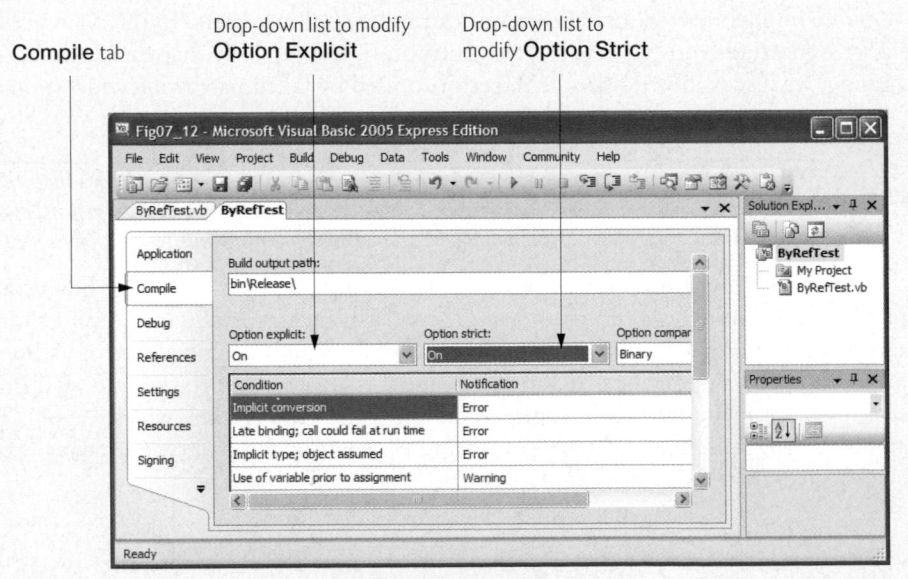

Fig. 7.8 | Modifying Option Strict and Option Explicit.

or a method to force a conversion to occur. In Chapter 11 we discuss using operators known as cast operators to perform explicit conversions. Explicit conversion enables you to "take control" from the compiler. You essentially say, "I know this conversion might cause loss of information, but for my purposes here, that's fine."

The methods of class **Convert** can be used to explicitly convert data from one type to another. The name of each conversion method is the word To, followed by the name of the type to which the method converts its argument. For instance, to convert a String input by the user to type Double (to be stored in variable number of type Double), we use the statement

```
number = Convert.ToDouble(Console.ReadLine())
```

Likewise, many of the primitive types have a Parse method that they can use for conversions. For instance, method **Double.Parse** converts a string representation of a number to a value of type Double.

When **Option Strict** is **Off** (as it has been for all the code examples so far in this book), Visual Basic performs such type conversions implicitly, and thus you may not realize that a narrowing conversion is being performed. If the data being converted is incompatible with the new type, a runtime error occurs. Option Strict draws your attention to narrowing conversions so that they can be eliminated or handled properly.

 Error-Prevention Tip 7.3

From this point forward, all code examples have **Option Strict** *set to* **On**.

Setting **Option Strict** to **On** applies the change globally, to the entire project. You also can enable **Option Strict** within an individual code file by typing Option Strict On— Option statements must be placed at the start of the file above any declarations or Imports statements.

7.11 **Value Types and Reference Types**

As we discussed briefly in Chapter 4, all Visual Basic types can be categorized as either value types or reference types. A variable of a value type contains data of that type. Normally, value types are used for a single piece of data, such as an Integer or a Double value. By contrast, a variable of a reference type contains the address of the location in memory where the data referred to by that variable is stored. The actual object to which the variable refers can contain many individual pieces of data. Reference types are known as classes and are discussed in more detail in Chapters 9–11.

Both value types and reference types include primitive types and types that you can create. The primitive value types include the integral types (Byte, SByte, Short, UShort, Integer, UInteger, Long and ULong), the floating-point types (Single and Double) and types Boolean, Date, Decimal and Char. There is only one primitive reference type— String. Reference types can be created by declaring classes and modules, as well as interfaces and delegates, constructs that we will discuss in Chapters 11 and 13, respectively. The primitive reference type, String, actually represents the **String** class in the FCL. Value types can be created by declaring structures and enumerations. **Structures**, like classes, define types that contain members such as methods and instance variables. **Enumerations** may only contain sets of integral values. The primitive value types are defined using structures. Most of these structures have the same name as the Visual Basic primitive type (type `Double` is defined by structure **`Double`**), but others do not (type `Integer` is defined by structure **`Int32`**). These structures are part of the FCL, which is used by several languages—as a result, the naming of types in the various .NET languages may not always be identical to their underlying classes and structures in the FCL. User-defined types are discussed in greater detail in Chapter 9, Classes and Objects: A Deeper Look, Chapter 10, Object-Oriented Programming: Inheritance and Chapter 16, Strings, Characters and Regular Expressions. Figure 7.9 lists the primitive types, which form the building blocks for more complicated types, such as the `GradeBook` type we have defined in several examples in this book.

Type	Size in bits	Values	Standard	Name of FCL class or structure
Boolean	16	True or False		Boolean
Byte	8	0 to 255		Byte
SByte	8	–128 to 127		SByte
Char	16	One Unicode character	(Unicode character set)	Char
Date	64	1 January 0001 to 31 December 9999 12:00:00 AM to 11:59:59 PM		DateTime
Decimal	128	1.0E–28 to 7.9E+28		Decimal
Double	64	±5.0E–324 to ±1.7E+308	(IEEE 754 floating point)	Double
Integer	32	–2,147,483,648 to 2,147,483,647		Int32
Long	64	–9,223,372,036,854,775,808 to 9,223,372,036,854,775,807		Int64
Short	16	–32,768 to 32,767		Int16
Single	32	±1.5E–45 to ±3.4E+38	(IEEE 754 floating point)	Single
String		0 to ~2000000000 Unicode characters	(Unicode character set)	String
UInteger	32	0 to 4,294,967,295		UInt32
ULong	64	0 to 18,446,744,073,709,551,615		UInt64
UShort	16	0 to 65,535		UInt16

Fig. 7.9 | Primitive types.

Each value type in the table is accompanied by its size in bits (there are 8 bits to a byte) and its range of values. To promote portability, Microsoft chose to use internationally recognized standards for character formats (Unicode®, www.unicode.org) and floating-point numbers (IEEE 754, grouper.ieee.org/groups/754/). We discuss the Unicode character formats in Appendix E, Unicode®. In the far right column of the table, we display the name of the structure or class that defines the primitive type. Note that these are the names used for the methods of class Convert that we discussed in the previous section. For instance, to convert a value to type Integer, the name of the proper Convert class method would be Convert.ToInt32, not Convert.ToInteger.

7.12 Framework Class Library Namespaces

As we have seen, the FCL contains many predefined classes that are grouped into namespaces. Throughout the text, we have used Imports statements to specify the namespaces used in a program. For example, a program includes the declaration

```
Imports System.Windows.Forms
```

to specify that the program uses classes in this namespace, such as class MessageBox. This allows you to use the simple class name MessageBox, rather than the fully qualified class name System.Windows.Forms.MessageBox, in the code. A great strength of Visual Basic is the large number of classes in the FCL. Some key FCL namespaces are described in Fig. 7.10, which represents only a small portion of the reusable components in the FCL.

The set of namespaces available in the FCL is quite large. In addition to the namespaces summarized in Fig. 7.10, the FCL includes namespaces for complex graphics, Web services, printing, security and many other capabilities.

Namespace	Description
System.Windows.Forms	Contains the classes required to create and manipulate GUIs. (Various classes in this namespace are discussed in Chapter 13, Graphical User Interface Concepts: Part 1 and Chapter 14, Graphical User Interface Concepts: Part 2.)
System.IO	Contains classes that enable programs to input and output data. (You will learn more about this namespace in Chapter 18, Files and Streams.)
System.Data	Contains classes that enable programs to access and manipulate databases (i.e., an organized collection of data). (You will learn more about this namespace in Chapter 20, Database, SQL and ADO.NET.)
System.Web	Contains classes used for creating and maintaining Web applications, which are accessible over the Internet. (You will learn more about this namespace in Chapter 21, ASP.NET 2.0, Web Forms and Web Controls.)

Fig. 7.10 | FCL namespaces (a subset). (Part 1 of 2.)

Namespace	Description
System.Xml	Contains classes for creating and manipulating XML data. Data can be read from or written to XML files. (You will learn more about this namespace in Chapter 19, Extensible Markup Language (XML).)
System.Collections	Contains classes that define data structures for maintaining collections of data. (You will learn more about this namespace in Chapter 26, Collections.)
System.Net	Contains classes that enable programs to communicate via computer networks like the Internet. (You will learn more about this namespace in Chapter 23, Networking: Streams-Based Sockets and Datagrams.)
System.Text	Contains classes and interfaces that enable programs to manipulate characters and strings. (You will learn more about this namespace in Chapter 16, Strings, Characters and Regular Expressions.)
System.Threading	Contains classes that enable programs to perform several tasks concurrently, or at the same time. (You will learn more about this namespace in Chapter 15, Multithreading.)
System.Drawing	Contains classes that enable programs to perform basic graphics processing, such as displaying shapes and arcs. (You will learn more about this namespace in Chapter 17, Graphics and Multimedia.)

Fig. 7.10 | FCL namespaces (a subset). (Part 2 of 2.)

You can locate additional information about a predefined FCL class's methods in the Visual Studio .NET documentation by selecting **Help > Index**. In the window that appears there will be an index to the left. Enter .NET Framework in the **Filtered by** drop-down list, and enter the name of the class in the **Look for** field. You will be provided with links for general information about the class or for a listing of the class's members.

Good Programming Practice 7.2

The Visual Studio .NET documentation is easy to search and provides many details about each class. As you learn a class in this book, you should read about the class in the online documentation.

7.13 Passing Arguments: Pass-by-Value vs. Pass-by-Reference

Arguments are passed in one of two ways: **pass-by-value** and **pass-by-reference**. When an argument is passed by value, the program makes a **copy** of the argument's value and passes the copy to the called method. With pass-by-value, changes to the called method's copy do not affect the original variable's value in the caller. In contrast, when an argument is passed by reference, the caller gives the called method the ability to access and modify the caller's original data directly. Figure 7.11 demonstrates passing value-type arguments by value and by reference.

```vb
1   ' Fig. 7.11: ByRefTest.vb
2   ' Demonstrates passing by value and by reference.
3   Module ByRefTest
4      Sub Main()
5         Dim number1 As Integer = 2
6
7         Console.WriteLine("Passing a value-type argument by value:")
8         Console.WriteLine("Before calling SquareByValue, " & _
9            "number1 is {0}", number1)
10        SquareByValue(number1)   ' passes number1 by value
11        Console.WriteLine("After returning from SquareByValue, " & _
12           "number1 is {0}" & vbCrLf, number1)
13
14        Dim number2 As Integer = 2
15
16        Console.WriteLine("Passing a value-type argument" & _
17           " by reference:")
18        Console.WriteLine("Before calling SquareByReference, " & _
19           "number2 is {0}", number2)
20        SquareByReference(number2) ' passes number2 by reference
21        Console.WriteLine("After returning from " & _
22           "SquareByReference, number2 is {0}" & vbCrLf, number2)
23
24        Dim number3 As Integer = 2
25
26        Console.WriteLine("Passing a value-type argument" & _
27           " by reference, but in parentheses:")
28        Console.WriteLine("Before calling SquareByReference " & _
29           "using parentheses, number3 is {0}", number3)
30        SquareByReference((number3)) ' passes number3 by value
31        Console.WriteLine("After returning from " & _
32           "SquareByReference, number3 is {0}", number3)
33     End Sub ' Main
34
35     ' squares number by value (note ByVal keyword)
36     Sub SquareByValue(ByVal number As Integer)
37        Console.WriteLine("After entering SquareByValue, " & _
38           "number is {0}", number)
39        number *= number
40        Console.WriteLine("Before exiting SquareByValue, " & _
41           "number is {0}", number)
42     End Sub ' SquareByValue
43
44     ' squares number by reference (note ByRef keyword)
45     Sub SquareByReference(ByRef number As Integer)
46        Console.WriteLine("After entering SquareByReference" & _
47           ", number is {0}", number)
48        number *= number
```

Fig. 7.11 | ByVal and ByRef used to pass value-type arguments. (Part 1 of 2.)

```
49          Console.WriteLine("Before exiting SquareByReference" & _
50              ", number is {0}", number)
51      End Sub ' SquareByReference
52  End Module ' ByRefTest
```

```
Passing a value-type argument by value:
Before calling SquareByValue, number1 is 2
After entering SquareByValue, number is 2
Before exiting SquareByValue, number is 4
After returning from SquareByValue, number1 is 2

Passing a value-type argument by reference:
Before calling SquareByReference, number2 is 2
After entering SquareByReference, number is 2
Before exiting SquareByReference, number is 4
After returning from SquareByReference, number2 is 4

Passing a value-type argument by reference, but in parentheses:
Before calling SquareByReference using parentheses, number3 is 2
After entering SquareByReference, number is 2
Before exiting SquareByReference, number is 4
After returning from SquareByReference, number3 is 2
```

Fig. 7.11 | ByVal and ByRef used to pass value-type arguments. (Part 2 of 2.)

The program passes three value-type variables, number1, number2 and number3, in different ways to methods SquareByValue (lines 36–42) and SquareByReference (lines 45–51). Keyword ByVal in the method header of SquareByValue (line 36) indicates that value-type arguments should be passed by value. A parameter declared with keyword ByVal is known as a **value parameter**. When number1 is passed to SquareByValue (line 10), a copy of the value stored in number1 (i.e., 2) is passed to the method. Therefore, the value of number1 in the calling method, Main, is not modified when parameter number is squared in method SquareByValue (line 39)—only the local copy stored in parameter number gets modified.

Method SquareByReference uses **keyword ByRef** (line 45) to receive its value-type parameter by reference. A parameter declared with keyword ByRef is known as a **reference parameter**. When Main calls SquareByReference (line 20), a reference to the value stored in number2 is passed, which gives SquareByReference direct access to the value stored in the original variable. Thus, the value stored in number2 after SquareByReference finishes executing is the same as the final value of parameter number.

When arguments are enclosed in parentheses, (), the expression within the parentheses is evaluated. In line 30, the inner set of parentheses evaluates number3 to its value (2) and passes this value to the method, even if the method header includes keyword ByRef. Thus, the value of number3 does not change after it is passed to SquareByReference (line 30) via parentheses.

Passing value-type arguments with keyword ByRef is useful when methods need to alter argument values directly. However, passing by reference can weaken security, because the called method can modify the caller's data. We discuss some of the more complex subtleties of passing arguments by value and by reference in Section 8.16.

When you pass a variable of a reference type to a method that declares the corresponding parameter ByVal, a copy of the variable's value is passed. In this case, the value is actually a reference to an object, so the method is able to modify the object in memory. Thus, reference-type variables passed with keyword ByVal are effectively passed by reference. Although Visual Basic allows you to use keyword ByRef with reference-type parameters, it is usually not necessary to do so except with type String. Although they technically are reference types, String arguments cannot be modified directly when passed with keyword ByVal, due to some subtle details of the String type, which we discuss in Chapter 16, Strings, Characters and Regular Expressions. We discuss passing reference types by reference in Section 8.16.

 Error-Prevention Tip 7.4

When passing arguments by value, changes to the called method's copy do not affect the original variable's value. This prevents possible side effects that could hinder the development of correct and reliable software systems. Always pass value-type arguments by value unless you explicitly intend for the called method to modify the caller's data.

7.14 Scope of Declarations

You have seen declarations of various Visual Basic entities, such as classes, methods, variables and parameters. Declarations introduce names that are used to refer to such entities. A declaration's **Scope** is the portion of the program that can refer to the declared entity by its name without qualification. Such an entity is said to be "in scope" for that portion of the program. This section introduces several important scope issues.

The basic scopes are as follows:

1. **Block scope**—The scope of a variable declared in a block is from the point of the declaration to the end of the block (e.g., a variable declared in a control statement's body is in scope only until the end of that control statement).

2. **Method scope**—The scope of a method's local-variable declaration or parameter is from the point at which the declaration appears to the end of that method. This is similar to block scope.

3. **Module scope**—The scope of a class's members or a module's members is the entire body of the class or module. This enables non-Shared methods of a class to use all of the class's members. (Note that Shared methods of a class can access only the class's Shared variables and Shared methods.) All module members are implicitly Shared, so all methods of a module can access all variables and other methods of the module.

4. **Namespace scope**—Elements declared in a namespace (i.e., classes, modules, interfaces, delegates, enumerations, structures and other namespaces) are accessible to all other elements in the same namespace. By default, all elements of a project are part of a namespace that uses the project's name. This enables, for example, a module method in the project to create an object of a class that is also part of the project.

Any block may contain variable declarations. If a local variable or parameter in a method has the same name as a field of the class, the field is "hidden" until the block terminates execution—this is called **shadowing**. In Chapter 9, we discuss how to access shadowed members. Keep in mind that although a variable may not be in scope, it may still exist. A variable's **lifetime** is the period during which the variable exists in memory. Some variables exist briefly, some are created and destroyed repeatedly, yet others are maintained through the entire execution of a program. Variables normally exist as long as their container exists—for instance, a local variable of a method will exist as long as the method itself exists in memory.

Error-Prevention Tip 7.5

Use different names for fields and local variables to help prevent subtle logic errors that occur when a method is called and a local variable of the method shadows a field of the same name in the class.

The application in Figs. 7.12 and 7.13 demonstrates scoping issues with fields and local variables. When the application begins execution, module `ScopeTest`'s `Main` method (Fig. 7.13, lines 4–7) creates an object of class `Scope` (line 5) and calls the object's `Begin` method (line 6) to produce the program's output (shown in Fig. 7.13).

```vb
 1   ' Fig. 7.12: Scope.vb
 2   ' Scope class demonstrates instance and local variable scopes.
 3   Public Class Scope
 4      ' instance variable that is accessible to all methods of this class
 5      Private x As Integer = 1
 6
 7      ' method Begin creates and initializes local variable x and
 8      ' calls methods UseLocalVariable and UseInstanceVariable
 9      Public Sub Begin()
10         ' method's local variable x shadows instance variable x
11         Dim x As Integer = 5
12
13         Console.WriteLine("local x in method Begin is " & x)
14
15         UseLocalVariable() ' UseLocalVariable has local x
16         UseInstanceVariable() ' uses class Scope's instance variable x
17         UseLocalVariable() ' UseLocalVariable reinitializes local x
18         UseInstanceVariable() ' Scope's instance variable x retains value
19
20         Console.WriteLine(vbCrLf & "local x in method Begin is " & x)
21      End Sub ' Begin
22
23      ' create and initialize local variable x during each call
24      Sub UseLocalVariable()
25         Dim x As Integer = 25 ' initialized in each call
26
27         Console.WriteLine( _
28            vbCrLf & "local x on entering method UseLocalVariable is " & x)
29         x += 1 ' modifies this method's local variable x
30         Console.WriteLine("local variable x before exiting method " & _
31            "UseLocalVariable is " & x)
32      End Sub ' UseLocalVariable
```

Fig. 7.12 | Scoping rules in a class. (Part 1 of 2.)

```
33
34        ' modify class Scope's instance variable x during each call
35     Sub UseInstanceVariable()
36        Console.WriteLine(vbCrLf & "instance variable" & _
37           " x on entering method UseInstanceVariable is " & x)
38        x *= 10 ' modifies class Scope's instance variable x
39        Console.WriteLine("instance variable " & _
40           "x before exiting method UseInstanceVariable is " & x)
41     End Sub ' UseInstanceVariable
42  End Class ' Scope
```

Fig. 7.12 | Scoping rules in a class. (Part 2 of 2.)

```
1    ' Fig. 7.13: ScopeTest.vb
2    ' Testing class Scope.
3    Module ScopeTest
4       Sub Main()
5          Dim testScope As New Scope()
6          testScope.Begin()
7       End Sub ' Main
8    End Module ' ScopeTest
```

```
local x in method Begin is 5

local x on entering method UseLocalVariable is 25
local variable x before exiting method UseLocalVariable is 26

instance variable x on entering method UseInstanceVariable is 1
instance variable x before exiting method UseInstanceVariable is 10

local x on entering method UseLocalVariable is 25
local variable x before exiting method UseLocalVariable is 26

instance variable x on entering method UseInstanceVariable is 10
instance variable x before exiting method UseInstanceVariable is 100

local x in method Begin is 5
```

Fig. 7.13 | Module to test class Scope.

In class Scope, line 5 declares and initializes the instance variable x to 1. This instance variable is shadowed (hidden) in any block (or method) that declares a local variable named x. Method Begin (lines 9–21) declares a local variable x (line 11) and initializes it to 5. This local variable's value is output to show that the instance variable x (whose value is 1) is shadowed in method Begin. The program declares two other methods—UseLocalVariable (lines 24–32) and UseInstanceVariable (lines 35–41)—that each take no arguments and do not return results. Method Begin calls each method twice (lines 15–18). Method UseLocalVariable declares local variable x (line 25). When UseLocalVariable is first called (line 15), it creates local variable x and initializes it to 25 (line 25), outputs the value of x (lines 27–28), increments x (line 29) and outputs the value of x again (lines 30–31). When UseLocalVariable is called a second time (line 17), it recreates local variable x and reinitializes it to 25, so the output of each UseLocalVariable call is identical.

Method `UseInstanceVariable` does not declare any local variables. Therefore, when it refers to x, instance variable x (line 5) of the class is used. When method `UseInstance-Variable` is first called (line 16), it outputs the value (1) of instance variable x (lines 36–37), multiplies the instance variable x by 10 (line 38) and outputs the value (10) of instance variable x again (lines 39–40) before returning. The next time method `UseInstanceVariable` is called (line 18), the instance variable has its modified value, 10, so the method outputs 10, then 100. Finally, in method `Begin`, the program outputs the value of local variable x again (line 20) to show that none of the method calls modified `Begin`'s local variable x, because the methods all referred to variables named x in other scopes.

7.15 Case Study: Random Number Generation

We now take a brief and hopefully entertaining diversion into a popular programming application—simulation and game playing. In this and the next section, we develop a game-playing program with multiple methods. The program employs many of the control statements presented thus far in the book and introduces several new concepts.

There is something in the air of a gambling casino that invigorates people—from the high rollers at the plush mahogany-and-felt craps tables to the quarter poppers at the one-armed bandits. It is the element of chance, the possibility that luck will convert a pocketful of money into a mountain of wealth. Unfortunately, that rarely happens because the odds, of course, favor the casinos. The element of chance can be introduced through class **Random** (located in namespace `System`).

Class *Random* and Method *Next*

Consider the following statements:

```
Dim randomObject As New Random()
Dim randomNumber As Integer = randomObject.Next()
```

The first statement declares `randomObject` as a reference to an object of type `Random` and creates a new `Random` object.

The second statement declares `Integer` variable `randomNumber` and assigns to it the value returned by calling `Random` method **Next**. Method `Next` generates a positive `Integer` value greater than or equal to zero and less than the constant `Int32.MaxValue` (2,147,483,647). If `Next` truly produces values at random, every value in this range has an equal chance (or **probability**) of being chosen when `Next` is called. The values returned by `Next` are actually **pseudo-random numbers**, or a sequence of values produced by a complex mathematical calculation. This calculation requires a **seed value**. If the seed value is different each time the program is run, the series of values will be different as well (so that the generated numbers are indeed random). When we create a `Random` object, the seed is based on the current time. Alternatively, we can pass a seed value as an argument in the parentheses after `New Random`. Passing in the same seed twice results in the same series of random numbers. Using the current time of day as the seed value is effective because the time is likely to change for each `Random` object we create.

The range of values produced by `Next` is often different from what is needed in a particular application. For example, a program that simulates coin-tossing might require only 0 for "heads" and 1 for "tails." A program that simulates the rolling of a six-sided die would require random integers in the range 1–6. Similarly, a program that randomly predicts the next type of spaceship (out of four possibilities) that flies across the horizon in a video game might require random integers from 1 to 4.

Scaling and Shifting of Random Numbers

By passing an argument to method Next as follows

```
value = 1 + randomObject.Next(6)
```

we can produce integers in the range 1–6. When a single argument is passed to Next, the values returned by Next will be in the range from 0 to (but not including) the value of that argument. This is called scaling. The number 6 is the scaling factor. We shift the range of numbers produced by adding 1 to our previous result, so that the return values are between 1 and 6 rather than 0 and 5.

Visual Basic simplifies the process of specifying a range of random numbers by allowing you to pass two arguments to Next. For example, the preceding statement also could be written as

```
value = randomObject.Next(1, 7)
```

Note that we must use 7 as the second argument to method Next to produce integers in the range from 1–6. The first argument indicates the minimum value in our desired range, whereas the second is equal to 1 + the maximum value desired. Figure 7.14 demonstrates the use of class Random and method Next by simulating 20 rolls of a six-sided die and showing the value of each roll. Note that all the values are in the range from 1 to 6, inclusive.

```vb
1  ' Fig. 7.14: RandomInteger.vb
2  ' Generating random integers.
3  Module RandomInteger
4     Sub Main()
5        Dim randomObject As New Random() ' create Random object
6        Dim randomNumber As Integer
7
8        ' generate 20 random numbers between 1 and 6
9        For i As Integer = 1 To 20
10          randomNumber = randomObject.Next(1, 7)
11          Console.Write(randomNumber & " ")
12
13          If i Mod 5 = 0 Then ' is i a multiple of 5?
14             Console.WriteLine()
15          End If
16       Next
17    End Sub ' Main
18 End Module ' RandomInteger
```

```
1 1 3 1 1
2 1 1 3 6
6 3 4 6 6
2 2 3 6 5
```

Fig. 7.14 | Random integers from 1 to 6 created by calling method Next of class Random.

The program in Fig. 7.15 uses class Random to simulate rolling four six-sided dice. We then use some of the functionality from this program in another example (Fig. 7.17) to demonstrate that the numbers generated by Next occur with approximately equal likelihood.

Using Buttons on a GUI

Before we discuss the use of Random in this application, let us analyze the GUI controls we use and the flow of control in this example. The names of the GUI controls are indicated in the output of Fig. 7.15. In this example, we use four PictureBoxes. You used Picture-Boxes in Chapters 2 and 5. In these examples, you used the PictureBox's Image property to display an image. We will do the same, but set the control's Image property programmatically, so that different die images can be displayed based on the random numbers generated.

In this example, we also use our first Button control. Like the other controls we have used, the Button control can be simply dragged and dropped onto the Form from the **Toolbox**, and its sizing handles can be used to increase or decrease the size of the Button. The Text property of the Button has been set to **Roll** and the font size of the Button's text has been set to 12, using the same **Font** dialog as you would for Label controls. Name the control btnRoll. Recall that we have used prefixes for our other controls, to make identifying the type of control easier during coding. For Buttons, we will use the btn prefix.

```vb
1   ' Fig. 7.15: RollDice.vb
2   ' Rolling four dice.
3   Imports System.IO
4
5   Public Class FrmRollDice
6       ' declare Random object reference
7       Dim randomObject As New Random()
8
9       ' display results of four rolls
10      Private Sub btnRoll_Click(ByVal sender As System.Object, _
11          ByVal e As System.EventArgs) Handles btnRoll.Click
12          ' method randomly assigns a face to each die
13          DisplayDie(picDie1)
14          DisplayDie(picDie2)
15          DisplayDie(picDie3)
16          DisplayDie(picDie4)
17      End Sub ' btnRoll_Click
18
19      ' get a random die image
20      Sub DisplayDie(ByVal picDie As PictureBox)
21          ' generate random integer in range 1 to 6
22          Dim face As Integer = randomObject.Next(1, 7)
23
24          ' load corresponding image
25          picDie.Image = Image.FromFile( _
26              Directory.GetCurrentDirectory & "\Images\die" & face & ".png")
27      End Sub ' DisplayDie
28  End Class ' FrmRollDice
```

Fig. 7.15 | Demonstrating four die rolls with graphical output. (Part 1 of 2.)

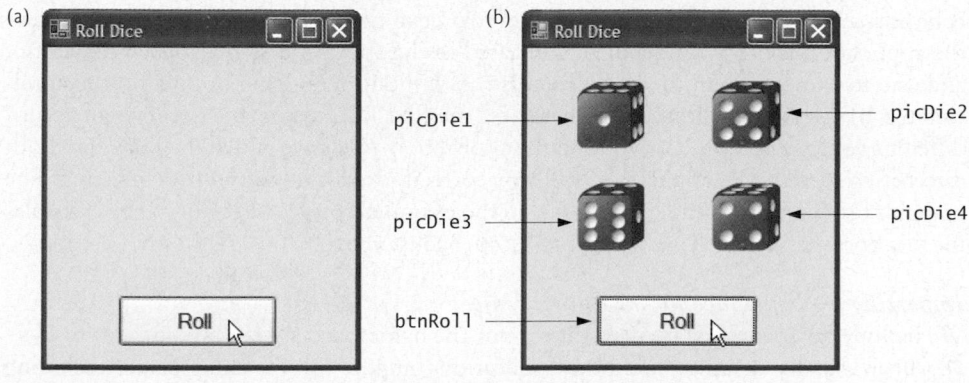

Fig. 7.15 | Demonstrating four die rolls with graphical output. (Part 2 of 2.)

Creating a *Click Event Handler*

For this example, the random die images will be displayed whenever btnRoll is clicked. To enable such functionality, we need to add an event handler for our Button's Click event. To do so, simply double click the Button in design view. This will create the empty event handler in your code. In Chapter 5 we created an event handler for the Form's Load event, which is executed when the Form is loaded. An event handler for a Button's Click event executes whenever the Button is clicked. The event handler with code added to its body is defined in lines 10–17. The name of the event handler is btnRoll_Click. Note that the event handler is a subroutine—the event handler performs actions in response to an event, but does not return a value. The first argument to this method represents the object that is associated with the event; the second argument is an object that contains information about the event. Event-handler names created by the IDE normally begin with the object's name, followed by an underscore and the name of the event. From here on, if you see a method in an example named using this convention, you can assume that it is an event handler. Event handlers are discussed in more detail in Chapter 13.

Displaying Random Images in a *PictureBox*

The body of our event handler calls method DisplayDie four times, once for each PictureBox on the Form. Calling DisplayDie (lines 13–16) causes four dice to appear as if they are being rolled each time **Roll** is clicked. When this program runs, the dice images do not appear until the user clicks **Roll** for the first time.

Method DisplayDie specifies the correct image for the face value calculated by method Next (line 22). Note that we declare randomObject as an instance variable of Frm-RollDice (line 7). This allows the same Random object to be used each time DisplayDie executes. We set the Image property (line 25) to display one of the die images (the image is selected using random values) in the current PictureBox (passed as an argument). We set the property's value with an assignment statement (lines 25–26). Note that we specify the image to display through method **FromFile** in class **Image** (contained in the System.Drawing namespace). Method **GetCurrentDirectory** of class **Directory** (contained in the System.IO namespace) returns the current directory. Recall that when the application is compiled, an executable (.exe file) is created. This is the file that is executed when the application is run, so `GetCurrentDirectory` returns the location of this file. It is important to note that there are actually two `.exe` files created—one to execute when the application is run with debugging (located in the application's `bin\Debug` directory), and one to execute when the application is run without debugging (located in the application's `bin\Release` directory). Therefore, method `GetCurrentDirectory` can return different values based on how you run the application. We have added the images to both directories so that the application will run correctly with and without debugging. The graphics used in this example are located in the example's project directory. The examples for this book are available at www.deitel.com/books/vbhtp3.

Importing a Namespace for an Entire Project

We include an `Imports` statement (line 3) for the namespace `System.IO` but not for `System.Drawing`. By default, Windows applications import several namespaces, including `System`, `System.Drawing`, and `System.Windows.Forms`. These namespaces are imported for the entire project, eliminating the need for `Imports` statements in individual project files. You can see which namespaces have been imported into a project by double clicking the **My Project** folder in the **Solution Explorer**, and then selecting **References** in the page that appears. You will be presented with a list of the application's references to assemblies in the **References** area of the window, and a list of the namespaces defined in those references in the **Imported namespaces** area (Fig. 7.16). The namespaces that have been checked are those that are imported for the entire project. Some of the namespaces imported by default are not used in this example. For instance, we do not yet use namespace `System.Collections`, which allows you to create collections of objects (see

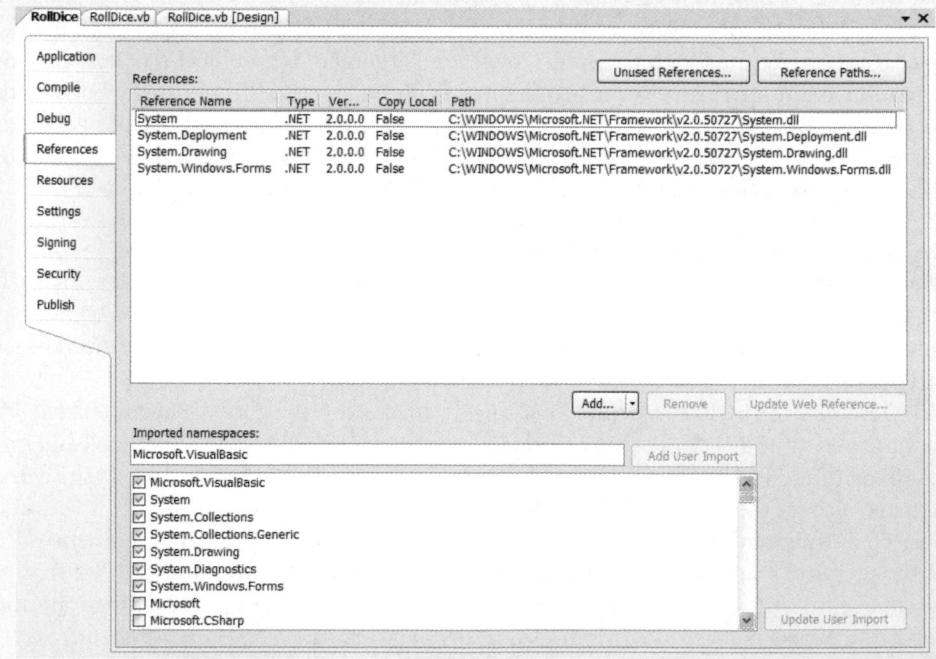

Fig. 7.16 | Imported namespaces in a project.

Chapter 26, Collections). Do not confuse importing namespaces for an entire application with adding references to an application. Adding a reference to an application causes a library (.dll) file to be included into your application. This compiled code can contain several namespaces. An Imports statement indicates that you will be using a specific namespace from a library file.

The Windows application in Fig. 7.17 enables the reader to repeatedly roll 12 dice to show that the numbers generated by class Random occur with approximately equal frequencies. The program displays the cumulative frequencies of each face in a TextBox control, and the die faces are displayed using 12 PictureBoxes.

The TextBox control is located toward the bottom of the GUI. This control can be used both for displaying data to the user and inputting data from the user. The data in the TextBox can be accessed and modified via the control's Text property. This TextBox's name is txtDisplay (we use the txt prefix for TextBoxes) and the font size has been set to 9. Finally, the TextBox's Multiline property has been set to True, so that multiple lines of text can be displayed.

Figure 7.17 contains two screenshots. The one on the left shows the program when it initially executes, and the one on the right shows the program after the user has clicked **Roll** over 200 times. If the values produced by method Next are indeed random, the frequencies of the face values (1–6) should be approximately the same (as Figure 7.17(b) illustrates).

To show that the die rolls occur with approximately equal likelihood, the program in Fig. 7.17 has been modified to keep some simple statistics. We declare counters for each of the possible rolls in lines 7–12. Note that the counters are instance variables. Lines 37–49 display the frequency of each roll as percentages using the P format specifier.

```vb
1    ' Fig. 7.17: RollTwelveDice.vb
2    ' Rolling 12 dice with frequency chart.
3    Imports System.IO
4
5    Public Class FrmRollTwelveDice
6       Dim randomObject As New Random() ' generate random number
7       Dim ones As Integer ' count of die face 1
8       Dim twos As Integer ' count of die face 2
9       Dim threes As Integer ' count of die face 3
10      Dim fours As Integer ' count of die face 4
11      Dim fives As Integer ' count of die face 5
12      Dim sixes As Integer ' count of die face 6
13
14      ' display result of twelve rolls
15      Private Sub btnRoll_Click(ByVal sender As System.Object, _
16         ByVal e As System.EventArgs) Handles btnRoll.Click
17
18         ' assign random faces to 12 dice using DisplayDie
19         DisplayDie(picDie1)
20         DisplayDie(picDie2)
21         DisplayDie(picDie3)
22         DisplayDie(picDie4)
23         DisplayDie(picDie5)
```

Fig. 7.17 | Random class used to simulate rolling 12 six-sided dice. (Part 1 of 3.)

```vbnet
24          DisplayDie(picDie6)
25          DisplayDie(picDie7)
26          DisplayDie(picDie8)
27          DisplayDie(picDie9)
28          DisplayDie(picDie10)
29          DisplayDie(picDie11)
30          DisplayDie(picDie12)
31
32          Dim total As Integer = ones + twos + threes + fours + fives + sixes
33          Dim output As String
34
35          ' display frequencies of faces
36          output = ("Face" & vbTab & vbTab & "Frequency" & vbTab & "Percent")
37          output &= (vbCrLf & "1" & vbTab & vbTab & ones & _
38              vbTab & vbTab & String.Format("{0:P}", ones / total))
39          output &= (vbCrLf & "2" & vbTab & vbTab & twos & vbTab & _
40              vbTab & String.Format("{0:P}", twos / total))
41          output &= (vbCrLf & "3" & vbTab & vbTab & threes & vbTab & _
42              vbTab & String.Format("{0:P}", threes / total))
43          output &= (vbCrLf & "4" & vbTab & vbTab & fours & vbTab & _
44              vbTab & String.Format("{0:P}", fours / total))
45          output &= (vbCrLf & "5" & vbTab & vbTab & fives & vbTab & _
46              vbTab & String.Format("{0:P}", fives / total))
47          output &= (vbCrLf & "6" & vbTab & vbTab & sixes & vbTab & _
48              vbTab & String.Format("{0:P}", sixes / total) & vbCrLf)
49          txtDisplay.Text = output
50      End Sub ' btnRoll_Click
51
52      ' display a single die image
53      Sub DisplayDie(ByVal picDie As PictureBox)
54          Dim face As Integer = randomObject.Next(1, 7)
55
56          picDie.Image = Image.FromFile(Directory.GetCurrentDirectory & _
57              "\Images\die" & face & ".png")
58
59          ' maintain count of die faces
60          Select Case face
61              Case 1 ' die face 1
62                  ones += 1
63              Case 2 ' die face 2
64                  twos += 1
65              Case 3 ' die face 3
66                  threes += 1
67              Case 4 ' die face 4
68                  fours += 1
69              Case 5 ' die face 5
70                  fives += 1
71              Case 6 ' die face 6
72                  sixes += 1
73          End Select
74      End Sub ' DisplayDie
75  End Class ' FrmRollTwelveDice
```

Fig. 7.17 | Random class used to simulate rolling 12 six-sided dice. (Part 2 of 3.)

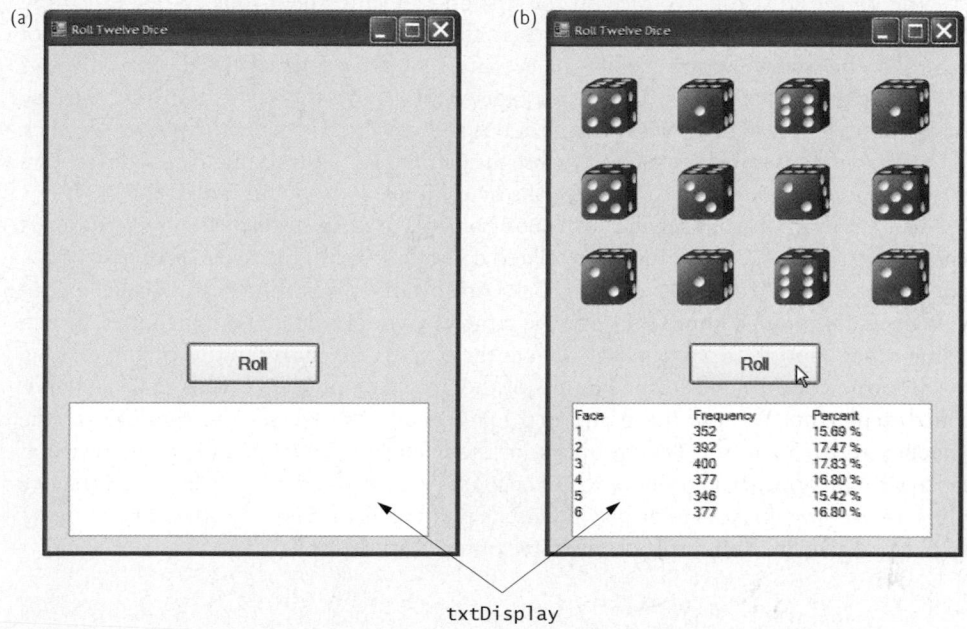

(a)   (b)

txtDisplay

Fig. 7.17 | Random class used to simulate rolling 12 six-sided dice. (Part 3 of 3.)

As the program output demonstrates, method Next can be used to effectively simulate the rolling of a six-sided die. Over the course of many die rolls, each of the possible faces from 1–6 appears with equal likelihood, or approximately one-sixth of the time. Note that *no* Case Else is provided in the Select...Case statement (lines 60–73), because we know that the values generated are in the range 1–6. In Chapter 8, Arrays, we show the power of arrays by explaining how to replace the entire Select...Case statement in this program with a single-line statement.

Run the program several times and observe the results. Note that a different sequence of random numbers is obtained each time the program is executed, causing the resulting frequencies to vary.

7.16 Case Study: A Game of Chance

One of the most popular games of chance is a dice game known as "craps." The rules of the game are straightforward:

A player rolls two dice. Each die has six faces. Each face contains 1, 2, 3, 4, 5 or 6 spots. After the dice have come to rest, the sum of the spots on the two upward faces is calculated. If the sum is 7 or 11 on the first throw, the player wins. If the sum is 2, 3 or 12 on the first throw (called "craps"), the player loses (i.e., the "house" wins). If the sum is 4, 5, 6, 8, 9 or 10 on the first throw, that sum becomes the player's "point." To win, players must continue rolling the dice until they "make their point" (i.e., roll their point value). The player loses by rolling a 7 before making the point.

The application in Fig. 7.18 simulates the game of craps.

The player must roll two dice on the first and all subsequent rolls. When executing the application, click the **Play** Button to play the game. The form displays the results of each roll. The screen captures depict the execution of two games. Figure 7.18(a) displays the Form before the game has begun, while Fig. 7.18(b) shows the application after the **Play** Button has been clicked. In this example, a 6 is rolled, which is made the point. We click **Roll** again and a 7 is rolled, causing us to lose the game (Fig. 7.18(c)). Figure 7.18(d) shows another example game, where the user wins by rolling a 7 on the first roll.

This program introduces the **GroupBox** control, used to display the user's point. A GroupBox is a container used to group related controls. Within the GroupBox pointDice-Group, we add two PictureBoxes, which are controls that display images. A GroupBox can be dragged and dropped onto the Form the same way you would any other control. When adding other controls to a GroupBox (such as the two PictureBoxes in this example), drag and drop the controls within the bounds of the GroupBox on the Form. The GroupBox is named grpPoint. We use the prefix grp for GroupBoxes. We set the font size of the GroupBox to 9.75 and the **Text** property of the GroupBox to **Point**. This is the text that displays in the upper-left corner of the GroupBox. Note in the output of Fig. 7.18 that we will be modifying this text to display the user's point value. If you leave the Text property blank, the GroupBox will display as a simple border without any text.

```
 1    ' Fig. 7.18: CrapsGame.vb
 2    ' Playing a craps game.
 3    Imports System.IO
 4
 5    Public Class FrmCrapsGame
 6        ' die-roll constants
 7        Enum DiceNames
 8            SNAKE_EYES = 2
 9            TREY = 3
10            LUCKY_SEVEN = 7
11            CRAPS = 7
12            YO_LEVEN = 11
13            BOX_CARS = 12
14        End Enum
15
16        ' file-name and directory constants
17        Const FILE_PREFIX As String = "/images/die"
18        Const FILE_SUFFIX As String = ".png"
19
20        Dim myPoint As Integer ' total point
21        Dim myDie1 As Integer ' die1 face
22        Dim myDie2 As Integer ' die2 face
23        Dim randomObject As New Random() ' generate random number
24
25        ' begins new game and determines point
26        Private Sub btnPlay_Click(ByVal sender As System.Object, _
27            ByVal e As System.EventArgs) Handles btnPlay.Click
28
29            ' initialize variables for new game
30            myPoint = 0
```

Fig. 7.18 | Craps game using class Random. (Part 1 of 3.)

```vbnet
31          grpPoint.Text = "Point"
32          lblStatus.Text = ""
33
34          ' remove point-die images
35          picPointDie1.Image = Nothing
36          picPointDie2.Image = Nothing
37
38          Dim sum As Integer = RollDice() ' roll dice and calculate sum
39
40          ' check die roll
41          Select Case sum
42             Case DiceNames.LUCKY_SEVEN, DiceNames.YO_LEVEN
43                btnRoll.Enabled = False ' disable Roll button
44                lblStatus.Text = "You Win!!!"
45             Case DiceNames.SNAKE_EYES, DiceNames.TREY, DiceNames.BOX_CARS
46                btnRoll.Enabled = False ' disable Roll button
47                lblStatus.Text = "Sorry. You Lose."
48             Case Else
49                myPoint = sum
50                grpPoint.Text = "Point is " & sum
51                lblStatus.Text = "Roll Again!"
52                DisplayDie(picPointDie1, myDie1)
53                DisplayDie(picPointDie2, myDie2)
54                btnPlay.Enabled = False ' disable Play button
55                btnRoll.Enabled = True ' enable Roll button
56          End Select
57       End Sub ' btnPlay_Click
58
59    ' determines outcome of next roll
60    Private Sub btnRoll_Click(ByVal sender As System.Object, _
61       ByVal e As System.EventArgs) Handles btnRoll.Click
62
63          Dim sum As Integer = RollDice() ' roll dice and calculate sum
64
65          ' check outcome of roll
66          If sum = myPoint Then ' win
67             lblStatus.Text = "You Win!!!"
68             btnRoll.Enabled = False ' disable Roll button
69             btnPlay.Enabled = True ' enable Play button
70          ElseIf sum = DiceNames.CRAPS Then ' lose
71             lblStatus.Text = "Sorry. You Lose."
72             btnRoll.Enabled = False ' disable Roll button
73             btnPlay.Enabled = True ' enable Play button
74          End If
75       End Sub ' btnRoll_Click
76
77    ' display die image
78    Sub DisplayDie(ByVal picDie As PictureBox, _
79       ByVal face As Integer)
80          ' assign die image to picture box
81          picDie.Image = Image.FromFile(Directory.GetCurrentDirectory & _
82             FILE_PREFIX & face & FILE_SUFFIX)
83       End Sub ' DisplayDie
```

Fig. 7.18 | Craps game using class **Random**. (Part 2 of 3.)

```
84
85        ' generate random die rolls
86        Function RollDice() As Integer
87            ' determine random integer
88            myDie1 = randomObject.Next(1, 7)
89            myDie2 = randomObject.Next(1, 7)
90
91            ' display rolls
92            DisplayDie(picDie1, myDie1)
93            DisplayDie(picDie2, myDie2)
94
95            Return myDie1 + myDie2 ' return sum
96        End Function ' RollDice
97    End Class ' FrmCrapsGame
```

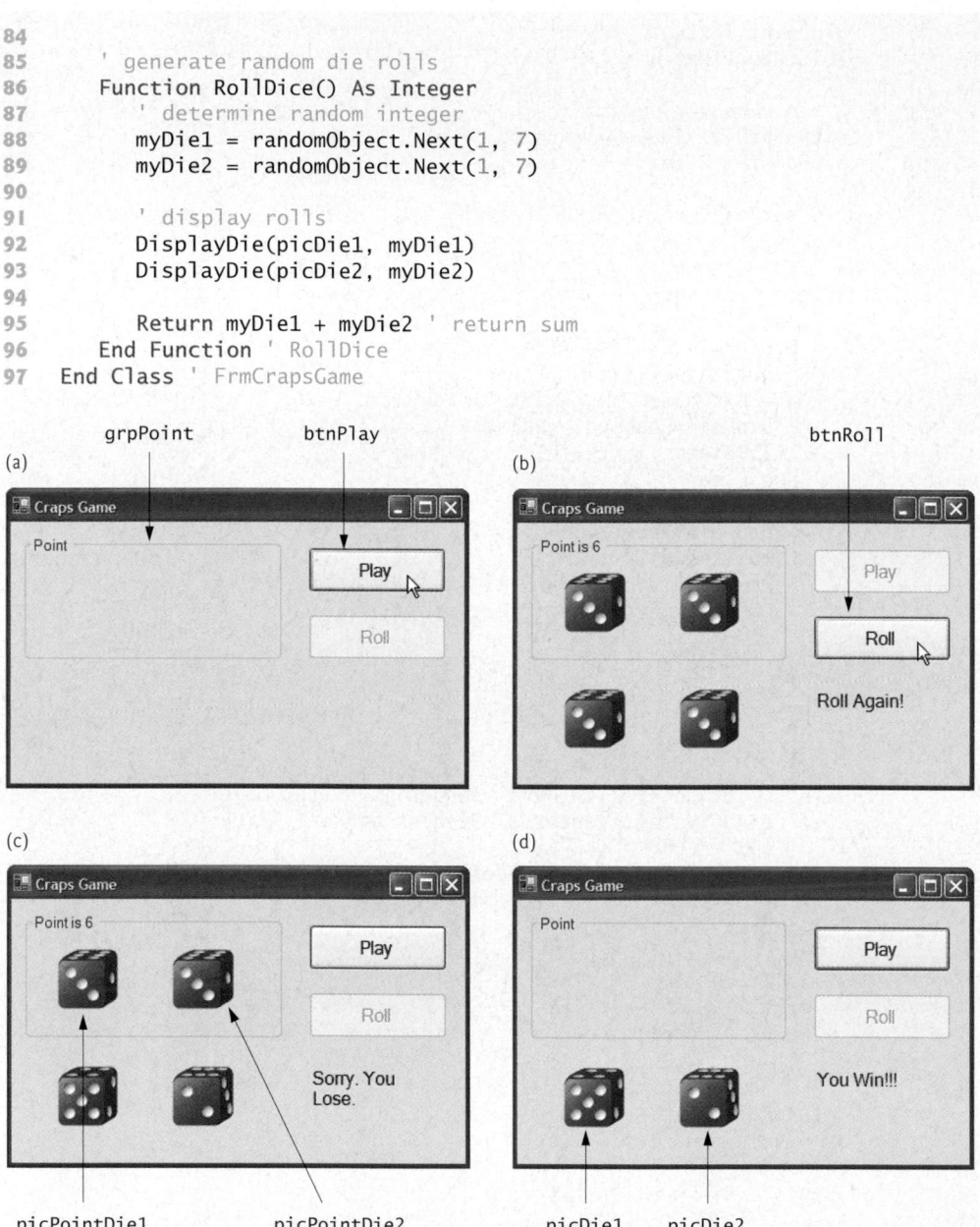

Fig. 7.18 | Craps game using class Random. (Part 3 of 3.)

Enumerations and Constants

Before introducing any method declarations, the program includes several declarations, including our first enumeration in lines 7–14 and our first constant identifiers in lines 17–18. Constant identifiers and Enumerations enhance program readability by providing descriptive identifiers for constant numbers or Strings. Constant identifiers and Enumerations help you ensure that values are consistent throughout a program. Recall that keyword Const creates a single constant identifier; Enumerations are used to define groups of related constants. In this case, we create Constant identifiers for the file names that are used throughout the program and create an Enumeration of descriptive names for the various dice combinations in craps (i.e., SNAKE_EYES, TREY, LUCKY_SEVEN, CRAPS, YO_LEVEN and BOX_CARS). Note that multiple enumeration members can have the same value—in this example, LUCKY_SEVEN and CRAPS both have the value 7. We use two identifiers for program clarity; on the first roll, a seven causes the player to win (LUCKY_SEVEN), and on subsequent rolls, a seven causes the player to lose (CRAPS). Constant identifiers must be assigned constant values and cannot be modified after they are declared.

After the constant-identifier declarations and the declarations for several instance variables (lines 20–23), method btnPlay_Click is declared (lines 26–57). It is the event handler for btnPlay's Click event. When the user clicks the **Play** button, method btnPlay_Click sets up a new game by initializing several values (lines 30–32). Note that line 32 sets our status Label's Text property to "". This is known as the **empty string** (i.e., a string that does not contain any characters). Nothing appears on the screen when an empty string is displayed. Setting the Image property of picPointDie1 and picPointDie2 to Nothing (lines 35–36) causes the PictureBoxes to appear blank. Method btnPlay_Click executes the game's opening roll by calling RollDice (line 38). Internally, RollDice (lines 86–96) generates two random numbers and calls method DisplayDie (lines 78–83), which loads an appropriate die image in the PictureBox passed to it.

The Select...Case statement (lines 41–56) analyzes the roll returned by RollDice to determine how play should continue (i.e., by terminating the game with a win or loss, or by enabling subsequent rolls). If the user does not win or lose on the first roll, the GroupBox's text is set to display the point value (line 50) and the property images are displayed in the GroupBox's PictureBoxes (lines 52–53). Depending on the value of the roll, Buttons **Roll** and **Play** become either enabled or disabled (lines 43, 46 and 54–55). Disabling a Button means that no action will be performed when the Button is clicked. Buttons can be enabled and disabled by setting the Button's Enabled property to True or False, respectively.

If button **Roll** is enabled, clicking it invokes method btnRoll_Click (lines 60–75), which executes an additional roll of the dice. Method btnRoll_Click then analyzes the roll, letting users know whether they have won or lost.

7.17 Method Overloading

Visual Basic provides several ways of allowing methods to have variable sets of parameters. **Method overloading** allows you to create multiple methods with the same name but different **signatures**—that is, different numbers and types of parameters, or with different orderings of the parameters (by type). When an overloaded method is called, the compiler selects the proper method by examining the number, types and order (by type) of the arguments. Often, method overloading is used to create several methods with the same name that perform similar tasks on different types of data.

Good Programming Practice 7.3

Overloading methods that perform closely related tasks can make programs clearer.

The program in Fig. 7.19 uses overloaded method Square to calculate the square of both an Integer and a Double.

If the compiler looked only at method names during compilation, the code in Fig. 7.19 would be ambiguous—the compiler would not know how to differentiate between the two Square methods. The compiler uses a process known as **overload resolution** to determine which method to call. This process first searches for all methods that *could* be used on the basis of the number and type of arguments that are present. Although it might seem that only one method would match, it is important to remember that Visual Basic converts variables as necessary when they are passed as arguments. Once all matching methods are found, the compiler then selects the closest match.

Note that at line 12 we use method Convert.ToInt32, which converts its argument to a value of type Integer. This explicit conversion is needed because the exponent (^) operator expects operands of type Double, and implicitly converts its operands to that type. This version of method Square returns an Integer value, so Convert.ToInt32 performs this conversion. Recall that because we are now using **Option Strict**, such conversion is required to compile the application.

In Fig. 7.19, the compiler might use the logical name "Square of Integer" for the Square method that specifies an Integer parameter (line 10) and "Square of Double" for the Square method that specifies a Double parameter (line 15). If a method ExampleSub's declaration begins as

```
 1   ' Fig. 7.19: Overload2.vb
 2   ' Using overloaded methods with identical signatures and
 3   ' different return types.
 4   Module Overload2
 5      Sub Main() ' call Square methods with Integer and Double
 6         Console.WriteLine("The square of Integer 7 is " & Square(7) & _
 7            vbCrLf & "The square of Double 7.5 is " & Square(7.5))
 8      End Sub ' Main
 9
10      ' method takes a Double and returns an Integer
11      Function Square(ByVal value As Double) As Integer
12         Return Convert.ToInt32(value ^ 2)
13      End Function ' Square
14
15      ' method takes a Double and returns a Double
16      Function Square(ByVal value As Double) As Double
17         Return value ^ 2
18      End Function ' Square
19   End Module ' Overload2
```

Error List					
⊗ 1 Error	⚠ 0 Warnings	ⓘ 0 Messages			☒
Description ▲		File	Line	Column	Project
⊗ 1 'Public Function Square(value As Double) As Integer' and 'Public Function Square(value As Double) As Double' cannot overload each other because they differ only by return types.		Overload2.vb	11	13	Overload2

Fig. 7.19 | Syntax error generated from overloaded methods with identical parameter lists and different return types.

```
Function ExampleSub(ByVal a As Integer, ByVal b As Double) _
    As Integer
```

the compiler might use the logical name "ExampleSub of Integer and Double." Similarly, if the parameters are specified as

```
Function ExampleSub(ByVal a As Double, ByVal b As Integer) _
    As Integer
```

the compiler might use the logical name "ExampleSub of Double and Integer." The order of the parameters (by type) is important to the compiler; it considers the preceding two ExampleSub methods to be distinct.

So far, the logical method names used by the compiler have not mentioned the methods' return types. This is because method calls cannot be distinguished by return type. The program in Fig. 7.19 illustrates the syntax error that is generated when two methods have the same signature and different return types. Overloaded methods with different parameter lists can have different return types. Overloaded methods need not have the same number of parameters.

Common Programming Error 7.9

Creating overloaded methods with identical parameter lists and different return types is a compilation error.

7.18 **Optional Parameters**

Methods can have **optional parameters**. Declaring a parameter as optional allows the calling method to vary the number of arguments to pass. Optional parameters specify a default value that is assigned to the parameter if the optional argument is not passed. Overloaded methods are generally more flexible than methods with optional parameters. For instance, you can specify different return types for overloaded methods.

You can create methods with one or more optional parameters. All optional parameters, however, must be placed to the right of the method's non-optional parameters.

Common Programming Error 7.10

Declaring a non-Optional parameter to the right of an Optional parameter is a syntax error.

When a parameter is declared as optional, the caller has the *option* of passing that particular argument. Optional parameters are specified in the method header with keyword Optional. For example, the method header

```
Sub ExampleMethod(ByVal value1 As Boolean, Optional _
    ByVal value2 As Integer = 0)
```

specifies the last parameter as Optional. Any call to ExampleMethod must pass at least one argument (the Boolean), or else a syntax error is generated. If the caller chooses, a second argument (the Integer) can be passed to ExampleMethod. Consider the following calls to ExampleMethod:

```
ExampleMethod()
ExampleMethod(True)
ExampleMethod(False, 10)
```

The first call to ExampleMethod generates a syntax error because a minimum of one argument is required for this method. The second call to ExampleMethod is valid because one argument (the Boolean) is being passed—the Optional argument, corresponding to parameter value2, is not specified in the method call. The last call to ExampleMethod also is valid: False is passed as the one required argument, and 10 is passed as the Optional argument.

In the call that passes only one argument (True) to ExampleMethod, parameter value2 defaults to 0, which is the value specified in the method header. Optional parameters must specify a **default value**, using the equals sign followed by the value. For example, the header for ExampleMethod sets 0 as the default value for value2. Default values can be used only with parameters declared as Optional.

 Common Programming Error 7.11

Not specifying a default value for an Optional parameter is a syntax error.

The example in Fig. 7.20 demonstrates the use of optional parameters. The program calculates the result of raising a base to an exponent, both of which are specified by the user. Method Power (lines 23–33) specifies that its second parameter is Optional. If the user does not specify an exponent, the Optional argument is omitted, and the default parameter value, 2, is used.

```vb
1   ' Fig. 7.20: Power.vb
2   ' Calculates the power of a value, demonstrates optional parameters.
3   Public Class FrmPower
4      ' reads input and displays result
5      Private Sub btnCalculate_Click(ByVal sender As System.Object, _
6         ByVal e As System.EventArgs) Handles btnCalculate.Click
7
8         Dim value As Integer
9
10        ' call version of Power depending on power input
11        If Not txtPower.Text = "" Then
12           value = Power(Convert.ToInt32(txtBase.Text), _
13              Convert.ToInt32(txtPower.Text))
14        Else
15           value = Power(Convert.ToInt32(txtBase.Text))
16           txtPower.Text = Convert.ToString(2)
17        End If
18
19        lblOutput.Text = Convert.ToString(value)
20     End Sub ' btnCalculate_Click
21
22     ' use iteration to calculate power
23     Function Power(ByVal base As Integer, _
24        Optional ByVal exponent As Integer = 2) As Integer
25
26        Dim total As Integer = 1 ' initialize total
27
```

Fig. 7.20 | Optional argument demonstration with method Power. (Part 1 of 2.)

```
28          For i As Integer = 1 To exponent ' calculate power
29              total *= base
30          Next
31
32          Return total ' return result
33      End Function ' Power
34  End Class ' FrmPower
```

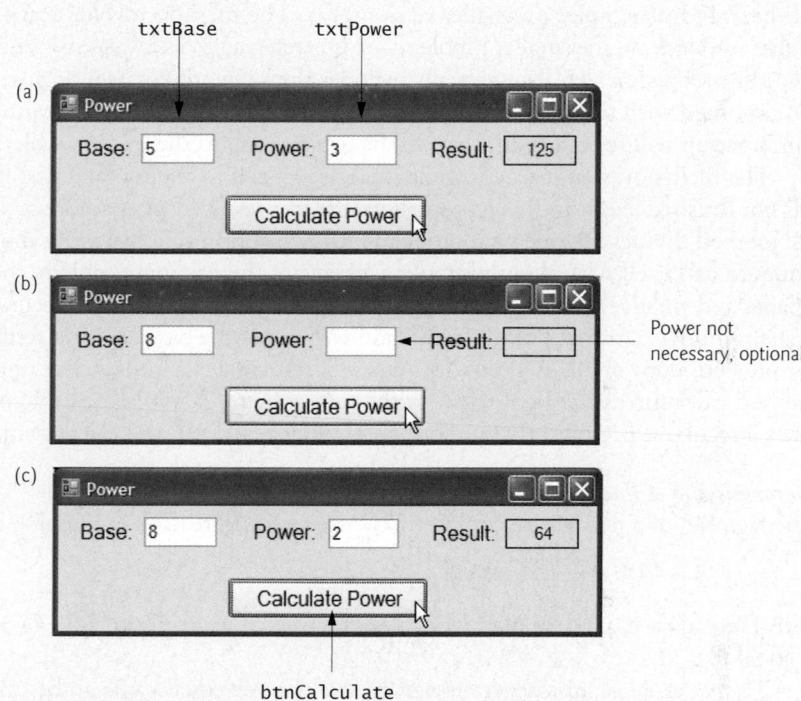

Fig. 7.20 | Optional argument demonstration with method Power. (Part 2 of 2.)

In this example, we use TextBoxes to input data from the user. When the **Calculate Power** Button is clicked, line 11 determines whether txtPower contains a value. If true (as in Fig. 7.20(a)), the values in the TextBoxes are converted to Integers and passed to Power. Otherwise, txtBase's value is converted to an Integer and passed as the first of two arguments to Power in line 15. An example of this is shown in Fig. 7.20(b), where we clicked the **Calculate Power** Button without entering an exponent value. The second argument, 2, is provided by the compiler (using the default value of the Optional argument) and is not visible to you in the call. Line 16 displays the value 2 in txtPower, for clarity (Fig. 7.20(c)).

7.19 Recursion

It is sometimes useful for methods to call themselves—a **recursive method** is a method that calls itself either directly or indirectly (i.e., through another method). In this section, we present a simple example of recursion.

Let us first consider recursion conceptually. Recursive problem-solving approaches have a number of elements in common. A recursive method is called to solve a problem. The method actually knows how to solve only the simplest case(s)—the **base case(s)**. If the method is called with a base case, it returns a result. If the method is called with a more complex problem, it divides the problem into two conceptual pieces—a piece that the method knows how to perform (i.e., base case), and a piece that it does not know how to perform. To make recursion feasible, the latter piece must resemble the original problem but be a slightly simpler or smaller version of it. The method invokes (calls) a fresh copy of itself to work on the smaller problem—this is referred to as a **recursive call**, or **recursion step**. The recursion step also normally includes the keyword Return, because its result will be combined with the portion of the problem that the method knew how to solve. Such a combination will form a result that will be passed back to the original caller.

The recursion step executes while the original call to the method is still "open" (i.e., has not finished executing). The recursion step can result in many more recursive calls, as the method divides each new subproblem into two conceptual pieces. As the method continues to call itself with slightly simpler versions of the original problem, the sequence of smaller and smaller problems must converge on a base case, so that the recursion can eventually terminate. At that point, the method recognizes the base case and returns a result to the previous copy of the method. A sequence of returns ensues up the line until the original method call returns the final result to the caller. As an example of these concepts, let us write a recursive program that performs a popular mathematical calculation.

Determining a Factorial Value Recursively

The factorial of a nonnegative integer n, written $n!$ (and read "n factorial"), is the product

$$n \cdot (n-1) \cdot (n-2) \cdot \ldots \cdot 1$$

with $1!$ equal to 1, and $0!$ defined as 1. For example, $5!$ is the product $5 \cdot 4 \cdot 3 \cdot 2 \cdot 1$, which is equal to 120.

The factorial of an integer number greater than or equal to 0 can be calculated **iteratively** (nonrecursively) using a For...Next statement, as follows:

```
Dim counter, factorial As Integer = 1

For counter = number To 1 Step -1
   factorial *= counter
Next
```

We arrive at a recursive definition of the factorial method by observing the following relationship:

$$n! = n \cdot (n-1)!$$

For example, $5!$ is clearly equal to $5 \cdot 4!$, as is shown by the following:

$$5! = 5 \cdot 4 \cdot 3 \cdot 2 \cdot 1$$
$$5! = 5 \cdot (4 \cdot 3 \cdot 2 \cdot 1)$$
$$5! = 5 \cdot (4!)$$

A recursive evaluation of $5!$ would proceed as in Fig. 7.21. Figure 7.21(a) shows how the succession of recursive calls proceeds until $1!$ is evaluated to be 1, which terminates the

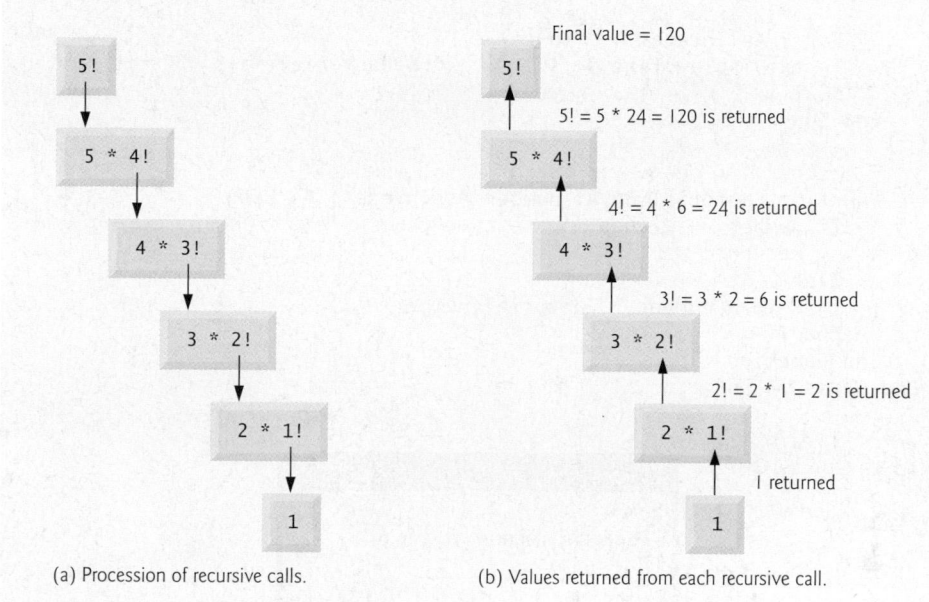

(a) Procession of recursive calls.   (b) Values returned from each recursive call.

Fig. 7.21 | Recursive evaluation of 5!.

recursion. Figure 7.21(b) depicts the values that are returned from each recursive call to its caller until the final value is calculated and returned.

The program in Fig. 7.22 recursively calculates and prints factorials. The recursive method Factorial (lines 19–25) first tests (line 20) to determine whether its terminating condition is true (i.e., number is less than or equal to 1). This determines whether the parameter is one of the base cases (0 or 1). If number is less than or equal to 1, Factorial returns 1, no further recursion is necessary and the method returns. If number is greater than 1, line 23 expresses the problem as the product of number and a recursive call to Factorial, evaluating the factorial of number - 1. Note that calculating Factorial(number - 1) is slightly simpler than the original calculation, Factorial(number).

```vb
1    ' Fig. 7.22: Factorial.vb
2    ' Calculating factorials using recursion.
3    Public Class FrmFactorial
4       ' calculate factorial
5       Private Sub btnCalculate_Click(ByVal sender As System.Object, _
6          ByVal e As System.EventArgs) Handles btnCalculate.Click
7
8          ' convert text in TextBox to Integer
9          Dim value As Integer = Convert.ToInt32(txtInput.Text)
10         txtDisplay.Text = "" ' reset TextBox
11
```

Fig. 7.22 | Recursive factorial program. (Part 1 of 2.)

```
12            ' call Factorial to perform calculation
13            For i As Integer = 0 To value
14                txtDisplay.Text &= i & "! = " & Factorial(i) & vbCrLf
15            Next
16        End Sub ' btnCalculate_Click
17
18        ' recursively generates factorial of number
19        Function Factorial(ByVal number As Integer) As Long
20            If number <= 1 Then ' base case
21                Return 1
22            Else
23                Return number * Factorial(number - 1)
24            End If
25        End Function ' Factorial
26    End Class ' FrmFactorial
```

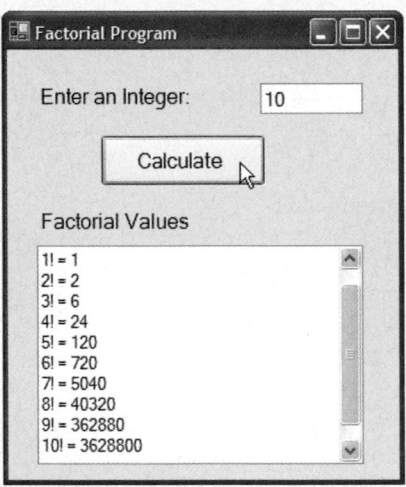

Fig. 7.22 | Recursive factorial program. (Part 2 of 2.)

We have set the output TextBox's **ScrollBars** property to Vertical, to display a vertical scrollbar. This allows us to display more outputs than will fit in the space allocated for the TextBox. Method Factorial (line 19) receives a parameter of type Integer and returns a result of type Long. Type **Long** is designed to store integer values in a range much larger than that of type Integer. As is seen in the output window of Fig. 7.22, factorial values grow quickly. We choose type Long to enable the program to calculate factorials greater than 12!. Unfortunately, the values produced by the Factorial method increase at such a rate that the range of even the Long type is quickly exceeded. This points to a weakness in most programming languages—they are not easily extended to handle the unique requirements of various applications, such as the evaluation of large factorials. Recall that Visual Basic is an extensible language—programmers with unique requirements can extend the language by defining new classes. You could create a HugeInteger class that would enable a program to calculate the factorials of arbitrarily large numbers— we create a HugeInteger class in Chapter 22, Web Services.

Common Programming Error 7.12

Forgetting to return a value from a recursive method can result in logic errors.

Common Programming Error 7.13

*Omitting the base case or writing the recursion step so that it does not converge on the base case will cause **infinite recursion**, eventually exhausting memory. This is analogous to the problem of an infinite loop in an iterative (nonrecursive) solution.*

7.20 (Optional) Software Engineering Case Study: Identifying Class Operations in the ATM System

In the Software Engineering Case Study sections at the ends of Chapters 4–6, we performed the first few steps in the object-oriented design of our ATM system. In Chapter 4, we identified the classes that we will likely need to implement and we created our first class diagram. In Chapter 5, we described some attributes of our classes. In Chapter 6, we examined our objects' states and modeled the objects' state transitions and activities. In this section, we determine some of the class operations (or behaviors) needed to implement the ATM system.

Identifying Operations

An operation is a service that objects of a class provide to clients of the class. Consider the operations of some real-world objects. A radio's operations include setting its station and volume (typically invoked by a person adjusting the radio's controls). A car's operations include accelerating (invoked by the driver pressing the accelerator pedal), decelerating (invoked by the driver pressing the brake pedal or releasing the gas pedal), turning, and shifting gears. Software objects can offer operations as well—for example, a software graphics object might offer operations for drawing a circle, drawing a line, drawing a square and the like. A spreadsheet software object might offer operations like printing the spreadsheet, totaling the elements in a row or column and graphing information in the spreadsheet as a bar chart or pie chart.

We can derive many of the operations of the classes in our ATM system by examining the verbs and verb phrases in the requirements document. We then relate each of these to particular classes in our system (Fig. 7.23). The verb phrases in Fig. 7.23 help us determine the operations of our classes.

Class	Verbs and verb phrases
ATM	executes financial transactions
BalanceInquiry	[none in the requirements document]
Withdrawal	[none in the requirements document]
Deposit	[none in the requirements document]
BankDatabase	authenticates a user, retrieves an account balance, credits an account by a deposit amount, debits an account by a withdrawal amount

Fig. 7.23 | Verbs and verb phrases for each class in the ATM system. (Part 1 of 2.)

Class	Verbs and verb phrases
Account	retrieves an account balance, credits an account by a deposit amount, debits an account by a withdrawal amount
Screen	displays a message to the user
Keypad	receives numeric input from the user
CashDispenser	dispenses cash, indicates whether it contains enough cash to satisfy a withdrawal request
DepositSlot	receives a deposit envelope

Fig. 7.23 | Verbs and verb phrases for each class in the ATM system. (Part 2 of 2.)

Modeling Operations

To identify operations, we examine the verb phrases listed for each class in Fig. 7.23. The "executes financial transactions" phrase associated with class ATM implies that class ATM instructs transactions to execute. Therefore, classes BalanceInquiry, Withdrawal and Deposit each need an operation to provide this service to the ATM. We place this operation (which we have named Execute) in the third compartment of the three transaction classes in the updated class diagram of Fig. 7.24. During an ATM session, the ATM object will invoke the Execute operation of each transaction object to tell it to execute.

The UML represents operations (which are implemented as methods in Visual Basic) by listing the operation name, followed by a comma-separated list of parameters in parentheses, a colon and the return type:

operationName(parameter1 , parameter2 , …, parameterN) : returnType

Each parameter in the comma-separated parameter list consists of a parameter name, followed by a colon and the parameter type:

parameterName : parameterType

For the moment, we do not list the parameters of our operations—we will identify and model the parameters of some of the operations shortly. For some of the operations, we do not yet know the return types, so we also omit them from the diagram. These omissions are perfectly normal at this point. As our design and implementation proceed, we will add the remaining return types.

Operations of Class *BankDatabase* and Class *Account*

Figure 7.23 lists the phrase "authenticates a user" next to class BankDatabase—the database is the object that contains the account information necessary to determine whether the account number and PIN entered by a user match those of an account held at the bank. Therefore, class BankDatabase needs an operation that provides an authentication service to the ATM. We place the operation AuthenticateUser in the third compartment of class BankDatabase (Fig. 7.24). However, an object of class Account, not class BankDatabase, stores the account number and PIN that must be accessed to authenticate a user, so class Account must provide a service to validate a PIN obtained through user input

Fig. 7.24 | Classes in the ATM system with attributes and operations.

against a PIN stored in an `Account` object. Therefore, we add a `ValidatePIN` operation to class `Account`. Note that we specify a return type of `Boolean` for the `AuthenticateUser` and `ValidatePIN` operations. Each operation returns a value indicating either that the operation was successful in performing its task (i.e., a return value of `True`) or that it was not successful (i.e., a return value of `False`).

Figure 7.23 lists several additional verb phrases for class `BankDatabase`: "retrieves an account balance," "credits an account by a deposit amount" and "debits an account by a withdrawal amount." Like "authenticates a user," these phrases refer to services that the database must provide to the ATM, because the database holds all the account data used to authenticate a user and perform ATM transactions. However, `Account` objects actually perform the operations to which these phrases refer. Thus, class `BankDatabase` and class `Account` both need operations that correspond to each of these phrases. Recall from Section 4.9 that, because a bank account contains sensitive information, we do not allow the ATM to access accounts directly. The database acts as an intermediary between the ATM and the account data, preventing unauthorized access. As we will see in Section 8.17, class ATM invokes the operations of class BankDatabase, each of which in turn invokes operations (which are the Get accessors of ReadOnly properties) in class Account.

The phrase "retrieves an account balance" suggests that classes BankDatabase and Account each need an operation that gets the balance. However, recall that Fig. 5.32 specified two attributes in class Account to represent a balance—availableBalance and totalBalance. A balance inquiry requires access to both balance attributes so that it can display them to the user, but a withdrawal needs to check only the value of available-Balance. To allow objects in the system to obtain these balance attributes individually from a specific Account object in the BankDatabase, we add operations GetAvailable-Balance and GetTotalBalance to the third compartment of class BankDatabase (Fig. 7.24). We specify a return type of Decimal for each of these operations, because the balances which they retrieve are of type Decimal.

Once the BankDatabase knows which Account to access, the BankDatabase must be able to obtain each balance attribute individually from that Account. For this purpose, we could add operations GetAvailableBalance and GetTotalBalance to the third compartment of class Account (Fig. 7.24). However, in Visual Basic, simple operations such as getting the value of an attribute are typically performed by a property's Get accessor (at least when that particular class "owns" the underlying attribute). This design is for a Visual Basic application, so rather than modeling operations GetAvailableBalance and Get-TotalBalance, we model Decimal properties AvailableBalance and TotalBalance in class Account. Properties are placed in the second compartment of a class diagram. These properties replace the availableBalance and totalBalance attributes that we modeled for class Account in Fig. 5.32. Recall from Chapter 4 that a property's accessors are implied, thus they are not modeled in a class diagram. Figure 7.23 does not mention the need to set the balances, so Fig. 7.24 shows properties AvailableBalance and TotalBalance as ReadOnly properties (i.e., they have only Get accessors). To indicate a ReadOnly property, we follow the property's type with "{ReadOnly}."

You may be wondering why we modeled AvailableBalance and TotalBalance *properties* in class Account, but modeled GetAvailableBalance and GetTotalBalance *operations* in class BankDatabase. Since there can be many Account objects in the BankDatabase, the ATM must specify which Account to access when invoking BankDatabase operations GetAvailableBalance and GetTotalBalance. The ATM does this by passing an account number argument to each BankDatabase operation. The Get accessors of the properties you have seen in Visual Basic code cannot receive arguments. Thus, we modeled GetAvailableBalance and GetTotalBalance as operations in class BankDatabase so that we could specify parameters to which the ATM can pass arguments. Also, the underlying balance attributes are not owned by the BankDatabase, so Get accessors are not appropriate here. We discuss the parameters for the BankDatabase operations shortly.

The phrases "credits an account by a deposit amount" and "debits an account by a withdrawal amount" indicate that classes BankDatabase and Account must perform operations to update an account during a deposit and withdrawal, respectively. We therefore assign Credit and Debit operations to classes BankDatabase and Account. You may recall that crediting an account (as in a deposit) adds an amount only to the Account's total balance. Debiting an account (as in a withdrawal), on the other hand, subtracts the amount from both the total and available balances. We hide these implementation details inside class Account. This is a good example of encapsulation and information hiding.

If this were a real ATM system, classes BankDatabase and Account would also provide a set of operations to allow another banking system to update a user's account balance after either confirming or rejecting all or part of a deposit. Operation ConfirmDepositAmount, for example, would add an amount to the Account's available balance, thus making deposited funds available for withdrawal. Operation RejectDepositAmount would subtract an amount from the Account's total balance to indicate that a specified amount, which had recently been deposited through the ATM and added to the Account's total balance, was invalidated (or checks may have "bounced"). The bank would invoke operation Reject-DepositAmount after determining either that the user failed to include the correct amount of cash or that any checks did not clear (i.e., they "bounced"). While adding these operations would make our system more complete, we do not include them in our class diagrams or implementation because they are beyond the scope of the case study.

Operations of Class *Screen*

Class Screen "displays a message to the user" at various times in an ATM session. All visual output occurs through the screen of the ATM. The requirements document describes many types of messages (e.g., a welcome message, an error message, a thank-you message) that the screen displays to the user. The requirements document also indicates that the screen displays prompts and menus to the user. However, a prompt is really just a message describing what the user should input next, and a menu is essentially a type of prompt consisting of a series of messages (i.e., menu options) displayed consecutively. Therefore, rather than assign class Screen an individual operation to display each type of message, prompt and menu, we simply create one operation that can display any message specified by a parameter. We place this operation (DisplayMessage) in the third compartment of class Screen in our class diagram (Fig. 7.24). Note that we do not worry about the parameter of this operation at this time—we model the parameter momentarily.

Operations of Class *Keypad*

From the phrase "receives numeric input from the user" listed by class Keypad in Fig. 7.23, we conclude that class Keypad should perform a GetInput operation. Because the ATM's keypad, unlike a computer keyboard, contains only the numbers 0–9, we specify that this operation returns an integer value. Recall from the requirements document that in different situations the user may be required to enter a different type of number (e.g., an account number, a PIN, the number of a menu option, a deposit amount as a number of cents). Class Keypad simply obtains a numeric value for a client of the class—it does not determine whether the value meets any specific criteria. Any class that uses this operation must verify that the user enters appropriate numbers, and if not, display error messages via class Screen). [*Note:* When we implement the system, we simulate the ATM's keypad with a computer keyboard, and for simplicity we assume that the user does not enter nonnumeric input using keys on the computer keyboard that do not appear on the ATM's keypad. In Chapter 16, Strings, Characters and Regular Expressions, you will learn how to examine inputs to determine if they are of particular types.]

Operations of Class *CashDispenser* and Class *DepositSlot*

Figure 7.23 lists "dispenses cash" for class CashDispenser. Therefore, we create operation DispenseCash and list it under class CashDispenser in Fig. 7.24. Class CashDispenser also "indicates whether it contains enough cash to satisfy a withdrawal request." Thus, we include `IsSufficientCashAvailable`, an operation that returns a value of type `Boolean`, in class `CashDispenser`. Figure 7.23 also lists "receives a deposit envelope" for class `DepositSlot`. The deposit slot must indicate whether it received an envelope, so we place the operation `IsDepositEnvelopeReceived`, which returns a `Boolean` value, in the third compartment of class `DepositSlot`. [*Note:* A real hardware deposit slot would most likely send the ATM a signal to indicate that an envelope was received. We simulate this behavior, however, with an operation in class `DepositSlot` that class `ATM` can invoke to find out whether the deposit slot received an envelope.]

Operations of Class *ATM*

We do not list any operations for class `ATM` at this time. We are not yet aware of any services that class `ATM` provides to other classes in the system. When we implement the system in Visual Basic (Appendix J), however, operations of this class, and additional operations of the other classes in the system, may become apparent.

Identifying and Modeling Operation Parameters

So far, we have not been concerned with the parameters of our operations—we have attempted to gain only a basic understanding of the operations of each class. Let's now take a closer look at some operation parameters. We identify an operation's parameters by examining what data the operation requires to perform its assigned task.

Consider class `BankDatabase`'s `AuthenticateUser` operation. To authenticate a user, this operation must know the account number and PIN supplied by the user. Thus we specify that operation `AuthenticateUser` takes integer parameters `userAccountNumber` and `userPIN`, which the operation must compare to the account number and PIN of an `Account` object in the database. We prefix these parameter names with "user" to avoid confusion between the operation's parameter names and the attribute names that belong to class `Account`. We list these parameters in the class diagram in Fig. 7.25 that models only class `BankDatabase`. [*Note:* It is perfectly normal to model only one class in a class diagram. In this case, we are most concerned with examining the parameters of this one class in particular, so we omit the other classes. In class diagrams later in the case study, in which parameters are no longer the focus of our attention, we omit the parameters to save space. Remember, however, that the operations listed in these diagrams still have parameters.]

Recall that the UML models each parameter in an operation's comma-separated parameter list by listing the parameter name, followed by a colon and the parameter type. Figure 7.25 thus specifies, for example, that operation `AuthenticateUser` takes two parameters—`userAccountNumber` and `userPIN`, both of type `Integer`.

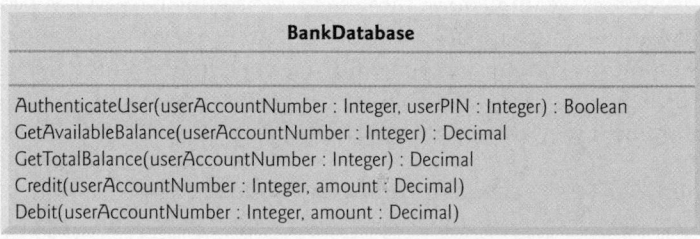

Fig. 7.25 | Class `BankDatabase` with operation parameters.

Class BankDatabase operations GetAvailableBalance, GetTotalBalance, Credit and Debit also each require a userAccountNumber parameter to identify the account to which the database must apply the operations, so we include these parameters in the class diagram. In addition, operations Credit and Debit each require a Decimal parameter amount to specify the amount of money to be credited or debited, respectively.

The class diagram in Fig. 7.26 models the parameters of class Account's operations. Operation ValidatePIN requires only a userPIN parameter, which contains the user-specified PIN to be compared with the PIN associated with the account. Like their counterparts in class BankDatabase, operations Credit and Debit in class Account each require a Decimal parameter amount that indicates the amount of money involved in the operation. Note that class Account's operations do not require an account number parameter—each of these operations can be invoked only on the Account object in which they are executing, so including a parameter to specify an Account is unnecessary.

Figure 7.27 models class Screen with a parameter specified for operation Display-Message. This operation requires only a String parameter message that indicates the text to be displayed.

The class diagram in Fig. 7.28 specifies that operation DispenseCash of class Cash-Dispenser takes a Decimal parameter amount to indicate the amount of cash (in dollars) to be dispensed. Operation IsSufficientCashAvailable also takes a Decimal parameter amount to indicate the amount of cash in question.

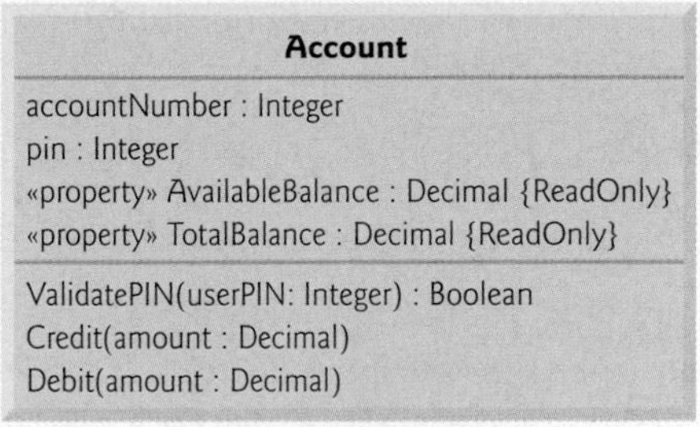

Account
accountNumber : Integer
pin : Integer
«property» AvailableBalance : Decimal {ReadOnly}
«property» TotalBalance : Decimal {ReadOnly}
ValidatePIN(userPIN: Integer) : Boolean
Credit(amount : Decimal)
Debit(amount : Decimal)

Fig. 7.26 | Class Account with operation parameters.

Screen
DisplayMessage(message : String)

Fig. 7.27 | Class Screen with an operation parameter.

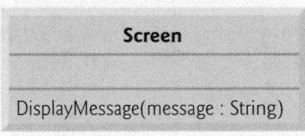

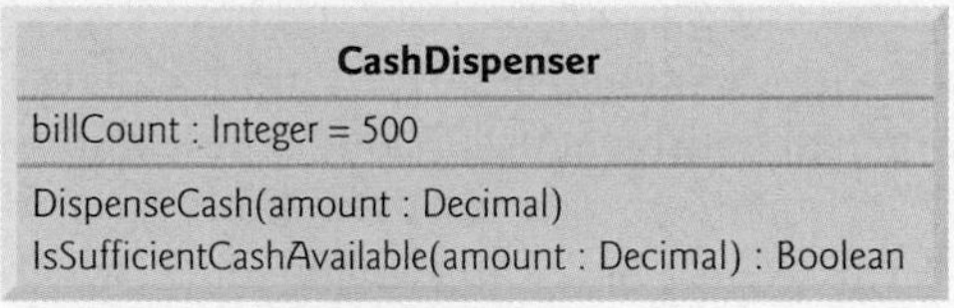

CashDispenser
billCount : Integer = 500
DispenseCash(amount : Decimal)
IsSufficientCashAvailable(amount : Decimal) : Boolean

Fig. 7.28 | Class CashDispenser with operation parameters.

Note that we do not discuss parameters for operation Execute of classes Balance-Inquiry, Withdrawal and Deposit, operation GetInput of class Keypad and operation IsDepositEnvelopeReceived of class DepositSlot. At this point in our design process, we cannot determine whether these operations require additional data to perform their tasks, so we leave their parameter lists empty. As we progress through the case study, we may decide to add parameters to these operations.

In this section, we have determined many of the operations performed by the classes in the ATM system. We have identified the parameters and return types of some of the operations. As we continue our design process, the number of operations belonging to each class may vary—we might find that new operations are needed or that some current ones are unnecessary—and we might determine that some of our class operations need additional parameters and different return types. Again, all of this is perfectly normal.

Software Engineering Case Study Self-Review Exercises

7.1 Which of the following is not a behavior?
a) reading data from a file
b) printing output
c) text output
d) obtaining input from the user

7.2 If you were to add to the ATM system an operation that returns the amount attribute of class Withdrawal, how and where would you specify this operation in the class diagram of Fig. 7.24?

7.3 Describe the meaning of the following operation listing that might appear in a class diagram for an object-oriented design of a calculator:

```
Add( x : Integer, y : Integer ) : Integer
```

Answers to Software Engineering Case Study Self-Review Exercises

7.1 c.

7.2 An operation that retrieves the amount attribute of class Withdrawal would typically be implemented as a Get accessor of a property of class Withdrawal. The following would replace attribute amount in the attribute (i.e., second) compartment of class Withdrawal:

```
«property» Amount : Decimal
```

7.3 This is an operation named Add that takes Integer parameters x and y and returns an Integer value. This operation would most likely sum its parameters x and y and return the result.

7.21 **Wrap-Up**

In this chapter, you studied methods in greater depth. You learned the difference between subroutines and functions, and when to use each type of method. You also learned the difference between non-Shared and Shared methods and how to call Shared methods by preceding the method name with the name of the class in which it appears and a dot (.). You learned how to declare named constants using both enumerations and constant variables. You learned about how arguments can be implicitly converted to the type of their corresponding parameters. We demonstrated using **Option Strict**, which causes the compiler to check all conversions and requires you to perform an explicit conversion for all narrowing conversions that could cause data loss or program termination. We discussed how Visual

Basic performs method calls using a stack data structure. You saw how to use class Random to generate random numbers that can be used for simulations and game playing. You also learned about the scope of instance variables and local variables in classes and methods, respectively. You enhanced your GUI skills, using PictureBoxes, GroupBoxes, Buttons and TextBoxes, and created event handlers for Buttons. Finally, you learned that multiple methods in one class can be overloaded by providing methods with the same name and different signatures. Such methods can be used to perform the same or similar tasks using different types or different numbers of parameters.

In Chapter 8, you will learn how to maintain lists and tables of data in arrays. You will see a more elegant implementation of the application that rolls a die several times and two enhanced versions of the GradeBook case study that you studied in Chapters 4–7.

Summary

Section 7.1 Introduction
- Experience has shown that the best way to develop and maintain a large program is to construct it from small, simple pieces. This technique is called divide and conquer.

Section 7.2 Modules, Classes and Methods
- Although the same method can be executed from multiple points in a program, the actual statements that define the method are written only once.
- A method is invoked by a method call. The method call specifies the method name and provides information, called arguments, that the callee requires to do its job.
- When the method completes its task, it returns control to the caller (i.e., the calling method). In some cases, the method also returns a result to the caller.

Section 7.3 Subroutines: Methods That Do Not Return a Value
- Subroutines are methods that perform tasks but don't return a value.
- The format of a subroutine declaration is

```
Sub method-name(parameter-list)
    declarations and statements
End Sub
```

- Control returns to the caller when execution reaches the End Sub statement.

Section 7.4 Functions: Methods That Return a Value
- Functions are methods that perform tasks and return a value.
- The Return statement terminates execution of a method and can optionally return a result.
- The format of a function declaration is

```
Function method-name(parameter-list) As return-type
    declarations and statements
End Function
```

- A function's return type indicates the type of the result returned from the function to its caller.
- Functions return exactly one value. When a Return statement is executed, control returns immediately to the point at which that function was invoked.

Section 7.5 **Shared Methods and Class Math**

- Shared methods are associated with the class, but not with any specific object of the class; they perform tasks that do not depend on the contents of any object.

- You call a Shared method by specifying the name of the class or module in which the method is declared, followed by the dot (.) separator and the method name.

- Any variable declared with keyword Const is constant—its value cannot be changed after the variable is initialized. Constants are implicitly Shared.

- There are variables for which each object of a class does not have a separate instance of the member. That is the case with Shared members. When objects of a class containing Shared variables are created, all the objects of that class share one copy of the class's Shared variables. Together, the instance variables and Shared variables of a class are known as the class's fields.

Section 7.6 **GradeBook** Case Study: Declaring Methods with Multiple Parameters

- When a method has more than one parameter, the parameters are specified as a comma-separated list.

- There must be one argument in the method call for each parameter in the method declaration (except in the case of Optional parameters). The type of each argument must be consistent with the type of the corresponding parameter.

- Methods can return at most one value, but the returned value could be a reference to an object that contains many values.

Section 7.7 Notes on Declaring and Using Methods

- There are three ways to call a method: using a method name by itself to call another method of the same class or module, using a variable that contains a reference to an object followed by a dot (.) and the method name to call a method of the referenced object, and using the class or module name and a dot (.) to call a Shared method of a class or module (all methods of a module are implicitly Shared).

- Control can be returned to the statement that calls a method by using the Return statement or by reaching the end of the method (End Sub or End Function). If the method does not return a result but uses a Return statement to return control to the calling method, the Return statement cannot include an expression. If the method does return a result, the statement

        Return *expression*

evaluates the *expression*, then returns the result to the caller.

Section 7.8 Method Call Stack and Activation Records

- Stacks are known as last-in, first-out (LIFO) data structures—the last item pushed (inserted) on the stack is the first item popped (removed) from the stack.

- When a program calls a method, the called method must know how to return to its caller, so the return address of the calling method is pushed onto the method call stack. If a series of nested method calls occurs, the successive return addresses are pushed onto the stack in last-in, first-out order so that each method can return to its caller.

- The method call stack also contains the memory for the local variables used in each invocation of a method during a program's execution. This data is known as the activation record or stack frame of the method call. When a method call is made, the activation record for that method call is pushed onto the method call stack. When the method returns to its caller, the activation record for this method call is popped off the stack and those local variables are no longer known to the program.

Section 7.9 Implicit Argument Conversions
- An important feature of argument passing is implicit argument conversion—converting an argument's value to the type that a method expects to receive in its corresponding parameter.
- In a widening conversion, data of one type is converted to data of another type without losing data. In a narrowing conversion, there is potential for data loss during the conversion.
- Conversions occur not only for values passed as arguments to methods, but also for expressions containing values of two or more types. In such expressions, each value is converted to the "widest" type in the expression.

Section 7.10 Option Strict and Data-Type Conversions
- **Option Explicit** forces you to explicitly declare all variables before they are used in a program.
- **Option Strict** causes the compiler to check all conversions and requires you to perform an explicit conversion for all narrowing conversions that could cause data loss or program termination.
- The methods in class Convert convert data between types explicitly.

Section 7.11 Value Types and Reference Types
- Both value types and reference types include primitive types and types that you can create. The primitive value types include the integral types (Byte, SByte, Short, UShort, Integer, UInteger, Long and ULong), the floating-point types (Single and Double) and types Boolean, Date, Decimal and Char. There is only one primitive reference type—String.
- Reference types can be created by defining classes, modules, interfaces and delegates. Value types can be created by defining structures and enumerations.

Section 7.12 Framework Class Library Namespaces
- A great strength of Visual Basic is the large number of classes in the FCL. The set of namespaces available in the FCL is quite large. The FCL includes namespaces for graphics, input/output, database processing, GUI development, Web services and many other capabilities.

Section 7.13 Passing Arguments: Pass-by-Value vs. Pass-by-Reference
- When an argument is passed by value, the program makes a copy of the argument's value and passes that copy to the called method. With pass-by-value, changes to the called method's copy do not affect the original variable's value.
- When an argument is passed by reference, the caller gives the called method the ability to access and modify the caller's original data directly.

Section 7.14 Scope of Declarations
- The scope of a declaration is the portion of the program that can refer to the declared entity by its name, without qualification.
- If a local variable or parameter in a method has the same name as a field, the member is "hidden" until the block terminates execution—this is called shadowing.

Section 7.15 Case Study: Random Number Generation
- The element of chance can be introduced through class Random (located in namespace System).
- Class Random's Next method generates pseudo-random numbers based on a complex mathematical calculation that requires a seed value. If the seed value is different each time the program is run, the series of values will be different as well.
- A Button's Click event handler executes whenever the Button is clicked.
- The data in a TextBox can be accessed and modified via the control's Text property.

Section 7.16 Case Study: A Game of Chance

- A GroupBox is a container used to group related controls.

- Constant identifiers and Enumerations enhance program readability by providing descriptive identifiers for constant numbers or Strings.

- Enumerations are used to define groups of related constants.

- Disabling a Button causes no action to be performed when the Button is clicked. Buttons can be enabled and disabled by setting the Button's Enabled property to True or False, respectively.

Section 7.17 Method Overloading

- Method overloading allows you to create multiple methods with the same name but differing numbers and types of parameters, or with different orders of the parameters (by type).

- Overloaded methods are distinguished by their signatures, which are a combination of the method's name and parameter types, and the order of the parameters (by type).

Section 7.18 Optional Parameters

- Methods can have optional parameters. Declaring a parameter as Optional allows the calling method to vary the number of arguments to pass.

- Optional parameters specify a default value that is assigned to the parameter if the optional argument is not passed.

- For an Optional parameter, the caller has the *option* of passing that particular argument.

- You can create methods with one or more optional parameters. All optional parameters, however, must be placed to the right of the method's non-optional parameters.

- Default values can be used only with parameters declared as Optional.

Section 7.19 Recursion

- A recursive method calls itself either directly or indirectly (i.e., through another method).

- A recursive method knows how to solve only the simplest case(s)—the base case(s). If the method is called with a base case, it returns a result. If the method is called with a more complex problem, it divides the problem into a base case and recursion step that resembles the original problem but is a slightly simpler or smaller version of it. The recursion step executes while the original call to the method is still "open." The recursion step can result in many more recursive calls as the method divides each new subproblem into two conceptual pieces. Since the method continues to call itself with simpler versions of the original problem, the sequence of smaller and smaller problems must converge on a base case, so that the recursion can eventually terminate. At that point, the method recognizes the base case and returns a result to the previous copy of the method. A sequence of returns ensues until the original method call returns the final result to the caller.

Terminology

activation record
argument conversion
base case(s) in recursion
block
block scope
ByRef keyword
class method
Click event of a Button
Const keyword
Convert class

Convert.ToInt32 method
copy of an argument
default value for Optional parameter
divide-and-conquer approach
Double structure
Double.Parse method
empty string
Enabled property of class Button
Enum keyword
enumeration

Exit Function statement
Exit Sub statement
explicit conversion
field of a class
floating-point type
formal parameter
FromFile method of class Image
function
GetCurrentDirectory method of class
    Directory
GroupBox control
implicit argument conversion
infinite recursion
Int32 structure
Int32.MaxValue constant
integral type
iteratively (nonrecursively) solve a problem
last-in, first-out (LIFO)
lifetime of a variable
Long primitive type
method call stack
method overloading
method scope
module scope
namespace scope
narrowing conversion
Next method of class Random
Object class
Option Explicit
Option Strict
Optional keyword

optional parameter
overload resolution
overloaded methods
P format specifier for displaying percentages
pass-by-reference
pass-by-value
pop off a stack
pseudo-random numbers
push onto a stack
recursion
recursion step
recursive call
recursive method
reference parameter
return a value from a method
Return statement
return type of a method
scaling factor
scope of a declaration
seed value to generate pseudo-random numbers
shadowing an instance variable
Shared method
shifted random integers
signature of a method
stack data structure
stack frame
stack overflow
strong typing
subroutine
value parameter
widening conversion

Self-Review Exercises

7.1   Fill in the blanks in each of the following statements:
    a) Methods can be declared in _____ and _____.
    b) A method is invoked with a(n) _____.
    c) A variable known only within the method in which it is declared is called a(n)
       _____.
    d) The _____ statement in a called function can be used to pass the value of an expression back to the calling method.
    e) A method declared with keyword _____ does not return a value.
    f) The _____ of a variable is the portion of the program in which the variable can be referenced without qualification.
    g) Control can be returned from a called subroutine to a caller with the _____ or _____ statements.
    h) The _____ method in class Random produces random numbers.
    i) A method that calls itself either directly or indirectly is a(n) _____ method.
    j) A recursive method typically has two components—one that provides a means for the recursion to terminate by testing for a(n) _____ case, and one that expresses the problem as a recursive call for a problem slightly simpler or smaller than the original call.

    k) It is possible to have several methods with the same name that operate on different types or numbers of arguments. This is called method _____.

    l) A method that performs a task that does not depend on the contents of an object is normally declared as a(n) _____ method.

    m) When a program calls a method, the called method must know how to return to its caller, so the return address of the calling method is pushed onto the _____.

    n) Recursion terminates when a(n) _____ is reached.

    o) The _____ is a comma-separated list containing the declarations of the parameters received by the called method.

    p) The _____ is the type of the result returned from a called function.

    q) A Button's _____ event occurs when a Button is clicked.

7.2 State whether each of the following is *true* or *false*. If *false*, explain why.

    a) Math method Abs rounds its parameter to the smallest integer not less than its parameter.

    b) Math method Exp is the exponential method that calculates e^x.

    c) A recursive method is one that calls itself.

    d) Conversion of a data item from type Single to type Double is an example of a widening conversion.

    e) Variables of type Char cannot be converted to type Integer.

    f) When a method recursively calls itself, it is known as the base case.

    g) Forgetting to return a value from a recursive method when one is needed results in a logic error.

    h) **Option Explicit** causes the compiler to check all conversions and requires you to perform an explicit conversion for all narrowing conversions that could cause data loss or program termination.

    i) Visual Basic supports Optional parameters.

    j) When an argument is passed by value, the program makes a copy of the argument's value and passes the copy to the called method.

7.3 Write an application that tests whether the examples of the Math class method calls shown in Fig. 7.4 actually produce the indicated results.

7.4 Give the method header for each of the following:

    a) Method Hypotenuse, which takes two double-precision, floating-point arguments, side1 and side2, and returns a double-precision, floating-point result.

    b) Method Smallest, which takes three integers, x, y and z, and returns an integer.

    c) Method Instructions, which does not take any arguments and does not return a value.

    d) Method IntegerToSingle, which takes an integer argument, number, and returns a floating-point result.

7.5 Find the error in each of the following program segments and explain how the error can be corrected:

    a)
```
Sub General1()
    Console.WriteLine("Inside method General1")

    Sub General2()
        Console.WriteLine("Inside method General2")
    End Sub ' General2
End Sub ' General1
```

    b)
```
Function Sum(ByVal x As Integer, ByVal y As Integer) As Integer
    Dim result As Integer
    result = x + y
End Function ' Sum
```

```
c) Sub Printer1(ByVal value As Single)
      Dim value As Single
      Console.WriteLine(value)
   End Sub ' Printer1
d) Sub Product()
      Dim a As Integer = 6
      Dim b As Integer = 5
      Dim result As Integer = a * b
      Console.WriteLine("Result is " & result)
       Return result
   End Sub ' Product
e) Function Sum(ByVal value As Integer) As Integer
      If value = 0 Then
         Return 0
      Else
         value += Sum(value - 1)
      End If
   End Function ' Sum
```

Answers to Self-Review Exercises

7.1   a) classes, modules. b) method call. c) local variable. d) Return. e) Sub. f) scope. g) Return, End Sub. h) Next. i) recursive. j) base. k) overloading. l) Shared. m) method call stack. n) base case. o) parameter list. p) return-value type. q) Click.

7.2   a) False. Math method Abs returns the absolute value of a number. b) True. c) True. d) True. e) False. Type Char variables can be converted to type Integer with a narrowing conversion. f) False. A method recursively calling itself is known as a recursive call or recursion step. g) True. h) False. **Option Strict** causes the compiler to check all conversions and requires you to perform an explicit conversion for all narrowing conversions that could cause data loss or program termination. **Option Explicit** forces you to explicitly declare all variables before they are used in a program. i) True. j) True.

7.3   The following code demonstrates the use of some Math library method calls:

```
1  ' Exercise 7.3 Solution: MathTest.vb
2  ' Testing the Math class methods
3  Module MathTest
4     Sub Main()
5        Console.WriteLine("Math.Abs(23.7) = " & _
6           Convert.ToString(Math.Abs(23.7)))
7        Console.WriteLine("Math.Abs(0.0) = " & _
8           Convert.ToString(Math.Abs(0.0)))
9        Console.WriteLine("Math.Abs(-23.7) = " & _
10          Convert.ToString(Math.Abs(-23.7)))
11       Console.WriteLine("Math.Ceiling(9.2) = " & _
12          Convert.ToString(Math.Ceiling(9.2)))
13       Console.WriteLine("Math.Ceiling(-9.8) = " & _
14          Convert.ToString(Math.Ceiling(-9.8)))
15       Console.WriteLine("Math.Cos(0.0) = " & _
16          Convert.ToString(Math.Cos(0.0)))
17       Console.WriteLine("Math.Exp(1.0) = " & _
18          Convert.ToString(Math.Exp(1.0)))
```

```vbnet
19            Console.WriteLine("Math.Exp(2.0) = " & _
20               Convert.ToString(Math.Exp(2.0)))
21            Console.WriteLine("Math.Floor(9.2) = " & _
22               Convert.ToString(Math.Floor(9.2)))
23            Console.WriteLine("Math.Floor(-9.8) = " & _
24               Convert.ToString(Math.Floor(-9.8)))
25            Console.WriteLine("Math.Log(2.7182818284590451) = " & _
26               Convert.ToString(Math.Log(2.7182818284590451)))
27            Console.WriteLine("Math.Log(7.3890560989306504) = " & _
28               Convert.ToString(Math.Log(7.3890560989306504)))
29            Console.WriteLine("Math.Max(2.3, 12.7) = " & _
30               Convert.ToString(Math.Max(2.3, 12.7)))
31            Console.WriteLine("Math.Max(-2.3, -12.7) = " & _
32               Convert.ToString(Math.Max(-2.3, -12.7)))
33            Console.WriteLine("Math.Min(2.3, 12.7) = " & _
34               Convert.ToString(Math.Min(2.3, 12.7)))
35            Console.WriteLine("Math.Min(-2.3, -12.7) = " & _
36               Convert.ToString(Math.Min(-2.3, -12.7)))
37            Console.WriteLine("Math.Pow(2, 7) = " & _
38               Convert.ToString(Math.Pow(2, 7)))
39            Console.WriteLine("Math.Pow(9, .5) = " & _
40               Convert.ToString(Math.Pow(9, 0.5)))
41            Console.WriteLine("Math.Sin(0.0) = " & _
42               Convert.ToString(Math.Sin(0.0)))
43            Console.WriteLine("Math.Sqrt(9.0) = " & _
44               Convert.ToString(Math.Sqrt(9.0)))
45            Console.WriteLine("Math.Sqrt(2.0) = " & _
46               Convert.ToString(Math.Sqrt(2.0)))
47            Console.WriteLine("Math.Tan(0.0) = " & _
48               Convert.ToString(Math.Tan(0.0)))
49       End Sub ' Main
50    End Module ' MathTest
```

```
Math.Abs(23.7) = 23.7
Math.Abs(0.0) = 0
Math.Abs(-23.7) = 23.7
Math.Ceiling(9.2) = 10
Math.Ceiling(-9.8) = -9
Math.Cos(0.0) = 1
Math.Exp(1.0) = 2.71828182845905
Math.Exp(2.0) = 7.38905609893065
Math.Floor(9.2) = 9
Math.Floor(-9.8) = -10
Math.Log(2.7182818284590451) = 1
Math.Log(7.3890560989306504) = 2
Math.Max(2.3, 12.7) = 12.7
Math.Max(-2.3, -12.7) = -2.3
Math.Min(2.3, 12.7) = 2.3
Math.Min(-2.3, -12.7) = -12.7
Math.Pow(2, 7) = 128
Math.Pow(9, .5) = 3
Math.Sin(0.0) = 0
Math.Sqrt(9.0) = 3
Math.Sqrt(2.0) = 1.4142135623731
Math.Tan(0.0) = 0
```

7.4 a) `Function Hypotenuse(ByVal side1 As Double, _`
             `ByVal side2 As Double) As Double`
     b) `Function Smallest(ByVal x As Integer, _`
             `ByVal y As Integer, ByVal z As Integer) As Integer`
     c) `Sub Instructions()`
     d) `Function IntegerToSingle(ByVal number As Integer) As Single`

7.5 a) Error: Method `General2` is declared in method `General1`.
        Correction: Move the declaration of `General2` out of the declaration of `General1`.
     b) Error: The method is supposed to return an `Integer`, but does not.
        Correction: Replace the statement `result = x + y` with

```
Return x + y
```

or add the following statement at the end of the method body:

```
Return result
```

     c) Error: Parameter `value` is redefined in the method declaration.
        Correction: Delete the declaration `Dim value As Single`.
     d) Error: The method returns a value, but is declared as a subroutine.
        Correction: Change the method to a function with return type `Integer`.
     e) Error: The result of `value += Sum(value - 1)` is not returned by this recursive method, resulting in a logic error.
        Correction: Rewrite the statement in the `Else` clause as

```
Return value + Sum(value - 1)
```

Exercises

7.6   A gas pump calculates the cost of gas at a local gas station. The station charges $2.09 per gallon for regular grade gas, $2.16 per gallon for special grade gas and $2.26 per gallon for super grade gas. Create an application that simulates the functionality of the gas pump. The user enters the number of gallons to purchase and clicks the desired grade (each grade is represented by a Button whose Text properties are set to **Regular**, **Special** and **Super+**). The Click event handler for each Button calls a method to compute the total cost from the number of gallons entered and the selected grade. [*Note:* You can use the Text property of each Button to pass the selected grade to your method.]

7.7   A lottery commission offers four different lottery games to play: Three-number, Four-number, Five-number and Five-number + 1 lotteries. Each game has independent numbers. Develop an application that randomly picks numbers for all four games and displays the generated numbers in a GUI. Declare a method that generates a random number based on a range given, and returns the random number as a String. The games are played as follows:
     a) Three-number lotteries require players to choose three numbers in the range 0–9.
     b) Four-number lotteries require players to choose four numbers, in the range 0–9.
     c) Five-number lotteries require players to choose five numbers in the range 1–39.
     d) Five-number + 1 lotteries require players to choose five numbers in the range 1–49 and an additional number in the range 1–42.

7.8   Develop an application that calculates a salesperson's commission from the number of items sold. Assume that all items have a fixed price of $10 per unit. Use a Select...Case statement to implement the following sales commission schedule:
     a) Up to 50 items sold = 6% commission
     b) Between 51 and 100 items sold = 7% commission
     c) Between 101 and 150 items sold = 8% commission
     d) More than 150 items sold = 9% commission

Create an application that inputs the number of items sold and contains a **Calculate** Button. When this Button is clicked, three methods should be called—one to calculate gross sales, one to calculate the commission percentage based on the commission schedule above and one to calculate the salesperson's earnings. Earnings are defined as gross sales multiplied by commission percentage, divided by 100 (because we are working with a percentage value). The data returned by these three methods should be displayed in the GUI.

7.9   What is the value of x after each of the following statements is performed?

    a) `x = Math.Abs(7.5)`
    a) `x = Math.Floor(7.5)`
    b) `x = Math.Abs(0.0)`
    c) `x = Math.Ceiling(0.0)`
    d) `x = Math.Abs(-6.4)`
    e) `x = Math.Ceiling(-6.4)`
    f) `x = Math.Ceiling(-Math.Abs(-8 + Math.Floor(-5.5)))`

7.10   A parking garage charges a $2.00 minimum fee to park for up to three hours. The garage charges an additional $0.50 per hour for each hour *or part thereof* in excess of three hours. The maximum charge for any given 24-hour period is $10.00. Assume that no car parks for longer than 24 hours at a time. Write a program that calculates and displays the parking charges for each customer who parked a car in this garage yesterday. You should enter in a `TextBox` the hours parked for each customer. The program should display the charge for the current customer. The program should use the method `CalculateCharges` to determine the charge for each customer. Use the techniques described in the chapter to read the `Double` value from a `TextBox`. [*Note:* You may need to use methods `Convert.ToDouble` and `Convert.ToDecimal` when doing calculations with the number of hours and charges, respectively.]

7.11   Write a method `IntegerPower(base, exponent)` that returns the value of

    $base^{exponent}$

For example, `IntegerPower(3, 4) = 3 * 3 * 3 * 3`. Assume that `exponent` is a positive integer and that `base` is an integer. Method `IntegerPower` should use a `For...Next` statement to control the calculation. Do not use any `Math` library methods or the exponentiation operator, `^`. Incorporate this method into a Windows application that reads integer values from `TextBox`es for `base` and `exponent` from the user and performs the calculation by calling method `IntegerPower`. [*Note:* You may need to use method `Convert.ToString` to display numeric output in a `Label`.]

7.12   Declare a method `Hypotenuse` that calculates the length of the hypotenuse of a right triangle when the other two sides are given. The method should take two arguments of type `Double` and return the hypotenuse as a `Double`. Incorporate this method into a Windows application that reads integer values for `side1` and `side2` from `TextBox`es and performs the calculation with the `Hypotenuse` method. Determine the length of the hypotenuse for each of the following triangles:

Triangle	Side 1	Side 2
1	3.0	4.0
2	5.0	12.0
3	8.0	15.0

7.13   Write a method `SquareOfAsterisks` that displays a solid square of asterisks whose side is specified in integer parameter `side`. For example, if `side` is 4, `SquareOfAsterisks` displays

```
* * * *
* * * *
* * * *
* * * *
```

Incorporate this method into a Windows application that reads an integer value for side from the user and performs the drawing with SquareOfAsterisks. This method should obtain the side of the square from a TextBox and should print to a Label. Display a space after each asterisk to make the shape appear more like a square on the screen.

7.14 Modify the method created in Exercise 7.13 to form the square out of whatever character is contained in parameter fillCharacter. Thus, if side is 5 and fillCharacter is "#", this method should print

Display a space after each fill character to make the shape appear more like a square on the screen.

7.15 Write a Windows application that simulates coin tossing. Let the program toss the coin each time the user presses the **Toss** button. Count the number of times each side of the coin appears. Display the results. The program should call a separate method Flip, which takes no arguments and returns False for tails and True for heads. [*Note:* If the program simulates the coin tossing realistically, each side of the coin should appear approximately half the time.]

7.16 Computers are playing an increasing role in education. Write a program that will help an elementary school student learn multiplication. Use the Next method from an object of type Random to produce two positive one-digit integers. It should display a question, such as

```
How much is 6 times 7?
```

The student should then type the answer into a TextBox. Your program should check the student's answer. If it is correct, display "Very good!" in a Label, then ask another multiplication question. If the answer is incorrect, display "No. Please try again." in the same Label, then let the student try the same question again until the student finally gets it right. A separate method should be used to generate each new question. This method should be called once when the program begins execution and then each time the user answers a question correctly.

7.17 (*Towers of Hanoi*) Legend has it that in a temple in the Far East, priests are attempting to move a stack of disks from one peg to another. The initial stack had 64 disks threaded onto one peg and arranged from bottom to top by decreasing size. The priests are attempting to move the stack from this peg to a second peg, under the constraints that exactly one disk is moved at a time and that at no time may a larger disk be placed above a smaller disk. A third peg is available for temporarily holding disks. Figure 7.29 shows the Towers of Hanoi with four disks. Supposedly, the world will end when the priests complete their task, so there is little incentive for us to facilitate their efforts.

Let us assume that the priests are attempting to move the disks from peg 1 to peg 3. We wish to develop an algorithm that prints the precise sequence of peg-to-peg disk transfers.

If we were to approach this problem with conventional techniques, we would find ourselves hopelessly knotted up in managing the disks. However, if we approach the problem with recursion in mind, it becomes simpler. Moving n disks can be viewed in terms of moving only $n - 1$ disks (and hence the recursion) as follows:

    a) Move $n - 1$ disks from peg 1 to peg 2, using peg 3 as a temporary holding area.

    b) Move the last disk (the largest) from peg 1 to peg 3.

    c) Move the $n - 1$ disks from peg 2 to peg 3, using peg 1 as a temporary holding area.

The process ends when the last task involves moving $n = 1$ disk (i.e., the base case). This is accomplished by moving the disk without the need for a temporary holding area.

Write a program to solve the Towers of Hanoi problem. Allow the user to enter the number of disks in a TextBox. Use a recursive Tower method with four parameters:

    a) The number of disks to be moved

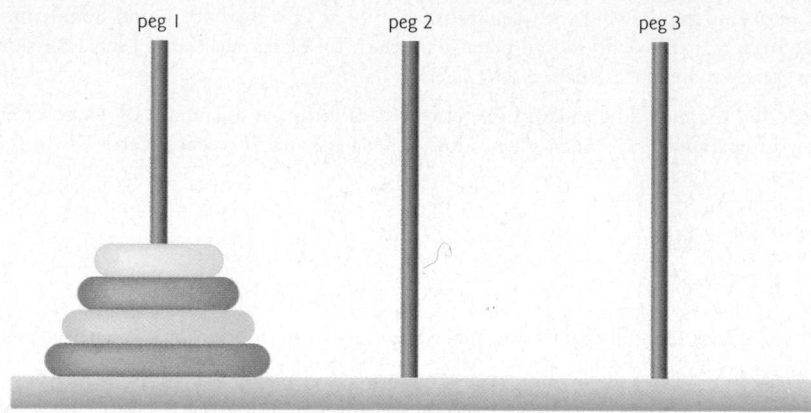

Fig. 7.29 | Towers of Hanoi for the case with four disks.

    b) The peg on which the disks are threaded initially
    c) The peg to which this stack of disks is to be moved
    d) The peg to be used as a temporary holding area

Your program should display in a `TextBox` with scrolling functionality the precise instructions for moving the disks from the starting peg to the destination peg. For example, to move a stack of three disks from peg 1 to peg 3, your program should print the following series of moves:

1 → 3 (This means move one disk from peg 1 to peg 3.)
1 → 2
3 → 2
1 → 3
2 → 1
2 → 3
1 → 3

8

Arrays

*Now go, write it before them
in a table,
and note it in a book.*
—Isaiah 30:8

*With sobs and tears he sorted
out
Those of the largest size ...*
—Lewis Carroll

*Attempt the end, and never
stand to doubt;
Nothing's so hard, but search
will find it out.*
—Robert Herrick

*Begin at the beginning, ...
and go on till you come to
the end: then stop.*
—Lewis Carroll

*To go beyond is as wrong as
to fall short*
—Confucius

OBJECTIVES

In this chapter you will learn:

- To use the array data structure; arrays are objects.
- How arrays are used to store, sort and search lists and tables of values.
- To declare, initialize and refer to individual elements of arrays.
- To pass arrays to methods using **ByVal** and **ByRef**.
- To sort and search arrays.
- To declare and manipulate multidimensional arrays, especially rectangular arrays and jagged arrays.
- To create variable-length parameter lists.
- To use the **For Each**...**Next** statement to iterate through the elements of arrays without using a loop counter.

8.1 Introduction

This chapter introduces basic concepts and features of data structures. **Arrays** are simple data structures consisting only of data items of the same type. Arrays normally are "static" entities, in that they typically remain the same size once they are created, although you can use the ReDim statement to resize an array at execution time. We begin by creating and accessing arrays; we then perform more complex manipulations of arrays, including searching and sorting. We discuss arrays with one dimension and with multiple dimensions. Chapter 24, Data Structures and Chapter 26, Collections introduce dynamic data structures, such as lists, queues, stacks and trees, which typically grow and shrink as programs execute. Chapter 26 also presents Visual Basic's predefined data structures, including lists, queues, stacks and trees.

8.2 Arrays

An array is a group of variables (called **elements**) containing values that all have the same type. Array names follow the same conventions that apply to other variable names. To refer to a particular element in an array, we specify the name of the array and the **position number** of the element to which we refer. Position numbers are values that indicate specific locations within arrays.

Figure 8.1 shows a logical representation of an integer array called c. This array contains 12 elements, any one of which can be referred to by giving the name of the array followed by the position number of the element in parentheses (). The first element in every array is the **zeroth element**. Thus, the elements of array c are c(0), c(1), c(2) and so on. The highest position number in array c is 11, which is 1 less than 12—the number of elements in the array.

The position number in parentheses more formally is called an **index** (or a **subscript**). An index must be a non-negative integer or integer expression. If a program uses an expression as an index, the expression is evaluated first to determine the index. For example, if variable value1 is equal to 5, and variable value2 is equal to 6, then the statement

```
c(value1 + value2) += 2
```

adds 2 to array element c(11). Note that an **indexed array name** (i.e., the array name followed by an index enclosed in parentheses) is an *lvalue*—it can be used on the left side of an assignment statement to place a new value into an array element.

Let us examine array c in Fig. 8.1 more closely. The name of the array is c. The 12 elements of the array are referred to as c(0) through c(11)—pronounced as "c sub zero" through "c sub 11," where "sub" derives from "subscript." The value of c(0) is -45, the value of c(1) is 6, the value of c(2) is 0, the value of c(7) is 62 and the value of c(11) is 78. Values stored in arrays can be employed in calculations. For example, to determine the

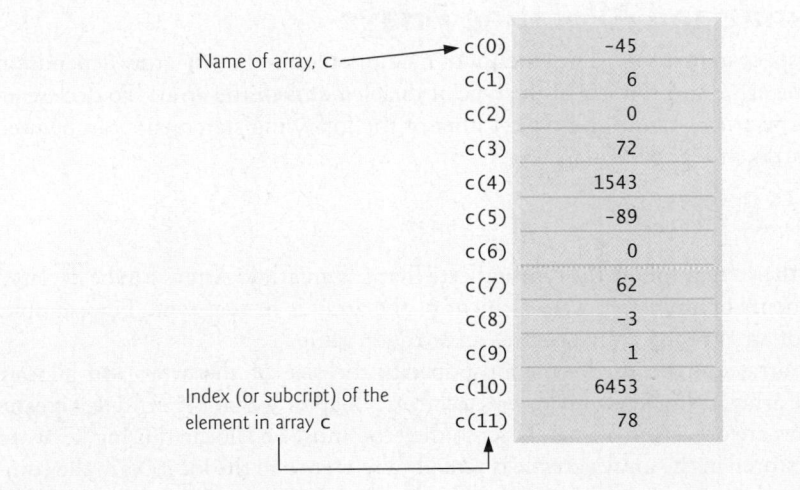

Fig. 8.1 | Array consisting of 12 elements.

total of the values contained in the first three elements of array c and then store the result in variable sum, we would write

```
sum = c(0) + c(1) + c(2)
```

To divide the value of c(6) by 2 and assign the result to the variable result, we would write

```
result = c(6) \ 2
```

Common Programming Error 8.1

It is important to note the difference between the "seventh element of the array" and "array element seven." Array indices begin at 0, which means that the "seventh element of the array" has the index 6, whereas "array element seven" has the index 7 and is actually the eighth element of the array. This confusion is a common source of "off-by-one" errors. We will avoid such terminology; instead, we refer to all array elements simply by their indexed names—such as c(0) rather than "the first element of c."

Every array in Visual Basic "knows" its own length. The length of array c (i.e., 12) is determined by the following expression:

```
c.Length
```

All arrays have access to the methods and properties of class `System.Array`, including the `Length` property. For instance, method `GetUpperBound` returns the index of the last element in the array. Method `GetUpperBound` takes one argument indicating a dimension of the array (e.g., 0 for the first dimension, 1 for the second dimension, etc.). We discuss arrays with multiple dimensions in Section 8.11. For one-dimensional arrays, such as c, the argument passed to `GetUpperBound` is 0. For example, the expression

```
c.GetUpperBound(0)
```

returns 11. Note that the value returned by method `GetUpperBound` is one less than the value of the array's `Length` property.

8.3 Declaring and Allocating Arrays

Arrays occupy space in memory. The amount of memory required by an array depends on the length of the array and the size of the type of the elements in the array. To declare an array, provide the array's name and type. Either of the following statements can be used to declare the array in Fig. 8.1:

```
Dim c As Integer()
Dim c() As Integer
```

The parentheses that follow the type indicate that c is an array. Arrays can be declared to contain elements of any type; every element of the array is of that type. For example, every element of an `Integer` array contains an `Integer` value.

Before an array can be used, you must specify the size of the array and allocate memory for the array, using keyword New. Recall from Chapter 4 that keyword New creates an object. Arrays are objects in Visual Basic, so they too must be allocated using keyword New. The value stored in the array variable is actually a reference to the location in the computer's memory where the array object is stored. All non-primitive and non-structure type variables (such as arrays) are reference variables (normally called references). The statement

```
c = New Integer(11) {}
```

allocates memory for the array c after it has been declared. In our example, the number 11 defines the upper bound for the array. **Array bounds** determine what indices can be used to access an element in the array. Here the array bounds are 0 (which is implicit in the preceding statement and is always the lower bound of every array) and 11—an index outside these bounds cannot be used to access elements in the array c. Note that the actual size of the array is one larger (12) than the upper bound specified in the allocation. We also can explicitly specify the array bounds, as in

```
c = New Integer(0 To 11) {}
```

The **explicit array bounds** specified in the preceding statement indicate that the lower bound of the array is 0 and the upper bound is 11. Note that the size of the array is still 12.

Common Programming Error 8.2

Explicitly setting the lower bound of an array to a value other than 0 is a compilation error.

The required braces ({ and }) are called an **initializer list** and specify the initial values of the elements in the array. When the initializer list is empty, the elements in the array are initialized to the default value for the type of the elements of the array. Again, the default value is 0 for numeric primitive data-type variables, False for Boolean variables and Nothing for references. The initializer list also can contain a comma-separated list specifying the initial values of the elements in the array. For instance,

```
Dim numbers As Integer()
numbers = New Integer() {1, 2, 3, 6}
```

declares and allocates an array containing four Integer values. Visual Basic can determine the array bounds from the number of elements in the initializer list—it is not necessary to specify the upper bound of the array when a non-empty initializer list is present. When you explicitly state the upper bound and a non-empty initializer list, make sure that the upper bound of the array is one less than the number of elements in the initializer list; otherwise, a compilation error occurs.

The two preceding statements can be combined into a single statement, as in

```
Dim numbers As Integer() = New Integer() {1, 2, 3, 6}
```

8.4 Examples Using Arrays

This section presents several examples that demonstrate the declaration, allocation and initialization of arrays, as well as various common manipulations of array elements. The examples in this section use arrays that contain elements of type Integer.

8.4.1 Allocating an Array

The program in Fig. 8.2 uses the New operator to allocate an array of 10 Integer elements, which are initially zero (the default value for Integer variables). The program displays the array elements in tabular format in a console window.

```
 1   ' Fig. 8.2: CreateArray.vb
 2   ' Declaring and allocating an array.
 3   Module CreateArray
 4      Sub Main()
 5         Dim array As Integer() ' declare array variable
 6
 7         ' allocate memory for 10-element array using explicit array bounds
 8         array = New Integer(0 To 9) {}
 9
10         Console.WriteLine("Index " & vbTab & "Value")
11
12         ' display values in array
13         For i As Integer = 0 To array.GetUpperBound(0)
14            Console.WriteLine(i & vbTab & array(i))
15         Next
16
17         Console.WriteLine(vbCrLf & "The array contains " & _
18            array.Length & " elements.")
19      End Sub ' Main
20   End Module ' CreateArray
```

```
Index   Value
0       0
1       0
2       0
3       0
4       0
5       0
6       0
7       0
8       0
9       0

The array contains 10 elements.
```

Fig. 8.2 | Creating an array.

Line 5 declares array—a variable capable of storing a reference to an array of Integers. Line 8 allocates an array of 10 elements (with explicit array bounds 0 to 9) using New and assigns it to array. Line 10 displays the headings for the columns. The columns represent the index for each array element and the value of each array element, respectively.

Lines 13–15 use a For statement to display the index number (i) and the value of each array element (array(i)). We use zero-based counting (recall that array indices start at 0), so that the loop accesses every array element. Also note, in the header of the For statement, the expression array.GetUpperBound(0), used to retrieve the upper bound of the array (in this case, 9). The Length property (line 18) returns the number of elements in the array.

8.4.2 Initializing the Values in an Array

The program in Fig. 8.3 creates two integer arrays of 10 elements each and sets the values of the elements, using an initializer list and a For statement, respectively. The arrays are displayed in tabular format.

```
 1    ' Fig. 8.3: InitArray.vb
 2    ' Initializing arrays.
 3    Module InitArray
 4       Sub Main()
 5          ' initializer list specifies the number of elements
 6          ' and the value of each element
 7          Dim array1 As Integer() = New Integer() _
 8             {32, 27, 64, 18, 95, 14, 90, 70, 60, 37}
 9
10          ' allocate array2 based on length of array1
11          Dim array2 As Integer() = New Integer(array1.GetUpperBound(0)) {}
12
13          ' set values in array2 by a calculation
14          For i As Integer = 0 To array2.GetUpperBound(0)
15             array2(i) = 2 + 2 * i ' generate 2, 4, 6, ..., 20
16          Next
17
18          Console.WriteLine("Index " & vbTab & "Array1" & vbTab & "Array2")
19
20          ' display values for both arrays side by side
21          For i As Integer = 0 To array1.GetUpperBound(0)
22             Console.WriteLine(i & vbTab & array1(i) & vbTab & array2(i))
23          Next
24       End Sub ' Main
25    End Module ' InitArray
```

Index	Array1	Array2
0	32	2
1	27	4
2	64	6
3	18	8
4	95	10
5	14	12
6	90	14
7	70	16
8	60	18
9	37	20

Fig. 8.3 | Initializing array elements with an array initializer and a For statement.

Lines 7–8 combine the declaration and allocation of array1 into one statement, allocate the 10 elements of array1 with New, and initialize the values in array1, using an initializer list. Line 11 declares and allocates array2, whose size is determined by the expression array1.GetUpperBound(0), meaning that array1 and array2, in this particular program, have the same upper bound (9) and the same size (10).

The For statement in lines 14–16 initializes the elements in array2 to the even integers 2, 4, 6, ..., 20. These numbers are generated by multiplying each successive value of the loop counter by 2 and adding 2 to the product. The For statement in lines 21–23 displays the values in the arrays.

8.4.3 Summing the Elements of an Array

Often, the elements of an array represent a series of values that are employed in a calculation. For example, if the elements of an array represent a group of students' exam grades, the instructor might wish to total the elements of the array, then calculate the class average for the exam. The program in Fig. 8.4 sums the values contained in a 10-element integer array.

Lines 5–6 declare, allocate and initialize the 10-element array `array`. Line 11, in the body of the `For` statement, performs the addition. Alternatively, the values supplied as initializers for `array` could have been read into the program. For example, the user could enter the values through a `TextBox`, or the values could be read from a file on disk. Information about reading values into a program from a file can be found in Chapter 18, Files and Streams.

8.4.4 Using Arrays to Analyze Survey Results

Our next example uses arrays to summarize data collected in a survey. Consider the following problem statement:

> *Forty students were asked to rate on a scale of 1 to 10 the quality of the food in the student cafeteria, with 1 being "awful" and 10 being "excellent." Place the 40 responses in an integer array and determine the frequency of each rating.*

This exercise represents a typical array-processing application (Fig. 8.5). We wish to summarize the number of responses of each type (i.e., 1–10). Array `responses` (lines 6–8) is a 40-element integer array containing the students' responses to the survey. Using an 11-element array `frequency`, we can count the number of occurrences of each response. We ignore `frequency(0)` because it is more natural to have a survey response of 1 result in frequency(1) being incremented rather than incrementing `frequency(0)`. We can use each response directly as an index on the `frequency` array. Each element of the array is used as a counter for one of the possible types of survey responses—`frequency(1)` counts the number of students who rated the food as 1, `frequency(2)` counts the number of students who rated the food as 2, and so on.

```vb
 1   ' Fig. 8.4: SumArray.vb
 2   ' Computing the sum of the elements in an array.
 3   Module SumArray
 4      Sub Main()
 5         Dim array As Integer() = New Integer() _
 6            {1, 2, 3, 4, 5, 6, 7, 8, 9, 10}
 7         Dim total As Integer = 0
 8
 9         ' sum the array element values
10         For i As Integer = 0 To array.GetUpperBound(0)
11            total += array(i)
12         Next
13
14         Console.WriteLine("Total of array elements: " & total)
15      End Sub ' Main
16   End Module ' SumArray
```

```
Total of array elements: 55
```

Fig. 8.4 | Computing the sum of the elements in an array.

```vb
 1    ' Fig. 8.5: StudentPoll.vb
 2    ' Using arrays to display poll results.
 3    Module StudentPoll
 4       Sub Main()
 5          ' student response array (more typically, input at run time)
 6          Dim responses As Integer() = New Integer() _
 7             {1, 2, 6, 4, 8, 5, 9, 7, 8, 10, 1, 6, 3, 8, 6, 10, 3, 8, 2, _
 8             7, 6, 5, 7, 6, 8, 6, 7, 5, 6, 6, 5, 6, 7, 5, 6, 4, 8, 6, 8, 10}
 9
10          ' response frequency array (indices 0 through 10)
11          Dim frequency As Integer() = New Integer(10) {}
12
13          ' count frequencies
14          For answer As Integer = 0 To responses.GetUpperBound(0)
15             frequency(responses(answer)) += 1
16          Next
17
18          Console.WriteLine("Rating " & vbTab & "Frequency ")
19
20          ' display output, ignore element 0 of frequency
21          For rating As Integer = 1 To frequency.GetUpperBound(0)
22             Console.WriteLine(rating & vbTab & frequency(rating))
23          Next
24       End Sub ' Main
25    End Module ' StudentPoll
```

```
Rating  Frequency
1       2
2       2
3       2
4       2
5       5
6       11
7       5
8       7
9       1
10      3
```

Fig. 8.5 | Simple student-poll analysis program.

The For statement (lines 14–16) reads the responses from the array responses one at a time and increments one of the 10 counters in the frequency array (frequency(1) to frequency(10); we ignore frequency(0) because the survey responses are limited to the range 1–10). The key statement in the loop appears in line 15. This statement increments the appropriate frequency counter as determined by the value of responses(answer).

Let us consider several iterations of the For statement. When the counter answer is 0, responses(answer) is the value of responses(0) (i.e., 1—see line 7). Therefore, frequency(responses(answer)) is interpreted as frequency(1), meaning that the counter frequency(1) is incremented by one. In evaluating the expression frequency(responses(answer)), Visual Basic starts with the value in the innermost set of parentheses (answer, currently 0). The value of answer is plugged into the expression, and Visual Basic evaluates the next set of parentheses (responses(answer)). That value is used as the index for the frequency array to determine which counter to increment (in this case, the 1 counter).

When answer is 1, responses(answer) is the value of responses(1) (i.e., 2—see line 7). As a result, frequency(responses(answer)) is interpreted as frequency(2), causing array element 2 to be incremented.

When answer is 2, responses(answer) is the value of responses(2) (i.e., 6—see line 7), so frequency(responses(answer)) is interpreted as frequency(6), causing array element 6 to be incremented, and so on. Note that, regardless of the number of responses processed in the survey, only an 11-element array (in which we ignore element zero) is required to summarize the results, because all the response values are between 1 and 10, and the index values for an 11-element array are 0–10. Note that, in the output in Fig. 8.5, the numbers in the frequency column correctly total 40 (the elements of the frequency array were initialized to zero when the array was allocated with New).

If the data contained the out-of-range value 13, the program would attempt to add 1 to frequency(13). This is outside the bounds of the array. In languages like C and C++, such a dangerous out-of-bounds reference would be allowed. The program would "walk" past the end of the array to where it thought element number 13 was located and would add 1 to whatever happened to be stored at that memory location. This could modify another variable in the program, possibly causing incorrect results or even premature program termination. Visual Basic provides mechanisms that prevent accessing elements outside the bounds of arrays.

Common Programming Error 8.3

Referencing an element outside the array bounds is a runtime error.

Error-Prevention Tip 8.1

When a program is executed, array element indices are checked for validity (i.e., all indices must be greater than or equal to 0 and less than the length of the array). If an attempt is made to use an invalid index to access an element, Visual Basic generates an IndexOutOfRangeException exception. Exceptions are discussed in detail in Chapter 12, Exception Handling.

Error-Prevention Tip 8.2

When looping through an array, the array index should remain between 0 and the upper bound of the array (i.e., the value returned by method GetUpperBound). The initial and final values used in the repetition statement should prevent accessing elements outside this range.

8.4.5 Using Bar Charts to Display Array Data Graphically

Many programs present data to users in a visual or graphical format. For example, numeric values are often displayed as bars in a bar chart. In such a chart, longer bars represent proportionally larger numeric values. Figure 8.6 displays numeric data graphically by creating a bar chart that shows each numeric value as a bar of asterisks (*).

The program reads numbers from an array and graphs the information as a bar chart. Each number is printed, and a bar consisting of the corresponding number of asterisks is

```
1   ' Fig. 8.6: BarChart.vb
2   ' Using data to create bar chart.
3   Module BarChart
4      Sub Main()
5         ' create data array
6         Dim array1 As Integer() = New Integer() _
7            {19, 3, 15, 7, 11, 9, 13, 5, 17, 1}
8
9         Console.WriteLIne("Element " & "Value " & vbTab & "Bar Chart")
10
11        ' display a bar of the bar chart for each element in the array
12        For i As Integer = 0 To array1.GetUpperBound(0)
13           Console.Write(i & vbTab & array1(i) & vbTab)
14
15           For j As Integer = 1 To array1(i)
16              Console.Write("*") ' display one asterisk
17           Next
18
19           Console.WriteLine()
20        Next
21     End Sub ' Main
22   End Module ' BarChart
```

```
Element Value    Bar Chart
0       19       ********************
1       3        ***
2       15       ****************
3       7        *******
4       11       ***********
5       9        *********
6       13       *************
7       5        *****
8       17       *****************
9       1        *
```

Fig. 8.6 | Bar chart printing program.

displayed beside the number. The nested For loops (lines 12–20) display the bars. Note the end value (array1(i)) of the inner For statement at line 15. Each time the inner For statement is reached (line 15), it counts from 1 to array1(i), using a value in array1 to determine the final value of the control variable j—the number of asterisks to display.

8.4.6 Using the Elements of an Array as Counters

Sometimes programs use a series of counter variables to summarize data, such as the results of a survey. In Chapter 7, we used a series of counters in our die-rolling program to track the number of occurrences of each face on a six-sided die as the program rolled the die 12 times. We indicated that there is a more elegant way of doing what we did in Fig. 7.17 for writing the dice-rolling program. An array version of this application is shown in Fig. 8.7. The images of the dice are included in this example's directory.

```
 1   ' Fig. 8.7: RollDie.vb
 2   ' Rolling 12 dice with frequency chart.
 3   Imports System.IO
 4
 5   Public Class FrmRollDie
 6      Dim randomNumber As Random = New Random()
 7      Dim frequency As Integer() = New Integer(6) {}
 8
 9      ' event handler for btnRoll button
10      Private Sub btnRoll_Click(ByVal sender As System.Object, _
11         ByVal e As System.EventArgs) Handles btnRoll.Click
12
13         ' pass PictureBox to a method that assigns a face to each die
14         DisplayDie(picDie1)
15         DisplayDie(picDie2)
16         DisplayDie(picDie3)
17         DisplayDie(picDie4)
18         DisplayDie(picDie5)
19         DisplayDie(picDie6)
20         DisplayDie(picDie7)
21         DisplayDie(picDie8)
22         DisplayDie(picDie9)
23         DisplayDie(picDie10)
24         DisplayDie(picDie11)
25         DisplayDie(picDie12)
26
27         Dim total As Double = 0
28
29         ' total the die faces (used in percentage calculations)
30         For i As Integer = 1 To frequency.GetUpperBound(0)
31            total += frequency(i)
32         Next
33
34         txtDisplay.Text = "Face" & vbTab & "Frequency" & _
35            vbTab & "Percent" & vbCrLf
36
37         ' output frequency values
38         For i As Integer = 1 To frequency.GetUpperBound(0)
39            txtDisplay.Text &= i & vbTab & frequency(i) & _
40               vbTab & vbTab & String.Format("{0:N}", _
41               frequency(i) / total * 100) & "%" & vbCrLf
42         Next
43      End Sub ' btnRoll_Click
44
45      ' simulate roll, display proper image and increment frequency
46      Sub DisplayDie(ByVal picDie As PictureBox)
47         Dim face As Integer = 1 + randomNumber.Next(6)
48
49         ' set appropriate die image in Image property
50         picDie.Image = _
51            Image.FromFile(Directory.GetCurrentDirectory & _
52            "\Images\die" & face & ".png")
```

Fig. 8.7 | Using arrays to eliminate a Select Case statement. (Part 1 of 2.)

```
53              frequency(face) += 1 ' increment appropriate frequency counter
54         End Sub ' DisplayDie
55    End Class ' FrmRollDie
```

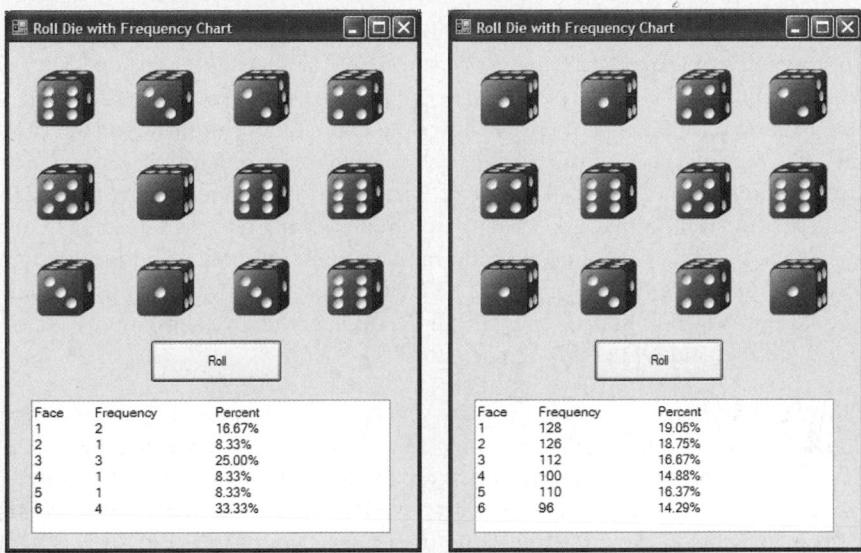

Fig. 8.7 | Using arrays to eliminate a Select Case statement. (Part 2 of 2.)

Lines 60–73 of Fig. 7.17 are replaced by line 53 of Fig. 8.7, which uses face's value as the index for array frequency to determine which element should be incremented during each iteration of the loop. The random number calculation at line 47 produces numbers from 1to 6 (the values for a six-sided die); thus, the frequency array must have seven elements to allow the index values 1–6. We ignore element 0 of array frequency. Lines 34–42 replace lines 36–49 from Fig. 7.17. We can loop through array frequency; therefore, we do not have to enumerate each line of text to display in the PictureBox, as we did in Fig. 7.17.

8.5 Case Study: Card Shuffling and Dealing Simulation

The examples in the chapter thus far have used arrays containing elements of primitive types. Recall from Section 8.2 that the elements of an array can be of either primitive types or reference types. This section uses random number generation and an array of reference-type elements, namely references to objects representing playing cards, to develop a class that simulates card shuffling and dealing. You can then use this class to implement applications that play specific card games. The exercises at the end of the chapter use the classes developed here to build a simple poker application.

First, we develop class Card (Fig. 8.8), which represents a playing card that has a face (e.g., "Ace", "Deuce", "Three", ..., "Jack", "Queen", "King") and a suit (e.g., "Hearts", "Diamonds", "Clubs", "Spades"). Next, we develop the DeckOfCards class (Fig. 8.9), which creates a deck of 52 playing cards in which each element is a Card object. We then build a test application DeckOfCardsTest (Fig. 8.10) that demonstrates class DeckOf-Cards's card shuffling and dealing capabilities.

Class *Card*

Class Card (Fig. 8.8) contains two String instance variables—face and suit—that are used to store references to the face name and suit name for a specific Card. The constructor for the class (lines 8–11) receives two Strings that it uses to initialize face and suit. Method ToString (lines 14–16) creates a String consisting of the face of the card, the String " of " and the suit of the card. Recall from Chapter 3 that the & operator can be used to concatenate (i.e., combine) several Strings to form one larger String. Card's ToString method can be invoked explicitly to obtain a string representation of a Card object (e.g., "Ace of Spades"). The ToString method of an object is called implicitly when an object is output as a String. For this behavior to occur, ToString must be declared with the header shown in line 14 of Fig. 8.8. We discuss the special method ToString in Chapter 9, Classes and Objects: A Deeper Look.

Class *DeckOfCards*

Class DeckOfCards (Fig. 8.9) declares an instance variable array named deck, which consists of Card objects (line 4). Like primitive-type array declarations, the declaration of an array of objects includes the name of the array variable, followed by the keyword As, the type of the elements in the array and parentheses (e.g., deck As Card()). Class DeckOf-Cards also declares an integer instance variable currentCard (line 5) representing the next Card to be dealt from the deck array and a named constant NUMBER_OF_CARDS (line 6) indicating the number of Cards in the deck (52).

The class's constructor instantiates the deck array (line 15) with upper bound NUMBER_OF_CARDS - 1. When first created, the elements of the deck array are Nothing by default, so the constructor uses a For statement (lines 20–22) to fill the deck array with Cards. This statement initializes control variable count to 0 and loops while count is less

```vb
 1   ' Fig. 8.8: Card.vb
 2   ' Card class represents a playing card.
 3   Public Class Card
 4      Private face As String ' face of card ("Ace", "Deuce", ...)
 5      Private suit As String ' suit of card ("Hearts", "Diamonds", ...)
 6
 7      ' two-argument constructor initializes card's face and suit
 8      Public Sub New(ByVal cardFace As String, ByVal cardSuit As String)
 9         face = cardFace ' initialize face of card
10         suit = cardSuit ' initialize suit of card
11      End Sub ' New
12
13      ' return String representation of Card, Overrides defined in Ch 9
14      Public Overrides Function ToString() As String
15         Return face & " of " & suit
16      End Function ' ToString
17   End Class ' Card
```

Fig. 8.8 | Card class represents a playing card.

than or equal to deck.GetUpperBound(0), causing count to take on each integer value from 0 to 51 (the indices of the deck array). Each Card is instantiated and initialized with two Strings—one from the faces array (which contains the Strings "Ace" through "King") and one from the suits array (which contains the Strings "Hearts", "Diamonds", "Clubs" and "Spades"). The calculation count Mod 13 always results in a value from 0 to 12 (the 13 indices of the faces array in lines 11–12), and the calculation count \ 13 always results in a value from 0 to 3 (the four indices of the suits array in line 13). When the deck array is initialized, it contains the Cards with faces "Ace" through "King" in order for each suit.

```vb
1    ' Fig. 8.9: DeckOfCards.vb
2    ' DeckOfCards class represents a deck of playing cards.
3    Public Class DeckOfCards
4       Private deck As Card() ' array of Card objects
5       Private currentCard As Integer ' index of next Card to be dealt
6       Private Const NUMBER_OF_CARDS As Integer = 52 ' number of cards
7       Private randomNumbers As Random ' random number generator
8
9       ' constructor fills deck of Cards
10      Public Sub New()
11         Dim faces As String() = {"Ace", "Deuce", "Three", "Four", "Five", _
12            "Six", "Seven", "Eight", "Nine", "Ten", "Jack", "Queen", "King"}
13         Dim suits As String() = {"Hearts", "Diamonds", "Clubs", "Spades"}
14
15         deck = New Card(NUMBER_OF_CARDS - 1) {} ' create array of Cards
16         currentCard = 0 ' set currentCard so first Card dealt is deck(0)
17         randomNumbers = New Random() ' create random number generator
18
19         ' populate deck with Card objects
20         For count As Integer = 0 To deck.GetUpperBound(0)
21            deck(count) = New Card(faces(count Mod 13), suits(count \ 13))
22         Next
23      End Sub ' New
24
25      ' shuffle deck of Cards with simple one-pass algorithm
26      Public Sub Shuffle()
27         ' after shuffling, dealing should start at deck(0) again
28         currentCard = 0 ' reinitialize currentCard
29
30         ' for each Card, pick another random Card and swap them
31         For first As Integer = 0 To deck.GetUpperBound(0)
32            ' select a random number between 0 and 51
33            Dim second As Integer = randomNumbers.Next(NUMBER_OF_CARDS)
34
35            ' swap current Card with randomly selected Card
36            Dim temp As Card = deck(first)
37            deck(first) = deck(second)
38            deck(second) = temp
39         Next
40      End Sub ' Shuffle
```

Fig. 8.9 | DeckOfCards class represents a deck of playing cards that can be shuffled and dealt one at a time. (Part 1 of 2.)

```
41
42        ' deal one Card
43        Public Function DealCard() As Card
44           ' determine whether Cards remain to be dealt
45           If currentCard <= deck.GetUpperBound(0) Then
46              Dim lastCard = currentCard ' store current card number
47              currentCard += 1 ' increment current card number
48              Return deck(lastCard)
49           Else
50              Return Nothing
51           End If
52        End Function ' DealCard
53     End Class ' DeckOfCards
```

Fig. 8.9 | `DeckOfCards` class represents a deck of playing cards that can be shuffled and dealt one at a time. (Part 2 of 2.)

Method `Shuffle` (lines 26–40) shuffles the `Cards` in the deck. The method loops through all 52 `Cards` (array indices 0 to 51). For each `Card`, a number between 0 and 51 is picked randomly to select another `Card` (line 33). Next, the current `Card` object and the randomly selected `Card` object are swapped in the array (lines 36–38). The extra variable `temp` temporarily stores one of the two `Card` objects being swapped. The swap cannot be performed with only the two statements

```
deck(first) = deck(second)
deck(second) = deck(first)
```

If `deck(first)` is the `"Ace"` of `"Spades"` and `deck(second)` is the `"Queen"` of `"Hearts"`, after the first assignment, both array elements contain the `"Queen"` of `"Hearts"` and the `"Ace"` of `"Spades"` is lost—hence, the extra variable `temp` is needed. After the `For` loop terminates, the `Card` objects are randomly ordered. Only 52 swaps are made in a single pass of the entire array, and the array of `Card` objects is shuffled!

Method `DealCard` (lines 43–52) deals one `Card` in the array. Recall that `currentCard` indicates the index of the next `Card` to be dealt (i.e., the `Card` at the top of the deck). Thus, line 45 compares `currentCard` to the upper bound (51) of the deck array. If the deck is not empty (i.e., `currentCard` is less than or equal to 51), line 46 assigns `currentCard` (the index of the card that will be returned) to temporary variable `lastCard`, line 47 increments `currentCard` to prepare for the next call to `DealCard` and line 48 returns `deck(lastCard)`, which represents the top card of the deck for this call to `DealCard`. Otherwise, `DealCard` returns `Nothing` to indicate that the deck is empty.

Shuffling and Dealing Cards

The application in Fig. 8.10 demonstrates the card dealing and shuffling capabilities of class `DeckOfCards` (Fig. 8.9). Line 5 creates a `DeckOfCards` object named `cards`. Recall that the `DeckOfCards` constructor creates the deck with the 52 `Card` objects in order by suit and face. Line 6 invokes `cards`'s `Shuffle` method to randomly rearrange the `Card` objects. The `For` statement in lines 9–13 deals all 52 `Cards` in the deck and prints them in four columns of 13 `Cards` each. Lines 10–12 deal and print four `Card` objects (on one line), each obtained by invoking `cards`'s `DealCard` method. When `Console.WriteLine` outputs

```
1   ' Fig. 8.10: DeckOfCardsTest.vb
2   ' Card shuffling and dealing application.
3   Module DeckOfCardsTest
4      Sub Main()
5         Dim cards As New DeckOfCards()
6         cards.Shuffle() ' place Cards in random order
7
8         ' print all 52 Cards in the order in which they are dealt
9         For i As Integer = 0 To 12
10           Console.WriteLine("{0, -18} {1, -18} {2, -18} {3, -18}", _
11              cards.DealCard(), cards.DealCard(), cards.DealCard(), _
12              cards.DealCard())
13        Next
14     End Sub ' Main
15  End Module ' DeckOfCardsTest
```

Five of Spades	Nine of Spades	Seven of Hearts	Eight of Clubs
Jack of Spades	Seven of Clubs	Queen of Spades	Ace of Diamonds
Ace of Clubs	Five of Hearts	Ten of Diamonds	Queen of Diamonds
Nine of Diamonds	Four of Hearts	Six of Spades	Six of Diamonds
Ace of Hearts	King of Spades	Jack of Diamonds	Seven of Spades
Four of Spades	Seven of Diamonds	Ten of Spades	Eight of Spades
Deuce of Spades	King of Diamonds	Deuce of Hearts	Nine of Hearts
Three of Clubs	King of Hearts	Six of Hearts	Queen of Hearts
Eight of Hearts	Ten of Hearts	Five of Clubs	King of Clubs
Five of Diamonds	Jack of Clubs	Jack of Hearts	Eight of Diamonds
Six of Clubs	Deuce of Clubs	Ace of Spades	Three of Hearts
Four of Diamonds	Ten of Clubs	Nine of Clubs	Three of Spades
Queen of Clubs	Deuce of Diamonds	Three of Diamonds	Four of Clubs

Fig. 8.10 | Card shuffling and dealing (all 52 cards are dealt).

a Card with the {0, -18} format specifier, the Card's ToString method (declared in lines 14–16 of Fig. 8.8) is implicitly invoked, and the result is output left justified (because of the minus sign in -18) in a field of width 18. Again, we explain ToString in detail in Chapter 9.

8.6 Passing an Array to a Method

To pass an array argument to a method, specify the name of the array without using parentheses. For example, if array hourlyTemperatures has been declared as

```
Dim hourlyTemperatures As Integer() = New Integer(24) {}
```

the method call

```
DayData(hourlyTemperatures)
```

passes array hourlyTemperatures to method DayData.

Every array object "knows" its own upper bound (i.e., the value returned by the method GetUpperBound), so when you pass an array object to a method, you do not need to pass the upper bound of the array as a separate argument.

For a method to receive an array through a method call, the method's parameter list must specify that an array will be received. For example, the method header for DayData might be written as

```
Sub DayData(ByVal temperatureData As Integer())
```

indicating that DayData expects to receive an Integer array in parameter temperatureData. In Visual Basic, arrays always are passed by reference, yet it is normally inappropriate to use keyword ByRef in the method definition header. We discuss this subtle (and somewhat complex) issue in more detail in Section 8.16.

Although entire arrays are always passed by reference, individual array elements can be passed in the same manner as simple variables of that type. For instance, array element values of primitive types, such as Integer, can be passed either by value or by reference, depending on the method definition. To pass an array element to a method, use the indexed name of the array element as an argument in the method call. The program in Fig. 8.11 demonstrates the difference between passing an entire array and passing an array element.

The For...Next statement in lines 12–14 displays the five elements of integer array array1 (line 5). Line 16 passes array1 to method ModifyArray (lines 42–46), which then multiplies each element by 2 (line 44). To illustrate that array1's elements were modified in the called method (i.e., as enabled by passing by reference), the For...Next statement in lines 20–22 displays the five elements of array1. As the output indicates, the elements of array1 are indeed modified by ModifyArray.

To show the value of array1(3) before the call to ModifyElementByVal, lines 24–27 display the value of array1(3). Line 29 invokes method ModifyElementByVal (lines 50–56) and passes array1(3). When array1(3) is passed by value, the Integer value in position 3 of array array1 (now an 8) is copied and is passed to method ModifyElementByVal, where it becomes the value of parameter element. Method ModifyElementByVal then multiplies element by 2 (line 53). The parameter element of ModifyElementByVal is a local variable that is destroyed when the method terminates. Thus, when control is returned to Main, the unmodified value of array1(3) is displayed.

```
1    ' Fig. 8.11: PassArray.vb
2    ' Passing arrays and individual array elements to methods.
3    Module PassArray
4       Sub Main()
5          Dim array1 As Integer() = New Integer() {1, 2, 3, 4, 5}
6
7          Console.WriteLine("EFFECTS OF PASSING AN ENTIRE ARRAY " & _
8             "BY REFERENCE:" & vbCrLf & vbCrLf & _
9             "The values of the original array are:")
10
11         ' display original elements of array1
12         For i As Integer = 0 To array1.GetUpperBound(0)
13            Console.Write("   " & array1(i))
14         Next
15
```

Fig. 8.11 | Passing arrays and individual array elements to methods. (Part 1 of 3.)

```
16        ModifyArray(array1) ' array is passed by reference
17        Console.WriteLine(vbCrLf & "The values of the modified array are:")
18
19        ' display modified elements of array1
20        For i As Integer = 0 To array1.GetUpperBound(0)
21           Console.Write("   " & array1(i))
22        Next
23
24        Console.WriteLine(vbCrLf & vbCrLf & _
25           "EFFECTS OF PASSING AN ARRAY ELEMENT BY VALUE:" & _
26           vbCrLf & vbCrLf & "array1(3) before ModifyElementByVal: " & _
27           array1(3))
28
29        ModifyElementByVal(array1(3)) ' array element passed by value
30        Console.WriteLine("array1(3) after ModifyElementByVal: " & _
31           array1(3))
32        Console.WriteLine(vbCrLf & "EFFECTS OF PASSING AN " & _
33           "ARRAY ELEMENT BY REFERENCE: " & vbCrLf & vbCrLf & _
34           "array1(3) before ModifyElementByRef: " & array1(3))
35
36        ModifyElementByRef(array1(3)) ' array element passed by reference
37        Console.WriteLine("array1(3) after ModifyElementByRef: " & _
38           array1(3))
39     End Sub ' Main
40
41     ' method modifies array it receives (note ByVal)
42     Sub ModifyArray(ByVal arrayParameter As Integer())
43        For j As Integer = 0 To arrayParameter.GetUpperBound(0)
44           arrayParameter(j) *= 2 ' double the array element
45        Next
46     End Sub ' ModifyArray
47
48     ' method modifies integer passed to it
49     ' original is not modified (note ByVal)
50     Sub ModifyElementByVal(ByVal element As Integer)
51        Console.WriteLine("Value received in ModifyElementByVal: " & _
52           element)
53        element *= 2 ' double the array element
54        Console.WriteLine("Value calculated in ModifyElementByVal: " & _
55           element)
56     End Sub ' ModifyElementByVal
57
58     ' method modifies integer passed to it
59     ' original is modified (note ByRef)
60     Sub ModifyElementByRef(ByRef element As Integer)
61        Console.WriteLine("Value received in ModifyElementByRef: " & _
62           element)
63        element *= 2 ' double the array element
64        Console.WriteLine("Value calculated in ModifyElementByRef: " & _
65           element)
66     End Sub ' ModifyElementByRef
67  End Module ' PassArray
```

Fig. 8.11 | Passing arrays and individual array elements to methods. (Part 2 of 3.)

```
EFFECTS OF PASSING AN ENTIRE ARRAY BY REFERENCE:

The values of the original array are:
  1   2   3   4   5
The values of the modified array are:
  2   4   6   8  10

EFFECTS OF PASSING AN ARRAY ELEMENT BY VALUE:

array1(3) before ModifyElementByVal: 8
Value received in ModifyElementByVal: 8
Value calculated in ModifyElementByVal: 16
array1(3) after ModifyElementByVal: 8

EFFECTS OF PASSING AN ARRAY ELEMENT BY REFERENCE:

array1(3) before ModifyElementByRef: 8
Value received in ModifyElementByRef: 8
Value calculated in ModifyElementByRef: 16
array1(3) after ModifyElementByRef: 16
```

Fig. 8.11 | Passing arrays and individual array elements to methods. (Part 3 of 3.)

Lines 32–38 demonstrate the effects of method `ModifyElementByRef` (lines 60–66). This method performs the same calculation as `ModifyElementByVal`, multiplying `element` by 2. In this case, `array1(3)` is passed by reference, meaning that the value of `array1(3)` displayed (lines 37–38) is the same as the value calculated in the method (i.e., the original value in the caller is modified by the called method).

Common Programming Error 8.4

When passing an array to a method, including an empty pair of parentheses after the array name is a syntax error.

8.7 For Each...Next Repetition Statement

Visual Basic provides the **For Each...Next** repetition statement for iterating through the values in a data structure, such as an array, without using a loop counter. When used with one-dimensional arrays, For Each...Next behaves like a For...Next statement that iterates through the range of indices from 0 to the value returned by GetUpperBound(0). Instead of a counter, For Each...Next uses a variable to represent the value of each element. The program in Fig. 8.12 uses the For Each...Next statement to determine the minimum value in a one-dimensional array of grades.

The header of the For Each repetition statement (line 10) specifies an `Integer` variable (grade) and an array (gradeArray). The For Each statement iterates through all the elements in gradeArray, sequentially assigning each value to variable grade. The values are compared to variable lowGrade (line 11), which stores the lowest grade in the array.

For one-dimensional arrays, the repetition of the For Each...Next statement begins with the element whose index is zero, then iterates through all the indices. In this case, grade takes on the successive values as they are ordered in the initializer list in line 6. When all the grades have been processed, lowGrade is displayed. Although many array calcula-

```
1   ' Fig. 8.12: ForEach.vb
2   ' Program uses For Each...Next to find the minimum grade.
3   Module ForEach
4      Sub Main()
5         Dim gradeArray As Integer() = New Integer() _
6            {77, 68, 86, 73, 98, 87, 89, 81, 70, 90, 86, 81}
7         Dim lowGrade As Integer = 100
8
9         ' use For Each...Next to find the minimum grade
10        For Each grade As Integer In gradeArray
11           If grade < lowGrade Then
12              lowGrade = grade
13           End If
14        Next
15
16        Console.WriteLine("The minimum grade is: {0}", lowGrade)
17     End Sub ' Main
18  End Module ' ForEach
```

```
The minimum grade is: 68
```

Fig. 8.12 | Using For Each...Next with an array.

tions are handled best with a counter, For Each is useful when the indices of the elements are not important.

8.8 GradeBook Case Study: Using an Array to Store Grades

This section further evolves class GradeBook, introduced in Chapter 4 and expanded in Chapters 5–6. Recall that this class represents a grade book used by a professor to store and analyze a set of student grades. Previous versions of the class process a set of grades entered by the user, but do not maintain the individual grade values in instance variables of the class. Thus, repeat calculations require the user to reenter the same grades. One way to solve this problem would be to store each grade entered in an instance of the class. For example, we could create instance variables grade1, grade2, ..., grade10 in class GradeBook to store 10 student grades. However, the code to total the grades and determine the class average would be cumbersome, and the class would not be able to process any more than 10 grades at a time. In this section, we solve the problem by storing the grades in an array.

Storing Student Grades in an Array in Class GradeBook
The version of class GradeBook (Fig. 8.13) presented here uses an array of Integers to store the grades of several students on a single exam. This eliminates the need to repeatedly input the same set of grades. Array grades is declared as an instance variable in line 5—therefore, each GradeBook object maintains its own set of grades. The class's constructor (lines 8–11) has two parameters—the name of the course and an array of grades. When an application (e.g., class GradeBookTest in Fig. 8.14) creates a GradeBook object, the application passes an existing Integer array to the constructor, which assigns the array's refer-

ence to instance variable grades (line 10). The size of the array grades is determined by the class that passes the array to the constructor. Thus, a GradeBook object can process a variable number of grades. The grade values in the passed array could have been input from a user or read from a file on disk (as discussed in Chapter 18). In our test application, we simply initialize an array with a set of grade values (Fig. 8.14, lines 6–7). Once the grades are stored in instance variable grades of class GradeBook, all the class's methods can access the elements of grades as needed to perform various calculations.

Method ProcessGrades (lines 31–43) contains a series of method calls that result in the output of a report summarizing the grades. Line 32 calls method OutputGrades to print the contents of the array grades. Lines 124–127 in method OutputGrades use a For statement to output each student's grade. Lines 125–126 use counter variable student's value to output each grade next to a particular student number (see the output in Fig. 8.14). Although array indices start at 0, a professor would typically number students starting at 1. Thus, lines 125–126 output student + 1 as the student number to produce grade labels "Student 1: ", "Student 2: ", and so on.

```vb
 1   ' Fig. 8.13: GradeBook.vb
 2   ' GradeBook class uses an array to store test grades.
 3   Public Class GradeBook
 4      Private courseNameValue As String ' name of course
 5      Private grades As Integer() ' array of student grades
 6
 7      ' two-argument constructor initializes courseNameValue and grades
 8      Public Sub New(ByVal name As String, ByVal gradesArray As Integer())
 9         CourseName = name ' initializes courseNameValue via property
10         grades = gradesArray ' store reference to gradesArray
11      End Sub ' New
12
13      ' property CourseName
14      Public Property CourseName() As String
15         Get
16            Return courseNameValue
17         End Get
18
19         Set(ByVal name As String)
20            courseNameValue = name
21         End Set
22      End Property ' Course Name
23
24      ' display a welcome message to the GradeBook user
25      Public Sub DisplayMessage()
26         Console.WriteLine("Welcome to the grade book for " & vbCrLf & _
27            CourseName & vbCrLf)
28      End Sub ' DisplayMessage
29
30      ' perform various operations on the data
31      Public Sub ProcessGrades()
32         OutputGrades() ' output grades array
33
```

Fig. 8.13 | GradeBook class using an array to store test grades. (Part 1 of 3.)

```vb
34          ' call method GetAverage to calculate the average grade
35          Console.WriteLine("Class average is {0:F2}", GetAverage())
36
37          ' call methods GetMinimum and GetMaximum
38          Console.WriteLine("Lowest grade is {0}", GetMinimum())
39          Console.WriteLine("Highest grade is {0}", GetMaximum())
40
41          ' call OutputBarChart to print grade distribution chart
42          OutputBarChart()
43       End Sub ' ProcessGrades
44
45       ' find minimum grade
46       Public Function GetMinimum() As Integer
47          Dim lowGrade As Integer = grades(0) ' assume grades(0) is smallest
48
49          ' loop through grades array
50          For Each grade As Integer In grades
51             ' if grade lower than lowGrade, assign it to lowGrade
52             If grade < lowGrade Then
53                lowGrade = grade ' new lowest grade
54             End If
55          Next
56
57          Return lowGrade ' return lowest grade
58       End Function ' GetMinimum
59
60       ' find maximum grade
61       Public Function GetMaximum() As Integer
62          Dim highGrade As Integer = grades(0) ' assume grades(0) is largest
63
64          ' loop through grades array
65          For Each grade As Integer In grades
66             ' if grade greater than highGrade, assign it to highGrade
67             If grade > highGrade Then
68                highGrade = grade ' new highest grade
69             End If
70          Next
71
72          Return highGrade ' return highest grade
73       End Function ' GetMaximum
74
75       ' determine average grade for test
76       Public Function GetAverage() As Double
77          Dim total As Integer = 0 ' initialize total
78
79          ' sum grades for one student
80          For Each grade As Integer In grades
81             total += grade
82          Next
83
84          ' return average of grades
85          Return (total / grades.Length)
86       End Function ' GetAverage
```

Fig. 8.13 | GradeBook class using an array to store test grades. (Part 2 of 3.)

```
87
88        ' output bar chart displaying grade distribution
89      Public Sub OutputBarChart()
90         Console.WriteLine(vbCrLf & "Grade distribution:")
91
92         ' stores frequency of grades in each range of 10 grades
93         Dim frequency As Integer() = New Integer(10) {}
94
95         ' for each grade, increment the appropriate frequency
96         For Each grade As Integer In grades
97            frequency(grade \ 10) += 1
98         Next
99
100        ' for each grade frequency, print bar in chart
101        For count As Integer = 0 To frequency.GetUpperBound(0)
102           ' output bar label ( "00-09: ", ..., "90-99: ", "100: " )
103           If count = 10 Then
104              Console.Write("{0, 5:D}: ", 100)
105           Else
106              Console.Write("{0, 2:D2}-{1, 2:D2}: ", _
107                 count * 10, count * 10 + 9)
108           End If
109
110           ' print bar of asterisks
111           For stars As Integer = 0 To frequency(count) - 1
112              Console.Write("*")
113           Next
114
115           Console.WriteLine() ' start a new line of output
116        Next
117     End Sub ' OutputBarChart
118
119     ' output the contents of the grades array
120     Public Sub OutputGrades()
121        Console.WriteLine("The grades are:" & vbCrLf)
122
123        ' output each student's grade
124        For student As Integer = 0 To grades.GetUpperBound(0)
125           Console.WriteLine("Student {0, 2:D}: {1, 3:D}", _
126              student + 1, grades(student))
127        Next
128
129        Console.WriteLine()
130     End Sub ' OutputGrades
131  End Class ' GradeBook
```

Fig. 8.13 | GradeBook class using an array to store test grades. (Part 3 of 3.)

Method ProcessGrades next calls method GetAverage (line 35) to obtain the average of the grades in the array. Method GetAverage (lines 76–86) uses a For Each statement to total the values in array grades before calculating the average. The loop control variable declaration in the For Each's header (e.g., grade As Integer) indicates that for each iteration, the Integer variable grade takes on the next successive value in the array grades. The averaging calculation in line 85 uses grades.Length to determine the number of grades being averaged.

Lines 38–39 in method ProcessGrades call methods GetMinimum and GetMaximum to determine the lowest and highest grades of any student on the exam, respectively. Each of these methods uses a For Each statement to loop through array grades. Lines 50–55 in method GetMinimum loop through the array, and lines 52–54 compare each grade to lowGrade. If a grade is less than lowGrade, lowGrade is set to that grade. When line 57 executes, lowGrade contains the lowest grade in the array. Method GetMaximum (lines 61–73) works similarly to method GetMinimum.

Finally, line 42 in method ProcessGrades calls method OutputBarChart to print a distribution chart of the grade data using a technique similar to that in Fig. 8.6. Lines 96–98 calculate the frequency of grades in each category. Line 106 passes to the method Console.Write the format string "{0, 2:D2}-{1, 2:D2}", which indicates that arguments 0 and 1 (the first two arguments after the format string) should take the format D2 (base 10 decimal number format using two digits) for display purposes—thus, 8 would be converted to 08 and 10 would remain as 10. Recall that the number 2 before the colon indicates that the result should be output right justified in a field of width 2. The dash that separates the curly braces } and { is printed to display the range of the grades (see the output of Fig. 8.14).

Line 93 declares and creates array frequency of 11 Integers to store the frequency of grades in each grade category. For each grade in array grades, lines 96–98 increment the appropriate element of the frequency array. To determine which element to increment, line 97 divides the current grade by 10 using integer division. For example, if grade is 85, line 97 increments frequency[8] to update the count of grades in the range 80–89. Lines 101–116 next print the bar chart (see the output of Fig. 8.14) based on the values in the frequency array. Like lines 15–17 of Fig. 8.6, lines 111–113 of Fig. 8.13 use a value in array frequency to determine the number of asterisks to display in each bar.

Class *GradeBookTest* That Demonstrates Class *GradeBook*

The application in Fig. 8.14 creates an object of class GradeBook (Fig. 8.13) using the Integer array gradesArray (declared and initialized in lines 6–7). Lines 8–9 pass a course name and gradesArray to the GradeBook constructor. Line 10 displays a welcome message, and line 11 invokes the GradeBook object's ProcessGrades method. The output presents an analysis of the 10 grades in gradeBooks.

Software Engineering Observation 8.1

A test harness (or test application) is responsible for creating an object of the class being tested and providing it with data. This data could come from any of several sources. Test data can be placed directly into an array with an array initializer, it can be entered by the user at the keyboard, it can be read from a file (as you will see in Chapter 18), or it can arrive over a network (as you will see in Chapter 23). After passing this data to the class's constructor to instantiate the object, the test harness should call the object's methods to verify that they work properly.

```
 1    ' Fig. 8.14: GradeBookTest.vb
 2    ' Create GradeBook object using any array of grades.
 3    Module GradeBookTest
 4       Sub Main()
 5          ' array of student grades
 6          Dim gradesArray As Integer() = _
 7             {87, 68, 94, 100, 83, 78, 85, 91, 76, 87}
 8          Dim gradeBooks As New GradeBook( _
 9             "CS101 Introduction to Visual Basic Programming", gradesArray)
10          gradeBooks.DisplayMessage()
11          gradeBooks.ProcessGrades()
12       End Sub ' Main
13    End Module ' GradeBookTest
```

```
Welcome to the grade book for
CS101 Introduction to Visual Basic Programming

The grades are:

Student  1:  87
Student  2:  68
Student  3:  94
Student  4: 100
Student  5:  83
Student  6:  78
Student  7:  85
Student  8:  91
Student  9:  76
Student 10:  87

Class average is 84.90
Lowest grade is 68
Highest grade is 100

Grade distribution:
00-09:
10-19:
20-29:
30-39:
40-49:
50-59:
60-69: *
70-79: **
80-89: ****
90-99: **
  100: *
```

Fig. 8.14 | GradeBookTest creates a GradeBook object using an array of grades, then invokes method ProcessGrades to analyze them.

8.9 Sorting an Array with Method Sort of Class Array

Sorting data (i.e., arranging the data in ascending or descending order) is one of the most popular computing applications. For example, a bank sorts all checks by account number, so that it can prepare individual bank statements at the end of each month. Telephone companies sort their lists of accounts by last name and, within last-name listings, by first name, to make it easy to find phone numbers. Virtually every organization must sort some data and, often, massive amounts of it.

Recall that all arrays have access to the methods and properties of class Array (in namespace System). Class Array provides methods for creating, modifying, sorting and searching arrays. By default, Shared method **Sort** of class Array sorts an array's elements into ascending order. The Windows application in Fig. 8.15 demonstrates method Sort by sorting an array of 10 randomly generated elements (which may contain duplicates).

```vb
1   ' Fig. 8.15: SortTest.vb
2   ' Program creates random numbers and sorts them.
3   Imports System
4
5   Public Class FrmSortTest
6      Dim integerArray As Integer() = New Integer(9) {}
7
8      ' creates random generated numbers
9      Private Sub btnCreate_Click(ByVal sender As System.Object, _
10        ByVal e As System.EventArgs) Handles btnCreate.Click
11
12        Dim output As String = ""
13        Dim randomNumber As Random = New Random()
14
15        txtSorted.Text = "" ' clear txtSorted TextBox
16
17        ' create 10 random numbers and append to output
18        For i As Integer = 0 To integerArray.GetUpperBound(0)
19           integerArray(i) = randomNumber.Next(100)
20           output &= (integerArray(i) & vbCrLf)
21        Next
22
23        txtOriginal.Text = output ' display numbers
24        btnSort.Enabled = True ' enable Sort button
25     End Sub ' btnCreate_Click
26
27     ' sorts randomly generated numbers
28     Private Sub btnSort_Click(ByVal sender As System.Object, _
29        ByVal e As System.EventArgs) Handles btnSort.Click
30
31        Dim output As String = ""
32
33        Array.Sort(integerArray) ' sort array integerArray
34
35        ' creates string with sorted numbers
36        For i As Integer = 0 To integerArray.GetUpperBound(0)
37           output &= (integerArray(i) & vbCrLf)
38        Next
39
40        txtSorted.Text = output ' display numbers
41        btnSort.Enabled = False ' disable Sort button
42     End Sub ' btnSort_Click
43  End Class ' FrmSortTest
```

Fig. 8.15 | Sorting an array with method Array.Sort. (Part 1 of 2.)

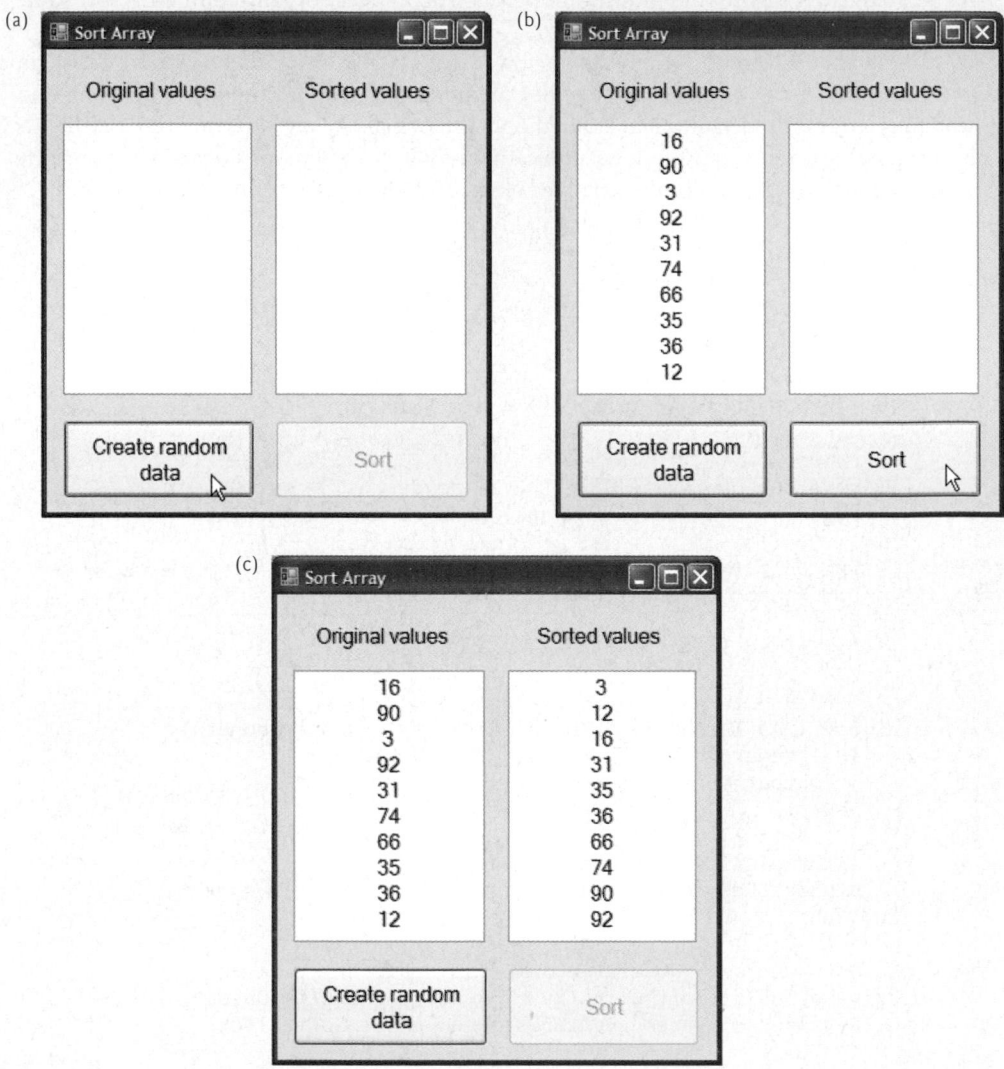

Fig. 8.15 | Sorting an array with method `Array.Sort`. (Part 2 of 2.)

The program contains methods `btnCreate_Click` and `btnSort_Click`. Method `btnCreate_Click` (lines 9–25) assigns 10 random values to the elements of `integerArray` and displays the contents of the array in the `txtOriginal` TextBox. Method `btnSort_Click` (lines 28–42) sorts `array` by calling `Shared` method `Sort` of class `Array`, which takes an array as its argument and sorts the elements in the array in ascending order. To sort an array in descending order, first call method `Sort` to sort the array, then call `Shared` method **Reverse** of class `Array` to reverse the order of the elements in the array. Like method `Sort`, method `Reverse` takes an array as its argument. In Exercise 8.6, you are asked to modify the program in Fig. 8.15 to display an array of values in both ascending and descending order.

8.10 Searching Arrays

Often it is necessary to determine whether an array contains a value that matches a certain key value. The process of locating a particular element value in an array is called searching. In this section, we use two searching techniques—the simple linear search and the more efficient (but more complex) binary search.

8.10.1 Searching an Array with Linear Search

Module LinearSearch in Fig. 8.16 contains a function for performing a linear search. Function Search simply compares each element of an array with a search key. If the search key is found, the method returns the index value of the matching element. If the search key is not found, the method returns -1. The value -1 is a good choice because it is not a valid index number. If the elements of the array being searched are unordered, it is just as likely that the value will be found in the front half of the array as in the back half, so on average the method will have to compare the search key with half the elements of the array.

Figure 8.17 uses function Search in module LinearSearch to search a 20-element array filled with random values created when the user clicks btnCreate. The user types a search key in a TextBox (named txtInput) and clicks btnSearch to start the search.

```
 1   ' Fig. 8.16: LinearSearch.vb
 2   ' Linear search of an array.
 3   Module LinearSearch
 4      ' iterates through array
 5      Function Search(ByVal key As Integer, _
 6         ByVal numbers As Integer()) As Integer
 7
 8         ' statement iterates linearly through array
 9         For i As Integer= 0 To numbers.GetUpperBound(0)
10            If numbers(i) = key Then
11               Return i
12            End If
13         Next
14
15         Return -1 ' indicates the key was not found
16      End Function ' Search
17   End Module ' LinearSearch
```

Fig. 8.16 | Method for performing a linear search.

```
 1   ' Fig. 8.17: LinearSearchTest.vb
 2   ' Linear search of an array.
 3   Public Class FrmLinearSearchTest
 4      Dim array1 As Integer() = New Integer(19) {}
 5
 6      ' create random data
 7      Private Sub btnCreate_Click(ByVal sender As System.Object, _
 8         ByVal e As System.EventArgs) Handles btnCreate.Click
 9
```

Fig. 8.17 | Linear search of an array. (Part 1 of 3.)

```
10          Dim randomNumber As Random = New Random()
11          Dim output As String = ("Index" & vbTab & "Value" & vbCrLf)
12
13          ' create string containing 20 random numbers
14          For i As Integer = 0 To array1.GetUpperBound(0)
15             array1(i) = randomNumber.Next(1000)
16             output &= (i & vbTab & array1(i) & vbCrLf)
17          Next
18
19          txtData.Text = output ' display numbers
20          txtInput.Text = "" ' clear search key text box
21          btnSearch.Enabled = True ' enable search button
22       End Sub ' btnCreate_Click
23
24       ' search array for search key
25       Private Sub btnSearch_Click(ByVal sender As System.Object, _
26          ByVal e As System.EventArgs) Handles btnSearch.Click
27
28          ' if search key text box is empty, display
29          ' message and exit method
30          If txtInput.Text = "" Then
31             MessageBox.Show("You must enter a search key.", "Error", _
32                MessageBoxButtons.OK, MessageBoxIcon.Error)
33             Exit Sub
34          End If
35
36          Dim searchKey As Integer = Convert.ToInt32(txtInput.Text)
37          Dim element As Integer = LinearSearch.Search(searchKey, array1)
38
39          If element <> -1 Then
40             lblResult.Text = "Found value in index " & element
41          Else
42             lblResult.Text = "Value not found"
43          End If
44       End Sub ' btnSearch_Click
45    End Class ' FrmLinearSearchTest
```

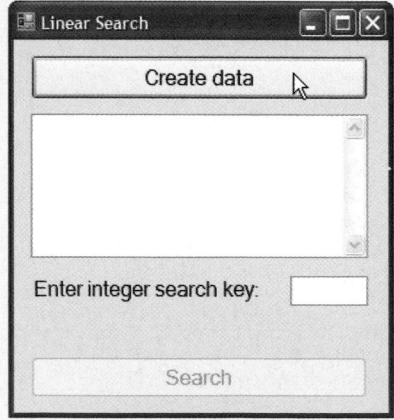

Fig. 8.17 | Linear search of an array. (Part 2 of 3.)

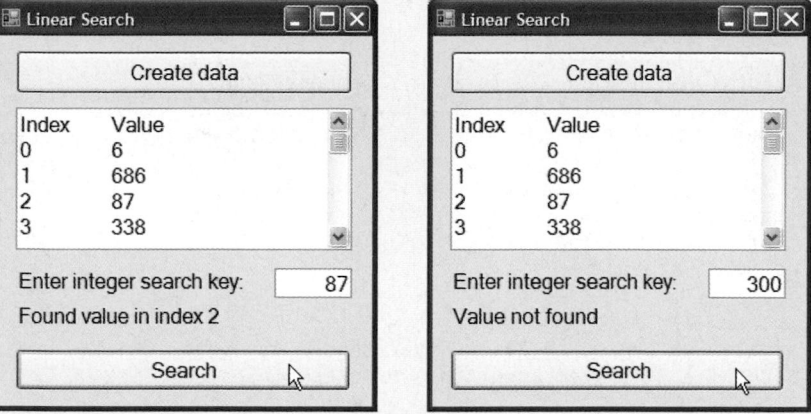

Fig. 8.17 | Linear search of an array. (Part 3 of 3.)

8.10.2 Searching a Sorted Array with Method BinarySearch of Class Array

The linear search method works well for small or unsorted arrays. However, for large unsorted arrays, linear searching is inefficient. If the array is sorted, the high-speed binary search technique can be used. Class Array provides method **BinarySearch**, which searches a sorted array for a value using binary search.

Figure 8.18 uses method BinarySearch of class Array to perform a binary search for a key value. The method receives two arguments—integer array array1 (the array to search) and integer searchKey (the search key). If the value is found, method Binary-Search returns the index of the search key; otherwise, it returns a negative number.

```vb
1   ' Fig. 8.18: BinarySearchTest.vb
2   ' Binary search of an array using Array.BinarySearch.
3   Imports System
4
5   Public Class FrmBinarySearchTest
6      Dim array1 As Integer() = New Integer(19) {}
7
8      ' create random data
9      Private Sub btnCreate_Click(ByVal sender As System.Object, _
10        ByVal e As System.EventArgs) Handles btnCreate.Click
11
12        Dim randomNumber As Random = New Random()
13        Dim output As String = ("Index" & vbTab & "Value" & vbCrLf)
14
15        ' create random array elements
16        For i As Integer = 0 To array1.GetUpperBound(0)
17           array1(i) = randomNumber.Next(1000)
18        Next
19
```

Fig. 8.18 | Binary search of an array. (Part 1 of 3.)

```
20        Array.Sort(array1) ' sort array to enable binary searching
21
22        ' display sorted array elements
23        For i As Integer = 0 To array1.GetUpperBound(0)
24           output &= (i & vbTab & array1(i) & vbCrLf)
25        Next
26
27        txtData.Text = output ' displays numbers
28        txtInput.Text = "" ' clear search key text box
29        btnSearch.Enabled = True ' enable search button
30     End Sub ' btnCreate_Click
31
32     ' search array for search key
33     Private Sub btnSearch_Click(ByVal sender As System.Object, _
34        ByVal e As System.EventArgs) Handles btnSearch.Click
35
36        ' if search key text box is empty, display
37        ' message and exit method
38        If txtInput.Text = "" Then
39           MessageBox.Show("You must enter a search key.", "Error", _
40              MessageBoxButtons.OK, MessageBoxIcon.Error)
41           Exit Sub
42        End If
43
44        Dim searchKey As Integer = Convert.ToInt32(txtInput.Text)
45        Dim element As Integer = Array.BinarySearch(array1, searchKey)
46
47        If element >= 0 Then
48           lblResult.Text = "Found Value in index " & element
49        Else
50           lblResult.Text = "Value Not Found"
51        End If
52     End Sub ' btnSearch_Click
53  End Class ' FrmBinarySearchTest
```

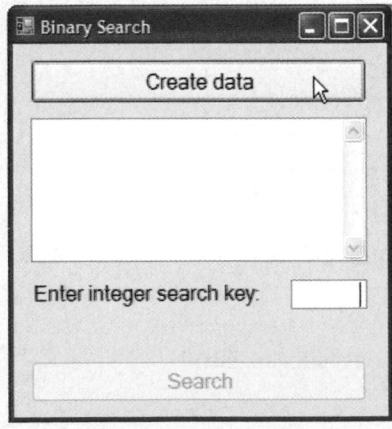
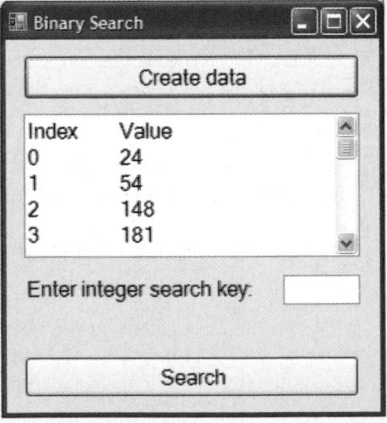

Fig. 8.18 | Binary search of an array. (Part 2 of 3.)

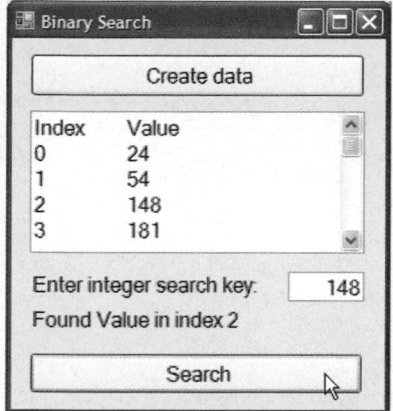 

Fig. 8.18 | Binary search of an array. (Part 3 of 3.)

For method BinarySearch to perform correctly, the array passed to it must be sorted. Line 20 invokes method Sort to sort the randomly generated array elements in ascending order. Line 44 obtains the search key and converts it to an integer. Line 45 then passes the sorted array and the search key to method BinarySearch, and assigns the value returned by BinarySearch to variable element. If the search key is found, the value of variable element is greater than or equal to 0; otherwise, the value of variable element is less than 0. The If statement in lines 47–51 displays the search result.

8.11 Rectangular Arrays

So far, we have studied **one-dimensional** (or **single-subscripted**) arrays—arrays that contain one row of values. In this section, we introduce **multidimensional** (also called **multiple-subscripted**) arrays, which require two or more indices to identify particular elements. We concentrate on **two-dimensional** (also called **double-subscripted**) arrays, or arrays that contain multiple rows of values. There are two types of two-dimensional arrays—**rectangular** and **jagged**. We discuss jagged arrays in Section 8.14. Rectangular arrays often represent **tables** of values consisting of information arranged in **rows** and **columns**. Each row is the same size, and each column is the same size (hence the term "rectangular"). To identify a particular table element, we specify two indices—by convention, the first identifies the element's row, the second the element's column. Figure 8.19 illustrates a rectangular array, a, containing three rows and four columns. A rectangular array with m rows and n columns is called an **m-by-n array**; the array in Fig. 8.19 is referred to as a 3-by-4 array.

Every element in array a is identified in Fig. 8.19 by an element name of the form a(i, j), where a is the name of the array and i and j are the indices that uniquely identify the row and column of each element in array a. Array indices are zero-based, so the names of the elements in the first row all have a first index of 0; the names of the elements in the fourth column all have a second index of 3.

Declaring and Initializing Rectangular Arrays
A two-dimensional rectangular array numbers with two rows and two columns can be declared and initialized with

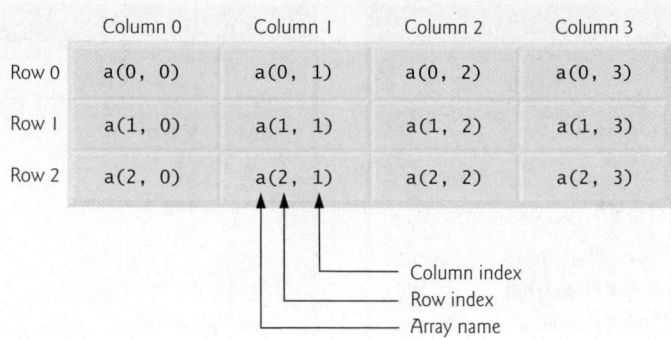

Fig. 8.19 | Two-dimensional array with three rows and four columns.

```
Dim numbers As Integer(,) = New Integer(1,1) {}

numbers(0, 0) = 1 ' leftmost element in row 0
numbers(0, 1) = 2 ' rightmost element in row 0
numbers(1, 0) = 3 ' leftmost element in row 1
numbers(1, 1) = 4 ' rightmost element in row 1
```

Alternatively, the initialization can be written on one line, as shown below:

```
Dim numbers As Integer(,) = New Integer(,) {{1, 2}, {3, 4}}
```

The values are grouped by row in braces, with 1 and 2 initializing numbers(0,0) and numbers(0,1), respectively, and 3 and 4 initializing numbers(1,0) and numbers(1,1), respectively. The compiler determines the number of rows by counting the number of subinitializer lists (represented by the sets of data in curly braces) in the main initializer list. Then the compiler determines the number of columns in each row by counting the number of initializer values in the subinitializer list for that row. In rectangular arrays, each row has the same number of values.

The program in Fig. 8.20 demonstrates the initialization of a rectangular array (array1) and the use of nested For...Next loops to traverse the arrays (i.e., to manipulate every array element).

The program declares a rectangular array in method Main. The allocation of rectangular array1 (line 7) provides six initializers in two sublists. The first sublist initializes row 0 of the array to the values 1, 2 and 3; the second sublist initializes row 1 of the array to the values 4, 5 and 6.

```
1   ' Fig. 8.20: RectangularArray.vb
2   ' Initializing a rectangular array.
3   Module RectangularArray
4      Sub Main()
5         ' create rectangular array
6         Dim array1 As Integer(,)
7         array1 = New Integer(,) {{1, 2, 3}, {4, 5, 6}}
```

Fig. 8.20 | Initializing a rectangular array (Part 1 of 2.).

```
 8
 9        Console.WriteLine("Values in rectangular array1 by row are ")
10
11            ' output array1 elements
12            For i As Integer = 0 To array1.GetUpperBound(0)
13                For j As Integer = 0 To array1.GetUpperBound(1)
14                    Console.Write(array1(i, j) & "   ")
15                Next
16
17                Console.WriteLine()
18            Next
19        End Sub ' Main
20    End Module ' RectangularArray
```

```
Values in rectangular array1 by row are
1   2   3
4   5   6
```

Fig. 8.20 | Initializing a rectangular array (Part 2 of 2.).

The nested For...Next statements in lines 12–18 display the elements of rectangular array array1, traversing the array in two dimensions. The outer For...Next statement traverses the rows; the inner For...Next statement traverses the columns within a row. Each For...Next statement calls method GetUpperBound to obtain the upper bound of the dimension it traverses. Note that the dimensions are zero-based, meaning that the rows are dimension 0 (line 12) and the columns are dimension 1 (line 13).

8.12 GradeBook Case Study: Using a Rectangular Array

In Section 8.8, we presented class GradeBook (Fig. 8.13), which used a one-dimensional array to store student grades on a single exam. In most semesters, students take several exams. Professors are likely to want to analyze grades across the entire semester, both for a single student and for the class as a whole.

Storing Student Grades in a Rectangular Array in Class *GradeBook*

Figure 8.21 contains a version of class GradeBook that uses a rectangular array grades to store the grades of several students on multiple exams. Each row of the array represents a single student's grades for the entire course, and each column represents a grade on one of the exams the students took during the course. An application such as GradeBookTest (Fig. 8.22) passes the array as an argument to the GradeBook constructor. In this example, we use a 10-by-3 array containing ten students' grades on three exams. Five methods perform various array manipulations to process the grades. Each method is similar to its counterpart in the earlier one-dimensional array version of class GradeBook (Fig. 8.13). Method GetMinimum (lines 45–61) determines the lowest grade of any student for the semester. Method GetMaximum (lines 64–80) determines the highest grade of any student for the semester. Method GetAverage (lines 83–93) determines a particular student's semester average. Method OutputBarChart (lines 96–126) outputs a bar chart of the distribution of all student grades for the semester. Method OutputGrades (lines 129–156) outputs the rectangular array in a tabular format, along with each student's semester average.

Methods GetMinimum, GetMaximum, OutputBarChart and OutputGrades each loop through array grades by using nested For statements—for example, the nested For statement (lines 50–58) from the declaration of method GetMinimum. The outer For statement iterates through the rows of two-dimensional array grades. To find the lowest overall grade, the inner For statement compares the current array element to variable lowGrade. For example, on the first iteration of the outer For, row 0 of grades is used. The inner For statement then loops through elements in row 0 and compares each grade value with low-Grade. If a grade is less than lowGrade, lowGrade is set to that grade. On the second iteration of the outer For statement, row 1 of grades is used, and the elements of this row are compared with variable lowGrade. This repeats until all the rows of grades have been traversed. When execution of the nested statement is complete, lowGrade contains the lowest grade in the two-dimensional array. Method GetMaximum works similarly to method Get-Minimum.

```vb
 1    ' Fig. 8.21: GradeBook.vb
 2    ' Grade book using a rectangular array to store grades.
 3    Public Class GradeBook
 4       Private courseNameValue As String ' name of course
 5       Private grades As Integer(,) ' rectangular array of student grades
 6
 7       ' two-argument constructor initializes courseNameValue and Grades
 8       Public Sub New(ByVal name As String, ByVal gradesArray As Integer(,))
 9          CourseName = name ' initializes courseNameValue via property
10          grades = gradesArray ' store grades
11       End Sub ' New
12
13       ' property CourseName
14       Public Property CourseName() As String
15          Get
16             Return courseNameValue
17          End Get
18
19          Set(ByVal name As String)
20             courseNameValue = name
21          End Set
22       End Property ' Course Name
23
24       ' display a welcome message to the GradeBook user
25       Public Sub DisplayMessage()
26          Console.WriteLine("Welcome to the grade book for " & vbCrLf & _
27             CourseName & vbCrLf)
28       End Sub ' DisplayMessage
29
30       ' perform various operations on the data
31       Public Sub ProcessGrades()
32          OutputGrades() ' output grades array
33
34          ' call methods GetMinimum and GetMaximum
35          Console.WriteLine("Lowest grade in the grade book is {0}", _
36             GetMinimum())
```

Fig. 8.21 | GradeBook class using a rectangular array to store grades. (Part 1 of 4.)

```vb
37          Console.WriteLine("Highest grade in the grade book is {0}", _
38              GetMaximum())
39
40          ' call OutputBarChart to print grade distribution chart
41          OutputBarChart()
42      End Sub ' ProcessGrades
43
44      ' find minimum grade
45      Public Function GetMinimum() As Integer
46          ' assume first element of grades array is smallest
47          Dim lowGrade As Integer = grades(0,0)
48
49          ' loop through grades array
50          For i As Integer = 0 To grades.GetUpperBound(0)
51              ' loop through columns of current row
52              For j As Integer = 0 To grades.GetUpperBound(1)
53                  ' if grade lower than lowGrade, assign it to lowGrade
54                  If grades(i,j) < lowGrade Then
55                      lowGrade = grades(i,j) ' new lowest grade
56                  End If
57              Next
58          Next
59
60          Return lowGrade ' return lowest grade
61      End Function ' GetMinimum
62
63      ' find maximum grade
64      Public Function GetMaximum() As Integer
65          ' assume first element of grades array is largest
66          Dim highGrade As Integer = grades(0,0)
67
68          ' loop through grades array
69          For i As Integer = 0 To grades.GetUpperBound(0)
70              ' loop through columns of current row
71              For j As Integer = 0 To grades.GetUpperBound(1)
72                  ' if grade greater than highGrade, assign it to highGrade
73                  If grades(i,j) > highGrade Then
74                      highGrade = grades(i,j) ' new highest grade
75                  End If
76              Next
77          Next
78
79          Return highGrade ' return highest grade
80      End Function ' GetMaximum
81
82      ' determine average grade for particular student's grades
83      Public Function GetAverage(ByVal row As Integer) As Double
84          Dim total As Integer = 0 ' initialize total
85
86          ' sum grades for one student
87          For column As Integer = 0 To grades.GetUpperBound(1)
88              total += grades(row, column)
89          Next
```

Fig. 8.21 | GradeBook class using a rectangular array to store grades. (Part 2 of 4.)

```
90
91         ' return average of grades
92         Return (total / (grades.GetUpperBound(1) + 1))
93     End Function ' GetAverage
94
95     ' output bar chart displaying grade distribution
96     Public Sub OutputBarChart()
97         Console.WriteLine(vbCrLf & "Overall grade distribution:")
98
99         ' stores frequency of grades in each range of 10 grades
100        Dim frequency As Integer() = New Integer(10) {}
101
102        ' for each grade, increment the appropriate frequency
103        For i As Integer = 0 To grades.GetUpperBound(0)
104            For j As Integer = 0 To grades.GetUpperBound(1)
105                frequency(grades(i,j) \ 10) += 1
106            Next
107        Next
108
109        ' for each grade frequency, print bar in chart
110        For count As Integer = 0 To frequency.GetUpperBound(0)
111            ' output bar label ( "00-09: ", ..., "90-99: ", "100: " )
112            If count = 10 Then
113                Console.Write("{0, 5:D}: ", 100)
114            Else
115                Console.Write("{0, 2:D2}-{1, 2:D2}: ", _
116                    count * 10, count * 10 + 9)
117            End If
118
119            ' print bar of asterisks
120            For stars As Integer = 0 To frequency(count) - 1
121                Console.Write("*")
122            Next
123
124            Console.WriteLine() ' start a new line of output
125        Next
126    End Sub ' OutputBarChart
127
128    ' output the contents of the grades array
129    Public Sub OutputGrades()
130        Console.WriteLine("The grades are:" & vbCrLf)
131        Console.Write("              ") ' align column heads
132
133        ' create a column heading for each of the tests
134        For test As Integer = 0 To grades.GetUpperBound(1)
135            Console.Write("Test {0:D}  ", test + 1)
136        Next
137
138        Console.WriteLine("Average") ' student average column heading
139
140        ' create rows/columns of text representing array grades
141        For student As Integer = 0 To grades.GetUpperBound(0)
142            Console.Write("Student {0, 2:D}", student + 1)
```

Fig. 8.21 | GradeBook class using a rectangular array to store grades. (Part 3 of 4.)

```
143
144            ' output student's grades
145            For counter As Integer = 0 To grades.GetUpperBound(1)
146                Console.Write("{0, 8:D}", grades(student, counter))
147            Next
148
149            ' call method GetAverage to calculate student's average grade;
150            ' pass row of grades as the argument to GetAverage
151            Dim average As Double = GetAverage(student)
152            Console.WriteLine("{0, 9:F2}", average)
153        Next
154
155        Console.WriteLine()
156    End Sub ' OutputGrades
157 End Class ' GradeBook
```

Fig. 8.21 | GradeBook class using a rectangular array to store grades. (Part 4 of 4.)

Method OutputBarChart in Fig. 8.21 is nearly identical to the one in Fig. 8.13. However, to output the overall grade distribution for a whole semester, the method here uses a nested For statement (lines 103–107) to create the one-dimensional array frequency based on all the grades in the rectangular array. The rest of the code in each of the two OutputBarChart methods that displays the chart is identical.

Method OutputGrades (lines 129–156) also uses nested For statements to output values of the array grades, in addition to each student's semester average. The output in Fig. 8.22 shows the result, which resembles the tabular format of a professor's physical grade book. Lines 134–136 (Fig. 8.21) print the column headings for each test. We use a counter-controlled For statement here so that we can identify each test with a number. Similarly, the For statement in lines 141–153 first outputs a row label using a counter variable to identify each student (line 142). Although array indices start at 0, note that lines 135 and 142 output test + 1 and student + 1, respectively, to produce test and student numbers starting at 1 (see Fig. 8.22). The inner For statement in lines 145–147 loops through a specific row of array grades and outputs each student's test grades. Finally, line 151 obtains each student's semester average by passing the current row number (i.e., student) to method GetAverage.

Method GetAverage (lines 83–93) takes one argument—an integer which specifies the row number of a particular student. When line 151 calls GetAverage, the argument is student, which specifies that a particular row number of the rectangular array grades should be passed to GetAverage. Method GetAverage calculates the sum of the array elements, divides the total by the number of test results and returns the floating-point result as a Double value (line 92).

Class *GradeBookTest* That Demonstrates Class *GradeBook*

The application in Fig. 8.22 creates an object of class GradeBook (Fig. 8.21) using the rectangular array of Integers named gradesArray (declared and initialized in lines 6–9). Lines 11–12 pass a course name and gradesArray to the GradeBook constructor. Lines 13–14 then invoke gradeBooks's DisplayMessage and ProcessGrades methods to display a welcome message and obtain a report summarizing the students' grades for the semester, respectively.

```vb
 1   ' Fig. 8.22: GradeBookTest.vb
 2   ' Create GradeBook object using a rectangular array of grades.
 3   Module GradeBookTest
 4      Sub Main()
 5         ' array of student grades
 6         Dim gradesArray As Integer(,)
 7         gradesArray = New Integer(,) {{87, 96, 70}, {68, 87, 90}, _
 8            {94, 37, 90}, {100, 81, 82}, {83, 65, 85}, {78, 87, 65}, _
 9            {85, 75, 83}, {91, 59, 100}, {76, 72, 84}, {87, 93, 73}}
10
11         Dim gradeBooks As New GradeBook( _
12            "CS101 Introduction to Visual Basic Programming", gradesArray)
13         gradeBooks.DisplayMessage()
14         gradeBooks.ProcessGrades()
15      End Sub ' Main
16   End Module ' GradeBookTest
```

```
Welcome to the grade book for
CS101 Introduction to Visual Basic Programming

The grades are:

            Test 1  Test 2  Test 3  Average
Student  1      87      96      70    84.33
Student  2      68      87      90    81.67
Student  3      94      37      90    73.67
Student  4     100      81      82    87.67
Student  5      83      65      85    77.67
Student  6      78      87      65    76.67
Student  7      85      75      83    81.00
Student  8      91      59     100    83.33
Student  9      76      72      84    77.33
Student 10      87      93      73    84.33

Lowest grade in the grade book is 37
Highest grade in the grade book is 100

Overall grade distribution:
00-09:
10-19:
20-29:
30-39: *
40-49:
50-59: *
60-69: ***
70-79: ******
80-89: ***********
90-99: ******
  100: **
```

Fig. 8.22 | Creates GradeBook object using a rectangular array of grades, then invokes method processGrades to analyze them.

8.13 **Variable-Length Parameter Lists**

It is possible to create methods that receive a variable number of arguments, using keyword **ParamArray**. The program in Fig. 8.23 calls programmer-defined method AnyNumberOfArguments three times, passing a different number of values each time. The values passed into method AnyNumberOfArguments are stored in one-dimensional Integer array array1, which is declared using ParamArray.

We call method AnyNumberOfArguments in lines 5–7, passing a different number of arguments each time. The method is defined in lines 11–29 and applies keyword ParamArray to array1 in line 11. The If statement in lines 15–28 determines whether the number of arguments passed to the method is zero. If not, lines 19–27 display array1's elements and their sum. All arguments passed to the ParamArray array must be of the same type as the array or a type that can be implicitly converted to the type of the array, otherwise a compilation error occurs (when **Option Strict** is **On**). Though we used an Integer array in this example, any type of array can be used.

```vb
1   ' Fig. 8.23: ParamArrayTest.vb
2   ' Using ParamArray to create variable-length parameter lists.
3   Module ParamArrayTest
4      Sub Main()
5         AnyNumberOfArguments()
6         AnyNumberOfArguments(2, 3)
7         AnyNumberOfArguments(7, 8, 9, 10, 11, 12)
8      End Sub ' Main
9
10     ' receives any number of arguments in array
11     Sub AnyNumberOfArguments(ByVal ParamArray array1 As Integer())
12        Dim total As Integer = 0
13
14        ' check number of arguments
15        If array1.Length = 0 Then
16           Console.WriteLine("Method AnyNumberOfArguments" & _
17              " received 0 arguments.")
18        Else
19           Console.Write("The total of ")
20
21           ' total array elements
22           For i As Integer = 0 To array1.GetUpperBound(0)
23              Console.Write(array1(i) & " ")
24              total += array1(i)
25           Next
26
27           Console.WriteLine("is {0}.", total)
28        End If
29     End Sub ' AnyNumberOfArguments
30  End Module ' ParamArrayTest
```

```
Method AnyNumberOfArguments received 0 arguments.
The total of 2 3 is 5.
The total of 7 8 9 10 11 12 is 57.
```

Fig. 8.23 | Creating variable-length parameter lists .

In the last chapter, we discussed method overloading. Programmers often prefer to use method overloading rather than write methods with variable-length parameter lists.

Common Programming Error 8.5

Attempting to declare a parameter variable to the right of the ParamArray *array variable is a syntax error.*

Common Programming Error 8.6

Using ByRef *with* ParamArray *is a syntax error.*

8.14 Jagged Arrays

Jagged arrays are maintained as arrays of arrays. Unlike rectangular arrays, rows in jagged arrays can be of different lengths. The program in Fig. 8.24 demonstrates the initialization of a jagged array (array1) and the use of nested For...Next loops to traverse the array.

The program declares a jagged array in method Main. The declaration and allocation of the jagged array array1 (line 6) create a jagged array of three arrays (specified by the 2 in the first set of parentheses after keyword Integer). Lines 7–9 initialize each subarray so that the first subarray contains the values 1 and 2, the second contains the value 3 and the last contains the values 4, 5 and 6.

```vb
1   ' Fig. 8.24: JaggedArray.vb
2   ' Initializing a jagged array.
3   Module JaggedArray
4      Sub Main()
5         ' create jagged array
6         Dim array1 As Integer()() = New Integer(2)() {} ' three rows
7         array1(0) = New Integer() {1, 2} ' row 0 is a single array
8         array1(1) = New Integer() {3} ' row 1 is a single array
9         array1(2) = New Integer() {4, 5, 6} ' row 2 is a single array
10
11        Console.WriteLine("Values in jagged array1 by row are ")
12
13        ' output array1 elements
14        For i As Integer = 0 To array1.GetUpperBound(0)
15           For j As Integer = 0 To array1(i).GetUpperBound(0)
16              Console.Write(array1(i)(j) & "   ")
17           Next
18
19           Console.WriteLine()
20        Next
21     End Sub ' Main
22  End Module ' JaggedArray
```

```
Values in jagged array1 by row are
1   2
3
4   5   6
```

Fig. 8.24 | Initializing a jagged array .

The nested For...Next statements in lines 14–20 behave similarly to those that manipulate the rectangular array in Fig. 8.20. However, in a jagged array, the second dimension is actually an index into the one-dimensional array that represents the current row. In the example, the inner For...Next statement (lines 15–17) uses GetUpperBound with the argument 0 to determine the number of columns in each row. In this case, we call GetUpperBound on a single row—array(i). Arrays of more than two dimensions can be traversed using one nested For...Next statement for each dimension.

8.15 Changing the Size of an Array at Execution Time: Using the ReDim Statement

The number of elements in an array can be changed at execution time. For example, when an array is used to store information about all the employees in a company, the size of the array would change when the company hires a new employee or when an employee leaves the company. The ReDim statement enables you to dynamically change the array size, but not the type of the array elements, nor the number of dimensions in the array. Figure 8.25 demonstrates the ReDim statement.

```vb
1   ' Fig. 8.25: ReDimTest.vb
2   ' Resize an array using the ReDim statement.
3   Module ReDimTest
4      Sub Main()
5         ' create and initialize a 5-element array
6         Dim array As Integer() = {1, 2, 3, 4, 5}
7         Dim arrayCopy As Integer() = array
8
9         ' display array length and the elements in array
10        Console.Write("The original array has {0} elements: ", _
11           array.Length)
12        DisplayArray(array)
13
14        ' change the size of the array without the Preserve keyword
15        ReDim array(6)
16
17        ' display new array length and the elements in array
18        Console.Write("New array (without Preserve) has {0} elements: ", _
19           array.Length)
20        DisplayArray(array)
21
22        ' change the size of the array with the Preserve keyword
23        ReDim Preserve arrayCopy(6)
24        arrayCopy(6) = 7 ' assign 7 to array element 6
25
26        ' display new array length and the elements in array
27        Console.Write("New array (with Preserve) has {0} elements: ", _
28           arrayCopy.Length)
29        DisplayArray(arrayCopy)
30     End Sub ' Main
31
```

Fig. 8.25 | Using ReDim statements to change the array size. (Part 1 of 2.)

```
32        ' display array elements
33        Sub DisplayArray(ByVal array As Integer())
34           For Each number As Integer In array
35              Console.Write("{0} ", number)
36           Next
37
38           Console.WriteLine()
39        End Sub ' DisplayArray
40     End Module ' ReDimTest
```

```
The original array has 5 elements: 1 2 3 4 5
New array (without Preserve) has 7 elements: 0 0 0 0 0 0 0
New array (with Preserve) has 7 elements: 1 2 3 4 5 0 7
```

Fig. 8.25 | Using ReDim statements to change the array size. (Part 2 of 2.)

Line 6 creates and initializes a five-element array array. Line 7 creates a copy of the array named arrayCopy. Lines 10–12 display the size and elements of the original array. Line 15 uses a ReDim statement to change the upper bound of array to 6, so that the array now contains seven elements. The ReDim statement contains keyword ReDim, followed by the name of the array to be resized and the new upper bound in parentheses. The output of Fig. 8.25 shows that after the ReDim statement is executed, the size of the array is changed to 7 and the value of each element is reinitialized to the default value of the type of the array element (i.e., 0 for Integers). To save the original data stored in an array, follow the ReDim keyword with the optional **Preserve** keyword. Line 23 uses Preserve in the ReDim statement to indicate that the existing array elements are to be preserved in the now larger array after the array is resized. If the new array is smaller than the original array, the existing elements that are outside the bounds of the new array are discarded. If the new array is larger than the original array, all the existing elements are preserved in the now larger array, and the extra elements are initialized to the default value of the type of the array element. For example, after line 23 is executed, the value of arrayCopy(5) is 0. Line 24 assigns the value 7 to arrayCopy(6), so that the now larger array arrayCopy contains elements 1, 2, 3, 4, 5, 0 and 7.

In Chapter 26, Collections, we introduce class ArrayList from the System.Collections namespace. An ArrayList is a dynamically resizable array-like data structure that mimics the functionality of conventional arrays. Additional ArrayList capabilities include inserting elements, searching for elements, removing elements and sorting elements.

8.16 Passing Arrays: ByVal vs. ByRef

A variable that "stores" an object, such as an array, does not actually store the object itself. Instead, the variable stores a reference to the object (i.e., the address of the location in the computer's memory where the object is stored). Recall that in Chapters 4–6, we discussed two types of variables—value types and reference types. The distinction between value-type variables and reference-type variables raises some subtle issues that you must understand to create secure, stable programs.

Effects of **ByVal** on Value-Type Parameters and Reference-Type Parameters

When used to declare a value-type parameter, keyword ByVal causes the value of the argument to be copied to a local variable in the method. Changes to the local variable are reflected in the local copy of the variable, but not in the original variable in the calling program. If the argument passed using keyword ByVal is of a reference type, the value copied is a reference to the original object in the computer's memory. Thus, reference types (like arrays and other objects) passed via keyword ByVal are actually passed by reference, meaning that changes made to the objects in called methods are actually made to the original objects in the callers.

> **Performance Tip 8.1**
>
> *Passing arrays and other objects by reference makes sense for performance reasons. If arrays were passed by value, a copy of each element would be passed. For large, frequently passed arrays, this would waste time and consume considerable storage for the copies of the arrays—both of these problems cause poor performance.*

Passing Reference Type Parameters Using **ByRef**

Visual Basic also allows methods to pass references with keyword ByRef. This is a subtle capability, which, if misused, can lead to problems. For instance, when a reference-type object like an array is passed with ByRef, the called method actually gains control over the original reference in the caller, allowing the called method to replace the reference with one to a different object or even with Nothing. Such behavior can lead to unpredictable effects, which can be disastrous in business-critical and mission-critical applications. The program in Fig. 8.26 demonstrates the subtle difference between passing a reference ByVal and passing a reference ByRef.

Lines 6–7 declare two Integer array variables, firstArray and firstArrayCopy (we make the copy so that we can determine whether the reference firstArray gets overwritten by method FirstDouble). Line 10 allocates an array containing Integer values 1, 2 and 3 and stores the array reference in variable firstArray. The assignment statement at line 11 copies the reference firstArray to the reference variable firstArrayCopy, causing these variables to reference the same array object. The For...Next statement in lines 17–19 prints the contents of firstArray before it is passed to method FirstDouble at line 21 so we can verify that this array is passed by reference (i.e., the called method indeed changes the array's contents in Main).

```
 1    ' Fig. 8.26: ArrayReferenceTest.vb
 2    ' Testing the effects of passing array references using ByVal and ByRef.
 3    Module ArrayReferenceTest
 4       Sub Main()
 5          ' declare array references
 6          Dim firstArray As Integer()
 7          Dim firstArrayCopy As Integer()
 8
 9          ' allocate firstArray and copy its reference
10          firstArray = New Integer() {1, 2, 3}
11          firstArrayCopy = firstArray ' reference preceding array
```

Fig. 8.26 | Passing an array reference with ByVal and ByRef. (Part 1 of 3.)

```vb.net
12
13      Console.WriteLine("Passing an array reference using ByVal.")
14      Console.Write("Contents of firstArray before calling FirstDouble: ")
15
16      ' print contents of firstArray
17      For i As Integer = 0 To firstArray.GetUpperBound(0)
18         Console.Write(firstArray(i) & " ")
19      Next
20
21      FirstDouble(firstArray) ' pass firstArray using ByVal
22      Console.Write(vbCrLf & "Contents of firstArray after " & _
23         "calling FirstDouble: ")
24
25      ' print contents of firstArray
26      For i As Integer = 0 To firstArray.GetUpperBound(0)
27         Console.Write(firstArray(i) & " ")
28      Next
29
30      ' was reference to firstArray changed by FirstDouble?
31      If firstArray Is firstArrayCopy Then
32         Console.WriteLine(vbCrLf & "The references are equal.")
33      Else
34         Console.WriteLine(vbCrLf & "The references are not equal.")
35      End If
36
37      ' declare array references
38      Dim secondArray As Integer()
39      Dim secondArrayCopy As Integer()
40
41      ' allocate secondArray and copy its reference
42      secondArray = New Integer() {1, 2, 3}
43      secondArrayCopy = secondArray
44
45      Console.WriteLine(vbCrLf & "Passing an array " & _
46         "reference using ByRef.")
47      Console.Write("Contents of secondArray before " & _
48         "calling SecondDouble: ")
49
50      ' print contents of secondArray before method call
51      For i As Integer = 0 To secondArray.GetUpperBound(0)
52         Console.Write(secondArray(i) & " ")
53      Next
54
55      SecondDouble(secondArray) ' pass secondArray using ByRef
56      Console.Write(vbCrLf & "Contents of secondArray " & _
57         "after calling SecondDouble: ")
58
59      ' print contents of secondArray after method call
60      For i As Integer = 0 To secondArray.GetUpperBound(0)
61         Console.Write(secondArray(i) & " ")
62      Next
63
```

Fig. 8.26 | Passing an array reference with ByVal and ByRef. (Part 2 of 3.)

```
64          ' was reference secondArray changed by SecondDouble
65          If secondArray Is secondArrayCopy Then
66             Console.WriteLine(vbCrLf & "The references are equal.")
67          Else
68             Console.WriteLine(vbCrLf & "The references are not equal.")
69          End If
70       End Sub ' Main
71
72       ' method modifies elements of array and assigns
73       ' new reference (note ByVal)
74       Sub FirstDouble(ByVal array As Integer())
75          ' double each element value in caller's array
76          For i As Integer = 0 To array.GetUpperBound(0)
77             array(i) *= 2 ' double the ith element
78          Next
79
80          ' create a new array and assign its reference to the variable array
81          array = New Integer() {11, 12, 13}
82       End Sub ' FirstDouble
83
84       ' method modifies elements of array and assigns
85       ' new reference (note ByRef)
86       Sub SecondDouble(ByRef array As Integer())
87          ' double each element value in caller's array
88          For i As Integer = 0 To array.GetUpperBound(0)
89             array(i) *= 2 ' double the ith element
90          Next
91
92          ' create a new array and assign its reference to the variable array
93          array = New Integer() {11, 12, 13} ' lose the 2, 4, 6 array
94       End Sub ' SecondDouble
95    End Module ' ArrayReferenceTest
```

```
Passing an array reference using ByVal.
Contents of firstArray before calling FirstDouble: 1 2 3
Contents of firstArray after calling FirstDouble: 2 4 6
The references are equal.

Passing an array reference using ByRef.
Contents of secondArray before calling SecondDouble: 1 2 3
Contents of secondArray after calling SecondDouble: 11 12 13
The references are not equal.
```

Fig. 8.26 | Passing an array reference with ByVal and ByRef. (Part 3 of 3.)

The For...Next statement in method FirstDouble (lines 76–78) multiplies the values of all the elements in the array by 2. Line 81 allocates a new array containing the values 11, 12 and 13; the reference for this array then is assigned to parameter array (in an attempt to overwrite reference firstArray in Main—this, of course, does not happen, because the reference firstArray was passed ByVal). After method FirstDouble executes, the For...Next statement in lines 26–28 prints the contents of firstArray, demonstrating that the values of the elements have been changed by the method FirstDouble (and confirming that in Visual Basic arrays are always passed by reference). The `If` statement in lines 31–35 uses the `Is` operator to compare references `firstArray` (which we just attempted to overwrite) and `firstArrayCopy`. Visual Basic provides operator `Is` for comparing references to determine whether they are referencing the same object. The expression at line 31 is true if the operands to the binary operator `Is` reference the same object. In this case, the object represented is the array allocated in line 10—not the array allocated in method `FirstDouble` (line 81). Visual Basic also provides operator `IsNot` for comparing two references. If two references refer to the same objects, operator `IsNot` returns `False`; otherwise it returns `True`. Line 81 modifies only the parameter `array`, not the variable `firstArray` because `firstArray` was passed with keyword `ByVal`. We will see in a moment the effect of passing an array with keyword `ByRef`.

Lines 38–69 in method `Main` perform similar tests, using array variables `secondArray` and `secondArrayCopy` and method `SecondDouble` (lines 86–94). Method `SecondDouble` performs the same operations as `FirstDouble`, but receives its array argument with `ByRef`. In this case, the reference stored in `secondArray` after the method call is a reference to the array allocated at line 93 of `SecondDouble`, demonstrating that a reference passed with `ByRef` can be modified by the called method so that the reference actually points to a different object, in this case the array that is allocated in method `SecondDouble`. The `If` statement in lines 65–69 determines that `secondArray` and `secondArrayCopy` no longer represent the same array.

Software Engineering Observation 8.2

Using `ByVal` to receive a reference-type object parameter does not cause the object to pass by value—the object still passes by reference. `ByVal` causes only the object's reference to pass by value. This prevents a called method from overwriting a reference in the caller. In the vast majority of cases, protecting the caller's reference from modification is the desired behavior. If you encounter a situation where you truly want the called method to modify the caller's reference, pass the reference-type object `ByRef`.

8.17 (Optional) Software Engineering Case Study: Collaboration Among Objects in the ATM System

When two objects communicate with each other to accomplish a task, they are said to collaborate. A **collaboration** consists of an object of one class sending a **message** to an object of another class. Messages are sent in Visual Basic via method calls. In this section, we concentrate on the collaborations (interactions) among the objects in our ATM system.

In Section 7.20, we determined many of the operations of the classes in our system. In this section, we concentrate on the messages that invoke these operations. To identify the collaborations in the system, we return to the requirements document of Section 3.10. Recall that this document specifies the activities that occur during an ATM session (e.g., authenticating a user, performing transactions). The steps used to describe how the system must perform each of these tasks are our first indication of the collaborations in our system. As we proceed through this and the remaining Software Engineering Case Study sections, we may discover additional collaborations.

Identifying the Collaborations in a System
We begin to identify the collaborations in the system by carefully reading the sections of the requirements document that specify what the ATM should do to authenticate a user

and to perform each transaction type. For each action or step described in the requirements document, we decide which objects in our system must interact to achieve the desired result. We identify one object as the sending object (i.e., the object that sends the message) and another as the receiving object (i.e., the object that offers that operation to clients of the class). We then select one of the receiving object's operations (identified in Section 7.20) that must be invoked by the sending object to produce the proper behavior. For example, the ATM displays a welcome message when idle. We know that an object of class `Screen` displays a message to the user via its `DisplayMessage` operation. Thus, we decide that the system can display a welcome message by employing a collaboration between the ATM and the `Screen` in which the ATM sends a `DisplayMessage` message to the `Screen` by invoking the `DisplayMessage` operation of class `Screen`. [*Note:* To avoid repeating the phrase "an object of class...," we refer to each object simply by using its class name preceded by an article (e.g., "a," "an" or "the")—for example, "the ATM" refers to an object of class ATM.]

Figure 8.27 lists the collaborations that can be derived from the requirements document. For each sending object, we list the collaborations in the order in which they are discussed in the requirements document. We list each collaboration involving a unique sender, message and recipient only once, even though the collaboration may occur several times during an ATM session. For example, the first row in Fig. 8.27 indicates that the ATM collaborates with the `Screen` whenever the ATM needs to display a message to the user.

Let's consider the collaborations in Fig. 8.27. Before allowing a user to perform any transactions, the ATM must prompt the user to enter an account number, then to enter a PIN. It accomplishes each of these tasks by sending a `DisplayMessage` message to the `Screen`. Both of these actions refer to the same collaboration between the ATM and the `Screen`, which is already listed in Fig. 8.27. The ATM obtains input in response to a prompt by sending a `GetInput` message to the `Keypad`. Next, the ATM must determine whether the user-specified account number and PIN match those of an account in the database. It does so by sending an `AuthenticateUser` message to the `BankDatabase`. Recall that the `BankDatabase` cannot authenticate a user directly—only the user's `Account` (i.e., the `Account` that contains the account number specified by the user) can access the user's PIN

An object of class...	sends the message...	to an object of class...
ATM	DisplayMessage	Screen
	GetInput	Keypad
	AuthenticateUser	BankDatabase
	Execute	BalanceInquiry
	Execute	Withdrawal
	Execute	Deposit
BalanceInquiry	GetAvailableBalance	BankDatabase
	GetTotalBalance	BankDatabase
	DisplayMessage	Screen

Fig. 8.27 | Collaborations in the ATM system. (Part 1 of 2.)

An object of class...	sends the message...	to an object of class...
Withdrawal	DisplayMessage	Screen
	GetInput	Keypad
	GetAvailableBalance	BankDatabase
	IsSufficientCashAvailable	CashDispenser
	Debit	BankDatabase
	DispenseCash	CashDispenser
Deposit	DisplayMessage	Screen
	GetInput	Keypad
	IsDepositEnvelopeReceived	DepositSlot
	Credit	BankDatabase
BankDatabase	ValidatePIN	Account
	AvailableBalance (Get)	Account
	TotalBalance (Get)	Account
	Debit	Account
	Credit	Account

Fig. 8.27 | Collaborations in the ATM system. (Part 2 of 2.)

to authenticate the user. Figure 8.27 therefore lists a collaboration in which the Bank-Database sends a ValidatePIN message to an Account.

After the user is authenticated, the ATM displays the main menu by sending a series of DisplayMessage messages to the Screen and obtains input containing a menu selection by sending a GetInput message to the Keypad. We have already accounted for these collaborations. After the user chooses a type of transaction to perform, the ATM executes the transaction by sending an Execute message to an object of the appropriate transaction class (i.e., a BalanceInquiry, a Withdrawal or a Deposit). For example, if the user chooses to perform a balance inquiry, the ATM sends an Execute message to a BalanceInquiry.

Further examination of the requirements document reveals the collaborations involved in executing each transaction type. A BalanceInquiry retrieves the amount of money available in the user's account by sending a GetAvailableBalance message to the BankDatabase, which sends a Get message to an Account's AvailableBalance property to access the available balance. Similarly, the BalanceInquiry retrieves the amount of money on deposit by sending a GetTotalBalance message to the BankDatabase, which sends a Get message to an Account's TotalBalance property to access the total balance on deposit. To display both measures of the user's balance at the same time, the BalanceInquiry sends DisplayMessage messages to the Screen.

A Withdrawal sends DisplayMessage messages to the Screen to display a menu of standard withdrawal amounts (i.e., $20, $40, $60, $100, $200). The Withdrawal sends a GetInput message to the Keypad to obtain the user's menu selection. Next, the Withdrawal determines whether the requested withdrawal amount is less than or equal to the user's account balance. The Withdrawal can obtain the amount of money available in the user's account by sending a GetAvailableBalance message to the BankDatabase. The

Withdrawal then tests whether the cash dispenser contains enough cash by sending an IsSufficientCashAvailable message to the CashDispenser. A Withdrawal sends a Debit message to the BankDatabase to decrease the user's account balance. The Bank-Database in turn sends the same message to the appropriate Account. Recall that debiting an Account decreases both the total balance and the available balance. To dispense the requested amount of cash, the Withdrawal sends a DispenseCash message to the CashDispenser. Finally, the Withdrawal sends a DisplayMessage message to the Screen, instructing the user to take the cash.

A Deposit responds to an Execute message first by sending a DisplayMessage message to the Screen to prompt the user for a deposit amount. The Deposit sends a Get-Input message to the Keypad to obtain the user's input. The Deposit then sends a DisplayMessage message to the Screen to tell the user to insert a deposit envelope. To determine whether the deposit slot received an incoming deposit envelope, the Deposit sends an IsDepositEnvelopeReceived message to the DepositSlot. The Deposit updates the user's account by sending a Credit message to the BankDatabase, which subsequently sends a Credit message to the user's Account. Recall that crediting an Account increases the total balance but not the available balance.

Interaction Diagrams

Now that we have identified a set of possible collaborations between the objects in our ATM system, let us graphically model these interactions. The UML provides several types of **interaction diagrams** that model the behavior of a system by modeling how objects interact with one another. The **communication diagram** emphasizes *which objects* participate in collaborations. [*Note:* Communication diagrams were called **collaboration diagrams** in earlier versions of the UML.] Like the communication diagram, the **sequence diagram** shows collaborations among objects, but it emphasizes *when* messages are sent between objects.

Communication Diagrams

Figure 8.28 shows a communication diagram that models the ATM executing a Balance-Inquiry. Objects are modeled in the UML as rectangles containing names in the form objectName : ClassName. In this example, which involves only one object of each type, we disregard the object name and list only a colon followed by the class name. Specifying the name of each object in a communication diagram is recommended when modeling multiple objects of the same type. Communicating objects are connected with solid lines, and messages are passed between objects along these lines in the direction shown by arrows with filled arrowheads. The name of the message, which appears next to the arrow, is the name of an operation (i.e., a method) belonging to the receiving object—think of the name as a service that the receiving object provides to sending objects (its "clients").

The filled arrow in Fig. 8.28 represents a message—or **synchronous call**—in the UML and a method call in Visual Basic. This arrow indicates that the flow of control is

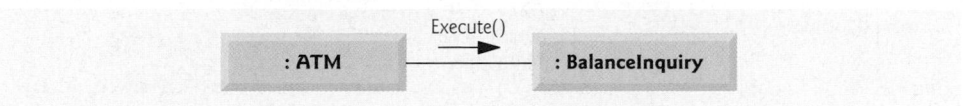

Fig. 8.28 | Communication diagram of the ATM executing a BalanceInquiry.

from the sending object (the ATM) to the receiving object (a BalanceInquiry). Since this is a synchronous call, the sending object may not send another message, or do anything at all, until the receiving object processes the message and returns control (and possibly a return value) to the sending object. The sender just waits. For example, in Fig. 8.28, the ATM calls method Execute of a BalanceInquiry and may not send another message until Execute finishes and returns control to the ATM. [*Note:* If this were an asynchronous call, represented by a stick arrowhead, the sending object would not have to wait for the receiving object to return control—it would continue sending additional messages immediately following the asynchronous call. Such calls are beyond the scope of this book.]

Sequence of Messages in a Communication Diagram

Figure 8.29 shows a communication diagram that models the interactions among objects in the system when an object of class BalanceInquiry executes. We assume that the object's accountNumber attribute contains the account number of the current user. The collaborations in Fig. 8.29 begin after the ATM sends an Execute message to a BalanceInquiry (i.e., the interaction modeled in Fig. 8.28). The number to the left of a message name indicates the order in which the message is passed. The sequence of messages in a communication diagram progresses in numerical order from least to greatest. In this diagram, the numbering starts with message 1 and ends with message 3. The Balance-Inquiry first sends a GetAvailableBalance message to the BankDatabase (message 1), then sends a GetTotalBalance message to the BankDatabase (message 2). Within the parentheses following a message name, we can specify a comma-separated list of the names of the arguments sent with the message (i.e., arguments in a Visual Basic method call)— the BalanceInquiry passes attribute accountNumber with its messages to the BankDatabase to indicate which Account's balance information to retrieve. Recall from Fig. 7.24

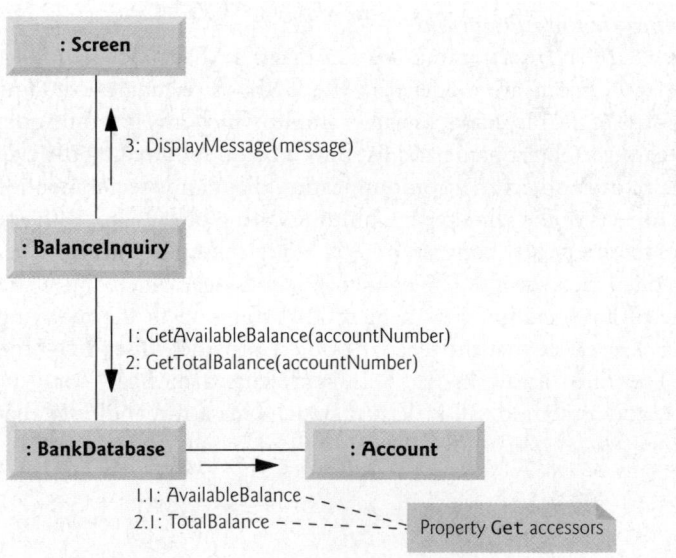

Fig. 8.29 | Communication diagram for executing a BalanceInquiry.

that operations GetAvailableBalance and GetTotalBalance of class BankDatabase each require a parameter to identify an account. The BalanceInquiry next displays the available balance and the total balance to the user by passing a DisplayMessage message to the Screen (message 3) that includes a parameter indicating the message to be displayed.

Note that Fig. 8.29 models two additional messages passing from the BankDatabase to an Account (message 1.1 and message 2.1). To provide the ATM with the two balances of the user's Account (as requested by messages 1 and 2), the BankDatabase must send Get messages to the Account's AvailableBalance and TotalBalance properties. A message passed within the handling of another message is called a **nested message**. The UML recommends using a decimal numbering scheme to indicate nested messages. For example, message 1.1 is the first message nested in message 1—the BankDatabase sends the Get message to the Account's AvailableBalance property during BankDatabase's processing of a GetAvailableBalance message. [*Note:* If the BankDatabase needed to pass a second nested message while processing message 1, the second message would be numbered 1.2.] A message may be passed only when all the nested messages from the previous message have been passed. For example, the BalanceInquiry passes message 3 to the Screen only after messages 2 and 2.1 have been passed, in that order.

The nested numbering scheme used in communication diagrams helps clarify precisely when and in what context each message is passed. For example, if we numbered the five messages in Fig. 8.29 using a flat numbering scheme (i.e., 1, 2, 3, 4, 5), someone looking at the diagram might not be able to determine that BankDatabase passes the Get message to an Account's AvailableBalance property (message 1.1) *during* the BankDatabase's processing of message 1, as opposed to *after* completing the processing of message 1. The nested decimal numbers make it clear that the Get message (message 1.1) is passed to an Account's AvailableBalance property within the handling of the GetAvailableBalance message (message 1) by the BankDatabase.

Sequence Diagrams

Communication diagrams emphasize the participants in collaborations but model their timing a bit awkwardly. A sequence diagram helps model the timing of collaborations more clearly. Figure 8.30 shows a sequence diagram modeling the sequence of interactions that occur when a Withdrawal executes. The dotted line extending down from an object's rectangle is that object's **lifeline**, which represents the progression of time. Actions typically occur along an object's lifeline in chronological order from top to bottom—an action near the top of the sequence diagram is performed before one near the bottom.

Message passing in sequence diagrams is similar to message passing in communication diagrams. An arrow with a filled arrowhead extending from the sending object to the receiving object represents a message between two objects. The arrowhead points to an activation on the receiving object's lifeline. An **activation**, shown as a thin vertical rectangle, indicates that an object is executing. When an object returns control, a return message, represented as a dashed line with a stick arrowhead, extends from the activation of the object returning control to the activation of the object that initially sent the message; to eliminate clutter, we omit the return-message arrows—the UML allows this practice to make diagrams more readable. Like communication diagrams, sequence diagrams can indicate message parameters between the parentheses following a message name.

The sequence of messages in Fig. 8.30 begins when a `Withdrawal` prompts the user to choose a withdrawal amount by sending a `DisplayMessage` message to the `Screen`. The `Withdrawal` then sends a `GetInput` message to the `Keypad`, which obtains input from the user. We have already modeled the control logic involved in a `Withdrawal` in the activity diagram of Fig. 6.25, so we do not show this logic in the sequence diagram of Fig. 8.30. Instead, we model the best-case scenario in which the balance of the user's account is greater than or equal to the chosen withdrawal amount, and the cash dispenser contains a sufficient amount of cash to satisfy the request. For information on how to model control logic in a sequence diagram, please refer to the Web resources and recommended readings listed at the end of Section 3.10.

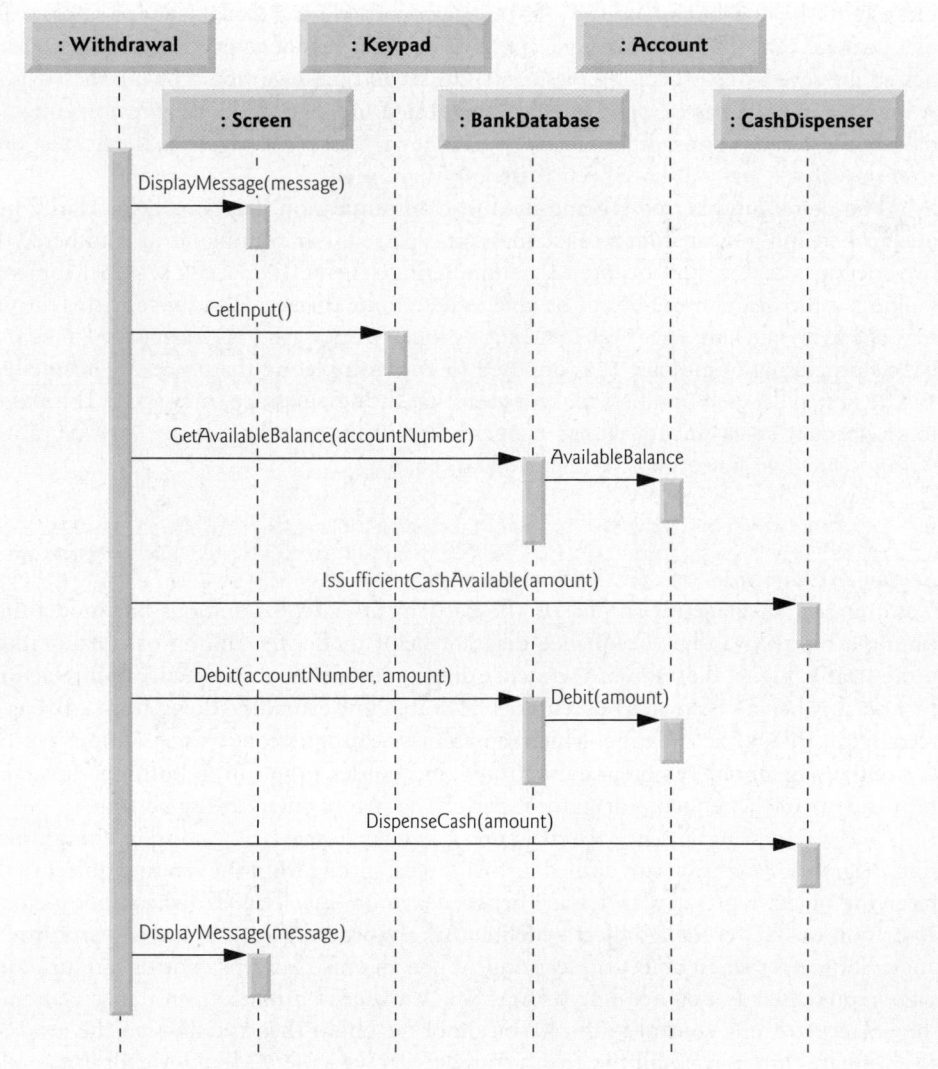

Fig. 8.30 | Sequence diagram that models a `Withdrawal` executing.

After obtaining a withdrawal amount, the Withdrawal sends a GetAvailableBalance message to the BankDatabase, which in turn sends a Get message to the Account's AvailableBalance property. Assuming that the user's account has enough money available to permit the transaction, the Withdrawal next sends an IsSufficientCashAvailable message to the CashDispenser. Assuming that there is enough cash available, the Withdrawal decreases the balance of the user's account (i.e., both the total balance and the available balance) by sending a Debit message to the BankDatabase. The BankDatabase responds by sending a Debit message to the user's Account. Finally, the Withdrawal sends a DispenseCash message to the CashDispenser and a DisplayMessage message to the Screen, telling the user to remove the cash from the machine.

We have identified collaborations among objects in the ATM system and modeled some of these collaborations using UML interaction diagrams—communication diagrams and sequence diagrams. In the next Software Engineering Case Study section (Section 9.14), we enhance the structure of our model to complete a preliminary object-oriented design, then we begin implementing the ATM system in Visual Basic.

Software Engineering Case Study Self-Review Exercises

8.1 A(n) _____ consists of an object of one class sending a message to an object of another class.
    a) association
    b) aggregation
    c) collaboration
    d) composition

8.2 Which form of interaction diagram emphasizes *what* collaborations occur? Which form emphasizes *when* collaborations occur?

8.3 Create a sequence diagram that models the interactions among objects in the ATM system that occur when a Deposit executes successfully, and explain the sequence of messages modeled by the diagram.

Answers to Software Engineering Case Study Self-Review Exercises

8.1 c.

8.2 Communication diagrams emphasize *what* collaborations occur. Sequence diagrams emphasize *when* collaborations occur.

8.3 Figure 8.31 presents a sequence diagram that models the interactions between objects in the ATM system that occur when a Deposit executes successfully. Figure 8.31 indicates that a Deposit first sends a DisplayMessage message to the Screen (to ask the user to enter a deposit amount). Next the Deposit sends a GetInput message to the Keypad to receive the amount of the deposit from the user. The Deposit then prompts the user (to enter a deposit envelope) by sending a DisplayMessage message to the Screen. The Deposit next sends an IsDepositEnvelopeReceived message to the DepositSlot to confirm that the deposit envelope has been received by the ATM. Finally, the Deposit increases the total balance (but not the available balance) of the user's Account by sending a Credit message to the BankDatabase. The BankDatabase responds by sending the same message to the user's Account.

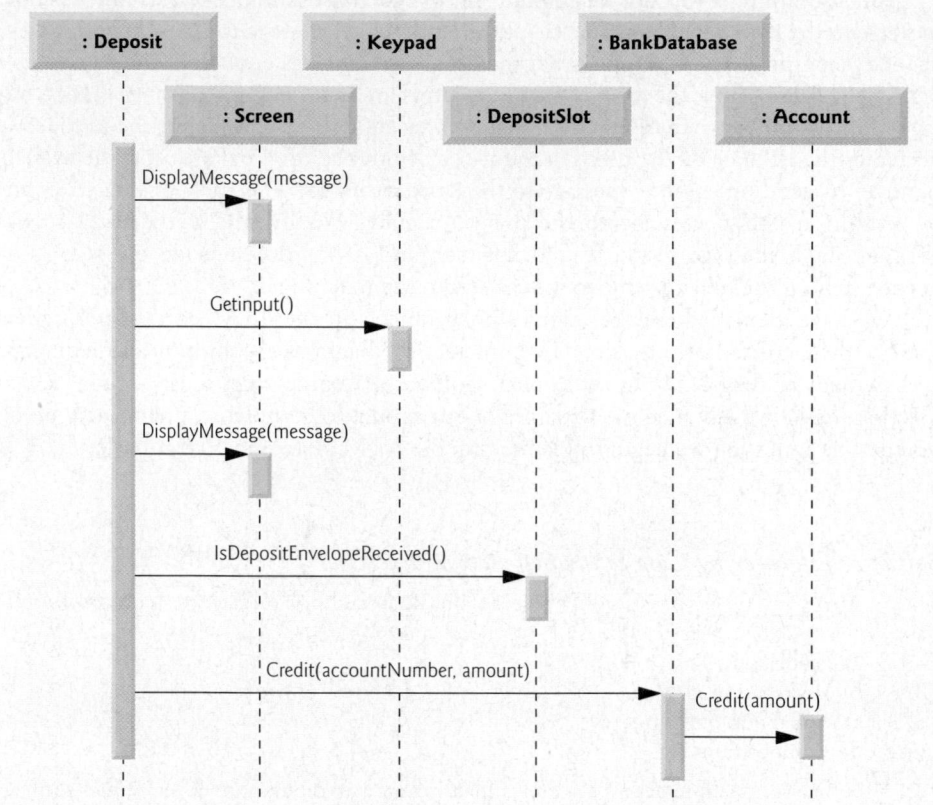

Fig. 8.31 | Sequence diagram that models a `Deposit` executing.

8.18 **Wrap-Up**

This chapter began our discussion of data structures, exploring the use of arrays to store data in and retrieve data from lists and tables of values. The chapter examples demonstrated how to declare an array, initialize an array and refer to individual elements of an array. We showed how to pass arrays to methods using `ByVal` and `ByRef`. We also showed how to use the `For Each...Next` statement to iterate through the values in an array without using an index. We used method `Sort` of class `Array` to sort an array and method `Binary-Search` of class `Array` to search an array for a specific value. We explained how to declare and manipulate rectangular arrays and jagged arrays. We wrote methods that use variable-length parameter lists. Finally, we demonstrated how to use the `ReDim` statement to dynamically change an array's size.

Chapter 24, Data Structures introduces dynamic data structures, such as lists, queues, stacks and trees, that can grow and shrink as programs execute. Chapter 25, Generics, presents one of Visual Basic 2005's new features—generics—which provides the means to create general models of methods and classes that can be declared once but used with many different types. Chapter 26, Collections, introduces Visual Basic's predefined data structures, which you can use instead of building your own.

We have now introduced the basic concepts of classes, objects, control statements, methods and arrays. In Chapter 9, we take a deeper look at classes and objects.

Summary

Section 8.1 Introduction
- Arrays are data structures consisting of data items of the same type.

Section 8.2 Arrays
- An array is a group of variables (called elements) that all have the same type.
- To refer to a particular element in an array, we specify the name of the array and the position number of the element to which we refer.
- Every array begins with a zeroth element (i.e., element 0).
- The position number in parentheses more formally is called an index (or a subscript). An index must be a non-negative integer or integer expression.
- An indexed array name (i.e., the array name followed by an index enclosed in parentheses) is an *lvalue*—it can be used on the left side of an assignment statement to place a new value into an array element.
- Every array in Visual Basic "knows" its own length. The length of an array named c is determined by the expression c.Length.
- All arrays have access to the methods and properties of class System.Array, including the Length property.
- Method GetUpperBound returns the index of the last element in the array.

Section 8.3 Declaring and Allocating Arrays
- To declare an array, you provide the array's name and type—for example, Dim c As Integer(). The parentheses that follow the type indicate that c is an array.
- The declaration of an array creates a variable that can store a reference to any array but does not actually create the array in memory.
- Arrays can be declared to contain any type.
- Before an array can be used, you must specify the size of the array and allocate memory for the array, using keyword New.
- Array bounds determine what indices can be used to access an element in the array.
- The initializer list enclosed in braces ({ and }) specifies the initial values of the elements in the array. The initializer list can be a comma-separated list specifying the initial values of the elements in the array.
- When the initializer list is empty, the elements in the array are initialized to the default value for the type of the elements of the array.

Section 8.4 Examples Using Arrays
- All the elements of any array must be of the same type.
- Visual Basic provides mechanisms that prevent accessing elements outside the bounds of arrays.

Section 8.6 Passing an Array to a Method
- To pass an array argument to a method, specify the name of the array without using parentheses.

- Every array object "knows" its own upper bound (i.e., the value returned by the method `GetUpperBound`), so when you pass an array object to a method, you do not need to pass the upper bound of the array as a separate argument.

- For a method to receive an array through a method call, the method's parameter list must specify that an array will be received.

- In Visual Basic, arrays always are passed by reference, yet it is normally inappropriate to use keyword `ByRef` in the method definition header.

- To pass an array element to a method, use the indexed name of the array element as an argument in the method call.

Section 8.7 *For Each...Next Repetition Statement*

- Visual Basic provides the `For Each...Next` repetition statement for iterating through the values in a data structure, such as an array.

- When used with one-dimensional arrays, `For Each...Next` behaves like a `For...Next` statement that iterates through the range of indices from 0 to the value returned by `GetUpperBound(0)`.

Section 8.9 *Sorting an Array with Method* **Sort** *of Class* **Array**

- Sorting data (i.e., arranging the data in some particular order, such as ascending or descending order) is one of the most popular computing applications.

- Class Array provides methods for creating, modifying, sorting and searching arrays.

- `Shared` method `Sort` of class `Array` takes an array as its argument and sorts the elements in the array in ascending order.

- To sort an array in descending order, first call method `Sort` of class array to sort the array, then call method `Reverse` of class `Array` to reverse the order of the elements in the array.

Section 8.10 *Searching Arrays*

- Often it is necessary to determine whether an array contains a value that matches a certain key value. The process of locating a particular element value in an array is called searching.

- The linear search method works well for small or unsorted arrays. However, it is inefficient for large unsorted arrays. If the array is sorted, the high-speed binary search technique can be used.

- The `Array` class provides method `BinarySearch`, which searches a sorted array for a value using binary search.

Section 8.11 *Rectangular Arrays*

- One-dimensional arrays contain one row of values.

- Multidimensional arrays require two or more indices to identify particular elements.

- There are two types of two-dimensional arrays—rectangular and jagged.

- Rectangular arrays with two indices often represent tables of values consisting of information arranged in rows and columns. Each row is the same size, and each column is the same size (hence the term "rectangular").

Section 8.13 *Variable-Length Parameter Lists*

- Methods can be created to receive a variable number of arguments using keyword `ParamArray`.

- All arguments passed to the `ParamArray` array must be of the same type as the array, otherwise a compilation error occurs (when **Option Strict** is **On**).

Section 8.14 *Jagged Arrays*

- Jagged arrays are maintained as arrays of arrays. Unlike rectangular arrays, rows in jagged arrays can be of different lengths.

- In a jagged array, the second dimension is actually an index into the one-dimensional array that represents the current row.
- Arrays of more than two dimensions can be traversed using one nested For…Next statement for each dimension.

Section 8.15 Using the **ReDim** Statement to Change the Size of an Array at Execution Time

- The ReDim statement enables you to dynamically change the array size, but not the type of the array elements, nor the number of dimensions in the array.
- The ReDim statement contains keyword ReDim, followed by the name of the array to be resized and the new upper bound in parentheses.
- The ReDim statement changes the size of the array and reinitializes the value of the elements to the default value of the type of the array element.
- To save the original data stored in an array, follow the ReDim keyword with the optional Preserve keyword. If the new array is smaller than the original array, the existing elements that are outside the bounds of the new array are discarded. If the new array is larger than the original array, all the existing elements are preserved in the now larger array, and the extra elements are initialized to the default value of the type of the array element.

Section 8.16 Passing Arrays: **ByVal** vs. **ByRef**

- If an argument passed using keyword ByVal is of a reference type, the value copied is a reference to the original object in the computer's memory. Thus, reference types (like arrays and other objects) passed via keyword ByVal are actually passed by reference, meaning that changes made to the objects in called methods are actually made to the original objects in the callers.
- Visual Basic also allows methods to pass references with keyword ByRef.
- When a reference-type object like an array is passed with ByRef, the called method actually gains control over the original reference in the caller, allowing the called method to replace the original reference in the caller with a reference to a different object or even with Nothing. Such behavior can lead to unpredictable effects, which can be disastrous in business-critical and mission-critical applications.
- Visual Basic provides operator Is for comparing references to determine whether they are referencing the same object.
- Visual Basic also provides operator IsNot for comparing two references. If two references refer to the same object, operator IsNot returns False; otherwise it returns True.

Terminology

allocate an array with New
array
array as an object
array bounds
array declaration
array element
array element passed by value
array initialized to zeros
array of arrays
bar chart
binary search
BinarySearch method of class Array

braces ({ and })
column
declaration and initialization of array
double-subscripted array
element
exception for invalid array indexing
explicit array bounds
For Each...Next statement
GetUpperBound method
ignoring array element zero
index
IndexOutOfRange exception

Self-Review Exercises

8.1 Fill in the blanks in each of the following statements:
 a) Lists and tables of values can be stored in _____.
 b) An array is a group of variables containing values that all have the same _____.
 c) The number that refers to a particular element of an array is called its _____.
 d) The process of placing the elements of an array in order is called _____ the array.
 e) Determining whether an array contains a certain value is called _____ the array.
 f) Arrays that use two or more indices are referred to as _____ arrays.
 g) Keyword _____ in a method definition header indicates that the method receives a variable number of arguments.
 h) _____ arrays are maintained as arrays of arrays.
 i) All arrays have access to the methods and properties of class _____.
 j) When an invalid array reference is made, a(n) _____ exception is thrown.

8.2 State whether each of the following is *true* or *false*. If *false*, explain why.
 a) An array can store many different types of values.
 b) An array index normally should be of type Double.
 c) Method GetUpperBound returns the highest numbered index in an array.
 d) There are two types of two-dimensional arrays—square and jagged.
 e) To determine the number of elements in an array, we can use the NumberOfElements property.
 f) The linear search works well for unsorted arrays.
 g) In an *m*-by-*n* array, the *m* stands for the number of columns and the *n* stands for the number of rows.

Answers to Self-Review Exercises

8.1   a) arrays. b) type. c) index, subscript or position number. d) sorting. e) searching. f) multidimensional. g) `ParamArray`. h) Jagged. i) `System.Array`. j) `IndexOutOfRangeException`.

8.2   a) False. An array can store only values of the same type. b) False. An array index must be a non-negative integer or integer expression. c) True. d) False. The two different types are called rectangular and jagged. e) False. To determine the number of elements in an array, we can use the `Length` property. f) True. g) False. In an *m*-by-*n* array, the *m* stands for the number of rows and the *n* stands for the number of columns.

Exercises

8.3   Write statements to accomplish each of the following tasks:
  a) Display the value of element 6 of array `numbers`.
  b) Using a `For...Next` statement, assign the value 8 to each of the five elements of one-dimensional `Integer` array `values`.
  c) Total the 100 elements of floating-point array `results`.
  d) Copy 11-element array `source` into the first portion of 34-element array `sourceCopy`.
  e) Determine the smallest and largest values contained in 99-element floating-point array `data`.

8.4   Use a one-dimensional array to solve the following problem: A company pays its salespeople on a commission basis. The salespeople receive $200 per week, plus 9% of their gross sales for that week. For example, a salesperson who grosses $5000 in sales in a week receives $200 plus 9% of $5000, or a total of $650. Write a program (using an array of counters) that determines how many of the salespeople earned salaries in each of the following ranges (assume that each salesperson's salary is truncated to an integer amount):
  a) $200–299
  b) $300–399
  c) $400–499
  d) $500–599
  e) $600–699
  f) $700–799
  g) $800–899
  h) $900–999
  i) $1000 and over

8.5   Use a one-dimensional array to solve the following problem: Read in 20 numbers, each of which is between 10 and 100, inclusive. As each number is read, print it only if it is not a duplicate of a number already read. Provide for the "worst case" (in which all 20 numbers are different). Use the smallest possible array to solve this problem.

8.6   Modify the sorting example of Fig. 8.15 so that it lists three columns of data headed "Original values," "Values sorted in ascending order" and "Values sorted in descending order"; your program should display in the last two columns the values sorted in ascending and descending order, respectively.

8.7   *(Telephone-Number Word Generator)* Standard telephone keypads contain the digits zero through nine. The numbers two through nine each have three letters associated with them (Fig. 8.32). Many people find it difficult to memorize phone numbers, so they use the correspondence between digits and letters to develop seven-letter words that correspond to their phone numbers. For example, a person whose telephone number is 686-2377 might use the correspondence indicated in Fig. 8.32 to develop the seven-letter word "NUMBERS." Every seven-letter word cor-

Digit	Letters
2	A B C
3	D E F
4	G H I
5	J K L
6	M N O
7	P R S
8	T U V
9	W X Y

Fig. 8.32 | Telephone keypad digits and letters.

responds to exactly one seven-digit telephone number. A restaurant wishing to increase its takeout business could surely do so with the number 825-3688 (i.e., "TAKEOUT").

Every seven-letter phone number corresponds to many different seven-letter combinations. Unfortunately, most of these represent unrecognizable juxtapositions of letters. It is possible, however, that the owner of a barbershop would be pleased to know that the shop's telephone number, 424-7288, corresponds to "HAIRCUT." The owner of a liquor store would, no doubt, be delighted to find that the store's number, 233-7226, corresponds to "BEERCAN." A veterinarian with the phone number 738-2273 would be pleased to know that the number corresponds to the letters "PETCARE." An automotive dealership would be pleased to know that the dealership number, 639-2277, corresponds to "NEWCARS."

Write a Windows application (Fig. 8.33) that allows the user to enter a seven-digit number in a TextBox, and displays every possible seven-letter word combination corresponding to that number in a multiple line TextBox when the user clicks the **Generate Words** button. There are 2,187 (3^7) such combinations. Avoid phone numbers with the digits 0 and 1.

8.8 *(Flag Quiz Application)* A geography teacher would like to quiz students on their knowledge of the flags of various countries. The teacher has asked you to write an application that displays a flag and allows students to select the corresponding country by clicking the appropriate buttons. The application should inform the user of whether the answer is correct and display the next flag. The application should display five flags randomly chosen from the flags of Australia, Brazil, China, Italy, Russia, South Africa, Spain and the United States (these images are included with the book's examples). When the application is run, a given flag should be displayed only once.

8.9 *(Airline Reservations System)* A small airline has just purchased a computer for its new automated reservations system. You have been asked to develop the new system. You are to write an application to assign seats on each flight of the airline's only plane (capacity: 10 seats).

Your application should display the following alternatives: Please type 1 for First Class and Please type 2 for Economy. If the user types 1, your application should assign a seat in the first-class section (seats 1–5). If the user types 2, your application should assign a seat in the economy section (seats 6–10). Your application should then display a boarding pass indicating the person's seat number and whether it is in the first-class or economy section of the plane.

Use a one-dimensional array of primitive type Boolean to represent the seating chart of the plane. Initialize all the elements of the array to False to indicate that all the seats are empty. As

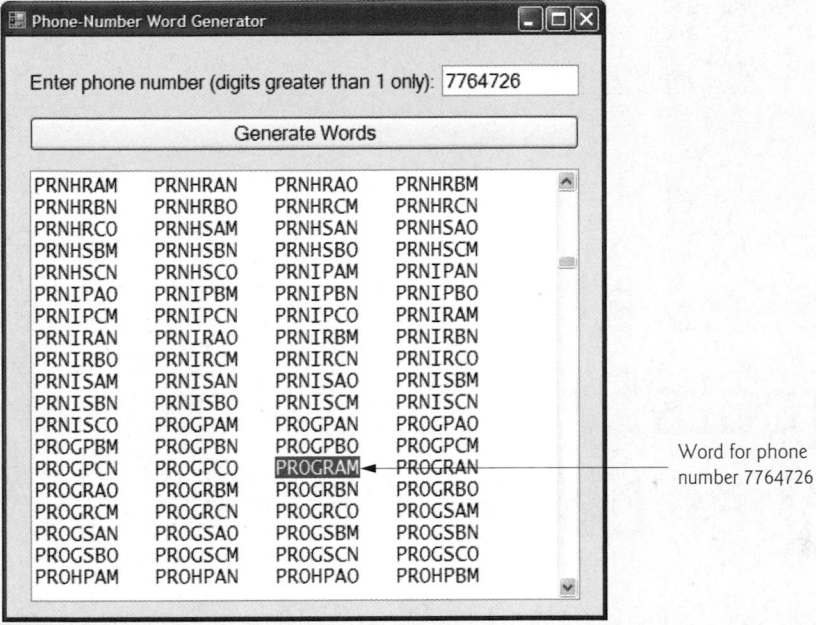

Fig. 8.33 | Windows application to generate the words for a phone number.

each seat is assigned, set the corresponding elements of the array to True to indicate that the seat is no longer available.

Your application should never assign a seat that has already been assigned. When the economy section is full, your application should ask the person if it is acceptable to be placed in the first-class section (and vice versa). If yes, make the appropriate seat assignment. If no, display the message "Next flight leaves in 3 hours."

8.10 *(Total Sales)* Use a two-dimensional array to solve the following problem: A company has four salespeople (1 to 4) who sell five different products (1 to 5). Once a day, each salesperson passes in a slip for each type of product sold. Each slip contains the following:

a) The salesperson number
b) The product number
c) The total dollar value of that product sold that day

Thus, each salesperson passes in between zero and five sales slips per day. Assume that the information from all of the slips for last month is available. Write an application that will read all this information for last month's sales and summarize the total sales by salesperson and by product. All totals should be stored in the two-dimensional array sales. After processing all the information for last month, display the results in tabular format, with each column representing a particular salesperson and each row representing a particular product. Cross-total each row to get the total sales of each product for last month. Cross-total each column to get the total sales by salesperson for last month. Your tabular output should include these cross-totals to the right of the totaled rows and to the bottom of the totaled columns.

9

Classes and Objects: A Deeper Look

OBJECTIVES

In this chapter you will learn:

- What class scope is and how it affects access to class members.

- To create overloaded constructors that can initialize objects of a class in a variety of ways.

- To use partial classes to enable one class to span multiple source-code files.

- How composition enables you to construct classes that are "made out of" other classes.

- To use Me to refer to the current object's members.

- How garbage collection eliminates most "memory leaks."

- How Shared class variables help conserve memory.

- How to create constant members with Const (at compile time) and ReadOnly (at runtime).

- To use the **Object Browser** to discover the capabilities of the classes in the Framework Class Library (FCL).

9.1 Introduction

In the preceding chapters, we introduced the basic concepts and terminology of object-oriented programming (OOP) in Visual Basic. This chapter takes a deeper look at classes. We introduce class scope and discuss how it affects where class members can be accessed. We demonstrate that constructors can be overloaded to allow clients to initialize objects of a class in several ways. We discuss how partial classes enable one class to span multiple source-code files. We explain composition—a capability that allows a class to have references to objects of other classes as members. We show how to use the Me reference to refer to the current object's members. The chapter presents garbage collection and discusses how it eliminates most "memory leaks." In addition, we discuss Shared class variables that are shared among all objects of a class. We then present the differences between constant members created with Const and ReadOnly. Finally, we show how to use the **Object Browser** to discover the capabilities of the classes in the Framework Class Library (FCL). Chapters 10 and 11 introduce inheritance and polymorphism, respectively—two key OOP technologies.

9.2 Time Class Case Study

We begin with a substantial application that uses most of the object-oriented programming concepts presented in Chapters 4–8. We introduce class Object, the ultimate "ancestor" of all classes in Visual Basic. Also, we explain method ToString, which can be used to obtain a String representation of any Visual Basic object.

Time Class Declaration

The application consists of classes Time (Fig. 9.1) and FrmTimeTest (Fig. 9.2). Class Time contains the information needed to represent a specific time in two popular formats. Class FrmTimeTest represents a GUI for class Time.

```vb
 1  ' Fig. 9.1: Time.vb
 2  ' Represents time to clients in 12-hour and 24-hour clock formats.
 3  Class Time
 4     Inherits Object ' if omitted, Object is inherited implicitly
 5
 6     ' declare Integer instance variables for the hour, minute and second
 7     Private hourValue As Integer ' 0 - 23
 8     Private minuteValue As Integer ' 0 - 59
 9     Private secondValue As Integer ' 0 - 59
10
11     ' Time constructor initializes instance variables
12     ' when a Time object is created
13     Public Sub New()
14        SetTime(12, 0, 0) ' initialize hour to noon; minute, second to 0
15     End Sub ' New
16
17     ' set a new time value using universal time, check validity of the
18     ' data, set invalid hour to noon, set invalid minute, second to zero
19     Public Sub SetTime(ByVal hh As Integer, _
20        ByVal mm As Integer, ByVal ss As Integer)
21        Hour = hh ' set hourValue using Hour property
22        Minute = mm ' set minuteValue using Minute property
23        Second = ss ' set secondValue using Second property
24     End Sub ' SetTime
25
26     ' property Hour
27     Public Property Hour() As Integer
28        Get ' return hourValue
29           Return hourValue
30        End Get
31
32        Set(ByVal value As Integer) ' set hourValue
33           If (value >= 0 AndAlso value < 24) Then ' in range 0-23
34              hourValue = value ' value is valid
35           Else ' value is invalid
36              hourValue = 12 ' set to default of noon
37           End If
38        End Set
39     End Property ' Hour
40
41     ' property Minute
42     Public Property Minute() As Integer
43        Get ' return minuteValue
44           Return minuteValue
45        End Get
46
```

Fig. 9.1 | Time class declaration maintains the time in 24-hour format. (Part 1 of 2.)

```
47          Set(ByVal value As Integer) ' set minuteValue
48             If (value >= 0 AndAlso value < 60) Then ' in range 0-59
49                minuteValue = value ' value is valid
50             Else ' value is invalid
51                minuteValue = 0 ' set to default of 0
52             End If
53          End Set
54       End Property ' Minute
55
56       ' property Second
57       Public Property Second() As Integer
58          Get ' return secondValue
59             Return secondValue
60          End Get
61
62          Set(ByVal value As Integer) ' set secondValue
63             If (value >= 0 AndAlso value < 60) Then ' in range 0-59
64                secondValue = value ' value is valid
65             Else ' value is invalid
66                secondValue = 0 ' set to default of 0
67             End If
68          End Set
69       End Property ' Second
70
71       ' convert Time to a String in universal-time (24-hour clock) format
72       Public Function ToUniversalString() As String
73          Return String.Format("{0}:{1:D2}:{2:D2}", Hour, Minute, Second)
74       End Function ' ToUniversalString
75
76       ' convert Time to a String in standard-time (12-hour clock) format
77       Public Overrides Function ToString() As String
78          Dim suffix As String ' AM or PM suffix
79          Dim standardHour As Integer ' a standard hour in the range 1-12
80
81          ' determine whether the 12-hour clock suffix should be AM or PM
82          If Hour < 12 Then
83             suffix = "AM" ' note space preceding AM
84          Else
85             suffix = "PM" ' note space preceding PM
86          End If
87
88          ' convert hour from universal-time format to standard-time format
89          If (Hour = 12 OrElse Hour = 0) Then
90             standardHour = 12
91          Else
92             standardHour = Hour Mod 12 ' 1 through 11, AM or PM
93          End If
94
95          Return String.Format("{0}:{1:D2}:{2:D2} {3}", _
96             standardHour, Minute, Second, suffix)
97       End Function ' ToString
98    End Class ' Time
```

Fig. 9.1 | Time class declaration maintains the time in 24-hour format. (Part 2 of 2.)

In Fig. 9.1, lines 3–4 begin the Time class declaration, indicating that class Time inherits from class **Object** of namespace System. Recall from Chapter 7 that it is not necessary to add an assembly reference for namespace System because it is implicitly added to all projects. Visual Basic programmers use inheritance to quickly create new classes from existing classes (and, as we will see in the next chapter, to organize groups of related classes). The Inherits keyword (line 4) followed by class name Object indicates that class Time inherits the attributes and behaviors of class Object. In fact, every class (except Object) inherits either directly or indirectly from Object. If you do not include line 4, the Visual Basic compiler includes it implicitly. A complete understanding of inheritance is not necessary to understand the concepts and programs in this chapter. We explore inheritance in detail in Chapter 10.

Lines 3 and 98 delimit with keywords Class and End Class, respectively, the body of the Time class declaration. Any information that we place in this body is contained within the class's scope. Class Time declares three Private Integer instance variables—hourValue, minuteValue and secondValue (lines 7–9)—that represent the time in universal-time format (24-hour clock format). We prefer to list the instance variables of a class first, so that, when reading the code, you see the name and type of each instance variable before it is used in the class's methods.

It is possible to have Private methods and Public instance variables. Private methods are called **utility methods,** or **helper methods,** because they can be called only by other methods of the class to support the operation of those methods. Using Public instance variables in a class is an uncommon and dangerous programming practice. Providing such access to a class's instance variables is unsafe; other parts of the program could accidentally or maliciously set these members to invalid values, producing potentially disastrous results.

Time Class Properties

Class Time (Fig. 9.1) declares properties Hour (lines 27–39), Minute (lines 42–54) and Second (lines 57–69) to access instance variables hourValue, minuteValue and secondValue, respectively. Each of these properties contains a Get accessor and a Set accessor. The Set accessors (lines 32–38, 47–53 and 62–68) strictly control the setting of the instance variables to ensure that they contain valid values. An attempt to set any instance variable to an incorrect value causes the instance variable to be set to its default value—12 (noon) for the hour and 0 for the minute and second—leaving the instance variable in a consistent state. Each Get accessor (lines 28–30, 43–45 and 58–60) returns the appropriate instance variable's value.

Time Class Methods

Class Time contains the following Public methods—the constructor New (lines 13–15), SetTime (lines 19–24), ToUniversalString (lines 72–74) and ToString (lines 77–97). Constructor New calls (in line 14) method SetTime (discussed shortly) with the hour value specified as 12, and the minute and second values specified as 0 to indicate that the default time should be noon. Visual Basic initializes Integer variables to 0 by default, so if we did not provide a constructor for class Time, instance variables hourValue, minuteValue and secondValue would each be initialized to 0, making the default time midnight. For some classes that would be fine, but we want our Time objects to be initialized to noon.

Constructors are implemented as Sub procedures, not as Functions, because Sub procedures cannot return values. Generally, constructors are declared Public. Private constructors are useful but are beyond the scope of the book. As we will see, a class can have many overloaded constructors—all share the same name, New, but each must have different numbers and/or types of parameters.

Method SetTime (lines 19–24) uses properties Hour, Minute and Second to ensure that instance variables hourValue, minuteValue and secondValue have valid values. For example, the hourValue must be greater than or equal to 0 and less than 24, because universal-time format represents hours as integers from 0 to 23. Similarly, both the minuteValue and secondValue must fall between 0 and 59. Any values outside these ranges are invalid and default to 12 for the hourValue or 0 for the minuteValue and secondValue, ensuring that a Time object always contains valid data; that is, the object remains in a consistent state. When a user calls SetTime with invalid arguments, the program should indicate that the attempted time setting was invalid. This can be done by "throwing an exception"—we discuss exception handling in Chapter 12.

Method ToUniversalString (lines 72–74) takes no arguments and returns a String in universal-time format, consisting of the Hour property value, two digits for the Minute property value and two digits for the Second property value. For example, if the time were 1:30:07 PM, method ToUniversalString would return the String "13:30:07". Note that format specifier D2 formats a single digit integer value with a leading 0.

Method ToString (lines 77–97) takes no arguments and returns a String in standard-time format, consisting of the Hour, Minute and Second property values separated by colons and followed by an AM or PM indicator (e.g., 1:27:06 PM). Lines 82–93 determine the proper formatting for the hour—hours from 0 to 11 print with AM, hours from 12 to 23 print with PM, hour 0 prints as 12 (midnight), hours 1–12 print as is and hours 13–23 print as 1–11 (PM).

Note that method ToString contains the keyword **Overrides** (line 77) in its declaration. Recall that every class in Visual Basic (such as class Time) inherits either directly or indirectly from class Object, which is the root of the class hierarchy. Section 10.7 summarizes class Object's seven methods, including method ToString, which returns a String representation of an object. The default implementation of ToString that every class inherits (directly or indirectly) from class Object returns the namespace and the class name of the object's class. This implementation is primarily a placeholder that can be overridden by a derived class to specify a more appropriate String representation of the data in a derived class object. For class Time, we choose to override (i.e., redefine) the ToString method to return a String which represents the Time object in standard-time (i.e., 12-hour clock) format.

After defining the class, we can use it as a type in declarations such as

```
Dim sunset As Time ' reference to object of class Time
```

Using the Time Class

Class FrmTimeTest (Fig. 9.2) provides a GUI for testing class Time. The GUI contains three text boxes in which the user can enter values for the Time object's Hour, Minute and Second properties, respectively. Class FrmTimeTest creates an object of class Time (line 4) and assigns its reference to variable time. When the object is instantiated, New allocates the memory for the Time object, then calls the Time constructor (method New in lines 13–15

of Fig. 9.1) to initialize the object's instance variables. The constructor invokes method
SetTime of class Time to initialize each of the properties, setting the time to noon.

Common Programming Error 9.1

*Using a reference (which, as you know, is initialized to the default value Nothing) before it refers
to an actual object results in a NullReferenceException at execution time and causes the program to terminate prematurely. We discuss how to handle exceptions to make programs more
robust in Chapter 12, Exception Handling.*

```
1   ' Fig. 9.2: FrmTimeTest.vb
2   ' Demonstrates Properties.
3   Public Class FrmTimeTest
4      Dim time As New Time() ' construct Time with zero arguments
5
6      ' invoked when user clicks the Add 1 to Second button
7      Private Sub btnAddSecond_Click(ByVal sender As System.Object, _
8         ByVal e As System.EventArgs) Handles btnAddSecond.Click
9         time.Second = (time.Second + 1) Mod 60 ' add 1 to Second
10        txtSetSecond.Text = time.Second
11
12        ' add one minute if 60 seconds have passed
13        If time.Second = 0 Then
14           time.Minute = (time.Minute + 1) Mod 60 ' add 1 to Minute
15           txtSetMinute.Text = time.Minute
16
17           ' add one hour if 60 minutes have passed
18           If time.Minute = 0 Then
19              time.Hour = (time.Hour + 1) Mod 24 ' add 1 to Hour
20              txtSetHour.Text = time.Hour
21           End If
22        End If
23
24        UpdateDisplay() ' update the text in lblOutput1 and lblOutput2
25     End Sub ' btnAddSecond_Click
26
27     ' handle event when txtSetHour's text changes
28     Private Sub txtSetHour_TextChanged(ByVal sender As System.Object, _
29        ByVal e As System.EventArgs) Handles txtSetHour.TextChanged
30        time.Hour = txtSetHour.Text
31        UpdateDisplay() ' update the text in lblOutput1 and lblOutput2
32     End Sub ' txtSetHour_TextChanged
33
34     ' handle event when txtSetMinute's text changes
35     Private Sub txtSetMinute_TextChanged(ByVal sender As System.Object, _
36        ByVal e As System.EventArgs) Handles txtSetMinute.TextChanged
37        time.Minute = txtSetMinute.Text
38        UpdateDisplay() ' update the text in lblOutput1 and lblOutput2
39     End Sub ' txtSetMinute_TextChanged
40
41     ' handle event when txtSetSecond's text changes
42     Private Sub txtSetSecond_TextChanged(ByVal sender As System.Object, _
43        ByVal e As System.EventArgs) Handles txtSetSecond.TextChanged
```

Fig. 9.2 | Graphical user interface for class Time. (Part 1 of 2.)

```
44          time.Second = txtSetSecond.Text
45          UpdateDisplay() ' update the text in lblOutput1 and lblOutput2
46       End Sub ' txtSetSecond_Textchanged
47
48       ' update time display
49       Private Sub UpdateDisplay()
50          txtSetHour.Text = time.Hour
51          txtSetMinute.Text = time.Minute
52          txtSetSecond.Text = time.Second
53          lblOutput1.Text = ("Hour: " & time.Hour & "; Minute: " & _
54             time.Minute & "; Second: " & time.Second)
55          lblOutput2.Text = ("Standard time is: " & time.ToString() & _
56             "; Universal Time is: " & time.ToUniversalString())
57       End Sub ' UpdateDisplay
58    End Class ' FrmTimeTest
```

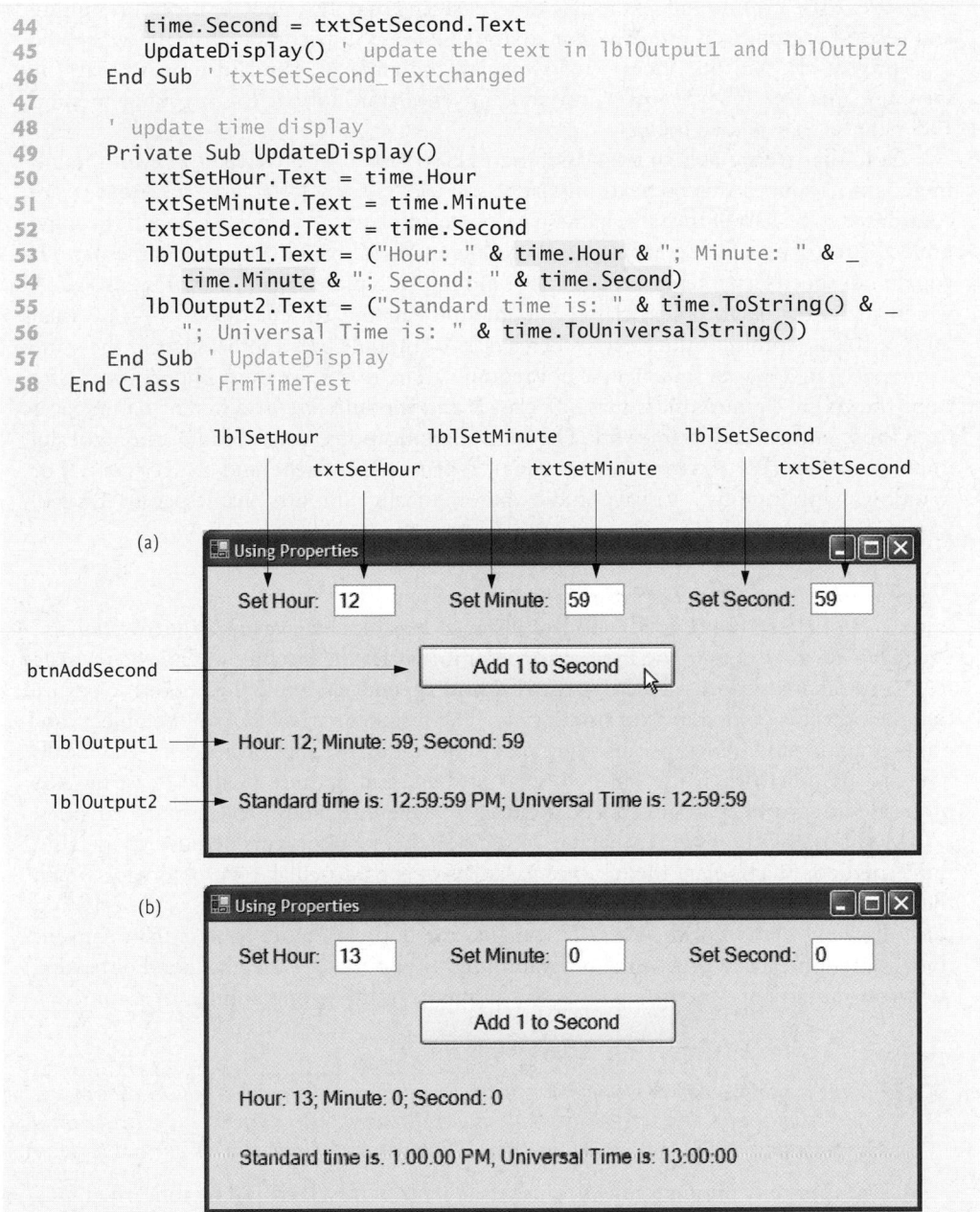

Fig. 9.2 | Graphical user interface for class Time. (Part 2 of 2.)

Lines 28–46 declare three methods that use the Time object's Hour, Minute and Second properties to alter the corresponding instance variable values. The GUI also contains a button that enables the user to increment the Second property value by 1 without having to use the corresponding text box. Method btnAddSecond_Click (lines 7–25) uses properties to determine and set the new time, ensuring that the values for the hour, minute and second are updated properly. For example, `23:59:59` becomes `00:00:00` when the user presses the button. Lines 55–56 display the time in standard-time format (by invoking method `ToString` of `Time`) and universal-time format (by invoking method `ToUniversalString` of `Time`).

Note that we are able to use class `Time` in class `FrmTimeTest` (Fig. 9.2) even though there is no `Imports` statement to import class `Time`. Classes `Time` and `FrmTimeTest` are considered to be part of the same namespace by default because we placed then in the same project directory. In fact, every class and module in Visual Basic is part of a namespace. If you do not specify a namespace for a class or module, it is placed in the **default namespace**, which includes the compiled classes and modules in the current directory—in Visual Studio, this is a project's directory. When a class or module uses another class in the same namespace, an `Imports` statement is not required. The reason we must import the classes from the .NET Framework is that our classes and modules are in different namespaces from those in the .NET Framework. For console applications, Visual Studio automatically imports namespaces `System`, `System.Data`, `System.Deployment` and `System.Xml`. For Windows applications, Visual Studio automatically imports namespaces `System`, `System.Deployment`, `System.Drawing` and `System.Windows.Forms`.

Notes on the *Time* Class Declaration

Lines 7–9 of class `Time` (Fig. 9.1) declare instance variables `hourValue`, `minuteValue` and `secondValue` as `Private`. The `Time` constructor initializes the instance variable `hourValue` to 12 and the instance variables `minuteValue` and `secondValue` to 0 (i.e., noon) to ensure that the object is created in a consistent state. The instance variables of a `Time` object cannot contain invalid values, because they are `Private`, because the constructor (which calls `SetTime`) is called when the `Time` object is created, and because method `SetTime` uses properties to scrutinize all subsequent attempts by a client to modify the instance variables.

Methods `ToUniversalString` and `ToString` take no arguments because, by default, these methods manipulate the instance variables of the particular `Time` object for which they are invoked. Any method of a class can access all the instance variables of the class and can call every method of the class. This makes method calls more concise than conventional function calls in procedural programming. It also reduces the likelihood of passing the wrong arguments, the wrong types of arguments or the wrong number of arguments.

> **Software Engineering Observation 9.1**
>
> *Using an object-oriented programming approach often simplifies method calls by reducing, or even eliminating, the arguments that must be passed. This benefit of object-oriented programming derives from the encapsulation of instance variables within an object.*

Classes simplify programming because the clients of the class need be concerned only with its `Public` operations. Clients are neither aware of, nor involved in, a class's implementation. Interfaces change less frequently than implementations. When an implementation changes, implementation-dependent code must change accordingly. By hiding the implementation, we eliminate the possibility that the clients of the class will become dependent on the class's implementation details.

You do not always have to create classes from scratch. Rather, you can derive classes by inheritance from other classes that provide capabilities required by the new classes.

Classes also can include references to objects of other classes as members—this is called composition. Such software reuse can greatly enhance your productivity. Section 9.7 discusses composition. Chapter 10 discusses inheritance.

9.3 **Class Scope**

In Section 7.16, we discussed method scope; now, we consider class scope. A class's instance variables and methods belong to its scope. Within a class's scope, class members are accessible to all of the class's methods and properties and can be referenced simply by name (without an object reference). Outside a class's scope, class members cannot be referenced directly by name. Those class members that are visible (such as `Public` members) can be accessed through a "handle" (i.e., members can be referenced via names of the form *objectReferenceName.memberName* or *ClassName.memberName* for `Shared` members). For example, line 56 of Fig. 9.2 accessess a `Time` object's method with the method call `time.ToUniversalString()`.

   If a variable is defined in a method, only that method can access the variable (i.e., the variable is a local variable of that method). Such variables have block scope. If a method defines a local variable that has the same name as an instance variable, the local variable hides the instance variable in that method's scope—this is called shadowing. A shadowed instance variable can be accessed in a method of that class by preceding its name with the keyword `Me` and the dot separator, as in `Me.hourValue`. Section 9.8 discusses keyword `Me`.

9.4 **Default and Parameterless Constructors**

If a class does not define constructors, the compiler provides a default constructor. This constructor contains no code (i.e., the constructor body is empty) and takes no parameters. You can also provide a constructor—called a parameterless constructor—that contains code (but, again, takes no parameters), as we demonstrated in class `Time` (lines 13–15 of Fig. 9.1), and as we will see again in the next example. If you provide any constructors for a class, the compiler will not provide a default constructor for that class.

Common Programming Error 9.2

If `Public` *constructors are provided for a class, but none of them is a parameterless constructor, and an attempt is made to call a constructor with no arguments to initialize an object of the class, a compilation error occurs. A constructor can be called with no arguments only if there are no constructors for the class (in which case the default constructor is called) or if the class includes a parameterless constructor provided by the programmer.*

9.5 **Time Class Case Study: Overloaded Constructors**

Like methods, constructors of a class can be overloaded. To do so, provide a separate method declaration with the same name (`New`) for each version of the method but different numbers, types and/or orders of parameters.

Class Time with Overloaded Constructors

The `Time` constructor in Fig. 9.1 initialized `hourValue` to 12 and `minuteValue` and `secondValue` to 0 (i.e., noon) with a call to the class's `SetTime` method. Recall that the declaration in line 4 of Fig. 9.2 supplied no arguments to the `Time` class constructor. Suppose you would like to create Time objects with any legitimate hour, minute and/or second values. Class Time of Fig. 9.3 includes five overloaded constructors to provide several ways to initialize Time objects. Each constructor calls method SetTime of the Time object, which uses the Set accessors of properties Hour, Minute and Second to ensure that the object begins in a consistent state by setting out-of-range hour, minute and second values to 12, 0 and 0, respectively. The compiler invokes the appropriate constructor by matching the number, types and order of the arguments specified in the constructor call with the number, types and order of the parameters specified in each constructor method declaration.

```vb
1   ' Fig. 9.3: Time.vb
2   ' Represents time and contains overloaded constructors.
3   Class Time
4      ' declare Integer instance variables for the hour, minute and second
5      Private hourValue As Integer ' 0 - 23
6      Private minuteValue As Integer ' 0 - 59
7      Private secondValue As Integer ' 0 - 59
8
9      ' constructor initializes hour to 12, minute to 0 and second to 0
10     ' to ensure that each Time object starts in a consistent state
11     Public Sub New() ' parameterless constructor
12        SetTime(12) ' initialize hour to noon; minute and second to 0
13     End Sub ' New
14
15     ' Time constructor: hour supplied;
16     ' minute and second default to 0
17     Public Sub New(ByVal hh As Integer)
18        SetTime(hh) ' call SetTime with one argument
19     End Sub ' New
20
21     ' Time constructor: hour and minute supplied;
22     ' second defaults to 0
23     Public Sub New(ByVal hh As Integer, ByVal mm As Integer)
24        SetTime(hh, mm) ' call SetTime with two arguments
25     End Sub ' New
26
27     ' Time constructor: hour, minute and second supplied
28     Public Sub New(ByVal hh As Integer, _
29        ByVal mm As Integer, ByVal ss As Integer)
30        SetTime(hh, mm, ss) ' call SetTime with three arguments
31     End Sub ' New
32
33     ' Time constructor: another Time object supplied
34     Public Sub New(ByVal tt As Time)
35        SetTime(tt.Hour, tt.Minute, tt.Second)
36     End Sub ' New
37
38     ' set a new time value using universal time, check validity of the
39     ' data, set invalid hour to 12, set invalid minute/second to zero
40     Public Sub SetTime(Optional ByVal hh As Integer = 12, _
41        Optional ByVal mm As Integer = 0, Optional ByVal ss As Integer = 0)
42        Hour = hh ' set hourValue using the Hour property
```

Fig. 9.3 | Overloaded constructors and Optional arguments. (Part 1 of 3.)

```vbnet
43          Minute = mm ' set minuteValue using the Minute property
44          Second = ss ' set secondValue using the Second property
45       End Sub ' SetTime
46
47       ' property Hour
48       Public Property Hour() As Integer
49          Get ' return hourValue
50             Return hourValue
51          End Get
52
53          Set(ByVal value As Integer) ' set hourValue
54             If (value >= 0 AndAlso value < 24) Then ' in range 0-23
55                hourValue = value ' value is valid
56             Else ' value is invalid
57                hourValue = 12 ' set to default of noon
58             End If
59          End Set
60       End Property ' Hour
61
62       ' property Minute
63       Public Property Minute() As Integer
64          Get ' return minuteValue
65             Return minuteValue
66          End Get
67
68          Set(ByVal value As Integer) ' set minuteValue
69             If (value >= 0 AndAlso value < 60) Then ' in range 0-59
70                minuteValue = value ' value is valid
71             Else ' value is invalid
72                minuteValue = 0 ' set to default of 0
73             End If
74          End Set
75       End Property ' Minute
76
77       ' property Second
78       Public Property Second() As Integer
79          Get ' return secondValue
80             Return secondValue
81          End Get
82
83          Set(ByVal value As Integer) ' set secondValue
84             If (value >= 0 AndAlso value < 60) Then ' in range 0-59
85                secondValue = value ' value is valid
86             Else ' value is invalid
87                secondValue = 0 ' set to default of 0
88             End If
89          End Set
90       End Property ' Second
91
92       ' convert Time to a String in universal-time (24-hour clock) format
93       Public Function ToUniversalString() As String
94          Return String.Format("{0}:{1:D2}:{2:D2}", Hour, Minute, Second)
95       End Function ' ToUniversalString
```

Fig. 9.3 | Overloaded constructors and `Optional` arguments. (Part 2 of 3.)

```
 96
 97      ' convert Time to a String in standard-time (12-hour clock) format
 98      Public Overrides Function ToString() As String
 99         Dim suffix As String ' AM or PM suffix
100         Dim standardHour As Integer ' a standard hour in the range 1-12
101
102         ' determine whether the 12-hour clock suffix should be AM or PM
103         If Hour < 12 Then
104            suffix = " AM" ' note space preceding AM
105         Else
106            suffix = " PM" ' note space preceding PM
107         End If
108
109         ' convert hour from universal-time format to standard-time format
110         If (Hour = 12 OrElse Hour = 0) Then
111            standardHour = 12
112         Else
113            standardHour = Hour Mod 12 ' 1 through 11, AM or PM
114         End If
115
116         Return String.Format("{0}:{1:D2}:{2:D2}", standardHour, Minute, _
117            Second) & suffix
118      End Function ' ToString
119   End Class ' Time
```

Fig. 9.3 | Overloaded constructors and `Optional` arguments. (Part 3 of 3.)

Class *Time's* Constructors

Because most of the code in class `Time` is identical to that in Fig. 9.1, this section concentrates only on the overloaded constructors. Lines 11–13 define the parameterless constructor that calls `SetTime` (line 12), initializing the time to noon. Lines 17–19 define a `Time` constructor with a single `Integer` parameter, representing the hour. Lines 23–25 define a `Time` constructor with two `Integer` parameters, representing the hour and minute. Lines 28–31 define a `Time` constructor with three `Integer` parameters representing the hour, minute and second. Lines 34–36 define a `Time` constructor that receives a reference to another `Time` object. When this last constructor—sometimes called a copy constructor—is called, the values from the `Time` argument are copied to initialize the new object's hour-`Value`, `minuteValue` and `secondValue`. Class `Time` declares these values as `Private` (lines 5–7), but the new `Time` object's constructor obtains these values via the `Public` properties of its `Time` parameter by using the expressions `tt.Hour`, `tt.Minute` and `tt.Second`. In fact, line 35 could have accessed the argument `Time` object's instance variables directly with the expressions `tt.hourValue`, `tt.minuteValue` and `tt.secondValue`.

Software Engineering Observation 9.2

When one object of a class has a reference to another object of the same class, the first object can access all of the second object's data, methods and properties (including those that are `Private`).

Although the parameter to the constructor in lines 34–36 is passed by value, this does not make a copy of the `Time` object that is passed as the constructor's argument. Rather, it makes a copy of the reference to the `Time` object passed as the argument.

Software Engineering Observation 9.3

Visual Basic classes are reference types, so all Visual Basic objects are passed to methods by reference.

Note that each constructor receives a different number and/or different types of parameters. Also, recall that if a method has one or more `Optional` parameters, the caller has the option of passing a value for each parameter. Method `SetTime` declares three `Optional` parameters—hh, mm and ss (lines 40–41). Lines 12 and 18 call method `SetTime` with one argument, which indicates that the default values for the `Optional` `minuteValue` and `secondValue` parameters should be used. Line 24 calls method `SetTime` with two arguments, which indicates that the default value for the `Optional` parameter `second-Value` is used. Lines 30 and 35 call method `SetTime` with all three arguments, so that no default values are used.

Common Programming Error 9.3

A constructor can call other class methods that use instance variables not yet initialized. Using instance variables before they have been initialized can lead to logic errors.

Using Class Time's Overloaded Constructors

Figure 9.4 (`TimeTest.vb`) demonstrates class `Time`'s overloaded constructors. Lines 6–11 create six `Time` objects that invoke various constructors of the class. Line 6 invokes the parameterless constructor by placing an empty set of parentheses after the class name. Lines 7–11 demonstrate passing arguments to the `Time` constructors. Line 7 invokes the constructor at lines 17–19 of Fig. 9.3. Line 8 invokes the constructor at lines 23–25 of Fig. 9.3. Lines 9–10 invoke the constructor at lines 28–31 of Fig. 9.3. Line 11 invokes the constructor at lines 34–36 of Fig. 9.3.

```vb
 1    ' Fig. 9.4: TimeTest.vb
 2    ' Overloading constructors.
 3    Module TimeTest
 4       Sub Main()
 5          ' use overloaded constructors
 6          Dim time1 As New Time() ' constructor with zero parameters
 7          Dim time2 As New Time(2) ' constructor with one parameter
 8          Dim time3 As New Time(21, 34) ' constructor with two parameters
 9          Dim time4 As New Time(12, 25, 42) ' three valid arguments
10          Dim time5 As New Time(27, 74, 99) ' three invalid arguments
11          Dim time6 As New Time(time4) ' copy another Time object
12
13          ' invoke time1 methods
14          Console.WriteLine("Constructed with: " & vbCrLf & _
15             "time1: all arguments defaulted" & vbCrLf & vbTab & _
16             time1.ToUniversalString() & vbCrLf & vbTab & _
17             time1.ToString())
18          ' invoke time2 methods
19          Console.WriteLine( _
20             "time2: hour specified; minute and second defaulted" & _
21             vbCrLf & vbTab & time2.ToUniversalString() & _
```

Fig. 9.4 | Overloading constructors. (Part 1 of 2.)

```
22            vbCrLf & vbTab & time2.ToString())
23        ' invoke time3 methods
24        Console.WriteLine( _
25           "time3: hour and minute specified; second defaulted" & _
26           vbCrLf & vbTab & time3.ToUniversalString() & _
27           vbCrLf & vbTab & time3.ToString())
28        ' invoke time4 methods
29        Console.WriteLine("time4: hour, minute and second specified" & _
30           vbCrLf & vbTab & time4.ToUniversalString() & _
31           vbCrLf & vbTab & time4.ToString())
32        ' invoke time5 methods
33        Console.WriteLine( _
34           "time5: invalid hour, minute and second specified" & _
35           vbCrLf & vbTab & time5.ToUniversalString() & _
36           vbCrLf & vbTab & time5.ToString())
37        ' invoke time6 methods
38        Console.WriteLine( "time6: Time object copied from time4" & _
39           vbCrLf & vbTab & time6.ToUniversalString() & _
40           vbCrLf & vbTab & time6.ToString())
41     End Sub ' Main
42  End Module ' TimeTest
```

```
Constructed with:
time1: all arguments defaulted
        12:00:00
        12:00:00 PM
time2: hour specified; minute and second defaulted
        2:00:00
        2:00:00 AM
time3: hour and minute specified; second defaulted
        21:34:00
        9:34:00 PM
time4: hour, minute and second specified
        12:25:42
        12:25:42 PM
time5: invalid hour, minute and second specified
        12:00:00
        12:00:00 PM
time6: Time object copied from time4
        12:25:42
        12:25:42 PM
```

Fig. 9.4 | Overloading constructors. (Part 2 of 2.)

Each Time constructor can be written to include a copy of the appropriate statements from method SetTime. This might be slightly more efficient, because it eliminates the extra SetTime call. However, consider what would happen if you change the representation of the time from three Integer values (requiring 12 bytes of memory) to a single Integer value representing the total number of elapsed seconds since midnight (requiring only 4 bytes of memory). Placing identical code in the Time constructors and method SetTime makes such a change in the class declaration more difficult. If the implementation of SetTime changes, the implementation of all the Time constructors would need to change accordingly. If, on the other hand, the Time constructors call method SetTime directly, any changes to the implementation of SetTime must be made only once, thus reducing the likelihood of a programming error when altering the implementation.

Software Engineering Observation 9.4

If a method of a class provides functionality required by a constructor (or other method) of the class, call that method from the constructor (or other method). This simplifies the maintenance of the code and reduces the likelihood of code errors.

9.6 Partial Classes

Visual Basic allows a class declaration to span multiple source-code files. The separate portions of the class declaration in each file are known as **partial classes**. We have already created applications that use partial classes—in each GUI application, the code that is auto-generated by the IDE (i.e., the code that declares and creates GUI components in the code-behind file) is marked with the **Partial** modifier and stored in a separate source file. For example, in the GUI application in Fig. 9.2, the lines 2–3 of the auto-generated partial class (stored in FrmTimeTest.Designer.vb) are:

```
Partial Public Class FrmTimeTest
    Inherits System.Windows.Forms.Form
```

which indicates that the code in this file is part of class FrmTimeTest. The partial class is stored in a file named FrmTimeTest.Designer.vb. To view the file FrmTimeTest.Designer.vb, click the **Show All Files** button on the **Solution Explorer** toolbar and then click the plus sign (+) to the left of the FrmTimeTest.vb in the **Solution Explorer** window.

When a class declaration specifies the Partial modifier, any class declarations with the same class name in the program will be combined with the partial class declaration to form a single class declaration at compile time. Partial classes must be declared in the same namespace and assembly. If members (e.g., instance variables, methods and properties) in one source file conflict with those in other source files, compilation errors will occur.

Error-Prevention Tip 9.1

When combining all partial classes, at least one class declaration must have a Partial *modifier. Otherwise, a compilation error occurs.*

Most of the classes you have seen to this point are small. In real applications, classes can grow to be quite large and might be developed by a team of programmers. Partial classes provide a convenient way to split a large class into small, manageable pieces. With partial classes, several developers can work on the same class at once.

9.7 Composition

A class can have references to objects of other classes as members. Such a capability is called **composition** and is sometimes referred to as a *has-a* relationship. For example, an object of class AlarmClock needs to know the current time and the time when it is supposed to sound its alarm, so it is reasonable to include two references to Time objects as members of the AlarmClock object.

Software Engineering Observation 9.5

One form of software reuse is composition, in which a class has as members references to objects of other classes.

Our example of composition contains two classes—Day (Fig. 9.5) and Employee (Fig. 9.6)—and module CompositionTest (Fig. 9.7) to demonstrate them. Class Day (Fig. 9.5) encapsulates information relating to a specific date. Lines 4–6 declare Integers monthValue, dayValue and yearValue. Lines 10–15 declare the constructor, which receives as parameters values for the month, day and year, then assigns these values to the class's properties to ensure that the parameter values are valid.

```vb
1   ' Fig. 9.5: Day.vb
2   ' Encapsulates month, day and year.
3   Class Day
4      Private monthValue As Integer ' 1-12
5      Private dayValue As Integer ' 1-31 based on month
6      Private yearValue As Integer ' any year (could validate)
7
8      ' constructor confirms proper value for month, then calls
9      ' method CheckDay to confirm proper value for day
10     Public Sub New(ByVal mm As Integer, _
11        ByVal dd As Integer, ByVal yy As Integer)
12        Month = mm
13        Day = dd
14        Year = yy
15     End Sub ' New
16
17     ' property Month
18     Public Property Month() As Integer
19        Get
20           Return monthValue
21        End Get
22
23        Set(ByVal mm As Integer)
24           ' ensure month value is valid (in the range 1-12)
25           If (mm > 0 AndAlso mm <= 12) Then
26              monthValue = mm
27           Else
28              monthValue = 1 ' to ensure consistent state
29
30              ' inform user of error
31              Console.WriteLine("Invalid month (" & mm & _
32                 ") set to 1.")
33           End If
34        End Set
35     End Property ' Month
36
37     ' property Day
38     Public Property Day() As Integer
39        Get
40           Return dayValue
41        End Get
42
```

Fig. 9.5 | Day class encapsulates day, month and year information. (Part 1 of 2.)

```
43          Set(ByVal dd As Integer)
44              dayValue = CheckDay(dd) ' validate dayPassed
45          End Set
46       End Property ' Day
47
48       ' property Year
49       Public Property Year() As Integer
50          Get
51              Return yearValue
52          End Get
53
54          Set(ByVal yy As Integer)
55              yearValue = yy
56          End Set
57       End Property ' Year
58
59       ' confirm proper day value based on month and year
60       Private Function CheckDay(ByVal testDayValue As Integer) As Integer
61          Dim daysPerMonth() As Integer = _
62              {0, 31, 28, 31, 30, 31, 30, 31, 31, 30, 31, 30, 31}
63
64          ' validate day
65          If (testDayValue > 0 AndAlso _
66              testDayValue <= daysPerMonth(Month)) Then
67              Return testDayValue
68          End If
69
70          ' check for leap year in February
71          If (Month = 2 AndAlso testDayValue = 29 AndAlso _
72              ((Year Mod 400 = 0) OrElse _
73              (Year Mod 4 = 0 AndAlso Year Mod 100 <> 0))) Then
74              Return testDayValue
75          End If
76
77          ' inform user of error
78          Console.WriteLine("Invalid day (" & testDayValue & ") set to 1. ")
79          Return 1 ' leave object in consistent state
80       End Function ' CheckDay
81
82       ' create string containing month/day/year format
83       Public Overrides Function ToString() As String
84          Return (Month & "/" & Day & "/" & Year)
85       End Function ' ToString
86    End Class ' Day
```

Fig. 9.5 | Day class encapsulates day, month and year information. (Part 2 of 2.)

The Set accessor (lines 23–34) of property Month ensures that the month value is in the range 1–12. The Set accessor (lines 43–45) of property Day invokes utility function CheckDay to validate the day value. The Year property does not perform the validation of the year value. We assume that the Year is a valid four-digit year, such as 2005; however, we could have validated the year as well.

Function CheckDay (lines 60–80) validates whether the day is correct based on the current Month and Year. Lines 65–68 determine whether the day is a valid day for the particular month. If not, lines 71–75 determine whether the Month is February, the day is 29 and the Year is a leap year. A year is a leap year if it is divisible by 400 (tested at line 72), or if it is divisible by 4 and not divisible by 100 (tested at line 73). If lines 71–75 do not return a correct value for day, line 79 returns 1 to maintain the date in a consistent state.

Using Class **Day** in Class **Employee**

Class Employee (Fig. 9.6) holds information relating to an employee's birthday and hire date using instance variables firstName, lastName, birthDate and hireDate (lines 4–7). Members birthDate and hireDate are references to Day objects, each of which contains instance variables month, day and year. In this example, class Employee is *composed of* two references to Day objects. The Employee constructor (lines 10–23) takes eight arguments (first, last, birthMonth, birthDay, birthYear, hireMonth, hireDay and hireYear). Line 19 passes arguments birthMonth, birthDay and birthYear to the Day constructor to create the birthDate object. Similarly, line 22 passes arguments hireMonth, hireDay and hireYear to the Day constructor to create the hireDate object.

Testing Class **Employee**

Module CompositionTest (Fig. 9.7) contains Main, which tests the classes in Figs. 9.5–9.6. Lines 5–6 instantiate an Employee object ("Bob Blue" with birthday 7/24/1949 and hire date 3/12/1988), and line 7 displays the Employee information to the user.

```
 1  ' Fig. 9.6: Employee.vb
 2  ' Represent employee name, birthday and hire date.
 3  Class Employee
 4     Private firstName As String
 5     Private lastName As String
 6     Private birthDate As Day ' member object reference
 7     Private hireDate As Day ' member object reference
 8
 9     ' Employee constructor
10     Public Sub New(ByVal first As String, ByVal last As String, _
11        ByVal birthMonth As Integer, ByVal birthDay As Integer, _
12        ByVal birthYear As Integer, ByVal hireMonth As Integer, _
13        ByVal hireDay As Integer, ByVal hireYear As Integer)
14
15        firstName = first
16        lastName = last
17
18        ' create Day instance for employee birthday
19        birthDate = New Day(birthMonth, birthDay, birthYear)
20
21        ' create Day instance for employee hire date
22        hireDate = New Day(hireMonth, hireDay, hireYear)
23     End Sub ' New
24
```

Fig. 9.6 | Employee class encapsulates employee name, birthday and hire date. (Part 1 of 2.)

```
25        ' return employee information as String
26        Public Overrides Function ToString() As String
27           Return (lastName & ", " & firstName & " Hired: " _
28              & hireDate.ToString() & " Birthday: " & birthDate.ToString())
29        End Function ' ToString
30     End Class ' Employee
```

Fig. 9.6 | `Employee` class encapsulates employee name, birthday and hire date. (Part 2 of 2.)

```
1     ' Fig. 9.7: CompositionTest.vb
2     ' Demonstrate an object with member object reference.
3     Module CompositionTest
4        Sub Main()
5           Dim employee As New Employee( _
6              "Bob", "Blue", 7, 24, 1949, 3, 12, 1988)
7           Console.WriteLine(employee.ToString())
8        End Sub ' Main
9     End Module ' CompositionTest
```

```
Blue, Bob Hired: 3/12/1988 Birthday: 7/24/1949
```

Fig. 9.7 | Composition demonstration.

9.8 Using the Me Reference to Access the Current Object

Every object of a class shares the class's method declarations. We have seen that an object's methods can manipulate the object's data. But how do methods know which object's instance variables to manipulate? Every object has access to itself through a reference called `Me` (a Visual Basic keyword). On every method call, the compiler passes an object's `Me` reference as an implicit argument to each of the object's non-`Shared` methods. The `Me` reference can then be used to access a particular object's members implicitly or explicitly. (Section 9.10 introduces `Shared` class members and explains why the `Me` reference is *not* implicitly passed to `Shared` methods.)

Class `Time` (Fig. 9.8) defines `Private` instance variables `hour`, `minute` and `second` (lines 4–6). The constructor (lines 9–14) receives three `Integer` arguments to initialize a `Time` object. For this example, we use parameter names (lines 9–10) that are identical to the class's instance variable names (lines 4–6). When a method has a parameter or local variable with the same name as one of the class's instance variables, the instance variable is shadowed (hidden) in the method's scope. However, the method can use the `Me` reference to refer explicitly to shadowed instance variables. Lines 11–13 of Fig. 9.8 demonstrate this feature.

Method `BuildString` (lines 17–20) returns a `String` created by a statement that uses the `Me` reference first explicitly then implicitly. Line 18 uses the `Me` reference explicitly to call method `ToUniversalString`, whereas line 19 calls the same method using the `Me` reference implicitly. Note that both lines generate identical outputs.

Error-Prevention Tip 9.2

For a method in which a parameter has the same name as an instance variable, use reference `Me` *to access the instance variable explicitly; otherwise, the method parameter is referenced.*

```
 1   ' Fig. 9.8: Time.vb
 2   ' Encapsulate time using Me reference.
 3   Class Time
 4      Private hour As Integer
 5      Private minute As Integer
 6      Private second As Integer
 7
 8      ' Time constructor
 9      Public Sub New(ByVal hour As Integer, _
10         ByVal minute As Integer, ByVal second As Integer)
11         Me.hour = hour ' set instance variable to parameter
12         Me.minute = minute ' set instance variable to parameter
13         Me.second = second ' set instance variable to parameter
14      End Sub ' New
15
16      ' create String using Me explicitly then implicitly
17      Public Function BuildString() As String
18         Return "Me.ToUniversalString(): " & Me.ToUniversalString() _
19            & vbCrLf & "ToUniversalString(): " & ToUniversalString()
20      End Function ' BuildString
21
22      ' convert to String in universal-time format
23      Public Function ToUniversalString() As String
24         Return String.Format("{0:D2}:{1:D2}:{2:D2}", hour, minute, second)
25      End Function ' ToUniversalString
26   End Class ' Time
```

Fig. 9.8 | Class using the Me reference.

Error-Prevention Tip 9.3

Avoid parameter names that conflict with instance variable names to prevent subtle, hard-to-find bugs.

Module MeTest (Fig. 9.9) demonstrates the Me reference. Line 5 instantiates a Time object. Line 6 invokes method BuildString, then displays the results to the user.

```
 1   ' Fig. 9.9: MeTest.vb
 2   ' Demonstrates Me reference.
 3   Module MeTest
 4      Sub Main()
 5         Dim time As New Time(12, 30, 19)
 6         Console.WriteLine(time.BuildString())
 7      End Sub ' Main
 8   End Module ' MeTest
```

```
Me.ToUniversalString(): 12:30:19
ToUniversalString(): 12:30:19
```

Fig. 9.9 | Me reference demonstration.

9.9 Garbage Collection

Every object you create uses various system resources, including the memory that holds the object itself. We need a disciplined way to give resources back to the system when they are no longer needed, so as to avoid "resource leaks." The Common Language Runtime (CLR) performs automatic garbage collection to reclaim the memory occupied by objects that are no longer in use. When there are no more references to an object, the object is marked for garbage collection by the CLR. The memory for such an object can be reclaimed when the runtime executes its garbage collector, which is responsible for retrieving the memory of objects that are no longer used, so that the memory can be used for other objects. Therefore, whereas memory leaks are common in other languages like C and C++ (because memory is not automatically reclaimed in those languages), they are much less likely in Visual Basic (but some can still happen in subtle ways). Resources like memory that are allocated and reclaimed by the CLR are known as managed resources.

Other types of resource leaks can occur. For example, an application could open a file on disk to modify the file's contents. If the application does not close the file, no other application may be allowed to use the file until the application that opened the file finishes. An application that no longer needs a file should close it immediately so that other programs can access the file. Resources like files, network connections and database connections that the *programmer* must manage are known as unmanaged resources (because they are not managed by the CLR). Such resources are typically scarce and should be released as soon as they are no longer needed by a program.

To help prevent resource leaks for unmanaged resources, the garbage collector calls a special method named `Finalize` on each object before it is removed from memory. Recall from Section 9.2 that all classes inherit the methods of class `Object`, one of which is `Finalize`. You will learn more about class `Object` in Chapter 10, Object-Oriented Programming: Inheritance. The `Finalize` method is called by the garbage collector to perform termination housekeeping on an object (such as releasing unmanaged resources used by the object) just before the garbage collector reclaims the object's memory. Method `Finalize` does not take parameters and does not return a value. In Section 9.10, we demonstrate a situation in which method `Finalize` is called by the garbage collector.

Unfortunately, `Finalize` is not ideal for releasing unmanaged resources because the garbage collector is unpredictable—it is not guaranteed to execute at a specified time. In some cases the garbage collector may *never* execute before a program terminates. Thus, it is unclear if, or when, method `Finalize` will be called. Unmanaged resources might not be released for a long time, which would prevent these scarce resources from being used by other programs. For this reason, most programmers should avoid method `Finalize`.

In Chapter 11, we discuss interfaces. As will be explained, an interface describes methods that a class must implement. The FCL provides interface `IDisposable`, which contains a method named `Dispose` that a client can invoke to immediately release the resources used by an object. When a program creates an object of a class that implements interface `IDisposable`, the client should call that object's `Dispose` method as soon as the client is done using the object. This ensures that the resources used by the object are released promptly so they can be reused. The following URL links to a Microsoft Developer Network (MSDN) TV interview describing `IDisposable`:

```
msdn.microsoft.com/msdntv/episode.aspx?xml=episodes/en/
    20030501CLRBA/manifest.xml
```

The following URL provides detailed information on memory management in .NET:

```
www.gotdotnet.com/team/libraries/whitepapers/resourcemanagement/
    resourcemanagement.aspx
```

Software Engineering Observation 9.6

A class that uses unmanaged resources, such as files on disk, should provide a method that clients of the class can call explicitly to release the resources. Many Visual Basic library classes provide Close *or* Dispose *methods for this purpose.*

9.10 Shared Class Members

Each object of a class has its own copy of all the instance variables of the class. However, in certain cases, all class objects should share only one copy of a particular variable. A program contains only one copy of a Shared class variable in memory, no matter how many objects of the class have been instantiated. A Shared class variable represents class-wide information—all class objects share the same piece of data. The declaration of a Shared member begins with the keyword Shared.

Let us use a video game example to explain the need for Shared class-wide data. Suppose we have a video game in which Martians attack other space creatures. A Martian tends to be brave and willing to attack other space creatures when it is aware that there are at least four other Martians present. If there are fewer than five Martians present, a Martian becomes cowardly. For this reason, each Martian must know the martianCount. We could endow class Martian with a martianCount instance variable. If we were to do this, then every Martian would have a separate copy of the instance variable, and every time we create a Martian, we would have to update the instance variable martianCount in every Martian. The redundant copies waste space, and updating those copies is time-consuming. Worse yet, while we are updating the individual copies of martianCount, there will be periods of time during which some of these copies have not yet been updated, so we could have inconsistent bravery behavior among the Martians. Instead, we declare martianCount to be Shared so that martianCount is class-wide data. Each Martian can then see the martianCount as if it were instance data of that Martian, but Visual Basic maintains only one copy of the Shared martianCount to save space. We also save time, in that the Martian constructor increments only the Shared martianCount—there is only one copy, so we do not have to increment separate copies of martianCount for each Martian object. This also prevents inconsistent bravery behavior among the Martians.

Performance Tip 9.1

When a single copy of the data will suffice, use Shared *class variables rather than instance variables to save storage and simplify program logic.*

Shared class members have class scope. A class's Public Shared members can be accessed through the class name using the dot separator (e.g., *className.sharedMember-Name*). A class's Private Shared class members can be accessed by clients only indirectly through non-Private methods of the class. Shared class members are available as soon as the class is loaded into memory at execution time; like other variables with class scope, they exist for the duration of program execution, even when no objects of that class exist. To allow clients to access a Private Shared class member when no objects of the class exist, you must provide a non-Private Shared method or property.

Unlike non-Shared methods, a Shared method has no Me reference, because Shared class members exist independently of any class objects and even when there are no objects of that class. So a Shared method cannot access non-Shared class members.

Common Programming Error 9.4

Using the Me *reference in a* Shared *method or* Shared *property is a compilation error.*

Shared Constructors

When Shared variables require more complex initialization than can be accomplished in a Shared variable declaration, you can create a **Shared** constructor to initialize them. A Shared constructor is declared like an instance constructor, but is preceded by the Shared modifier and can be used only to initialize Shared variables. A Shared constructor is implicitly Public, must be declared with no parameters, cannot call other constructors of the class and is guaranteed to execute before a program creates any objects of the class or accesses any Shared class members. A class can have both a Shared constructor and a non-Shared parameterless constructor.

Common Programming Error 9.5

Explicitly declaring a Shared *constructor* Public *is a compilation error, because a* Shared *constructor is* Public *implicitly.*

Class Employee with Shared Variables

Class Employee (Fig. 9.10) demonstrates a Private Shared class variable and a Public Shared Property. The Shared class variable countValue is initialized to zero by default (line 6). It maintains a count of the number of Employee objects that have been instantiated and currently reside in memory, including objects that have already been marked for garbage collection but have not yet been reclaimed by the garbage collector.

When objects of class Employee exist, Shared member countValue can be used in any method of an Employee object—in this example, the constructor (lines 9–15) increments countValue (line 12) and method Finalize (lines 18–23) decrements countValue (line

```vb
1    ' Fig. 9.10: Employee.vb
2    ' Class Employee uses Shared variable.
3    Class Employee
4       Private firstNameValue As String ' employee first name
5       Private lastNameValue As String ' employee last name
6       Private Shared countValue As Integer ' Employee objects in memory
7
8       ' Employee constructor
9       Public Sub New(ByVal first As String, ByVal last As String)
10          firstNameValue = first
11          lastNameValue = last
12          countValue += 1 ' increment shared count of employees
13          Console.WriteLine("Employee object constructor for " & _
14             firstNameValue & " " & lastNameValue)
15       End Sub ' New
16
```

Fig. 9.10 | Employee class objects share Shared variable. (Part 1 of 2.)

```
17          ' finalizer method decrements Shared count of employees
18          Protected Overrides Sub Finalize()
19             countValue -= 1 ' decrement countValue
20             Console.WriteLine("Employee object finalizer for " & _
21                firstNameValue & " " & lastNameValue & "; count = " & _
22                countValue)
23          End Sub ' Finalize
24
25          ' return first name
26          Public ReadOnly Property FirstName() As String
27             Get
28                Return firstNameValue
29             End Get
30          End Property ' FirstName
31
32          ' return last name
33          Public ReadOnly Property LastName() As String
34             Get
35                Return lastNameValue
36             End Get
37          End Property ' LastName
38
39          ' property Count
40          Public Shared ReadOnly Property Count() As Integer
41             Get
42                Return countValue
43             End Get
44          End Property ' Count
45       End Class ' Employee
```

Fig. 9.10 | `Employee` class objects share `Shared` variable. (Part 2 of 2.)

19). (Note that method `Finalize` is declared using keywords `Protected` and `Over-rides`—method `Finalize`'s header must contain these keywords, which we discuss in Chapters 10–11.) If no objects of class `Employee` exist, member `countValue` can be referenced through a call to Property `Count` (lines 40–44)—this `Property` is `Shared`, and therefore we do not have to instantiate an `Employee` object to call the `Get` method of the `Property`. Also, by declaring property `Count` as `ReadOnly`, we prevent clients from changing the value of `countValue` directly, thus ensuring that clients can change `count-Value`'s value only under the tight control of class `Employee`'s constructors and finalizer.

Testing *Shared* Variables

Module `SharedTest` (Fig. 9.11) demonstrates the `Shared` members of Fig. 9.10. Lines 5–6 use the `ReadOnly Shared Property Count` of class `Employee` to obtain the current value of `countValue`. No `Employee` objects exist yet, so we must call `Count` using the class name `Employee`. Lines 8–9 then instantiate two `Employee` objects, causing `countValue` to be incremented by 2. Lines 13–14 print the `countValue` by using `ReadOnly Shared Property Count`. Lines 17–21 display the names of the employees. Lines 24–25 set these objects' references to `Nothing`, so that `employee1` and `employee2` no longer refer to the `Employee` objects. This "marks" the objects for garbage collection, because there are no more references to these objects in the program.

Common Programming Error 9.6

A compilation error occurs if a Shared *method calls an instance (non-*Shared*) method in the same class by using only the name of the method. Similarly, a compilation error occurs if a* Shared *method attempts to access an instance variable in the same class by using only the name of the variable.*

```vb
 1  ' Fig. 9.11: SharedTest.vb
 2  ' Demonstrates Shared members.
 3  Module SharedTest
 4     Sub Main()
 5        Console.WriteLine("Employees before instantiation: " & _
 6           Employee.Count) ' Count is a Shared property
 7
 8        Dim employee1 As New Employee("Susan", "Baker") ' call constructor
 9        Dim employee2 As New Employee("Bob", "Blue") ' call constructor
10
11        ' output number of employees after instantiation
12        ' (use Shared property)
13        Console.WriteLine(vbCrLf & "Employees after instantiation " & _
14           "(via Employee.Count): " & Employee.Count)
15
16        ' display names of first and second employees (using properties)
17        Console.WriteLine(vbCrLf & "Display names of employees " & _
18           "(using properties)" & vbCrLf & "Employee 1: " & _
19           employee1.FirstName & " " & employee1.LastName & vbCrLf & _
20           "Employee 2: " & employee2.FirstName & " " & _
21           employee2.LastName & vbCrLf)
22
23        Console.WriteLine("Marking employees for garbage collection")
24        employee1 = Nothing ' mark employee1 for garbage collection
25        employee2 = Nothing ' mark employee2 for garbage collection
26
27        Console.WriteLine()
28        Console.WriteLine("Explicitly invoking the garbage collector")
29        System.GC.Collect() ' request garbage collection
30     End Sub ' Main
31  End Module ' SharedTest
```

```
Employees before instantiation: 0
Employee object constructor for Susan Baker
Employee object constructor for Bob Blue

Employees after instantiation (via Employee.Count): 2

Display names of employees (using properties)
Employee 1: Susan Baker
Employee 2: Bob Blue

Marking employees for garbage collection

Explicitly invoking the garbage collector
Employee object finalizer for Bob Blue; count = 1
Employee object finalizer for Susan Baker; count = 0
```

Fig. 9.11 | Shared class member demonstration.

Normally, the garbage collector is not invoked directly by the user. Either the garbage collector reclaims the memory for objects when it deems garbage collection is appropriate, or the operating system recovers the unneeded memory when the program terminates. Line 29 uses `Public Shared` method `Collect` from class `GC` (namespace `System`) to request that the garbage collector execute. Before the garbage collector releases the memory occupied by the two `Employee` objects, it invokes method `Finalize` for each `Employee` object, which decrements the `countValue` value by a total of 2.

The last two lines of the sample output show that the `Employee` object for `Bob Blue` was finalized before the `Employee` object for `Susan Baker`. However, the output of this program on your system could differ. The garbage collector is not guaranteed to collect objects in a specific order, nor is it guaranteed to run at all before the program terminates.

9.11 Const and ReadOnly Members

Visual Basic allows you to create constants—members whose values cannot change during program execution. To create a constant instance variable of a class, declare that member as either `Const` or `ReadOnly`. An instance variable declared as `Const` must be initialized in its declaration; an instance variable declared as `ReadOnly` can be initialized either in its declaration or in the class constructor. `Const` values must be initialized at compile time; whereas `ReadOnly` values are not initialized until runtime. Neither a `Const` nor a `ReadOnly` value can be modified once initialized.

 Error-Prevention Tip 9.4

If a variable's value should never change, making it a constant prevents it from changing. This helps eliminate errors that might occur if the value of the variable were to change.

 Common Programming Error 9.7

Declaring an instance variable as `Const` but failing to initialize it in that declaration is a compilation error.

 Common Programming Error 9.8

Assigning a value to a `Const` instance variable is a compilation error.

`Const` members must be initialized at compile time; thus, they can be initialized only to constant values, such as integers, string literals, characters and other `Const` members. Constant members with values that cannot be determined at compile time must be declared `ReadOnly`. Recall that a `ReadOnly` member can be assigned a value only once, either when it is declared or within the class's constructor (the `Shared` constructor for `Shared ReadOnly` members and a non-`Shared` constructor for non-`Shared ReadOnly` members).

 Common Programming Error 9.9

Declaring an instance variable as `ReadOnly` and attempting to use it before it is initialized is a logic error.

 Common Programming Error 9.10

A `Shared ReadOnly` variable cannot be initialized in an instance constructor for that class, and a `ReadOnly` instance variable cannot be initialized in a `Shared` constructor for that class. Attempting to define a `ReadOnly` variable in an inappropriate constructor is a compilation error.

Common Programming Error 9.11

Declaring a Const member as Shared is a compilation error, because a Const member is Shared implicitly.

Common Programming Error 9.12

Declaring a ReadOnly member as Const is a compilation error, because these two keywords are not allowed to be combined in a variable declaration.

Class *CircleConstants* with *Const* and *ReadOnly* Instance Variables

Class CircleConstants (Fig. 9.12) demonstrates constants. Line 4 creates constant PI using keyword Const and assigns to PI the Double value 3.14159—an approximation of π. We could have used pre-defined constant PI of class Math (Math.PI) as the value, but we wanted to demonstrate how you can create your own Const instance variables. The compiler must be able to determine a Const's value to be able to initialize a Const instance variable with that value. The value 3.14159 is acceptable (line 4), but the expression

```
Convert.ToDouble("3.14159")
```

generates a compilation error if used in place of that value. Although this expression uses a constant value (String literal "3.14159") as an argument and produces the same numeric value, a compilation error occurs, because the compiler cannot evaluate executable code (such as a method call). This restriction is lifted with ReadOnly members, which are initialized at runtime. Note that line 9 assigns the value of the constructor parameter radiusValue to ReadOnly member RADIUS at runtime. We could also have used a method call, such as Convert.ToDouble, to assign a value to this ReadOnly member.

Using *Const* and *ReadOnly*

Module ConstAndReadOnly (Fig. 9.13) demonstrates the Const and ReadOnly values. Line 5 creates a Random object that is used in line 8 to generate a random Integer in the range 1–20 that corresponds to a circle's radius. This enables each program execution to produce different output. The random value is passed to the CircleConstants constructor to initialize a CircleConstants object. Lines 11–13 access the ReadOnly variable RADIUS through a reference to object circle, and compute and display the circle's circumference.

```vb
1   ' Fig. 9.12: CircleConstants.vb
2   ' Encapsulate constants PI and radius.
3   Class CircleConstants
4      Public Const PI As Double = 3.14159 ' PI is a Const instance variable
5      Public ReadOnly RADIUS As Integer ' radius is uninitialized constant
6
7      ' constructor of class CircleConstants
8      Public Sub New(ByVal radiusValue As Integer)
9         RADIUS = radiusValue ' initialize ReadOnly constant
10     End Sub ' New
11   End Class ' CircleConstants
```

Fig. 9.12 | Constants used in class CircleConstants.

```
1    ' Fig. 9.13: ConstAndReadOnly.vb
2    ' Demonstrates Const and ReadOnly members.
3    Module ConstAndReadOnly
4       Sub Main()
5          Dim random As New Random() ' create Random object
6
7          ' create CircleConstants object with random radius
8          Dim circle As New CircleConstants(random.Next(1, 20))
9
10         ' calculate the circle's circumference
11         Console.WriteLine("Radius = " & circle.RADIUS & vbCrLf & _
12            "Circumference = " & String.Format("{0:F3}", _
13            2 * CircleConstants.PI * circle.RADIUS))
14      End Sub ' Main
15   End Module ' ConstAndReadOnly
```

```
Radius = 9
Circumference = 56.549
```

Fig. 9.13 | Const and ReadOnly class members demonstration.

This calculation employs the Public Const member PI, which we access in line 13 through its class name CircleConstants. Recall that Const members are implicitly Shared; thus we can access a Const member with its class name followed by the dot separator even when no objects of the class are present.

ReadOnly *and* WriteOnly *Properties*

Recall from Chapter 4 that not all properties need to have Get and Set accessors—a property with only a Get accessor is called a read-only property and must be declared using keyword ReadOnly; a property with only a Set accessor is called a write-only property and must be declared using keyword WriteOnly.

9.12 Object Browser

Now we present a feature that Visual Studio provides to facilitate the design of object-oriented applications—the **Object Browser**. The **Object Browser** lists all the libraries that are available to the application, including the Framework Class Library (FCL) classes and programmer-defined classes. Developers use the **Object Browser** to learn about the functionality provided by specific classes. To open the **Object Browser**, right click any Visual Basic class or method in the code editor and select **Go To Definition** (Figs. 9.14–9.15). Figure 9.16 shows the **Object Browser** after the user selects class Random in Fig. 9.14. Figure 9.17 shows the **Object Browser** after the user selects method Next of class Random in Fig. 9.15. The **Object Browser** lists all non-Private members provided by class Random in the upper-right portion of the window, which offers developers instant access to information regarding the services of the selected class. You can also view the details of method Next by clicking the method name in the upper-right portion of the windows in Figure 9.16.

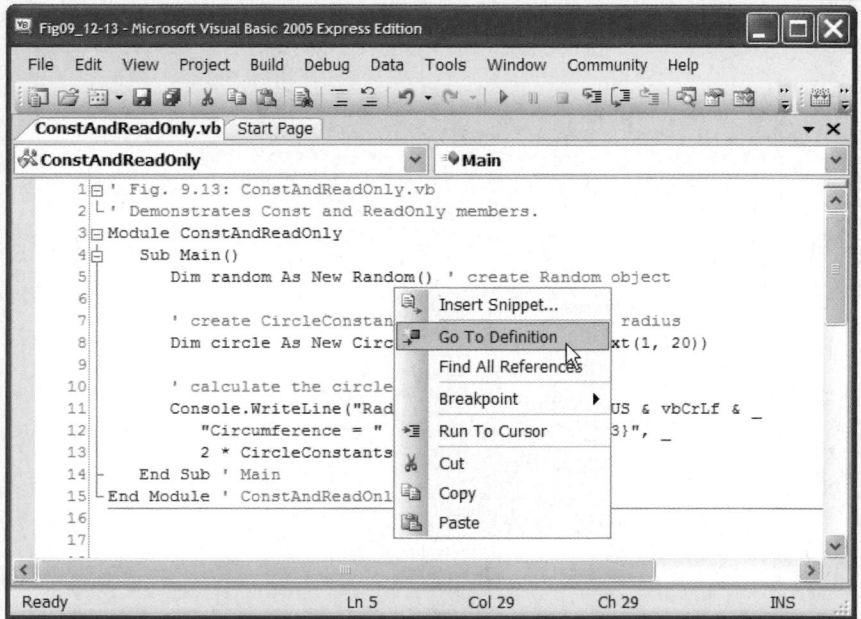

Fig. 9.14 | Invoking the **Object Browser** by right clicking class Random and selecting **Go To Definition**.

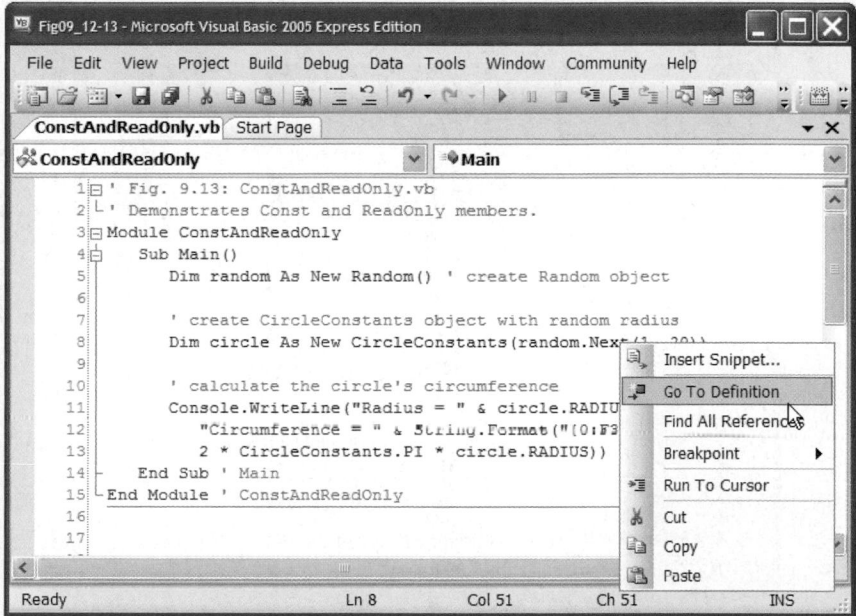

Fig. 9.15 | Invoking the **Object Browser** by right clicking method Next and selecting **Go To Definition**.

Classes available to the application are listed here   Non-**Private** members of the selected class are listed here   Details of a particular member are listed here (or a summary of the class if a specific member is not selected)

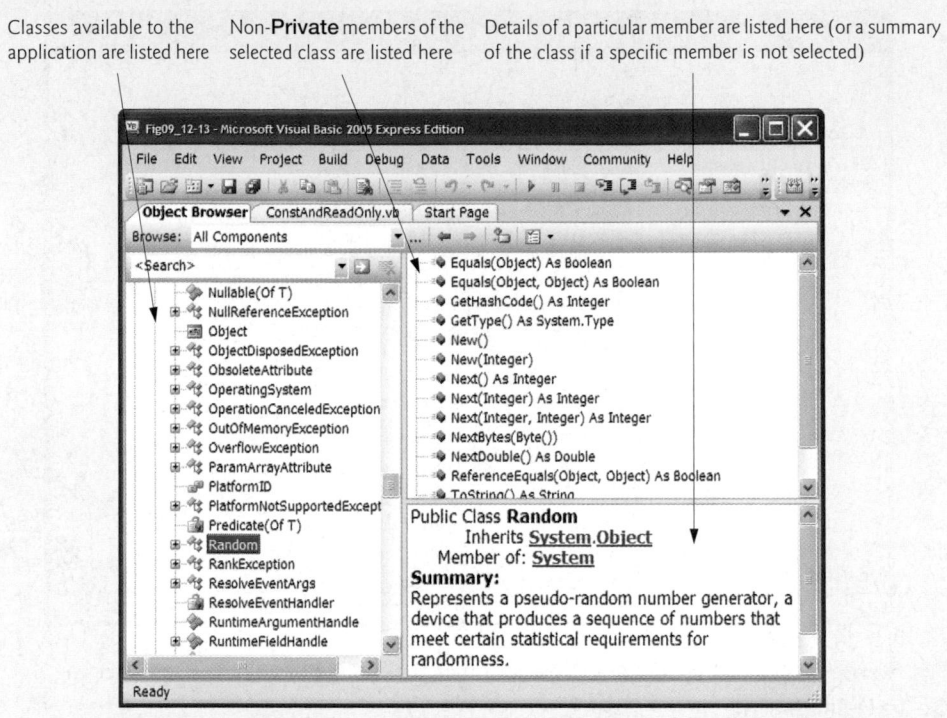

Fig. 9.16 | **Object Browser** when user selects class Random from the code editor.

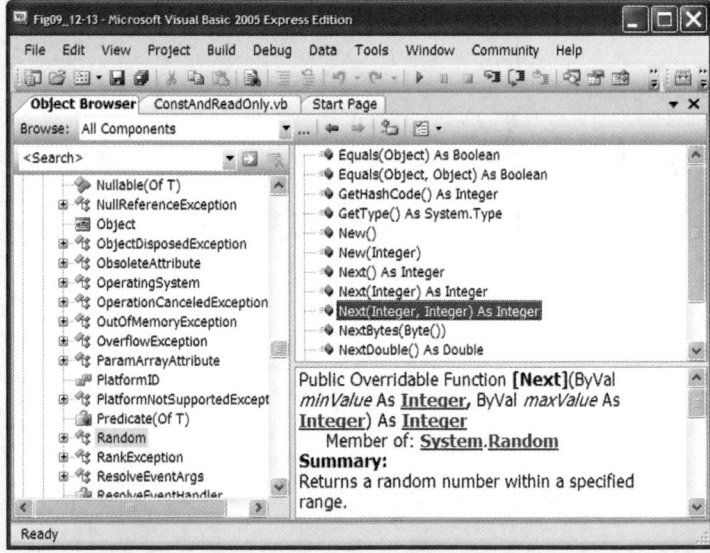

Fig. 9.17 | **Object Browser** when user selects class Random's Next method from the code editor.

9.13 Time Class Case Study: Creating Class Libraries

We have seen that classes from preexisting libraries, such as .NET's Framework Class Library (FCL), can be imported into Visual Basic applications. Each class in the FCL belongs to a namespace that contains a group of related classes. Class libraries and namespaces facilitate software reuse by enabling applications to add classes from other namespaces (as we have done in most examples). This section demonstrates how to create your own class libraries for reuse.

Making a Class Reusable

Before a class can be imported into multiple applications, it must be placed in an assembly to make it reusable. The steps for creating an assembly are as follows:

1. Create a **Class Library** project.

2. Add the reusable class(es) to the project. [*Note:* You can also create reusable classes from scratch.]

3. Ensure that each reusable class is declared `Public`—only `Public` classes can be imported for use in other projects; non-`Public` classes are typically placed in a library to support the `Public` reusable classes in that library.

4. Compile the project to create the assembly that contains the reusable class(es).

5. In an application that requires the class library, add a reference to the class library. Then specify an `Imports` statement for the class library and use its class(es) in your application.

Next, we present the five steps in detail.

Step 1: Creating a Class Library Project

In this example, we'd like to place class `Time` of Fig. 9.1 into a class library to make it a reusable class. To create a class library in Visual Basic 2005 Express, select **File > New Project...** and choose **Class Library** from the list of templates, as shown in Fig. 9.18. Name your project `TimeLibrary`, then click **OK**.

When you create a **Class Library** project, Visual Basic automatically includes the file `Class1.vb` in the project. You can modify the `Public` class in this file to create a reusable class. However, we'll be using the file from the `Time` class in Fig. 9.1, so you can select `Class1.vb` in the **Solution Explorer** and press *Delete* to remove it from the project.

Step 2: Adding Class **Time** to the Project

Next, you must add the file that contains class `Time` to the project. Right click **TimeLibrary** in the **Solution Explorer**. In the menu that appears, select **Add > Existing Item...** to display the **Add Existing Item** dialog box. Locate the `Time.vb` file from Fig. 9.1, select it and click the **Add** button to add the file to this **Class Library** project. [*Note:* We assume that you downloaded the book's examples and placed them on your `C:\` drive. If so, the file is located in the directory `C:\examples\ch09\Fig09_01-02\TimeTest\`.]

Step 3: Adding Class **Time** to the Project

Recall that only `Public` classes can be imported for use in other projects. Thus, you must add the `Public` access modifier to class `Time` to make it reusable. The new version of class `Time` is shown in Fig. 9.19. Notice that line 3 now contains `Public`.

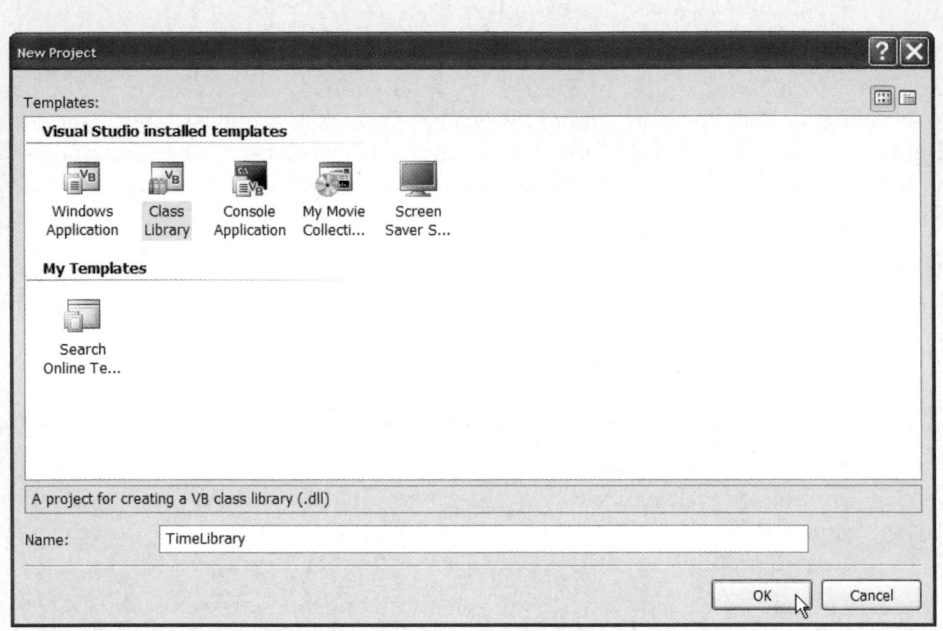

Fig. 9.18 | Creating a **Class Library** Project.

```
 1   ' Fig. 9.19: Time.vb
 2   ' Represents time to clients in 12-hour and 24-hour clock formats.
 3   Public Class Time
 4      Inherits Object ' if not specified, compiler includes it implicitly
 5
 6      ' declare Integer instance variables for the hour, minute and second
 7      Private hourValue As Integer ' 0 - 23
 8      Private minuteValue As Integer ' 0 - 59
 9      Private secondValue As Integer ' 0 - 59
10
11      ' Time constructor initializes instance variables
12      ' when a Time object is created
13      Public Sub New()
14         SetTime(12, 0, 0) ' initialize hour to noon; minute, second to 0
15      End Sub ' New
16
17      ' set a new time value using universal time, check validity of the
18      ' data, set invalid hour to noon, set invalid minute, second to zero
19      Public Sub SetTime(ByVal hh As Integer, _
20         ByVal mm As Integer, ByVal ss As Integer)
21         Hour = hh ' set hourValue using Hour property
22         Minute = mm ' set minuteValue using Minute property
23         Second = ss ' set secondValue using Second property
24      End Sub ' SetTime
25
```

Fig. 9.19 | Creating reusable class `Time`. (Part 1 of 3.)

```
26      ' property Hour
27      Public Property Hour() As Integer
28         Get ' return hourValue
29            Return hourValue
30         End Get
31
32         Set(ByVal value As Integer) ' set hourValue
33            If (value >= 0 AndAlso value < 24) Then ' in range 0-23
34               hourValue = value ' value is valid
35            Else ' value is invalid
36               hourValue = 12 ' set to default of noon
37            End If
38         End Set
39      End Property ' Hour
40
41      ' property Minute
42      Public Property Minute() As Integer
43         Get ' return minuteValue
44            Return minuteValue
45         End Get
46
47         Set(ByVal value As Integer) ' set minuteValue
48            If (value >= 0 AndAlso value < 60) Then ' in range 0-59
49               minuteValue = value ' value is valid
50            Else ' value is invalid
51               minuteValue = 0 ' set to default of 0
52            End If
53         End Set
54      End Property ' Minute
55
56      ' property Second
57      Public Property Second() As Integer
58         Get ' return secondValue
59            Return secondValue
60         End Get
61
62         Set(ByVal value As Integer) ' set secondValue
63            If (value >= 0 AndAlso value < 60) Then ' in range 0-59
64               secondValue = value ' value is valid
65            Else ' value is invalid
66               secondValue = 0 ' set to default of 0
67            End If
68         End Set
69      End Property ' Second
70
71      ' convert Time to a String in universal-time (24-hour clock) format
72      Public Function ToUniversalString() As String
73         Return String.Format("{0}:{1:D2}:{2:D2}", Hour, Minute, Second)
74      End Function ' ToUniversalString
75
76      ' convert Time to a String in standard-time (12-hour clock) format
77      Public Overrides Function ToString() As String
78         Dim suffix As String ' AM or PM suffix
```

Fig. 9.19 | Creating reusable class Time. (Part 2 of 3.)

```
79        Dim standardHour As Integer ' a standard hour in the range 1-12
80
81        ' determine whether the 12-hour clock suffix should be AM or PM
82        If Hour < 12 Then
83           suffix = "AM" ' note space preceding AM
84        Else
85           suffix = "PM" ' note space preceding PM
86        End If
87
88        ' convert hour from universal-time format to standard-time format
89        If (Hour = 12 OrElse Hour = 0) Then
90           standardHour = 12
91        Else
92           standardHour = Hour Mod 12 ' 1 through 11, AM or PM
93        End If
94
95        Return String.Format("{0}:{1:D2}:{2:D2} {3}", _
96           standardHour, Minute, Second, suffix)
97     End Function ' ToString
98  End Class ' Time
```

Fig. 9.19 | Creating reusable class `Time`. (Part 3 of 3.)

Step 4: Building the `TimeLibrary`

To create the assembly containing the reusable class, select **Build > Build TimeLibrary**. When you build a **Class Library** project, the compiler creates a `.dll` file, known as a dynamic link library—a type of assembly that you can reference from other applications. This assembly is located in the project's `bin\Release` directory. By default, the name of the file is the class library's name followed by the `.dll` extension—`TimeLibrary.dll` in this example. The assembly file contains the reusable class `Time`, which can now be imported into other projects. Save your project and remember where you saved it on your system, so you can locate the `TimeLibrary.dll` file in the next step. Note that class libraries are not executable, so if you attempt to execute the class library by selecting **Debug > Start**, you'll receive an error message.

Step 5: Create an Application, Add a Reference to the Class Library's Assembly and Import the Library's Namespace

Once the class is compiled and stored in an assembly, it can be imported into a program for reuse. Module `TimeLibraryTest` (Fig. 9.20) uses class `Time` from the assembly `TimeLibrary.dll` to create a `Time` object, set its time and display the time.

```
1  ' Fig. 9.20: TimeLibraryTest.vb
2  ' Demonstrating class Time in TimeLibrary.
3  Imports TimeLibrary ' import namespace TimeLibrary
4
5  Module TimeLibraryTest
6     Sub Main()
7        Dim time As New Time() ' call Time constructor
```

Fig. 9.20 | Module `TimeLibraryTest` references `TimeLibrary.dll`. (Part 1 of 2.)

```
 8
 9          Console.WriteLine("The initial universal time is: " & _
10              time.ToUniversalString() & vbCrLf & _
11              "The initial standard time is: " & time.ToString())
12
13          time.SetTime(13, 27, 6) ' set time with valid settings
14          Console.WriteLine(vbCrLf & "Universal time after setTime is: " & _
15              time.ToUniversalString() & vbCrLf & _
16              "Standard time after setTime is: " & time.ToString())
17
18          time.SetTime(99, 99, 99) ' set time with invalid settings
19          Console.WriteLine(vbCrLf & _
20              "After attempting invalid settings: " & vbCrLf & _
21              "Universal time: " & time.ToUniversalString() & _
22              vbCrLf & "Standard time: " & time.ToString())
23      End Sub ' Main
24   End Module ' TimeLibraryTest
```

```
The initial universal time is: 12:00:00
The initial standard time is: 12:00:00 PM

Universal time after setTime is: 13:27:06
Standard time after setTime is: 1:27:06 PM

After attempting invalid settings:
Universal time: 12:00:00
Standard time: 12:00:00 PM
```

Fig. 9.20 | Module `TimeLibraryTest` references `TimeLibrary.dll`. (Part 2 of 2.)

When you create a **Class Library** project, the classes in that library are automatically placed in a namespace that has the same name as the library itself. Thus, class `Time` is located in namespace `TimeLibrary`—part of the assembly `TimeLibrary.dll`. Before you can use the classes in the namespace `TimeLibrary`, you must reference its assembly. Select **Project > Add Reference....** The **Add Reference** dialog that appears contains a list of class libraries from the .NET Framework. Some class libraries, like the one containing the `System` namespace, are so common that they are added to your application implicitly. Additional libraries can be selected from this dialog. In the dialog, click the **Browse** tab, then locate and select the `TimeLibrary.dll` file (located in the `bin\Release` directory of the `TimeLibrary` project we created in *Steps 1–4*) as shown in Fig. 9.21. Click **OK** to add the reference to the project.

After adding the reference, you can use keyword `Imports` followed by the namespace name `TimeLibrary` (line 3) to inform the compiler that you are using classes from this namespace. Module `TimeLibraryTest` and class `Time` are in different namespaces, so the `Imports` statement at line 3 allows module `TimeLibraryTest` to use class `Time`.

The `Imports` statement at line 3 is not required if you refer to class `Time` with its fully qualified name—`TimeLibrary.Time`—which includes the namespace name and the class name. For example, line 7 could be written as

```
Dim time As New TimeLibrary.Time()
```

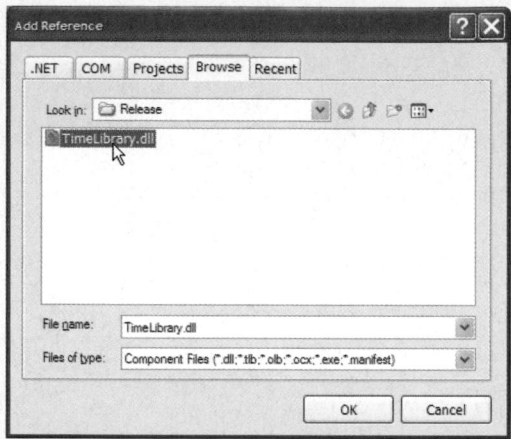

Fig. 9.21 | Adding a Reference.

You can use this fully qualified name in your programs, or you can import the class and use its simple name (the unqualified class name—Time). If another namespace also contains a Time class, fully qualified class names can be used to distinguish between the two Time classes and prevent a name conflict (also called a name collision).

9.14 (Optional) Software Engineering Case Study: Starting to Program the Classes of the ATM System

In the Software Engineering Case Study sections in Chapters 1 and 3–8, we introduced the fundamentals of object orientation and developed an object-oriented design for our ATM system. In Chapters 4–8, we introduced object-oriented programming in Visual Basic. In Chapter 9, we took a deeper look at the details of programming with classes. We now begin implementing our object-oriented design by converting class diagrams to Visual Basic code. In the final Software Engineering Case Study section (Section 11.8), we modify the code to incorporate the object-oriented concepts of inheritance and polymorphism. We present the full Visual Basic code implementation in Appendix J.

Visibility

We now apply access modifiers to the members of our classes. In Chapter 9, we introduced access modifiers Public and Private. Access modifiers determine the visibility or accessibility of an object's attributes and operations to other objects. Before we can begin implementing our design, we must consider which attributes and methods of our classes should be Public and which should be Private.

In Chapter 9, we observed that attributes normally should be Private and that methods invoked by clients of a class should be Public. Methods that are called only by other methods of the class as "utility functions," however, should be Private. The UML employs visibility markers for modeling the visibility of attributes and operations. Public visibility is indicated by placing a plus sign (+) before an operation or an attribute; a minus sign (–) indicates private visibility. Figure 9.22 shows our updated class diagram with visibility markers included. [*Note:* We do not include any operation parameters in Fig. 9.22.

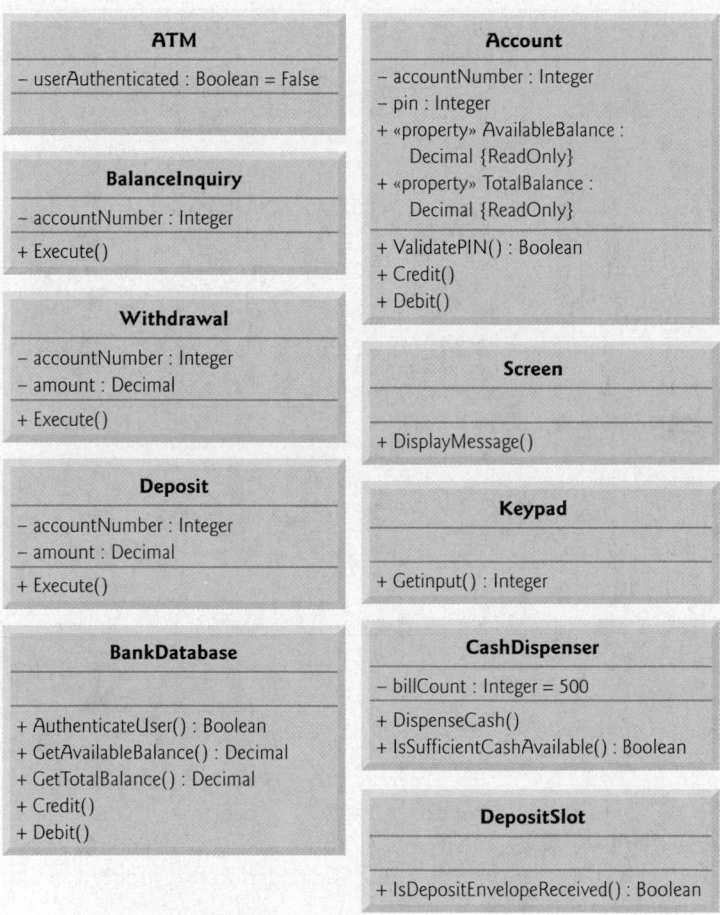

Fig. 9.22 | Class diagram with visibility markers.

This is perfectly normal. Adding visibility markers does not affect the parameters already modeled in the class diagrams of Figs. 7.25–7.28.]

Navigability

Before we begin implementing our design in Visual Basic, we introduce an additional UML notation. The class diagram in Fig. 9.23 further refines the relationships among classes in the ATM system by adding navigability arrows to the association lines. Navigability arrows (represented as arrows with stick arrowheads in the class diagram) indicate in which direction an association can be traversed and are based on the collaborations modeled in communication and sequence diagrams (see Section 8.17). When implementing a system designed using the UML, you use navigability arrows to help determine which objects need references to other objects. For example, the navigability arrow pointing from class ATM to class BankDatabase indicates that we can navigate from the former to the latter, thereby enabling the ATM to invoke the BankDatabase's operations. However, since Fig. 9.23 does not contain a navigability arrow pointing from class BankDatabase to

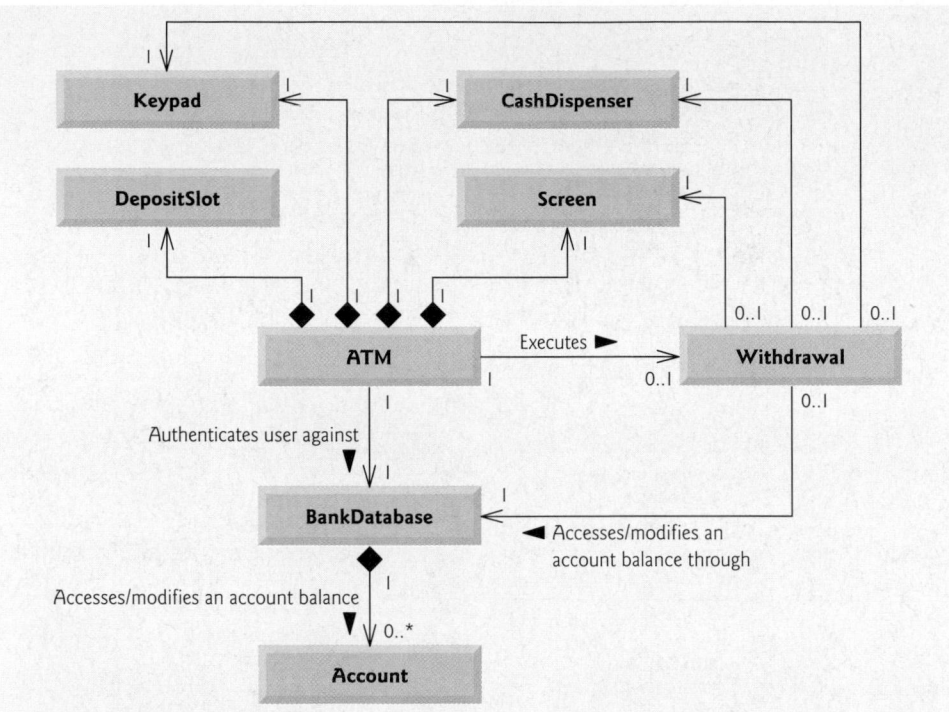

Fig. 9.23 | Class diagram with navigability arrows.

class ATM, the BankDatabase cannot access the ATM's operations. Note that associations in a class diagram that have navigability arrows at both ends or do not have navigability arrows at all indicate **bidirectional navigability**—navigation can proceed in either direction across the association.

Like the class diagram of Fig. 4.22, the one in Fig. 9.23 omits classes BalanceInquiry and Deposit to keep the diagram simple. The navigability of the associations in which these classes participate closely parallels the navigability of class Withdrawal's associations. Recall from Section 4.9 that BalanceInquiry has an association with class Screen. We can navigate from class BalanceInquiry to class Screen along this association, but we cannot navigate from class Screen to class BalanceInquiry. Thus, if we were to model class BalanceInquiry in Fig. 9.23, we would place a navigability arrow at class Screen's end of this association. Also recall that class Deposit associates with classes Screen, Keypad and DepositSlot. We can navigate from class Deposit to each of these classes, but not vice versa. We therefore would place navigability arrows at the Screen, Keypad and DepositSlot ends of these associations. [*Note:* We model these additional classes and associations in our final class diagram in Section 11.8, after we have simplified the structure of our system by incorporating the object-oriented concept of inheritance.]

Implementing the ATM System from Its UML Design
We are now ready to begin implementing the ATM system. We first convert the classes in the diagrams of Fig. 9.22 and Fig. 9.23 into Visual Basic code. This code will represent

the "skeleton" of the system. In Chapter 11, we modify the code to incorporate the object-oriented concept of inheritance. In Appendix J, ATM Case Study Code, we present the complete working Visual Basic code that implements our object-oriented design.

As an example, we begin to develop the code for class Withdrawal from our design of class Withdrawal in Fig. 9.22. We use this figure to determine the attributes and operations of the class. We use the UML model in Fig. 9.23 to determine the associations among classes. We follow the following four guidelines for each class:

1. Use the name located in the first compartment of a class in a class diagram to declare the class as a Public class with an empty parameterless constructor. We include this constructor simply as a placeholder to remind us that most classes will need one or more constructors. In Appendix J, when we complete a working version of this class, we add any necessary arguments and code to the body of the constructor. Class Withdrawal initially yields the code in Fig. 9.24. [*Note:* If we find that the class's instance variables require only default initialization, we will remove the empty parameterless constructor because it is unnecessary.]

2. Use the attributes located in the class's second compartment to declare the instance variables. The Private attributes accountNumber and amount of class Withdrawal yield the code in Fig. 9.25.

3. Use the associations described in the class diagram to declare references (or pointers, where appropriate) to other objects. According to Fig. 9.23, Withdrawal can access one object of class Screen, one object of class Keypad, one object of class CashDispenser and one object of class BankDatabase. Class Withdrawal must

```vb
1   ' Class Withdrawal represents an ATM withdrawal transaction
2   Public Class Withdrawal
3      ' parameterless constructor
4      Public Sub New()
5         ' constructor body code
6      End Sub ' New
7   End Class ' Withdrawal
```

Fig. 9.24 | Initial Visual Basic code for class Withdrawal based on Figs. 9.22 and 9.23.

```vb
1    ' Class Withdrawal represents an ATM withdrawal transaction
2    Public Class Withdrawal
3       ' attributes
4       Private accountNumber As Integer ' account to withdraw funds from
5       Private amount As Decimal ' amount to withdraw from account
6
7       ' parameterless constructor
8       Public Sub New()
9          ' constructor body code
10      End Sub ' New
11   End Class ' Withdrawal
```

Fig. 9.25 | Visual Basic code incorporating Private variables for class Withdrawal based on Figs. 9.22 and 9.23.

maintain references to these objects for sending messages to them, so lines 8–11 of Fig. 9.26 declare four references as Private instance variables. In the implementation of class Withdrawal in Appendix J, a constructor initializes these instance variables with references to the actual objects.

4. Use the operations located in the third compartment of Fig. 9.22 to declare the shells of the methods. If we have not yet specified a return type for an operation, we declare the method with keyword Sub. Refer to the class diagrams of Figs. 7.25–7.28 to declare any necessary parameters. Adding the Public operation Execute (which has an empty parameter list) in class Withdrawal yields the code in line 19 of Fig. 9.27. [*Note:* We code the bodies of methods when we implement the complete ATM system in Appendix J.]

```
 1    ' Class Withdrawal represents an ATM withdrawal transaction
 2    Public Class Withdrawal
 3       ' attributes
 4       Private accountNumber As Integer ' account to withdraw funds from
 5       Private amount As Decimal ' amount to withdraw
 6
 7       ' references to associated objects
 8       Private screenHandle As Screen ' ATM's screen
 9       Private keypadHandle As Keypad ' ATM's keypad
10       Private cashDispenserHandle As CashDispenser ' ATM's cash dispenser
11       Private bankDatabaseHandle As BankDatabase ' account info database
12
13       ' parameterless constructor
14       Public Sub New()
15          ' constructor body code
16       End Sub ' New
17    End Class ' Withdrawal
```

Fig. 9.26 | Visual Basic code incorporating Private reference handles for the associations of class Withdrawal based on Figs. 9.22 and 9.23.

```
 1    ' Class Withdrawal represents an ATM withdrawal transaction
 2    Public Class Withdrawal
 3       ' attributes
 4       Private accountNumber As Integer ' account to withdraw funds from
 5       Private amount As Decimal ' amount to withdraw
 6
 7       ' references to associated objects
 8       Private screenHandle As Screen ' ATM's screen
 9       Private keypadHandle As Keypad ' ATM's keypad
10       Private cashDispenserHandle As CashDispenser ' ATM's cash dispenser
11       Private bankDatabaseHandle As BankDatabase ' account info database
12
```

Fig. 9.27 | Visual Basic code incorporating method Execute in class Withdrawal based on Figs. 9.22 and 9.23. (Part 1 of 2.)

```
13        ' parameterless constructor
14        Public Sub New()
15            ' constructor body code
16        End Sub ' New
17
18        ' operations
19        Public Sub Execute()
20            ' Execute method body code
21        End Sub ' Execute
22    End Class ' Withdrawal
```

Fig. 9.27 | Visual Basic code incorporating method `Execute` in class `Withdrawal` based on Figs. 9.22 and 9.23. (Part 2 of 2.)

Software Engineering Observation 9.7

Many UML modeling tools can convert UML-based designs into Visual Basic code, considerably speeding the implementation process. For more information on these "automatic" code generators, refer to the Web resources listed at the end of Section 3.10.

This concludes our discussion of the basics of generating class files from UML diagrams. In the final Software Engineering Case Study section (Section 11.8), we demonstrate how to modify the code in Fig. 9.27 to incorporate the object-oriented concepts of inheritance and polymorphism in Chapter 11.

Software Engineering Case Study Self-Review Exercises

9.1 State whether the following statement is *true* or *false*, and if *false*, explain why: If an attribute of a class is marked with a minus sign (-) in a class diagram, the attribute is not directly accessible outside of the class.

9.2 In Fig. 9.23, the association between the `ATM` and the `Screen` indicates that:
a) we can navigate from the `Screen` to the `ATM`
b) we can navigate from the `ATM` to the `Screen`
c) Both a and b; the association is bidirectional
d) None of the above

9.3 Write Visual Basic code to begin implementing the design for class `Account`.

Answers to Software Engineering Case Study Self-Review Exercises

9.1 True. The minus sign (-) indicates private visibility. We've mentioned "friendship" as an exception to private visibility. Friendship is discussed in Chapter 10.

9.2 b.

9.3 The design for class `Account` yields the code in Fig. 9.28. Note that we include `Private` instance variables `availableBalance` and `totalBalance` to store the data that properties `AvailableBalance` and `TotalBalance`, and methods `Credit` and `Debit` will manipulate.

9.15 Wrap-Up

This chapter investigated the object-oriented programming concepts of classes, objects, methods and instance variables in more depth. The `Time` class case study presented a complete class declaration consisting of `Private` data, overloaded constructors for initializa-

```vbnet
1    ' Represents a bank account.
2    Public Class Account
3       Private accountNumber As Integer ' account number
4       Private pin As Integer ' PIN for authentication
5       Private availableBalance As Decimal ' available withdrawal amount
6       Private totalBalance As Decimal ' funds available + pending deposit
7
8       ' parameterless constructor
9       Public Sub New()
10          ' constructor body code
11      End Sub ' New
12
13      ' validates user PIN
14      Public Function ValidatePIN() As Boolean
15          ' ValidatePIN method body code
16      End Function ' ValidatePIN
17
18      ' property AvailableBalance
19      Public ReadOnly Property AvailableBalance() As Decimal
20          ' AvailableBalance property body code
21      End Property ' AvailableBalance
22
23      ' property TotalBalance
24      Public ReadOnly Property TotalBalance() As Decimal
25          ' TotalBalance property body code
26      End Property ' TotalBalance
27
28      ' credits the account
29      Public Sub Credit()
30          ' Credit method body code
31      End Sub ' Credit
32
33      ' debits the account
34      Public Sub Debit()
35          ' Debit method body code
36      End Sub ' Debit
37   End Class ' Account
```

Fig. 9.28 | Visual Basic code for class Account based on Figs. 9.22 and 9.23.

tion flexibility, properties with Set and Get accessors for manipulating the class's data, and methods that returned String representations of a Time object in two different formats.

We showed how the Me reference is used implicitly in a class's non-Shared methods to access the class's instance variables and non-Shared methods. We also showed how to use the Me reference explicitly to access the class's shadowed instance variables explicitly.

You learned that a class can have references to objects of other classes as members—a concept known as composition. We discussed how garbage collection reclaims the memory of objects that are no longer needed. You learned how to execute the garbage collector to invoke the method Finalize on each object before it is removed from memory. We explained the motivation for Shared instance variables in a class, and demonstrated how to declare and use Shared variables and methods in your own classes. You learned how to declare and initialize Const and ReadOnly variables. We showed how to use the

Object Browser to learn the functionality provided by the classes of the Framework Class Library. We also showed how to create a class library for reuse and how to use the classes of the library in an application.

In the next chapter, we continue our discussion of classes by introducing a form of software reuse called inheritance. We will see that classes often share common attributes and behaviors. In such cases, it is possible to define those attributes and behaviors in a common "base" class and "inherit" those capabilities into new class declarations.

Summary

Section 9.1 Introduction
- Composition allows a class to have references to objects of other classes as members.

Section 9.2 *Time Class Case Study*
- Programmers use inheritance to create new classes from existing classes. The Inherits keyword followed by class name Object indicates that a class inherits existing pieces of class Object (of namespace System). Every class (except Object) inherits from Object implicitly if explicit inheritance from Object is not indicated.

- Keywords Class and End Class delimit the body of a class declaration. Any information placed in this body is part of the class's scope.

- Constructors are implemented as Sub procedures, not as Functions, because constructors cannot return values. Generally, constructors are Public.

- If you do not specify a namespace for a class or module, it is placed in the default namespace, which includes the compiled classes and modules in the current directory.

- When a class or module uses another class or module in the same namespace, an Imports statement is not required.

- You must import the classes from the .NET Framework because your classes and modules are in difference namespaces from those in the .NET Framework.

- Any method of a class can access all the instance variables of the class and can call every method of the class. This reduces the number of arguments needed in a method call, making method calls more concise than conventional function calls in procedural programming. It also reduces the likelihood of passing the wrong arguments, the wrong types of arguments or the wrong number of arguments.

- Classes simplify programming, because the clients need be concerned only with the Public operations encapsulated in the object. Usually, such operations are designed to be client-oriented.

- Clients are neither aware of, nor involved in, a class's implementation. Interfaces change less frequently than implementations. When an implementation changes, implementation-dependent code must change accordingly. By hiding the implementation, we eliminate the possibility that other parts of the program will become dependent on the class implementation details.

Section 9.3 Class Scope
- A class's instance variables and methods belong to that class's scope. Within a class's scope, class members are accessible to all of the class's methods and can be referenced by name.

- Outside a class's scope, class members cannot be referenced directly by name. Public class members can be accessed through a "handle," such as a reference to an object of the class (or also through the class name if the member is Shared).

- If a variable is defined in a method, the variable is a local variable to that method and can be used only in the method's body. Such variables are said to have block scope.

- If a method defines a local variable that has the same name as an instance variable, the local variable hides the instance variable in the method's scope—this is called shadowing.

- A shadowed instance variable can be accessed in a method of that class by preceding its name with the keyword Me and the dot separator.

Section 9.4 Default and Parameterless Constructors

- Overloaded constructors provide multiple ways to initialize objects of a class.

- If a class does not define constructors, the compiler provides a default constructor for the class. This constructor contains no code and takes no parameters.

- You can define a parameterless constructor for a class that is similar to a default constructor except that it is defined by you and would typically contain statements in its body.

Section 9.5 Time Class Case Study: Overloaded Constructors

- Like methods, constructors of a class can be overloaded.

- The compiler invokes the appropriate overloaded constructor by matching the number, types and order of the arguments specified in the constructor call with the number, types and order of the parameters specified in the various constructor declarations.

- A copy constructor initializes an object by copying values from another object of the same class.

Section 9.6 Partial Classes

- Visual Basic allows a class declaration to span multiple source-code files. The separate portions of the class declaration in each file are known as partial classes. At least one partial class declaration for a given class must be marked with the Partial modifier.

- When a class declaration specifies the Partial modifier, any class declarations with the same class name in the program are combined at compile time to form a single class declaration.

- Partial classes must be declared in the same namespace and assembly.

- If class members in one partial class source file conflict with those in other source files for the same class, compilation errors will occur.

- Partial classes provide a convenient way to split a class into small, manageable pieces that enable several developers to work on the same class at once.

Section 9.7 Composition

- A class can have references to objects of other classes as members. Such a capability is called composition and is sometimes referred to as a *has-a* relationship.

Section 9.8 Using the Me Reference to Access the Current Object

- Every object of a class shares the class's method declarations.

- Every object has access to itself through a reference called Me. The compiler passes an object's Me reference as an implicit argument to each of the object's non-Shared methods. The Me reference can then be used to access a particular object's members implicitly or explicitly.

- When a method has a parameter or local variable with the same name as one of the class's instance variables, the instance variable is hidden in that method's scope. However, the method can use the Me reference to refer to hidden instance variables explicitly.

Section 9.9 Garbage Collection

- The Common Language Runtime (CLR) performs automatic garbage collection to reclaim the memory occupied by objects that are no longer in use. When there are no more references to an object, it is marked for garbage collection by the CLR. The memory for such an object can be reclaimed when the runtime executes its garbage collector, which is responsible for retrieving the memory of objects that are no longer being used, so that the memory can be used for other objects.

- Managed resources like memory are allocated and reclaimed by the CLR.

- Resources like files, network connections and database connections that the programmer must manage are known as unmanaged resources.

- To help prevent resource leaks for unmanaged resources, the garbage collector calls a special method named Finalize on each object before it is removed from memory.

- The Finalize method is called by the garbage collector to perform termination housekeeping on an object (such as releasing unmanaged resources used by the object) just before the garbage collector reclaims the object's memory.

- Method Finalize is not ideal for releasing unmanaged resources because the garbage collector is unpredictable—it is not guaranteed to execute at a specified time. In fact, the garbage collector may never execute before a program terminates.

- The FCL provides interface IDisposable, which contains a method named Dispose that a client can invoke to immediately release the resources used by an object.

Section 9.10 *Shared Class Members*

- A program contains only one copy of a Shared class variable in memory, no matter how many objects of the class have been instantiated. A Shared class variable represents class-wide information—all class objects share the same piece of data.

- The declaration of a Shared member begins with the keyword Shared.

- Shared class members are accessible in all methods of a class, both Shared and non-Shared.

- A class's Public Shared members can be accessed by clients through the class name using the dot separator.

- A class's Private Shared members can be accessed by clients only through non-Private methods of the class.

- Shared class members are available as soon as the class is loaded into memory at execution time and exist for the duration of program execution, even when no objects of the class exist.

- To allow clients to access a Private Shared class member when no objects of the class exist, you must provide a non-Private Shared method or property.

- A Shared method cannot access non-Shared class members. Unlike non-Shared methods, a Shared method has no Me reference, because Shared variables and Shared methods exist independently of any class objects and even when there are no objects of that class.

- Normally, the garbage collector is not invoked directly by the user. Either the garbage collector reclaims the memory for objects when it deems garbage collection is appropriate, or the operating system recovers the unneeded memory when the program terminates. Public Shared method Collect from class GC of namespace System requests that the garbage collector execute.

- When Shared variables require more complex initialization than can be accomplished in a Shared variable declaration, you can create a Shared constructor to initialize those variables.

- A Shared constructor is declared like an instance constructor, but is preceded by the Shared modifier and can be used only to initialize Shared variables.

- A Shared constructor is implicitly Public, must be declared with no parameters, cannot call other constructors and is guaranteed to execute before a program creates any objects of the class. Explicitly declaring a Shared constructor Public is a compilation error.

Section 9.11 *Const and ReadOnly Members*

- To create a constant instance variable in a class, declare that member as either Const or ReadOnly.

- An instance variable declared as Const must be initialized in its declaration.

- An instance variable declared as ReadOnly can be initialized either in its declaration or in the class constructor.

- Const values must be initialized at compile time, but ReadOnly values are not initialized until runtime. Neither a Const nor a ReadOnly value can be modified once initialized.

- Const members must be initialized at compile time and therefore they can be initialized only to other constant values, such as integers, string literals, characters and other Const members.

- Constant members with values that cannot be determined at compile time must be declared with the keyword ReadOnly.

- A Shared constructor can be used to initialize Shared ReadOnly members, and a non-Shared (instance) constructor can be used to initialize non-Shared ReadOnly members.

- A property with only a Get accessor is called a read-only property and must be declared using keyword ReadOnly. A property with only a Set accessor is called a write-only property and must be declared using keyword WriteOnly.

Section 9.12 *Object Browser*

- The **Object Browser** lists all the libraries that are available to the application, including the Framework Class Library (FCL) classes and programmer-defined classes.

- Developers use the **Object Browser** to learn about the functionality provided by specific classes.

- To open the **Object Browser**, right click any Visual Basic class or method in the code editor and select **Go To Definition**.

Section 9.13 *Time Class Case Study: Creating Class Libraries*

- Class libraries and namespaces facilitate software reuse by enabling applications to add classes from other namespaces.

- Before a class can be used in multiple applications, it must be declared Public and placed in a class library to make it reusable.

- When you compile a class library project, the compiler will create a .dll file, known as a dynamic link library—a type of assembly that you can reference from other applications.

Terminology

assembly
body of class declaration
class library
class scope
"class-wide" information
Collect method of System.GC
composition
Const keyword
constructor overloading
copy constructor

default namespace
.dll file
dynamic link library
explicit use of Me reference
Finalize method
garbage collection
garbage collector
GC namespace of System
has-a relationship
helper method

hide an instance variable	ReadOnly keyword
implementation-dependent code	reclaim memory
implementation hiding	reference to a new object
inheritance relationship	resource leak
initialize Shared class variables	reusable component
initializer	service of a class
managed resource	shadowing a variable
Me reference	Shared class variable
memory leak	Shared constructor
non-Public method	Shared keyword
Object Browser	Shared method
Object class	software reuse
overloaded constructor	termination housekeeping
Overrides keyword	ToString method
parameterless constructor	unmanaged resource
partial class	utility method
Partial modifier	validity checking
Private Shared member	write-only property
Public Shared member	WriteOnly keyword
read-only property	

Self-Review Exercises

9.1   Fill in the blanks in each of the following:
   a) A(n) _____ variable represents class-wide information.
   b) _____ allow a class declaration to span multiple source-code files.
   c) The keyword _____ specifies that an object or variable is not modifiable after it is initialized at runtime.
   d) A method declared Shared cannot access _____ class members.

9.2   State whether each of the following is *true* or *false*. If *false* explain why.
   a) Every class in Visual Basic inherits either directly or indirectly from class Object, which is the root of the class hierarchy.
   b) The Me reference of an object is a reference to that object.
   c) Setting objects to Nothing in a specific order guarantees that those objects are finalized in that order.
   d) A Shared member of a class can be referenced when no object of that type exists.
   e) A Shared member of a class can be referenced through an instance of the class.
   f) ReadOnly variables must be initialized either in a declaration or in the class constructor.

Answers to Self-Review Exercises

9.1   a) Shared. b) Partial classes. c) ReadOnly. d) non-Shared.

9.2   a) True. b) True. c) False. The garbage collector does not guarantee that resources are reclaimed in a specific order or even that they will be reclaimed before the program terminates. d) True. e) True. f) True.

Exercises

9.3   *(Enhancing Class* Day*)* Modify the Day class of Fig. 9.5 to provide validations of the initial values for instance variables monthValue, dayValue and yearValue. For the purposes of this exercise, ensure that the year is between 1900 and 2100. Also provide a method NextDay to increment the day by 1. The Day object should always remain in a consistent state. Write a console application that tests the NextDay method and illustrates that it works correctly. Be sure to test the following cases:

a) Incrementing into the next month.

b) Incrementing into the next year.

9.4 *(Savings Account Class)* Create class SavingsAccount. Use a Shared class variable to store the annualInterestRate for all account holders. Each object of the class contains a Private instance variable savingsBalance indicating the amount the saver currently has on deposit. Provide the CalculateMonthlyInterest method to calculate the monthly interest by multiplying the savingsBalance by the annualInterestRate divided by 12; this interest should be added to savingsBalance and returned to the method caller. Provide a Shared method ModifyInterestRate that sets the annualInterestRate to a new value. Write a console application to test class SavingsAccount. Instantiate two SavingsAccount objects, saver1 and saver2, with balances of $2000.00 and $3000.00, respectively. Set annualInterestRate to 4%, then calculate the monthly interest and print the amounts of interest earned and the new balances for each of the savers. Then set the annualInterestRate to 5% and calculate the next month's interest and print the amounts of interest earned and the new balances for each of the savers.

9.5 *(Date Format Class)* Create a DateFormat class with the following capabilities:

a) Output the date in multiple formats such as

```
MM/DD/YYYY
June 14, 2001
DDD YYYY
```

b) Use overloaded constructors to create DateFormat objects initialized with dates of the formats in part a).

9.6 *(Square Class)* Write a class that implements a Square shape. Class Square should contain a Side property for accessing Private data. Provide a constructor that takes a Side length as a value. Also provide the following methods:

a) Perimeter returns 4 × Side.

b) Area returns Side × Side.

c) Diagonal returns the square root of the expression (2 × Side^2).

Test your new Square class in a module.

9.7 *(Tic-Tac-Toe)* Create a class TicTacToe that enables you to write a complete GUI application to play the game of Tic-Tac-Toe. The class contains a 3-by-3 Integer array as Private data. The constructor should initialize the empty board to all zeros. Allow two human players. Wherever the first player moves, display an X in the specified Label; place an O in a Label wherever the second player moves. Each move must be to an empty Label. Players move by clicking one of nine Labels. [*Note:* To create a Click event handler for a Label, you could double click that Label in the **Design** view. This is similar to how you create a Click event handler for a Button.] After each move determine whether the game has been won or if it is a draw via a GameStatus method. [*Hint:* Use constants of an enumeration with the following statuses: WIN, DRAW, CONTINUE.] If you feel ambitious, modify your program so that the computer is the opponent. Also, allow players to specify whether they want to go first or second. [*Note:* If you feel exceptionally ambitious, develop a program that plays three-dimensional Tic-Tac-Toe on a 4-by-4-by-4 board. *Caution:* This is a challenging project that could take weeks of effort!]

9.8 *(Enhancing Class Time)* Modify class Time of Fig. 9.1 to include the Tick method that increments the time stored in a Time object by one second. Also provide method IncrementMinute to increment the minute and method IncrementHour to increment the hour. The Time object should always remain in a consistent state. Write a GUI application that is similar to the output of Fig. 9.2, but with two more buttons—**Add 1 to Minute** and **Add 1 to Hour**. The Tick method, the Increment-

Minute method and the IncrementHour method should be called when you click the **Add 1 to Second** button, the **Add 1 to Minute** button and the **Add 1 to Hour** button, respectively. Be sure to test the following cases:

a) incrementing into the next minute.

b) incrementing into the next hour.

c) incrementing into the next day (i.e., 11:59:59 PM to 12:00:00 AM).

9.9 *(Modifying the Internal Data Representation of a Class)* It would be perfectly reasonable for the Time class of Fig. 9.1 to represent the time internally as the number of seconds since midnight rather than the three integer values hourValue, minuteValue and secondValue. Clients could use the same Public methods and get the same results. Modify the Time class of Fig. 9.1 to implement the Time as the number of seconds since midnight and show that there is no change visible to the clients of the class.

9.10 *(Account Information Application)* A bank wants you to create a GUI application that will allow bank employees to view the clients' information. The application interface should have four Labels and four TextBoxes, which are used to display first name, last name, account number and account balance, respectively. The interface should also have two Buttons, **Previous** and **Next**, which allow the bank manager to search through each client's information backwards and forwards, respectively. The application GUI is shown in Fig. 9.29. Create a Customer class to represent the client with first name, last name, account number and account balance. When the GUI application is loaded, create an array of Customer objects, and display the first client's information to the manager. If the current client is the first in the array, the last client in the array is displayed when the manager clicks the **Previous** button. If the current client is the last in the array, the first client in the array is displayed when the manager clicks the **Next** button.

9.11 *(Microwave Oven Application)* An electronics company is considering building microwave ovens. The company has asked you to develop a GUI application that simulates a microwave oven. The oven will contain a keypad that allows the user to specify the microwave cook time and display it for the user. Once a time is entered, the user clicks the **Start** button to begin the cooking process. The microwave's glass window changes color (from gray to yellow) to simulate the oven's light, which remains on while the food cooks, and a timer counts down one second at a time. Once the time expires, the color of the microwave's glass window returns to gray (indicating that the microwave's light is now off) and the microwave displays the text Done!. The application GUI is shown in Fig. 9.30. The user can click the **Clear** button at any time to stop the microwave and enter a new time. The user should be able to enter a number of hours no greater than 9, a number of minutes no greater than 59 and a number of seconds no greater than 59; otherwise, the invalid cook time

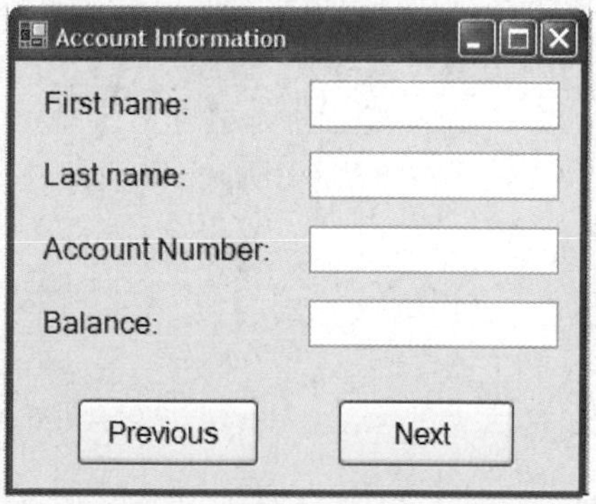

Fig. 9.29 | **Account Information** application GUI.

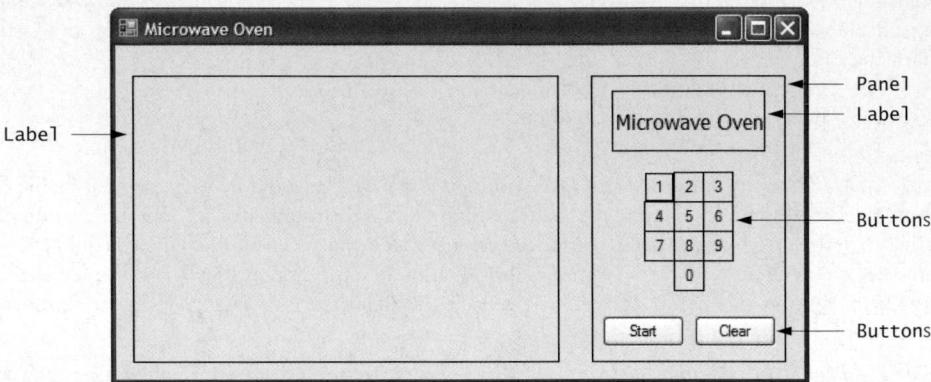

Fig. 9.30 | **Microwave Oven** application GUI.

will be set to zero. A beep will be sounded whenever a button is clicked and when the microwave oven has finished a countdown. [*Hint:* Use a Timer control to implement the timer countdown. To add a Timer, click the Timer control in the **Toolbox**, and drag and drop it anywhere on the Form. Note that the Timer does not actually appear on the Form; it appears below the **Designer View** in an area called the component tray. A Timer generates a Tick event every millisecond (1/1000 of a second). Double click the Timer control in the component tray to generate the empty event handler for the Tick event. A Timer can be started and stopped by setting its Enabled property to True and False, respectively. The statement

```
Beep() ' sound beep
```

causes the computer to make a beep sound.]

10

Object-Oriented Programming: Inheritance

*Say not you know
another entirely,
till you have divided an
inheritance with him.*
—Johann Kasper Lavater

*This method is to define as
the number of a class the
class of all classes similar to
the given class.*
—Bertrand Russell

*Good as it is to inherit
a library, it is better to
collect one.*
—Augustine Birrell

*Save base authority from
others' books.*
—William Shakespeare

OBJECTIVES

In this chapter you will learn:

- What inheritance is and how it promotes software reusability.

- The notions of base classes and derived classes.

- To use keyword **Inherits** to create a class that inherits attributes and behaviors from another class.

- To use the access modifier **Protected** in a base class to give derived class methods access to base class members.

- To access base class members from a derived class with **MyBase**.

- How constructors are used in inheritance hierarchies.

- To access the current object with **Me** and **MyClass**.

- The methods of class **Object**—the direct or indirect base class of all classes in Visual Basic.

10.1 Introduction

This chapter continues our discussion of object-oriented programming (OOP) by introducing one of its primary features, inheritance, a form of software reuse in which a new class is created by absorbing an existing class's members and embellishing them with new or modified capabilities. With inheritance, you can save time during program development by reusing proven and debugged high-quality software. This increases the likelihood that a system will be implemented effectively.

When creating a class, rather than declaring completely new members, you can designate that the new class will inherit the members of an existing class. The existing class is called the base class, and the new class is the derived class. (The Java programming language refers to the base class as the superclass and the derived class as the subclass.) A derived class can become the base class for future derived classes.

A derived class normally adds its own instance variables, Shared variables, properties and methods. Therefore, a derived class is more specific than its base class and represents a more specialized group of objects. Typically, the derived class exhibits the behaviors of its base class and additional behaviors that are specific to the derived class. [*Note:* A class's instance variables and Shared variables are referred to collectively as the class's fields.]

The direct base class is the class from which the derived class explicitly inherits. An indirect base class is inherited from two or more levels up in the class hierarchy. In Visual Basic, the class hierarchy begins with class `Object` (in namespace `System`), which *every* class in Visual Basic directly or indirectly extends (or "inherits from"). Section 10.7 lists the seven methods of class `Object`, which every other class inherits. In the case of single inheritance, a class is derived from one direct base class. Visual Basic, unlike C++, does not support multiple inheritance (which occurs when a class is derived from more than one direct base class). In Chapter 11, Object-Oriented Programming: Polymorphism, we explain how you can use Interfaces to realize many of the benefits of multiple inheritance while avoiding the associated problems.

We distinguish between the *is-a* relationship and the *has-a* relationship. *Is-a* represents inheritance. In an *is-a* relationship, an object of a derived class also can be treated as an object of its base class. For example, a car *is a* vehicle. By contrast, the *has-a* relationship represents composition (see Chapter 9). In a *has-a* relationship, an object contains one or more object references as members. For example, a car *has a* steering wheel (and a car object has a reference to a steering wheel object).

New classes can inherit from classes in class libraries. Organizations develop their own class libraries and can take advantage of others available worldwide. Some day, most new software will probably be constructed from standardized reusable components, just as automobiles and most computer hardware items are constructed today. This will facilitate the development of more powerful, abundant and economical software.

10.2 Base Classes and Derived Classes

Often, an object of one class *is an* object of another class as well. For example, in geometry, a rectangle *is a* quadrilateral (as are squares, parallelograms and trapezoids). Thus, in Visual Basic, class Rectangle can be said to inherit from class Quadrilateral. In this context, class Quadrilateral is a base class and class Rectangle is a derived class. A rectangle *is a* specific type of quadrilateral, but it is incorrect to claim that every quadrilateral *is a* rectangle—the quadrilateral could be a parallelogram or some other shape. Figure 10.1 lists several simple examples of base classes and derived classes—note that base classes tend to be "more general" and derived classes tend to be "more specific."

Every derived class object *is an* object of its base class, and one base class can have many derived classes, so the set of objects represented by a base class is typically larger than the set of objects represented by any of its derived classes. For example, the base class Vehicle represents all vehicles, including cars, trucks, boats, bicycles and so on. By contrast, derived class Car represents a smaller, more specific subset of vehicles.

Inheritance relationships form tree-like hierarchical structures. A base class exists in a hierarchical relationship with its derived classes. When classes participate in inheritance

Base class	Derived classes
Student	GraduateStudent, UndergraduateStudent
Shape	Circle, Triangle, Rectangle
Loan	CarLoan, HomeImprovementLoan, MortgageLoan
Employee	Faculty, Staff
BankAccount	CheckingAccount, SavingsAccount

Fig. 10.1 | Inheritance examples.

relationships, they become "affiliated" with other classes. A class becomes either a base class, supplying members to other classes, or a derived class, inheriting its members from other classes. In some cases, a class is both a base class and a derived class.

CommunityMember *Inheritance Hierarchy*

Let's develop a sample class hierarchy (Fig. 10.2), also called an inheritance hierarchy. A university community has thousands of members, including employees, students and alumni. Employees are either faculty members or staff members. Faculty members are either administrators (such as deans and department chairpersons) or teachers. The hierarchy could contain many other classes. For example, students can be graduate or undergraduate students. Undergraduate students can be freshmen, sophomores, juniors or seniors.

Each arrow in the inheritance hierarchy diagram of Fig. 10.2 represents an *is-a* relationship. As we follow the arrows in this class hierarchy, we can state, for instance, that "an Employee *is a* CommunityMember" and "a Teacher *is a* Faculty member." Community-Member is the direct base class of Employee, Student and Alumnus, and is an indirect base class of all the other classes in the diagram. Starting from the bottom of the diagram, you can follow the arrows and apply the *is-a* relationship up to the topmost base class. For example, an Administrator *is a* Faculty member, *is an* Employee and *is a* Community-Member.

Shape *Inheritance Hierarchy*

Now consider the Shape inheritance hierarchy in Fig. 10.3. This hierarchy begins with base class Shape, which is inherited by derived classes TwoDimensionalShape and Three-DimensionalShape—Shapes are either TwoDimensionalShapes or ThreeDimensional-Shapes. The third level of the hierarchy contains some more specific types of TwoDimensionalShapes and ThreeDimensionalShapes. As in Fig. 10.2, we can follow the arrows from the bottom of the diagram to the topmost base class in this class hierarchy to identify several *is-a* relationships. For example, a Triangle *is a* TwoDimensionalShape and *is a* Shape, while a Sphere *is a* ThreeDimensionalShape and *is a* Shape. Note that this hierarchy could contain many other classes. For example, ellipses and trapezoids also are TwoDimensionalShapes, and cylinders also are ThreeDimensionalShapes.

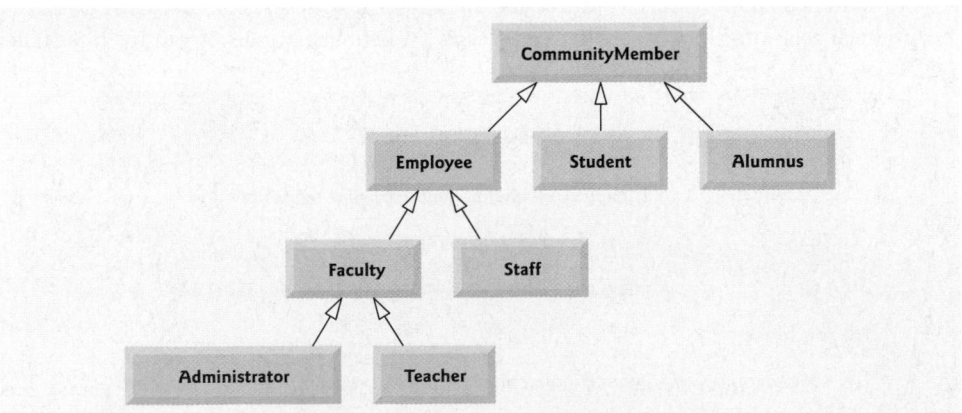

Fig. 10.2 | Inheritance hierarchy for university CommunityMembers.

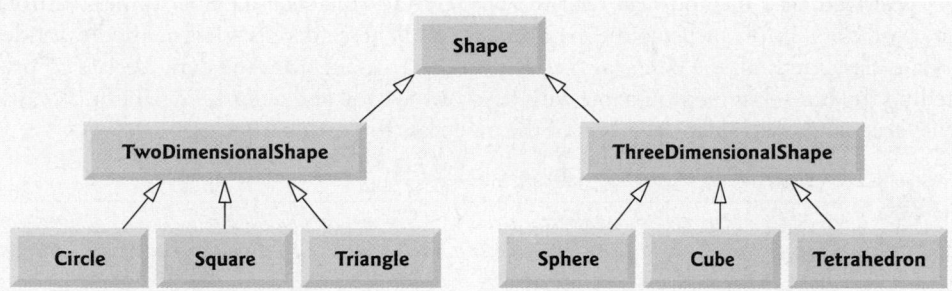

Fig. 10.3 | Inheritance hierarchy for Shapes.

Notes on Inheritance Relationships
Not every class relationship is an inheritance relationship. In Chapter 9, we discussed the *has-a* relationship, in which classes have members that are references to objects of other classes. Such relationships create classes by composition of existing classes. For example, given the classes Employee, BirthDate and TelephoneNumber, it is improper to say that an Employee *is a* BirthDate or that an Employee *is a* TelephoneNumber. However, an Employee *has a* BirthDate, and an Employee *has a* TelephoneNumber.

It is possible to treat base class objects and derived class objects similarly—their commonalities are expressed in the members of the base class. Objects of all classes that inherit a common base class can be treated as objects of that base class (i.e., such objects have an *is-a* relationship with the base class). However, base class objects cannot be treated as objects of their derived classes. For example, all cars are vehicles, but not all vehicles are cars (the other vehicles could be trucks, planes or bicycles, for example). Later in this chapter and in Chapter 11, we consider many examples that use the *is-a* relationship.

One problem with inheritance is that a derived class can inherit methods that it does not need or should not have. Even when a base class method is appropriate for a derived class, the derived class often needs a customized version of the method. In such cases, the derived class can override (redefine) the base class method with an implementation appropriate for the derived class, as we will see often in the chapter's code examples.

10.3 Protected Members

Chapter 9 discussed access modifiers Public and Private. A class's Public members are accessible wherever the program has a reference to an object of that class or one of its derived classes. A class's Private members are accessible only within the class itself. A base class's Private members are not inherited by its derived classes. This section introduces the access modifier Protected. In Section 10.8, we discuss the access modifier **Friend**.

Protected access offers an intermediate level of access between Public and Private access. A base class's Protected members can be accessed only by members of that base class and by members of its derived classes.

All Public and Protected base class members retain their original access modifier when they become members of the derived class (i.e., Public members of the base class become Public members of the derived class, and Protected members of the base class become Protected members of the derived class).

Derived class methods can refer to `Public` and `Protected` members inherited from the base class simply by using the member names. When a derived class method overrides a base class method, the base class version can be accessed from the derived class by preceding the base class method name with keyword `MyBase` and a dot (`.`) separator. We discuss accessing overridden members of the base class in Section 10.4.

Software Engineering Observation 10.1

Derived class methods cannot directly access `Private` members of their base class. A derived class can change the state of `Private` base class instance variables only through non-`Private` methods provided in the base class and inherited by the derived class.

Software Engineering Observation 10.2

Declaring `Private` instance variables helps programmers test, debug and correctly modify systems. If a derived class could access its base class's `Private` instance variables, classes that inherit from that derived class could access the instance variables as well. This would propagate access to what should be `Private` instance variables, and the benefits of information hiding would be lost.

10.4 Relationship between Base Classes and Derived Classes

In this section, we use a business-oriented inheritance hierarchy containing types of employees in a company's payroll application to discuss the relationship between a base class and a derived class. Commission employees (who will be represented as objects of a base class) are paid a percentage of their sales, while base-salaried commission employees (who will be represented as objects of a derived class) receive a base salary plus a percentage of their sales. We divide our discussion of the relationship between commission employees and base-salaried commission employees into a carefully paced series of five examples:

1. In the first example, we create class `CommissionEmployee`, which contains as `Private` instance variables a first name, last name, social security number, commission rate (percentage) and gross (i.e., total) sales amount.

2. The second example defines class `BasePlusCommissionEmployee`, which contains as `Private` instance variables a first name, last name, social security number, commission rate, gross sales amount *and* a base salary. We create the class by writing every line of code that the class requires—we will soon see that it is much more efficient to create this class simply by inheriting from class `CommissionEmployee`, then adding appropriate attributes and behaviors.

3. The third example defines a new version of class `BasePlusCommissionEmployee` that inherits directly from class `CommissionEmployee` (i.e., a `BasePlus-CommissionEmployee` *is a* `CommissionEmployee` who also has a base salary) and attempts to access class `CommissionEmployee`'s `Private` members—this results in compilation errors, because the derived class does not have access to the base class's `Private` data.

4. The fourth example shows that if `CommissionEmployee`'s data is declared as `Protected`, a new version of class `BasePlusCommissionEmployee` that inherits from class `CommissionEmployee` *can* access that data directly. For this purpose, we de-

fine a new version of class CommissionEmployee with Protected data. Both the inherited and noninherited BasePlusCommissionEmployee classes contain identical functionality, but we show how the version of BasePlusCommissionEmployee that inherits from class CommissionEmployee is easier to create and manage.

5. After we discuss the convenience of using protected data, we create the fifth example, which sets the CommissionEmployee data members back to Private to enforce good software engineering. This example demonstrates that derived class BasePlusCommissionEmployee can use base class CommissionEmployee's Public properties and methods to manipulate (in a carefully controlled manner) CommissionEmployee's Private data.

10.4.1 Creating and Using a CommissionEmployee Class

We begin by declaring class CommissionEmployee (Fig. 10.4). Lines 3–4 begin the class declaration and indicate that class CommissionEmployee Inherits from class Object (from namespace System). Visual Basic programmers use inheritance to create classes from existing classes. In fact, every class in Visual Basic (except Object) inherits from an existing class. Because class CommissionEmployee is derived from class Object, class CommissionEmployee inherits the methods of class Object—class Object does not have any fields. In fact, every Visual Basic class directly or indirectly inherits Object's methods. If a class does not specify that it inherits another class, the new class implicitly inherits Object. For this reason, programmers typically do not include "Inherits Object" in their code—we do so in this example for demonstration purposes, but then we omit "Inherits Object" in all subsequent examples.

The Public services of class CommissionEmployee include a constructor (lines 13–22), properties FirstName (lines 25–33), LastName (lines 36–44), SocialSecurityNumber (lines 47–55), GrossSales (lines 58–70) and CommissionRate (lines 73–85), and methods CalculateEarnings (lines 88–90) and ToString (lines 93–100). Lines 25–85 declare Public properties for manipulating the class's instance variables firstNameValue, lastNameValue, socialSecurityNumberValue, grossSalesValue and commissionRateValue (declared in lines 6–10). Class CommissionEmployee declares each of its instance variables as Private, so objects of other classes cannot directly access these variables. Properties GrossSales and CommissionRate validate their arguments before assigning the values to instance variables grossSalesValue and commissionRateValue, respectively.

```vb
 1   ' Fig. 10.4: CommmissionEmployee.vb
 2   ' CommissionEmployee class represents a commission employee.
 3   Public Class CommissionEmployee
 4      Inherits Object ' optional
 5
 6      Private firstNameValue As String ' first name
 7      Private lastNameValue As String ' last name
 8      Private socialSecurityNumberValue As String ' social security number
 9      Private grossSalesValue As Decimal ' gross weekly sales
10      Private commissionRateValue As Decimal ' commission percentage
```

Fig. 10.4 | CommissionEmployee class represents an employee paid a percentage of gross sales. (Part 1 of 3.)

```vbnet
11
12      ' five-argument constructor
13      Public Sub New(ByVal first As String, ByVal last As String, _
14        ByVal ssn As String, ByVal sales As Decimal, ByVal rate As Decimal)
15
16         ' implicit call to Object constructor occurs here
17         FirstName = first
18         LastName = last
19         SocialSecurityNumber = ssn
20         GrossSales = sales ' validate and store gross sales
21         CommissionRate = rate ' validate and store commission rate
22      End Sub ' New
23
24      ' property FirstName
25      Public Property FirstName() As String
26         Get
27            Return firstNameValue
28         End Get
29
30         Set(ByVal first As String)
31            firstNameValue = first ' no validation
32         End Set
33      End Property ' FirstName
34
35      ' property LastName
36      Public Property LastName() As String
37         Get
38            Return lastNameValue
39         End Get
40
41         Set(ByVal last As String)
42            lastNameValue = last ' no validation
43         End Set
44      End Property ' LastName
45
46      ' property SocialSecurityNumber
47      Public Property SocialSecurityNumber() As String
48         Get
49            Return socialSecurityNumberValue
50         End Get
51
52         Set(ByVal ssn As String)
53            socialSecurityNumberValue = ssn ' no validation
54         End Set
55      End Property ' SocialSecurityNumber
56
57      ' property GrossSales
58      Public Property GrossSales() As Decimal
59         Get
60            Return grossSalesValue
61         End Get
```

Fig. 10.4 | CommissionEmployee class represents an employee paid a percentage of gross sales. (Part 2 of 3.)

```
62
63        Set(ByVal sales As Decimal)
64          If sales < 0.0 Then ' validate gross sales
65            grossSalesValue = 0
66          Else
67            grossSalesValue = sales
68          End If
69        End Set
70      End Property ' GrossSales
71
72      ' property CommissionRate
73      Public Property CommissionRate() As Decimal
74        Get
75          Return commissionRateValue
76        End Get
77
78        Set(ByVal rate As Decimal)
79          If rate > 0.0 AndAlso rate < 1.0 Then ' validate rate
80            commissionRateValue = rate
81          Else
82            commissionRateValue = 0
83          End If
84        End Set
85      End Property ' CommissionRate
86
87      ' calculate earnings
88      Public Function CalculateEarnings() As Decimal
89        Return commissionRateValue * grossSalesValue
90      End Function ' CalculateEarnings
91
92      ' return String representation of CommissionEmployee object
93      Public Overrides Function ToString() As String
94        Return ("commission employee: " & firstNameValue & " " & _
95          lastNameValue & vbCrLf & "social security number: " & _
96          socialSecurityNumberValue & vbCrLf & "gross sales: " & _
97          String.Format("{0:C}", grossSalesValue) & vbCrLf & _
98          "commission rate: " & String.Format("{0:F}", _
99          commissionRateValue))
100     End Function ' ToString
101   End Class ' CommissionEmployee
```

Fig. 10.4 | CommissionEmployee class represents an employee paid a percentage of gross sales. (Part 3 of 3.)

Constructors are not inherited, so class CommissionEmployee does not inherit class Object's constructor. However, class CommissionEmployee's constructor calls class Object's constructor implicitly. In fact, the first task of any derived class constructor is to call its direct base class's constructor, either explicitly or implicitly (if no constructor call is specified), to ensure that the instance variables inherited from the base class are initialized properly. The syntax for calling a base class constructor explicitly is discussed in Section 10.4.3. If the code does not include an explicit call to the base class constructor, Visual Basic implicitly calls the base class's default or parameterless constructor. The comment in line 16 of Fig. 10.4 indicates where the implicit call to the base class `Object`'s default constructor is made (you do not need to write the code for this call). `Object`'s default constructor does nothing. Note that even if a class does not have constructors, the default constructor that the compiler implicitly declares for the class will call the base class's default or parameterless constructor.

After the implicit call to `Object`'s constructor occurs, lines 17–21 of `Commission-Employee`'s constructor assign values to the class's instance variables. Note that we do not validate the values of arguments `first`, `last` and `ssn` before assigning them to the corresponding instance variables. We could validate the first and last names—perhaps by ensuring that they are of a reasonable length. Similarly, a social security number could be validated to ensure that it contains nine digits, with or without dashes (e.g., `123-45-6789` or `123456789`).

Method `CalculateEarnings` (lines 88–90) calculates a `CommissionEmployee`'s earnings. Line 89 multiplies the `commissionRateValue` by the `grossSalesValue` and returns the result.

Method `ToString` (lines 93–100) of class `CommissionEmployee` Overrides (redefines) class `Object`'s `ToString` method. When invoked, `CommissionEmployee`'s `ToString` method returns a `String` containing information about the `CommissionEmployee`. Without overriding `ToString` in class `CommissionEmployee`, the default implementation would return `"CommissionEmployeeTest.CommissionEmployee"`, where `CommissionEmployeeTest` is the default namespace (which is the same as the project name).

A base class method must be declared **Overridable** if it is to be overridden in a derived class. Method `ToString` of class `Object` is declared Overridable, so derived class `CommissionEmployee` can override this method. To view the method header for `ToString`, select **Help > Index...**, and enter "`Object.ToString` method" in the search text box. The page displayed contains a description of method `ToString`, which includes the following header:

```
Public Overridable Function ToString() As String
```

Common Programming Error 10.1

It is a compilation error to attempt to override a method that is not declared Overridable.

Common Programming Error 10.2

It is a compilation error to override a method with a method that has a different access modifier than the method being overridden.

Testing Class CommissionEmployee

Figure 10.5 tests class `CommissionEmployee`. Lines 6–7 instantiate a `CommissionEmployee` object and invoke `CommissionEmployee`'s constructor (lines 13–22 of Fig. 10.4) to initialize it with `"Sue"` as the first name, `"Jones"` as the last name, `"222-22-2222"` as the social security number, `10000` as the gross sales amount and `0.06` as the commission rate. Lines 10–16 access `CommissionEmployee`'s `Public` properties for output. Lines 18–19 change the values of properties `GrossSales` and `CommissionRate`. Lines 22–24 call `CommissionEmployee`'s `ToString` method to output the string representation of the updated `CommissionEmployee`. Lines 27–28 display the `CommissionEmployee`'s earnings, calculated by the object's `CalculateEarnings` method using the updated values of instance variables `grossSalesValue` and `commissionRateValue`.

```vb
 1   ' Fig. 10.5: CommissionEmployeeTest.vb
 2   ' Testing class CommissionEmployee.
 3   Module CommissionEmployeeTest
 4      Sub Main()
 5         ' instantiate CommissionEmployee object
 6         Dim employee As New CommissionEmployee( _
 7            "Sue", "Jones", "222-22-2222", 10000, 0.06D)
 8
 9         ' get commission employee data
10         Console.WriteLine("Employee information obtained by properties:" _
11            & vbCrLf & "First name is " & employee.FirstName & vbCrLf & _
12            "Last name is " & employee.LastName & vbCrLf & _
13            "Social Security Number is " & employee.SocialSecurityNumber)
14         Console.WriteLine("Gross sales is {0:C}", employee.GrossSales)
15         Console.WriteLine("Commission rate is {0:F}", _
16            employee.CommissionRate)
17
18         employee.GrossSales = 500 ' set gross sales
19         employee.CommissionRate = 0.1D ' set commission rate to 10%
20
21         ' get new employee information
22         Console.WriteLine(vbCrLf & _
23            "Updated employee information obtained by ToString: " & _
24            vbCrLf & employee.ToString() & vbCrLf)
25
26         ' display the employee's earnings
27         Console.WriteLine("Employee's earnings: {0:C}", _
28            employee.CalculateEarnings())
29      End Sub ' Main
30   End Module ' CommissionEmployeeTest
```

```
Employee information obtained by properties:
First name is Sue
Last name is Jones
Social Security Number is 222-22-2222
Gross sales is $10,000.00
Commission rate is 0.06

Updated employee information obtained by ToString:
commission employee: Sue Jones
social security number: 222-22-2222
gross sales: $500.00
commission rate: 0.10

Employee's earnings: $50.00
```

Fig. 10.5 | CommissionEmployee class test program.

10.4.2 Creating a BasePlusCommissionEmployee Class without Using Inheritance

We now discuss the second part of our introduction to inheritance by declaring and testing a completely new and independent class BasePlusCommissionEmployee (Fig. 10.6), which contains a first name, last name, social security number, gross sales amount, commission rate *and* base salary.

```vb
1   ' Fig. 10.6: BasePlusCommissionEmployee.vb
2   ' BasePlusCommissionEmployee class represents an employee that receives
3   ' a base salary in addition to a commission.
4   Public Class BasePlusCommissionEmployee
5      Private firstNameValue As String ' first name
6      Private lastNameValue As String ' last name
7      Private socialSecurityNumberValue As String ' social security number
8      Private grossSalesValue As Decimal ' gross weekly sales
9      Private commissionRateValue As Decimal ' commission percentage
10     Private baseSalaryValue As Decimal ' base salary per week
11
12     ' six-argument constructor
13     Public Sub New(ByVal first As String, ByVal last As String, _
14        ByVal ssn As String, ByVal sales As Decimal, _
15        ByVal rate As Decimal, ByVal salary As Decimal)
16
17        ' implicit call to Object constructor occurs here
18        FirstName = first
19        LastName = last
20        SocialSecurityNumber = ssn
21        GrossSales = sales ' validate and store gross sales
22        CommissionRate = rate ' validate and store commission rate
23        BaseSalary = salary ' validate and store base salary
24     End Sub ' New
25
26     ' property FirstName
27     Public Property FirstName() As String
28        Get
29           Return firstNameValue
30        End Get
31
32        Set(ByVal first As String)
33           firstNameValue = first ' no validation
34        End Set
35     End Property ' FirstName
36
37     ' property LastName
38     Public Property LastName() As String
39        Get
40           Return lastNameValue
41        End Get
42
43        Set(ByVal last As String)
44           lastNameValue = last ' no validation
45        End Set
46     End Property ' LastName
47
```

Fig. 10.6 | BasePlusCommissionEmployee class represents an employee who receives a base salary in addition to a commission. (Part 1 of 3.)

```
48          ' property SocialSecurityNumber
49          Public Property SocialSecurityNumber() As String
50             Get
51                Return socialSecurityNumberValue
52             End Get
53
54             Set(ByVal ssn As String)
55                socialSecurityNumberValue = ssn ' no validation
56             End Set
57          End Property ' SocialSecurityNumber
58
59          ' property GrossSales
60          Public Property GrossSales() As Decimal
61             Get
62                Return grossSalesValue
63             End Get
64
65             Set(ByVal sales As Decimal)
66                If sales < 0.0 Then ' validate gross sales
67                   grossSalesValue = 0
68                Else
69                   grossSalesValue = sales
70                End If
71             End Set
72          End Property ' GrossSales
73
74          ' property CommissionRate
75          Public Property CommissionRate() As Decimal
76             Get
77                Return commissionRateValue
78             End Get
79
80             Set(ByVal rate As Decimal)
81                If rate > 0.0 AndAlso rate < 1.0 Then ' validate rate
82                   commissionRateValue = rate
83                Else
84                   commissionRateValue = 0
85                End If
86             End Set
87          End Property ' CommissionRate
88
89          ' property BaseSalary
90          Public Property BaseSalary() As Decimal
91             Get
92                Return baseSalaryValue
93             End Get
94
95             Set(ByVal salary As Decimal)
96                If salary < 0.0 Then ' validate base salary
97                   baseSalaryValue = 0
```

Fig. 10.6 | BasePlusCommissionEmployee class represents an employee who receives a base salary in addition to a commission. (Part 2 of 3.)

```vbnet
 98           Else
 99               baseSalaryValue = salary
100           End If
101       End Set
102   End Property ' BaseSalary
103
104   ' calculate earnings
105   Public Function CalculateEarnings() As Decimal
106       Return baseSalaryValue + (commissionRateValue * grossSalesValue)
107   End Function ' CalculateEarnings
108
109   ' return String representation of BasePlusCommissionEmployee object
110   Public Overrides Function ToString() As String
111       Return ("base-plus-commission employee: " & firstNameValue & " " & _
112           lastNameValue & vbCrLf & "social security number: " & _
113           socialSecurityNumberValue & vbCrLf & "gross sales: " & _
114           String.Format("{0:C}", grossSalesValue) & vbCrLf & _
115           "commission rate: " & String.Format("{0:F}", _
116           commissionRateValue) & vbCrLf & "base salary: " & _
117           String.Format("{0:C}", baseSalaryValue))
118   End Function ' ToString
119 End Class ' BasePlusCommissionEmployee
```

Fig. 10.6 | BasePlusCommissionEmployee class represents an employee who receives a base salary in addition to a commission. (Part 3 of 3.)

Defining Class BasePlusCommissionEmployee

Class BasePlusCommissionEmployee's Public services include a BasePlusCommissionEmployee constructor (lines 13–24), properties FirstName (lines 27–35), LastName (lines 38–46), SocialSecurityNumber (lines 49–57), GrossSales (lines 60–72), CommissionRate (lines 75–87) and BaseSalary (lines 90–102), and methods CalculateEarnings (lines 105–107) and ToString (lines 110–118). Lines 27–102 declare Public properties for the class's Private instance variables firstNameValue, lastNameValue, socialSecurityNumberValue, grossSalesValue, commissionRateValue and baseSalaryValue (declared in lines 5–10). These variables, properties and methods comprise all the necessary features of a base-salaried commission employee. Note the similarity between this class and class CommissionEmployee (Fig. 10.4)—in this example, we do not yet exploit that similarity.

Note that class BasePlusCommissionEmployee does not specify "Inherits Object," so the class implicitly inherits Object. Also, like class CommissionEmployee's constructor (lines 13–22 of Fig. 10.4), class BasePlusCommissionEmployee's constructor invokes class Object's default constructor implicitly, as noted in the comment in line 17 (Fig. 10.6).

Class BasePlusCommissionEmployee's CalculateEarnings method (lines 105–107) computes the earnings of a base-salaried commission employee. Line 106 returns the result of adding the base salary to the product of the commission rate and the gross sales. Class BasePlusCommissionEmployee overrides Object method ToString (lines 110–118) to return a String containing the BasePlusCommissionEmployee's information.

Testing Class BasePlusCommissionEmployee

Figure 10.7 tests class BasePlusCommissionEmployee. Lines 6–7 instantiate a BasePlusCommissionEmployee object and pass "Bob", "Lewis", "333-33-3333", 5000, 0.04 and

```vb
1    ' Fig. 10.7: BasePlusCommissionEmployeeTest.vb
2    ' Testing class BasePlusCommissionEmployee.
3    Module BasePlusCommissionEmployeeTest
4       Sub Main()
5          ' instantite BasePlusCommissionEmployee object
6          Dim employee As New BasePlusCommissionEmployee( _
7             "Bob", "Lewis", "333-33-3333", 5000, 0.04D, 300)
8
9          ' get base-salaried commission employee data
10         Console.WriteLine("Employee information obtained by properties:" _
11            & vbCrLf & "First name is " & employee.FirstName & vbCrLf & _
12            "Last name is " & employee.LastName & vbCrLf & _
13            "Social Security Number is " & employee.SocialSecurityNumber)
14         Console.WriteLine("Gross sales is {0:C}", employee.GrossSales)
15         Console.WriteLine("Commission rate is {0:F}", _
16            employee.CommissionRate)
17         Console.WriteLine("Base salary is {0:C}", employee.BaseSalary)
18
19         employee.BaseSalary = 1000 ' set base salary
20
21         ' get new employee information
22         Console.WriteLine(vbCrLf & _
23            "Updated employee information obtained by ToString: " & _
24            vbCrLf & employee.ToString() & vbCrLf)
25
26         ' display the employee's earnings
27         Console.WriteLine("Employee's earnings: $" & _
28            employee.CalculateEarnings())
29      End Sub ' Main
30   End Module ' BasePlusCommissionEmployeeTest
```

```
Employee information obtained by properties:
First name is Bob
Last name is Lewis
Social Security Number is 333-33-3333
Gross sales is $5,000.00
Commission rate is 0.04
Base salary is $300.00

Updated employee information obtained by ToString:
base-plus-commission employee: Bob Lewis
social security number: 333-33-3333
gross sales: $5,000.00
commission rate: 0.04
base salary: $1,000.00

Employee's earnings: $1200.00
```

Fig. 10.7 | BasePlusCommissionEmployee test program.

300 to the constructor as the first name, last name, social security number, gross sales, commission rate and base salary, respectively. Lines 10–17 use BasePlus-CommissionEmployee's properties to retrieve the values of the object's instance variables for output. Line 19 changes the BaseSalary property. Property BaseSalary's Set accessor

(Fig. 10.6, lines 95–101) ensures that instance variable baseSalaryValue is not assigned a negative value, because an employee's base salary cannot be negative. Line 24 of Fig. 10.7 invokes the object's ToString method explicitly to get the object's string representation.

Exploring the Similarities between Class BasePlusCommissionEmployee and Class CommissionEmployee

Much of the code for class BasePlusCommissionEmployee (Fig. 10.6) is similar, if not identical, to the code for class CommissionEmployee (Fig. 10.4). For example, both classes contain Private instance variables firstNameValue, lastNameValue, socialSecurityNumberValue, grossSalesValue and commissionRateValue, and properties FirstName, LastName, SocialSecurityNumber, GrossSales and CommissionRate to manipulate these variables. The BasePlusCommissionEmployee constructor is *almost* identical to that of class CommissionEmployee, except that BasePlusCommissionEmployee's constructor also sets the BaseSalary property. The other additions to class BasePlusCommissionEmployee are Private instance variable baseSalaryValue and property BaseSalary. Class BasePlusCommissionEmployee's ToString method is nearly identical to that of class CommissionEmployee except that BasePlusCommissionEmployee's ToString also outputs the value of instance variable baseSalaryValue.

   To form class BasePlusCommissionEmployee, we copied the code from class CommissionEmployee and pasted it into class BasePlusCommissionEmployee, then modified class BasePlusCommissionEmployee to include a base salary and methods that manipulate the base salary. This "copy-and-paste" approach is often error prone and time consuming. Worse yet, it can spread many physical copies of the same code throughout a system, creating a code-maintenance nightmare. Is there a way to "absorb" the instance variables and methods of one class in a way that makes them part of other classes without duplicating code? Indeed there is—using the elegant object-oriented programming technique of inheritance that we demonstrate in the next section.

Software Engineering Observation 10.3

Copying and pasting code from one class to another can spread errors among multiple source code files. To avoid duplicating code (and possibly errors), use inheritance, rather than the "copy-and-paste" approach, where you want one class to "absorb" the members of another class.

Software Engineering Observation 10.4

With inheritance, the common instance variables and methods of all the classes in the hierarchy are declared in a base class. When changes are required for these common features, software developers need to make the changes only in the base class—derived classes then inherit the changes. Without inheritance, the changes would need to be made to all the source code files that contain copies of the code in question.

10.4.3 Creating a CommissionEmployee– BasePlusCommissionEmployee Inheritance Hierarchy

Now we declare class BasePlusCommissionEmployee (Fig. 10.9), which inherits from class CommissionEmployee (Fig. 10.8). Class CommissionEmployee is almost identical to Fig. 10.4, except that method CalculateEarnings (Fig. 10.8, lines 88–90) is now declared Overridable so that a derived class of CommissionEmployee can override method CalculateEarnings to provide an appropriate earnings calculation. A BasePlusCommission-

Employee object *is a* CommissionEmployee (because inheritance passes on the capabilities of class CommissionEmployee), but class BasePlusCommissionEmployee also has instance variable baseSalaryValue (Fig. 10.9, line 6). Note that Fig. 10.9 does not redeclare the base class instance variables (lines 6–10 of Fig. 10.8)—these are nevertheless present in the derived class (through inheritance). Even though they are present, they are declared Private in the base class, so as we will see in a moment, we will have to make special provision to access this base class information from the derived class. Keyword Inherits in line 4 of the class declaration (Fig. 10.9) indicates inheritance. As a derived class, BasePlusCommission-Employee inherits the Public (and Protected, if there were any) instance variables and methods of class CommissionEmployee. The constructor of class CommissionEmployee is not inherited. Thus, the Public services of BasePlusCommissionEmployee include its constructor (lines 9–16), Public methods and properties inherited from class Commission-Employee, property BaseSalary (lines 19–31), method CalculateEarnings (lines 34–37) and method ToString (lines 40–49).

```vb
1    ' Fig. 10.8: CommissionEmployee.vb
2    ' CommissionEmployee class represents a commission employee.
3    Public Class CommissionEmployee
4       Inherits Object ' optional
5
6       Private firstNameValue As String ' first name
7       Private lastNameValue As String ' last name
8       Private socialSecurityNumberValue As String ' social security number
9       Private grossSalesValue As Decimal ' gross weekly sales
10      Private commissionRateValue As Decimal ' commission percentage
11
12      ' five-argument constructor
13      Public Sub New(ByVal first As String, ByVal last As String, _
14         ByVal ssn As String, ByVal sales As Decimal, ByVal rate As Decimal)
15
16         ' implicit call to Object constructor occurs here
17         FirstName = first
18         LastName = last
19         SocialSecurityNumber = ssn
20         GrossSales = sales ' validate and store gross sales
21         CommissionRate = rate ' validate and store commission rate
22      End Sub ' New
23
24      ' property FirstName
25      Public Property FirstName() As String
26         Get
27            Return firstNameValue
28         End Get
29
30         Set(ByVal first As String)
31            firstNameValue = first ' no validation
32         End Set
33      End Property ' FirstName
34
```

Fig. 10.8 | CommissionEmployee class with Overridable method CalculateEarnings. (Part 1 of 3.)

```
35    ' property LastName
36    Public Property LastName() As String
37       Get
38          Return lastNameValue
39       End Get
40
41       Set(ByVal last As String)
42          lastNameValue = last ' no validation
43       End Set
44    End Property ' LastName
45
46    ' property SocialSecurityNumber
47    Public Property SocialSecurityNumber() As String
48       Get
49          Return socialSecurityNumberValue
50       End Get
51
52       Set(ByVal ssn As String)
53          socialSecurityNumberValue = ssn ' no validation
54       End Set
55    End Property ' SocialSecurityNumber
56
57    ' property GrossSales
58    Public Property GrossSales() As Decimal
59       Get
60          Return grossSalesValue
61       End Get
62
63       Set(ByVal sales As Decimal)
64          If sales < 0.0 Then ' validate gross sales
65             grossSalesValue = 0
66          Else
67             grossSalesValue = sales
68          End If
69       End Set
70    End Property ' GrossSales
71
72    ' property CommissionRate
73    Public Property CommissionRate() As Decimal
74       Get
75          Return commissionRateValue
76       End Get
77
78       Set(ByVal rate As Decimal)
79          If rate > 0.0 AndAlso rate < 1.0 Then ' validate rate
80             commissionRateValue = rate
81          Else
82             commissionRateValue = 0
83          End If
84       End Set
85    End Property ' CommissionRate
```

Fig. 10.8 | CommissionEmployee class with Overridable method CalculateEarnings. (Part 2 of 3.)

```
86
87       ' calculate earnings
88       Public Overridable Function CalculateEarnings() As Decimal
89          Return commissionRateValue * grossSalesValue
90       End Function ' CalculateEarnings
91
92       ' return String representation of CommissionEmployee object
93       Public Overrides Function ToString() As String
94          Return ("commission employee: " & firstNameValue & " " & _
95             lastNameValue & vbCrLf & "social security number: " & _
96             socialSecurityNumberValue & vbCrLf & "gross sales: " & _
97             String.Format("{0:C}", grossSalesValue) & vbCrLf & _
98             "commission rate: " & String.Format("{0:F}", _
99             commissionRateValue))
100      End Function ' ToString
101   End Class ' CommissionEmployee
```

Fig. 10.8 | CommissionEmployee class with Overridable method CalculateEarnings.
(Part 3 of 3.)

```
1    ' Fig. 10.9: BasePlusCommissionEmployee.vb
2    ' BasePlusCommissionEmployee inherits from class CommissionEmployee.
3    Public Class BasePlusCommissionEmployee
4       Inherits CommissionEmployee
5
6       Private baseSalaryValue As Decimal ' base salary per week
7
8       ' six-argument constructor
9       Public Sub New(ByVal first As String, ByVal last As String, _
10         ByVal ssn As String, ByVal sales As Decimal, _
11         ByVal rate As Decimal, ByVal salary As Decimal)
12
13         ' use MyBase to invoke CommissionEmployee constructor explicitly
14         MyBase.New(first, last, ssn, sales, rate)
15         BaseSalary = salary ' validate and store base salary
16      End Sub ' New
17
18      ' property BaseSalary
19      Public Property BaseSalary() As Decimal
20         Get
21            Return baseSalaryValue
22         End Get
23
24         Set(ByVal salary As Decimal)
25            If salary < 0.0 Then ' validate base salary
26               baseSalaryValue = 0
27            Else
28               baseSalaryValue = salary
29            End If
30         End Set
31      End Property ' BaseSalary
```

Fig. 10.9 | Private base class members cannot be accessed in a derived class. (Part 1 of 2.)

```
32
33      ' calculate earnings
34      Public Overrides Function CalculateEarnings() As Decimal
35          ' not allowed: attempts to access private base class members
36          Return baseSalaryValue + (commissionRateValue * grossSalesValue)
37      End Function ' CalculateEearnings
38
39      ' return String representation of BasePlusCommissionEmployee object
40      Public Overrides Function ToString() As String
41          ' not allowed: attempts to access private base class members
42          Return ("base-plus-commission employee: " & firstNameValue & " " & _
43              lastNameValue & vbCrLf & "social security number: " & _
44              socialSecurityNumberValue & vbCrLf & "gross sales: " & _
45              String.Format("{0:C}", grossSalesValue) & vbCrLf & _
46              "commission rate: " & String.Format("{0:F}", _
47              commissionRateValue) & vbCrLf & "base salary: " & _
48              String.Format("{0:C}", baseSalaryValue))
49      End Function ' ToString
50  End Class ' BasePlusCommissionEmployee
```

	Description	File	Line	Column
❌ 1	'BasePlusCommissionEmployee.CommissionEmployee.commissionRateValue' is not accessible in this context because it is 'Private'.	BasePlusCommissionEmployee.vb	36	33
❌ 2	'BasePlusCommissionEmployee.CommissionEmployee.grossSalesValue' is not accessible in this context because it is 'Private'.	BasePlusCommissionEmployee.vb	36	55
❌ 3	'BasePlusCommissionEmployee.CommissionEmployee.firstNameValue' is not accessible in this context because it is 'Private'.	BasePlusCommissionEmployee.vb	42	51
❌ 4	'BasePlusCommissionEmployee.CommissionEmployee.lastNameValue' is not accessible in this context because it is 'Private'.	BasePlusCommissionEmployee.vb	43	10
❌ 5	'BasePlusCommissionEmployee.CommissionEmployee.socialSecurityNumberValue' is not accessible in this context because it is 'Private'.	BasePlusCommissionEmployee.vb	44	10
❌ 6	'BasePlusCommissionEmployee.CommissionEmployee.grossSalesValue' is not accessible in this context because it is 'Private'.	BasePlusCommissionEmployee.vb	45	33
❌ 7	'BasePlusCommissionEmployee.CommissionEmployee.commissionRateValue' is not accessible in this context because it is 'Private'.	BasePlusCommissionEmployee.vb	47	10

Error List — ❌ 7 Errors | ⚠ 0 Warnings | ⓘ 0 Messages

Fig. 10.9 | `Private` base class members cannot be accessed in a derived class. (Part 2 of 2.)

Each derived class constructor must implicitly or explicitly call its base class constructor to ensure that the instance variables inherited from the base class are initialized properly. BasePlusCommissionEmployee's six-argument constructor (lines 9–16 of Fig. 10.9) explicitly calls class CommissionEmployee's five-argument constructor to initialize the base class portion of a BasePlusCommissionEmployee object (i.e., variables firstNameValue, lastNameValue, socialSecurityNumberValue, grossSalesValue and commissionRateValue). Line 14 in BasePlusCommissionEmployee's six-argument constructor invokes the CommissionEmployee's five-argument constructor (declared at lines 13–22 of Fig. 10.8) by using the base class constructor call syntax—keyword **MyBase**, followed by the dot (.) separator, followed by New and a set of parentheses containing the arguments to the base class constructor. The arguments first, last, ssn, sales and rate (which were received by the derived class constructor) are used to initialize base class members firstNameValue, lastNameValue, socialSecurityNumberValue, grossSalesValue and commissionRateValue, respectively. If the BasePlusCommissionEmployee constructor did not invoke Commission-

Employee's constructor explicitly, Visual Basic would attempt to invoke class Commission-Employee's parameterless or default constructor—but the class does not have such a constructor, so the compiler would issue an error. The explicit base class constructor call in line 14 (Fig. 10.9) *must* be the first statement in the derived class constructor's body. When a base class contains a default or parameterless constructor, you can use MyBase.New() to call that constructor explicitly, but this is unnecessary and is rarely done.

The compiler issues errors for line 36 of Fig. 10.9 because base class CommissionEm-ployee's instance variables commissionRateValue and grossSalesValue are Private—derived class BasePlusCommissionEmployee's methods are not allowed to access base class CommissionEmployee's Private members. Note that we use red text in Fig. 10.9 (and else-where in the book) to indicate erroneous code. The compiler issues additional errors at lines 42–47 of BasePlusCommissionEmployee's ToString method for the same reason. The errors in BasePlusCommissionEmployee could have been prevented by using the properties inherited from class CommissionEmployee. For example, line 36 could have used properties CommissionRate and GrossSales to access CommissionEmployee's Private instance vari-ables commissionRateValue and grossSalesValue, respectively. Lines 42–47 also could have used appropriate properties to retrieve the values of the base class's instance variables.

10.4.4 CommissionEmployee–BasePlusCommissionEmployee Inheritance Hierarchy Using Protected Instance Variables

To enable class BasePlusCommissionEmployee to directly access base class instance vari-ables firstNameValue, lastNameValue, socialSecurityNumberValue, grossSalesValue and commissionRateValue, we can declare those members as Protected in the base class. As we discussed in Section 10.3, a base class's Protected members *are* inherited by all de-rived classes of that base class and are directly accessible by derived classes.

Defining Base Class CommissionEmployee with Protected Data
Class CommissionEmployee (Fig. 10.10) modifies Fig. 10.8 to declare instance variables firstNameValue, lastNameValue, socialSecurityNumberValue, grossSalesValue and

```vb
1   ' Fig. 10.10: CommissionEmployee.vb
2   ' CommissionEmployee class represents a commission employee.
3   Public Class CommissionEmployee
4      Inherits Object ' optional
5
6      Protected firstNameValue As String ' first name
7      Protected lastNameValue As String ' last name
8      Protected socialSecurityNumberValue As String ' social security number
9      Protected grossSalesValue As Decimal ' gross weekly sales
10     Protected commissionRateValue As Decimal ' commission percentage
11
12     ' five-argument constructor
13     Public Sub New(ByVal first As String, ByVal last As String, _
14        ByVal ssn As String, ByVal sales As Decimal, ByVal rate As Decimal)
15
16        ' implicit call to Object constructor occurs here
17        FirstName = first
```

Fig. 10.10 | CommissionEmployee class with Protected instance variables. (Part 1 of 3.)

```
18            LastName = last
19            SocialSecurityNumber = ssn
20            GrossSales = sales ' validate and store gross sales
21            CommissionRate = rate ' validate and store commission rate
22        End Sub ' New
23
24        ' property FirstName
25        Public Property FirstName() As String
26            Get
27                Return firstNameValue
28            End Get
29
30            Set(ByVal first As String)
31                firstNameValue = first ' no validation
32            End Set
33        End Property ' FirstName
34
35        ' property LastName
36        Public Property LastName() As String
37            Get
38                Return lastNameValue
39            End Get
40
41            Set(ByVal last As String)
42                lastNameValue = last ' no validation
43            End Set
44        End Property ' LastName
45
46        ' property SocialSecurityNumber
47        Public Property SocialSecurityNumber() As String
48            Get
49                Return socialSecurityNumberValue
50            End Get
51
52            Set(ByVal ssn As String)
53                socialSecurityNumberValue = ssn ' no validation
54            End Set
55        End Property ' SocialSecurityNumber
56
57        ' property GrossSales
58        Public Property GrossSales() As Decimal
59            Get
60                Return grossSalesValue
61            End Get
62
63            Set(ByVal sales As Decimal)
64                If sales < 0.0 Then ' validate gross sales
65                    grossSalesValue = 0
66                Else
67                    grossSalesValue = sales
68                End If
69            End Set
70        End Property ' GrossSales
```

Fig. 10.10 | CommissionEmployee class with Protected instance variables. (Part 2 of 3.)

```
71
72       ' property CommissionRate
73       Public Property CommissionRate() As Decimal
74          Get
75             Return commissionRateValue
76          End Get
77
78          Set(ByVal rate As Decimal)
79             If rate > 0.0 AndAlso rate < 1.0 Then ' validate rate
80                commissionRateValue = rate
81             Else
82                commissionRateValue = 0
83             End If
84          End Set
85       End Property ' CommissionRate
86
87       ' calculate earnings
88       Public Overridable Function CalculateEarnings() As Decimal
89          Return commissionRateValue * grossSalesValue
90       End Function ' CalculateEarnings
91
92       ' return String representation of CommissionEmployee object
93       Public Overrides Function ToString() As String
94          Return ("commission employee: " & firstNameValue & " " & _
95             lastNameValue & vbCrLf & "social security number: " & _
96             socialSecurityNumberValue & vbCrLf & "gross sales: " & _
97             String.Format("{0:C}", grossSalesValue) & vbCrLf & _
98             "commission rate: " & String.Format("{0:F}", _
99             commissionRateValue))
100      End Function ' ToString
101   End Class ' CommissionEmployee
```

Fig. 10.10 | CommissionEmployee class with Protected instance variables. (Part 3 of 3.)

commissionRateValue as Protected (Fig. 10.10, lines 6–10) rather than Private. The rest of the class declaration in Fig. 10.10 is identical to the one in Fig. 10.8.

We could have declared the base class CommissionEmployee's instance variables first-NameValue, lastNameValue, socialSecurityNumberValue, grossSalesvalue and commissionRateValue as Public to enable derived class BasePlusCommissionEmployee to access the base class instance variables. Doing this is dangerous because it allows unrestricted access to the instance variables, greatly increasing the chance of errors. With Protected base class instance variables, the derived class gains access to the instance variables, but classes that are not derived classes of this base class cannot access these variables directly.

Modifying Derived Class BasePlusCommissionEmployee
We now modify class BasePlusCommissionEmployee (Fig. 10.9) so that it inherits from the version of class CommissionEmployee in Fig. 10.10. Because class BasePlusCommissionEmployee inherits from this new version of class CommissionEmployee, objects of class BasePlusCommissionEmployee (Fig. 10.11) inherit CommissionEmployee's Protected instance variables firstNameValue, lastNameValue, socialSecurityNumberValue, grossSalesValue and commissionRateValue—all these variables are now Protected members

```vb
1   ' Fig. 10.11: BasePlusCommissionEmployee.vb
2   ' BasePlusCommissionEmployee inherits from class CommissionEmployee.
3   Public Class BasePlusCommissionEmployee
4      Inherits CommissionEmployee
5
6      Private baseSalaryValue As Decimal ' base salary per week
7
8      ' six-argument constructor
9      Public Sub New(ByVal first As String, ByVal last As String, _
10        ByVal ssn As String, ByVal sales As Decimal, _
11        ByVal rate As Decimal, ByVal salary As Decimal)
12
13          ' use MyBase reference to CommissionEmployee constructor explicitly
14         MyBase.New(first, last, ssn, sales, rate)
15         BaseSalary = salary ' validate and store base salary
16      End Sub ' New
17
18      ' property BaseSalary
19      Public Property BaseSalary() As Decimal
20         Get
21            Return baseSalaryValue
22         End Get
23
24         Set(ByVal salary As Decimal)
25            If salary < 0.0 Then ' validate base salary
26               baseSalaryValue = 0
27            Else
28               baseSalaryValue = salary
29            End If
30         End Set
31      End Property ' BaseSalary
32
33      ' calculate earnings
34      Public Overrides Function CalculateEarnings() As Decimal
35         Return baseSalaryValue + (commissionRateValue * grossSalesValue)
36      End Function ' CalculateEarnings
37
38      ' return String representation of BasePlusCommissionEmployee object
39      Public Overrides Function ToString() As String
40         Return ("base-plus-commission employee: " & firstNameValue & " " & _
41            lastNameValue & vbCrLf & "social security number: " & _
42            socialSecurityNumberValue & vbCrLf & "gross sales: " & _
43            String.Format("{0:C}", grossSalesValue) & vbCrLf & _
44            "commission rate: " & String.Format("{0:F}", _
45            commissionRateValue) & vbCrLf & "base salary: " & _
46            String.Format("{0:C}", baseSalaryValue))
47      End Function ' ToString
48   End Class ' BasePlusCommissionEmployee
```

Fig. 10.11 | BasePlusCommissionEmployee inherits Protected instance variables from CommissionEmployee.

of BasePlusCommissionEmployee. As a result, the compiler does not generate errors when compiling line 35 of method CalculateEarnings and lines 40–45 of method ToString (so in Fig. 10.11 we have removed the two "not allowed" comments from Fig. 10.9 and we have changed all red text to black). If another class inherits BasePlusCommission-Employee, the new derived class also inherits the Protected members.

Class BasePlusCommissionEmployee does not inherit class CommissionEmployee's constructor. However, class BasePlusCommissionEmployee's six-argument constructor (lines 9–16) calls class CommissionEmployee's five-argument constructor explicitly. Base-PlusCommissionEmployee's constructor does this because CommissionEmployee does not provide a parameterless constructor that could be invoked implicitly and, more important, because arguments are being passed to the base class constructor.

Testing the Modified *BasePlusCommissionEmployee* Class

Figure 10.12 uses a BasePlusCommissionEmployee object to perform the same tasks that Fig. 10.7 performed on an object of the first version of class BasePlusCommissionEmploy-ee (Fig. 10.6). Note that the outputs of the two programs are identical. We declared the first class BasePlusCommissionEmployee without using inheritance and declared this version of BasePlusCommissionEmployee using inheritance—nevertheless, both classes provide the same functionality. Note that the code for class BasePlusCommissionEmployee (Fig. 10.11), which is 48 lines, is considerably shorter than the code for the noninherited version of the class (Fig. 10.6), which is 119 lines, because the inherited version absorbs much of its functionality from base class CommissionEmployee, whereas the noninherited version absorbs only class Object's functionality.

```vb
1    ' Fig. 10.12: BasePlusCommissionEmployeeTest.vb
2    ' Testing class BasePlusCommissionEmployee.
3    Module BasePlusCommissionEmployeeTest
4       Sub Main()
5          ' instantiate BasePlusCommissionEmployee object
6          Dim employee As New BasePlusCommissionEmployee( _
7             "Bob", "Lewis", "333-33-3333", 5000, 0.04D, 300)
8
9          ' get base-salaried commission employee data
10         Console.WriteLine("Employee information obtained by properties:" _
11            & vbCrLf & "First name is " & employee.FirstName & vbCrLf & _
12            "Last name is " & employee.LastName & vbCrLf & _
13            "Social Security Number is " & employee.SocialSecurityNumber)
14         Console.WriteLine("Gross sales is {0:C}", employee.GrossSales)
15         Console.WriteLine("Commission rate is {0:F}", _
16            employee.CommissionRate)
17         Console.WriteLine("Base salary is {0:C}", employee.BaseSalary)
18
19         employee.BaseSalary = 1000 ' set base salary
20
21         ' get new employee information
22         Console.WriteLine(vbCrLf & _
23            "Updated employee information obtained by ToString: " & _
24            vbCrLf & employee.ToString() & vbCrLf)
25
```

Fig. 10.12 | Protected base class members inherited into derived class BasePlusCommissionEmployee. (Part 1 of 2.)

```
26              ' display the employee's earnings
27          Console.WriteLine("Employee's earnings: $" & _
28             employee.CalculateEarnings())
29      End Sub ' Main
30    End Module ' BasePlusCommissionEmployeeTest
```

```
Employee information obtained by properties:
First name is Bob
Last name is Lewis
Social Security Number is 333-33-3333
Gross sales is $5,000.00
Commission rate is 0.04
Base salary is $300.00

Updated employee information obtained by ToString:
base-plus-commission employee: Bob Lewis
social security number: 333-33-3333
gross sales: $5,000.00
commission rate: 0.04
base salary: $1,000.00

Employee's earnings: $1200.00
```

Fig. 10.12 | Protected base class members inherited into derived class BasePlusCommissionEmployee. (Part 2 of 2.)

Notes on Using *Protected* Data

In this example, we declare base class instance variables as Protected so that derived classes can inherit and access them. Inheriting Protected instance variables slightly improves performance, because we can directly access the variables in the derived class without incurring the overhead of calling property Set or Get accessors. In most cases, however, it is better to use Private instance variables to encourage proper software engineering, and leave code optimization issues to the compiler. Your code will be easier to maintain, modify and debug.

Using Protected instance variables creates several potential problems. First, the derived class object can set an inherited variable's value directly without using a Set accessor. Therefore, a derived class object can assign an invalid value to the variable, thus leaving the object in an inconsistent state. For example, if we were to declare Commission-Employee's instance variable grossSalesValue as Protected, a derived class object could then assign a negative value to grossSalesValue. Another problem with using Protected instance variables is that derived class methods are more likely to be written so that they depend on the base class's data implementation. In practice, derived classes should depend only on the base class services (i.e., non-Private methods and properties) and not on the base class data implementation. With Protected instance variables in the base class, all the derived classes of the base class may need to be modified if the base class implementation changes. For example, if for some reason we were to change the names of instance variables firstNameValue and lastNameValue to first and last, then we would have to do so for all occurrences in which a derived class directly references base class instance variables firstNameValue and lastNameValue. In such a case, the software is said to be fragile or brittle, because a small change in the base class can "break" derived class implementations.

We should be able to change the base class implementation while still providing the same services to the derived classes. Of course, if the base class services change, we must reimplement our derived classes.

Software Engineering Observation 10.5

Use the Protected access modifier on a method when a base class is to provide the method to its derived classes but not to other clients.

10.4.5 CommissionEmployee–BasePlusCommissionEmployee Inheritance Hierarchy Using Private Instance Variables

We now reexamine our hierarchy once more, this time using better software engineering practices. Class CommissionEmployee (Fig. 10.13) declares instance variables firstName-Value, lastNameValue, socialSecurityNumberValue, grossSalesValue and commissionRateValue as Private (lines 4–8) and provides Public properties FirstName, LastName, SocialSecurityNumber, GrossSales and CommissionRate for manipulating these values. Note that methods CalculateEarnings (lines 86–88) and ToString (lines 91–97) use the class's properties to obtain the values of the Private instance variables. If we decide to change the instance variable names, the CalculateEarnings and ToString declarations will not require modification—only the bodies of the Get and Set accessors that directly manipulate the instance variables will need to change. These changes would occur solely within the base class—no changes to the derived class would be needed. Localizing the effects of changes is good software engineering. Derived class BasePlusCommissionEmployee (Fig. 10.14) inherits CommissionEmployee's non-Private properties and methods and can access the Private base class members via those properties and methods.

Software Engineering Observation 10.6

Declaring base class instance variables Private (as opposed to Protected) enables the base class implementation of these instance variables to change without affecting derived class implementations.

Error-Prevention Tip 10.1

When possible, do not include Protected instance variables in a base class. Instead, include non-Private properties and methods that carefully access Private instance variables. This will ensure that objects of the derived classes of this base class maintain consistent states of the base class instance variables.

```
 I    ' Fig. 10.13: CommmissionEmployee.vb
 2    ' CommissionEmployee class represents a commission employee.
 3    Public Class CommissionEmployee
 4       Private firstNameValue As String ' first name
 5       Private lastNameValue As String ' last name
 6       Private socialSecurityNumberValue As String ' social security number
 7       Private grossSalesValue As Decimal ' gross weekly sales
 8       Private commissionRateValue As Decimal ' commission percentage
```

Fig. 10.13 | CommissionEmployee class uses properties to manipulate its Private instance variables. (Part 1 of 3.)

```vbnet
 9
10     ' five-argument constructor
11     Public Sub New(ByVal first As String, ByVal last As String, _
12        ByVal ssn As String, ByVal sales As Decimal, ByVal rate As Decimal)
13
14        ' implicit call to Object constructor occurs here
15        FirstName = first
16        LastName = last
17        SocialSecurityNumber = ssn
18        GrossSales = sales ' validate and store gross sales
19        CommissionRate = rate ' validate and store commission rate
20     End Sub ' New
21
22     ' property FirstName
23     Public Property FirstName() As String
24        Get
25           Return firstNameValue
26        End Get
27
28        Set(ByVal first As String)
29           firstNameValue = first ' no validation
30        End Set
31     End Property ' FirstName
32
33     ' property LastName
34     Public Property LastName() As String
35        Get
36           Return lastNameValue
37        End Get
38
39        Set(ByVal last As String)
40           lastNameValue = last ' no validation
41        End Set
42     End Property ' LastName
43
44     ' property SocialSecurityNumber
45     Public Property SocialSecurityNumber() As String
46        Get
47           Return socialSecurityNumberValue
48        End Get
49
50        Set(ByVal ssn As String)
51           socialSecurityNumberValue = ssn ' no validation
52        End Set
53     End Property ' SocialSecurityNumber
54
55     ' property GrossSales
56     Public Property GrossSales() As Decimal
57        Get
58           Return grossSalesValue
59        End Get
```

Fig. 10.13 | CommissionEmployee class uses properties to manipulate its Private instance variables. (Part 2 of 3.)

```
60
61          Set(ByVal sales As Decimal)
62             If sales < 0.0 Then ' validate gross sales
63                grossSalesValue = 0
64             Else
65                grossSalesValue = sales
66             End If
67          End Set
68       End Property ' GrossSales
69
70       ' property CommissionRate
71       Public Property CommissionRate() As Decimal
72          Get
73             Return commissionRateValue
74          End Get
75
76          Set(ByVal rate As Decimal)
77             If rate > 0.0 AndAlso rate < 1.0 Then ' validate rate
78                commissionRateValue = rate
79             Else
80                commissionRateValue = 0
81             End If
82          End Set
83       End Property ' CommissionRate
84
85       ' calculate earnings
86       Public Overridable Function CalculateEarnings() As Decimal
87          Return CommissionRate * GrossSales
88       End Function ' CalculateEarnings
89
90       ' return String representation of CommissionEmployee object
91       Public Overrides Function ToString() As String
92          Return ("commission employee: " & FirstName & " " & _
93             LastName & vbCrLf & "social security number: " & _
94             SocialSecurityNumber & vbCrLf & "gross sales: " & _
95             String.Format("{0:C}", GrossSales) & vbCrLf & _
96             "commission rate: " & String.Format("{0:F}", CommissionRate))
97       End Function ' ToString
98    End Class ' CommissionEmployee
```

Fig. 10.13 | CommissionEmployee class uses properties to manipulate its Private instance variables. (Part 3 of 3.)

Class BasePlusCommissionEmployee (Fig. 10.14) has several changes to its method implementations that distinguish it from class BasePlusCommissionEmployee (Fig. 10.11). Methods CalculateEarnings (Fig. 10.14, lines 34–36) and ToString (lines 39–42) both use property BaseSalary to obtain the base salary value, rather than accessing baseSalaryValue directly. If we decide to rename instance variable baseSalaryValue, only the bodies of property BaseSalary will need to change.

Class BasePlusCommissionEmployee's CalculateEarnings method (Fig. 10.14, lines 34–36) overrides class CommissionEmployee's CalculateEarnings method (Fig. 10.13, lines 86–88) to calculate the earnings of a base-salaried commission employee. The new

```vbnet
1   ' Fig. 10.14: BasePlusCommissionEmployee.vb
2   ' BasePlusCommissionEmployee inherits from class CommissionEmployee.
3   Public Class BasePlusCommissionEmployee
4      Inherits CommissionEmployee
5
6      Private baseSalaryValue As Decimal ' base salary per week
7
8      ' six-argument constructor
9      Public Sub New(ByVal first As String, ByVal last As String, _
10        ByVal ssn As String, ByVal sales As Decimal, _
11        ByVal rate As Decimal, ByVal salary As Decimal)
12
13        ' use MyBase reference to CommissionEmployee constructor explicitly
14        MyBase.New(first, last, ssn, sales, rate)
15        BaseSalary = salary ' validate and store base salary
16      End Sub ' New
17
18      ' property BaseSalary
19      Public Property BaseSalary() As Decimal
20        Get
21           Return baseSalaryValue
22        End Get
23
24        Set(ByVal salary As Decimal)
25           If salary < 0.0 Then ' validate base salary
26              baseSalaryValue = 0
27           Else
28              baseSalaryValue = salary
29           End If
30        End Set
31      End Property ' BaseSalary
32
33      ' calculate earnings
34      Public Overrides Function CalculateEarnings() As Decimal
35        Return BaseSalary + MyBase.CalculateEarnings()
36      End Function ' CalculateEarnings
37
38      ' return String representation of BasePlusCommissionEmployee object
39      Public Overrides Function ToString() As String
40        Return ("base-plus-" & MyBase.ToString() & vbCrLf & _
41           "base salary: " & String.Format("{0:C}", BaseSalary))
42      End Function ' ToString
43   End Class ' BasePlusCommissionEmployee
```

Fig. 10.14 | BasePlusCommissionEmployee class Inherits CommissionEmployee, which provides only Private instance variables.

version obtains the portion of the employee's earnings based on commission alone by calling CommissionEmployee's CalculateEarnings method with the expression MyBase.CalculateEarnings() (Fig. 10.14, line 35). BasePlusCommissionEmployee's CalculateEarnings method then adds the base salary to this value to calculate the total earnings of the derived-class employee. Note the syntax used to invoke an overridden base class method from a derived class—place the keyword MyBase and a dot (.) separator before the base class method name. By having BasePlusCommissionEmployee's Calculate-Earnings method invoke CommissionEmployee's CalculateEarnings method to calculate part of a BasePlusCommissionEmployee object's earnings, we avoid duplicating the code and reduce code maintenance problems.

Common Programming Error 10.3

When a base class method is overridden in a derived class, the derived class version often calls the base class version to do a portion of the work. Failure to prefix the base class method name with the keyword MyBase and a dot (.) separator when referencing the base class's method causes the derived class method to call itself, creating an error called infinite recursion.

Similarly, BasePlusCommissionEmployee's ToString method (Fig. 10.14, lines 39–42) overrides class CommissionEmployee's ToString method (Fig. 10.13, lines 91–97) to return a string representation that is appropriate for a base-salaried commission employee. The derived class creates part of a BasePlusCommissionEmployee object's string representation (i.e., the string "base-plus-commission employee" and the values of class CommissionEmployee's Private instance variables) by appending "base-plus-" in front of the string returned by calling CommissionEmployee's ToString method with the expression MyBase.ToString() (Fig. 10.14, line 40). BasePlusCommissionEmployee's ToString method then outputs the remainder of a BasePlusCommissionEmployee object's string representation (i.e., the value of class BasePlusCommissionEmployee's base salary).

Figure 10.15 performs the same manipulations on a BasePlusCommissionEmployee object as did Fig. 10.7 and Fig. 10.12. Although each "base-salaried commission employee" class behaves identically, class BasePlusCommissionEmployee (Fig. 10.14) is the best engineered. By using inheritance and by calling methods that hide the data and ensure consistency, we have efficiently constructed a well-engineered class.

```vb
 1    ' Fig. 10.15: BasePlusCommissionEmployeeTest.vb
 2    ' Testing class BasePlusCommissionEmployee.
 3    Module BasePlusCommissionEmployeeTest
 4       Sub Main()
 5          ' instantiate BasePlusCommissionEmployee object
 6          Dim employee As New BasePlusCommissionEmployee( _
 7             "Bob", "Lewis", "333-33-3333", 5000, 0.04D, 300)
 8
 9          ' get base-salaried commission employee data
10          Console.WriteLine("Employee information obtained by properties:" _
11             & vbCrLf & "First name is " & employee.FirstName & vbCrLf & _
12             "Last name is " & employee.LastName & vbCrLf & _
13             "Social Security Number is " & employee.SocialSecurityNumber)
14          Console.WriteLine("Gross sales is {0:C}", employee.GrossSales)
15          Console.WriteLine("Commission rate is {0:F}", _
16             employee.CommissionRate)
17          Console.WriteLine("Base salary is {0:C}", employee.BaseSalary)
18
19          employee.BaseSalary = 1000 ' set base salary
20
```

Fig. 10.15 | Base class Private instance variables are accessible to a derived class via the Public or Protected properties and methods inherited by the derived class. (Part 1 of 2.)

```
21          ' get new employee information
22          Console.WriteLine(vbCrLf & _
23              "Updated employee information obtained by ToString: " & _
24              vbCrLf & employee.ToString() & vbCrLf)
25
26          ' display the employee's earnings
27          Console.WriteLine("Employee's earnings: $" & _
28              employee.CalculateEarnings())
29      End Sub ' Main
30  End Module ' BasePlusCommissionEmployeeTest
```

```
Employee information obtained by properties:
First name is Bob
Last name is Lewis
Social Security Number is 333-33-3333
Gross sales is $5,000.00
Commission rate is 0.04
Base salary is $300.00

Updated employee information obtained by ToString:
base-plus-commission employee: Bob Lewis
social security number: 333-33-3333
gross sales: $5,000.00
commission rate: 0.04
base salary: $1,000.00

Employee's earnings: $1200.00
```

Fig. 10.15 | Base class `Private` instance variables are accessible to a derived class via the `Public` or `Protected` properties and methods inherited by the derived class. (Part 2 of 2.)

In this section, you studied five example programs that were carefully designed to teach key capabilities for good software engineering with inheritance. You learned how to use the keyword `Inherits` to create a derived class using inheritance, how to use `Protected` base class members to enable a derived class to access inherited base class instance variables and how to override base class methods to provide versions that are more appropriate for derived class objects. Also, you applied software engineering techniques from Chapter 9 and 10 to create classes that are easy to maintain, modify and debug.

10.5 Constructors in Derived Classes

As we explained in the preceding section, instantiating a derived class object begins a chain of constructor calls in which the derived class constructor, before performing its own tasks, invokes its direct base class's constructor either explicitly (via the `MyBase` reference) or implicitly (calling the base class's default or parameterless constructor). Similarly, if the base class is derived from another class (as is every class except `Object`), the base class constructor invokes the constructor of the next class up the hierarchy, and so on. The last constructor called in the chain is always the constructor for class `Object`. The original derived class constructor's body finishes executing last. Each base class's constructor manipulates the base class instance variables that the derived class object inherits. For example, let's reconsider the CommissionEmployee–BasePlusCommissionEmployee hierarchy from Figs. 10.13 and 10.14. When a program creates a BasePlusCommissionEmployee object, the BasePlus-CommissionEmployee constructor is called. That constructor, before executing its full body code, immediately calls CommissionEmployee's constructor, which in turn calls Object's constructor. Class Object's constructor has an empty body, so it immediately returns control to the CommissionEmployee's constructor, which then initializes the Private instance variables of CommissionEmployee that are part of the BasePlusCommissionEmployee object. When the CommissionEmployee's constructor completes execution, it returns control to the BasePlusCommissionEmployee's constructor, which initializes the BasePlusCommissionEmployee object's baseSalaryValue.

Our next example revisits the commission employee hierarchy by redeclaring class CommissionEmployee (Fig. 10.16) and class BasePlusCommissionEmployee (Fig. 10.17) with each class's constructor printing a message when invoked, enabling us to observe the order in which the constructors in the hierarchy execute.

```vbnet
1   ' Fig. 10.16: CommissionEmployee.vb
2   ' CommissionEmployee class represents a commission employee.
3   Public Class CommissionEmployee
4      Private firstNameValue As String ' first name
5      Private lastNameValue As String ' last name
6      Private socialSecurityNumberValue As String ' social security number
7      Private grossSalesValue As Decimal ' gross weekly sales
8      Private commissionRateValue As Decimal ' commission percentage
9
10     ' five-argument constructor
11     Public Sub New(ByVal first As String, ByVal last As String, _
12        ByVal ssn As String, ByVal sales As Decimal, ByVal rate As Decimal)
13
14        ' implicit call to Object constructor occurs here
15        FirstName = first
16        LastName = last
17        SocialSecurityNumber = ssn
18        GrossSales = sales ' validate and store gross sales
19        CommissionRate = rate ' validate and store commission rate
20        Console.WriteLine(vbCrLf & _
21           "CommissionEmployee constructor:" & vbCrLf & "{0}", Me)
22     End Sub ' New
23
24     ' property FirstName
25     Public Property FirstName() As String
26        Get
27           Return firstNameValue
28        End Get
29
30        Set(ByVal first As String)
31           firstNameValue = first ' no validation
32        End Set
33     End Property ' FirstName
34
```

Fig. 10.16 | CommissionEmployee's constructor outputs text. (Part 1 of 3.)

```vbnet
35        ' property LastName
36        Public Property LastName() As String
37           Get
38              Return lastNameValue
39           End Get
40
41           Set(ByVal last As String)
42              lastNameValue = last ' no validation
43           End Set
44        End Property ' LastName
45
46        ' property SocialSecurityNumber
47        Public Property SocialSecurityNumber() As String
48           Get
49              Return socialSecurityNumberValue
50           End Get
51
52           Set(ByVal ssn As String)
53              socialSecurityNumberValue = ssn ' no validation
54           End Set
55        End Property ' SocialSecurityNumber
56
57        ' property GrossSales
58        Public Property GrossSales() As Decimal
59           Get
60              Return grossSalesValue
61           End Get
62
63           Set(ByVal sales As Decimal)
64              If sales < 0.0 Then ' validate gross sales
65                 grossSalesValue = 0
66              Else
67                 grossSalesValue = sales
68              End If
69           End Set
70        End Property ' GrossSales
71
72        ' property CommissionRate
73        Public Property CommissionRate() As Decimal
74           Get
75              Return commissionRateValue
76           End Get
77
78           Set(ByVal rate As Decimal)
79              If rate > 0.0 AndAlso rate < 1.0 Then ' validate rate
80                 commissionRateValue = rate
81              Else
82                 commissionRateValue = 0
83              End If
84           End Set
85        End Property ' CommissionRate
86
```

Fig. 10.16 | CommissionEmployee's constructor outputs text. (Part 2 of 3.)

```
87        ' calculate earnings
88        Public Overridable Function CalculateEarnings() As Decimal
89           Return CommissionRate * GrossSales
90        End Function ' CalculateEarnings
91
92        ' return String representation of CommissionEmployee object
93        Public Overrides Function ToString() As String
94           Return ("commission employee: " & FirstName & " " & _
95              LastName & vbCrLf & "social security number: " & _
96              SocialSecurityNumber & vbCrLf & "gross sales: " & _
97              String.Format("{0:C}", GrossSales) & vbCrLf & _
98              "commission rate: " & String.Format("{0:F}", CommissionRate))
99        End Function ' ToString
100   End Class ' CommissionEmployee
```

Fig. 10.16 | CommissionEmployee's constructor outputs text. (Part 3 of 3.)

Class CommissionEmployee (Fig. 10.16) contains the same features as the version of the class shown in Fig. 10.13. We have modified the constructor (lines 11–22) to output text upon its invocation (lines 20–21). Note that outputting Me with the {0} format string (line 21) implicitly invokes the ToString method of the CommissionEmployee object being constructed to obtain the object's string representation.

Class BasePlusCommissionEmployee (Fig. 10.17) is almost identical to Fig. 10.14, except that BasePlusCommissionEmployee's constructor also outputs text when invoked (lines 16–17). Again, we output Me using the {0} format string (line 17) to implicitly invokes the ToString method, this time to obtain the BasePlusCommissionEmployee object's string representation.

```
1    ' Fig. 10.17: BasePlusCommissionEmployee.vb
2    ' BasePlusCommissionEmployee inherits from class CommissionEmployee.
3    Public Class BasePlusCommissionEmployee
4       Inherits CommissionEmployee
5
6       Private baseSalaryValue As Decimal ' base salary per week
7
8       ' six-argument constructor
9       Public Sub New(ByVal first As String, ByVal last As String, _
10         ByVal ssn As String, ByVal sales As Decimal, _
11         ByVal rate As Decimal, ByVal salary As Decimal)
12
13         ' use MyBase reference to CommissionEmployee constructor explicitly
14         MyBase.New(first, last, ssn, sales, rate)
15         BaseSalary = salary ' validate and store base salary
16         Console.WriteLine(vbCrLf & _
17            "BasePlusCommissionEmployee constructor:" & vbCrLf & "{0}", Me)
18      End Sub ' New
19
```

Fig. 10.17 | BasePlusCommissionEmployee's constructor outputs text. (Part 1 of 2.)

```
20        ' property BaseSalary
21        Public Property BaseSalary() As Decimal
22           Get
23              Return baseSalaryValue
24           End Get
25
26           Set(ByVal salary As Decimal)
27              If salary < 0.0 Then ' validate base salary
28                 baseSalaryValue = 0
29              Else
30                 baseSalaryValue = salary
31              End If
32           End Set
33        End Property ' BaseSalary
34
35        ' calculate earnings
36        Public Overrides Function CalculateEarnings() As Decimal
37           Return BaseSalary + MyBase.CalculateEarnings()
38        End Function ' earnings
39
40        ' return String representation of BasePlusCommissionEmployee object
41        Public Overrides Function ToString() As String
42           Return ("base-plus-" & MyBase.ToString() & vbCrLf & _
43              "base salary: " & String.Format("{0:C}", BaseSalary))
44        End Function ' ToString
45     End Class ' BasePlusCommissionEmployee
```

Fig. 10.17 | BasePlusCommissionEmployee's constructor outputs text. (Part 2 of 2.)

Figure 10.18 demonstrates the order in which constructors are called for objects of classes that are part of an inheritance hierarchy. Method Main begins by instantiating CommissionEmployee object employee1 (lines 6–7). Next, lines 10–11 instantiate BasePlusCommissionEmployee object employee2. This invokes the CommissionEmployee constructor, which prints output with the values passed from the BasePlusCommissionEmployee constructor, then performs the output specified in the BasePlusCommissionEmployee constructor.

```
 1     ' Fig. 10.18: Constructor.vb
 2     ' Display order in which base class and derived class constructors
 3     ' and finalizers are called.
 4     Module Constructor
 5        Sub Main()
 6           Dim employee1 As New CommissionEmployee( _
 7              "Bob", "Lewis", "333-33-3333", 5000, 0.04D)
 8           Console.WriteLine()
 9
10           Dim employee2 As New BasePlusCommissionEmployee( _
11              "Lisa", "Jones", "555-55-5555", 2000, 0.06D, 800)
12        End Sub ' Main
13     End Module ' Constructor
```

Fig. 10.18 | Constructor call order using Me. (Part 1 of 2.)

```
CommissionEmployee constructor:
commission employee: Bob Lewis
social security number: 333-33-3333
gross sales: $5,000.00
commission rate: 0.04

CommissionEmployee constructor:
base-plus-commission employee: Lisa Jones
social security number: 555-55-5555
gross sales: $2,000.00
commission rate: 0.06
base salary: $0.00

BasePlusCommissionEmployee constructor:
base-plus-commission employee: Lisa Jones
social security number: 555-55-5555
gross sales: $2,000.00
commission rate: 0.06
base salary: $800.00
```

Fig. 10.18 | Constructor call order using Me. (Part 2 of 2.)

Analyzing the Output

The outputs of the CommissionEmployee constructor and BasePlusCommissionEmployee constructor calls each contain values for the first name, last name, social security number, gross sales, commission rate *and* base salary of the BasePlusCommissionEmployee. When constructing a BasePlusCommissionEmployee object, the Me reference used in the body of both the CommissionEmployee and BasePlusCommissionEmployee constructors refers to the BasePlusCommissionEmployee object being constructed. When a program invokes method ToString on an object, the version of ToString that executes is always the version defined in that object's class. This is an example of polymorphism, a key aspect of object-oriented programming that we discuss in detail in Chapter 11. Reference Me refers to the current BasePlusCommissionEmployee object being constructed, so BasePlusCommission-Employee's ToString method executes even when ToString is invoked from the body of class CommissionEmployee's constructor. This would not be the case if the Commission-Employee constructor were called to initialize a new CommissionEmployee object. When the CommissionEmployee constructor invokes method ToString for the BasePlusCommission-Employee being constructed, the program displays 0 for the BaseSalary value, because the BasePlusCommissionEmployee constructor's body has not yet initialized the BaseSalary. The BasePlusCommissionEmployee constructor output shows the proper BaseSalary value (i.e., 800.00), because this line is output after the BaseSalary is initialized.

Using *MyClass* in Class *CommissionEmployee's* Constructor

To force CommissionEmployee's ToString method to execute when the CommissionEmployee's constructor is called, we use the MyClass reference. Reference **MyClass** is similar to Me, except that a method call with MyClass always invokes the version of the method defined in that particular class—the method called is not affected by the runtime type of the object. For example, if we replace Me in line 21 of Fig. 10.16 with

```
MyClass.ToString()
```

then `CommissionEmployee`'s `ToString` will be executed (even though the runtime type of the object is `BasePlusCommissionEmployee`). Thus, the output of the `CommissionEmployee`'s constructor call will not display the base salary value (Fig. 10.19).

Recall that `Shared` class variables and `Shared` class methods exist independently of any class objects. They also exist when there are no objects of that class. Hence, the `MyClass` reference cannot be used in a `Shared` method because such a method can be called even when there are no objects of the corresponding class.

10.6 Software Engineering with Inheritance

Novice programmers sometimes have difficulty appreciating the scope of the problems faced by developers who work on large-scale software projects in industry. People experienced with such projects say that effective software reuse improves the software-development process. Object-oriented programming facilitates software reuse, potentially shortening development and maintenance efforts.

This section discusses customizing existing software with inheritance. When a new class inherits from an existing class, the new class inherits the non-`Private` members of the existing class. We can customize the new class to meet our needs by including additional members and by overriding base class members. Doing this does not require the derived class programmer to change the base class's source code. Visual Basic simply requires access to the base class's assembly file so that it can compile and execute any program that uses or inherits the base class. This is attractive to independent software vendors (ISVs) because they develop proprietary classes for sale or license and make them available to users in MSIL format. Users then can derive new classes from these library classes rapidly and without accessing the ISVs' proprietary source code.

 Software Engineering Observation 10.7

Despite the fact that inheriting from a class does not require access to the class's source code, developers often insist on seeing the source code to see how the class is implemented. They want to ensure that they are extending a solid class that performs well and is implemented securely.

```
CommissionEmployee constructor:
commission employee: Bob Lewis
social security number: 333-33-3333
gross sales: $5,000.00
commission rate: 0.04

CommissionEmployee constructor:
commission employee: Lisa Jones
social security number: 555-55-5555
gross sales: $2,000.00
commission rate: 0.06

BasePlusCommissionEmployee constructor:
base-plus-commission employee: Lisa Jones
social security number: 555-55-5555
gross sales: $2,000.00
commission rate: 0.06
base salary: $800.00
```

Fig. 10.19 | Constructor call order using `MyClass`.

The availability of substantial class libraries helps deliver the maximum benefits of software reuse through inheritance. Application designers build their applications with these libraries, and library designers are compensated when their libraries are included with the applications. The standard Visual Basic class libraries tend to be general purpose. Many special-purpose class libraries exist and more are being created.

Software Engineering Observation 10.8

At the design stage in an object-oriented system, the designer often finds that certain classes are closely related. The designer should "factor out" common instance variables and methods and place them in a base class. Then the designer should use inheritance to develop derived classes, specializing them with capabilities beyond those inherited from the base class.

Performance Tip 10.1

If derived classes are larger than they need to be (i.e., contain too much functionality), memory and processing resources may be wasted. Extend the base class that contains the functionality that is closest to what you need.

Reading derived class declarations can be confusing, because inherited members are not declared explicitly in the derived classes, but are nevertheless present in them. A similar problem exists in documenting derived class members.

10.7 Class Object

As we have mentioned, all classes inherit directly or indirectly from the Object class (namespace System), so its seven methods are inherited by all other classes. Figure 10.20 summarizes Object's methods.

Method	Description
Equals	Compares two objects for equality; returns True if they are equal and False otherwise. The method takes any Object as an argument. When objects of a class must be compared for equality, the class should override method Equals to compare the contents of the two objects. The method's implementation should meet the following requirements: • It should return False if the argument is Nothing. • It should return True if an object is compared to itself, as in object1.Equals(object1). • It should return True only if both object1.Equals(object2) and object2.Equals(object1) would return True. • For three objects, if object1.Equals(object2) returns True and object2.Equals(object3) returns True, then object1.Equals(object3) should also return True. • A class that overrides Equals must also override GetHashCode to ensure that equal objects have identical hashcodes. The default Equals implementation determines only whether two references *refer to the same object* in memory.

Fig. 10.20 | Object methods that are inherited by all classes. (Part I of 2.)

Method	Description
Finalize	This Protected method (introduced in Section 9.9) is called by the garbage collector on an object just before the garbage collector reclaims the object's memory. It is not guaranteed that the garbage collector will reclaim an object, so it cannot be guaranteed that the object's Finalize method will execute. The method must specify an empty parameter list and must not return a value. The default implementation of this method is a placeholder that does nothing.
GetHashCode	A hashtable is a data structure that relates one object, called the key, to another object, called the value. We discuss class Hashtable in Chapter 26, Collections. When initially inserting a value into a hashtable, the key's GetHashCode method is called. The hashcode value returned is used by the hashtable to determine the location at which to insert the corresponding value. The key's hashcode is also used by the hashtable to locate the key's corresponding value.
GetType	Every object in Visual Basic knows its own type at execution time. Method GetType (used in Section 11.5) returns an object of class Type (namespace System) that contains information about the object's type, such as its class name (obtained from Type property FullName).
MemberwiseClone	This Protected method, which takes no arguments and returns an Object reference, makes a copy of the object on which it is called. The implementation of this method performs a **shallow copy**—instance variable values in one object are copied into another object of the same type. For reference types, only the references are copied.
ReferenceEquals	This Shared method takes two Object arguments and returns True if two objects are the same instance or if they are Nothing references. Otherwise, it returns False.
ToString	This method (introduced in Section 9.2) returns a String representation of an object. The default implementation of this method returns the namespace followed by a dot and the class name of the object's class.

Fig. 10.20 | Object methods that are inherited by all classes. (Part 2 of 2.)

We discuss most of Object's methods throughout this book (as indicated in the table). To learn more about these methods from the **Help** menu, select **Help > Index…**, and enter "Object class" in the search text box.

10.8 Friend Members

Another intermediate level of member access is Friend access. A class's Friend members can be accessed only by code in the same assembly. In a program or an assembly that consists of one class declaration, declaring a member with Friend access has no specific effect. However, if a program uses multiple classes from the same assembly, these classes can access each other's Friend members directly through references to objects of the appropriate classes. Unlike Public access, any other programs that are declared outside the assembly cannot access these Friend members. To access a non-Shared Friend member within the same assembly, you would first have to create an object of the class that declares the Friend member, then invoke the Friend member using the dot (.) separator. You can access a Friend member that is also Shared via the name of the class that declares the Friend member and a dot (.) separator. Note that you can also have Protected Friend members that are accessible both from code in the same assembly and by subclasses of the class in which the Protected Friend members are declared.

10.9 Wrap-Up

This chapter introduced inheritance—the ability to create a class by absorbing an existing class's members and embellishing them with new capabilities. Through a series of examples using an employee inheritance hierarchy, you learned the notions of base classes and derived classes and used keyword Inherits to create derived classes that inherit members from base classes. We introduced the access modifiers Protected and Friend. Derived class methods can access Protected base class members. Friend members are accessible to classes declared in the same assembly as the class that declares the Friend members. You learned how to access base class members with MyBase and how to access the current object with the Me and MyClass references. You also saw the order in which constructors are called for objects of classes that are part of an inheritance hierarchy. Finally, you learned about the methods of class Object—the direct or indirect base class of all classes.

In Chapter 11, Object-Oriented Programming: Polymorphism, we build on our discussion of inheritance by introducing polymorphism—an object-oriented concept that enables us to write programs that handle, in a simple and more general manner, objects of a wide variety of classes related by inheritance. After studying Chapter 11, you will be familiar with classes, objects, encapsulation, inheritance and polymorphism—the most essential aspects of object-oriented programming.

Summary

Section 10.1 Introduction

- Inheritance is a form of software reuse in which a new class is created by absorbing an existing class's members and embellishing them with new or modified capabilities.

- When creating a class, rather than declaring completely new members, you can designate that the new class inherits the members of an existing class. The existing class is called the base class, and the new class is the derived class.

- A derived class is more specific than its base class and normally represents a more specialized group of objects.

- The direct base class is the base class from which the derived class explicitly inherits.

- An indirect base class is inherited from two or more levels up in the class hierarchy.

- An *is-a* relationship represents inheritance. In an *is-a* relationship, an object of a derived class also can be treated as an object of its base class, but not vice versa.

- A *has-a* relationship represents composition. In a *has-a* relationship, an object contains references to objects of other classes.

Section 10.2 Base Classes and Derived Classes

- A class can be either a base class, supplying members to other classes, or a derived class, inheriting some of its members from other classes.

- A derived class can override (redefine) a base class method with an appropriate implementation.

Section 10.3 Protected Members

- A base class's Protected members can be accessed by members of that base class and by members of its derived classes.

- When a derived class method overrides a base class method, the base class method can be accessed from the derived class by preceding the base class method name with MyBase and a dot (.).

- Derived class methods cannot directly access Private members of their base class.

Section 10.4.1 Creating and Using a CommissionEmployee Class

- Every class directly or indirectly inherits class Object's methods. If a class does not specify that it inherits another class, the new class implicitly inherits Object.

- Declaring instance variables as Private and providing Public properties to manipulate and validate the instance variables help enforce good software engineering.

- A base class method must be declared Overridable if it is to be overridden in a derived class.

- A derived class method uses keyword Overrides to indicate that it overrides (redefines) the corresponding method declared in the base class.

Section 10.4.2 Creating a BasePlusCommissionEmployee Class without Using Inheritance

- With inheritance, the common instance variables and methods of all the classes in the hierarchy are declared in a base class.

Section 10.4.3 Creating a CommissionEmployee–BasePlusCommissionEmployee Inheritance Hierarchy

- Each derived class constructor must implicitly or explicitly call its base class constructor to ensure that the instance variables inherited from the base class are initialized properly.

- A derived class can explicitly invoke a constructor of its base class by using the base class constructor call syntax—keyword MyBase, followed by the dot (.) separator, followed by New and a set of parentheses containing the base class constructor arguments.

Section 10.4.4 CommissionEmployee–BasePlusCommissionEmployee Inheritance hierarchy Using Protected Instance Variables

- Declaring Public instance variables is poor software engineering because it allows unrestricted access to the instance variables, greatly increasing the chance of errors.

- With Protected instance variables, a derived class gets access to the instance variables, but classes that are not derived classes cannot access these variables directly.

- With Protected instance variables, a derived class object can set an inherited variable directly.

- With Protected instance variables in the base class, all the derived classes of the base class may need to be modified if the base class implementation changes.

Section 10.5 Constructors in Derived Classes

- When a program creates a derived class object, the derived class constructor immediately calls the base class constructor (explicitly via MyBase, or implicitly).

- A method call with MyClass always invokes the version of the method defined in that particular class—the method called is not affected by the runtime type of the object.

- The MyClass reference cannot be used in a Shared method because such a method can be called when no objects exist.

Section 10.6 Software Engineering with Inheritance

- When a new class inherits from an existing class, the new class inherits the non-Private members of the existing class.

- Object-oriented programming facilitates software reuse, potentially shortening development and maintenance effort.

- The availability of substantial and useful class libraries helps deliver the maximum benefits of software reuse through inheritance.

Section 10.7 Class *Object*

- Method Equals of Object compares two objects for equality and returns True if they are equal and False otherwise.

- The default Equals implementation determines whether two references refer to the same object in memory.

- Method Finalize of Object is called by the garbage collector on an object just before the garbage collector reclaims the object's memory.

- Every object knows its own type. Method GetType of Object returns an object of class Type (namespace System) that contains information about the object's type, such as its class name (obtained from Type property FullName).

- Method ToString of Object returns a String representation of an object. The default implementation of this method returns the namespace and class name of the object's class.

- The default implementation of method MemberwiseClone of Object performs a so-called shallow copy—instance variable values in one object are copied into another object of the same type.

Section 10.8 *Friend* Members

- A class's Friend members can be accessed only by code in the same assembly.

- To access a non-Shared Friend member within the same assembly, create an object of the class that declares the Friend member, then invoke the Friend member using the dot (.) separator.

- To access a Friend member that is Shared, use the name of the class that declares the Friend member followed by the dot (.) separator.

- You can also have Protected Friend members that are accessible both from code in the same assembly and by subclasses of the class in which the Protected Friend members are declared.

Terminology

base class	composition
base class constructor	constructor call order
base class constructor call syntax	deep copy
base class default constructor	derived class
base class parameterless constructor	derived class constructor
brittle software	direct base class
class hierarchy	Equals method of class Object
class library	field of a class
cloning an object	Finalize method of Object

fragile software
`Friend` access modifier
`FullName` property of `Type`
`GetHashCode` method of class `Object`
`GetType` method of class `Object`
has-a relationship
hierarchical relationship
hierarchy diagram of classes
indirect base class
inheritance
inheritance hierarchy
inherited member
inherited method
`Inherits` keyword
invoke a base class constructor
invoke a base class method
is-a relationship
`MemberwiseClone` method of class `Object`
`MyBase` keyword
`MyClass` keyword

object of a base class
object of a derived class
`Overridable` keyword
override a base class method in a derived class
`Overrides` keyword
`Private` base class member
`Protected` base class member
`Protected` keyword
`Public` base class member
`ReferenceEquals` method of `Object`
reusable component
shallow copy
single inheritance
software reuse
standardized reusable components
subclass
superclass
`ToString` method of class `Object`
`Type` class

Self-Review Exercises

10.1 Fill in the blanks in each of the following statements:

a) _____ is a form of software reusability in which new classes acquire the members of existing classes and enhance those classes with new capabilities.

b) A base class's _____ members can be accessed only in the base class declaration and in derived class declarations.

c) In a(n) _____ relationship, an object of a derived class can also be treated as an object of its base class.

d) In a(n) _____ relationship, a class object has references to objects of other classes as members.

e) In single inheritance, a base class exists in a(n) _____ relationship with its derived classes.

f) A base class's _____ members are accessible anywhere that the application has a reference to an object of that base class or to an object of any of its derived classes.

g) When an object of a derived class is instantiated, a base class _____ is called implicitly or explicitly.

h) Derived class constructors can call base class constructors via the _____ keyword.

10.2 State whether each of the following is *true* or *false*. If a statement is *false*, explain why.

a) Base class constructors are not inherited by derived classes.

b) A *has-a* relationship is implemented via inheritance.

c) A `Car` class has *is-a* relationships with the `SteeringWheel` and `Brakes` classes.

d) Inheritance encourages the reuse of proven high-quality software.

e) When a derived class redefines a base class method by using the same signature and return type, the derived class is said to overload that base class method.

Answers to Self-Review Exercises

10.1 a) Inheritance. b) `Protected`. c) *is-a* or inheritance. d) *has-a* or composition. e) hierarchical. f) `Public`. g) constructor. h) `MyBase`.

10.2 a) True. b) False. A *has-a* relationship is implemented via composition. An *is-a* relationship is implemented via inheritance. c) False. These are examples of *has-a* relationships. Class Car has an *is-a* relationship with class Vehicle. d) True. e) False. This is known as overriding, not overloading.

Exercises

10.3 Many applications written with inheritance could be written with composition instead, and vice versa. Rewrite class BasePlusCommissionEmployee (Fig. 10.14) of the CommissionEmployee–BasePlusCommissionEmployee hierarchy to use composition rather than inheritance.

10.4 Discuss the ways in which inheritance promotes software reuse, saves time during application development and helps prevent errors.

10.5 Draw a UML class diagram for an inheritance hierarchy for students at a university similar to the hierarchy shown in Fig. 10.2. Use Student as the base class of the hierarchy, then extend Student with classes UndergraduateStudent and GraduateStudent. Continue to extend the hierarchy as deeply (i.e., as many levels) as possible. For example, Freshman, Sophomore, Junior and Senior might extend UndergraduateStudent, and DoctoralStudent and MastersStudent might be derived classes of GraduateStudent. After drawing the hierarchy, discuss the relationships that exist between the classes. [*Note:* You do not need to write any code for this exercise.]

10.6 The world of shapes is much richer than the shapes included in the inheritance hierarchy of Fig. 10.3. Write down all the shapes you can think of—both two-dimensional and three-dimensional—and form them into a more complete Shape hierarchy with as many levels as possible. Your hierarchy should have class Shape at the top. Class TwoDimensionalShape and class ThreeDimensionalShape should extend Shape. Add additional derived classes, such as Quadrilateral and Sphere, at their correct locations in the hierarchy as necessary.

10.7 Some programmers prefer not to use Protected access, because they believe it breaks the encapsulation of the base class. Discuss the relative merits of using Protected access vs. using Private access in base classes.

10.8 Write an inheritance hierarchy for classes Quadrilateral, Trapezoid, Parallelogram, Rectangle and Square. Use Quadrilateral as the base class of the hierarchy. Make the hierarchy as deep (i.e., as many levels) as possible. Specify the instance variables, properties and methods for each class. The Private instance variables of Quadrilateral should be the *x-y* coordinate pairs for the four endpoints of the Quadrilateral. Write an application that instantiates objects of your classes and outputs each object's area (except Quadrilateral).

10.9 (*Package Inheritance Hierarchy*) Package-delivery services, such as FedEx®, DHL® and UPS®, offer a number of different shipping options, each with specific costs associated. Create an inheritance hierarchy to represent various types of packages. Use Package as the base class of the hierarchy, then include classes TwoDayPackage and OvernightPackage that derive from Package. Base class Package should include Private instance variables representing the name, address, city, state and ZIP code for the package's sender and recipient, and instance variables that store the weight (in ounces) and cost per ounce to ship the package. Package's constructor should initialize these Private instance variables with Public properties. Ensure that the weight and cost per ounce contain positive values. Package should provide a Public method CalculateCost that returns a Decimal indicating the cost associated with shipping the package. Package's CalculateCost method should determine the cost by multiplying the weight by the cost per ounce. Derived class TwoDayPackage should inherit the functionality of base class Package, but also include an instance variable that represents a flat fee that the shipping company charges for two-day delivery service. TwoDayPackage's constructor should receive a value to initialize this instance variable. TwoDayPackage should redefine method CalculateCost so that it computes the shipping cost by adding the flat fee to the weight-based cost calculated by base class Package's CalculateCost method. Class OvernightPackage should inherit directly from class Package and contain an instance variable representing an additional fee per ounce charged for overnight-delivery service. OvernightPackage should redefine method CalculateCost so that it adds the additional fee per ounce to the standard cost per ounce before calculating the shipping cost. Write a test application that creates objects of each type of Package and tests method CalculateCost.

10.10 *(Account Inheritance Hierarchy)* Create an inheritance hierarchy that a bank might use to represent customer bank accounts. All customers at this bank can deposit (i.e., credit) money into their accounts and withdraw (i.e., debit) money from their accounts. More specific types of accounts also exist. Savings accounts, for instance, earn interest on the money they hold. Checking accounts, on the other hand, charge a fee per transaction.

Create base class Account and derived classes SavingsAccount and CheckingAccount that inherit from class Account. Base class Account should include one Private instance variable of type Decimal to represent the account balance. The class should provide a constructor that receives an initial balance and uses it to initialize the instance variable with a Public property. The property should validate the initial balance to ensure that it is greater than or equal to 0.0. If not, the balance should be set to 0.0, and the set accessor should display an error message, indicating that the initial balance was invalid. The class should provide two Public methods. Method Credit should add an amount to the current balance. Method Debit should withdraw money from the Account and ensure that the debit amount does not exceed the Account's balance. If it does, the balance should be left unchanged, and the method should print the message "Debit amount exceeded account balance." The class should also provide a get accessor in property Balance that returns the current balance.

Derived class SavingsAccount should inherit the functionality of an Account, but also include a Decimal instance variable indicating the interest rate (percentage) assigned to the Account. SavingsAccount's constructor should receive the initial balance, as well as an initial value for the interest rate. SavingsAccount should provide Public method CalculateInterest that returns a Decimal indicating the amount of interest earned by an account. Method CalculateInterest should determine this amount by multiplying the interest rate by the account balance. [*Note:* SavingsAccount should inherit methods Credit and Debit without redefining them.]

Derived class CheckingAccount should inherit from base class Account and include a Decimal instance variable that represents the fee charged per transaction. CheckingAccount's constructor should receive the initial balance, as well as a parameter indicating a fee amount. Class CheckingAccount should redefine methods Credit and Debit so that they subtract the fee from the account balance whenever either transaction is performed successfully. CheckingAccount's versions of these methods should invoke the base-class Account version to perform the updates to an account balance. CheckingAccount's Debit method should charge a fee only if money is actually withdrawn (i.e., the debit amount does not exceed the account balance). [*Hint:* Define Account's Debit method so that it returns a bool indicating whether money was withdrawn. Then use the return value to determine whether a fee should be charged.]

After defining the classes in this hierarchy, write an application that creates objects of each class and tests their methods. Add interest to the SavingsAccount object by first invoking its CalculateInterest method, then passing the returned interest amount to the object's Credit method.

Object-Oriented Programming: Polymorphism

OBJECTIVES

In this chapter you will learn:

- What polymorphism is.
- To use overridden methods to effect polymorphism.
- To distinguish between abstract and concrete classes.
- To declare abstract methods to create abstract classes.
- How polymorphism makes systems extensible and maintainable.
- To determine an object's type at execution time.
- To declare and implement interfaces.

11.1 Introduction

We now continue our study of object-oriented programming by explaining and demonstrating **polymorphism** with inheritance hierarchies. Polymorphism enables us to "program in the general" rather than "program in the specific." In particular, polymorphism enables us to write programs that process objects that share the same base class in a class hierarchy as simply as if they were all objects of the base class. Yet, as we send method calls in this general way, the specific objects "do the right thing."

Consider the following example of polymorphism. Suppose we create a program that simulates the movement of several types of animals for a biological study. Classes `Fish`, `Frog` and `Bird` represent the three types of animals under investigation. Imagine that each of these classes inherits base class `Animal`, which contains a method move and maintains the animal's current location as *x-y* coordinates. Each derived class implements method move. Our program maintains an array of references to objects of the various Animal derived classes. To simulate the animals' movements, the program sends each object the same message—move—once per second. However, each specific type of Animal responds to the move message in a unique way—a Fish might swim two feet, a Frog might jump three feet and a Bird might fly ten feet. The program issues the same move message to each animal object generically, but each object knows how to modify its *x-y* coordinates appropriately for its specific type of movement. Relying on each object to know how to "do the right thing" (i.e., what is appropriate for that type of object) in response to the same method call is the key concept of polymorphism. The same message (in this case, move) sent to a variety of objects has "many forms" of results—hence the term polymorphism.

With polymorphism, we can design and implement systems that are easily extensible—new classes can be added with little or no modification to the general portions of the program, as long as the new classes are part of the inheritance hierarchy that the program processes generically. The only parts of a program that must be altered to accommodate new classes are those that require direct knowledge of the new classes that you add to the hierarchy. For example, if we inherit from class Animal to create class Tortoise (which might respond to a move message by crawling one inch), we need to write only the Tortoise class (with a move method) and the part of the simulation that instantiates Tortoise objects. The portions of the simulation that process each Animal generically can remain the same.

This chapter has several key parts. First, we discuss common examples of polymorphism. We then provide a live-code example demonstrating polymorphic behavior. As you will soon see, you will use base class references to conveniently manipulate both base class objects and derived class objects polymorphically.

We then present a case study that revisits the employee hierarchy of Section 10.4.5. We develop a simple payroll application that polymorphically calculates the weekly pay of several different types of employees using each employee's CalculateEarnings method. Though the earnings of each type of employee are calculated in a specific way, polymorphism allows us to process the employees "in the general." We add two new classes to the hierarchy—SalariedEmployee (for people paid a fixed weekly salary) and HourlyEmployee (for people paid an hourly salary and "time-and-a-half" for overtime). We declare a common set of functionality for all the classes in the updated hierarchy in a so-called abstract class, Employee, from which classes SalariedEmployee, HourlyEmployee and CommissionEmployee inherit directly, and from which class BasePlusCommissionEmployee inherits indirectly. As you will see, when we invoke each employee's CalculateEarnings method off a base class Employee reference, the correct earnings calculation is performed due to Visual Basic's polymorphic capabilities.

Occasionally, when performing polymorphic processing, we need to program "in the specific." Our Employee case study demonstrates that a program can determine an object's type at execution time and act on that object accordingly. The case study uses these capabilities to determine whether a particular employee object *is a* BasePlusCommissionEmployee, and, in that specific case, we increase the employee's base salary by 10%.

The chapter continues with an introduction to interfaces. An interface describes a set of methods that can be called on an object, but does not provide concrete implementations for the methods. Programmers can declare classes that **implement** (i.e., declare the methods of) one or more interfaces. Each interface method must be declared in all the classes that implement the interface. Once a class implements an interface, all objects of that class have an *is-a* relationship with the interface type, and all objects of the class are guaranteed to provide the functionality described by the interface. This is true of all derived classes of that class as well.

Interfaces are particularly useful for assigning common functionality to possibly unrelated classes. This allows objects of unrelated classes to be processed polymorphically—objects of classes that implement the same interface can respond to the same method calls. To demonstrate creating and using interfaces, we modify our payroll application to create a general accounts payable application that can calculate payments due not only for company employees, but also for invoice amounts to be billed for purchased goods. As you will see, interfaces enable polymorphic capabilities similar to those possible with inheritance.

11.2 Polymorphic Video Game

Suppose we design a video game that manipulates objects of many different types, including objects of classes Martian, Venutian, Plutonian, SpaceShip and LaserBeam. Imagine that each class inherits from the common base class called SpaceObject, which contains method draw. Each derived class implements this method in a manner appropriate to that class. A screen-manager program maintains a collection (e.g., a SpaceObject array) of references to objects of the various classes. To refresh the screen, the screen manager periodically sends each object the same message—namely, draw. However, each object responds in a unique way. For example, a Martian object might draw itself in red with the appropriate number of antennae. A SpaceShip object might draw itself as a bright silver flying saucer. A LaserBeam object might draw itself as a bright red beam across the screen. The same message (in this case, draw) sent to a variety of objects has "many forms" of results.

A screen manager might use polymorphism to facilitate adding new classes to a system with minimal modifications to the system's code. Suppose that we want to add Mercurian objects to our video game. To do so, we must build a class Mercurian that inherits from SpaceObject and provides its own draw method implementation. When objects of class Mercurian appear in the SpaceObject collection, the screen manager code invokes method draw, exactly as it does for the other objects in the collection, regardless of their types. So the new Mercurian class simply "plugs right in" without any modification of the screen manager code by the programmer. Thus, without modifying the system (other than to build new classes and modify the code that creates new objects), programmers can use polymorphism to include types that were not envisioned when the system was created.

With polymorphism, calls to methods of the same method name, signature and return type can be used to cause different actions to occur, depending on the type of objects on which the method is invoked. This gives you tremendous expressive capability, as you will soon see.

> **Software Engineering Observation 11.1**
>
> *Polymorphism promotes extensibility: Software that invokes polymorphic behavior is independent of the object types to which messages are sent. New object types that can respond to existing method calls can be incorporated into a system without requiring modification of the base system. Only client code that instantiates new objects must be modified to accommodate new types.*

11.3 **Demonstrating Polymorphic Behavior**

Section 10.4 created a commission employee class hierarchy, in which class `BasePlusCommissionEmployee` inherited from class `CommissionEmployee`. The examples in that section manipulated `CommissionEmployee` and `BasePlusCommissionEmployee` objects by using references to them to invoke their methods. We aimed base class references at base class objects and derived class references at derived class objects. These assignments are natural and straightforward—base class references are intended to refer to base class objects, and derived class references are intended to refer to derived class objects. However, as you will soon see, some "crossover" assignments are possible.

In the next example, we aim a base class reference at a derived class object. We then show how invoking a method on a derived class object via a base class reference invokes the derived class functionality—*the type of the actual referenced object, not the type of the reference, determines which method is called.* This example demonstrates the key concept that an object of a derived class can be treated as an object of its base class, yet still "do the right thing." This enables various interesting manipulations. A program can create an array of base class references that refer to objects of many derived class types. This is allowed because each derived class object *is an* object of its base class. For instance, we can assign the reference of a `BasePlusCommissionEmployee` object to a base class `CommissionEmployee` variable because a `BasePlusCommissionEmployee` *is a* `CommissionEmployee`—so we can treat a `BasePlusCommissionEmployee` as a `CommissionEmployee`.

As you will learn later in the chapter, we cannot treat a base class object as a derived class object because a base class object is not an object of any of its derived classes. For example, we cannot assign the reference of a `CommissionEmployee` object to a derived class `BasePlusCommissionEmployee` variable because a `CommissionEmployee` is not a `BasePlusCommissionEmployee`—a `CommissionEmployee` does not have a `baseSalary` instance variable and does not have property `BaseSalary`. The *is-a* relationship applies only from a derived class to its direct (and indirect) base classes, but not vice versa.

The compiler *does* allow the assignment of a base class reference to a derived class variable if we explicitly cast the base class reference to the derived class type—a technique we discuss in detail in Section 11.5. Why would we ever want to perform such an assignment? A base class reference can be used to invoke only the methods declared in the base class—attempting to invoke derived-class-only methods through a base class reference results in compilation errors. If a program needs to perform a derived class-specific operation on a derived class object referenced by a base class variable, the program must first cast the base class reference to a derived class reference through a technique known as downcasting. This enables the program to invoke derived class methods that are not in the base class, but only off a derived class reference. We demonstrate downcasting in Section 11.5.

Figure 11.1 shows three ways to use base class and derived class variables to store references to base class and derived class objects. The first two are straightforward—as in Section 10.4, we assign a base class reference to a base class variable, and we assign a derived class reference to a derived class variable. Then we demonstrate the relationship between derived classes and base classes (i.e., the *is-a* relationship) by assigning a derived class reference to a base class variable. [*Note:* This program uses the `CommissionEmployee` and `BasePlusCommissionEmployee` classes from Fig. 10.13 and Fig. 10.14, respectively.]

In Fig. 11.1, lines 10–11 create a `CommissionEmployee` object and assign its reference to a `CommissionEmployee` variable. Lines 14–15 create a `BasePlusCommissionEmployee` object and assign its reference to a BasePlusCommissionEmployee variable. These assignments are natural—for example, a CommissionEmployee variable's primary purpose is to hold a reference to a CommissionEmployee object. Lines 18–20 use reference commissionEmployee1 to invoke ToString explicitly. Because commissionEmployee1 refers to a CommissionEmployee object, base class CommissionEmployee's version of ToString is called, as is evident from the output. Similarly, lines 24–26 use basePlusCommissionEmployee to invoke ToString explicitly on the BasePlusCommissionEmployee object. This invokes derived class BasePlusCommissionEmployee's version of ToString, as is also evident from the output.

Lines 29–30 then assign to a base class CommissionEmployee variable commissionEmployee2 the reference to derived class object basePlusCommissionEmployee, which

```vb
 1  ' Fig. 11.1: PolymorphismTest.vb
 2  ' Assigning base class and derived class references to base class and
 3  ' derived class variables.
 4  Module PolymorphismTest
 5     Sub Main()
 6        Dim commissionEmployee1 As CommissionEmployee
 7        Dim basePlusCommissionEmployee As BasePlusCommissionEmployee
 8
 9        ' assign base class reference to base class variable
10        commissionEmployee1 = New CommissionEmployee( _
11           "Sue", "Jones", "222-22-2222", 10000, 0.06D)
12
13        ' assign derived class reference to derived class variable
14        basePlusCommissionEmployee = New BasePlusCommissionEmployee( _
15           "Bob", "Lewis", "333-33-3333", 5000, 0.04D, 300)
16
17        ' invoke ToString on base class object using base class variable
18        Console.WriteLine("Call CommissionEmployee's ToString with " & _
19           "base class reference to base class object: " & vbCrLf & _
20           commissionEmployee1.ToString() & vbCrLf)
21
22        ' invoke ToString on derived class object using
23        ' derived class variable
24        Console.WriteLine("Call BasePlusCommissionEmployee's ToString " & _
25           "with derived class reference to derived class object: " & _
26           vbCrLf & basePlusCommissionEmployee.ToString() & vbCrLf)
27
28        ' assign derived class reference to base class variable
29        Dim commissionEmployee2 As CommissionEmployee = _
30           basePlusCommissionEmployee
31
32        ' invoke ToString on derived class object using base class variable
33        Console.WriteLine("Call BasePlusCommissionEmployee's ToString " & _
34           "with base class reference to derived class object: " & _
35           vbCrLf & commissionEmployee2.ToString())
36     End Sub ' Main
37  End Module ' PolymorphismTest
```

Fig. 11.1 | Assigning base class and derived class references to base class and derived class variables. (Part 1 of 2.)

```
Call CommissionEmployee's ToString with base class reference to base class
object:
commission employee: Sue Jones
social security number: 222-22-2222
gross sales: 10,000.00
commission rate: 0.06

Call BasePlusCommissionEmployee's ToString with derived class reference to
derived class object:
commission employee: Bob Lewis
social security number: 333-33-3333
gross sales: 5,000.00
commission rate: 0.04
base salary: 300.00

Call BasePlusCommissionEmployee's ToString with base class reference to
derived class object:
commission employee: Bob Lewis
social security number: 333-33-3333
gross sales: 5,000.00
commission rate: 0.04
base salary: 300.00
```

Fig. 11.1 | Assigning base class and derived class references to base class and derived class variables. (Part 2 of 2.)

lines 33–35 use to invoke method ToString. A base class variable that contains a reference to a derived class object and that is used to call a method (which is in both the base class and the derived class) actually calls the derived class version of the method (polymorphically). Hence, commissionEmployee2.ToString() in line 35 actually calls class BasePlusCommissionEmployee's ToString method. The compiler allows this "crossover" because an object of a derived class *is an* object of its base class (but not vice versa). When the compiler encounters a method call made through a variable, it determines whether the method can be called by checking the variable's class type. If that class contains the proper method declaration (or inherits one), the compiler allows the call to be compiled. At execution time, the type of the object to which the variable refers determines the actual version of the method to use. This is polymorphic behavior.

11.4 Abstract Classes and Methods

When we think of a class type, we assume that programs will create objects of that type. In some cases, however, it is useful to declare classes for which you never intend to instantiate objects. Such classes are called **abstract classes**. Because they are used only as base classes in inheritance hierarchies, we refer to them as **abstract base classes**. These classes cannot be used to instantiate objects, because, as we will soon see, abstract classes are incomplete. We demonstrate abstract classes in Section 11.5.

The purpose of an abstract class is primarily to provide an appropriate base class from which other classes can inherit and thus share a common design. In the Shape hierarchy of Fig. 10.3, for example, derived classes inherit the notion of what it means to be a Shape—possibly including common properties such as Location, Color and Border-

Thickness, and behaviors such as Draw, Move, Resize and ChangeColor. Classes that can be used to instantiate objects are called **concrete classes**. Such classes provide implementations of every method they declare (some of the implementations can be inherited). For example, we could derive concrete classes Circle, Square and Triangle from abstract base class TwoDimensionalShape. Similarly, we could derive concrete classes Sphere, Cube and Tetrahedron from abstract base class ThreeDimensionalShape. Abstract base classes are too general to create real objects—they specify only what is common among derived classes. We need to be more specific before we can create objects. For example, if you send the Draw message to abstract class TwoDimensionalShape, it knows that two-dimensional shapes should be *drawable*, but it does not know *what specific shape to draw*, so it cannot implement a real Draw method. Concrete classes provide the specifics that make it reasonable to instantiate objects.

Abstract Classes in Inheritance Hierarchies

Not all inheritance hierarchies contain abstract classes. However, programmers often write client code that uses only abstract base class types to reduce the client code's dependencies on a range of specific derived class types. For example, a programmer can write a method with a parameter of an abstract base class type. When called, such a method can be passed an object of any concrete class that directly or indirectly inherits the base class specified as the parameter's type.

Abstract classes sometimes constitute several levels of the hierarchy. For example, the Shape hierarchy of Fig. 10.3 begins with abstract class Shape. The next level of the hierarchy contains abstract classes TwoDimensionalShape and ThreeDimensionalShape. The next level of the hierarchy declares concrete classes for TwoDimensionalShapes (Circle, Square and Triangle) and ThreeDimensionalShapes (Sphere, Cube and Tetrahedron).

Declaring Abstract Classes and Abstract Methods

You make a class abstract by declaring it with keyword MustInherit. An abstract class normally contains one or more **abstract methods**. An abstract method is one with keyword MustOverride in its declaration, as in

```
Public MustOverride Sub Draw() ' abstract method
```

Abstract methods do not provide implementations. A class that contains any abstract methods must be declared as an abstract (i.e., MustInherit) class even if it contains some concrete (non-abstract) methods. Each concrete derived class of an abstract base class must provide concrete implementations of all the base class's abstract methods. Constructors and Shared methods cannot be inherited, so they cannot be declared MustOverride.

Software Engineering Observation 11.2

An abstract class declares common attributes and behaviors of the various classes in a class hierarchy. An abstract class typically contains one or more abstract methods that derived classes must override if the derived classes are to be concrete. The instance variables and concrete methods of an abstract class are subject to the normal rules of inheritance.

Common Programming Error 11.1

Attempting to instantiate an object of an abstract class is a compilation error.

> **Common Programming Error 11.2**
>
> *Failure to implement a base class's abstract methods in a derived class is a compilation error unless the derived class is also declared* MustInherit *(i.e., the derived class is also abstract).*

Although we cannot instantiate objects of abstract base classes, soon you will see that we *can* use abstract base classes to declare variables that can hold references to objects of any concrete classes derived from those abstract classes. Programs typically use such variables to manipulate derived class objects polymorphically.

Using Abstract Classes and Methods to Achieve Polymorphism

Consider another polymorphism application. A drawing program needs to display many shapes, including new shape types that you might add to the system even after writing the drawing program. The drawing program might need to display shapes, such as Circles, Triangles, Rectangles or others, that derive from abstract base class Shape. The drawing program uses Shape variables to manage the objects that are displayed. To draw any object in this inheritance hierarchy, the drawing program uses a base class Shape variable containing a reference to a derived class object to invoke the object's Draw method. This method is declared MustOverride in base class Shape, so each concrete derived class *must* implement method Draw in a manner specific to that shape. Each object in the Shape hierarchy "knows" how to draw itself. The drawing program does not have to worry about the type of each object or whether the drawing program has ever encountered objects of that type.

Polymorphism is particularly effective for implementing so-called layered software systems. Each of the physical devices in an operating system, for example, operates quite differently from the others. Even so, the same commands can be used to read or write data from and to the various devices. For each device, the operating system uses a piece of software called a device driver to control all communication between the system and the device. The write message sent to a device driver object needs to be interpreted specifically in the context of that driver and how it manipulates devices of that specific type. However, the write call itself really is no different from the write to any other device in the system—place some number of bytes from memory onto that device. An object-oriented operating system might use an abstract base class to provide an "interface" appropriate for all device drivers. Then, through inheritance from that abstract base class, derived classes are formed that all behave similarly. The device driver methods are declared as abstract methods in the abstract base class. The implementations of these abstract methods are provided in the concrete derived classes that correspond to the specific types of device drivers. New devices are always being developed, and often long after the operating system has been released. When you buy a new device, it comes with a device driver provided by the device vendor. The device is immediately operational after you connect it to your computer and install the driver. This is another nice example of how polymorphism makes systems extensible.

It is common in object-oriented programming to declare an **iterator class** that can traverse all the objects in a collection, such as an array (Chapter 8) or an ArrayList (Chapter 26, Collections). For example, a program can print an ArrayList of objects by creating an iterator object and using it to obtain the next list element each time the iterator is called. Iterators often are used in polymorphic programming to traverse a collection that contains references to objects from various levels of an inheritance hierarchy. (Chapter 26 presents a thorough treatment of ArrayLists, collections and iterators.) An ArrayList of objects of class TwoDimensionalShape, for example, could contain objects from derived classes Square, Circle, Triangle and so on. Calling method Draw for each TwoDimensionalShape object off a TwoDimensionalShape variable would polymorphically draw each object correctly on the screen.

11.5 Case Study: Payroll System Class Hierarchy Using Polymorphism

This section reexamines the CommissionEmployee–BasePlusCommissionEmployee hierarchy that we explored in Section 10.4. Now we use an abstract method and polymorphism to perform payroll calculations based on the type of employee. We create an enhanced employee hierarchy to solve the following problem:

> *A company pays its employees on a weekly basis. The employees are of four types: Salaried employees are paid a fixed weekly salary regardless of the number of hours worked, hourly employees are paid by the hour and receive overtime pay (1.5 times the regular hourly salary) for all hours worked in excess of 40 hours, commission employees are paid a percentage of their sales, and base-plus-commission employees receive a base salary plus a percentage of their sales. For the current pay period, the company has decided to reward base-plus-commission employees by adding 10% to their base salaries. The company wants to implement a Visual Basic application that performs its payroll calculations polymorphically.*

We use abstract class Employee to represent the general concept of an employee. The classes that inherit from Employee are SalariedEmployee, CommissionEmployee and HourlyEmployee. Class BasePlusCommissionEmployee inherits from CommissionEmployee. The UML class diagram in Fig. 11.2 shows our polymorphic employee inheritance hierarchy. Note that abstract class name Employee is italicized, as per UML convention; concrete class names are not italicized.

Abstract base class Employee declares the "interface" to the hierarchy—that is, the set of methods that a program can invoke on all Employee objects. We use the term "interface" here in a general sense to refer to the various ways programs can communicate with objects of any Employee derived class. Be careful not to confuse the general notion of an "interface" with the formal notion of a Visual Basic interface, the subject of Section 11.7. Each employee, regardless of the way his or her earnings are calculated, has a first name, a last

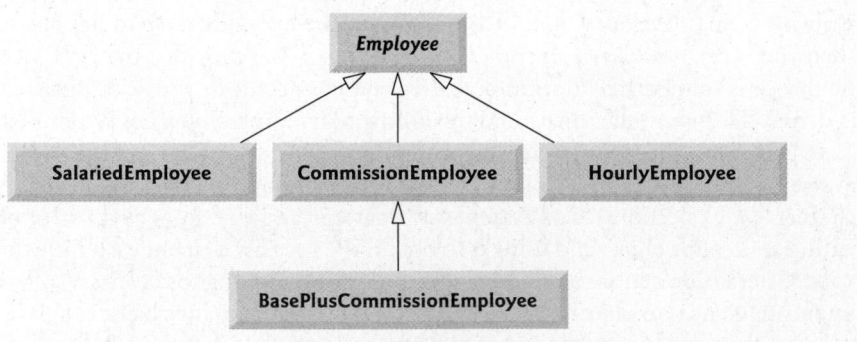

Fig. 11.2 | Employee hierarchy UML class diagram.

name and a social security number, so Public properties FirstName, LastName and SocialSecurityNumber appear in abstract base class Employee.

The following sections implement the Employee class hierarchy. The first five sections show the abstract base class Employee and the concrete derived classes SalariedEmployee, CommissionEmployee, HourlyEmployee and the indirectly derived concrete class Base-PlusCommissionEmployee. The last section shows a test program that builds objects of these classes and processes the objects polymorphically.

11.5.1 Creating Abstract Base Class Employee

In this example, class Employee will provide methods CalculateEarnings and ToString, and properties that manipulate an Employee's instance variables. A CalculateEarnings method certainly applies generically to all employees. But each earnings calculation depends on the employee's class. So we declare CalculateEarnings as MustOverride in base class Employee because a default implementation does not make sense for that method—there is not enough information to determine what amount CalculateEarnings should return. Each derived class overrides CalculateEarnings with an appropriate implementation. To calculate an employee's earnings, the program assigns to a base class Employee variable a reference to the employee's object, then invokes the CalculateEarnings method on that variable. We will maintain an array of Employee variables, each of which holds a reference to an Employee object (of course, there cannot be Employee objects because Employee is an abstract class—thanks to inheritance, however, all objects of all derived classes of Employee may nevertheless be thought of as Employee objects). The program iterates through the array and calls method CalculateEarnings for each Employee object. Visual Basic processes these method calls polymorphically. Including abstract method CalculateEarnings in class Employee forces every directly derived concrete class of Employee to override CalculateEarnings. This enables the designer of the class hierarchy to demand that each derived concrete class provide an appropriate pay calculation.

Method ToString in class Employee returns a String containing the first name, last name and social security number of the employee. As we will see, each derived class of Employee overrides method ToString to create a string representation of an object of that class that contains the employee's type (e.g., "salaried employee:") followed by the rest of the employee's information.

The diagram in Fig. 11.3 shows the five classes of the hierarchy down the left side and methods CalculateEarnings and ToString across the top. For each class, the diagram shows the desired results of each method. [*Note:* We do not list base class Employee's properties because they are not overridden in any of the derived classes—each of these properties is inherited and used "as is" by each of the derived classes.]

Class Employee (Fig. 11.4) includes a constructor that takes the first name, last name and social security number as arguments (lines 9–14); Get accessors that return the first name, last name and social security number (lines 18–20, 29–31 and 40–42, respectively); Set accessors that set the first name, last name and social security number (lines 22–24, 33–35 and 44–46, respectively); method ToString (lines 50–53), which returns the string representation of an Employee; and abstract (MustOverride) method CalculateEarnings (line 56), which must be implemented by concrete derived classes. Note that the SocialSecurityNumber property does not validate the social security number in this example. In business-critical applications, such validation should be provided.

	CalculateEarnings	ToString
Employee	MustOverride	*FirstName LastName* social security number: *SSN*
Salaried-Employee	*WeeklySalary*	salaried employee: *FirstName LastName* social security number: *SSN* weekly salary: *WeeklySalary*

Hourly-Employee	*If Hours <= 40*
	    Wage *Hours*
	 If Hours > 40
	    *40 * Wage +*
	    *((Hours − 40) **
	    *Wage * 1.5)*
		hourly employee: *FirstName LastName*
		 social security number: *SSN*
		 hourly wage: *Wage*; hours worked: *Hours*

Commission-Employee	*CommissionRate * GrossSales*	commission employee: *FirstName LastName* social security number: *SSN* gross sales: *GrossSales*; commission rate: *CommissionRate*
BasePlus-Commission-Employee	*(CommissionRate * GrossSales) + BaseSalary*	base-salaried commission employee: *FirstName LastName* social security number: *SSN* gross sales: *GrossSales*; commission rate: *CommissionRate*; base salary: *BaseSalary*

Fig. 11.3 | Polymorphic interface for the `Employee` hierarchy classes.

```
1   ' Fig. 11.4: Employee.vb
2   ' Employee abstract base class.
3   Public MustInherit Class Employee
4       Private firstNameValue As String
5       Private lastNameValue As String
6       Private socialSecurityNumberValue As String
7
8       ' three-argument constructor
9       Public Sub New(ByVal first As String, ByVal last As String, _
10          ByVal ssn As String)
11          FirstName = first
12          LastName = last
13          SocialSecurityNumber = ssn
14      End Sub ' New
15
16      ' property FirstName
17      Public Property FirstName() As String
18          Get
19              Return firstNameValue
20          End Get
```

Fig. 11.4 | `Employee` abstract base class. (Part 1 of 2.)

```
21
22          Set(ByVal first As String)
23              firstNameValue = first
24          End Set
25      End Property ' FirstName
26
27      ' property LastName
28      Public Property LastName() As String
29          Get
30              Return lastNameValue
31          End Get
32
33          Set(ByVal last As String)
34              lastNameValue = last
35          End Set
36      End Property ' LastName
37
38      ' property SocialSecurityNumber
39      Public Property SocialSecurityNumber() As String
40          Get
41              Return socialSecurityNumberValue
42          End Get
43
44          Set(ByVal ssn As String)
45              socialSecurityNumberValue = ssn
46          End Set
47      End Property ' SocialSecurityNumber
48
49      ' return String representation of Employee object
50      Public Overrides Function ToString() As String
51          Return (String.Format("{0} {1}", FirstName, LastName) & vbCrLf & _
52              "social security number: " & SocialSecurityNumber)
53      End Function ' ToString
54
55      ' abstract method overridden by derived class
56      Public MustOverride Function CalculateEarnings() As Decimal
57  End Class ' Employee
```

Fig. 11.4 | Employee abstract base class. (Part 2 of 2.)

Why did we decide to declare CalculateEarnings as a MustOverride method? It simply does not make sense to provide an implementation of this method in class Employee. We cannot calculate the earnings for a general Employee—we first must know the specific Employee type to determine the appropriate earnings calculation. By declaring this method MustOverride, we indicate that each concrete derived class *must* provide an appropriate CalculateEarnings implementation and that a program will be able to use base class Employee variables to invoke method CalculateEarnings polymorphically for any type of Employee.

11.5.2 Creating Concrete Derived Class SalariedEmployee

Class SalariedEmployee (Fig. 11.5) inherits class Employee (line 4) and overrides CalculateEarnings (lines 31–33), which makes SalariedEmployee a concrete class. The

```vb
1   ' Fig. 11.5: SalariedEmployee.vb
2   ' SalariedEmployee class inherits Employee
3   Public Class SalariedEmployee
4      Inherits Employee
5
6      Private weeklySalaryValue As Decimal ' employee's weekly salary
7
8      ' four-argument constructor
9      Public Sub New(ByVal first As String, ByVal last As String, _
10        ByVal ssn As String, ByVal salary As Decimal)
11        MyBase.New(first, last, ssn) ' pass to Employee constructor
12        WeeklySalary = salary ' validate and store salary
13     End Sub ' New
14
15     ' property WeeklySalary
16     Public Property WeeklySalary() As Decimal
17        Get
18           Return weeklySalaryValue
19        End Get
20
21        Set(ByVal salary As Decimal)
22           If salary < 0.0 Then ' validate salary
23              weeklySalaryValue = 0
24           Else
25              weeklySalaryValue = salary
26           End If
27        End Set
28     End Property ' WeeklySalary
29
30     ' calculate earnings; override abstract method CalculateEarnings
31     Public Overrides Function CalculateEarnings() As Decimal
32        Return WeeklySalary
33     End Function ' CalculateEarnings
34
35     ' return String representation of SalariedEmployee object
36     Public Overrides Function ToString() As String
37        Return ("salaried employee: " & MyBase.ToString() & vbCrLf & _
38           String.Format("weekly salary {0:C}", WeeklySalary))
39     End Function ' ToString
40  End Class ' SalariedEmployee
```

Fig. 11.5 | SalariedEmployee class derived from class Employee.

class includes a constructor (lines 9–13) that takes a first name, a last name, a social security number and a weekly salary as arguments; a WeeklySalary property that has a Get accessor (lines 17–19) to return weeklySalaryValue's value and a Set accessor (lines 21–27) to assign a new non-negative value to instance variable weeklySalaryValue; a method CalculateEarnings (lines 31–33) to calculate a SalariedEmployee's earnings; and a method ToString (lines 36–39) that returns a String including the employee's type, namely, "salaried employee: ", followed by employee-specific information produced by base class Employee's ToString method, and the value of SalariedEmployee's WeeklySalary property. Class SalariedEmployee's constructor passes the first name, last name and social security number to base class Employee's constructor (line 11). Method CalculateEarnings overrides abstract method CalculateEarnings of Employee with a concrete implementation that returns the SalariedEmployee's weekly salary. If we do not implement CalculateEarnings, class SalariedEmployee must be declared MustOverride—otherwise, a compilation error occurs (and, of course, we want SalariedEmployee to be a concrete class).

SalariedEmployee's ToString method (lines 36–39) overrides Employee method ToString. If class SalariedEmployee did not override ToString, the class would have inherited Employee's ToString method. In that case, SalariedEmployee's ToString method would simply return the employee's full name and social security number, which does not adequately represent a SalariedEmployee. To produce a complete string representation of a SalariedEmployee, the derived class's ToString method returns "salaried employee: " followed by the base class Employee-specific information (i.e., first name, last name and social security number) obtained by invoking the base class's ToString (line 37)—a nice example of code reuse. The string representation of a SalariedEmployee also contains the employee's weekly salary obtained from the WeeklySalary property.

11.5.3 Creating Concrete Derived Class HourlyEmployee

Class HourlyEmployee (Fig. 11.6) also inherits class Employee (line 4). The class includes a constructor (lines 10–16) that takes as arguments a first name, a last name, a social security number, an hourly wage and the number of hours worked. Lines 24–30 and 39–45

```vbnet
1   ' Fig. 11.6: HourlyEmployee.vb
2   ' HourlyEmployee class inherits Employee.
3   Public Class HourlyEmployee
4      Inherits Employee
5
6      Private wageValue As Decimal ' wage per hour
7      Private hoursValue As Decimal ' hours worked for week
8
9      ' five-argument constructor
10     Public Sub New(ByVal first As String, ByVal last As String, _
11        ByVal ssn As String, ByVal hourlyWage As Decimal, _
12        ByVal hoursWorked As Decimal)
13        MyBase.New(first, last, ssn) ' pass to Employee constructor
14        Wage = hourlyWage ' validate and store hourly wage
15        Hours = hoursWorked ' validate and store hours worked
16     End Sub ' New
17
18     ' property Wage
19     Public Property Wage() As Decimal
20        Get
21           Return wageValue
22        End Get
23
24        Set(ByVal hourlyWage As Decimal)
25           If hourlyWage < 0 Then ' validate hourly wage
26              wageValue = 0
```

Fig. 11.6 | HourlyEmployee class derived from class Employee. (Part 1 of 2.)

```
27              Else
28                  wageValue = hourlyWage
29              End If
30          End Set
31      End Property ' Wage
32
33      ' property Hours
34      Public Property Hours() As Decimal
35          Get
36              Return hoursValue
37          End Get
38
39          Set(ByVal hoursWorked As Decimal)
40              If (hoursWorked >= 0.0) AndAlso (hoursWorked <= 168.0) Then
41                  hoursValue = hoursWorked ' valid weekly hours
42              Else
43                  hoursValue = 0
44              End If
45          End Set
46      End Property ' Hours
47
48      ' calculate earnings; override abstract method CalculageEarnings
49      Public Overrides Function CalculateEarnings() As Decimal
50          If Hours <= 40 Then ' no overtime
51              Return Wage * Hours
52          Else
53              Return 40 * Wage + ((Hours - 40) * Wage * 1.5D)
54          End If
55      End Function ' CalculateEarnings
56
57      ' return String representation of HourlyEmployee object
58      Public Overrides Function ToString() As String
59          Return ("hourly employee: " & MyBase.ToString() & vbCrLf & _
60              String.Format("hourly wage: {0:C}; hours worked: {1}", _
61              Wage, Hours))
62      End Function ' ToString
63  End Class ' HourlyEmployee
```

Fig. 11.6 | HourlyEmployee class derived from class Employee. (Part 2 of 2.)

declare Set accessors that assign new values to instance variables wageValue and hours-Value, respectively. The Set accessor of property Wage (lines 24–30) ensures that wage-Value is non-negative, and the Set accessor of property Hours (lines 39–45) ensures that hoursValue is between 0 and 168 (the total number of hours in a week). Properties Wage and Hours also include Get accessors (lines 20–22 and 35–37) to return the values of wage-Value and hoursValue, respectively. Method CalculateEarnings (lines 49–55) calculates an HourlyEmployee's earnings. Method ToString (lines 58–62) returns the employee's type, namely, "hourly employee: ", and employee-specific information, including the full name, the social security number, and the values of properties Wage and Hours. Note that the HourlyEmployee constructor, like the SalariedEmployee constructor, passes the first name, last name and social security number to the base class Employee constructor (line 13). In addition, method ToString calls base class method ToString (line 59) to obtain the Employee-specific information (i.e., first name, last name and social security number)—this is another nice example of code reuse.

11.5.4 Creating Concrete Derived Class CommissionEmployee

Class CommissionEmployee (Fig. 11.7) inherits class Employee (line 4). The class includes a constructor (lines 10–15) that takes a first name, a last name, a social security number, a sales amount and a commission rate; Get accessors (lines 19–21 and 34–36) that retrieve the values of instance variables grossSalesValue and commissionRateValue, respectively; Set accessors (lines 23–29 and 38–44) that assign new values to these instance variables; method CalculateEarnings (lines 48–50) to calculate a CommissionEmployee's earnings; and method ToString (lines 53–57), which returns the employee's type, namely, "commission employee: " and employee-specific information, including the full name and social security number, and the values of properties GrossSales and CommissionRate. The CommissionEmployee's constructor also passes the first name, last name and social security number to the Employee constructor (line 12) to initialize Employee's Private instance variables. Method ToString calls base class method ToString (line 54) to obtain the Employee-specific information (i.e., first name, last name and social security number).

```vb
1    ' Fig. 11.7: CommissionEmployee.vb
2    ' CommissionEmployee class inherits Employee.
3    Public Class CommissionEmployee
4       Inherits Employee
5
6       Private grossSalesValue As Decimal
7       Private commissionRateValue As Decimal
8
9       ' five-argument constructor
10      Public Sub New(ByVal first As String, ByVal last As String, _
11         ByVal ssn As String, ByVal sales As Decimal, ByVal rate As Decimal)
12         MyBase.New(first, last, ssn) ' pass to Employee constructor
13         GrossSales = sales ' validate and store gross sales
14         CommissionRate = rate ' validate and store commission rate
15      End Sub ' New
16
17      ' property GrossSales
18      Public Property GrossSales() As Decimal
19         Get
20            Return grossSalesValue
21         End Get
22
23         Set(ByVal sales As Decimal)
24            If sales < 0 Then ' validate gross sales
25               grossSalesValue = 0
26            Else
27               grossSalesValue = sales
28            End If
29         End Set
30      End Property ' GrossSales
31
```

Fig. 11.7 | CommissionEmployee class derived from Employee. (Part 1 of 2.)

```vbnet
32        ' property CommissionRate
33     Public Property CommissionRate() As Decimal
34        Get
35           Return commissionRateValue
36        End Get
37
38        Set(ByVal rate As Decimal)
39           If rate > 0.0 AndAlso rate < 1.0 Then ' validate commission rate
40              commissionRateValue = rate
41           Else
42              commissionRateValue = 0
43           End If
44        End Set
45     End Property ' CommissionRate
46
47        ' calculate earnings; override abstract method CalculateEarnings
48     Public Overrides Function CalculateEarnings() As Decimal
49        Return CommissionRate * GrossSales
50     End Function ' CalculateEarnings
51
52        ' return String representation of CommissionEmployee object
53     Public Overrides Function ToString() As String
54        Return ("commission employee: " & MyBase.ToString() & vbCrLf & _
55           String.Format("gross sales: {0:C}; commission rate: {1}", _
56           GrossSales, CommissionRate))
57     End Function ' ToString
58  End Class ' CommissionEmployee
```

Fig. 11.7 | CommissionEmployee class derived from Employee. (Part 2 of 2.)

11.5.5 Creating Indirect Concrete Derived Class BasePlusCommissionEmployee

Class BasePlusCommissionEmployee (Fig. 11.8) inherits class CommissionEmployee (line 4) and therefore is an indirect derived class of class Employee. Class BasePlusCommission-Employee has a constructor (lines 9–14) that takes as arguments a first name, a last name, a social security number, a sales amount, a commission rate and a base salary. It then passes the first name, last name, social security number, sales amount and commission rate to the CommissionEmployee constructor (line 12) to initialize the inherited members. BasePlus-CommissionEmployee also contains a property BaseSalary whose Set accessor (lines 22–28) assigns a new value to instance variable baseSalaryValue, and whose Get accessor (lines 18–20) returns baseSalaryValue. Method CalculateEarnings (lines 32–34) calculates a BasePlusCommissionEmployee's earnings. Note that line 33 in method CalculateEarnings calls base class CommissionEmployee's CalculateEarnings method to calculate the commission-based portion of the employee's earnings. This is another nice example of code reuse. BasePlusCommissionEmployee's ToString method (lines 37–40) creates a String representation of a BasePlusCommissionEmployee that contains "base-salaried", followed by the String obtained by invoking base class CommissionEmploy-ee's ToString method (another example of code reuse), then the base salary. The result is a String beginning with "base-salaried commission employee" followed by the rest of the BasePlusCommissionEmployee's information. Recall that CommissionEmployee's

```vbnet
1   ' Fig. 11.8: BasePlusCommissionEmployee.vb
2   ' BasePlusCommissionEmployee class inherits CommissionEmployee.
3   Public Class BasePlusCommissionEmployee
4      Inherits CommissionEmployee
5
6      Private baseSalaryValue As Decimal ' base salary
7
8      ' six-argument constructor
9      Public Sub New(ByVal first As String, ByVal last As String, _
10        ByVal ssn As String, ByVal sales As Decimal, _
11        ByVal rate As Decimal, ByVal salary As Decimal)
12        MyBase.New(first, last, ssn, sales, rate)
13        BaseSalary = salary
14     End Sub ' New
15
16     ' property BaseSalary
17     Public Property BaseSalary() As Decimal
18        Get
19           Return baseSalaryValue
20        End Get
21
22        Set(ByVal salary As Decimal)
23           If salary < 0 Then ' validate salary
24              baseSalaryValue = 0
25           Else
26              baseSalaryValue = salary
27           End If
28        End Set
29     End Property ' BaseSalary
30
31     ' calculate earnings; override method CalculateEarnings
32     Public Overrides Function CalculateEarnings() As Decimal
33        Return BaseSalary + MyBase.CalculateEarnings()
34     End Function ' CalculateEarnings
35
36     ' return String representation of BasePlusCommissionEmployee object
37     Public Overrides Function ToString() As String
38        Return ("base-salaried " & MyBase.ToString() & _
39           String.Format("; base salary: {0:C}", BaseSalary))
40     End Function ' ToString
41  End Class ' BasePlusCommissionEmployee
```

Fig. 11.8 | BasePlusCommissionEmployee derived from CommissionEmployee.

ToString method obtains the employee's first name, last name and social security number by invoking the ToString method of its base class (i.e., Employee)—another example of code reuse. Note that BasePlusCommissionEmployee's ToString initiates a chain of method calls that spans all three levels of the Employee hierarchy.

11.5.6 Demonstrating Polymorphic Processing, Expression TypeOf...Is, TryCast and Downcasting

To test our Employee hierarchy, the program in Fig. 11.9 creates an object of each of the four concrete classes SalariedEmployee, HourlyEmployee, CommissionEmployee and

```vb
 1   ' Fig. 11.9: PayrollSystemTest.vb
 2   ' Employee hierarchy test program.
 3   Module PayrollSystemTest
 4      Sub Main()
 5         ' create derived class objects
 6         Dim salariedEmployee As New SalariedEmployee( _
 7            "John", "Smith", "111-11-1111", 800)
 8         Dim hourlyEmployee As New HourlyEmployee( _
 9            "Karen", "Price", "222-22-2222", 16.75D, 40)
10         Dim commissionEmployee As New CommissionEmployee( _
11            "Sue", "Jones", "333-33-3333", 10000, 0.06D)
12         Dim basePlusCommissionEmployee As New BasePlusCommissionEmployee( _
13            "Bob", "Lewis", "444-44-4444", 5000, 0.04D, 300)
14
15         ' display each employee's info non-polymorphically
16         Console.WriteLine("Employees processed individually:" & vbCrLf)
17         Console.WriteLine(salariedEmployee.ToString() & vbCrLf & _
18            String.Format("earned: {0:C}", _
19            salariedEmployee.CalculateEarnings()) & vbCrLf)
20         Console.WriteLine(hourlyEmployee.ToString() & vbCrLf & _
21            String.Format("earned: {0:C}", _
22            hourlyEmployee.CalculateEarnings()) & vbCrLf)
23         Console.WriteLine(commissionEmployee.ToString() & vbCrLf & _
24            String.Format("earned: {0:C}", _
25            commissionEmployee.CalculateEarnings()) & vbCrLf)
26         Console.WriteLine(basePlusCommissionEmployee.ToString() & _
27            vbCrLf & String.Format("earned: {0:C}", _
28            basePlusCommissionEmployee.CalculateEarnings()) & vbCrLf)
29
30         ' create four-element Employee array
31         Dim employees() As Employee = {salariedEmployee, hourlyEmployee, _
32            commissionEmployee, basePlusCommissionEmployee}
33
34         Console.WriteLine("Employees processed polymorphically:" & vbCrLf)
35
36         ' polymorphically process each element in array employees
37         For Each currentEmployee As Employee In employees
38            Console.WriteLine(currentEmployee.ToString())
39
40            ' determine if currentEmployee is a BasePlusCommissionEmployee
41            If (TypeOf currentEmployee Is BasePlusCommissionEmployee) Then
42
43               ' downcast Employee reference to BasePlusCommissionEmployee
44               Dim employee As BasePlusCommissionEmployee = _
45                  TryCast(currentEmployee, BasePlusCommissionEmployee)
46
47               employee.BaseSalary *= 1.1D
48               Console.WriteLine(String.Format( _
49                  "new base salary with 10% increase is: {0:C}", _
50                  employee.BaseSalary))
51            End If
52
```

Fig. 11.9 | Employee class hierarchy test program. (Part 1 of 3.)

```
53            Console.Write(String.Format("earned {0:C}", _
54               currentEmployee.CalculateEarnings()) & vbCrLf & vbCrLf)
55         Next
56
57         ' get type name of each object in employees array
58         For i As Integer = 0 To employees.Length - 1
59            Console.WriteLine(String.Format("Employee {0} is a {1}", _
60               i, employees(i).GetType().FullName))
61         Next
62      End Sub ' Main
63   End Module ' PayrollSystemTest
```

```
Employees processed individually:

salaried employee: John Smith
social security number: 111-11-1111
weekly salary $800.00
earned: $800.00

hourly employee: Karen Price
social security number: 222-22-2222
hourly wage: $16.75; hours worked: 40
earned: $670.00

commission employee: Sue Jones
social security number: 333-33-3333
gross sales: $10,000.00; commission rate: 0.06
earned: $600.00

base-salaried commission employee: Bob Lewis
social security number: 444-44-4444
gross sales: $5,000.00; commission rate: 0.04; base salary: $300.00
earned: $500.00

Employees processed polymorphically:

salaried employee: John Smith
social security number: 111-11-1111
weekly salary $800.00
earned $800.00

hourly employee: Karen Price
social security number: 222-22-2222
hourly wage: $16.75; hours worked: 40
earned $670.00

commission employee: Sue Jones
social security number: 333-33-3333
gross sales: $10,000.00; commission rate: 0.06
earned $600.00
```

(continued on next page...)

Fig. 11.9 | Employee class hierarchy test program. (Part 2 of 3.)

(continued from previous page...)

```
base-salaried commission employee: Bob Lewis
social security number: 444-44-4444
gross sales: $5,000.00; commission rate: 0.04; base salary: $300.00
new base salary with 10% increase is: $330.00
earned $530.00

Employee 0 is a PayrollSystem.SalariedEmployee
Employee 1 is a PayrollSystem.HourlyEmployee
Employee 2 is a PayrollSystem.CommissionEmployee
Employee 3 is a PayrollSystem.BasePlusCommissionEmployee
```

Fig. 11.9 | Employee class hierarchy test program. (Part 3 of 3.)

BasePlusCommissionEmployee. The program manipulates these objects, first via variables of each object's own type, then polymorphically, using an array of Employee variables. While processing the objects polymorphically, the program increases the base salary of each BasePlusCommissionEmployee by 10%—this requires that the program determine each object's type at execution time. Finally, the program polymorphically determines and outputs the type of each object in the Employee array. Lines 6–13 create objects of each of the four concrete Employee derived classes. Lines 16–28 output (non-polymorphically) the string representation and earnings of each of these objects.

Lines 31–32 create and initialize array employees with four Employees. This statement is valid because, through inheritance, a SalariedEmployee *is an* Employee, an HourlyEmployee *is an* Employee, a CommissionEmployee *is an* Employee and a BasePlusCommissionEmployee *is an* Employee. Therefore, we can assign the references of SalariedEmployee, HourlyEmployee, CommissionEmployee and BasePlusCommissionEmployee objects to base class Employee variables, even though Employee is an abstract class.

Lines 37–55 iterate through array employees and invoke methods ToString and CalculateEarnings with Employee variable currentEmployee, which is assigned the reference to a different Employee in the array during each iteration. The output illustrates that the appropriate methods for each class are indeed invoked. All calls to method ToString and CalculateEarnings are resolved at execution time, based on the type of the object to which currentEmployee refers. This process is known as late binding. For example, line 38 explicitly invokes method ToString of the object to which currentEmployee refers. As a result of late binding, Visual Basic decides which class's ToString method to call at execution time rather than at compile time. Recall that only the methods of class Employee can be called via an Employee variable (and Employee, of course, includes the methods of class Object). (Section 10.7 discussed the set of methods that all classes inherit from class Object.) A base class reference can be used to invoke only methods of the base class, even though those method calls polymorphically invoke derived class method implementations when sent to derived class objects.

Using Expression TypeOf...Is to Determine Object Type
We perform special processing on BasePlusCommissionEmployee objects—as we encounter these objects, we increase their base salary by 10%. When processing objects polymorphically, we typically do not need to worry about the specifics, but to adjust the base salary,

we do have to determine the specific type of Employee object at execution time. Line 41 uses a TypeOf...Is expression to determine whether a particular Employee object's type is BasePlusCommissionEmployee. The condition in line 41 is true if the object referenced by currentEmployee *is a* BasePlusCommissionEmployee. This would also be true for any object of a BasePlusCommissionEmployee derived class (if there are any) because of the *is-a* relationship a derived class has with its base class.

Using TryCast to Downcast from a Base Class to a Derived Class Type

Lines 44–45 use keyword **TryCast** to downcast currentEmployee from base class type Employee to derived class type BasePlusCommissionEmployee—this cast returns an object only if the object has an *is a* relationship with type BasePlusCommissionEmployee. The condition at line 41 ensures that this is the case. If the *is a* relationship does not exist, TryCast returns Nothing. This cast is required if we are to access derived class BasePlusCommissionEmployee property BaseSalary on the current Employee object—as you will see momentarily, attempting to invoke a derived-class-only method or property directly on a base class reference is a compilation error. Note that we did not need to use both TypeOf...Is and TryCast. We could have simply used TryCast, then tested the value of variable employee to ensure that it was not Nothing before attempting to execute the statements in lines 47–50. We used both here so that we could demonstrate the new Visual Basic 2005 TryCast keyword.

Common Programming Error 11.3

Assigning a base class variable to a derived class variable (without an explicit cast) is a compilation error.

Error-Prevention Tip 11.1

If at execution time the reference of a derived class object has been assigned to a variable of one of its direct or indirect base classes, it is acceptable to cast the reference stored in that base class variable back to a reference of the derived class type. Before performing such a cast, use the Typeof...Is expression to ensure that the object is indeed an object of an appropriate derived class type. You can then use TryCast to downcast from the base class type to the derived class type.

When downcasting an object, TryCast returns Nothing if at execution time the object being converted does not have an *is-a* relationship with the target type. An object can be cast only to its own type or to one of its base class types; otherwise, a compilation error occurs.

If the Typeof...Is expression in line 41 is True, the body of the If statement (lines 44–50) performs the special processing required for the BasePlusCommissionEmployee object. Using BasePlusCommissionEmployee variable employee, lines 47–50 access derived-class-only property BaseSalary to retrieve and update the employee's base salary with the 10% raise.

Lines 53–54 invoke method CalculateEarnings on currentEmployee, which calls the appropriate derived class object's CalculateEarnings method polymorphically. Note that obtaining the earnings of the SalariedEmployee, HourlyEmployee and CommissionEmployee polymorphically in lines 53–54 produces the same result as obtaining these employees' earnings non-polymorphically in lines 16–25. However, the earnings amount obtained for the BasePlusCommissionEmployee in lines 53–54 is higher than that obtained in lines 26–28, due to the 10% increase in its base salary.

Lines 58–61 display each employee's type as a string. Every object in Visual Basic knows its own class and can access this information through method `GetType`, which all classes inherit from class `Object`. Figure 10.20 lists the `Object` methods that are inherited directly or indirectly by all classes. Method `GetType` returns an object of class `Type` (namespace `System`), which contains information about the object's type, including its fully qualified class name. For more information on the `Type` class, please read `msdn.microsoft.com/library/en-us/cpref/html/frlrfsystemtypeclasstopic.asp`. Line 60 invokes method `GetType` on the object to get a `Type` object that represents the object's type at execution time. Then line 60 uses the `FullName` property of the object returned by `GetType` to get the class's name fully qualified name (see the last four lines of the program's output).

Notes on Downcasting

We avoid several compilation errors by downcasting an `Employee` variable to a `BasePlus-CommissionEmployee` variable in lines 44–45. If we remove the cast expression from line 45 and attempt to assign `Employee` variable `currentEmployee` directly to `BasePlusCommissionEmployee` variable `employee`, we would receive a compilation error (when **Option Strict** is **On**). This error indicates that the attempt to assign the base class variable `currentEmployee` to derived class variable `basePlusCommissionEmployee` is not allowed. The compiler prevents this assignment because a `CommissionEmployee` is not a `BasePlus-CommissionEmployee`—the *is-a* relationship applies only between the derived class and its base classes, not vice versa.

Similarly, if lines 47 and 50 were to use base class variable `currentEmployee`, rather than derived class variable `employee`, to access derived-class-only property `BaseSalary`, we would receive a compilation error on each of these lines. Attempting to invoke derived-class-only methods and properties on a base class reference is not allowed. While lines 47 and 50 execute only if the `Typeof...If` expression in line 41 returns `True` to indicate that `currentEmployee` has been assigned a reference to a `BasePlusCommissionEmployee` object, we cannot attempt to invoke derived class `BasePlusCommissionEmployee` property `BaseSalary` on base class `Employee` reference `currentEmployee`. The compiler would generate errors in lines 47 and 50, because property `BaseSalary` is not a base class property and cannot be accessed using a base class variable. Although the actual method or property that is called depends on the object's type at execution time, a variable can be used to invoke only those methods and properties that are members of that variable's type, which the compiler verifies. Using a base class `Employee` variable, we can invoke only methods and properties found in class `Employee` (Fig. 11.4)—methods `CalculateEarnings` and `ToString`, and properties `FirstName`, `LastName` and `SocialSecurityNumber`.

11.5.7 Summary of the Allowed Assignments between Base Class and Derived Class Variables

Now that you have seen a complete application that processes diverse derived class objects polymorphically, we summarize what you can and cannot do with base class and derived class objects and variables. Although a derived class object also *is a* base class object, the two objects are nevertheless different. As discussed previously, derived class objects can be treated as if they are base class objects. However, the derived class can have additional derived-class-only members. For this reason, assigning a base class reference to a derived class variable is not allowed without a cast—such an assignment would leave the derived-class-only members undefined for the base class object.

We have discussed four ways to assign base class and derived class references to variables of base class and derived class types:

1. Assigning a base class reference to a base class variable is straightforward.

2. Assigning a derived class reference to a derived class variable is straightforward.

3. Assigning a derived class reference to a base class variable is safe, because the derived class object *is an* object of its base class. However, this reference can be used to refer only to base class members. Referring to a derived-class-only member through the base class variable is a compilation error.

4. Attempting to assign a base class reference to a derived class variable is a compilation error (when **Option Strict** is **On**). To avoid this error, the base class reference must be cast to a derived class type explicitly. At execution time, if the object to which the reference refers is not a derived class object, an exception will occur. (For more on exception handling, see Chapter 12, Exception Handling.) The `TypeOf...Is` expression can be used to ensure that such a cast is performed only if the object is a derived class object. Then a `TryCast` can be used to perform the downcast operation.

11.6 NotOverridable Methods and NotInheritable Classes

A method that is declared `NotOverridable` in a base class cannot be overridden in a derived class. A method that is declared `Overridable` in a base class can be declared `NotOverridable` in a derived class—this prevents overriding the method in classes that inherit from the derived class. All classes derived from the class that contains the `NotOverridable` method use that class's method implementation. Methods that are declared `Private` are implicitly `NotOverridable`.

A class that is declared `NotInheritable` cannot be a base class (i.e., a class cannot inherit from a `NotInheritable` class). All methods in a `NotInheritable` class are implicitly `NotOverridable`. A `NotInheritable` class is the opposite of a `MustInherit` class. A `NotInheritable` class is a concrete class that cannot act as a base class, whereas a `MustInherit` class is an abstract class that is intended as a base class. Class `String` is a `NotInheritable` class.

Common Programming Error 11.4

Attempting to inherit a `NotInheritable` class is a compilation error.

11.7 Case Study: Creating and Using Interfaces

Our next example reexamines the payroll system of Section 11.5. Suppose that the company involved wishes to perform several accounting operations in an accounts payable application In addition to calculating the earnings that must be paid to each employee, the company also wants to calculate the payment due on each of several invoices (i.e., bills for goods and services purchased). Though applied to unrelated things (i.e., employees and invoices), both operations have to do with obtaining some kind of payment amount. For an employee, the payment refers to the employee's earnings. For an invoice, the payment refers to the total cost of the goods and services listed on the invoice. Can we calculate such different things as the payments due for employees and invoices in a single application polymorphically? Does Visual Basic have a capability that forces possibly unrelated classes to implement a set of common methods (e.g., a method that calculates a payment amount)? Visual Basic interfaces offer exactly this capability.

Interfaces define and standardize the ways in which things such as people and systems can interact with one another. For example, the controls on a radio serve as an interface between radio users and a radio's internal components. The controls allow users to perform only a limited set of operations (e.g., changing the station, adjusting the volume, choosing between AM and FM), and different radios may implement the controls in different ways (e.g., using push buttons, dials, voice commands). The interface specifies *what* operations a radio permits users to perform but does not specify *how* the operations are implemented. Similarly, the interface between a driver and a car with a manual transmission includes the steering wheel, the gear shift, and the clutch, gas and brake pedals. This same interface is found in nearly all manual transmission cars, enabling someone who knows how to drive one particular manual transmission car to drive just about any manual transmission car. The components of each individual car may look a bit different, but the components' general purpose is the same—to allow people to drive the car.

Software objects also communicate via interfaces. A Visual Basic interface describes a set of methods that can be called on an object, to tell the object to perform some task or return some piece of information, for example. An interface is often used in place of a `MustInherit` class when there is no default implementation to inherit—that is, no instance variables and no default method and property implementations. The next example introduces an interface named `IPayable` to describe the functionality of any object that must be capable of being paid and thus must offer a method to determine the proper payment amount due. An **interface declaration** begins with the keyword `Interface` and can contain abstract methods and properties, but cannot contain instance variables, concreate methods or concrete properties. Unlike classes, interfaces may not specify any implementation details, such as concrete method declarations and instance variables. All members declared in an interface are implicitly `Public`, and may not specify an access modifier.

Common Programming Error 11.5

It is a compilation error to explicitly declare interface methods `Public`.

Common Programming Error 11.6

In Visual Basic, an `Interface` can be declared only as `Public` or `Friend`; the declaration of an `Interface` as `Private` or `Protected` is an error.

To use an interface, a concrete class must specify that it `Implements` the interface and must implement each method in the interface with the signature and return type specified in the interface declaration. A class that does not implement all the methods of the interface is an abstract class and must be declared `MustInherit`. Implementing an interface is like signing a contract with the compiler that states, "I will declare all the methods specified by the interface or I will declare my class `MustInherit`."

Common Programming Error 11.7

Failing to implement any method of an interface in a concrete class that Implements *the interface results in a syntax error indicating that the class must be declared* MustInherit.

An interface is typically used when unrelated classes need to share common methods and properties. This allows objects of unrelated classes to be processed polymorphically— objects of classes that implement the same interface have an *is-a* relationship with the interface type and can respond to the same method calls. Programmers can create an interface that describes the desired functionality, then implement this interface in any classes that require that functionality. For example, in the accounts payable application that we develop in the next several subsections, we implement interface IPayable in any class that must be able to calculate a payment amount (e.g., Employee, Invoice).

11.7.1 Developing an IPayable Hierarchy

To build an application that can determine payments for employees and invoices alike, we will first create interface IPayable. Interface IPayable contains method GetPaymentAmount, which returns a Decimal amount that must be paid for an IPayable object, and method ToString, which returns the String representation of an IPayable object. Method GetPaymentAmount is a general purpose version of the Employee hierarchy's CalculateEarnings method—method CalculateEarnings calculates a payment amount specifically for an Employee, while GetPaymentAmount can be applied more generally to unrelated objects. After declaring interface IPayable, we will introduce class Invoice, which implements interface IPayable. We then modify class Employee so that it, too, implements interface IPayable. Finally, we update Employee derived class SalariedEmployee to "fit" into the IPayable hierarchy (i.e., we rename SalariedEmployee method CalculateEarnings as GetPaymentAmount).

Good Programming Practice 11.1

When declaring a method in an interface, choose a method name that describes the method's purpose in a general manner, because the method may be implemented by many unrelated classes.

Classes Invoice and Employee both represent things for which the company must be able to calculate a payment amount. Both classes implement IPayable, so a program can invoke method GetPaymentAmount on Invoice objects and Employee objects alike. As you will soon see, this enables the polymorphic processing of Invoices and Employees required for our accounts payable application.

The UML class diagram in Fig. 11.10 shows the class and interface hierarchy used in our accounts payable application. The hierarchy begins with interface IPayable. The UML distinguishes an interface from other classes by placing the word "interface" in guillemets (« ») above the interface name. The UML expresses the relationship between a class and an interface through an association known as a **realization**. A class is said to "realize," or implement, an interface. A class diagram models a realization as a dashed arrow with a hollow arrowhead pointing from the implementing classes to the interface. The diagram in Fig. 11.10 indicates that class Invoice realizes (i.e., implements) interface IPayable. Class Employee also realizes interface IPayable, but it is not required to provide method implementations, because it is an abstract class (note that it appears in italics). Concrete class SalariedEmployee inherits from Employee and inherits its base class's

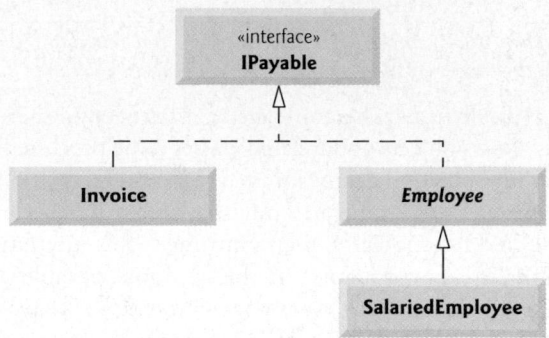

Fig. 11.10 | IPayable interface hierarchy UML class diagram.

realization relationship with interface IPayable, so SalariedEmployee must implement the method(s) of IPayable.

11.7.2 Declaring Interface IPayable

The declaration of interface IPayable begins in Fig. 11.11 at line 3. Interface IPayable contains Public methods GetPaymentAmount (line 4) and ToString (line 5). Note that the methods are not explicitly declared Public. Interface methods are implicitly Public. Also note that we explicitly declare the ToString method. Unlike a class, an interface does not inherit from Object, so it does not implicitly have a ToString method. You must explicitly declare ToString in the interface if a program must call this method through an IPayable variable. Interfaces can have any number of methods. Although methods GetPaymentAmount and ToString have no parameters, interface methods can have parameters.

11.7.3 Creating Class Invoice

We now create class Invoice (Fig. 11.12) to represent a simple invoice that contains billing information for only one kind of part. The class declares Private instance variables partNumberValue, partDescriptionValue, quantityValue and pricePerItemValue (in lines 6–9) that indicate the part number, a description of the part, the quantity of the part ordered and the price per item, respectively. Class Invoice also contains a constructor (lines 12–18), and properties PartNumber (lines 21–29), PartDescription(lines 32–40), Quantity (lines 43–55) and PricePerItem (lines 58–70) that manipulate the class's instance variables. Note that the Set accessors of properties Quantity and PricePerItem ensure that quantityValue and pricePerItemValue are assigned only non-negative values.

```
1   ' Fig. 11.11: IPayable.vb
2   ' IPayable interface declaration.
3   Public Interface IPayable
4       Function GetPaymentAmount() As Decimal ' calculate payment
5       Function ToString() As String ' display Payable object
6   End Interface ' IPayable
```

Fig. 11.11 | IPayable interface declaration.

Line 4 of Fig. 11.12 indicates that class `Invoice` implements interface `IPayable`. Class `Invoice` also implicitly inherits from `Object`. A derived class cannot inherit from more than one base class, but can inherit from a base class and implement zero or more interfaces. To implement more than one interface, use a comma-separated list of interface names after keyword `Implements` in the class declaration, as in:

```
Public Class ClassName
   Inherits BaseClassName
   Implements IFirstInterface, ISecondInterface, ...
```

```vb
 1   ' Fig. 11.12: Invoice.vb
 2   ' Invoice class implements IPayable.
 3   Public Class Invoice
 4      Implements IPayable
 5
 6      Private partNumberValue As String
 7      Private partDescriptionValue As String
 8      Private quantityValue As Integer
 9      Private pricePerItemValue As Decimal
10
11      ' four-argument constructor
12      Public Sub New(ByVal part As String, ByVal description As String, _
13         ByVal count As Integer, ByVal price As Decimal)
14         PartNumber = part
15         PartDescription = description
16         Quantity = count ' validate quantity
17         PricePerItem = price ' validate price per item
18      End Sub ' New
19
20      ' property PartNumber
21      Public Property PartNumber() As String
22         Get
23            Return partNumberValue
24         End Get
25
26         Set(ByVal part As String)
27            partNumberValue = part
28         End Set
29      End Property ' PartNumber
30
31      ' property PartDescription
32      Public Property PartDescription() As String
33         Get
34            Return partDescriptionValue
35         End Get
36
37         Set(ByVal description As String)
38            partDescriptionValue = description
39         End Set
40      End Property ' PartDescription
41
```

Fig. 11.12 | `Invoice` class that implements interface `IPayable`. (Part 1 of 2.)

```
42    ' property Quantity
43    Public Property Quantity() As Integer
44       Get
45          Return quantityValue
46       End Get
47
48       Set(ByVal count As Integer)
49          If count < 0 Then ' validate quantity
50             quantityValue = 0
51          Else
52             quantityValue = count
53          End If
54       End Set
55    End Property ' Quantity
56
57    ' property PricePerItem
58    Public Property PricePerItem() As Decimal
59       Get
60          Return pricePerItemValue
61       End Get
62
63       Set(ByVal price As Decimal)
64          If price < 0 Then ' validate price
65             pricePerItemValue = 0
66          Else
67             pricePerItemValue = price
68          End If
69       End Set
70    End Property ' PricePerItem
71
72    ' function required to carry out contract with interface IPayable
73    Public Function GetPaymentAmount() As Decimal _
74       Implements IPayable.GetPaymentAmount
75       Return Quantity * PricePerItem ' calculate total cost
76    End Function ' GetPaymentAmount
77
78    ' return String representation of Invoice object
79    Public Overrides Function ToString() As String _
80       Implements IPayable.ToString
81       Return ("invoice:" & vbCrLf & "part number: " & PartNumber & _
82          "(" & PartDescription & ")" & vbCrLf & "quantity: " & _
83          Quantity & vbCrLf & _
84          String.Format("price per item: {0:C}", PricePerItem))
85    End Function ' ToString
86 End Class ' Invoice
```

Fig. 11.12 | Invoice class that implements interface IPayable. (Part 2 of 2.)

Inherits *BaseClassName* is optional if the class implicitly inherits from class Object. All objects of a class that implements multiple interfaces have the *is-a* relationship with each implemented interface type.

Class Invoice implements the methods in interface IPayable. Method GetPayment-Amount is declared in lines 73–76. Line 74 contains keyword Implements followed by

IPayable.GetPaymentAmount to indicate that the method in lines 73–76 is the implementation of the interface's GetPaymentAmount method. Line 75 calculates the total payment required to pay the invoice by multiplying the values of quantityValue and pricePerItemValue (obtained through the appropriate properties) and returning the result.

Method ToString (lines 79–85) returns the String representation of an Invoice object. Recall that all classes directly or indirectly inherit from class Object. Therefore, class Invoice implicitly inherits Object's ToString method. However, we want to declare a customized ToString method in Invoice that returns a String containing the values of an Invoice's instance variables. Line 79 indicates that Invoice's ToString method overrides the one defined in base class Object. We also must satisfy the requirements of the IPayable interface, which Invoice implements. Line 80 contains the keyword Implements followed by IPayable.ToString to indicate that this version of ToString also serves as the required implementation of IPayable's ToString method. Note that it is possible for the same method to both override a method of a base class and implement a method of an interface. Implementing methods GetPaymentAmount and ToString in class Invoice satisfies the implementation requirement for the methods of interface IPayable—concrete class Invoice fulfills the interface contract with the compiler.

11.7.4 Modifying Class Employee to Implement Interface IPayable

We now modify class Employee to implement interface IPayable. Figure 11.13 contains the modified Employee class. This class declaration is identical to that of Fig. 11.4 with only three exceptions. First, line 4 of Fig. 11.13 indicates that class Employee now implements interface IPayable. Second, we must implement method ToString (lines 52–56) declared in the IPayable interface, which also overrides the version declared in base class Object. Third, since Employee now implements interface IPayable, we rename CalculateEarnings to GetPaymentAmount throughout the Employee hierarchy. As with method CalculateEarnings in the Employee class of Fig. 11.4, however, it does not make sense to implement method GetPaymentAmount in abstract class Employee because we cannot calculate the earnings payment owed to a general Employee—first we must know the specific type of Employee. In Fig. 11.4, we declared method CalculateEarnings as MustOverride for this reason, so class Employee had to be declared MustInherit. This forced each concrete Employee derived class to override CalculateEarnings with an implementation.

```
 1    ' Fig. 11.13: Employee.vb
 2    ' Employee abstract base class implements IPayable.
 3    Public MustInherit Class Employee
 4       Implements IPayable
 5
 6       Private firstNameValue As String
 7       Private lastNameValue As String
 8       Private socialSecurityNumberValue As String
 9
10       ' three-argument constructor
11       Public Sub New(ByVal first As String, ByVal last As String, _
12          ByVal ssn As String)
13          FirstName = first
```

Fig. 11.13 | Employee class that implements interface IPayable. (Part 1 of 2.)

gram that uses an array of Shape references to objects of each concrete class in the hierarchy. The program should print a text description of the object to which each array element refers. Also, in the loop that processes all the shapes in the array, determine whether each shape is a TwoDimensionalShape or a ThreeDimensionalShape. If a shape is a TwoDimensionalShape, display its area. If a shape is a ThreeDimensionalShape, display its area and volume.

11.11   *(Shape Hierarchy Modification)* Reimplement the program of Exercise 11.10 such that classes TwoDimensionalShape and ThreeDimensionalShape implement an IShape interface rather than inherit MustInherit class Shape.

11.12   Modify Exercise 10.10 so that class Account is abstract. Make property InterestRate abstract. For all three derived classes, define this property. If an invalid interest rate is entered (less than 0% or greater than 100%), set a default interest rate. Make the default different for each class.

12

Exception Handling

It is common sense to take a
method and try it. If it fails,
admit it frankly and try
another. But above all, try
something.
—Franklin Delano Roosevelt

O! throw away the
worser part of it,
And live the purer
with the other half.
—William Shakespeare

If they're running and they
don't look where they're going
I have to come out from
somewhere and catch them.
—J. D. Salinger

And oftentimes
excusing of a fault
Doth make the fault the
worse by the excuse.
—William Shakespeare

O infinite virtue! com'st thou
smiling from the world's great
snare uncaught?
—William Shakespeare

OBJECTIVES

In this chapter you will learn:

- What exceptions are and how they are handled.
- When to use exception handling.
- To use **Try** blocks to delimit code in which exceptions might occur.
- To **Throw** exceptions to indicate a problem.
- To use **Catch** blocks to specify exception handlers.
- To use the **Finally** block to release resources.
- The .NET exception class hierarchy.
- **Exception** properties.
- To create user-defined exceptions.

12.1 Introduction

In this chapter, we introduce exception handling. An exception is an indication of a problem that occurs during a program's execution. The name "exception" comes from the fact that, although the problem can occur, it occurs infrequently. If the "rule" is that a statement normally executes correctly, then the occurrence of a problem represents the "exception to the rule." Exception handling enables you to create applications that can resolve (or handle) exceptions. In many cases, handling an exception allows a program to continue executing as if no problems were encountered. However, more severe problems may prevent a program from continuing normal execution, instead requiring the program to notify the user of the problem, then terminate in a controlled manner. The features presented in this chapter help you to write clear, robust and more fault-tolerant programs (i.e., programs that are able to deal with problems that may arise and continue executing). The style and details of Visual Basic exception handling are based in part on the work of Andrew Koenig and Bjarne Stroustrup in the C++ community. "Best practices" for exception handling in Visual Basic 2005 are specified in the Visual Studio documentation.[1]

Error-Prevention Tip 12.1

Exception handling helps improve a program's fault tolerance.

---

1.   "Best Practices for Handling Exceptions [Visual Basic]," *.NET Framework Developer's Guide*, Visual Studio .NET Online Help (`msdn2.microsoft.com/library/seyhszts(en-us,vs.80).aspx`).

This chapter begins with an overview of exception-handling concepts and demonstrations of basic exception-handling techniques. The chapter also overviews .NET's exception-handling class hierarchy. Programs typically request and release resources (such as files on disk) during program execution. Often, the supply of these resources is limited, or the resources can be used by only one program at a time. We demonstrate a part of the exception-handling mechanism that enables a program to use a resource, then guarantee that the resource will be released for use by other programs, even if an exception occurs. The chapter demonstrates several properties of class `System.Exception` (the base class of all exception classes) and discusses how you can create and use your own exception classes.

12.2 Exception Handling Overview

Programs frequently test conditions to determine how program execution should proceed. Consider the following pseudocode:

> *Perform a task*
>
> *If the preceding task did not execute correctly*
>   *Perform error processing*
>
> *Perform next task*
>
> *If the preceding task did not execute correctly*
>   *Perform error processing*
>
> …

In this pseudocode, we begin by performing a task; then we test whether that task executed correctly. If not, we perform error processing. Otherwise, we continue with the next task. Although this form of error handling works, intermixing program logic with error-handling logic can make programs difficult to read, modify, maintain and debug—especially in large applications.

Exception handling enables you to remove error-handling code from the "main line" of the program's execution, improving program clarity and enhancing modifiability. You can decide to handle any exceptions you choose—all exceptions, all exceptions of a certain type or all exceptions of a group of related types (i.e., exception types that are related through an inheritance hierarchy). Such flexibility reduces the likelihood that errors will be overlooked, thus making programs more robust.

With programming languages that do not support exception handling, programmers often delay writing error-processing code and sometimes forget to include it. This results in less robust software products. Visual Basic enables you to deal with exception handling easily from the beginning of a project.

12.3 Example: Divide by Zero Without Exception Handling

First we demonstrate what happens when errors arise in a console application that does not use exception handling. Figure 12.1 inputs two integers from the user, then divides the first integer by the second using integer division to obtain an `Integer` result. In this example, we will see that an exception is *thrown* (i.e., an exception occurs) when a method detects a problem and is unable to handle it.

```
 I    ' Fig. 12.1: DivideByZeroNoExceptionHandling.vb
 2    ' An application that attempts to divide by zero.
 3    Module DivideByZeroNoExceptionHandling
 4       Sub Main()
 5          ' get numerator and denominator
 6          Console.Write("Please enter an integer numerator: ")
 7          Dim numerator As Integer = Convert.ToInt32(Console.ReadLine())
 8          Console.Write("Please enter an integer denominator: ")
 9          Dim denominator As Integer = Convert.ToInt32(Console.ReadLine())
10
11          ' divide the two integers, then display the result
12          Dim result As Integer = numerator \ denominator
13          Console.WriteLine(vbCrLf & _
14             "Result: {0:D} \ {1:D} = {2:D}", numerator, denominator, result)
15       End Sub ' Main
16    End Module ' DivideByZeroNoExceptionHandling
```

```
Please enter an integer numerator: 100
Please enter an integer denominator: 7

Result: 100 \ 7 = 14
```

```
Please enter an integer numerator: 100
Please enter an integer denominator: 0

Unhandled Exception: System.DivideByZeroException:
   Attempted to divide by zero.
   at DivideByZeroNoExceptionHandling.Main()
      in C:\examples\ch12\Fig12_01\DivideByZeroNoExceptionHandling\
      DivideByZeroNoExceptionHandling.vb:line 12
```

```
Please enter an integer numerator: 100
Please enter an integer denominator: hello

Unhandled Exception: System.FormatException:
   Input string was not in a correct format.
   at System.Number.StringToNumber(String str, NumberStyles options,
      NumberBuffer& number, NumberFormatInfo info, Boolean parseDecimal)
   at System.Number.ParseInt32(String s, NumberStyles style,
      NumberFormatInfo info)
   at System.Convert.ToInt32(String value)
   at DivideByZeroNoExceptionHandling.Main()
      in C:\examples\ch12\Fig12_01\DivideByZeroNoExceptionHandling\
      DivideByZeroNoExceptionHandling.vb:line 9
```

Fig. 12.1 | Integer division without exception handling.

Running the Application

In most of the examples we have created so far, the application appears to run the same with or without debugging. As we discuss shortly, the example in Fig. 12.1 might cause errors, depending on the user's input. If you run this application using the **Debug > Start Debugging** menu option, the program pauses at the line where an exception occurs and allows you to analyze the current state of the program and debug it. We discuss the Exception Assistant in Section 12.4.3. We discuss debugging in detail in Appendix C.

In this example, we do not wish to debug the application; we simply want to see what happens when errors arise. For this reason, we execute this application from a Command Prompt window. Select **Start > All Programs > Accessories > Command Prompt** to open a Command Prompt window, then use the `cd` command to change to the application's `bin\Debug` directory. If this application resides in the directory `C:\examples\ch12\ Fig12_01\DivideByZeroNoExceptionHandling` on your system, you would provide the cd command with the argument

```
C:\examples\ch12\Fig12_01\DivideByZeroNoExceptionHandling\bin\Debug
```

in the Command Prompt, then press *Enter* to change to the application's `Debug` directory. To execute the application, type

```
DivideByZeroNoExceptionHandling.exe
```

in the Command Prompt, then press *Enter*. If an error arises during execution, a dialog is displayed indicating that the application has encountered a problem and needs to close. The dialog also asks whether you'd like to send information about this error to Microsoft. Since we are creating this error for demonstration purposes, you should click **Don't Send**. [*Note:* On some systems a **Just-In-Time Debugging** dialog is displayed instead. If this occurs, simply click the **No** button to dismiss the dialog.] At this point, an error message describing the problem is displayed in the Command Prompt. We formatted the error messages in Fig. 12.1 for readability. [*Note:* Selecting **Debug > Start Without Debugging** (or *<Ctrl> F5*) to run the application from Visual Studio executes the application's so-called release version. The error messages produced by this version of the application may differ from those shown in Fig. 12.1 due to optimizations that the compiler performs to create an application's release version.]

Analyzing the Results

The first sample execution in Fig. 12.1 shows a successful division. In the second sample execution, the user enters 0 as the denominator. Note that several lines of information are displayed in response to the invalid input. This information—known as a stack trace—includes the exception name (`System.DivideByZeroException`) in a descriptive message indicating the problem that occurred and the path of execution that led to the exception, method by method. This information helps you debug a program. The first line of the error message specifies that a `DivideByZeroException` has occurred. When division by zero in integer arithmetic occurs, the CLR throws a `DivideByZeroException` (namespace System). The text after the name of the exception, "`Attempted to divide by zero,`" indicates that this exception occurred as a result of an attempt to divide by zero. Division by zero is not allowed in integer arithmetic. [*Note:* Division by zero with floating-point values is allowed. Such a calculation results in the value infinity, which is represented either by constant **Double.PositiveInfinity** or constant **Double.NegativeInfinity**, depending on whether the numerator is positive or negative. These values are displayed as Infinity or

-Infinity. If both the numerator and denominator are zero, the result of the calculation is the constant `Double.NaN` ("not a number"), which is returned when a calculation's result is undefined.]

Each "at" line in the stack trace indicates a line of code in the method that was executing when the exception occurred. The "at" line contains the namespace, class name and method name in which the exception occurred (`DivideByZeroNoExceptionHandling.Main`), the location and name of the file in which the code resides (`C:\examples\ch12\Fig12_01\DivideByZeroNoExceptionHandling\DivideByZeroNoException Handling.vb:line 12`) and the line of code where the exception occurred. In this case, the stack trace indicates that the `DivideByZeroException` occurred when the program was executing line 12 of method `Main`. The first "at" line in the stack trace indicates the exception's throw point—the initial point at which the exception occurred (i.e., line 12 in `Main`). This information makes it easy for you to see where the exception originated, and what method calls were made to get to that point in the program.

Now, let's look at a more detailed stack trace. In the third sample execution, the user enters the string `"hello"` as the denominator. This causes a `FormatException`, and another stack trace is displayed. Our earlier examples that input numeric values assumed that the user would input an integer value. However, a user could erroneously input a noninteger value. A `FormatException` (namespace `System`) occurs, for example, when Convert method `ToInt32` receives a string that does not represent a valid integer. Starting from the last "at" line in the stack trace, we see that the exception was detected in line 9 of method `Main`. The stack trace also shows the other methods that led to the exception being thrown—`Convert.ToInt32`, `Number.ParseInt32` and `Number.StringToNumber`. To perform its task, `Convert.ToInt32` calls method `Number.ParseInt32`, which in turn calls `Number.StringToNumber`. The throw point occurs in `Number.StringToNumber`, as indicated by the first "at" line in the stack trace.

In Fig. 12.1, the program also terminates when exceptions occur and stack traces are displayed. This does not always happen—sometimes a program may continue executing even though an exception has occurred and a stack trace has been printed. In such cases, the application may produce incorrect results. The next section demonstrates how to handle exceptions to enable the program to run to normal completion.

12.4 Example: Handling `DivideByZeroExceptions` and `FormatExceptions`

Let us consider a simple example of exception handling. The application in Fig. 12.2 uses exception handling to process any `DivideByZeroExceptions` and `FormatExceptions` that might arise. The application displays two `TextBoxes` in which the user can type integers. When the user presses **Click To Divide**, the program invokes event handler `btnDivide_Click` (lines 6–33), which obtains the user's input, converts the input values to type `Integer` and divides the first number (numerator) by the second number (denominator). Assuming that the user provides integers as input and does not specify 0 as the denominator, `btnDivide_Click` displays the division result in `lblOutput`. However, if the user inputs a noninteger value or supplies 0 as the denominator, an exception occurs. This program demonstrates how to catch and handle (i.e., deal with) such exceptions—in this case, displaying an error message and allowing the user to enter another set of values.

Before we discuss the program's details in Sections 12.4.1–12.4.5, let's consider the sample output windows in Fig. 12.2. The window in Fig. 12.2(a) shows a successful calculation, in which the user enters the numerator 100 and the denominator 7. Note that the result (14) is an Integer, because integer division always yields an Integer result. The next two windows, Fig. 12.2(b and c), demonstrate the result of an attempt to divide by zero. In integer arithmetic, the CLR tests for division by zero and, if the denominator is

```vb
1   ' Fig. 12.2: DivideByZeroTest.vb
2   ' Exception handlers for FormatException and DivideByZeroException.
3   Public Class frmDivideByZeroTest
4      ' obtain 2 integers from the user
5      ' and divide numerator by denominator
6      Private Sub btnDivide_Click(ByVal sender As System.Object, _
7         ByVal e As System.EventArgs) Handles btnDivide.Click
8
9         lblOutput.Text = "" ' clear Label lblOutput
10
11        ' retrieve user input and calculate quotient
12        Try
13           ' Convert.ToInt32 generates FormatException
14           ' if argument is not an integer
15           Dim numerator As Integer = Convert.ToInt32(txtNumerator.Text)
16           Dim denominator As Integer = Convert.ToInt32(txtDenominator.Text)
17
18           ' division generates DivideByZeroException
19           ' if denominator is 0
20           Dim result As Integer = numerator \ denominator
21
22           ' display result in lblOutput
23           lblOutput.Text = result.ToString()
24        Catch formatExceptionParameter As FormatException
25           MessageBox.Show("You must enter two integers.", _
26              "Invalid Number Format", MessageBoxButtons.OK, _
27              MessageBoxIcon.Error)
28        Catch divideByZeroExceptionParameter As DivideByZeroException
29           MessageBox.Show(divideByZeroExceptionParameter.Message, _
30              "Attempted to Divide by Zero", MessageBoxButtons.OK, _
31              MessageBoxIcon.Error)
32        End Try
33     End Sub ' btnDivide_Click
34  End Class ' frmDivideByZeroTest
```

(a)

Fig. 12.2 | FormatException and DivideByZeroException exception handlers. (Part 1 of 2.)

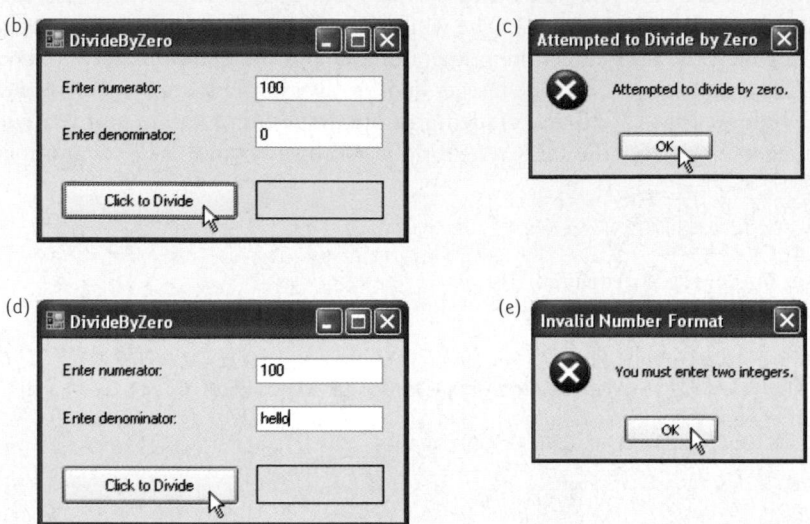

Fig. 12.2 | `FormatException` and `DivideByZeroException` exception handlers. (Part 2 of 2.)

zero, generates a `DivideByZeroException`. The program detects the exception and displays the error message dialog in Fig. 12.2(c) indicating the attempt to divide by zero. The last two output windows, Fig. 12.2(d) and Fig. 12.2(e), depict the result of inputting a non-`Integer` value—in this case, the user enters "`hello`" in the second `TextBox`, as shown in Fig. 12.2(d). When the user clicks **Click To Divide**, the program attempts to convert the input `Strings` into `Integer` values using method `Convert.ToInt32` (lines 15–16). If an argument passed to `Convert.ToInt32` cannot be converted to an `Integer` value, the method throws a `FormatException`. The program catches the exception and displays the error message dialog in Fig. 12.2(e) indicating that the user must enter two `Integers`.

12.4.1 Enclosing Code in a Try Block

Now we consider the user interactions and flow of control that yield the results shown in the sample output windows. The user inputs values into the `TextBoxes` that represent the numerator and denominator, then presses **Click To Divide**. At this point, the program invokes method `btnDivide_Click`. Line 9 assigns the empty string to `lblOutput` to clear any prior result in preparation for a new calculation. Lines 12–23 define a `Try block` enclosing the code that might throw exceptions, as well as the code that is skipped when an exception occurs. For example, the program should not display a new result in `lblOutput` (line 23) unless the calculation in line 20 completes successfully.

The two statements that read the `Integers` from the `TextBoxes` (lines 15–16) call method `Convert.ToInt32` to convert `Strings` to `Integer` values. This method throws a `FormatException` if it cannot convert its `String` argument to an `Integer`. If lines 15–16 convert the values properly (i.e., no exceptions occur), then line 20 divides the `numerator` by the `denominator`. If denominator is 0, line 20 causes the CLR to throw a `DivideByZeroException`. If line 20 does not cause an exception to be thrown, then the result is assigned to variable `result` and line 23 displays the result of the division.

12.4.2 Catching Exceptions

Exception-handling code appears in a **Catch block**. In general, when an exception occurs in a Try block, a corresponding Catch block catches the exception and handles it. The Try block in this example is followed by two Catch blocks—one that handles a Format-Exception (lines 24–27) and one that handles a DivideByZeroException (lines 28–31). A Catch block specifies an exception parameter representing the exception that the Catch block can handle. The Catch block can use the parameter's identifier (which is chosen by the programmer) to interact with a caught exception object. The type of the Catch's parameter is the type of the exception that the Catch block handles. Optionally, you can include a Catch block that does not specify an exception type or an identifier—such a Catch block catches all exception types. At least one Catch block or a **Finally block** (discussed in Section 12.6) must immediately follow a Try block.

In Fig. 12.2, the first Catch block (lines 23–27) catches FormatExceptions (thrown by method Convert.ToInt32), and the second Catch block (lines 28–31) catches Divide-ByZeroExceptions (thrown by the CLR). If an exception occurs, the program executes only the first matching Catch block. Both exception handlers in this example display an error message dialog. After either Catch block terminates, program control continues with the first statement after the last Catch block (the end of the method, in this example). We will soon take a deeper look at how this flow of control works in exception handling.

12.4.3 Uncaught Exceptions

An **uncaught exception** is an exception for which there is no matching Catch block. You saw the results of uncaught exceptions in the second and third outputs of Fig. 12.1. Recall that when exceptions occur in that example, the application terminates early (after displaying the exception's stack trace). The result of an uncaught exception depends on how you execute the program—Fig. 12.1 demonstrated the results of an uncaught exception when an application is executed in a Command Prompt. If you run the application from Visual Studio with debugging and the runtime environment detects an uncaught exception, the application pauses, and a window called the Exception Assistant appears indicating where the exception occurred, the type of the exception and links to helpful information on handling the exception. Figure 12.3 shows the Exception Assistant that is displayed if the user attempts to divide by zero in the application of Fig. 12.1.

12.4.4 Termination Model of Exception Handling

When a method called in a program or the CLR detects a problem, the method or the CLR throws an exception. Recall that the point in the program at which an exception occurs is called the throw point—this is an important location for debugging purposes (as we demonstrate in Section 12.7). If an exception occurs in a Try block (such as a Format-Exception being thrown as a result of the code in line 16 in Fig. 12.2), the Try block terminates immediately, and program control transfers to the first of the following Catch blocks in which the exception parameter's type matches the type of the thrown exception. In Fig. 12.2, the first Catch block catches FormatExceptions (which occur if input of an invalid type is entered); the second Catch block catches DivideByZeroExceptions (which occur if an attempt is made to divide by zero). After the exception is handled, program control does not return to the throw point because the Try block has expired (which also

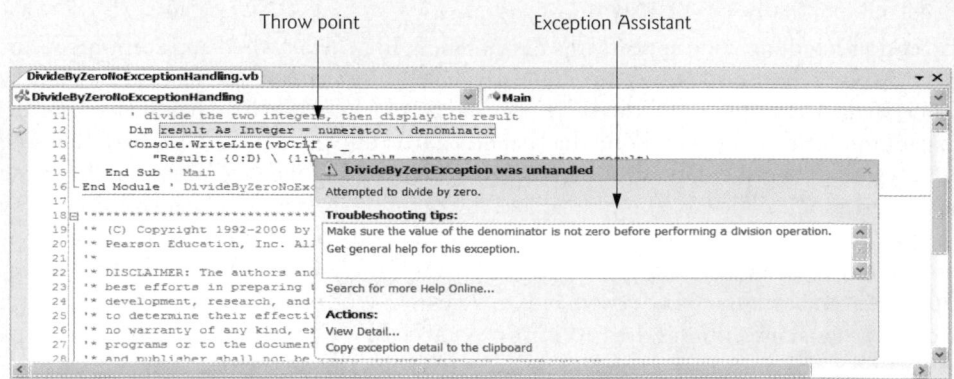

Fig. 12.3 | Exception Assistant.

causes any of its local variables to go out of scope). Rather, control resumes after the last Catch block. This is known as the **termination model of exception handling**. [*Note:* Some languages use the **resumption model of exception handling**, in which after an exception is handled, control resumes just after the throw point.]

 Common Programming Error 12.1

Logic errors can occur if you assume that after an exception is handled, control will return to the first statement after the throw point.

If no exceptions occur in the Try block, the program of Fig. 12.2 successfully completes the Try block by ignoring the Catch blocks in lines 24–27 and 28–31, and passing over line 32. Then the program executes the first statement following the Try and Catch blocks. In this example, the program reaches the end of event handler btnDivide_Click (line 33), so the method terminates, and the program awaits the next user interaction.

The Try block and its corresponding Catch and Finally blocks together form a **Try statement**. It is important not to confuse the terms "Try block" and "Try statement"—the term "Try block" refers to the block of code following the keyword Try (but before any Catch or Finally blocks), while the term "Try statement" includes all the code from the opening Try keyword to the closing End Try. This includes the Try block, as well as any associated Catch blocks and Finally block, if there is one.

As with any other block of code, when a Try block terminates, local variables defined in the block go out of scope. If a Try block terminates due to an exception, the CLR searches for the first Catch block that can process the type of exception that occurred. The CLR locates the matching Catch by comparing the type of the thrown exception to each Catch's parameter type. A match occurs if the types are identical or if the thrown exception's type is a derived class of the Catch's parameter type. Once an exception is matched to a Catch block, the code in that block executes and the other Catch blocks in the Try statement are ignored.

12.4.5 Flow of Control When Exceptions Occur

In the sample output of Fig. 12.2(b), the user inputs 0 as the denominator. When the division in line 20 executes, a DivideByZeroException occurs. When the exception occurs, the `Try` block expires (terminates). Next, the CLR attempts to locate a matching `Catch` block. In this case, the first `Catch` block does not match—the exception type in the `Catch`-handler declaration is not the same as the type of the thrown exception, and `FormatException` is not a base class of `DivideByZeroException`. Therefore the program continues to search for a matching `Catch` block, which it finds in line 28. Line 29 displays the value of property `Message` of class `Exception`, which contains the error message. Note that our program never "sets" this error message attribute. This is done by the CLR when it creates the exception object.

In the sample output of Fig. 12.2(d), the user inputs `hello` as the denominator. When line 16 executes, `Convert.ToInt32` cannot convert this `String` to an `Integer`, so `Convert.ToInt32` throws a `FormatException` object to indicate that the method was unable to convert the `String` to an `Integer`. Once again, the `Try` block terminates, and the program attempts to locate a matching `Catch` block. A match occurs with the `Catch` block in line 24, so the exception handler executes and the program ignores all other exception handlers following the `Try` block.

Common Programming Error 12.2

Specifying a comma-separated list of parameters in a `Catch` block is a syntax error. A `Catch` block can have at most one parameter.

12.5 .NET Exception Hierarchy

In Visual Basic, the exception-handling mechanism allows only objects of class `Exception` (namespace `System`) and its derived classes to be thrown and caught. Visual Basic programs may interact with software components written in other .NET languages (such as C++) that do not restrict exception types. Such exceptions are wrapped by the CLR as `Exception` objects, so they can be caught by a `Catch` clause of type `Exception`.

This section overviews several of the .NET Framework's exception classes and focuses exclusively on exceptions that derive from class `Exception`. In addition, we discuss how to determine whether a particular method throws exceptions.

12.5.1 Classes ApplicationException and SystemException

Class `Exception` of namespace `System` is the base class of the .NET Framework exception class hierarchy. Two of the most important classes derived from `Exception` are `ApplicationException` and `SystemException`. `ApplicationException` is a base class that you can extend to create exception classes that are specific to their applications. We show how to create user-defined exception classes in Section 12.8. Programs can recover from most `ApplicationException`s and continue execution.

The CLR generates `SystemException`s, which can occur at any point during program execution. Many of these exceptions can be avoided if applications are coded properly. For example, if a program attempts to access an out-of-range array index, the CLR throws an exception of type `IndexOutOfRangeException` (a derived class of `SystemException`). Similarly, an exception occurs when a program uses an object reference to manipulate an object that does not yet exist (i.e., the reference has the value `Nothing`). Attempting to use a `Nothing` reference causes a `NullReferenceException` (another derived class of `System-Exception`). You saw earlier in this chapter that a `DivideByZeroException` occurs in integer division when a program attempts to divide by zero.

Other `SystemException` types thrown by the CLR include `OutOfMemoryException`, `StackOverflowException` and `ExecutionEngineException`. These are thrown when the something goes wrong that causes the CLR to become unstable. In some cases, such exceptions cannot even be caught. In general, it is best to simply log such exceptions (possibly by writing information about the problem to a file) then terminate your application.

A benefit of the exception class hierarchy is that a `Catch` block can catch exceptions of a particular type or—because of the *is-a* relationship of inheritance—can use a base-class type to catch exceptions in a hierarchy of related exception types. For example, Section 12.4.2 discussed the `Catch` block with no parameter, which catches exceptions of all types (including those that are not derived from `Exception`). A `Catch` block that specifies a parameter of type `Exception` can catch all exceptions that derive from `Exception`, because `Exception` is the base class of all exception classes. The advantage of this approach is that the exception handler can access the caught exception's information via the parameter in the `Catch`. We demonstrated accessing the information in an exception in line 29 of Fig. 12.2. We'll say more about accessing exception information in Section 12.7.

Using inheritance with exceptions enables a `Catch` block to catch related exceptions using a concise notation. A set of exception handlers could catch each derived-class exception type individually, but catching the base-class exception type is more concise. However, this technique makes sense only if the handling behavior is the same for a base class and all of its derived classes. Otherwise, catch each derived-class exception individually.

Common Programming Error 12.3

It is a compilation error if a `Catch` block that catches a base-class exception is placed before a `Catch` block for any of that class's derived-class types. If this were allowed, the base-class `Catch` block would catch all base-class and derived-class exceptions, so the derived-class exception handler would never execute.

12.5.2 Determining Which Exceptions a Method Throws

How do we determine that an exception might occur in a program? For methods of the .NET Framework classes, read the detailed descriptions of the methods in the online documentation (accessible through the IDE's **Help** menu). If a method throws an exception, its description contains a section called **Exceptions** that specifies the types of exceptions the method throws and briefly describes possible causes for the exceptions. For example, search for "`Convert.ToInt32` method" in the **Index** of the Visual Studio online documentation (use the **.NET Framework** filter). Select the document entitled **Convert.ToInt32 Method**. In the document that describes the method, click the link **Convert.ToInt32(String)**. In the document that appears, the **Exceptions** section (near the bottom of the document) indicates that method `Convert.ToInt32` throws two exception types—`FormatException` and `OverflowException`—and describes the reason why each might occur.

Software Engineering Observation 12.1

If a method throws exceptions, statements that invoke the method directly or indirectly should be placed in `Try` blocks, and those exceptions should be caught and handled.

It is more difficult to determine when the CLR throws exceptions. Such information appears in the *Visual Basic Language Specification 8.0* (`www.microsoft.com/downloads/ details.aspx?familyid=6d50d709-eaa4-44d7-8af3-e14280403e6e`). This document defines Visual Basic's syntax and specifies cases in which exceptions are thrown. Figure 12.2 demonstrated that the CLR throws a DivideByZeroException in integer arithmetic when a program attempts to divide by zero. Section 11.13.6 of the language specification discusses the division operator and when DivideByZeroExceptions occur.

12.6 Finally Block

Programs frequently request and release resources dynamically (i.e., at execution time). For example, a program that reads a file from disk first makes a file-open request (as we'll see in Chapter 18, Files and Streams). If that request succeeds, the program reads the contents of the file. Operating systems typically prevent more than one program from manipulating a file at once. Therefore, when a program finishes processing a file, the program should close the file (i.e., release the resource) so other programs can use it. If the file is not closed, a resource leak occurs. In such a case, the file resource is not available to other programs, possibly because a program using the file has not closed it.

In languages such as C and C++, in which the programmer (not the runtime) is responsible for dynamic memory management, the most common type of resource leak is a memory leak. A memory leak occurs when a program allocates memory (as Visual Basic programmers do via keyword New), but does not deallocate the memory when it is no longer needed. Normally, this is not an issue in Visual Basic, because the CLR garbage collects memory that is no longer needed by an executing program (Section 9.9). However, other kinds of resource leaks (such as unclosed files) can occur.

Error-Prevention Tip 12.2

The CLR does not completely eliminate memory leaks. The CLR will not garbage collect an object until the program contains no more references to that object. Thus, memory leaks can occur if you inadvertently keep references to unwanted objects.

Moving Resource Release Code to a Finally Block

Typically, exceptions occur when processing resources that require explicit release. For example, a program that processes a file might receive IOExceptions during the processing. For this reason, file processing code normally appears in a Try block. Regardless of whether a program experiences exceptions while processing a file, the program should close the file when it is no longer needed. Suppose a program places all resource request and resource release code in a Try block. If no exceptions occur, the Try block executes normally and releases the resources after using them. However, if an exception occurs, the Try block may expire before the resource-release code can execute. We could duplicate all the resource release code in each of the Catch blocks, but this would make the code more difficult to modify and maintain. We could also place the resource release code after the Try statement; however, if the Try block terminates due to a return statement, code following the Try statement would never execute.

To address these problems, Visual Basic's exception handling mechanism provides the optional Finally block, which is guaranteed to execute regardless of whether the Try block executes successfully or an exception occurs. This makes the Finally block an ideal location in which to place resource-release code for resources that are acquired and manipulated in the corresponding Try block. If the Try block executes successfully, the Finally block executes immediately after the Try block terminates. If an exception occurs in the

```
53      ' throws exception and catches it locally
54      Sub ThrowExceptionWithCatch()
55         ' try block throws exception
56         Try
57            Console.WriteLine("In ThrowExceptionWithCatch")
58            Throw New Exception("Exception in ThrowExceptionWithCatch")
59         Catch exceptionParameter As Exception
60            Console.WriteLine("Message: " & exceptionParameter.Message)
61         Finally
62            Console.WriteLine("finally executed in ThrowExceptionWithCatch")
63         End Try
64
65         Console.WriteLine("End of ThrowExceptionWithCatch")
66      End Sub ' ThrowExceptionWithCatch
67
68      ' throws exception and does not catch it locally
69      Sub ThrowExceptionWithoutCatch()
70         ' throw exception, but do not catch it
71         Try
72            Console.WriteLine("In ThrowExceptionWithoutCatch")
73            Throw New Exception("Exception in ThrowExceptionWithoutCatch")
74         Finally
75            Console.WriteLine("finally executed in " & _
76               "ThrowExceptionWithoutCatch")
77         End Try
78
79         ' unreachable code; logic error
80         Console.WriteLine("End of ThrowExceptionWithoutCatch")
81      End Sub ' ThrowExceptionWithoutCatch
82
83      ' throws exception, catches it and rethrows it
84      Sub ThrowExceptionCatchRethrow()
85         ' try block throws exception
86         Try
87            Console.WriteLine("In ThrowExceptionCatchRethrow")
88            Throw New Exception("Exception in ThrowExceptionCatchRethrow")
89         Catch exceptionParameter As Exception
90            Console.WriteLine("Message: " & exceptionParameter.Message)
91
92            ' rethrow exception for further processing
93            Throw
94
95            ' code placed here would be unreachable; logic error
96         Finally
97            Console.WriteLine("finally executed in " & _
98               "ThrowExceptionCatchRethrow")
99         End Try
100
101        ' any code placed here is never reached
102        Console.WriteLine("End of ThrowExceptionCatchRethrow")
103     End Sub ' ThrowExceptionCatchRethrow
104  End Module ' UsingExceptions
```

Fig. 12.4 | `Finally` always executes, regardless of whether an exception occurs. (Part 2 of 3.)

```
Calling DoesNotThrowException
In DoesNotThrowException
finally executed in DoesNotThrowException
End of DoesNotThrowException

Calling ThrowExceptionWithCatch
In ThrowExceptionWithCatch
Message: Exception in ThrowExceptionWithCatch
finally executed in ThrowExceptionWithCatch
End of ThrowExceptionWithCatch

Calling ThrowExceptionWithoutCatch
In ThrowExceptionWithoutCatch
finally executed in ThrowExceptionWithoutCatch
Caught exception from ThrowExceptionWithoutCatch in Main

Calling ThrowExceptionCatchRethrow
In ThrowExceptionCatchRethrow
Message: Exception in ThrowExceptionCatchRethrow
finally executed in ThrowExceptionCatchRethrow
Caught exception from ThrowExceptionCatchRethrow in Main
```

Fig. 12.4 | **Finally** always executes, regardless of whether an exception occurs. (Part 3 of 3.)

Throw statement. Just as with exceptions thrown by the FCL's methods and the CLR, this indicates to client applications that an error has occurred. A Throw statement specifies an object to be thrown. The operand of a Throw statement can be of type Exception or of any type derived from class Exception.

Common Programming Error 12.5

It is a compilation error if the argument of a Throw—an exception object—is not of class Exception or one of its derived classes.

The String passed to the constructor becomes the exception object's error message. When a Throw statement in a Try block executes, the Try block expires immediately, and program control continues with the first matching Catch block (lines 59–60) following the Try block. In this example, the type thrown (Exception) matches the type specified in the Catch, so line 60 outputs a message indicating the exception that occurred. Then, the Finally block (lines 61–62) executes and outputs a message. At this point, program control continues with the first statement after the end of the Finally block (line 65), which outputs a message indicating that the end of the method has been reached. Program control then returns to Main. In line 60, note that we use the exception object's Message property to retrieve the error message associated with the exception (i.e., the message passed to the Exception constructor). Section 12.7 discusses several properties of class Exception.

Lines 19–24 of Main define a Try statement in which Main invokes method ThrowExceptionWithoutCatch (lines 69–81). The Try block enables Main to catch any exceptions thrown by ThrowExceptionWithoutCatch. The Try block in lines 71–73 of ThrowExceptionWithoutCatch begins by outputting a message. Next, the Try block throws an Exception (line 73) and expires immediately.

Normally, program control would continue at the first Catch following this Try block. However, this Try block does not have any Catch blocks. Therefore, the exception is not caught in method `ThrowExceptionWithoutCatch`. Program control proceeds to the `Finally` block (lines 74–76), which outputs a message. At this point, program control returns to `Main`—any statements appearing after the `Finally` block (e.g., line 80) do not execute. In this example, such statements could cause logic errors, because the exception thrown in line 73 is not caught. In `Main`, the `Catch` block in lines 21–23 catches the exception and displays a message indicating that the exception was caught in `Main`.

Rethrowing Exceptions

Lines 31–36 of `Main` define a `Try` statement in which `Main` invokes method `ThrowExceptionCatchRethrow` (lines 84–103). The `Try` statement enables `Main` to catch any exceptions thrown by `ThrowExceptionCatchRethrow`. The `Try` statement in lines 86–99 of `ThrowExceptionCatchRethrow` begins by outputting a message. Next, the `Try` block throws an `Exception` (line 88). The `Try` block expires immediately, and program control continues at the first `Catch` (lines 89–95) following the `Try` block. In this example, the type thrown (`Exception`) matches the type specified in the `Catch`, so line 90 outputs the exception's message, which in this case indicates where the exception was thrown. Line 93 uses the `Throw` statement to *rethrow* the exception. This indicates that the `Catch` block performed partial processing of the exception and now is passing the exception back to the calling method (in this case, `Main`) for further processing.

You can also rethrow an exception with a version of the `Throw` statement which takes an operand that is the reference to the exception that was caught. It's important to note, however, that this form of `Throw` statement resets the throw point, so the original throw point's stack trace information is lost. Section 12.7 demonstrates using a `Throw` statement with an operand from a `Catch` block. In that section, you will see that after an exception is caught, you can create and throw a different type of exception object from the `Catch` block and you can include the original exception as part of the new exception object. Class library designers often do this to customize the exception types thrown from methods in their class libraries or to provide additional debugging information.

The exception handling in method `ThrowExceptionCatchRethrow` does not complete, because the the method rethrows the exception with the `Throw` statement in line 93. This causes method `ThrowExceptionCatchRethrow` to terminate and return control to `Main`. Once again, the `Finally` block (lines 96–98) executes and outputs a message before control returns to `Main`. When control returns to `Main`, the `Catch` block in lines 33–35 catches the exception and displays a message indicating that the exception was caught. Then the program terminates.

Returning After a `Finally` Block

Note that the next statement to execute after a `Finally` block terminates depends on the exception-handling state. If the `Try` block successfully completes, or if a `Catch` block catches and handles an exception, the program continues its execution with the next statement after the `Finally` block. However, if an exception is not caught, or if a `Catch` block rethrows an exception, program control continues in the next enclosing `Try` block, which could be in the calling method or in one of its callers. It also is possible to nest a `Try` statement in a `Try` block; in such a case, the outer `Try` statement's `Catch` blocks would process any exceptions that were not caught in the inner `Try` statement. If a `Try` block executes and has a corresponding `Finally` block, the `Finally` block executes even if the `Try` block terminates due to a `Return` statement—the `Return` occurs after executing the `Finally` block.

Common Programming Error 12.6

Throwing an exception from a Finally block can be dangerous. If an uncaught exception is awaiting processing when the Finally block executes, and the Finally block throws a new exception that is not caught in the Finally block, the first exception is lost, and the new exception is passed to the next enclosing Try block.

Error-Prevention Tip 12.4

When placing code that can throw an exception in a Finally block, always enclose the code in a Try statement that catches the appropriate exception types. This prevents the loss of any uncaught and rethrown exceptions that occur before the Finally block executes.

Software Engineering Observation 12.2

Do not place Try blocks around every statement that might throw an exception, because this can make programs difficult to read. It is better to place one Try block around a significant portion of code, and follow this Try block with Catch blocks that handle each of the possible exceptions. Then follow the Catch blocks with a single Finally block. Separate Try blocks should be used when it is important to distinguish between multiple statements that can throw the same exception type.

The *Using Statement*

Recall from earlier in this section that resource-release code should be placed in a Finally block to ensure that a resource is released, regardless of whether exceptions occurred when the resource was used in the corresponding Try block. An alternative notation—the **Using** statement—simplifies writing code in which you obtain a resource, use the resource in a Try block and release the resource in a corresponding Finally block. For example, a file-processing application (Chapter 18) could process a file with a Using statement to ensure that the file is closed properly when it is no longer needed. The resource must be an object that implements the IDisposable interface and therefore has a Dispose method. The general form of a Using statement is

```
Using exampleObject As New ExampleObject()
    exampleObject.SomeMethod()
End Using
```

where ExampleObject is a class that implements the IDisposable interface. This code creates an object of type ExampleObject and uses it in a statement, then calls its Dispose method to release any resources used by the object. The Using statement implicitly places the code in its body in a Try block with a corresponding Finally block that calls the object's Dispose method. For instance, the preceding code is equivalent to

```
Dim exampleObject As New ExampleObject()

Try
    exampleObject.SomeMethod()
Finally
    If Not (exampleObject Is Nothing) Then
        exampleObject.Dispose()
    End If
End Try
```

Note that the If statement ensures that exampleObject still references an object; otherwise, a NullReferenceException might occur. You can read more about the Using statement in Section 10.13 of the *Visual Basic Language Specification*.

12.7 Exception Properties

As we discussed in Section 12.5, exception types derive from class Exception, which has several properties. These frequently are used in error messages indicating a caught exception. Two important properties are Message and **StackTrace**.

Property Message stores the error message associated with an Exception object. This message can be a default message associated with the exception type or a customized message passed to an Exception object's constructor when the Exception object is thrown.

Property StackTrace contains a (normally lengthy) String that represents the method-call stack. Recall that the runtime environment at all times keeps a list of open method calls that have been made but have not yet returned. The StackTrace represents the series of methods that have not finished processing at the time the exception occurs.

Error-Prevention Tip 12.5

A stack trace shows the complete method-call stack at the time an exception occurred. This enables you to view the series of method calls that led to the exception. Information in the stack trace includes the names of the methods on the call stack at the time of the exception, the names of the classes in which the methods are defined and the names of the namespaces in which the classes are defined. The IDE creates program database (PDB) files to maintain the debugging information for your projects. If the PDB file that contains the debugging information for the method is available, the stack trace also includes line numbers; the first line number indicates the throw point, and subsequent line numbers indicate the locations from which the methods in the stack trace were called.

Property *InnerException*

Another property used frequently by class-library programmers is InnerException. Typically, class library programmers "wrap" exception objects caught in their code so they then can throw new exception types that are specific to their libraries. For example, a programmer implementing an accounting system might have some account-number processing code in which account numbers are input as Strings but represented as Integers in the code. Recall that a program can convert Strings to Integer values with Convert.ToInt32, which throws a FormatException when it encounters an invalid number format. When an invalid account number format occurs, the accounting system programmer might wish to employ a different error message than the default message supplied by FormatException or might wish to indicate a new exception type, such as InvalidAccountNumberFormatException. In such cases, the programmer would provide code to catch the FormatException, then create an appropriate type of Exception object in the Catch block and pass the original exception as one of the constructor arguments. The original exception object becomes the InnerException of the new exception object. When an InvalidAccountNumberFormatException occurs in code that uses the accounting system library, the Catch block that catches the exception can obtain a reference to the original exception via property InnerException. Thus the exception indicates both that the user specified an invalid account number and that the problem was an invalid number format.

If the `InnerException` property is `Nothing`, this indicates that the exception was not caused by another exception.

Other **Exception** Properties

Class `Exception` provides other properties, including `HelpLink`, `Source` and `TargetSite`. Property `HelpLink` specifies the location of the help file that describes the problem that occurred. This property is `Nothing` if no such file exists. Property `Source` specifies the name of the application where the exception occurred. Property `TargetSite` specifies the method where the exception originated.

Demonstrating **Exception** Properties and Stack Unwinding

Our next example (Fig. 12.5) demonstrates properties `Message`, `StackTrace` and `Inner-Exception`, and method `ToString`, of class `Exception`. In addition, the example introduces **stack unwinding**—when an exception is thrown but not caught in a particular scope, the method-call stack is "unwound," and an attempt is made to catch the exception in the next outer `Try` block. We keep track of the methods on the call stack as we discuss property `StackTrace` and the stack-unwinding mechanism. To see the proper stack trace, you should execute this program using steps similar to those presented in Section 12.3.

Program execution begins with `Main`, which becomes the first method on the method call stack. Line 9 of the `Try` block in `Main` invokes `Method1` (declared in lines 29–31), which becomes the second method on the stack. If `Method1` throws an exception, the `Catch` block in lines 10–24 handles the exception and outputs information about the exception that occurred. Line 30 of `Method1` invokes `Method2` (lines 34–36), which becomes the third method on the stack. Then line 35 of `Method2` invokes `Method3` (lines 39–48), which becomes the fourth method on the stack.

```vb
1   ' Fig. 12.5: Properties.vb
2   ' Stack unwinding and Exception class properties.
3   ' Demonstrates using properties Message, StackTrace and InnerException.
4   Module Properties
5      Sub Main()
6         ' call Method1; any Exception generated is caught
7         ' in the catch block that follows
8         Try
9            Method1()
10        Catch exceptionParameter As Exception
11           ' output the string representation of the Exception, then output
12           ' properties InnerException, Message and StackTrace
13           Console.WriteLine("exceptionParameter.ToString: " & _
14              vbCrLf & "{0}" & vbCrLf, _
15              exceptionParameter.ToString())
16           Console.WriteLine("exceptionParameter.Message: " & _
17              vbCrLf & "{0}" & vbCrLf, _
18              exceptionParameter.Message)
19           Console.WriteLine("exceptionParameter.StackTrace: " & _
20              vbCrLf & "{0}" & vbCrLf, _
21              exceptionParameter.StackTrace)
```

Fig. 12.5 | `Exception` properties and stack unwinding. (Part 1 of 3.)

```
22          Console.WriteLine("exceptionParameter.InnerException: " & _
23             vbCrLf & "{0}" & vbCrLf, _
24             exceptionParameter.InnerException.ToString())
25       End Try
26    End Sub ' Main
27
28    ' calls Method2
29    Sub Method1()
30       Method2()
31    End Sub ' Method1
32
33    ' calls Method3
34    Sub Method2()
35       Method3()
36    End Sub ' Method2
37
38    ' throws an Exception containing an InnerException
39    Sub Method3()
40       ' attempt to convert string to integer
41       Try
42          Convert.ToInt32("Not an integer")
43       Catch formatExceptionParameter As FormatException
44          ' wrap FormatException in new Exception
45          Throw New Exception("Exception occurred in Method3", _
46             formatExceptionParameter)
47       End Try
48    End Sub ' Method3
49 End Module ' Properties
```

```
exceptionParameter.ToString:
System.Exception: Exception occurred in Method3 --->
   System.FormatException: Input string was not in a correct format.
   at System.Number.StringToNumber(String str, NumberStyles options,
      NumberBuffer& number, NumberFormatInfo info, Boolean parseDecimal)
   at System.Number.ParseInt32(String s, NumberStyles style,
      NumberFormatInfo info)
   at System.Convert.ToInt32(String value)
   at Properties.Method3() in C:\examples\ch12\Fig12_04\Properties\
      Properties.vb:line 42
   --- End of inner exception stack trace ---
   at Properties.Method3() in C:\examples\ch12\Fig12_04\Properties\
      Properties.vb:line 45
   at Properties.Method2() in C:\examples\ch12\Fig12_04\Properties\
      Properties.vb:line 35
   at Properties.Method1() in C:\examples\ch12\Fig12_04\Properties\
      Properties.vb:line 30
   at Properties.Main() in C:\examples\ch12\Fig12_04\Properties\
      Properties.vb:line 9

exceptionParameter.Message:
Exception occurred in Method3
```

(continued on next page...)

Fig. 12.5 | Exception properties and stack unwinding (Part 2 of 3.)

```
exceptionParameter.StackTrace:
   at Properties.Method3() in C:\examples\ch12\Fig12_04\Properties\
      Properties.vb:line 45
   at Properties.Method2() in C:\examples\ch12\Fig12_04\Properties\
      Properties.vb:line 35
   at Properties.Method1() in C:\examples\ch12\Fig12_04\Properties\
      Properties.vb:line 30
   at Properties.Main() in C:\examples\ch12\Fig12_04\Properties\
      Properties.vb:line 9

exceptionParameter.InnerException:
System.FormatException: Input string was not in a correct format.
   at System.Number.StringToNumber(String str, NumberStyles options,
      NumberBuffer& number, NumberFormatInfo info, Boolean parseDecimal)
   at System.Number.ParseInt32(String s, NumberStyles style,
      NumberFormatInfo info)
   at System.Convert.ToInt32(String value)
   at Properties.Method3() in C:\examples\ch12\Fig12_04\Properties\
      Properties.vb:line 42
```

Fig. 12.5 | Exception properties and stack unwinding. (Part 3 of 3.)

At this point, the method-call stack (from top to bottom) for the program is:

```
Method3
Method2
Method1
Main
```

The method called most recently (Method3) appears at the top of the stack; the first method called (Main) appears at the bottom. The Try statement (lines 41–47) in Method3 invokes Convert.ToInt32 (line 42), which attempts to convert a String to an Integer. At this point, Convert.ToInt32 becomes the fifth and final method on the call stack.

Throwing an *Exception* with an *InnerException*

Because the argument to Convert.ToInt32 is not in Integer format, line 42 throws a FormatException that is caught in line 43 of Method3. When the exception occurs, the call to Convert.ToInt32 terminates, so the method is removed (or unwound) from the method-call stack. The Catch block in Method3 then creates and throws an Exception object. The first argument to the Exception constructor is the custom error message for our example, "Exception occurred in Method3". The second argument is the InnerException—the FormatException that was caught. The StackTrace for this new exception object reflects the point at which the exception was thrown (line 45). Now Method3 terminates, because the exception thrown in the Catch block is not caught in the method body. Thus, control returns to the statement that invoked Method3 in the prior method in the call stack (Method2). This removes, or unwinds, Method3 from the method-call stack.

When control returns to line 35 in Method2, the CLR determines that line 35 is not in a Try block. Therefore the exception cannot be caught in Method2, and Method2 terminates. This unwinds Method2 from the call stack and returns control to line 30 in Method1.

Here again, line 30 is not in a Try block, so Method1 cannot catch the exception. The method terminates and is unwound from the call stack, returning control to line 9 in Main, which *is* located in a Try block. The Try block in Main expires and the Catch block (lines 10–24) catches the exception. The Catch block uses method ToString and properties Message, StackTrace and InnerException to create the output. Note that stack unwinding continues until a Catch block catches the exception or the program terminates.

Displaying Information About the Exception

The first block of output (which we reformatted for readability) in Fig. 12.5 contains the exception's String representation, which is returned from method ToString. The String begins with the name of the exception class followed by the Message property value. The next four items present the stack trace of the InnerException object. The remainder of the block of output shows the StackTrace for the exception thrown in Method3. Note that the StackTrace represents the state of the method-call stack at the throw point of the exception, rather than at the point where the exception eventually is caught. Each Stack-Trace line that begins with "at" represents a method on the call stack. These lines indicate the method in which the exception occurred, the file in which the method resides and the line number of the throw point in the file. Note that the inner-exception information includes the inner exception stack trace.

Error-Prevention Tip 12.6

When catching and rethrowing an exception, provide additional debugging information in the rethrown exception. To do so, create an Exception object containing more specific debugging information, then pass the original caught exception to the new exception object's constructor to initialize the InnerException property.

The next block of output (two lines) simply displays the Message property's value (Exception occurred in Method3) of the exception thrown in Method3.

The third block of output displays the StackTrace property of the exception thrown in Method3. Note that this StackTrace property contains the stack trace starting from line 45 in Method3, because that is the point at which the Exception object was created and thrown. The stack trace always begins with the exception's throw point.

Finally, the last block of output displays the String representation of the InnerException property, which includes the namespace and class name of the exception object, as well as its Message and StackTrace properties.

12.8 User-Defined Exception Classes

In many cases, you can use existing exception classes from the .NET Framework Class Library to indicate exceptions that occur in your programs. However, in some cases, you might wish to create new exception classes specific to the problems that occur in your programs. User-defined exception classes should derive directly or indirectly from class ApplicationException of namespace System.

Good Programming Practice 12.1

Associating each type of malfunction with an appropriately named exception class improves program clarity.

Software Engineering Observation 12.3

Before creating a user-defined exception class, investigate the existing exceptions in the .NET Framework Class Library to determine whether an appropriate exception type already exists.

Figures 12.6 and 12.7 demonstrate a user-defined exception class. Class `Negative-NumberException` (Fig. 12.6) is a user-defined exception class representing exceptions that occur when a program performs an illegal operation on a negative number, such as attempting to calculate its square root.

According to Microsoft's "Best Practices for Handling Exceptions [Visual Basic]," user-defined exceptions should extend class `ApplicationException`, have a class name that ends with "Exception" and define three constructors: a parameterless constructor; a constructor that receives a `String` argument (the error message); and a constructor that receives a `String` argument and an `Exception` argument (the error message and the inner exception object). Defining these three constructors makes your exception class more flexible, allowing other programmers to easily use and extend it.

`NegativeNumberException`s most frequently occur during arithmetic operations, so it seems logical to derive class `NegativeNumberException` from class `ArithmeticException`. However, class `ArithmeticException` derives from class `SystemException`—the category of exceptions thrown by the CLR. Recall that user-defined exception classes should inherit from `ApplicationException` rather than `SystemException`.

Class `SquareRootForm` (Fig. 12.7) demonstrates our user-defined exception class. The application enables the user to input a numeric value, then invokes method `SquareRoot` (lines 6–14) to calculate the square root of that value. To perform this calculation, `SquareRoot` invokes class `Math`'s `Sqrt` method, which receives a `Double` value as its argument. Normally, if the argument is negative, method `Sqrt` returns `NaN`. In this program, we would like to prevent the user from calculating the square root of a negative number. If the numeric value that the user enters is negative, the `SquareRoot` method throws a

```
 1    ' Fig. 12.6: NegativeNumberException.vb
 2    ' NegativeNumberException represents exceptions caused by
 3    ' illegal operations performed on negative numbers.
 4    Public Class NegativeNumberException : Inherits ApplicationException
 5       ' default constructor
 6       Public Sub New()
 7          MyBase.New("Illegal operation for a negative number")
 8       End Sub ' New
 9
10       ' constructor for customizing error message
11       Public Sub New(ByVal messageValue As String)
12          MyBase.New(messageValue)
13       End Sub ' New
14
15       ' constructor for customizing the exception's error
16       ' message and specifying the InnerException object
17       Public Sub New(ByVal messageValue As String, ByVal inner As Exception)
18          MyBase.New(messageValue, inner)
19       End Sub ' New
20    End Class ' NegativeNumberException
```

Fig. 12.6 | `ApplicationException` derived class thrown when a program performs an illegal operation on a negative number.

NegativeNumberException (lines 9–10). Otherwise, SquareRoot invokes class Math's method Sqrt to compute the square root (line 12).

When the user inputs a value and clicks the **Calculate Square Root** button, the program invokes event handler SquareRootButton_Click (lines 17–37). The Try statement (lines 23–36) attempts to invoke SquareRoot using the value input by the user. If the user input is not a valid number, a FormatException occurs, and the Catch block in lines 28–31 processes the exception. If the user inputs a negative number, method SquareRoot throws a NegativeNumberException (lines 9–10); the Catch block in lines 32–35 catches and handles this type of exception.

```vb
1  ' Fig. 12.7: SquareRootTest.vb
2  ' Demonstrating a user-defined exception class.
3  Public Class frmSquareRootTest
4     ' computes square root of parameter; throws
5     ' NegativeNumberException if parameter is negative
6     Public Function SquareRoot(ByVal value As Double) As Double
7        ' if negative operand, throw NegativeNumberException
8        If value < 0 Then
9           Throw New NegativeNumberException( _
10             "Square root of negative number not permitted")
11       Else
12          Return Math.Sqrt(value) ' compute square root
13       End If
14    End Function ' SquareRoot
15
16    ' obtain user input, convert to double, calculate square root
17    Private Sub btnSquareRoot_Click(ByVal sender As System.Object, _
18       ByVal e As System.EventArgs) Handles btnSquareRoot.Click
19
20       lblOutput.Text = "" ' clear lblOutput
21
22       ' catch any NegativeNumberException thrown
23       Try
24          Dim result As Double = _
25             SquareRoot(Convert.ToDouble(txtInput.Text))
26
27          lblOutput.Text = result.ToString()
28       Catch formatExceptionParameter As FormatException
29          MessageBox.Show(formatExceptionParameter.Message, _
30             "Invalid Number Format", MessageBoxButtons.OK, _
31             MessageBoxIcon.Error)
32       Catch negativeNumberExceptionParameter As NegativeNumberException
33          MessageBox.Show(negativeNumberExceptionParameter.Message, _
34             "Invalid Operation", MessageBoxButtons.OK, _
35             MessageBoxIcon.Error)
36       End Try
37    End Sub ' btnSquareRoot_Click
38 End Class ' frmSquareRootTest
```

Fig. 12.7 | SquareRootForm class throws an exception if an error occurs when calculating the square root. (Part 1 of 2.)

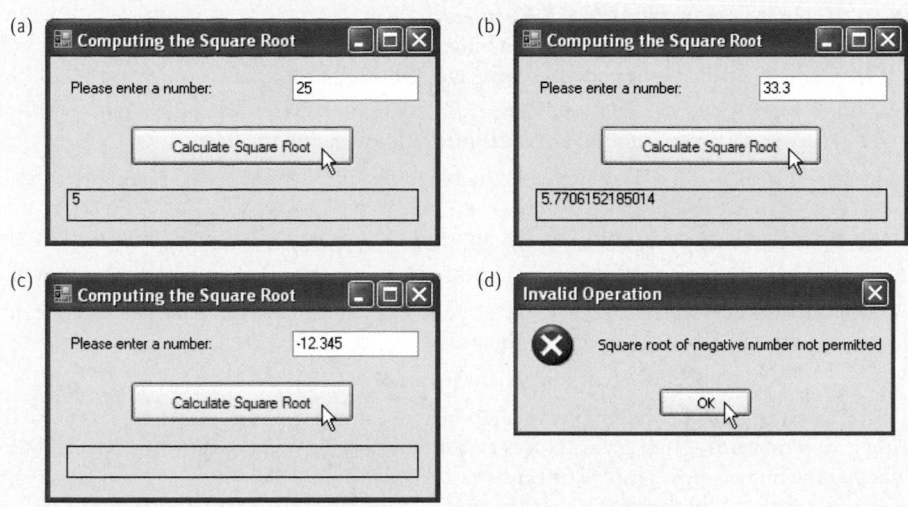

Fig. 12.7 | `SquareRootForm` class throws an exception if an error occurs when calculating the square root. (Part 2 of 2.)

12.9 Wrap-Up

In this chapter, you learned how to use exception handling to deal with errors in an application. We showed how exception handling enables you to remove error-handling code from the "main line" of the program's execution. You saw exception handling in the context of a divide-by-zero example. You learned how to use `Try` blocks to enclose code that may throw an exception, and how to use `Catch` blocks to deal with exceptions that may arise. We discussed the termination model of exception handling, in which after an exception is handled, program control does not return to the throw point. We also discussed several important classes of the .NET `Exception` hierarchy, including `ApplicationException` (from which user-defined exception classes are derived) and `SystemException`. You learned how to use the `Finally` block to release resources whether or not an exception occurs, and how to throw and rethrow exceptions with the `Throw` statement. We also discussed how the `Using` statement can be used to automate the process of releasing a resource. You then learned how to obtain information about an exception using `Exception` properties `Message`, `StackTrace` and `InnerException`, and method `ToString`. You learned how to create your own exception classes. In the next two chapters, we present an in-depth treatment of graphical user interfaces. In these chapters and throughout the rest of the book, we use exception handling to make our examples more robust.

Summary

Section 12.1 Introduction
- An exception is an indication of a problem that occurs during a program's execution.
- Exception handling enables you to create applications that can resolve (or handle) exceptions.

Section 12.2 Exception Handling Overview

- Intermixing program logic with error-handling logic can make programs difficult to read, modify, maintain and debug—especially in large applications.

- Exception handling enables you to remove error-handling code from the "main line" of the program's execution, improving program clarity and enhancing modifiability.

- Visual Basic enables you to deal with exception handling easily from the beginning of a project.

Section 12.3 Example: Divide by Zero Without Exception Handling

- An exception is thrown when a method or the CLR detects a problem and is unable to handle it.

- A stack trace includes the name of the exception in a descriptive message that indicates the problem that occurred and the complete method-call stack at the time the exception occurred.

- Division by zero is not allowed in integer arithmetic.

- Division by zero with floating-point values results in the value infinity, which is represented by either constant `Double.PositiveInfinity` or constant `Double.NegativeInfinity`, depending on whether the numerator is positive or negative. If both the numerator and denominator are zero, the result of the calculation is the constant `Double.NaN`, which stands for "not a number."

- When division by zero occurs in integer arithmetic, a `DivideByZeroException` is thrown.

- A `FormatException` occurs when `Convert` method `ToInt32` receives a string that does not represent a valid integer.

Section 12.4 Example: Handling `DivideByZeroExceptions` and `FormatExceptions`

- A `Try` block encloses the code that might throw exceptions, as well as the code that should not execute if an exception occurs.

- A `Catch` block can specify an identifier of the exception type that the `Catch` block can handle.

- At least one `Catch` block and/or a `Finally` block must immediately follow the `Try` block.

- An uncaught exception is an exception that occurs for which there is no matching `Catch` block.

- When a method called in a program detects an exception, or when the CLR detects a problem, the method or the CLR throws an exception.

- The point in the program at which an exception occurs is called the throw point.

- If an exception occurs in a `Try` block, the `Try` block terminates immediately, and program control transfers to the first of the following `Catch` blocks in which the exception parameter's type matches the type of the thrown exception.

- After the exception is handled, program control does not return to the throw point because the `Try` block has expired (which also causes any of its local variables to be lost). Instead control resumes after the last `Catch` block. This is known as the termination model of exception handling.

- The `Try` block and its corresponding `Catch` and `Finally` blocks together form a `Try` statement.

- The CLR locates the matching `Catch` by comparing the thrown exception's type to each `Catch`'s exception-parameter type. A match occurs if the types are identical or if the thrown exception's type is a derived class of the exception-parameter type.

- Once an exception is matched to a `Catch` block, that `Catch` block executes and the other `Catch` blocks are ignored.

Section 12.5 .NET `Exception` Hierarchy

- The Visual Basic exception-handling mechanism allows objects only of class `Exception` and its derived classes to be thrown and caught.

- Class Exception of namespace System is the base class of the .NET Framework Class Library exception class hierarchy.

- Two of the most important classes derived from Exception are ApplicationException and SystemException.

- ApplicationException is the base class that you should extend to create exception classes that are specific to your applications.

- The CLR generates SystemExceptions, which can occur at any point during the execution of the program. Many of these exceptions can be avoided if applications are coded properly.

- A benefit of using the exception class hierarchy is that a Catch block can catch exceptions of a particular type or—because of the *is-a* relationship of inheritance—can use a base-class type to catch exceptions in a hierarchy of related exception types.

- A Catch block that specifies an exception parameter of type Exception can catch all exceptions that derive from Exception, because Exception is the base class of all exception classes.

- Using inheritance with exceptions enables an exception handler to catch related exceptions using a concise notation.

Section 12.6 *Finally Block*

- The most common type of resource leak is a memory leak.

- A memory leak occurs when a program allocates memory but does not deallocate the memory when it is no longer needed. Normally, this is not an issue in Visual Basic, because the CLR garbage collects memory that is no longer needed by an executing program.

- Visual Basic's exception handling mechanism provides the Finally block, which is guaranteed to execute if program control enters the corresponding Try block.

- The Finally block executes regardless of whether the corresponding Try block executes successfully or an exception occurs. This makes the Finally block an ideal location in which to place resource-release code for resources acquired and manipulated in the corresponding Try block.

- If the Try block executes successfully, the Finally block executes immediately after the Try block terminates. If an exception occurs in the Try block, the Finally block executes immediately after a Catch block completes.

- If the exception is not caught by a Catch block associated with the Try block, or if a Catch block associated with the Try block throws an exception, the Finally block executes before the exception is processed by the next enclosing Try block (if there is one).

- The Throw statement can be used to rethrow an exception, indicating that a Catch block performed partial processing of the exception and now is passing the exception back to the calling method for further processing.

- If a Try block executes and has a corresponding Finally block, the Finally block always executes—even if the Try block terminates due to a Return statement. The Return occurs after the execution of the Finally block.

- The Using statement simplifies writing code in which you obtain a resource, use the resource in a Try block and release the resource in a corresponding Finally block.

Section 12.7 *Exception Properties*

- Property Message of class Exception stores the error message associated with an Exception object.

- Property StackTrace of class Exception contains a String that represents the method-call stack.

- Another Exception property used frequently by class library programmers is InnerException. Typically, you use this property to "wrap" exception objects caught in your code so that you then can throw new exception types specific to your libraries.

Panel properties	Description
AutoScroll	Indicates whether scrollbars appear when the Panel is too small to display all of its controls. The default value is False.
BorderStyle	Sets the border of the Panel. The default value is None; other options are Fixed3D and FixedSingle.
Controls	The set of controls that the Panel contains.

Fig. 13.22 | Panel properties.

that they also have borders by changing their BorderStyle property. Figures 13.21–13.22 list the common properties of GroupBoxes and Panels, respectively.

Look-and-Feel Observation 13.4

Panels and GroupBoxes can contain other Panels and GroupBoxes for more complex layouts.

Look-and-Feel Observation 13.5

You can organize a GUI by anchoring and docking controls inside a GroupBox or Panel. The GroupBox or Panel can then be anchored or docked inside a Form. This divides controls into functional "groups" that can be arranged easily.

To create a GroupBox, drag its icon from the **Toolbox** onto the Form. Then drag new controls from the **Toolbox** into the GroupBox. These controls are added to the GroupBox's Controls property and become part of the GroupBox. The GroupBox's Text property specifies the caption.

To create a Panel, drag its icon from the **Toolbox** onto the Form. You can then add controls directly to the Panel by dragging them from the **Toolbox** onto the Panel. To enable the scrollbars, set the Panel's AutoScroll property to True. If the Panel is resized and cannot display all of its controls, scrollbars appear (Fig. 13.23). The scrollbars can be used to view all the controls in the Panel—both at design time and at execution time. In Fig. 13.23, we set the Panel's BorderStyle property to FixedSingle so that you can see the Panel in the Form.

The program in Fig. 13.24 uses a GroupBox and a Panel to arrange Buttons. When these Buttons are clicked, their event handlers change the text on a Label.

The GroupBox (named grpMain) has two Buttons—btnHi (which displays the text **Hi**) and btnBye (which displays the text **Bye**). The Panel (named pnlMain) also has two Buttons, btnLeft (which displays the text **Far Left**) and btnRight (which displays the text **Far Right**). The pnlMain has its AutoScroll property set to True, allowing scrollbars to appear when the contents of the Panel require more space than the Panel's visible area. The Label (named lblMessage) is initially blank. To add controls to grpMain or pblMain, Visual Studio calls method Add of each container's Controls property. This code is placed in the partial class located in the file FrmGroupBoxPanelExample.Designer.vb.

The event handlers for the four Buttons are located in lines 5–26. We added a line in each event handler (lines 7, 13, 19 and 25) to change the text of lblMessage to indicate which Button the user pressed.

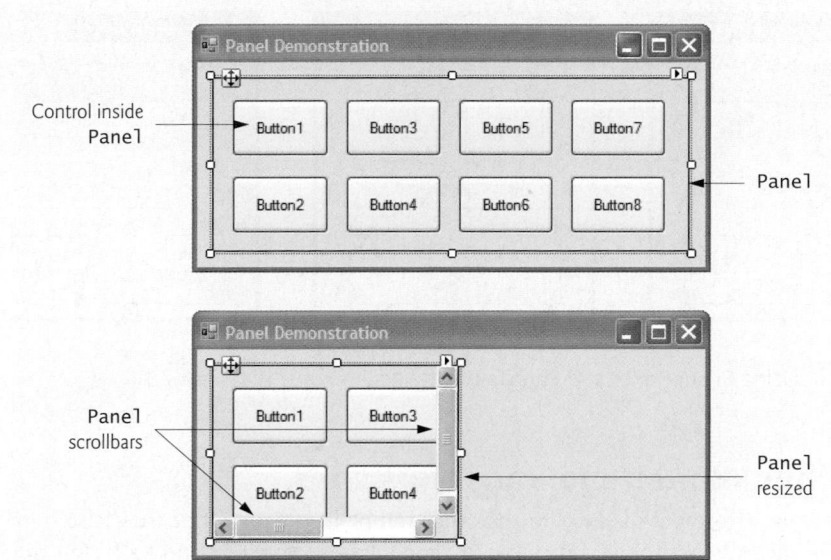

Fig. 13.23 | Creating a Panel with scrollbars.

```
 I   ' Fig. 13.24: FrmGroupboxPanelExample.vb
 2   ' Using GroupBoxes and Panels to hold Buttons.
 3   Public Class FrmGroupBoxPanelExample
 4      ' event handler for btnHi's Click event
 5      Private Sub btnHi_Click(ByVal sender As System.Object, _
 6         ByVal e As System.EventArgs) Handles btnHi.Click
 7         lblMessage.Text = "Hi pressed" ' change text in Label
 8      End Sub ' btnHi_Click
 9
10      ' event handler for btnBye's Click event
11      Private Sub btnBye_Click(ByVal sender As System.Object, _
12         ByVal e As System.EventArgs) Handles btnBye.Click
13         lblMessage.Text = "Bye pressed" ' change text in Label
14      End Sub ' btnBye_Click
15
16      ' event handler for btnLeft's Click event
17      Private Sub btnLeft_Click(ByVal sender As System.Object, _
18         ByVal e As System.EventArgs) Handles btnLeft.Click
19         lblMessage.Text = "Far left pressed" ' change text in Label
20      End Sub ' btnLeft_Click
21
22      ' event handler for btnRIght's Click event
23      Private Sub btnRight_Click(ByVal sender As System.Object, _
24         ByVal e As System.EventArgs) Handles btnRight.Click
25         lblMessage.Text = "Far right pressed" ' change text in Label
26      End Sub ' btnRight_Click
27   End Class ' FrmGroupBoxPanelExample
```

Fig. 13.24 | Using GroupBoxes and Panels to arrange Buttons. (Part I of 2.)

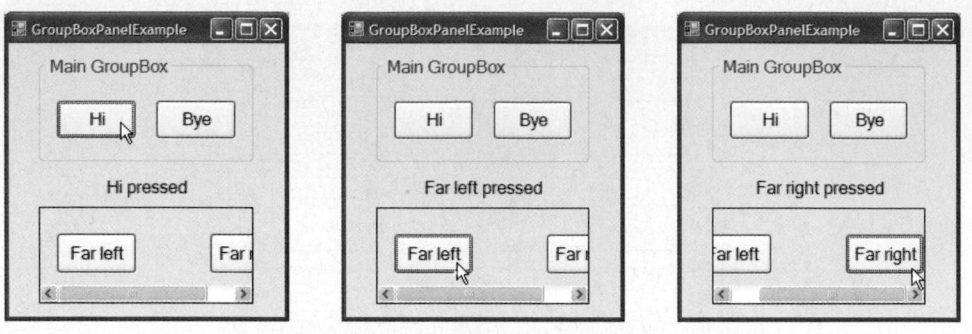

Fig. 13.24 | Using GroupBoxes and Panels to arrange Buttons. (Part 2 of 2.)

13.7 CheckBoxes and RadioButtons

Visual Basic has two types of state buttons that can be in the on/off or true/false states—CheckBoxes and RadioButtons. Like class Button, classes CheckBox and RadioButton are derived from class ButtonBase.

CheckBoxes

A CheckBox is a small square that either is blank or contains a check mark. When the user clicks a CheckBox to select it, a check mark appears in the box. If the user clicks the CheckBox again to deselect it, the check mark is removed. Any number of CheckBoxes can be selected at a time. A list of common CheckBox properties and events appears in Fig. 13.25.

CheckBox properties and events	Description
Common Properties	
Checked	Indicates whether the CheckBox is checked (contains a check mark) or unchecked (blank). This property returns a Boolean value.
CheckState	Indicates whether the CheckBox is checked or unchecked with a value from the CheckState enumeration (Checked, Unchecked or Indeterminate). Indeterminate is used when it is unclear whether the state should be Checked or Unchecked. For example, in Microsoft Word, when you select a paragraph that contains several character formats, then go to **Format > Font**, some of the CheckBoxes appear in the Indeterminate state. When CheckState is set to Indeterminate, the CheckBox is usually shaded.
Text	Specifies the text displayed to the right of the CheckBox.

Fig. 13.25 | CheckBox properties and events. (Part 1 of 2.)

CheckBox properties and events	Description
Common Events	
CheckedChanged	Generated when the Checked property changes. This is a CheckBox's default event. When a user double clicks the CheckBox control in design view, an empty event handler for this event is generated.
CheckStateChanged	Generated when the CheckState property changes.

Fig. 13.25 | CheckBox properties and events. (Part 2 of 2.)

The program in Fig. 13.26 allows the user to select CheckBoxes to change a Label's font style. The event handler for one CheckBox applies bold, and the event handler for the other applies italic. If both CheckBoxes are selected, the font style is set to bold and italic. Initially, neither CheckBox is checked.

```vb
 1   ' Fig. 13.26: FrmCheckBoxTest.vb
 2   ' Using CheckBoxes to toggle italic and bold styles.
 3   Public Class FrmCheckBoxTest
 4      ' toggle the font style between bold and
 5      ' not bold based on the current setting
 6      Private Sub chkBold_CheckedChanged(ByVal sender As System.Object, _
 7         ByVal e As System.EventArgs) Handles chkBold.CheckedChanged
 8         lblOutput.Font = _
 9            New Font(lblOutput.Font.Name, lblOutput.Font.Size, _
10               lblOutput.Font.Style Xor FontStyle.Bold)
11      End Sub ' chkBold_CheckedChanged
12
13      ' toggle the font setting between italic and
14      ' not italic based on the current setting
15      Private Sub chkItalic_CheckedChanged(ByVal sender As System.Object, _
16         ByVal e As System.EventArgs) Handles chkItalic.CheckedChanged
17         lblOutput.Font = _
18            New Font(lblOutput.Font.Name, lblOutput.Font.Size, _
19               lblOutput.Font.Style Xor FontStyle.Italic)
20      End Sub ' chkItalic_CheckedChanged
21   End Class ' FrmCheckBoxTest
```

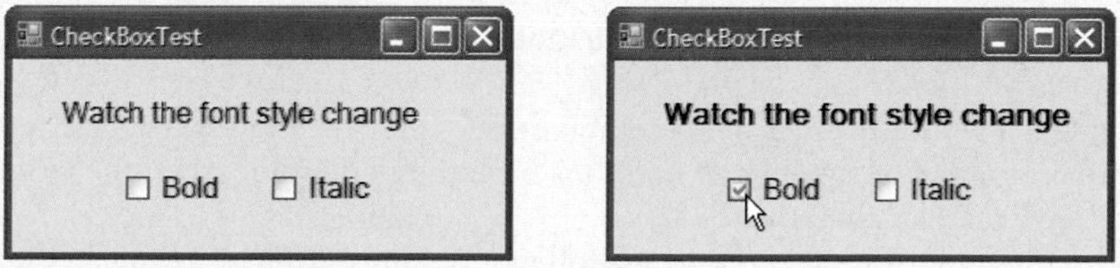

Fig. 13.26 | Using CheckBoxes to change font styles. (Part 1 of 2.)

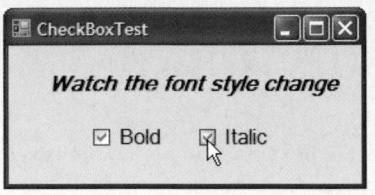 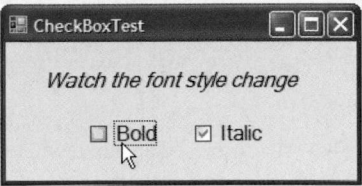

Fig. 13.26 | Using CheckBoxes to change font styles. (Part 2 of 2.)

The chkBold has its Text property set to Bold. The chkItalic has its Text property set to Italic. The Text property of lblOutput is set to Watch the font style change. After creating the controls, we define their event handlers. Double clicking the CheckBoxes at design time creates empty CheckedChanged event handlers.

To change the font style on a Label, you must set its Font property to a new **Font object** (lines 8–10 and 17–19). The Font constructor that we use here takes the font name, size and style as arguments. The first two arguments—lblOutput.Font.Name and lblOutput.Font.Size—use lblOutput's original font name and size. The style is specified with a member of the **FontStyle enumeration**, which contains Regular, Bold, Italic, Strikeout and Underline. (The Strikeout style displays text with a line through it.) A Font object's **Style** property is read-only, so it can be set only when the Font object is created.

Styles can be combined via **bitwise operators**—operators that perform manipulations on bits of information. Recall from Chapter 1 that all data is represented in the computer as combinations of 0s and 1s. Each 0 or 1 represents a bit. FontStyle has a System.Flag-Attribute, meaning that the FontStyle bit values are selected in a way that allows us to combine different FontStyle elements to create compound styles, using bitwise operators. These styles are not mutually exclusive, so we can combine different styles and remove them without affecting the combination of previous FontStyle elements. We can combine these various font styles using either the Or operator or the Xor operator. When the Or operator is applied to two bits, if at least one bit of the two has the value 1, then the result is 1. Combining styles using the Or operator works as follows. Assume that Font-Style.Bold is represented by bits 01 and that FontStyle.Italic is represented by bits 10. When we use the Or operator to combine the styles, we obtain the bits 11.

```
01   =   Bold
10   =   Italic
--
11   =   Bold and Italic
```

The Or operator helps create style combinations. However, what happens if we want to undo a style combination, as we did in Fig. 13.26?

The Xor operator enables us to combine styles and to undo existing style settings. When Xor is applied to two bits, if both bits have the same value, then the result is 0. If both bits are different, then the result is 1.

Combining styles using Xor works as follows. Assume, again, that FontStyle.Bold is represented by bits 01 and that FontStyle.Italic is represented by bits 10. When we use Xor on both styles, we obtain the bits 11.

```
01  =  Bold
10  =  Italic
--
11  =  Bold and Italic
```

Now suppose that we would like to remove the `FontStyle.Bold` style from the previous combination of `FontStyle.Bold` and `FontStyle.Italic`. The easiest way to do so is to reapply the `Xor` operator to the compound style and `FontStyle.Bold`.

```
11  =  Bold and Italic
01  =  Bold
--
10  =  Italic
```

This is a simple example. The advantages of using bitwise operators to combine `FontStyle` values become more evident when we consider that there are five different `FontStyle` values (`Bold`, `Italic`, `Regular`, `Strikeout` and `Underline`), resulting in 16 different `FontStyle` combinations. Using bitwise operators to combine font styles greatly reduces the amount of code required to check all possible font combinations.

In Fig. 13.26, we need to set the `FontStyle` so that the text appears in bold if it was not bold originally, and vice versa. Note that line 10 uses the `Xor` operator to do this. If `lblOutput.Font.Style` is bold, then the resulting style is not bold. If the text is originally italic, the resulting style is bold and italic rather than just bold. The same applies for `FontStyle.Italic` in line 19.

If we did not use bitwise operators to compound `FontStyle` elements, we would have to test for the current style and change it accordingly. For example, in event handler `chkBold_CheckChanged`, we could test for the regular style and make it bold, test for the bold style and make it regular, test for the italic style and make it bold italic, and test for the italic bold style and make it italic. This is cumbersome because for every new style we add, we double the number of combinations. Adding a `CheckBox` for underline would require testing eight additional styles. Adding a `CheckBox` for strikeout would require testing 16 additional styles.

RadioButtons
Radio buttons (defined with class `RadioButton`) are similar to `CheckBox`es in that they also have two states—**selected** and **not selected** (also called **deselected**). However, `RadioButtons` normally appear as a **group**, in which only one `RadioButton` can be selected at a time. Selecting one `RadioButton` in the group forces all the others to be deselected. Therefore, `RadioButtons` are used to represent a set of **mutually exclusive** options (i.e., a set in which multiple options cannot be selected at the same time).

Look-and-Feel Observation 13.6

Use `RadioButtons` when the user should choose only one option in a group.

Look-and-Feel Observation 13.7

Use `CheckBoxes` when the user should be able to choose multiple options (or no options at all) in a group.

All RadioButtons added to a container are part of the same group. To separate them into several groups, the RadioButtons must be added to GroupBoxes or Panels. The common properties and a common event of class RadioButton are listed in Fig. 13.27.

Software Engineering Observation 13.2

Forms, GroupBoxes and Panels act as logical groups for RadioButtons. The RadioButtons within each group are mutually exclusive to each other, but not to those in different logical groups.

The program in Fig. 13.28 uses RadioButtons to enable users to select options for a MessageBox. After selecting the desired attributes, the user presses the **Display** Button to display the MessageBox. A Label in the lower-left corner shows the result of the MessageBox (i.e., which Button the user clicked—**Yes, No, Cancel,** etc.).

To store the user's choices, we create and initialize the iconType and buttonType objects (lines 5–6). Object iconType is of type MessageBoxIcon, and can have values Asterisk, Error, Exclamation, Hand, Information, None, Question, Stop and Warning. The sample output shows only the Error, Exclamation, Information and Question icons.

RadioButton properties and an event	Description
Common Properties	
Checked	Indicates whether the RadioButton is checked.
Text	Specifies the RadioButton's text.
Common Event	
CheckedChanged	Generated every time the RadioButton is checked or unchecked. When you double click a RadioButton control in design view, an empty event handler for this event is generated.

Fig. 13.27 | RadioButton properties and an event.

```
1   ' Fig. 13.28: FrmRadioButtonsTest.vb
2   ' Using RadioButtons to set message window options.
3   Public Class FrmRadioButtonsTest
4      ' create variables that store the user's choice of options
5      Private iconType As MessageBoxIcon
6      Private buttonType As MessageBoxButtons
7
8      ' set button type to OK
9      Private Sub radOk_CheckedChanged(ByVal sender As System.Object, _
10        ByVal e As System.EventArgs) Handles radOk.CheckedChanged
11        buttonType = MessageBoxButtons.OK
12     End Sub ' radOk_CheckedChanged
13
```

Fig. 13.28 | Using RadioButtons to set message-window options. (Part 1 of 4.)

```
14      ' set button type to OKCancel
15      Private Sub radOkCancel_CheckedChanged(ByVal sender As System.Object, _
16         ByVal e As System.EventArgs) Handles radOkCancel.CheckedChanged
17         buttonType = MessageBoxButtons.OKCancel
18      End Sub ' radOkCancel_CheckedChanged
19
20      ' set button type to AbortRetryIgnore
21      Private Sub radAbortRetryIgnore_CheckedChanged( _
22         ByVal sender As System.Object, ByVal e As System.EventArgs) _
23         Handles radAbortRetryIgnore.CheckedChanged
24         buttonType = MessageBoxButtons.AbortRetryIgnore
25      End Sub ' radAbortRetryIgnore_CheckedChanged
26
27      ' set button type to YesNoCancel
28      Private Sub radYesNoCancel_CheckedChanged( _
29         ByVal sender As System.Object, ByVal e As System.EventArgs) _
30         Handles radYesNoCancel.CheckedChanged
31         buttonType = MessageBoxButtons.YesNoCancel
32      End Sub ' radYesNoCancel_CheckedChanged
33
34      ' set button type to YesNo
35      Private Sub radYesNo_CheckedChanged(ByVal sender As System.Object, _
36         ByVal e As System.EventArgs) Handles radYesNo.CheckedChanged
37         buttonType = MessageBoxButtons.YesNo
38      End Sub ' radYesNo_CheckedChanged
39
40      ' set button type to RetryCancel
41      Private Sub radRetryCancel_CheckedChanged( _
42         ByVal sender As System.Object, ByVal e As System.EventArgs) _
43         Handles radRetryCancel.CheckedChanged
44         buttonType = MessageBoxButtons.RetryCancel
45      End Sub ' radRetryCancel_CheckedChanged
46
47      ' set icon type to Asterisk
48      Private Sub radAsterisk_CheckedChanged(ByVal sender As System.Object, _
49         ByVal e As System.EventArgs) Handles radAsterisk.CheckedChanged
50         iconType = MessageBoxIcon.Asterisk
51      End Sub ' radAsterisk_CheckedChanged
52
53      ' set icon type to Error
54      Private Sub radError_CheckedChanged(ByVal sender As System.Object, _
55         ByVal e As System.EventArgs) Handles radError.CheckedChanged
56         iconType = MessageBoxIcon.Error
57      End Sub ' radError_CheckedChanged
58
59      ' set icon type to Exclamation
60      Private Sub radExclamation_CheckedChanged( _
61         ByVal sender As System.Object, ByVal e As System.EventArgs) _
62         Handles radExclamation.CheckedChanged
63         iconType = MessageBoxIcon.Exclamation
64      End Sub ' radExclamation_CheckedChanged
65
```

Fig. 13.28 | Using RadioButtons to set message-window options. (Part 2 of 4.)

```
66    ' set icon type to Hand
67    Private Sub radHand_CheckedChanged(ByVal sender As System.Object, _
68       ByVal e As System.EventArgs) Handles radHand.CheckedChanged
69       iconType = MessageBoxIcon.Hand
70    End Sub ' radHand_CheckedChanged
71
72    ' set icon type to Information
73    Private Sub radInformation_CheckedChanged( _
74       ByVal sender As System.Object, ByVal e As System.EventArgs) _
75       Handles radInformation.CheckedChanged
76       iconType = MessageBoxIcon.Information
77    End Sub ' radInformation_CheckedChanged
78
79    ' set icon type to Question
80    Private Sub radQuestion_CheckedChanged(ByVal sender As System.Object, _
81       ByVal e As System.EventArgs) Handles radQuestion.CheckedChanged
82       iconType = MessageBoxIcon.Question
83    End Sub ' radQuestion_CheckedChanged
84
85    ' set icon type to Stop
86    Private Sub radStop_CheckedChanged(ByVal sender As System.Object, _
87       ByVal e As System.EventArgs) Handles radStop.CheckedChanged
88       iconType = MessageBoxIcon.Stop
89    End Sub ' radStop_CheckedChanged
90
91    ' set icon type to Warning
92    Private Sub radWarning_CheckedChanged(ByVal sender As System.Object, _
93       ByVal e As System.EventArgs) Handles radWarning.CheckedChanged
94       iconType = MessageBoxIcon.Warning
95    End Sub ' radWarning_CheckedChanged
96
97    ' display MessageBox and Button user pressed
98    Private Sub btnDisplay_Click(ByVal sender As System.Object, _
99       ByVal e As System.EventArgs) Handles btnDisplay.Click
100      ' display MessageBox and store
101      ' the value of the Button that was pressed
102      Dim result As DialogResult = MessageBox.Show( _
103         "This is your Custom MessageBox.", _
104         "Custon MessageBox", buttonType, iconType, 0, 0)
105
106      ' check to see which Button was pressed in the MessageBox
107      ' change text displayed accordingly
108      Select Case result
109         Case Windows.Forms.DialogResult.OK
110            lblDisplay.Text = "OK was pressed"
111         Case Windows.Forms.DialogResult.Cancel
112            lblDisplay.Text = "Cancel was pressed"
113         Case Windows.Forms.DialogResult.Abort
114            lblDisplay.Text = "Abort was pressed"
115         Case Windows.Forms.DialogResult.Retry
116            lblDisplay.Text = "Retry was pressed"
117         Case Windows.Forms.DialogResult.Ignore
118            lblDisplay.Text = "Ignore was pressed"
```

Fig. 13.28 | Using RadioButtons to set message-window options. (Part 3 of 4.)

```
119            Case Windows.Forms.DialogResult.Yes
120                lblDisplay.Text = "Yes was pressed"
121            Case Windows.Forms.DialogResult.No
122                lblDisplay.Text = "No was pressed"
123        End Select
124    End Sub ' btnDisplay_Click
125 End Class ' FrmRadioButtonsTest
```

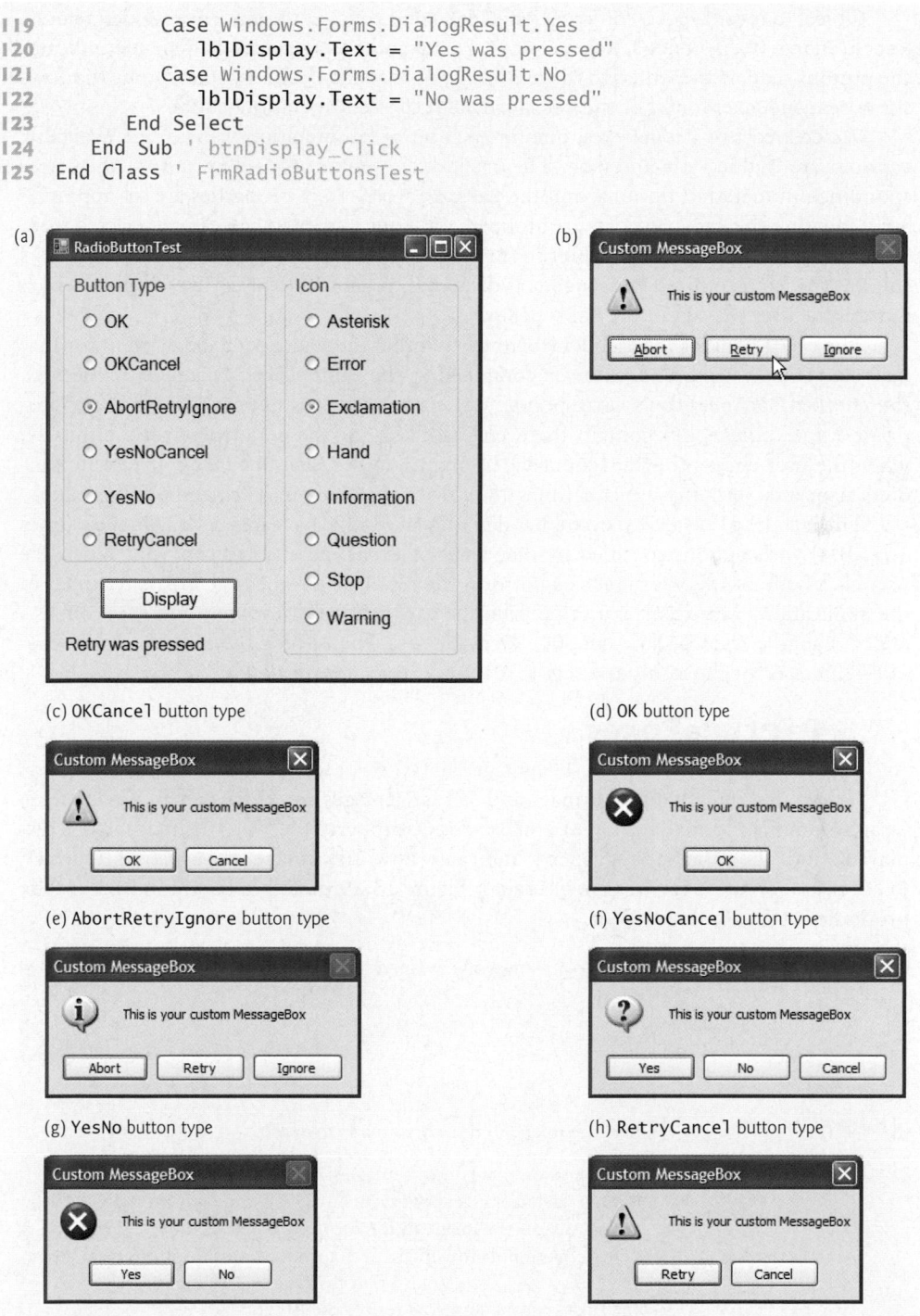

(a)

(b)

(c) OKCancel button type

(d) OK button type

(e) AbortRetryIgnore button type

(f) YesNoCancel button type

(g) YesNo button type

(h) RetryCancel button type

Fig. 13.28 | Using RadioButtons to set message-window options. (Part 4 of 4.)

Object `buttonType` is of type `MessageBoxButtons`, and can have values `Abort-RetryIgnore`, `OK`, `OKCancel`, `RetryCancel`, `YesNo` and `YesNoCancel`. The name indicates the options that are presented to the user in the `MessageBox`. The sample output windows show `MessageBoxes` for all of the `MessageBoxButtons` enumeration values.

We created two `GroupBoxes`, one for each set of enumeration values. The `GroupBox` captions are **Button Type** and **Icon**. The `GroupBoxes` contain `RadioButtons` for the corresponding enumeration options, and the `RadioButtons`' `Text` properties are set appropriately. Because the `RadioButtons` are grouped, only one `RadioButton` can be selected from each `GroupBox`. There is also a `Button` (`btnDisplay`) labeled **Display**. When a user clicks this `Button`, a customized `MessageBox` is displayed. A `Label` (`lblDisplay`) displays which `Button` the user pressed in the `MessageBox`.

The event handler for each `RadioButton` handles the `CheckedChanged` event for that `RadioButton`. When a `RadioButton` contained in the **Button Type** `GroupBox` is checked, the checked `RadioButton`'s corresponding event handler sets `buttonType` to the appropriate value. Lines 9–45 contain the event handling for these `RadioButtons`. Similarly, when the user checks the `RadioButtons` belonging to the **Icon** `GroupBox`, the event handlers associated with these events (lines 48–95) set `iconType` to its corresponding value.

The `btnDisplay_Click` event handler (lines 98–124) creates a `MessageBox` (lines 102–104) with options specified by the values of `iconType` and `buttonType`. When the user clicks one of the `MessageBox`'s buttons, the result of the message box is returned to the application. This result is a value from the **DialogResult enumeration** that contains `Abort`, `Cancel`, `Ignore`, `No`, `None`, `OK`, `Retry` or `Yes`. The `Select Case` statement in lines 108–123 tests for the result and sets `lblDisplay.Text` appropriately.

13.8 PictureBoxes

A `PictureBox` displays an image. The image can be one of several formats, such as bitmap, GIF (Graphics Interchange Format) and JPEG. (Images are discussed in Chapter 17, Graphics and Multimedia.) A `PictureBox`'s `Image` property specifies the image that is displayed, and the `SizeMode` property indicates how the image is displayed (`Normal`, `StretchImage`, `Autosize` or `CenterImage`). Figure 13.29 describes common `PictureBox` properties and a common event.

PictureBox properties and an event	Description
Common Properties	
Image	Sets the image to display in the `PictureBox`.
SizeMode	Enumeration that controls image sizing and positioning. Values are `Normal` (default), `StretchImage`, `AutoSize` and `CenterImage`. `Normal` places the image in the top-left corner of the `PictureBox`; `CenterImage` puts the image in the middle. Both options truncate the image if it is too large. `StretchImage` resizes the image to fit in the `PictureBox`. `AutoSize` resizes the `PictureBox` to fit the image.

Fig. 13.29 | `PictureBox` properties and an event. (Part 1 of 2.)

PictureBox properties and an event	Description
Common Event	
Click	Occurs when the user clicks the control. Double clicking this control design mode generates an empty event handler for this event.

Fig. 13.29 | `PictureBox` properties and an event. (Part 2 of 2.)

Figure 13.30 uses a `PictureBox` named `picImage` to display one of three bitmap images—`image0`, `image1` or `image2`. These images are located in the project's `bin/Debug` and `bin/Release` directories in the subdirectory `images`. Whenever a user clicks the **Next Image** Button, the image changes to the next image in sequence. When the last image is displayed and the user clicks the **Next Image** Button, the first image is displayed again. Event handler `btnNext_Click` (lines 10–17) uses `Integer` variable `imageNum` to store the number of the image we want to display. We then set the `Image` property of `picImage` to an `Image` (lines 15–16).

13.9 ToolTips

In Chapter 2, we discussed tool tips—the helpful text that appears when the mouse hovers over a GUI control. The tool tips displayed in Visual Studio serve as useful reminders of each toolbar icon's functionality. Many programs use tool tips to remind users of each control's purpose. For example, Microsoft Word has tool tips that help users determine the purpose of the application's icons. This section demonstrates how to use the `ToolTip` component to add tool tips to your applications. Figure 13.31 describes common properties and a common event of class `ToolTip`.

```vb
1   ' Fig. 13.30: FrmPictureBoxTest.vb
2   ' Using a PictureBox to display images.
3   Imports System.IO
4
5   Public Class FrmPictureBoxTest
6      ' determines which image is displayed
7      Private imageNum As Integer = -1
8
9      ' change image whenever Next Button is clicked
10     Private Sub btnNext_Click(ByVal sender As System.Object, _
11        ByVal e As System.EventArgs) Handles btnNext.Click
12        imageNum = (imageNum + 1) Mod 3 ' imageNum cycles from 0 to 2
13
14        ' create Image object from file, display in PicutreBox
15        picImage.Image = Image.FromFile(Directory.GetCurrentDirectory() & _
16           "\images\image" & imageNum & ".bmp")
17     End Sub ' btnNext_Click
18  End Class ' FrmPictureBoxTest
```

Fig. 13.30 | Using a `PictureBox` to display images. (Part 1 of 2.)

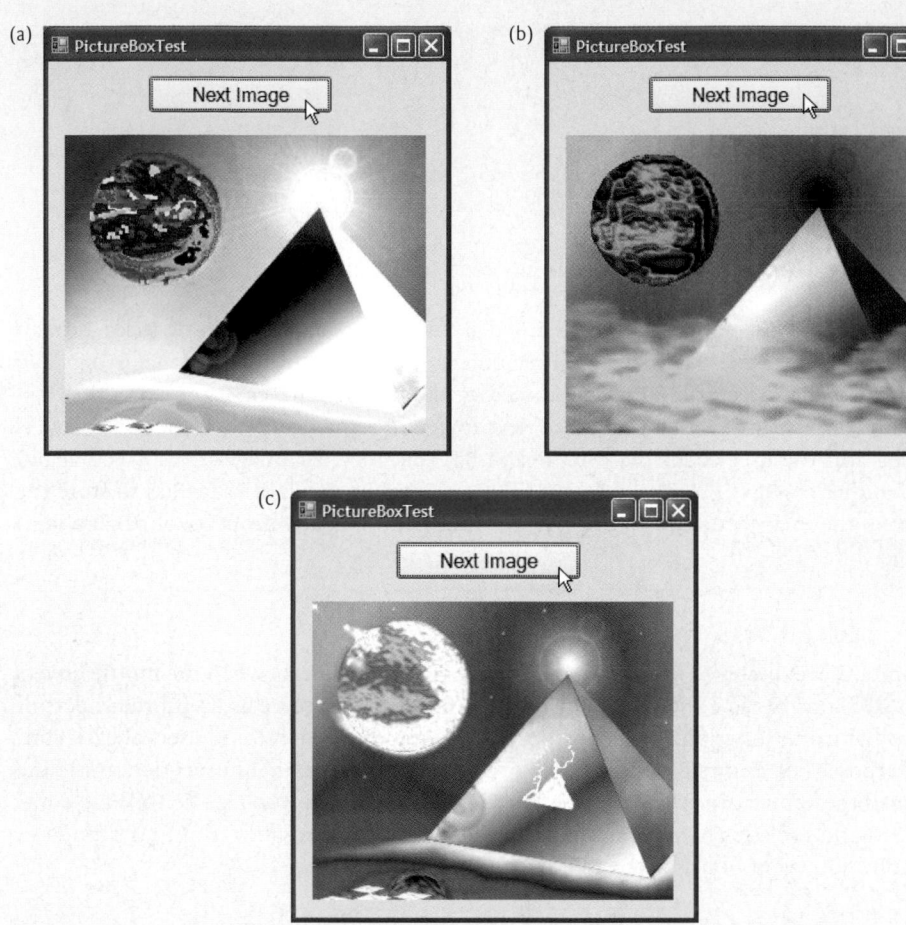

Fig. 13.30 | Using a `PictureBox` to display images. (Part 2 of 2.)

ToolTip properties and an event	Description
Common Properties	
AutoPopDelay	The amount of time (in milliseconds) that the tool tip appears while the mouse is over a control.
InitialDelay	The amount of time (in milliseconds) that a mouse must hover over a control before a tool tip appears.
ReshowDelay	The amount of time (in milliseconds) between which two different tool tips appear (when the mouse is moved from one control to another).

Fig. 13.31 | `ToolTip` properties and an event. (Part 1 of 2.)

ToolTip properties and an event	Description
Common Event	
Draw	Raised when the tool tip is displayed. This event allows programmers to modify the appearance of the tool tip.

Fig. 13.31 | `ToolTip` properties and an event. (Part 2 of 2.)

When you add a `ToolTip` component from the **Toolbox**, it appears in the component tray—the gray region below the `Form` in **Design** mode. Once a `ToolTip` is added to a `Form`, a new property appears in the **Properties** window for the `Form`'s other controls. This property appears in the **Properties** window as **ToolTip on**, followed by the name of the `ToolTip` component. For instance, if our `Form`'s `ToolTip` were named `helpfulToolTip`, you would set a control's **ToolTip on helpfulToolTip** property value to specify the control's tool tip text. Figure 13.32 demonstrates the `ToolTip` component. For this example, we create a GUI containing two `Label`s so that we can demonstrate a different tool tip for each `Label`. To make the sample outputs clearer, we set the `BorderStyle` property of each `Label` to `FixedSingle`, which displays a solid border. Since there is no event-handling code in this example, the class in Fig. 13.32 is empty.

In this example, we named the `ToolTip` component `labelsToolTip`. Figure 13.33 shows the `ToolTip` in the component tray. We set the tool tip text for the first `Label` to "`First Label`" and the tool tip text for the second `Label` to "`Second Label`." Figure 13.34 demonstrates setting the tool tip text for the first `Label`.

13.10 NumericUpDown Control

At times, we will want to restrict a user's input choices to a specific range of numeric values. This is the purpose of the `NumericUpDown` control. This control appears as a `TextBox`, with two small `Button`s on the right side—one with an up arrow and one with a down

```
1    ' Fig. 13.32: FrmToolTipExample.vb
2    ' Demonstrating the ToolTip component.
3    Public Class FrmToolTipDemonstration
4        ' no event handlers needed for this example
5    End Class
```

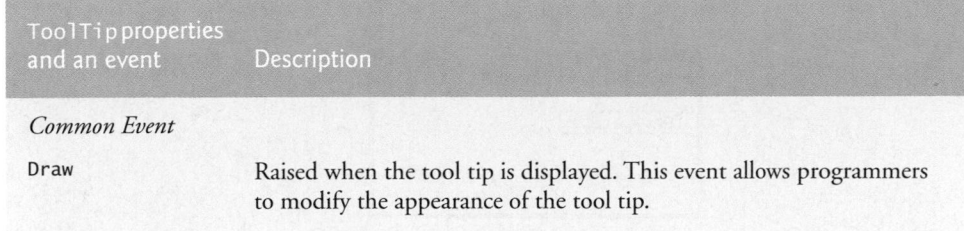

Fig. 13.32 | Demonstrating the `ToolTip` component.

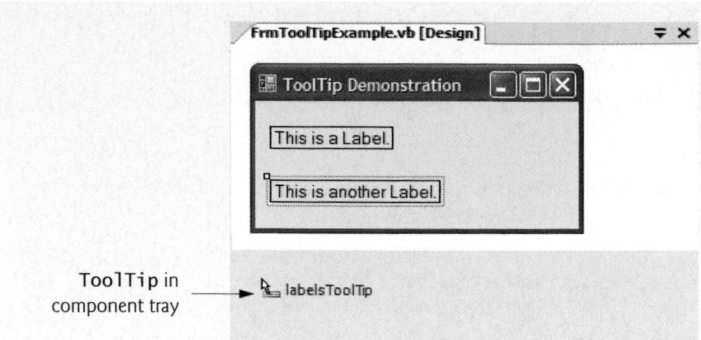

Fig. 13.33 | ToolTip component in the component tray.

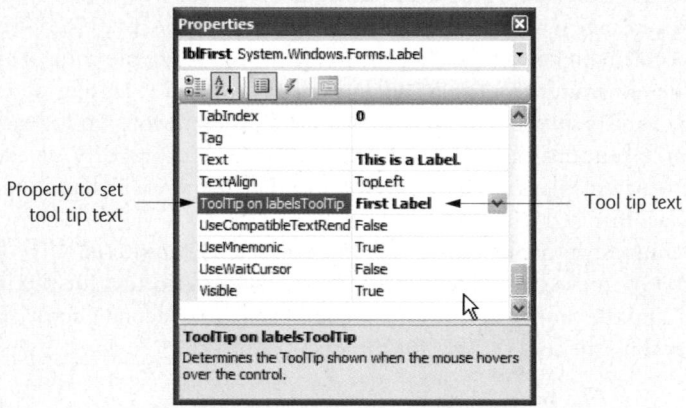

Fig. 13.34 | Setting a control's tool tip text.

arrow. By default, a user can type numeric values into this control as if it were a TextBox or click the up and down arrows to increase or decrease the value in the control, respectively. The largest and smallest values in the range are specified with the Maximum and Minimum properties, respectively (both of type Decimal). The Increment property (also of type Decimal) specifies by how much the current number in the control changes when the user clicks the control's up and down arrows. Figure 13.35 describes common properties and a common event of class NumericUpDown.

NumericUpDown properties and an event	Description
Common Properties	
Increment	Specifies by how much the current number in the control changes when the user clicks the control's up and down arrows.

Fig. 13.35 | NumericUpDown properties and an event. (Part 1 of 2.)

NumericUpDown properties and an event	Description
Maximum	Largest value in the control's range.
Minimum	Smallest value in the control's range.
UpDownAlign	Modifies the alignment of the up and down Buttons on the NumericUpDown control. This property can be used to display these Buttons to either the left or the right of the control.
Value	The numeric value currently displayed in the control.
Common Event	
ValueChanged	This event is raised when the value in the control is changed. It is the default event for the NumericUpDown control.

Fig. 13.35 | NumericUpDown properties and an event. (Part 2 of 2.)

Figure 13.36 demonstrates using a NumericUpDown control for a GUI that calculates interest rate. The calculations performed in this application are similar to those performed in Fig. 6.8. TextBoxes are used to input the principal and interest rate amounts, and a NumericUpDown control is used to input the number of years for which we want to calculate interest.

```vb
1   ' Fig. 13.36: FrmInterestCalculator.vb
2   ' Demonstrating the NumericUpDown control.
3   Public Class FrmInterestCalculator
4
5      Private Sub btnCalculate_Click(ByVal sender As System.Object, _
6         ByVal e As System.EventArgs) Handles btnCalculate.Click
7         ' declare variables to store user input
8         Dim principal As Decimal ' store principal
9         Dim rate As Double ' store interest rate
10        Dim year As Integer ' store number of years
11        Dim amount As Decimal ' store amount
12
13        ' retrieve user input
14        principal = Convert.ToDecimal(txtPrincipal.Text)
15        rate = Convert.ToDouble(txtInterest.Text)
16        year = Convert.ToInt32(updYear.Value)
17
18        ' set output header
19        txtDisplay.Text = "Year" & vbTab & "Amount on Deposit" & vbCrLf
20
21        ' calculate amount after each year and append to output
22        For yearCounter As Integer = 1 To year
23           amount = principal * Convert.ToDecimal( _
24              Math.Pow(1 + rate / 100, yearCounter))
```

Fig. 13.36 | Demonstrating the NumericUpDown control. (Part 1 of 2.)

```
25              txtDisplay.Text &= (yearCounter & vbTab & _
26                 String.Format("{0:C}", amount) & vbCrLf)
27          Next
28      End Sub ' btnCalculate_Click
29   End Class ' FrmInterestCalculator
```

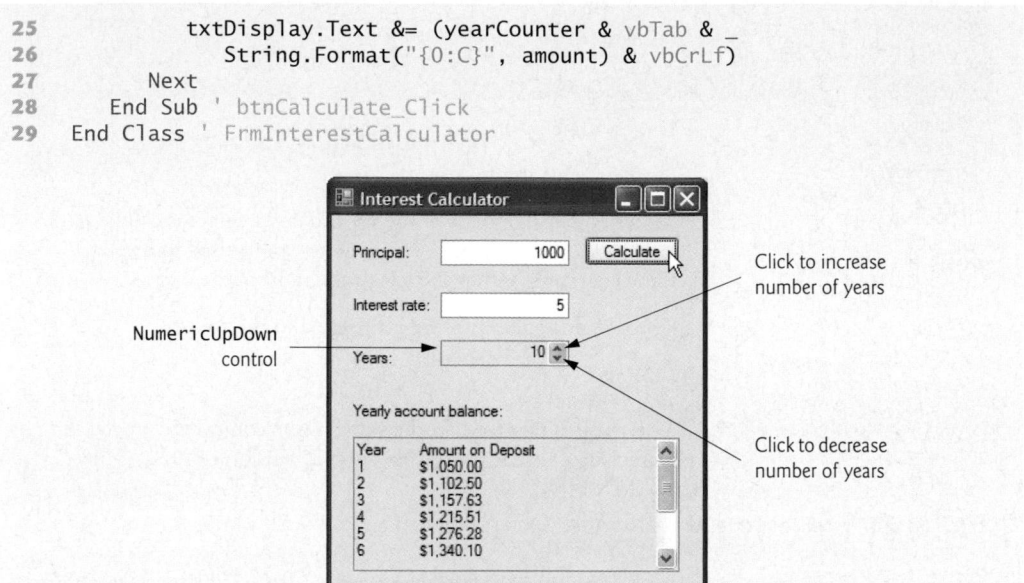

Fig. 13.36 | Demonstrating the NumericUpDown control. (Part 2 of 2.)

For the NumericUpDown control named updYear, we set the Minimum property to 1 and the Maximum property to 10. We left the Increment property's default value (1). These settings specify that users can enter a number of years in the range 1 to 10 in increments of 1. If we had set the Increment to 0.5, we could also input values such as 1.5 or 2.5. We set the NumericUpDown's **ReadOnly property** to True to indicate that the user cannot type a number into the control to make a selection. Thus, the user must click the up and down arrows (or use the arrow keys on the keyboard) to modify the value in the control. By default, the ReadOnly property is set to False. The output for this application is displayed in a multiline read-only TextBox with a vertical scrollbar so that the user can scroll through the entire output.

13.11 Mouse-Event Handling

This section explains how to handle mouse events, such as clicks, presses and moves, which are generated when the user interacts with a control via the mouse. Mouse events can be handled for any control that derives from class System.Windows.Forms.Control. For most mouse events, information about the event is passed to the event-handling method through an object of class **MouseEventArgs**, and the delegate used to create the mouse-event handlers is **MouseEventHandler**. Each mouse-event-handling method for these events requires an Object and a MouseEventArgs object as arguments.

Class MouseEventArgs contains information related to the mouse event, such as the mouse pointer's x- and y-coordinates, the mouse button pressed (Right, Left or Middle) and the number of times the mouse was clicked. Note that the x- and y-coordinates of the MouseEventArgs object are relative to the control that generated the event—that is point *(0,0)* represents the upper-left corner of the control where the mouse event occurred. Several common mouse events are described in Fig. 13.37.

Mouse events and event arguments	
Mouse Events with Event Argument of Type EventArgs	
MouseEnter	Occurs when the mouse cursor enters the control's boundaries.
MouseLeave	Occurs when the mouse cursor leaves the control's boundaries.
Mouse Events with Event Argument of Type MouseEventArgs	
MouseDown	Occurs when a mouse button is pressed while the mouse cursor is within a control's boundaries.
MouseHover	Occurs when the mouse cursor hovers within the control's boundaries.
MouseMove	Occurs when the mouse cursor is moved while in the control's boundaries.
MouseUp	Occurs when a mouse button is released when the cursor is within the control's boundaries.
Class MouseEventArgs *Properties*	
Button	Specifies which mouse button was pressed (Left, Right, Middle or none).
Clicks	The number of times the mouse button was clicked.
X	The *x*-coordinate within the control where the event occurred.
Y	The *y*-coordinate within the control where the event occurred.

Fig. 13.37 | Mouse events and event arguments.

Figure 13.38 uses mouse events to draw on a Form. Whenever the user drags the mouse (i.e., moves the mouse while a mouse button is pressed), small circles appear on the Form at the position where each mouse event occurs during the drag operation.

Line 4 declares variable shouldPaint, which determines whether to draw on the Form. We want to draw only while the mouse button is pressed (i.e., held down). Thus, when the user clicks or holds down a mouse button, the system generates a MouseDown event, and the event handler FrmPainter_MouseDown (lines 7–11) sets shouldPaint to True. When the user releases the mouse button, the system generates a MouseUp event, shouldPaint is set to False in the FrmPainter_MouseUp event handler (lines 14–18) and the program stops drawing. Unlike MouseMove events, which occur continuously as the user moves the mouse, the system generates a MouseDown event only when a mouse button is first pressed and generates a MouseUp event only when a mouse button is released.

```vb
1   ' Fig 13.38: FrmPainter.vb
2   ' Using the mouse to draw on a Form.
3   Public Class FrmPainter
4       Private shouldPaint As Boolean = False ' determines whether to paint
5
```

Fig. 13.38 | Using the mouse to draw on a Form. (Part 1 of 2.)

```
 6      ' should paint when mouse button is pressed down
 7      Private Sub FrmPainter_MouseDown(ByVal sender As System.Object, _
 8         ByVal e As System.Windows.Forms.MouseEventArgs) _
 9         Handles MyBase.MouseDown
10         shouldPaint = True
11      End Sub ' FrmPainter_MouseDown
12
13      ' stop painting when mouse button is released
14      Private Sub FrmPainter_MouseUp(ByVal sender As System.Object, _
15         ByVal e As System.Windows.Forms.MouseEventArgs) _
16         Handles MyBase.MouseUp
17         shouldPaint = False
18      End Sub ' FrmPainter_MouseUp
19
20      ' draw circle whenever mouse moves with its button held down
21      Private Sub FrmPainter_MouseMove(ByVal sender As System.Object, _
22         ByVal e As System.Windows.Forms.MouseEventArgs) _
23         Handles MyBase.MouseMove
24         ' check if mouse button is being pressed
25         If (shouldPaint) Then
26            ' draw a circle where the mouse pointer is present
27            Dim g As Graphics = CreateGraphics()
28            g.FillEllipse( _
29               New SolidBrush(Color.BlueViolet), e.X, e.Y, 4, 4)
30            g.Dispose()
31         End If
32      End Sub ' FrmPainter_MouseMove
33   End Class ' FrmPainter
```

Fig. 13.38 | Using the mouse to draw on a Form. (Part 2 of 2.)

Whenever the mouse moves over a control, the MouseMove event for that control occurs. Inside the FrmPainter_MouseMove event handler (lines 21–32), the program draws only if shouldPaint is True (i.e., a mouse button is pressed). Line 27 calls inherited Form method CreateGraphics to create a **Graphics** object that allows the program to draw on the Form. Class Graphics provides methods that draw various shapes. For example, lines 28–29 use method **FillEllipse** to draw a circle. The first parameter to method FillEllipse in this case is an object of class **SolidBrush**, which specifies the solid color that will fill the shape. The color is provided as an argument to class SolidBrush's constructor. Type **Color** contains many predefined color constants—we selected Color.BlueViolet. FillEllipse draws an oval in a bounding rectangle that is specified by the *x*- and *y*-coordinates of its upper-left corner, its width and its height—the final four arguments to the method. The *x*- and *y*-coordinates represent the location of the mouse event and can be taken from the mouse-event arguments (e.X and e.Y). To draw a circle, we set the width and height of the bounding rectangle so that they are equal—in this example, both are 4 pixels. Line 30 invokes the Graphics object's Dispose method to return the Graphics object's resources back to the system. Graphics, SolidBrush and Color are all part of the System.Drawing namespace. We discuss class Graphics and its methods in depth in Chapter 17, Graphics and Multimedia.

13.12 Keyboard-Event Handling

Key events occur when keyboard keys are pressed and released. Such events can be handled for any control that inherits from System.Windows.Forms.Control. There are three key events—KeyPress, KeyUp and KeyDown. The KeyPress event occurs when the user presses a key that represents an ASCII character. The specific key can be determined with property KeyChar of the event handler's KeyPressEventArgs argument. ASCII is a 128-character set of alphanumeric symbols, a full listing of which can be found in Appendix D.

The KeyPress event does not indicate whether modifier keys (e.g., *Shift, Alt* and *Ctrl*) were pressed when a key event occurred. If this information is important, the KeyUp or KeyDown events can be used. The KeyEventArgs argument for each of these events contains information about modifier keys. Often, modifier keys are used in conjunction with the mouse to select or highlight information. Figure 13.39 lists important key-event information. Several properties return values from the Keys enumeration, which provides constants that specify the various keys on a keyboard. Like the FontStyle enumeration (Section 13.7), the Keys enumeration has the System.FlagAttribute, so the enumeration's constants can be combined to indicate multiple keys pressed at the same time.

Keyboard events and event arguments	
Key Events with Event Arguments of Type KeyEventArgs	
KeyDown	Generated when a key is initially pressed.
KeyUp	Generated when a key is released.
Key Event with Event Argument of Type KeyPressEventArgs	
KeyPress	Generated when a key is pressed.
Class KeyPressEventArgs *Properties*	
KeyChar	Returns the ASCII character for the key pressed.
Handled	Indicates whether the KeyPress event was handled.
Class KeyEventArgs *Properties*	
Alt	Indicates whether the *Alt* key was pressed.

Fig. 13.39 | Keyboard events and event arguments. (Part 1 of 2.)

Keyboard events and event arguments	
Control	Indicates whether the *Ctrl* key was pressed.
Shift	Indicates whether the *Shift* key was pressed.
Handled	Indicates whether the event was handled.
KeyCode	Returns the key code for the key as a value from the Keys enumeration. This does not include modifier-key information. It is used to test for a specific key.
KeyData	Returns the key code for a key combined with modifier information as a Keys value. This property contains all the information about the pressed key.
KeyValue	Returns the key code as an int, rather than as a value from the Keys enumeration. This property is used to obtain a numeric representation of the pressed key. The int value is known as a Windows virtual key code.
Modifiers	Returns a Keys value indicating any pressed modifier keys (*Alt*, *Ctrl* and *Shift*). This property is used to determine modifier-key information only.

Fig. 13.39 | Keyboard events and event arguments. (Part 2 of 2.)

Figure 13.40 demonstrates the use of the key-event handlers to display a key pressed by a user. The program is a Form with two Labels that displays the pressed key on one Label and modifier-key information on the other.

```
1   ' Fig. 13.40: FrmKeyDemo.vb
2   ' Displaying information about the key the user pressed.
3   Public Class FrmKeyDemo
4
5      ' display the character pressed using KeyChar
6      Private Sub FrmKeyDemo_KeyPress(ByVal sender As System.Object, _
7         ByVal e As System.Windows.Forms.KeyPressEventArgs) _
8         Handles MyBase.KeyPress
9
10        lblChar.Text = "Key pressed: " & e.KeyChar
11     End Sub ' FrmKeyDemo_KeyPress
12
13     ' display modifier keys, key code, key data and key value
14     Private Sub FrmKeyDemo_KeyDown(ByVal sender As System.Object, _
15        ByVal e As System.Windows.Forms.KeyEventArgs) _
16        Handles MyBase.KeyDown
17
18        If e.Alt Then ' key is Alt
19           lblKeyInfo.Text = "Alt: Yes" & vbCrLf
20        Else ' key is not Alt
21           lblKeyInfo.Text = "Alt: No" & vbCrLf
22        End If
23
```

Fig. 13.40 | Demonstrating keyboard events. (Part I of 2.)

```
24        If e.Shift Then ' key is Shift
25            lblKeyInfo.Text &= "Shift: Yes" & vbCrLf
26        Else ' key is not Shift
27            lblKeyInfo.Text &= "Shift: No" & vbCrLf
28        End If
29
30        If e.Control Then ' key is Control
31            lblKeyInfo.Text &= "Control: Yes" & vbCrLf
32        Else ' key is not Control
33            lblKeyInfo.Text &= "Control: No" & vbCrLf
34        End If
35
36        ' diplay key code, key data and key value
37        lblKeyInfo.Text &= "KeyCode: " & e.KeyCode.ToString() & vbCrLf & _
38            "KeyData: " & e.KeyData.ToString() & vbCrLf & _
39            "KeyValue: " & e.KeyValue.ToString()
40    End Sub ' FrmKeyDemo_KeyDown
41
42    ' clear Labels when keys are released
43    Private Sub FrmKeyDemo_KeyUp(ByVal sender As System.Object, _
44        ByVal e As System.Windows.Forms.KeyEventArgs) Handles MyBase.KeyUp
45
46        lblChar.Text = ""
47        lblKeyInfo.Text = ""
48    End Sub ' FrmKeyDemo_KeyUp
49  End Class ' FrmKeyDemo
```

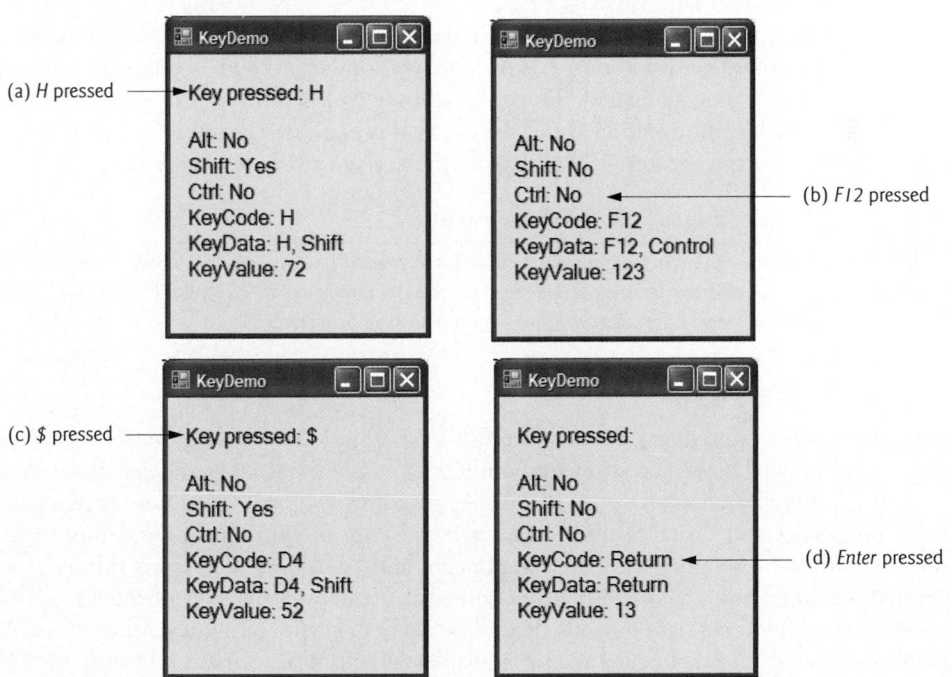

Fig. 13.40 | Demonstrating keyboard events. (Part 2 of 2.)

Initially, the two `Labels` (`lblChar` and `lblKeyInfo`) contain `"Just Press"` and `"A Key..."`. Control `lblChar` displays the character value of the key pressed, whereas `lblKeyInfo` displays information relating to the pressed key. Because the `KeyDown` and `KeyPress` events convey different information, the `Form` (`FrmKeyDemo`) handles both.

The `KeyPress` event handler (lines 6–11) accesses the `KeyChar` property of the `KeyPressEventArgs` object. This returns the pressed key as a `Char`, which we then display in `lblChar` (line 10). If the pressed key is not an ASCII character, then the `KeyPress` event will not occur, and `lblChar` will not display any text. ASCII is a common encoding format for letters, numbers, punctuation marks and other characters. It does not support keys such as the **function keys** (like *F1*) or the modifier keys (*Alt*, *Ctrl* and *Shift*).

The `KeyDown` event handler (lines 14–40) displays information from its `KeyEventArgs` object. The event handler tests for the *Alt*, *Shift* and *Ctrl* keys by using the `Alt`, `Shift` and `Control` properties, each of which returns a `Boolean` value—`True` if the corresponding key is pressed and `False` otherwise. The event handler then displays the `KeyCode`, `KeyData` and `KeyValue` properties.

The `KeyCode` property returns a `Keys` enumeration value (line 37). The `KeyCode` property returns the pressed key, but does not provide any information about modifier keys. Thus, both a capital "A" and a lowercase "a" are represented as the *A* key.

The `KeyData` property (line 38) also returns a `Keys` enumeration value, but this property includes data about modifier keys. Thus, if "A" is input, the `KeyData` shows that both the *A* key and the *Shift* key were pressed. Lastly, `KeyValue` (line 39) returns the key code of the pressed key as an `Integer`. This `Integer` is the key code, which provides an `Integer` value for a wide range of keys and for mouse buttons. The key code is useful when one is testing for non-ASCII keys (such as *F12*).

The `KeyUp` event handler (lines 43–48) clears both `Labels` when the key is released. As we can see from the output, non-ASCII keys are not displayed in `lblChar`, because the `KeyPress` event is not generated. However, the `KeyDown` event is still generated, and `lblKeyInfo` displays information about the key that is pressed. The `Keys` enumeration can be used to test for specific keys by comparing the key pressed to a specific `KeyCode`.

 Software Engineering Observation 13.3

To make a control react when a particular key is pressed (such as Enter*), handle a key event for that control and test for the pressed key. To allow a* Button *to be clicked when the user presses the* Enter *key on a* Form*, set the* Form's `AcceptButton` *property.*

13.13 Wrap-Up

This chapter introduced several common GUI controls. We discussed event handling in detail, and showed how to create event handlers. We also discussed how delegates are used to connect event handlers to the events of specific controls. You learned how to use a control's properties and Visual Studio to specify the layout of your GUI. We demonstrated several controls, beginning with `Labels`, `Buttons` and `TextBoxes`. You learned how to use `GroupBoxes` and `Panels` to organize other controls. We demonstrated `CheckBoxes` and `RadioButtons`, which are state buttons that allow users to select among several options. We displayed images in `PictureBox` controls, displayed helpful text on a GUI with `ToolTip` components and specified a range of input values for users with a `NumericUpDown` control. We then demonstrated how to handle mouse and keyboard events. The next chapter introduces additional GUI controls. You will learn how to add menus to your GUIs and create Windows applications that display multiple Forms.

Summary

Section 13.1 Introduction
- A graphical user interface (GUI) allows a user to interact visually with a program.
- By providing different applications with a consistent set of intuitive user-interface components, GUIs enable users to become productive with each application faster.
- GUIs are built from GUI controls—objects that can display information on the screen or enable users to interact with an application via the mouse, keyboard or some other form of input.

Section 13.2 Windows Forms
- Windows Forms are used to create the GUIs for programs.
- A Form is a graphical element that appears on the desktop; it can be a dialog, a window or an MDI (multiple document interface) window.
- A component is an instance of a class that implements the IComponent interface, which defines the behaviors that components must implement.
- A control has a graphical representation at runtime.
- Some components lack graphical representations (e.g., class Timer of namespace System.Windows.Forms). Such components are not visible at runtime.
- When there are several windows on the screen, the active window is the frontmost and has a highlighted title bar—typically darker than the other windows on the screen. A window becomes the active window when the user clicks somewhere inside it.
- The active window is said to "have the focus."
- A Form is a container for controls and components.

Section 13.3 Event Handling
- A user interacts with an application's GUI to indicate the tasks that the application can perform on the user's behalf.
- GUIs are event driven.
- When the user interacts with a control, the interaction—known as an event—drives the program to perform a task. Common events include clicking a Button, typing in a TextBox, selecting an item from a menu, closing a window and moving the mouse.
- A method that performs a task in response to an event is called an event handler, and the overall process of responding to events is known as event handling.

Section 13.3.1 A Simple Event-Driven GUI
- By convention, event-handler methods are named as *controlName_eventName*.
- An event handler executes only when the user performs the specific event.
- Each event handler receives two parameters when it is called. The first—an Object reference named sender—is a reference to the object that generated the event. The second is a reference to an event arguments object of type EventArgs (or one of its derived classes), which is typically named e. This object contains additional information about the event that occurred.
- EventArgs is the base class of all classes that represent event information.

Section 13.3.2 Another Look at the Visual Studio Generated Code

- Visual Studio generates the code that creates and initializes the GUI you build in the GUI design window. This auto-generated code is placed in the `Designer.vb` file of the `Form`.

- The auto-generated code that defines the GUI is part of the `Form`'s class. The use of the `Partial` modifier in the class declaration allows the class to be split among multiple files.

- The `Designer.vb` file contains the declarations of the controls you create in **Design** mode. By default, all variable declarations for controls created through Visual Basic's design window have a `Friend` access modifier.

- The `Designer.vb` file includes the `Dispose` method for releasing resources and method `InitializeComponent`, which sets the properties of the `Form` and its controls.

- Visual Studio uses the code in `InitializeComponent` to create the GUI you see in design view. Changing the code in this method may prevent Visual Studio from displaying the GUI properly.

Section 13.3.3 Delegates and the Event-Handling Mechanism

- The control that generates an event is known as the event sender.

- An event-handling method—known as the event receiver—responds to a particular event that a control generates.

- When an event occurs, the event sender calls its event receiver to perform a task.

- The .NET event-handling mechanism allows you to choose your own names for event-handling methods. However, each event-handling method must declare the proper parameters to receive information about the event it handles.

- Event handlers are connected to a control's events via special objects called delegates.

- A delegate object holds a reference to a method. The method's signature must match the signature specified by the delegate type's declaration.

- GUI controls have predefined delegates that correspond to every event they can generate.

- An event uses a delegate object like a method call.

- Since each event handler is declared as a delegate, the event sender can simply call the appropriate delegate when an event occurs. The delegate's job is to invoke the appropriate method.

Section 13.3.4 Other Ways to Create Event Handlers

- Double clicking a control on the `Form` creates an event handler for a control's default event.

- Typically, controls can generate many different events, and each can have its own event handler.

- You can create additional event handlers through the **Properties** window.

- If you select a control on the `Form`, then click the **Events** icon (the lightning bolt icon) in the **Properties** window, all the events for that control are listed in the window. You can double click an event's name to display the event handler in the editor, if the event handler already exists, or to create the corresponding event handler.

- You can select an event, then use the drop-down list to its right to choose an existing method that will be used as the event handler for that event. The methods that appear in this drop-down list are the class's methods that have the proper signature to be an event handler for the selected event.

Section 13.3.5 Locating Event Information

- Read the Visual Studio documentation to learn about the different events raised by a control.

- To do this, select **Help > Index**. In the window that appears, select **.NET Framework** in the **Filtered by:** drop-down list and enter the name of the control's class in the **Index** window. To ensure that you are selecting the proper class, enter the fully qualified class name.

- Once you select a control's class in the documentation, a list of all the class's members are displayed. This list includes the events the class can generate.
- Click the name of an event to view its description and examples of its use.

Section 13.4 Control Properties and Layout

- Controls derive from class Control (of namespace System.Windows.Forms).
- The Focus method transfers the focus to a control and makes it the active control.
- The Enabled property indicates whether the user can interact with a control to generate an event.
- A programmer can hide a control from the user without disabling the control by setting the Visible property to False or by calling method Hide.
- Anchoring causes controls to remain at a fixed distance from the sides of the container even when the container is resized.
- Docking attaches a control to a container such that the control stretches across an entire side.
- Forms have a Padding property that specifies the distance between the docked controls and the Form edges.
- The Anchor and Dock properties of a Control are set with respect to the Control's parent container, which could be a Form or other parent container (such as a Panel).
- The minimum and maximum Form (or other Control) sizes can be set via properties MinimumSize and MaximumSize, respectively.
- When dragging a control across a Form, blue lines (known as snap lines) appear to help you position the control with respect to other controls and the Form's edges.
- Visual Studio also provides the **Format** menu, which contains several options for modifying your GUI's layout.

Section 13.5 *Labels, TextBoxes and Buttons*

- Labels provide text information (as well as optional images) that the user cannot directly modify.
- A textbox (class TextBox) is an area in which text can be displayed by a program or the user can type text via the keyboard.
- A password TextBox is a TextBox that hides the information entered by the user. As the user types characters, the password TextBox masks the user input by displaying a character you specify (usually *). If you set the PasswordChar property, the TextBox becomes a password TextBox.
- The user clicks a button to trigger a specific action in a program or to select an option.
- All the button classes derive from class ButtonBase (namespace System.Windows.Forms), which defines common button features.

Section 13.6 *GroupBoxes and Panels*

- GroupBoxes and Panels arrange controls on a GUI.
- GroupBoxes and Panels are typically used to group several controls of similar functionality or several controls that are related in a GUI.
- GroupBoxes can display a caption (i.e., text) and do not include scrollbars, whereas Panels can include scrollbars and do not include a caption.
- GroupBoxes have thin borders by default; Panels can be set so that they also have borders, by changing their BorderStyle property.
- The controls of a GroupBox or Panel are added to the container's Controls property.
- To enable a Panel's scrollbars, set the Panel's AutoScroll property to True. If the Panel is resized and cannot display all of its controls, scrollbars appear.

Section 13.7 *CheckBoxes and RadioButtons*

- CheckBoxes and RadioButtons can be in the on/off or true/false states.

- Classes CheckBox and RadioButton are derived from class ButtonBase.

- A CheckBox is a small square that either is blank or contains a check mark. When a CheckBox is selected, a check mark appears in the box. Any number of CheckBoxes can be selected at a time.

- Styles can be combined via bitwise operators, such as the Or operator or the Xor operator.

- RadioButtons (defined with class RadioButton) are similar to CheckBoxes in that they also have two states—selected and not selected (also called deselected).

- RadioButtons normally appear as a group, in which only one RadioButton can be selected at a time. The selection of one RadioButton in the group forces all the others to be deselected. Therefore, RadioButtons are used to represent a set of mutually exclusive options.

- All RadioButtons added to a container become part of the same group.

Section 13.8 *PictureBoxes*

- A PictureBox displays the image specified by the Image property.

- The SizeMode property indicates how the image is displayed (Normal, StretchImage, Autosize or CenterImage).

Section 13.9 *ToolTips*

- Tool tips help you become familiar with the IDE's features and serve as useful reminders of each toolbar icon's functionality. This property appears in the **Properties** window as **ToolTip on** followed by the name of the ToolTip component.

- Once a ToolTip is added to a Form, a new property appears in the **Properties** window for the other controls on the Form.

- The ToolTip component can be used to add tool tips to your application.

- The component tray is the gray region below the Form in **Design** mode.

Section 13.10 *NumericUpDown Control*

- The NumericUpDown control restricts a user's input choices to a specific range of numeric values.

- The NumericUpDown control appears as a TextBox, with two small Buttons on the right side, one with an up arrow and one with a down arrow. By default, a user can type numeric values into this control as if it were a TextBox or click the up and down arrows to increase or decrease the value in the control, respectively.

- The largest and smallest values in the range are specified with the Maximum and Minimum properties, respectively (both are of type Decimal).

- The Increment property (of type Decimal) specifies by how much the current number in the control changes when the user clicks the control's up and down arrows.

- Setting a NumericUpDown control's ReadOnly property to True specifies that the user can only use the up and down arrows to modify the value in the NumericUpDown control.

Section 13.11 *Mouse-Event Handling*

- Mouse events, such as clicks, presses and moves, are generated when the mouse interacts with any control that derives from class System.Windows.Forms.Control.

- Class MouseEventArgs contains information related to the mouse event, such as the *x*- and *y*-coordinates of the mouse pointer, the mouse button pressed (Right, Left or Middle) and the number of times the mouse was clicked.

- Whenever the user clicks or holds down a mouse button, the system generates a MouseDown event.
- When the user releases the mouse button (to complete a "click" operation), the system generates a single MouseUp event.
- Moving the mouse over a control causes a MouseMove event for that control.

Section 13.12 Keyboard-Event Handling

- Key events KeyPress, KeyUp and KeyDown occur when various keys on the keyboard are pressed and released.
- The KeyPress event occurs when the user presses a key that represents an ASCII character. The specific key can be determined with property KeyChar of the event handler's KeyPressEventArgs argument.
- The KeyPress event does not indicate whether modifier keys (e.g., *Shift*, *Alt* and *Ctrl*) were pressed when a key event occurred. If this information is important, the KeyUp or KeyDown events can be used.
- The KeyEventArgs argument for each Key event contains information about modifier keys. Several properties return values from the Keys enumeration, which provides constants that specify the various keys on a keyboard.
- The KeyCode property returns the pressed key, but does not provide any information about modifier keys.
- The KeyData property returns a Keys enumeration value, including data about modifier keys.

Terminology

active control
active window
anchor a control
bitwise operator
Button properties and events
Button property of class MouseEventArgs
ButtonBase class
checkbox
CheckBox class
Checked property of class CheckBox
Checked property of class RadioButton
CheckedChanged event of class CheckBox
CheckedChanged event of class RadioButton
CheckState property of class CheckBox
CheckStateChanged event of class CheckBox
Color structure
component
component tray
container
Control class
Controls property of a container
default event
delegate
Delegate keyword
deselected state
DialogResult enumeration

dock a control
Dock property of class Control
Enabled property of class Control
event
event-driven programming
event handler
event handling
event receiver
event sender
FillEllipse method of class Graphics
FlatStyle property of class Button
focus
Focus method of class Control
Font class
FontStyle enumeration
Graphics class
Handles clause
Height property of structure Size
IComponent interface
Increment property of class NumericUpDown
key code
key event
KeyChar property of class KeyPressEventArgs
KeyCode property of class KeyEventArgs
KeyData property of class KeyEventArgs
KeyDown event of class Control

KeyEventArgs class
KeyPress event of class Control
KeyPressEventArgs class
Keys enumeration
KeyUp event of class Control
KeyValue property of class KeyEventArgs
Maximum property of class NumericUpDown
MaximumSize property of class Control
Minimum property of class NumericUpDown
MinimumSize property of class Control
modifier key
mouse click
mouse event
mouse move
mouse press
MouseDown event of class Control
MouseEventArgs class
MouseEventHandler delegate
MouseMove event of class Control
MouseUp event of class Control
multiple document interface (MDI) window
mutual exclusion
"not-selected" state
NumericUpDown class
Padding property of class Control

Panel class
password TextBox
PasswordChar property of class TextBox
radio button
radio button group
RadioButton class
ReadOnly property of class NumericUpDown
selected state
Size property of class Control
Size structure
snap line
SolidBrush class
state button
Style property of class Font
TabIndex property of class Control
TabStop property of class Control
ToolTip class
UpDownAlign property of class NumericUpDown
Value property of class NumericUpDown
Visible property of class Control
widget
Width property of structure Size
window gadget
Windows Form

Self-Review Exercises

13.1   State whether each of the following is *true* or *false*. If *false*, explain why.
a) The KeyData property includes data about modifier keys.
b) Windows Forms commonly are used to create GUIs.
c) A Form is a container.
d) All Forms, components and controls are classes.
e) CheckBoxes are used to represent a set of mutually exclusive options.
f) A Label displays text that a user running an application can edit.
g) Button presses generate events.
h) All mouse events use the same event arguments class.
i) The NumericUpDown control is used to specify a range of input values.
j) A control's tool tip text is set with the ToolTip property of class Control.

13.2   Fill in the blanks in each of the following statements:
a) The active control is said to have the _____.
b) The Form acts as a(n) _____ for the controls that are added.
c) GUIs are _____ driven.
d) Every method that handles the same event must have the same _____.
e) A(n) _____ TextBox masks user input with a character used repeatedly.
f) Class _____ and class _____ help arrange controls on a GUI and provide logical groups for radio buttons.
g) Typical mouse events include _____, _____ and _____.
h) _____ events are generated when a key on the keyboard is pressed or released.
i) The modifier keys are _____, _____ and _____.

Answers To Self-Review Exercises

13.1 a) True. b) True. c) True. d) True. e) False. RadioButtons are used to represent a set of mutually exclusive options. f) False. A Label's text cannot be edited by the user. g) True. h) False. Some mouse events use EventArgs, others use MouseEventArgs. i) True. j) False. A control's tool tip text is set using a ToolTip component that must be added to the application.

13.2 a) focus. b) container. c) event. d) signature. e) password. f) GroupBox, Panel. g) mouse clicks, mouse presses, mouse moves. h) Key. i) *Shift, Ctrl, Alt.*

Exercises

13.3 Extend the program in Fig. 13.26 to include a CheckBox for every font-style option. [*Hint:* Use Xor rather than test for every bit explicitly.]

13.4 Create the GUI in Fig. 13.41 (you do not have to provide functionality).

13.5 Create the GUI in Fig. 13.42 (you do not have to provide functionality).

13.6 Write a temperature-conversion program that converts from Fahrenheit to Celsius. The Fahrenheit temperature should be entered from the keyboard (via a TextBox). A Label should be used to display the converted temperature. Use the following formula for the conversion:

$$Celsius = (5 / 9) \times (Fahrenheit - 32)$$

Fig. 13.41 | Calculator GUI.

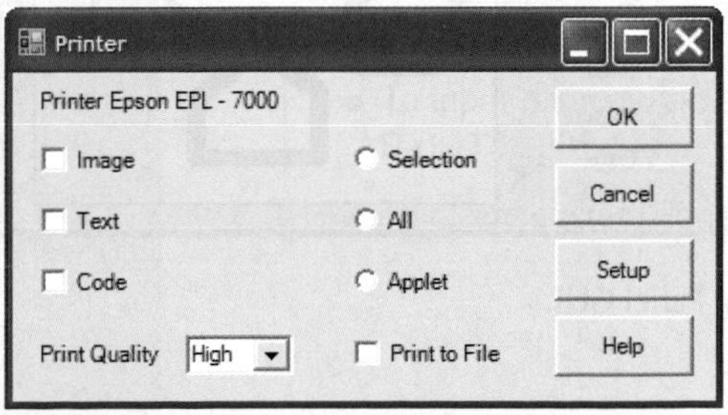

Fig. 13.42 | Printer GUI.

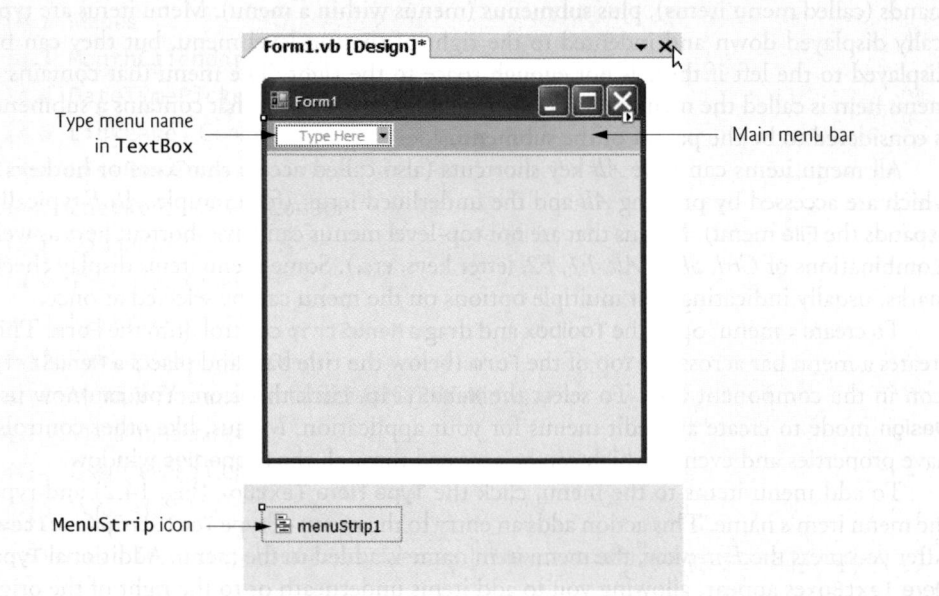

Fig. 14.2 | Editing menus in Visual Studio.

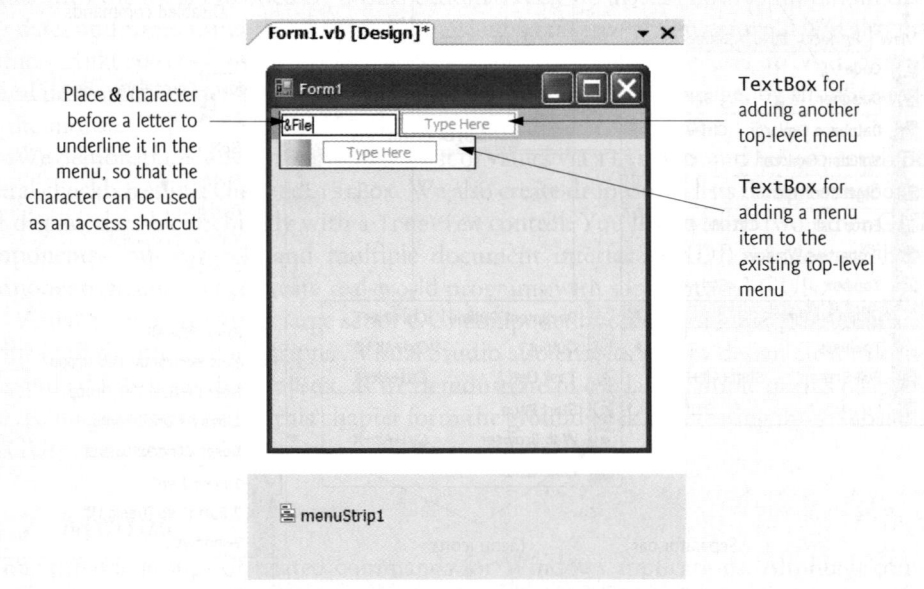

Fig. 14.3 | Adding ToolStripMenuItems to a MenuStrip.

To create an access shortcut (or keyboard shortcut), type an ampersand (&) before the character to be underlined. For example, to create the **File** menu item with the letter **F** underlined, type &File. To display an ampersand, type &&. To add other shortcut keys (like those shown in Fig. 14.1) for menu items, set the **ShortcutKeys** property of the appropriate ToolStripMenuItems. To do this, select the down arrow to the right of this property in the **Properties** window. In the window that appears (Fig. 14.4), use the **Check-Boxes** and drop-down list to select the shortcut keys. When you are finished, click elsewhere on the screen. You can hide the shortcut keys by setting property ShowShortcutKeys to False, and you can modify how the control keys are displayed in the menu item by modifying property **ShortcutKeyDisplayString**.

Look-and-Feel Observation 14.1

Buttons can have access shortcuts. Place the & symbol immediately before the desired character in the Button's text. To press the button by using its access key in the running application, press Alt and the underlined character.

You can remove a menu item by selecting it and pressing the *Delete* key. Menu items can be grouped logically by separator bars, which are inserted by right clicking a menu item and selecting **Insert > Separator** or by typing "-" for the text of a menu item.

You can also add TextBoxes and ComboBoxes (drop-down lists) as menu items. When adding an item in **Design** mode, you may have noticed that before you click to enter text for a new item, you are provided with a drop-down list. Clicking the down arrow (Fig. 14.5) allows you to select the type of item to add—**MenuItem** (of type ToolStrip-MenuItem, the default), **ComboBox** (of type ToolStripComboBox) and **TextBox** (of type ToolStripTextBox). We focus on ToolStripMenuItems. [*Note:* If you view this drop-down list for menu items that are not on the top level, a fourth option appears, allowing you to insert a separator bar.]

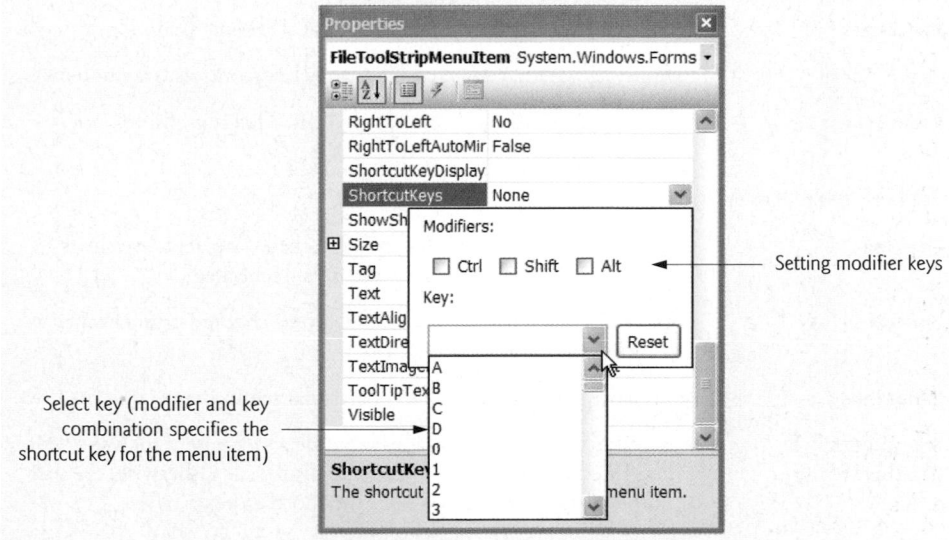

Fig. 14.4 | Setting a menu item's shortcut keys.

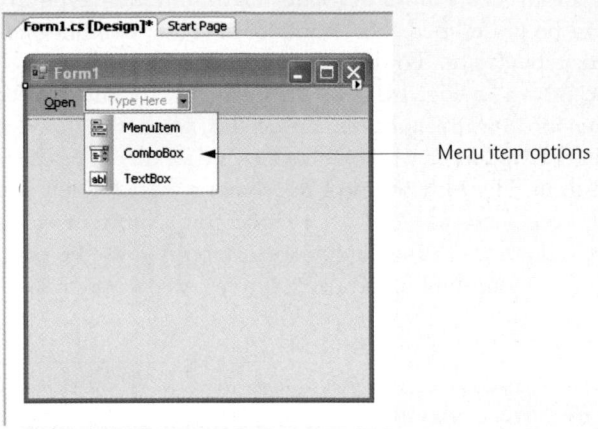

Fig. 14.5 | Menu item options.

ToolStripMenuItems generate a Click event when selected. To create an empty Click event handler, double click the menu item in **Design** mode. Common actions in response to these events include displaying dialogs and setting application properties. Common menu properties and a common event of MenuStrip and ToolStripMenuItem are summarized in Fig. 14.6.

MenuStrip and ToolStripMenuItem properties and an event	Description
MenuStrip Properties	
MenuItems	Contains the top-level menu items for this MenuStrip.
HasChildren	Indicates whether MenuStrip has any child controls (menu items).
RightToLeft	Causes text to display from right to left. This is useful for languages that are read from right to left.
ToolStripMenuItem Properties	
Checked	Indicates whether a menu item is checked. The default value is False, meaning that the menu item is unchecked.
CheckOnClick	Indicates that a menu item should appear checked or unchecked as the item is clicked.
MenuItems	Lists the submenu items for a particular menu item.
ShortcutKey-DisplayString	Specifies text that should appear beside a menu item for a shortcut key. If left blank, the key names are displayed. Otherwise, the text in this property is displayed for the shortcut key.

Fig. 14.6 | MenuStrip and ToolStripMenuItem properties and an event. (Part 1 of 2.)

MenuStrip and ToolStripMenuItem properties and an event	Description
ShortcutKeys	Specifies the shortcut key for the menu item.
ShowShortcutKeys	Indicates whether a shortcut key is shown beside the menu item text. The default is True, which displays the shortcut key.
Text	Specifies the menu item's text. To create an *Alt* access shortcut, precede a character with & (e.g., &File to specify a menu named **File** with the letter **F** underlined).
Common ToolStripMenuItem Event	
Click	Generated when an item is clicked or a shortcut key is used to select a menu item.

Fig. 14.6 | MenuStrip and ToolStripMenuItem properties and an event. (Part 2 of 2.)

Look-and-Feel Observation 14.2

*It is a convention to place an ellipsis (...) after the name of a menu item that, when selected, displays a dialog (e.g. **Save As**...). A menu item that causes an immediate action without prompting the user for more information (e.g., **Save**) should not have an ellipsis following its name.*

Class FrmMenuTest (Fig. 14.7) creates a simple menu on a Form. The Form has a top-level **File** menu with menu items **About** (which displays a MessageBox) and **Exit** (which terminates the program). The program also includes a **Format** menu, which contains menu items that change the format of the text on a Label. The **Format** menu has submenus **Color** and **Font**, which change the color and font of the text on a Label.

```
1   ' Fig. 14.7: FrmMenuTest.vb
2   ' Using Menus to change font colors and styles.
3   Public Class FrmMenuTest
4
5      ' display MessageBox when About MenuItem is selected
6      Private Sub aboutToolStripMenuItem_Click( _
7         ByVal sender As System.Object, ByVal e As System.EventArgs) _
8         Handles aboutToolStripMenuItem.Click
9
10        MessageBox.Show("This is an example" & vbCrLf & "of using menus.", _
11           "About", MessageBoxButtons.OK, MessageBoxIcon.Information)
12     End Sub ' aboutToolStripMenuItem_Click
13
14     ' exit program when Exit MenuItem is selected
15     Private Sub exitToolStripMenuItem_Click( _
16        ByVal sender As System.Object, ByVal e As System.EventArgs) _
17        Handles exitToolStripMenuItem.Click
18
```

Fig. 14.7 | Menus for changing text font and color. (Part 1 of 4.)

```vb
19          Application.Exit()
20       End Sub ' exitToolStripMenuItem_Click
21
22       ' reset checkmarks for Color MenuItems
23       Private Sub ClearColor()
24          ' clear all checkmarks
25          blackToolStripMenuItem.Checked = False
26          blueToolStripMenuItem.Checked = False
27          redToolStripMenuItem.Checked = False
28          greenToolStripMenuItem.Checked = False
29       End Sub ' ClearColor
30
31       ' update Menu state and color display black
32       Private Sub blackToolStripMenuItem_Click( _
33          ByVal sender As System.Object, ByVal e As System.EventArgs) _
34          Handles blackToolStripMenuItem.Click
35
36          ClearColor() ' reset checkmarks for Color MenuItems
37          lblDisplay.ForeColor = Color.Black ' set Color to Black
38          blackToolStripMenuItem.Checked = True
39       End Sub ' blackToolStripMenuItem_Click
40
41       ' update Menu state and color display blue
42       Private Sub blueToolStripMenuItem_Click( _
43          ByVal sender As System.Object, ByVal e As System.EventArgs) _
44          Handles blueToolStripMenuItem.Click
45
46          ClearColor() ' reset checkmarks for Color MenuItems
47          lblDisplay.ForeColor = Color.Blue ' set Color to Blue
48          blueToolStripMenuItem.Checked = True
49       End Sub ' blueToolStripMenuItem_Click
50
51       ' update Menu state and color display red
52       Private Sub redToolStripMenuItem_Click( _
53          ByVal sender As System.Object, ByVal e As System.EventArgs) _
54          Handles redToolStripMenuItem.Click
55
56          ClearColor() ' reset checkmarks for Color MenuItems
57          lblDisplay.ForeColor = Color.Red ' set Color to Red
58          redToolStripMenuItem.Checked = True
59       End Sub ' redToolStripMenuItem_Click
60
61       ' update Menu state and color display green
62       Private Sub greenToolStripMenuItem_Click( _
63          ByVal sender As System.Object, ByVal e As System.EventArgs) _
64          Handles greenToolStripMenuItem.Click
65
66          ClearColor() ' reset checkmarks for Color MenuItems
67          lblDisplay.ForeColor = Color.Green ' set Color to Green
68          greenToolStripMenuItem.Checked = True
69       End Sub ' greenToolStripMenuItem_Click
70
```

Fig. 14.7 | Menus for changing text font and color. (Part 2 of 4.)

```vbnet
71     ' reset checkmarks for Font MenuItems
72     Private Sub ClearFont()
73        timesToolStripMenuItem.Checked = False
74        courierToolStripMenuItem.Checked = False
75        comicToolStripMenuItem.Checked = False
76     End Sub ' ClearFont
77
78     ' update Menu state and set Font to Times New Roman
79     Private Sub timesToolStripMenuItem_Click( _
80        ByVal sender As System.Object, ByVal e As System.EventArgs) _
81        Handles timesToolStripMenuItem.Click
82
83        ClearFont() 'reset checkmarks for Font MenuItems
84        timesToolStripMenuItem.Checked = True
85
86        ' set Times New Roman font
87        lblDisplay.Font = _
88           New Font("Times New Roman", 14, lblDisplay.Font.Style)
89     End Sub ' timesToolStripMenuItem_Click
90
91     ' update Menu state and set Font to Courier New
92     Private Sub courierToolStripMenuItem_Click( _
93        ByVal sender As System.Object, ByVal e As System.EventArgs) _
94        Handles courierToolStripMenuItem.Click
95
96        ClearFont() ' reset checkmarks for Font MenuItems
97        courierToolStripMenuItem.Checked = True
98
99        ' set Courier font
100       lblDisplay.Font = _
101          New Font("Courier New", 14, lblDisplay.Font.Style)
102    End Sub ' courierToolStripMenuItem_Click
103
104    ' update Menu state and set Font to Comic Sans MS
105    Private Sub comicToolStripMenuItem_Click( _
106       ByVal sender As System.Object, ByVal e As System.EventArgs) _
107       Handles comicToolStripMenuItem.Click
108
109       ClearFont() ' reset checkmarks for Font MenuItems
110       comicToolStripMenuItem.Checked = True
111
112       ' set Comic Sans MS font
113       lblDisplay.Font = _
114          New Font("Comic Sans MS", 14, lblDisplay.Font.Style)
115    End Sub ' comicToolStripMenuItem_Click
116
117    ' toggle checkmark and toggle bold style
118    Private Sub boldToolStripMenuItem_Click( _
119       ByVal sender As System.Object, ByVal e As System.EventArgs) _
120       Handles boldToolStripMenuItem.Click
121       ' toggle menu item checkmark
122       boldToolStripMenuItem.Checked = Not boldToolStripMenuItem.Checked
123
```

Fig. 14.7 | Menus for changing text font and color. (Part 3 of 4.)

```
124          ' use Xor to toggle bold, keep all other styles
125          lblDisplay.Font = New Font(lblDisplay.Font.FontFamily, 14, _
126             lblDisplay.Font.Style Xor FontStyle.Bold)
127       End Sub ' boldToolStripMenuItem_Click
128
129       ' toggle checkmark and toggle italic style
130       Private Sub italicToolStripMenuItem_Click( _
131          ByVal sender As System.Object, ByVal e As System.EventArgs) _
132          Handles italicToolStripMenuItem.Click
133          ' toggle menu item checkmark
134          italicToolStripMenuItem.Checked = _
135             Not italicToolStripMenuItem.Checked
136
137          ' use Xor to toggle italic, keep all other styles
138          lblDisplay.Font = New Font(lblDisplay.Font.FontFamily, 14, _
139             lblDisplay.Font.Style Xor FontStyle.Italic)
140       End Sub ' italicToolStripMenuItem_Click
141    End Class ' FrmMenuTest
```

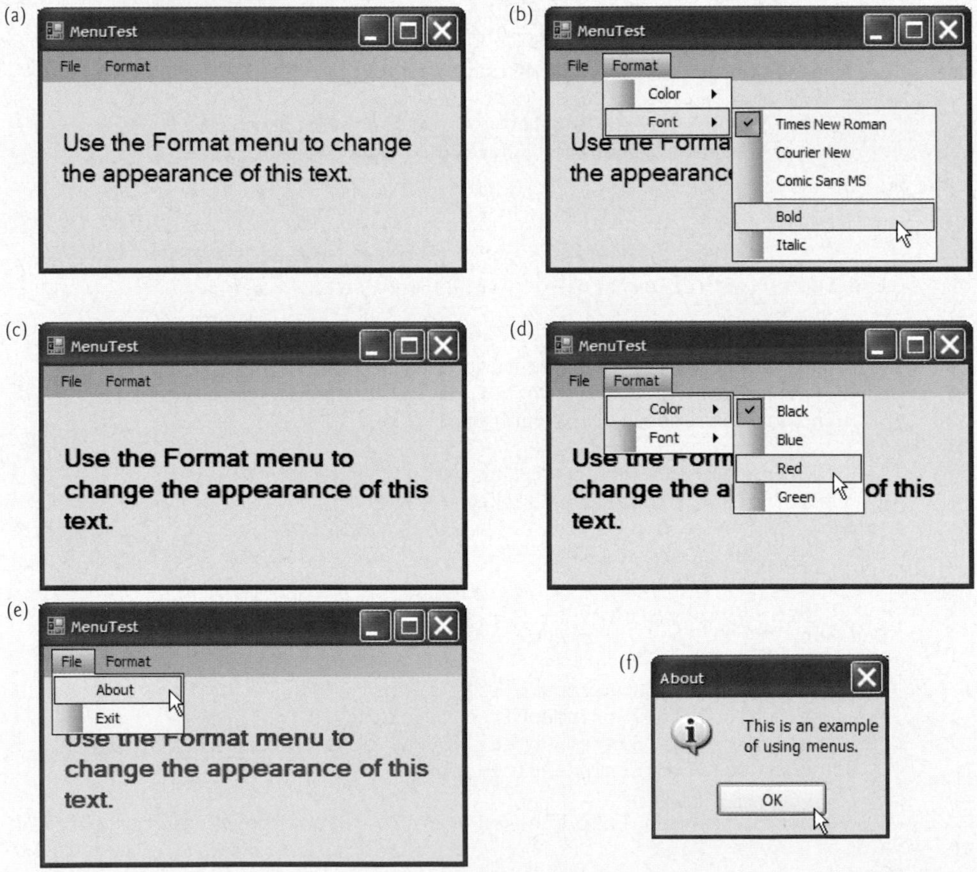

Fig. 14.7 | Menus for changing text font and color. (Part 4 of 4.)

To create this GUI, begin by dragging the MenuStrip from the **ToolBox** onto the Form. Then use **Design** mode to create the menu structure shown in the sample outputs. The **File** menu (fileToolStripMenuItem) has menu items **About** (aboutToolStripMenuItem) and **Exit** (exitToolStripMenuItem); the **Format** menu (formatToolStripMenuItem) has two submenus. The first submenu, **Color** (colorToolStripMenuItem), contains menu items **Black** (blackToolStripMenuItem), **Blue** (blueToolStripMenuItem), **Red** (redToolStripMenuItem) and **Green** (greenToolStripMenuItem). The second submenu, **Font** (fontToolStripMenuItem), contains menu items **Times New Roman** (timesToolStripMenuItem), **Courier New** (courierToolStripMenuItem), **Comic Sans MS** (comicToolStripMenuItem), a separator bar (dashToolStripMenuItem), **Bold** (boldToolStripMenuItem) and **Italic** (italicToolStripMenuItem).

The **About** menu item in the **File** menu displays a MessageBox when clicked (lines 6–12). The **Exit** menu item closes the application through Shared method **Exit** of class Application (line 19). Class Application's Shared methods control program execution. Method Exit causes our application to terminate.

We made the items in the **Color** submenu (**Black**, **Blue**, **Red** and **Green**) mutually exclusive—the user can select only one at a time (we explain how we did this shortly). To indicate that a menu item is selected, we will set each **Color** menu item's Checked property to True. This causes a check to appear to the left of a menu item.

Each **Color** menu item has its own Click event handler. The event handler for color **Black** is blackToolStripMenuItem_Click (lines 32–39). Similarly, the event handlers for colors **Blue**, **Red** and **Green** are blueToolStripMenuItem_Click (lines 42–49), redToolStripMenuItem_Click (lines 52–59) and greenToolStripMenuItem_Click (lines 62–69), respectively. The **Color** menu items must be mutually exclusive, so each event handler calls method ClearColor (lines 23–29) before setting its corresponding Checked property to True. Method ClearColor sets the Checked property of each color MenuItem to False, effectively preventing more than one menu item from being selected at a time. In the designer, we initially set the **Black** menu item's Checked property to True, because at the start of the program, the text on the Form is black.

Software Engineering Observation 14.1

The mutual exclusion of menu items is not enforced by the MenuStrip. You must program this behavior.

The **Font** menu contains three menu items for fonts (**Times New Roman**, **Courier New** and **Comic Sans MS**) and two menu items for font styles (**Bold** and **Italic**). We added a separator bar between the font and font-style menu items to indicate that these are separate options. A Font object can specify only one font at a time but can set multiple styles at once (e.g., a font can be both bold and italic). We set the font menu items to display checks. As with the **Color** menu, we must enforce mutual exclusion of these items in our event handlers.

Event handlers for font menu items **Times New Roman**, **Courier New** and **Comic Sans MS** are timesToolStripMenuItem_Click (lines 79–89), courierToolStripMenuItem_Click (lines 92–102) and comicToolStripMenuItem_Click (lines 105–115), respectively. These event handlers behave in a manner similar to that of the event handlers for the **Color** menu items. Each event handler clears the Checked properties for all the font menu items by calling method ClearFont (lines 72–76), then sets to True the Checked property of the menu item that raised the event. This enforces the mutual exclusion of the font menu items. In the designer, we initially set the **Times New Roman** menu item's Checked property to True, because this is the original font for the text on the Form. The event handlers for the **Bold** and **Italic** menu items (lines 118–127 and 130–140) use the Xor operator to combine font styles, as we discussed in Chapter 13.

14.3 MonthCalendar Control

Many applications manipulate dates and times. The .NET Framework provides two controls that allow an application to retrieve date and time information—MonthCalendar and DateTimePicker (Section 14.4).

The MonthCalendar control (Fig. 14.8) displays a monthly calendar on the Form. The user can select a date from the currently displayed month or can use the provided links to navigate to another month. When a date is selected, it is highlighted. Multiple dates can be selected by clicking dates on the calendar while holding down the *Shift* key. The default event for this control is **DateChanged**, which is generated when a new date is selected. Properties are provided that allow you to modify the appearance of the calendar, how many dates can be selected at once, and the minimum and maximum dates that may be selected. MonthCalendar properties and a common event are summarized in Fig. 14.9.

Fig. 14.8 | MonthCalendar control.

MonthCalendar properties and an event	Description
MonthCalendar Properties	
FirstDayOfWeek	Sets which day of the week is the first displayed for each week in the calendar.
MaxDate	The last date that can be selected.
MaxSelectionCount	The maximum number of dates that can be selected at once.
MinDate	The first date that can be selected.

Fig. 14.9 | MonthCalendar properties and an event. (Part 1 of 2.)

MonthCalendar properties and an event	Description
MonthlyBoldedDates	An array of dates that will displayed in bold in the calendar.
SelectionEnd	The last of the dates selected by the user.
SelectionRange	The dates selected by the user.
SelectionStart	The first of the dates selected by the user.
Common MonthCalendar Event	
DateChanged	Generated when a date is selected in the calendar.

Fig. 14.9 | MonthCalendar properties and an event. (Part 2 of 2.)

14.4 DateTimePicker Control

The **DateTimePicker** control (see output of Fig. 14.11) is similar to the MonthCalendar control, but displays the calendar when the user clicks the down arrow. The DateTimePicker can be used to retrieve date and time information from the user. The DateTimePicker is also more customizable than a MonthCalendar control—more properties are provided to edit the look-and-feel of the drop-down calendar. Property **Format** specifies the user's selection options using the **DateTimePickerFormat** enumeration. The values in this enumeration are **Long** (displays the date in long format, as in **Friday, July 1, 2005**), **Short** (displays the date in short format, as in **7/1/2005**), **Time** (displays a time value, as in **11:48:02 PM**) and **Custom** (indicates that a custom format will be used). If value Custom is used, the display in the DateTimePicker is specified using property **CustomFormat**. The default event for this control is **ValueChanged**, which occurs when the selected value (whether a date or a time) is changed. DateTimePicker properties and a common event are summarized in Fig. 14.10.

DateTimePicker properties and an event	Description
DateTimePicker Properties	
CalendarForeColor	Sets the text color for the calendar.
CalendarMonth-Background	Sets the calendar's background color.
CustomFormat	Sets the custom format string for the user's options.
Format	Sets the format of the date and/or time used for the user's options.
MaxDate	The maximum date and time that can be selected.

Fig. 14.10 | DateTimePicker properties and an event. (Part 1 of 2.)

DateTimePicker properties and an event	Description
MinDate	The minimum date and time that can be selected.
ShowCheckBox	Indicates whether a CheckBox should be displayed to the left of the selected date and time.
ShowUpDown	Used to indicate that the control should have up and down Buttons. This is helpful for instances when the DateTimePicker is used to select a time—the Buttons can be used to increase or decrease hour, minute and second values.
Value	The data selected by the user.
Common DateTimePicker Event	
ValueChanged	Generated when the Value property changes, including when the user selects a new date or time.

Fig. 14.10 | DateTimePicker properties and an event. (Part 2 of 2.)

Figure 14.11 demonstrates using the DateTimePicker control to select an item's drop-off date. Many companies use such functionality. For instance, several online DVD-rental companies specify the day a movie is sent out, and the estimated time that the movie will arrive at your home. In this application, the user selects a drop-off day, and then an estimated arrival date is displayed. The date is always two days after drop off, three days if a Sunday is reached (mail is not delivered on Sunday).

```vb
1   ' Fig. 14.11: FrmDateTimePickerForm.vb
2   ' Using a DateTimePicker to select a drop off date.
3   Public Class FrmDateTimePickerTest
4      ' set DateTimePicker's MinDate and MaxDate properties
5      Private Sub FrmDateTimePickerTest_Load(ByVal sender As System.Object, _
6         ByVal e As System.EventArgs) Handles MyBase.Load
7         ' user cannot select days before today
8         dropOffDateTimePicker.MinDate = DateTime.Today
9
10        ' user can select days up to one year from now
11        dropOffDateTimePicker.MaxDate = DateTime.Today.AddYears(1)
12     End Sub ' FrmDateTimePickerTest_Load
13
14     ' display delivery date
15     Private Sub dropOffDateTimePicker_ValueChanged( _
16        ByVal sender As System.Object, ByVal e As System.EventArgs) _
17        Handles dropOffDateTimePicker.ValueChanged
18
19        Dim dropOffDate As DateTime = dropOffDateTimePicker.Value
20
```

Fig. 14.11 | Demonstrating DateTimePicker. (Part 1 of 2.)

```
21          ' add an extra day when items are dropped off Friday-Sunday
22        If dropOffDate.DayOfWeek = DayOfWeek.Friday Or _
23           dropOffDate.DayOfWeek = DayOfWeek.Saturday Or _
24           dropOffDate.DayOfWeek = DayOfWeek.Sunday Then
25           ' estimate three days for delivery
26           lblOutput.Text = dropOffDate.AddDays(3).ToLongDateString()
27        Else ' otherwise estimate only two days for delivery
28           lblOutput.Text = dropOffDate.AddDays(2).ToLongDateString()
29        End If
30     End Sub ' dateTimePickerDropOff_ValueChanged
31  End Class ' FrmDateTimePickerTest
```

Fig. 14.11 | Demonstrating DateTimePicker. (Part 2 of 2.)

The DateTimePicker (dropOffDateTimePicker) has its Format property set to Long, so the user can select a date and not a time in this application. When the user selects a date, the ValueChanged event occurs. The event handler for this event (lines 15–30) first retrieves the selected date from the DateTimePicker's **Value** property (line 19). Lines 22–24 use the DateTime structure's **DayOfWeek** property to determine the day of the week on which the selected date falls. The day values are represented using the **DayOfWeek** enumeration. Lines 26 and 28 use DateTime's **AddDays** method to increase the date by three days or two days, respectively. Then a string representing the delivery date is obtained by calling method **ToLongDateString**.

In this application, we do not want the user to be able to select a drop-off day before the current day, or one that is more than a year into the future. To enforce this, we set the DateTimePicker's **MinDate** and **MaxDate** properties when the Form is loaded (lines 8 and

11). Property Today returns the current day, and method **AddYears** (with an argument of 1) is used to specify a date one year in the future.

Let's take a closer look at the output. This application begins by displaying the current date (Fig. 14.11(a)). In Fig. 14.11(b), we select the 12th of July. In Fig. 14.11(c), the estimated arrival date is displayed as the 14th. Figure 14.11(d) shows that the 12th, after it is selected, is highlighted in the calendar.

14.5 LinkLabel Control

The LinkLabel control displays links to other resources, such as files or Web pages (Fig. 14.12). A LinkLabel appears as underlined text (colored blue by default). When the mouse moves over the link, the pointer changes to a hand; this is similar to the behavior of a hyperlink in a Web page. The link can change color to indicate whether the link is new, previously visited or active. When clicked, the LinkLabel generates a LinkClicked event. Class LinkLabel is derived from class Label and therefore inherits all of class Label's functionality. Figure 14.13 lists several LinkLabel properties and a common event.

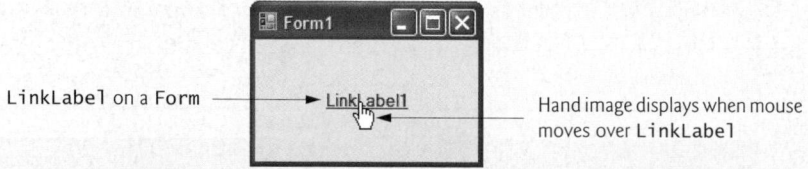

Fig. 14.12 | LinkLabel control in running program.

LinkLabel properties and an event	Description
Common Properties	
ActiveLinkColor	Specifies the color of the link when clicked.
LinkArea	Specifies which portion of text in the LinkLabel is part of the link.
LinkBehavior	Specifies the link's behavior, such as how the link appears when the mouse is placed over it.
LinkColor	Specifies the original color of all links before they have been visited. The default color is set by the system, but is usually blue.
LinkVisited	If True, the link appears as though it has been visited (its color is changed to that specified by property VisitedLinkColor). The default value is False.
Text	Specifies the control's text.
UseMnemonic	If True, the & character can be used in the Text property to create a shortcut (similar to the *Alt* shortcut in menus).

Fig. 14.13 | LinkLabel properties and an event. (Part 1 of 2.)

LinkLabel properties and an event	Description
VisitedLinkColor	Specifies the color of visited links. The default color is set by the system, but is usually purple.
Common Event (event argument type is LinkLabelLinkClickedEventArgs*)*	
LinkClicked	Generated when the link is clicked.

Fig. 14.13 | LinkLabel properties and an event. (Part 2 of 2.)

Look-and-Feel Observation 14.3

A LinkLabel *is the preferred control for indicating that the user can click a link to jump to a resource such as a Web page, though other controls can perform similar tasks.*

Class FrmLinkLabelTest (Fig. 14.14) uses three LinkLabels to link to the C: drive, the Deitel Web site (www.deitel.com) and the Notepad application, respectively. The Text properties of the LinkLabel's lnklblCDrive, lnklblDeitel and lnklblNotepad describe each link's purpose.

```
1   ' Fig. 14.14: FrmLinkLabelTest.vb
2   ' Using LinkLabels to create hyperlinks.
3   Public Class FrmLinkLabelTest
4      ' browse C:\ drive
5      Private Sub lnklblCDrive_LinkClicked(ByVal sender As System.Object, _
6         ByVal e As System.Windows.Forms.LinkLabelLinkClickedEventArgs) _
7         Handles lnklblCDrive.LinkClicked
8
9         lnklblCDrive.LinkVisited = True ' change LinkColor after click
10        System.Diagnostics.Process.Start("C:\")
11     End Sub ' lnklblCDrive_LinkClicked
12
13        ' browse www.deitel.com in Internet Explorer
14     Private Sub lnklblDeitel_LinkClicked(ByVal sender As System.Object, _
15        ByVal e As System.Windows.Forms.LinkLabelLinkClickedEventArgs) _
16        Handles lnklblDeitel.LinkClicked
17
18        lnklblDeitel.LinkVisited = True ' change LinkColor after click
19        System.Diagnostics.Process.Start( _
20           "IExplore", "http://www.deitel.com")
21     End Sub ' lnklblDeitel_LinkClicked
22
23        ' run the Notepad application
24     Private Sub lnklblNotepad_LinkClicked(ByVal sender As System.Object, _
25        ByVal e As System.Windows.Forms.LinkLabelLinkClickedEventArgs) _
26        Handles lnklblNotepad.LinkClicked
27
```

Fig. 14.14 | LinkLabels used to link to a drive, a Web page and an application. (Part 1 of 2.)

```
28        lnklblNotepad.LinkVisited = True ' change LinkColor after click
29        System.Diagnostics.Process.Start("notepad")
30     End Sub ' lnklblNotepad_LinkClicked
31  End Class ' FrmLinkLabelTest
```

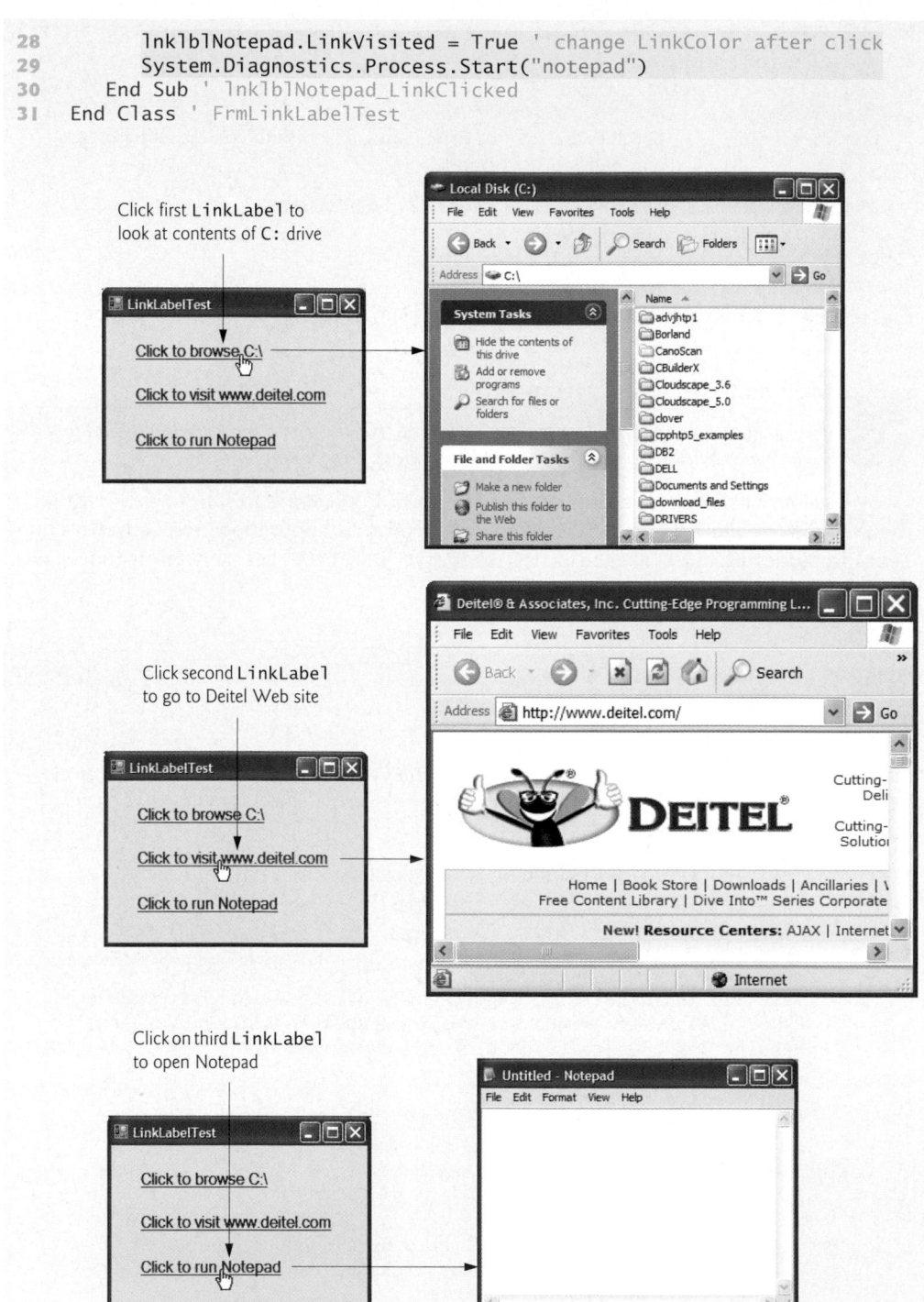

Fig. 14.14 | LinkLabels used to link to a drive, a Web page and an application. (Part 2 of 2.)

The event handlers for the LinkLabels call method Start of class Process (namespace System.Diagnostics), which allows you to execute other programs from an application. Method Start can take one argument, the file to open (a String), or two arguments, the application to run and its command-line arguments (two Strings). Method Start's arguments can be in the same form as if they were provided for input to the Windows **Run** command (**Start > Run...**). For applications that are known to Windows (such as Notepad), full path names are not required, and the .exe extension often can be omitted. To open a file that has a file type that Windows recognizes, simply use the file's full path name. The Windows operating system must be able to use the application associated with the given file's extension to open the file.

The event handler for lnklblCDrive's LinkClicked event browses the C: drive (lines 5–11). Line 9 sets the LinkVisited property to True, which changes the link's color from blue to purple (the LinkVisited colors can be configured through the **Properties** window in Visual Studio). The event handler then passes "C:\" to method Start (line 10), which opens a **Windows Explorer** window.

The event handler for lnklblDeitel's LinkClicked event (lines 14–21) opens the Web page www.deitel.com in Internet Explorer. We achieve this by passing the Web page address as a String (lines 19–20), which opens Internet Explorer. Line 18 sets the LinkVisited property to True.

The event handler for lnklblNotepad's LinkClicked event (lines 24–30) opens the Notepad application. Line 28 sets the LinkVisited property to True so that the link appears as a visited link. Line 29 passes the argument "notepad" to method Start, which runs notepad.exe. Note that in line 29, the .exe extension is not required—Windows can determine whether it recognizes the argument given to method Start as an executable file.

14.6 ListBox Control

The ListBox control allows the user to view and select from multiple items in a list. The CheckedListBox control (Section 14.7) extends a ListBox by including CheckBoxes next to each item in the list. This allows users to place checks on multiple items at once, as is possible with CheckBox controls. (Users also can select multiple items from a ListBox by setting the ListBox's SelectionMode property, which is discussed shortly.) Figure 14.15 displays a ListBox and a CheckedListBox. In both controls, scrollbars appear if the number of items exceeds the ListBox's viewable area.

Figure 14.16 lists common ListBox properties and methods, and a common event. The SelectionMode property determines the number of items that can be selected. This property has the possible values None, One, MultiSimple and MultiExtended (from the SelectionMode enumeration)—the differences among these settings are explained in Fig. 14.16. The SelectedIndexChanged event occurs when the user selects a new item.

Both the ListBox and CheckedListBox have properties Items, SelectedItem and SelectedIndex. Property Items returns all the list items as a collection. Collections are a common way of managing lists of Objects in the .NET framework. Many .NET GUI components (e.g., ListBoxes) use collections to expose lists of internal objects (e.g., items contained within a ListBox). We discuss collections further in Chapter 26. The collection returned by property Items is represented as an object of type ObjectCollection. Property SelectedItem returns the ListBox's currently selected item. If the user can select multiple items, use collection SelectedItems to obtain all the selected items as a collection.

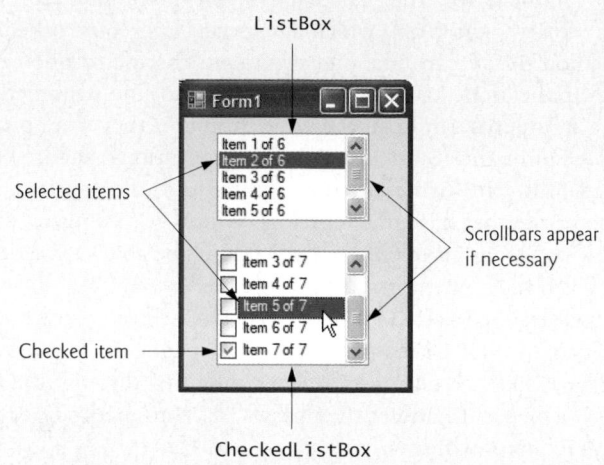

Fig. 14.15 | ListBox and CheckedListBox on a Form.

ListBox properties, methods and an event	Description
Common Properties	
Items	The collection of items in the ListBox.
MultiColumn	Indicates whether the ListBox can break a list into multiple columns, which eliminates vertical scrollbars from the display.
SelectedIndex	Returns the index of the selected item, or -1 if no items have been selected. If the user selects multiple items, this property returns only one of the selected indices. For this reason, if multiple items are selected, you should use property SelectedIndices.
SelectedIndices	Returns a collection containing the indices of all selected items.
SelectedItem	Returns a reference to the selected item. If multiple items are selected, it returns the item with the lowest index number.
SelectedItems	Returns a collection of the selected item(s).
SelectionMode	Determines the number of items that can be selected and the means through which multiple items can be selected. Values None, One, MultiSimple (multiple selection allowed) or MultiExtended (multiple selection allowed using a combination of arrow keys or mouse clicks and *Shift* and *Ctrl* keys).
Sorted	Indicates whether items are sorted alphabetically. Setting this property's value to True sorts the items. The default value is False.

Fig. 14.16 | ListBox properties, methods and an event. (Part 1 of 2.)

ListBox properties, methods and an event	Description
Common Methods	
ClearSelected	Deselects all items in the ListBox.
GetSelected	Takes an index as an argument, and returns True if the corresponding item is selected.
Common Event	
SelectedIndexChanged	Generated when the selected index changes.

Fig. 14.16 | ListBox properties, methods and an event. (Part 2 of 2.)

Property **SelectedIndex** returns the index of the selected item—if there could be more than one, use property **SelectedIndices**. If no items are selected, property Selected-Index returns -1. Method **GetSelected** takes an index and returns True if the corresponding item is selected.

To add items to a ListBox or to a CheckedListBox, we must add objects to its Items collection. This can be accomplished by calling method Add to add a String to the ListBox's or CheckedListBox's Items collection. For example, we could write

> *myListBox*.Items.Add(*myListItem*)

to add String *myListItem* to ListBox *myListBox*. To add multiple objects, you can either call method Add multiple times or call method AddRange to add an array of objects. Classes ListBox and CheckedListBox each call the submitted object's ToString method to determine the Label for the corresponding object's entry in the list. This allows you to add non-String objects to a ListBox or a CheckedListBox that later can be returned through properties SelectedItem and SelectedItems.

Alternatively, you can add items to ListBoxes and CheckedListBoxes visually by examining the Items property in the **Properties** window. Clicking the ellipsis button opens the **String Collection Editor**, which contains a text area for adding items; each item appears on a separate line (Fig. 14.17). Visual Studio then writes code to add these Strings to the Items collection inside method InitializeComponent in the Form's Designer.vb file.

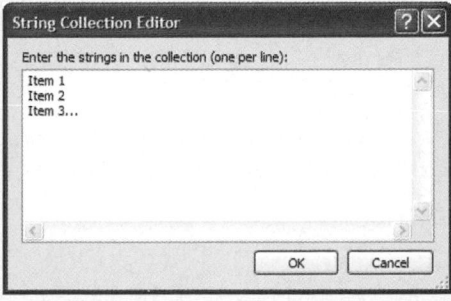

Fig. 14.17 | String Collection Editor.

Figure 14.18 uses class FrmListBoxTest to add, remove and clear items from ListBox lstDisplay. Class FrmListBoxTest uses TextBox txtInput to allow the user to enter new items. When the user clicks the **Add** Button, the new item appears in lstDisplay. Similarly, if the user selects an item and clicks **Remove**, the item is deleted. When clicked, **Clear** deletes all entries in lstDisplay. The user terminates the application by clicking **Exit**.

The btnAdd_Click event handler (lines 6–11) calls method **Add** of the ListBox's Items collection. This method takes an Object as the item to add to lstDisplay. In this case, the Object used is the text entered by the user—txtInput.Text (line 9). After the item is added, txtInput.Text is cleared (line 10).

The btnRemove_Click event handler (lines 14–21) uses method **RemoveAt** to remove an item from the ListBox. Lines 18–20 first use property SelectedIndex to determine which index is selected. If SelectedIndex is not –1 (i.e., an item is selected) line 19 removes the item that corresponds to the selected index.

```
1   ' Fig. 14.18: FrmListBoxTest.vb
2   ' Program to add, remove and clear ListBox items
3   Public Class FrmListBoxTest
4      ' add to lstDisplay the item the user enters in txtInput,
5      ' then clear txtInput
6      Private Sub btnAdd_Click(ByVal sender As System.Object, _
7         ByVal e As System.EventArgs) Handles btnAdd.Click
8
9         lstDisplay.Items.Add(txtInput.Text)
10        txtInput.Clear()
11     End Sub ' btnAdd_Click
12
13     ' remove an item from lstDisplay if one is selected
14     Private Sub btnRemove_Click(ByVal sender As System.Object, _
15        ByVal e As System.EventArgs) Handles btnRemove.Click
16
17        ' if an item is selected, remove that item
18        If lstDisplay.SelectedIndex <> -1 Then
19           lstDisplay.Items.RemoveAt(lstDisplay.SelectedIndex)
20        End If
21     End Sub ' btnRemove_Click
22
23     ' clear all the items in lstDisplay
24     Private Sub btnClear_Click(ByVal sender As System.Object, _
25        ByVal e As System.EventArgs) Handles btnClear.Click
26
27        lstDisplay.Items.Clear()
28     End Sub ' btnClear_Click
29
30     ' terminate the application
31     Private Sub btnExit_Click(ByVal sender As System.Object, _
32        ByVal e As System.EventArgs) Handles btnExit.Click
33
34        Application.Exit()
35     End Sub ' btnExit_Click
36  End Class ' FrmListBoxTest
```

Fig. 14.18 | Program that adds, removes and clears ListBox items. (Part 1 of 2.)

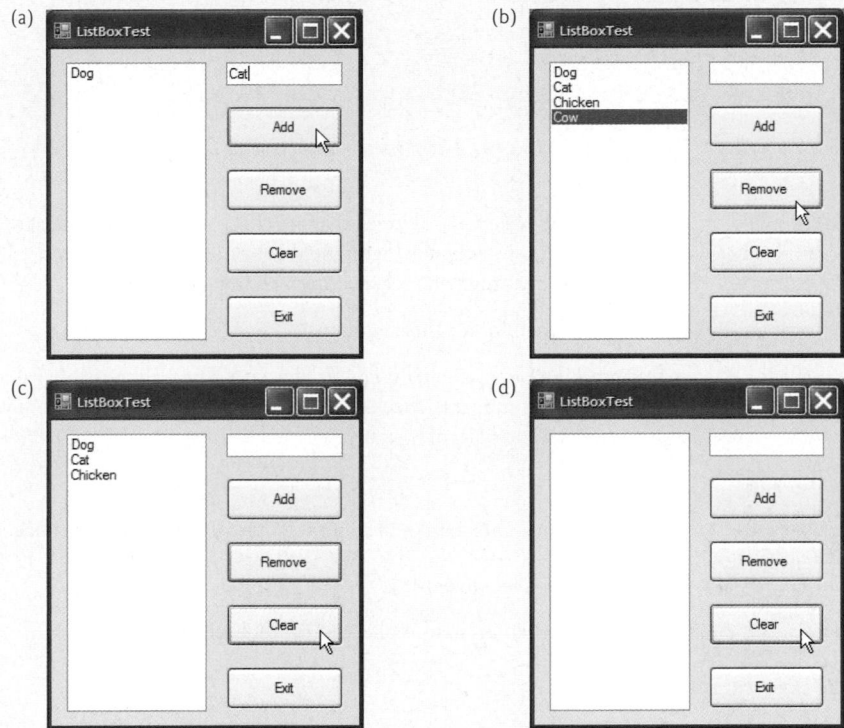

Fig. 14.18 | Program that adds, removes and clears ListBox items. (Part 2 of 2.)

The btnClear_Click event handler (lines 24–28) calls method Clear of the Items collection (line 27) to remove all the entries in lstDisplay. Finally, event handler btnExit_Click (lines 31–35) terminates the application by calling method Application.Exit (line 34).

14.7 CheckedListBox Control

The CheckedListBox control derives from class ListBox and includes a CheckBox next to each item. As in ListBoxes, items can be added via methods Add and AddRange or through the **String Collection Editor**. CheckedListBoxes imply that multiple items can be selected, and the only possible values for the SelectionMode property are None and One. One allows multiple selection, because CheckBoxes imply that there are no logical restrictions on the items—the user can select as many items as required. Thus, the only choice is whether to give the user multiple selection or no selection at all. This keeps the CheckedListBox's behavior consistent with that of CheckBoxes. Figure 14.19 lists some common properties, a common method and a common event of class CheckedListBox.

Common Programming Error 14.1

*The IDE displays an error message if you attempt to set the SelectionMode property to Multi-Simple or MultiExtended in the **Properties** window of a CheckedListBox. If this value is set programmatically, a runtime error occurs.*

CheckedListBox properties, methods and an event	Description
Common Properties	*(All the ListBox properties, methods and events are inherited by CheckedListBox.)*
CheckedItems	Contains the collection of items that are checked. This is distinct from the selected item, which is highlighted (but not necessarily checked). There can be at most one selected item at any given time.
CheckedIndices	Returns indices for all checked items.
SelectionMode	Determines how many items can be checked. The only possible values are One (allows multiple checks to be placed) or None (does not allow any checks to be placed).
Common Method	
GetItemChecked	Takes an index and returns True if the corresponding item is checked.
Common Event (Event arguments ItemCheckEventArgs)	
ItemCheck	Generated when an item is checked or unchecked.
ItemCheckEventArgs Properties	
CurrentValue	Indicates whether the current item is checked or unchecked. Possible values are Checked, Unchecked and Indeterminate.
Index	Returns the zero-based index of the item that changed.
NewValue	Specifies the new state of the item.

Fig. 14.19 | CheckedListBox properties, a method and an event.

Event **ItemCheck** occurs when a user checks or unchecks a CheckedListBox item. Event argument properties CurrentValue and NewValue return CheckState values for the current and new state of the item, respectively. A comparison of these values allows you to determine whether the CheckedListBox item was checked or unchecked. The CheckedListBox control inherits the SelectedItems and SelectedIndices properties from class ListBox. It also includes properties CheckedItems and CheckedIndices, which return information about the checked items and indices.

In Fig. 14.20, class FrmCheckedListBoxTest uses a CheckedListBox and a ListBox to display a user's book selections. The CheckedListBox allows the user to select multiple titles. In the **String Collection Editor**, we added items for some Deitel books—C++, Java, Visual Basic, Internet & WWW, Perl, Python, Wireless Internet and Advanced Java (the acronym HTP stands for "How to Program"). The ListBox (named lstDisplay) displays the user's selections.

When the user checks or unchecks an item in chklstInput, an ItemCheck event occurs and event handler chklstItem_ItemCheck (lines 5–20) executes. An If...Else statement (lines 15–19) determines whether the user checked or unchecked an item in the

```
 1    ' Fig. 14.20: FrmCheckedListBoxTest.vb
 2    ' Using the checked ListBox to add items to a display ListBox
 3    Public Class FrmCheckedListBoxTest
 4       ' add an item to or remove an item from lstDisplay
 5       Private Sub chklstItem_ItemCheck( _
 6          ByVal sender As System.Object, _
 7          ByVal e As System.Windows.Forms.ItemCheckEventArgs) _
 8          Handles chklstItem.ItemCheck
 9
10          ' obtain selected item
11          Dim item As String = chklstItem.SelectedItem.ToString()
12
13          ' if the selected item is checked add it to lstDisplay;
14          ' otherwise, remove it from lstDisplay
15          If e.NewValue = CheckState.Checked Then
16             lstDisplay.Items.Add(item)
17          Else
18             lstDisplay.Items.Remove(item)
19          End If
20       End Sub ' chklstItem_ItemCheck
21    End Class ' FrmCheckedListBoxTest
```

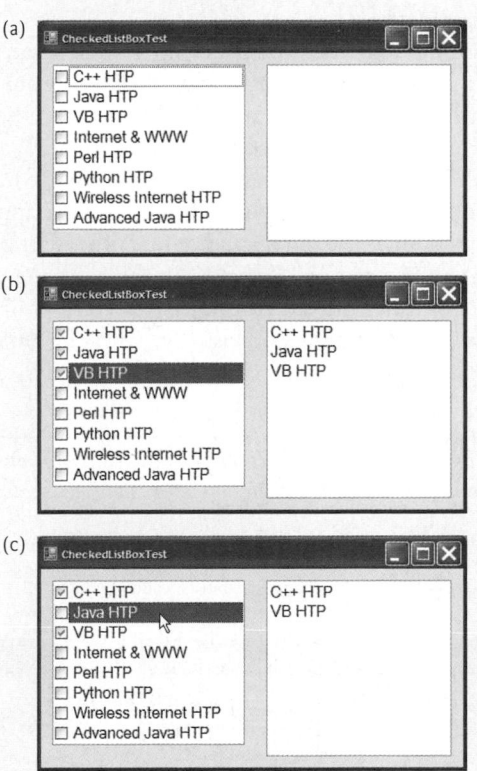

Fig. 14.20 | CheckedListBox and ListBox used in a program to display a user selection. (Part 1 of 2.)

(d)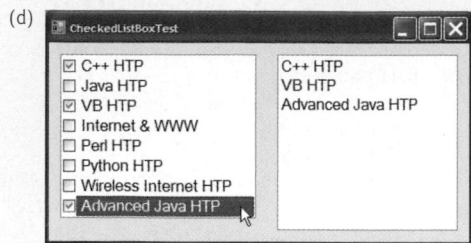

Fig. 14.20 | CheckedListBox and ListBox used in a program to display a user selection. (Part 2 of 2.)

CheckedListBox. Line 15 uses the ItemCheckEventArgs property NewValue to determine whether the item is being checked (CheckState.Checked). If the user checks an item, line 16 adds the checked entry to lstDisplay. If the user unchecks an item, line 18 removes the corresponding item from lstDisplay. This event handler was created by selecting the CheckedListBox in **Design** mode, viewing the control's events in the **Properties** window and double clicking the ItemCheck event.

14.8 ComboBox Control

The **ComboBox** control combines TextBox features with a **drop-down list**—a GUI component that contains a list from which a value can be selected. A ComboBox usually appears as a TextBox with a down arrow to its right. By default, the user can enter text into the Text-Box or click the down arrow to display a list of predefined items. If a user chooses an element from this list, that element is displayed in the TextBox. If the list contains more elements than can be displayed in the drop-down list, a scrollbar appears. The maximum number of items that a drop-down list can display at one time is set by property **MaxDrop-DownItems**. Figure 14.21 shows a sample ComboBox in three different states.

As with the ListBox control, you can add objects to collection Items programmatically, using methods Add and AddRange, or visually, with the **String Collection Editor**. Figure 14.22 lists common properties and a common event of class ComboBox.

Look-and-Feel Observation 14.4

Use a ComboBox to save space on a GUI. It has the disadvantage, however, that unlike with a ListBox, the user cannot see available items without expanding the drop-down list.

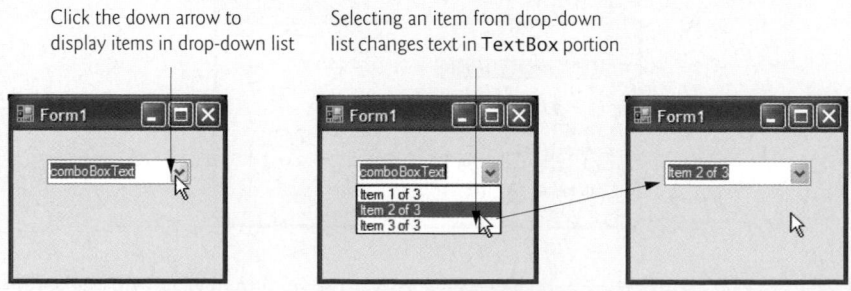

Click the down arrow to display items in drop-down list

Selecting an item from drop-down list changes text in **TextBox** portion

Fig. 14.21 | ComboBox demonstration.

ComboBox properties and an event	Description
Common Properties	
DropDownStyle	Determines the ComboBox type. Value Simple means that the text portion is editable, and the list portion is always visible. Value DropDown (the default) means that the text portion is editable, but the user must click an arrow button to see the list portion. Value DropDownList means that the text portion is not editable, and the user must click the arrow button to see the list portion.
Items	The collection of items in the ComboBox control.
MaxDropDownItems	Specifies the maximum number of items (between 1 and 100) that the drop-down list can display. If the number of items exceeds the maximum number of items to display, a scrollbar appears.
SelectedIndex	Returns the index of the selected item, or -1 if there is no selected item.
SelectedItem	Returns a reference to the selected item.
Sorted	Indicates whether items are sorted alphabetically. Setting this property's value to True sorts the items. The default is False.
Common Event	
SelectedIndexChanged	Generated when the selected index changes (such as when a different item is selected). This is the default event when control is double clicked in the designer.

Fig. 14.22 | ComboBox properties and an event.

Property **DropDownStyle** determines the type of ComboBox and is represented as a value of the **ComboBoxStyle** enumeration, which contains values Simple, DropDown and DropDownList. Option **Simple** does not display a drop-down arrow. Instead, a scrollbar appears next to the control, allowing the user to select a choice from the list. The user also can type in a selection. Style **DropDown** (the default) displays a drop-down list when the down arrow is clicked (or the down-arrow key is pressed). The user can type a new item in the ComboBox. The last style is **DropDownList**, which displays a drop-down list but does not allow the user to type in the ComboBox.

The ComboBox control has properties **Items** (a collection), **SelectedItem** and **SelectedIndex**, which are similar to the corresponding properties in ListBox. There can be at most one selected item in a ComboBox. If no items are selected, then SelectedIndex is -1. When the selected item changes, a **SelectedIndexChanged** event occurs.

Class FrmComboBoxTest (Fig. 14.23) allows users to select a shape to draw—circle, ellipse, square or pie (in both filled and unfilled versions)—by using a ComboBox. The ComboBox in this example is uneditable, so the user cannot type in the ComboBox.

Look-and-Feel Observation 14.5

Make lists (such as ComboBoxes) editable only if the program is designed to accept user-submitted elements. Otherwise, the user might try to enter a custom item that is improper for the purposes of your application.

After creating ComboBox cboImage, make it uneditable by setting its DropDownStyle to DropDownList in the **Properties** window. Next, add items Circle, Square, Ellipse, Pie, Filled Circle, Filled Square, Filled Ellipse and Filled Pie to the Items collection using the **String Collection Editor**. Whenever the user selects an item from cboImage,

```vb
1   ' Fig. 14.23: FrmComboBoxTest.vb
2   ' Using ComboBox to select a shape to draw.
3   Public Class FrmComboBoxTest
4      ' get index of selected shape, then draw the shape
5      Private Sub cboImage_SelectedIndexChanged( _
6         ByVal sender As System.Object, ByVal e As System.EventArgs) _
7         Handles cboImage.SelectedIndexChanged
8         ' create graphics object, Pen and SolidBrush
9         Dim myGraphics As Graphics = MyBase.CreateGraphics()
10
11        ' create Pen using color DarkRed
12        Dim myPen As Pen = New Pen(Color.DarkRed)
13
14        ' create SolidBrush using color DarkRed
15        Dim mySolidBrush As SolidBrush = New SolidBrush(Color.DarkRed)
16
17        ' clear drawing area setting it to color white
18        myGraphics.Clear(Color.White)
19
20        ' find index, draw proper shape
21        Select Case cboImage.SelectedIndex
22           Case 0 ' case Circle is selected
23              myGraphics.DrawEllipse(myPen, 50, 50, 150, 150)
24           Case 1 ' case Rectangle is selected
25              myGraphics.DrawRectangle(myPen, 50, 50, 150, 150)
26           Case 2 ' case Ellipse is selected
27              myGraphics.DrawEllipse(myPen, 50, 85, 150, 115)
28           Case 3 ' case Pie is selected
29              myGraphics.DrawPie(myPen, 50, 50, 150, 150, 0, 45)
30           Case 4 ' case Filled Circle is selected
31              myGraphics.FillEllipse(mySolidBrush, 50, 50, 150, 150)
32           Case 5 ' case Filled Rectangle is selected
33              myGraphics.FillRectangle(mySolidBrush, 50, 50, 150, 150)
34           Case 6 ' case Filled Ellipse is selected
35              myGraphics.FillEllipse(mySolidBrush, 50, 85, 150, 115)
36           Case 7 ' case Filled Pie is selected
37              myGraphics.FillPie(mySolidBrush, 50, 50, 150, 150, 0, 45)
38        End Select
39
40        myGraphics.Dispose() ' release the Graphics object
41     End Sub ' cboImage_SelectedIndexChanged
42  End Class ' FrmComboBoxTest
```

Fig. 14.23 | ComboBox used to draw a selected shape. (Part 1 of 2.)

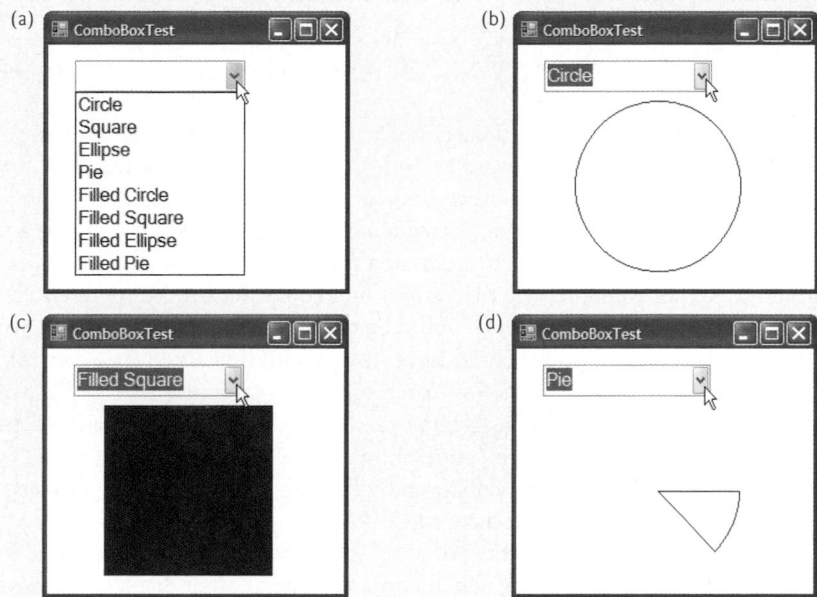

Fig. 14.23 | ComboBox used to draw a selected shape. (Part 2 of 2.)

a SelectedIndexChanged event occurs and event handler cboImage_SelectedIndex-Changed (lines 5–41) executes. Lines 9–15 create a Graphics object, a Pen and a Solid-Brush, which are used to draw on the Form. The Graphics object (line 9) allows a pen or brush to draw on a component using one of several Graphics methods. The Pen object (line 12) is used by methods DrawEllipse, DrawRectangle and DrawPie (lines 23, 25, 27 and 29) to draw the outlines of their corresponding shapes. The SolidBrush object (line 15) is used by methods FillEllipse, FillRectangle and FillPie (lines 31, 33, 35 and 37) to fill their corresponding solid shapes. Line 18 colors the entire Form White, using Graphics method **Clear**. These methods are discussed in greater detail in Chapter 17.

The application draws a shape based on the selected item's index. The Select Case statement (lines 21–38) uses cboImage.SelectedIndex to determine which item the user selected. Graphics method **DrawEllipse** (line 23) takes a Pen, the *x*- and *y*-coordinates of the center and the width and height of the ellipse to draw. The origin of the coordinate system is in the upper-left corner of the Form; the *x*-coordinate increases to the right, and the *y*-coordinate increases toward the bottom of the Form. A circle is a special case of an ellipse with equal width and height. Line 23 draws a circle. Line 27 draws an ellipse that has different values for width and height.

Class Graphics method **DrawRectangle** (line 25) takes a Pen, the *x*- and *y*-coordinates of the upper-left corner and the width and height of the rectangle to draw. Method **DrawPie** (line 29) draws a pie as a portion of an ellipse. The ellipse is bounded by a rectangle. Method DrawPie takes a Pen, the *x*- and *y*-coordinates of the upper-left corner of the rectangle, its width and height, the start angle (in degrees) and the sweep angle (in degrees) of the pie. Angles increase clockwise. The **FillEllipse** (lines 31 and 35), **FillRectangle** (line 33) and **FillPie** (line 37) methods are similar to their unfilled counterparts, except that they take a `SolidBrush` instead of a `Pen`. Some of the drawn shapes are illustrated in the screen shots of Fig. 14.23.

14.9 **TreeView Control**

The `TreeView` control displays **nodes** hierarchically in a **tree**. Traditionally, nodes are objects that contain values and can refer to other nodes. A **parent node** contains **child nodes**, and the child nodes can be parents to other nodes. Two child nodes that have the same parent node are considered **sibling nodes**. A tree is a collection of nodes, usually organized in a hierarchical manner. The first parent node of a tree is the **root** node (a `TreeView` can have multiple roots). For example, the file system of a computer can be represented as a tree. The top-level directory (perhaps `C:\`) would be the root, each subfolder of `C:\` would be a child node and each child folder could have its own children. `TreeView` controls are useful for displaying hierarchal information, such as the file structure that we just mentioned. We cover nodes and trees in greater detail in Chapter 24, Data Structures. Figure 14.24 displays a sample `TreeView` control on a `Form`.

A parent node can be expanded or collapsed by clicking the plus box or minus box to its left. Nodes without children do not have these boxes.

The nodes in a `TreeView` are instances of class **TreeNode**. Each `TreeNode` has a **Nodes** collection (type **TreeNodeCollection**), which contains a list of other `TreeNodes`—known as its children. The `Parent` property returns a reference to the parent node (or `Nothing` if the node is a root node). Figure 14.25 and Fig. 14.26 list the common properties of `Tree-Views` and `TreeNodes`, common `TreeNode` methods and a common `TreeView` event.

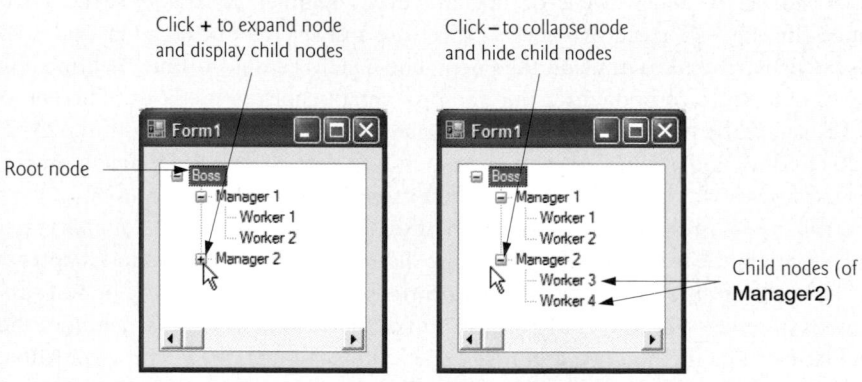

Fig. 14.24 | `TreeView` displaying a sample tree.

TreeView properties and an event	Description
Common Properties	
CheckBoxes	Indicates whether CheckBoxes appear next to nodes. A value of True displays CheckBoxes. The default value is False.

Fig. 14.25 | `TreeView` properties and an event. (Part 1 of 2.)

TreeView properties and an event	Description
ImageList	Specifies an ImageList object containing the node icons. An Image-List object is a collection that contains Image objects.
Nodes	Lists the collection of TreeNodes in the control. It contains methods Add (adds a TreeNode object), Clear (deletes the entire collection) and Remove (deletes a specific node). Removing a parent node deletes all of its children.
SelectedNode	The selected node.
Common Event (Event arguments TreeViewEventArgs)	
AfterSelect	Generated after selected node changes.

Fig. 14.25 | TreeView properties and an event. (Part 2 of 2.)

TreeNode properties and methods	Description
Common Properties	
Checked	Indicates whether the TreeNode is checked (CheckBoxes property must be set to True in the parent TreeView).
FirstNode	Specifies the first node in the Nodes collection (i.e., the first child in the tree).
FullPath	Indicates the path of the node, starting at the root of the tree.
ImageIndex	Specifies the index of the image shown when the node is deselected.
LastNode	Specifies the last node in the Nodes collection (i.e., the last child in the tree).
NextNode	Next sibling node.
Nodes	Collection of TreeNodes contained in the current node (i.e., all the children of the current node). The Nodes collection has methods Add (adds a TreeNode object), Clear (deletes the entire collection) and Remove (deletes a specific node). Removing a parent node deletes all of its children.
Parent	Parent node of the current node.
PrevNode	Previous sibling node.
SelectedImageIndex	Specifies the index of the image to use when the node is selected.
Text	Specifies the TreeNode's text.

Fig. 14.26 | TreeNode properties and methods. (Part 1 of 2.)

TreeNode properties and methods	Description
Common Methods	
Collapse	Collapses a node.
Expand	Expands a node.
ExpandAll	Expands all the children of a node.
GetNodeCount	Returns the number of child nodes.

Fig. 14.26 | TreeNode properties and methods. (Part 2 of 2.)

To add nodes to the TreeView visually, click the ellipsis next to the Nodes property in the **Properties** window. This opens the **TreeNode Editor** (Fig. 14.27), which displays an empty tree representing the TreeView. There are Buttons to create a root, and to add or delete a node. To the right are the properties of current node. Here you can rename the node.

To add nodes programmatically, first create a root node. Create a new TreeNode object and pass it a String to display. Then call method Add to add this new TreeNode to the TreeView's Nodes collection. Thus, to add a root node to TreeView *myTreeView*, write

  myTreeView.Nodes.Add(*rootLabel*)

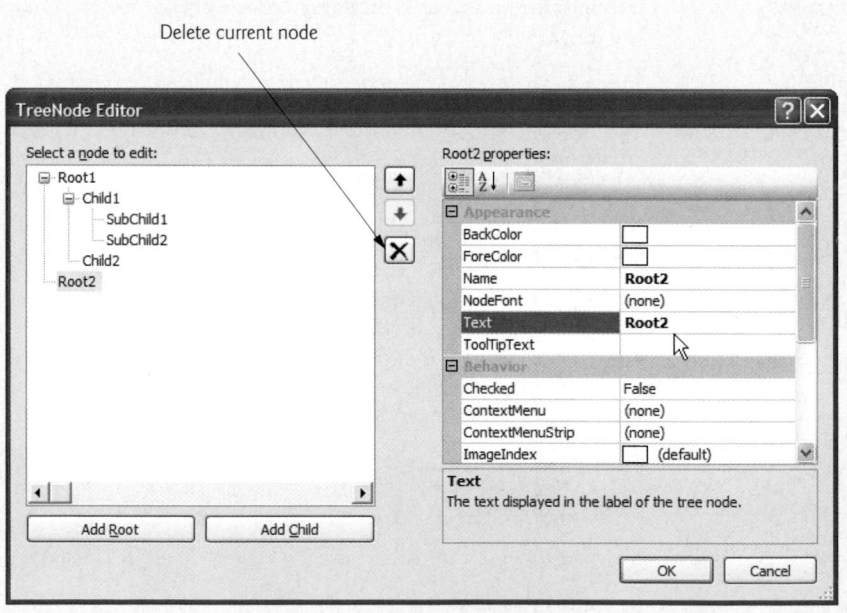

Fig. 14.27 | TreeNode Editor.

where *myTreeView* is the `TreeView` to which we are adding nodes, and *rootLabel* is the text to display in *myTreeView*. To add children to a root node, add new `TreeNodes` to its `Nodes` collection. We select the appropriate root node from the `TreeView` by writing

> *myTreeView*.`Nodes`(*myIndex*)

where *myIndex* is the root node's index in *myTreeView*'s `Nodes` collection. We add nodes to child nodes through the same process by which we added root nodes to *myTreeView*. To add a child to the root node at index *myIndex*, write

> *myTreeView*.`Nodes`(*myIndex*).`Nodes`.`Add`(*childNodeText*)

Class `FrmTreeViewDirectoryStructure` (Fig. 14.28) uses a `TreeView` to display the contents of a directory chosen by the user. A `TextBox` and a `Button` are used to specify the directory. First, enter the full path of the directory you want to display. Then click the `Button` to set the specified directory as the root node in the `TreeView`. Each subdirectory of this directory becomes a child node. This layout is similar to the one used in **Windows Explorer**. Folders can be expanded or collapsed by clicking the plus or minus boxes that appear to their left.

```vb
 1  ' Fig. 14.28: FrmTreeViewDirectoryStructure.vb
 2  ' Using TreeView to display directory structure.
 3  Imports System.IO
 4
 5  Public Class FrmTreeViewDirectoryStructure
 6     ' clear treDirectory, then call PopulateTreeView
 7     Private Sub btnEnter_Click(ByVal sender As System.Object, _
 8        ByVal e As System.EventArgs) Handles btnEnter.Click
 9
10        treDirectory.Nodes.Clear() ' clear all nodes
11
12        ' if the directory specified by the user exists, fill in the
13        ' TreeView; otherwise, display an error message
14        If (Directory.Exists(txtInput.Text)) Then
15           ' add full path name to directoryTreeView
16           treDirectory.Nodes.Add(txtInput.Text)
17
18           ' insert subfolders
19           PopulateTreeView(txtInput.Text, treDirectory.Nodes(0))
20        Else ' display error MessageBox if directory not found
21           MessageBox.Show(txtInput.Text & " could not be found.", _
22              "Directory Not Found", MessageBoxButtons.OK, _
23              MessageBoxIcon.Error)
24        End If
25     End Sub ' btnEnter
26
27     ' populate current node with subdirectories
28     Private Sub PopulateTreeView( _
29        ByVal directoryValue As String, ByVal parentNode As TreeNode)
30        ' array stores all subdirectories in the directory
31        Dim directoryArray As String() = _
32           Directory.GetDirectories(directoryValue)
```

Fig. 14.28 | `TreeView` used to display directories. (Part 1 of 2.)

```
33
34          ' populate current node with subdirectories
35          Try
36              ' check to see if any subdirectories are present
37              If directoryArray.Length <> 0 Then
38                  ' for every subdirectory, create new TreeNode,
39                  ' add as a child of current node and recursively
40                  ' populate child nodes with subdirectories
41                  For Each directory As String In directoryArray
42                      ' obtain last part of path name from the full path name
43                      ' by finding the last occurence of "\" and returning the
44                      ' part of the path name that comes after this occurrence
45                      Dim directoryName As String = directory.Substring( _
46                          directory.LastIndexOf("\") + 1)
47
48                      ' create TreeNode for current directory
49                      Dim myNode As TreeNode = New TreeNode(directoryName)
50
51                      ' add current directory node to parent node
52                      parentNode.Nodes.Add(myNode)
53
54                      ' recursively populate every subdirectory
55                      PopulateTreeView(directory, myNode)
56                  Next
57              End If
58          Catch e As UnauthorizedAccessException
59              parentNode.Nodes.Add("Access denied")
60          End Try
61      End Sub ' PopulateTreeView
62  End Class ' FrmTreeViewDirectoryStructure
```

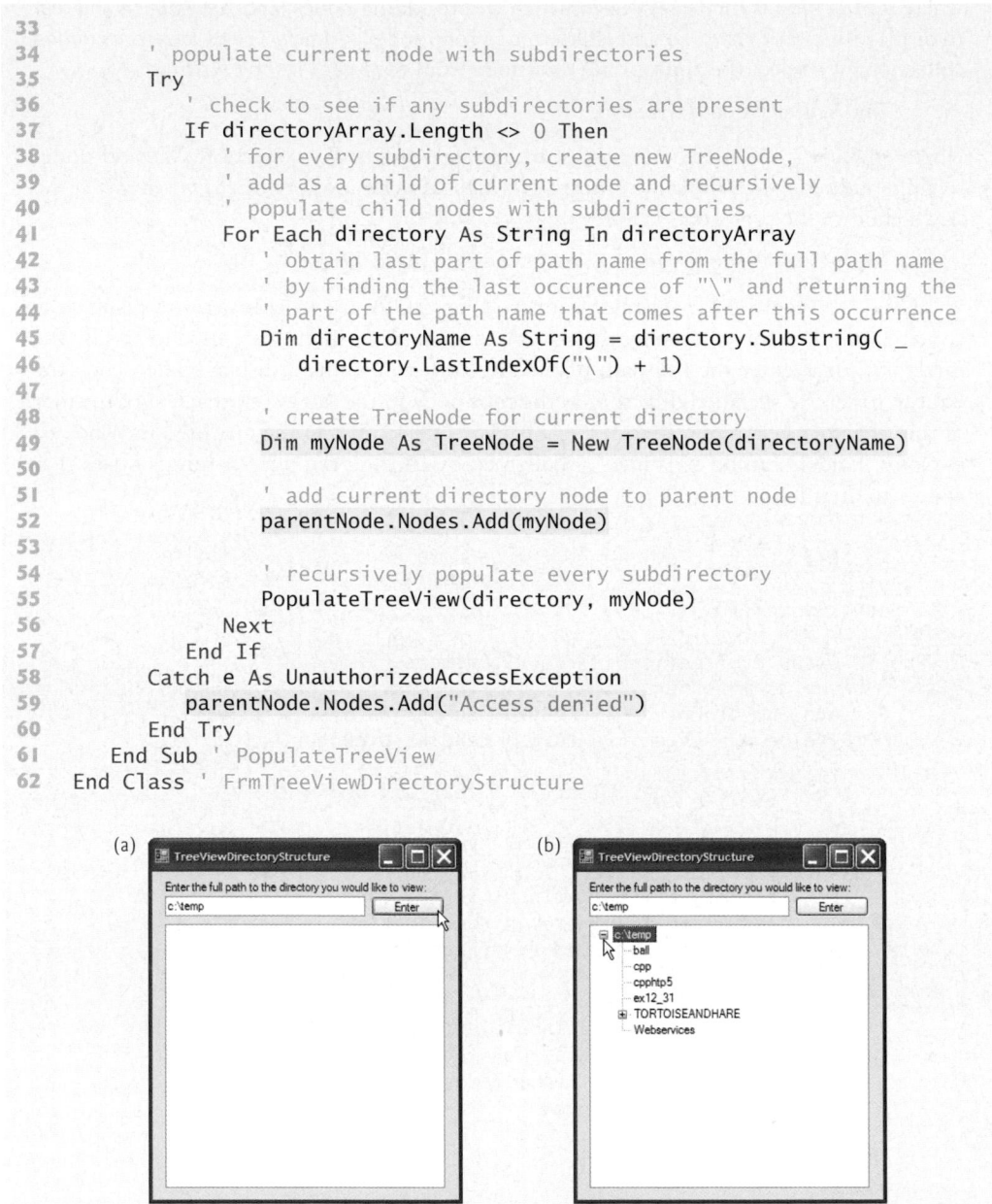

Fig. 14.28 | `TreeView` used to display directories. (Part 2 of 2.)

When the user clicks the `btnEnter`, all the nodes in `treDirectory` are cleared (line 10). Then the path entered in `txtInput` is used to create the root node. Line 16 adds the directory to `treDirectory` as the root node, and line 19 calls method `PopulateTreeView` (lines 28–61), which receives as arguments a directory (as a `String`) and a parent node (as a TreeNode). Method PopulateTreeView then creates child nodes corresponding to the subdirectories of the directory it receives as an argument.

PopulateTreeView (lines 28–61) obtains a list of subdirectories, using method **Get-Directories** of class Directory (namespace System.IO) in lines 31–32. Method GetDirectories receives the current directory (as a String) and returns an array of Strings representing its subdirectories. If a directory is not accessible for security reasons, an UnauthorizedAccessException is thrown. Lines 58–59 catch this exception and add a node containing "Access Denied."

If there are accessible subdirectories, lines 45–46 use the Substring method to increase readability by shortening the full path name to just the directory name. Next, each String in the directoryArray is used to create a new child node (line 49). We use method Add (line 52) to add each child node to the parent. PopulateTreeView calls itself recursively on each subdirectory (line 55), which eventually populates the TreeView with the entire directory structure. Note that our recursive algorithm may cause a delay when the program loads directories with many subdirectories. However, once the folder names are added to the appropriate Nodes collection, they can be expanded and collapsed without delay. In the next section, we present an alternative algorithm to solve this problem.

14.10 ListView Control

The ListView control is similar to a ListBox in that both display lists from which the user can select one or more items (an example of a ListView can be found in Fig. 14.31). The important difference between the two classes is that a ListView can display icons next to the list items (controlled by its ImageList property). Property **MultiSelect** (a Boolean) determines whether multiple items can be selected. CheckBoxes can be included by setting property **CheckBoxes** (a Boolean) to True, making the ListView similar in appearance to a CheckedListBox. The **View** property specifies the layout of the ListBox. Property **Activation** determines the method by which the user selects a list item. Figure 14.29 presents some of the ListView class's common properties and its ItemActivate event.

ListView properties and an event	Description
Common Properties	
Activation	Determines how the user activates an item. This property takes a value in the ItemActivation enumeration. Possible values are OneClick (single-click activation), TwoClick (double-click activation, item changes color when selected) and Standard (double-click activation, item does not change color).
CheckBoxes	Indicates whether items appear with CheckBoxes. True displays CheckBoxes. The default is False.
LargeImageList	Specifies the ImageList containing large icons for display.
Items	Returns the collection of ListViewItems in the control.

Fig. 14.29 | ListView properties and an event. (Part 1 of 2.)

ListView properties and an event	Description
MultiSelect	Determines whether multiple selection is allowed. The default is True, which enables multiple selection.
SelectedItems	Gets the collection of selected items.
SmallImageList	Specifies the ImageList containing small icons for display.
View	Determines appearance of ListViewItems. Possible values are LargeIcon (large icon displayed, items can be in multiple columns), SmallIcon (small icon displayed, items can be in multiple columns), List (small icons displayed, items appear in a single column), Details (like List, but multiple columns of information can be displayed per item) and Tile (large icons displayed, information provided to right of icon, valid only in Windows XP or later).
Common Event	
ItemActivate	Generated when an item in the ListView is activated. Does not contain the specifics of the item activated.

Fig. 14.29 | ListView properties and an event. (Part 2 of 2.)

ListView allows you to define the images used as icons for ListView items. To display images, an ImageList component is required. Create one by dragging it to a Form from the **ToolBox**. Then select the **Images** property in the **Properties** window to display the **Image Collection Editor** (Fig. 14.30). Here you can browse for images that you wish to add to the ImageList, which contains an array of Images. Once the images have been defined, set property SmallImageList of the ListView to the new ImageList object. Property SmallImageList specifies the image list for the small icons. Property LargeImageList sets the ImageList for large icons. The items in a ListView are each of type ListViewItem. Icons for the ListView items are selected by setting the item's ImageIndex property to the appropriate index.

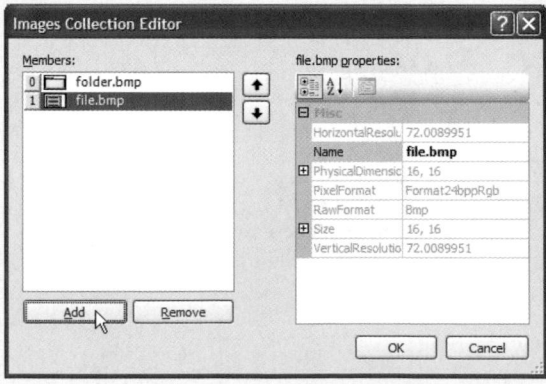

Fig. 14.30 | **Image Collection Editor** window for an ImageList component.

Class FrmListViewTest (Fig. 14.31) displays files and folders in a ListView, along with small icons representing each file or folder. If a file or folder is inaccessible because of permission settings, a MessageBox appears. The program scans the contents of the directory as it browses, rather than indexing the entire drive at once.

```vb
1   ' Fig. 14.31: FrmListViewTest.vb
2   ' Displaying directories and their contents in ListView.
3   Imports System.IO
4
5   Public Class FrmListViewTest
6      ' store current directory
7      Private currentDirectory As String = Directory.GetCurrentDirectory()
8
9      ' display files/subdirectories of current directory
10     ' (i.e., the one from which the application is executed)
11     Private Sub FrmListViewTest_Load(ByVal sender As Object, _
12        ByVal e As System.EventArgs) Handles Me.Load
13        ' set Image list
14        Dim folderImage As Image = Image.FromFile( _
15           currentDirectory & "\images\folder.bmp")
16
17        Dim fileImage As Image = Image.FromFile( _
18           currentDirectory & "\images\file.bmp")
19
20        fileFolder.Images.Add(folderImage)
21        fileFolder.Images.Add(fileImage)
22
23        ' load current directory into browserListView
24        LoadFilesInDirectory(currentDirectory)
25        lblDisplay.Text = currentDirectory
26     End Sub ' FrmListViewTest_Load
27
28     ' browse directory user clicked or go up one level
29     Private Sub lvwBrowser_Click(ByVal sender As System.Object, _
30        ByVal e As System.EventArgs) Handles lvwBrowser.Click
31        ' ensure an item is selected
32        If lvwBrowser.SelectedItems.Count <> 0 Then
33           ' if first item selected, go up one level
34           If lvwBrowser.Items(0).Selected Then
35              ' create DirectoryInfo object for directory
36              Dim directoryObject As DirectoryInfo = _
37                 New DirectoryInfo(currentDirectory)
38
39              ' if directory has parent, load it
40              If directoryObject.Parent IsNot Nothing Then
41                 LoadFilesInDirectory(directoryObject.Parent.FullName)
42                 lblDisplay.Text = currentDirectory
43              End If
44           Else ' selected directory or file
45              ' directory or file chosen
46              Dim chosen As String = lvwBrowser.SelectedItems(0).Text
```

Fig. 14.31 | ListView displaying files and folders. (Part 1 of 3.)

```
47
48                    ' if item selected is directory, load selected directory
49                If Directory.Exists(currentDirectory & "\" & chosen) Then
50                    ' if currently in C:\, do not need '\'; otherwise we do
51                    If currentDirectory = "C:\" Then
52                        LoadFilesInDirectory(currentDirectory & chosen)
53                    Else
54                        LoadFilesInDirectory(currentDirectory & "\" & chosen)
55                    End If
56
57                    ' update displayLabel
58                    lblDisplay.Text = currentDirectory
59                End If
60            End If
61        End If
62    End Sub ' lvwBrowser_Click
63
64    ' display files/subdirectories of current directory
65    Private Sub LoadFilesInDirectory( _
66        ByVal currentDirectoryValue As String)
67        ' load directory information and display
68        Try
69            ' clear ListView and set first item
70            lvwBrowser.Items.Clear()
71            lvwBrowser.Items.Add("Go Up One Level")
72
73            ' update current directory
74            currentDirectory = currentDirectoryValue
75            Dim newCurrentDirectory As DirectoryInfo = _
76                New DirectoryInfo(currentDirectory)
77
78            ' put files and directories into arrays
79            Dim directoryArray As DirectoryInfo() = _
80                newCurrentDirectory.GetDirectories()
81            Dim fileArray As FileInfo() = newCurrentDirectory.GetFiles()
82
83            ' add directory names to ListView
84            For Each dir As DirectoryInfo In directoryArray
85                ' add directory to ListView
86                Dim newDirectoryItem As ListViewItem = _
87                    lvwBrowser.Items.Add(dir.Name)
88
89                newDirectoryItem.ImageIndex = 0 ' set directory image
90            Next
91
92            ' add file names to ListView
93            For Each file As FileInfo In fileArray
94                ' add file to ListView
95                Dim newFileItem As ListViewItem = _
96                    lvwBrowser.Items.Add(file.Name)
97
```

Fig. 14.31 | ListView displaying files and folders. (Part 2 of 3.)

```
98              newFileItem.ImageIndex = 1 ' set file image
99          Next
100      Catch e As UnauthorizedAccessException
101          MessageBox.Show("Warning: Some files may not be " & _
102              "visible due to permission settings", _
103              "Attention", 0, MessageBoxIcon.Warning)
104      End Try
105   End Sub ' LoadFilesInDirectory
106 End Class ' FrmListViewTest
```

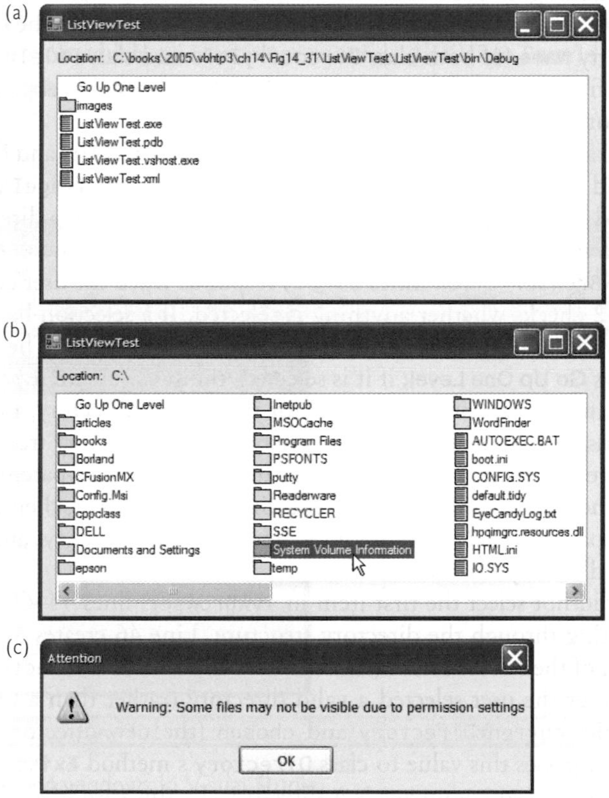

(a)

(b)

(c)

Fig. 14.31 | ListView displaying files and folders. (Part 3 of 3.)

To display icons beside list items, create an ImageList for the ListView lvwBrowser. First, drag and drop an ImageList on the Form and open the **Image Collection Editor**. Select our two simple bitmap images, provided in the bin\Debug and bin\Release folders of this example—one for a folder (array index 0) and the other for a file (array index 1). Then set the object lvwBrowser property SmallImageList to the new ImageList in the **Properties** window.

Method LoadFilesInDirectory (lines 65–105) populates lvwBrowser with the directory passed to it (currentDirectoryValue). It clears lvwBrowser and adds the element "Go Up One Level". When the user clicks this element, the program attempts to move up one level (we see how shortly). The method then creates a DirectoryInfo object ini-

application can have many child windows, there is only one parent window. Furthermore, a maximum of one child window can be active at once. Child windows cannot be parents themselves and cannot be moved outside their parent. In all other ways (closing, minimizing, resizing, etc.), a child window behaves like any other window. A child window's functionality can be different from the functionality of other child windows of the parent. For example, one child window might allow the user to edit images, another might allow the user to edit text and a third might display network traffic graphically, but all could belong to the same MDI parent. Figure 14.37 depicts a sample MDI application.

To create an MDI Form, create a new Form and set its **IsMdiContainer** property to True. The Form changes appearance, as in Fig. 14.38.

Next, create a child Form class to be added to the Form. To do this, right click the project in the **Solution Explorer**, select **Add > Windows Form...** and name the file. Edit the

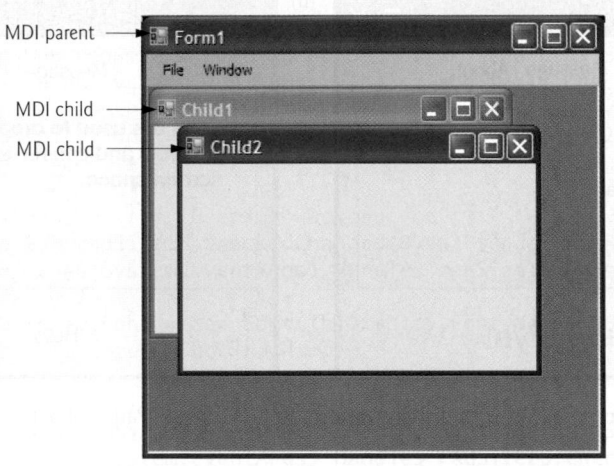

Fig. 14.37 | MDI parent window and MDI child windows.

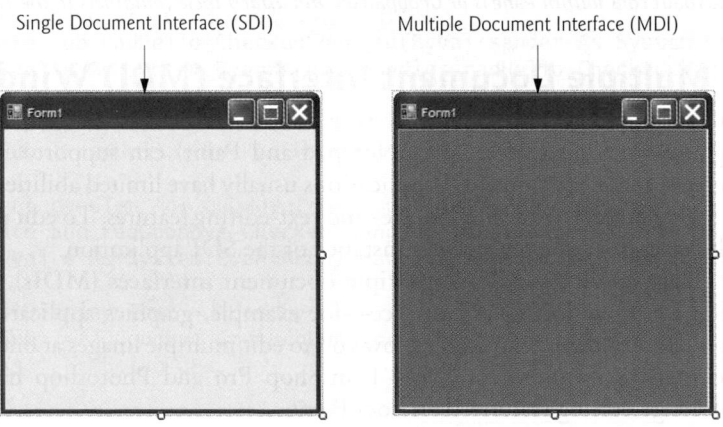

Fig. 14.38 | SDI and MDI forms.

Form as you like. To add the child Form to the parent, we must create a new child Form object, set its **MdiParent** property to the parent Form and call the child Form's Show method. In general, to add a child Form to a parent, you would write

Dim childForm As New *ChildFormClass*()
childForm.MdiParent = *parentForm*
childForm.Show()

In most cases, the parent Form creates the child, so the *parentForm* reference is Me. The code to create a child usually resides in an event handler, which creates a new window in response to a user action. Menu selections (such as **File > New > Window**) are commonly used to create new child windows.

Class Form property **MdiChildren** returns an array of child Form references. This is useful if the parent window wants to check the status of all its children (for example, ensuring that all are saved before the parent closes). Property **ActiveMdiChild** returns a reference to the active child window; it returns Nothing if there are no active child windows. Other features of MDI windows are described in Fig. 14.39.

MDI Form properties, a method and an event	Description
Common MDI Child Properties	
IsMdiChild	Indicates whether a Form is an MDI child. If True, the Form is an MDI child (read-only property).
MdiParent	Specifies the MDI parent Form of the child.
Common MDI Parent Properties	
ActiveMdiChild	Returns the Form that is the currently active MDI child (returns Nothing if no children are active).
IsMdiContainer	Indicates whether a Form can be an MDI parent. If True, the Form can be an MDI parent. The default value is False.
MdiChildren	Returns the MDI children as an array of Forms.
Common Method	
LayoutMdi	Arranges child forms in an MDI parent Form. The method takes as a parameter an MdiLayout enumeration constant (ArrangeIcons, Cascade, TileHorizontal or TileVertical). Figure 14.42 depicts the effects of these values.
Common Event	
MdiChildActivate	Generated when an MDI child is closed or activated.

Fig. 14.39 | MDI parent and MDI child properties, a method and an event.

Child windows can be minimized, maximized and closed independently of each other and the parent window. Figure 14.40 shows two images—one containing two minimized child windows and a second containing a maximized child window. When the parent is minimized or closed, the child windows are minimized or closed as well. Note that the title bar in Fig. 14.40(b) is **Form1 - [Child2]**. When a child window is maximized, its title bar text is inserted into the parent window's title bar. When a child window is minimized or maximized, its title bar displays a restore icon, which can be used to return the child window to its previous size (i.e., its size before it was minimized or maximized).

Visual Basic provides a property that helps track which child windows are open in an MDI container. Property `MdiWindowListItem` of class `MenuStrip` specifies which menu, if any, displays a list of open child windows. When a new child window is opened, an entry is added to the list (as in the first screen of Figure 14.41). If nine or more child windows are open, the list includes the option **More Windows...**, which allows the user to select a window from a list in a dialog.

 Good Programming Practice 14.1

When creating MDI applications, include a menu that displays a list of the open child windows. This helps the user select a child window quickly, rather than having to search for it in the parent window.

MDI containers allow you to organize child windows by calling method `LayoutMdi` of the parent `Form`. Method `LayoutMdi` receives as its argument one of the `MdiLayout` enumeration constants—`ArrangeIcons`, `Cascade`, `TileHorizontal` and `TileVertical`. Tiled windows completely fill the parent and do not overlap; such windows can be arranged horizontally (value `TileHorizontal`) or vertically (value `TileVertical`). Cascaded windows (value `Cascade`) overlap—each is the same size and displays a visible title bar, if possible. Value `ArrangeIcons` arranges the icons for any minimized child windows. If minimized windows are scattered around the parent window, value `ArrangeIcons` orders them neatly at the bottom-left corner of the parent window. Figure 14.42 illustrates the values of the `MdiLayout` enumeration.

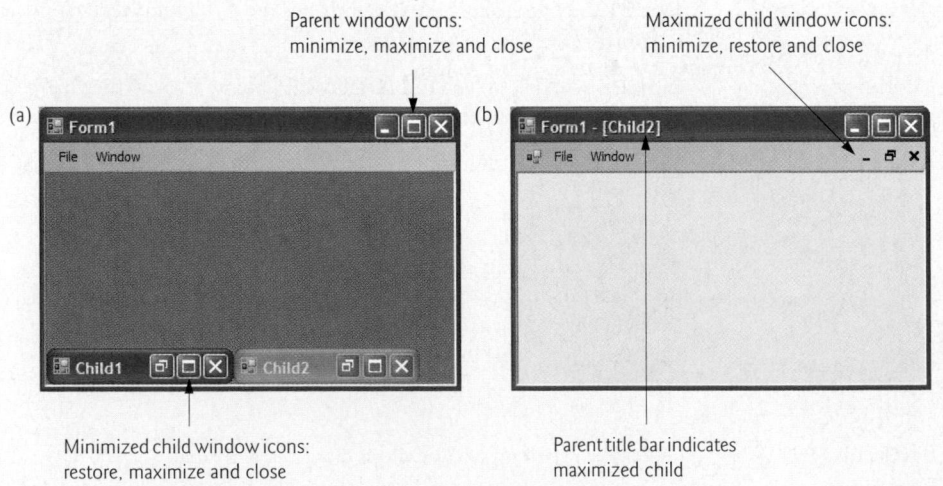

Fig. 14.40 | Minimized and maximized child windows.

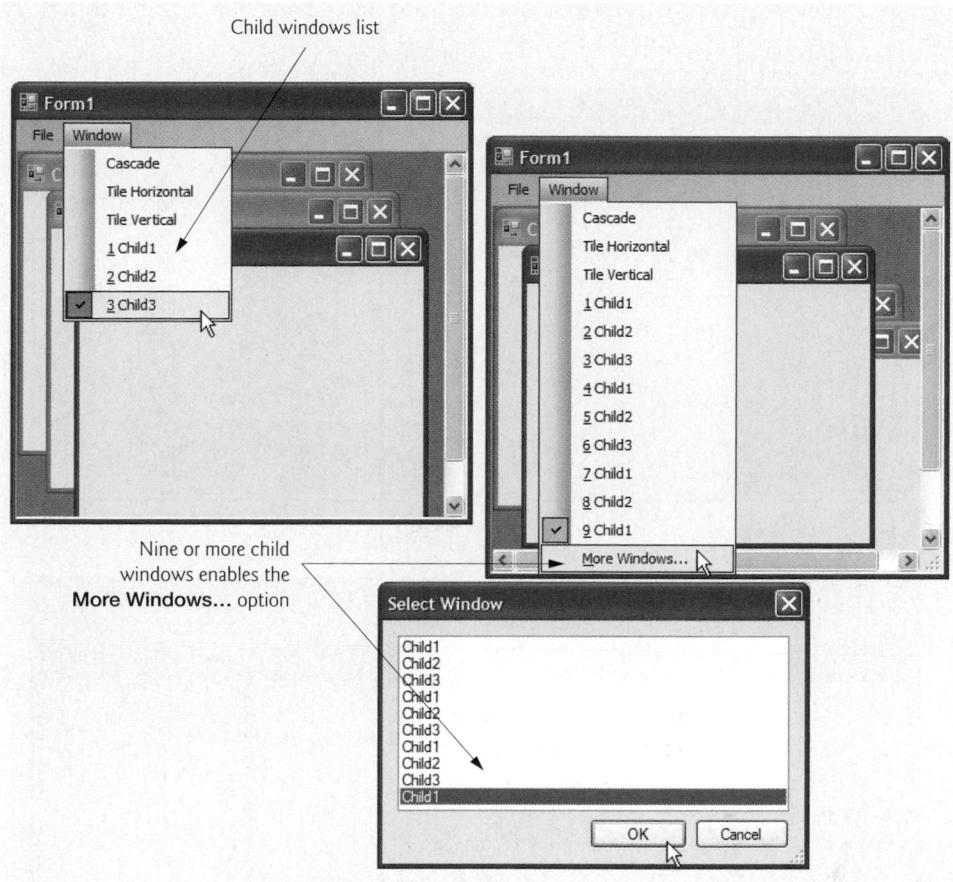

Fig. 14.41 | `MenuStrip` property `MdiWindowListItem` example.

Class `FrmUsingMDI` (Fig. 14.43) demonstrates MDI windows. Class `FrmUsingMDI` uses three instances of child `FrmChild` (Fig. 14.44), each containing a `PictureBox` that displays an image. The parent MDI `Form` contains menus that enable users to create and arrange child `Forms`.

FrmUsingMDI

Figure 14.43 presents class `FrmUsingMDI`—the application's MDI parent `Form`. This `Form`, which is created first, contains two top-level menus. The first of these menus, **File** (`fileToolStripMenuItem`), contains both an **Exit** item (`exitToolStripMenuItem`) and a **New** submenu (`newToolStripMenuItem`) consisting of items for each child window. The second menu, **Window** (`windowToolStripMenuItem`), provides options for laying out the MDI children, plus a list of the active MDI children.

In the **Properties** window, we set the `Form`'s `IsMdiContainer` property to `True`, making the `Form` an MDI parent. In addition, we set the `MenuStrip`'s `MdiWindowListItem` property to `windowToolStripMenuItem` so that the **Window** menu can list the open MDI child windows.

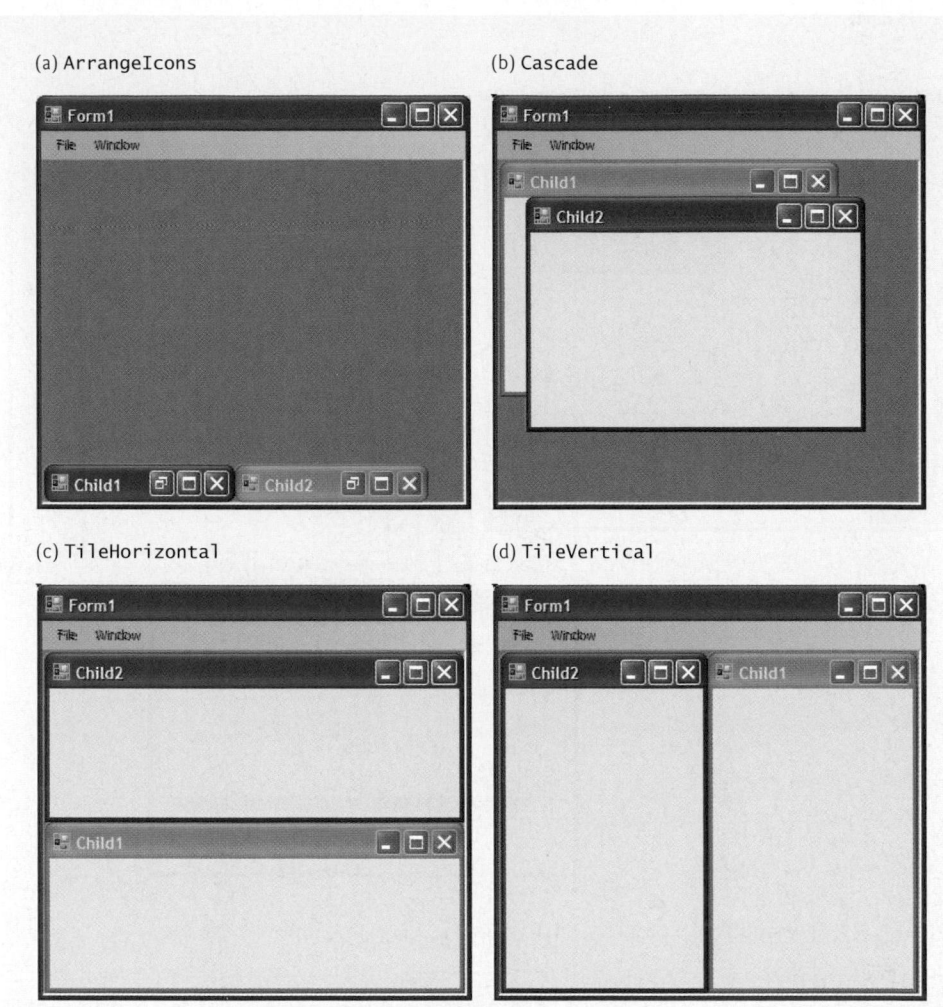

Fig. 14.42 | MdiLayout enumeration values.

```
 1   ' Fig. 14.43: FrmUsingMDI.vb
 2   ' MDI parent and child windows.
 3   Public Class FrmUsingMDI
 4      ' create Child 1 window when child1ToolStripMenuItem is clicked
 5      Private Sub child1ToolStripMenuItem_Click( _
 6         ByVal sender As System.Object, ByVal e As System.EventArgs) _
 7         Handles child1ToolStripMenuItem.Click
 8         ' create new child
 9         Dim child As New FrmChild("Child 1", "\images\vcsharphtp2_238h.jpg")
10         child.MdiParent = Me ' set parent
11         child.Show() ' display child
12      End Sub ' child1ToolStripMenuItem_Click
```

Fig. 14.43 | MDI parent-window class. (Part 1 of 3.)

```vbnet
13
14      ' create Child 2 window when child2ToolStripMenuItem is clicked
15      Private Sub child2ToolStripMenuItem_Click( _
16         ByVal sender As System.Object, ByVal e As System.EventArgs) _
17         Handles child2ToolStripMenuItem.Click
18         ' create new child
19         Dim child As New FrmChild("Child 2", "\images\vcsharpfp2_238h.jpg")
20         child.MdiParent = Me ' set parent
21         child.Show() ' display child
22      End Sub ' child2ToolStripMenuItem_Click
23
24      ' create Child 3 window when child3ToolStripMenuItem is clicked
25      Private Sub child3ToolStripMenuItem_Click( _
26         ByVal sender As System.Object, ByVal e As System.EventArgs) _
27         Handles child3ToolStripMenuItem.Click
28         ' create new child
29         Dim child As New FrmChild("Child 3", "\images\vbhtp3_238h.jpg")
30         child.MdiParent = Me ' set parent
31         child.Show() ' display child
32      End Sub ' child3ToolStripMenuItem_Click
33
34      ' exit application
35      Private Sub exitToolStripMenuItem_Click( _
36         ByVal sender As System.Object, ByVal e As System.EventArgs) _
37         Handles exitToolStripMenuItem.Click
38
39         Application.Exit()
40      End Sub ' exitToolStripMenuItem_Click
41
42      ' set Cascade layout
43      Private Sub cascadeToolStripMenuItem_Click( _
44         ByVal sender As System.Object, ByVal e As System.EventArgs) _
45         Handles cascadeToolStripMenuItem.Click
46
47         Me.LayoutMdi(MdiLayout.Cascade)
48      End Sub ' cascadeToolStripMenuItem_Click
49
50      ' set TileHorizontal layout
51      Private Sub tileHorizontalToolStripMenuItem_Click( _
52         ByVal sender As System.Object, ByVal e As System.EventArgs) _
53         Handles tileHorizontalToolStripMenuItem.Click
54
55         Me.LayoutMdi(MdiLayout.TileHorizontal)
56      End Sub ' tileHorizontalToolStripMenuItem_Click
57
58      ' set TileVertical layout
59      Private Sub tileVerticalToolStripMenuItem_Click( _
60         ByVal sender As System.Object, ByVal e As System.EventArgs) _
61         Handles tileVerticalToolStripMenuItem.Click
62
63         Me.LayoutMdi(MdiLayout.TileVertical)
64      End Sub ' tileVerticalToolStripMenuItem_Click
65   End Class ' FrmUsingMDI
```

Fig. 14.43 | MDI parent-window class. (Part 2 of 3.)

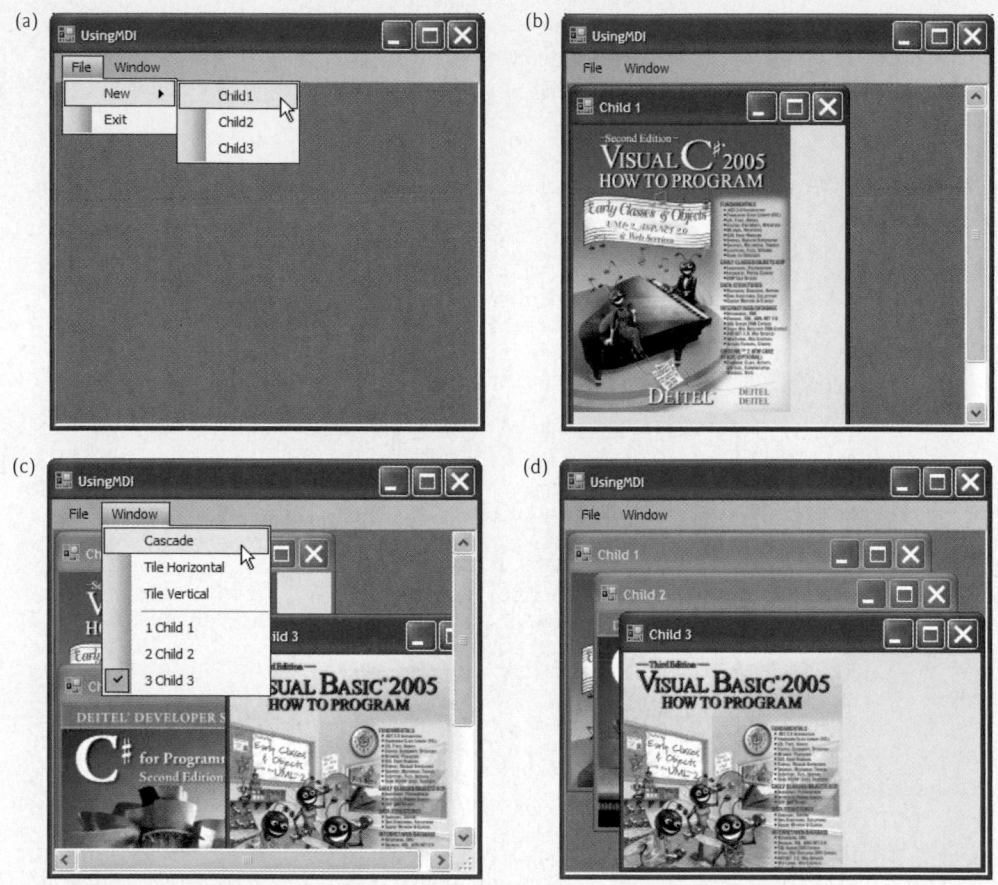

Fig. 14.43 | MDI parent-window class. (Part 3 of 3.)

The **Cascade** menu item's (cascadeToolStripMenuItem) event handler (lines 43–48) cascades the child windows by calling the parent Form's LayoutMdi method with the argument MdiLayout.Cascade (line 47). The **Tile Horizontal** menu item's (tileHorizontal-ToolStripMenuItem) event handler (lines 51–56) arranges the child windows horizontally by calling the parent Form's LayoutMdi method with the argument MdiLayout.TileHorizontal (line 55). Finally, the **Tile Vertical** menu item's (tileVerticalToolStripMenu-Item) event handler (lines 59–64) arranges the child windows vertically by calling the parent Form's LayoutMdi method with the argument MdiLayout.TileVertical (line 63).

FrmChild

At this point, the application is still incomplete—we must define the MDI child class. To do this, right click the project in the **Solution Explorer** and select **Add > Windows Form...**. Then name the new class in the dialog as FrmChild (Fig. 14.44). Next, add a PictureBox (picDisplay) to FrmChild. In the constructor, line 8 sets the title bar text. Lines 11–12 set picDisplay's Image property to an Image by using method FromFile (a Shared method of class Image).

```
 1   ' Fig. 14.44: FrmChild.vb
 2   ' Child window of MDI parent.
 3   Imports System.IO
 4
 5   Public Class FrmChild
 6      Public Sub New(ByVal title As String, ByVal fileName As String)
 7         InitializeComponent() ' ensure that Designer generated code executes
 8         Text = title ' set title text
 9
10         ' set image to display in pictureBox
11         picDisplay.Image = Image.FromFile( _
12            Directory.GetCurrentDirectory() & fileName)
13      End Sub ' New
14   End Class ' FrmChild
```

Fig. 14.44 | MDI child `FrmChild`.

The parent MDI `Form` (Fig. 14.43) creates new child windows using class `FrmChild`. The event handlers in lines 5–32 create a new child `Form` corresponding to the menu item clicked. Lines 9, 19 and 29 create new instances of `FrmChild`. Lines 10, 20 and 30 set each child's `MdiParent` property to the parent `Form` (`Me`). Lines 11, 21 and 31 call method `Show` to display each child `Form`.

14.13 Visual Inheritance

Chapter 10 discussed how to create classes by inheriting from other classes. We have also used inheritance to create `Forms` that display a GUI, by deriving our new `Form` classes from class `System.Windows.Forms.Form` (the code that indicates the inheritance relationship appears in the `Form`'s `Designer.vb` file). This is an example of *visual inheritance*. The derived `Form` class contains the functionality of its `Form` base class, including any base-class properties, methods, variables and controls. The derived class also inherits all visual aspects—such as size, component layout, spacing between GUI components, colors and fonts—from its base class.

Visual inheritance enables you to achieve visual consistency across your applications by giving them a common look-and-feel. This also reduces the learning curve as your users move between applications. For example, you could define a base `Form` that contains a product's logo, a specific background color, a predefined menu bar and other elements. You then could use the base `Form` throughout an application for uniformity and branding.

Class `FrmVisualInheritance` (Fig. 14.45) derives from `Form`. The output depicts the workings of the `Form`. The GUI contains two `Labels` with the text **Bugs, Bugs, Bugs** and **Copyright 2006, by Deitel & Associates, Inc.**, as well as one `Button` displaying the text **Learn More**. When a user presses the **Learn More** `Button`, the event handler `btnLearnMore_Click` (lines 5–12) displays a `MessageBox` that provides some informative text.

To allow other `Forms` to inherit from `FrmVisualInheritance`, we must package it as a class library in a `.dll` file. To do so, right click the project name in the **Solution Explorer** and select **Properties**, then choose the **Application** tab. In the **Application type** drop-down list, change **Windows Application** to **Class Library**. Building the project produces the `.dll`. The name of the solution that contains `FrmVisualInheritance` becomes parts of the class's fully qualified name—in this case, `VisualInheritance.FrmVisualInheritance`.

```
 1    ' Fig. 14.45: FrmVisualInheritance.vb
 2    ' Base Form for use with visual inheritance.
 3    Public Class FrmVisualInheritance
 4       ' display MessageBox when Button is clicked
 5       Private Sub btnLearnMore_Click(ByVal sender As System.Object, _
 6          ByVal e As System.EventArgs) Handles btnLearnMore.Click
 7
 8          MessageBox.Show( _
 9             "Bugs, Bugs, Bugs is a product of deitel.com", _
10             "Learn More", MessageBoxButtons.OK, _
11             MessageBoxIcon.Information)
12       End Sub ' btnLearnMore_Click
13    End Class ' FrmVisualInheritance
```

Fig. 14.45 | Class `FrmVisualInheritance`, which inherits from class `Form`, contains a `Button` (**Learn More**).

To visually inherit from `FrmVisualInheritance`, first create a new Windows application. In this application, add a reference to the `.dll` you just created (located in the `bin/Release` folder of the solution containing Fig. 14.45). Then open the `Designer.vb` file for the new application's `Form` and modify the line

```
Inherits System.Windows.Forms.Form
```

to indicate that the application's `Form` should inherit from class `FrmVisualInheritance` instead. The `Inherits` line in the `Designer.vb` file should now appear as follows:

```
Inherits VisualInheritance.FrmVisualInheritance
```

Note that you must either specify `FrmVisualInheritance`'s fully qualified name or use an `Imports` declaration to indicate that the new application uses classes from the namespace `VisualInheritance`. In **Design** view, the new application's `Form` now displays the inherited controls of the base class `FrmVisualInheritance` (as shown in Fig. 14.46). You can now add more components to the `Form`.

Class `FrmVisualInheritanceTest` (Fig. 14.47) derives from `FrmVisualInheritance` (Fig. 14.45). The GUI contains the components inherited from `FrmVisualInheritance` and a `Button` with the text **About this Program**. When the user presses this `Button`, the event handler `btnAbout_Click` (lines 5–12) displays another `MessageBox` providing different informative text.

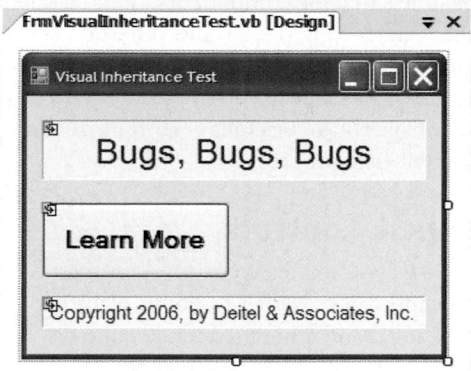

Fig. 14.46 | Form demonstrating visual inheritance.

```
1   ' Fig. 14.47: FrmVisualInheritanceTest.vb
2   ' Derived Form using visual inheritance.
3   Public Class FrmVisualInheritanceTest
4       ' display MessageBox when Button is clicked
5       Private Sub btnAbout_Click(ByVal sender As System.Object, _
6           ByVal e As System.EventArgs) Handles btnAbout.Click
7
8           MessageBox.Show( _
9               "This program was created by Deitel & Associates", _
10              "About this Program", MessageBoxButtons.OK, _
11              MessageBoxIcon.Information)
12      End Sub ' btnAbout_Click
13  End Class ' FrmVisualInheritanceTest
```

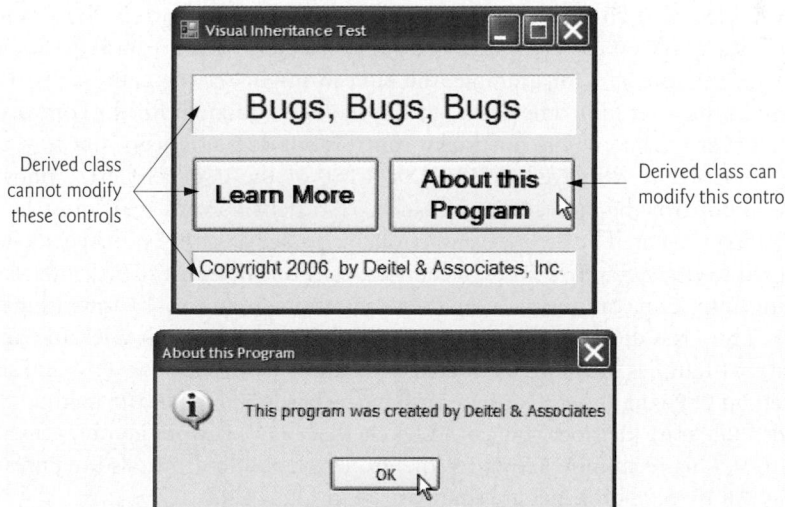

Fig. 14.47 | Class FrmVisualInheritanceTest, which inherits from class FrmVisualInheritance, contains an additional Button.

Figure 14.47 demonstrates that the components, their layouts and the functionality of base-class FrmVisualInheritance (Fig. 14.45) are inherited by FrmVisualInheritance-Test. If a user clicks the button **Learn More**, the base class event handler btnLearnMore_Click displays a MessageBox. FrmVisualInheritance uses a Private access modifier to declare its controls (in its Designer.vb file), so class FrmVisualInheritanceTest cannot modify the inherited controls.

14.14 User-Defined Controls

The .NET Framework allows you to create custom controls. These custom controls appear in the user's **Toolbox** and can be added to Forms, Panels or GroupBoxes in the same way that we add Buttons, Labels and other predefined controls. The simplest way to create a custom control is to derive a class from an existing control, such as a Label. This is useful if you want to add functionality to an existing control rather than reimplement the existing control to include the desired functionality. For example, you can create a new type of Label that behaves like a normal Label but has a different appearance. You accomplish this by inheriting from class Label and overriding method OnPaint.

All controls contain method OnPaint, which the system calls when a component must be redrawn (such as when the component is resized). Method OnPaint is passed a **Paint-EventArgs** object, which contains graphics information—property **Graphics** is the graphics object used to draw, and property **ClipRectangle** defines the rectangular boundary of the control. Whenever the system raises the Paint event, polymorphism enables the system to call the new control's OnPaint. The base class's OnPaint method is not called, so you must call it explicitly from the derived class's OnPaint implementation before performing any customized painting operation. In most cases, you want to do this to ensure that the original painting code executes in addition to the code you define in the custom control's class, so that the control will be displayed correctly.

To create a new control that is composed of existing controls, use class UserControl. Controls added to a custom control are called constituent controls. For example, you could create a UserControl composed of a Button, a Label and a TextBox, each associated with some functionality (for example, the Button might set the Label's text to the text contained in the TextBox). The UserControl acts as a container for the controls added to it. The UserControl contains constituent controls but does not determine how these constituent controls are displayed. Method OnPaint of the UserControl cannot be overridden. To control the appearance of each constituent control, you must handle each control's Paint event. The Paint event handler is passed a PaintEventArgs object, which can be used to draw graphics (lines, rectangles, etc.) on the constituent controls.

Using another technique, you can create a brand new control by inheriting from class Control. This class does not define any specific behavior; that task is left to you. Instead, class Control handles the items associated with all controls, such as events and sizing handles. Method OnPaint should contain a call to the base class's OnPaint method. Inside the overridden OnPaint method, you can add code that draws custom graphics when drawing the control. This technique allows for the greatest flexibility, but also requires the most planning. All three approaches are summarized in Fig. 14.48.

We create a "clock" control in Fig. 14.49. This is a UserControl composed of a Label and a Timer—whenever the Timer raises an event (once per second in this example), the Timer's event handler updates the Label to reflect the current time.

Custom control techniques and PaintEventArgs properties	Description
Custom Control Techniques	
Inherit from Windows Forms control	You can do this to add functionality to a pre-existing control. If you override method OnPaint, call the base class's OnPaint method. Note that you only can add to the original control's appearance, not redesign it.
Create a UserControl	You can create a UserControl composed of multiple pre-existing controls (e.g., to combine their functionality). Note that you cannot override the OnPaint methods of custom controls. Instead, you must place drawing code in a Paint event handler. Again, note that you only can add to the original control's appearance, not redesign it
Inherit from class Control	Define a brand-new control. Override method OnPaint, then call base class method OnPaint and include methods to draw the control. With this method you can customize control appearance and functionality.
PaintEventArgs Properties	
Graphics	The graphics object of the control. It is used to draw on the control.
ClipRectangle	Specifies the rectangle indicating the boundary of the control.

Fig. 14.48 | Custom control creation.

```
 1   ' Fig. 14.49: ClockUserControl.vb
 2   ' User-defined control with a timer and a Label.
 3   Public Class ClockUserControl
 4      ' update label for each clock tick
 5      Private Sub tmrClock_Tick(ByVal sender As System.Object, _
 6         ByVal e As System.EventArgs) Handles tmrClock.Tick
 7         ' get current time (Now), convert to String
 8         lblDisplay.Text = DateTime.Now.ToLongTimeString()
 9      End Sub ' tmrClock_Tick
10   End Class ' ClockUserControl
```

Fig. 14.49 | UserControl-defined clock.

`Timers` (`System.Windows.Forms` namespace) are invisible components that reside on a `Form`, generating `Tick` events at set intervals. The interval is set by the `Timer`'s `Interval` property, which defines the number of milliseconds (thousandths of a second) between events. By default, timers are disabled and do not generate events.

This application contains a user control (`ClockUserControl`) and a `Form` that displays the user control. We begin by creating a Windows application. Next, we create a User-Control class for the project by selecting **Project > Add User Control...**. This displays a dialog from which we can select the type of control to add—**User Control** is already selected. We then name the file (and the class) `ClockUserControl`. Our empty `Clock-UserControl` is displayed as a gray rectangle.

You can treat this control like a Windows Form, meaning that you can add controls using the **ToolBox** and set properties using the **Properties** window. However, rather than creating an application's Form, you are simply creating a new control composed of other controls. Add a `Label` (`lblDisplay`) and a `Timer` (`tmrClock`) to the `UserControl`. Set the `Timer`'s `Interval` property to 1000 milliseconds and set `lblDisplay`'s text with each event (lines 5–9). To generate events, `tmrClock` must be enabled by setting property `Enabled` to `True` in the **Properties** window.

Line 8 sets `lblDisplay`'s text to the current time. Structure `DateTime` (namespace `System`) contains property `Now`, which is the current time. Method `ToLongTimeString` converts `Now` to a `String` containing the current hour, minute and second followed by AM or PM. Once you build the project containing the custom user control, the control is automatically added to the IDE's **Toolbox**. You may need to switch to the application's `Form` in the Designer before the custom user control appears in the **Toolbox**.

To use the custom control, simply drag it onto the `Form` and run the Windows application. We gave the `ClockUserControl` object a white background to make it stand out in the `Form`. Figure 14.49 shows the output of `FrmUserControlTest`, which contains our `ClockUserControl`. There are no event handlers in `FrmUserControlTest`, so we show only the code for `ClockUserControl`.

Sharing Custom Controls with Other Developers
Visual Studio allows you to share custom controls with other developers. To create a User-Control that can be exported to other solutions, do the following:

1. Create a new **Class Library** project.

2. Delete the file `Class1.vb` that is initially provided with the project.

3. Right click the project in the **Solution Explorer** and select **Add > User Control...**. In the dialog that appears, name the user control file and click **Add**.

4. In the project, add controls and functionality to the `UserControl` (Fig. 14.50).

5. Build the project. Visual Studio creates a `.dll` file for the `UserControl` in the solution's `bin/Release` directory. The file is not executable; class libraries are used to define classes that are reused in other executable applications.

6. Create a new Windows application.

7. In the new Windows application, right click the **Toolbox** and select **Choose Items...**. In the **Choose Toolbox Items** dialog that appears, click **Browse...** and locate the `.dll` file for the class library you created in *Steps 1–5*. The item will then

appear in the **Choose Toolbox Items** dialog (Fig. 14.51). If it is not already checked, check this item. Click **OK** to add the item to the **Toolbox**. This control can now be added to the Form as if it were any other control (Fig. 14.52).

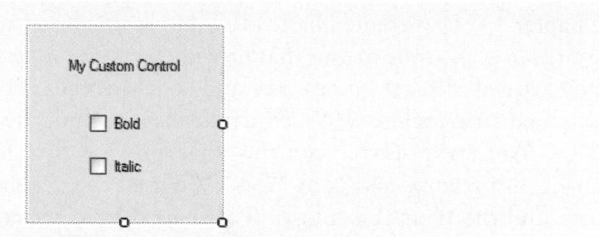

Fig. 14.50 | Custom-control creation.

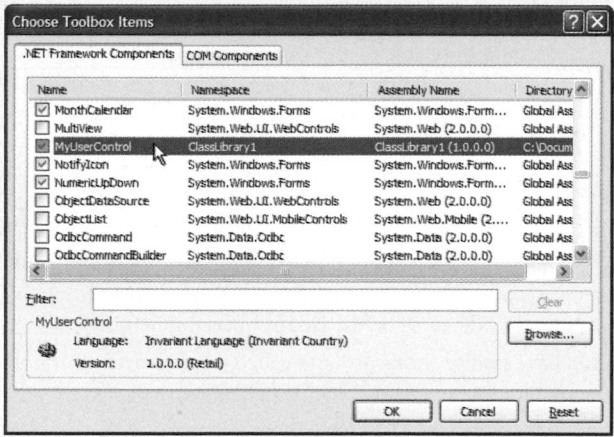

Fig. 14.51 | Custom control added to the **ToolBox**.

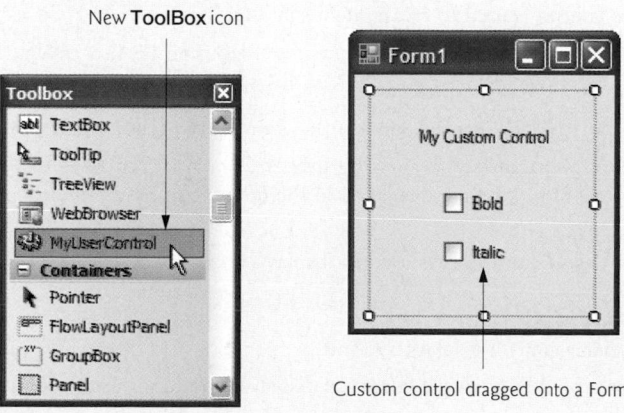

Fig. 14.52 | Custom control added to a Form.

14.15 Wrap-Up

Many of today's commercial applications provide GUIs that are easy to use and manipulate. The demand for user-friendly GUIs makes sophisticated GUI design an essential programming skill. Visual Studio's IDE makes GUI development quick and easy. In Chapter 13, we presented basic GUI development techniques. In Chapter 14, we demonstrated how to create menus that provide users easy access to an application's functionality. You learned the DateTimePicker and MonthCalendar controls, which allow users to input date and time values. We used LinkLabels to link the user to an application or a Web page. You used several controls that provide lists of data to the user—ListBoxes, CheckedListBoxes and ListViews. We used the ComboBox control to create drop-down lists, and the TreeView control to display data in hierarchical form. We then introduced complex GUIs that use tabbed windows and multiple document interfaces. The chapter concluded with demonstrations of visual inheritance and creating custom controls.

The next chapter explores multithreading, which enables you to create applications in which several activities can proceed in parallel.

Summary

Section 14.2 Menus

- Menus provide groups of related commands and organize them without "cluttering" the GUI.
- An expanded menu lists various menu items and submenus (menus within a menu).
- A menu that contains a menu item is called the menu item's parent menu. A menu item that contains a submenu is considered to be the parent of the submenu.
- All menu items can have *Alt* key shortcuts (also called access shortcuts or hotkeys), which are accessed by pressing *Alt* and the underlined letter.
- Menus that are not top-level menus can have shortcut keys as well (combinations of *Ctrl, Shift, Alt, F1, F2*, letter keys, etc.).
- Some menu items display check marks, indicating that multiple options on the menu can be selected at once.
- The MenuStrip control is used to create menus in a GUI.
- Top-level menus and their menu items are represented using ToolStripMenuItems.
- To create an access shortcut, type an ampersand (&) before the character to be underlined.
- To add other shortcut keys, set the ShortcutKeys property of the ToolStripMenuItem.
- You can hide the shortcut keys by setting property ShowShortcutKeys to False, and you can modify how the control keys are displayed in the menu item by modifying property ShortcutKeyDisplayString.
- A menu item's Checked property is used to display a check to the left of the menu item.

Section 14.3 MonthCalendar Control

- The MonthCalendar control displays a monthly calendar.
- The user can select a date from the currently displayed month or use the links to navigate to another month.
- A MonthCalendar's DateChanged event occurs when a new date is selected.

Section 14.4 *DateTimePicker Control*
- The DateTimePicker control can be used to retrieve date and/or time information from the user.
- DateTimePicker property Format specifies the user's selection options by using constants from the DateTimePickerFormat enumeration.
- The DateTimePicker's ValueChanged event occurs when the selected value changes.

Section 14.5 *LinkLabel Control*
- The LinkLabel control displays links to other resources, such as files or Web pages.
- A LinkLabel appears as underlined text (colored blue by default). When the mouse moves over the link, the pointer changes to a hand; this is similar to a hyperlink in a Web page.
- The link can change color to indicate whether the link is new, previously visited or active.
- When clicked, the LinkLabel generates a LinkClicked event.

Section 14.6 *ListBox Control*
- The ListBox control allows the user to view and select items in a list.
- ListBox property SelectionMode determines the number of items that can be selected. This property has the possible values None, One, MultiSimple and MultiExtended (from the SelectionMode enumeration).
- The SelectedIndexChanged event of class ListBox occurs when the user selects a new item.
- Property Items returns all the list items as a collection.
- Property SelectedItem returns the currently selected item.
- To add items to a ListBox, add objects to its Items collection. Call method Add to add a String to the ListBox's Items collection.
- You can add items to ListBoxes and CheckedListBoxes visually by examining the Items property in the **Properties** window.

Section 14.7 *CheckedListBox Control*
- The CheckedListBox control extends a ListBox by including CheckBoxes next to each item.
- Items can be added to a CheckedListBox control via methods Add and AddRange or through the **String Collection Editor.**
- CheckedListBoxes imply that multiple items can be selected.
- An ItemCheck event occurs whenever a user checks or unchecks a CheckedListBox item.

Section 14.8 *ComboBox Control*
- The ComboBox control combines TextBox features with a drop-down list.
- MaxDropDownItems specifies the maximum number of items that a drop-down list can display.
- As with the ListBox control, you can add objects to collection Items programmatically, using methods Add and AddRange, or visually, with the **String Collection Editor.**
- Property DropDownStyle determines the type of ComboBox and is represented as a value of the ComboBoxStyle enumeration, which contains values Simple, DropDown and DropDownList.
- There can be at most one selected item in a ComboBox (if none are selected, then the property SelectedIndex contains -1).
- When the selected item changes in a ComboBox, a SelectedIndexChanged event occurs.

Section 14.9 *TreeView Control*
- The TreeView control displays nodes hierarchically in a tree.

- Traditionally, nodes are objects that contain values and can refer to other nodes.
- A parent node contains child nodes, and the child nodes can be parents to other nodes.
- Two child nodes that have the same parent node are considered sibling nodes.
- A tree is a collection of nodes, usually organized in a hierarchical manner. The first parent node of a tree is the root node.
- TreeView controls are useful for displaying hierarchical information.
- In a TreeView, a parent node can be expanded or collapsed by clicking the plus box or minus box to its left. Nodes without children do not have these boxes.
- The nodes displayed in a TreeView are instances of class TreeNode.
- Each TreeNode has a Nodes collection (of type TreeNodeCollection), which contains a list of the node's children.
- To add nodes to a TreeView visually, click the ellipsis next to the Nodes property in the **Properties** window, then use the **TreeNode Editor**, which displays an empty tree representing the TreeView.
- To add nodes programmatically, create a root TreeNode object and pass it a String to display. Then call method Add to add this new TreeNode to the TreeView's Nodes collection.

Section 14.10 *ListView Control*
- The ListView control is similar to a ListBox in that both display lists from which the user can select one or more items. The important difference between the two classes is that a ListView can display icons next to list items.
- Property MultiSelect (a Boolean) determines whether multiple items can be selected.
- To display images in a ListView, an ImageList component is required.
- Property SmallImageList of class ListView sets the ImageList for the small icons.
- Property LargeImageList of class ListView sets the ImageList for large icons.
- The items in a ListView are each of type ListViewItem.

Section 14.11 *TabControl Control*
- A TabControl creates tabbed windows. This allows you to organize more complex GUIs.
- TabPage objects are containers for other controls.
- Only one TabPage is displayed at a time.
- You can add TabControls visually by dragging and dropping them on a Form in **Design** mode. You can also right click the TabControl in **Design** mode and select **Add Tab**, or click the TabPages property in the **Properties** window and add tabs in the dialog that appears.
- Each TabPage raises a Click event when its tab is clicked.

Section 14.12 *Multiple Document Interface (MDI) Windows*
- Multiple document interface (MDI) programs enable users to edit multiple documents at once.
- The application window of an MDI program is called the parent window, and each window inside the application is referred to as a child window.
- Child windows cannot be parents themselves and cannot be moved outside their parent.
- To create an MDI Form, create a new Form and set its IsMdiContainer property to True.
- To add a child Form to the parent, create a new child Form object, set its MdiParent property to the parent Form and call the child Form's Show method.
- Child windows can be minimized, maximized and closed independently of each other and of the parent window.

- Property `MdiWindowListItem` of class `MenuStrip` specifies which menu, if any, displays a list of open child windows.

- MDI containers allow you to organize the placement of child windows. The child windows in an MDI application can be arranged by calling method `LayoutMdi` of the parent `Form`.

Section 14.13 Visual Inheritance

- Visual inheritance allows you to create a new `Form` by inheriting from an existing `Form`. The derived `Form` class contains the functionality of its base class.

- Visual inheritance enables you to achieve visual consistency across applications by reusing code.

- A `Form` can inherit from another `Form` as long as that `Form` (or its compiled `.dll`) is included in the project.

Section 14.14 User-Defined Controls

- The .NET Framework allows you to create custom controls.

- Custom controls appear in the user's **Toolbox** and can be added to `Forms`, `Panels` or `GroupBoxes` in the same way that `Buttons`, `Labels` and other predefined controls are added.

- The simplest way to create a custom control is to derive a class from an existing control, such as a `Label`. This is useful if you want to add functionality to an existing control rather than reimplement the existing control to include the desired functionality.

- To create a new control composed of existing controls, use class `UserControl`.

- Controls added to a custom control are called constituent controls.

- You can create a brand-new control by inheriting from class `Control`.

- `Timers` are invisible components that reside on a `Form`, generating `Tick` events at set intervals. The interval is set by the `Timer`'s `Interval` property, which defines the number of milliseconds (thousandths of a second) between events.

- A `Timer`'s `Enabled` property must be set to `True` before the `Timer` will generate events.

Terminology

Activation property of class `ListView`
ActiveMdiChild property of class Form
Add method of class `ObjectCollection`
AddDays method of structure `DateTime`
AddYears method of structure `DateTime`
ArrangeIcons value of enumeration `MdiLayout`
Cascade value of enumeration `MdiLayout`
cascaded window
CheckBoxes property of class `ListView`
Checked property of class `ToolStripMenuItem`
CheckedListBox class
child node
child window
Clear method of class `Graphics`
Clear method of class `ObjectCollection`
Click event of class `ToolStripMenuItem`
ClipRectangle property of class
    `PaintEventArgs`
ComboBox class
ComboBoxStyle enumeration

constituent controls
custom controls
Custom value of enumeration
    `DateTimePickerFormat`
CustomFormat property of class `DateTimePicker`
DateChanged event of class `MonthCalendar`
DateTime structure
DateTimePicker class
DateTimePickerFormat enumeration
DayOfWeek enumeration
DayOfWeek property of class `DateTime`
DirectoryInfo class
DrawEllipse method of class `Graphics`
DrawPie method of class `Graphics`
DrawRectangle method of class `Graphics`
drop-down list
DropDown value of enumeration `ComboBoxStyle`
DropDownList value of enumeration
    `ComboBoxStyle`
DropDownStyle property of class `ComboBox`

TileHorizontal value of enumeration
    MdiLayout
TileVertical value of enumeration MdiLayout
Time value of enumeration
    DateTimePickerFormat
Timer class
ToLongDateString method of structure
    DateTime
ToLongTimeString method of structure
    DateTime
ToolStripMenuItem class

tree
TreeNode class
TreeNodeCollection type
TreeView class
TreeViewEventArgs class
UserControl class
Value property of class DateTimePicker
ValueChanged event of class DateTimePicker
View property of class ListView
visual inheritance

Self-Review Exercises

14.1 State whether each of the following is *true* or *false*. If *false*, explain why.
    a) Menus organize groups of related classes.
    b) Menu items can display ComboBoxes, checkmarks and access shortcuts.
    c) The ListBox control allows only single selection (like a RadioButton).
    d) A ComboBox control typically has a drop-down list.
    e) Deleting a parent node in a TreeView control deletes its child nodes.
    f) The user can select only one item in a ListView control.
    g) A TabPage can act as a container for RadioButtons.
    h) An MDI child window can have MDI children.
    i) MDI child windows can be moved outside the boundaries of their parent window.
    j) There are two basic ways to create a customized control.

14.2 Fill in the blanks in each of the following statements:
    a) Method _____ of class Process can open files and Web pages, similar to the **Run...** command in Windows.
    b) If more elements appear in a ComboBox than can fit, a(n) _____ appears.
    c) The top-level node in a TreeView is the _____ node.
    d) A(n) _____ and a(n) _____ can display icons contained in an ImageList control.
    e) The _____ property of class MenuStrip allows a menu to display a list of active child windows.
    f) Class _____ allows you to combine several controls into a single custom control.
    g) The _____ saves space by layering TabPages on top of each other.
    h) The _____ window layout option makes all MDI windows the same size and layers them so that every title bar is visible (if possible).
    i) _____ are typically used to display hyperlinks to other resources, files or Web pages.

Answers to Self-Review Exercises

14.1 a) False. Menus organize groups of related commands. b) True. c) False. The ListBox control allows single or multiple selection. d) True. e) True. f) False. The user can select one or more items. g) True. h) False. Only an MDI parent window can have MDI children. An MDI parent window cannot be an MDI child. i) False. MDI child windows cannot be moved outside their parent window. j) False. There are three ways—derive from an existing control, derive a new control from class UserControl (to create a control that contains other controls) or derive a new control from class Control (to create a control from scratch).

14.2 a) Start. b) scrollbar. c) root. d) ListView, TreeView. e) MdiWindowListItem. f) UserControl. g) TabControl. h) Cascade. i) LinkLabels.

Exercises

14.3 Write a program that displays the names of 15 states in a ComboBox. When an item is selected from the ComboBox, remove it.

14.4 Modify your solution to Exercise 14.3 to add a ListBox. When the user selects an item from the ComboBox, remove the item from the ComboBox and add it to the ListBox. Your program should check to ensure that the ComboBox contains at least one item. If it does not, display a message, using a message box, then terminate program execution when the user dismisses the message box.

14.5 Write a program that allows the user to enter Strings in a TextBox. Add each String the user inputs to a ListBox. As each String is added to the ListBox, ensure that the Strings are in sorted order. [*Note:* Use property Sorted.]

14.6 Create a file browser (similar to Windows Explorer) based on the programs in Fig. 14.14, Fig. 14.28 and Fig. 14.31. The file browser should have a TreeView that allows the user to browse directories. There should also be a ListView that displays the contents (all subdirectories and files) of the directory being browsed. Double clicking a file in the ListView should open it, and double clicking a directory in either the ListView or the TreeView should browse it. If a file or directory cannot be accessed because of its permission settings, notify the user.

14.7 Create an MDI text editor. Each child window should contain a multiline RichTextBox. The MDI parent should have a **Format** menu with submenus to control the size, font and color of the text in the active child window. Each submenu should have at least three options. In addition, the parent should have a **File** menu with menu items **New** (create a new child), **Close** (close the active child) and **Exit** (exit the application). The parent should have a **Window** menu to display a list of the open child windows and their layout options.

14.8 Create a UserControl called LoginPasswordUserControl. The LoginPasswordUserControl contains a Label (loginLabel) that displays String "Login:", a TextBox (loginTextBox) where the user inputs a login name, a Label (passwordLabel) that displays the String "Password:" and finally, a TextBox (passwordTextBox) where a user inputs a password (do not forget to set property PasswordChar to "*" in the TextBox's **Properties** window). LoginPasswordUserControl must provide Public read-only properties Login and Password that allow an application to retrieve the user input from a login TextBox and a password TextBox. Use the new control in an application that displays the values input by the user in LoginPasswordUserControl.

14.9 A restaurant wants an application that calculates a table's bill. The application should display all the menu items from Fig. 14.53 in four ComboBoxes. Each ComboBox should contain a category of food offered by the restaurant (Beverage, Appetizer, Main Course and Dessert). The user can choose from one of these ComboBoxes to add an item to a table's bill. As each item is selected in the ComboBoxes, add the price of the item to the bill. The user can click the Clear Button to restore the Subtotal:, Tax: and Total: fields to $0.00.

14.10 Create an application that contains three TabPages. On the first TabPage, place a CheckedListBox with six items. On the second TabPage, place six TextBoxes. On the last TabPage, place six LinkLabels. The user's selections on the first TabPage should specify which of the six LinkLabels will be displayed. To hide or display a LinkLabel's value, use its Visible property. Use the second TabPage to modify the Web page that is opened by the LinkLabels. [*Note:* To change the LinkLabels' Visible properties, you will need to change the currently displayed TabPage to the last one. To do this, use the TabPage's SelectedTab property.]

14.11 Create an MDI application with child windows that each have a Panel for drawing. Add menus to the MDI application that allow the user to modify the size and color of the paint brush. When running this application, be aware that the Panel will be cleared if one of the windows overlaps another.

Name	Category	Price
Soda	Beverage	$1.95
Tea	Beverage	$1.50
Coffee	Beverage	$1.25
Mineral Water	Beverage	$2.95
Juice	Beverage	$2.50
Milk	Beverage	$1.50
Buffalo Wings	Appetizer	$5.95
Buffalo Fingers	Appetizer	$6.95
Potato Skins	Appetizer	$8.95
Nachos	Appetizer	$8.95
Mushroom Caps	Appetizer	$10.95
Shrimp Cocktail	Appetizer	$12.95
Chips and Salsa	Appetizer	$6.95
Seafood Alfredo	Main Course	$15.95
Chicken Alfredo	Main Course	$13.95
Chicken Picatta	Main Course	$13.95
Turkey Club	Main Course	$11.95
Lobster Pie	Main Course	$19.95
Prime Rib	Main Course	$20.95
Shrimp Scampi	Main Course	$18.95
Turkey Dinner	Main Course	$13.95
Stuffed Chicken	Main Course	$14.95
Apple Pie	Dessert	$5.95
Sundae	Dessert	$3.95
Carrot Cake	Dessert	$5.95
Mud Pie	Dessert	$4.95
Apple Crisp	Dessert	$5.95

Fig. 14.53 | Food items and prices.

15

Multithreading

OBJECTIVES

In this chapter you will learn:

- What threads are and why they are useful.
- How threads enable you to implement and manage concurrent activities.
- The life cycle of a thread.
- Thread priorities and scheduling.
- To create and execute **Thread**s.
- Thread synchronization.
- What producer/consumer relationships are and how they are implemented with multithreading.
- To ensure that the User Interface thread performs all GUI modifications that are initiated by other threads in a Windows application.

15.1 Introduction

It would be nice if we could perform one action at a time and perform it well, but that is usually difficult to do. The human body performs a great variety of operations in parallel—or, as we will say throughout this chapter, concurrently. Respiration, blood circulation, digestion, walking and talking, for example, can occur concurrently. All the senses—sight, touch, smell, taste and hearing—can be employed at once. Computers, too, perform operations concurrently—compiling a program, sending a file to a printer and receiving electronic mail messages can all occur in parallel.

Ironically, most programming languages do not enable programmers to specify concurrent activities. Rather, programming languages generally provide only a simple set of control statements that enable programmers to perform one action at a time, proceeding to the next action after the previous one has finished. Historically, the type of concurrency that computers perform today has generally been implemented as operating-system "primitives" available only to highly experienced "systems programmers."

The Ada programming language, developed by the United States Department of Defense, made concurrency primitives widely available to defense contractors building military command-and-control systems. However, Ada has not been widely used in academia and commercial industry.

The FCL provides concurrency primitives. You specify that applications contain "threads of execution," each of which designates a portion of a program that may execute concurrently with other threads—this capability is called multithreading. Multithreading is available to all .NET programming languages, including Visual Basic, Visual C# and Visual C++. The FCL's multithreading capabilities are located in the `System.Threading` namespace.

> **Performance Tip 15.1**
>
> *A problem with single-threaded applications is that lengthy activities must complete before other activities can begin. In a multithreaded application, threads can be distributed across multiple processors (if they are available) so that multiple tasks are performed concurrently, allowing the application to operate more efficiently. Multithreading can also increase performance on single-processor systems that simulate concurrency—when one thread cannot proceed, another can use the processor.*

This chapter discusses many applications of **concurrent programming**. When programs download large files, such as audio clips or video clips over the Internet, users do not want to wait until an entire clip downloads before starting the playback. To solve this problem, we can put multiple threads to work—one thread downloads a clip, while another plays the clip. These activities proceed concurrently. To avoid choppy playback, we **synchronize** the threads so that the player thread does not begin until there is a sufficient amount of the clip in memory to keep the player thread busy.

Another example of multithreading is the CLR's automatic **garbage collection**. C and C++ require programmers to explicitly reclaim dynamically allocated memory. The CLR's garbage-collector thread reclaims dynamically allocated memory that is no longer needed.

 Good Programming Practice 15.1

Set an object reference to Nothing when the program no longer needs that object. This enables the garbage collector to determine at the earliest possible moment that the object can be garbage collected. If such an object has other references to it, that object cannot be collected. Note that you still cannot predict when, or if, the garbage collector will actually reclaim the memory.

Writing multithreaded programs can be tricky. Although the human mind can perform functions concurrently, people find it difficult to jump between parallel "trains of thought." To see why multithreading can be difficult to program and understand, try the following experiment: Open three books to page 1 and try reading the books concurrently. Read a few words from the first book, then read a few words from the second book, then read a few words from the third book, then loop back and read the next few words from the first book, etc. After this experiment, you will appreciate the challenges of multithreading—switching between books, reading briefly, remembering your place in each book, moving the book you are reading closer so you can see it, pushing aside books you are not reading and, amid all this chaos, trying to comprehend the content of the books!

15.2 Thread States: Life Cycle of a Thread

At any time, a thread is said to be in one of several **thread states** that are illustrated in the UML state diagram of Fig. 15.1. This section discusses these states and the transitions between states. Two classes critical for multithreaded applications are `Thread` and `Monitor`, both of the `System.Threading` namespace. This section also discusses several methods of classes `Thread` and `Monitor` that cause state transitions. Several of the terms introduced here are discussed in detail in later sections.

A `Thread` object begins its life cycle in the *Unstarted* state when the program creates the object and passes a `ThreadStart` delegate to the object's constructor. (For more information on delegates, see Chapter 13.) The `ThreadStart` delegate, which specifies the actions the thread will perform during its life cycle, must be initialized with a method that takes no arguments and does not return a value. [*Note:* .NET 2.0 also includes a `ParameterizedThreadStart` delegate to which you can pass a method that takes arguments. For more information on this delegate, visit the site `msdn2.microsoft.com/en-us/library/system.threading.parameterizedthreadstart.aspx`.] The thread remains in the *Unstarted* state until the Thread's `Start` method is called, which places the thread in the *Running* state and immediately returns control to the method that called `Start`. Then the newly *Running* thread and any other threads in the program can execute concurrently on a multiprocessor system or share the processor on a system with a single processor.

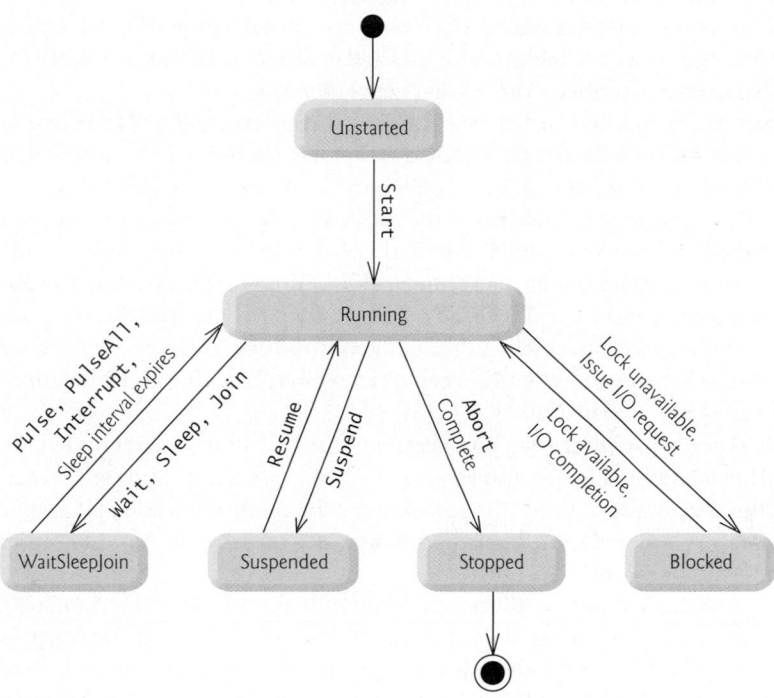

Fig. 15.1 | Thread life cycle.

While in the *Running* state, the thread may not actually be executing all the time. The thread executes in the *Running* state only when the operating system assigns a processor to the thread. When a *Running* thread receives a processor for the first time, the thread begins executing the method specified by its ThreadStart delegate.

A *Running* thread enters the *Stopped* (or *Aborted*) state when its ThreadStart delegate terminates, which normally indicates that the thread has completed its task. Note that a program can force a thread into the *Stopped* state by calling Thread method Abort on the appropriate Thread object. Method Abort throws a ThreadAbortException in the thread, normally causing the thread to terminate. When a thread is in the *Stopped* state and there are no references to the thread object, the garbage collector can remove the thread object from memory. [*Note:* Internally, when a thread's Abort method is called, the thread actually enters the *AbortRequested* state before entering the *Stopped* state. The thread remains in the *AbortRequested* state while waiting to receive the pending ThreadAbortException. When Abort is called, a thread in the *WaitSleepJoin*, *Suspended* or *Blocked* state resides in its current state and the *AbortRequested* state, and cannot receive the ThreadAbortException until it leaves its current state.]

A thread is considered to be *Blocked* if it is unable to use a processor, even if one is available. For example, a thread becomes blocked when it issues an input/output (I/O) request. The thread is blocked from executing by the operating system until it can complete the thread's I/O request. At that point, the thread returns to the *Running* state so that it can resume execution. Another case in which a thread becomes blocked is in thread synchronization (Section 15.5). A thread being synchronized must acquire a lock on an object by calling `Monitor` method `Enter`. If a lock is not available, the thread is blocked until the desired lock becomes available. [*Note: Blocked* is not an actual state in .NET. It is a conceptual state that describes a thread that is not *Running*.]

There are three ways in which a *Running* thread enters the *WaitSleepJoin* state. If a thread encounters code that it cannot execute yet, the thread can call `Monitor` method `Wait` to enter the *WaitSleepJoin* state (we'll present several examples of this in this chapter). Once in this state, a thread returns to the *Running* state when another thread invokes `Monitor` method `Pulse` or `PulseAll`. Method `Pulse` moves the next waiting thread back to the *Running* state. Method `PulseAll` moves all waiting threads back to the *Running* state.

A *Running* thread can call `Thread` method `Sleep` to enter the *WaitSleepJoin* state for a period of milliseconds specified as the argument to `Sleep`. A sleeping thread returns to the *Running* state when its designated sleep time expires. Sleeping threads cannot use a processor even if one is available.

Any thread that enters the *WaitSleepJoin* state by calling `Monitor` method `Wait` or by calling `Thread` method `Sleep` also leaves the *WaitSleepJoin* state and returns to the *Running* state if the sleeping or waiting `Thread`'s `Interrupt` method is called by another thread in the program. The `Interrupt` method causes a `ThreadInterruptionException` to be thrown in the interrupted thread.

A thread that cannot continue executing until another thread terminates is called the dependent thread. The dependent thread calls the other thread's `Join` method to "join" the two threads. When two threads are "joined," the dependent thread leaves the *WaitSleepJoin* state and re-enters the *Running* state when the other thread finishes execution (enters the *Stopped* state).

If a *Running* `Thread`'s `Suspend` method is called, the *Running* thread enters the *Suspended* state. A *Suspended* thread returns to the *Running* state when another thread in the program invokes the *Suspended* thread's `Resume` method. [*Note:* Internally, when a thread's `Suspend` method is called, the thread actually enters the *SuspendRequested* state before entering the *Suspended* state. The thread remains in the *SuspendRequested* state while waiting to respond to the `Suspend` request. A thread that is in the *WaitSleepJoin* state or is blocked when its `Suspend` method is called resides in its current state and the *SuspendRequested* state, and cannot respond to the `Suspend` request until it leaves its current state.] Methods `Suspend` and `Resume` are now deprecated and should not be used. In Section 15.9, we show how to emulate these methods using thread synchronization.

If a thread's `IsBackground` property is set to `True`, the thread resides in the *Background* state (not shown in Fig. 15.1). A thread can reside in the *Background* state and any other state simultaneously. A process cannot terminate until all foreground threads (threads not in the *Background* state) finish executing and enter the *Stopped* state. However, if the only threads remaining in a process are *Background threads*, the CLR terminates each thread by invoking its `Abort` method, and the process terminates.

15.3 Thread Priorities and Thread Scheduling

Every thread has a priority in the range between `ThreadPriority.Lowest` and `ThreadPriority.Highest`. These values come from the `ThreadPriority` enumeration (namespace `System.Threading`), which consists of the values `Lowest`, `BelowNormal`, `Normal`, `AboveNormal` and `Highest`. By default, each thread has priority `Normal`.

The Windows operating system supports a concept called timeslicing that enables threads of equal priority to share a processor. Without timeslicing, each thread in a set of equal-priority threads runs to completion (unless the thread leaves the *Running* state and enters the *WaitSleepJoin*, *Suspended* or *Blocked* state) before the thread's peers get a chance to execute. With timeslicing, each thread receives a brief burst of processor time, called a quantum, during which the thread can execute. At the completion of the quantum, even if the thread has not finished executing, the processor is taken away from that thread and given to the next thread of equal priority, if one is available.

The job of the thread scheduler is to keep the highest-priority thread running at all times and, if there is more than one highest-priority thread, to ensure that all such threads execute for a quantum in round-robin fashion. Figure 15.2 illustrates the multilevel priority queue for threads. In Fig. 15.2, assuming a single-processor computer, threads A and B each execute for a quantum in round-robin fashion until both threads complete execution. This means that A gets a quantum of time to run. Then B gets a quantum. Then A gets another quantum. Then B gets another quantum. This continues until one thread completes. The processor then devotes all its power to the thread that remains (unless another thread of that priority is started). Next, thread C runs to completion. Threads D, E and F each execute for a quantum in round-robin fashion until they all complete execution. This process continues until all the threads run to completion. Depending on the operating system, new higher-priority threads could postpone—possibly indefinitely—the execution of lower-priority threads. Such indefinite postponement often is referred to more colorfully as starvation.

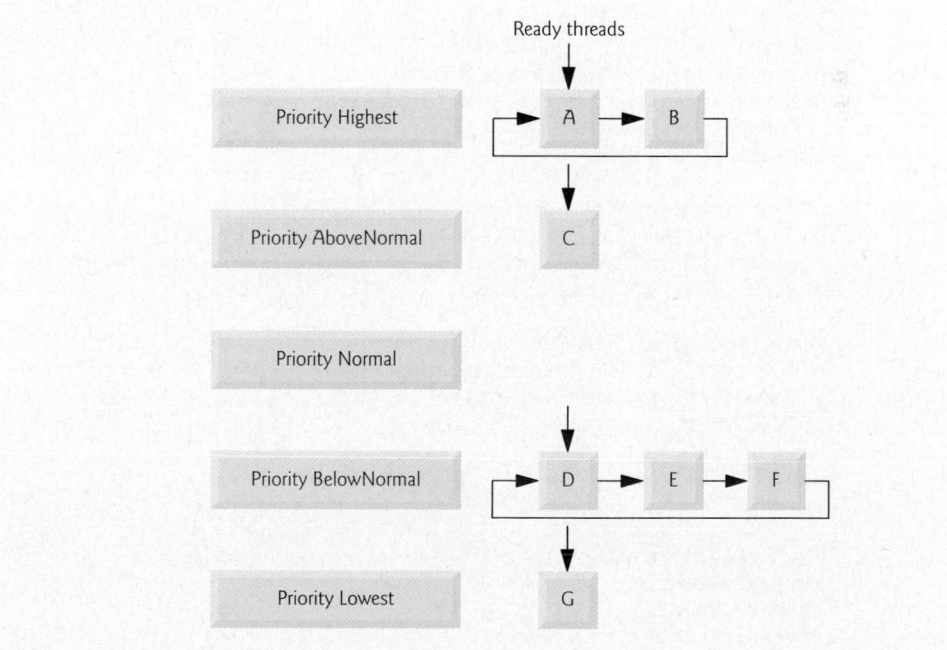

Fig. 15.2 | Thread-priority scheduling.

A thread's priority can be adjusted through the thread's `Priority` property, which accepts values from the `ThreadPriority` enumeration. If the value specified is not one of the valid thread-priority constants, an `ArgumentException` occurs.

A thread executes until it dies, becomes *Blocked* for I/O (or some other reason), calls `Sleep`, calls `Monitor` method `Wait` or `Join`, is preempted by a thread of higher priority or has its **quantum expire**. A thread with a higher priority than the *Running* thread can become *Running* (and hence preempt the first *Running* thread) if a sleeping thread wakes up, if I/O completes for a thread that *Blocked* for that I/O, if either `Pulse` or `PulseAll` is called on an object on which `Wait` was called, if a thread is `Resumed` from the *Suspended* state or if a thread to which the high-priority thread was joined completes.

15.4 Creating and Executing Threads

Figure 15.3 shows how to construct `Thread` objects and demonstrates class `Thread`'s `Shared` method `Sleep`. The program creates three threads of execution, each with the default priority `Normal`. Each thread displays a message indicating that it is going to sleep for a random interval of from 0 to 5000 milliseconds, then goes to sleep. When each thread awakens, it displays its name, indicates that it is done sleeping, terminates and enters the *Stopped* state. You will see that method `Main` (i.e., the `Main` *thread of execution*) terminates

```vb
1   ' Fig. 15.3: ThreadTester.vb
2   ' Multiple threads printing at different intervals.
3   Imports System.Threading
4
5   Module ThreadTester
6      Sub Main()
7         ' Create and name each thread. Use MessagePrinter's
8         ' Print method as argument to ThreadStart delegate.
9         Dim printer1 As New MessagePrinter
10        Dim thread1 As New Thread(New ThreadStart( _
11           AddressOf printer1.Print))
12        thread1.Name = "thread1"
13
14        Dim printer2 As New MessagePrinter
15        Dim thread2 As New Thread(New ThreadStart( _
16           AddressOf printer2.Print))
17        thread2.Name = "thread2"
18
19        Dim printer3 As New MessagePrinter
20        Dim thread3 As New Thread(New ThreadStart( _
21           AddressOf printer3.Print))
22        thread3.Name = "thread3"
23
24        Console.WriteLine("Starting threads in Main")
25
26        ' call each thread's Start method to place each
27        ' thread in Running state
28        thread1.Start()
29        thread2.Start()
30        thread3.Start()
```

Fig. 15.3 | Threads sleeping and printing. (Part 1 of 2.)

```vb
31
32          Console.WriteLine("Threads started, Main ends" & vbCrLf)
33      End Sub ' Main
34
35      ' Print method of this class used to control threads
36      Class MessagePrinter
37          Private sleepTime As Integer
38          Private Shared random As New Random
39
40          ' constructor to initialize a MessagePrinter object
41          Sub New()
42              ' pick random sleep time between 0 and 5 seconds
43              sleepTime = random.Next(5001)
44          End Sub ' New
45
46          ' method Print controls thread that prints messages
47          Public Sub Print()
48              ' obtain reference to currently executing thread
49              Dim current As Thread = Thread.CurrentThread
50
51              ' indicate that thread is going to sleep
52              Console.WriteLine(current.Name & " going to sleep for " & _
53                  sleepTime & " milliseconds")
54              Thread.Sleep(sleepTime) ' sleep for sleepTime milliseconds
55
56              ' display the thread's name
57              Console.WriteLine(current.Name + " done sleeping")
58          End Sub ' Print
59      End Class ' MessagePrinter
60  End Module ' ThreadTester
```

```
Starting threads in Main
thread1 going to sleep for 1603 milliseconds
thread2 going to sleep for 2355 milliseconds
thread3 going to sleep for 285 milliseconds
Threads started, Main ends

thread3 done sleeping
thread1 done sleeping
thread2 done sleeping
```

```
Starting threads in Main
thread1 going to sleep for 4245 milliseconds
thread2 going to sleep for 1466 milliseconds
Threads started, Main ends

thread3 going to sleep for 1929 milliseconds
thread2 done sleeping
thread3 done sleeping
thread1 done sleeping
```

Fig. 15.3 | Threads sleeping and printing. (Part 2 of 2.)

before the application terminates. The program consists of method `Main` (lines 6–33), which creates the three threads, and class `MessagePrinter` (lines 36–59), which defines a `Print` method containing the actions each thread will perform.

Objects of class `MessagePrinter` control the life cycle of each of the three threads created in class `ThreadTester`'s `Main` method. Class `MessagePrinter` consists of instance variable `sleepTime` (line 37), `Shared` variable `random` (line 38), a constructor (lines 41–44) and a `Print` method (lines 47–58). Variable `sleepTime` stores a random integer value chosen when a new `MessagePrinter` object's constructor is called. Each thread controlled by a `MessagePrinter` object sleeps for the amount of time specified by the corresponding `MessagePrinter` object's `sleepTime`.

The `MessagePrinter` constructor (lines 41–44) initializes `sleepTime` to a random number of milliseconds from 0 up to, but not including, 5001 (i.e., from 0 to 5000).

Method `Print` begins by obtaining a reference to the currently executing thread (line 49) via class `Thread`'s `Shared` property `CurrentThread`. The currently executing thread is the one that invoked method `Print`. Next, lines 52–53 display a message indicating the name of the currently executing thread and stating that the thread is going to sleep for a certain number of milliseconds. Note that line 52 uses the currently executing thread's `Name` property to obtain the thread's name (set in method `Main` when each thread is created). Line 54 invokes `Shared` `Thread` method `Sleep` to place the thread in the *WaitSleep-Join* state. At this point, the thread loses the processor, and the system allows another thread to execute if one is ready to run. When the thread awakens, it re-enters the *Running* state and waits to be assigned a processor by the thread scheduler. When the `Message-Printer` object enters the *Running* state again, line 57 outputs the thread's name in a message indicating that the thread is done sleeping, and method `Print` terminates.

Module `ThreadTester`'s `Main` method (lines 6–33) creates three `MessagePrinter` objects (lines 9, 14 and 19). Lines 10–11, 15–16 and 20–21 create and initialize three `Thread` objects. Each `Thread`'s constructor receives as an argument a `ThreadStart` delegate. A `ThreadStart` delegate represents a method with no arguments and no return value that specifies the actions a thread will perform. Lines 10–11 initialize the `ThreadStart` delegate for `thread1` with `printer1`'s `Print` method. The `AddressOf` operator creates a delegate that references a specific method—in this case `printer1.Print`. When `thread1` enters the *Running* state for the first time, `thread1` will invoke `printer1`'s `Print` method to perform the tasks specified in method `Print`'s body. Thus, `thread1` will print its name, display the amount of time for which it will go to sleep, sleep for that amount of time, wake up and display a message indicating that the thread is done sleeping. At that point, method `Print` will terminate. A thread completes its task when the method specified by its `ThreadStart` delegate terminates, at which point the thread enters the *Stopped* state. When `thread2` and `thread3` enter the *Running* state for the first time, they invoke the `Print` methods of `printer2` and `printer3`, respectively. Threads `thread2` and `thread3` perform the same tasks as `thread1` by executing the `Print` methods of the objects to which `printer2` and `printer3` refer (each of which has its own randomly chosen sleep time). Lines 12, 17 and 22 set each `Thread`'s `Name` property, which we use for output purposes.

Error-Prevention Tip 15.1

Naming threads helps in the debugging of a multithreaded program. Visual Studio .NET's debugger provides a **Threads** *window that displays the name of each thread and enables you to view the execution of any thread in the program.*

Lines 28–30 invoke each Thread's Start method to place the threads in the *Running* state. Method Start returns immediately from each invocation, then line 32 outputs a message indicating that the threads were started, and the Main thread of execution terminates. The program itself does not terminate, however, because there are still non-background threads that are alive (i.e., the threads are *Running* and have not yet reached the *Stopped* state). The program will not terminate until its last non-background thread dies. When the system assigns a processor to a thread, the thread enters the *Running* state and calls the method specified by the thread's ThreadStart delegate. In this program, each thread invokes method Print of the appropriate MessagePrinter object to perform the tasks discussed previously.

Note that the sample outputs for this program show each thread and the thread's sleep time in milliseconds as the thread goes to sleep. The thread with the shortest sleep time normally awakens first, then indicates that it is done sleeping and terminates. In Section 15.8, we discuss multithreading issues that could prevent the thread with the shortest sleep time from awakening first. Notice in the second sample output that thread1 and thread2 were able to report their sleep times before Main could output its final message. This means that the main thread's quantum ended before it could finish executing Main, and thread1 and thread2 each got a chance to execute.

15.5 Thread Synchronization and Class Monitor

Often, multiple threads of execution manipulate shared data. If threads with access to shared data simply read that data, then any number of threads can access the data simultaneously without problems. However, when multiple threads share data and the data is modified by one or more of the threads, then indeterminate results may occur. If one thread is in the process of updating the data and another thread tries to update it too, the data will reflect only the later update. If the data is an array or other data structure in which the threads could update separate parts of the data concurrently, it is possible that part of the data will reflect the information from one thread while another part of the data will reflect information from another thread. When this happens, the program has difficulty determining when the data has been updated properly.

The problem can be solved by giving one thread at a time exclusive access to code that manipulates the shared data. During this time, other threads wishing to manipulate the data are kept waiting. When the thread with exclusive access to the data completes its data manipulations, one of the waiting threads is allowed to proceed. In this fashion, each thread accessing the shared data excludes all other threads from doing so simultaneously. This is called mutual exclusion or thread synchronization.

Visual Basic programmers use the .NET Framework's monitors to perform synchronization. Class Monitor provides the methods for locking objects to implement synchronized access to shared data. Locking an object means that only one thread can access that object at a time. When a thread wishes to acquire exclusive control over an object, the thread invokes the Monitor method Enter to acquire the lock on the data object. Each object has a SyncBlock that maintains the state of the object's lock. Methods of class Monitor use the data in an object's SyncBlock to determine the state of the lock for that object. After acquiring the lock for an object, a thread can manipulate that object's data. While the object is locked, all other threads attempting to acquire the lock on that object are blocked from acquiring the lock—such threads enter the *Blocked* state. When the thread that locked the shared object no longer requires the lock, that thread invokes Monitor method `Exit` to release the lock. This updates the SyncBlock of the shared object to indicate that the lock for the object is available again. At this point, if there is a thread that was previously blocked from acquiring the lock on the shared object, that thread acquires the lock to begin its processing of the object. If all threads with access to an object attempt to acquire the object's lock before manipulating the object, only one thread at a time will be allowed to manipulate the object. This helps ensure the integrity of the data.

Error-Prevention Tip 15.2

All code that modifies a shared object should first lock the object to ensure that only one thread at a time has access to the shared object.

Common Programming Error 15.1

Deadlock occurs when a waiting thread (let us call this thread1) cannot proceed because it is waiting (either directly or indirectly) for another thread (let us call this thread2) to proceed, while simultaneously thread2 cannot proceed because it is waiting (either directly or indirectly) for thread1 to proceed. Two threads are waiting for each other, so the actions that would enable either thread to continue execution never occur.

Visual Basic provides another means of manipulating an object's lock—the `SyncLock` statement. Wrapping a block of code in `SyncLock... End SyncLock`, as in

```
SyncLock objectReference
    ' code that requires synchronization goes here
End SyncLock
```

obtains the lock on the object to which the *objectReference* refers; thus, only one thread at a time can execute the code in a `SyncLock` statement. The *objectReference* is the same reference that normally would be passed to `Monitor` methods `Enter`, `Exit`, `Pulse` and `PulseAll`. When a `SyncLock` statement terminates for any reason, Visual Basic releases the lock on the object to which the *objectReference* refers. We explain `SyncLock` further in Section 15.8.

If a thread that owns the lock on an object determines that it cannot continue with its task until some condition is satisfied, the thread should call `Monitor` method `Wait` and pass as an argument the object on which the thread will wait until the thread can perform its task. Calling method `Monitor.Wait` from a thread releases the lock the thread has on the object that `Wait` receives as an argument and places that thread in the *WaitSleepJoin* state for that object. A thread in the *WaitSleepJoin* state of a specific object leaves that state when a separate thread invokes `Monitor` method `Pulse` or `PulseAll` with that object as an argument. Method `Pulse` transitions the object's first waiting thread from the *WaitSleepJoin* state to the *Running* state. Method `PulseAll` transitions all threads in the object's *WaitSleepJoin* state to the *Running* state. The transition to the *Running* state enables the thread (or threads) to get ready to continue executing.

There is a difference between threads waiting to acquire an object's lock and threads waiting in an object's *WaitSleepJoin* state. Threads that call `Monitor` method `Wait` with an object as an argument are placed in that object's *WaitSleepJoin* state. Threads that are simply waiting to acquire the lock enter the conceptual *Blocked* state and wait until the object's lock becomes available. Then a *Blocked* thread can acquire the object's lock.

`Monitor` methods `Enter`, `Exit`, `Wait`, `Pulse` and `PulseAll` all take a reference to an object—usually the keyword `Me`—as their argument.

Common Programming Error 15.2

A thread in the WaitSleepJoin *state cannot re-enter the* Running *state to continue execution until a separate thread invokes* Monitor *method* Pulse *or* PulseAll *with the appropriate object as an argument. If this does not occur, the waiting thread will wait forever—essentially the equivalent of deadlock.*

Error-Prevention Tip 15.3

When multiple threads manipulate a shared object using monitors, ensure that if one thread calls Monitor *method* Wait *to enter the* WaitSleepJoin *state for the shared object, a separate thread eventually will call* Monitor *method* Pulse *to transition the thread waiting on the shared object back to the* Running *state. If multiple threads may be waiting for the shared object, a separate thread can call* Monitor *method* PulseAll *as a safeguard to ensure that all waiting threads have another opportunity to perform their tasks. If this is not done, indefinite postponement or deadlock could occur.*

Performance Tip 15.2

Synchronization to achieve correctness in multithreaded programs can make programs run more slowly, as a result of monitor overhead and the frequent transitioning of threads between the Running, WaitSleepJoin *and* Running *states. There is not much to say, however, for highly efficient but incorrect multithreaded programs!*

15.6 Producer/Consumer Relationship without Thread Synchronization

In a **producer/consumer relationship**, the *producer* portion of an application generates data and the *consumer* portion of the application uses that data. In a multithreaded producer/consumer relationship, a **producer thread** calls a **produce method** to generate data and place it in a shared region of memory called a **buffer**. A **consumer thread** calls a **consume method** to read the data. If the producer wishes to put the next data in the buffer but determines that the consumer has not yet read the previous data from the buffer, the producer thread should call Wait. Otherwise, the consumer would never see the previous data, which would be lost to that application. When the consumer thread reads the data, it should call Pulse to allow a waiting producer to proceed, since there is now free space in the buffer. If a consumer thread finds the buffer empty or finds that the previous data has already been read, the consumer should call Wait. Otherwise, the consumer might read "garbage" from the buffer or might process a previous data item more than once—each of these possibilities results in a logic error in the application. When the producer places the next data into the buffer, the producer should call Pulse to allow the consumer thread to proceed and read that data.

Let us consider how logic errors can arise if we do not synchronize access among multiple threads manipulating shared data. Consider a producer/consumer relationship in which a producer thread writes a sequence of numbers (we use 1–10) into a **shared buffer**—a memory location shared between multiple threads. The consumer thread reads this data from the shared buffer, then displays the data. We display in the program's output the values that the producer writes (produces) and the consumer reads (consumes). Figures 15.4–15.8 demonstrate a producer thread and a consumer thread accessing a single shared Integer variable without any synchronization. The producer thread writes to the variable; the consumer thread reads from it. We would like each value the producer thread writes to the shared variable to be consumed exactly once by the consumer thread. However, the threads in this example are not synchronized. Therefore, data can be lost if the producer places new data in the variable before the consumer consumes the previous data. Also, data can be incorrectly repeated if the consumer consumes data again before the producer produces the next value. If the consumer attempts to read before the producer produces the first value, the consumer reads garbage. To show these possibilities, the consumer thread in the example keeps a total of all the values it reads. The producer thread produces values from 1 to 10. If the consumer reads each value produced once and only once, the total will be 55. However, when you execute this program several times, you'll see that the total is rarely, if ever, 55. Also, to emphasize our point, the producer and consumer threads in the example each sleep for random intervals of up to three seconds between performing their tasks. Thus, we do not know exactly when the producer thread will attempt to write a new value, nor do we know when the consumer thread will attempt to read a value.

The program consists of interface IBuffer (Fig. 15.4), three classes—Producer (Fig. 15.5), Consumer (Fig. 15.6), UnsynchronizedBuffer (Fig. 15.7), and one module—UnsynchronizedBufferTest (Fig. 15.8). Interface IBuffer declares an Integer property called Buffer. Any implementation of IBuffer must provide a Get and a Set accessor for this property to allow the producer and consumer to access the shared data stored in the buffer.

Class Producer (Figure 15.5) consists of instance variable sharedLocation (line 8) of type IBuffer, instance variable randomSleepTime (line 9) of type Random, a constructor (lines 12–15) to initialize the instance variables and a Produce method (lines 18–28). The constructor initializes instance variable sharedLocation to refer to the IBuffer object received from method Main as the parameter sharedBuffer. The producer thread in this program executes the tasks specified in method Produce of class Producer. The For statement in method Produce (lines 21–24) loops ten times. Each iteration of the loop first invokes Thread method Sleep to place the producer thread in the *WaitSleepJoin* state for a random time interval between 0 and 3 seconds. When the thread awakens, line 23 assigns the value of control variable count to sharedLocation's Buffer property. When the loop completes, lines 26–27 display a line of text in the console window indicating that the thread has finished producing data and the thread is terminating. The Produce method then terminates, and the producer thread enters the *Stopped* state.

Class Consumer (Figure 15.6) consists of instance variable sharedLocation (line 8) of type IBuffer, instance variable randomSleepTime (line 9) of type Random, a constructor (lines 12–15) to initialize the instance variables and a Consume method (lines 18–31). The constructor initializes sharedLocation to refer to the IBuffer object received from Main as the parameter shared. The consumer thread in this program performs the tasks specified in class Consumer's Consume method. The method contains a for statement (lines 23–

```vb
1   ' Fig. 15.4: IBuffer.vb
2   ' Interface for a shared Integer buffer.
3   Public Interface IBuffer
4      Property Buffer() As Integer ' property to access the buffer
5   End Interface ' IBuffer
```

Fig. 15.4 | IBuffer interface used in producer/consumer examples.

```
 1     ' Fig. 15.5: Producer.vb
 2     ' Producer produces ten integer values in the shared buffer.
 3     Imports System.Threading
 4
 5     ' class Producer's Produce method controls a thread that
 6     ' stores values from 1 to 10 in sharedLocation
 7     Public Class Producer
 8        Private sharedLocation As IBuffer
 9        Private randomSleepTime As Random
10
11        ' constructor
12        Public Sub New(ByVal sharedBuffer As IBuffer, ByVal random As Random)
13           sharedLocation = sharedBuffer
14           randomSleepTime = random
15        End Sub ' New
16
17        ' store values 1-10 in object sharedLocation
18        Public Sub Produce()
19           ' sleep for random interval up to 3000 milliseconds
20           ' then set sharedLocation's Buffer property
21           For count As Integer = 1 To 10
22              Thread.Sleep(randomSleepTime.Next(1, 3001))
23              sharedLocation.Buffer = count
24           Next count
25
26           Console.WriteLine(Thread.CurrentThread.Name & " done producing." & _
27              vbCrLf & "Terminating " & Thread.CurrentThread.Name & ".")
28        End Sub ' Produce
29     End Class ' Producer
```

Fig. 15.5 | Producer represents the producer thread in a producer/consumer relationship.

26) that loops ten times. Each iteration of the loop invokes Thread method Sleep to put the consumer thread into the *WaitSleepJoin* state for a random time interval between 0 and 3 seconds. Next, line 25 gets the value of sharedLocation's Buffer property and adds the value to variable sum. When the loop completes, lines 28–30 display a line in the console window indicating the sum of all values read. Again, ideally the total should be 55, but because access to the shared data is not synchronized, this sum will almost never appear. The Consume method then terminates, and the consumer thread enters the *Stopped* state.

We use method Sleep in this example's threads to emphasize the fact that in multi-threaded applications, it is unclear when each thread will perform its task and for how long it will perform that task when it has the processor. Normally, these thread-scheduling issues are the job of the computer's operating system. In this program, our thread's tasks are quite simple—for the producer, loop ten times and perform an assignment statement; for the consumer, loop ten times and add a value to variable sum. Without the Sleep method call, and if the producer executes first, the producer would most likely complete its task before the consumer ever gets a chance to execute. If the consumer executes first, it would consume -1 ten times, then terminate before the producer could produce the first real value.

Class UnsynchronizedBuffer (Figure 15.7) implements interface IBuffer (line 7) and consists of instance variable bufferValue (line 10) and property Buffer (lines 13–24),

```
Consumer reads 3 (buffers occupied: 0)
buffers:    1    2    3
            ---- ---- ----
            WR

All buffers empty. Consumer waits.
Producer writes 4 (buffers occupied: 1)
buffers:    4    2    3
            ---- ---- ----
            R    W

Producer writes 5 (buffers occupied: 2)
buffers:    4    5    3
            ---- ---- ----
            R         W

Consumer reads 4 (buffers occupied: 1)
buffers:    4    5    3
            ---- ---- ----
                 R    W

Producer writes 6 (buffers occupied: 2)
buffers:    4    5    6
            ---- ---- ----
            W         R

Producer writes 7 (buffers occupied: 3)
buffers:    7    5    6
            ---- ---- ----
                 WR

All buffers full. Producer waits.
Consumer reads 5 (buffers occupied: 2)
buffers:    7    5    6
            ---- ---- ----
                 W    R

Consumer reads 6 (buffers occupied: 1)
buffers:    7    5    6
            ---- ---- ----
            R    W

Producer writes 8 (buffers occupied: 2)
buffers:    7    8    6
            ---- ---- ----
            R         W

Consumer reads 7 (buffers occupied: 1)
buffers:    7    8    6
            ---- ---- ----
                 R    W

Consumer reads 8 (buffers occupied: 0)
buffers:    7    8    6
            ---- ---- ----
                 WR
```

Fig. 15.12 | Producer and consumer threads accessing a circular buffer. (Part 3 of 4.)

```
Producer writes 9 (buffers occupied: 1)
buffers:   7    8    9
         ---- ---- ----
           W         R

Producer writes 10 (buffers occupied: 2)
buffers:   10   8    9
         ---- ---- ----
                W    R
Producer done producing.
Terminating Producer.

Consumer reads 9 (buffers occupied: 1)
buffers:   10   8    9
         ---- ---- ----
           R    W

Consumer reads 10 (buffers occupied: 0)
buffers:   10   8    9
         ---- ---- ----
                WR
Consumer read values totaling: 55.
Terminating Consumer.
```

Fig. 15.12 | Producer and consumer threads accessing a circular buffer. (Part 4 of 4.)

15.9 **Multithreading with GUIs**

The nature of multithreaded programming prevents you from knowing exactly when a thread will execute. GUI controls are not thread safe—if multiple threads manipulate a control, the results may not be correct. To ensure that threads manipulate controls in a thread-safe manner, all interactions with them should be performed by the User Interface thread (also known as the UI thread)—the thread that creates and maintains the GUI. Class Control provides method Invoke to help with this process. Method Invoke specifies GUI processing statements that the UI thread should execute. The method receives as its arguments a Delegate representing a method that will modify the GUI and an optional array of objects representing the parameters to the method. At some point after Invoke is called, the UI thread will execute the method represented by the Delegate, passing to the contents of the object array as the method's arguments.

Our next example (Figs. 15.13–15.14) uses separate threads to modify the content displayed in a Windows GUI. This example also demonstrates how to use thread synchronization to suspend a thread (i.e., temporarily prevent it from executing) and to resume a suspended thread. The GUI for the application contains three Labels and three Check-Boxes. Each thread in the program displays random characters in a particular Label. The user can temporarily suspend a thread by clicking the appropriate CheckBox and can resume the thread's execution by clicking the same CheckBox again.

Class RandomLetters (Fig. 15.13) contains method Run (lines 28–49), which takes no arguments and does not return any values. Line 30 uses Shared Thread property current-Thread to determine the currently executing thread, then uses the thread's Name property to get the thread's name. Each executing thread is assigned a name that includes the number of the thread in the Main method (see the output of Fig. 15.14). Lines 32–48 are an infinite loop, which is in a separate thread from the main thread. When the application window is closed in this example, all the threads created by the main thread are closed as well, including threads (such as this one) that are executing infinite loops. In each iteration of the loop, the thread sleeps for a random interval from 0 to 1 second (line 34).

```vb
1    ' Fig. 15.13: RandomLetters.vb
2    ' Writes a random letter to a label
3    Imports System.Threading
4
5    Public Class RandomLetters
6       Private Shared generator As New Random() ' for random letters
7       Private suspended As Boolean = False ' true if thread is suspended
8       Private output As Label ' Label for output
9       Private threadName As String ' name of the current thread
10
11      ' constructor
12      Public Sub New(ByVal label As Label)
13         output = label
14      End Sub ' New
15
16      ' delegate that allows method DisplayCharacter to be called
17      ' in the thread that creates and maintains the GUI
18      Delegate Sub DisplayDelegate(ByVal displayChar As Char)
19
20      ' method DisplayCharacter sets the Label's Text property
21      ' in a thread-safe manner
22      Private Sub DisplayCharacter(ByVal displayChar As Char)
23         ' output character in Label
24         output.Text = threadName + ": " + displayChar
25      End Sub ' DisplayCharacter
26
27      ' place random characters in GUI
28      Public Sub Run()
29         ' get name of executing thread
30         threadName = Thread.CurrentThread.Name
31
32         While True ' infinite loop; will be terminated from outside
33            ' sleep for up to 1 second
34            Thread.Sleep(generator.Next(1001))
35
36            SyncLock Me ' obtain lock
37               While suspended ' loop until not suspended
38                  Monitor.Wait(Me) ' suspend thread execution
39               End While
40            End SyncLock
41
42            ' select random uppercase letter
43            Dim displayChar As Char = ChrW(generator.Next(26) + 65)
44
```

Fig. 15.13 | Class RandomLetters outputs random letters and can be suspended. (Part 1 of 2.)

```
45                    ' display character on corresponding Label
46                    output.Invoke(New DisplayDelegate(AddressOf DisplayCharacter), _
47                        New Object() {displayChar})
48             End While
49         End Sub ' Run
50
51         ' change the suspended/running state
52         Public Sub Toggle()
53             suspended = Not suspended ' toggle bool controlling state
54
55             ' change label color on suspend/resume
56             If suspended Then
57                 output.BackColor = Color.Red
58             Else
59                 output.BackColor = Color.LightGreen
60             End If
61
62             SyncLock Me ' obtain lock
63                 If Not suspended Then ' if thread resumed
64                     Monitor.Pulse(Me)
65                 End If
66             End SyncLock
67         End Sub ' Toggle
68     End Class ' RandomLetters
```

Fig. 15.13 | Class RandomLetters outputs random letters and can be suspended. (Part 2 of 2.)

When the thread awakens, line 36 locks this RandomLetters object. so we can determine whether the thread has been suspended (i.e., the user clicked the corresponding CheckBox). Lines 37–39 loop while the Boolean variable suspended remains True. Line 38 calls Monitor method Wait on this RandomLetters object to temporarily release the lock and place this thread into the *WaitSleepJoin* state. When this thread is Pulsed (i.e., the user clicks the corresponding CheckBox again), it moves back to the *Running* state. If suspended is False, the thread resumes execution. If suspended is still True, the loop executes again and the thread re-enters the *WaitSleepJoin* state.

Line 43 generates a random uppercase character. Lines 46–47 call method Invoke passing to it a New DisplayDelegate containing the method DisplayCharacter and a New array of Objects that contains the randomly generated letter. Line 18 declares a Delegate type named DisplayDelegate, which represents methods that take a Char argument and do not return a value. Method DisplayCharacter (lines 22–25) meets those requirements—it receives a Char parameter named displayChar and does not return a value. The call to Invoke in lines 46–47 will cause the UI thread to call DisplayCharacter with the randomly generated letter as the argument. At that time, line 24 will replace the text in the Label associated with this RandomLetters object with the name of the Thread executing this RandomLetters object's GenerateRandomCharacters method and the randomly generated letter.

When the user clicks the CheckBox to the right of a Label, the corresponding thread should be suspended (temporarily prevented from executing) or resumed (allowed to continue executing). Suspending and resuming a thread can be implemented by using thread synchronization and `Monitor` methods `Wait` and `Pulse`. Lines 52–67 declare method `Toggle`, which will change the suspended/resumed state of the current thread. Line 53 reverses the value of `Boolean` variable `suspended`. Lines 56–60 change the background color of the `Label` by assigning a color to `Label` property `BackColor`. If the thread is suspended, the background color will be `Color.Red`. If the thread is running, the background color will be `Color.LightGreen`. Method `Toggle` is called from the event handler in Fig. 15.14, so its tasks will be performed in the UI thread—thus, there is no need to use `Invoke` for lines 57 and 59. Line 62 locks this `RandomLetters` object so we can determine whether the thread should resume execution. If so, line 64 calls method `Pulse` on this `RandomLetters` object to alert the thread that was placed in the *WaitSleepJoin* state by the `Wait` method call in line 38.

Note that the `If` statement in line 63 does not have an associated `Else`. If this condition fails, it means that the thread has just been suspended. When this happens, a thread executing in line 37 will enter the `while` loop and line 38 will suspend the thread with a call to method `Wait`.

Class `frmGUIThreads` (Fig. 15.14) displays three `Label`s and three `CheckBox`es. A separate thread of execution is associated with each `Label` and `CheckBox` pair. Each thread randomly displays letters from the alphabet in its corresponding `Label` object. Lines 14, 21 and 28 create three new `RandomLetters` objects. Lines 15–16, 22–23 and 29–30 create three new `Thread`s that will execute the `RandomLetters` objects' `GenerateRandomCharacters` methods. Lines 17, 24 and 31 assign each `Thread` a name, and lines 18, 25 and 32 `Start` the `Thread`s.

```
1   ' Fig. 15.14: frmGUIThreads.vb
2   ' Demonstrates using threads in a GUI
3   Imports System.Threading
4
5   Public Class frmGUIThreads
6      Private letter1 As RandomLetters ' first randomLetters object
7      Private letter2 As RandomLetters ' second randomLetters object
8      Private letter3 As RandomLetters ' third randomLetters object
9
10     Private Sub frmGUIThreads_Load(ByVal sender As System.Object, _
11        ByVal e As System.EventArgs) Handles MyBase.Load
12
13        ' create first thread
14        letter1 = New RandomLetters(lblThread1)
15        Dim firstThread As New Thread(New ThreadStart( _
16           AddressOf letter1.Run))
17        firstThread.Name = "Thread 1"
18        firstThread.Start()
19
20        ' create second thread
21        letter2 = New RandomLetters(lblTread2)
22        Dim secondThread As New Thread(New ThreadStart( _
23           AddressOf letter2.Run))
24        secondThread.Name = "Thread 2"
25        secondThread.Start()
```

Fig. 15.14 | `GUIThreads` demonstrates multithreading in a GUI application. (Part 1 of 2.)

```
26
27          ' create third thread
28          letter3 = New RandomLetters(lblThread3)
29          Dim thirdThread As New Thread(New ThreadStart( _
30             AddressOf letter3.Run))
31          thirdThread.Name = "Thread 3"
32          thirdThread.Start()
33       End Sub ' frmGUIThreads_Load
34
35       ' close all threads associated with this application
36       Private Sub frmGUIThreads_FormClosing(ByVal sender As System.Object, _
37          ByVal e As System.Windows.Forms.FormClosingEventArgs) _
38          Handles MyBase.FormClosing
39          System.Environment.Exit(System.Environment.ExitCode)
40       End Sub ' frmGUIThreads_FormClosing
41
42       Private Sub chkThread_CheckedChanged(ByVal sender As System.Object, _
43          ByVal e As System.EventArgs) Handles chkThread1.CheckedChanged, _
44          chkThread3.CheckedChanged, chkThread2.CheckedChanged
45          If sender.Equals(chkThread1) Then
46             letter1.Toggle()
47          ElseIf sender.Equals(chkThread2) Then
48             letter2.Toggle()
49          ElseIf sender.Equals(chkThread3) Then
50             letter3.Toggle()
51          End If
52       End Sub ' chkThread_CheckedChanged
53    End Class ' frmGUIThreads
```

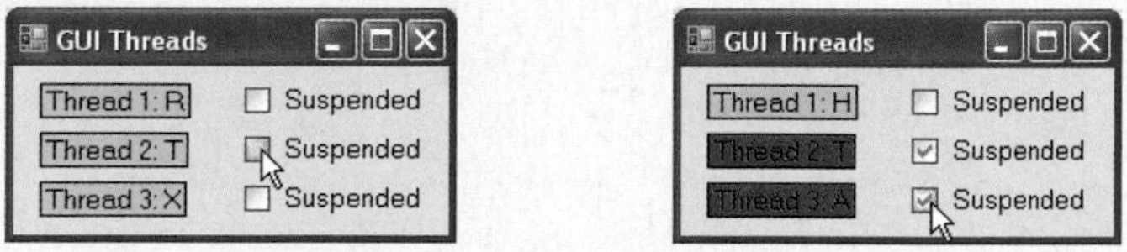

Fig. 15.14 | GUIThreads demonstrates multithreading in a GUI application. (Part 2 of 2.)

If the user clicks the **Suspended** CheckBox next to a Label, event handler chkThread_CheckedChanged (lines 42–52) determines which CheckBox was clicked and calls its associated RandomLetters object's Toggle method to suspend or resume the thread.

Lines 36–40 define the frmGUIThreads_FormClosing event handler, which calls method Exit of class System.Environment with the ExitCode property as an argument. This causes all other threads in this application to terminate. Otherwise, only the UI thread would be terminated when the user closes this application; Thread1, Thread2 and Thread3 would continue executing forever.

15.10 **Wrap-Up**

In this chapter, you learned the capabilities of the .NET framework that enable you to specify concurrent tasks in your programs. We discussed how to create threads of execution using class Thread and ThreadStart delegates—both from the System.Threading namespace.

We discussed several applications of concurrent programming. In particular, you learned about problems that may occur when multiple threads share the same data. To emphasize these issues, we presented an unsynchronized example of the producer/consumer relationship in which a producer thread placed values in a shared buffer and a consumer thread consumed those values. We then demonstrated the producer/consumer relationship again and showed how to synchronize threads using the capabilities of class Monitor. This ensured that the shared data was accessed and manipulated properly by the producer and consumer threads. You also learned how to enable threads to operate more efficiently by using a circular buffer that provided extra locations in which the producer could place values and from which the consumer could retrieve those values.

Next, you learned that GUI components are not thread safe, so all changes to GUI components should be performed in the user interface thread that creates and maintains the GUI. We showed how to use Control method Invoke and a delegate to allow a thread to specify the tasks the user interface thread should perform on GUI components. This enabled multiple threads to modify GUI components in a thread-safe manner. In the next chapter, you will learn about the .NET framework's string, character and regular expression processing capabilities.

Summary

Section 15.1 Introduction

- Computers perform operations concurrently—compiling a program, sending a file to a printer and receiving electronic mail messages can all occur in parallel.

- Historically, the type of concurrency that computers perform today has generally been implemented as operating system "primitives" available only to experienced "systems programmers."

- The Ada programming language, developed by the United States Department of Defense, made concurrency primitives widely available.

- The FCL provides concurrency primitives in the System.Threading namespace.

- Each thread designates a portion of a program that may execute concurrently with other threads—this capability is called multithreading.

- An example of multithreading is the CLR's a garbage-collector thread, which reclaims dynamically allocated memory that is no longer needed.

Section 15.2 Thread States: Life Cycle of a Thread

- At any time, a thread is in one of several thread states.

- A Thread object begins its life cycle in the *Unstarted* state when the program creates the object and passes a ThreadStart delegate to the object's constructor.

- A ThreadStart delegate, which specifies the actions the thread will perform during its life cycle, must be initialized with a method that takes no arguments and does not return a value.

- A thread remains in the *Unstarted* state until the program calls the Thread's Start method, which places the thread in the *Running* state and immediately returns control to the part of the program that called Start.

- While in the *Running* state, a thread may not actually be executing all the time. The thread executes in the *Running* state only when the operating system assigns a processor to it.

- When a *Running* thread receives a processor for the first time, the thread begins executing the method specified by its ThreadStart delegate.

- A *Running* thread enters the *Stopped* (or *Aborted*) state when its `ThreadStart` delegate terminates, which normally indicates that the thread has completed its task.

- A program can force a thread into the *Stopped* state by calling `Thread` method `Abort` on the appropriate `Thread` object. Method `Abort` throws a `ThreadAbortException` in the thread, normally causing the thread to terminate.

- When a thread is in the *Stopped* state and there are no references to the thread object, the garbage collector can remove the thread object from memory.

- A thread is considered to be *Blocked* if it is unable to use a processor even if one is available.

- If a thread encounters code that it cannot execute yet, it can call `Monitor` method `Wait` to enter the *WaitSleepJoin* state. Once in this state, a thread returns to the *Running* state when another thread invokes `Monitor` method `Pulse` or `PulseAll`. Method `Pulse` moves the next waiting thread back to the *Running* state; `PulseAll` moves all waiting threads back.

- A *Running* thread can call `Thread` method `Sleep` to enter the *WaitSleepJoin* state for a specified period of milliseconds. The thread returns to the *Running* state when its sleep time expires.

- Any thread that enters the *WaitSleepJoin* state also returns to the *Running* state if the Thread's `Interrupt` method is called by another thread in the program. This causes a `ThreadInterruptionException` to be thrown in the interrupted thread.

- A thread that cannot continue executing until another thread terminates is called the dependent thread. The dependent thread calls the other thread's `Join` method to "join" the two threads. The dependent thread leaves the *WaitSleepJoin* state and re-enters the *Running* state when the other thread finishes execution (enters the *Stopped* state).

- If a *Running* Thread's `Suspend` method is called, it enters the *Suspended* state. A *Suspended* thread returns to the *Running* state when another thread in the program invokes the *Suspended* thread's `Resume` method. Methods `Suspend` and `Resume` are now deprecated.

- If a thread's `IsBackground` property is set to `True`, the thread resides in the *Background* state. A thread can reside in the *Background* state and any other state simultaneously.

- A process must wait for all foreground threads to enter the *Stopped* state before it can terminate. If the only threads remaining in a process are *Background threads*, the CLR terminates them by invoking their `Abort` methods, and the process terminates.

Section 15.3 Thread Priorities and Thread Scheduling

- Every thread has a priority in the range between `ThreadPriority.Lowest` and `ThreadPriority.Highest`. These values come from the `ThreadPriority` enumeration (namespace `System.Threading`), which consists of the values `Lowest`, `BelowNormal`, `Normal`, `AboveNormal` and `Highest`. By default, each thread has priority `Normal`.

- The Windows operating system supports a concept called timeslicing that enables threads of equal priority to share a processor.

- Without timeslicing, each thread in a set of equal-priority threads runs to completion (unless the thread leaves the *Running* state and enters the *WaitSleepJoin*, *Suspended* or *Blocked* state) before the thread's peers get a chance to execute.

- With timeslicing, each thread receives a brief burst of processor time, called a quantum, during which the thread can execute. At the completion of the quantum, the processor is taken away from that thread and given to the next thread of equal priority, if one is available.

- The job of the thread scheduler is to keep the highest-priority thread running at all times and, if there is more than one highest-priority thread, to ensure that all such threads execute for a quantum in round-robin fashion.

- A thread's priority can be adjusted with the `Priority` property, which accepts values from the `ThreadPriority` enumeration. If the value specified is not one of the valid thread-priority constants, an `ArgumentException` occurs.

- A thread executes until it dies, becomes *Blocked*, calls `Sleep`, calls `Monitor` method `Wait` or `Join`, is preempted by a thread of higher priority or has its quantum expire.

- A thread with a higher priority than the *Running* thread can preempt the *Running* thread.

Section 15.4 Creating and Executing Threads

- `Thread` Shared property `CurrentThread` returns the currently executing thread.

- `Thread` property `Name` specifies the name of the thread.

- `Thread`'s Shared method `Sleep` places a thread into the *WaitSleepJoin* state for a specified number of milliseconds. At this point, the thread loses the processor, and the system allows another thread to execute if one is ready to run. When the thread awakens, it re-enters the *Running* state and waits for the thread scheduler to assign a processor to the thread.

- A `Thread` constructor receives as an argument a `ThreadStart` delegate that represents a method with no arguments and no return type, and specifies the actions the thread will perform.

- `Thread` method `Start` places a thread in the *Running* state. Method `Start` returns immediately.

- When the system assigns a processor to a thread for the first time, the thread calls the method specified by the thread's `ThreadStart` delegate.

Section 15.5 Thread Synchronization and Class `Monitor`

- When multiple threads share data and that data is modified by one or more of the threads, indeterminate results may occur. The problem can be solved by giving one thread at a time exclusive access to code that manipulates the shared data. During this time, other threads wishing to manipulate the data are kept waiting. When the thread with exclusive access to the data completes its data manipulations, one of the waiting threads is allowed to proceed. In this fashion, each thread accessing the shared data excludes all other threads from doing so simultaneously. This is called mutual exclusion or thread synchronization.

- Class `Monitor` provides the methods for locking objects to implement synchronized access to shared data. Locking an object means that only one thread can access that object at a time.

- When a thread wishes to acquire exclusive control over an object, the thread invokes the `Monitor` method `Enter` to acquire the lock on that data object.

- Each object has a SyncBlock that maintains the state of that object's lock. Methods of class `Monitor` use the data in an object's SyncBlock to determine the state of the lock for that object.

- While an object is locked, all other threads attempting to acquire the lock on that object are blocked from acquiring the lock—such threads enter the *Blocked* state.

- When the thread that locked a shared object no longer requires the lock, that thread invokes `Monitor` method `Exit` to release the lock. This updates the SyncBlock of the shared object to indicate that the lock for the object is available again. If a thread was previously blocked from acquiring the lock on the shared object, that thread acquires the lock to begin its processing of the object.

- Visual Basic provides another means of manipulating an object's lock—keyword `SyncLock`. Enclosing a block of code in `SyncLock...End SyncLock` obtains the lock on the object specified after keyword `SyncLock`. This is the same object that normally would be passed to class `Monitor`'s methods. When a lock block terminates for any reason, Visual Basic releases the lock on the object.

- If a thread that owns the lock on an object determines that it cannot continue executing until some condition is satisfied, the thread should call `Monitor` method `Wait` and pass as an argument the object on which the thread will wait. This releases the lock the thread has on that object and places the thread into the *WaitSleepJoin* state for that object.

- A thread in the *WaitSleepJoin* state of a specific object leaves that state when a separate thread invokes `Monitor` method `Pulse` or `PulseAll` with the object on which the thread is waiting as an argument. Method `Pulse` transitions the object's first waiting thread to the *Running* state; `PulseAll` transitions all the object's waiting threads to the *Running* state.

- There is a difference between threads waiting to acquire an object's lock and threads waiting in the *WaitSleepJoin* state. Threads that call `Monitor` method `Wait` with an object as an argument are placed in the *WaitSleepJoin* state. Threads that are simply waiting to acquire the object's lock enter the conceptual *Blocked* state and wait until the lock becomes available.

Section 15.6 Producer/Consumer Relationship without Thread Synchronization
- In a producer/consumer relationship, the producer portion of an application generates data, and the consumer portion of an application uses that data.

- In a multithreaded producer/consumer relationship, a producer thread calls a produce method to generate data and place it in a shared region of memory called a buffer. A consumer thread calls a consume method to read that data. If the producer wishes to put the next data into the buffer but determines that the consumer has not yet read the previous data from the buffer, the producer thread should call `Wait`. Otherwise, the consumer would never see the previous data, which would be lost to that application. When the consumer thread was read the data, it calls `Pulse` to allow a waiting producer to proceed since there is now free space in the buffer. If a consumer thread finds the buffer empty or finds that the previous data has already been read, the consumer should call `Wait`. Otherwise, the consumer might read "garbage" from the buffer, or the consumer might process a previous data item more than once—each of these possibilities results in a logic error in the application. When the producer has placed the next data into the buffer, it calls `Pulse` to allow the consumer thread to proceed and read that data.

Section 15.7 Producer/Consumer Relationship with Thread Synchronization
- A condition variable is used to determine when a thread must wait to perform its task.

Section 15.8 Producer/Consumer Relationship: Circular Buffer
- If producer and consumer threads operate at different speeds, one will spend more (or most) of its time waiting. If the producer thread produces values faster than the consumer can consume those values, then the producer thread waits for the consumer, because there are no other locations in memory to place the next value. Similarly, if the consumer consumes faster than the producer can produce values, the consumer waits until the producer places the next value into the shared location in memory.

- When threads operate at the same relative speeds, they may become "out of sync," over a period of time causing one thread to wait for the other. When threads wait, programs become less productive, user-interactive programs become less responsive and network applications suffer longer delays because the processor is not used efficiently.

- To minimize the waiting for threads that share resources and operate at the same relative speeds, we can implement a circular buffer that provides extra locations in which the producer can place values (if it "gets ahead" of the consumer) and from which the consumer can retrieve those values (while it is "catching up" to the producer).

- A circular buffer would be inappropriate if the producer and consumer operate at different speeds. If the consumer always executes faster than the producer, then a buffer with one location is sufficient. Additional locations would waste memory. If the producer always executes faster, a buffer with an infinite number of locations would be required to absorb the extra production.

- The key to using a circular buffer is to define it with enough extra cells to handle the anticipated "extra" production.

Section 15.9 Multithreading with GUIs
- To ensure that threads manipulate GUI components in a thread-safe manner, all interactions with GUI components should be performed by the User Interface thread. Class `Control` provides method `Invoke` to help with this process. Method `Invoke` specifies GUI processing statements that the UI thread should execute. The method receives as its arguments a `delegate` representing a method that will modify the GUI and an optional array of `objects` representing the parameters to the method. At some point after `Invoke` is called, the UI thread will execute the method represented by the `delegate`, passing to the contents of the `object` array as the method's arguments.

- Suspending and resuming a thread can be implemented by using thread synchronization and `Monitor` methods `Wait` and `Pulse`.

Terminology

Abort method of class `Thread`
Aborted state
Abort Requested state
`AboveNormal` constant of the `ThreadPriority` enumeration
accessing shared data with synchronization
acquire the lock for an object
`AddressOf` operator
Background state
`BelowNormal` constant of the `ThreadPriority` enumeration
Blocked state
Blocked thread
buffer
circular buffer
concurrency
concurrent producer and consumer threads
concurrent programming
condition variable
consumer thread
`CurrentThread` property of class `Thread`
deadlock
`Enter` method of class `Monitor`
`Exit` method of class `Monitor`
foreground thread
garbage collection
garbage-collector thread
`Highest` constant of the `ThreadPriority` enumeration
indefinite postponement
I/O completion
I/O request
I/O blocking
`Interrupt` method of class `Thread`
`Invoke` method of class `Control`

`IsBackground` method of class `Thread`
`Join` method of class `Thread`
life cycle of a thread
locking objects
`Lowest` constant of the `ThreadPriority` enumeration
`Monitor` class
multilevel priority queue
multithreading
mutual exclusion
`Name` property of class `Thread`
`Normal` constant of the `ThreadPriority` enumeration
perform operations in parallel
`Priority` property of class `Thread`
priority scheduling
producer thread
producer/consumer relationship
`Pulse` method of class `Monitor`
`PulseAll` method of class `Monitor`
quantum
quantum expiration
release a lock
resume a suspended thread
`Resume` method of class `Thread`
Running state
scheduling
shared buffer
sleep interval expires
`Sleep` method of class `Thread`
sleeping thread
`Start` method of class `Thread`
starvation
suspend a thread
`Suspend` method of class `Thread`

Suspended state
SuspendRequested state
SyncBlock
synchronized block of code
SyncLock keyword
System.Threading namespace
Thread class
thread of execution
thread-priority scheduling
thread safe

thread scheduler
thread state
ThreadAbortException
ThreadPriority enumeration
ThreadStart delegate
timeslicing
Unstarted state
User Interface (UI) thread
Wait method of class Monitor
WaitSleepJoin state

Self-Review Exercises

15.1 Fill in the blanks in each of the following statements:

a) Monitor methods _____ and _____ acquire and release the lock on an object.

b) Among a group of equal-priority threads, each thread receives a brief burst of time called a(n) _____, during which the thread has the processor and can perform its tasks.

c) Visual Basic provides a(n) _____ thread to reclaim dynamically allocated memory.

d) Four reasons a thread that is alive is not in the *Running* state are _____, _____, _____ and _____.

e) A thread enters the _____ state when the method that controls the thread's life cycle terminates.

f) A thread's priority must be one of the ThreadPriority constants _____, _____, _____, _____ and _____.

g) To wait for a designated number of milliseconds then resume execution, a thread should call the _____ method of class Thread.

h) Method _____ of class Monitor transitions a thread from the *WaitSleepJoin* state to the *Running* state.

i) A(n) _____ block automatically acquires the lock on an object as program control enters the block and releases the lock on that object when the block terminates.

j) Class Monitor provides methods that _____ access to shared data.

15.2 State whether each of the following is *true* or *false*. If *false*, explain why.

a) A thread cannot execute if it is in the *Stopped* state.

b) A higher-priority thread entering (or re-entering) the *Running* state will preempt threads of lower priority.

c) The code that a thread executes is defined in its Main method.

d) A thread in the *WaitSleepJoin* state always returns to the *Running* state when Monitor method Pulse is called.

e) Method Sleep of class Thread does not consume processor time while a thread sleeps.

f) A blocked thread can be placed in the *Running* state by Monitor method Pulse.

g) Class Monitor's Wait, Pulse and PulseAll methods can be used in any block of code.

h) The programmer must place a call to Monitor method Exit in a SyncLock block to relinquish the lock.

i) When Monitor class method Wait is called within a SyncLock block, the lock for that block is released and the thread that called Wait is placed in the *WaitSleepJoin* state.

Answers to Self-Review Exercises

15.1 a) Enter, Exit. b) timeslice or quantum. c) garbage collector. d) waiting, sleeping, suspended, blocked for input/output. e) *Stopped*. f) Lowest, BelowNormal, Normal, AboveNormal, Highest. g) Sleep. h) Pulse. i) SyncLock. j) synchronize.

15.2 a) True. b) True. c) False. The code that a thread executes is defined in the method specified by the thread's ThreadStart delegate. d) False. A thread may be in the *WaitSleepJoin* state for several reasons. Calling Pulse moves a thread from the *WaitSleepJoin* state to the *Running* state only if the thread entered the *WaitSleepJoin* state as the result of a call to Monitor method Wait. e) True. f) False. A thread is blocked by the operating system and returns to the *Running* state when the operating system determines that the thread can continue executing (e.g., when an I/O request completes or when a lock the thread attempted to acquire becomes available). g) False. Class Monitor methods can be called only if the thread performing the call currently owns the lock on the object each method receives as an argument. h) False. A SyncLock block implicitly relinquishes the lock when the thread completes execution of the SyncLock block. i) True.

Exercises

15.3 *(Bouncing Ball)* Write a program that bounces a blue ball inside a Panel (pnlBall). Draw the ball using the FillEllipse method of class Graphics (as demonstrated in Fig. 13.39). The ball should be created and begin moving in response to a MouseClick event. When the ball hits the edge of the Panel, it should bounce off the edge.

Create a class called Ball to represent the ball. (You'll use this class to create multiple balls in subsequent exercises.) The class should maintain instance variables for the following information:

a) current *x*-coordinate
b) current *y*-coordinate
c) horizontal velocity (i.e., the number of pixels the ball will move horizontally each time its position changes)
d) vertical velocity (i.e., the number of pixels the ball will move vertically each time its position changes)
e) radius
f) color
g) width of Panel in which the ball will bounce
h) height of the Panel in which the ball will bounce

Use variables of type Single to maintain the ball's coordinates, radius and velocity. Class Ball should provide a constructor to initialize the instance variables, and ReadOnly properties to access the ball's *x*-coordinate, *y*-coordinate, radius and color. Class Ball should also provide a Run method that will be used by a Thread to control the ball's movement. Method Run should contain an infinite loop that changes the ball's coordinates every 20 milliseconds. This method should also determine whether the ball needs to bounce in another direction.

Create a Form that contains a Panel in which the ball will be drawn. The Form should create a Ball when the user clicks the mouse in the Panel. The initial coordinates of the Ball should be the coordinates where the user clicked. Choose random horizontal and vertical velocities for the ball. Use a Thread to redraw the ball every 20 milliseconds. Once again, create a method with an infinite loop that the thread can use for this purpose. This drawing Thread should be separate from the one that moves the ball.

Recall from Section 15.9 that all GUI changes must be performed in the User Interface thread. A separate thread will be used to initiate the refreshing of the GUI, so you must declare a Delegate that Control method Invoke can use to perform the update. Declare the following Delegate in your Form class:

```
Delegate Sub RefreshDelegate()
```

Then use this delegate as follows each time the thread updates the Panel:

```
Invoke(New RefreshDelegate(AddressOf pnlBall.Refresh))
```

This invokes the Panel's Refresh method, which causes a Paint event that will redraw the Ball in the User Interface thread. Remember to terminate all Threads when the user closes the application.

15.4   *(Enhanced Bouncing Ball)* Modify the program in Exercise 15.3 to add a new ball each time the user clicks the mouse. Provide for a maximum of 10 balls. There should be a separate Thread to control the movements of each ball. A separate Thread should periodically redraw all of the balls. Randomly choose the color and size for each new ball. Reuse the Ball class from Exercise 15.3 for this exercise.

15.5   *(Bouncing Balls with Shadows)* Modify the program in Exercise 15.4 to add shadows. As a ball moves, draw a solid black oval at the bottom of the Panel. You may consider adding a 3-D effect by increasing or decreasing the size of the shadow depending on the vertical position of the ball. Reuse the Ball class from Exercise 15.3 for this exercise.

15.6   *(Bouncing Balls with Collision Detection; Caution: Difficult)* Modify the program in Exercise 15.4 or Exercise 15.5 to bounce the balls off each other when they collide. A collision should occur between two balls when the distance between their centers is less than the sum of their radii. When a collision between two balls occurs, use the following equations to modify each ball's velocity:

$$distance = \sqrt{(x1 - x2)^2 + (y1 - y2)^2}$$

$$overlap = (\ radius1 + radius2\ ) - distance$$

$$xVelocity1 = xVelocity1 + (\ x1 - x2\ ) * (\ overlap\ /\ distance\ ) * 0.5$$

$$yVelocity1 = yVelocity1 + (\ y1 - y2\ ) * (\ overlap\ /\ distance\ ) * 0.5$$

$$xVelocity2 = xVelocity2 + (\ x2 - x1\ ) * (\ overlap\ /\ distance\ ) * 0.5$$

$$yVelocity2 = yVelocity2 + (\ y2 - y1\ ) * (\ overlap\ /\ distance\ ) * 0.5$$

[*Note:* Ensure that *distance* does not equal zero.] This exercise requires that you modify both the Ball class and your Form class from Exercise 15.4 or Exercise 15.5.

16

Strings, Characters and Regular Expressions

OBJECTIVES

In this chapter you will learn:

- To create and manipulate immutable character String objects of class `String`.

- To create and manipulate mutable character String objects of class `StringBuilder`.

- To manipulate character objects of structure `Char`.

- To use regular expressions in conjunction with classes `Regex` and `Match`.

16.1 Introduction

This chapter introduces the FCL's string and character processing capabilities, and demonstrates how to use regular expressions to search for patterns in text. The techniques presented in this chapter can be employed in text editors, word processors, page-layout software, computerized typesetting systems and other kinds of text-processing software. Previous chapters presented some basic string-processing capabilities. In this chapter, we discuss in detail the text-processing capabilities of class `String` and type `Char` from the `System` namespace and class `StringBuilder` from the `System.Text` namespace.

We begin with an overview of the fundamentals of characters and strings in which we discuss character literals and string literals. We then provide examples of class `String`'s many constructors and methods. The examples demonstrate how to determine the length of strings, copy strings, access individual characters in strings, search strings, obtain substrings from larger strings, compare strings, concatenate strings, replace characters in strings and convert strings to uppercase or lowercase letters.

Next we introduce class `StringBuilder`, which is used to build strings dynamically. We demonstrate `StringBuilder` capabilities for determining and specifying the size of a `StringBuilder` object, as well as appending, inserting, removing and replacing characters in a `StringBuilder` object. We then introduce the character-testing methods of the `Char` structure that enable a program to determine whether a character is a digit, a letter, a lowercase letter, an uppercase letter, a punctuation mark or a symbol other than a punctuation mark. Such methods are useful for validating individual characters in user input. In addition, type Char provides methods for converting a character to uppercase or lowercase.

The chapter concludes with a discussion of regular expressions. We discuss classes Regex and Match from the System.Text.RegularExpressions namespace as well as the symbols that are used to form regular expressions. We then demonstrate how to find patterns in a string, match entire strings to patterns, replace characters in a string that match a pattern and split strings at delimiters specified as a pattern.

16.2 Fundamentals of Characters and Strings

Characters are the fundamental building blocks of Visual Basic source code. Every program is composed of characters that, when grouped together meaningfully, create a sequence that the compiler interprets as instructions describing how to accomplish a task. In addition to normal characters, a program also can contain character literals, also called character constants. A character literal is a character that is represented internally as an integer value, called a *character code*. For example, the integer value 97 corresponds to the character literal "a"c, and the integer value 122 corresponds to the character literal "z"c. The letter c following the closing double quote is Visual Basic's syntax for a character literal. Character literals are established according to the Unicode character set, an international character set that contains many more symbols and letters than the ASCII character set (listed in Appendix D). To learn more about Unicode, see Appendix E.

A string is a series of characters treated as a single unit. These characters can be uppercase letters, lowercase letters, digits and various special characters: +, -, *, /, $ and others. A string is an object of class String in the System namespace. We write string literals, also called string constants, as sequences of characters in double quotation marks, as follows:

```
"John Q. Doe"
"9999 Main Street"
"Waltham, Massachusetts"
"(201) 555-1212"
```

A declaration can assign a String literal to a String variable. The declaration

```
Dim color As String = "blue"
```

initializes String variable color to refer to the String literal object "blue".

Performance Tip 16.1

If there are multiple occurrences of the same String literal in an application, a single copy of the String literal object will be referenced from each location in the program that uses that String literal. It is possible to share the object in this manner because String literal objects are implicitly constant. Such sharing conserves memory.

Common Programming Error 16.1

Assigning Nothing to a String variable can lead to logic errors if you attempt to compare Nothing to an empty String. The keyword Nothing is a null reference, not an empty String (which is a String that is of length 0 and contains no characters).

16.3 String Constructors

Class String provides eight constructors for initializing Strings. Figure 16.1 demonstrates three of the constructors.

Lines 6–7 declare the String variables originalString, string1, string2, string3 and string4. Lines 8–9 allocate the Char array characterArray, which contains nine characters. Line 12 assigns the String literal "Welcome to VB programming!" to variable originalString. Line 13 sets string1 to refer to the same String literal as originalString.

Line 14 assigns a new String to string2, using the String constructor that takes a character array as an argument. The new String contains a copy of the characters in array characterArray.

Software Engineering Observation 16.1

In most cases, it is not necessary to make a copy of an existing String. All Strings are immutable—their character contents cannot be changed after they are created. Also, if there are one or more references to a String (or any object, for that matter), the object cannot be reclaimed by the garbage collector. When a new value is assigned to a String variable, the variable simply refers to a different String object in memory.

Line 15 assigns a new String to string3, using the String constructor that takes a Char array and two Integer arguments. The second argument specifies the starting index

```
1    ' Fig. 16.1: StringConstructor.vb
2    ' Demonstrating String class constructors.
3
4    Module StringConstructor
5       Sub Main()
6          Dim originalString, string1, string2, _
7             string3, string4 As String
8          Dim characterArray() As Char = _
9             {"b"c, "i"c, "r"c, "t"c, "h"c, " "c, "d"c, "a"c, "y"c}
10
11          ' string initialization
12          originalString = "Welcome to VB programming!"
13          string1 = originalString
14          string2 = New String(characterArray)
15          string3 = New String(characterArray, 6, 3)
16          string4 = New String("C"c, 5)
17
18          Console.WriteLine("string1 = " & """" & string1 & """" & _
19             vbCrLf & "string2 = " & """" & string2 & """" & vbCrLf & _
20             "string3 = " & """" & string3 & """" & vbCrLf & _
21             "string4 = " & """" & string4 & """" & vbCrLf)
22       End Sub ' Main
23    End Module ' StringConstructor
```

```
string1 = "Welcome to VB programming!"
string2 = "birth day"
string3 = "day"
string4 = "CCCCC"
```

Fig. 16.1 | String constructors.

position (the **offset**) from which characters in the array are to be copied. The third argument specifies the number of characters (the **count**) to be copied from the specified starting position in the array. The new String contains a copy of the specified characters in the array. If the offset or count causes the program to access an element outside the character array's bounds, an ArgumentOutOfRangeException is thrown.

Line 16 assigns a new String to string4, using the String constructor that takes as arguments a character and an Integer specifying the number of times to repeat that character in the String. Lines 18–21 output the contents of variables string1, string2, string3 and string4.

16.4 String Indexer, Length Property and CopyTo Method

Figure 16.2 uses the String indexer to access individual characters in a String, and demonstrates String property Length, which returns the length of the String. The program also uses String method CopyTo to copy a specified number of characters from a String into a Char array. This application determines the length of a String, reverses the order of the characters in the String and copies a series of characters from the String to a character array.

```vb
1   ' Fig. 16.2: StringMethods.vb
2   ' Using the indexer, property Length and method CopyTo
3   ' of class String.
4
5   Module StringMethods
6      Sub Main()
7         Dim string1 As String
8         Dim characterArray() As Char
9
10        string1 = "hello there"
11        characterArray = New Char(5) {}
12
13        ' output string1
14        Console.WriteLine("string1: """ & string1 & """")
15
16        ' test Length property
17        Console.WriteLine("Length of string1: " & string1.Length)
18
19        ' loop through characters in string1 and display reversed
20        Console.Write("The string reversed is: ")
21
22        Dim i As Integer
23
24        For i = string1.Length - 1 To 0 Step -1
25           Console.Write(string1(i))
26        Next i
27
28        ' copy characters from string1 into characterArray
29        string1.CopyTo(0, characterArray, 0, 5)
30        Console.Write(vbCrLf & "The character array is: ")
```

Fig. 16.2 | String indexer, Length property and CopyTo method. (Part 1 of 2.)

```
31
32          For i = 0 To characterArray.Length - 1
33             Console.Write(characterArray(i))
34          Next i
35
36          Console.WriteLine(vbCrLf)
37       End Sub ' Main
38    End Module ' StringMethods
```

```
string1: "hello there"
Length of string1: 11
The string reversed is: ereht olleh
The character array is: hello
```

Fig. 16.2 | String indexer, Length property and CopyTo method. (Part 2 of 2.)

Line 17 uses String property Length to determine the number of characters in string1. Like arrays, Strings always know their own size.

Lines 24–26 output the characters of string1 in reverse order using the String indexer, which treats a String as an array of Chars and returns the character at a specific index in the String. The indexer receives an integer argument as the index and returns the character at that index. As with arrays, the first element of a String is considered to be at position 0.

Common Programming Error 16.2

Attempting to access a character that is outside the bounds of a String (i.e., an index less than 0 or an index greater than or equal to the String's length) results in an IndexOutOfRangeException.

Line 29 uses String method CopyTo to copy the characters of a String (string1) into a character array (characterArray). CopyTo's first argument is the index from which the method begins copying characters in the String. The second argument is the character array into which the characters are copied. The third argument is the index specifying the starting location at which the method begins placing the copied characters into the character array. The last argument is the number of characters that the method will copy from the String. Lines 32–34 output the Char array contents one character at a time.

16.5 Comparing Strings

The next two examples demonstrate the various methods for comparing Strings. To understand how one String can be "greater than" or "less than" another String, consider the process of alphabetizing a series of last names. The reader would, no doubt, place "Jones" before "Smith", because the first letter of "Jones" comes before the first letter of "Smith" in the alphabet. The alphabet is more than just a set of 26 letters—it is an ordered list of characters in which each letter occurs in a specific position. For example, Z is more than just a letter of the alphabet; Z is specifically the 26th letter of the alphabet.

Computers can order characters alphabetically because the characters are represented internally as Unicode numeric codes. When comparing two Strings, the string comparison methods simply compare the numeric codes of the characters in the Strings.

*Comparing Strings with = and **String** Methods **Equals** and **CompareTo***

Class String provides several ways to compare Strings. Figure 16.3 demonstrates method Equals, method CompareTo and the equality operator (=).

The condition in the If statement (line 18) uses String method Equals to compare string1 and the String literal "hello" to determine whether they are equal. Method Equals (inherited by String from class Object) tests any two objects for equality (i.e., whether the objects have the same contents). The method returns True if the objects are equal and False otherwise. In this instance, the preceding condition returns True because string1 references the String literal object "hello". Method Equals uses a lexicographical comparison—the integer Unicode values that represent each character in each String are compared. Comparing "hello" with "HELLO" would return False because the

```
 1   ' Fig. 16.3: StringCompare.vb
 2   ' Comparing Strings
 3
 4   Module StringCompare
 5      Sub Main()
 6         Dim string1 As String = "hello"
 7         Dim string2 As String = "good bye"
 8         Dim string3 As String = "Happy Birthday"
 9         Dim string4 As String = "happy birthday"
10
11         ' output values of four strings
12         Console.WriteLine("string1 = """ & string1 & """" & vbCrLf & _
13            "string2 = """ & string2 & """" & vbCrLf & _
14            "string3 = """ & string3 & """" & vbCrLf & _
15            "string4 = """ & string4 & "" & vbCrLf)
16
17         ' test for equality using Equals method
18         If string1.Equals("hello") Then
19            Console.WriteLine("string1 equals ""hello""")
20         Else
21            Console.WriteLine("string1 does not equal ""hello""")
22         End If
23
24         ' test for equality with =
25         If string1 = "hello" Then
26            Console.WriteLine("string1 equals ""hello""")
27         Else
28            Console.WriteLine("string1 does not equal ""hello""")
29         End If
30
31         ' test for equality comparing case
32         If String.Equals(string3, string4) Then ' static method
33            Console.WriteLine("string3 equals string4")
34         Else
35            Console.WriteLine("string3 does not equal string4")
36         End If
37
```

Fig. 16.3 | String test to determine equality. (Part 1 of 2.)

```
38            ' test CompareTo
39            Console.WriteLine(vbCrLf & "string1.CompareTo( string2 ) is " & _
40                string1.CompareTo(string2) & vbCrLf & _
41                "string2.CompareTo( string1 ) is " & _
42                string2.CompareTo(string1) & vbCrLf & _
43                "string1.CompareTo( string1 ) is " & _
44                string1.CompareTo(string1) & vbCrLf & _
45                "string3.CompareTo( string4 ) is " & _
46                string3.CompareTo(string4) & vbCrLf & _
47                "string4.CompareTo( string3 ) is " & _
48                string4.CompareTo(string3) & vbCrLf)
49        End Sub ' Main
50    End Module ' StringCompare
```

```
string1 = "hello"
string2 = "good bye"
string3 = "Happy Birthday"
string4 = "happy birthday"

string1 equals "hello"
string1 equals "hello"
string3 does not equal string4

string1.CompareTo( string2 ) is 1
string2.CompareTo( string1 ) is -1
string1.CompareTo( string1 ) is 0
string3.CompareTo( string4 ) is 1
string4.CompareTo( string3 ) is -1
```

Fig. 16.3 | String test to determine equality. (Part 2 of 2.)

numeric representations of lowercase letters are different from the numeric representations of corresponding uppercase letters.

The condition in the second If statement (line 25) uses the equality operator (=) to compare string1 with the String literal "hello" for equality. In Visual Basic, the equality operator also uses a lexicographical comparison to compare two Strings. Thus, the condition in the If statement evaluates to True because the values of string1 and "hello" are equal.

Line 32 compares string3 and string4 for equality to illustrate that comparisons are indeed case sensitive. Shared method Equals is used to compare the values of two Strings. "Happy Birthday" does not equal "happy birthday", so the condition of the If statement fails, and the message "string3 does not equal string4" is output (line 35).

Lines 39–48 use String method CompareTo to compare Strings. Method CompareTo returns 0 if the Strings are equal, -1 if the String that invokes CompareTo is less than the String passed as an argument and 1 if the String that invokes CompareTo is greater than the String passed as an argument. Method CompareTo uses a lexicographical comparison.

Note that CompareTo considers string3 to be larger than string4. The only difference between these two Strings is that string3 contains two uppercase letters in positions where string4 contains lowercase letters.

Using **String** *Methods* **StartsWith** *and* **EndsWith**

The application in Fig. 16.4 shows how to test whether a String begins or ends with a given String. Method StartsWith determines whether a String starts with the String passed to it as an argument. Method EndsWith determines whether a String ends with the String passed to it as an argument. Class StringStartEnd's Main method defines an array of Strings (called strings), which contains "started", "starting", "ended" and "ending". The remainder of method Main tests the elements of the array to determine whether they start or end with a particular set of characters.

Line 11 uses method StartsWith, which takes a String argument. The condition in the If statement determines whether the String at index i of the array starts with the characters "st". If so, the method returns True, and lines 12–13 output a message.

Line 21 uses method EndsWith, which also takes a String argument. The condition in the If statement determines whether the String at index i of the array ends with the characters "ed". If so, the method returns True, and lines 22–23 output a message.

```vb
 1   ' Fig. 16.4: StringStartEnd.vb
 2   ' Demonstrating StartsWith and EndsWith methods.
 3
 4   Module StringStartEnd
 5      Sub Main()
 6         Dim strings As String() = _
 7            {"started", "starting", "ended", "ending"}
 8
 9         ' test every string to see if it starts with "st"
10         For i As Integer = 0 To strings.Length - 1
11            If strings(i).StartsWith("st") Then
12               Console.WriteLine( _
13                  """" & strings(i) & """" & " starts with ""st""")
14            End If
15         Next i
16
17         Console.WriteLine("")
18
19         ' test every string to see if it ends with "ed"
20         For i As Integer = 0 To strings.Length - 1
21            If strings(i).EndsWith("ed") Then
22               Console.WriteLine( _
23                  """" & strings(i) & """" & " ends with ""ed""")
24            End If
25         Next i
26
27         Console.WriteLine("")
28      End Sub ' Main
29   End Module ' StringStartEnd
```

```
"started" starts with "st"
"starting" starts with "st"

"started" ends with "ed"
"ended" ends with "ed"
```

Fig. 16.4 | StartsWith and EndsWith methods.

16.6 **Locating Characters and Substrings in `Strings`**

In many applications, it is necessary to search for a character or set of characters in a `String`. For example, a programmer creating a word processor would want to provide capabilities for searching through documents. Figure 16.5 demonstrates some of the many versions of `String` methods `IndexOf`, `IndexOfAny`, `LastIndexOf` and `LastIndexOfAny`, which search for a specified character or substring in a `String`. This example searches the `String` `letters` which is initialized with "abcdefghijklmabcdefghijklm" (line 6).

```vb
1   ' Fig. 16.5: StringIndexMethods.vb
2   ' Using String searching methods.
3
4   Module StringIndexMethods
5      Sub Main()
6         Dim letters As String = "abcdefghijklmabcdefghijklm"
7         Dim searchLetters As Char() = {"c"c, "a"c, "$"c}
8
9         ' test IndexOf to find a character in a string
10        Console.WriteLine("First 'c' is located at index " & _
11           letters.IndexOf("c"c))
12        Console.WriteLine("First 'a' starting at 1 is located at index " _
13           & letters.IndexOf("a"c, 1))
14        Console.WriteLine("First '$' in the 5 positions starting at 3 " & _
15           "is located at index " & letters.IndexOf("$"c, 3, 5))
16
17        ' test LastIndexOf to find a character in a string
18        Console.WriteLine(vbCrLf & "Last 'c' is located at index " & _
19           letters.LastIndexOf("c"c))
20        Console.WriteLine("Last 'a' up to position 25 is located at " & _
21           "index " & letters.LastIndexOf("a"c, 25))
22        Console.WriteLine("Last '$' in the 5 positions starting at 15 " & _
23           "is located at index " & letters.LastIndexOf("$"c, 15, 5))
24
25        ' test IndexOf to find a substring in a string
26        Console.WriteLine(vbCrLf & _
27           "First ""def"" is located at index " & letters.IndexOf("def"))
28        Console.WriteLine("First ""def"" starting at 7 is located at " & _
29           "index " & letters.IndexOf("def", 7))
30        Console.WriteLine("First ""hello"" in the 15 positions " & _
31           "starting at 5 is located at index " & _
32           letters.IndexOf("hello", 5, 15))
33
34        ' test LastIndexOf to find a substring in a string
35        Console.WriteLine(vbCrLf & "Last ""def"" is located at index " & _
36           letters.LastIndexOf("def"))
37        Console.WriteLine("Last ""def"" up to position 25 is located " & _
38           "at index" & letters.LastIndexOf("def", 25))
39        Console.WriteLine("Last ""hello"" in the 15 positions " & _
40           "ending at 20 is located at index " & _
41           letters.LastIndexOf("hello", 20, 15))
42
```

Fig. 16.5 | Searching for characters and substrings in `Strings`. (Part 1 of 2.)

```
43              ' test IndexOfAny to find first occurrence of character in array
44              Console.WriteLine(vbCrLf & "First 'c', 'a' or '$' is " & _
45                 "located at index " & letters.IndexOfAny(searchLetters))
46              Console.WriteLine("First 'c', 'a' or '$' starting at 7 is " & _
47                 "located at index " & letters.IndexOfAny(searchLetters, 7))
48              Console.WriteLine("First 'c', 'a' or '$' in the 5 positions " & _
49                 "starting at 7 is located at index " & _
50                 letters.IndexOfAny(searchLetters, 7, 5))
51
52              ' test LastIndexOfAny to find last occurrence of character
53              ' in array
54              Console.WriteLine(vbCrLf & "Last 'c', 'a' or '$' is " & _
55                 "located at index " & letters.LastIndexOfAny(searchLetters))
56              Console.WriteLine("Last 'c', 'a' or '$' up to position 1 is " & _
57                 "located at index " & letters.LastIndexOfAny(searchLetters, 1))
58              Console.WriteLine("Last 'c', 'a' or '$' in the 5 positions " & _
59                 "ending at 25 is located at index " & _
60                 letters.LastIndexOfAny(searchLetters, 25, 5))
61        End Sub ' Main
62     End Module ' StringIndexMethods
```

```
First 'c' is located at index 2
First 'a' starting at 1 is located at index 13
First '$' in the 5 positions starting at 3 is located at index -1

Last 'c' is located at index 15
Last 'a' up to position 25 is located at index 13
Last '$' in the 5 positions starting at 15 is located at index -1

First "def" is located at index 3
First "def" starting at 7 is located at index 16
First "hello" in the 15 positions starting at 5 is located at index -1

Last "def" is located at index 16
Last "def" up to position 25 is located at index 16
Last "hello" in the 15 positions ending at 20 is located at index -1

First 'c', 'a' or '$' is located at index 0
First 'c', 'a' or '$' starting at 7 is located at index 13
First 'c', 'a' or '$' in the 5 positions starting at 7 is located at index -1

Last 'c', 'a' or '$' is located at index 15
Last 'c', 'a' or '$' up to position 1 is located at index 0
Last 'c', 'a' or '$' in the 5 positions ending at 25 is located at index -1
```

Fig. 16.5 | Searching for characters and substrings in Strings. (Part 2 of 2.)

Lines 11, 13 and 15 use method IndexOf to locate the first occurrence of a character in a String. If it finds a character, IndexOf returns the index of the specified character in the String; otherwise, IndexOf returns –1. Line 13 uses a version of method IndexOf that takes two arguments—the character to search for and the starting index in the String at which the search should begin. The method does not examine any characters before the starting index (in this case, 1). Line 15 uses another version of method IndexOf that takes three arguments—the character to search for, the index at which to start searching and the number of characters to search.

Lines 19, 21 and 23 use method LastIndexOf to locate the last occurrence of a character in a String. Method LastIndexOf searches from the end of the String toward the beginning. If it finds the character, LastIndexOf returns the index of the specified character in the String; otherwise, LastIndexOf returns –1. There are three versions of LastIndexOf. Line 19 uses the version of method LastIndexOf that takes as an argument the character for which to search. Line 21 uses the version of method LastIndexOf that takes two arguments—the character for which to search and the highest index from which to begin searching backward for the character. The expression in line 23 uses a third version of method LastIndexOf that takes three arguments—the character for which to search, the starting index from which to start searching backward and the number of characters (the portion of the String) to search.

Lines 26–41 use versions of IndexOf and LastIndexOf that take a String instead of a character as the first argument. These versions of the methods perform identically to the ones described above except that they search for sequences of characters (or substrings) that are specified by their String arguments.

Lines 44–60 use methods IndexOfAny and LastIndexOfAny, which take an array of characters as the first argument. These versions of the methods also perform identically to those described above except that they return the index of the first occurrence of any of the characters in the character array argument.

Common Programming Error 16.3

In the overloaded methods LastIndexOf and LastIndexOfAny that take three parameters, the second argument must be greater than or equal to the third argument; otherwise, an exception occurs. This might seem counterintuitive, but remember that the search moves from the end of the string toward the beginning.

16.7 **Extracting Substrings from Strings**

Class String provides two Substring methods, which are used to create a new String by copying part of an existing String. Each method returns a new String. Figure 16.6 demonstrates both methods.

Line 11 uses the Substring method that takes one Integer argument. The argument specifies the starting index from which the method copies characters in the original String. The substring returned contains a copy of the characters from the starting index to the end of the String. If the index specified in the argument is outside the bounds of the String, an ArgumentOutOfRangeException occurs.

The second version of method Substring (line 15) takes two Integer arguments. The arguments specify the starting index from which to copy characters and the length of the substring to copy. The substring returned contains a copy of the specified characters from the original String. If the starting index plus the length is greater than the number of characters in the String, an ArgumentOutOfRangeException occurs.

```
1    ' Fig. 16.6: SubString.vb
2    ' Demonstrating the String Substring method.
3
```

Fig. 16.6 | Substrings generated from Strings. (Part 1 of 2.)

```
 4    Module SubString
 5       Sub Main()
 6          Dim letters As String = "abcdefghijklmabcdefghijklm"
 7          Dim output As String = ""
 8
 9          ' invoke Substring method and pass it one parameter
10          Console.WriteLine("Substring from index 20 to end is """ & _
11             letters.Substring(20) & """")
12
13          ' invoke Substring method and pass it two parameters
14          Console.WriteLine("Substring from index 0 of length 6 is """ & _
15             letters.Substring(0, 6) & """")
16       End Sub ' Main
17    End Module ' SubString
```

```
Substring from index 20 to end is "hijklm"
Substring from index 0 of length 6 is "abcdef"
```

Fig. 16.6 | Substrings generated from Strings. (Part 2 of 2.)

16.8 Concatenating Strings

Like the & operator, the String class's Shared method Concat (Fig. 16.7) can be used to concatenate two Strings. The method returns a new String containing the combined characters from both original Strings. Line 13 appends the characters from string2 to the end of a copy of string1, using method Concat. The original Strings are not modified.

```
 1    ' Fig. 16.7: SubConcatenation.vb
 2    ' Demonstrating String class Concat method.
 3
 4    Module StringConcatenation
 5       Sub Main()
 6          Dim string1 As String = "Happy "
 7          Dim string2 As String = "Birthday"
 8
 9          Console.WriteLine("string1 = """ & string1 & """" & _
10             vbCrLf & "string2 = """ & string2 & """")
11          Console.WriteLine(vbCrLf & _
12             "Result of string.Concat( string1, string2 ) = " & _
13             String.Concat(string1, string2))
14          Console.WriteLine("string1 after concatenation = " & string1)
15       End Sub ' Main
16    End Module ' StringConcatenation
```

```
string1 = "Happy "
string2 = "Birthday"

Result of string.Concat( string1, string2 ) = Happy Birthday
string1 after concatenation = Happy
```

Fig. 16.7 | Concat Shared method.

16.9 **Miscellaneous String Methods**

Class String provides several methods that return modified copies of Strings. Figure 16.8 demonstrates String methods Replace, ToLower, ToUpper and Trim. None of these methods modifies the original String.

Line 18 uses String method Replace to return a new String, replacing every occurrence in string1 of character 'e' with character 'E'. Method Replace takes two arguments—a Char for which to search and another Char with which to replace all matching

```vb
1   ' Fig. 16.8: StringMethods2.vb
2   ' Demonstrating String methods Replace, ToLower, ToUpper, Trim,
3   ' and ToString.
4
5   Module StringMethods2
6      Sub Main()
7         Dim string1 As String = "cheers!"
8         Dim string2 As String = "GOOD BYE "
9         Dim string3 As String = "   spaces      "
10
11         Console.WriteLine("string1 = """ & string1 & """" & vbCrLf & _
12            "string2 = """ & string2 & """" & vbCrLf & _
13            "string3 = """ & string3 & """")
14
15         ' call method Replace
16         Console.WriteLine( _
17            vbCrLf & "Replacing ""e"" with ""E"" in string1: """ & _
18            string1.Replace("e"c, "E"c) & """")
19
20         ' call ToLower and ToUpper
21         Console.WriteLine(vbCrLf & "string1.ToUpper() = """ & _
22            string1.ToUpper() & """" & vbCrLf & "string2.ToLower() = """ & _
23            string2.ToLower() & """")
24
25         ' call Trim method
26         Console.WriteLine( _
27            vbCrLf & "string3 after trim = """ & string3.Trim() & """")
28
29         Console.WriteLine(vbCrLf & "string1 = """ & string1 & """")
30      End Sub ' Main
31   End Module ' StringMethods2
```

```
string1 = "cheers!"
string2 = "GOOD BYE "
string3 = "   spaces      "

Replacing "e" with "E" in string1: "chEErs!"

string1.ToUpper() = "CHEERS!"
string2.ToLower() = "good bye "

string3 after trim = "spaces"

string1 = "cheers!"
```

Fig. 16.8 | String methods Replace, ToLower, ToUpper and Trim.

occurrences of the first argument. This method is also overloaded to receive two String parameters. If there are no occurrences of the first argument in the String, the method returns the original String.

String method ToUpper returns a new String (line 22) that replaces any lowercase letters in string1 with their uppercase equivalent. If there are no characters to convert to uppercase, the method returns the original String. Line 23 uses String method ToLower to return a new String in which any uppercase letters in string2 are replaced by their lowercase equivalents. As with ToUpper, if there are no characters to convert to lowercase, method ToLower returns the original String.

Line 27 uses String method Trim to remove all whitespace characters that appear at the beginning and end of a String. The method returns a new String that contains the original String, but omits leading or trailing whitespace characters. Another version of method Trim takes a character array and returns a String that does not contain the characters in the array argument at the start or end of the String. Line 29 demonstrates that string1 did not change.

16.10 Class StringBuilder

The String class provides many capabilities for processing Strings. However, a String's contents can never change. Operations that seem to concatenate Strings are in fact creating new Strings (e.g., the &= operator creates a new String and assigns it to the String variable on the left side of the operator).

The next several sections discuss the features of class StringBuilder (namespace System.Text), used to create and manipulate dynamic string information—that is, mutable strings. Every StringBuilder can store the number of characters specified by its capacity. Exceeding the capacity of a StringBuilder makes the capacity expand to accommodate the additional characters. As we will see, members of class StringBuilder, such as methods Append and AppendFormat, can be used for concatenation like the operators &, and &= for class String.

Performance Tip 16.2

Objects of class String are constant strings, whereas object of class StringBuilder are mutable sequences of characters. The CLR can perform certain optimizations with Strings (such as referring to one String with many variables) because it knows the Strings will not change.

Performance Tip 16.3

When you have a choice between using a String or a StringBuilder to represent a sequence of characters, always use a String if the contents of the object will not change. When appropriate, using Strings instead of StringBuilder objects improves performance.

Class StringBuilder provides six overloaded constructors. Class StringBuilderConstructor (Fig. 16.9) demonstrates three of them.

Line 9 employs the parameterless StringBuilder constructor to create a StringBuilder that contains no characters and has a default initial capacity of 16 characters. Line 10 uses the StringBuilder constructor that takes an Integer argument to create a StringBuilder that contains no characters and has the initial capacity specified in the Integer argument (i.e., 10). Line 11 uses the StringBuilder constructor that takes a String argument to create a StringBuilder containing the characters of the String argument. The

```
 1    ' Fig. 16.9: StringBuilderConstructor.vb
 2    ' Demonstrating StringBuilder class constructors.
 3    Imports System.Text
 4
 5    Module StringBuilderConstructor
 6       Sub Main()
 7          Dim buffer1, buffer2, buffer3 As StringBuilder
 8
 9          buffer1 = New StringBuilder()
10          buffer2 = New StringBuilder(10)
11          buffer3 = New StringBuilder("hello")
12
13          Console.WriteLine("buffer1 = """ & buffer1.ToString() & """")
14          Console.WriteLine("buffer2 = """ & buffer2.ToString() & """")
15          Console.WriteLine("buffer3 = """ & buffer3.ToString() & """")
16       End Sub ' Main
17    End Module ' StringBuilderConstructor
```

```
buffer1 = ""
buffer2 = ""
buffer3 = "hello"
```

Fig. 16.9 | StringBuilder class constructors.

initial capacity is the smallest power of two greater than or equal to the number of characters in the argument String, with a minimum of 16. Lines 13–15 use StringBuilder method ToString to obtain String representations of the StringBuilders' contents.

16.11 Length and Capacity Properties, EnsureCapacity Method and Indexer of Class StringBuilder

Class StringBuilder provides the Length and Capacity properties to return the number of characters currently in a StringBuilder and the number of characters that a String-Builder can store without allocating more memory, respectively. These properties also can increase or decrease the length or the capacity of the StringBuilder.

Method EnsureCapacity allows you to reduce the number of times a String-Builder's capacity must be increased. Method EnsureCapacity doubles the String-Builder instance's current capacity. If this doubled value is greater than the value you wish to ensure, that value becomes the new capacity. Otherwise, EnsureCapacity alters the capacity by making it equal to the requested number. For example, if the current capacity is 17 and we wish to make it 40, 17 multiplied by 2 is not greater than or equal to 40, so the call will result in a new capacity of 40. If the current capacity is 23 and we wish to make it 40, 23 will be multiplied by 2 to result in a new capacity of 46. Both 40 and 46 are greater than or equal to 40, so a capacity of 40 is indeed ensured by method EnsureCapacity. Figure 16.10 demonstrates these methods and properties.

The program contains one StringBuilder, called buffer. Line 7 uses the String-Builder constructor that takes a String argument to instantiate a StringBuilder and initialize its value to "Hello, how are you?". Lines 10–12 output the content, length and capacity of the StringBuilder. In the output window, note that the capacity of the

```vb
 1    ' Fig. 16.10: StringBuilderFeatures.vb
 2    ' Demonstrating some features of class StringBuilder.
 3    Imports System.Text
 4
 5    Module StringBuilderFeatures
 6       Sub Main()
 7          Dim buffer As New StringBuilder("Hello, how are you?")
 8
 9          ' use Length and Capacity properties
10          Console.WriteLine( _
11             "buffer = " & buffer.ToString() & vbCrLf & "Length = " & _
12             buffer.Length & vbCrLf & "Capacity = " & buffer.Capacity)
13
14          buffer.EnsureCapacity(75) ' ensure a capacity of at least 75
15          Console.WriteLine(vbCrLf & "New capacity = " & buffer.Capacity)
16
17          ' truncate StringBuilder by setting Length property
18          buffer.Length = 10
19          Console.Write(vbCrLf & "New length = " & _
20             buffer.Length & vbCrLf & "buffer = ")
21
22          ' use StringBuilder indexer
23          For i As Integer = 0 To buffer.Length - 1
24             Console.Write(buffer(i))
25          Next i
26
27          Console.WriteLine()
28       End Sub ' Main
29    End Module ' StringBuilderFeatures
```

```
buffer = Hello, how are you?
Length = 19
Capacity = 32

New capacity = 75

New length = 10
buffer = Hello, how
```

Fig. 16.10 | StringBuilder size manipulation.

StringBuilder is initially 32. Remember, the StringBuilder constructor that takes a String argument creates a StringBuilder object with an initial capacity that is the smallest power of two greater than or equal to the number of characters in the String passed as an argument.

Line 14 expands the capacity of the StringBuilder to a minimum of 75 characters. The current capacity (32) multiplied by two is less than 75, so method EnsureCapacity increases the capacity to 75. If new characters are added to a StringBuilder so that its length exceeds its capacity, the capacity grows to accommodate the additional characters in the same manner as if method EnsureCapacity had been called.

Line 18 uses property Length to set the length of the StringBuilder to 10. If the specified length is less than the current number of characters in the StringBuilder, the contents of the StringBuilder are truncated to the specified length. If the specified length is greater than the number of characters currently in the StringBuilder, null characters (characters with the numeric representation 0) are appended to the StringBuilder until the total number of characters in the StringBuilder is equal to the specified length. Lines 23–25 use the StringBuilder indexer to output the characters in the StringBuilder one character at a time.

16.12 Append and AppendFormat Methods of Class StringBuilder

Class StringBuilder provides 19 overloaded Append methods for appending values of various types to the end of a StringBuilder's contents. There are versions of this method for each of the primitive types and for character arrays, Strings and Objects. Remember that method ToString produces a String representation of any Object, so any Object's string representation can be appended to a StringBuilder. Each of the methods takes an argument, converts it to a String and appends it to the StringBuilder. Figure 16.11 demonstrates several Append methods.

```vb
1   ' Fig. 16.11: StringBuilderAppend.vb
2   ' Demonstrating StringBuilder Append methods.
3   Imports System.Text
4
5   Module StringBuilderAppend
6      Sub Main()
7         Dim objectValue As Object = "hello"
8         Dim stringValue As String = "good bye"
9         Dim characterArray As Char() = {"a"c, "b"c, "c"c, "d"c, "e"c, "f"c}
10        Dim booleanValue As Boolean = True
11        Dim characterValue As Char = "Z"c
12        Dim integerValue As Integer = 7
13        Dim longValue As Long = 1000000
14        Dim floatValue As Single = 2.5F ' F indicates that 2.5 is a float
15        Dim doubleValue As Double = 33.333
16        Dim buffer As New StringBuilder()
17
18        ' use method Append to append values to buffer
19        buffer.Append(objectValue)
20        buffer.Append("  ")
21        buffer.Append(stringValue)
22        buffer.Append("  ")
23        buffer.Append(characterArray)
24        buffer.Append("  ")
25        buffer.Append(characterArray, 0, 3)
26        buffer.Append("  ")
27        buffer.Append(booleanValue)
28        buffer.Append("  ")
29        buffer.Append(characterValue)
30        buffer.Append("  ")
31        buffer.Append(integerValue)
32        buffer.Append("  ")
```

Fig. 16.11 | Append methods of StringBuilder. (Part 1 of 2.)

```
33          buffer.Append(longValue)
34          buffer.Append("  ")
35          buffer.Append(floatValue)
36          buffer.Append("  ")
37          buffer.Append(doubleValue)
38
39          Console.WriteLine("buffer = " & buffer.ToString() & vbCrLf)
40      End Sub ' Main
41  End Module ' StringBuilderAppend
```

```
buffer = hello  good bye  abcdef  abc  True  Z  7  1000000  2.5  33.333
```

Fig. 16.11 | Append methods of `StringBuilder`. (Part 2 of 2.)

Lines 19–37 use 10 different overloaded `Append` methods to append the `String` representations of the variables created in lines 7–16 to the end of the `StringBuilder`. `Append` behaves similarly to the `&` operator, which is used to concatenate `String`s.

Class `StringBuilder` also provides method `AppendFormat`, which converts a `String` to a specified format, then appends it to the `StringBuilder`. The example in Fig. 16.12 demonstrates this method.

```
1   ' Fig. 16.12: StringBuilderAppendFormat.vb
2   ' Demonstrating method AppendFormat.
3   Imports System.Text
4
5   Module StringBuilderAppendFormat
6       Sub Main()
7           Dim buffer As New StringBuilder()
8           Dim string1, string2 As String
9
10          ' formatted string
11          string1 = "This {0} costs: {1:C}." & vbCrLf
12
13          ' string1 argument array
14          Dim objectArray(2) As Object
15
16          objectArray(0) = "car"
17          objectArray(1) = 1234.56
18
19          ' append to buffer formatted string with argument
20          buffer.AppendFormat(string1, objectArray)
21
22          ' formatted string
23          string2 = "Number:{0:d3}." & vbCrLf & _
24              "Number right aligned with spaces:{0, 4}." & vbCrLf & _
25              "Number left aligned with spaces:{0, -4}."
26
27          ' append to buffer formatted string with argument
28          buffer.AppendFormat(string2, 5)
29
```

Fig. 16.12 | `StringBuilder`'s `AppendFormat` method. (Part 1 of 2.)

```
30              ' display formatted strings
31          Console.WriteLine(buffer.ToString())
32      End Sub ' Main
33  End Module ' StringBuilderAppendFormat
```

```
This car costs: $1,234.56.
Number:005.
Number right aligned with spaces:    5.
Number left aligned with spaces:5    .
```

Fig. 16.12 | StringBuilder's AppendFormat method. (Part 2 of 2.)

Line 11 creates a String that contains formatting information. The information enclosed within the braces specifies how to format a specific piece of information. Formats have the form {X[,Y][:FormatString]}, where X is the number of the argument to be formatted, counting from zero. Y is an optional argument, which can be positive or negative, indicating how many characters should be in the formatted String. If the resulting String has fewer characters than the number Y, the String will be padded with spaces to make up for the difference. A positive integer aligns the String to the right; a negative integer aligns it to the left. The optional FormatString applies a particular format to the argument—currency, decimal or scientific, among others. In this case, {0} means that the first argument's String representation will be included in the formatted String. {1:C} specifies that the second argument will be formatted as a currency value.

Line 20 shows a version of AppendFormat that takes two parameters—a String specifying the format and an array of objects to serve as the arguments to the format String. The argument referred to by {0} is in the object array at index 0.

Lines 23–25 define another String used for formatting. The first format {0:D3}, specifies that the first argument will be formatted as a three-digit decimal, meaning any number that has fewer than three digits will have leading zeros, so the total number of formatted digits will be 3. The next format, {0, 4}, specifies that the formatted String should have four characters and should be right aligned. The third format, {0, -4}, specifies that the String should be aligned to the left. For more formatting options, please refer to the online help documentation.

Line 28 uses a version of AppendFormat that takes two parameters—a String containing a format and an object to which the format is applied. In this case, the object is the number 5. The output of Fig. 16.12 displays the result of applying these versions of AppendFormat with their respective arguments.

16.13 Insert, Remove and Replace Methods of Class StringBuilder

Class StringBuilder provides 18 overloaded Insert methods to allow values of various types to be inserted at any position in a StringBuilder. There are versions of Insert for each of the primitive types and for character arrays, Strings and Objects. Each version takes its second argument, converts it to a String and inserts the String into the String-Builder at the index specified by the first argument. The index must be greater than or equal to 0 and less than the length of the StringBuilder; otherwise, an ArgumentOutOf-RangeException occurs.

Class `StringBuilder` also provides method `Remove` for deleting characters in a `StringBuilder`. Method `Remove` takes two arguments—the index at which to begin deletion and the number of characters to delete. The sum of the starting subscript and the number of characters to be deleted must always be less than the `StringBuilder`'s length; otherwise, an `ArgumentOutOfRangeException` occurs. Figure 16.13 demonstrates the `Insert` and `Remove` methods. Lines 20–37 use nine different overloaded `Insert` methods to insert the `String` representations of the variables created in lines 7–17 at index 0 in the `StringBuilder`.

```vb
 1  ' Fig. 16.13: StringBuilderInsertRemove.vb
 2  ' Insert and Remove methods of class StringBuilder.
 3  Imports System.Text
 4
 5  Module StringBuilderInsertRemove
 6     Sub Main()
 7        Dim objectValue As Object = "hello"
 8        Dim stringValue As String = "good bye"
 9        Dim characterArray As Char() = _
10           {"a"c, "b"c, "c"c, "d"c, "e"c, "f"c}
11        Dim booleanValue As Boolean = True
12        Dim characterValue As Char = "K"c
13        Dim integerValue As Integer = 7
14        Dim longValue As Long = 10000000
15        Dim floatValue As Single = 2.5F ' F indicates that 2.5 is a float
16        Dim doubleValue As Double = 33.333
17        Dim buffer As New StringBuilder()
18
19        ' insert values into buffer
20        buffer.Insert(0, objectValue)
21        buffer.Insert(0, "   ")
22        buffer.Insert(0, stringValue)
23        buffer.Insert(0, "   ")
24        buffer.Insert(0, characterArray)
25        buffer.Insert(0, "   ")
26        buffer.Insert(0, booleanValue)
27        buffer.Insert(0, "   ")
28        buffer.Insert(0, characterValue)
29        buffer.Insert(0, "   ")
30        buffer.Insert(0, integerValue)
31        buffer.Insert(0, "   ")
32        buffer.Insert(0, longValue)
33        buffer.Insert(0, "   ")
34        buffer.Insert(0, floatValue)
35        buffer.Insert(0, "   ")
36        buffer.Insert(0, doubleValue)
37        buffer.Insert(0, "   ")
38
39        Console.WriteLine("buffer after inserts: " & vbCrLf & _
40           buffer.ToString() & vbCrLf)
41
42        buffer.Remove(10, 1) ' delete 2 in 2.5
```

Fig. 16.13 | `StringBuilder` text insertion and removal. (Part 1 of 2.)

```
43          buffer.Remove(4, 4) ' delete .333 in 33.333
44
45          Console.WriteLine("buffer after Removes:" & vbCrLf & _
46              buffer.ToString())
47      End Sub ' Main
48  End Module ' StringBuilderInsertRemove
```

```
buffer after inserts:
  33.333  2.5  10000000  7  K  True  abcdef  good bye  hello

buffer after Removes:
  33  .5  10000000  7  K  True  abcdef  good bye  hello
```

Fig. 16.13 | StringBuilder text insertion and removal. (Part 2 of 2.)

Another useful StringBuilder method is Replace, which searches for a specified String or character and substitutes another String or character in its place. Figure 16.14 demonstrates Replace.

Line 13 uses method Replace to replace all instances of the String "Jane" with the String "Greg" in builder1. An overloaded version of this method takes two characters as parameters and replaces each occurrence of the first character with the second character. Line 14 uses an overload of Replace that takes four parameters—two characters and two Integers. The method replaces all instances of the first character with the second char-

```
1   ' Fig. 16.14: StringBuilderReplace.vb
2   ' Demonstrating method Replace.
3   Imports System.Text
4
5   Module StringBuilderReplace
6       Sub Main()
7           Dim builder1 As New StringBuilder("Happy Birthday Jane")
8           Dim builder2 As New StringBuilder("good bye greg")
9
10          Console.WriteLine("Before replacements:" & vbCrLf & _
11              builder1.ToString() & vbCrLf & builder2.ToString())
12
13          builder1.Replace("Jane", "Greg")
14          builder2.Replace("g"c, "G"c, 0, 5)
15
16          Console.WriteLine(vbCrLf & "After replacements:" & vbCrLf & _
17              builder1.ToString() & vbCrLf & builder2.ToString())
18      End Sub ' Main
19  End Module ' StringBuilderReplace
```

```
Happy Birthday Jane
good bye greg

After replacements:
Happy Birthday Greg
Good bye greg
```

Fig. 16.14 | StringBuilder text replacement.

acter, beginning at the index specified by the first `Integer` and continuing for a count specified by the second `Integer`. In this case, `Replace` looks at only five characters, starting with the character at index 0. As the output illustrates, this version of `Replace` replaces g with G in the word "good", but not in "greg"—the gs in "greg" are not in the range indicated by the `Integer` arguments (i.e., between indexes 0 and 4).

16.14 Char Methods

Visual Basic provides a type called a structure that is similar to a class. Although structures and classes are comparable in many ways, structures represent value types. Like classes, structures include methods and properties. Both use the same access modifiers (such as `Public`, `Protected` and `Private`) and access members via the member access operator (.). Classes are created by using the keyword `Class`, but structures are created using the keyword **Structure**.

Many of the primitive types that we have used in this book are actually aliases for different structures. For instance, an `Integer` is defined by structure `System.Int32`, a `Long` by `System.Int64` and so on. These structures derive from class **ValueType**, which in turn derives from class `Object`. In this section, we present structure **Char**, which is the structure for characters.

Most `Char` methods are `Shared`, take at least one character argument and perform either a test or a manipulation on the character. We present several of these methods in the next example. Figure 16.15 demonstrates `Shared` methods that test characters to determine whether they are of a specific character type and `Shared` methods that perform case conversions on characters.

This Windows application contains a prompt, a `TextBox` in which the user can input a character, a button that the user can press after entering a character and a second `TextBox` that displays the output of our analysis. When the user clicks the **Analyze Character** button, event handler `btnAnalyze_Click` (lines 7–28) converts the entered data from a `String` to a `Char`, using method `Convert.ToChar` (line 11).

Line 15 uses `Char` method `IsDigit` to determine whether `character` is a digit. If so, the method returns `True`; otherwise, it returns `False`. Line 16 uses `Char` method `IsLetter` to determine whether `character` is a letter. Line 18 uses `Char` method `IsLetterOrDigit` to determine whether `character` is a letter or a digit.

```
1   ' Fig. 16.15: SharedCharMethods.vb
2   ' Demonstrates Shared character testing methods
3   ' from Char structure
4
5   Public Class SharedCharMethods
6      ' handle btnAnalyze_Click
7      Private Sub btnAnalyze_Click( ByVal sender As System.Object, _
8         ByVal e As System.EventArgs) Handles btnAnalyze.Clickstructure
9
10        If txtInput.Text.Length > 0 Then
11           ' convert string entered to type char
12           Dim character As Char = Convert.ToChar(txtInput.Text)
13           Dim output As String
```

Fig. 16.15 | Char's Shared character-testing and case-conversion methods. (Part 1 of 2.)

```
14
15            output = "is digit: " & Char.IsDigit(character) & vbCrLf
16            output &= "is letter: " & Char.IsLetter(character) & vbCrLf
17            output &= "is letter or digit: " & _
18               Char.IsLetterOrDigit(character) & vbCrLf
19            output &= "is lowercase: " & Char.IsLower(character) & vbCrLf
20            output &= "is uppercase: " & Char.IsUpper(character) & vbCrLf
21            output &= "to uppercase: " & Char.ToUpper(character) & vbCrLf
22            output &= "to lowercase: " & Char.ToLower(character) & vbCrLf
23            output &= "is punctuation: " & _
24               Char.IsPunctuation(character) & vbCrLf
25            output &= "is symbol: " & Char.IsSymbol(character)
26            txtOutput.Text = output
27         End If
28      End Sub ' btnAnalyze_Click
29   End Class ' SharedCharMethods
```

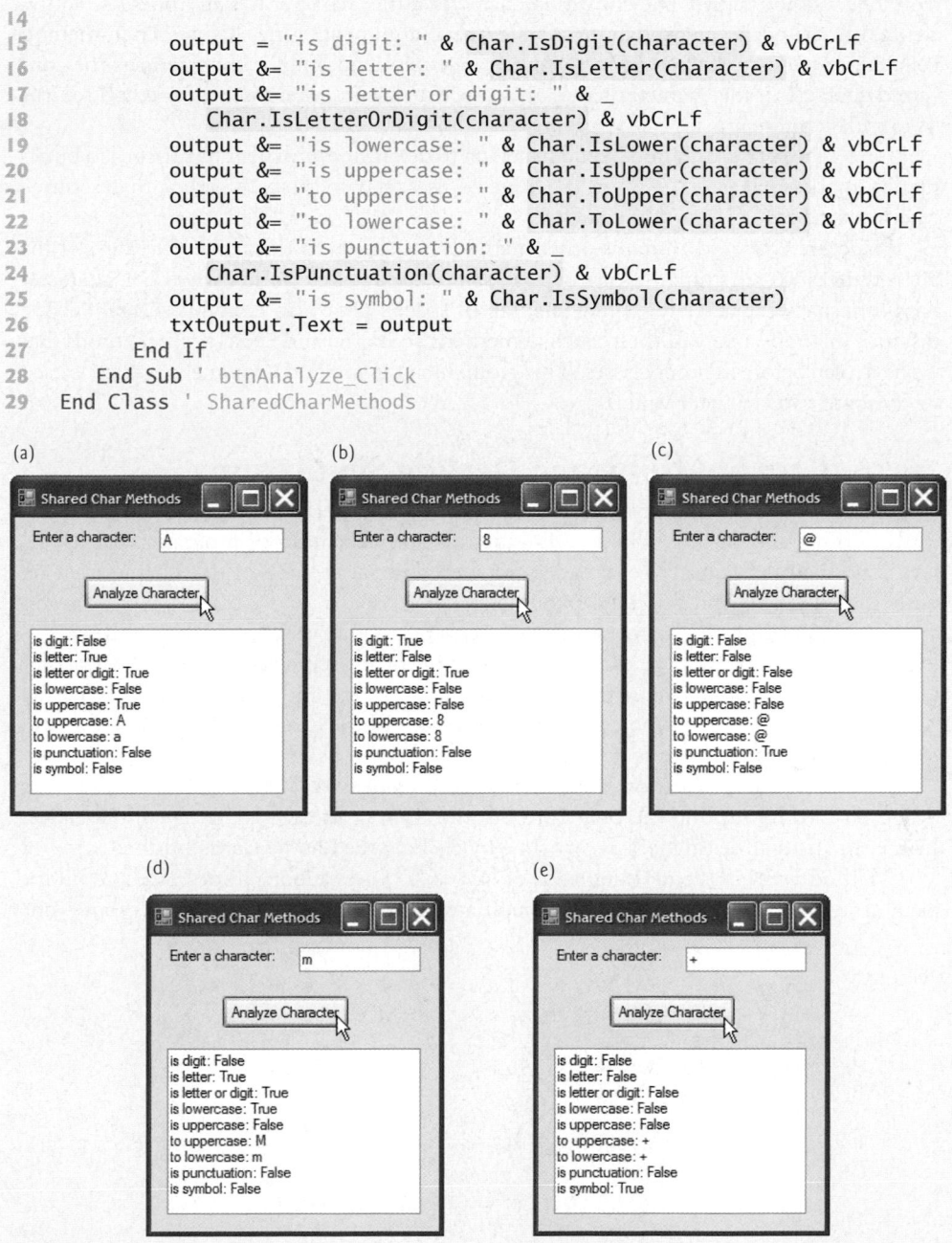

Fig. 16.15 | Char's Shared character-testing and case-conversion methods. (Part 2 of 2.)

Line 19 uses Char method IsLower to determine whether character is a lowercase letter. Line 20 uses Char method IsUpper to determine whether character is an uppercase letter. Line 21 uses Char method ToUpper to convert character to its uppercase equivalent. The method returns the converted character if the character has an uppercase equivalent; otherwise, the method returns its original argument. Line 22 uses Char method ToLower to convert character to its lowercase equivalent. The method returns the converted character if the character has a lowercase equivalent; otherwise, the method returns its original argument.

Line 24 uses Char method IsPunctuation to determine whether character is a punctuation mark, such as "!", ":" or ")". Line 24 uses Char method IsSymbol to determine whether character is a symbol, such as "+", "=" or "^".

Structure Char also contains other methods not shown in this example. Many of the Shared methods are similar—for instance, IsWhiteSpace determines whether a character is a whitespace character (e.g., newline, tab or space). Char also contains several Public instance methods; many of these, such as methods ToString and Equals, are methods that we have seen before in other classes. This group includes method CompareTo, which is used to compare two character values.

16.15 Card Shuffling and Dealing Simulation

In this section, we use random-number generation to develop a program that simulates card shuffling and dealing. These techniques can form the basis of programs that implement specific card games. We include several exercises at the end of this chapter that require card shuffling and dealing capabilities.

Class Card (Fig. 16.16) contains two String instance variables—face and suit— that store references to the face value and suit name of a specific card. The constructor for the class receives two Strings that it uses to initialize face and suit. Method ToString (lines 12–14) creates a String consisting of the face of the card and the suit of the card to identify the card when it is dealt.

The DeckForm application (Fig. 16.17) creates a deck of 52 Card objects. Users can deal each card by clicking the **Deal Card** button. Each dealt card is displayed in a Label. Users can also shuffle the deck at any time by clicking the **Shuffle Cards** button.

Method frmDeck_Load (lines 8–22 of Fig. 16.17) uses a loop (lines 19–21) to fill the deck array with Cards. Each Card is instantiated and initialized with two Strings—one

```vb
1   ' Fig. 16.16: Card.vb
2   ' Stores suit and face information on each card.
3   Public Class Card
4      Private face As String
5      Private suit As String
6
7      Public Sub New(ByVal faceValue As String, ByVal suitValue As String)
8         face = faceValue
9         suit = suitValue
10     End Sub ' New
11
12     Public Overrides Function ToString() As String
13        Return face & " of " & suit
14     End Function ' ToString
15  End Class ' Card
```

Fig. 16.16 | Card class.

from the faces array (Strings "Ace" through "King") and one from the suits array ("Hearts", "Diamonds", "Clubs" or "Spades"). The calculation i Mod 13 always results in a value from 0 to 12 (the 13 subscripts of the faces array), and the calculation i \ 13 always results in an Integer value from 0 to 3 (the four subscripts in the suits array). The initialized deck array contains the cards with faces Ace through King for each suit.

When the user clicks the **Deal Card** button, event handler btnDeal_Click (lines 25–39) invokes method DealCard (defined in lines 62–73) to get the next card in the deck array. If the deck is not empty, the method returns a Card object reference; otherwise, it returns Nothing. If the reference is not Nothing, lines 33–34 display the Card in lblDisplay and display the card number in lblStatus. If DealCard returns Nothing, the String

```vb
 1   ' Fig. 16.17: DeckForm.vb
 2   ' Simulating card shuffling and dealing.
 3   Public Class frmDeck
 4      Private deck(51) As Card ' deck of 52 cards
 5      Private currentCard As Integer ' count which card was just dealt
 6
 7      ' handles form at load time
 8      Private Sub frmDeck_Load( ByVal sender As System.Object, _
 9         ByVal e As System.EventArgs) Handles MyBase.Load
10
11         Dim faces As String() = _
12            {"Ace", "Deuce", "Three", "Four", "Five", "Six", "Seven", _
13            "Eight", "Nine", "Ten", "Jack", "Queen", "King"}
14         Dim suits As String() = {"Hearts", "Diamonds", "Clubs", "Spades"}
15
16         currentCard = -1 ' no cards have been dealt
17
18         ' initialize deck
19         For i As Integer = 0 To deck.Length - 1
20            deck(i) = New Card(faces(i Mod 13), suits(i \ 13))
21         Next i
22      End Sub ' frmDeck_Load
23
24   ' deal a card
25      Private Sub btnDeal_Click( ByVal sender As System.Object, _
26         ByVal e As System.EventArgs) Handles btnDeal.Click
27
28         Dim dealt As Card = DealCard()
29
30         ' if dealt card is Nothing, then no cards left
31         ' player must shuffle cards
32         If Not (dealt Is Nothing) Then
33            lblDisplay.Text = dealt.ToString()
34            lblStatus.Text = "Card #: " & currentCard
35         Else
36            lblDisplay.Text = "NO MORE CARDS TO DEAL"
37            lblStatus.Text = "Shuffle cards to continue"
38         End If
39      End Sub ' btnDeal_Click
40
```

Fig. 16.17 | Card shuffling and dealing simulation. (Part 1 of 3.)

```vb
41      ' shuffle cards
42      Private Sub Shuffle()
43         Dim randomNumber As New Random()
44         Dim temporaryValue As Card
45
46         currentCard = -1
47
48         ' swap each card with randomly selected card (0-51)
49         For i As Integer = 0 To deck.Length - 1
50            Dim j As Integer = randomNumber.Next(52)
51
52            ' swap cards
53            temporaryValue = deck(i)
54            deck(i) = deck(j)
55            deck(j) = temporaryValue
56         Next i
57
58         btnDeal.Enabled = True ' shuffled deck can now deal cards
59      End Sub ' Shuffle
60
61      ' deal a card if the deck is not empty
62      Private Function DealCard() As Card
63         ' if there is a card to deal then deal it;
64         ' otherwise, signal that cards need to be shuffled by
65         ' disabling dealButton and returning Nothing
66         If currentCard + 1 < deck.Length Then
67            currentCard += 1 ' increment count
68            Return deck(currentCard) ' return new card
69         Else
70            btnDeal.Enabled = False ' empty deck cannot deal cards
71            Return Nothing ' do not return a card
72         End If
73      End Function ' DealCard
74
75      ' handles btnShuffle Click
76      Private Sub btnShuffle_Click( ByVal sender As System.Object, _
77         ByVal e As System.EventArgs) Handles btnShuffle.Click
78
79         lblDisplay.Text = "SHUFFLING..."
80         Shuffle()
81         lblDisplay.Text = "DECK IS SHUFFLED"
82      End Sub ' btnShuffle_Click
83   End Class ' frmDeck
```

Fig. 16.17 | Card shuffling and dealing simulation. (Part 2 of 3.)

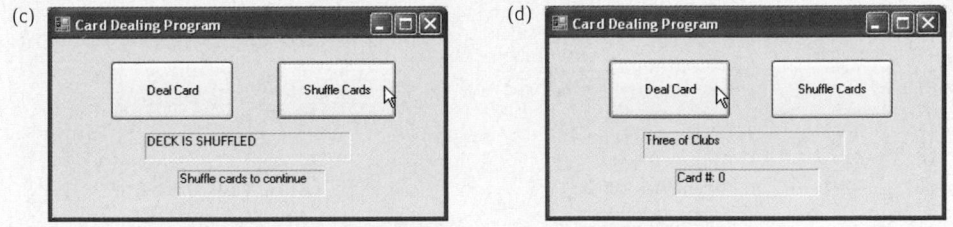

Fig. 16.17 | Card shuffling and dealing simulation. (Part 3 of 3.)

"NO MORE CARDS TO DEAL" is displayed in lblDisplay, and the String "Shuffle cards to continue" is displayed in lblStatus.

When the user clicks the **Shuffle Cards** button, event handler btnShuffle_Click (lines 76–82) invokes method Shuffle (defined in lines 42–59) to shuffle the cards. The method loops through all 52 cards (array subscripts 0–51). For each card, the method randomly picks a number between 0 and 51. Then the current Card object and the randomly selected Card object are swapped in the array. To shuffle the cards, method Shuffle makes a total of only 52 swaps during a single pass of the entire array. When the shuffling is complete, lblDisplay displays the String "DECK IS SHUFFLED".

16.16 **Regular Expressions and Class RegEx**

Regular expressions are specially formatted Strings used to find (and possibly replace) patterns in text. They can be useful during information validation, to ensure that data is in a particular format. For example, a United States ZIP code must consist of five digits, and a last name must start with a capital letter. Compilers use regular expressions to validate the syntax of programs. If the program code does not match the regular expression, the compiler indicates that there is a syntax error.

The .NET Framework provides several classes to help developers recognize and manipulate regular expressions. Class Regex (of the System.Text.RegularExpressions namespace) represents an immutable regular expression. Regex *method* Match returns an object of *class* Match that represents a single regular-expression match. Regex also provides method Matches, which finds all matches of a regular expression in an arbitrary String and returns an object of the class MatchCollection object containing all the Matches. A collection is a data structure similar to an array and can be used with a For Each statement to iterate through the collection's elements. We discuss collections in more detail in Chapter 26, Collections. To use class Regex, add an Imports statement for the package System.Text.RegularExpressions.

Regular Expression Character Classes

The table in Fig. 16.18 specifies some character classes that can be used with regular expressions. Do not confuse a character class with a Visual Basic class declaration. A character class is simply an escape sequence that represents a group of characters that might appear in a String.

A word character is any alphanumeric character or underscore. A whitespace character is a space, a tab, a carriage return, a newline or a form feed. A digit is any numeric character. Regular expressions are not limited to the character classes in Fig. 16.18. As you

Character class	Matches	Character class	Matches
\d	any digit	\D	any non-digit
\w	any word character	\W	any non-word character
\s	any whitespace	\S	any non-whitespace

Fig. 16.18 | Character classes.

will see in our first example, regular expressions can use other notations to search for complex patterns in Strings.

16.16.1 Regular Expression Example

The program in Fig. 16.19 tries to match birthdays to a regular expression. For demonstration purposes, the expression matches only birthdays that do not occur in April and that belong to people whose names begin with "J".

Line 8 creates a Regex object and passes a regular-expression pattern string to the Regex constructor. The first character in the regular expression, "J", is a literal character. Any String matching this regular expression is required to start with "J". In a regular expression, the dot character "." matches any single character except a newline character. When the dot character is followed by an asterisk, as in ".*", the regular expression

```
1   ' Fig. 16.19: RegexMatches.vb
2   ' Demonstrating Class Regex.
3   Imports System.Text.RegularExpressions
4
5   Module RegexMatches
6      Sub Main()
7         ' create regular expression
8         Dim expression As New Regex("J.*\d[0-35-9]-\d\d-\d\d")
9
10        Dim string1 As String = "Jane's Birthday is 05-12-75" & vbCrLf & _
11           "Dave's Birthday is 11-04-68" & vbCrLf & _
12           "John's Birthday is 04-28-73" & vbCrLf & _
13           "Joe's Birthday is 12-17-77"
14
15        ' match regular expression to string and
16        ' print out all matches
17        For Each myMatch As Match In expression.Matches(string1)
18           Console.WriteLine(myMatch)
19        Next myMatch
20     End Sub ' Main
21  End Module ' RegexMatches
```

```
Jane's Birthday is 05-12-75
Joe's Birthday is 12-17-77
```

Fig. 16.19 | Regular expressions checking birthdays.

matches any number of unspecified characters except newlines. In general, when the regular-expression operator "*" is applied to a pattern, the pattern will match zero or more occurrences. By contrast, applying the regular-expression operator "+" to a pattern causes the pattern to match one or more occurrences. For example, both "A*" and "A+" will match "A", but only "A*" will match an empty String.

As indicated in Fig. 16.18, "\d" matches any numeric digit. To specify sets of characters other than those that belong to a predefined character class, characters can be listed in square brackets, []. For example, the pattern "[aeiou]" matches any vowel. Ranges of characters are represented by placing a dash (-) between two characters. In the example, "[0-35-9]" matches only digits in the ranges specified by the pattern—any digit between 0 and 3 or between 5 and 9; therefore, it matches any digit except 4. You can also specify that a pattern should match anything other than the characters in the brackets. To do so, place ^ as the first character in the brackets. It is important to note that "[^4]" is not the same as "[0-35-9]"; "[^4]" matches any non-digit and digits other than 4.

Although the "-" character indicates a range when it is enclosed in square brackets, instances of the "-" character outside grouping expressions are treated as literal characters. Thus, the regular expression in line 8 searches for a String that starts with the letter "J", followed by any number of characters, followed by a two-digit number (of which the second digit cannot be 4), followed by a dash, another two-digit number, a dash and another two-digit number.

Lines 17–19 use a For Each statement to iterate through the MatchCollection returned by the expression object's Matches method, which received string1 as an argument. The elements in the MatchCollection are Match objects, so the For Each statement declares variable myMatch to be of type Match. For each Match, line 18 outputs the text that matched the regular expression. The output in Fig. 16.19 indicates the two matches that were found in string1. Note that both matches conform to the pattern specified by the regular expression.

Quantifiers

The asterisk (*) in line 8 of Fig. 16.19 is more formally called a quantifier. Figure 16.20 lists various quantifiers that you can place after a pattern in a regular expression and the purpose of each quantifier.

Quantifier	Matches
*	Matches zero or more occurrences of the preceding pattern.
+	Matches one or more occurrences of the preceding pattern.
?	Matches zero or one occurrences of the preceding pattern.
{n}	Matches exactly n occurrences of the preceding pattern.
{n,}	Matches at least n occurrences of the preceding pattern.
{n,m}	Matches between n and m (inclusive) occurrences of the preceding pattern.

Fig. 16.20 | Quantifiers used in regular expressions.

We have already discussed how the asterisk (*) and plus (+) quantifiers work. The question mark (?) quantifier matches zero or one occurrences of the pattern that it quantifies. A set of braces containing one number ({n}) matches exactly n occurrences of the pattern it quantifies. We demonstrate this quantifier in the next example. Including a comma after the number enclosed in braces matches at least n occurrences of the quantified pattern. The set of braces containing two numbers ({n,m}) matches between n and m occurrences (inclusively) of the pattern it qualifies. All of the quantifiers are greedy—they will match as many occurrences of the pattern as possible until the pattern fails to make a match. If a quantifier is followed by a question mark (?), the quantifier becomes lazy and will match as few occurrences as possible as long as there is a successful match.

16.16.2 Validating User Input with Regular Expressions

The Windows application in Fig. 16.21 presents a more involved example that uses regular expressions to validate name, address and telephone number information input by a user.

When a user clicks the **OK** button, the program checks to make sure that none of the fields is empty (lines 10–13). If one or more fields are empty, the program displays a message to the user (lines 15–16) that all fields must be filled in before the program can validate the input information. Line 17 calls txtLastName's Focus method so that the user can begin typing in that TextBox. The program then exits the event handler (line 18). If there are no empty fields, lines 22–88 validate the user input. Lines 22–29 validate the last name by calling Shared method Match of class Regex, passing both the string to validate and the regular expression as arguments. Method Match returns a Match object. This object contains a Success property that indicates whether method Match's first argument matched the pattern specified by the regular expression in the second argument. If the value of Success is False (i.e., there was no match), lines 25–26 display an error message, line 27 sets the focus back to txtLastName so that the user can retype the input, and line 28 terminates the event handler. If there is a match, the event handler proceeds to validate the first name. This process continues for each TextBox's contents until the event handler validates the user input in all the TextBoxes or until a validation fails. If all of the fields contain valid information, the program displays a message dialog stating this, and the program terminates when the user dismisses the dialog.

```
1   ' Fig. 16.21: Validate.vb
2   ' Validate user information using regular expressions.
3   Imports System.Text.RegularExpressions
4
5   Public Class frmValidate
6      ' handles btnOk Click event
7      Private Sub btnOk_Click(ByVal sender As System.Object, _
8         ByVal e As System.EventArgs) Handles btnOk.Click
9         ' ensures no TextBoxes are empty
10        If txtLastName.Text = "" Or txtFirstName.Text = "" Or _
11           txtAddress.Text = "" Or txtCity.Text = "" Or _
12           txtState.Text = "" Or txtZipCode.Text = "" Or _
13           txtPhone.Text = "" Then
```

Fig. 16.21 | Validating user information using regular expressions. (Part 1 of 4.)

```
14          ' display popup box
15          MessageBox.Show("Please fill in all fields", "Error", _
16             MessageBoxButtons.OK, MessageBoxIcon.Error)
17          txtLastName.Focus() ' set focus to txtLastName
18          Return
19       End If
20
21       ' if last name format invalid show message
22       If Not Regex.Match(txtLastName.Text, _
23          "^[A-Z][a-zA-Z]*$").Success Then
24          ' last name was incorrect
25          MessageBox.Show("Invalid last name", "Message", _
26             MessageBoxButtons.OK, MessageBoxIcon.Error)
27          txtLastName.Focus()
28          Return
29       End If
30
31       ' if first name format invalid show message
32       If Not Regex.Match(txtFirstName.Text, _
33          "^[A-Z][a-zA-Z]*$").Success Then
34          ' first name was incorrect
35          MessageBox.Show("Invalid first name", "Message", _
36             MessageBoxButtons.OK, MessageBoxIcon.Error)
37          txtFirstName.Focus()
38          Return
39       End If
40
41       ' if address format invalid show message
42       If Not Regex.Match(txtAddress.Text, _
43          "^[0-9]+\s+([a-zA-Z]+|[a-zA-Z]+\s[a-zA-Z]+)$").Success Then
44          ' address was incorrect
45          MessageBox.Show("Invalid address", "Message", _
46             MessageBoxButtons.OK, MessageBoxIcon.Error)
47          txtAddress.Focus()
48          Return
49       End If
50
51       ' if state format invalid show message
52       If Not Regex.Match(txtCity.Text, _
53          "^([a-zA-Z]+|[a-zA-Z]+\s[a-zA-Z]+)$").Success Then
54          ' city was incorrect
55          MessageBox.Show("Invalid city", "Message", _
56             MessageBoxButtons.OK, MessageBoxIcon.Error)
57          txtCity.Focus()
58          Return
59       End If
60
61       ' if state format invalid show message
62       If Not Regex.Match(txtState.Text, _
63          "^([a-zA-Z]+|[a-zA-Z]+\s[a-zA-Z]+)$").Success Then
64          ' state was incorrect
65          MessageBox.Show("Invalid state", "Message", _
66             MessageBoxButtons.OK, MessageBoxIcon.Error)
```

Fig. 16.21 | Validating user information using regular expressions. (Part 2 of 4.)

```
67              txtState.Focus()
68              Return
69          End If
70
71          ' if zip code format invalid show message
72          If Not Regex.Match(txtZipCode.Text, "^\d{5}$").Success Then
73              ' zip was incorrect
74              MessageBox.Show("Invalid zip code", "Message", _
75                  MessageBoxButtons.OK, MessageBoxIcon.Error)
76              txtZipCode.Focus()
77              Return
78          End If
79
80          ' if phone number format invalid show message
81          If Not Regex.Match(txtPhone.Text, _
82              "^[1-9]\d{2}-[1-9]\d{2}-\d{4}$").Success Then
83              ' phone number was incorrect
84              MessageBox.Show("Invalid phone number", "Message", _
85                  MessageBoxButtons.OK, MessageBoxIcon.Error)
86              txtPhone.Focus()
87              Return
88          End If
89
90          ' information is valid, signal user and exit application
91          Me.Hide() ' hide main window while MessageBox displays
92          MessageBox.Show("Thank You!", "Information Correct", _
93              MessageBoxButtons.OK, MessageBoxIcon.Information)
94          Application.Exit()
95      End Sub ' btnOk_Click
96  End Class ' frmValidate
```

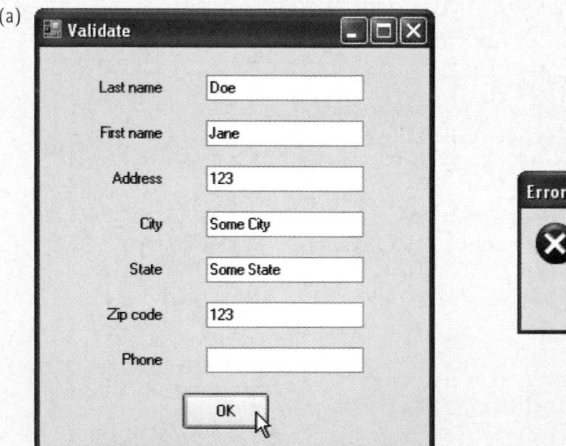

Fig. 16.21 | Validating user information using regular expressions. (Part 3 of 4.)

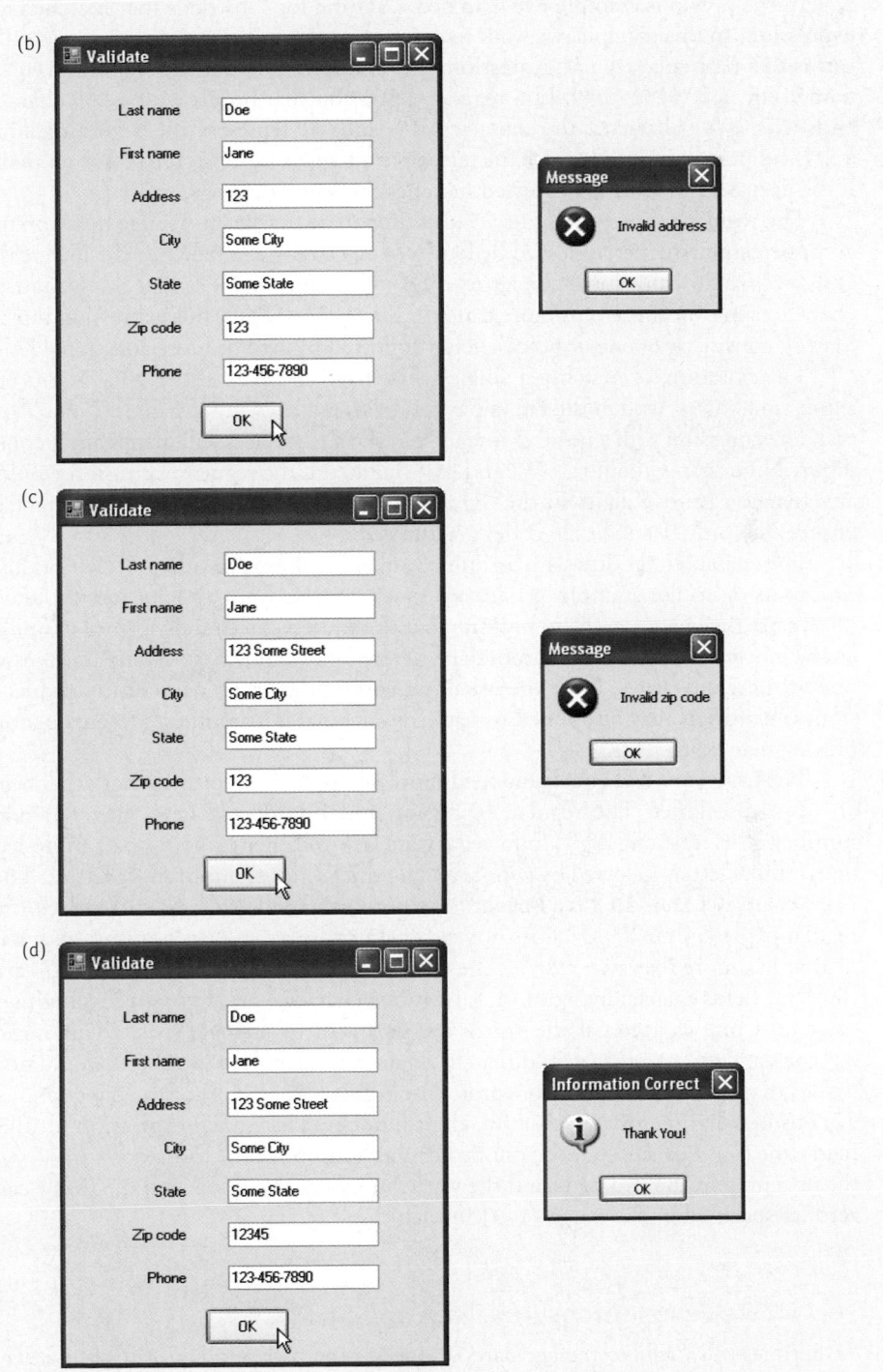

Fig. 16.21 | Validating user information using regular expressions. (Part 4 of 4.)

In the previous example, we searched a `String` for substrings that matched a regular expression. In this example, we want to ensure that the entire `String` in each `TextBox` conforms to a particular regular expression. For example, we want to accept `"Smith"` as a last name, but not `"9@Smith#"`. In a regular expression that begins with a `"^"` character and ends with a `"$"` character, the characters `"^"` and `"$"` represent the beginning and end of a `String`, respectively. These characters force a regular expression to return a match only if the entire `String` being processed matches the regular expression.

The regular expression in line 23 uses the square bracket and range notation to match an uppercase first letter, followed by letters of any case—a-z matches any lowercase letter, and A-Z matches any uppercase letter. The * quantifier signifies that the second range of characters may occur zero or more times in the `String`. Thus, this expression matches any `String` consisting of one uppercase letter followed by zero or more additional letters.

The notation `\s` matches a single whitespace character (lines 43, 53 and 63). The expression `\d{5}`, used in the **Zip** (zip code) field, matches any five digits (line 72). In general, an expression with a positive integer x in the curly braces will match any x consecutive digits. Note that without the `"^"` and `"$"` characters, the regular expression would match any five consecutive digits in the `String`. By including the `"^"` and `"$"` characters, we ensure that only five-digit zip codes are allowed.

The character `"|"` (lines 43, 53 and 63) matches the expression to its left or the expression to its right. For example, `Hi (John|Jane)` matches both `Hi John` and `Hi Jane`. In line 43, we use the character `"|"` to indicate that the address can contain a word of one or more characters *or* a word of one or more characters followed by a space and another word of one or more characters. Note the use of parentheses to group parts of the regular expression. Quantifiers may be applied to patterns enclosed in parentheses to create more complex regular expressions.

The **Last name** and **First name** fields both accept `Strings` of any length that begin with an uppercase letter. The regular expression for the **Address** field (line 43) matches a number of at least one digit, followed by a space and then either one or more letters, or one or more letters followed by a space and another series of one or more letters. Therefore, `"10 Broadway"` and `"10 Main Street"` are both valid addresses. As currently formed, the regular expression in line 43 does not match an address that does not start with a number or that has more than two words. The regular expressions for the **City** (line 53) and **State** (line 63) fields match any word of at least one character or, alternatively, any two words of at least one character if the words are separated by a single space. This means both `Waltham` and `West Newton` would match. Again, these regular expressions would not accept names that have more than two words. The regular expression for the **Zip code** field (line 72) ensures that the zip code is a five-digit number. The regular expression for the **Phone** field (line 82) indicates that the phone number must be of the form xxx-yyy-yyyy, where the xs represent the area code and the ys the number. The first x and the first y cannot be zero, as specified by the range `[1-9]` in each case.

16.16.3 Regex methods `Replace` and `Split`

Sometimes it is useful to replace parts of one `String` with another or to split a `String` according to a regular expression. For this purpose, the `Regex` class provides `Shared` and instance versions of methods `Replace` and `Split`, which are demonstrated in Fig. 16.22.

```vb
 1   ' Fig. 16.22: RegexSubstitution.vb
 2   ' Using Regex method Replace.
 3   Imports System.Text.RegularExpressions
 4
 5   Module RegexSubstitution
 6      Sub Main()
 7         Dim testString1 As String = _
 8            "This sentence ends in 5 stars *****"
 9         Dim output As String = ""
10         Dim testString2 As String = "1, 2, 3, 4, 5, 6, 7, 8"
11         Dim testRegex1 As New Regex("\d")
12         Dim result() As String
13
14         Console.WriteLine("Original string: " & testString1)
15         testString1 = Regex.Replace(testString1, "\*", "^")
16         Console.WriteLine("^ substituted for *: " & testString1)
17         testString1 = Regex.Replace(testString1, "stars", "carets")
18         Console.WriteLine("""carets"" substituted for ""stars"": " & _
19            testString1)
20         Console.WriteLine("Every word replaced by ""word"": " & _
21            Regex.Replace(testString1, "\w+", "word"))
22         Console.WriteLine(vbCrLf & "Original string: " & testString2)
23         Console.WriteLine("Replace first 3 digits by ""digit"": " & _
24            testRegex1.Replace(testString2, "digit", 3))
25         Console.Write("string split at commas [")
26
27         result = Regex.Split(testString2, ",\s")
28
29         For Each resultString As String In result
30            output &= """" & resultString & """, "
31         Next resultString
32
33         ' Delete ", " at the end of output string
34         Console.WriteLine(output.Substring(0, output.Length - 2) + "]")
35      End Sub ' Main
36   End Module ' RegexSubstitution
```

```
Original string: This sentence ends in 5 stars *****
^ substituted for *: This sentence ends in 5 stars ^^^^^
"carets" substituted for "stars": This sentence ends in 5 carets ^^^^^
Every word replaced by "word": word word word word word word ^^^^^

Original string: 1, 2, 3, 4, 5, 6, 7, 8
Replace first 3 digits by "digit": digit, digit, digit, 4, 5, 6, 7, 8
string split at commas ["1", "2", "3", "4", "5", "6", "7", "8"]
```

Fig. 16.22 | Regex methods `Replace` and `Split`.

Method `Replace` replaces text in a `String` with new text wherever the original `String` matches a regular expression. We use two versions of this method in Fig. 16.22. The first version (line 15) is `Shared` and takes three parameters—the `String` to modify, the `String` containing the regular expression to match and the replacement `String`. Here, `Replace` replaces every instance of "*" in `testString1` with "∧". Note that the regular expression ("*") precedes character * with a backslash, \. Normally, * is a quantifier indicating that a regular expression should match any number of occurrences of a preceding pattern. However, in line 15, we want to find all occurrences of the literal character *; to do this, we must escape character * with a \. By escaping a special regular-expression character with a \, we tell the regular-expression matching engine to find the actual character * rather than use it as a quantifier. Line 17 replaces every occurrence of "stars" in `testString1` with "carets". Line 21 replaces every word in `testString1` with "word".

The second version of method `Replace` (line 24) is an instance method that uses the regular expression passed to the constructor for `testRegex1` (line 11) to perform the replacement operation. Line 11 instantiates `testRegex1` with argument "\d". The call to instance method `Replace` in line 24 takes three arguments—a `String` to modify, a `String` containing the replacement text and an `Integer` specifying the number of replacements to make. In this case, line 24 replaces the first three instances of a digit ("\d") in `testString2` with the text "digit".

Method `Split` divides a `String` into several substrings. The original `String` is broken at delimiters that match a specified regular expression. Method `Split` returns an array containing the substrings. In line 27, we use the `Shared` version of method `Split` to separate a `String` of comma-separated integers. The first argument is the `String` to split; the second argument is the regular expression that represents the delimiter. The regular expression ",\s*" separates the substrings at each comma. By matching any whitespace characters (\s* in the regular expression), we eliminate extra spaces from the resulting substrings.

16.17 Wrap-Up

In this chapter, you learned about the FCL's string and character processing capabilities. We overviewed the fundamentals of characters and strings. You saw how to determine the length of strings, copy strings, access the individual characters in strings, search strings, obtain substrings from larger strings, compare strings, concatenate strings, replace characters in strings and convert strings to uppercase or lowercase letters.

We showed how to use class `StringBuilder` to build sequences of characters dynamically. You learned how to determine and specify the size of a `StringBuilder` object, and how to append, insert, remove and replace characters in a `StringBuilder` object. We then introduced the character-testing methods of type `Char` that enable a program to determine whether a character is a digit, a letter, a lowercase letter, an uppercase letter, a punctuation mark or a symbol other than a punctuation mark, and the methods for converting a character to uppercase or lowercase.

Finally, we discussed classes `Regex` and `Match` from the `System.Text.Regular-Expressions` namespace. We also discussed the symbols that are used to form regular expressions. You learned how to find patterns in a string and match entire strings to patterns with `Regex` method `Match`, how to replace characters in a string with `Regex` method `Replace` and how to split strings at delimiters with `Regex` method `Split`. In the next chapter, you will learn how to add graphics and other multimedia capabilities to your Windows applications.

Summary

Section 16.2 Fundamentals of Characters and Strings
- Characters are the fundamental building blocks of Visual Basic source code. Every program is composed of characters that, when grouped together meaningfully, create a sequence that the compiler interprets as instructions describing how to accomplish a task.
- A character literal is a character represented internally as an integer value, called a character code. For example, the integer value 97 corresponds to the character literal "a"c. The letter c following the closing double quote is Visual Basic's syntax for a character literal.
- Character literals are established according to the Unicode character set.
- A string is a series of characters treated as a single unit. These characters can be uppercase letters, lowercase letters, digits and various special characters: +, -, *, /, $ and others.
- A string is an object of class String in the System namespace. We write string literals, also called string constants, as sequences of characters in double quotation marks.
- A declaration can assign a String literal to a String variable.

Section 16.3 **String** Constructors
- Class String provides eight constructors for initializing Strings.

Section 16.4 **String** Indexer, **Length** Property and **CopyTo** Method
- The String indexer provides access to individual characters in a String.
- String property Length returns the length of the String.
- String method CopyTo copies a specified number of characters from a String into a Char array. CopyTo's first argument is the index from which the method begins copying characters in the String. The second argument is the character array into which the characters are copied. The third argument is the index specifying the starting location at which the method begins placing the copied characters into the character array. The last argument is the number of characters that the method will copy from the String.
- The String indexer receives an integer argument as the index and returns the character at that index. As with arrays, the first element of a String is considered to be at position 0.

Section 16.5 Comparing **Strings**
- Computers can order characters alphabetically because the characters are represented internally as Unicode numeric codes. When comparing two Strings, the string comparison methods simply compare the numeric codes of the characters in the Strings.
- String method Equals compares two Strings to determine whether they are equal, and returns True if the objects are equal and False otherwise. Method Equals uses a lexicographical comparison—the integer Unicode values that represent each character in each String are compared.
- The equality operator (=) can be used to compare two Strings for equality. This operator also uses a lexicographical comparison to compare two Strings.
- String method CompareTo returns 0 if two Strings are equal, -1 if the String that invokes CompareTo is less than the String passed as an argument and 1 if the String that invokes CompareTo is greater than the String passed as an argument. Method CompareTo uses a lexicographical comparison.
- String method StartsWith determines whether a String starts with the String passed to it as an argument.
- String method EndsWith determines whether a String ends with the String passed to it as an argument.

Section 16.6 Locating Characters and Substrings in *Strings*

- String method IndexOf locates the first occurrence of a character in a String. If it finds the character, IndexOf returns the character's index in the String; otherwise, IndexOf returns –1.

- String method LastIndexOf locates the last occurrence of a character in a String. Method LastIndexOf searches from the end of the String toward the beginning. If it finds the character, LastIndexOf returns the character's index in the String; otherwise, LastIndexOf returns –1.

- There are also versions of IndexOf and LastIndexOf that take Strings rather than characters as their first argument.

- String methods IndexOfAny and LastIndexOfAny each take an array of characters as the first argument. These methods return the index of the first occurrence of any of the characters in the character array argument.

Section 16.7 Extracting Substrings from *Strings*

- Class String provides two Substring methods that are used to create a new String by copying part of an existing String. Each method returns a new String.

- One Substring method takes one Integer argument that specifies the starting index from which the method copies characters in the original String.

- The second version of method Substring takes two Integer arguments. The arguments specify the starting index from which to copy characters and the length of the substring to copy.

Section 16.8 Concatenating *Strings*

- Like the & operator, the String class's Shared method Concat can be used to concatenate two Strings. The method returns a new String containing the combined characters from both original Strings. The original Strings are not modified.

Section 16.9 Miscellaneous *String* Methods

- Class String provides several methods that return modified copies of Strings. None of these methods modifies the original String.

- String method Replace takes two arguments—a Char for which to search and another Char with which to replace all matching occurrences of the first argument. This method is also overloaded to receive two String parameters. If there are no occurrences of the first argument in the String, the method returns the original String.

- String method ToUpper returns a new String that replaces any lowercase letters in a String with their uppercase equivalent. If there are no characters to convert to uppercase, the method returns the original String.

- String method ToLower returns a new String in which any uppercase letters in a String are replaced by their lowercase equivalents. As with ToUpper, if there are no characters to convert to lowercase, method ToLower returns the original String.

- String method Trim removes all whitespace characters that appear at the beginning and end of a String. The method returns a new String that contains the original String, but omits leading or trailing whitespace characters.

Section 16.10 Class *StringBuilder*

- A String's contents can never change. Operations that seem to concatenate Strings are in fact creating new Strings.

- Class StringBuilder (namespace System.Text) is used to create and manipulate dynamic string information.

- A StringBuilder can store the number of characters specified by its capacity. Exceeding the capacity of a StringBuilder makes the capacity expand to accommodate the additional characters.
- Class StringBuilder provides six overloaded constructors.

Section 16.11 *Length and Capacity Properties, EnsureCapacity Method and Indexer of Class StringBuilder*

- Class StringBuilder provides the Length and Capacity properties to return the number of characters currently in a StringBuilder and the number of characters that a StringBuilder can store without allocating more memory, respectively. These properties also can increase or decrease the length or the capacity of the StringBuilder.
- Method EnsureCapacity allows you to reduce the number of times that a StringBuilder's capacity must be increased. Method EnsureCapacity doubles the StringBuilder instance's current capacity. If this doubled value is greater than the value you wish to ensure, that value becomes the new capacity. Otherwise, the capacity is set to the requested number.
- The StringBuilder constructor that takes a String argument creates a StringBuilder object with an initial capacity that is the smallest power of two greater than or equal to the number of characters in the String passed as an argument.

Section 16.12 *Append and AppendFormat Methods of Class StringBuilder*

- Class StringBuilder provides 19 overloaded Append methods for appending values of various types to the end of a StringBuilder's contents. There are versions of this method for each of the primitive types and for character arrays, Strings and Objects.
- StringBuilder method AppendFormat converts a String to a specified format, then appends it to the StringBuilder.

Section 16.13 *Insert, Remove and Replace Methods of Class StringBuilder*

- Class StringBuilder provides 18 overloaded Insert methods to allow values of various types to be inserted at any position in a StringBuilder. There are versions of Insert for each of the primitive types and for character arrays, Strings and Objects. Each version takes its second argument, converts it to a String and inserts the String into the StringBuilder at the index specified by the first argument. The index must be greater than or equal to 0 and less than the length of the StringBuilder; otherwise, an ArgumentOutOfRangeException occurs.
- StringBuilder method Remove deletes characters in a StringBuilder. Method Remove takes two arguments—the index at which to begin deletion and the number of characters to delete. The sum of the starting subscript and the number of characters to be deleted must always be less than the StringBuilder's length; otherwise, an ArgumentOutOfRangeException occurs.
- StringBuilder method Replace searches for a specified String or character and substitutes another String or character in its place.

Section 16.14 *Char Methods*

- Visual Basic provides a type called a structure that is similar to a class. Although structures and classes are comparable in many ways, structures represent value types.
- Like classes, structures include methods and properties. Both use the same access modifiers (such as Public, Protected and Private) and access members via the member access operator (.).
- Classes are created by using the keyword Class, but structures are created using the keyword Structure.
- Many of the primitive types that we have used in this book are actually aliases for different structures. For instance, an Integer is defined by structure System.Int32, a Long by System.Int64 and so on.

- Structures derive from class ValueType, which in turn derives from class Object.
- Most Char methods are Shared, take at least one character argument and perform either a test or a manipulation on the character.
- Method Convert.ToChar converts a String to a Char.
- Char method IsDigit determines whether a character is a digit.
- Char method IsLetter determines whether a character is a letter.
- Char method IsLetterOrDigit determines whether a character is a letter or a digit.
- Char method IsLower determines whether a character is a lowercase letter.
- Char method IsUpper determines whether a character is an uppercase letter.
- Char method ToUpper converts a character to its uppercase equivalent. The method returns the converted character if the character has an uppercase equivalent; otherwise, the method returns its original argument.
- Char method ToLower converts a character to its lowercase equivalent. The method returns the converted character if the character has a lowercase equivalent; otherwise, the method returns its original argument.
- Char method IsPunctuation determines whether a character is a punctuation mark.
- Char method IsSymbol determines whether a character is a symbol.
- Char method IsWhiteSpace determines whether a character is a whitespace character.

Section 16.16 Regular Expressions and Class **Regex**
- Regular expressions are specially formatted Strings used to find patterns in text.
- The .NET Framework provides several classes to help developers recognize and manipulate regular expressions.
- Class Regex (of the System.Text.RegularExpressions namespace) represents an immutable regular expression.
- Regex *method* Match returns an object of *class* Match representing a single regular-expression match.
- Regex method Matches finds all matches of a regular expression in an arbitrary String and returns an object of the class MatchCollection object containing all the Matches.
- A collection is a data structure similar to an array and can be used with a For Each statement to iterate through the collection's elements.
- A character class is simply an escape sequence that represents a group of characters that might appear in a String.
- A word character is any alphanumeric character or underscore.
- A whitespace character is a space, a tab, a carriage return, a newline or a form feed.
- A digit is any numeric character.

Section 16.16.1 Regular Expression Example
- In a regular expression, the dot character "." matches any single character except a newline character. When the dot character is followed by an asterisk, as in ".*", the regular expression matches any number of unspecified characters except newlines.
- In general, when the regular-expression operator "*" is applied to a pattern, the pattern will match zero or more occurrences.
- Applying the regular-expression operator "+" to a pattern causes the pattern to match one or more occurrences.

- The regular expression "\d" matches any numeric digit.
- To specify sets of characters other than those that belong to a predefined character class, characters can be listed in square brackets, []. For example, the pattern "[aeiou]" matches any vowel.
- Ranges of characters are represented by placing a dash (-) between two characters.
- To specify that a pattern should match anything other than the characters in the brackets, place ∧ as the first character in the brackets.
- Although the "-" character indicates a range when it is enclosed in square brackets, instances of the "-" character outside grouping expressions are treated as literal characters.
- The elements in a MatchCollection are Match objects.
- The asterisk (*) is more formally called a quantifier.
- The question mark (?) quantifier matches zero or one occurrences of the pattern it quantifies.
- A set of braces containing one number ({n}) matches exactly n occurrences of the pattern it quantifies. Including a comma after the number enclosed in braces matches at least n occurrences of the quantified pattern. The set of braces containing two numbers ({n,m}) matches between n and m occurrences (inclusively) of the pattern it qualifies.
- All of the quantifiers are greedy—they will match as many occurrences of the pattern as possible until the pattern fails to make a match.
- If a quantifier is followed by a question mark (?), the quantifier becomes lazy and will match as few occurrences as possible as long as there is a successful match.

Section 16.16.2 Validating User Input with Regular Expressions
- Match property Success indicates whether method Match's first argument matched the pattern specified by the regular expression in the second argument. If the value of Success is False, there was no match.
- In a regular expression that begins with a "∧" character and ends with a "$" character, the characters "∧" and "$" represent the beginning and end of a String, respectively. These characters force a regular expression to return a match only if the entire String being processed matches the regular expression.
- The notation \s matches a single whitespace character.
- The expression \d{5} matches any five digits. In general, an expression with a positive integer x in the curly braces will match any x consecutive digits.
- The character "|" matches the expression to its left or the expression to its right.
- Parentheses can be used to group parts of a regular expression.
- Quantifiers may be applied to patterns enclosed in parentheses to create more complex regular expressions.

Section 16.16.3 Regex methods Replace and Split
- Sometimes it is useful to replace parts of one String with another or to split a String according to a regular expression. For this purpose, the Regex class provides Shared and instance versions of methods Replace and Split.
- Method Replace replaces text in a String with new text wherever the original String matches a regular expression.
- Method Split divides a String into several substrings. The original String is broken at delimiters that match a specified regular expression.

Terminology

\d (regular expressions)	IsPunctuation method of structure Char
\w (regular expressions)	IsSymbol method of structure Char
\s (regular expressions)	IsUpper method of structure Char
\D (regular expressions)	IsWhiteSpace method of structure Char
\W (regular expressions)	LastIndexOf method of class String
\S (regular expressions)	LastIndexOfAny method of class String
$ (regular expressions)	lazy quantifier
^ (regular expressions)	Length property of class String
& operator	Length property of class StringBuilder
&= concatenation operator	lexicographical comparison
= equality operator	Match class
alphabetizing	MatchCollection class
Append method of class StringBuilder	quantifier in a regular expression
AppendFormat method of class StringBuilder	random-number generation
ArgumentOutOfRangeException	Regex class for regular expressions
Capacity property of StringBuilder	Remove method of class StringBuilder
Char array	Replace method of class Regex
Char structure	Replace method of class String
Chars property of class String	Replace method of class StringBuilder
character	special characters
character class, in regular expressions	Split method of class Regex
character constant	StartsWith method of class String
character literal	String class
CompareTo method of class String	string literal
CompareTo method of structure Char	StringBuilder class
Concat method of class String	Structure keyword
CopyTo method of class String	Substring method of class String
Enabled property of class Control	Success property of class Match
EndsWith method of class String	System namespace
EnsureCapacity method of class StringBuilder	System.Text namespace
Equals method of class String	System.Text.RegularExpressions namespace
Equals method of structure Char	ToLower method of class String
format string	ToLower method of structure Char
greedy quantifier	ToString method of StringBuilder
immutable String	ToUpper method of class String
IndexOf method of class String	ToUpper method of structure Char
IndexOfAny method of class String	trailing whitespace characters
Insert method of class StringBuilder	Trim method of class String
IsDigit method of structure Char	Unicode character set
IsLetter method of structure Char	ValueType class
IsLetterOrDigit method of structure Char	whitespace character
IsLower method of structure Char	word character

Self-Review Exercises

16.1 State whether each of the following is *true* or *false*. If *false*, explain why.

    a) When Strings are compared with =, the result is True if the Strings contain the same values.

    b) A String can be modified after it is created.

c) StringBuilder method EnsureCapacity sets the StringBuilder instance's length to the argument's value.

d) Method Equals and the equality operator work the same for Strings.

e) Method Trim removes all whitespace at the beginning and the end of a String.

f) A regular expression matches a String to a pattern.

g) It is always better to use Strings rather than StringBuilders because Strings containing the same value will reference the same object in memory.

h) String method ToUpper capitalizes just the first letter of the String.

i) The expression \d in a regular expression denotes a letter.

16.2 Fill in the blanks in each of the following statements:

a) Operators _____ and _____ can be used to concatenate Strings.

b) Method Equals of class String uses a(n) _____ comparison of Strings.

c) Class Regex is located in namespace _____.

d) StringBuilder method _____ first formats the specified String, then appends it to the end of the StringBuilder's contents.

e) If the arguments to a Substring method call are out of range, an exception of type _____ occurs.

f) Regex method _____ changes all occurrences of a pattern in a String to a specified String.

g) A C in a format string means to output the number as _____.

h) Regular-expression quantifier _____ matches zero or more occurrences of an expression.

i) Regular-expression operator _____ inside square brackets will not match any of the characters in that set of brackets.

Answers to Self-Review Exercises

16.1 a) True. b) False. Strings are immutable; they cannot be modified after they are created. However, many methods return new Strings containing modified copies of existing Strings. c) False. EnsureCapacity sets the instance's capacity to double either the current capacity or the value of its argument, whichever is larger. d) True. e) True. f) True. g) False. StringBuilder should be used when a program needs to modify a sequence of characters repeatedly. h) False. String method ToUpper capitalizes all letters in the String. i) False. The expression \d in a regular expression denotes a digit.

16.2 a) &, &=. b) lexicographical. c) System.Text.RegularExpressions. d) AppendFormat e) ArgumentOutOfRangeException. f) Replace. g) currency. h) *. i) ^.

Exercises

16.3 Modify the program in Fig. 16.17 so that the card-dealing method deals a five-card poker hand. Then write the following additional methods:

a) Determine whether the hand contains a pair.

b) Determine whether the hand contains two pairs.

c) Determine whether the hand contains three of a kind (e.g., three jacks).

d) Determine whether the hand contains four of a kind (e.g., four aces).

e) Determine whether the hand contains a flush (i.e., all five cards of the same suit).

f) Determine whether the hand contains a straight (i.e., five cards of consecutive face values).

g) Determine whether the hand contains a full house (i.e., two cards of one face value and three cards of another face value).

16.4 Write an application that uses String method CompareTo to compare two Strings input by the user. Output whether the first String is less than, equal to or greater than the second.

16.5 Write an application that uses random-number generation to create sentences. Use four arrays of Strings, called article, noun, verb and preposition. Create a sentence by selecting a word at random from each array in the following order: article, noun, verb, preposition, article, noun. As each word is picked, concatenate it to the previous words in the sentence. The words should be separated by spaces. When the sentence is output, it should start with a capital letter and end with a period. The program should generate 10 sentences and output them to a text area.

The arrays should be filled as follows: The article array should contain the articles "the", "a", "one", "some" and "any"; the noun array should contain the nouns "boy", "girl", "dog", "town" and "car"; the verb array should contain the past-tense verbs "drove", "jumped", "ran", "walked" and "skipped"; and the preposition array should contain the prepositions "to", "from", "over", "under" and "on".

After the preceding program is written, modify the program to produce a short story consisting of several of these sentences. (How about the possibility of a random term-paper writer!)

16.6 (*Pig Latin*) Write an application that encodes English language phrases into pig Latin. Pig Latin is a form of coded language often used for amusement. Many variations exist in the methods used to form pig Latin phrases. For simplicity, use the following algorithm:

To translate an English word into a pig Latin word, place the first letter of the English word at the end of the word and add the letters "ay." Thus, the word "jump" becomes "umpjay," the word "the" becomes "hetay" and the word "computer" becomes "omputercay." Blanks between words remain blanks. Assume the following: The English phrase consists of words separated by blanks, there are no punctuation marks and all words have two or more letters. Enable the user to input a sentence. Use techniques discussed in this chapter to divide the sentence into separate words. Method GetPigLatin should translate a single word into pig Latin. Keep a running display of all the converted sentences in a text area.

16.7 Write a program that reads a five-letter word from the user and produces all possible three-letter words that can be derived from the letters of the five-letter word. For example, the three-letter words produced from the word "bathe" include the commonly used words "ate," "bat," "bet," "tab," "hat," "the" and "tea."

Graphics and Multimedia

OBJECTIVES

In this chapter you will learn:

- To understand graphics contexts and graphics objects.
- To manipulate colors and fonts.
- To understand and use GDI+ `Graphics` methods to draw lines, rectangles, `String`s and images.
- To use class `Image` to manipulate and display images.
- To draw complex shapes from simple shapes with class `GraphicsPath`.
- To use Windows Media Player to play audio or video in a Visual Basic application.
- To use Microsoft Agent to add interactive animated characters to a Visual Basic application.

17.1 Introduction

In this chapter, we overview the FCL's tools for drawing two-dimensional shapes and for controlling colors and fonts. The FCL supports graphics that enable programmers to visually enhance their Windows applications. The many sophisticated drawing capabilities are part of namespace `System.Drawing` and the other namespaces that make up the .NET resource **GDI+**. GDI+ is an application programming interface (API) that provides classes for creating two-dimensional vector graphics (a way to describe graphics that makes them easy to manipulate with high-performance techniques), manipulating fonts and inserting images.

We begin with an introduction to the .NET framework's drawing capabilities. We then present more powerful drawing capabilities, such as changing the styles of the lines used to draw shapes and controlling the colors and patterns of the filled shapes.

Later in this chapter, we explore techniques for manipulating images and creating smooth animations. We also discuss class `Image`, which can store and manipulate images of various formats. We explain how to combine the graphical rendering capabilities covered in the early sections of the chapter with those for image manipulation. The chapter ends with several multimedia examples in which you build an animation, use the Windows Media Player control and use Microsoft Agent—a technology for adding interactive animated characters to applications or Web pages.

17.2 Drawing Classes and the Coordinate System

Figure 17.1 depicts a portion of namespace `System.Drawing`, including several graphics classes and structures covered in this chapter. Namespaces `System.Drawing` and `System.Drawing.Drawing2D` contain the most commonly used GDI+ components.

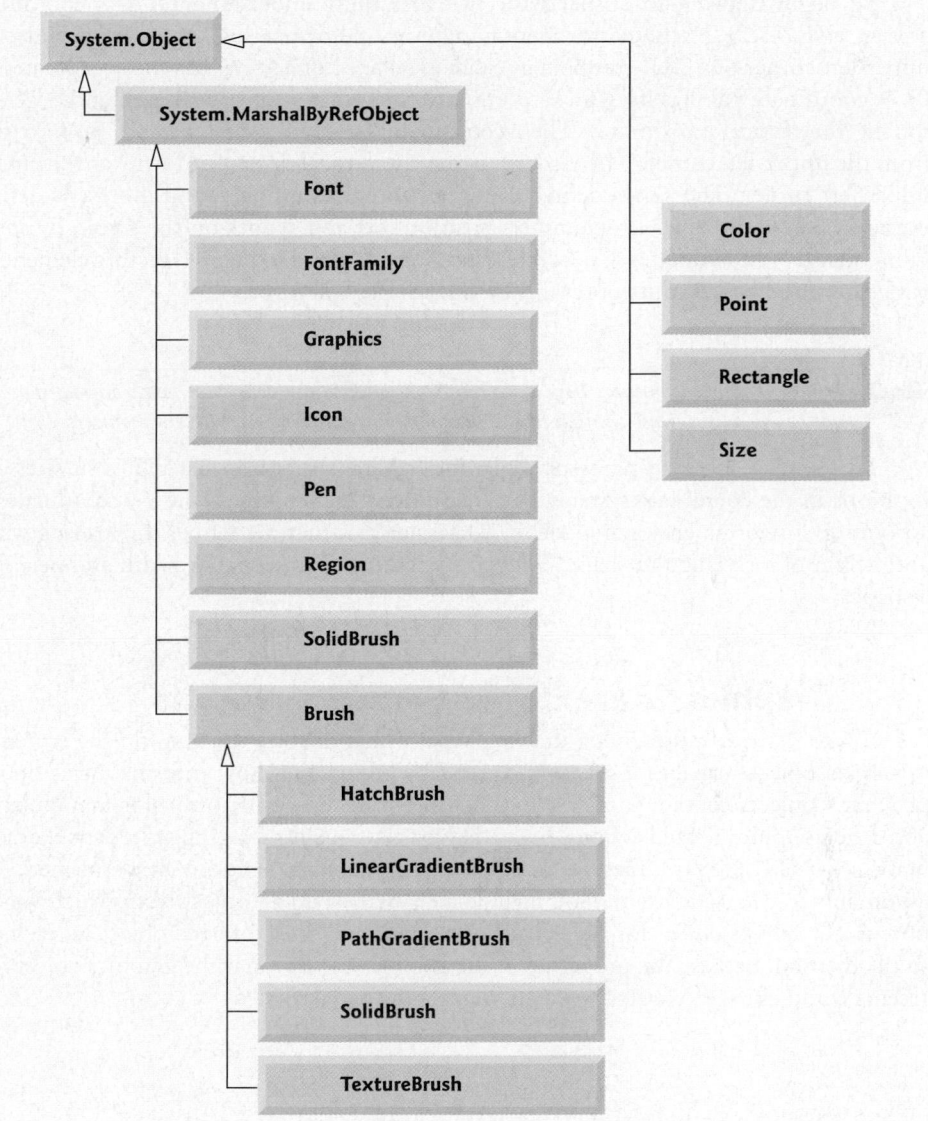

Fig. 17.1 | System.Drawing namespace's classes and structures.

Class **Graphics** contains methods used for drawing Strings, lines, rectangles and other shapes on a Control. The drawing methods of class Graphics usually require a **Pen** or **Brush** object to render a specified shape. The Pen draws shape outlines; the Brush draws solid objects.

The **Color** structure contains numerous Shared properties that set the colors of various graphical components, plus methods that allow users to create new colors. Class **Font** contains properties that define unique fonts. Class **FontFamily** contains methods for obtaining font information.

To begin drawing in Visual Basic, we first must understand GDI+'s **coordinate system** (Fig. 17.2), a scheme for identifying every point on the screen. By default, the upper-left corner of a GUI component (such as a Panel or a Form) has the coordinates (0, 0). A coordinate pair has both an *x-coordinate* (the **horizontal coordinate**) and a *y-coordinate* (the **vertical coordinate**). The *x*-coordinate is the horizontal distance (to the right) from the upper-left corner. The *y*-coordinate is the vertical distance (downward) from the upper-left corner. The *x*-axis defines every horizontal coordinate, and the *y*-axis defines every vertical coordinate. Programmers position text and shapes on the screen by specifying their (*x*, *y*) coordinates. Coordinate units are measured in pixels ("picture elements"), which are the smallest units of **resolution** on a display monitor.

Portability Tip 17.1

Different display monitors have different resolutions, so the density of pixels on monitors will vary. This might cause the sizes of graphics to appear different on different monitors.

The System.Drawing namespace provides several structures that represent sizes and locations in the coordinate system. The **Point** structure represents the *x-y* coordinates of a point on a two-dimensional plane. The **Rectangle** structure defines the loading width and height of a rectangular shape. The Size structure represents the width and height of a shape.

17.3 Graphics Contexts and Graphics Objects

A **graphics context** represents a drawing surface that enables drawing on the screen. A Graphics object manages a graphics context by controlling how information is drawn. Graphics objects contain methods for drawing, font manipulation, color manipulation and other graphics-related actions. Every derived class of System.Windows.Forms.Form inherits a virtual OnPaint method in which most graphics operations are performed. The arguments to the OnPaint method include a **PaintEventArgs** object from which we can obtain a Graphics object for the Form. We must obtain the Graphics object on each call to the method, because the properties of the graphics context that the graphics object represents could change. Method OnPaint triggers the Control's **Paint** event.

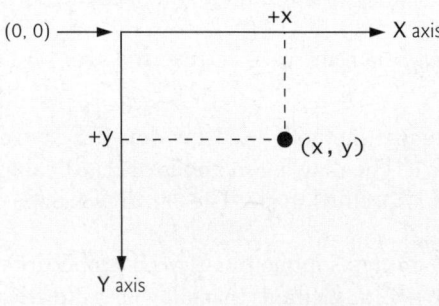

Fig. 17.2 | GDI+ coordinate system. Units are measured in pixels.

When drawing on a Form, you can override method OnPaint to retrieve a Graphics object from argument PaintEventArgs or to create a new Graphics object associated with the appropriate surface. We demonstrate these drawing techniques later in the chapter.

To override the inherited OnPaint method, use the following method header:

```
Protected Overrides Sub OnPaint(PaintEventArgs e)
```

Next, extract the incoming Graphics object from argument PaintEventArg, as in:

```
Dim graphicsObject As Graphics = e.Graphics
```

Variable graphicsObject can now be used to draw shapes and Strings on the Form.

Calling the OnPaint method raises the Paint event. Instead of overriding the OnPaint method, programmers can add an event handler for the Paint event. Visual Studio .NET generates the Paint event handler in this form:

```
Protected Sub MyEventHandler_Paint( _
    ByVal sender As Object, ByVal e As PaintEventArgs)
```

Programmers seldom call the OnPaint method directly, because drawing graphics is an **event-driven process**. An event—such as covering, uncovering or resizing a window—calls the OnPaint method of that Form. Similarly, when any control (such as a TextBox or Label) is displayed, that control's OnPaint method is called.

You can force a call to OnPaint by calling a Control's **Invalidate** method. This method refreshes a control and implicitly repaints all its graphical components. Class Control has several overloaded Invalidate methods that allow programmers to update portions of a control.

Performance Tip 17.1

Calling the Invalidate method to refresh the Control can be inefficient if only a small portion of a Control needs refreshing. Calling Invalidate with a Rectangle parameter refreshes only the area designated by the rectangle. This improves program performance.

Controls, such as Labels and Buttons, do not have their own graphics contexts, but you can create them. To draw on a control, first create a graphics object by invoking the control's CreateGraphics method, as in:

```
Dim graphicsObject As Graphics = controlName.CreateGraphics();
```

Now you can use the methods provided in class Graphics to draw on the control.

17.4 Color Control

Colors can enhance a program's appearance and help convey meaning. For example, a red traffic light indicates stop, yellow indicates caution and green indicates go. Structure Color defines methods and constants used to manipulate colors.

Every color can be created from a combination of alpha, red, green and blue components (called **ARGB values**). All four ARGB components are Bytes that represent integer values in the range 0 to 255. The alpha value determines the opacity of the color. For example, the alpha value 0 represents a transparent color, and the value 255 represents an opaque color. Alpha values between 0 and 255 result in a weighted blending effect of the color's **RGB value** with that of any background color, causing a semitransparent effect. The first number in the RGB value defines the amount of red in the color, the second defines the amount of green and the third defines the amount of blue. The larger the value, the greater the amount of that color. Programmers can choose from almost 17 million colors. If a computer cannot display all these colors, it will display the color closest to the one specified. Figure 17.3 summarizes some predefined `Color` constants (all are `Public` and `Shared`), and Fig. 17.4 describes several `Color` methods and properties. For a complete list of the predefined `Color` constants, methods and properties, see `Color` structure's online documentation (`msdn2.microsoft.com/en-us/library/system.drawing.color`).

Constants in structure `Color`	RGB value	Constants in structure `Color`	RGB value
Orange	255, 200, 0	White	255, 255, 255
Pink	255, 175, 175	Gray	128, 128, 128
Cyan	0, 255, 255	DarkGray	64, 64, 64
Magenta	255, 0, 255	Red	255, 0, 0
Yellow	255, 255, 0	Green	0, 255, 0
Black	0, 0, 0	Blue	0, 0, 255

Fig. 17.3 | `Color` structure `Shared` constants and their RGB values.

Structure `Color` methods and properties	Description
Common Methods	
FromArgb	A `Shared` method that creates a color based on red, green and blue values expressed as `int`s from 0 to 255. The overloaded version allows specification of alpha, red, green and blue values.
FromName	A `Shared` method that creates a color from a name, passed as a `String`.
Common Properties	
A	A byte between 0 and 255, representing the alpha component.
R	A byte between 0 and 255, representing the red component.
G	A byte between 0 and 255, representing the green component.
B	A byte between 0 and 255, representing the blue component.

Fig. 17.4 | `Color` structure members.

The table in Fig. 17.4 describes two `FromArgb` method calls. One takes three `Integer` arguments, and one takes four `Integer` arguments (all argument values must be between 0 and 255, inclusive). Both take `Integer` arguments specifying the amount of red, green and blue. The overloaded version also allows the user to specify the alpha component; the three-argument version defaults the alpha to 255 (opaque). Both methods return a `Color` object. `Color` properties `A`, `R`, `G` and `B` return bytes that represent `Integer` values from 0 to 255, corresponding to the amounts of alpha, red, green and blue, respectively.

Programmers draw shapes and `Strings` with `Brushes` and `Pens`. A `Pen`, which functions similarly to an ordinary pen, is used to draw lines. Most drawing methods require a `Pen` object. The overloaded `Pen` constructors allow programmers to specify the colors and widths of the lines they wish to draw. The `System.Drawing` namespace also provides a `Pens` class containing predefined `Pens`.

All classes derived from `MustInherit` class `Brush` define objects that color the interiors of graphical shapes. For example, the `SolidBrush` constructor takes a `Color` object—the color to draw. In most `Fill` methods, `Brushes` fill a space with a color, pattern or image. Figure 17.5 summarizes various `Brushes` and their functions.

Manipulating Colors

Figure 17.6 demonstrates several of the methods and properties described in Fig. 17.4. It displays two overlapping rectangles, allowing you to experiment with color values, color names and alpha values (for transparency).

Class	Description
HatchBrush	Fills a region with a pattern. The pattern is defined by a member of the **HatchStyle enumeration**, a foreground color (with which the pattern is drawn) and a background color.
LinearGradientBrush	Fills a region with a gradual blend of one color to another. Linear gradients are defined along a line. They can be specified by the two colors, the angle of the gradient and either the width of a rectangle or two points.
SolidBrush	Fills a region with one color that is specified by a `Color` object.
TextureBrush	Fills a region by repeating a specified `Image` across the surface.

Fig. 17.5 | Classes that derive from class `Brush`.

```
1   ' Fig 17.6: FrmShowColors.vb
2   ' Color value and alpha demonstration.
3   Public Class FrmShowColors
4       ' color for back rectangle
5       Private backgroundColor As Color = Color.Wheat
6
```

Fig. 17.6 | Color value and alpha demonstration. (Part 1 of 3.)

```vbnet
 7      ' color for front rectangle
 8      Private foregroundColor As Color = Color.FromArgb(100, 0, 0, 255)
 9
10      ' override Form's OnPaint method
11      Protected Overrides Sub OnPaint(ByVal e As PaintEventArgs)
12         Dim graphicsObject As Graphics = e.Graphics ' get graphics object
13
14         ' create text brush
15         Dim textBrush As New SolidBrush(Color.Black)
16
17         ' create solid brush
18         Dim brush As New SolidBrush(Color.White)
19
20         ' draw white background
21         graphicsObject.FillRectangle(brush, 4, 4, 275, 180)
22
23         ' display name of backColor
24         graphicsObject.DrawString( _
25            BackColor.Name, Me.Font, textBrush, 40, 5)
26
27         ' set brush color and display back rectangle
28         brush.Color = backgroundColor
29         graphicsObject.FillRectangle(brush, 45, 20, 150, 120)
30
31         ' display Argb values of front color
32         graphicsObject.DrawString("Alpha: " & foregroundColor.A & _
33            " Red: " & foregroundColor.R & " Green: " & _
34            foregroundColor.G & " Blue: " & foregroundColor.B, Me.Font, _
35            textBrush, 55, 165)
36
37         ' set brush color and display front rectangle
38         brush.Color = foregroundColor
39         graphicsObject.FillRectangle(brush, 65, 35, 170, 130)
40      End Sub ' OnPaint
41
42      ' change Form's background color
43      Private Sub btnColorName_Click(ByVal sender As System.Object, _
44         ByVal e As System.EventArgs) Handles btnColorName.Click
45         ' set backColor to color specified in text box
46         backgroundColor = Color.FromName(txtColorName.Text)
47         Invalidate() ' refresh Form
48      End Sub ' btnColorName_Click
49
50      ' change Form's foreground color
51      Private Sub btnColorValue_Click(ByVal sender As System.Object, _
52         ByVal e As System.EventArgs) Handles btnColorValue.Click
53         ' obtain new front color from text boxes
54         foregroundColor = Color.FromArgb( _
55            Convert.ToInt32(txtAlpha.Text), Convert.ToInt32(txtRed.Text), _
56            Convert.ToInt32(txtGreen.Text), Convert.ToInt32(txtBlue.Text))
57         Invalidate() ' refresh Form
58      End Sub ' btnColorValue_Click
59   End Class ' FrmShowColors
```

Fig. 17.6 | Color value and alpha demonstration. (Part 2 of 3.)

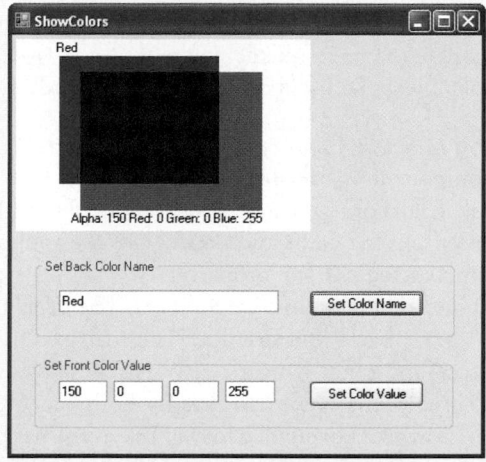

Fig. 17.6 | Color value and alpha demonstration. (Part 3 of 3.)

When the application begins executing, its Form is displayed. This results in a call to FrmShowColors's OnPaint method to paint the Form's contents. Line 12 gets a reference to PaintEventArgs e's Graphics object and assigns it to graphicsObject. Lines 15 and 18 create a black and a white SolidBrush for drawing solid shapes on the Form. Class **Solid-Brush** derives from MustInherit class Brush, so a SolidBrush can be passed to any method that expects a Brush parameter.

Line 21 uses Graphics method FillRectangle to draw a solid white rectangle using the SolidBrush created in line 18. FillRectangle takes as parameters a Brush, the *x*- and *y*-coordinates of the rectangle's upper-left corner, and the width and height of the rectangle. Lines 24–25 display the Name property of BackColor with Graphics method **Draw-String**. There are several overloaded DrawString methods; the version demonstrated in lines 24–25 takes as arguments the String to display, the display Font, the Brush to use for drawing and the *x*- and *y*-coordinates of the location for the String's first character.

Lines 28–29 assign the backgroundColor value to brush's Color property and display a rectangle. Lines 32–35 extract and display foregroundColor's ARGB values and draw a string containing those values. Lines 38–39 assign the foregroundColor value to brush's Color property, then draw a filled rectangle in the foregroundColor that overlaps the rectangle drawn at line 29.

Button event handler btnColorName_Click (lines 43–48) uses class Color's Shared method **FromName** to create a new Color object from the color name that a user enters in a TextBox. This Color is assigned to backgroundColor (line 46). Then line 47 invokes the Form's Invalidate method to indicate that the Form should be repainted, which results in a call to OnPaint to update the Form on the screen.

Button event handler btnColorValue_Click (lines 51–58) uses Color method From-Argb to construct a new Color object from the ARGB values that a user specifies via Text-Boxes, then assigns the newly created Color to foregroundColor. Line 57 invokes the Form's Invalidate method to indicate that the Form should be repainted, which results in a call to OnPaint to update the Form on the screen.

Changing the alpha value of the foregroundColor from 0 to 255, makes the effects of alpha blending apparent. The sample output shows that the red back rectangle blends with the blue front rectangle to create purple where they overlap. Note that you cannot modify an existing Color object. To use a different color, create a new Color object.

Using the ColorDialog to Select Colors from a Color Palette

The predefined GUI component **ColorDialog** is a dialog box that allows users to select from a palette of available colors or to create custom colors. Figure 17.7 demonstrates the ColorDialog. When a user selects a color and presses **OK**, the application retrieves the user's selection via the ColorDialog's **Color** property.

The GUI for this application contains two Buttons. The btnBackgroundColor allows the user to change the Form's background color. The btnTextColor allows the user to change the button text colors. Line 5 creates a Private Shared ColorDialog named colorChooser, which is used in the event handlers for both Buttons.

Lines 8–17 define the btnBackgroundColor_Click event handler. The method sets the ColorDialog's **FullOpen** property to True (line 11), so the dialog displays all available

```vb
1    ' Fig. 17.7: FrmShowColorsComplex.vb
2    ' ColorDialog used to change background and text color.
3    Public Class FrmShowColorsComplex
4        ' create ColorDialog object
5        Private Shared colorChooser As New ColorDialog()
6
7        ' change background color
8        Private Sub btnBackgroundColor_Click(ByVal sender As System.Object, _
9            ByVal e As System.EventArgs) Handles btnBackgroundColor.Click
10           ' show ColorDialog and get result
11           colorChooser.FullOpen = True
12           Dim result As DialogResult = colorChooser.ShowDialog()
13
14           If result = Windows.Forms.DialogResult.OK Then
15               Me.BackColor = colorChooser.Color ' set background color
16           End If
17       End Sub ' btnBackgroundColor_Click
18
19       ' change text color
20       Private Sub btnTextColor_Click(ByVal sender As System.Object, _
21           ByVal e As System.EventArgs) Handles btnTextColor.Click
22           ' get chosen color
23           Dim result As DialogResult = colorChooser.ShowDialog()
24
25           If result = Windows.Forms.DialogResult.OK Then
26               ' assign forecolor to result of dialog
27               btnBackgroundColor.ForeColor = colorChooser.Color
28               btnTextColor.ForeColor = colorChooser.Color
29           End If
30       End Sub ' btnTextColor_Click
31   End Class ' FrmShowColorsComplex
```

Fig. 17.7 | ColorDialog used to change background and text color. (Part 1 of 2.)

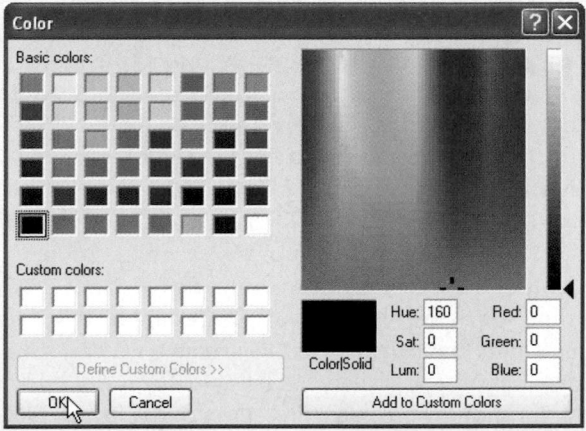

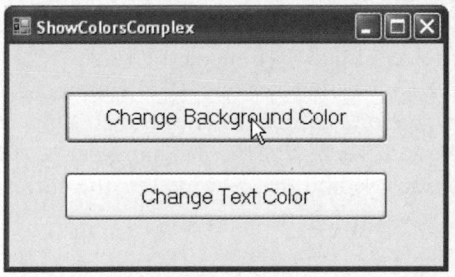 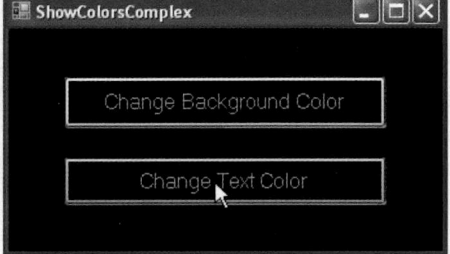

Fig. 17.7 | `ColorDialog` used to change background and text color. (Part 2 of 2.)

colors, as shown in the screen capture in Fig. 17.7. When `FullOpen` is `False`, the dialog shows only the color swatches. Line 12 invokes `colorChooser`'s `ShowDialog` method to display the dialog. The dialog's `Color` property stores the user's selection. If the user clicks **OK**, line 15 modifies the background color of the form by setting its `BackColor` property to the dialog's `Color` property.

Lines 20–30 define the `btnTextColor_Click` event handler. If the user clicks **OK** in the dialog, lines 27–28 set the text color of both buttons to the selected color.

Users are not restricted to the `ColorDialog`'s 48 color swatches. To create a custom color, users can click anywhere in the `ColorDialog`'s large rectangle, which displays various color shades. Adjust the slider, hue and other features to refine the color. When finished, click the **Add to Custom Colors** button, which adds the custom color to a square in the **Custom Colors** section of the dialog. Clicking **OK** sets the `Color` property of the `Color-Dialog` to that color.

17.5 Font Control

This section introduces methods and constants related to font control. The properties of `Font` objects cannot be modified. If you need a different `Font`, you must create a new `Font` object. There are many overloaded versions of the Font constructor for initializing Font objects. Some properties of class Font are summarized in Fig. 17.8.

Note that the Size property returns the font size as measured in design units, whereas SizeInPoints returns the font size as measured in points (the more common measurement). Design units allow the font size to be specified in one of several units of measurement, such as inches or millimeters. Some versions of the Font constructor accept a GraphicsUnit argument. GraphicsUnit is an enumeration that allows you to specify the unit of measurement that describes the font size. Members of the GraphicsUnit enumeration include Point (1/72 inch), Display (1/75 inch), Document (1/300 inch), Millimeter, Inch and Pixel. If this argument is provided, the Size property contains the size of the font as measured in the specified design unit, and the SizeInPoints property contains the corresponding size of the font in points. For example, if we create a Font having size 1 and specify the unit of measurement as GraphicsUnit.Inch, the Size property will be 1 and the SizeInPoints property will be 72, because there are 72 points in an inch. The default measurement for the font size is GraphicsUnit.Point (thus, the Size and SizeInPoints properties will be equal).

Class Font has several constructors. Most require a font name, which is a String representing a font currently supported by the system. Common fonts include Microsoft SansSerif and Serif. Most Font constructors also require as arguments the font size and font style. The font style is specified with a constant from the FontStyle enumeration (Bold, Italic, Regular, Strikeout and Underline, or a combination of these). You can combine font styles with the Or operator, as in FontStyle.Italic Or FontStyle.Bold, which makes a font both italic and bold. Graphics method DrawString sets the current drawing font—the font in which the text displays—to its Font argument.

Property	Description
Bold	Returns True if the font is bold.
FontFamily	Returns the font's FontFamily—a grouping structure to organize fonts and define their similar properties.
Height	Returns the height of the font.
Italic	Returns True if the font is italic.
Name	Returns the font's name as a String.
Size	Returns a float value indicating the current font size measured in design units (design units are any specified unit of measurement for the font).
SizeInPoints	Returns a float value indicating the current font size measured in points.
Strikeout	Returns True if the font is in strikeout format.
Underline	Returns True if the font is underlined.

Fig. 17.8 | Font class read-only properties.

> ### Common Programming Error 17.1
> *Specifying a font that is not available on a system is a logic error. If this occurs, the system's default font is substituted.*

Drawing Strings in Different Fonts

The program in Fig. 17.9 displays text in different fonts and sizes. The program uses the Font constructor to initialize the Font objects (lines 11, 15, 19 and 23). Each call to the Font constructor passes a font name (e.g., Arial, Times New Roman, Courier New or Tahoma) as a String, a font size (a float) and a FontStyle object (style). Graphics method DrawString sets the font and draws the text at the specified location. Note that line 7 creates a DarkBlue SolidBrush object (brush). All Strings drawn with that brush appear in DarkBlue.

```vb
1   ' Fig. 17.9 FrmUsingFonts.vb
2   ' Fonts and FontStyles.
3   Public Class FrmUsingFonts
4      ' demonstrate various font and style settings
5      Protected Overrides Sub OnPaint(ByVal paintEvent As PaintEventArgs)
6         Dim graphicsObject As Graphics = paintEvent.Graphics
7         Dim brush As New SolidBrush(Color.DarkBlue)
8
9         ' arial, 12 pt bold
10        Dim style As FontStyle = FontStyle.Bold
11        Dim arial As New Font("Arial", 12, style)
12
13        ' times new roman, 12 pt regular
14        style = FontStyle.Regular
15        Dim timesNewRoman As New Font("Times New Roman", 12, style)
16
17        ' courier new, 16 pt bold and italic
18        style = FontStyle.Bold Or FontStyle.Italic
19        Dim courierNew As New Font("Courier New", 16, style)
20
21        ' tahoma, 18 pt strikeout
22        style = FontStyle.Strikeout
23        Dim tahoma As New Font("Tahoma", 18, style)
24
25        graphicsObject.DrawString(arial.Name & _
26           " 12 point bold.", arial, brush, 10, 10)
27
28        graphicsObject.DrawString(timesNewRoman.Name & _
29           " 12 point plain.", timesNewRoman, brush, 10, 30)
30
31        graphicsObject.DrawString(courierNew.Name & _
32           " 16 point bold and italic.", courierNew, brush, 10, 50)
33
34        graphicsObject.DrawString(tahoma.Name & _
35           " 18 point strikeout.", tahoma, brush, 10, 70)
36     End Sub ' OnPaint
37  End Class ' FrmUsingFonts
```

Fig. 17.9 | Fonts and FontStyles. (Part 1 of 2.)

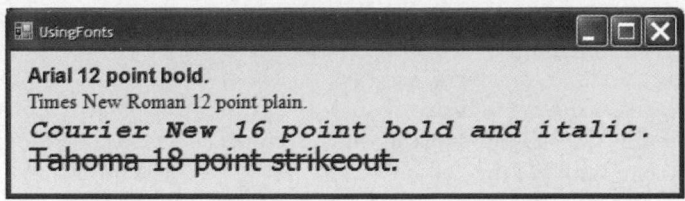

Fig. 17.9 | `Font`s and `FontStyle`s. (Part 2 of 2.)

Font Metrics

You can determine precise information about a font's **metrics** (or properties), such as **height**, **descent** (the amount characters dip below the baseline), **ascent** (the amount characters rise above the baseline) and **leading** (the difference between the ascent of one line and the descent of the previous line). Figure 17.10 illustrates these font metrics.

Class `FontFamily` defines characteristics common to a group of related fonts. Class `FontFamily` provides several methods used to determine the font metrics shared by members of a particular family. These methods are summarized in Fig. 17.11.

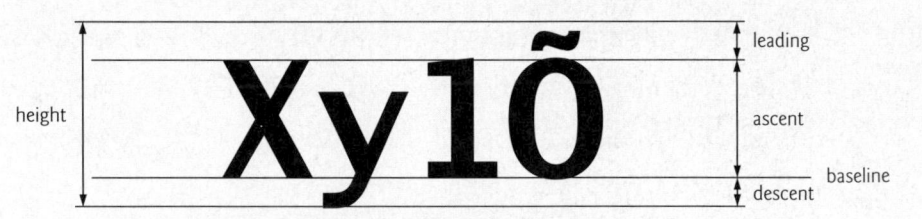

Fig. 17.10 | Font metrics illustration.

Method	Description
GetCellAscent	Returns an Integer representing the ascent of a font as measured in design units.
GetCellDescent	Returns an Integer representing the descent of a font as measured in design units.
GetEmHeight	Returns an Integer representing the height of a font as measured in design units.
GetLineSpacing	Returns an Integer representing the distance between two consecutive lines of text as measured in design units.

Fig. 17.11 | `FontFamily` methods that return font-metric information.

The program in Fig. 17.12 displays the metrics of two fonts. Line 10 creates Font object arial and sets it to 10-point Arial font. Line 11 uses Font property FontFamily to obtain object arial's FontFamily object. Lines 14–15 output the String representation of the font. Lines 17–27 then use methods of class FontFamily to obtain the ascent, descent, height and leading of the font and draw strings containing this information. Lines 30–50 repeat the process for font sansSerif, a Font object derived from the MS Sans Serif FontFamily.

```vb
1   ' Fig 17.12: FrmUsingFontMetrics.vb
2   ' Displaying font metric information
3   Public Class FrmUsingFontMetrics
4      ' displays font information
5      Protected Overrides Sub OnPaint(ByVal paintEvent As PaintEventArgs)
6         Dim graphicsObject As Graphics = paintEvent.Graphics
7         Dim brush As New SolidBrush(Color.DarkBlue)
8
9         ' Arial font metrics
10        Dim arial As New Font("Arial", 10)
11        Dim family As FontFamily = arial.FontFamily
12
13        ' display Arial font metrics
14        graphicsObject.DrawString("Current Font: " & _
15           arial.ToString(), arial, brush, 10, 10)
16
17        graphicsObject.DrawString("Ascent: " & _
18           family.GetCellAscent(FontStyle.Regular), arial, brush, 10, 30)
19
20        graphicsObject.DrawString("Descent: " & _
21           family.GetCellDescent(FontStyle.Regular), arial, brush, 10, 50)
22
23        graphicsObject.DrawString("Height: " & _
24           family.GetEmHeight(FontStyle.Regular), arial, brush, 10, 70)
25
26        graphicsObject.DrawString("Leading: " & _
27           family.GetLineSpacing(FontStyle.Regular), arial, brush, 10, 90)
28
29        ' display Sans Serif font metrics
30        Dim sanSerif As New Font("Microsoft Sans Serif", _
31           12, FontStyle.Italic)
32        family = sanSerif.FontFamily
33
34        graphicsObject.DrawString("Current Font: " & _
35           sanSerif.ToString(), sanSerif, brush, 10, 130)
36
37        graphicsObject.DrawString("Ascent: " & _
38           family.GetCellAscent(FontStyle.Regular), _
39           sanSerif, brush, 10, 150)
40
41        graphicsObject.DrawString("Descent: " & _
42           family.GetCellDescent(FontStyle.Regular), _
43           sanSerif, brush, 10, 170)
```

Fig. 17.12 | FontFamily class used to obtain font-metric information. (Part 1 of 2.)

```
44
45          graphicsObject.DrawString("Height: " & _
46             family.GetEmHeight(FontStyle.Regular), sanSerif, brush, 10, 190)
47
48          graphicsObject.DrawString("Leading: " & _
49             family.GetLineSpacing(FontStyle.Regular), _
50             sanSerif, brush, 10, 210)
51      End Sub ' OnPaint
52   End Class ' FrmUsingFontMetrics
```

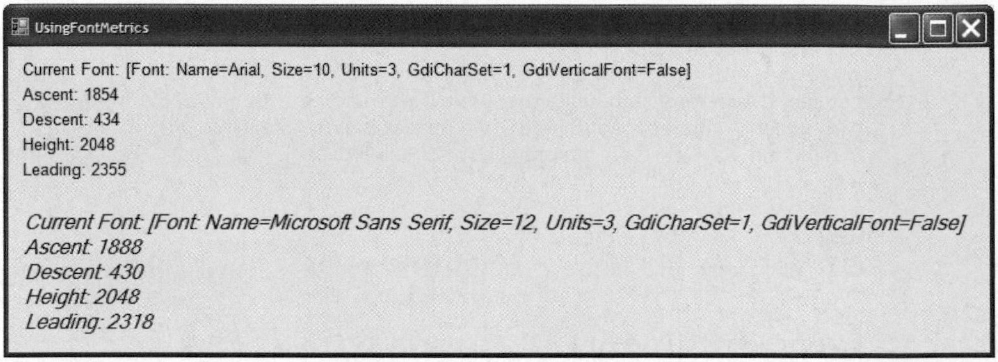

```
UsingFontMetrics                                          _ □ X

Current Font: [Font: Name=Arial, Size=10, Units=3, GdiCharSet=1, GdiVerticalFont=False]
Ascent: 1854
Descent: 434
Height: 2048
Leading: 2355


Current Font: [Font: Name=Microsoft Sans Serif, Size=12, Units=3, GdiCharSet=1, GdiVerticalFont=False]
Ascent: 1888
Descent: 430
Height: 2048
Leading: 2318
```

Fig. 17.12 | FontFamily class used to obtain font-metric information. (Part 2 of 2.)

17.6 Drawing Lines, Rectangles and Ovals

This section presents Graphics methods for drawing lines, rectangles and ovals. Each of the drawing methods has several overloaded versions. Methods that draw hollow shapes typically require as arguments a Pen and four ints. Methods that draw solid shapes typically require as arguments a Brush and four ints. The first two Integer arguments represent the coordinates of the upper-left corner of the shape (or its enclosing area), and the last two ints indicate the shape's (or enclosing area's) width and height. Figure 17.13 summarizes several Graphics methods and their parameters. [*Note:* Many of these methods are overloaded—consult the online Graphics class documentation for a complete listing (msdn2.microsoft.com/en-us/library/system.drawing.graphics).]

Graphics Drawing Methods and Descriptions

`DrawLine(ByVal p As Pen, ByVal x1 As Integer, ByVal y1 As Integer, _`
`    ByVal x2 As Integer, ByVal y2 As Integer)`
Draws a line from (x1, y1) to (x2, y2). The Pen determines the line's color, style and width.

`DrawRectangle(ByVal p As Pen, ByVal x As Integer, ByVal y As Integer, _`
`    ByVal width As Integer, ByVal height As Integer)`
Draws a rectangle of the specified width and height. The top-left corner of the rectangle is at point (x, y). The Pen determines the rectangle's color, style and border width.

Fig. 17.13 | Graphics methods that draw lines, rectangles and ovals. (Part 1 of 2.)

Graphics Drawing Methods and Descriptions

```
FillRectangle(ByVal b As Brush, ByVal x As Integer, ByVal y As Integer, _
    ByVal width As Integer, ByVal height As Integer)
```
Draws a solid rectangle of the specified width and height. The top-left corner of the rectangle is at point (x, y). The Brush determines the fill pattern inside the rectangle.

```
DrawEllipse(ByVal p As Pen, ByVal x As Integer, ByVal y As Integer, _
    ByVal width As Integer, ByVal height As Integer)
```
Draws an ellipse inside a bounding rectangle of the specified width and height. The top-left corner of the bounding rectangle is located at (x, y). The Pen determines the color, style and border width of the ellipse.

```
FillEllipse(ByVal b As Brush, ByVal x As Integer, ByVal y As Integer, _
    ByVal width As Integer, ByVal height As Integer)
```
Draws a filled ellipse inside a bounding rectangle of the specified width and height. The top-left corner of the bounding rectangle is located at (x, y). The Brush determines the pattern inside the ellipse.

Fig. 17.13 | `Graphics` methods that draw lines, rectangles and ovals. (Part 2 of 2.)

The application in Fig. 17.14 draws lines, rectangles and ellipses. In this application, we also demonstrate methods that draw filled and unfilled shapes.

```
 1    ' Fig. 17.14: FrmLinesRectanglesOvals.vb
 2    ' Demonstrating lines, rectangles and ovals.
 3    Public Class FrmLinesRectanglesOvals
 4       ' override Form OnPaint method
 5       Protected Overrides Sub OnPaint(ByVal paintEvent As PaintEventArgs)
 6          ' get graphics object
 7          Dim g As Graphics = paintEvent.Graphics
 8          Dim brush As New SolidBrush(Color.Blue)
 9          Dim pen As New Pen(Color.Black)
10
11          ' create filled rectangle
12          g.FillRectangle(brush, 90, 30, 150, 90)
13
14          ' draw lines to connect rectangles
15          g.DrawLine(pen, 90, 30, 110, 40)
16          g.DrawLine(pen, 90, 120, 110, 130)
17          g.DrawLine(pen, 240, 30, 260, 40)
18          g.DrawLine(pen, 240, 120, 260, 130)
19
20          ' draw top rectangle
21          g.DrawRectangle(pen, 110, 40, 150, 90)
22
23          ' set brush to red
24          brush.Color = Color.Red
25
```

Fig. 17.14 | Demonstration of methods that draw lines, rectangles and ellipses. (Part 1 of 2.)

```
26            ' draw base Ellipse
27           g.FillEllipse(brush, 280, 75, 100, 50)
28
29            ' draw connecting lines
30           g.DrawLine(pen, 380, 55, 380, 100)
31           g.DrawLine(pen, 280, 55, 280, 100)
32
33            ' draw Ellipse outline
34           g.DrawEllipse(pen, 280, 30, 100, 50)
35      End Sub ' OnPaint
36   End Class ' FrmLinesRectanglesOvals
```

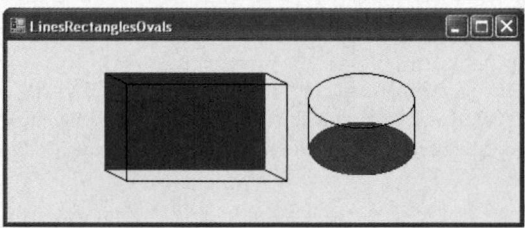

Fig. 17.14 | Demonstration of methods that draw lines, rectangles and ellipses. (Part 2 of 2.)

Methods **FillRectangle** and **DrawRectangle** (lines 12 and 21) draw rectangles on the screen. For each method, the first argument specifies the drawing object to use. The FillRectangle method uses a Brush object (in this case, an instance of SolidBrush—a class that derives from Brush), whereas the DrawRectangle method uses a Pen object. The next two arguments specify the coordinates of the upper-left corner of the bounding rect-angle, which represents the area in which the rectangle will be drawn. The fourth and fifth arguments specify the rectangle's width and height. Method DrawLine (lines 15–18) takes a Pen and two pairs of ints, specifying the start and end of a line. The method then draws a line, using the Pen object.

Methods **FillEllipse** and **DrawEllipse** (lines 27 and 34) each provide overloaded versions that take five arguments. In both methods, the first argument specifies the drawing object to use. The next two arguments specify the upper-left coordinates of the bounding rectangle representing the area in which the ellipse will be drawn. The last two arguments specify the bounding rectangle's width and height, respectively. Figure 17.15 depicts an

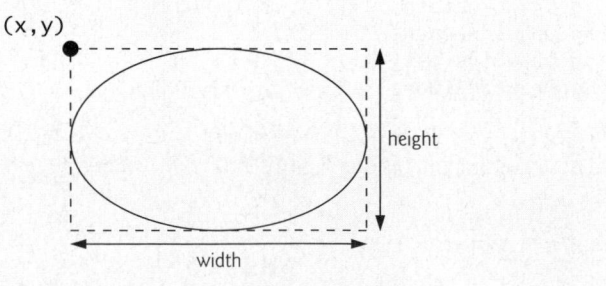

Fig. 17.15 | Ellipse bounded by a rectangle.

ellipse bounded by a rectangle. The ellipse touches the midpoint of each of the four sides of the bounding rectangle. The bounding rectangle is not displayed on the screen.

17.7 **Drawing Arcs**

Arcs are portions of ellipses and are measured in degrees, beginning at a *starting angle* and continuing for a specified number of degrees called the *arc angle*. An arc is said to *sweep* (traverse) its arc angle, beginning from its starting angle. Arcs that sweep in a clockwise direction are measured in positive degrees, whereas arcs that sweep in a counterclockwise direction are measured in negative degrees. Figure 17.16 depicts two arcs. Note that the arc at the left of the figure sweeps upward from zero degrees to approximately –110 degrees. Similarly, the arc at the right of the figure sweeps downward from zero degrees to approximately 110 degrees.

Note the dashed boxes around the arcs in Fig. 17.16. Each arc is drawn as part of an oval (the rest of which is not visible). When drawing an oval, we specify the oval's dimensions in the form of a bounding rectangle that encloses the oval. The boxes in Fig. 17.16 correspond to these bounding rectangles. The `Graphics` methods used to draw arcs—`DrawArc`, `DrawPie` and `FillPie`—are summarized in Fig. 17.17.

The program in Fig. 17.18 draws six images (three arcs and three filled pie slices) to demonstrate the arc methods listed in Fig. 17.17. To illustrate the bounding rectangles that determine the sizes and locations of the arcs, the arcs are displayed inside red rectangles that have the same *x-y* coordinates, width and height arguments as those that define the bounding rectangles for the arcs.

Fig. 17.16 | Positive and negative arc angles.

Graphics methods and descriptions

Note: Many of these methods are overloaded—consult the documentation for a complete listing.

```
DrawArc(ByVal p As Pen, ByVal x As Integer, ByVal y As Integer, _
    ByVal width As Integer, ByVal height As Integer, _
    ByVal startAngle As Integer, ByVal sweepAngle As Integer)
```
Draws an arc beginning from angle `startAngle` (in degrees) and sweeping `sweepAngle` degrees. The ellipse is defined by a bounding rectangle of `width`, `height` and upper-left corner (x,y). The `Pen` determines the color, border width and style of the arc.

Fig. 17.17 | `Graphics` methods for drawing arcs. (Part 1 of 2.)

Graphics methods and descriptions

```
DrawPie(ByVal p As Pen, ByVal x As Integer, ByVal y As Integer, _
   ByVal width As Integer, ByVal height As Integer, _
   ByVal startAngle As Integer, ByVal sweepAngle As Integer)
```
Draws a pie section of an ellipse beginning from angle startAngle (in degrees) and sweeping sweepAngle degrees. The ellipse is defined by a bounding rectangle of width, height and upper-left corner (x,y). The Pen determines the color, border width and style of the arc.

```
FillPie(ByVal b As Brush, ByVal x As Integer, ByVal y As Integer, _
   ByVal width As Integer, ByVal height As Integer, _
   ByVal startAngle As Integer, ByVal sweepAngle As Integer)
```
Functions similarly to DrawPie, except draws a solid arc (i.e., a sector). The Brush determines the fill pattern for the solid arc.

Fig. 17.17 | Graphics methods for drawing arcs. (Part 1 of 2.)

```
1   ' Fig. 17.18: FrmDrawingArcs.vb
2   ' Drawing various arcs on a Form.
3   Public Class FrmDrawArcs
4      ' draw arcs
5      Private Sub FrmDrawArcs_Paint(ByVal sender As Object, _
6         ByVal e As System.Windows.Forms.PaintEventArgs) Handles Me.Paint
7         ' get graphics object
8         Dim graphicsObject As Graphics = e.Graphics
9         Dim rectangle1 As New Rectangle(15, 35, 80, 80)
10        Dim brush1 As New SolidBrush(Color.Firebrick)
11        Dim pen1 As New Pen(brush1, 1)
12        Dim brush2 As New SolidBrush(Color.DarkBlue)
13        Dim pen2 As New Pen(brush2, 1)
14
15        ' start at 0 and sweep 360 degrees
16        graphicsObject.DrawRectangle(pen1, rectangle1)
17        graphicsObject.DrawArc(pen2, rectangle1, 0, 360)
18
19        ' start at 0 and sweep 110 degrees
20        rectangle1.Location = New Point(100, 35)
21        graphicsObject.DrawRectangle(pen1, rectangle1)
22        graphicsObject.DrawArc(pen2, rectangle1, 0, 110)
23
24        ' start at 0 and sweep -270 degrees
25        rectangle1.Location = New Point(185, 35)
26        graphicsObject.DrawRectangle(pen1, rectangle1)
27        graphicsObject.DrawArc(pen2, rectangle1, 0, -270)
28
29        ' start at 0 and sweep 360 degrees
30        rectangle1.Location = New Point(15, 120)
31        rectangle1.Size = New Size(80, 40)
32        graphicsObject.DrawRectangle(pen1, rectangle1)
33        graphicsObject.FillPie(brush2, rectangle1, 0, 360)
34
```

Fig. 17.18 | Drawing various arcs on a Form. (Part 1 of 2.)

```
35          ' start at 270 and sweep -90 degrees
36          rectangle1.Location = New Point(100, 120)
37          graphicsObject.DrawRectangle(pen1, rectangle1)
38          graphicsObject.FillPie(brush2, rectangle1, 270, -90)
39
40          ' start at 0 and sweep -270 degrees
41          rectangle1.Location = New Point(185, 120)
42          graphicsObject.DrawRectangle(pen1, rectangle1)
43          graphicsObject.FillPie(brush2, rectangle1, 0, -270)
44       End Sub ' FrmDrawArcs_Paint
45    End Class ' FrmDrawArcs
```

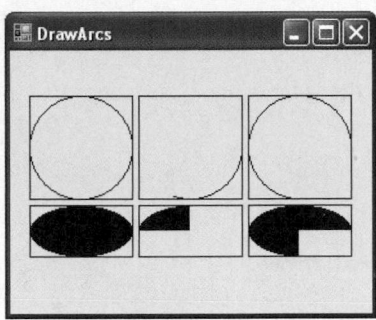

Fig. 17.18 | Drawing various arcs on a Form. (Part 2 of 2.)

Lines 9–13 create the objects that we need to draw arcs—a Graphics object, a Rectangle, SolidBrushes and Pens. Lines 16–17 then draw a rectangle and an arc inside the rectangle. The arc sweeps 360 degrees, forming a circle. Line 20 changes the location of the Rectangle by setting its Location property to a new Point. The Point constructor takes as arguments the *x*- and *y*-coordinates of the new point. The Location property determines the upper-left corner of the Rectangle. After drawing the rectangle, the program draws an arc that starts at 0 degrees and sweeps 110 degrees. Because the angles increase in a clockwise direction, the arc sweeps downward. Lines 25–27 perform similar functions, except that the specified arc sweeps –270 degrees. The Size property of a Rectangle determines the arc's height and width.

Line 31 sets the Size property to a new Size object, which changes the size of the rectangle. The remainder of the program is similar to the portions described above, except that a SolidBrush is used with method FillPie. The resulting arcs, which are filled, can be seen in the bottom half of the sample output (Fig. 17.18).

17.8 Drawing Polygons and Polylines

Polygons are multisided shapes. There are several Graphics methods used to draw polygons—DrawLines draws a series of connected lines, DrawPolygon draws a closed polygon and FillPolygon draws a solid polygon. These methods are described in Fig. 17.19. The program in Fig. 17.20 allows users to draw polygons and connected lines via the methods listed in Fig. 17.19.

Method	Description
DrawLines	Draws a series of connected lines. The coordinates of each point are specified in an array of Point objects. If the last point is different from the first point, the figure is not closed.
DrawPolygon	Draws a polygon. The coordinates of each point are specified in an array of Point objects. If the last point is different from the first point, those two points are connected to close the polygon.
FillPolygon	Draws a solid polygon. The coordinates of each point are specified in an array of Point objects. If the last point is different from the first point, those two points are connected to close the polygon.

Fig. 17.19 | Graphics methods for drawing polygons.

```
1   ' Fig. 17.20: FrmDrawPolygons.vb
2   ' Demonstrating polygons.
3   Public Class FrmDrawPolygons
4       ' contains list of polygon vertices
5       Private points As New ArrayList()
6
7       ' initialize default pen and brush
8       Private pen As New Pen(Color.DarkBlue)
9       Private brush As New SolidBrush(Color.DarkBlue)
10
11      ' draw panel mouse down event handler
12      Private Sub pnlDraw_MouseDown(ByVal sender As Object, _
13          ByVal e As System.Windows.Forms.MouseEventArgs) _
14          Handles pnlDraw.MouseDown
15          ' add mouse position to vertex list
16          points.Add(New Point(e.X, e.Y))
17          pnlDraw.Invalidate() ' refresh panel
18      End Sub ' FrmDrawPolygons_MouseDown
19
20      ' draw panel Paint event handler
21      Private Sub pnlDraw_Paint(ByVal sender As Object, _
22          ByVal e As System.Windows.Forms.PaintEventArgs) _
23          Handles pnlDraw.Paint
24          ' get graphics object for panel
25          Dim graphicsObject As Graphics = e.Graphics
26
27          ' if arraylist has 2 or more points, display shape
28          If points.Count > 1 Then
29              ' get array for use in drawing functions
30              Dim pointArray As Point() = _
31                  CType(points.ToArray(points(0).GetType()), Point())
32
```

Fig. 17.20 | Polygon-drawing demonstration. (Part 1 of 3.)

```vbnet
33                If radLineOption.Checked Then
34                    graphicsObject.DrawLines(pen, pointArray)
35                ElseIf radPolygonOption.Checked Then
36                    graphicsObject.DrawPolygon(pen, pointArray)
37                ElseIf radFilledPolygonOption.Checked Then
38                    graphicsObject.FillPolygon(brush, pointArray)
39                End If
40            End If
41        End Sub ' pnlDraw_Paint
42
43        ' clear all points in the polygon
44        Private Sub btnClear_Click(ByVal sender As System.Object, _
45            ByVal e As System.EventArgs) Handles btnClear.Click
46            points.Clear() ' remove points
47            pnlDraw.Invalidate() ' refresh panel
48        End Sub ' btnClear_Click
49
50        ' change pen and brush colors
51        Private Sub btnColor_Click(ByVal sender As System.Object, _
52            ByVal e As System.EventArgs) Handles btnColor.Click
53            ' create new color dialog
54            Dim dialogColor As New ColorDialog()
55
56            ' show dialog and obtain result
57            Dim result As DialogResult = dialogColor.ShowDialog()
58
59            ' return if user cancels
60            If result = Windows.Forms.DialogResult.Cancel Then
61                Return
62            End If
63
64            pen.Color = dialogColor.Color ' set pen to color
65            brush.Color = dialogColor.Color ' set brush
66            pnlDraw.Invalidate() ' refresh panel
67        End Sub ' btnColor_Click
68
69        ' cause Paint event
70        Private Sub radLineOption_CheckedChanged( _
71            ByVal sender As System.Object, ByVal e As System.EventArgs) _
72            Handles radLineOption.CheckedChanged
73
74            pnlDraw.Invalidate() ' refresh panel
75        End Sub ' radLineOption
76
77        ' cause Paint event
78        Private Sub radPolygonOption_CheckedChanged( _
79            ByVal sender As System.Object, ByVal e As System.EventArgs) _
80            Handles radPolygonOption.CheckedChanged
81
82            pnlDraw.Invalidate() ' refresh panel
83        End Sub ' radPolygonOption
84
```

Fig. 17.20 | Polygon-drawing demonstration. (Part 2 of 3.)

```
85        ' cause Paint event
86        Private Sub radFilledPolygonOption_CheckedChanged( _
87           ByVal sender As System.Object, ByVal e As System.EventArgs) _
88           Handles radFilledPolygonOption.CheckedChanged
89
90           pnlDraw.Invalidate() ' refresh panel
91        End Sub ' radFilledPolygonOption
92     End Class ' FrmDrawPolygons
```

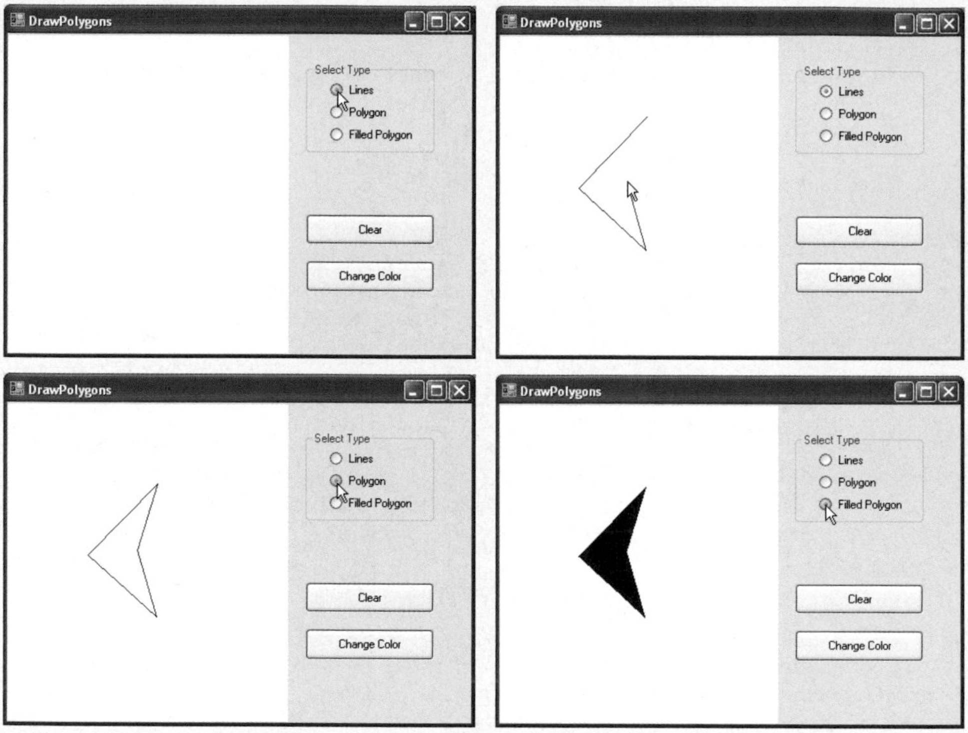

Fig. 17.20 | Polygon-drawing demonstration. (Part 3 of 3.)

To allow the user to specify a variable number of points, line 5 declares `ArrayList` `points` as a container for our `Point` objects. An `ArrayList` is similar to an array, but an `ArrayList` can grow dynamically to accommodate more elements. Lines 8–9 declare the `Pen` and `Brush` used to color our shapes. The `MouseDown` event handler (lines 12–18) for `pnlDraw` stores mouse-click locations in `points` with `ArrayList` method `Add` (line 16). The event handler then calls method `Invalidate` of `pnlDraw` (line 17) to ensure that the panel refreshes to accommodate the new point. Method `pnlDraw_Paint` (lines 21–41) handles the `Panel`'s `Paint` event. It obtains the `Panel`'s `Graphics` object (line 25) and, if the `ArrayList` `points` contains two or more `Points` (line 28), displays the polygon with the method the user selected via the GUI radio buttons (lines 33–39). In lines 30–31, we extract an array from the `ArrayList` via method `ToArray`. Method `ToArray` can take a single argument to determine the type of the returned array; we obtain the type from the first element in the `ArrayList` by calling the element's `GetType` method.

Note that line 31 uses Visual Basic's CType function to convert the Object array returned by ToArray into an array of type Point. This is required because implicit conversions are not allowed if **Option Strict** is turned on (as is the case in this chapter). A conversion performed with the CType function is also known as a *cast operation*.

Method btnClear_Click (lines 44–48) handles the **Clear** button's Click event by calling ArrayList method Clear (causing the old list to be erased) and refreshing the display. Event handler btnColor_Click (51–67) allows the user to select a new drawing color with a ColorDialog, using the techniques demonstrated in Fig. 17.7. Lines 70–91 define the event handlers for each radio button's CheckedChanged event. Each method invalidates pnlDraw to ensure that the panel is repainted to reflect the selected shape type.

17.9 Advanced Graphics Capabilities

The FCL offers many other graphics capabilities. The Brush hierarchy, for example, also includes HatchBrush, LinearGradientBrush, PathGradientBrush and TextureBrush.

Gradients, Line Styles and Fill Patterns

The program in Fig. 17.21 demonstrates several graphics features, such as dashed lines, thick lines and the ability to fill shapes with various patterns. These represent just a few of the additional capabilities of the System.Drawing namespace.

Lines 7–73 define the DrawShapesForm Paint event handler. Lines 14–15 create a LinearGradientBrush (namespace System.Drawing.Drawing2D) object named linearBrush to enable users to draw with a color gradient. The LinearGradientBrush used in this example takes four arguments—a Rectangle, two Colors and a member of enumeration LinearGradientMode. Linear gradients are defined along a line that determines the gradient endpoints. This line can be specified either by the starting and ending points or by the diagonal of a rectangle. The first argument, Rectangle drawArea1, represents the endpoints of the linear gradient—the upper-left corner is the starting point, and the bottom-right corner is the ending point. The second and third arguments specify the colors the gradient will use. In this case, the color of the ellipse will gradually change from Color.Blue to Color.Yellow. The last argument, a type from the enumeration LinearGradientMode, specifies the linear gradient's direction. In our case, we use LinearGradientMode.ForwardDiagonal, which creates a gradient from the upper-left to the lower-right corner. We then use Graphics method FillEllipse in line 18 to draw an ellipse with linearBrush; the color gradually changes from blue to yellow, as described above.

```
 1   ' Fig. 17.21: FrmDrawShapes.vb
 2   ' Drawing various shapes on a Form.
 3   Imports System.Drawing.Drawing2D
 4
 5   Public Class FrmDrawShapes
 6      ' draw various shapes on Form
 7      Private Sub FrmDrawShapes_Paint(ByVal sender As Object, _
 8         ByVal e As System.Windows.Forms.PaintEventArgs) Handles Me.Paint
 9         ' references to object we will use
10         Dim graphicsObject As Graphics = e.Graphics
11
```

Fig. 17.21 | Shapes drawn on a form. (Part 1 of 3.)

```vb
12      ' ellipse rectangle and gradient brush
13      Dim drawArea1 As New Rectangle(5, 35, 30, 100)
14      Dim linearBrush As New LinearGradientBrush(drawArea1, Color.Blue, _
15          Color.Yellow, LinearGradientMode.ForwardDiagonal)
16
17      ' draw ellipse filled with a blue-yellow gradient
18      graphicsObject.FillEllipse(linearBrush, 5, 30, 65, 100)
19
20      ' pen and location for red outline rectangle
21      Dim thickRedPen As New Pen(Color.Red, 10)
22      Dim drawArea2 As New Rectangle(80, 30, 65, 100)
23
24      ' draw thick rectangle outline in red
25      graphicsObject.DrawRectangle(thickRedPen, drawArea2)
26
27      ' bitmap texture
28      Dim textureBitmap As New Bitmap(10, 10)
29
30      ' get bitmap graphics
31      Dim graphicsObject2 As Graphics = Graphics.FromImage(textureBitmap)
32
33      ' brush and pen used throughout program
34      Dim solidColorBrush As New SolidBrush(Color.Red)
35      Dim coloredPen As New Pen(solidColorBrush)
36
37      ' fill textureBitmap with yellow
38      solidColorBrush.Color = Color.Yellow
39      graphicsObject2.FillRectangle(solidColorBrush, 0, 0, 10, 10)
40
41      ' draw small black rectangle in textureBitmap
42      coloredPen.Color = Color.Black
43      graphicsObject2.DrawRectangle(coloredPen, 1, 1, 6, 6)
44
45      ' draw small blue rectangle in textureBitmap
46      solidColorBrush.Color = Color.Blue
47      graphicsObject2.FillRectangle(solidColorBrush, 1, 1, 3, 3)
48
49      ' draw small red square in textureBitmap
50      solidColorBrush.Color = Color.Red
51      graphicsObject2.FillRectangle(solidColorBrush, 4, 4, 3, 3)
52
53      ' create textured brush and
54      ' display textured rectangle
55      Dim texturedBrush As New TextureBrush(textureBitmap)
56      graphicsObject.FillRectangle(texturedBrush, 155, 30, 75, 100)
57
58      ' draw pie-shaped arc in white
59      coloredPen.Color = Color.White
60      coloredPen.Width = 6
61      graphicsObject.DrawPie(coloredPen, 240, 30, 75, 100, 0, 270)
62
63      ' draw lines in green and yellow
64      coloredPen.Color = Color.Green
```

Fig. 17.21 | Shapes drawn on a form. (Part 2 of 3.)

```
65          coloredPen.Width = 5
66          graphicsObject.DrawLine(coloredPen, 395, 30, 320, 150)
67
68          ' draw a rounded, dashed yellow line
69          coloredPen.Color = Color.Yellow
70          coloredPen.DashCap = DashCap.Round
71          coloredPen.DashStyle = DashStyle.Dash
72          graphicsObject.DrawLine(coloredPen, 320, 30, 395, 150)
73      End Sub ' FrmDrawShapes_Paint
74  End Class ' FrmDrawShapes
```

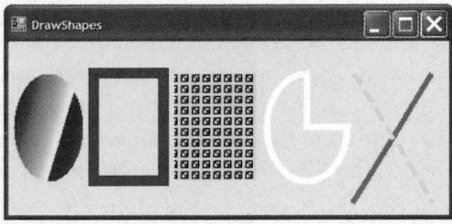

Fig. 17.21 | Shapes drawn on a form. (Part 3 of 3.)

In line 21, we create Pen object thickRedPen. We pass to thickRedPen's constructor Color.Red and Integer argument 10, indicating that we want thickRedPen to draw red lines that are 10 pixels wide.

Line 28 creates a new **Bitmap** image, which initially is empty. Class Bitmap can produce images in color and gray scale; this particular Bitmap is 10 pixels wide and 10 pixels tall. Method **FromImage** (line 31) is a Shared member of class Graphics and retrieves the Graphics object associated with an Image, which may be used to draw on an image. Lines 38–51 draw on the Bitmap a pattern consisting of black, blue, red and yellow rectangles and lines. A TextureBrush is a brush that fills the interior of a shape with an image rather than a solid color. In lines 55–56, TextureBrush object textureBrush fills a rectangle with our Bitmap. The TextureBrush constructor used in line 55 takes as an argument an image that defines its texture.

Next, we draw a pie-shaped arc with a thick white line. Lines 59–60 set coloredPen's color to White and modify its width to be 6 pixels. We then draw the pie on the form by specifying the Pen, the x-coordinate, y-coordinate, the width and height of the bounding rectangle and the start and sweep angles.

Lines 64–66 draw a 5-pixel-wide green line. Finally, lines 70–71 use enumerations **DashCap** and **DashStyle** (namespace System.Drawing.Drawing2D) to specify settings for a dashed line. Line 70 sets the **DashCap** property of coloredPen (not to be confused with the DashCap enumeration) to a member of the DashCap enumeration. The DashCap enumeration specifies the styles for the start and end of a dashed line. In this case, we want both ends of the dashed line to be rounded, so we use **DashCap.Round**. Line 71 sets the **DashStyle** property of coloredPen (not to be confused with the DashStyle enumeration) to **DashStyle.Dash**, indicating that we want our line to consist entirely of dashes.

General Paths

Our next example demonstrates a general path. A general path is a shape constructed from straight lines and complex curves. An object of class **GraphicsPath** (namespace System.Drawing.Drawing2D) represents a general path. The GraphicsPath class provides functionality that enables the creation of complex shapes from vector-based primitive graphics objects. A GraphicsPath object consists of figures defined by simple shapes. The start point of each vector-graphics object (such as a line or an arc) added to the path is connected by a straight line to the endpoint of the previous object. When called, the **Close-Figure** method attaches the final vector-graphic object endpoint to the initial starting point for the current figure by a straight line, then starts a new figure. Method StartFigure begins a new figure within the path without closing the previous figure.

The program in Fig. 17.22 draws general paths in the shape of five-pointed stars. Lines 15–16 define two Integer arrays, representing the *x*- and *y*-coordinates of the points in the star, and line 19 defines GraphicsPath object star. A loop (lines 22–25) then creates lines to connect the points of the star and adds these lines to star. We use GraphicsPath method **AddLine** to append a line to the shape. The arguments of AddLine specify the coordinates for the line's endpoints; each new call to AddLine adds a line from the previous point to the current point. Line 27 uses GraphicsPath method CloseFigure to complete the shape.

```vb
1   ' Fig. 17.22: FrmDrawStars.vb
2   ' Using paths to draw stars on the form.
3   Imports System.Drawing.Drawing2D
4
5   Public Class FrmDrawStars
6      ' create path and draw stars along it
7      Private Sub FrmDrawStars_Paint(ByVal sender As Object, _
8         ByVal e As System.Windows.Forms.PaintEventArgs) Handles Me.Paint
9
10        Dim graphicsObject As Graphics = e.Graphics
11        Dim random As New Random()
12        Dim brush As New SolidBrush(Color.DarkMagenta)
13
14        ' x and y points of the path
15        Dim xPoints As Integer() = {55, 67, 109, 73, 83, 55, 27, 37, 1, 43}
16        Dim yPoints As Integer() = {0, 36, 36, 54, 96, 72, 96, 54, 36, 36}
17
18        ' create graphics path for star
19        Dim star As New GraphicsPath()
20
21        ' create star from series of points
22        For i As Integer = 0 To 8 Step 2
23           star.AddLine(xPoints(i), yPoints(i), _
24              xPoints(i + 1), yPoints(i + 1))
25        Next
26
27        star.CloseFigure() ' close the shape
28
29        ' translate the origin to (150, 150)
30        graphicsObject.TranslateTransform(150, 150)
31
```

Fig. 17.22 | Paths used to draw stars on a form. (Part 1 of 2.)

```
32          ' rotate the origin and draw stars in random colors
33          For i As Integer = 1 To 18
34             graphicsObject.RotateTransform(20)
35
36             brush.Color = Color.FromArgb(random.Next(200, 255), _
37                random.Next(255), random.Next(255), random.Next(255))
38
39             graphicsObject.FillPath(brush, star)
40          Next
41       End Sub ' FrmDrawStars_Paint
42    End Class ' FrmDrawStars
```

Fig. 17.22 | Paths used to draw stars on a form. (Part 2 of 2.)

Line 30 sets the origin of the Graphics object. The arguments to method Trans-lateTransform indicate that the origin should be translated to the coordinates (150, 150). The loop in lines 33–40 draws the star 18 times, rotating it around the origin. Line 34 uses Graphics method **RotateTransform** to move to the next position on the form; the argument specifies the rotation angle in degrees. Graphics method FillPath (line 39) then draws a filled version of the star with the Brush created in lines 36–37. The application determines the SolidBrush's color randomly, using Random method Next.

17.10 Introduction to Multimedia

The FCL offers many convenient ways to include images and animations in programs. People who entered the computing field decades ago used computers primarily to perform arithmetic calculations. As the discipline evolves, we are realizing the importance of computers' data-manipulation capabilities. We are seeing many exciting new three-dimensional applications. Multimedia programming is an entertaining and innovative field, but one that presents many challenges

Multimedia applications demand extraordinary computing power. Today's ultrafast processors make multimedia-based applications commonplace. As the market for multimedia explodes, users are purchasing the faster processors, larger memories and wider communications bandwidths needed to support multimedia applications. This benefits the computer and communications industries, which provide the hardware, software and services fueling the multimedia revolution.

In the remaining sections of this chapter, we introduce basic image processing and other multimedia features and capabilities. Section 17.11 discusses how to load, display and scale images; Section 17.12 demonstrates image animation; Section 17.13 presents the video capabilities of the Windows Media Player control; and Section 17.14 explores Microsoft Agent technology.

17.11 Loading, Displaying and Scaling Images

Visual Basic's multimedia capabilities include graphics, images, animations and video. Previous sections demonstrated vector-graphics capabilities; this section presents image manipulation. The application in Fig. 17.23 loads an Image (System.Drawing namespace), then allows the user to scale the Image to a specified width and height.

Line 4 declares Image variable image. Line 11 in the Form's Load event handler uses Shared Image method **FromFile** to load an image from a file on disk. Line 12 uses the Form's **CreateGraphics** method to create a Graphics object for drawing on the Form. Method CreateGraphics is inherited from class Control. When you click the **Set** Button,

```vb
1   ' Fig. 17.23: FrmDisplayLogo.vb
2   ' Displaying and resizing an image
3   Public Class FrmDisplayLogo
4       Private imageValue As Image
5       Private graphicsObject As Graphics
6
7       ' load image and obtain Graphics object
8       Private Sub FrmDisplayLogo_Load(ByVal sender As Object, _
9           ByVal e As System.EventArgs) Handles Me.Load
10
11          imageValue = Image.FromFile("images\Logo.gif")
12          graphicsObject = Me.CreateGraphics()
13      End Sub ' FrmDisplayLogo_Load
14
15      ' get new width and height of image, then redraw it
16      Private Sub btnSet_Click(ByVal sender As System.Object, _
17          ByVal e As System.EventArgs) Handles btnSet.Click
18          ' get user input
19          Dim Width As Integer = Convert.ToInt32(widthTextBox.Text)
20          Dim Height As Integer = Convert.ToInt32(heightTextBox.Text)
21
22          ' if dimensions specified are too large
23          ' display problem
24          If Width > 375 Or Height > 225 Then
25              MessageBox.Show(" Height or Width too large")
26              Return
27          End If
28
29          ' clear the Form then draw the image
30          graphicsObject.Clear(Me.BackColor)
31          graphicsObject.DrawImage(imageValue, 5, 5, Width, Height)
32      End Sub ' btnSet_Click
33  End Class ' FrmDisplayLogo
```

Fig. 17.23 | Image resizing. (Part 1 of 2.)

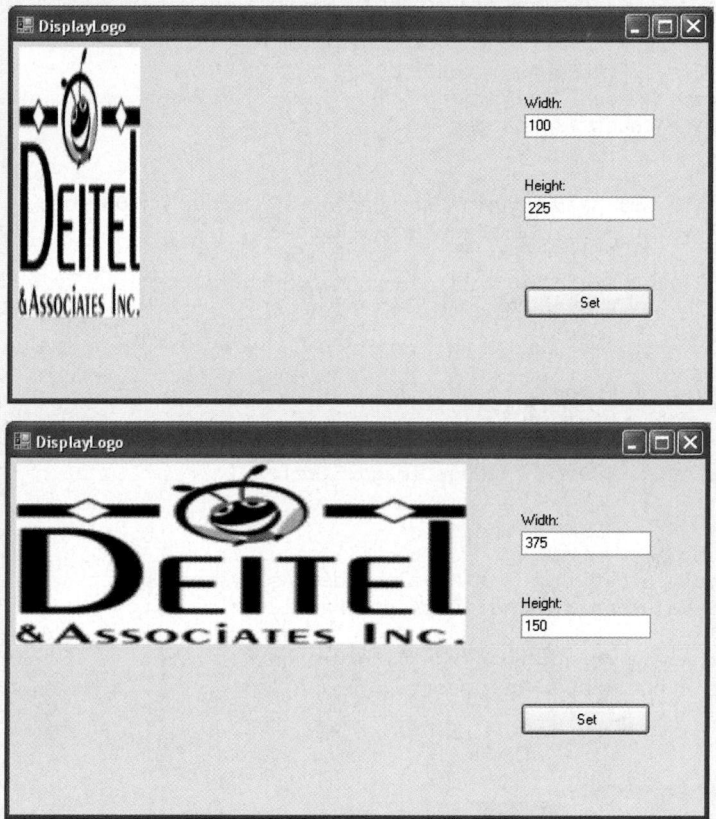

Fig. 17.23 | Image resizing. (Part 2 of 2.)

lines 24–27 validate the width and height to ensure that they are not too large. If the parameters are valid, line 30 calls Graphics method Clear to paint the entire Form in the current background color. Line 31 calls Graphics method DrawImage, passing as arguments the image to draw, the *x*-coordinate of the image's upper-left corner, the *y*-coordinate of the image's upper-left corner, the width of the image and the height of the image. If the width and height do not correspond to the image's original dimensions, the image is scaled to fit the new width and height.

17.12 Animating a Series of Images

The next example animates a series of images stored in an array. The application uses the same technique to load and display Images as shown in Fig. 17.23.

The animation in Fig. 17.24 uses a PictureBox, which contains the images that we animate. We use a Timer to cycle through the images and display a new image every 50 milliseconds. Variable count keeps track of the current image number and increases by 1 every time we display a new image. The array includes 30 images (numbered 0–29); when the application reaches image 29, it returns to image 0. The 30 images are located in the images folder inside the project's bin/Debug and bin/Release directories.

```vb
1   ' Fig. 17.24: FrmLogoAnimator.vb
2   ' Program that animates a series of images.
3   Public Class FrmLogoAnimator
4      Private images(29) As Image
5      Private count As Integer = -1
6
7      ' load images
8      Private Sub FrmLogoAnimator_Load(ByVal sender As Object, _
9         ByVal e As System.EventArgs) Handles Me.Load
10
11         For i As Integer = 0 To images.Length - 1
12            images(i) = Image.FromFile("images\deitel" & i & ".gif")
13         Next
14
15         picLogo.Image = images(0) ' display first image
16
17         ' set PictureBox to be the same size as Image
18         picLogo.Size = picLogo.Image.Size
19      End Sub ' FrmLogoAnimator_Load
20
21      ' display new image every 50 milliseconds
22      Private Sub timer_Tick(ByVal sender As System.Object, _
23         ByVal e As System.EventArgs) Handles timer.Tick
24
25         count = (count + 1) Mod images.Length ' increment counter
26         picLogo.Image = images(count) ' display next image
27      End Sub ' timer_Tick
28   End Class ' FrmLogoAnimator
```

Fig. 17.24 | Animation of a series of images.

Lines 11–13 load each of 30 images and place them in an array of Images (declared in line 4). Line 15 places the first image in the PictureBox. Line 18 modifies the size of the PictureBox so that it is equal to the size of the Image it is displaying. The event handler for timer's Tick event (line 22–27) responds to each event by displaying the next image from the array.

Performance Tip 17.2

It is more efficient to load an animation's frames as one image than to load each image separately. (A painting program, such as Adobe Photoshop® or Jasc® Paint Shop Pro™, can be used to combine the animation's frames into one image.) If the images are being loaded separately from the Web, each loaded image requires a separate connection to the site on which the images are stored; this process can result in poor performance.

Chess Example

The following chess example demonstrates techniques for two-dimensional **collision detection**, selecting single frames from a multiframe image, and **regional invalidation**, refreshing only the parts of the screen that have changed, to increase performance. Two-dimensional collision detection enables a program to detect whether two shapes overlap or whether a point is contained within a shape. In the next example, we demonstrate the simplest form of collision detection, which determines whether a point (the mouse-click location) is contained within a rectangle (a chess-piece image).

Class `ChessPiece` (Fig. 17.25) represents the individual chess pieces. Lines 5–12 define a `Public` enumeration of constants that identify each chess-piece type. The constants also serve to identify the location of each piece in the chess-piece image file. Rectangle object `targetRectangle` (line 18) identifies the image location on the chessboard. The x and y properties of the rectangle are assigned in the `ChessPiece` constructor, and all chess-piece images have a width and height of 75 pixels.

```
1    ' Fig. 17.25 : ChessPiece.cs
2    ' Class that represents chess piece attributes.
3    Public Class ChessPiece
4        ' define chess-piece type constants
5        Public Enum Types
6            KING
7            QUEEN
8            BISHOP
9            KNIGHT
10           ROOK
11           PAWN
12       End Enum ' Types
13
14       Private currentType As Integer ' this object's type
15       Private pieceImage As Bitmap ' this object's image
16
17       ' default display location
18       Private targetRectangle As New Rectangle(0, 0, 75, 75)
19
20       ' constructor
21       Public Sub New(ByVal type As Integer, ByVal xLocation As Integer, _
22           ByVal yLocation As Integer, ByVal sourceImage As Bitmap)
23
24           currentType = type ' set current type
25           targetRectangle.X = xLocation ' set current x location
26           targetRectangle.Y = yLocation ' set current y location
27
28           ' obtain pieceImage from section of sourceImage
29           pieceImage = sourceImage.Clone( _
30               New Rectangle(type * 75, 0, 75, 75), _
31               System.Drawing.Imaging.PixelFormat.DontCare)
32       End Sub ' New
33
```

Fig. 17.25 | Class that represents chess-piece attributes. (Part 1 of 2.)

```
34        ' draw chess piece
35        Public Sub Draw(ByVal graphicsObject As Graphics)
36            graphicsObject.DrawImage(pieceImage, targetRectangle)
37        End Sub ' end method Draw
38
39        ' obtain this piece's location rectangle
40        Public Function GetBounds() As Rectangle
41            Return targetRectangle
42        End Function ' end method GetBounds
43
44        ' set this piece's location
45        Public Sub SetLocation( _
46            ByVal xLocation As Integer, ByVal yLocation As Integer)
47
48            targetRectangle.X = xLocation
49            targetRectangle.Y = yLocation
50        End Sub ' end method SetLocation
51    End Class ' ChessPiece
```

Fig. 17.25 | Class that represents chess-piece attributes. (Part 2 of 2.)

The ChessPiece constructor (lines 21–32) receives the chess-piece type, its x and y location and the Bitmap containing all chess-piece images. Rather than loading the chess-piece image within the class, we allow the calling class to pass the image. This increases the flexibility of the class by allowing the user to change images. Lines 29–31 extract a sub-image that contains only the current piece's bitmap data. Our chess-piece images are defined in a specific manner: One image contains six chess-piece images, each defined within a 75-pixel block, resulting in a total image size of 450-by-75. We obtain a single image via Bitmap's Clone method, which allows us to specify a rectangle-image location and the desired pixel format. The location is a 75-by-75 pixel block with its upper-left corner x equal to 75 * type, and the corresponding y equal to 0. For the pixel format, we specify constant DontCare, causing the format to remain unchanged.

Method Draw (lines 35–37) causes the ChessPiece to draw pieceImage in the targetRectangle using the Graphics object passed as Draw's argument. Method GetBounds (lines 40–52) returns the targetRectangle object for use in collision detection, and method SetLocation (lines 45–50) allows the calling class to specify a new piece location.

Class FrmChessGame (Fig. 17.26) defines the game and graphics code for our chess game. Lines 4–8 define instance variables the program requires. ArrayList chessTile (line 4) stores the board tile images. ArrayList chessPieces (line 5) stores all active ChessPiece objects, and Integer selectedIndex (line 6) identifies the index in chessPieces of the currently selected piece. The board (line 7) is an 8-by-8, two-dimensional Integer array corresponding to the squares of a chess board. Each board element is an integer from 0 to 3 that corresponds to an index in chessTile and is used to specify the chessboard-square image. Const TILESIZE (line 8) defines the size of each tile in pixels.

The chess game GUI consists of Form ChessGame, the area in which we draw the tiles; Panel pieceBox, the area in which we draw the pieces (note that pieceBox's background color is set to "transparent"); and a Menu that allows the user to begin a new game. Although the pieces and tiles could have been drawn on the same form, doing so would decrease performance. We would be forced to refresh the board and all the pieces every time we refreshed the control.

```vb
 1   ' Fig. 17.26: FrmChessGame.vb
 2   ' Chess Game graphics code.
 3   Public Class FrmChessGame
 4      Private chessTile As New ArrayList() ' for tile images
 5      Private chessPieces As New ArrayList() ' for chess pieces
 6      Private selectedIndex As Integer = -1 ' index for selected piece
 7      Private board(,) As Integer = New Integer(7, 7) {} ' board array
 8      Private Const TILESIZE As Integer = 75 ' chess tile size in pixels
 9
10      ' load tile bitmaps and reset game
11      Private Sub FrmChessGame_Load(ByVal sender As Object, _
12         ByVal e As System.EventArgs) Handles Me.Load
13         ' load chess board tiles
14         chessTile.Add(Bitmap.FromFile("images\lightTile1.png"))
15         chessTile.Add(Bitmap.FromFile("images\lightTile2.png"))
16         chessTile.Add(Bitmap.FromFile("images\darkTile1.png"))
17         chessTile.Add(Bitmap.FromFile("images\darkTile2.png"))
18
19         ResetBoard() ' initialize board
20         Invalidate() ' refresh form
21      End Sub ' FrmChessGame_Load
22
23      ' initialize pieces to start and rebuild board
24      Private Sub ResetBoard()
25         Dim current As Integer = -1
26         Dim piece As ChessPiece
27         Dim random As New Random()
28         Dim light As Boolean = False
29         Dim type As Integer
30
31         chessPieces.Clear() ' ensure empty arraylist
32
33         ' load whitepieces image
34         Dim whitePieces As Bitmap = _
35            CType(Image.FromFile("images\whitePieces.png"), Bitmap)
36
37         ' load blackpieces image
38         Dim blackPieces As Bitmap = _
39            CType(Image.FromFile("images\blackPieces.png"), Bitmap)
40
41         ' set whitepieces to be drawn first
42         Dim selected As Bitmap = whitePieces
43
44         ' traverse board rows in outer loop
45         For row As Integer = 0 To board.GetUpperBound(0)
46            ' if at bottom rows, set to black pieces images
47            If row > 5 Then
48               selected = blackPieces
49            End If
```

Fig. 17.26 | Chess-game code. (Part 1 of 6.)

```vb
50
51                   ' traverse board columns in inner loop
52              For column As Integer = 0 To board.GetUpperBound(1)
53                 ' if first or last row, organize pieces
54              If row = 0 OrElse row = 7 Then
55                  Select Case column
56                     Case 0, 7 ' set current piece to rook
57                        current = ChessPiece.Types.ROOK
58                     Case 1, 6 ' set current piece to knight
59                        current = ChessPiece.Types.KNIGHT
60                     Case 2, 5 ' set current piece to bishop
61                        current = ChessPiece.Types.BISHOP
62                     Case 3 ' set current piece to king
63                        current = ChessPiece.Types.KING
64                     Case 4 ' set current piece to queen
65                        current = ChessPiece.Types.QUEEN
66                  End Select
67
68                  ' create current piece at start position
69                  piece = New ChessPiece(current, _
70                     column * TILESIZE, row * TILESIZE, selected)
71
72                  chessPieces.Add(piece) ' add piece to arraylist
73              End If
74
75                 ' if second or seventh row, organize pawns
76              If row = 1 OrElse row = 6 Then
77                  piece = New ChessPiece(ChessPiece.Types.PAWN, _
78                     column * TILESIZE, row * TILESIZE, selected)
79                  chessPieces.Add(piece) ' add piece to arraylist
80              End If
81
82              type = random.Next(0, 2) ' determine board piece type
83
84              If light Then ' set light tile
85                 board(row, column) = type
86                 light = False
87              Else ' set dark tile
88                 board(row, column) = type + 2
89                 light = True
90              End If
91           Next column
92
93           light = Not light ' account for new row tile color switch
94        Next row
95     End Sub ' ResetBoard
96
97     ' display board in form OnPaint event
98     Private Sub FrmChessGame_Paint(ByVal sender As Object, _
99        ByVal e As System.Windows.Forms.PaintEventArgs) Handles Me.Paint
100       Dim graphicsObject As Graphics = e.Graphics ' obtain graphics object
101       graphicsObject.TranslateTransform(0, 24) ' adjust origin
102
```

Fig. 17.26 | Chess-game code. (Part 2 of 6.)

```
103         For row As Integer = 0 To board.GetUpperBound(0)
104             For column As Integer = 0 To board.GetUpperBound(1)
105                 ' draw image specified in board array
106                 graphicsObject.DrawImage( _
107                     CType(chessTile(board(row, column)), Image), _
108                     New Point(TILESIZE * column, (TILESIZE * row)))
109             Next column
110         Next row
111     End Sub ' FrmChessGame_Paint
112
113     ' return index of piece that intersects point
114     ' optionally exclude a value
115     Private Function CheckBounds(ByVal pointValue As Point, _
116         ByVal exclude As Integer) As Integer
117         Dim rectangleValue As Rectangle ' current bounding rectangle
118
119         For i As Integer = 0 To chessPieces.Count - 1
120             ' get piece rectangle
121             rectangleValue = GetPiece(i).GetBounds()
122
123             ' check if rectangle contains point
124             If rectangleValue.Contains(pointValue) And i <> exclude Then
125                 Return i
126             End If
127         Next
128
129         Return -1
130     End Function ' CheckBounds
131
132     ' handle picBoard Paint event
133     Private Sub picBoard_Paint(ByVal sender As Object, _
134         ByVal e As System.Windows.Forms.PaintEventArgs) _
135         Handles picBoard.Paint
136         ' draw all pieces
137         For i As Integer = 0 To chessPieces.Count - 1
138             GetPiece(i).Draw(e.Graphics)
139         Next
140     End Sub ' picBoard_Paint
141
142     ' handle picBoard MouseDown event
143     Private Sub picBoard_MouseDown(ByVal sender As Object, _
144         ByVal e As System.Windows.Forms.MouseEventArgs) _
145         Handles picBoard.MouseDown
146         ' determine selected piece
147         selectedIndex = CheckBounds(New Point(e.X, e.Y), -1)
148     End Sub ' picBoard_MouseDown
149
150     ' if piece is selected, move it
151     Private Sub picBoard_MouseMove(ByVal sender As Object, _
152         ByVal e As System.Windows.Forms.MouseEventArgs) _
153         Handles picBoard.MouseMove
154
```

Fig. 17.26 | Chess-game code. (Part 3 of 6.)

```
155          If selectedIndex > -1 Then
156             Dim region As New Rectangle(e.X - TILESIZE * 2, _
157                e.Y - TILESIZE * 2, TILESIZE * 4, TILESIZE * 4)
158
159             ' set piece center to mouse
160             GetPiece(selectedIndex).SetLocation( _
161                e.X - TILESIZE \ 2, e.Y - TILESIZE \ 2)
162
163             picBoard.Invalidate(region) ' refresh region
164          End If
165       End Sub ' picBoard_MouseMove
166
167       ' on mouse up deselect piece and remove taken piece
168       Private Sub picBoard_MouseUp(ByVal sender As Object, _
169          ByVal e As System.Windows.Forms.MouseEventArgs) _
170          Handles picBoard.MouseUp
171
172          Dim remove As Integer = -1
173
174          ' if chess piece was selected
175          If selectedIndex > -1 Then
176             Dim current As New Point(e.X, e.Y)
177             Dim newPoint As New Point( _
178                current.X - (current.X Mod TILESIZE), _
179                current.Y - (current.Y Mod TILESIZE))
180
181             ' check bounds with point, exclude selected piece
182             remove = CheckBounds(current, selectedIndex)
183
184             ' snap piece into center of closest square
185             GetPiece(selectedIndex).SetLocation(newPoint.X, newPoint.Y)
186             selectedIndex = -1 ' deselect piece
187
188             ' remove taken piece
189             If remove > -1 Then
190                chessPieces.RemoveAt(remove)
191             End If
192          End If
193
194          picBoard.Invalidate() ' ensure artifact removal
195       End Sub ' picBoard_MouseUp
196
197       ' helper function to convert
198       ' ArrayList object to ChessPiece
199       Private Function GetPiece(ByVal i As Integer) As ChessPiece
200          Return CType(chessPieces(i), ChessPiece)
201       End Function ' GetPiece
202
203       ' handle NewGame menu option click
204       Private Sub newGameItem_Click(ByVal sender As System.Object, _
205          ByVal e As System.EventArgs) Handles newGameItem.Click
206
```

Fig. 17.26 | Chess-game code. (Part 4 of 6.)

```
207        ResetBoard() ' reinitialize board
208        Invalidate() ' refresh form
209     End Sub ' newGameItem_Click
210  End Class ' FrmChessGame
```

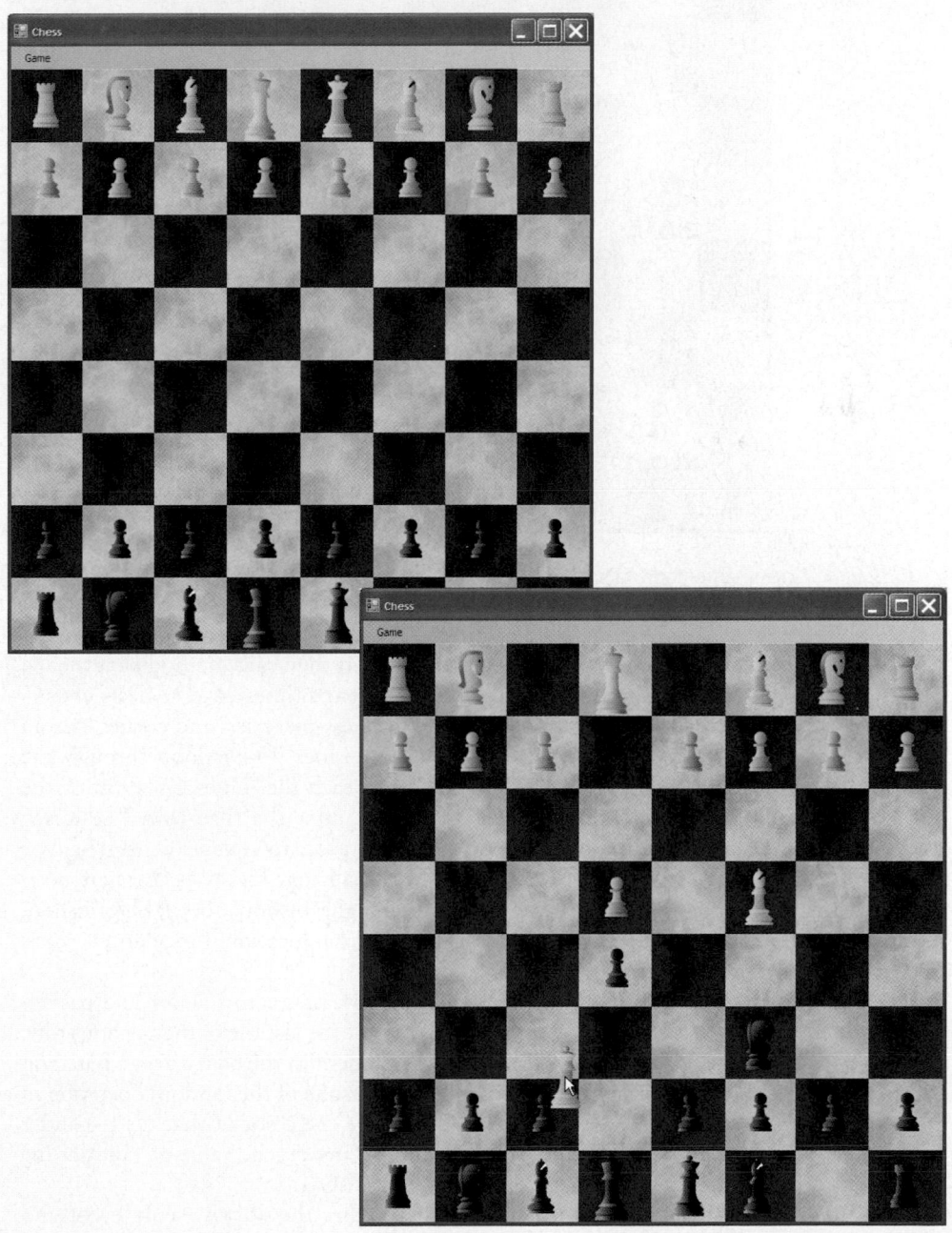

Fig. 17.26 | Chess-game code. (Part 5 of 6.)

Fig. 17.26 | Chess-game code. (Part 6 of 6.)

The `ChessGame_Load` event handler (lines 11–21) loads four tile images into `chessTile`—two light tiles and two dark tiles for variety. It then calls method `ResetBoard` to refresh the `Form` and begin the game. Method `ResetBoard` (lines 24–95) clears `chess-Pieces`, loads images for both the black and the white chess-piece sets and creates `Bitmap` `selected` to define the currently selected `Bitmap` set. Lines 45–94 loop through the board's 64 positions, setting the tile color and piece for each tile. Lines 47–49 cause the currently selected image to switch to the `blackPieces` after the fifth row. If the row counter is on the first or last row, lines 55–66 add a new piece to `chessPieces`. The type of the piece is based on the current column we are initializing. Pieces in chess are positioned in the following order, from left to right: rook, knight, bishop, queen, king, bishop, knight and rook. Lines 76–80 add a new pawn at the current location if the current row is second or seventh.

A chessboard is defined by alternating light and dark tiles across a row in a pattern where the color that starts each row is equal to the color of the last tile of the previous row. Lines 82–90 assign the current board-tile color to an element in the `board` array. Based on the alternating value of `Boolean` variable `light` and the results of the random operation in line 82, we assign an `Integer` to the board to determine the color of that tile—0 and 1 represent light tiles; 2 and 3 represent dark tiles. Line 93 inverts the value of `light` at the end of each row to maintain the staggered effect of a chessboard.

Method `FrmChessGame_Paint` (lines 98–111) handles the `Form`'s `Paint` event and draws the tiles according to their values in the `board` array. Since the default height of a `MenuStrip` is 24 pixels, we use the `TranslateTransform` method of class `Graphics` to shift the origin of the Form down 24 pixels (line 101). This shift prevents the top row of tiles from being hidden behind the MenuStrip. Method picBoard_Paint (lines 133–140), which handles the Paint event for the picBoard Panel, iterates through each element of the chessPieces ArrayList and calls its Draw method.

The picBoard MouseDown event handler (lines 143–148) calls CheckBounds (declared in lines 115–130) with the location of the mouse to determine whether the user has selected a piece.

The picBoard MouseMove event handler (lines 151–165) moves the selected piece with the mouse. Lines 156–157 define a region of the Panel that spans two tiles in every direction from the pointer. As mentioned previously, Invalidate is slow. This means that the picBoard MouseMove event handler might be called several times before the Invalidate method completes. If a user working on a slow computer moves the mouse quickly, the application could leave behind **artifacts**. An artifact is any unintended visual abnormality in a graphical program. By causing the program to refresh a two-square rectangle, which should suffice in most cases, we achieve a significant performance enhancement over an entire component refresh during each MouseMove event. Lines 160–161 set the selected piece location to the mouse-cursor position, adjusting the location to center the image on the mouse. Line 163 invalidates the region defined in lines 156–157 so that it will be refreshed.

Lines 168–195 define the picBoard MouseUp event handler. If a piece has been selected, lines 175–192 determine the index in chessPieces of any piece collision, remove the collided piece, snap (align) the current piece to a valid location and deselect the piece. We check for piece collisions to allow the chess piece to "take" other chess pieces. Line 182 checks whether any piece (excluding the currently selected piece) is beneath the current mouse location. If a collision is detected, the returned piece index is assigned to remove. Line 185 determine the closest valid chess tile and "snaps" the selected piece to that location. If remove contains a positive value, line 190 removes the object at that index from the chessPieces ArrayList. Finally, the entire Panel is invalidated in line 194 to display the new piece location and remove any artifacts created during the move.

Method CheckBounds (lines 115–130) is a collision-detection helper method; it iterates through ArrayList chessPieces and returns the index of any piece's rectangle that contains the point passed to the method (the mouse location, in this example). CheckBounds uses Rectangle method Contains to determine whether a point is in the Rectangle. Method CheckBounds optionally can exclude a single piece index (to ignore the selected index in the picBoard MouseUp event handler, in this example).

Lines 199–201 define helper function GetPiece, which simplifies the conversion from objects in ArrayList chessPieces to ChessPiece types. Event handler newGameItem_Click (lines 204–209) handles the NewGame menu-item click event, calls RefreshBoard to reset the game and invalidates the entire form.

17.13 Windows Media Player

The Windows Media Player control enables an application to play video and sound in many multimedia formats. These include MPEG (Motion Pictures Experts Group) audio and video, AVI (audio-video interleave) video, WAV (Windows wave-file format) audio and MIDI (Musical Instrument Digital Interface) audio. Users can find pre-existing audio and video on the Internet, or they can create their own files, using available sound and graphics packages.

The application in Fig. 17.27 demonstrates the Windows Media Player control. To use this control, you must add the control to the **Toolbox**. First select **Tools > Choose Toolbox Items…** to display the **Choose Toolbox Items** dialog. Click the **COM components** tab, then scroll down and select the option **Windows Media Player**. Click the **OK** button to dismiss the dialog. The Windows Media Player control now appears at the bottom of the **Toolbox**.

The Windows Media Player control provides several buttons that allow the user to play the current file, pause, stop, play the previous file, rewind, forward and play the next file. The control also includes a volume control and trackbars to select a specific position in the media file.

```vb
 1   ' Fig. 17.27: FrmMediaPlayer.vb
 2   ' Windows Media Player control used to play media files.
 3   Public Class FrmMediaPlayer
 4      ' open new media file in Windows Media Player
 5      Private Sub openItem_Click(ByVal sender As System.Object, _
 6         ByVal e As System.EventArgs) Handles openItem.Click
 7
 8         openMediaFileDialog.ShowDialog()
 9
10         ' load and play the media clip
11         player.URL = openMediaFileDialog.FileName
12      End Sub ' openItem_Click
13
14      ' exit program when exit menu item is clicked
15      Private Sub exitItem_Click(ByVal sender As System.Object, _
16         ByVal e As System.EventArgs) Handles exitItem.Click
17
18         Application.Exit()
19      End Sub ' exitItem_Click
20   End Class ' FrmMediaPlayer
```

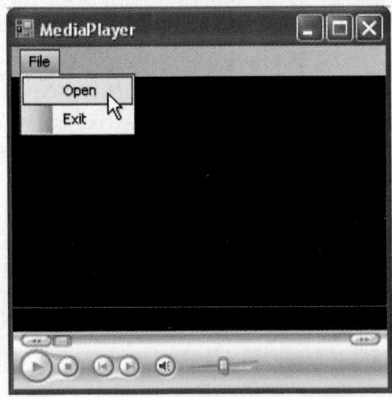

Fig. 17.27 | Windows Media Player demonstration. (Part 1 of 2.)

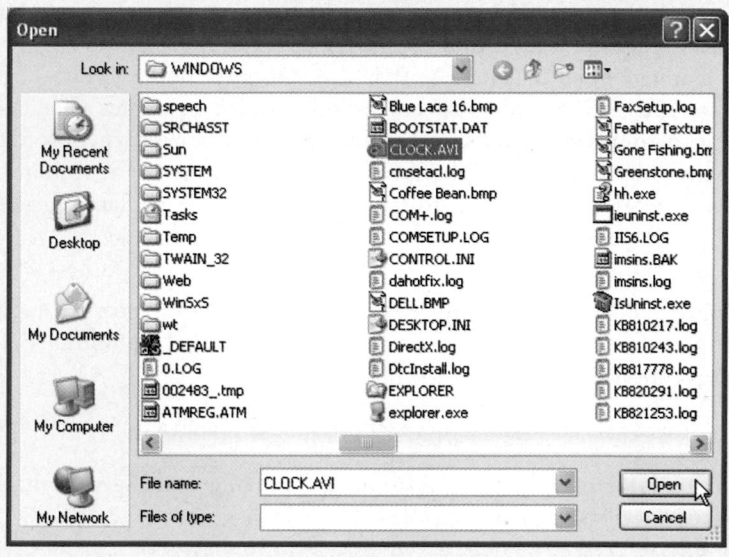

Fig. 17.27 | Windows Media Player demonstration. (Part 2 of 2.)

Our application provides a **File** menu containing the **Open** and **Exit** menu items. When a user chooses **Open** from the **File** menu, event handler openItem_Click (lines 5–12) executes. An OpenFileDialog box displays (line 8) to allow the user to select a file. The program then sets the URL property of the player (the Windows Media Player control object of type **AxMediaPlayer**) to the name of the file chosen by the user. The URL property specifies the file that Windows Media Player is currently using.

The exitItem_Click event handler (lines 15–19) executes when the user selects **Exit** from the **File** menu. This event handler simply calls Application method Exit to terminate the application. We provide sample audio and video files in the directory that contains this example.

17.14 Microsoft Agent

Microsoft Agent is a technology used to add interactive animated characters to Windows applications or Web pages. Microsoft Agent characters can speak and respond to user input via speech recognition and synthesis. Microsoft employs its Agent technology in applications such as Word, Excel and PowerPoint. Agents in these programs aid users in finding answers to questions and in understanding how the applications function.

The Microsoft Agent control provides programmers with access to four predefined characters—Genie (a genie), Merlin (a wizard), Peedy (a parrot) and Robby (a robot). Each character has a unique set of animations that programmers can use in their applications to illustrate different points and functions. For instance, the Peedy character-animation set includes different flying animations, which the programmer might use to move Peedy on the screen. Microsoft provides basic information on Agent technology at

www.microsoft.com/msagent

Microsoft Agent technology enables users to interact with applications and Web pages through speech, the most natural form of human communication. To understand speech, the control uses a **speech-recognition engine**—an application that translates vocal sound input from a microphone to language that the computer understands. The Microsoft Agent control also uses a **text-to-speech engine**, which generates characters' spoken responses. A text-to-speech engine is an application that translates typed words into audio sound that users hear through headphones or speakers connected to a computer. Microsoft provides speech-recognition and text-to-speech engines for several languages at

> www.microsoft.com/msagent/downloads/user.asp

Programmers can even create their own animated characters with the help of the **Microsoft Agent Character Editor** and the **Microsoft Linguistic Sound Editing Tool**. These products are available free for download from

> www.microsoft.com/msagent/downloads/developer.asp

This section introduces the basic capabilities of the Microsoft Agent control. For complete details on downloading this control, visit

> www.microsoft.com/msagent/downloads/user.asp

The following example, Peedy's Pizza Palace, was developed by Microsoft to illustrate the capabilities of the Microsoft Agent control. Peedy's Pizza Palace is an online pizza shop where users can place their orders via voice input. The Peedy character interacts with users by helping them choose toppings and calculating the totals for their orders. You can view this example at

> www.microsoft.com/agent2/sdk/samples/html/peedypza.htm

To run the example, you must go to www.microsoft.com/msagent/downloads/user.asp and download and install the Peedy character file, a text-to-speech engine and a speech-recognition engine.

When the window opens, Peedy introduces himself (Fig. 17.28), and the words he speaks appear in a cartoon bubble above his head. Note that Peedy's animations correspond to the words he speaks.

Programmers can synchronize character animations with speech output to illustrate a point or to convey a character's mood. For instance, Fig. 17.29 depicts Peedy's *Pleased* animation. The Peedy character-animation set includes 85 different animations, each of which is unique to the Peedy character.

Look-and-Feel Observation 17.1

Agent characters remain on top of all active windows while a Microsoft Agent application is running. Their motions are not limited by the boundaries of the browser or the application window.

Peedy also responds to input from the keyboard and mouse. Figure 17.30 shows what happens when a user clicks Peedy with the mouse pointer. Peedy jumps up, ruffles his feathers and exclaims, "Hey, that tickles!" or "Be careful with that pointer!" Users can relocate Peedy on the screen by dragging him with the mouse. However, even when the user moves Peedy to a different part of the screen, he continues to perform his preset animations and location changes.

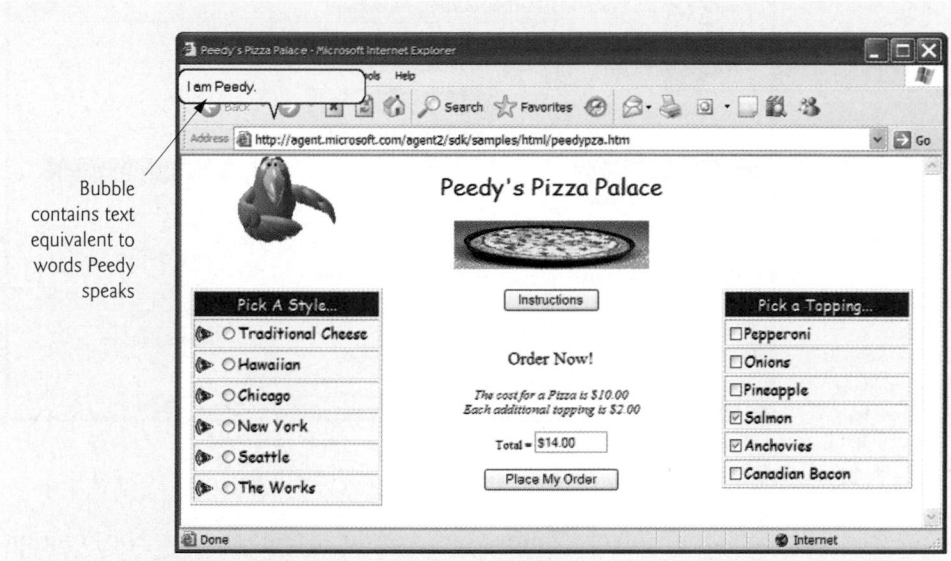

Bubble contains text equivalent to words Peedy speaks

Fig. 17.28 | Peedy introducing himself when the window opens.

Fig. 17.29 | Peedy's *Pleased* animation.

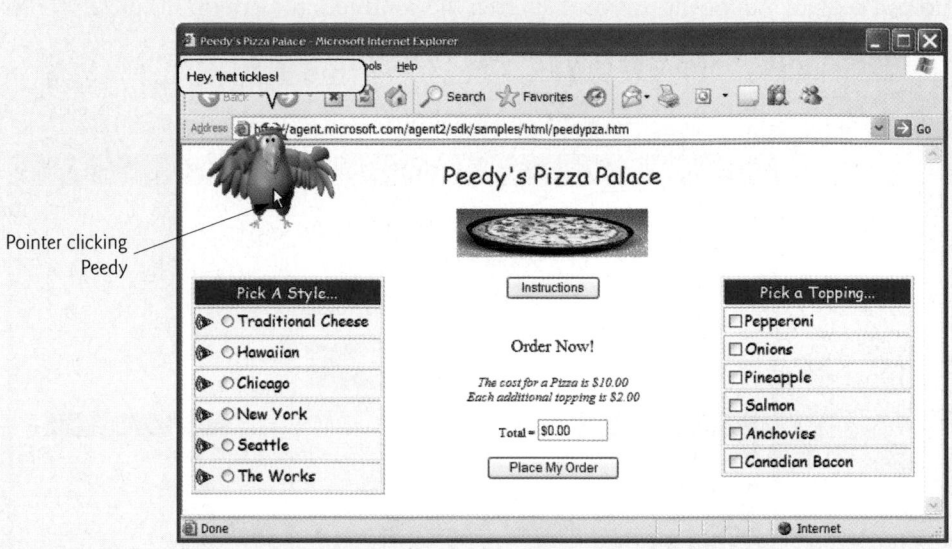

Fig. 17.30 | Peedy's reaction when he is clicked.

Many location changes involve animations. For instance, Peedy can hop from one screen location to another, or he can fly (Fig. 17.31).

Once Peedy completes the ordering instructions, a tool tip appears beneath him indicating that he is listening for a voice command (Fig. 17.32). You can enter the type of pizza to order either by speaking the style name into a microphone or by clicking the radio button corresponding to your choice.

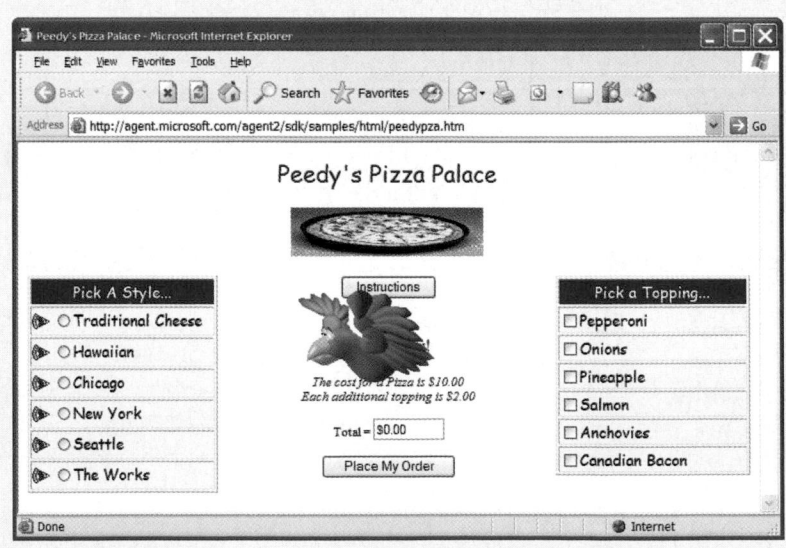

Fig. 17.31 | Peedy flying animation.

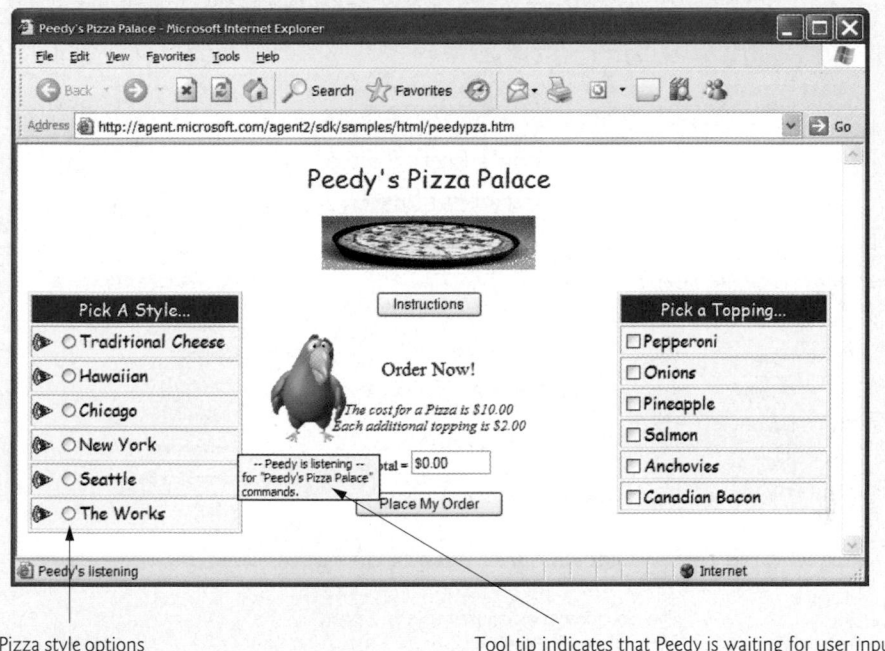

Pizza style options   Tool tip indicates that Peedy is waiting for user input

Fig. 17.32 | Peedy waiting for speech input.

If you choose speech input, a box appears below Peedy displaying the words that Peedy "heard" (i.e., the words translated to the program by the speech-recognition engine). Once he recognizes your input, Peedy gives you a description of the selected pizza. Figure 17.33 shows what happens when you choose **Seattle** as the pizza style.

Peedy then asks you to choose additional toppings. Again, you can either speak or use the mouse to make a selection. Checkboxes corresponding to toppings that come with the selected pizza style are checked for you. Figure 17.34 shows what happens when you choose anchovies as an additional topping. Peedy makes a wisecrack about your choice.

You can submit the order either by pressing the **Place My Order** button or by speaking "Place order" into the microphone. Peedy recounts the order while writing down the order items on his notepad (Fig. 17.35). He then calculates the figures on his calculator and reports the total price (Fig. 17.36).

Creating an Application That Uses Microsoft Agent
[*Note:* Before running this example, you must first download and install the Microsoft Agent control, a speech-recognition engine, a text-to-speech engine and the four character definitions from the Microsoft Agent Web site, as we discussed at the beginning of this section.]

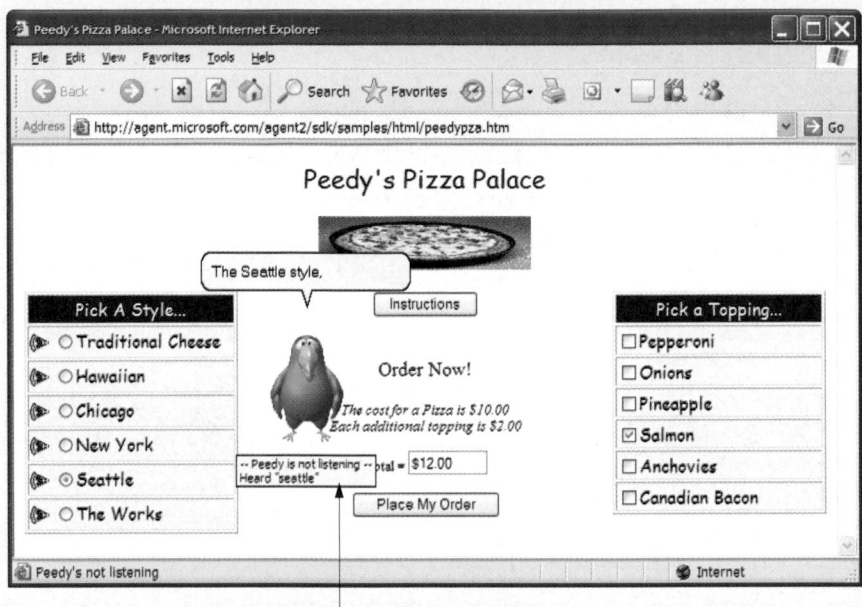

Fig. 17.33 | Peedy repeating a request for Seattle-style pizza.

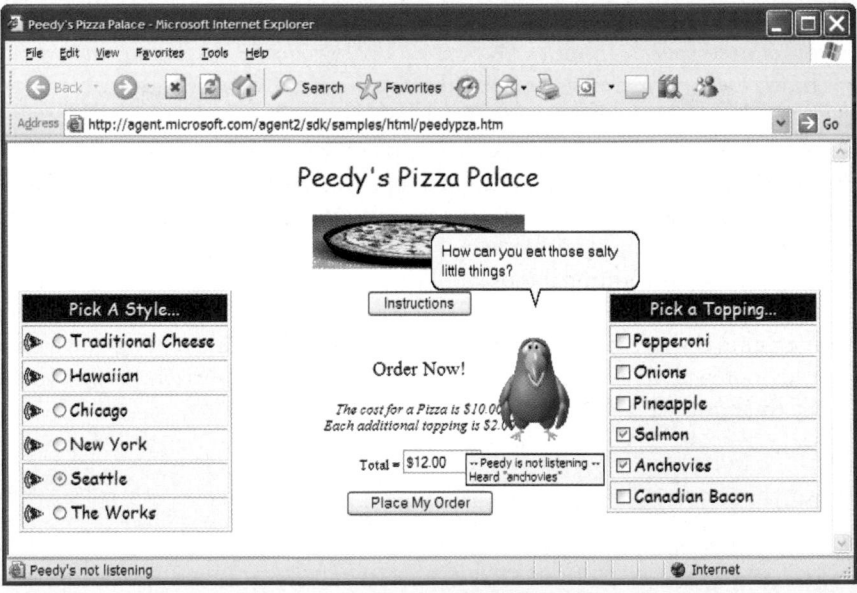

Fig. 17.34 | Peedy repeating a request for anchovies as an additional topping.

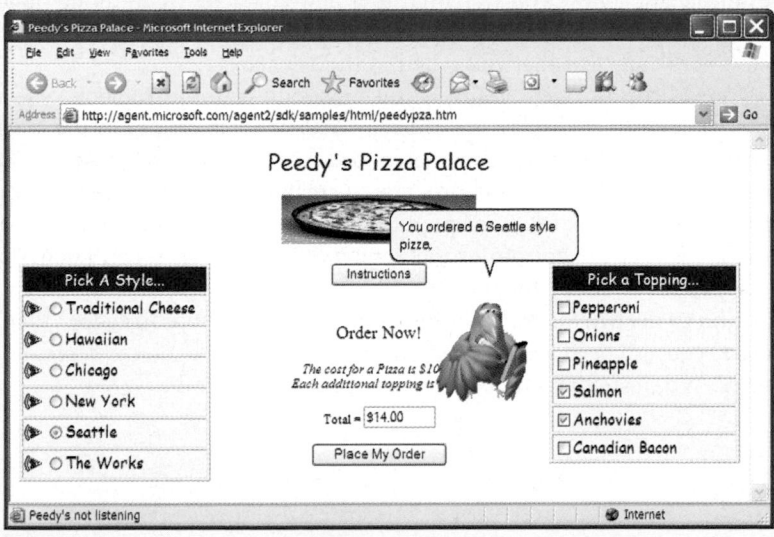

Fig. 17.35 | Peedy recounting the order.

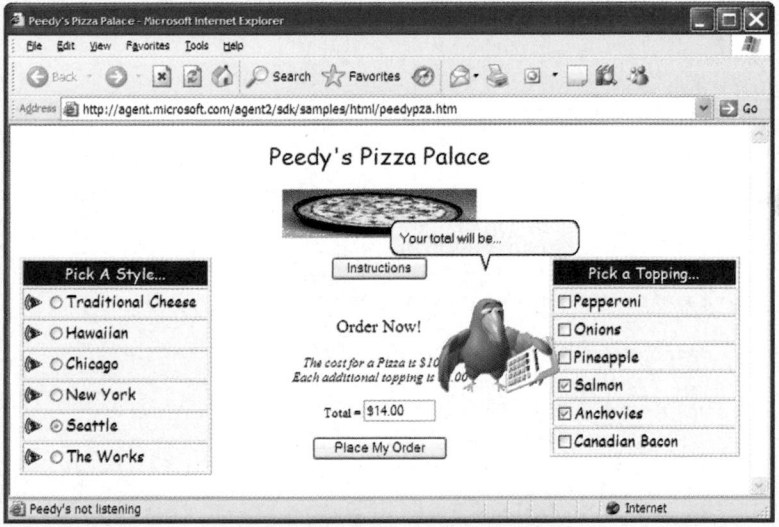

Fig. 17.36 | Peedy calculating the total.

The following example (Fig. 17.37) demonstrates how to build a simple application with the Microsoft Agent control. This application contains two drop-down lists from which the user can choose an Agent character and a character animation. When the user chooses from these lists, the chosen character appears and performs the selected animation. The application uses speech recognition and synthesis to control the character animations and speech—you can tell the character which animation to perform by pressing the *Scroll Lock* key, then speaking the animation name into a microphone.

The example also allows you to switch to a new character by speaking its name and creates a custom command, MoveToMouse. In addition, when you press the **Speak** Button, the characters speak any text that you typed in the TextBox.

To use the Microsoft Agent control, you must add it to the **Toolbox**. Select **Tools > Choose Toolbox Items...** to display the **Choose Toolbox Items** dialog. In the dialog, select the **COM Components** tab, then scroll down and select the **Microsoft Agent Control 2.0** option. When this option is selected properly, a small check mark appears in the box to the left of the option. Click **OK** to dismiss the dialog. The icon for the Microsoft Agent control now appears at the bottom of the **Toolbox**. Drag the **Microsoft Agent Control 2.0** control onto your Form and name the object mainAgent.

In addition to the Microsoft Agent object mainAgent (of type **AxAgent**) that manages the characters, you also need a variable of type **IAgentCtlCharacter** to represent the current character. We create this variable, named speaker, in line 11.

```vb
 1  ' Fig. 17.28: FrmAgent.vb
 2  ' Microsoft Agent demonstration.
 3  Imports System.IO
 4
 5  Public Class FrmAgent
 6     ' current agent object
 7     Private speaker As AgentObjects.IAgentCtlCharacter
 8
 9     ' parameterless constructor
10     Public Sub New()
11        InitializeComponent()
12
13        ' initialize the characters
14        Try
15           ' load characters into agent object
16           mainAgent.Characters.Load("Genie", _
17              "C:\windows\msagent\chars\Genie.acs")
18           mainAgent.Characters.Load("Merlin", _
19              "C:\windows\msagent\chars\Merlin.acs")
20           mainAgent.Characters.Load("Peedy", _
21              "C:\windows\msagent\chars\Peedy.acs")
22           mainAgent.Characters.Load("Robby", _
23              "C:\windows\msagent\chars\Robby.acs")
24
25           ' set current character to Genie and show him
26           speaker = mainAgent.Characters("Genie")
27           GetAnimationNames() ' obtain an animation name list
28           speaker.Show(0) ' display Genie
29           cboCharacter.SelectedText = "Genie"
30        Catch fileNotFound As FileNotFoundException
31           MessageBox.Show("Invalid character location", _
32              "Error", MessageBoxButtons.OK, MessageBoxIcon.Error)
33        End Try
34     End Sub ' New
35
```

Fig. 17.37 | Microsoft Agent demonstration. (Part 1 of 5.)

```vbnet
36        ' event handler for Speak Button
37        Private Sub btnSpeak_Click(ByVal sender As System.Object, _
38           ByVal e As System.EventArgs) Handles btnSpeak.Click
39           ' if TextBox is empty, have the character ask
40           ' user to type the words into the TextBox otherwise,
41           ' have the character say the words in the TextBox
42           If txtSpeech.Text = "" Then
43              speaker.Speak("Please, type the words you want me to speak", "")
44           Else
45              speaker.Speak(txtSpeech.Text, "")
46           End If
47        End Sub ' btnSpeak_Click
48
49        ' event handler for Agent control's ClickEvent
50        Private Sub mainAgent_ClickEvent(ByVal sender As Object, _
51           ByVal e As AxAgentObjects._AgentEvents_ClickEvent) _
52           Handles mainAgent.ClickEvent
53
54           speaker.Play("Confused")
55           speaker.Speak("Why are you poking me?", "")
56           speaker.Play("RestPose")
57        End Sub ' mainAgent_ClickEvent
58
59        ' ComboBox changed event, switch active agent character
60        Private Sub cboCharacter_SelectedIndexChanged( _
61           ByVal sender As System.Object, ByVal e As System.EventArgs) _
62           Handles cboCharacter.SelectedIndexChanged
63
64           ChangeCharacter(cboCharacter.Text)
65        End Sub ' cboCharacter_SelectedIndexChanged
66
67        ' utility method to change characters
68        Private Sub ChangeCharacter(ByVal name As String)
69           speaker.StopAll("Play")
70           speaker.Hide(0)
71           speaker = mainAgent.Characters(Name)
72
73           ' regenerate animation name list
74           GetAnimationNames()
75           speaker.Show(0)
76        End Sub ' ChangeCharacter
77
78        ' get animation names and store in ArrayList
79        Private Sub GetAnimationNames()
80           ' ensure thread safety
81           SyncLock (Me)
82              ' get animation names
83              Dim enumerator As IEnumerator = mainAgent.Characters( _
84                 speaker.Name).AnimationNames.GetEnumerator()
85
86              Dim voiceString As String
87
```

Fig. 17.37 | Microsoft Agent demonstration. (Part 2 of 5.)

```
 88              ' clear cboActions
 89              cboActions.Items.Clear()
 90              speaker.Commands.RemoveAll()
 91
 92              ' copy enumeration to ArrayList
 93              While enumerator.MoveNext()
 94                  ' remove underscores in speech string
 95                  voiceString = enumerator.Current.ToString()
 96                  voiceString = voiceString.Replace("_", "underscore")
 97
 98                  cboActions.Items.Add(enumerator.Current)
 99
100                  ' add all animations as voice enabled commands
101                  speaker.Commands.Add(enumerator.Current.ToString(), _
102                      enumerator.Current, voiceString, True, False)
103              End While
104
105              ' add custom command
106              speaker.Commands.Add("MoveToMouse", "MoveToMouse", _
107                  "MoveToMouse", True, True)
108          End SyncLock
109      End Sub ' GetAnimationNames
110
111      ' user selects new action
112      Private Sub cboActions_SelectedIndexChanged( _
113          ByVal sender As System.Object, ByVal e As System.EventArgs) _
114          Handles cboActions.SelectedIndexChanged
115
116          speaker.StopAll("Play")
117          speaker.Play(cboActions.Text)
118          speaker.Play("RestPose")
119      End Sub ' cboActions_SelectedIndexChanged
120
121      ' event handler for Agent commands
122      Private Sub mainAgent_Command(ByVal sender As Object, _
123          ByVal e As AxAgentObjects._AgentEvents_CommandEvent) _
124          Handles mainAgent.Command
125          ' get UserInput object
126          Dim command As AgentObjects.IAgentCtlUserInput = _
127              CType(e.userInput, AgentObjects.IAgentCtlUserInput)
128
129          ' change character if user speaks character name
130          If command.Voice = "Peedy" OrElse command.Voice = "Robby" OrElse _
131              command.Voice = "Merlin" OrElse command.Voice = "Genie" Then
132              ChangeCharacter(command.Voice)
133              Return
134          End If
135
136          ' send agent to mouse
137          If command.Voice = "MoveToMouse" Then
138              speaker.MoveTo( _
139                  Convert.ToInt16(Windows.Forms.Cursor.Position.X - 60), _
140                  Convert.ToInt16(Windows.Forms.Cursor.Position.Y - 60), 5)
```

Fig. 17.37 | Microsoft Agent demonstration. (Part 3 of 5)

```
141            Return
142        End If
143
144        ' play new animation
145        speaker.StopAll("Play")
146        speaker.Play(command.Name)
147    End Sub ' mainAgent_Command
148 End Class ' FrmAgent
```

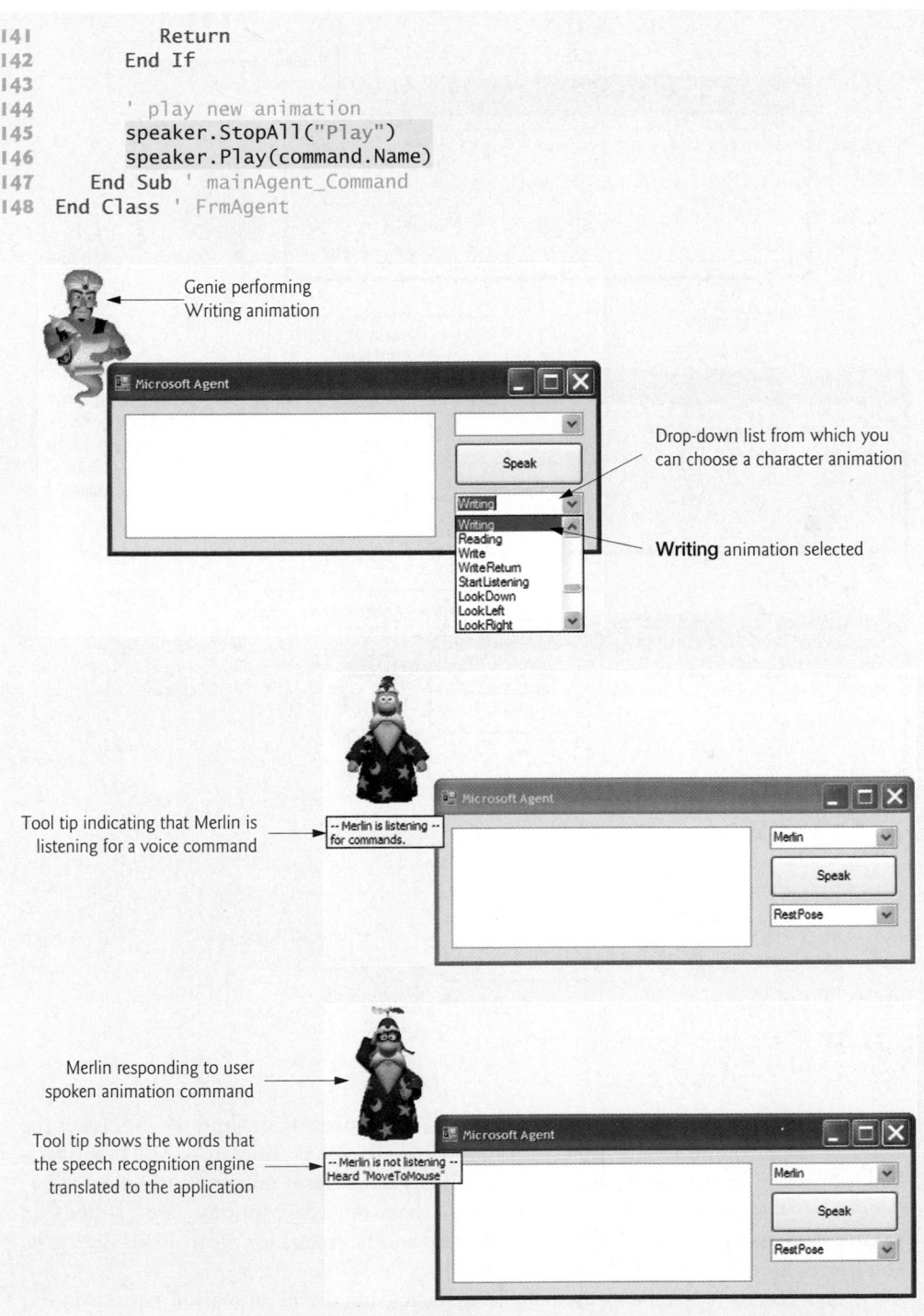

Genie performing Writing animation

Drop-down list from which you can choose a character animation

Writing animation selected

Tool tip indicating that Merlin is listening for a voice command

Merlin responding to user spoken animation command

Tool tip shows the words that the speech recognition engine translated to the application

Fig. 17.37 | Microsoft Agent demonstration. (Part 4 of 5.)

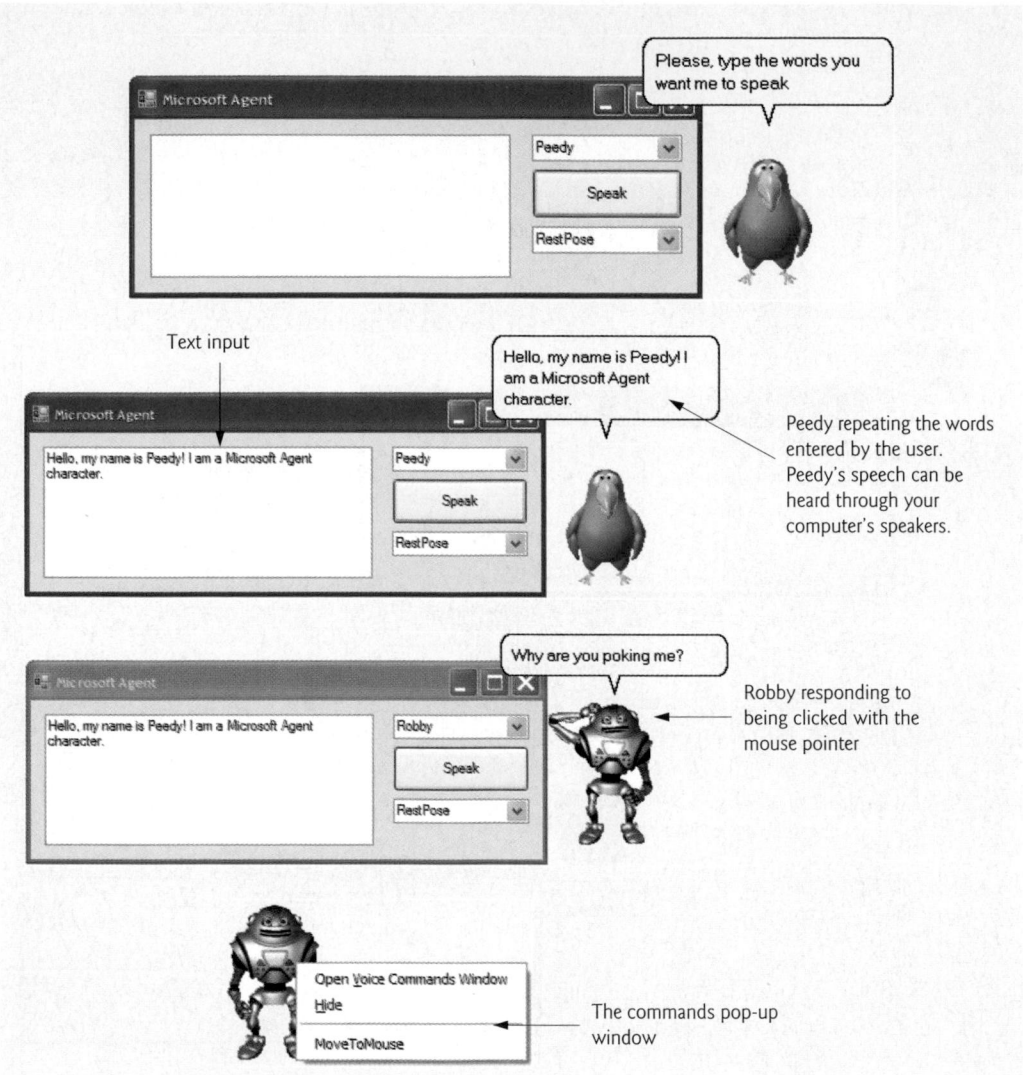

Fig. 17.37 | Microsoft Agent demonstration. (Part 5 of 5.)

When you execute this program, class `FrmAgent`'s constructor (lines 10–34) loads the character descriptions for the predefined animated characters (lines 16–23). If the specified location of the characters is incorrect, or if any character is missing, a `FileNotFound-Exception` is thrown. By default, the character descriptions are stored in `C:\Windows\msagent\chars`. If your system uses another name for the `Windows` directory, you'll need to modify the paths in lines 16–23.

Lines 26–28 set Genie as the default character, obtain all animation names via our utility method `GetAnimationNames` and call `IAgentCtlCharacter` method **Show** to display the character. We access characters through property **Characters** of `mainAgent`, which contains all the characters that have been loaded. We use the indexer of the `Characters` property to specify the name of the character we wish to load (Genie).

Responding to the Agent Control's `ClickEvent`

When a user clicks the character (i.e., pokes it with the mouse), event handler `mainAgent_ClickEvent` (lines 50–57) executes. First, `speaker` method **`Play`** plays an animation. This method accepts as an argument a `String` representing one of the predefined animations for the character (a list of animations for each character is available at the Microsoft Agent Web site; each character provides over 70 animations). In our example, the argument to `Play` is `"Confused"`—this animation is defined for all four characters, each of which expresses this emotion in a unique way. The character then speaks, `"Why are you poking me?"` via a call to method `Speak`. Finally, we play the `RestPose` animation, which returns the character to its neutral, resting pose.

Obtaining a Character's List of Animations and Defining Its Commands

The list of valid commands for a character is contained in property `Commands` of the `IAgentCtlCharacter` object (`speaker`, in this example). The commands for an Agent character can be viewed in the **Commands** pop-up window, which displays when the user right clicks an Agent character (the last screenshot in Fig. 17.37). Method `Add` of property `Commands` adds a new command to the command list. Method `Add` takes three `String` arguments and two `Boolean` arguments. The first `String` argument identifies the name of the command, which we use to identify the command programmatically. The second `String` defines the command name as it appears in the **Commands** pop-up window. The third `String` defines the voice input that triggers the command. The first `Boolean` specifies whether the command is active, and the second `Boolean` indicates whether the command is visible in the **Commands** pop-up window. A command is triggered when the user selects the command from the **Commands** pop-up window or speaks the voice input into a microphone. Command logic is handled in the `Command` event handler of the `AxAgent` control (`mainAgent`, in this example). In addition, Agent defines several global commands that have predefined functions (for example, speaking a character name causes that character to appear).

Method `GetAnimationNames` (lines 79–109) fills the `cboActions` ComboBox with the current character's animation listing and defines the valid commands that can be used with the character. The method contains a `SyncLock` block to prevent errors resulting from rapid character changes. The method uses an `IEnumerator` (lines 83–84) to obtain the current character's animations. Lines 89–90 clear the existing items in the ComboBox and the character's `Commands` property. Lines 93–103 iterate through all the items in the animation-name enumerator. For each animation, line 95 assigns the animation name to `String` `voiceString`. Line 96 removes any underscore characters (`_`) and replaces them with the `String` `"underscore"`; this changes the `String` so that a user can pronounce and employ it as a command activator. Line 98 adds the animation's name to the `cboActions` ComboBox. The `Add` method of the `Commands` property (lines 101–102) adds a new command to the current character. In this example, we add every animation name as a command. Each call to `Add` receives the animation name as both the name of the command and the string that appears in the **Commands** pop-up window. The third argument is the voice command, and the last two arguments enable the command but indicate that it is not available via the **Commands** pop-up window. Thus, the command can be activated only by voice input. Lines 106–107 create a new command, named MoveToMouse, which is visible in the **Commands** pop-up window.

Responding to Selections from the cboActions ComboBox

After the GetAnimationNames method has been called, the user can select a value from the cboActions ComboBox. Event handler cboActions_SelectedIndexChanged (lines 112–119) stops any current animation, then plays the animation that the user selects from the ComboBox, followed by the RestPose animation.

Speaking the Text Typed by the User

You can also type text in the TextBox and click **Speak**. This causes event handler btnSpeak_Click (line 37–47) to call speaker method Speak, supplying as an argument the text in speechTextBox. If the user clicks **Speak** without providing text, the character speaks, "Please, type the words you want me to speak".

Changing Characters

At any point in the program, the user can choose a different character from the cboCharacters ComboBox. When this happens, the SelectedIndexChanged event handler for cboCharacters (lines 60–65) executes. The event handler calls method ChangeCharacter (declared in lines 68–76) with the text in the cboCharacters as an argument. Method ChangeCharacter stops any current animation, then calls the Hide method of speaker (line 70) to remove the current character from view. Line 71 assigns the newly selected character to speaker, line 74 generates the character's animation names and commands, and line 75 displays the character via a call to method Show.

Responding to Commands

Each time a user presses the *Scroll Lock* key and speaks into a microphone or selects a command from the **Commands** pop-up window, event handler mainAgent_Command (lines 122–147) is called. This method receives an argument of type AxAgentObjects. _AgentEvents_CommandEvent, which contains a single property, userInput. This property returns an Object that can be converted to type AgentObjects.IAgentCtlUserInput. Lines 126–127 assigns the userInput object to an IAgentCtlUserInput object named command, which is used to identify the command, so that the program can respond appropriately. Lines 130–134 use method ChangeCharacter to change the current Agent character if the user speaks a character name. Microsoft Agent always will show a character when a user speaks its name; however, by controlling the character change, we can ensure that only one Agent character is displayed at a time. Lines 137–142 move the character to the current mouse location if the user invokes the MoveToMouse command. Agent method MoveTo takes *x*- and *y*-coordinate arguments and moves the character to the specified screen position, applying appropriate movement animations. For all other commands, we Play the command name as an animation in line 146.

17.15 Wrap-Up

This chapter began with an introduction to the .NET framework's drawing capabilities. We then presented more powerful drawing capabilities, such as changing the styles of the lines used to draw shapes and controlling the colors and patterns of filled shapes.

Next, you learned techniques for manipulating images and creating smooth animations. We discussed class Image, which can store and manipulate images of various formats. We explained how to combine the graphical rendering capabilities covered in the early sections of the chapter with those for image manipulation.

You also learned how to incorporate the Windows Media Player control in an application to play audio or video. Finally, we demonstrated Microsoft Agent—a technology for adding interactive animated characters to applications or Web pages—then showed how to incorporate Microsoft Agent in an application to add speech synthesis and recognition capabilities. In the next chapter, we discuss file-processing techniques that enable programs to store and retrieve data from persistent storage, such as your computer's hard disk. We also explore several types of streams included in Visual Studio .NET.

Summary

Section 17.1 Introduction
- The FCL contains many sophisticated drawing capabilities as part of namespace System.Drawing and the other namespaces that make up the .NET resource GDI+.
- GDI+ is an API that provides classes for creating two-dimensional vector graphics, manipulating fonts and inserting images.

Section 17.2 Drawing Classes and the Coordinate System
- Namespaces System.Drawing and System.Drawing.Drawing2D contain the most commonly used GDI+ components.
- Class Graphics contains methods used for drawing Strings, lines, rectangles and other shapes on a Control. These methods usually require a Pen or Brush object to render a shape. A Pen draws shape outlines; a Brush draws solid objects.
- The Color structure contains numerous Shared properties that set the colors of various graphical components, plus methods that allow users to create new colors.
- Class Font contains properties that define unique fonts.
- Class FontFamily contains methods for obtaining font information.
- GDI+'s coordinate system identifies points on the screen. The upper-left corner of a control has the coordinates (0, 0). The x-coordinate is the horizontal distance to the right from the upper-left corner. The y-coordinate is the vertical distance downward from the upper-left corner. The x-axis defines every horizontal coordinate, and the y-axis defines every vertical coordinate.
- Programmers position text and shapes on the screen by specifying their coordinates, which are measured in pixels—the smallest units of resolution on a display monitor.
- The Point structure represents the x-y coordinates of a point on a two-dimensional plane.
- The Rectangle structure defines the location, width and height of a rectangular shape.
- The Size structure represents the width and height of a shape.

Section 17.3 Graphics Contexts and Graphics Objects
- A graphics context represents a drawing surface that enables drawing on the screen. A Graphics object manages a graphics context by controlling how information is drawn.
- Every derived class of Form inherits a virtual OnPaint method in which most graphics operations are performed. The OnPaint method triggers the Control's Paint event. Instead of overriding the OnPaint method, you can add an event handler for the Paint event.

- You can force a call to `OnPaint` by calling a `Control`'s `Invalidate` method to indicate that the control should be refreshed.

- To draw on a control, first create a graphics object by invoking the control's `CreateGraphics` method, then use the `Graphics` object's methods to draw on the control.

Section 17.4 Color Control

- Structure `Color` defines methods and constants used to manipulate colors.

- Every color can be created from a combination of alpha, red, green and blue components (called ARGB values). All four ARGB values are integer values in the range 0–255.

- The alpha value determines the opacity of the color. The alpha value 0 represents a transparent color, and the value 255 represents an opaque color. Alpha values between 0 and 255 result in a weighted blending effect of the color's RGB value with that of any background color, causing a semitransparent effect.

- The first number in the RGB value defines the amount of red in the color, the second defines the amount of green and the third defines the amount of blue. The larger the value, the greater the amount of that particular color.

- Method `FromArgb` has three- and four-parameter versions (all argument values must be `Integer` between 0 and 255, inclusive). Both take `Integer` arguments specifying the amount of red, green and blue. The four-argument version also allows the user to specify the alpha component; the three-argument version defaults the alpha to 255 (opaque). Both methods return a `Color` object.

- A `Pen` is used to draw lines. Most drawing methods require a `Pen` object. The overloaded `Pen` constructors allow programmers to specify the colors and widths of the lines they wish to draw.

- The `System.Drawing` namespace provides a `Pens` class containing predefined `Pens`.

- Derived classes of `Brush` define objects that color the interiors of graphical shapes.

- The `SolidBrush` constructor takes a `Color` object representing the color to draw.

- `Fill` methods use `Brushes` to fill a space with a color, pattern or image.

- `Graphics` method `FillRectangle` draws a filled-in rectangle. `FillRectangle` takes as parameters a `Brush`, the *x*- and *y*-coordinates of the rectangle's upper-left corner and its width and height.

- There are several overloaded `DrawString` methods; one takes as arguments the `String` to display, the display `Font`, the `Brush` to use for drawing and the coordinates of the `String`'s first character.

- Class `Color`'s `Shared` method `FromName` creates a new `Color` object from a `String`.

- `ColorDialog` is a dialog box that allows users to select from a palette of available colors or to create custom colors. An application retrieves the user's selection via the `ColorDialog`'s `Color` property.

- Setting `ColorDialog`'s `FullOpen` property to `True` indicates that the dialog should display all available colors. When `FullOpen` is `False`, the dialog shows only color swatches.

Section 17.5 Font Control

- A `Font`'s `Size` property returns the font size as measured in design units, whereas property `SizeInPoints` returns the font size as measured in points. Design units allow the font size to be specified in one of several units of measurement, such as inches or millimeters.

- Some `Font` constructors accept a `GraphicsUnit` enumeration argument that allows you to specify the unit of measurement for the font size. Members of the `GraphicsUnit` enumeration include `Point` (1/72 inch), `Display` (1/75 inch), `Document` (1/300 inch), `Millimeter`, `Inch` and `Pixel`.

- Most `Font` constructors require a font name, the font size and the font style. The font style is specified with a constant from the `FontStyle` enumeration (`Bold`, `Italic`, `Regular`, `Strikeout` and `Underline`, or a combination of these). You can combine font styles with the | operator.

- You can determine a font's metrics, such as height, descent, ascent and leading.
- Class `FontFamily` defines characteristics common to a group of related fonts. Class `FontFamily` provides methods to determine the font metrics shared by members of a particular family.

Section 17.6 Drawing Lines, Rectangles and Ovals
- Methods that draw hollow shapes typically require as arguments a `Pen` and four `int`s. Methods that draw solid shapes typically require as arguments a `Brush` and four `int`s. The `int`s represent the bounding box of the shape.
- Methods `FillRectangle` and `DrawRectangle` draw rectangles. For each method, the first argument specifies the drawing object to use—for `FillRectangle` a `Brush` object and for `DrawRectangle` method a `Pen` object. The last four arguments represent the rectangle's bounding box.
- Method `DrawLine` takes a `Pen` and two pairs of `int`s that specify the start and end of a line. The method then draws a line, using the `Pen` object.
- Methods `FillEllipse` and `DrawEllipse` draw ellipse. For each method, the first argument specifies the drawing object to use. The last four arguments represent the ellipse's bounding box. The ellipse touches the midpoint of each of the four sides of the bounding rectangle.

Section 17.7 Drawing Arcs
- Arcs are portions of ellipses and are measured in degrees, beginning at a starting angle and continuing for a specified number of degrees called the arc angle. Arcs that sweep in a clockwise direction are measured in positive degrees. Arcs that sweep in a counterclockwise direction are measured in negative degrees.
- The `Point` constructor takes as arguments the *x*- and *y*-coordinates of the new point.
- The `Location` property determines the upper-left corner of the `Rectangle`.
- The `Size` property of a `Rectangle` determines the arc's height and width.

Section 17.8 Drawing Polygons and Polylines
- Polygons are multisided shapes. There are several `Graphics` methods used to draw polygons— `DrawLines` draws a series of connected points, `DrawPolygon` draws a closed polygon and `FillPolygon` draws a solid polygon.
- An `ArrayList` is similar to an array, but an `ArrayList` can grow dynamically to accommodate more elements.
- `ArrayList` method `ToArray` returns an array representing an `ArrayList`'s contents. The method takes a single argument that determine the type of the returned array.
- `ArrayList` method `Clear` erases the contents of an `ArrayList`.

Section 17.9 Advanced Graphics Capabilities
- The `Brush` hierarchy includes `HatchBrush`, `LinearGradientBrush`, `PathGradientBrush` and `TextureBrush`.
- Graphics features such as dashed lines, thick lines and the ability to fill shapes with various patterns represent just a few of the capabilities of the `System.Drawing` namespace.
- Class `LinearGradientBrush` (`System.Drawing.Drawing2D`) enables drawing with a color gradient. One of its constructors takes four arguments—a `Rectangle`, two `Color`s and a member of enumeration `LinearGradientMode`. All linear gradients are defined along a line that determines the gradient endpoints. This line can be specified either the starting and ending points or the diagonal of a rectangle. The `Rectangle` argument represents the endpoints of the linear gradient— the upper-left corner is the starting point and the bottom-right corner is the ending point. The

second and third arguments specify the colors the gradient will use. The last argument, a type from the enumeration `LinearGradientMode`, specifies the gradient's direction. `LinearGradient-Mode.ForwardDiagonal` creates a gradient from the upper-left to the lower-right corner.

- Class `Bitmap` can produce images in color and gray scale. `Graphics` method `FromImage` retrieves the `Graphics` object associated with an `Image`, which may be used to draw on the image.

- A `TextureBrush` is a brush that fills the interior of a shape with an image rather than a solid color. The `TextureBrush` constructor takes as an argument an image that defines its texture.

- Enumerations `DashCap` and `DashStyle` (`System.Drawing.Drawing2D` namespace) specify settings for a dashed line.

- The `DashCap` enumeration specifies the styles for the start and end of a dashed line.

- The `DashStyle` enumeration specifies the dash styles for a line.

- A `GraphicsPath` (`System.Drawing.Drawing2D` namespace) represents a general path. The class provides functionality for creating complex shapes from vector-based primitive graphics objects.

- `GraphicsPath` method `CloseFigure` attaches the final vector-graphic object endpoint to the initial starting point for the current figure by a straight line, then starts a new figure. Method `Start-Figure` begins a new figure within the path without closing the previous figure.

- `GraphicsPath` method `AddLine` appends a line to the shape.

- Method `TranslateTransform` sets the origin of a `Graphics` object.

- `Graphics` method `RotateTransform` enables you to rotate drawing positions around the origin.

- `Graphics` method `FillPath` draws a filled version of a `GraphicsPath`.

Section 17.10 Introduction to Multimedia
- Multimedia applications demand extraordinary computing power. Today's ultrafast processors make multimedia-based applications commonplace.

Section 17.11 Loading, Displaying and Scaling Images
- `Image` method `FromFile` loads an image from a file on disk.

- `Graphics` method `Clear` paints the entire `Form` in the current background color.

- `Graphics` method `DrawImage` receives as arguments the image to draw, the *x*- and *y*-coordinates of the image's upper-left corner, the width of the image and the height of the image. The image is scaled to fit the specified width and height.

Section 17.12 Animating a Series of Images
- Two-dimensional collision detection enables a program to detect whether two shapes overlap or whether a point is contained within a shape. `Rectangle` method `Contains` is useful for determining whether a point is inside a rectangular area.

- If a user working with graphics on a slow computer moves the mouse quickly, the application could leave behind artifacts (unintended visual abnormalities).

Section 17.13 Windows Media Player
- The Windows Media Player control enables an application to play video and sound in many multimedia formats, including MPEG, AVI, WAV and MIDI.

- To use the Windows Media Player control, you must add the control to the **Toolbox**. Select **Tools > Choose Toolbox Items...** to display the **Choose Toolbox Items** dialog. Click the **COM components** tab, then select the option **Windows Media Player**. Click the **OK** button to dismiss the dialog. The **Windows Media Player** control now appears at the bottom of the **Toolbox**.

- The Windows Media Player control provides several buttons that allow the user to play the current file, pause, stop, play the previous file, rewind, forward and play the next file. The control also includes a volume control and trackbars to select a specific position in the media file.

- The URL property of a Windows Media Player control object (type AxMediaPlayer) specifies the file that Windows Media Player is currently using.

Section 17.14 Microsoft Agent

- Microsoft Agent is a technology used to add interactive animated characters to Windows applications or Web pages. Microsoft Agent characters can speak and respond to user input via speech recognition and synthesis.

- There are four predefined characters—Genie (a genie), Merlin (a wizard), Peedy (a parrot) and Robby (a robot). Each has a unique set of animations.

- The control uses a speech-recognition engine to translate vocal sound input from a microphone to language that the computer understands. The Microsoft Agent control also uses a text-to-speech engine, which generates characters' spoken responses.

- Programmers can synchronize character animations with speech output to illustrate a point or to convey a character's mood.

- Agent characters also respond to input from the keyboard and mouse.

- You can issue spoken commands to an Agent character by pressing the *Scroll Lock* key, then speaking into a microphone.

- To use the Microsoft Agent control, you must add it to the **Toolbox**. Select **Tools > Choose Toolbox Items...** to display the **Choose Toolbox Items** dialog. In the dialog, select the **COM Components** tab, then select the **Microsoft Agent Control 2.0** option. Click **OK** to dismiss the dialog. The icon for the Microsoft Agent control now appears at the bottom of the **Toolbox**.

- A variable of type IAgentCtlCharacter represents the current Agent character in a program.

- By default, the character descriptions are stored in C:\Windows\msagent\chars.

- IAgentCtlCharacter method Show displays a character.

- AxAgent control property Characters contains all the characters that have been loaded. Use the indexer of the Characters property to specify the name of the character you want to access.

- When a user clicks a character, the AxAgent control's ClickEvent event handler executes.

- IAgentCtlCharacter method Play plays an animation. This method accepts as an argument a String representing one of the predefined animations for the character.

- The list of valid commands for a character is contained in property **Commands** of the IAgentCtlCharacter object. The commands for an Agent character can be viewed in the Commands pop-up window, which displays when the user right clicks an Agent character.

- Method Add of property Commands adds a new command to the command list. Method Add takes three String arguments and two Boolean arguments. The first String identifies the name of the command, which we use to identify the command programmatically. The second String defines the command name as it appears in the **Commands** pop-up window. The third String defines the voice input that triggers the command. The first Boolean specifies whether the command is active, and the second Boolean indicates whether the command is visible in the **Commands** pop-up window.

- A command is triggered when the user selects the command from the **Commands** pop-up window or speaks the voice input into a microphone. Command logic is handled in the Command event handler of the AxAgent control.

- IAgentCtlCharacter method Speak receives a String that the character is ro speak.

- IAgentCtlCharacter method MoveTo moves the character to the specified position on the screen.

Terminology

A property of structure `Color`
`AboutBox` method of `AxMediaPlayer`
`Add` method of class `ArrayList`
`AddLine` method of class `GraphicsPath`
animation
arc angle
ARGB values
artifact
`ArrayList` class
audio-video interleave (AVI)
`AxAgent` class
`AxMediaPlayer` class
B property of structure `Color`
bandwidth
`Bitmap` class
`Black` Shared property of structure `Color`
`Blue` Shared property of structure `Color`
`Bold` member of enumeration `FontStyle`
`Bold` property of class `Font`
bounding rectangle for an oval
`Brush` class
cast operation
`Characters` property of class `AxAgent`
`Clear` method of class `ArrayList`
closed polygon
`CloseFigure` method of class `GraphicsPath`
collision detection
color constants
color manipulation
`Color` methods and properties
`Color` property of class `ColorDialog`
`Color` structure
`ColorDialog` class
complex curve
connected lines
coordinate system
coordinates (0, 0)
`CreateGraphics` method of class `Graphics`
CType function
customizing the **Toolbox**
`Cyan` Shared property of structure `Color`
`DarkBlue` Shared property of structure `Color`
`DarkGray` Shared property of structure `Color`
`Dash` member of enumeration `DashStyle`
`DashCap` enumeration
`DashCap` property of class `Pen`
dashed lines
`DashStyle` enumeration
`DashStyle` property of class `Pen`

default font
degree
design units
`GetCellDescent` method of class `FontFamily`
`GetEmHeight` method of `FontFamily`
`GetLineSpacing` method of class `FontFamily`
`Display` member of enumeration `GraphicsUnit`
display monitor
`Document` member of enumeration `GraphicsUnit`
`DrawArc` method of class `Graphics`
`DrawEllipse` method of class `Graphics`
`DrawLine` method of class `Graphics`
`DrawLines` method of class `Graphics`
`DrawPie` method of class `Graphics`
`DrawPolygon` method of class `Graphics`
`DrawRectangle` method of class `Graphics`
`DrawString` method of class `Graphics`
event-driven process
fill a shape with color
fill shape
`FillEllipse` method of class `Graphics`
`FillPath` method of class `Graphics`
`FillPie` method of class `Graphics`
`FillPolygon` method of class `Graphics`
`FillRectangle` method of class `Graphics`
`FillRectangles` method of class `Graphics`
five-pointed star
font
font ascent
`Font` class
font control
font descent
font height
font leading
font manipulation
font metrics
font name
font size
font style
`Form` class
`FontFamily` class
`FontFamily` property of class `Font`
`FontStyle` enumeration
`ForwardDiagonal` member of enumeration `LinearGradientMode`
`FromArgb` method of structure `Color`
`FromImage` method of class `Graphics`
`FromFile` method of class `Image`

White Shared property of structure Color   *x*-coordinate
Windows Media Player   *y*-axis
Windows wave file format (WAV)   *y*-coordinate
x-axis   Yellow Shared property of structure Color

Self-Review Exercises

17.1 State whether each of the following is *true* or *false*. If *false*, explain why.
a) A Font object's size can be changed by setting its Size property.
b) In the GDI+ coordinate system, *x*-values increase from left to right.
c) Method FillPolygon draws a solid polygon with a specified Brush.
d) Method DrawArc allows negative angles.
e) Font property Size returns the size of the current font in centimeters.
f) Pixel coordinate (0, 0) is located at the exact center of the monitor.
g) A HatchBrush is used to draw lines.
h) A Color is defined by its alpha, red, green and violet content.
i) Every Control has an associated Graphics object.
j) Method OnPaint is inherited by every Form.

17.2 Fill in the blanks in each of the following statements:
a) Class _____ is used to draw lines of various colors and thicknesses.
b) Classes _____ and _____ define the fill for a shape in such a way that the fill gradually changes from one color to another.
c) Method _____ of class Graphics draws a line between two points.
d) ARGB is short for _____, _____, _____ and _____.
e) Font sizes usually are measured in units called _____.
f) Class _____ fills a shape using a pattern drawn in a Bitmap.
g) _____ _____ _____ allows an application to play multimedia files.
h) Class _____ defines a path consisting of lines and curves.
i) The FCL's drawing capabilities are part of the namespaces _____ and _____.
j) Method _____ loads an image from a disk into an Image object.

Answers to Self-Review Exercises

17.1 a) False. Size is a read-only property. b) True. c) True. d) True. e) False. It returns the size of the current Font in design units. f) False. The coordinate (0,0) corresponds to the upper-left corner of a GUI component on which drawing occurs. g) False. A Pen is used to draw lines, a Hatch-Brush fills a shape with a hatch pattern. h) False. A color is defined by its alpha, red, green and blue content. i) True. j) True.

17.2 a) Pen. b) LinearGradientBrush, PathGradientBrush. c) DrawLine. d) alpha, red, green, blue. e) points. f) TextureBrush. g) Windows Media Player h) GraphicsPath i) System.Drawing, System.Drawing.Drawing2D. j) FromFile.

Exercises

17.3 Write a program that draws eight concentric circles. The circles should be separated from one another by 10 pixels. Use the DrawArc method.

17.4 Write a program that draws 100 lines with random lengths, positions, thicknesses and colors.

17.5 Write a program that draws a tetrahedron (a pyramid). Use class GraphicsPath and method DrawPath.

17.6 Write a program that allows the user to draw "free-hand" images with the mouse in a PictureBox. Allow the user to change the drawing color and width of the pen. Provide a button that allows the user to clear the PictureBox.

17.7 Write a program that repeatedly flashes an image on the screen. Do this by interspersing the image with a plain background-color image.

17.8 (*Eight Queens*) A puzzler for chess buffs is the Eight Queens problem. Simply stated: Is it possible to place eight queens on an empty chessboard so that no queen is "attacking" any other (i.e., so that no two queens are in the same row, in the same column or along the same diagonal)?

Create a GUI that allows the user to drag-and-drop each queen on the board. Use the graphical features of Fig. 17.26. Provide eight queen images to the right of the board (Fig. 17.38) that the user can drag-and-drop on the board. When a queen is dropped on the board, its corresponding image to the right should not be visible. If a queen is in conflict with another queen when placed on the board, display a message box and remove that queen from the board.

Fig. 17.38 | GUI for the Eight Queens exercise.

18

Files and Streams

OBJECTIVES

In this chapter you will learn:

- To create, read, write and update files.
- The .NET framework streams class hierarchy.
- To use classes **File** and **Directory** to obtain information about files and directories on your computer.
- To become familiar with sequential-access file processing.
- To use classes **FileStream**, **StreamReader** and **StreamWriter** to read text from and write text to files.
- To use classes **FileStream** and **BinaryFormatter** to read objects from and write objects to files.

Consciousness ... does not appear to itself chopped up in bits. ... A "river" or a "stream" are the metaphors by which it is most naturally described.
—William James

I read part of it all the way through.
—Samuel Goldwyn

I can only assume that a "Do Not File" document is filed in a "Do Not File" file.
—Senator Frank Church
Senate Intelligence
Subcommittee Hearing, 1975

18.1 Introduction

Variables and arrays offer only temporary storage of data—the data is lost when a local variable "goes out of scope" or when the program terminates. By contrast, files (and databases, which we cover in Chapter 20, Database, SQL and ADO.NET) are used for long-term retention of large amounts of data, even after the program that created the data terminates. Data maintained in files is often called **persistent data**. Computers store files on **secondary storage devices**, such as magnetic disks, optical disks and magnetic tapes. In this chapter, we explain how to create, update and process data files.

We begin with an overview of the data hierarchy from bits to files. Next, we overview some of the FCL's file-processing classes. We then present two examples that show how you can determine information about the files and directories on your computer. The remainder of the chapter shows how to write to and read from text files that are human readable and binary files that store entire objects in binary format.

18.2 Data Hierarchy

Ultimately, all data items that computers process are reduced to combinations of 0s and 1s. This occurs because it is simple and economical to build electronic devices that can assume two stable states—one state represents 0 and the other represents 1. It is remarkable that the impressive functions performed by computers involve only the most fundamental manipulations of 0s and 1s!

The smallest data item that computers support is called a **bit** (short for "binary digit"—a digit that can assume one of two values). Each data item, or bit, can assume either the value 0 or the value 1. Computer circuitry performs various simple bit manipulations, such as examining the value of a bit, setting the value of a bit and reversing a bit (from 1 to 0 or from 0 to 1).

Programming with data in the low-level form of bits is cumbersome. It is preferable to program with data in forms such as **decimal digits** (i.e., 0, 1, 2, 3, 4, 5, 6, 7, 8 and 9), **letters** (i.e., the uppercase letters A–Z and the lowercase letters a–z) and **special symbols** (i.e., $, @, %, &, *, (,), -, +, ", :, ?, / and many others). Digits, letters and special symbols are referred to as **characters**. The set of all characters used to write programs and represent data items on a particular computer is called that computer's **character set**. Because computers can process only 0s and 1s, every character in a computer's character set is represented as a pattern of 0s and 1s. **Bytes** are composed of eight bits. Visual Basic uses the **Unicode character set** (www.unicode.org) in which each character is composed of two bytes. Programmers create programs and data items with characters; computers manipulate and process these characters as patterns of bits.

Just as characters are composed of bits, fields are composed of characters. A **field** is a group of characters that conveys meaning. For example, a field consisting of uppercase and lowercase letters can represent a person's name.

Data items processed by computers form a **data hierarchy** (Fig. 18.1), in which data items become larger and more complex in structure as we progress up the hierarchy from bits to characters to fields to larger data aggregates.

Typically, a **record** (which can be represented as a Class) is composed of several related fields. In a payroll system, for example, a record for a particular employee might include the following fields:

1. Employee identification number

2. Name

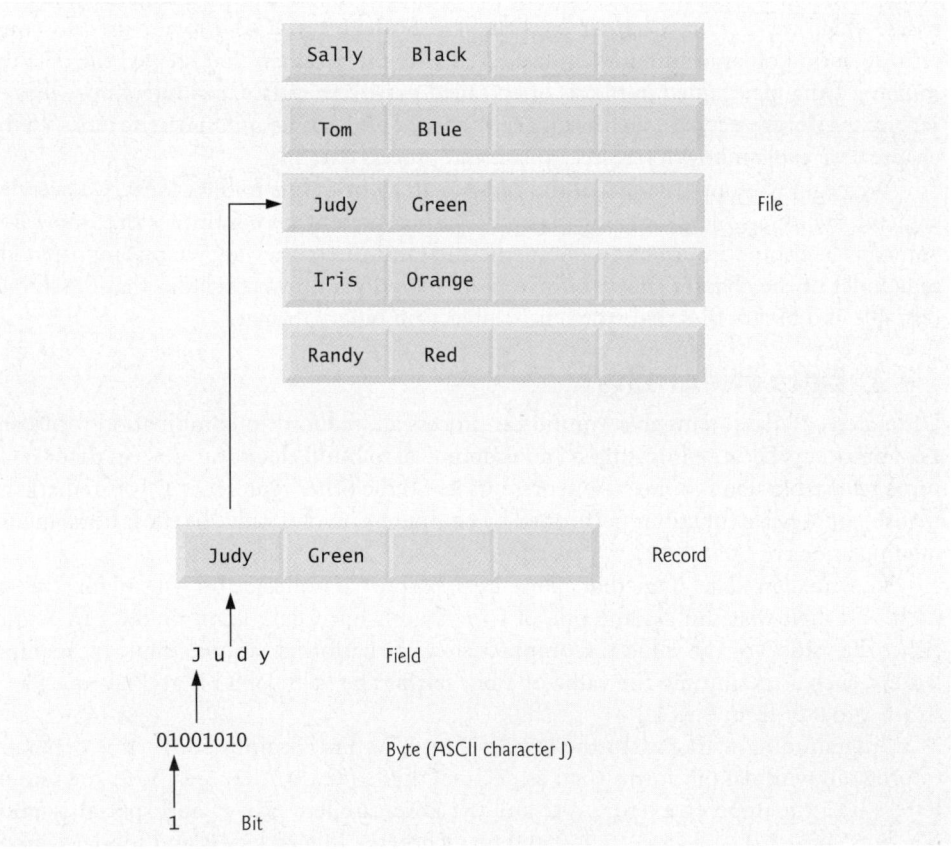

Fig. 18.1 | Data hierarchy.

3. Address

4. Hourly pay rate

5. Number of exemptions claimed

6. Year-to-date earnings

7. Amount of taxes withheld

In the preceding example, each field is associated with the same employee. A data file is a group of related records.[1] A company's payroll file normally contains one record for each employee. A payroll file for a small company might contain only 22 records, whereas one for a large company might contain 100,000 records. Companies typically have many files, some containing millions, billions or even trillions of characters of information.

To facilitate the retrieval of specific records from a file, at least one field in each record is chosen as a **record key**, which identifies a record as belonging to a particular person or entity and distinguishes that record from all others. For example, in a payroll record, the employee identification number normally would be the record key.

There are many ways to organize records in a file. A common organization is called a **sequential file,** in which records typically are stored in order by a record-key field. In a payroll file, records usually are placed in order by employee identification number. The first employee record in the file contains the lowest employee identification number, and subsequent records contain increasingly higher ones.

Most businesses use many different files to store data. For example, a company might have payroll files, accounts-receivable files (listing money due from clients), accounts-payable files (listing money due to suppliers), inventory files (listing facts about all the items handled by the business) and many other files. Related files often are stored in a **database**. A collection of programs designed to create and manage databases is called a **database management system (DBMS)**. We discuss databases in Chapter 20.

18.3 Files and Streams

Visual Basic views a file as a sequential **stream** of bytes (Fig. 18.2). Depending on the operating system, each file ends either with an **end-of-file marker** or at a specific byte number that is recorded in a system-maintained administrative data structure. For example, the Windows keeps track of the number of bytes in a file. When you open a file from a Visual Basic program, an object is created and a stream is associated with the object. When a program executes, the runtime environment creates three stream objects that are accessible via properties `Console.Out`, `Console.In` and `Console.Error`, respectively. These objects facilitate communication between a program and a particular file or device. `Console.In` refers to the **standard input stream object**, which enables a program to input data from the keyboard. `Console.Out` refers to the **standard output stream object**, which enables a program to output data to the screen. `Console.Error` refers to the **standard error stream object**, which enables a program to output error messages to the screen. We have been using `Console.Out` and `Console.In` in our console applications—`Console` methods `Write` and

---

1. Generally, a file can contain arbitrary data in arbitrary formats. In some operating systems, a file is viewed as nothing more than a collection of bytes, and any organization of the bytes in a file (such as organizing the data into records) is a view created by the application programmer.

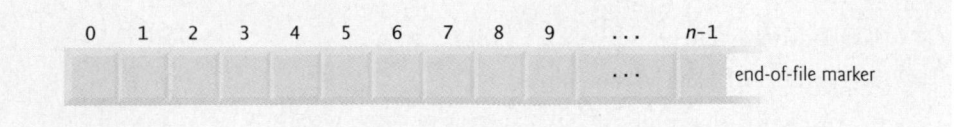

Fig. 18.2 | Visual Basic's view of an n-byte file.

`WriteLine` use `Console.Out` to perform output, and `Console` methods `Read` and `ReadLine` use `Console.In` to perform input.

There are many file-processing classes in the FCL. The `System.IO` namespace includes stream classes such as `StreamReader` (for text input from a file), `StreamWriter` (for text output to a file) and `FileStream` (for both input from and output to a file). These stream classes inherit from the `MustInherit` classes `TextReader`, `TextWriter` and `Stream`, respectively. Actually, properties `Console.In` and `Console.Out` are of type `TextReader` and `TextWriter`, respectively. The system creates objects of `TextReader` and `TextWriter` classes to initialize `Console` properties `Console.In` and `Console.Out`.

`MustInherit` class `Stream` provides functionality for representing streams that are made of bytes. Classes `FileStream`, `MemoryStream` and `BufferedStream` (all in namespace `System.IO`) inherit from class `Stream`. Class `FileStream` can be used to write data to and read data from files. Class `MemoryStream` enables the transfer of data directly to and from memory—this is much faster than reading from and writing to external devices. Class `BufferedStream` uses buffering to transfer data to or from a stream. Buffering is an I/O performance-enhancement technique, in which each output operation is directed to a region in memory, called a buffer, that is large enough to hold the data from many output operations. Then actual transfer to the output device is performed more efficiently in one large physical output operation each time the buffer fills. The output operations directed to the output buffer in memory are often called logical output operations. Buffering can also be used to speed input operations by initially reading more data than is required into a buffer, so that subsequent reads get data from memory rather than an external device.

In this chapter, we use key stream classes to implement file processing programs that create and manipulate sequential-access files. In Chapter 23, Networking: Streams-Based Sockets and Datagrams, we use stream classes to implement networking applications.

18.4 Classes `File` and `Directory`

Information is stored in files, which are organized in directories. Classes `File` and `Directory` enable programs to manipulate files and directories on disk. Class `File` can determine information about files and can be used to open files for reading or writing. We discuss techniques for writing to and reading from files in subsequent sections.

Figure 18.3 lists several of class `File`'s `Shared` methods for manipulating and determining information about files. We demonstrate several of these methods in Fig. 18.5.

Class `Directory` provides capabilities for manipulating directories. Figure 18.4 lists some of class `Directory`'s `Shared` methods for directory manipulation. Figure 18.5 demonstrates several of these methods, as well. The `DirectoryInfo` object returned by method `CreateDirectory` contains information about a directory. Much of the information contained in class `DirectoryInfo` also can be accessed via the methods of class `Directory`.

File class Shared methods and descriptions	
AppendText	Returns a StreamWriter that appends text to an existing file or creates a file if one does not exist.
Copy	Copies a file to a new file.
Create	Creates a file and returns its associated FileStream.
CreateText	Creates a text file and returns its associated StreamWriter.
Delete	Deletes the specified file.
Exists	Returns True if the specified file exists and False otherwise.
GetCreationTime	Returns a DateTime object representing when the file was created.
GetLastAccessTime	Returns a DateTime object representing when the file was last accessed.
GetLastWriteTime	Returns a DateTime object representing when the file was last modified.
Move	Moves the specified file to a specified location.
Open	Returns a FileStream associated with the specified file and equipped with the specified read/write permissions.
OpenRead	Returns a read-only FileStream associated with the specified file.
OpenText	Returns a StreamReader associated with the specified file.
OpenWrite	Returns a read/write FileStream associated with the specified file.

Fig. 18.3 | File class Shared methods (partial list).

Directory class Shared methods and descriptions	
CreateDirectory	Creates a directory and returns its associated DirectoryInfo object.
Delete	Deletes the specified directory.
Exists	Returns True if the specified directory exists and False otherwise.
GetDirectories	Returns a String array containing the names of the subdirectories in the specified directory.
GetFiles	Returns a String array containing the names of the files in the specified directory.
GetCreationTime	Returns a DateTime object representing when the directory was created.
GetLastAccessTime	Returns a DateTime object representing when the directory was last accessed.

Fig. 18.4 | Directory class Shared methods. (Part 1 of 2.)

Directory class Shared methods and descriptions	
GetLastWriteTime	Returns a DateTime object representing when items were last written to the directory.
Move	Moves the specified directory to a specified location.

Fig. 18.4 | Directory class Shared methods. (Part 2 of 2.)

Demonstrating Classes *File* and *Directory*

Class FrmFileTest (Fig. 18.5) uses File and Directory methods to access file and directory information. This Form contains the control txtInput, in which the user enters a file or directory name. For each key that the user presses while typing in the TextBox, the program calls event handler txtInput_KeyDown (lines 8–58). If the user presses the *Enter* key (line 12), this method displays either the file's or the directory's contents, depending on the text the user input. (If the user does not press the *Enter* key, this method returns without displaying any content.) Line 19 uses File method Exists to determine whether the user-specified text is the name of an existing file. If so, line 22 invokes Private method GetInformation (lines 61–80), which calls File methods GetCreationTime (line 69), GetLastWriteTime (line 73) and GetLastAccessTime (line 77) to access file information. When method GetInformation returns, line 27 instantiates a StreamReader for reading text from the file. The StreamReader constructor takes as an argument a String containing the name of the file to open. Line 28 calls StreamReader method ReadToEnd to read the entire contents of the file as a String, then appends the String to txtOutput.

```vb
1   ' Fig 18.5: FrmFileTest.vb
2   ' Using classes File and Directory.
3   Imports System.IO
4
5   ' displays contents of files and directories
6   Public Class FrmFileTest
7      ' invoked when user presses key
8      Private Sub txtInput_KeyDown(ByVal sender As System.Object, _
9         ByVal e As System.Windows.Forms.KeyEventArgs) _
10        Handles txtInput.KeyDown
11        ' determine whether user pressed Enter key
12        If e.KeyCode = Keys.Enter Then
13           Dim fileName As String ' name of file or directory
14
15           ' get user-specified file or directory
16           fileName = txtInput.Text
17
18           ' determine whether fileName is a file
19           If File.Exists(fileName) Then
20              ' get file's creation date,
21              ' modification date, etc.
22              txtOutput.Text = GetInformation(fileName)
```

Fig. 18.5 | Testing classes File and Directory. (Part 1 of 3.)

```
23
24                  ' display file contents through StreamReader
25              Try
26                  ' obtain reader and file contents
27                  Dim stream As New StreamReader(fileName)
28                  txtOutput.Text &= stream.ReadToEnd()
29                  ' handle exception if StreamReader is unavailable
30              Catch ex As System.IO.IOException
31                  MessageBox.Show("Error reading from file", "File Error", _
32                      MessageBoxButtons.OK, MessageBoxIcon.Error)
33              End Try
34              ' determine whether fileName is a directory
35          ElseIf Directory.Exists(fileName) Then
36              Dim directoryList() As String ' array for directories
37
38              ' get directory's creation date,
39              ' modification date, etc.
40              txtOutput.Text = GetInformation(fileName)
41
42              ' obtain file/directory list of specified directory
43              directoryList = Directory.GetDirectories(fileName)
44
45              txtOutput.Text &= vbCrLf & vbCrLf & _
46                  "Directory contents:" & vbCrLf
47
48              ' output directoryList contents
49              For Each directoryName As String In directoryList
50                  txtOutput.Text &= directoryName & vbCrLf
51              Next
52          Else
53              ' notify user that neither file nor directory exists
54              MessageBox.Show(txtInput.Text & " does not exist", _
55                  "File Error", MessageBoxButtons.OK, MessageBoxIcon.Error)
56          End If
57      End If
58  End Sub ' txtInput_KeyDown
59
60  ' get information on file or directory
61  Private Function GetInformation(ByVal fileName As String) As String
62      Dim information As String
63
64      ' output that file or directory exists
65      information = fileName & " exists" & vbCrLf & vbCrLf
66
67      ' output when file or directory was created
68      information &= "Created: " & _
69          File.GetCreationTime(fileName) & vbCrLf
70
71      ' output when file or directory was last modified
72      information &= "Last modified: " & _
73          File.GetLastWriteTime(fileName) & vbCrLf
74
```

Fig. 18.5 | Testing classes File and Directory. (Part 2 of 3.)

```
75          ' output when file or directory was last accessed
76          information &= "Last accessed: " & _
77             File.GetLastAccessTime(fileName) & vbCrLf & vbCrLf
78
79          Return information
80      End Function ' GetInformation
81  End Class ' FrmFileTest
```

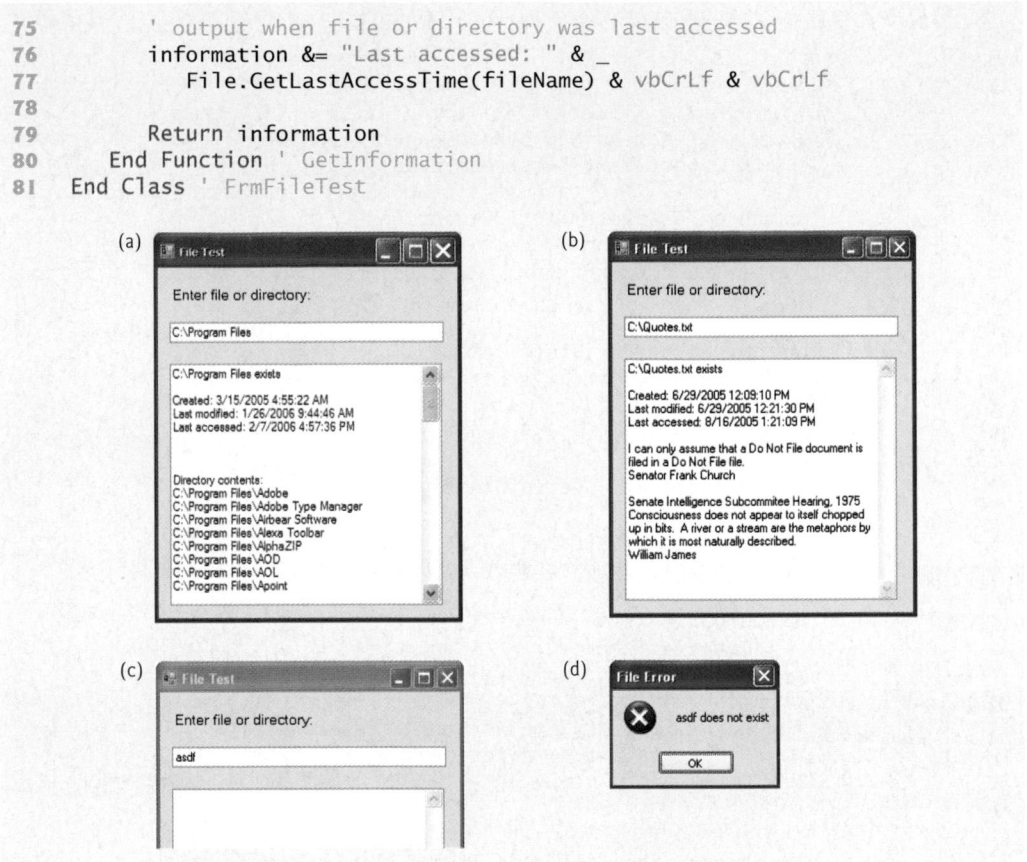

Fig. 18.5 | Testing classes `File` and `Directory`. (Part 3 of 3.)

If line 19 determines that the user-specified text is not a file, line 35 determines whether it is a directory using `Directory` method **Exists**. If the user specified an existing directory, line 40 invokes method `GetInformation` to access the directory information. Line 43 calls `Directory` method **GetDirectories** to obtain a `String` array containing the names of subdirectories in the specified directory. Lines 49–51 display each element in the `String` array. If line 35 determines that the user-specified text is not a directory name, lines 54–55 notify the user (via a `MessageBox`) that the name the user entered does not exist as a file or directory.

Finding Directories with Regular Expressions
We now consider another example that uses the FCL's file- and directory-manipulation capabilities. Class `FrmFileSearch` (Fig. 18.6) uses classes `File` and `Directory`, and regular-expression capabilities, to report the number of files of each file type that exist in the specified directory path. The program also serves as a "clean-up" utility—when a file that has the `.bak` filename extension (i.e., a backup file) is encountered, the program displays a `MessageBox` asking the user whether that file should be removed, then responds appropriately to the user's input.

When the user presses the *Enter* key or clicks the **Search Directory** button, the program invokes method btnSearch_Click (lines 26–58), which searches recursively through the directory path that the user provides. If the user inputs text in the TextBox, line 31 calls Directory method Exists to determine whether that text is a valid directory path and name. If not, lines 39–40 notify the user of the error.

If the user specifies a valid directory, line 48 passes the directory name as an argument to Private method SearchDirectory (lines 61–134). This method locates files that match the regular expression defined in lines 67–68. This regular expression matches any sequence of numbers or letters followed by a period and one or more letters. Note the substring of format (?<extension>\w+) in the argument to the Regex constructor (line 68). This indicates that the part of the string that matches \w+ (i.e., the filename extension that appears after a period in the file name) should be placed in the regular-expression variable named extension. This variable's value is retrieved later from Match object matchResult to obtain the filename extension so that we can summarize the types of files in the directory.

```vb
1    ' Fig 18.6: FrmFileSearch.vb
2    ' Using regular expressions to determine file types.
3    Imports System.IO
4    Imports System.Text.RegularExpressions
5    Imports System.Collections.Specialized
6
7    Public Class FrmFileSearch
8       Dim currentDirectory As String = Directory.GetCurrentDirectory()
9       Dim directoryList() As String ' subdirectories
10      Dim fileArray() As String
11
12      ' store extensions found and number found
13      Dim found As New NameValueCollection()
14
15      ' invoked when user types in text box
16      Private Sub txtInput_KeyDown(ByVal sender As System.Object, _
17         ByVal e As System.Windows.Forms.KeyEventArgs) _
18         Handles txtInput.KeyDown
19         ' determine whether user pressed Enter
20         If e.KeyCode = Keys.Enter Then
21            btnSearch_Click(sender, e)
22         End If
23      End Sub ' txtInput_KeyDown
24
25      ' invoked when user clicks "Search Directory" button
26      Private Sub btnSearch_Click(ByVal sender As System.Object, _
27         ByVal e As System.EventArgs) Handles btnSearch.Click
28         ' check for user input; default is current directory
29         If txtInput.Text <> "" Then
30            ' verify that user input is valid directory name
31            If Directory.Exists(txtInput.Text) Then
32               currentDirectory = txtInput.Text
```

Fig. 18.6 | Regular expression used to determine file types. (Part 1 of 4.)

```
33
34              ' reset input text box and update display
35              lblDirectory.Text = _
36                 "Current Directory:" & vbCrLf & currentDirectory
37           Else
38              ' show error if user does not specify valid directory
39              MessageBox.Show("Invalid Directory", "Error", _
40                 MessageBoxButtons.OK, MessageBoxIcon.Error)
41           End If
42        End If
43
44        ' clear text boxes
45        txtInput.Text = ""
46        txtOutput.Text = ""
47
48        SearchDirectory(currentDirectory) ' search directory
49
50        ' summarize and print results
51        For Each current As String In found
52           txtOutput.Text &= "* Found " & found(current) & _
53              " " & current & " files." & vbCrLf
54        Next current
55
56        ' clear output for new search
57        found.Clear()
58     End Sub ' btnSearch_Click
59
60     ' search directory using regular expression
61     Private Sub SearchDirectory(ByVal currentDirectory As String)
62        ' for file name without directory path
63        Try
64           Dim fileName As String = ""
65
66           ' regular expression for extensions matching pattern
67           Dim regularExpression As New Regex( _
68              "[a-zA-Z0-9]+\.(?<extension>\w+)")
69
70           ' stores regular-expression match result
71           Dim matchResult As Match
72
73           Dim fileExtension As String ' holds file extensions
74
75           ' number of files with given extension in directory
76           Dim extensionCount As Integer
77
78           ' get directories
79           directoryList = Directory.GetDirectories(currentDirectory)
80
81           ' get list of files in current directory
82           fileArray = Directory.GetFiles(currentDirectory)
83
```

Fig. 18.6 | Regular expression used to determine file types. (Part 2 of 4.)

```vbnet
84               ' iterate through list of files
85              For Each myFile As String In fileArray
86                  ' remove directory path from file name
87                  fileName = myFile.Substring(myFile.LastIndexOf("\") + 1)
88
89                  ' obtain result for regular-expression search
90                  matchResult = regularExpression.Match(fileName)
91
92                  ' check for match
93                  If matchResult.Success Then
94                      fileExtension = matchResult.Result("${extension}")
95                  Else
96                      fileExtension = "[no extension]"
97                  End If
98
99                  ' store value from container
100                 If found(fileExtension) Is Nothing Then
101                     found.Add(fileExtension, "1")
102                 Else
103                     extensionCount = Int32.Parse(found(fileExtension)) + 1
104                     found(fileExtension) = extensionCount.ToString()
105                 End If
106
107                 ' search for backup( .bak ) files
108                 If fileExtension = "bak" Then
109                     ' prompt user to delete ( .bak ) file
110                     Dim result As DialogResult = MessageBox.Show( _
111                         "Found backup file " & fileName & ". Delete?", _
112                         "Delete Backup", MessageBoxButtons.YesNo, _
113                         MessageBoxIcon.Question)
114
115                     ' delete file if user clicked 'yes'
116                     If result = Windows.Forms.DialogResult.Yes Then
117                         File.Delete(myFile)
118                         extensionCount = Int32.Parse(found("bak")) - 1
119                         found("bak") = extensionCount.ToString()
120                     End If
121                 End If
122             Next myFile
123
124             ' recursive call to search files in subdirectory
125             For Each myDirectory As String In directoryList
126                 SearchDirectory(myDirectory)
127             Next myDirectory
128             ' handle exception if files have unauthorized access
129         Catch ex As UnauthorizedAccessException
130             MessageBox.Show("Some files may not be visible" & _
131                 " due to permission settings", "Warning", _
132                 MessageBoxButtons.OK, MessageBoxIcon.Information)
133         End Try
134     End Sub ' SearchDirectory
135 End Class ' FrmFileSearch
```

Fig. 18.6 | Regular expression used to determine file types. (Part 3 of 4.)

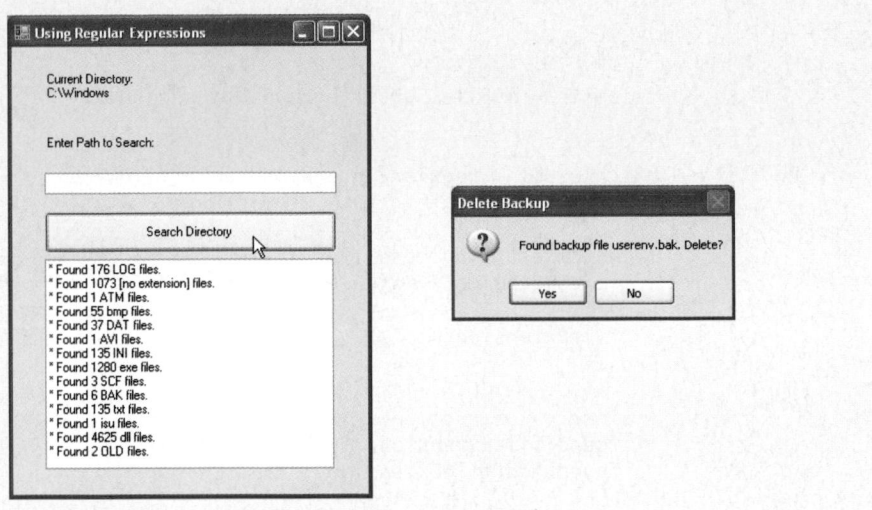

Fig. 18.6 | Regular expression used to determine file types. (Part 4 of 4.)

Line 79 calls `Directory` method `GetDirectories` to retrieve the names of all the subdirectories that belong to the current directory. Line 82 calls `Directory` method `GetFiles` to store in `String` array `fileArray` the names of the files in the current directory. The loop in lines 85–122 searches for all files with extension `.bak`. The loop at lines 125–127 then calls `SearchDirectory` recursively (line 126) for each subdirectory in the current directory. Line 87 eliminates the directory path, so the program can test only the file name when using the regular expression. Line 90 uses `Regex` method `Match` to match the regular expression with the file name, then assigns the result to `Match` object `matchResult`. If the match is successful, line 94 uses `Match` method `Result` to assign to `fileExtension` the value of the regular-expression variable `extension` from object `matchResult`. If the match is unsuccessful, line 96 sets `fileExtension` to `"[no extension]"`.

Class `FrmFileSearch` uses an instance of class `NameValueCollection` (declared in line 13) to store each filename-extension type and the number of files for each type. A `NameValueCollection` (namespace `System.Collections.Specialized`) contains a collection of key-value pairs of `Strings`, and provides method `Add` to add a key-value pair to the collection. The indexer for this class can index according to the order in which the items were added or according to the keys. Line 100 uses `NameValueCollection` `found` to determine whether this is the first occurrence of the filename extension (the expression returns `Nothing` if the collection does not contain a key-value pair for the specified `fileExtension`). If this is the first occurrence, line 101 adds that extension to `found` as a key with the value 1. Otherwise, line 103 increments the value associated with the extension in `found` to indicate another occurrence of the file extension, and line 104 assigns the new value to the key-value pair.

Line 108 determines whether `fileExtension` equals "bak"—that is, whether the file is a backup file. If so, lines 110–113 prompt the user to indicate whether the file should be deleted; if the user clicks **Yes** (line 116), lines 117–119 delete the file and decrement the value for the "bak" file type in `found`.

Lines 125–127 call method SearchDirectory for each subdirectory. Using recursion, we ensure that the program performs the same logic for finding .bak files in each subdirectory. After each subdirectory has been checked for .bak files, method SearchDirectory completes, and lines 51–54 display the results.

18.5 Creating a Sequential-Access Text File

Visual Basic imposes no structure on files. Thus, the concept of a "record" does not exist in Visual Basic files. This means that you must structure files to meet the requirements of your applications. In the next few examples, we use text and special characters to organize our own concept of a "record."

Class *FrmBankUI*

The following examples demonstrate file processing in a bank-account maintenance application. These programs have similar user interfaces, so we used the Visual Studio Form designer to create reusable base class FrmBankUI (Fig. 18.7), which encapsulates the common GUI components (see the screen capture in Fig. 18.7). Class FrmBankUI contains four Labels and four TextBoxes. Method ClearTextBoxes (lines 17–27) clears the TextBoxes' contents. Method SetTextBoxValues (lines 30–49) sets the text in the TextBoxes. Method GetTextBoxValues (lines 52–66) gets the values from the TextBoxes.

```
 1   ' Fig. 18.7: FrmBankUI.vb
 2   ' A reusable Windows Form for the examples in this chapter.
 3
 4   Public Class FrmBankUI
 5      ' number of TextBoxes on Form
 6      Protected TextBoxCount As Integer = 4
 7
 8      ' enumeration constants specify TextBox indices
 9      Public Enum TextBoxIndices
10         ACCOUNT
11         FIRST
12         LAST
13         BALANCE
14      End Enum ' TextBoxIndices
15
16      ' clear all TextBoxes
17      Public Sub ClearTextBoxes()
18         ' iterate through every Control on form
19         For i As Integer = 0 To Controls.Count - 1
20            Dim myControl As Control = Controls(i) ' get control
21            ' determine whether Control is TextBox
22            If TypeOf myControl Is TextBox Then
23               ' clear Text property (set to empty string)
24               myControl.Text = ""
25            End If
26         Next i
27      End Sub ' ClearTextBoxes
28
```

Fig. 18.7 | Base class for GUIs in our file-processing applications. (Part 1 of 2.)

```
29        ' set text box values to string array values
30        Public Sub SetTextBoxValues(ByVal values() As String)
31           ' determine whether string array has correct length
32           If values.Length <> TextBoxCount Then
33              ' throw exception if not correct length
34              Throw New ArgumentException( _
35                 "There must be " & (TextBoxCount + 1) & _
36                 " strings in the array")
37              ' set array values if array has correct length
38           Else
39              ' set array values to text box values
40              txtAccount.Text = _
41                 values(Convert.ToInt32(TextBoxIndices.ACCOUNT))
42              txtFirstName.Text = _
43                 values(Convert.ToInt32(TextBoxIndices.FIRST))
44              txtLastName.Text = _
45                 values(Convert.ToInt32(TextBoxIndices.LAST))
46              txtBalance.Text = _
47                 values(Convert.ToInt32(TextBoxIndices.BALANCE))
48           End If
49        End Sub ' SetTextBoxValues
50
51        ' return text box values as string array
52        Public Function GetTextBoxValues() As String()
53           Dim values(TextBoxCount) As String
54
55           ' copy text box fields to string array
56           values(Convert.ToInt32(TextBoxIndices.ACCOUNT)) = _
57              txtAccount.Text
58           values(Convert.ToInt32(TextBoxIndices.FIRST)) = _
59              txtFirstName.Text
60           values(Convert.ToInt32(TextBoxIndices.LAST)) = _
61              txtLastName.Text
62           values(Convert.ToInt32(TextBoxIndices.BALANCE)) = _
63              txtBalance.Text
64
65           Return values
66        End Function ' GetTextBoxValues
67     End Class ' FrmBankUI
```

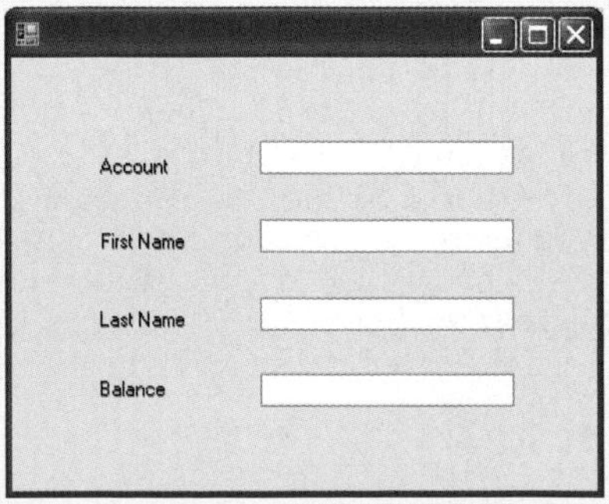

Fig. 18.7 | Base class for GUIs in our file-processing applications. (Part 2 of 2.)

To reuse class FrmBankUI, you must compile the GUI into a DLL (we called it Bank-Library) as described in Section 14.13. We provide the BankLibrary with the examples for this chapter. When you copy these examples to your system, you might need to delete the reference to BankLibrary and add it again, since the library most likely will reside in a different location on your system.

Class *Record*

Figure 18.8 contains class Record, which Fig. 18.9, Fig. 18.11 and Fig. 18.12 use to maintain the data in each record that is written to or read from a file. This class also belongs to the BankLibrary DLL, so it is located in the same project as class FrmBankUI.

Class Record contains Private instance variables accountValue, firstNameValue, lastNameValue and balanceValue (lines 6–9), which collectively represent all the information for a record. The parameterless constructor (lines 12–14) sets these members by

```vb
 1   ' Fig. 18.8: Record.vb
 2   ' Class that represents a data record.
 3   Imports System.Text
 4
 5   Public Class Record
 6      Private accountValue As Integer
 7      Private firstNameValue As String
 8      Private lastNameValue As String
 9      Private balanceValue As Decimal
10
11      ' parameterless constructor sets members to default values
12      Public Sub New()
13         MyClass.New(0, "", "", 0D)
14      End Sub ' New
15
16      ' overloaded constructor sets members to parameter values
17      Public Sub New(ByVal account As Integer, _
18         ByVal firstName As String, ByVal lastName As String, _
19         ByVal balance As Decimal)
20
21         accountValue = account
22         firstNameValue = firstName
23         lastNameValue = lastName
24         balanceValue = balance
25      End Sub ' New
26
27      ' property that gets and sets Account
28      Public Property Account() As Integer
29         Get
30            Return accountValue
31         End Get
32         Set(ByVal value As Integer)
33            accountValue = value
34         End Set
35      End Property ' Account
36
```

Fig. 18.8 | Record for sequential-access file-processing applications. (Part 1 of 2.)

```
37        ' property that gets and sets FirstName
38        Public Property FirstName() As String
39           Get
40              Return firstNameValue
41           End Get
42           Set(ByVal value As String)
43              firstNameValue = value
44           End Set
45        End Property ' FirstName
46
47        ' property that gets and sets LastName
48        Public Property LastName() As String
49           Get
50              Return lastNameValue
51           End Get
52           Set(ByVal value As String)
53              lastNameValue = value
54           End Set
55        End Property ' LastName
56
57        ' property that gets and sets Balance
58        Public Property Balance() As Decimal
59           Get
60              Return balanceValue
61           End Get
62           Set(ByVal value As Decimal)
63              balanceValue = value
64           End Set
65        End Property ' Balance
66     End Class ' Record
```

Fig. 18.8 | Record for sequential-access file-processing applications. (Part 2 of 2.)

calling the four-argument constructor with 0 for the account number, empty strings ("")
for the first and last names and 0D for the balance. The four-argument constructor (lines
17–25) sets these members to the specified parameter values. Class Record also provides
properties Account (lines 28–35), FirstName (lines 38–45), LastName (lines 48–55) and
Balance (lines 58–65) for accessing each record's account number, first name, last name
and balance, respectively.

Using a Character Stream to Create an Output File
Class FrmCreateFile (Fig. 18.9) uses instances of class Record to create a sequential-access
file that might be used in an accounts-receivable system—a program that organizes data
regarding money owed by a company's credit clients. For each client, the program obtains
an account number and the client's first name, last name and balance (i.e., the amount of
money that the client owes to the company for previously received goods and services).
The data obtained for each client constitutes a record for that client. In this application,
the account number is used as the record key—files are created and maintained in account-number order. This program assumes that the user enters records in account-number order. However, a comprehensive accounts-receivable system would provide a sorting
capability so that the user could enter the records in any order.

```vb
 1   ' Fig. 18.9: FrmCreateFile.vb
 2   ' Creating a sequential-access file.
 3   Imports System.IO
 4   Imports BankLibrary ' imports classes from Figs. 18.7 and 18.8
 5
 6   Public Class FrmCreateFile
 7      Private fileWriter As StreamWriter ' writes data to text file
 8      Private output As FileStream ' maintains connection to file
 9
10      ' event handler for Save Button
11      Private Sub btnSave_Click(ByVal sender As System.Object, _
12         ByVal e As System.EventArgs) Handles btnSave.Click
13         ' create dialog box enabling user to save file
14         Dim fileChooser As New SaveFileDialog()
15         Dim result As DialogResult = fileChooser.ShowDialog()
16         Dim fileName As String ' name of file to save data
17
18         fileChooser.CheckFileExists = False ' allow user to create file
19
20         ' exit event handler if user clicked "Cancel"
21         If result = Windows.Forms.DialogResult.Cancel Then
22            Return
23         End If
24
25         fileName = fileChooser.FileName ' get specified file name
26
27         ' show error if user specified invalid file
28         If fileName = "" Or fileName Is Nothing Then
29            MessageBox.Show("Invalid File Name", "Error", _
30               MessageBoxButtons.OK, MessageBoxIcon.Error)
31         Else
32            ' save file via FileStream if user specified valid file
33            Try
34               ' open file with write access
35               output = New FileStream( _
36                  fileName, FileMode.OpenOrCreate, FileAccess.Write)
37
38               ' sets file to where data is written
39               fileWriter = New StreamWriter(output)
40
41               ' disable Save button and enable Enter button
42               btnSave.Enabled = False
43               btnEnter.Enabled = True
44               ' handle exception if there is a problem opening the file
45            Catch ex As IOException
46               ' notify user if file does not exist
47               MessageBox.Show("Error opening file", "Error", _
48                  MessageBoxButtons.OK, MessageBoxIcon.Error)
49            End Try
50         End If
51      End Sub ' btnSave_Click
52
```

Fig. 18.9 | Creating and writing to a sequential-access file. (Part 1 of 4.)

```vbnet
53      ' event handler for Enter Button
54      Private Sub btnEnter_Click(ByVal sender As System.Object, _
55         ByVal e As System.EventArgs) Handles btnEnter.Click
56         ' store TextBox values string array
57         Dim values As String() = GetTextBoxValues()
58
59         ' Record containing TextBox values to serialize
60         Dim record As New Record()
61
62         ' determine whether TextBox account field is empty
63         If values(TextBoxIndices.ACCOUNT) <> "" Then
64            ' store TextBox values in Record and serialize Record
65            Try
66               ' get account number value from TextBox
67               Dim accountNumber As Integer = _
68                  Int32.Parse(values(TextBoxIndices.ACCOUNT))
69
70               ' determine whether accountNumber is valid
71               If accountNumber > 0 Then
72                  ' store TextBox fields in Record
73                  record.Account = accountNumber
74                  record.FirstName = values(TextBoxIndices.FIRST)
75                  record.LastName = values(TextBoxIndices.LAST)
76                  record.Balance = _
77                     Decimal.Parse(values(TextBoxIndices.BALANCE))
78
79                  ' write Record to file, fields separated by commas
80                  fileWriter.WriteLine( _
81                     record.Account & "," & record.FirstName & "," & _
82                     record.LastName & "," & record.Balance)
83               Else
84                  ' notify user if invalid account number
85                  MessageBox.Show("Invalid Account Number", "Error", _
86                     MessageBoxButtons.OK, MessageBoxIcon.Error)
87               End If
88               ' notify user if error occurs in serialization
89            Catch ex As IOException
90               MessageBox.Show("Error Writing to File", "Error", _
91                  MessageBoxButtons.OK, MessageBoxIcon.Error)
92               ' notify user if error occurs regarding parameter format
93            Catch ex As FormatException
94               MessageBox.Show("Invalid Format", "Error", _
95                  MessageBoxButtons.OK, MessageBoxIcon.Error)
96            End Try
97         End If
98
99         ClearTextBoxes() ' clear TextBox values
100     End Sub ' btnEnter_Click
101
102     ' event handler for Exit Button
103     Private Sub btnExit_Click(ByVal sender As System.Object, _
104        ByVal e As System.EventArgs) Handles btnExit.Click
```

Fig. 18.9 | Creating and writing to a sequential-access file. (Part 2 of 4.)

```
105          ' determine whether file exists
106       If output IsNot Nothing Then
107          Try
108             fileWriter.Close() ' close StreamWriter
109             output.Close() ' close file
110             ' notify user of error closing file
111          Catch ex As IOException
112             MessageBox.Show("Cannot close file", "Error", _
113                MessageBoxButtons.OK, MessageBoxIcon.Error)
114          End Try
115       End If
116
117       Application.Exit()
118    End Sub ' btnExit_Click
119 End Class ' FrmCreateFile
```

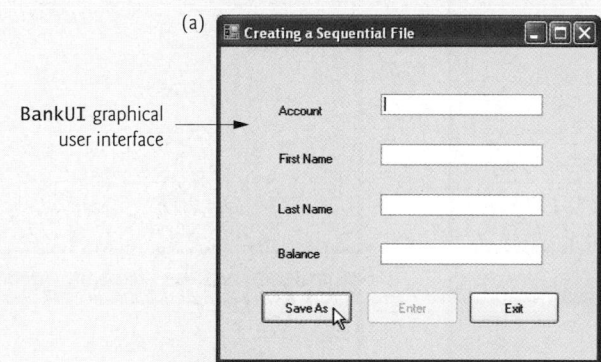

(a)

BankUI graphical user interface

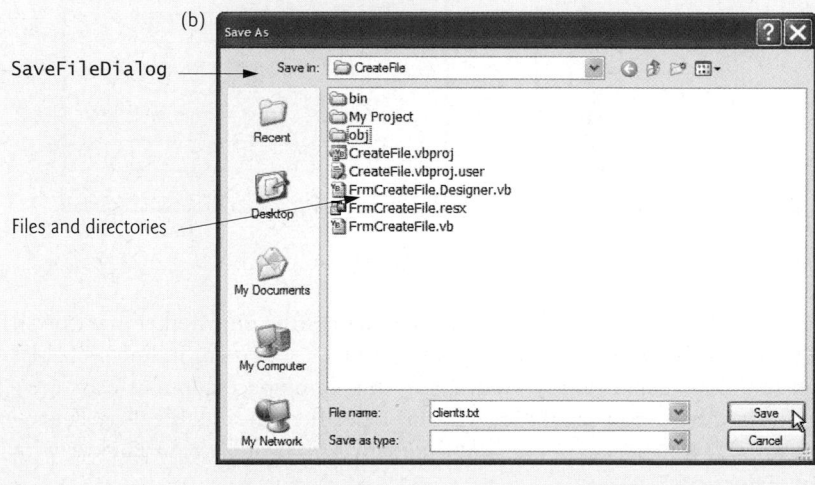

(b)

SaveFileDialog

Files and directories

Fig. 18.9 | Creating and writing to a sequential-access file. (Part 3 of 4.)

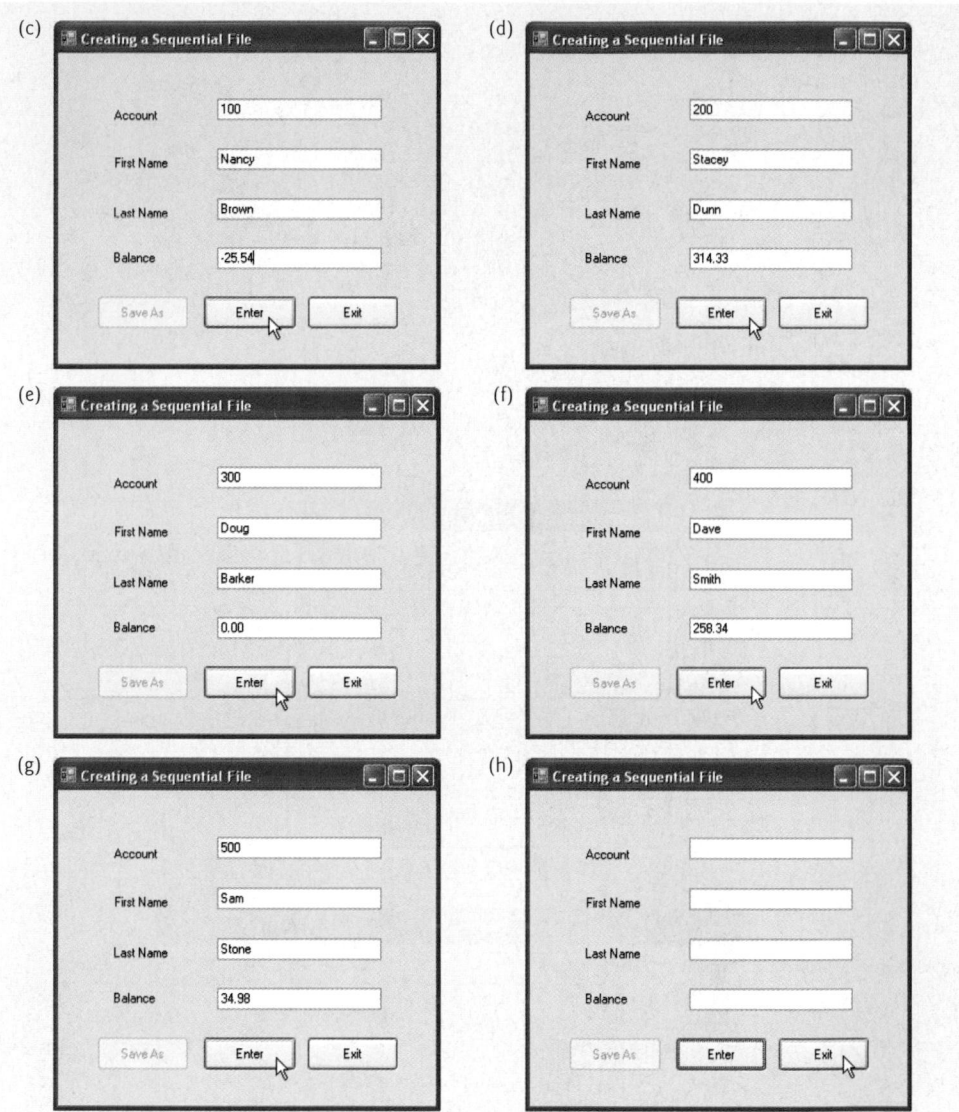

Fig. 18.9 | Creating and writing to a sequential-access file. (Part 4 of 4.)

Class FrmCreateFile either creates or opens a file (depending on whether one exists), then allows the user to write records to that file. The Imports statement in line 4 enables us to use the classes of the BankLibrary namespace; this namespace contains class Frm-BankUI, from which class FrmCreateFile inherits (specified in the file FrmCreate-File.Designer.vb). Class FrmCreateFile's GUI enhances that of class FrmBankUI with buttons **Save As**, **Enter** and **Exit**.

When the user clicks the **Save As** button, the program invokes the event handler btnSave_Click (lines 11–51). Line 14 instantiates a **SaveFileDialog** object (namespace System.Windows.Forms). Objects of this class are used for selecting files (see the second screen in Fig. 18.9). Line 15 calls SaveFileDialog method ShowDialog to display the dialog. When displayed, a SaveFileDialog prevents the user from interacting with any other window in the program until the user closes the SaveFileDialog by clicking either **Save** or **Cancel**. Dialogs that behave in this manner are called modal dialogs. The user selects the appropriate drive, directory and file name, then clicks **Save**. Method ShowDialog returns a DialogResult specifying which button (**Save** or **Cancel**) the user clicked to close the dialog. This is assigned to DialogResult variable result (line 15). Line 21 tests whether the user clicked **Cancel** by comparing this value to Windows.Forms.DialogResult.Cancel. If the values are equal, method btnSave_Click returns (line 22). Otherwise, line 25 uses SaveFileDialog property FileName to obtain the user-selected file.

You can open files to perform text manipulation by creating objects of class FileStream. In this example, we want the file to be opened for output, so lines 35–36 create a FileStream object. The FileStream constructor that we use receives three arguments—a String containing the path and name of the file to open, a constant describing how to open the file and a constant describing the file permissions. The constant FileMode.OpenOrCreate (line 36) indicates that the FileStream object should open the file if the file exists and create the file if it does not exist. There are other FileMode constants describing how to open files; we introduce these constants as we use them in examples. The constant FileAccess.Write (from the FileAccess enumeration) indicates that the program can only perform write operations with the FileStream object. There are two other constants for the third constructor parameter—FileAccess.Read for read-only access and FileAccess.ReadWrite for both read and write access. The StreamWriter object (line 39) is constructed with a FileStream argument that specifies the file to which the StreamWriter will output text. Class StreamWriter belongs to the System.IO namespace. Line 45 catches an IOException if there is a problem opening the file or creating the StreamWriter. If so, the program displays an error message (lines 47–48). If no exception occurs, the file is open for writing.

Common Programming Error 18.1

Failure to open a file before attempting to reference it in a program is a logic error.

After typing information in each TextBox, the user clicks the **Enter** button, which calls event handler btnEnter_Click (lines 54–100) to save the data from the TextBoxes into the user-specified file. If the user entered a valid account number (i.e., an integer greater than zero), lines 73–77 store the TextBox values in an object of type Record (created in line 60). If the user entered invalid data in one of the TextBoxes (such as non-numeric characters in the **Balance** field), the program throws a FormatException. The Catch block in lines 93–95 handles such exceptions by notifying the user (via a MessageBox) of the improper format.

If the user entered valid data, lines 80–82 write the record to the file by invoking method WriteLine of the StreamWriter object that was created at line 39. Method WriteLine writes a sequence of characters to a file. We separate each field with a comma in this example, and we place each record on its own line in the file.

When the user clicks the **Exit** button, event handler btnExit_Click (lines 103–118) exits the application. Line 108 closes the StreamWriter, line 109 closes the FileStream, then line 117 terminates the program. Note that the call to method Close is located in a

Try block. Method `Close` throws an `IOException` if the file or stream cannot be closed properly. In this case, it is important to notify the user that the information in the file or stream might be corrupted.

Performance Tip 18.1

Close each file explicitly when the program no longer needs to reference the file. This can reduce resource usage in programs that continue executing long after they finish using a specific file. The practice of explicitly closing files also improves program clarity.

Performance Tip 18.2

Releasing resources explicitly when they are no longer needed makes them immediately available for reuse by other programs, thus improving resource utilization.

In the sample execution for the program in Fig. 18.9, we entered information for the five accounts shown in Fig. 18.10. The program does not depict how the data records are rendered in the file. To verify that the file has been created successfully, we create a program in the next section to read and display the file. Since this is a text file, you can open it in any text editor to see its contents.

18.6 Reading Data from a Sequential-Access Text File

The preceding section demonstrated how to create a file for use in sequential-access applications. In this section, we discuss how to read (or retrieve) data sequentially from a file.

Class `FrmReadSequentialAccessFile` (Fig. 18.11) reads records from the file created in Fig. 18.9, then displays the contents of each record. Much of the code in this example is similar to that in Fig. 18.9, so we discuss only the unique aspects of the application.

Account Number	First Name	Last Name	Balance
100	Nancy	Brown	-25.54
200	Stacey	Dunn	314.33
300	Doug	Barker	0.00
400	Dave	Smith	258.34
500	Sam	Stone	34.98

Fig. 18.10 | Sample data for the program in Fig. 18.9.

```
1    ' Fig. 18.11: FrmReadSequentialAccessFile.vb
2    ' Reading a sequential-access file.
3    Imports System.IO
4    Imports BankLibrary ' imports classes from Figs. 18.7 and 18.8
5
6    Public Class FrmReadSequentialAccessFile
7        Private input As FileStream ' maintains connection to a file
```

Fig. 18.11 | Reading sequential-access files. (Part 1 of 4.)

```vbnet
 8        Private fileReader As StreamReader ' reads data from a text file
 9
10        ' invoked when user clicks the Open button
11        Private Sub btnOpen_Click(ByVal sender As System.Object, _
12           ByVal e As System.EventArgs) Handles btnOpen.Click
13           ' create dialog box enabling user to open file
14           Dim fileChooser As New OpenFileDialog()
15           Dim result As DialogResult = fileChooser.ShowDialog()
16           Dim fileName As String ' name of file containing data
17
18           ' exit event handler if user clicked Cancel
19           If result = Windows.Forms.DialogResult.Cancel Then
20              Return
21           End If
22
23           fileName = fileChooser.FileName ' get specified file name
24           ClearTextBoxes()
25
26           ' show error if user specified invalid file
27           If fileName = "" Or fileName Is Nothing Then
28              MessageBox.Show("Invalid File Name", "Error", _
29                 MessageBoxButtons.OK, MessageBoxIcon.Error)
30           Else
31              ' create FileStream to obtain read access to file
32              input = New FileStream(fileName, FileMode.Open, FileAccess.Read)
33
34              ' set file from where data is read
35              fileReader = New StreamReader(input)
36
37              btnOpen.Enabled = False ' disable Open File button
38              btnNext.Enabled = True ' enable Next Record button
39           End If
40        End Sub ' btnOpen_Click
41
42        ' invoked when user clicks Next button
43        Private Sub btnNext_Click(ByVal sender As System.Object, _
44           ByVal e As System.EventArgs) Handles btnNext.Click
45
46           Try
47              ' get next record available in file
48              Dim inputRecord As String = fileReader.ReadLine()
49
50              ' will store individual pieces of data
51              Dim inputFields() As String
52
53              If inputRecord IsNot Nothing Then
54                 inputFields = inputRecord.Split(",","c)
55
56                 Dim record As New Record(Convert.ToInt32( _
57                    inputFields(0)), inputFields(1), inputFields(2), _
58                    Convert.ToDecimal(inputFields(3)))
59
```

Fig. 18.11 | Reading sequential-access files. (Part 2 of 4.)

```
60              ' copy string array values to TextBox values
61              SetTextBoxValues(inputFields)
62          Else
63              fileReader.Close() ' close StreamReader
64              input.Close() ' close FileStream if no Records in file
65              btnOpen.Enabled = True ' enable Open File button
66              btnNext.Enabled = False ' disable Next Record button
67              ClearTextBoxes()
68
69              ' notify user if no Records in file
70              MessageBox.Show("No more records in file", "", _
71                  MessageBoxButtons.OK, MessageBoxIcon.Information)
72          End If
73      Catch ex As IOException
74          MessageBox.Show("Error Reading from File", "Error", _
75              MessageBoxButtons.OK, MessageBoxIcon.Error)
76      End Try
77   End Sub ' btnNext_Click
78 End Class ' FrmReadSequentialAccessFile
```

(a)

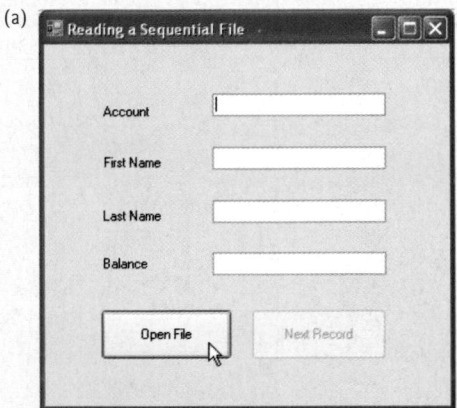

(b)

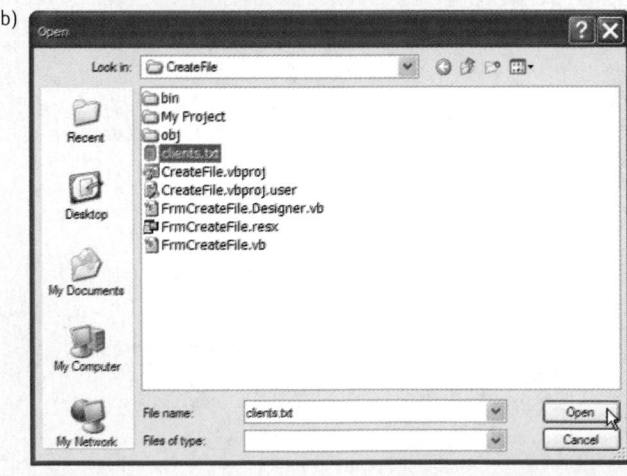

Fig. 18.11 | Reading sequential-access files. (Part 3 of 4.)

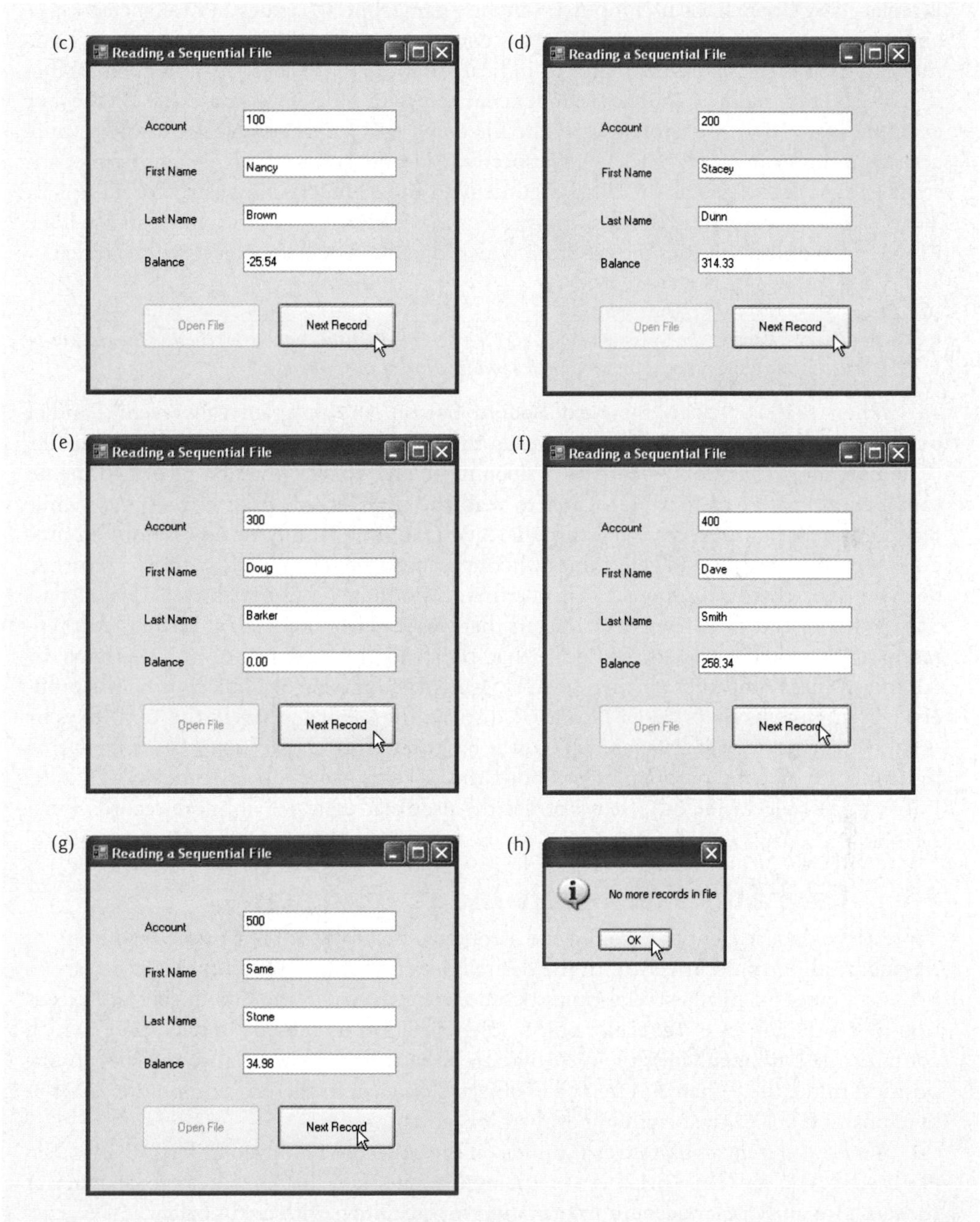

Fig. 18.11 | Reading sequential-access files. (Part 4 of 4.)

When the user clicks the **Open File** button, the program calls event handler btnOpen_Click (lines 11–40). Line 14 creates an `OpenFileDialog`, and line 15 calls its `ShowDialog` method to display the **Open** dialog (see the second screenshot in Fig. 18.11). The behavior and GUI for the **Save** and **Open** dialog types are identical, except that **Save** is replaced by **Open**. If the user inputs a valid file name, line 32 creates a `FileStream` object and assigns it to reference `input`. We pass constant `FileMode.Open` as the second argument to the `FileStream` constructor to indicate that the `FileStream` should open the file if it exists and throw a `FileNotFoundException` if the file does not exist. In the last example (Fig. 18.9), we wrote text to the file using a `FileStream` object with write-only access. In this example (Fig. 18.11), we specify read-only access to the file by passing constant `FileAccess.Read` as the third argument to the `FileStream` constructor (line 32). This `FileStream` object is used to create a `StreamReader` object in line 35. The `FileStream` object specifies the file from which the `StreamReader` object will read text.

 Error-Prevention Tip 18.1

Open a file with the `FileAccess.Read` file-open mode if the contents of the file should not be modified. This prevents unintentional modification of the contents.

When the user clicks the **Next Record** button, the program calls event handler `btnNext_Click` (lines 43–77), which reads the next record from the user-specified file. (The user must click **Next Record** after opening the file to view the first record.) Line 48 calls `StreamReader` method `ReadLine` to read the next record. If an error occurs while reading the file, an `IOException` is thrown (caught at line 73), and the user is notified (line 74–75). Otherwise, line 53 determines whether `StreamReader` method `ReadLine` returned `Nothing` (i.e., there is no more text in the file). If not, line 54 uses method `Split` of class `String` to separate the stream of characters that was read from the file into strings that represent the `Record`'s properties. Recall that the fields of each record are separated by commas. These properties are then stored by constructing a `Record` object using the properties as arguments (lines 56–58). Line 61 displays the `Record` values in the `TextBox`es by invoking method `SetTextBoxes`, which was inherited from class `FrmBankUI`. If `ReadLine` returns `Nothing`, the program closes both the `StreamReader` object (line 63) and the `FileStream` object (line 64), then notifies the user that there are no more records (lines 70–71).

18.7 Case Study: A Credit-Inquiry Program

To retrieve data sequentially from a file, programs normally start from the beginning of the file, reading consecutively until the desired data is found. It sometimes is necessary to process a file sequentially several times (from the beginning of the file) during the execution of a program. A `FileStream` object can reposition its file-position pointer (which contains the byte number of the next byte to be read from or written to the file) to any position in the file. When a `FileStream` object is opened, its file-position pointer is set to byte position 0 (i.e., the beginning of the file)

We now present a program that builds on the concepts employed in Fig. 18.11. Class `FrmCreditInquiry` (Fig. 18.12) is a credit-inquiry program that enables a credit manager to search for and display account information for customers with credit balances (i.e., customers to whom the company owes money), zero balances (i.e., customers who do not owe the company money) and debit balances (i.e., customers who owe the company money for previously received goods and services). We use a `RichTextBox` in the program to display the account information. `RichTextBox`es provide more functionality than regular `Text-Box`es—for example, `RichTextBox`es offer method `Find` for searching individual strings and method `LoadFile` for displaying file contents. Classes `RichTextBox` and `TextBox` both inherit from MustInherit class System.Windows.Forms.TextBoxBase. We chose a Rich-TextBox in this example because it displays multiple lines of text by default, whereas a regular TextBox displays only one. Alternatively, we could have specified that a TextBox object display multiple lines of text by setting its Multiline property to True.

```vb
 1  ' Fig. 18.12: FrmCreditInquiry.vb
 2  ' Read a file sequentially and display contents based on
 3  ' account type specified by user (credit, debit or zero balances).
 4  Imports System.IO
 5  Imports BankLibrary
 6
 7  Public Class FrmCreditInquiry
 8     Private input As FileStream ' maintains the connection to the file
 9     Private fileReader As StreamReader ' reads data from text file
10
11     ' name of file that stores credit, debit and zero balances
12     Private fileName As String
13
14     ' invoked when user clicks Open File button
15     Private Sub btnOpen_Click(ByVal sender As System.Object, _
16        ByVal e As System.EventArgs) Handles btnOpen.Click
17        ' create dialog box enabling user to open file
18        Dim fileChooser As New OpenFileDialog()
19        Dim result As DialogResult = fileChooser.ShowDialog()
20
21        ' exit event handler if user clicked Cancel
22        If result = Windows.Forms.DialogResult.Cancel Then
23           Return
24        End If
25
26        fileName = fileChooser.FileName ' get name from user
27
28        ' show error if user specified invalid file
29        If fileName = "" Or fileName Is Nothing Then
30           MessageBox.Show("Invalid File Name", "Error", _
31              MessageBoxButtons.OK, MessageBoxIcon.Error)
32        Else
33           ' create FileStream to obtain read access to file
34           input = New FileStream(fileName, FileMode.Open, FileAccess.Read)
35
36           ' set file from where data is read
37           fileReader = New StreamReader(input)
38
39           ' enable all GUI buttons, except for Open File button
40           btnOpen.Enabled = False
41           btnCredit.Enabled = True
42           btnDebit.Enabled = True
43           btnZero.Enabled = True
44        End If
45     End Sub ' btnOpen_Click
46
```

Fig. 18.12 | Credit-inquiry program. (Part 1 of 5.)

```vb
47          ' invoked when user clicks credit balances,
48          ' debit balances or zero balances button
49          Private Sub getBalances_Click( _
50             ByVal sender As System.Object, ByVal e As System.EventArgs) _
51             Handles btnCredit.Click, btnZero.Click, btnDebit.Click
52             ' convert sender explicitly to object of type button
53             Dim senderButton As Button = CType(sender, Button)
54
55             ' get text from clicked Button, which stores account type
56             Dim accountType As String = senderButton.Text
57
58             ' read and display file information
59             Try
60                ' go back to the beginning of the file
61                input.Seek(0, SeekOrigin.Begin)
62
63                txtDisplay.Text = "The accounts are:" & vbCrLf
64
65                ' traverse file until end of file
66                While True
67                   ' will store individual pieces of data
68                   Dim inputFields() As String
69
70                   Dim record As Record ' store each Record as file is read
71                   Dim balance As Decimal ' store each Record's balance
72
73                   ' get next Record available in file
74                   Dim inputRecord As String = fileReader.ReadLine()
75
76                   ' when at the end of file, exit method
77                   If inputRecord Is Nothing Then
78                      Return
79                   End If
80
81                   inputFields = inputRecord.Split(","c) ' parse input
82
83                   ' create Record from input
84                   record = New Record(Convert.ToInt32( _
85                      inputFields(0)), inputFields(1), inputFields(2), _
86                      Convert.ToDecimal(inputFields(3)))
87
88                   ' store record's last field in balance
89                   balance = record.Balance
90
91                   ' determine whether to display balance
92                   If ShouldDisplay(balance, accountType) Then
93                      ' display record
94                      Dim output As String = _
95                         record.Account & vbTab & _
96                         record.FirstName & vbTab & _
97                         record.LastName & vbTab
98
```

Fig. 18.12 | Credit-inquiry program. (Part 2 of 5.)

```
 99                     ' display balance with correct monetary format
100                     output &= String.Format("{0:F}", balance) & vbCrLf
101
102                     txtDisplay.Text &= output ' copy output to screen
103                  End If
104              End While
105              ' handle exception when file cannot be read
106           Catch ex As IOException
107              MessageBox.Show("Cannot Read File", "Error", _
108                 MessageBoxButtons.OK, MessageBoxIcon.Error)
109           End Try
110        End Sub ' getBalances_Click
111
112        ' determine whether to display given record
113        Private Function ShouldDisplay(ByVal balance As Decimal, _
114           ByVal accountType As String) As Boolean
115
116           If balance > 0 Then
117              ' display credit balances
118              If accountType = "Credit Balances" Then
119                 Return True
120              End If
121           ElseIf balance < 0 Then
122              ' display debit balances
123              If accountType = "Debit Balances" Then
124                 Return True
125              End If
126           Else ' balance = 0
127              ' display zero balances
128              If accountType = "Zero Balances" Then
129                 Return True
130              End If
131           End If
132
133           Return False
134        End Function ' ShouldDisplay
135
136        ' invoked when user clicks Done button
137        Private Sub btnDone_Click(ByVal sender As System.Object, _
138           ByVal e As System.EventArgs) Handles btnDone.Click
139           ' determine whether file exists
140           If input IsNot Nothing Then
141              ' close file and StreamReader
142              Try
143                 input.Close()
144                 fileReader.Close()
145                 ' handle exception if FileStream does not exist
146              Catch ex As IOException
147                 ' notify user of error closing file
148                 MessageBox.Show("Cannot close file", "Error", _
149                    MessageBoxButtons.OK, MessageBoxIcon.Error)
150              End Try
151           End If
```

Fig. 18.12 | Credit-inquiry program. (Part 3 of 5.)

```
152
153        Application.Exit()
154    End Sub ' btnDone_Click
155 End Class ' FrmCreditInquiry
```

(a)

(b)

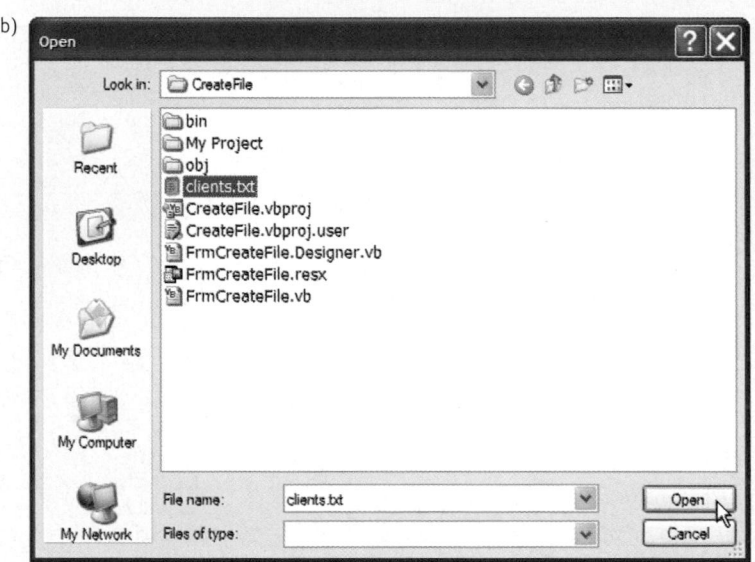

(c)

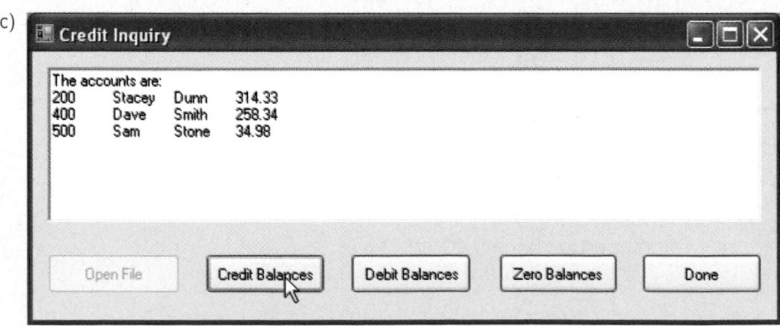

Fig. 18.12 | Credit-inquiry program. (Part 4 of 5.)

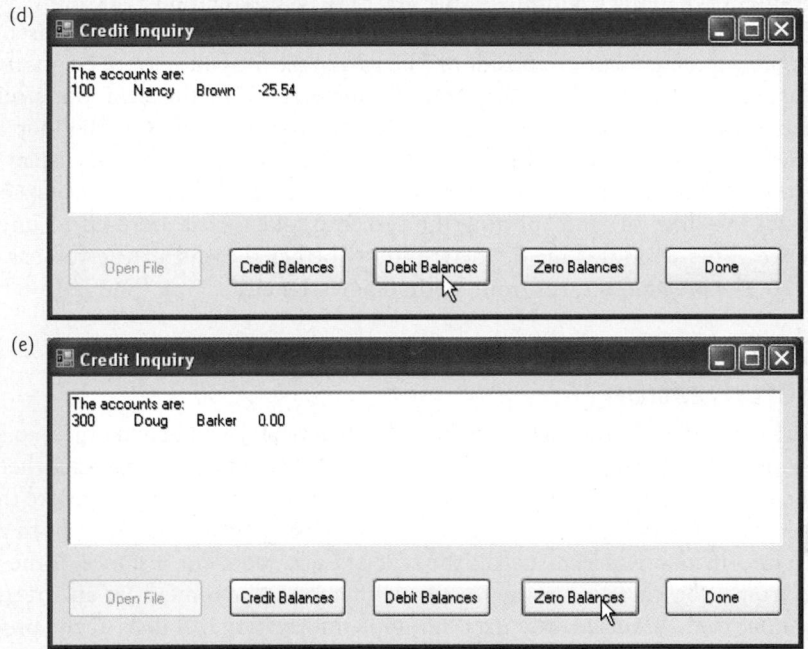

Fig. 18.12 | Credit-inquiry program. (Part 5 of 5.)

The program displays buttons that enable a credit manager to obtain credit information. The **Open File** button opens a file for gathering data. The **Credit Balances** button displays a list of accounts that have credit balances, the **Debit Balances** button displays a list of accounts that have debit balances and the **Zero Balances** button displays a list of accounts that have zero balances. The **Done** button exits the application.

When the user clicks the **Open File** button, the program calls the event handler btnOpen_Click (lines 15–45). Line 18 creates an OpenFileDialog, and line 19 calls its ShowDialog method to display the **Open** dialog, in which the user selects the file to open. Line 34 creates a FileStream object with read-only file access and assigns it to reference input. Line 37 creates a StreamReader object that we use to read text from the FileStream.

When the user clicks **Credit Balances**, **Debit Balances** or **Zero Balances**, the program invokes method getBalances_Click (lines 49–110). To create a single method that handles the events for multiple Buttons, select the Click event in the **Properties** window for one of the Buttons, type the name you wish to use for the event handler and press *Enter*. Then modify the Handles clause for the method so that it is followed by a comma separated list of the events the method handles, as shown in line 51. Line 53 uses Visual Basic's CType function to convert the sender parameter's type, which is an Object reference, to type Button. The sender parameter represents the control that generated the event. This conversion allows the event handler to use the properties and methods of the Button the user pressed. A conversion performed with the CType function is also known as a cast operation. Line 56 obtains the Button object's text, which the program uses to determine which type of accounts to display. Line 61 uses FileStream method Seek to reset the file-position pointer back to the beginning of the file. `FileStream` method `Seek` allows you to reset the file-position pointer by specifying the number of bytes it should be offset from the file's beginning, end or current position. The part of the file you want to be offset from is chosen using constants from the `SeekOrigin` enumeration. In this case, our stream is offset by 0 bytes from the file's beginning (`SeekOrigin.Begin`). Lines 66–104 loop using `Private` method `ShouldDisplay` (lines 113–134) to determine whether to display each record in the file. The loop obtains each record by repeatedly calling `StreamReader` method `ReadLine` (line 74) and splitting the text into tokens that are used to initialize object `record` (lines 81–86). Line 77 determines whether the end of the file has been reached. If so, the program returns from method `getBalances_Click` (line 78).

18.8 Serialization

Section 18.5 demonstrated how to write the individual fields of a `Record` object to a text file, and Section 18.6 demonstrated how to read those fields from a file and place their values in a `Record` object in memory. In the examples, `Record` was used to aggregate the information for one record. When the instance variables for a `Record` were output to a disk file, certain information was lost, such as the type of each value. For instance, if the value `"3"` is read from a file, there is no way to tell whether the value came from an `Integer`, a `String` or a `Decimal`. We have only data, not type information, on disk. If the program that is going to read this data "knows" what object type the data corresponds to, then the data can be read directly into objects of that type. For example, in Fig. 18.9, we know that we are inputting an `Integer` (the account number), followed by two `Strings` (the first and last names) and a `Decimal` (the balance). We also know that these values are separated by commas, with only one record on each line. Thus we are able to parse the strings and convert the account number to an `Integer` and the balance to a `Decimal`. Sometimes it would be easier to read or write entire objects. .NET provides such a mechanism, called object serialization. A serialized object is an object represented as a sequence of bytes that includes the object's data, as well as information about the object's type and the types of data stored in the object. After a serialized object has been written to a file, it can be read from the file and deserialized—that is, the type information and bytes that represent the object and its data can be used to recreate the object in memory.

Class `BinaryFormatter` (namespace `System.Runtime.Serialization.Formatters.Binary`) enables entire objects to be written to or read from a stream. `BinaryFormatter` method `Serialize` writes an object's representation to a file. `BinaryFormatter` method `Deserialize` reads this representation from a file and reconstructs the original object. Both methods throw a `SerializationException` if an error occurs during serialization or deserialization. Both methods require a `Stream` object (e.g., the `FileStream`) as a parameter so that the `BinaryFormatter` can access the correct stream. As you will see in Chapter 23, Networking: Streams-Based Sockets and Datagrams, serialization can be used to transmit objects between applications over a network.

In Sections 18.8 and 18.10, we create and manipulate sequential-access files using object serialization. Object serialization is performed with byte-based streams, so the sequential files created and manipulated will be binary files. Binary files are not human readable. For this reason, we write a separate application that reads and displays serialized objects.

18.9 Creating a Sequential-Access File Using Object Serialization

We begin by creating and writing serialized objects to a sequential-access file. In this section, we reuse much of the code from Section 18.5, so we focus only on the new features.

Defining the *RecordSerializable* Class

Let us begin by modifying our Record class (Fig. 18.8) so that objects of this class can be serialized. Class RecordSerializable (Fig. 18.13) is marked with the `<Serializable()>` attribute (line 5), which indicates to the CLR that objects of class RecordSerializable can be serialized. The classes for objects that we wish to write to or read from a stream must include this attribute in their declarations or must implement interface ISerializable (from namespace System.Runtime.Serialization). The remainder of class RecordSerializable is identical to class Record (Fig. 18.8).

```vb
1   ' Fig. 18.13: RecordSerializable.vb
2   ' Serializable class that represents a data record.
3
4   <Serializable()> _
5   Public Class RecordSerializable
6      Private accountValue As Integer
7      Private firstNameValue As String
8      Private lastNameValue As String
9      Private balanceValue As Decimal
10
11     ' default constructor sets members to default values
12     Public Sub New()
13        MyClass.New(0, "", "", 0D)
14     End Sub ' New
15
16     ' overloaded constructor sets members to parameter values
17     Public Sub New(ByVal account As Integer, ByVal firstName As String, _
18        ByVal lastName As String, ByVal balance As Decimal)
19
20        account = account
21        firstNameValue = firstName
22        lastNameValue = lastName
23        balanceValue = balance
24     End Sub ' New
25
26     ' property Account
27     Public Property Account() As Integer
28        Get
29           Return accountValue
30        End Get
31        Set(ByVal value As Integer)
32           accountValue = value
33        End Set
34     End Property ' Account
35
```

Fig. 18.13 | RecordSerializable class for serializable objects. (Part 1 of 2.)

```
36          ' property FirstName
37          Public Property FirstName() As String
38             Get
39                Return firstNameValue
40             End Get
41             Set(ByVal value As String)
42                firstNameValue = value
43             End Set
44          End Property ' FirstName
45
46          ' property LastName
47          Public Property LastName() As String
48             Get
49                Return lastNameValue
50             End Get
51             Set(ByVal value As String)
52                lastNameValue = value
53             End Set
54          End Property ' LastName
55
56          ' property Balance
57          Public Property Balance() As Decimal
58             Get
59                Return balanceValue
60             End Get
61             Set(ByVal value As Decimal)
62                balanceValue = value
63             End Set
64          End Property ' Balance
65       End Class ' RecordSerializable
```

Fig. 18.13 | RecordSerializable class for serializable objects. (Part 2 of 2.)

In a class that is marked with the <Serializable()> attribute or that implements interface ISerializable, you must ensure that every instance variable of the class is also serializable. All simple-type variables and Strings are serializable. For variables of reference types, you must check the class declaration (and possibly its base classes) to ensure that the type is serializable. By default, array objects are serializable. However, if the array contains references to other objects, those objects may or may not be serializable.

Using a Serialization Stream to Create an Output File

Now let's create a sequential-access file with serialization (Fig. 18.14). Line 10 creates a BinaryFormatter for writing serialized objects. Lines 38–39 open the FileStream to which this program writes the serialized objects. The String argument fileName that is passed to the FileStream's constructor represents the name and path of the file to be opened. This specifies the file to which the serialized objects will be written.

Common Programming Error 18.2

It is a logic error to open an existing file for output when the user wishes to preserve the file—the original file's contents will be lost.

```vb
1   ' Fig 18.14: FrmCreateFile.vb
2   ' Creating a sequential-access file using serialization.
3   Imports System.IO
4   Imports System.Runtime.Serialization.Formatters.Binary
5   Imports System.Runtime.Serialization
6   Imports BankLibrary
7
8   Public Class FrmCreateFile
9      ' object for serializing Records in binary format
10     Private formatter As New BinaryFormatter()
11     Private output As FileStream ' stream for writing to a file
12
13     ' handler for btnSave_Click
14     Private Sub btnSave_Click(ByVal sender As System.Object, _
15        ByVal e As System.EventArgs) Handles btnSave.Click
16        ' create dialog box enabling user to save file
17        Dim fileChooser As New SaveFileDialog()
18        Dim result As DialogResult = fileChooser.ShowDialog()
19        Dim fileName As String ' name of file to save data
20
21        fileChooser.CheckFileExists = False ' allow user to create file
22
23        ' exit event handler if user clicked "Cancel"
24        If result = Windows.Forms.DialogResult.Cancel Then
25           Return
26        End If
27
28        fileName = fileChooser.FileName ' get specified file name
29
30        ' show error if user specified invalid file
31        If fileName = "" Or fileName Is Nothing Then
32           MessageBox.Show("Invalid File Name", "Error", _
33              MessageBoxButtons.OK, MessageBoxIcon.Error)
34        Else
35           ' save file via FileStream if user specified valid file
36           Try
37              ' open file with write access
38              output = New FileStream( _
39                 fileName, FileMode.OpenOrCreate, FileAccess.Write)
40
41              ' disable Save button and enable Enter button
42              btnSave.Enabled = False
43              btnEnter.Enabled = True
44              ' handle exception if there is a problem opening the file
45           Catch ex As IOException
46              ' notify user if file does not exist
47              MessageBox.Show("Error opening file", "Error", _
48                 MessageBoxButtons.OK, MessageBoxIcon.Error)
49           End Try
50        End If
51     End Sub ' btnSave_Click
52
```

Fig. 18.14 | Sequential file created using serialization. (Part 1 of 4.)

```vbnet
53      ' handler for btnEnter_Click
54      Private Sub btnEnter_Click(ByVal sender As System.Object, _
55         ByVal e As System.EventArgs) Handles btnEnter.Click
56         ' store TextBox values string array
57         Dim values As String() = GetTextBoxValues()
58
59         ' Record containing TextBox values to serialize
60         Dim record As New RecordSerializable()
61
62         ' determine whether TextBox account field is empty
63         If values(TextBoxIndices.ACCOUNT) <> "" Then
64            ' store TextBox values in Record and serialize Record
65            Try
66               ' get account number value from TextBox
67               Dim accountNumber As Integer = _
68                  Int32.Parse(values(TextBoxIndices.ACCOUNT))
69
70               ' determine whether accountNumber is valid
71               If accountNumber > 0 Then
72                  ' store TextBox fields in Record
73                  record.Account = accountNumber
74                  record.FirstName = _
75                     values(TextBoxIndices.FIRST)
76                  record.LastName = _
77                     values(TextBoxIndices.LAST)
78                  record.Balance = _
79                     Decimal.Parse(values(TextBoxIndices.BALANCE))
80
81                  ' write Record to FileStream ( serialize object )
82                  formatter.Serialize(output, record)
83               Else
84                  ' notify user if invalid account number
85                  MessageBox.Show("Invalid Account Number", "Error", _
86                     MessageBoxButtons.OK, MessageBoxIcon.Error)
87               End If
88               ' notify user if error occurs in serialization
89            Catch ex As SerializationException
90               MessageBox.Show("Error Writing to File", "Error", _
91                  MessageBoxButtons.OK, MessageBoxIcon.Error)
92               ' notify user if error occurs regarding parameter format
93            Catch ex As FormatException
94               MessageBox.Show("Invalid Format", "Error", _
95                  MessageBoxButtons.OK, MessageBoxIcon.Error)
96            End Try
97         End If
98
99         ClearTextBoxes() ' clear TextBox values
100     End Sub ' btnEnter_Click
101
102     ' handler for btnSave_Click
103     Private Sub btnExit_Click(ByVal sender As System.Object, _
104        ByVal e As System.EventArgs) Handles btnExit.Click
```

Fig. 18.14 | Sequential file created using serialization. (Part 2 of 4.)

```
105           ' determine whether file exists
106       If output IsNot Nothing Then
107           ' close file
108          Try
109             output.Close()
110             ' notify user of error closing file
111          Catch ex As IOException
112             MessageBox.Show("Cannot close file", "Error", _
113                MessageBoxButtons.OK, MessageBoxIcon.Error)
114          End Try
115       End If
116
117       Application.Exit()
118     End Sub ' btnEnter_Click
119  End Class ' FrmCreateFile
```

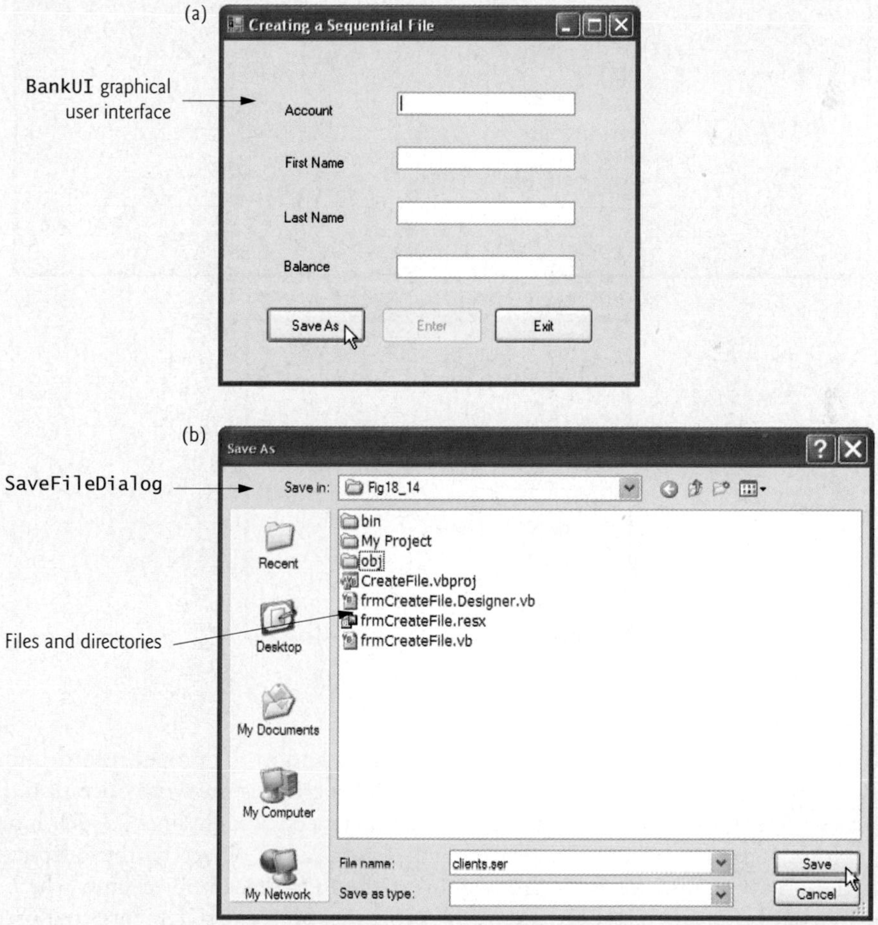

Fig. 18.14 | Sequential file created using serialization. (Part 3 of 4.)

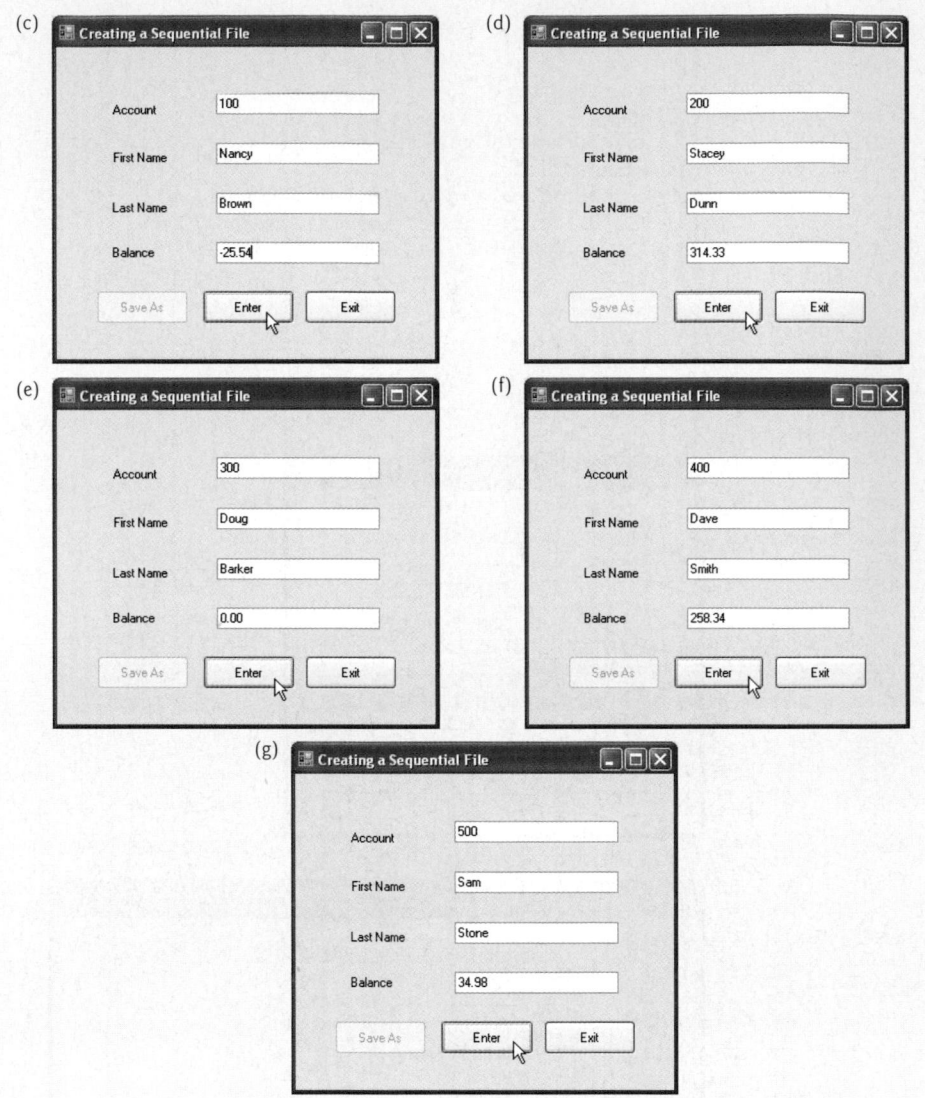

Fig. 18.14 | Sequential file created using serialization. (Part 4 of 4.)

This program assumes that data is input correctly and in the proper record-number order. Event handler btnEnter_Click (lines 54–100) performs the write operation. Line 60 creates a RecordSerializable object, which is assigned values in lines 73–79. Line 82 calls method Serialize to write the RecordSerializable object to the output file. Method Serialize receives as its first argument the FileStream object into which the BinaryFormatter writes its second argument. Note that only one statement is required to write the entire object.

In the sample execution for the program in Fig. 18.14, we entered information for five accounts—the same information shown in Fig. 18.10. The program does not show

how the data records actually appear in the file. Remember that we are now using binary files, which are not human readable. To verify that the file was created successfully, the next section presents a program to read the file's contents and deserialize the objects.

18.10 **Reading and Deserializing Data from a Sequential-Access Text File**

The preceding section showed how to create a sequential-access file using object serialization. In this section, we discuss how to read serialized objects sequentially from a file.

Figure 18.15 reads and displays the contents of the file created by the program in Fig. 18.14. Line 10 creates the BinaryFormatter that will be used to read objects. The program opens the file for input by creating a FileStream object (line 35). The name of the file to open is specified as the first argument to the FileStream constructor.

```vb
1   ' Fig. 18.15: FrmReadSequentialAccessFile.vb
2   ' Reading a sequential-access file using deserialization.
3   Imports System.IO
4   Imports System.Runtime.Serialization.Formatters.Binary
5   Imports System.Runtime.Serialization
6   Imports BankLibrary
7
8   Public Class FrmReadSequentialAccessFile
9      ' object for deserializing Record in binary format
10     Private reader As New BinaryFormatter()
11     Private input As FileStream ' stream for reading from a file
12
13     ' invoked when user clicks Open button
14     Private Sub btnOpen_Click(ByVal sender As System.Object, _
15        ByVal e As System.EventArgs) Handles btnOpen.Click
16        ' create dialog box enabling user to open file
17        Dim fileChooser As New OpenFileDialog()
18        Dim result As DialogResult = fileChooser.ShowDialog()
19        Dim fileName As String ' name of file containing data
20
21        ' exit event handler if user clicked Cancel
22        If result = Windows.Forms.DialogResult.Cancel Then
23           Return
24        End If
25
26        fileName = fileChooser.FileName ' get specified file name
27        ClearTextBoxes()
28
29        ' show error if user specified invalid file
30        If fileName = "" Or fileName Is Nothing Then
31           MessageBox.Show("Invalid File Name", "Error", _
32              MessageBoxButtons.OK, MessageBoxIcon.Error)
33        Else
34           ' create FileStream to obtain read access to file
35           input = New FileStream(fileName, FileMode.Open, FileAccess.Read)
36
```

Fig. 18.15 | Sequential file read using deserialzation. (Part 1 of 4.)

```vbnet
37              btnOpen.Enabled = False ' disable Open File button
38              btnNext.Enabled = True ' enable Next Record button
39          End If
40      End Sub ' btnOpen_Click
41
42      ' invoked when user clicks Next button
43      Private Sub btnNext_Click(ByVal sender As System.Object, _
44          ByVal e As System.EventArgs) Handles btnNext.Click
45          ' deserialize Record and store data in TextBoxes
46          Try
47              ' get next RecordSerializable available in file
48              Dim record As RecordSerializable = _
49                  CType(reader.Deserialize(input), RecordSerializable)
50
51              ' store Record values in temporary string array
52              Dim values() As String = { _
53                  record.Account.ToString(), record.FirstName.ToString(), _
54                  record.LastName.ToString(), record.Balance.ToString()}
55
56              ' copy string array values to TextBox values
57              SetTextBoxValues(values)
58              ' handle exception when there are no Records in file
59          Catch ex As SerializationException
60              input.Close() ' close FileStream if no Records in file
61              btnOpen.Enabled = True ' enable Open File button
62              btnNext.Enabled = False ' disable Next Record button
63
64              ClearTextBoxes()
65
66              ' notify user if no Records in file
67              MessageBox.Show("No more records in file", "", _
68                  MessageBoxButtons.OK, MessageBoxIcon.Information)
69          End Try
70      End Sub ' btnNext_Click
71  End Class ' FrmReadSequentialAccessFile
```

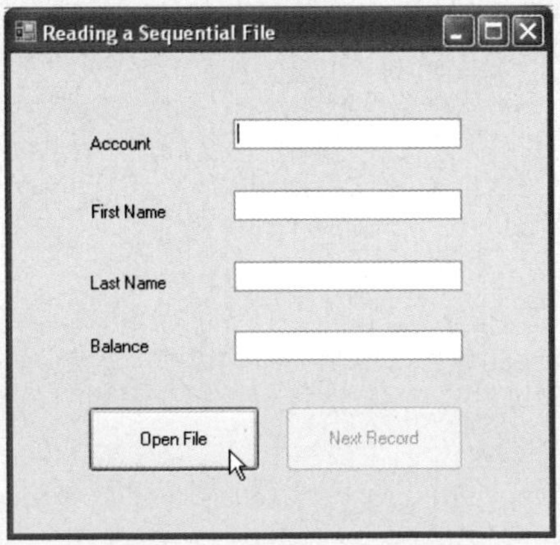

Fig. 18.15 | Sequential file read using deserialzation. (Part 2 of 4.)

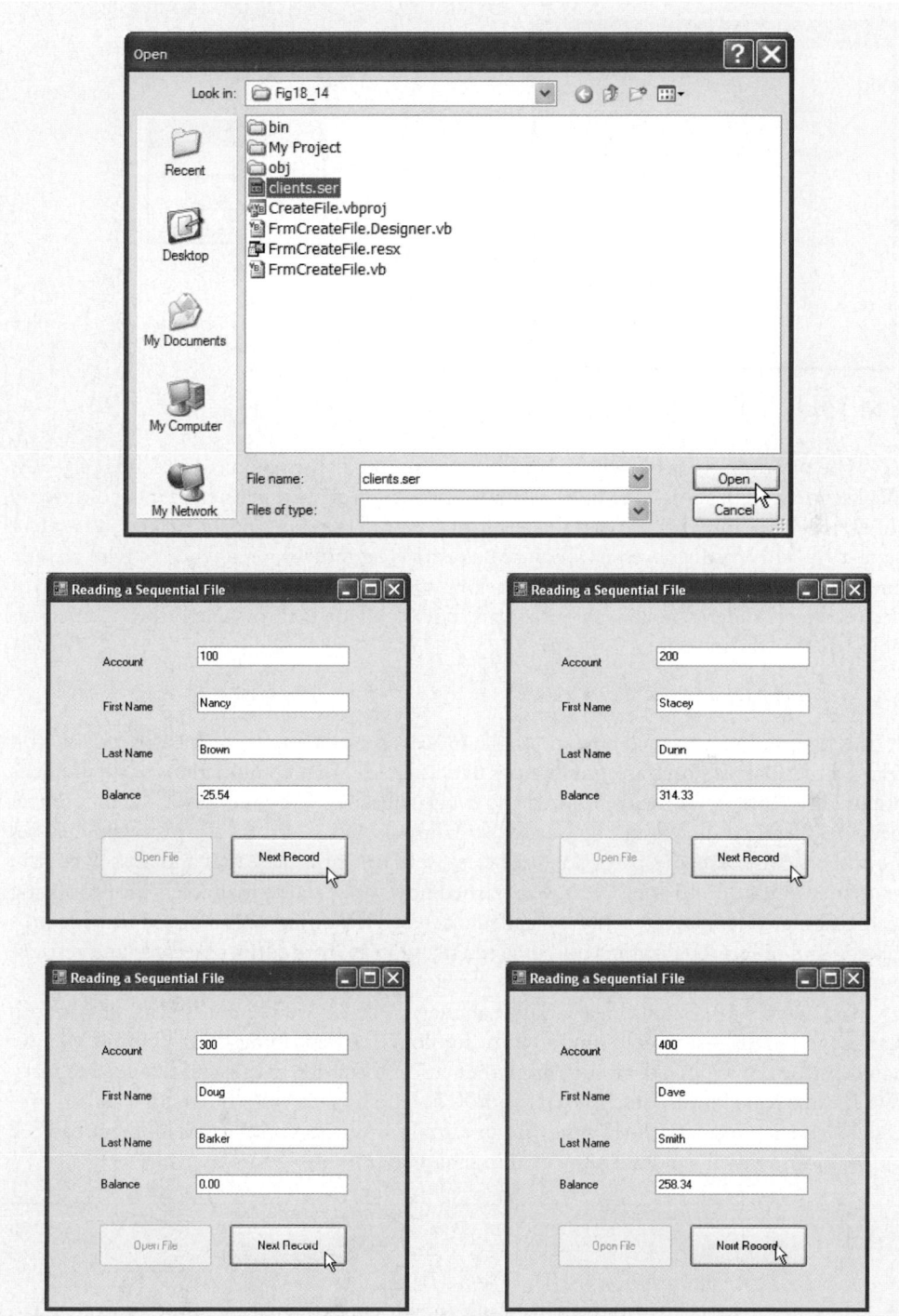

Fig. 18.15 | Sequential file read using deserialzation. (Part 3 of 4.)

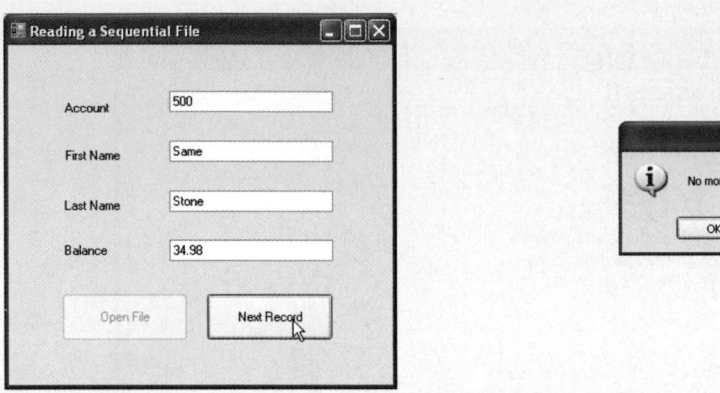

Fig. 18.15 | Sequential file read using deserialzation. (Part 4 of 4.)

The program reads objects from a file in event handler btnNext_Click (lines 43–70). We use method Deserialize (of the BinaryFormatter created in line 10) to read the data (lines 48–49). Note that we cast the result of Deserialize to type RecordSerializable (line 49)—this cast is necessary because Deserialize returns a reference of type object and we need to access properties that belong to class RecordSerializable. If an error occurs during deserialization, a SerializationException is thrown, and the FileStream object is closed (line 60).

18.11 Wrap-Up

In this chapter, you learned how to use file processing to manipulate persistent data. You learned that data is stored in computers as 0s and 1s, and that combinations of these values are used to form bytes, fields, records and eventually files. We overviewed the differences between character-based and byte-based streams, as well as several file-processing classes from the System.IO namespace. You used class File to manipulate files and class Directory to manipulate directories. Next, you learned how to use sequential-access file processing to manipulate records in text files. We then discussed the differences between text-file processing and object serialization, and used serialization to store entire objects in and retrieve entire objects from files.

In Chapter 19, Extensible Markup Language (XML), we present Extensible Markup Language (XML)—a widely supported technology for describing data. Using XML, we can describe any type of data, such as mathematical formulas, music and financial reports. We demonstrate how to describe data with XML and how to write programs that can process XML encoded data. XML is having an important impact on the development of Web applications, which we discuss in detail in Chapters 21 and 22.

Summary

Section 18.1 Introduction

- Files are used for long-term retention of large amounts of data, even after the program that created the data terminates.
- Data maintained in files is often called persistent data.

- Computers store files on secondary storage devices, such as magnetic disks, optical disks and magnetic tapes.
- File processing is one of a programming language's most important capabilities, because it enables a language to support commercial applications that typically process massive amounts of persistent data.

Section 18.2 Data Hierarchy
- All data items that computers process are reduced to combinations of 0s and 1s.
- The smallest data item that computers support is called a bit and can assume either the value 0 or the value 1.
- Digits, letters and special symbols are referred to as characters. The set of all characters used to write programs and represent data items on a particular computer is called that computer's character set. Every character in a computer's character set is represented as a pattern of 0s and 1s.
- Bytes are composed of eight bits.
- Characters in Visual Basic are Unicode characters composed of two bytes each.
- Just as characters are composed of bits, fields are composed of characters. A field is a group of characters that conveys meaning.
- Typically, a record is composed of several related fields.
- A data file is a group of related records.
- At least one field in each record is chosen as a record key, which identifies a record as belonging to a particular person or entity and distinguishes that record from all others.
- The most common type of file organization is a sequential file, in which records typically are stored in order by record-key field.
- A group of related files is called a database. A collection of programs designed to create and manage databases is called a database management system (DBMS).

Section 18.3 Files and Streams
- Visual Basic views each file as a sequential stream of bytes.
- Each file ends either with an end-of-file marker or at a specific byte number that is recorded in a system-maintained administrative data structure.
- Files are opened by creating an object that has a stream associated with it.
- Streams provide communication channels between files and programs.
- The System.IO namespace includes definitions for stream classes, such as StreamReader (for text input from a file), StreamWriter (for text output to a file) and FileStream (for both input from and output to a file).
- Class Stream provides functionality for representing streams as bytes. This class is a MustInherit class, so objects of this class cannot be instantiated.
- Classes FileStream, MemoryStream and BufferedStream (all from namespace System.IO) inherit from class Stream.
- Class FileStream can be used to read data to and write data from sequential-access files.
- Class MemoryStream enables the transfer of data directly to and from memory—this is much faster than other types of data transfer (e.g., to and from disk).
- Class BufferedStream uses buffering to transfer data to or from a stream. Buffering is an I/O performance-enhancement technique, in which each output operation is directed to a region in memory, called a buffer, that is large enough to hold the data from many output operations.

Then actual transfer to the output device is performed in one large physical output operation each time the buffer fills. The output operations directed to the output buffer in memory are often called logical output operations. Buffering can also be used to speed input operations.

Section 18.4 Classes `File` and `Directory`
- Information on computers is stored in files, which are organized in directories. Classes `File` and `Directory` enable programs to manipulate files and directories on disk.
- Class `File` provides `Shared` methods determining information about files and can be used to open files for reading or writing.
- Class `Directory` provides `Shared` methods for manipulating directories.
- The `DirectoryInfo` object returned by `Directory` method `CreateDirectory` contains information about a directory. Much of the information contained in class `DirectoryInfo` also can be accessed via the methods of class `Directory`.
- `File` method `Exists` determines whether a `String` is the name of an existing file.
- A `StreamReader` can be used to read text from a file. The `StreamReader` constructor takes as an argument a `String` containing the name of the file to open. `StreamReader` method `ReadToEnd` reads the entire contents of a file.
- `Directory` method `Exists` determines whether a `String` is the name of an existing directory.
- `Directory` method `GetDirectories` obtains a `String` array containing the names of subdirectories in the specified directory.
- A `NameValueCollection` (namespace `System.Collections.Specialized`) contains key-value pairs of `String`s, and provides method `Add` to add a key-value pair to the collection. The class's indexer can index according to the order in which the items were added or according to the keys.

Section 18.5 Creating a Sequential-Access Text File
- Visual Basic imposes no structure on files, so it does not recognize concepts like "record." This means that you must structure files to meet the requirements of your applications.
- When displayed, a `SaveFileDialog` prevents the user from interacting with any other window in the program until the user closes the `SaveFileDialog` by clicking either **Save** or **Cancel**. Dialogs that behave in this manner are called modal dialogs.
- There is a `FileStream` constructor that receives three arguments—a `String` containing the name of the file to be opened, a constant describing how to open the file and a constant describing the file permissions.
- The `StreamWriter` object is constructed with a `FileStream` argument that specifies the file to which `StreamWriter` outputs text.
- Class `StreamWriter` belongs to the `System.IO` namespace.

Section 18.6 Reading Data from a Sequential-Access Text File
- Data is stored in files so that it can be retrieved for processing when it is needed.
- To retrieve data sequentially from a file, programs normally start from the beginning of the file, reading data consecutively until the desired data is found. It sometimes is necessary to process a file sequentially several times during the execution of a program.
- An `OpenFileDialog` allows a user to select files to open. Method `ShowDialog` displays the dialog.

Section 18.7 Case Study: A Credit-Inquiry Program
- `FileStream` method `Seek` allows you to reset the file-position pointer by specifying the number of bytes it should be offset from the file's beginning, end or current position. The part of the file you want to be offset from is chosen using constants from the `SeekOrigin` enumeration.

Section 18.8 Serialization

- A serialized object is represented as a sequence of bytes that includes the object's data, as well as information about the object's type and the types of data stored in the object.
- After a serialized object has been written to a file, it can be read from the file and deserialized (recreated in memory).
- Class BinaryFormatter (namespace System.Runtime.Serialization.Formatters.Binary), enables entire serializable objects to be read from or written to a stream.
- BinaryFormatter methods Serialize and Deserialize write objects to and read objects from streams, respectively.
- Both method Serialize and method Deserialize require a Stream object (e.g., the FileStream) as a parameter so that the BinaryFormatter can access the correct file.

Section 18.9 Creating a Sequential-Access File Using Object Serialization

- Classes that are marked with the Serializable attribute indicate to the CLR that objects of the class can be serialized. Objects that we wish to write to or read from a stream must include this attribute in their class definitions.
- In a serializable class, you must ensure that every instance variable of the class is also serializable. By default, all simple-type variables are serializable. For reference-type variables, you must check the declaration of the class (and possibly its superclasses) to ensure that the type is serializable.

Section 18.10 Reading and Deserializing Data from a Sequential-Access Text File

- Method Deserialize (of class BinaryFormatter) reads a serialized object from a stream and reforms the object in memory.
- Method Deserialize returns a reference of type Object which must be cast to the appropriate type to manipulate the object.
- If an error occurs during deserialization, a SerializationException is thrown.

Terminology

binary digit (bit)	Delete method of class Directory
BinaryFormatter class	Delete method of class File
BinaryReader class	Deserialize method of class BinaryFormatter
BinaryWriter class	DialogResult enumeration
bit manipulation	Directory class
buffer	DirectoryInfo class
BufferedStream class	end-of-file marker
buffering	Error property of class Console
character	Exists method of class Directory
character set	field
close a file	file
Close method of class StreamWriter	File class
Console class	file-position pointer
Copy method of class File	file-processing programs
Create method of class File	FileAccess enumeration
CreateDirectory method of class Directory	FileStream class
CreateText method of class File	fixed-length records
data hierarchy	GetCreationTime method of class Directory
database	GetCreationTime method of class File
database management system (DBMS)	GetDirectories method of class Directory

GetFiles method of class `Directory`
GetLastAccessTime method of class `Directory`
GetLastAccessTime method of class `File`
GetLastWriteTime method of class `Directory`
GetLastWriteTime method of class `File`
In property of class `Console`
IOException
ISerializable interface
logical output operation
MemoryStream class
modal dialog
Move method of class `Directory`
Move method of class `File`
NameValueCollection class
object serialization
Open method of class `File`
OpenFileDialog class
OpenRead method of class `File`
OpenText method of class `File`
OpenWrite method of class `File`
Out property of class `Console`
pattern of 0s and 1s
persistent data
physical output operation
Read method of class `Console`
ReadLine method of class `Console`
ReadLine method of class `StreamReader`
record
record key

regular expression
SaveFileDialog class
secondary storage device
Seek method of class `FileStream`
SeekOrigin enumeration
sequential-access file
Serializable attribute
SerializationException
Serialize method of class `BinaryFormatter`
serialized object
OpenFileDialog
ShowDialog method of class OpenFileDialog
ShowDialog method of class SaveFileDialog
standard error stream object
standard input stream object
standard output stream object
Stream class
stream of bytes
StreamReader class
StreamWriter class
System.IO namespace
System.Runtime.Serialization.
    Formatters.Binary namespace
TextReader class
TextWriter class
Windows Control Library project
Write method of class `Console`
WriteLine method of class `Console`
WriteLine method of class `StreamWriter`

Self-Review Exercises

18.1 State whether each of the following is *true* or *false*. If *false*, explain why.
  a) Creating instances of classes `File` and `Directory` is not possible.
  b) Typically, a sequential file stores records in order by the record-key field.
  c) Class `StreamReader` inherits from class `Stream`.
  d) Any class can be serialized to a file.
  e) Method `Seek` of class `FileStream` always seeks relative to the beginning of a file.
  f) Classes `StreamReader` and `StreamWriter` are used with sequential-access files.
  g) You cannot instantiate objects of type `Stream`.

18.2 Fill in the blanks in each of the following statements:
  a) Ultimately, all data items processed by a computer are reduced to combinations of _____ and _____.
  b) The smallest data item a computer can process is called a(n) _____.
  c) A(n) _____ is a group of related records.
  d) Digits, letters and special symbols are collectively referred to as _____.
  e) A group of related files is called a(n) _____.
  f) `StreamReader` method _____ reads a line of text from a file.
  g) `StreamWriter` method _____ writes a line of text to a file.
  h) Method `Serialize` of class `BinaryFormatter` takes a(n) _____ and a(n) _____ as arguments.

i) The _____ namespace contains most of the FCL's file-processing classes.

j) The _____ namespace contains the `BinaryFormatter` class.

Answers to Self-Review Exercises

18.1   a) True. b) True. c) False. Class `StreamReader` inherits from class `TextReader`. d) False. Only classes with the `Serializable` attribute can be serialized. e) False. It seeks relative to the Seek-Origin enumeration member that is passed as one of the arguments. f.) True. g) True.

18.2   a) 0s, 1s. b) bit. c) file. d) characters. e) database. f) `ReadLine`. g) `WriteLine`. h) `Stream`, object. i) `System.IO`. j) `System.Runtime.Serialization.Formatters.Binary`.

Exercises

18.3   Create a program that stores student grades in a text file. The file should contain the name, ID number, class taken and grade of every student. Allow the user to load a grade file and display its contents in a read-only `TextBox`. The entries should be displayed in the following format:

```
LastName, FirstName:  ID# Class  Grade
```

We list some sample data below (note that strings should be enclosed in quotes):

```
Jones, Bob: 1 "Introduction to Computer Science" "A-"
Johnson, Sarah: 2 "Data Structures" "B+"
Smith, Sam: 3 "Data Structures" "C"
```

18.4   Modify the preceding program to use objects of a class that can be serialized to and deserialized from a file.

18.5   Create a program that combines the ideas of Fig. 18.9 and Fig. 18.11 to allow a user to write records to and read records from a file. Add an extra field of type `Boolean` to the record to indicate whether the account has overdraft protection.

18.6   *(Telephone-Number Word Generator)* Standard telephone keypads contain the digits 0 through 9. The numbers 2 through 9 each have three letters associated with them (Fig. 18.16). Many people find it difficult to memorize phone numbers, so they use the correspondence between digits and letters to develop seven-letter words that correspond to their phone numbers. For example, a person whose telephone number is 686-2377 might use the correspondence indicated in Fig. 18.16 to develop the seven-letter word "NUMBERS." Every seven-letter word corresponds to exactly one seven-digit telephone number. A restaurant wishing to increase its takeout business could surely do so with the number 825-3688 (i.e., "TAKEOUT").

Every seven-letter phone number corresponds to many different seven-letter words. Unfortunately, most of these words represent unrecognizable juxtapositions of letters. It is possible, how-

Digit	Letter	Digit	Letter
2	A B C	6	M N O
3	D E F	7	P R S
4	G H T	8	T U V
5	J K L	9	W X Y

Fig. 18.16 | Letters that correspond to the digits on a telephone keypad.

ever, that the owner of a barbershop would be pleased to know that the shop's telephone number, 424-7288, corresponds to "HAIRCUT." A veterinarian with the phone number 738-2273 would be pleased to know that the number corresponds to the letters "PETCARE." An automotive dealership would be pleased to know that its phone number, 639-2277, corresponds to "NEWCARS."

Write a GUI-based application (Fig. 18.17) that, given a seven-digit number, uses a Stream-Writer object to write to a file every possible seven-letter word combination corresponding to that number. There are 2,187 (3^7) such combinations. Avoid phone numbers with the digits 0 and 1.

18.7 *(Student Poll)* Figure 8.5 contains an array of survey responses that is hard-coded into the program. Suppose we wish to process survey results that are stored in a file. First, create a Windows Form that prompts the user for survey responses and outputs each response to a file. Use Stream-Writer to create a file called numbers.txt. Each integer should be written using method Write. Then add a TextBox that will output the frequency of survey responses. Modify the code in Fig. 8.5 to read the survey responses from numbers.txt. The responses should be read from the file by using a StreamReader. Class String's Split method should be used to split the input string into separate responses, then each response should be converted to an integer. The program should continue to read responses until it reaches the end of file. The results should be output to the TextBox.

Fig. 18.17 | Sample GUI for telephone-number word-generation application.

Extensible Markup Language (XML)

OBJECTIVES

In this chapter you will learn:

- To mark up data using XML.
- How XML namespaces help provide unique XML element and attribute names.
- To create DTDs and schemas for specifying and validating the structure of an XML document.
- To create and use simple XSL style sheets to render XML document data.
- To retrieve and modify XML data programmatically using .NET Framework classes.
- To validate XML documents against schemas using class `XmlReader`.
- To transform XML documents into XHTML using class `XslCompiledTransform`.

19.1 Introduction

The **Extensible Markup Language** (XML) was developed in 1996 by the **World Wide Web Consortium's** (W3C's) XML Working Group. XML is a widely supported **open technology** (i.e., nonproprietary technology) for describing data that has become the standard format for data exchanged between applications over the Internet.

The .NET Framework uses XML extensively. The Framework Class Library provides many XML-related classes, and much of Visual Studio's internal implementation also employs XML. Sections 19.2–19.6 introduce XML and XML-related technologies—XML namespaces for providing unique XML element and attribute names, and Document Type Definitions (DTDs) and XML Schemas for validating XML documents. These sections are required to support the use of XML in Chapters 20–22. Sections 19.7–19.10 present additional XML technologies and key .NET Framework classes for creating and manipulating XML documents programmatically—this material is optional but recommended if you plan to use XML in your own Visual Basic applications.

19.2 XML Basics

XML permits document authors to create **markup** (i.e., a text-based notation for describing data) for virtually any type of information. This enables document authors to create entirely new markup languages for describing any type of data, such as mathematical formulas, software-configuration instructions, chemical molecular structures, music, news, recipes and financial reports. XML describes data in a way that both human beings and computers can understand.

Figure 19.1 is a simple XML document that describes information for a baseball player. We focus on lines 5–11 to introduce basic XML syntax. You will learn about the other elements of this document in Section 19.3.

XML documents contain text that represents content (i.e., data), such as John (line 6 of Fig. 19.1), and **elements** that specify the document's structure, such as firstName (line 6 of Fig. 19.1). XML documents delimit elements with **start tags** and **end tags**. A start tag

```
 1   <?xml version = "1.0"?>
 2   <!-- Fig. 19.1: player.xml -->
 3   <!-- Baseball player structured with XML -->
 4
 5   <player>
 6      <firstName>John</firstName>
 7
 8      <lastName>Doe</lastName>
 9
10      <battingAverage>0.375</battingAverage>
11   </player>
```

Fig. 19.1 | XML that describes a baseball player's information.

consists of the element name in **angle brackets** (e.g., `<player>` and `<firstName>` in lines 5 and 6, respectively). An end tag consists of the element name preceded by a **forward slash** (/) in angle brackets (e.g., `</firstName>` and `</player>` in lines 6 and 11, respectively). An element's start and end tags enclose text that represents a piece of data (e.g., the `firstName` of the `player`—John—in line 6, which is enclosed by the `<firstName>` start tag and `</firstName>` end tag). Every XML document must have exactly one **root element** that contains all the other elements. In Fig. 19.1, `player` (lines 5–11) is the root element.

Some XML-based markup languages include XHTML (Extensible HyperText Markup Language—HTML's replacement for marking up Web content), MathML (for mathematics), VoiceXML™ (for speech), CML (Chemical Markup Language—for chemistry) and XBRL (Extensible Business Reporting Language—for financial data exchange). These markup languages are called XML **vocabularies** and provide a means for describing particular types of data in standardized, structured ways.

Massive amounts of data are currently stored on the Internet in a variety of formats (e.g., databases, Web pages, text files). Based on current trends, it is likely that much of this data, especially that which is passed between systems, will soon take the form of XML. Organizations see XML as the future of data encoding. Information technology groups are planning ways to integrate XML into their systems. Industry groups are developing custom XML vocabularies for most major industries that will allow computer-based business applications to communicate in common languages. For example, Web services, which we discuss in Chapter 22, allow Web-based applications to exchange data seamlessly through standard protocols based on XML.

The next generation of the Internet and World Wide Web is being built on a foundation of XML, which enables the development of more sophisticated Web-based applications. XML allows you to assign meaning to what would otherwise be random pieces of data. As a result, programs can "understand" the data they manipulate. For example, a Web browser might view a street address listed on a simple HTML Web page as a string of characters without any real meaning. In an XML document, however, this data can be clearly identified (i.e., marked up) as an address. A program that uses the document can recognize this data as an address and provide links to a map of that location, driving directions from that location or other location-specific information. Likewise, an application can recognize names of people, dates, ISBN numbers and any other type of XML-encoded data. Based on this data, the application can present users with other related information, providing a richer, more meaningful user experience.

Viewing and Modifying XML Documents

XML documents are highly portable. Viewing or modifying an XML document—which is a text file that ends with the `.xml` filename extension—does not require special software, although many software tools exist, and new ones are frequently released that make it more convenient to develop XML-based applications. Any text editor that supports ASCII/Unicode characters can open XML documents for viewing and editing. Also, most Web browsers can display XML documents in a formatted manner that shows the XML's structure. We demonstrate this using Internet Explorer in Section 19.3. One important characteristic of XML is that it is both human readable and machine readable.

Processing XML Documents

Processing an XML document requires software called an XML parser (or XML processor). A parser makes the document's data available to applications. While reading the contents of an XML document, a parser checks that the document follows the syntax rules specified by the W3C's XML Recommendation (`www.w3.org/XML`). XML syntax requires a single root element, a start tag and end tag for each element, and properly nested tags (i.e., the end tag for a nested element must appear before the end tag of the enclosing element). Furthermore, XML is case sensitive, so the proper capitalization must be used in elements. A document that conforms to this syntax is a well-formed XML document, and is syntactically correct. We present fundamental XML syntax in Section 19.3. If an XML parser can process an XML document successfully, that XML document is well formed. Parsers can provide access to XML-encoded data in well-formed documents only.

Often, XML parsers are built into software such as Visual Studio or available for download over the Internet. Popular parsers include Microsoft XML Core Services (MSXML), the Apache Software Foundation's Xerces (`xml.apache.org`) and the open-source Expat XML Parser (`expat.sourceforge.net`). In this chapter, we use MSXML.

Validating XML Documents

An XML document can optionally reference a Document Type Definition (DTD) or a schema that defines the proper structure of the XML document. When an XML document references a DTD or a schema, some parsers (called validating parsers) can read the DTD/schema and check that the XML document follows the structure defined by the DTD/schema. If the XML document conforms to the DTD/schema (i.e., the document has the appropriate structure), the XML document is valid. For example, if in Fig. 19.1 we were referencing a DTD that specifies that a `player` element must have `firstName`, `lastName` and `battingAverage` elements, then omitting the `lastName` element (line 8 in Fig. 19.1) would cause the XML document `player.xml` to be invalid. However, the XML document would still be well formed, because it follows proper XML syntax (i.e., it has one root element, and each element has a start tag and an end tag). By definition, a valid XML document is well formed. Parsers that cannot check for document conformity against DTDs/schemas are nonvalidating parsers—they determine only whether an XML document is well formed, not whether it is valid.

We discuss validation, DTDs and schemas, as well as the key differences between these two types of structural specifications, in Sections 19.5 and 19.6. For now, note that schemas are XML documents themselves, whereas DTDs are not. As you will learn in Section 19.6, this difference presents several advantages in using schemas over DTDs.

Software Engineering Observation 19.1

DTDs and schemas are essential for business-to-business (B2B) transactions and mission-critical systems. Validating XML documents ensures that disparate systems can manipulate data structured in standardized ways and prevents errors caused by missing or malformed data.

Formatting and Manipulating XML Documents

XML documents contain only data, not formatting instructions, so applications that process XML documents must decide how to manipulate or display each document's data. For example, a PDA (personal digital assistant) may render an XML document differently than a wireless phone or a desktop computer. You can use **Extensible Stylesheet Language** (**XSL**) to specify rendering instructions for different platforms. We discuss XSL in Section 19.7.

XML-processing programs can also search, sort and manipulate XML data using technologies such as XSL. Some other XML-related technologies are XPath (XML Path Language—a language for accessing parts of an XML document), XSL-FO (XSL Formatting Objects—an XML vocabulary used to describe document formatting) and XSLT (XSL Transformations—a language for transforming XML documents into other documents). We present XSLT in Section 19.7. We also introduce XPath in Section 19.7, then discuss it in greater detail in Section 19.8.

19.3 Structuring Data

In this section and throughout this chapter, we create our own XML markup. XML allows you to describe data precisely in a well-structured format.

XML Markup for an Article

In Fig. 19.2, we present an XML document that marks up a simple article using XML. The line numbers shown are for reference only and are not part of the XML document.

```
 1    <?xml version = "1.0"?>
 2    <!-- Fig. 19.2: article.xml -->
 3    <!-- Article structured with XML -->
 4
 5    <article>
 6       <title>Simple XML</title>
 7
 8       <date>May 5, 2005</date>
 9
10       <author>
11          <firstName>John</firstName>
12          <lastName>Doe</lastName>
13       </author>
14
15       <summary>XML is pretty easy.</summary>
16
```

Fig. 19.2 | XML used to mark up an article. (Part 1 of 2.)

```
17      <content>
18         In this chapter, we present a wide variety of examples that use XML.
19      </content>
20   </article>
```

Fig. 19.2 | XML used to mark up an article. (Part 2 of 2.)

This document begins with an XML declaration (line 1), which identifies the document as an XML document. The version attribute specifies the XML version to which the document conforms. The current XML standard is version 1.0. Though the W3C released a version 1.1 specification in February 2004, this newer version is not yet widely supported. The W3C may continue to release new versions as XML evolves to meet the requirements of different fields.

Portability Tip 19.1

Documents should include the XML declaration to identify the version of XML used. A document that lacks an XML declaration might be assumed to conform to the latest version of XML—when it does not, errors could result.

Common Programming Error 19.1

Placing whitespace characters before the XML declaration is an error.

XML comments (lines 2–3), which begin with <!-- and end with -->, can be placed almost anywhere in an XML document. XML comments can span to multiple lines—an end marker on each line is not needed; the end marker can appear on a subsequent line as long as there is exactly one end marker (-->) for each begin marker (<!--). Comments are used in XML for documentation purposes. Line 4 is a blank line. As in a Visual Basic program, blank lines, whitespaces and indentation are used in XML to improve readability. Later you will see that the blank lines are normally ignored by XML parsers.

Common Programming Error 19.2

In an XML document, each start tag must have a matching end tag; omitting either tag is an error. Soon, you will learn how such errors are detected.

Common Programming Error 19.3

XML is case sensitive. Using different cases for the start tag and end tag names for the same element is a syntax error.

In Fig. 19.2, article (lines 5–20) is the root element. The lines that precede the root element (lines 1–4) are the XML prolog. In an XML prolog, the XML declaration must appear before the comments and any other markup.

The elements we used in the example do not come from any specific markup language. Instead, we chose the element names and markup structure that best describe our particular data. You can invent elements to mark up your data. For example, element title (line 6) contains text that describes the article's title (e.g., Simple XML). Similarly, date (line 8), author (lines 10–13), firstName (line 11), lastName (line 12), summary (line 15) and content (lines 17–19) contain text that describes the date, author, the author's first name, the author's last name, a summary and the content of the document, respectively. XML element names can be of any length and may contain letters, digits, underscores, hyphens and periods. However, they must begin with either a letter or an underscore, and they should not begin with "xml" in any combination of uppercase and lowercase letters (e.g., XML, Xml, xMl) as this is reserved for use in the XML standards.

Common Programming Error 19.4

Using a whitespace character in an XML element name is an error.

Good Programming Practice 19.1

XML element names should be meaningful to humans and should not use abbreviations.

XML elements are **nested** to form hierarchies—with the root element at the top of the hierarchy. This allows document authors to create parent/child relationships between data. For example, elements title, date, author, summary and content are nested within article. Elements firstName and lastName are nested within author. Figure 19.21 shows the hierarchy of Fig. 19.2.

Common Programming Error 19.5

Nesting XML tags improperly is a syntax error. For example, <x><y>hello</x></y> is an error, because the </y> tag must precede the </x> tag.

Any element that contains other elements (e.g., article or author) is a **container element**. Container elements also are called **parent elements**. Elements nested inside a container element are **child elements** (or children) of that container element.

Viewing an XML Document in Internet Explorer

The XML document in Fig. 19.2 is simply a text file named article.xml. This document does not contain formatting information for the article. This is because XML is a technology for describing the structure of data. Formatting and displaying data from an XML document are application-specific issues. For example, when the user loads article.xml in Internet Explorer (IE), MSXML (Microsoft XML Core Services) parses and displays the document's data. Internet Explorer uses a built-in **style sheet** to format the data. Note that the resulting format of the data (Fig. 19.3) is similar to the format of the listing in Fig. 19.2. In Section 19.7, we show how to create style sheets to transform your XML data into various formats suitable for display.

Note the minus sign (–) and plus sign (+) in the screen shots of Fig. 19.3. Although these symbols are not part of the XML document, Internet Explorer places them next to every container element. A minus sign indicates that Internet Explorer is displaying the container element's child elements. Clicking the minus sign next to an element collapses that element (i.e., causes Internet Explorer to hide the container element's children and replace the minus sign with a plus sign). Conversely, clicking the plus sign next to an element expands that element (i.e., causes Internet Explorer to display the container element's children and replace the plus sign with a minus sign). This behavior is similar to viewing the directory structure using Windows Explorer. In fact, a directory structure often is modeled as a series of tree structures, in which the **root** of a tree represents a drive letter (e.g., C:), and **nodes** in the tree represent directories. Parsers often store XML data as tree structures to facilitate efficient manipulation, as discussed in Section 19.8.

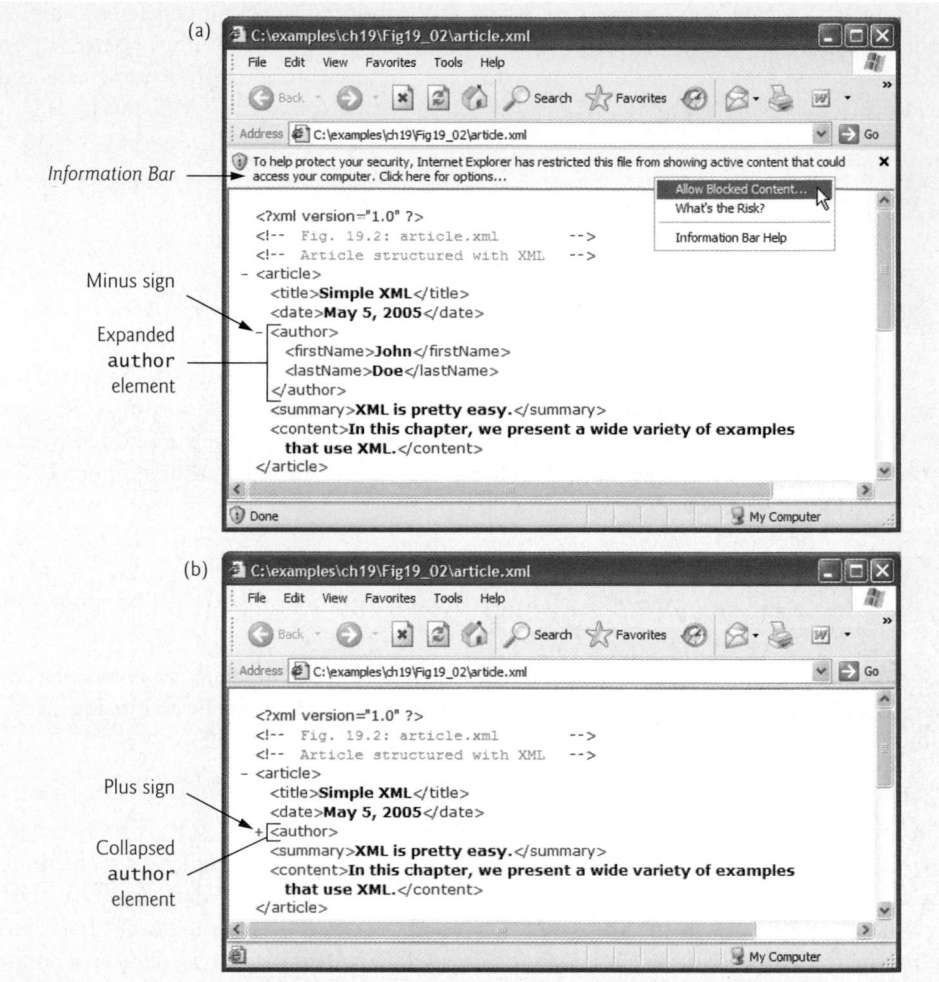

Fig. 19.3 | `article.xml` displayed by Internet Explorer.

[*Note:* In Windows XP Service Pack 2, by default Internet Explorer displays all the XML elements in expanded view, and clicking the minus sign (Fig. 19.3(a) does not do anything. So by default, Windows will not be able to collapse the element. To enable this functionality, right click the *Information Bar* just below the **Address** field and select **Allow Blocked Content...**. Then click **Yes** in the popup window that appears.]

XML Markup for a Business Letter

Now that we have seen a simple XML document, let's examine a more complex XML document that marks up a business letter (Fig. 19.4). Again, we begin the document with the XML declaration (line 1) that states the XML version to which the document conforms.

Line 5 specifies that this XML document references a DTD. Recall from Section 19.2 that DTDs define the structure of the data for an XML document. For example, a DTD specifies the elements and parent-child relationships between elements permitted in an XML document.

```
 1   <?xml version = "1.0"?>
 2   <!-- Fig. 19.4: letter.xml -->
 3   <!-- Business letter marked up as XML -->
 4
 5   <!DOCTYPE letter SYSTEM "letter.dtd">
 6
 7   <letter>
 8      <contact type = "sender">
 9         <name>Jane Doe</name>
10         <address1>Box 12345</address1>
11         <address2>15 Any Ave.</address2>
12         <city>Othertown</city>
13         <state>Otherstate</state>
14         <zip>67890</zip>
15         <phone>555-4321</phone>
16         <flag gender = "F" />
17      </contact>
18
19      <contact type = "receiver">
20         <name>John Doe</name>
21         <address1>123 Main St.</address1>
22         <address2></address2>
23         <city>Anytown</city>
24         <state>Anystate</state>
25         <zip>12345</zip>
26         <phone>555-1234</phone>
27         <flag gender = "M" />
28      </contact>
29
30      <salutation>Dear Sir:</salutation>
31
32      <paragraph>It is our privilege to inform you about our new database
33         managed with XML. This new system allows you to reduce the
34         load on your inventory list server by having the client machine
35         perform the work of sorting and filtering the data.
36      </paragraph>
37
38      <paragraph>Please visit our Web site for availability
39         and pricing.
40      </paragraph>
41
42      <closing>Sincerely,</closing>
43      <signature>Ms. Jane Doe</signature>
44   </letter>
```

Fig. 19.4 | Business letter marked up as XML.

Error-Prevention Tip 19.1

An XML document is not required to reference a DTD, but validating XML parsers can use a DTD to ensure that the document has the proper structure.

Portability Tip 19.2

Validating an XML document helps guarantee that independent developers will exchange data in a standardized form that conforms to the DTD.

The DTD reference (line 5) contains three items, the name of the root element that the DTD specifies (letter); the keyword SYSTEM (which denotes an **external DTD**—a DTD declared in a separate file, as opposed to a DTD declared locally in the same file); and the DTD's name and location (i.e., letter.dtd in the current directory). DTD document filenames typically end with the **.dtd** extension. We discuss DTDs and letter.dtd in detail in Section 19.5.

Several tools (many of which are free) validate documents against DTDs and schemas (discussed in Section 19.5 and Section 19.6, respectively). Microsoft's **XML Validator** is available free of charge from the **Download Sample** link at

msdn.microsoft.com/archive/en-us/samples/internet/
xml/xml_validator/default.asp

This validator can validate XML documents against both DTDs and Schemas. To install it, run the downloaded executable file xml_validator.exe and follow the steps to complete the installation. Once the installation is successful, open the validate_js.htm file located in your XML Validator installation directory in IE to validate your XML documents. We installed the XML Validator at C:\XMLValidator (Fig. 19.5). The output (Fig. 19.6) shows the results of validating the document using Microsoft's XML Validator. Visit www.w3.org/XML/Schema for a list of additional validation tools.

Root element letter (lines 7–44 of Fig. 19.4) contains the child elements contact, contact, salutation, paragraph, paragraph, closing and signature. In addition to being placed between tags, data also can be placed in **attributes**—name-value pairs that appear within the angle brackets of start tags. Elements can have any number of attributes (separated by spaces) in their start tags. The first contact element (lines 8–17) has an attribute named type with **attribute value** "sender", which indicates that this contact element identifies the letter's sender. The second contact element (lines 19–28) has attribute type with value "receiver", which indicates that this contact element identifies

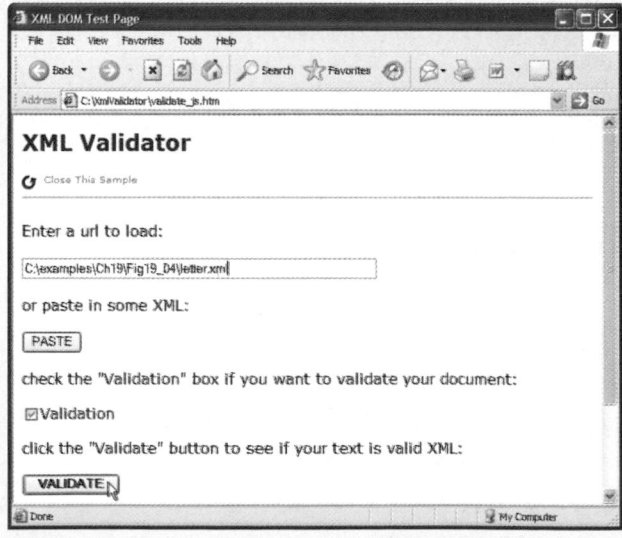

Fig. 19.5 | Validating an XML document with Microsoft's XML Validator.

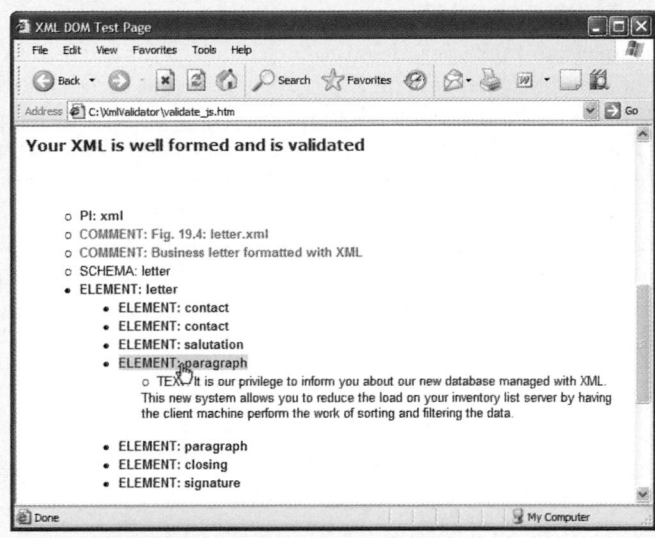

Fig. 19.6 | Validation result using Microsoft's XML Validator.

the letter's recipient. Like element names, attribute names are case sensitive, can be any length, may contain letters, digits, underscores, hyphens and periods, and must begin with either a letter or an underscore character. A `contact` element stores various items of information about a contact, such as the contact's name (represented by element `name`), address (represented by elements `address1`, `address2`, `city`, `state` and `zip`), phone number (represented by element `phone`) and gender (represented by attribute `gender` of element `flag`). Element `salutation` (line 30) marks up the letter's salutation. Lines 32–40 mark up the letter's body using two `paragraph` elements. Elements `closing` (line 42) and `signature` (line 43) mark up the closing sentence and the author's "signature," respectively.

> **Common Programming Error 19.6**
>
> *Failure to enclose attribute values in double ("") or single (' ') quotes is a syntax error.*

Line 16 introduces the **empty element** `flag`. An empty element is one that does not contain any content. Instead, an empty element sometimes contains data in attributes. Empty element `flag` contains an attribute that indicates the gender of the contact (represented by the parent `contact` element). Document authors can close an empty element either by placing a slash immediately preceding the right angle bracket, as shown in line 16, or by explicitly writing an end tag, as in line 22

```
<address2></address2>
```

Note that the `address2` element in line 22 is empty because there is no second part to this contact's address. However, we must include this element to conform to the structural rules specified in the XML document's DTD—`letter.dtd` (which we present in Section 19.5). This DTD specifies that each `contact` element must have an `address2` child element (even if it is empty). In Section 19.5, you will learn how DTDs indicate that certain elements are required while others are optional.

19.4 XML Namespaces

XML allows document authors to create custom elements. This extensibility can result in **naming collisions** among elements in an XML document that each have the same name. For example, we may use the element book to mark up data about a Deitel publication. A stamp collector may use the element book to mark up data about a book of stamps. Using both of these elements in the same document could create a naming collision, making it difficult to determine which kind of data each element contains.

An XML **namespace** is a collection of element and attribute names. Like Visual Basic namespaces, XML namespaces provide a means for document authors to unambiguously refer to elements with the same name (i.e., prevent collisions). For example,

```
<subject>Math</subject>
```

and

```
<subject>Cardiology</subject>
```

use element subject to mark up data. In the first case, the subject is something one studies in school, whereas in the second case, the subject is a field of medicine. Namespaces can differentiate these two subject elements. For example

```
<school:subject>Math</school:subject>
```

and

```
<medical:subject>Cardiology</medical:subject>
```

Both school and medical are **namespace prefixes**. A document author places a namespace prefix and colon (:) before an element name to specify the namespace to which that element belongs. Document authors can create their own namespace prefixes using virtually any name except the reserved namespace prefix xml. In the next subsections, we demonstrate how document authors ensure that namespaces are unique.

 Common Programming Error 19.7

Attempting to create a namespace prefix named xml in any mixture of uppercase and lowercase letters is a syntax error—the xml namespace prefix is reserved for internal use by XML itself.

Differentiating Elements with Namespaces

Figure 19.7 demonstrates namespaces. In this document, namespaces differentiate two distinct elements—the file element related to a text file and the file document related to an image file.

Lines 6–7 use the XML-namespace reserved attribute xmlns to create two namespace prefixes—text and image. Each namespace prefix is bound to a series of characters called a **Uniform Resource Identifier (URI)** that uniquely identifies the namespace. Document authors create their own namespace prefixes and URIs. A URI is a way to identifying a resource, typically on the Internet. Two popular types of URI are **Uniform Resource Name (URN)** and **Uniform Resource Locator (URL)**.

To ensure that namespaces are unique, document authors must provide unique URIs. In this example, we use the text urn:deitel:textInfo and urn:deitel:imageInfo as

```
 I   <?xml version = "1.0"?>
 2   <!-- Fig. 19.7: namespace.xml -->
 3   <!-- Demonstrating namespaces -->
 4
 5   <text:directory
 6      xmlns:text = "urn:deitel:textInfo"
 7      xmlns:image = "urn:deitel:imageInfo">
 8
 9      <text:file filename = "book.xml">
10         <text:description>A book list</text:description>
11      </text:file>
12
13      <image:file filename = "funny.jpg">
14         <image:description>A funny picture</image:description>
15         <image:size width = "200" height = "100" />
16      </image:file>
17   </text:directory>
```

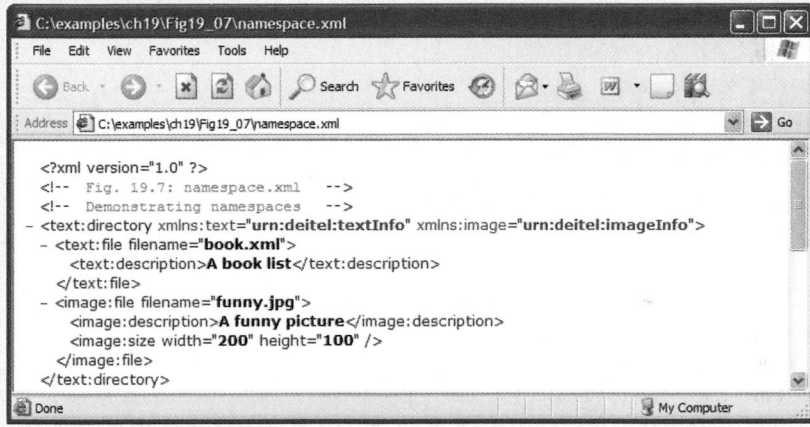

Fig. 19.7 | XML namespaces demonstration.

URIs. These URIs employ the URN scheme frequently used to identify namespaces. Under this naming scheme, a URI begins with "urn:", followed by a unique series of additional names separated by colons.

Another common practice is to use URLs, which specify the location of a file or a resource on the Internet. For example, www.deitel.com is the URL that identifies the home page of the Deitel & Associates Web site. Using URLs guarantees that the namespaces are unique because the domain names (e.g., www.deitel.com) are guaranteed to be unique. For example, lines 5–7 could be rewritten as

```
<text:directory
    xmlns:text = "http://www.deitel.com/xmlns-text"
    xmlns:image = "http://www.deitel.com/xmlns-image">
```

where URLs related to the Deitel & Associates, Inc. domain name serve as URIs to identify the text and image namespaces. The parser does not visit these URLs, nor do these URLs need to refer to actual Web pages. They each simply represent a unique series of characters used to differentiate URI names. In fact, any string can represent a namespace. For example, our `image` namespace URI could be `hgjfkdlsa4556`, in which case our prefix assignment would be

```
xmlns:image = "hgjfkdlsa4556"
```

Lines 9–11 use the `text` namespace prefix for elements `file` and `description`. Note that the end tags must also specify the namespace prefix `text`. Lines 13–16 apply namespace prefix `image` to the elements `file`, `description` and `size`. Note that attributes do not require namespace prefixes (although they can have them), because each attribute is already part of an element that specifies the namespace prefix. For example, attribute `filename` (line 9) is implicitly part of namespace `text` because its element (i.e., `file`) specifies the `text` namespace prefix.

Specifying a Default Namespace
To eliminate the need to place namespace prefixes in each element, document authors may specify a **default namespace** for an element and its children. Figure 19.8 demonstrates using a default namespace (`urn:deitel:textInfo`) for element `directory`.

```
1    <?xml version = "1.0"?>
2    <!-- Fig. 19.8: defaultnamespace.xml -->
3    <!-- Using default namespaces -->
4
5    <directory xmlns = "urn:deitel:textInfo"
6        xmlns:image = "urn:deitel:imageInfo">
7
8        <file filename = "book.xml">
9            <description>A book list</description>
10       </file>
11
12       <image:file filename = "funny.jpg">
13           <image:description>A funny picture</image:description>
14           <image:size width = "200" height = "100" />
15       </image:file>
16   </directory>
```

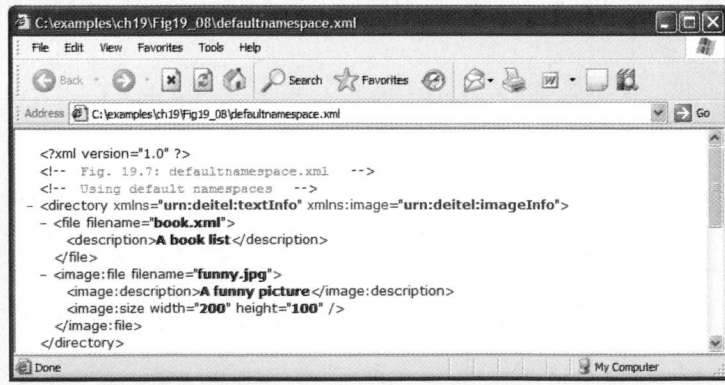

Fig. 19.8 | Default namespace demonstration.

Line 5 defines a default namespace using attribute xmlns with a URI as its value. Once we define this default namespace, child elements belonging to the namespace need not be qualified by a namespace prefix. Thus, element file (lines 8–10) is in the default namespace urn:deitel:textInfo. Compare this to lines 8–10 of Fig. 19.7, where we had to prefix the file and description element names with the namespace prefix text.

The default namespace applies to the directory element and all elements that are not qualified with a namespace prefix. However, we can use a namespace prefix to specify a different namespace for particular elements. For example, the file element in lines 12–15 includes the image namespace prefix, indicating that this element is in the urn:deitel:imageInfo namespace, not the default namespace.

Namespaces in XML Vocabularies

XML-based languages, such as XML Schema (Section 19.6), Extensible Stylesheet Language (XSL) (Section 19.7) and BizTalk (www.microsoft.com/biztalk), often use namespaces to identify their elements. Each of these vocabularies defines special-purpose elements that are grouped in namespaces. These namespaces help prevent naming collisions between predefined elements and user-defined elements.

19.5 Document Type Definitions (DTDs)

Document Type Definitions (DTDs) are one of two main types of documents you can use to specify XML document structure. Section 19.6 presents W3C XML Schema documents, which provide an improved method of specifying XML document structure.

Software Engineering Observation 19.2

XML documents can have many different structures, and for this reason an application cannot be certain whether a particular document it receives is complete, ordered properly, and not missing data. DTDs and schemas (Section 19.6) solve this problem by providing an extensible way to describe XML document structure. Applications should use DTDs or schemas to confirm whether XML documents are valid.

Software Engineering Observation 19.3

Many organizations and individuals are creating DTDs and schemas for a broad range of applications. These collections—called repositories—are available free for download from the Web (e.g., www.xml.org, www.oasis-open.org).

Creating a Document Type Definition

Figure 19.4 presented a simple business letter marked up with XML. Recall that line 5 of letter.xml references a DTD—letter.dtd (Fig. 19.9). This DTS specifies the business letter's element types and attributes, and their relationships to one another.

A DTD describes the structure of an XML document and enables an XML parser to verify whether an XML document is valid (i.e., whether its elements contain the proper attributes and appear in the proper sequence). DTDs allow users to check document structure and to exchange data in a standardized format. A DTD expresses the set of rules for document structure using an EBNF (Extended Backus-Naur Form) grammar. [*Note:* EBNF grammars are commonly used to define programming languages. For more information on EBNF grammars, please see en.wikipedia.org/wiki/EBNF or www.garshol.priv.no/download/text/bnf.html.]

```
 1   <!-- Fig. 19.9: letter.dtd      -->
 2   <!-- DTD document for letter.xml -->
 3
 4   <!ELEMENT letter ( contact+, salutation, paragraph+,
 5      closing, signature )>
 6
 7   <!ELEMENT contact ( name, address1, address2, city, state,
 8      zip, phone, flag )>
 9   <!ATTLIST contact type CDATA #IMPLIED>
10
11   <!ELEMENT name ( #PCDATA )>
12   <!ELEMENT address1 ( #PCDATA )>
13   <!ELEMENT address2 ( #PCDATA )>
14   <!ELEMENT city ( #PCDATA )>
15   <!ELEMENT state ( #PCDATA )>
16   <!ELEMENT zip ( #PCDATA )>
17   <!ELEMENT phone ( #PCDATA )>
18   <!ELEMENT flag EMPTY>
19   <!ATTLIST flag gender (M | F) "M">
20
21   <!ELEMENT salutation ( #PCDATA )>
22   <!ELEMENT closing ( #PCDATA )>
23   <!ELEMENT paragraph ( #PCDATA )>
24   <!ELEMENT signature ( #PCDATA )>
```

Fig. 19.9 | Document Type Definition (DTD) for a business letter.

Common Programming Error 19.8

For documents validated with DTDs, any document that uses elements, attributes or relation-ships not explicitly defined by a DTD is an invalid document.

Defining Elements in a DTD

The ELEMENT element type declaration in lines 4–5 defines the rules for element letter. In this case, letter contains one or more contact elements, one salutation element, one or more paragraph elements, one closing element and one signature element, in that sequence. The **plus sign (+) occurrence indicator** specifies that the DTD allows one or more occurrences of an element. Other occurence indicators include the **asterisk (*)**, which indicates an optional element that can occur zero or more times, and the **question mark (?)**, which indicates an optional element that can occur at most once (i.e., zero or one occurrence). If an element does not have an occurrence indicator, the DTD allows exactly one occurrence.

The contact element type declaration (lines 7–8) specifies that a contact element contains child elements name, address1, address2, city, state, zip, phone and flag— in that order. The DTD requires exactly one occurrence of each of these elements.

Defining Attributes in a DTD

Line 9 uses the **ATTLIST attribute-list declaration** to define an attribute named type for the contact element. Keyword **#IMPLIED** specifies that if the parser finds a contact element without a type attribute, the parser can choose an arbitrary value for the attribute or can ignore the attribute. Either way the document will still be valid (if the rest of the document is valid)—a missing type attribute will not invalidate the document. Other keywords that can be used in place of #IMPLIED in an ATTLIST declaration include #REQUIRED and #FIXED. Keyword #REQUIRED specifies that the attribute must be present in the element, and keyword #FIXED specifies that the attribute (if present) must have the given fixed value. For example,

```
<!ATTLIST address zip CDATA #FIXED "01757">
```

indicates that attribute zip (if present in element address) must have the value 01757 for the document to be valid. If the attribute is not present, then the parser, by default, uses the fixed value that the ATTLIST declaration specifies.

Character Data vs. Parsed Character Data

Keyword CDATA (line 9) specifies that attribute type contains character data (i.e., a string). A parser will pass such data to an application without modification.

Software Engineering Observation 19.4

DTD syntax cannot describe an element's (or attribute's) type. For example, a DTD cannot specify that a particular element or attribute can contain only integer data.

Keyword #PCDATA (line 11) specifies that an element (e.g., name) may contain parsed character data (i.e., data that is processed by an XML parser). Elements with parsed character data cannot contain markup characters, such as less than (<), greater than (>) or ampersand (&). The document author should replace any markup character in a #PCDATA element with the character's corresponding character entity reference. For example, the character entity reference < should be used in place of the less-than symbol (<), and the character entity reference > should be used in place of the greater-than symbol (>). A document author who wishes to use a literal ampersand should use the entity reference & instead—parsed character data can contain ampersands (&) only for inserting entities. See Appendix H, HTML/XHTML Special Characters for a list of other character entity references.

Common Programming Error 19.9

Using markup characters (e.g., <, > and &) in parsed character data is an error. Use character entity references (e.g., <, > and & instead).

Defining Empty Elements in a DTD

Line 18 defines an empty element named flag. Keyword EMPTY specifies that the element does not contain any data between its start and end tags. Empty elements commonly describe data via attributes. For example, flag's data appears in its gender attribute (line 19). Line 19 specifies that the gender attribute's value must be one of the enumerated values (M or F) enclosed in parentheses and delimited by a vertical bar (|) meaning "or." Note that line 19 also indicates that gender has a default value of M.

Well-Formed Documents vs. Valid Documents

In Section 19.3, we demonstrated how to use the Microsoft XML Validator to validate an XML document against its specified DTD. The validation revealed that the XML document letter.xml (Fig. 19.4) is well formed and valid—it conforms to letter.dtd (Fig. 19.9). Recall that a well-formed document is syntactically correct (i.e., each start tag has a corresponding end tag, the document contains only one root element, etc.), and a valid document contains the proper elements with the proper attributes in the proper sequence. An XML document cannot be valid unless it is well formed.

When a document fails to conform to a DTD or a schema, the Microsoft XML Validator displays an error message. For example, the DTD in Fig. 19.9 indicates that a `con-tact` element must contain the child element `name`. A document that omits this child element is still well formed, but is not valid. In such a scenario, Microsoft XML Validator displays the error message shown in Fig. 19.10.

19.6 W3C XML Schema Documents

In this section, we introduce schemas for specifying XML document structure and validating XML documents. Many developers in the XML community believe that DTDs are not flexible enough to meet today's programming needs. For example, DTDs lack a way of indicating what specific type of data (e.g., numeric, text) an element can contain and DTDs are not themselves XML documents. These and other limitations have led to the development of schemas.

Unlike DTDs, schemas do not use EBNF grammar. Instead, schemas use XML syntax and are actually XML documents that programs can manipulate. Like DTDs, schemas are used by validating parsers to validate documents.

In this section, we focus on the W3C's **XML Schema** vocabulary (note the capital "S" in "Schema"). We use the term XML Schema in the rest of the chapter whenever we refer to W3C's XML Schema vocabulary. For the latest information on XML Schema, visit `www.w3.org/XML/Schema`. For tutorials on XML Schema concepts beyond what we present here, visit `www.w3schools.com/schema/default.asp`.

A DTD describes an XML document's structure, not the content of its elements. For example,

```
<quantity>5</quantity>
```

contains character data. If the document that contains element `quantity` references a DTD, an XML parser can validate the document to confirm that this element indeed does contain `PCDATA` content. However, the parser cannot validate that the content is numeric; DTDs do not provide this capability. So, unfortunately, the parser also considers

```
<quantity>hello</quantity>
```

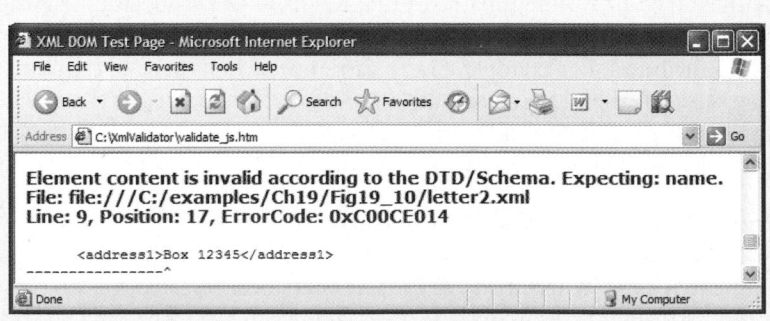

Fig. 19.10 | XML Validator displaying an error message.

to be valid. An application that uses the XML document containing this markup should test that the data in element `quantity` is numeric and take appropriate action if it is not.

XML Schema enables schema authors to specify that element `quantity`'s data must be numeric or, even more specifically, an integer. A parser validating the XML document against this schema can determine that 5 conforms and `hello` does not. An XML document that conforms to a schema document is **schema valid**, and one that does not conform is **schema invalid**. Schemas are XML documents and therefore must themselves be valid.

Validating Against an XML Schema Document
Figure 19.11 shows a schema-valid XML document named `book.xml`, and Fig. 19.12 shows the pertinent XML Schema document (`book.xsd`) that defines the structure for `book.xml`. By convention, schemas use the `.xsd` extension. We used an online XSD schema validator provided by Microsoft at

> apps.gotdotnet.com/xmltools/xsdvalidator

to ensure that the XML document in Fig. 19.11 conforms to the schema in Fig. 19.12. To validate the schema document itself (i.e., `book.xsd`) and produce the output shown in Fig. 19.12, we used an online XSV (XML Schema Validator) provided by the W3C at

> www.w3.org/2001/03/webdata/xsv

These tools are free and enforce the W3C's specifications regarding XML Schemas and schema validation. Section 19.12 lists several online XML Schema validators.

```
1   <?xml version = "1.0"?>
2   <!-- Fig. 19.11: book.xml -->
3   <!-- Book list marked up as XML -->
4
5   <deitel:books xmlns:deitel = "http://www.deitel.com/booklist">
6      <book>
7         <title>Visual Basic 2005 How to Program, 3/e</title>
8      </book>
9
10     <book>
11        <title>Visual C# 2005 How to Program</title>
12     </book>
13
14     <book>
15        <title>Java How to Program, 6/e</title>
16     </book>
17
18     <book>
19        <title>C++ How to Program, 5/e</title>
20     </book>
21
22     <book>
23        <title>Internet and World Wide Web How to Program, 3/e</title>
24     </book>
25  </deitel:books>
```

Fig. 19.11 | Schema-valid XML document describing a list of books.

```
 1   <?xml version = "1.0"?>
 2   <!-- Fig. 19.12: book.xsd              -->
 3   <!-- Simple W3C XML Schema document -->
 4
 5   <schema xmlns = "http://www.w3.org/2001/XMLSchema"
 6      xmlns:deitel = "http://www.deitel.com/booklist"
 7      targetNamespace = "http://www.deitel.com/booklist">
 8
 9      <element name = "books" type = "deitel:BooksType"/>
10
11      <complexType name = "BooksType">
12         <sequence>
13            <element name = "book" type = "deitel:SingleBookType"
14               minOccurs = "1" maxOccurs = "unbounded"/>
15         </sequence>
16      </complexType>
17
18      <complexType name = "SingleBookType">
19         <sequence>
20            <element name = "title" type = "string"/>
21         </sequence>
22      </complexType>
23   </schema>
```

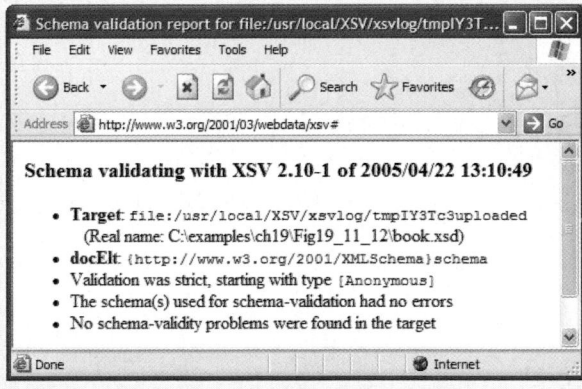

Fig. 19.12 | XML Schema document for book.xml.

Figure 19.11 contains markup describing several Deitel books. The books element (line 5) has the namespace prefix deitel, indicating that the books element is a part of the http://www.deitel.com/booklist namespace. Note that we declare the namespace prefix deitel in line 5.

Creating an XML Schema Document

Figure 19.12 presents the XML Schema document that specifies the structure of book.xml (Fig. 19.11). This document defines an XML-based language (i.e., a vocabulary) for writing XML documents about collections of books. The schema defines the elements, attributes and parent-child relationships that such a document can (or must) include. The schema also specifies the type of data that these elements and attributes may contain.

Root element **schema** (Fig. 19.12, lines 5–23) contains elements that define the structure of an XML document such as book.xml. Line 5 specifies as the default namespace the standard W3C XML Schema namespace URI—`http://www.w3.org/2001/XMLSchema`. This namespace contains predefined elements (e.g., root element **schema**) that comprise the XML Schema vocabulary—the language used to write an XML Schema document.

> **Portability Tip 19.3**
>
> *W3C XML Schema authors specify URI `http://www.w3.org/2001/XMLSchema` when referring to the XML Schema namespace. This namespace contains predefined elements that comprise the XML Schema vocabulary. Specifying this URI ensures that validation tools correctly identify XML Schema elements and do not confuse them with those defined by document authors.*

Line 6 binds the URI `http://www.deitel.com/booklist` to namespace prefix **deitel**. As we discuss momentarily, the schema uses this namespace to differentiate names created by us from names that are part of the XML Schema namespace. Line 7 also specifies `http://www.deitel.com/booklist` as the **targetNamespace** of the schema. This attribute identifies the namespace of the XML vocabulary that this schema defines. Note that the **targetNamespace** of book.xsd is the same as the namespace referenced in line 5 of book.xml (Fig. 19.11). This is what "connects" the XML document with the schema that defines its structure. When an XML schema validator examines book.xml and book.xsd, it will recognize that book.xml uses elements and attributes from the `http://www.deitel.com/booklist` namespace. The validator also will recognize that this namespace is the namespace defined in book.xsd (i.e., the schema's **targetNamespace**). Thus the validator knows where to look for the structural rules for the elements and attributes used in book.xml.

Defining an Element in XML Schema

In XML Schema, the **element** tag (line 9) defines an element to be included in an XML document that conforms to the schema. In other words, **element** specifies the actual *elements* that can be used to mark up data. Line 9 defines the books element, which we use as the root element in book.xml (Fig. 19.11). Attributes **name** and **type** specify the element's name and type, respectively. An element's type indicates the data that the element may contain. Possible types include XML Schema–defined types (e.g., `string`, `double`) and user-defined types (e.g., `BooksType`, which is defined in lines 11–16). Figure 19.13 lists several of XML Schema's many built-in types. For a complete list of built-in types, see Section 3 of the specification found at www.w3.org/TR/xmlschema-2.

In this example, books is defined as an element of type `deitel:BooksType` (line 9). `BooksType` is a user-defined type (lines 11–16) in the `http://www.deitel.com/booklist` namespace and therefore must have the namespace prefix `deitel`. It is not an existing XML Schema type.

Two categories of type exist in XML Schema—simple types and complex types. Simple and complex types differ only in that simple types cannot contain attributes or child elements and complex types can.

A user-defined type that contains attributes or child elements must be defined as a complex type. Lines 11–16 use element **complexType** to define `BooksType` as a complex type that has a child element named book. The **sequence** element (lines 12–15) allows you to specify the sequential order in which child elements must appear. The **element** (lines 13–14) nested within the **complexType** element indicates that a `BooksType` element (e.g.,

XML Schema type(s)	Description	Ranges or Structures	Examples
string	A character string.		"hello"
boolean	True or false.	true, false	true
decimal	A decimal numeral.	$i * (10^n)$, where i is an integer and n is an integer that is less than or equal to zero.	5, -12, -45.78
float	A floating-point number.	$m * (2^e)$, where m is an integer whose absolute value is less than 2^{24} and e is an integer in the range -149 to 104. Plus three additional numbers: positive infinity, negative infinity and not-a-number (NaN).	0, 12, -109.375, NaN
double	A floating-point number.	$m * (2^e)$, where m is an integer whose absolute value is less than 2^{53} and e is an integer in the range -1075 to 970. Plus three additional numbers: positive infinity, negative infinity and not-a-number (NaN).	0, 12, -109.375, NaN
long	A whole number.	-9223372036854775808 to 9223372036854775807, inclusive.	1234567890, -1234567890
int	A whole number.	-2147483648 to 2147483647, inclusive.	1234567890, -1234567890
short	A whole number.	-32768 to 32767, inclusive.	12, -345
date	A date consisting of a year, month and day.	yyyy-mm with an optional dd and an optional time zone, where yyyy is four digits long and mm and dd are two digits long.	2005-05-10
time	A time consisting of hours, minutes and seconds.	hh:mm:ss with an optional time zone, where hh, mm and ss are two digits long.	16:30:25-05:00

Fig. 19.13 | Some XML Schema types.

books) can contain child elements named book of type deitel:SingleBookType (defined in lines 18–22). Attribute minOccurs (line 14), with value 1, specifies that elements of type BooksType must contain a minimum of one book element. Attribute maxOccurs (line 14), with value **unbounded**, specifies that elements of type BooksType may have any number of book child elements.

Lines 18–22 define the complex type SingleBookType. An element of this type contains a child element named title. Line 20 defines element title to be of simple type string. Recall that elements of a simple type cannot contain attributes or child elements. The schema end tag (</schema>, line 23) declares the end of the XML Schema document.

A Closer Look at Types in XML Schema

Every element in XML Schema has a type. Types include the built-in types provided by XML Schema (Fig. 19.13) or user-defined types (e.g., SingleBookType in Fig. 19.12).

Every simple type defines a **restriction** on an XML Schema-defined type or a restriction on a user-defined type. Restrictions limit the possible values that an element can hold.

Complex types are divided into two groups—those with **simple content** and those with **complex content**. Both can contain attributes, but only complex content can contain child elements. Complex types with simple content must extend or restrict some other existing type. Complex types with complex content do not have this limitation. We demonstrate complex types with each kind of content in the next example.

The schema document in Fig. 19.14 creates both simple types and complex types. The XML document in Fig. 19.15 (laptop.xml) follows the structure defined in Fig. 19.14 to describe parts of a laptop computer. A document such as laptop.xml that conforms to a schema is known as an **XML instance document**—the document is an instance (i.e., example) of the schema.

Line 5 declares the default namespace to be the standard XML Schema namespace—any elements without a prefix are assumed to be in the XML Schema namespace. Line 6

```
 1   <?xml version = "1.0"?>
 2   <!-- Fig. 19.14: computer.xsd -->
 3   <!-- W3C XML Schema document   -->
 4
 5   <schema xmlns = "http://www.w3.org/2001/XMLSchema"
 6      xmlns:computer = "http://www.deitel.com/computer"
 7      targetNamespace = "http://www.deitel.com/computer">
 8
 9      <simpleType name = "gigahertz">
10         <restriction base = "decimal">
11            <minInclusive value = "2.1"/>
12         </restriction>
13      </simpleType>
14
15      <complexType name = "CPU">
16         <simpleContent>
17            <extension base = "string">
18               <attribute name = "model" type = "string"/>
19            </extension>
20         </simpleContent>
21      </complexType>
22
```

Fig. 19.14 | XML Schema document defining simple and complex types. (Part 1 of 2.)

```
23      <complexType name = "portable">
24        <all>
25          <element name = "processor" type = "computer:CPU"/>
26          <element name = "monitor" type = "int"/>
27          <element name = "CPUSpeed" type = "computer:gigahertz"/>
28          <element name = "RAM" type = "int"/>
29        </all>
30        <attribute name = "manufacturer" type = "string"/>
31      </complexType>
32
33      <element name = "laptop" type = "computer:portable"/>
34   </schema>
```

Fig. 19.14 | XML Schema document defining simple and complex types. (Part 2 of 2.)

```
 1   <?xml version = "1.0"?>
 2   <!-- Fig. 19.15: laptop.xml              -->
 3   <!-- Laptop components marked up as XML -->
 4
 5   <computer:laptop xmlns:computer = "http://www.deitel.com/computer"
 6      manufacturer = "IBM">
 7
 8      <processor model = "Centrino">Intel</processor>
 9      <monitor>17</monitor>
10      <CPUSpeed>2.4</CPUSpeed>
11      <RAM>256</RAM>
12   </computer:laptop>
```

Fig. 19.15 | XML document using the `laptop` element defined in `computer.xsd`.

binds the namespace prefix `computer` to the namespace `http://www.deitel.com/computer`. Line 7 identifies this namespace as the `targetNamespace`—the namespace being defined by the current XML Schema document.

To design the XML elements for describing laptop computers, we first create a simple type in lines 9–13 using the `simpleType` element. We name this `simpleType gigahertz` because it will be used to describe the clock speed of the processor in gigahertz. Simple types are restrictions of a type typically called a base type. For this `simpleType`, line 10 declares the base type as `decimal`, and we restrict the value to be at least 2.1 by using the `minInclusive` element in line 11.

Next, we declare a `complexType` named CPU that has `simpleContent` (lines 16–20). Remember that a complex type with simple content can have attributes but not child elements. Also recall that complex types with simple content must extend or restrict some XML Schema type or user-defined type. The `extension` element with attribute `base` (line 17) sets the base type to `string`. In this `complexType`, we extend the base type `string` with an attribute. The `attribute` element (line 18) gives the `complexType` an attribute of type `string` named `model`. Thus an element of type CPU must contain `string` text (because the base type is `string`) and may contain a `model` attribute that is also of type `string`.

Lastly we define type `portable`, which is a `complexType` with complex content (lines 23–31). Such types are allowed to have child elements and attributes. The element `all` (lines 24–29) encloses elements that must each be included once in the corresponding XML instance document. These elements can be included in any order. This complex type holds four elements—processor, monitor, CPUSpeed and RAM. They are given types CPU, int, gigahertz and int, respectively. When using types CPU and gigahertz, we must include the namespace prefix computer, because these user-defined types are part of the computer namespace (http://www.deitel.com/computer)—the namespace defined in the current document (line 7). Also, portable contains an attribute defined in line 30. The attribute element indicates that elements of type portable contain an attribute of type string named manufacturer.

Line 33 declares the actual element that uses the three types defined in the schema. The element is called laptop and is of type portable. We must use the namespace prefix computer in front of portable.

We have now created an element named laptop that contains child elements processor, monitor, CPUSpeed and RAM, and an attribute manufacturer. Figure 19.15 uses the laptop element defined in the computer.xsd schema. Once again, we used an online XSD schema validator (apps.gotdotnet.com/xmltools/xsdvalidator) to ensure that this XML instance document adheres to the schema's structural rules.

Line 5 declares namespace prefix computer. The laptop element requires this prefix because it is part of the http://www.deitel.com/computer namespace. Line 6 sets the laptop's manufacturer attribute, and lines 8–11 use the elements defined in the schema to describe the laptop's characteristics.

This section introduced W3C XML Schema documents for defining the structure of XML documents, and we validated XML instance documents against schemas using an online XSD schema validator. Section 19.9 demonstrates programmatically validating XML documents against schemas using .NET Framework classes. This allows you to ensure that a Visual Basic program manipulates only valid documents—manipulating an invalid document that is missing required pieces of data could cause errors in the program.

19.7 (Optional) Extensible Stylesheet Language and XSL Transformations

Extensible Stylesheet Language (XSL) documents specify how programs are to render XML document data. XSL is a group of three technologies—XSL-FO (XSL Formatting Objects), XPath (XML Path Language) and XSLT (XSL Transformations). XSL-FO is a vocabulary for specifying formatting, and XPath is a string-based language of expressions used by XML and many of its related technologies for effectively and efficiently locating structures and data (such as specific elements and attributes) in XML documents.

The third portion of XSL—XSL Transformations (XSLT)—is a technology for transforming XML documents into other documents—i.e., transforming the structure of the XML document data to another structure. XSLT provides elements that define rules for transforming one XML document to produce a different XML document. This is useful when you want to use data in multiple applications or on multiple platforms, each of which may be designed to work with documents written in a particular vocabulary. For example, XSLT allows you to convert a simple XML document to an XHTML (Extensible HyperText Markup Language) document that presents the XML document's data (or a subset of the data) formatted for display in a Web browser. (See Fig. 19.16 for a sample "before" and "after" view of such a transformation.) XHTML is the W3C technical recommendation that replaces HTML for marking up Web content. For more information on XHTML, see Appendix F, Introduction to XHTML: Part 1, and Appendix G, Introduction to XHTML: Part 2, and visit www.w3.org.

Transforming an XML document using XSLT involves two tree structures—the source tree (i.e., the XML document to be transformed) and the result tree (i.e., the XML document to be created). XPath is used to locate parts of the source tree document that match templates defined in an XSL style sheet. When a match occurs (i.e., a node matches a template), the matching template executes and adds its result to the result tree. When there are no more matches, XSLT has transformed the source tree into the result tree. The XSLT does not analyze every node of the source tree; it selectively navigates the source tree using XPath's `select` and `match` attributes. For XSLT to function, the source tree must be properly structured. Schemas, DTDs and validating parsers can validate document structure before using XPath and XSLTs.

A Simple XSL Example

Figure 19.16 lists an XML document that describes various sports. The output shows the result of the transformation (specified in the XSLT template of Fig. 19.17) rendered by Internet Explorer 6.

```
1   <?xml version = "1.0"?>
2   <?xml:stylesheet type = "text/xsl" href = "sports.xsl"?>
3
4   <!-- Fig. 19.16: sports.xml -->
5   <!-- Sports Database -->
6
7   <sports>
8      <game id = "783">
9         <name>Cricket</name>
10
11         <paragraph>
12            More popular among commonwealth nations.
13         </paragraph>
14      </game>
15
16      <game id = "239">
17         <name>Baseball</name>
18
19         <paragraph>
20            More popular in America.
21         </paragraph>
22      </game>
23
24      <game id = "418">
25         <name>Soccer (Futbol)</name>
26
27         <paragraph>
28            Most popular sport in the world.
29         </paragraph>
30      </game>
31   </sports>
```

Fig. 19.16 | XML document that describes various sports. (Part 1 of 2.)

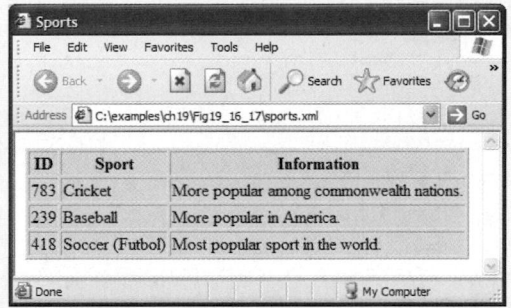

Fig. 19.16 | XML document that describes various sports. (Part 2 of 2.)

To perform transformations, an XSLT processor is required. Popular XSLT processors include Microsoft's MSXML and the Apache Software Foundation's Xalan 2 (xml.apache.org). The XML document shown in Fig. 19.16 is transformed into an XHTML document by MSXML when the document is loaded in Internet Explorer. MSXML is both an XML parser and an XSLT processor.

Line 2 (Fig. 19.16) is a **processing instruction** (PI) that references the XSL style sheet sports.xsl (Fig. 19.17). A processing instruction is embedded in an XML document and provides application-specific information to whichever XML processor the application uses. In this particular case, the processing instruction specifies the location of an XSLT document with which to transform the XML document. The characters <? and ?> (line 2, Fig. 19.16) delimit a processing instruction, which consists of a PI **target** (e.g., xml:stylesheet) and a PI **value** (e.g., type = "text/xsl" href = "sports.xsl"). The PI value's type attribute specifies that sports.xsl is a text/xsl file (i.e., a text file containing XSL content). The href attribute specifies the name and location of the style sheet to apply—in this case, sports.xsl in the current directory.

> **Software Engineering Observation 19.5**
>
> *XSL enables document authors to separate data presentation (specified in XSL documents) from data description (specified in XML documents).*

Figure 19.17 shows the XSL document for transforming the structured data of the XML document of Fig. 19.16 into an XHTML document for presentation. By convention, XSL documents have the filename extension .xsl.

Lines 6–7 begin the XSL style sheet with the **stylesheet** start tag. Attribute **version** specifies the XSLT version to which this document conforms. Line 7 binds namespace prefix xsl to the W3C's XSLT URI (i.e., http://www.w3.org/1999/XSL/Transform).

Lines 9–12 use element **xsl:output** to write an XHTML document type declaration (DOCTYPE) to the result tree (i.e., the XML document to be created). The DOCTYPE identifies XHTML as the type of the resulting document. Attribute method is assigned "xml", which indicates that XML is being output to the result tree. (Recall that XHTML is a type of XML.) Attribute **omit-xml-declaration** specifies whether the transformation should write the XML declaration to the result tree. In this case, we do not want to omit the XML declaration, so we assign to this attribute the value "no". Attributes doctype-system and doctype-public write the DOCTYPE DTD information to the result tree.

```
 1  <?xml version = "1.0"?>
 2  <!-- Fig. 19.17: sports.xsl -->
 3  <!-- A simple XSLT transformation -->
 4
 5  <!-- reference XSL style sheet URI -->
 6  <xsl:stylesheet version = "1.0"
 7     xmlns:xsl = "http://www.w3.org/1999/XSL/Transform">
 8
 9     <xsl:output method = "xml" omit-xml-declaration = "no"
10        doctype-system =
11           "http://www.w3c.org/TR/xhtml1/DTD/xhtml1-strict.dtd"
12        doctype-public = "-//W3C//DTD XHTML 1.0 Strict//EN"/>
13
14     <xsl:template match = "/"> <!-- match root element -->
15
16     <html xmlns = "http://www.w3.org/1999/xhtml">
17        <head>
18           <title>Sports</title>
19        </head>
20
21        <body>
22           <table border = "1" bgcolor = "wheat">
23              <thead>
24                 <tr>
25                    <th>ID</th>
26                    <th>Sport</th>
27                    <th>Information</th>
28                 </tr>
29              </thead>
30
31              <!-- insert each name and paragraph element value -->
32              <!-- into a table row. -->
33              <xsl:for-each select = "/sports/game">
34                 <tr>
35                    <td><xsl:value-of select = "@id"/></td>
36                    <td><xsl:value-of select = "name"/></td>
37                    <td><xsl:value-of select = "paragraph"/></td>
38                 </tr>
39              </xsl:for-each>
40           </table>
41        </body>
42     </html>
43
44     </xsl:template>
45  </xsl:stylesheet>
```

Fig. 19.17 | XSLT that creates elements and attributes in an XHTML document.

XSLT uses templates (i.e., xsl:template elements) to describe how to transform particular nodes from the source tree to the result tree. A template is applied to nodes that are specified in the required match attribute. Line 14 uses the match attribute to select the document root (i.e., the conceptual part of the document that contains the root element and everything below it) of the XML source document (i.e., sports.xml). The XPath character / (a forward slash) always selects the document root. Recall that XPath is a string-based language used to locate parts of an XML document easily. In XPath, a leading forward slash specifies that we are using **absolute addressing** (i.e., we are starting from the root and defining paths down the source tree). In the XML document of Fig. 19.16, the child nodes of the document root are the two processing instruction nodes (lines 1–2), the two comment nodes (lines 4–5) and the sports element node (lines 7–31). The template in Fig. 19.17, line 14, matches a node (i.e., the root node), so the contents of the template are now added to the result tree.

The MSXML processor writes the XHTML in lines 16–29 (Fig. 19.17) to the result tree exactly as it appears in the XSL document. Now the result tree consists of the DOCTYPE definition and the XHTML code from lines 16–29. Lines 33–39 use element **xsl:for-each** to iterate through the source XML document, searching for game elements. The xsl:for-each element is similar to Visual Basic's For Each statement. Attribute **select** is an XPath expression that specifies the nodes (called the **node set**) on which the xsl:for-each operates. Again, the first forward slash means that we are using absolute addressing. The forward slash between sports and game indicates that game is a child node of sports. Thus, the xsl:for-each finds game nodes that are children of the sports node. The XML document sports.xml contains only one sports node, which is also the document root node. After finding the elements that match the selection criteria, the xsl:for-each processes each element with the code in lines 34–38 (these lines produce one row in a table each time they execute) and places the result of lines 34–38 in the result tree.

Line 35 uses element **value-of** to retrieve attribute id's value and place it in a td element in the result tree. The XPath symbol @ specifies that id is an attribute node of the context node game. Lines 36–37 place the name and paragraph element values in td elements and insert them in the result tree. When an XPath expression has no beginning forward slash, the expression uses **relative addressing**. Omitting the beginning forward slash tells the **xsl:value-of select** statements to search for name and paragraph elements that are children of the context node, not the root node. Due to the last XPath expression selection, the current context node is game, which indeed has an id attribute, a name child element and a paragraph child element.

Using XSLT to Sort and Format Data

Figure 19.18 presents an XML document (sorting.xml) that marks up information about a book. Note that several elements of the markup describing the book appear out of order (e.g., the element describing Chapter 3 appears before the element describing Chapter 2). We arranged them this way purposely to demonstrate that the XSL style sheet referenced in line 5 (sorting.xsl) can sort the XML file's data for presentation purposes.

```
1   <?xml version = "1.0"?>
2   <!-- Fig. 19.18: sorting.xml -->
3   <!-- XML document containing book information -->
4
5   <?xml:stylesheet type = "text/xsl" href = "sorting.xsl"?>
6
7   <book isbn = "999-99999-9-X">
8      <title>Deitel&apos;s XML Primer</title>
```

Fig. 19.18 | XML document containing book information. (Part 1 of 2.)

```
9
10     <author>
11        <firstName>Jane</firstName>
12        <lastName>Blue</lastName>
13     </author>
14
15     <chapters>
16        <frontMatter>
17           <preface pages = "2" />
18           <contents pages = "5" />
19           <illustrations pages = "4" />
20        </frontMatter>
21
22        <chapter number = "3" pages = "44">Advanced XML</chapter>
23        <chapter number = "2" pages = "35">Intermediate XML</chapter>
24        <appendix number = "B" pages = "26">Parsers and Tools</appendix>
25        <appendix number = "A" pages = "7">Entities</appendix>
26        <chapter number = "1" pages = "28">XML Fundamentals</chapter>
27     </chapters>
28
29     <media type = "CD" />
30  </book>
```

Fig. 19.18 | XML document containing book information. (Part 2 of 2.)

Figure 19.19 presents an XSL document (sorting.xsl) for transforming sorting.xml (Fig. 19.18) to XHTML. Recall that an XSL document navigates a source tree and builds a result tree. In this example, the source tree is XML, and the output tree is XHTML. Line 14 of Fig. 19.19 matches the root element of the document in Fig. 19.18. Line 15 outputs an html start tag to the result tree. The <xsl:apply-templates/> element (line 16) specifies that the XSLT processor is to apply the xsl:templates defined in this XSL document to the current node's (i.e., the document root's) children. The content from the applied templates is output in the html element that ends at line 17. Lines 21–84 specify a template that matches element book. The template indicates how to format the information contained in book elements of sorting.xml (Fig. 19.18) as XHTML.

```
1   <?xml version = "1.0"?>
2   <!-- Fig. 19.19: sorting.xsl -->
3   <!-- Transformation of book information into XHTML -->
4
5   <xsl:stylesheet version = "1.0"
6      xmlns:xsl = "http://www.w3.org/1999/XSL/Transform">
7
8      <!-- write XML declaration and DOCTYPE DTD information -->
9      <xsl:output method = "xml" omit-xml-declaration = "no"
10        doctype-system = "http://www.w3.org/TR/xhtml11/DTD/xhtml11.dtd"
11        doctype-public = "-//W3C//DTD XHTML 1.1//EN"/>
12
```

Fig. 19.19 | XSL document that transforms sorting.xml into XHTML. (Part 1 of 3.)

```
13      <!-- match document root -->
14      <xsl:template match = "/">
15          <html xmlns = "http://www.w3.org/1999/xhtml">
16              <xsl:apply-templates/>
17          </html>
18      </xsl:template>
19
20      <!-- match book -->
21      <xsl:template match = "book">
22          <head>
23              <title>ISBN <xsl:value-of select = "@isbn"/> -
24                  <xsl:value-of select = "title"/></title>
25          </head>
26
27          <body>
28              <h1 style = "color: blue"><xsl:value-of select = "title"/></h1>
29              <h2 style = "color: blue">by
30                  <xsl:value-of select = "author/lastName"/>,
31                  <xsl:value-of select = "author/firstName"/></h2>
32
33              <table style = "border-style: groove; background-color: wheat">
34
35                  <xsl:for-each select = "chapters/frontMatter/*">
36                      <tr>
37                          <td style = "text-align: right">
38                              <xsl:value-of select = "name()"/>
39                          </td>
40
41                          <td>
42                              ( <xsl:value-of select = "@pages"/> pages )
43                          </td>
44                      </tr>
45                  </xsl:for-each>
46
47                  <xsl:for-each select = "chapters/chapter">
48                      <xsl:sort select = "@number" data-type = "number"
49                          order = "ascending"/>
50                      <tr>
51                          <td style = "text-align: right">
52                              Chapter <xsl:value-of select = "@number"/>
53                          </td>
54
55                          <td>
56                              <xsl:value-of select = "text()"/>
57                              ( <xsl:value-of select = "@pages"/> pages )
58                          </td>
59                      </tr>
60                  </xsl:for-each>
61
62                  <xsl:for-each select = "chapters/appendix">
63                      <xsl:sort select = "@number" data-type = "text"
64                          order = "ascending"/>
```

Fig. 19.19 | XSL document that transforms `sorting.xml` into XHTML. (Part 2 of 3.)

```
65                <tr>
66                    <td style = "text-align: right">
67                        Appendix <xsl:value-of select = "@number"/>
68                    </td>
69
70                    <td>
71                        <xsl:value-of select = "text()"/>
72                        ( <xsl:value-of select = "@pages"/> pages )
73                    </td>
74                </tr>
75            </xsl:for-each>
76        </table>
77
78        <br /><p style = "color: blue">Pages:
79            <xsl:variable name = "pagecount"
80                select = "sum(chapters//*/@pages)"/>
81            <xsl:value-of select = "$pagecount"/>
82            <br />Media Type: <xsl:value-of select = "media/@type"/></p>
83        </body>
84    </xsl:template>
85 </xsl:stylesheet>
```

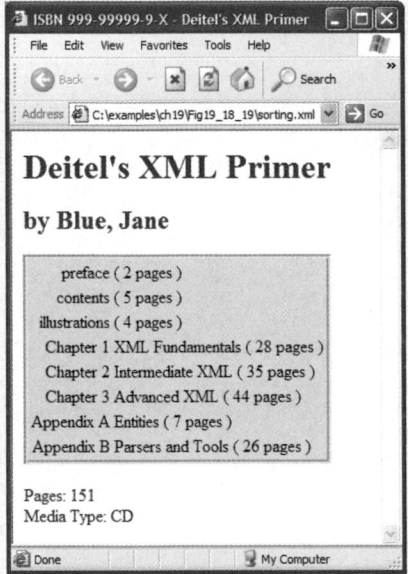

Fig. 19.19 | XSL document that transforms `sorting.xml` into XHTML. (Part 3 of 3.)

Lines 23–24 create the title for the XHTML document. We use the book's ISBN (from attribute `isbn`) and the contents of element `title` to create the string that appears in the browser window's title bar (**ISBN 999-99999-9-X - Deitel's XML Primer**).

Line 28 creates a header element that contains the book's title. Lines 29–31 create a header element that contains the book's author. Because the context node (i.e., the current node being processed) is `book`, the XPath expression `author/lastName` selects the author's last name, and the expression `author/firstName` selects the author's first name.

Line 35 selects each element (indicated by an asterisk) that is a child of element frontMatter. Line 38 calls node-set function name to retrieve the current node's element name (e.g., preface). The current node is the context node specified in the xsl:for-each (line 35). Line 42 retrieves the value of the pages attribute of the current node.

Line 47 selects each chapter element. Lines 48–49 use element xsl:sort to sort chapters by number in ascending order. Attribute select selects the value of attribute number in context node chapter. Attribute data-type, with value "number", specifies a numeric sort, and attribute order, with value "ascending", specifies ascending order. Attribute data-type also accepts the value "text" (line 63), and attribute order also accepts the value "descending". Line 56 uses node-set function text to obtain the text between the chapter start and end tags (i.e., the name of the chapter). Line 57 retrieves the value of the pages attribute of the current node. Lines 62–75 perform similar tasks for each appendix.

Lines 79–80 use an XSL variable to store the value of the book's total page count and output the page count to the result tree. Attribute name specifies the variable's name (i.e., pagecount), and attribute select assigns a value to the variable. Function sum (line 80) totals the values for all page attribute values. The two slashes between chapters and * indicate a recursive descent—the MSXML processor will search for elements that contain an attribute named pages in all descendant nodes of chapters. The XPath expression

```
//*
```

selects all the nodes in an XML document. Line 81 retrieves the value of the newly created XSL variable pagecount by placing a dollar sign in front of its name.

Summary of XSL Style Sheet Elements

This section's examples used several predefined XSL elements to perform various operations. Figure 19.20 lists these elements and several other commonly used XSL elements. For more information on these elements and XSL in general, see www.w3.org/Style/XSL.

Element	Description
`<xsl:apply-templates>`	Applies the templates of the XSL document to the children of the current node.
`<xsl:apply-templates match = "expression">`	Applies the templates of the XSL document to the children of *expression*. The value of the attribute match (i.e., *expression*) must be an XPath expression that specifies elements.
`<xsl:template>`	Contains rules to apply when a specified node is matched.
`<xsl:value-of select = "expression">`	Selects the value of an XML element and adds it to the output tree of the transformation. The required select attribute contains an XPath expression.
`<xsl:for-each select = "expression">`	Applies a template to every node selected by the XPath specified by the select attribute.

Fig. 19.20 | XSL style sheet elements. (Part 1 of 2.)

Element	Description
`<xsl:sort select = "expression">`	Used as a child element of an `<xsl:apply-templates>` or `<xsl:for-each>` element. Sorts the nodes selected by the `<xsl:apply-template>` or `<xsl:for-each>` element so that the nodes are processed in sorted order.
`<xsl:output>`	Has various attributes to define the format (e.g., XML, XHTML), version (e.g., 1.0, 2.0), document type and media type of the output document. This tag is a top-level element—it can be used only as a child element of an `xml:stylesheet`.
`<xsl:copy>`	Adds the current node to the output tree.

Fig. 19.20 | XSL style sheet elements. (Part 2 of 2.)

This section introduced Extensible Stylesheet Language (XSL) and showed how to create XSL transformations to convert XML documents from one format to another. We showed how to transform XML documents to XHTML documents for display in a Web browser. Recall that these transformations are performed by MSXML, Internet Explorer's built-in XML parser and XSLT processor. In most business applications, XML documents are transferred between business partners and are transformed to other XML vocabularies programmatically. In Section 19.10, we demonstrate how to perform XSL transformations using the XslCompiledTransform class provided by the .NET Framework.

19.8 (Optional) Document Object Model (DOM)

Although an XML document is a text file, retrieving data from the document using traditional sequential file processing techniques is neither practical nor efficient, especially for adding and removing elements dynamically.

Upon successfully parsing a document, some XML parsers store document data as tree structures in memory. Figure 19.21 illustrates the tree structure for the root element of the document article.xml discussed in Fig. 19.2. This hierarchical tree structure is called a Document Object Model (DOM) tree, and an XML parser that creates this type of structure is known as a DOM parser. Each element name (e.g., article, date, firstName) is represented by a node. A node that contains other nodes (called child nodes or children) is called a parent node (e.g., author). A parent node can have many children, but a child node can have only one parent node. Nodes that are peers (e.g., firstName and lastName) are called sibling nodes. A node's descendant nodes include its children, its children's children and so on. A node's ancestor nodes include its parent, its parent's parent and so on.

The DOM tree has a single root node, which contains all the other nodes in the document. For example, the root node of the DOM tree that represents article.xml (Fig. 19.2) contains a node for the XML declaration (line 1), two nodes for the comments (lines 2–3) and a node for the XML document's root element article (line 5).

Classes for creating, reading and manipulating XML documents are located in the FCL namespace System.Xml. This namespace also contains additional namespaces that provide other XML-related operations.

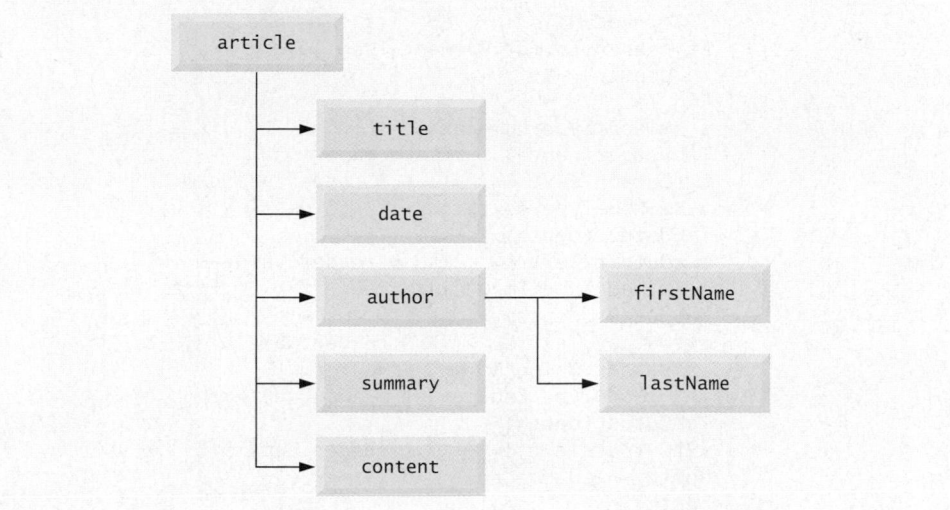

Fig. 19.21 | Tree structure for the document `article.xml` of Fig. 19.2.

Reading an XML Document with an *XmlReader*

In this section, we present several examples that use DOM trees. Our first example, the program in Fig. 19.22, loads the XML document presented in Fig. 19.2 and displays its data in a text box. This example uses class `XmlReader` to iterate through each node in the XML document.

```
1   ' Fig. 19.22: FrmXmlReaderTest.vb
2   ' Reading an XML document.
3   Imports System.Xml
4
5   Public Class FrmXmlReaderTest
6      ' read XML document and display its content
7      Private Sub FrmXmlReaderTest_Load(ByVal sender As System.Object, _
8         ByVal e As System.EventArgs) Handles MyBase.Load
9         ' create the XmlReader object
10        Dim settings As New XmlReaderSettings()
11        Dim reader As XmlReader = XmlReader.Create("article.xml", settings)
12
13        Dim depth As Integer = -1 ' tree depth is -1, no indentation
14
15        While reader.Read() ' display each node's content
16           Select Case (reader.NodeType)
17              Case XmlNodeType.Element ' XML Element, display its name
18                 depth += 1 ' increase tab depth
19                 TabOutput(depth) ' insert tabs
20                 txtOutput.Text &= "<" & reader.Name & ">" & vbCrLf
21
```

Fig. 19.22 | `XmlReader` iterating through an XML document. (Part 1 of 2.)

```
22                       ' if empty element, decrease depth
23                      If reader.IsEmptyElement Then
24                         depth -= 1
25                      End If
26              Case XmlNodeType.Comment ' XML Comment, display it
27                 TabOutput(depth) ' insert tabs
28                 txtOutput.Text &= "<!--" & reader.Value & "-->" & vbCrLf
29              Case XmlNodeType.Text ' XML Text, display it
30                 TabOutput(depth) ' insert tabs
31                 txtOutput.Text &= vbTab & reader.Value & vbCrLf
32              Case XmlNodeType.XmlDeclaration ' XML Declaration, display it
33                 TabOutput(depth) ' insert tabs
34                 txtOutput.Text &= "<?" & reader.Name & " " & _
35                    reader.Value & "?>" & vbCrLf
36              Case XmlNodeType.EndElement ' XML EndElement, display it
37                 TabOutput(depth) ' insert tabs
38                 txtOutput.Text &= "</" & reader.Name & ">" & vbCrLf
39                 depth -= 1 ' decrement depth
40           End Select
41        End While
42     End Sub ' FrmXmlReaderTest_Load
43
44     ' insert tabs
45     Private Sub TabOutput(ByVal number As Integer)
46        For i As Integer = 1 To number
47           txtOutput.Text &= vbTab
48        Next
49     End Sub ' TabOutput
50  End Class ' FrmXmlReaderTest
```

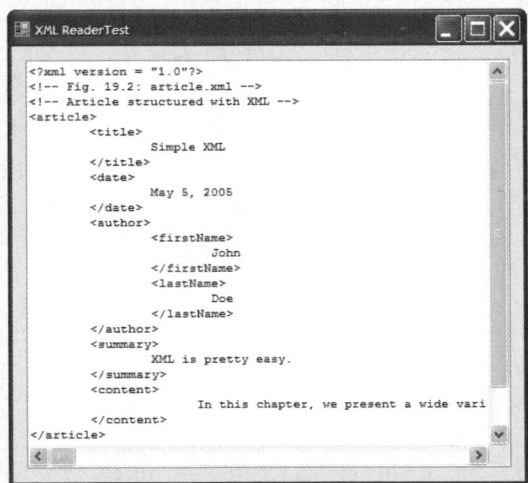

Fig. 19.22 | XmlReader iterating through an XML document. (Part 2 of 2.)

Line 3 imports the System.Xml namespace, which contains the XML classes used in this example. Class XmlReader is a MustInherit class that defines the interface for reading

XML documents. We cannot create an XmlReader object directly. Instead, we must invoke XmlReader's Shared method **Create** to obtain an XmlReader reference (line 11). Before doing so, however, we must prepare an XmlReaderSettings object that specifies how we would like the XmlReader to behave (line 10). In this example, we use the default settings of the properties of an XmlReaderSettings object. Later, you will learn how to set certain properties of the XmlReaderSettings class to instruct the XmlReader to perform validation, which it does not do by default. The Shared method Create receives as arguments the name of the XML document to read and an XmlReaderSettings object. In this example the XML document article.xml (Fig. 19.2) is opened when method Create is invoked in line 11. Once the XmlReader is created, the XML document's contents can be read programmatically.

Method **Read** of XmlReader reads one node from the DOM tree. By calling this method in the loop condition (line 15), reader reads all the document nodes. The Select Case statement (lines 16–40) processes each node. Either the Name property (lines 20, 34 and 38), which contains the node's name, or the Value property (lines 28 and 31), which contains the node's data, is formatted and concatenated to the String assigned to the TextBox's Text property. The XmlReader's NodeType property specifies whether the node is an element, comment, text, XML declaration or end element. Note that each Case specifies a node type using **XmlNodeType** enumeration constants. For example, XmlNode-Type.Element (line 17) indicates the start tag of an element.

The displayed output emphasizes the structure of the XML document. Variable depth (line 13) maintains the number of tab characters to indent each element. We increment the depth each time the program encounters an Element and decrement it each time the program encounters an EndElement or empty element. We use a similar technique in the next example to emphasize the tree structure of the XML document being displayed.

Displaying a DOM Tree Graphically in a TreeView Control

XmlReaders do not provide features for displaying their content graphically. In this example, we display an XML document's contents using a **TreeView** control. We use class **TreeNode** to represent each node in the tree. Class TreeView and class TreeNode are part of the System.Windows.Forms namespace. TreeNodes are added to the TreeView to emphasize the structure of the XML document.

The program in Fig. 19.23 demonstrates how to manipulate a DOM tree programmatically to display it graphically in a TreeView control. The GUI for this application contains a TreeView control named treeXML (declared in FrmXmlDom.Designer.vb). The application loads letter.xml (Fig. 19.24) into an XmlReader (line 17), then displays the document's tree structure in the TreeView control. [*Note:* The version of letter.xml in Fig. 19.24 is nearly identical to the one in Fig. 19.4, except that Fig. 19.24 does not reference a DTD as line 5 of Fig. 19.4 does.]

In FrmXmlDom's Load event handler (lines 9–22), lines 13–14 create an XmlReaderSettings object and set its **IgnoreWhitespace** property to True so that the insignificant whitespaces in the XML document are ignored. Line 17 then invokes Shared XmlReader method Create to parse and load letter.xml.

Line 18 creates the TreeNode tree (declared in line 6). This TreeNode is used as a graphical representation of a DOM tree node in the TreeView control. Line 19 assigns the XML document's name (i.e., letter.xml) to tree's Text property. Line 20 calls method

Add to add the new `TreeNode` to the `TreeView`'s Nodes collection. Line 21 calls our `Private` method `BuildTree` to update the `TreeView` so that it displays the complete DOM tree.

```vbnet
1   ' Fig. 19.23: FrmXmlDom.vb
2   ' Demonstrates DOM tree manipulation.
3   Imports System.Xml
4
5   Public Class FrmXmlDom
6      Private tree As TreeNode ' TreeNode reference
7
8      ' initialize instance variables
9      Private Sub FrmXmlDom_Load(ByVal sender As Object, _
10        ByVal e As EventArgs) Handles MyBase.Load
11        ' create Xml ReaderSettings and
12        ' set the IgnoreWhitespace property
13        Dim settings As New XmlReaderSettings()
14        settings.IgnoreWhitespace = True
15
16        ' create XmlReader object
17        Dim reader As XmlReader = XmlReader.Create("letter.xml", settings)
18        tree = New TreeNode() ' instantiate TreeNode
19        tree.Text = "letter.xml" ' assign name to TreeNode
20        treeXml.Nodes.Add(tree) ' add TreeNode to TreeView control
21        BuildTree(reader, tree) ' build node and tree hierarchy
22     End Sub ' FrmXmlDom_Load
23
24     ' construct TreeView based on DOM tree
25     Private Sub BuildTree(ByVal reader As XmlReader, _
26        ByVal treeNode As TreeNode)
27        ' treeNode to add to existing tree
28        Dim newNode As New TreeNode()
29
30        While reader.Read()
31           ' build tree based on node type
32           Select Case reader.NodeType
33              Case XmlNodeType.Text ' add Text node's value to tree
34                 newNode.Text = reader.Value
35                 treeNode.Nodes.Add(newNode)
36              Case XmlNodeType.EndElement ' move up tree
37                 treeNode = treeNode.Parent
38              Case XmlNodeType.Element ' add element name and traverse tree
39                 ' determine whether element contains information
40                 If Not reader.IsEmptyElement Then
41                    newNode.Text = reader.Name ' assign node text
42                    treeNode.Nodes.Add(newNode) ' add newNode as child
43                    treeNode = newNode ' set treeNode to last child
44                 Else ' do not traverse empty elements
45                    ' assign NodeType string to newNode and add it to tree
46                    newNode.Text = reader.NodeType.ToString()
47                    treeNode.Nodes.Add(newNode)
48                 End If
```

Fig. 19.23 | DOM structure of an XML document displayed in a `TreeView`. (Part 1 of 2.)

```
49              Case Else ' all other types, display node type
50                  newNode.Text = reader.NodeType.ToString()
51                  treeNode.Nodes.Add(newNode)
52          End Select
53
54          newNode = New TreeNode()
55      End While
56
57      ' update TreeView control
58      treeXml.ExpandAll() ' expand tree nodes in TreeView
59      treeXml.Refresh() ' force TreeView to update
60    End Sub ' BuildTree
61  End Class ' FrmXmlDom
```

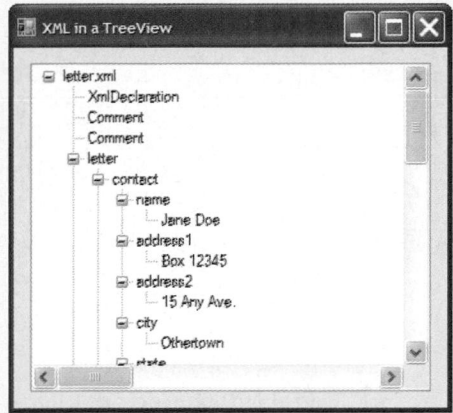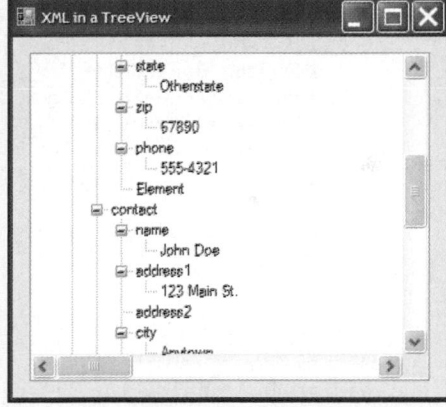

Fig. 19.23 | DOM structure of an XML document displayed in a `TreeView`. (Part 2 of 2.)

Method `BuildTree` (lines 25–60) receives an `XmlReader` for reading the XML document and a `TreeNode` referencing the current location in the tree (i.e., the `TreeNode` most recently added to the `TreeView` control). Line 28 declares `TreeNode` reference `newNode`, which will be used for adding new nodes to the `TreeView`. Lines 30–55 iterate through each node in the XML document's DOM tree.

The `Select Case` statement in lines 32–52 adds a node to the `TreeView`, based on the `XmlReader`'s current node. When a text node is encountered, the `Text` property of the new `TreeNode`—`newNode`—is assigned the current node's value (line 34). Line 35 adds this `TreeNode` to `treeNode`'s node list (i.e., adds the node to the `TreeView` control).

Line 36 matches an `EndElement` node type. This `Case` moves up the tree to the current node's parent because the end of an element has been encountered. Line 37 accesses `treeNode`'s **Parent** property to retrieve the node's current parent.

Line 38 matches `Element` node types. Each non-empty `Element` `NodeType` (line 40) increases the depth of the tree; thus, we assign the current `reader.Name` to the `newNode`'s `Text` property and add the `newNode` to `treeNode`'s node list (lines 41–42). Line 43 assigns the `newNode`'s reference to `treeNode` to ensure that `treeNode` refers to the last child `TreeNode` in the node list. If the current `Element` node is an empty element (line 44), we assign to the `newNode`'s `Text` property the string representation of the `NodeType` (line 46).

```
 I   <?xml version = "1.0"?>
 2   <!-- Fig. 19.24: letter.xml -->
 3   <!-- Business letter formatted with XML -->
 4
 5   <letter>
 6      <contact type = "sender">
 7         <name>Jane Doe</name>
 8         <address1>Box 12345</address1>
 9         <address2>15 Any Ave.</address2>
10         <city>Othertown</city>
11         <state>Otherstate</state>
12         <zip>67890</zip>
13         <phone>555-4321</phone>
14         <flag gender = "F" />
15      </contact>
16
17      <contact type = "receiver">
18         <name>John Doe</name>
19         <address1>123 Main St.</address1>
20         <address2></address2>
21         <city>Anytown</city>
22         <state>Anystate</state>
23         <zip>12345</zip>
24         <phone>555-1234</phone>
25         <flag gender = "M" />
26      </contact>
27
28      <salutation>Dear Sir:</salutation>
29
30      <paragraph>It is our privilege to inform you about our new database
31         managed with XML. This new system allows you to reduce the
32         load on your inventory list server by having the client machine
33         perform the work of sorting and filtering the data.
34      </paragraph>
35
36      <paragraph>Please visit our Web site for availability
37         and pricing.
38      </paragraph>
39
40      <closing>Sincerely,</closing>
41      <signature>Ms. Doe</signature>
42   </letter>
```

Fig. 19.24 | Business letter marked up as XML.

Next, the newNode is added to the treeNode node list (line 47). The default case (lines 49–51) assigns the string representation of the node type to the newNode Text property, then adds the newNode to the TreeNode node list.

After the entire DOM tree is processed, the TreeNode node list is displayed in the TreeView control (lines 58–59). TreeView method **ExpandAll** causes all the nodes of the tree to be displayed. TreeView method **Refresh** updates the display to show the newly added TreeNodes. Note that while the application is running, clicking nodes (i.e., the + or – boxes) in the TreeView either expands or collapses them.

Locating Data in XML Documents with XPath

Although XmlReader includes methods for reading and modifying node values, it is not the most efficient means of locating data in a DOM tree. The Framework Class Library provides class **XPathNavigator** in the **System.Xml.XPath** namespace for iterating through node lists that match search criteria, which are written as XPath expressions. Recall that XPath (XML Path Language) provides a syntax for locating specific nodes in XML documents effectively and efficiently. XPath is a string-based language of expressions used by XML and many of its related technologies (such as XSLT, discussed in Section 19.7).

Figure 19.25 uses an XPathNavigator to navigate an XML document and uses a TreeView control and TreeNode objects to display the XML document's structure. In this example, the TreeNode node list is updated each time the XPathNavigator is positioned to a new node, rather than displaying the entire DOM tree at once. Nodes are added to and deleted from the TreeView to reflect the XPathNavigator's location in the DOM tree. Figure 19.26 shows the XML document sports.xml that we use in this example. [*Note:* The versions of sports.xml presented in Fig. 19.26 and Fig. 19.16 are nearly identical. In the current example, we do not want to apply an XSLT, so we omit the processing instruction found in line 2 of Fig. 19.16.]

```vb
1   ' Fig. 19.25: FrmPathNavigator.vb
2   ' Demonstrates class XPathNavigator.
3   Imports System.Xml.XPath
4
5   Public Class FrmPathNavigator
6      Private xPath As XPathNavigator ' navigator to traverse document
7      Private document As XPathDocument ' document for use by XPathNavigator
8      Private tree As TreeNode ' TreeNode used by TreeView control
9
10     ' initialize variables and TreeView control
11     Private Sub FrmPathNavigator_Load(ByVal sender As Object, _
12        ByVal e As EventArgs) Handles MyBase.Load
13        document = New XPathDocument("sports.xml") ' load XML document
14        xPath = document.CreateNavigator() ' create navigator
15        tree = New TreeNode() ' create root node for TreeNodes
16
17        tree.Text = xPath.NodeType.ToString() ' root
18        treePath.Nodes.Add(tree) ' add tree
19
20        ' update TreeView control
21        treePath.ExpandAll() ' expand tree node in TreeView
22        treePath.Refresh() ' force TreeView update
23        treePath.SelectedNode = tree ' highlight root
24     End Sub ' FrmPathNavigator_Load
25
26     ' process btnSelect_Click event
27     Private Sub btnSelect_Click(ByVal sender As Object, _
28        ByVal e As EventArgs) Handles btnSelect.Click
29        Dim iterator As XPathNodeIterator ' enables node iteration
30
```

Fig. 19.25 | XPathNavigator navigating selected nodes. (Part 1 of 5.)

```
31            Try ' get specified node from ComboBox
32               iterator = xPath.Select(cboSelect.Text) ' select specified node
33               DisplayIterator(iterator) ' display selection
34            Catch argumentException As XPathException
35               MessageBox.Show(argumentException.Message, "Error", _
36                  MessageBoxButtons.OK, MessageBoxIcon.Error)
37            End Try
38         End Sub ' btnSelect_Click
39
40         ' traverse to first child on btnFirstChild_Click event
41         Private Sub btnFirstChild_Click(ByVal sender As Object, _
42            ByVal e As EventArgs) Handles btnFirstChild.Click
43            Dim newTreeNode As TreeNode
44
45            ' move to first child
46            If xPath.MoveToFirstChild() Then
47               newTreeNode = New TreeNode() ' create new node
48
49               ' set node's Text property to either navigator's name or value
50               DetermineType(newTreeNode, xPath)
51               tree.Nodes.Add(newTreeNode) ' add nodes to TreeNode node list
52               tree = newTreeNode ' assign tree newTreeNode
53
54               ' update TreeView control
55               treePath.ExpandAll() ' expand node in TreeView
56               treePath.Refresh() ' force TreeView to update
57               treePath.SelectedNode = tree ' highlight root
58            Else ' node has no children
59               MessageBox.Show("Current Node has no children.", _
60                  "", MessageBoxButtons.OK, MessageBoxIcon.Information)
61            End If
62         End Sub ' btnFirstChild_Click
63
64         ' traverse to node's parent on btnParent_Click event
65         Private Sub btnParent_Click(ByVal sender As Object, _
66            ByVal e As EventArgs) Handles btnParent.Click
67            ' move to parent
68            If xPath.MoveToParent() Then
69               tree = tree.Parent
70
71               ' get number of child nodes, not including sub trees
72               Dim count As Integer = tree.GetNodeCount(False)
73
74               ' remove all children
75               For i As Integer = 0 To count - 1
76                  tree.Nodes.Remove(tree.FirstNode) ' remove child node
77               Next
78
79               ' update TreeView control
80               treePath.ExpandAll() ' expand node in TreeView
81               treePath.Refresh() ' force TreeView to update
82               treePath.SelectedNode = tree ' highlight root
```

Fig. 19.25 | XPathNavigator navigating selected nodes. (Part 2 of 5.)

```vbnet
83          Else ' if node has no parent (root node)
84             MessageBox.Show("Current node has no parent.", "", _
85                MessageBoxButtons.OK, MessageBoxIcon.Information)
86          End If
87       End Sub ' btnParent_Click
88
89       ' find next sibling on btnNext_Click event
90       Private Sub btnNext_Click(ByVal sender As Object, _
91          ByVal e As EventArgs) Handles btnNext.Click
92          ' declare and initialize two TreeNodes
93          Dim newTreeNode As TreeNode = Nothing
94          Dim newNode As TreeNode = Nothing
95
96          ' move to next sibling
97          If xPath.MoveToNext() Then
98             newTreeNode = tree.Parent ' get parent node
99             newNode = New TreeNode() ' create new node
100
101             ' decide whether to display current node
102             DetermineType(newNode, xPath)
103             newTreeNode.Nodes.Add(newNode) ' add to parent node
104
105             tree = newNode ' set current position for display
106
107             ' update TreeView control
108             treePath.ExpandAll() ' expand node in TreeView
109             treePath.Refresh() ' force TreeView to update
110             treePath.SelectedNode = tree ' highlight root
111          Else ' node has no additional siblings
112             MessageBox.Show("Current node is last sibling.", "", _
113                MessageBoxButtons.OK, MessageBoxIcon.Information)
114          End If
115       End Sub ' btnNext_Click
116
117       ' get previous sibling on btnPrevious_Click
118       Private Sub btnPrevious_Click(ByVal sender As Object, _
119          ByVal e As EventArgs) Handles btnPrevious.Click
120          Dim parentTreeNode As TreeNode = Nothing
121
122          ' move to previous sibling
123          If xPath.MoveToPrevious() Then
124
125             parentTreeNode = tree.Parent ' get parent node
126             parentTreeNode.Nodes.Remove(tree) ' delete current node
127             tree = parentTreeNode.LastNode ' move to previous node
128
129             ' update TreeView control
130             treePath.ExpandAll() ' expand tree node in TreeView
131             treePath.Refresh() ' force TreeView to update
132             treePath.SelectedNode = tree ' highlight root
```

Fig. 19.25 | XPathNavigator navigating selected nodes. (Part 3 of 5.)

```
133          Else ' if current node has no previous siblings
134             MessageBox.Show("Current node is first sibling.", "", _
135                MessageBoxButtons.OK, MessageBoxIcon.Information)
136          End If
137       End Sub ' btnPrevious_Click
138
139       ' print values for XPathNodeIterator
140       Private Sub DisplayIterator(ByVal iterator As XPathNodeIterator)
141          txtSelect.Clear()
142
143          ' display selected node's values
144          While iterator.MoveNext()
145             txtSelect.Text &= iterator.Current.Value.Trim() & vbCrLf
146          End While
147       End Sub ' DisplayIterator
148
149       ' determine if TreeNode should display current node name or value
150       Private Sub DetermineType(ByVal node As TreeNode, _
151          ByVal xPath As XPathNavigator)
152
153          Select Case xPath.NodeType ' determine NodeType
154             Case XPathNodeType.Element ' if Element, get its name
155                ' get current node name, and remove whitespaces
156                node.Text = xPath.Name.Trim()
157             Case Else ' obtain node values
158                ' get current node value and remove whitespaces
159                node.Text = xPath.Value.Trim()
160          End Select
161       End Sub ' DetermineType
162    End Class ' FrmPathNavigator
```

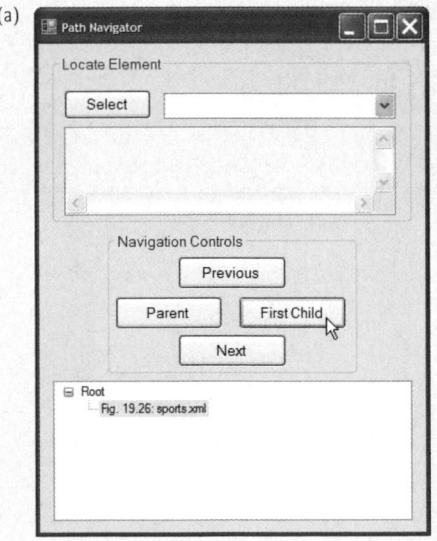

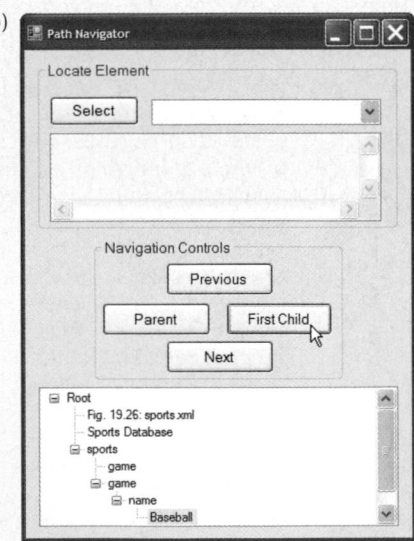

Fig. 19.25 | XPathNavigator navigating selected nodes. (Part 4 of 5.)

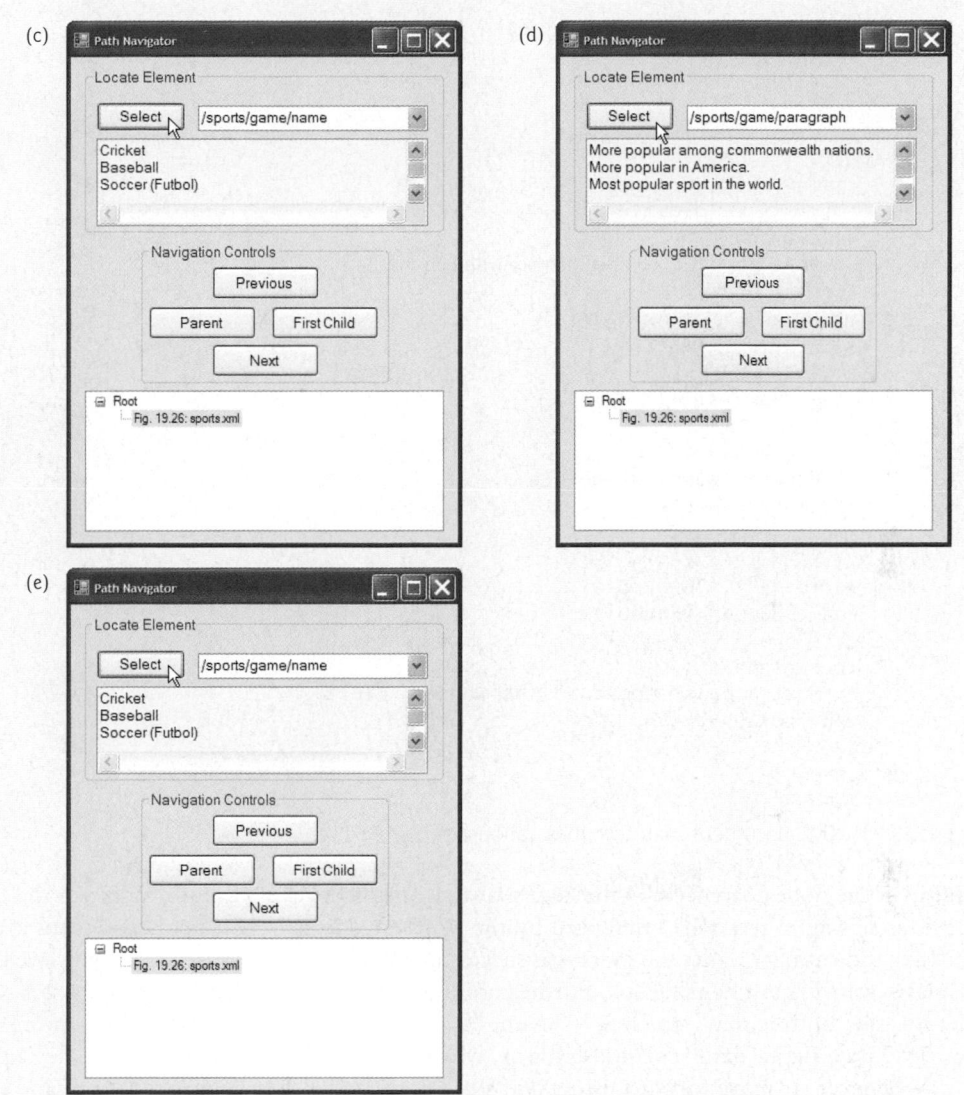

Fig. 19.25 | XPathNavigator navigating selected nodes. (Part 5 of 5.)

The program of Fig. 19.25 loads XML document sports.xml (Fig. 19.26) into an XPathDocument object by passing the document's file name to the XPathDocument constructor (line 13). Method **CreateNavigator** (line 14) creates and returns an XPathNavigator reference to the XPathDocument's tree structure.

The navigation methods of XPathNavigator are **MoveToFirstChild** (line 46), **MoveToParent** (line 68), **MoveToNext** (line 97) and **MoveToPrevious** (line 123). Each method performs the action that its name implies. Method MoveToFirstChild moves to the first child of the node referenced by the XPathNavigator, MoveToParent moves to the parent node of the node referenced by the XPathNavigator, MoveToNext moves to the next

```
 1   <?xml version = "1.0"?>
 2   <!-- Fig. 19.26: sports.xml -->
 3   <!-- Sports Database        -->
 4
 5   <sports>
 6      <game id = "783">
 7          <name>Cricket</name>
 8
 9          <paragraph>
10             More popular among commonwealth nations.
11          </paragraph>
12      </game>
13
14      <game id = "239">
15          <name>Baseball</name>
16
17          <paragraph>
18             More popular in America.
19          </paragraph>
20      </game>
21
22      <game id = "418">
23          <name>Soccer (Futbol)</name>
24
25          <paragraph>
26             Most popular sport in the world.
27          </paragraph>
28      </game>
29   </sports>
```

Fig. 19.26 | XML document that describes various sports.

sibling of the node referenced by the XPathNavigator and MoveToPrevious moves to the previous sibling of the node referenced by the XPathNavigator. Each method returns a Boolean indicating whether the move was successful. Whenever a move operation fails, we display a warning in a MessageBox. Furthermore, each method is called in the event handler of the button that matches its name (e.g., clicking the **First Child** button in Fig. 19.25(a) triggers btnFirstChild_Click, which calls MoveToFirstChild).

Whenever we move forward using XPathNavigator, as with MoveToFirstChild and MoveToNext, nodes are added to the TreeNode node list. The Private method Determine-Type (lines 150–161) determines whether to assign the Node's Name property or Value property to the TreeNode (lines 156 and 159). Whenever MoveToParent is called, all the children of the parent node are removed from the display. Similarly, a call to MoveToPrevious removes the current sibling node. Note that the nodes are removed only from the TreeView, not from the tree representation of the document.

The btnSelect_Click event handler (lines 27–38) corresponds to the **Select** button. XPathNavigator method Select (line 32) takes search criteria in the form of either an XPathExpression or a String that represents an XPath expression, and returns as an XPathNodeIterator object any node that matches the search criteria. Figure 19.27 summarizes the XPath expressions provided by this program's combo box. We show the result of some of these expressions in Figs. 19.25(b) (d).

XPath Expression	Description
/sports	Matches all sports nodes that are child nodes of the document root node.
/sports/game	Matches all game nodes that are child nodes of sports, which is a child of the document root.
/sports/game/name	Matches all name nodes that are child nodes of game. The game is a child of sports, which is a child of the document root.
/sports/game/paragraph	Matches all paragraph nodes that are child nodes of game. The game is a child of sports, which is a child of the document root.
/sports/game [name='Cricket']	Matches all game nodes that contain a child element whose name is Cricket. The game is a child of sports, which is a child of the document root.

Fig. 19.27 | XPath expressions and descriptions.

Method DisplayIterator (defined in lines 140–147) appends the node values from the given XPathNodeIterator to the txtSelect TextBox. Note that we call String method Trim to remove unnecessary whitespace. Method MoveNext (line 144) advances to the next node, which property Current (line 145) can access.

19.9 (Optional) Schema Validation with Class XmlReader

Recall from Section 19.6 that schemas provide a means for specifying XML document structure and validating XML documents. Such validation helps an application determine whether a particular document it receives is complete, ordered properly and not missing any data. In Section 19.6, we used an online XSD schema validator to verify that an XML document conforms to an XML Schema. In this section, we show how to perform the same type of validation programmatically using classes provided by the .NET Framework.

Validating an XML Document Programmatically
Class XmlReader can validate an XML document as it reads and parses the document. In this example, we demonstrate how to activate such validation. The program in Fig. 19.28 validates an XML document that the user chooses—either book.xml (Fig. 19.11) or fail.xml (Fig. 19.29)—against the XML Schema document book.xsd (Fig. 19.12).

```
 1   ' Fig. 19.28: FrmValidationTest.vb
 2   ' Validating XML documents against schemas.
 3   Imports System.Xml
 4   Imports System.Xml.Schema ' contains XmlSchemaSet class
```

Fig. 19.28 | Schema-validation example. (Part 1 of 2.)

```vbnet
5
6   Public Class FrmValidationTest
7       Private schemas As XmlSchemaSet ' schemas to validate against
8       Private valid As Boolean = True ' validation result
9
10      ' handle Validate Button Click event
11      Private Sub btnValidate_Click(ByVal sender As Object, _
12          ByVal e As EventArgs) Handles btnValidate.Click
13          schemas = New XmlSchemaSet() ' create the XmlSchemaSet class
14
15          ' add the schema to the collection
16          schemas.Add("http://www.deitel.com/booklist", "book.xsd")
17
18          ' set the validation settings
19          Dim settings As New XmlReaderSettings()
20          settings.ValidationType = ValidationType.Schema
21          settings.Schemas = schemas
22          AddHandler settings.ValidationEventHandler, _
23              AddressOf ValidationError
24
25          ' create the XmlReader object
26          Dim reader As XmlReader = XmlReader.Create(cboFiles.Text, settings)
27
28          ' parse the file
29          While reader.Read()
30              ' empty body
31          End While
32
33          If valid Then ' check validation result
34              lblConsole.Text = "Document is valid"
35          End If
36
37          valid = True ' reset variable
38          reader.Close() ' close reader stream
39      End Sub ' btnValidate_Click
40
41      ' event handler for validation error
42      Private Sub ValidationError(ByVal sender As Object, _
43          ByVal arguments As ValidationEventArgs)
44          lblConsole.Text = arguments.Message
45          valid = False ' validation failed
46      End Sub ' ValidationError
47  End Class ' FrmValidationTest
```

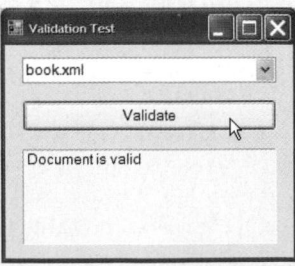

Fig. 19.28 | Schema-validation example. (Part 2 of 2.)

```
1   <?xml version = "1.0"?>
2   <!-- Fig. 19.29: fail.xml                              -->
3   <!-- XML file that does not conform to schema book.xsd -->
4
5   <deitel:books xmlns:deitel = "http://www.deitel.com/booklist">
6      <book>
7         <title>Visual Basic 2005 How to Program, 3/e</title>
8      </book>
9
10     <book>
11        <title>Visual C# 2005 How to Program</title>
12     </book>
13
14     <book>
15        <title>Java How to Program, 6/e</title>
16     </book>
17
18     <book>
19        <title>C++ How to Program, 5/e</title>
20        <title>Internet and World Wide Web How to Program, 3/e</title>
21     </book>
22
23     <book>
24        <title>XML How to Program</title>
25     </book>
26  </deitel:books>
```

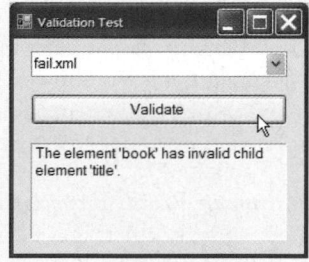

Fig. 19.29 | XML file that does not conform to the XML Schema document in Fig. 19.12.

Line 7 declares **XmlSchemaSet** variable schemas. An object of class XmlSchemaSet stores a collection of schemas against which an XmlReader can validate. Line 13 assigns a new XmlSchemaSet object to variable schemas, and line 16 calls this object's **Add** method to add a schema to the collection. Method Add receives as arguments a namespace URI that identifies the schema (http://www.deitel.com/booklist) and the name and location of the schema file (book.xsd in the current directory).

Lines 19–21 create and set the properties of an XmlReaderSettings object. Line 20 sets the XmlReaderSettings object's **ValidationType** property to the value **Validation-Type.Schema**, indicating that we want the XmlReader to perform validation with a schema as it reads an XML document. Line 21 sets the XmlReaderSettings object's **Schemas** property to schemas. This property sets the schema(s) used to validate the document read by the XmlReader.

Lines 22–23 register method ValidationError with the settings object's ValidationEventHandler. Method ValidationError (lines 42–46) is called if the document being read is found to be invalid or an error occurs (e.g., the document cannot be found). Failure to register a method with ValidationEventHandler causes an exception (XmlException) to be thrown when the XML document is found to be invalid or missing.

After setting the ValidationType property, Schemas property and ValidationEventHandler of the XmlReaderSettings object, we are ready to create a validating XmlReader. Line 26 creates an XmlReader that reads the file selected by the user from the cboFiles ComboBox and validates it against the book.xsd schema.

Validation is performed node-by-node by calling method Read of the XmlReader object (line 29). Because we set XmlReaderSettings property ValidationType to ValidationType.Schema, each call to Read validates the next node in the document. The loop terminates either when all the nodes have been validated or when a node fails validation.

Detecting an Invalid XML Document

The program in Fig. 19.28 validates the XML document book.xml (Fig. 19.12) against the book.xsd (Fig. 19.11) schema successfully. However, when the user selects the XML document of Fig. 19.29, validation fails—the book element in lines 18–21 contains more than one title element. When the program encounters the invalid node, it calls method ValidationError (lines 42–46 of Fig. 19.28), which displays a message explaining why validation failed.

19.10 (Optional) XSLT with Class XslCompiledTransform

Recall from Section 19.7 that XSLT elements define rules for converting one type of XML document to another type of XML document. We showed how to transform XML documents into XHTML documents and displayed these in Internet Explorer. The XSLT processor included in Internet Explorer (i.e., MSXML) performed the transformations.

Performing an XSL Transformation in Visual Basic Using the .NET Framework

Figure 19.30 applies the style sheet sports.xsl (Fig. 19.17) to sports.xml (Fig. 19.26) programmatically. The result of the transformation is written to an XHTML file on disk and displayed in a text box. Figure 19.30(c) shows the resulting XHTML document (sports.html) when you view it in Internet Explorer.

Line 5 imports for the **System.Xml.Xsl** namespace, which contains class **XslCompiledTransform** for applying XSLT style sheets to XML documents. Line 7 declares XslCompiledTransform reference transformer. An object of this type serves as an XSLT processor (like MSXML in earlier examples) to transform XML data from one format to another.

```
1    ' Fig. 19.30: FrmTransformTest.vb
2    ' Applying an XSLT style sheet to an XML document.
3    Imports System.Xml.Xsl ' contains class XslCompiledTransform
4
```

Fig. 19.30 | XSLT style sheet applied to an XML document. (Part 1 of 2.)

```
 5  Public Class FrmTransformTest
 6     ' applies the transformation
 7     Private transformer As XslCompiledTransform
 8
 9     ' initialize variables
10     Private Sub FrmTransformTest_Load(ByVal sender As Object, _
11        ByVal e As EventArgs) Handles MyBase.Load
12        transformer = New XslCompiledTransform() ' create transformer
13        transformer.Load("sports.xsl") ' load and compile the style sheet
14     End Sub ' FrmTransformTest_Load
15
16     ' transform XML data on Transform XML Button Click event
17     Private Sub btnTransform_Click(ByVal sender As Object, _
18        ByVal e As EventArgs) Handles btnTransform.Click
19        ' perform the transformation and store the result in new file
20        transformer.Transform("sports.xml", "sports.html")
21
22        ' read and display the XHTML document's text in a Textbox
23        txtConsole.Text = System.IO.File.ReadAllText("sports.html")
24     End Sub ' btnTransform_Click
25  End Class ' FrmTransformTest
```

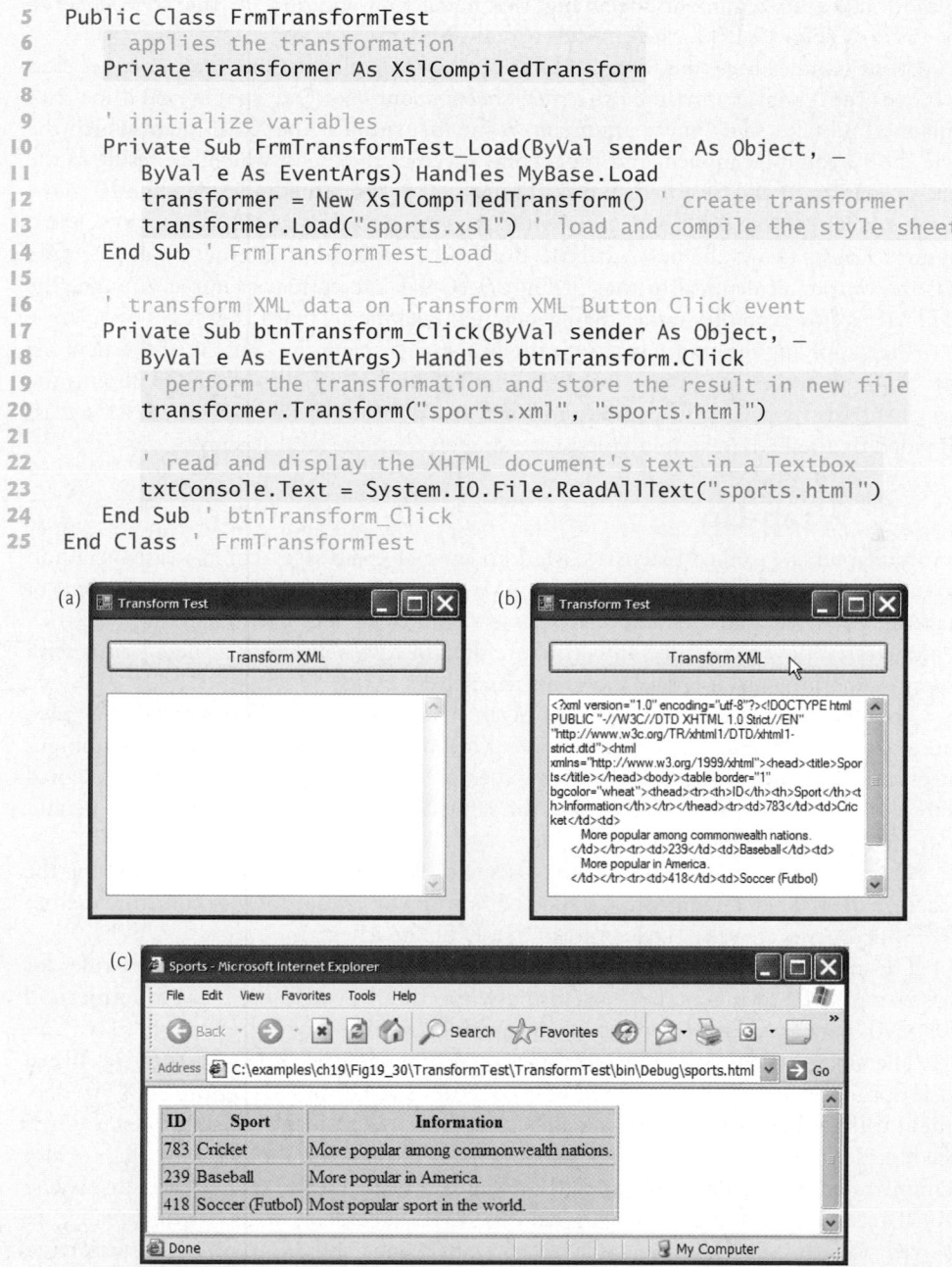

Fig. 19.30 | XSLT style sheet applied to an XML document. (Part 2 of 2.)

In event handler FrmTransformTest_Load (lines 10–14), line 12 creates a new XslCompiledTransform object. Then line 13 calls the XslCompiledTransform object's **Load** method, which parses and loads the style sheet that this application uses. This method takes an argument specifying the name and location of the style sheet—`sports.xsl` (Fig. 19.17) located in the current directory.

Event handler `btnTransform_Click` (lines 17–24) calls method `Transform` of class `XslCompiledTransform` to apply the style sheet (`sports.xsl`) to `sports.xml` (line 20). This method takes two `String` arguments—the first specifies the XML file to which the style sheet should be applied, and the second specifies the file in which the result of the transformation should be stored on disk. Thus the `Transform` method call in line 20 transforms `sports.xml` to XHTML and writes the result to disk as the file `sports.html`. Figure 19.30(c) shows the new XHTML document rendered in Internet Explorer. Note that the output is identical to that of Fig. 19.16—in the current example, though, the XHTML is stored on disk rather than generated dynamically by MSXML.

After applying the transformation, the program displays the content of the new file `sports.html` in the `txtConsole` TextBox, as shown in Fig. 19.30(b). Line 23 obtains the text of the file by passing its name to method `ReadAllText` of the `System.IO.File` class provided by the FCL to simplify file-processing tasks on the local system.

19.11 Wrap-Up

In this chapter, we studied Extensible Markup Language and several of its related technologies. We began by discussing some basic XML terminology, introducing the concepts of markup, XML vocabularies and XML parsers (validating and nonvalidating). We then demonstrated how to describe and structure data in XML, illustrating these points with examples marking up an article and a business letter.

The chapter discussed the concept of an XML namespace. You learned that each namespace has a unique name that provides a means for document authors to unambiguously refer to elements with the same name (i.e., prevent naming collisions). We presented examples of defining two namespaces in the same document, as well as setting the default namespace for a document.

We also discussed how to create DTDs and schemas for specifying and validating the structure of an XML document. We showed how to use various tools to confirm whether XML documents are valid (i.e., conform to a DTD or schema).

The chapter demonstrated how to create and use XSL documents to specify rules for converting XML documents between formats. Specifically, you learned how to format and sort XML data as XHTML for display in a Web browser.

The final sections of the chapter presented more advanced uses of XML in Visual Basic applications. We demonstrated how to retrieve and display data from an XML document using various FCL classes. We illustrated how a Document Object Model (DOM) tree represents each element of an XML document as a node in the tree. The chapter also demonstrated reading data from an XML document using the `XmlReader` class, displaying DOM trees graphically and locating data in XML documents with XPath. Finally, we showed how to use .NET Framework classes `XmlReader` and `XslCompiledTransform` to perform schema validation and XSL transformations, respectively.

In Chapter 20, we begin our discussion of databases, which organize data in such a way that the data can be selected and updated quickly. We introduce Structured Query Language (SQL) for writing simple database queries (i.e., searches) and ADO.NET for manipulating information in a database through Visual Basic. You will learn how to create XML documents based on data in a database.

19.12 **Web Resources**

www.w3.org/XML

The W3C (World Wide Web Consortium) facilitates the development of common protocols to ensure interoperability on the Web. Its XML page includes information about upcoming events, publications, software, discussion groups and the latest developments in XML.

www.xml.org

xml.org is a reference for XML, DTDs, schemas and namespaces.

www.w3.org/Style/XSL

This W3C site provides information on XSL, including such topics as XSL development, learning XSL, XSL-enabled tools, the XSL specification, FAQs and XSL history.

www.w3.org/TR

This is the W3C technical reports and publications site. It contains links to working drafts, proposed recommendations and other resources.

www.xmlbooks.com

This site provides a list of XML books recommended by Charles Goldfarb, one of the original designers of GML (General Markup Language), from which SGML, HTML and XML were derived.

www.xml-zone.com

The DevX XML Zone is a complete resource for XML information. This site includes FAQs, news, articles and links to other XML sites and newsgroups.

wdvl.internet.com/Authoring/Languages/XML

The Web Developer's Virtual Library XML site includes tutorials, FAQs, the latest news and extensive links to XML sites and software downloads.

www.xml.com

This site provides the latest news and information about XML, conference listings, links to XML Web resources organized by topic, tools and other resources.

msdn.microsoft.com/xml/default.aspx

The MSDN XML Development Center features articles on XML, Ask-the-Experts chat sessions, samples, demos, newsgroups and other helpful information.

www.oasis-open.org/cover/xml.html

This site includes links to several FAQs, online resources, industry initiatives, demos, conferences and tutorials.

www-106.ibm.com/developerworks/xml

The IBM developerWorks XML site is a great resource for developers that provides news, tools, a library, case studies and information about XML-related events and standards.

www.devx.com/projectcool/door/7051

The Project Cool DevX site includes several tutorials covering introductory through advanced XML topics.

www.ucc.ie/xml

This site provides a detailed XML FAQ. Developers can read responses to some popular questions or submit their own questions through the site.

www.w3.org/XML/Schema

This W3C site provides information on XML Schema, including links, tools, resources and the XML Schema specification.

tools.decisionsoft.com/schemaValidate.html

DecisionSoft provides a free online XML Schema validator from DecisionSoft.

www.sun.com/software/xml/developers/multischema/

The Web page for downloading the Sun Multi-Schema XML Validator (MSV), which validates XML documents against several kinds of schemas.

`en.wikipedia.org/wiki/EBNF`
This site provides detailed information about Extended Backus-Naur Form (EBNF).

`www.garshol.priv.no/download/text/bnf.html`
This site introduces Backus-Naur Form (BNF) and EBNF, and discusses the differences between these notations.

`www.w3schools.com/schema/default.asp`
This site provides an XML Schema tutorial.

`www.w3.org/2001/03/webdata/xsv`
This is an online tool for validating XML Schema documents.

`apps.gotdotnet.com/xmltools/xsdvalidator`
This is an online tool for validating XML documents against an XML Schema.

`www.w3.org/TR/xmlschema-2`
This is part 2 of the W3C XML Schema specification, which defines the types allowed in an XML Schema.

Summary

Section 19.1 Introduction

- XML is a portable, widely supported, open (i.e., nonproprietary) technology for data storage and exchange.
- The Framework Class Library provides an extensive set of XML-related classes. Much of Visual Studio's internal implementation also employs XML.

Section 19.2 XML Basics

- XML documents are readable by both humans and machines.
- XML permits document authors to create custom markup for any type of information. This enables document authors to create entirely new markup languages that describe specific types of data, including mathematical formulas, chemical molecular structures, music and recipes.
- An XML parser is responsible for identifying components of XML documents (typically files with the `.xml` extension) and then storing those components in a data structure for manipulation.
- An XML document can optionally reference a Document Type Definition (DTD) or schema that defines the XML document's structure.
- An XML document that conforms to a DTD/schema (i.e., has the appropriate structure) is valid.
- If an XML parser (validating or nonvalidating) can process an XML document successfully, that XML document is well formed.

Section 19.3 Structuring Data

- An XML document begins with an optional XML declaration, which identifies the document as an XML document. The `version` attribute specifies the version of XML syntax used in the document.
- XML comments begin with `<!--` and end with `-->`.
- An XML document contains text that represents its content (i.e., data) and elements that specify its structure. XML documents delimit an element with start and end tags.
- The root element of an XML document encompasses all its other elements.
- XML element names can be of any length and can contain letters, digits, underscores, hyphens and periods. However, they must begin with either a letter or an underscore, and they should not

begin with "xml" in any combination of uppercase and lowercase letters as this is reserved for use in the XML standards.

- When a user loads an XML document in Internet Explorer, MSXML parses the document, and Internet Explorer uses a style sheet to format the data for display.

- Internet Explorer displays minus (–) or plus (+) signs next to all container elements. A minus sign indicates that all child elements are being displayed. When clicked, a minus sign becomes a plus sign (which collapses the container element and hides all the children), and vice versa.

- Data can be placed between tags or in attributes (name-value pairs that appear within the angle brackets of start tags). Elements can have any number of attributes.

Section 19.4 XML Namespaces

- XML allows document authors to create their own markup, and as a result, naming collisions (i.e., two different elements that have the same name) can occur. XML namespaces provide a means for document authors to prevent collisions.

- Each namespace prefix is bound to a uniform resource identifier (URI) that uniquely identifies the namespace. A URI is a series of characters that differentiate names. Document authors create their own namespace prefixes. Any name can be used as a namespace prefix but the namespace prefix xml is reserved for use in XML standards.

- To eliminate the need to place a namespace prefix in each element, authors can specify a default namespace for an element and its children. We declare a default namespace using keyword xmlns with a URI (Uniform Resource Identifier) as its value.

- Document authors commonly use URLs (Uniform Resource Locators) for URIs, because domain names (e.g., deitel.com) in URLs must be unique.

Section 19.5 Document Type Definitions (DTDs)

- DTDs and schemas specify documents' element types and attributes, and their relationships to one another.

- DTDs and schemas enable an XML parser to verify whether an XML document is valid (i.e., its elements contain the proper attributes and appear in the proper sequence).

- A DTD expresses the set of rules for document structure using an EBNF (Extended Backus-Naur Form) grammar.

- In a DTD, an ELEMENT element type declaration defines the rules for an element. An ATTLIST attribute-list declaration defines attributes for a particular element.

Section 19.6 W3C XML Schema Documents

- Unlike DTDs, schemas do not use EBNF grammar. Instead, they use XML syntax and are themselves XML documents that programs can manipulate.

- Unlike DTDs, XML Schema documents can specify what type of data (e.g., numeric, text) an element can contain.

- An XML document that conforms to a schema document is schema valid.

- Two categories of types exist in XML Schema: simple types and complex types. Simple types cannot contain attributes or child elements; complex types can.

- Every simple type defines a restriction on an XML Schema–defined schema type or on a user-defined type.

- Complex types can have either simple content or complex content. Both simple content and complex content can contain attributes, but only complex content can contain child elements.

- Whereas complex types with simple content must extend or restrict some other existing type, complex types with complex content do not have this limitation.

Section 19.7 (Optional) Extensible Stylesheet Language and XSL Transformations

- XSL can convert XML into any text-based document. XSL documents have the extension `.xsl`.

- XPath is a string-based language of expressions used by XML and many of its related technologies for effectively and efficiently locating structures and data (such as specific elements and attributes) in XML documents.

- XPath is used to locate parts of the source tree document that match templates defined in an XSL style sheet. When a match occurs (i.e., a node matches a template), the matching template executes and adds its result to the result tree. When there are no more matches, XSLT has transformed the source tree into the result tree.

- The XSLT does not analyze every node of the source tree; it selectively navigates the source tree using XPath's `select` and `match` attributes.

- For XSLT to function, the source tree must be properly structured. Schemas, DTDs and validating parsers can validate document structure before using XPath and XSLTs.

- XSL style sheets can be connected directly to an XML document by adding an `xml:stylesheet` processing instruction to the XML document.

- Two tree structures are involved in transforming an XML document using XSLT—the source tree (the document being transformed) and the result tree (the result of the transformation).

- The XPath character / (a forward slash) always selects the document root. In XPath, a leading forward slash specifies that we are using absolute addressing.

- An XPath expression with no beginning forward slash uses relative addressing.

- XSL element `value-of` retrieves an attribute's value. The @ symbol specifies an attribute node.

- XSL node-set function `name` retrieves the current node's element name.

- XSL node-set function `text` retrieves the text between an element's start and end tags.

- The XPath expression //* selects all the nodes in an XML document.

Section 19.8 (Optional) Document Object Model (DOM)

- Upon successfully parsing a document, some XML parsers store document data as tree structures in memory. This hierarchical tree structure is called a Document Object Model (DOM) tree, and an XML parser that creates this type of structure is known as a DOM parser.

- In the DOM, each element name represents a node. A node that contains children is called a parent node. A parent node can have many children, but a child node can have only one parent node. Nodes that are peers are called sibling nodes.

- A node's descendant nodes include its children, its children's children and so on. A node's ancestor nodes include its parent, its parent's parent and so on.

- The DOM tree has a single root node that contains all the other nodes in the document.

- Namespace `System.Xml` contains classes for processing XML documents.

- Class `XmlReader` is an `MustInherit` class that defines the interface for reading XML documents.

- `XmlReader`'s `Shared` method `Create` obtains a new `XmlReader` object.

- An `XmlReaderSettings` object specifies how we would like the `XmlReader` to behave.

- By default, an `XmlReader` does not perform validation.

- Method `Create` receives as arguments the name of the XML document to read and an `XmlReaderSettings` object.

- An XML document is opened when method `Create` is invoked to create an `XmlReader` object. The document can then be read programmatically.

- Method `Read` of `XmlReader` reads one node from the DOM tree.

- The `Name` property contains the node's name, the `Value` property contains the node's data and the `NodeType` property contains the node's type (i.e., element, comment, text).

- A `TreeView` control can be used to display an XML document's contents graphically. Objects of class `TreeNode` represent each node in the tree.

- Class `XPathNavigator` in the `System.Xml.XPath` namespace can iterate through node lists that match search criteria written as XPath expressions.

- XPath provides a syntax for locating specific nodes in XML documents. XPath is a string-based language of expressions used by XML and many of its related technologies.

- `XPathNavigator` method `MoveToFirstChild` moves to the first child of the node referenced by the `XPathNavigator`. `MoveToParent` moves to the parent node of the node referenced by the `XPath-Navigator`, `MoveToNext` moves to the next sibling of the node referenced by the `XPathNavigator` and `MoveToPrevious` moves to the previous sibling of the node referenced by the `XPathNavigator`.

Section 19.9 (Optional) Schema Validation with Class *XmlReader*

- Class `XmlReader` can validate an XML document as it reads and parses the document.

- Class `XmlSchemaSet` stores a collection of schemas against which an `XmlReader` can validate.

- `XmlReader` Shared method `Create` returns a reference to an `XmlReader` object created based on an `XmlReaderSettings` object that specifies how the `XmlReader` is to behave.

- Setting `XmlReaderSettings`'s `ValidationType` property to `ValidationType.Schema` indicates that the `XmlReader` is to perform validation against an XML Schema as it reads an XML document.

- The `Schemas` property of an `XmlReaderSettings` object sets the schema(s) used to validate the document read by the `XmlReader`.

- If created with `XmlReaderSettings` property `ValidationType` set to `ValidationType.Schema`, an `XmlReader` validates each node in an XML document with each call to the object's `Read` method.

- When an `XmlReader` encounters an invalid node, the method registered with its `XmlReaderSettings` object's `ValidationEventHandler` is called.

Section 19.10 (Optional) XSLT with Class *XslCompiledTransform*

- The `System.Xml.Xsl` namespace contains class `XslCompiledTransform` for applying XSLT style sheets to XML documents.

- `XslCompiledTransform` method `Load` loads and compiles a style sheet.

- `XslCompiledTransform` method `Transform` applies the compiled style sheet to a specified XML document. This method takes two `string` arguments: the name of the XML file to which the style sheet should be applied and the name of the file to store the transformation result.

Terminology

Sections 19.1–19.6

/ forward slash (end tag of XML element)	attribute of XML element
`<!--` and `-->` XML comment delimiters	base attribute of element extension
`all` element	base attribute of element restriction
angle brackets (<>)	base type
asterisk (*) occurrence indicator	CDATA keyword
`ATTLIST` attribute-list declaration	character data

character entity reference
child element
complex content in XML Schema
complex type
complexType element
container element
default namespace
Document Type Definition (DTD)
.dtd filename extension
element element (XML Schema)
ELEMENT element type declaration
empty element
EMPTY keyword
end tag
Extensible HyperText Markup Language
    (XHTML)
Extensible Markup Language (XML)
Extensible Stylesheet Language (XSL)
extension element
external DTD
#FIXED keyword
forward slash character (/)
#IMPLIED keyword
markup
maxOccurs attribute of element element
Microsoft XML Core Services (MSXML)
minInclusive element
minOccurs attribute of element element
name attribute of element element
namespace prefix
nested element
node
nonvalidating XML parser
occurrence indicator
open technology
parent element
parsed character data
parser
#PCDATA keyword
plus sign (+) occurrence indicator
prolog of an XML document

question mark (?) occurrence indicator
#REQUIRED keyword
restriction on built-in schema type
root element (XML)
schema
schema element
schema-invalid XML document
schema repository
schema-valid XML document
simple content in XML Schema
simple type
simpleContent XML Schema element
simpleType XML Schema element
start tag
style sheet
SYSTEM keyword in XML
targetNamespace attribute of schema element
type attribute of element element
unbounded value of attribute maxOccurs
Uniform Resource Identifier (URI)
Uniform Resource Locator (URL)
Uniform Resource Name (URN)
valid XML document
validating XML parser
version attribute in an XML declaration
well-formed XML document
World Wide Web Consortium (W3C)
Xerces
XML comment
XML declaration
XML element
.xml filename extension
XML instance document
XML namespace
XML parser
XML processor
XML Schema
XML Validator
XML vocabulary
xmlns attribute in an XML document
.xsd filename extension

Sections 19.7–19.10
/ forward slash character (XPath)
@ XPath attribute symbol
<? and ?> XML delimiters
absolute addressing
Add method of XMLSchemaSet class
ancestor node
child node
context node

Create method of XmlReader class
CreateNavigator method of class
    XPathDocument
Current property of class XPathnodeIterator
data-type attribute of xsl:sort element
descendant node
Document Object Model (DOM)
document root

DOM parser
ExpandAll method of TreeView class
IgnoreWhitespace property of class
    XmlReaderSettings
Load method of XslCompiledTransform class
match attribute of xsl:template element
MoveNext method of class XPathNodeIterator
MoveToFirstChild method of class
    XPathNavigator
MoveToNext method of class XPathNavigator
MoveToParent method of class XPathNavigator
MoveToPrevious method of class
    XPathNavigator
name node-set function
node-set function
node set of an xsl:for-each element
order attribute of xsl:sort element
parent node
Parent property of TreeNode class
PI target
PI value
processing instruction (PI)
Read method of XmlReader class
recursive descent
Refresh method TreeView class
relative addressing
result tree (XSLT)
root node
Schemas property of XmlReaderSettings class
select attribute of xsl:for-each element
sibling node
source tree (XSLT)
stylesheet start tag
sum function (XSL)
System.Xml namespace

System.Xml.XPath namespace
System.Xml.Xsl namespace
text node-set function
TreeNode class
TreeView control
Transform method of class
    XslCompiledTransform
type attribute in a processing instruction
ValidationEventHandler of settings object
ValidationType property of class
    XmlReaderSettings
ValidationType.Schema
version attribute of xsl:stylesheet element
Xalan 2
XML Path Language (XPath)
XmlNodeType enumeration
XmlReader class
XmlReaderSettings class
XmlSchemaSet class
XPathDocument class
XPathExpression class
XPathNavigator class
XslCompiledTransform class
.xsl filename extension
XSL Formatting Objects (XSL-FO)
XSL style sheet
XSL template
XSL Transformations (XSLT)
XSL variable
xsl:for-each element
xsl:output element
xsl:sort element
xsl:stylesheet element
xsl:template element
xsl:value-of element

Self-Review Exercises
Sections 19.1–19.6

19.1 Which of the following are valid XML element names? (Select all that apply.)
    a) yearBorn
    b) year.Born
    c) year Born
    d) year-Born1
    e) 2_year_born
    f) _year_born_

19.2 State which of the following statements are *true* and which are *false*. If *false*, explain why.
    a) XML is a technology for creating markup languages.
    b) XML markup is delimited by forward and backward slashes (/ and \).
    c) All XML start tags must have corresponding end tags.

d) Parsers check an XML document's syntax.

e) XML does not support namespaces.

f) When creating XML elements, document authors must use the set of XML tags provided by the W3C.

g) The pound character (#), dollar sign ($), ampersand (&) and angle brackets (< and >) are examples of XML reserved characters.

19.3 Fill in the blanks for each of the following:

a) _____ help prevent naming collisions.

b) _____ embed application-specific information into an XML document.

c) _____ is Microsoft's XML parser.

d) XSL element _____ writes a DOCTYPE to the result tree.

e) XML Schema documents have root element _____.

f) XSL element _____ is the root element in an XSL document.

g) XSL element _____ selects specific XML elements using repetition.

19.4 State which of the following statements are *true* and which are *false*. If *false*, explain why.

a) XML is not case sensitive.

b) XML Schemas are better than DTDs, because DTDs lack a way of indicating what specific type of data (e.g., numeric, text) an element can contain and DTDs are not themselves XML documents.

c) DTDs are written using an XML vocabulary.

d) Schema is a technology for locating information in an XML document.

19.5 In Fig. 19.2, we subdivided the author element into more detailed pieces. How might you subdivide the date element? Use the date May 5, 2005, as an example.

Sections 19.7–19.10

19.6 Write a processing instruction that includes style sheet wap.xsl for use in Internet Explorer.

19.7 Fill in the blanks for each of the following:

a) Nodes that contain other nodes are called _____ nodes.

b) Nodes that are peers are called _____ nodes.

c) Class XmlReader is a(n) _____ class that defines the interface for reading XML documents.

19.8 Write an XPath expression that locates contact nodes in letter.xml (Fig. 19.4).

19.9 Describe method Select of class XPathNavigator.

Answers to Self-Review Exercises

Sections 19.1–19.6

19.1 a, b, d, f. [Choice c is incorrect because it contains a space. Choice e is incorrect because the first character is a number.]

19.2 a) True. b) False. In an XML document, markup text is delimited by tags enclosed in angle brackets (< and >) with a forward slash just after the < in the end tag. c) True. d) True. e) False. XML does support namespaces. f) False. When creating tags, document authors can use any valid name but should avoid ones that begin with the reserved word xml (also XML, Xml, etc.). g) False. XML reserved characters include the ampersand (&), the left-angle bracket (<) and the right-angle bracket (>), but not # and $.

19.3 a) Namespaces. b) Processing instructions. c) MSXML. d) xsl:output. e) schema. f) xsl:stylesheet. g) xsl:for-each.

19.4   a)   False. XML is case sensitive. b) True. c) False. DTDs use EBNF grammar, which is not XML syntax. d) False. XPath is a technology for locating information in an XML document. XML Schema provides a means for type checking XML documents and verifying their validity.

19.5   `<date>`
```
    <month>May</month>
    <day>5</day>
    <year>2005</year>
</date>.
```

Sections 19.7–19.10

19.6   `<?xsl:stylesheet type = "text/xsl" href = "wap.xsl"?>`

19.7   a) parent. b) sibling. c) `MustInherit`.

19.8   `/letter/contact`.

19.9   Method `Select` receives as an argument either an `XPathExpression` or a `string` containing an `XPathExpression`, to select nodes referenced by the navigator.

Exercises

Sections 19.1–19.6

19.10   *(Nutrition Information XML Document)* Create an XML document that marks up the nutrition facts for a package of Grandma White's cookies. A package of cookies has a serving size of 1 package and the following nutritional value per serving: 260 calories, 100 fat calories, 11 grams of fat, 2 grams of saturated fat, 5 milligrams of cholesterol, 210 milligrams of sodium, 36 grams of total carbohydrates, 2 grams of fiber, 15 grams of sugars and 5 grams of protein. Name this document `nutrition.xml`. Load the XML document into Internet Explorer. [*Hint:* Your markup should contain elements describing the product name, serving size/amount, calories, sodium, cholesterol, proteins, etc. Mark up each nutrition fact/ingredient listed above.]

19.11   *(Nutrition Information XML Schema)* Write an XML Schema document (`nutrition.xsd`) specifying the structure of the XML document created in Exercise 19.10.

Sections 19.7–19.10

19.12   *(Nutrition Information XSL Style Sheet)* Write an XSL style sheet for your solution to Exercise 19.10 that displays the nutritional facts in an XHTML table. Modify Fig. 19.30 (`TransformTest.cs`) to output an XHTML file, `nutrition.html`. Render `nutrition.html` in a Web browser.

19.13   *(Validation Against Multiple Schemas)* Alter Fig. 19.28 (`ValidationTest.cs`) to validate a selected XML file against multiple schemas—`book.xsd` and `nutrition.xsd` (Exercise 19.11). Allow the user to select either `book.xml`, `fail.xml` or `nutrition.xml` (Exercise 19.10). [*Hint:* You can add multiple schema documents to an `XmlSchemaSet`.]

19.14   *(XmlReaderTest Modification)* Modify `XmlReaderTest` (Fig. 19.22) to display `article.xml` (Fig. 19.2) in a `TreeView` instead of in a `TextBox`.

19.15   *(Sorting XSLT Modification)* Modify Fig. 19.19 (`sorting.xsl`) to sort by the number of pages rather than by chapter number. Save the modified document as `sorting_byPage.xsl`.

19.16   *(TransformTest Modification)* Modify `TransformTest` (Fig. 19.30) to use `sorting.xml` (Fig. 19.18), `sorting.xsl` (Fig. 19.19) and `sorting_byPage.xsl` (from Exercise 19.15). Display the result of transforming `sorting.xml` into two XHTML files, `sorting_byChapter.html` and `sorting_byPage.html`. [*Hint:* Remove the `xml:stylesheet` processing instruction from line 5 of `sorting.xml` before attempting to transform the file programmatically.]

20

Database, SQL and ADO.NET

It is a capital mistake to theorize before one has data.
—Arthur Conan Doyle

Now go, write it before them in a table, and note it in a book, that it may be for the time to come for ever and ever.
—Holy Bible, Isaiah 30:8

Get your facts first, and then you can distort them as much as you please.
—Mark Twain

I like two kinds of men: domestic and foreign.
—Mae West

OBJECTIVES

In this chapter you will learn:

- The relational database model.
- To write basic database queries in SQL.
- To add data sources to projects.
- To use the IDE's drag-and-drop capabilities to display database tables in applications.
- To use the classes of namespaces `System.Data` and `System.Data.SqlClient` to manipulate databases.
- To use ADO.NET's disconnected object model to store data from a database in local memory.
- To create XML documents from data sources.

20.1   Introduction

A database is an organized collection of data. Many strategies exist for organizing data to facilitate easy access and manipulation. A database management system (DBMS) provides mechanisms for storing, organizing, retrieving and modifying data for many users. Database management systems allow access to and storage of data independently of the internal representation of the data.

Today's most popular database systems are relational databases. A language called SQL—pronounced "sequel," or as its individual letters—is the international standard language used almost universally with relational databases to perform queries (i.e., to request information that satisfies given criteria) and to manipulate data. In this book, we pronounce SQL as "sequel."

Some popular relational database management systems (RDBMS) are Microsoft SQL Server, Oracle, Sybase, IBM DB2 and PostgreSQL. We provide URLs for these systems in Section 20.11, Web Resources. MySQL (www.mysql.com) is an increasingly popular open-source RDBMS that can be downloaded and used freely by non-commercial users. You may also be familiar with Microsoft Access—a relational database system that is part of Microsoft Office. In this chapter, we use Microsoft SQL Server 2005 Express— a version of SQL Server 2005 that is installed when you install Visual Basic 2005 Express. We will refer to SQL Server 2005 Express simply as SQL Server from this point forward.

A programming language connects to and interacts with a relational database via a database interface—software that facilitates communication between a database management system and a program. Visual Basic programs communicate with databases and manipulate their data through ADO.NET. The current version of ADO.NET is 2.0. Section 20.5 presents an overview of ADO.NET's object model and the relevant namespaces and classes that allow you to work with databases. However, as you will learn in subsequent sections, most of the work required to communicate with a database using ADO.NET 2.0 is performed by the IDE itself. You will work primarily with the IDE's visual programming tools and wizards, which simplify connecting to and manipulating a database. Throughout this chapter, we refer to ADO.NET 2.0 simply as ADO.NET.

This chapter introduces general concepts of relational databases and SQL, then explores ADO.NET and the IDE's tools for accessing data sources. The examples in Sections 20.6–20.9 demonstrate how to build applications that use databases to store information. In the next two chapters, you will see other practical database applications. Chapter 21, ASP.NET 2.0, Web Forms and Web Controls, presents a Web-based bookstore case study that retrieves user and book information from a database. Chapter 22, Web Services, uses a database to store airline reservation data for a Web service (i.e., a software component that can be accessed remotely over a network).

20.2 Relational Databases

A relational database is a logical representation of data that allows the data to be accessed independently of its physical structure. A relational database organizes data in tables. Figure 20.1 illustrates a sample Employees table that might be used in a personnel system. The table stores the attributes of employees. Tables are composed of rows and columns in which values are stored. This table consists of six rows and five columns. The Number column of each row in this table is the table's primary key—a column (or group of columns) in a table that requires a unique value that cannot be duplicated in other rows. This guarantees that a primary key value can be used to uniquely identify a row. A primary key that is composed of two or more columns is known as a composite key. Good examples of primary key columns in other applications are an employee ID number in a payroll system and a part number in an inventory system—values in each of these columns are guaranteed to be unique. The rows in Fig. 20.1 are displayed in order by primary key. In this case, the rows are listed in increasing (ascending) order, but they could also be listed in decreasing (descending) order or in no particular order at all. As we will demonstrate in an upcoming example, programs can specify ordering criteria when requesting data from a database.

Each column represents a different data attribute. Rows are normally unique (by primary key) within a table, but some column values may be duplicated between rows. For example, three different rows in the Employees table's Department column contain the number 413, indicating that these employees work in the same department.

Different database users are often interested in different data and different relationships among the data. Most users require only subsets of the rows and columns. To obtain these subsets, programs use SQL to define queries that select subsets of the data from a table. For example, a program might select data from the Employees table to create a query result that shows where each department is located, in increasing order by Department number (Fig. 20.2). SQL queries are discussed in Section 20.4. In Section 20.7, you will learn how to use the IDE's **Query Builder** to create SQL queries.

Table Employees

	Number	Name	Department	Salary	Location
	23603	Jones	413	1100	New Jersey
	24568	Kerwin	413	2000	New Jersey
Row	34589	Larson	642	1800	Los Angeles
	35761	Myers	611	1400	Orlando
	47132	Neumann	413	9000	New Jersey
	78321	Stephens	611	8500	Orlando

Primary key   Column

Fig. 20.1 | Employees table sample data.

Department	Location
413	New Jersey
611	Orlando
642	Los Angeles

Fig. 20.2 | Result of selecting distinct Department and Location data from the Employees table.

20.3 Relational Database Overview: Books Database

We now overview relational databases in the context of a simple Books database. The database stores information about some recent Deitel publications. First, we overview the tables of the Books database. Then we introduce database concepts, such as how to use SQL to retrieve information from the Books database and to manipulate the data. We provide the database file—Books.mdf—with the examples for this chapter (downloadable from www.deitel.com/books/vbhtp3/). SQL Server database files typically end with the .mdf ("master data file") filename extension. Section 20.6 explains how to use this file in an application.

Authors *Table of the* **Books** *Database*

The database consists of three tables: Authors, AuthorISBN and Titles. The Authors table (described in Fig. 20.3) consists of three columns that maintain each author's unique ID number, first name and last name, respectively. Figure 20.4 contains the data from the Authors table. We list the rows in order by the table's primary key—AuthorID. You will learn how to sort data by other criteria (e.g., in alphabetical order by last name) using SQL's ORDER BY clause in Section 20.4.3.

Titles *Table of the* **Books** *Database*

The Titles table (described in Fig. 20.5) consists of four columns that maintain information about each book in the database, including the ISBN, title, edition number and copyright year. Figure 20.6 contains the data from the Titles table.

Column	Description
AuthorID	Author's ID number in the database. In the Books database, this integer column is defined as an **identity** column, also known as an **autoincremented** column—for each row inserted in the table, the AuthorID value is increased by 1 automatically to ensure that each row has a unique AuthorID. This is the primary key.
FirstName	Author's first name (a string).
LastName	Author's last name (a string).

Fig. 20.3 | Authors table of the Books database.

AuthorID	FirstName	LastName
1	Harvey	Deitel
2	Paul	Deitel
3	Andrew	Goldberg
4	David	Choffnes

Fig. 20.4 | Data from the Authors table of the Books database.

Column	Description
ISBN	ISBN of the book (a string). The table's primary key. ISBN is an abbreviation for "International Standard Book Number"—a numbering scheme that publishers worldwide use to give every book a unique identification number.
Title	Title of the book (a string).
EditionNumber	Edition number of the book (an integer).
Copyright	Copyright year of the book (a string).

Fig. 20.5 | Titles table of the Books database.

ISBN	Title	Edition-Number	Copy-right
0131426443	C How to Program	4	2004
0131450913	Internet & World Wide Web How to Program	3	2004

Fig. 20.6 | Data from the Titles table of the Books database. (Part 1 of 2.)

ISBN	Title	Edition-Number	Copy-right
0131483986	Java How to Program	6	2005
0131525239	Visual C# 2005 How to Program	2	2006
0131828274	Operating Systems	3	2004
0131857576	C++ How to Program	5	2005
0131869000	Visual Basic 2005 How to Program	3	2006

Fig. 20.6 | Data from the Titles table of the Books database. (Part 2 of 2.)

AuthorISBN *Table of the* Books *Database*

The AuthorISBN table (described in Fig. 20.7) consists of two columns that maintain ISBNs for each book and their corresponding authors' ID numbers. This table associates authors with their books. The AuthorID column is a **foreign key**—a column in this table that matches the primary key column in another table (i.e., AuthorID in the Authors table). The ISBN column is also a foreign key—it matches the primary key column (i.e., ISBN) in the Titles table. Together the AuthorID and ISBN columns in this table form a composite primary key. Every row in this table uniquely matches one author to one book's ISBN. Figure 20.8 contains the data from the AuthorISBN table of the Books database.

Column	Description
AuthorID	The author's ID number, a foreign key to the Authors table.
ISBN	The ISBN for a book, a foreign key to the Titles table.

Fig. 20.7 | AuthorISBN table of the Books database.

AuthorID	ISBN	AuthorID	ISBN
1	0131869000	2	0131450913
1	0131525239	2	0131426443
1	0131483986	2	0131857576
1	0131857576	2	0131483986
1	0131426443	2	0131525239
1	0131450913	2	0131869000
1	0131828274	3	0131450913
2	0131828274	4	0131828274

Fig. 20.8 | Data from the AuthorISBN table of Books.

Foreign Keys

Foreign keys can be specified when creating a table. A foreign key helps maintain the **Rule of Referential Integrity**—every foreign key value must appear as another table's primary key value. This enables the DBMS to determine whether the `AuthorID` value for a particular row of the `AuthorISBN` table is valid. Foreign keys also allow related data in multiple tables to be selected from those tables—this is known as joining the data. (You will learn how to join data using SQL's `INNER JOIN` operator in Section 20.4.4.) There is a one-to-many relationship between a primary key and a corresponding foreign key (e.g., one author can write many books). This means that a foreign key can appear many times in its own table, but can appear only once (as the primary key) in another table. For example, the ISBN 0131450913 can appear in several rows of `AuthorISBN` (because this book has several authors), but can appear only once in `Titles`, where ISBN is the primary key.

*Entity-Relationship Diagram for the **Books** Database*

Figure 20.9 is an **entity-relationship (ER) diagram** for the `Books` database. This diagram shows the tables in the database and the relationships among them. The first compartment in each box contains the table's name. The names in italic font are primary keys (e.g., `AuthorID` in the `Authors` table). A table's primary key uniquely identifies each row in the table. Every row must have a value in the primary key column, and the value of the key must be unique in the table. This is known as the **Rule of Entity Integrity**. Note that the names `AuthorID` and `ISBN` in the `AuthorISBN` table are both italic—together these form a composite primary key for the `AuthorISBN` table.

Common Programming Error 20.1

Not providing a value for every column in a primary key breaks the Rule of Entity Integrity and causes the DBMS to report an error.

Common Programming Error 20.2

Providing the same value for the primary key in multiple rows breaks the Rule of Entity Integrity and causes the DBMS to report an error.

The lines connecting the tables in Fig. 20.9 represent the relationships among the tables. Consider the line between the `Authors` and `AuthorISBN` tables. On the `Authors` end of the line, there is a 1, and on the `AuthorISBN` end, there is an infinity symbol (∞). This indicates a one-to-many relationship—for each author in the `Authors` table, there can be an arbitrary number of ISBNs for books written by that author in the `AuthorISBN` table

Fig. 20.9 | Entity-relationship diagram for the `Books` database.

(i.e., an author can write any number of books). Note that the relationship line links the AuthorID column in the Authors table (where AuthorID is the primary key) to the AuthorID column in the AuthorISBN table (where AuthorID is a foreign key)—the line between the tables links the primary key to the matching foreign key.

> **Common Programming Error 20.3**
>
> *Providing a foreign-key value that does not appear as a primary-key value in another table breaks the Rule of Referential Integrity and causes the DBMS to report an error.*

The line between the Titles and AuthorISBN tables illustrates a one-to-many relationship—a book can be written by many authors. Note that the line between the tables links the primary key ISBN in table Titles to the corresponding foreign key in table AuthorISBN. The relationships in Fig. 20.9 illustrate that the sole purpose of the AuthorISBN table is to provide a many-to-many relationship between the Authors and Titles tables—an author can write many books, and a book can have many authors.

20.4 SQL

We now overview SQL in the context of the Books database. Later in the chapter, you will build Visual Basic applications that execute SQL queries and access their results using ADO.NET technology. Though the Visual Basic IDE provides visual tools that hide some of the SQL used to manipulate databases, it is nevertheless important to understand SQL basics. Knowing the types of operations you can perform will help you develop more advanced database-intensive applications.

Figure 20.10 lists some common SQL keywords used to form complete SQL statements—we discuss these keywords in the next several subsections. Other SQL keywords exist, but they are beyond the scope of this text. For additional information on SQL, please refer to the URLs listed in Section 20.11, Web Resources.

SQL keyword	Description
SELECT	Retrieves data from one or more tables.
FROM	Specifies the tables involved in a query. Required in every query.
WHERE	Specifies optional criteria for selection that determine the rows to be retrieved, deleted or updated.
ORDER BY	Specifies optional criteria for ordering rows (e.g., ascending, descending).
INNER JOIN	Specifies optional operator for merging rows from multiple tables.
INSERT	Inserts rows in a specified table.
UPDATE	Updates rows in a specified table.
DELETE	Deletes rows from a specified table.

Fig. 20.10 | Common SQL keywords.

20.4.1 Basic SELECT Query

Let us consider several SQL queries that retrieve information from database Books. A SQL query "selects" rows and columns from one or more tables in a database. Such selections are performed by queries with the **SELECT** keyword. The basic form of a **SELECT query** is

```
SELECT * FROM tableName
```

in which the asterisk (*) indicates that all the columns from the *tableName* table should be retrieved. For example, to retrieve all the data in the Authors table, use

```
SELECT * FROM Authors
```

Note that the rows of the Authors table are not guaranteed to be returned in any particular order. You will learn how to specify criteria for sorting rows in Section 20.4.3.

Most programs do not require all the data in a table. To retrieve only specific columns from a table, replace the asterisk (*) with a comma-separated list of the column names. For example, to retrieve only the columns AuthorID and LastName for all the rows in the Authors table, use the query

```
SELECT AuthorID, LastName FROM Authors
```

This query returns only the data listed in Fig. 20.11.

20.4.2 WHERE Clause

When users search a database for rows that satisfy certain **selection criteria** (formally called **predicates**), only rows that satisfy the selection criteria are selected. SQL uses the optional **WHERE clause** in a query to specify the selection criteria for the query. The basic form of a query with selection criteria is

```
SELECT columnName1, columnName2, ... FROM tableName WHERE criteria
```

For example, to select the Title, EditionNumber and Copyright columns from table Titles for which the Copyright date is more recent than 2004, use the query

```
SELECT Title, EditionNumber, Copyright
FROM Titles
WHERE Copyright > '2004'
```

Figure 20.12 shows the result of the preceding query.

AuthorID	LastName
1	Deitel
2	Deitel
3	Goldberg
4	Choffnes

Fig. 20.11 | AuthorID and LastName data from the Authors table.

Title	EditionNumber	Copyright
Java How to Program	6	2005
Visual C# 2005 How to Program	2	2006
C++ How to Program	5	2005
Visual Basic 2005 How to Program	3	2006

Fig. 20.12 | Titles with copyright dates after 2004 from table `Titles`.

The WHERE clause criteria can contain the relational operators <, >, <=, >=, = (equality), <> (inequality) and LIKE, as well as the logical operators AND, OR and NOT (discussed in Section 20.4.6). Operator **LIKE** is used for **pattern matching** with wildcard characters **percent** (%) and **underscore** (_). Pattern matching allows SQL to search for strings that match a given pattern.

A pattern that contains a percent character (%) searches for strings that have zero or more characters at the percent character's position in the pattern. For example, the following query locates the rows of all the authors whose last names start with the letter D:

```
SELECT AuthorID, FirstName, LastName
FROM Authors
WHERE LastName LIKE 'D%'
```

The preceding query selects the two rows shown in Fig. 20.13, because two of the four authors in our database have a last name starting with the letter D (followed by zero or more characters). The % in the WHERE clause's LIKE pattern indicates that any number of characters can appear after the letter D in the LastName column. Note that the pattern string is surrounded by single-quote characters.

An underscore (_) in the pattern string indicates a single wildcard character at that position in the pattern. For example, the following query locates the rows of all the authors whose last names start with any character (specified by _), followed by the letter h, followed by any number of additional characters (specified by %):

```
SELECT AuthorID, FirstName, LastName
FROM Authors
WHERE LastName LIKE '_h%'
```

The preceding query produces the row shown in Fig. 20.14, because only one author in our database has a last name that contains the letter h as its second letter.

AuthorID	FirstName	LastName
1	Harvey	Deitel
2	Paul	Deitel

Fig. 20.13 | Authors from the `Authors` table whose last names start with D.

AuthorID	FirstName	LastName
4	David	Choffnes

Fig. 20.14 | The only author from the Authors table whose last name contains h as the second letter.

20.4.3 ORDER BY Clause

The rows in the result of a query can be sorted into ascending or descending order by using the optional ORDER BY clause. The basic form of a query with an ORDER BY clause is

```
SELECT columnName1, columnName2, ... FROM tableName ORDER BY column ASC
SELECT columnName1, columnName2, ... FROM tableName ORDER BY column DESC
```

where ASC specifies ascending order (lowest to highest), DESC specifies descending order (highest to lowest) and *column* specifies the column on which the sort is based. For example, to obtain the list of authors in ascending order by last name (Fig. 20.15), use the query

```
SELECT AuthorID, FirstName, LastName
FROM Authors
ORDER BY LastName ASC
```

The default sorting order is ascending, so ASC is optional in the preceding query.

To obtain the same list of authors in descending order by last name (Fig. 20.16), use the query

```
SELECT AuthorID, FirstName, LastName
FROM Authors
ORDER BY LastName DESC
```

Multiple columns can be used for sorting with an ORDER BY clause of the form

```
ORDER BY column1 sortingOrder, column2 sortingOrder, ...
```

where *sortingOrder* is either ASC or DESC. Note that the *sortingOrder* does not have to be identical for each column. For example, the query

```
SELECT Title, EditionNumber, Copyright
FROM Titles
ORDER BY Copyright DESC, Title ASC
```

AuthorID	FirstName	LastName
4	David	Choffnes
1	Harvey	Deitel
2	Paul	Deitel
3	Andrew	Goldberg

Fig. 20.15 | Authors from table Authors in ascending order by LastName.

AuthorID	FirstName	LastName
3	Andrew	Goldberg
1	Harvey	Deitel
2	Paul	Deitel
4	David	Choffnes

Fig. 20.16 | Authors from table `Authors` in descending order by `LastName`.

returns the rows of the `Titles` table sorted first in descending order by copyright date, then in ascending order by title (Fig. 20.17). This means that rows with higher `Copyright` values are returned before rows with lower `Copyright` values, and any rows that have the same `Copyright` values are sorted in ascending order by title.

The `WHERE` and `ORDER BY` clauses can be combined in one query. For example, the query

```
SELECT ISBN, Title, EditionNumber, Copyright
FROM Titles
WHERE Title LIKE '%How to Program'
ORDER BY Title ASC
```

returns the `ISBN`, `Title`, `EditionNumber` and `Copyright` of each book in the `Titles` table that has a `Title` ending with "How to Program" and sorts them in ascending order by `Title`. The query results are shown in Fig. 20.18.

20.4.4 Merging Data from Multiple Tables: INNER JOIN

Database designers typically **normalize** databases—i.e., split related data into separate tables to ensure that a database does not store redundant data. For example, the `Books` database has tables `Authors` and `Titles`. We use an `AuthorISBN` table to store "links"

Title	EditionNumber	Copyright
Visual Basic 2005 How to Program	3	2006
Visual C# 2005 How to Program	2	2006
C++ How to Program	5	2005
Java How to Program	6	2005
C How to Program	4	2004
Internet & World Wide Web How to Program	3	2004
Operating Systems	3	2004

Fig. 20.17 | Data from `Titles` in descending order by `Copyright` and ascending order by `Title`.

ISBN	Title	EditionNumber	Copyright
0131426443	C How to Program	4	2004
0131857576	C++ How to Program	5	2005
0131450913	Internet & World Wide Web How to Program	3	2004
0131483986	Java How to Program	6	2005
0131869000	Visual Basic 2005 How to Program	3	2006
0131525239	Visual C# 2005 How to Program	2	2006

Fig. 20.18 | Books from table `Titles` whose titles end with `How to Program` in ascending order by `Title`.

between authors and titles. If we did not separate this information into individual tables, we would need to include author information with each entry in the `Titles` table. This would result in the database storing duplicate author information for authors who wrote more than one book.

Often, it is desirable to merge data from multiple tables into a single result. This is referred to as joining the tables, and is specified by an **INNER JOIN operator** in the query. An INNER JOIN merges rows from two tables by testing for matching values in a column that is common to the tables. The basic form of an INNER JOIN is:

```
SELECT columnName1, columnName2, ...
FROM table1 INNER JOIN table2
    ON table1.columnName = table2.columnName
```

The **ON clause** of the INNER JOIN specifies the columns from each table that are compared to determine which rows are merged. For example, the following query produces a list of authors accompanied by the ISBNs for books written by each author:

```
SELECT FirstName, LastName, ISBN
FROM Authors INNER JOIN AuthorISBN
    ON Authors.AuthorID = AuthorISBN.AuthorID
ORDER BY LastName, FirstName
```

The query combines the `FirstName` and `LastName` columns from table `Authors` and the `ISBN` column from table `AuthorISBN`, sorting the results in ascending order by `LastName` and `FirstName`. Note the use of the syntax *tableName.columnName* in the ON clause. This syntax (called a **qualified name**) specifies the columns from each table that should be compared to join the tables. The "*tableName.*" syntax is required if the columns have the same name in both tables. The same syntax can be used in any query to distinguish columns that have the same name in different tables.

 Common Programming Error 20.4

In a SQL query, failure to qualify names for columns that have the same name in two or more tables is an error.

As always, the query can contain an ORDER BY clause. Figure 20.19 depicts the results of the preceding query, ordered by LastName and FirstName.

20.4.5 INSERT Statement

The INSERT statement inserts a row into a table. The basic form of this statement is

```
INSERT INTO tableName ( columnName1, columnName2, ..., columnNameN )
VALUES ( value1, value2, ..., valueN )
```

where *tableName* is the table in which to insert the row. The *tableName* is followed by a comma-separated list of column names in parentheses (this list is not required if the INSERT operation specifies a value for every column of the table in the correct order). The list of column names is followed by the SQL keyword VALUES and a comma-separated list of values in parentheses. The values specified here must match up with the columns specified after the table name in both order and type (e.g., if *columnName1* is supposed to be the FirstName column, then *value1* should be a string in single quotes representing the first name). Always explicitly list the columns when inserting rows—if the order of the columns in the table changes, using only VALUES may cause an error. The INSERT statement

```
INSERT INTO Authors ( FirstName, LastName )
VALUES ( 'Sue', 'Smith' )
```

FirstName	LastName	ISBN
David	Choffnes	0131828274
Harvey	Deitel	0131869000
Harvey	Deitel	0131525239
Harvey	Deitel	0131483986
Harvey	Deitel	0131857576
Harvey	Deitel	0131426443
Harvey	Deitel	0131450913
Harvey	Deitel	0131828274
Paul	Deitel	0131869000
Paul	Deitel	0131525239
Paul	Deitel	0131483986
Paul	Deitel	0131857576
Paul	Deitel	0131426443
Paul	Deitel	0131450913
Paul	Deitel	0131828274
Andrew	Goldberg	0131450913

Fig. 20.19 | Authors and ISBNs for their books in ascending order by LastName and FirstName.

inserts a row into the Authors table. The statement indicates that the values 'Sue' and 'Smith' are provided for the FirstName and LastName columns, respectively.

We do not specify an AuthorID in this example because AuthorID is an identity column in the Authors table (see Fig. 20.3). For every row added to this table, SQL Server assigns a unique AuthorID value that is the next value in an autoincremented sequence (i.e., 1, 2, 3 and so on). In this case, Sue Smith would be assigned AuthorID number 5. Figure 20.20 shows the Authors table after the INSERT operation. Not every DBMS supports identity or autoincremented columns.

Common Programming Error 20.5

It is an error to specify a value for an identity column.

Common Programming Error 20.6

SQL uses the single-quote (') character to delimit strings. To specify a string containing a single quote (e.g., O'Malley) in a SQL statement, there must be two single quotes in the position where the single-quote character appears in the string (e.g., 'O''Malley'). The first of the two single-quote characters acts as an escape character for the second. Not escaping single-quote characters in a string that is part of a SQL statement is a syntax error.

20.4.6 UPDATE Statement

An UPDATE statement modifies data in a table. The basic form of the UPDATE statement is

```
UPDATE tableName
SET columnName1 = value1, columnName2 = value2, ..., columnNameN = valueN
WHERE criteria
```

where *tableName* is the table to update. The *tableName* is followed by keyword **SET** and a comma-separated list of column name-value pairs in the format *columnName = value*. The optional WHERE clause provides criteria that determine which rows to update. Though not required, the WHERE clause is typically used, unless a change is to be made to every row. The UPDATE statement

```
UPDATE Authors
SET LastName = 'Jones'
WHERE LastName = 'Smith' AND FirstName = 'Sue'
```

AuthorID	FirstName	LastName
1	Harvey	Deitel
2	Paul	Deitel
3	Andrew	Goldberg
4	David	Choffnes
5	Sue	Smith

Fig. 20.20 | Table Authors after an INSERT operation.

updates a row in the Authors table. Keyword AND is a logical operator that, like the Visual Basic And operator, returns true *if and only if* both of its operands are true. Thus, the preceding statement assigns to LastName the value Jones for the row in which LastName is equal to Smith *and* FirstName is equal to Sue. [*Note:* If there are multiple rows with the first name "Sue" and the last name "Smith," this statement modifies all such rows to have the last name "Jones."] Figure 20.21 shows the Authors table after the UPDATE operation has taken place. SQL also provides other logical operators, such as OR and NOT, which behave like their Visual Basic counterparts.

20.4.7 DELETE Statement

A **DELETE** statement removes rows from a table. The basic form of a DELETE statement is

```
DELETE FROM tableName WHERE criteria
```

where *tableName* is the table from which to delete. The optional WHERE clause specifies the criteria used to determine which rows to delete. The DELETE statement

```
DELETE FROM Authors
WHERE LastName = 'Jones' AND FirstName = 'Sue'
```

deletes the row for Sue Jones in the Authors table. DELETE statements can delete multiple rows if the rows all meet the criteria in the WHERE clause. Figure 20.22 shows the Authors table after the DELETE operation has taken place.

AuthorID	FirstName	LastName
1	Harvey	Deitel
2	Paul	Deitel
3	Andrew	Goldberg
4	David	Choffnes
5	Sue	Jones

Fig. 20.21 | Table Authors after an UPDATE operation.

AuthorID	FirstName	LastName
1	Harvey	Deitel
2	Paul	Deitel
3	Andrew	Goldberg
4	David	Choffnes

Fig. 20.22 | Table Authors after a DELETE operation.

SQL Wrap-Up

This concludes our SQL introduction. We demonstrated several commonly used SQL keywords, formed SQL queries that retrieved data from databases and formed other SQL statements that manipulated data in a database. Next, we introduce the ADO.NET object model, which allows Visual Basic applications to interact with databases. As you will see, ADO.NET objects manipulate databases using SQL statements like those presented here.

20.5 ADO.NET Object Model

The ADO.NET object model provides an API for accessing database systems programmatically. ADO.NET was created for the .NET framework to replace Microsoft's ActiveX Data Objects™ (ADO) technology. As will be discussed in the next section, the IDE features visual programming tools that simplify the process of using a database in your projects. While you may not need to work directly with many ADO.NET objects to develop simple applications, basic knowledge of how the ADO.NET object model works is important for understanding data access in Visual Basic.

Namespaces System.Data, System.Data.OleDb and System.Data.SqlClient

Namespace `System.Data` is the root namespace for the ADO.NET API. The other important ADO.NET namespaces, `System.Data.OleDb` and `System.Data.SqlClient`, contain classes that enable programs to connect with and manipulate data sources—locations that contain data, such as a database or an XML file. Namespace System.Data.OleDb contains classes that are designed to work with any data source, whereas System.Data.SqlClient contains classes that are optimized to work with Microsoft SQL Server databases. The chapter examples manipulate SQL Server 2005 Express databases, so we use the classes of namespace System.Data.SqlClient. SQL Server 2005 Express is provided with Visual Basic 2005 Express. It can also be downloaded from msdn.microsoft.com/vstudio/express/sql/default.aspx.

An object of class `SqlConnection` (namespace System.Data.SqlClient) represents a connection to a data source—specifically a SQL Server database. A SqlConnection object keeps track of the location of the data source and any settings that specify how the data source is to be accessed. A connection is either active (i.e., open and permitting data to be sent to and retrieved from the data source) or closed.

An object of class `SqlCommand` (namespace System.Data.SqlClient) represents a SQL command that a DBMS can execute on a database. A program can use SqlCommand objects to manipulate a data source through a SqlConnection. The program must open the connection to the data source before executing one or more SqlCommands and close the connection once no further access to the data source is required. A connection that remains active for some length of time to permit multiple data operations is known as a persistent connection.

Class `DataTable` (namespace System.Data) represents a table of data. A DataTable contains a collection of `DataRows` that represent the table's data. A DataTable also has a collection of `DataColumns` that describe the columns in a table. DataRow and DataColumn are both located in namespace System.Data. An object of class `System.Data.DataSet`, which consists of a set of DataTables and the relationships among them, represents a cache of data—data that a program stores temporarily in local memory. The structure of a DataSet mimics the structure of a relational database.

ADO.NET's Disconnected Model

An advantage of using class DataSet is that it is disconnected—the program does not need a persistent connection to the data source to work with data in a DataSet. Instead, the program connects to the data source to populate the DataSet (i.e., fill the DataSet's DataTables with data), but disconnects from the data source immediately after retrieving the desired data. The program then accesses and potentially manipulates the data stored in the DataSet. The program operates on this local cache of data, rather than the original data in the data source. If the program makes changes to the data in the DataSet that need to be permanently saved in the data source, the program reconnects to the data source to perform an update then disconnects promptly. Thus the program does not require any active, persistent connection to the data source.

An object of class SqlDataAdapter (namespace System.Data.SqlClient) connects to a SQL Server data source and executes SQL statements to both populate a DataSet and update the data source based on the current contents of a DataSet. A SqlDataAdapter maintains a SqlConnection object that it opens and closes as needed to perform these operations using SqlCommands. We demonstrate populating DataSets and updating data sources later in this chapter.

20.6 Programming with ADO.NET: Extracting Information from a Database

In this section, we demonstrate how to connect to a database, query the database and display the result of the query. You will notice that there is little code in this section. The IDE provides visual programming tools and wizards that simplify accessing data in your projects. These tools establish database connections and create the ADO.NET objects necessary to view and manipulate the data through GUI controls. The example in this section connects to the SQL Server Books database that we have discussed throughout this chapter. The Books.mdf file that contains the database can be found with the chapter's examples (www.deitel.com/books/vbhtp3).

20.6.1 Displaying a Database Table in a DataGridView

This example performs a simple query on the Books database that retrieves the entire Authors table and displays the data in a DataGridView (a control from namespace System.Windows.Forms that can display a data source in a GUI—see the sample outputs in Fig. 20.32 later in this section). First, we demonstrate how to connect to the Books database and include it as a data source in your project. Once the Books database is established as a data source, you can display the data from the Authors table in a DataGridView simply by dragging and dropping items in the project's **Design** view.

Step 1: Creating the Project
Create a new Windows Application named DisplayTable. Change name of the Form to FrmDisplayTable and change the source file name to FrmDisplayTable.vb. Then set the Form's **Text** property to Display Table.

Step 2: Adding a Data Source to the Project
To interact with a data source (e.g., a database), you must add it to the project using the **Data Sources window**, which lists the data that your project can access. Open the **Data**

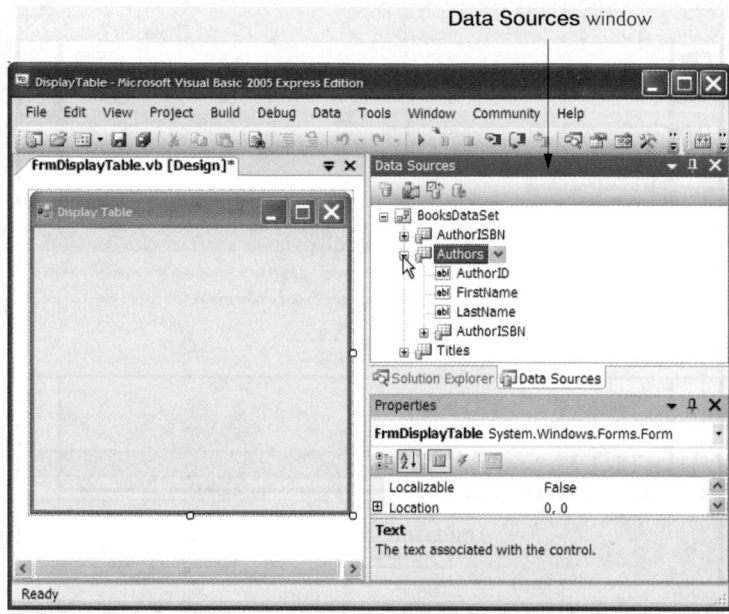

Fig. 20.29 | Viewing a data source listed in the **Data Sources** window.

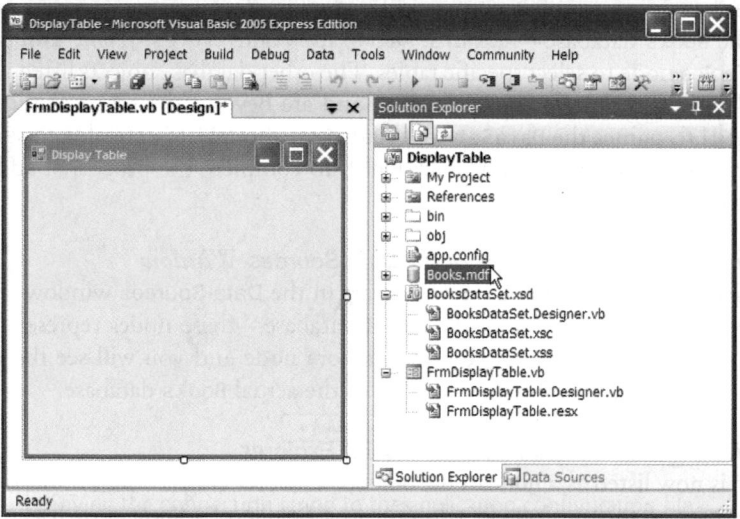

Fig. 20.30 | Viewing a database listed in the **Solution Explorer**.

Displaying the Authors Table

Now that you have added the Books database as a data source, you can display the data from the database's Authors table in your program. The IDE provides design tools that allow you to display data from a data source on a Form without writing any code. Simply drag and drop items from the **Data Sources** window onto a Form, and the IDE generates the GUI controls and code necessary to display the selected data source's content.

To display the Authors table of the Books database, drag the Authors node from the **Data Sources** window to the Form. Figure 20.31 presents the **Design** view after we performed this action and resized the Form and controls. The IDE generates two controls that appear on FrmDisplayTable—an AuthorsBindingNavigator and an AuthorsDataGrid-View. The IDE also generates several additional non-visual components that appear in the component tray—the gray region below the Form in **Design** view. We use the IDE's default names for these autogenerated components (and others throughout the chapter) to show exactly what the IDE creates. We briefly discuss the AuthorsBindingNavigator and AuthorsDataGridView controls here. The next section discusses all of the autogenerated components in detail and explains how the IDE uses these components to connect the GUI controls to the Authors table of the Books database.

A **DataGridView** displays data organized in rows and columns that correspond to the rows and columns of the underlying data source. In this case, the DataGridView displays the data of the Authors table, so the control has columns named AuthorID, FirstName and LastName. In **Design** view, the control does not display any rows of actual data below the column headers. The data is retrieved from the database and displayed in the DataGrid-View only at runtime. Execute the program. When the Form loads, the DataGridView contains four rows of data—one for each row of the Authors table (Fig. 20.32).

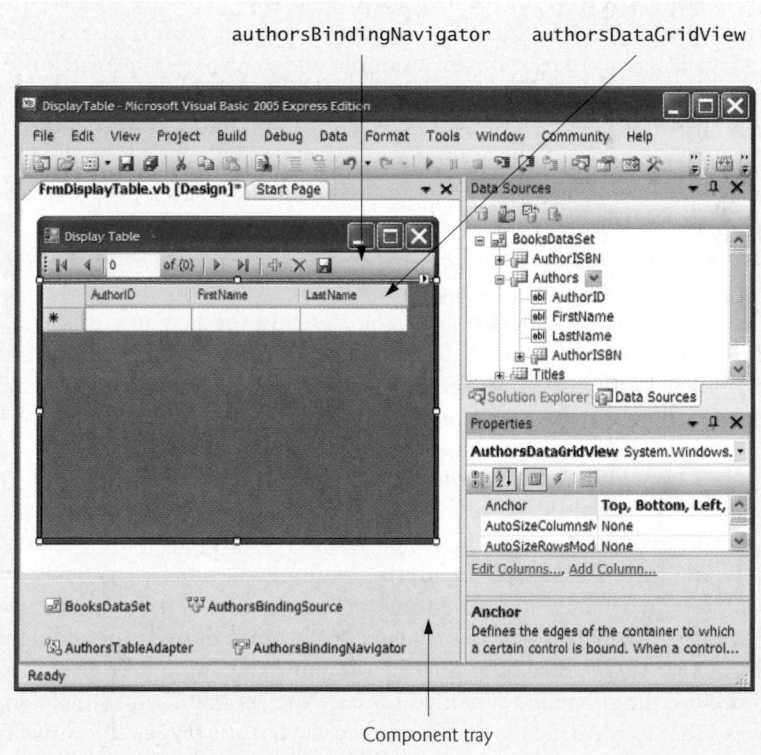

Fig. 20.31 | **Design** view after dragging the Authors data source node to the Form.

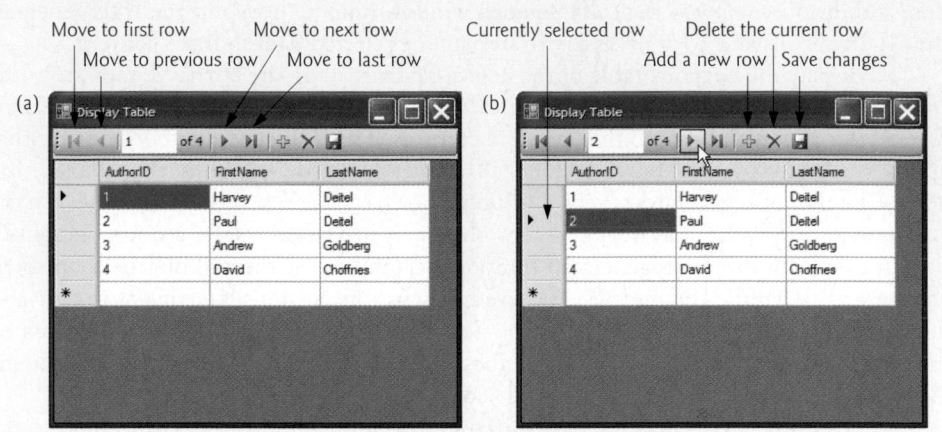

Fig. 20.32 | Displaying the Authors table in a DataGridView.

The strip of buttons below the title bar of the window is a **BindingNavigator**, which enables users to browse and manipulate data displayed by another GUI control (in this case, a DataGridView) on the Form. A BindingNavigator's buttons resemble the controls on a CD or DVD player and allow you to move to the first row of data, the preceding row, the next row and the last row. The control also displays the currently selected row number in a text box. You can use this text box to enter the number of a row that you want to select. The AuthorsBindingNavigator in this example allows you to "navigate" the Authors table displayed in the AuthorsDataGridView. Clicking the buttons or entering a value in the text box causes the DataGridView to select the appropriate row. An arrow in the Data-GridView's leftmost column indicates the currently selected row.

A BindingNavigator also has buttons that allow you to add a new row, delete a row and save changes back to the underlying data source (that is, the Authors table of the Books database). Clicking the button with the yellow plus icon (⊕) adds a new row to the DataGridView. However, simply typing values in the FirstName and LastName columns does not insert a new row in the Authors table. To add the new row to the database on disk, click the **Save** button (the button with the disk icon, 🖫). Clicking the button with the red **X** (✖) deletes the currently selected row from the DataGridView. Again, you must click the **Save** button to make the change in the database.

Changing the Database's Copy to Output Directory Property
By default, a new copy of the database file is used each time you run the application. Thus, any changes you make to the database when testing your application are lost. To allow changes to be made to the database file during testing, you must select Books.mdf in the **Solution Explorer**, then change its **Copy to Output Directory** property to **Copy if newer** in the **Properties** window. Now you can test BindingNavigator's buttons for adding and deleting records and see their results. Execute the program and add a new row, then save the changes and close the program. When you restart the program, you should see that the new row was saved to the database and appears in the DataGridView. Now delete the new row and click the **Save** button. Close and restart the program to see that the new row no longer exists in the database.

20.6.2 How Data Binding Works

The technique through which GUI controls are connected to data sources is known as data binding. The IDE allows controls, such as a DataGridView, to be bound to a data source, such as a DataSet that represents a table in a database. Any changes you make through the application to the underlying data source will automatically be reflected in the way the data is presented in the data-bound control (e.g., the DataGridView). Likewise, modifying the data in the data-bound control and saving the changes updates the underlying data source. In the current example, the DataGridView is bound to the DataTable of the BooksDataSet that represents the Authors table in the database. Dragging the Authors node from the **Data Sources** window to the Form caused the IDE to create this data binding for you, using several autogenerated components (i.e., objects) in the component tray. Figure 20.33 models these objects and their associations, which the following sections examine in detail to explain how data binding works.

BooksDataSet

As discussed in Section 20.6.1, adding the Books database to the project enabled the IDE to generate the BooksDataSet. Recall that a DataSet represents a cache of data that mimics the structure of a relational database. You can explore the structure of the BooksDataSet

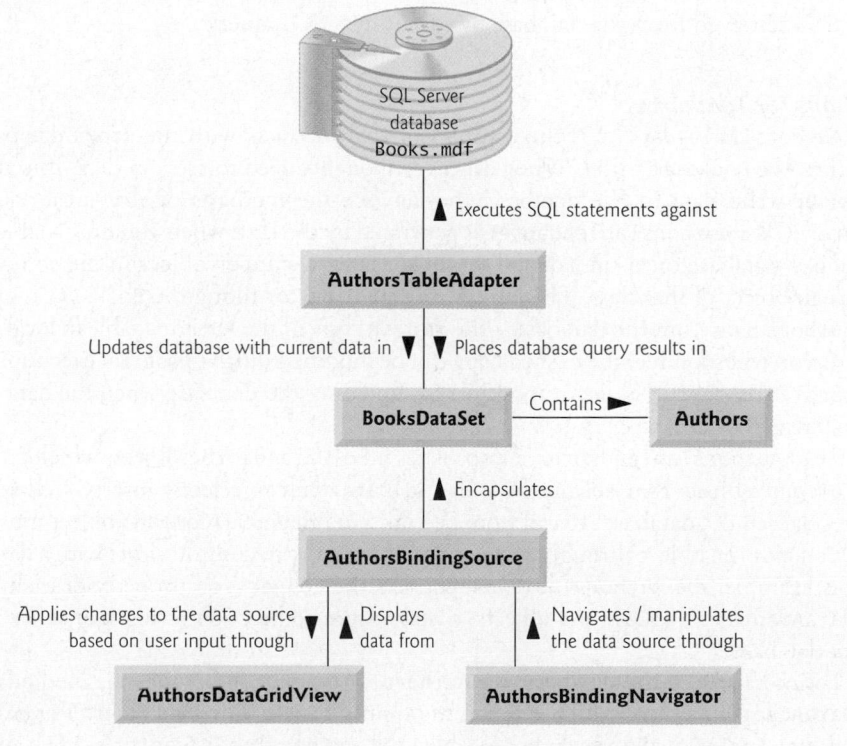

Fig. 20.33 | Data binding architecture used to display the Authors table of the Books database in a GUI.

in the **Data Sources** window. A DataSet's structure can be determined at execution time or at design time. An **untyped DataSet**'s structure (i.e., the tables that comprise it and the relationships among them) is determined at execution time based on the result of a specific query. Tables and column values are accessed using indices into collections of DataTables and DataRows, respectively. The type of each piece of data in an untyped DataSet is unknown at design time. BooksDataSet, however, is created by the IDE at design time as a **strongly typed DataSet**. BooksDataSet (a derived class of DataSet) contains objects of classes derived from DataTable that represent the tables in the Books database. BooksDataSet provides properties corresponding to these objects. The property names match the names of the underlying tables. For example, BooksDataSet.Authors represents a cache of the data in the Authors table. Each DataTable contains a collection of DataRows. Each DataRow contains members whose names and types correspond to those of the columns of the underlying database table. Thus, BooksDataSet.Authors(0).AuthorID refers to the AuthorID of the first row of the Authors table in the Books database. Note that zero-based indices are used to access DataRows in a DataTable.

The BooksDataSet object in the component tray is an object of the BooksDataSet class. When you indicate that you want to display the contents of the Authors table on the Form, the IDE generates a BooksDataSet object to store the data that Form will display. This is the data to which the DataGridView will be bound. The DataGridView does not display data from the database directly. Instead, it displays the contents of a BooksDataSet object. As we discuss shortly, the AuthorsTableAdapter fills the BooksDataSet object with data retrieved from the database by executing a SQL query.

AuthorsTableAdapter

The AuthorsTableAdapter is the component that interacts with the Books database on disk (i.e., the Books.mdf file). When other components need to retrieve data from the database or write data to the database, they invoke the methods of the AuthorsTableAdapter. Class AuthorsTableAdapter is generated by the IDE when you drag a table from the Books database onto the Form. The AuthorsTableAdapter object in the component tray is an object of this class. This object is responsible for filling the BooksDataSet with the Authors data from the database—this stores a copy of the Authors table in local memory. As you will soon see, the cached copy can be modified during program execution. The AuthorsTableAdapter is also responsible for updating the database when the data in the BooksDataSet changes.

Class AuthorsTableAdapter encapsulates a SqlDataAdapter object, which contains SqlCommand objects that specify how the SqlDataAdapter selects, inserts, updates and deletes data in the database. Recall from Section 20.5 that a SqlCommand object must have a SqlConnection object through which the SqlCommand can communicate with a database. In this example, the AuthorsTableAdapter sets the Connection property of each of the SqlDataAdapter's SqlCommand objects, based on the connection string that refers to the Books database.

To interact with the database, the AuthorsTableAdapter invokes the methods of its SqlDataAdapter, each of which executes the appropriate SqlCommand object. For example, to fill the BooksDataSet's Authors table, the AuthorsTableAdapter's Fill method invokes its SqlDataAdapter's Fill method, which executes a SqlCommand object representing the SELECT query

```
SELECT AuthorID, FirstName, LastName FROM Authors
```

This query selects all the rows and columns of the Authors table and places them in Books-DataSet.Authors. You will see an example of AuthorsTableAdapter's Fill method being invoked shortly.

AuthorsBindingSource and AuthorsDataGridView

The AuthorsBindingSource object (an object of class **BindingSource**) identifies a data source that a program can bind to a control and serves as an intermediary between a data-bound GUI control and its data source. In this example, the IDE uses a BindingSource object to connect the AuthorsDataGridView to BooksDataSet.Authors. To achieve this data binding, the IDE first sets AuthorsBindingSource's **DataSource** property to Books-DataSet. This property specifies the DataSet that contains the data to be bound. The IDE then sets the **DataMember** property to Authors. This property identifies a specific table within the DataSource. After configuring the AuthorsBindingSource object, the IDE assigns this object to AuthorsDataGridView's **DataSource** property to indicate what the DataGridView will display.

A BindingSource object also manages the interaction between a data-bound GUI control and its underlying data source. If you edit the data displayed in a DataGridView and want to save changes to the data source, your code must invoke the **EndEdit** method of the BindingSource object. This method applies the user's changes to the data (i.e., the pending changes) to the data source bound to that control. Note that this updates only the DataSet—an additional step is required to permanently update the database itself. You will see an example of this shortly, when we present the code generated by the IDE in the FrmDisplayTable.vb file.

AuthorsBindingNavigator

Recall that a BindingNavigator allows you to move through (i.e., navigate) and manipulate (i.e., add or delete rows) data bound to a control on a Form. A BindingNavigator communicates with a BindingSource (specified in the BindingNavigator's **BindingSource** property) to carry out these actions in the underlying data source (i.e., the DataSet). The BindingNavigator does not interact with the data-bound control. Instead, it invokes BindingSource methods that cause the data-bound control to update its presentation of the data. For example, when you click the BindingNavigator's button to add a new row, the BindingNavigator invokes a method of the BindingSource. The BindingSource then adds a new row to its associated DataSet. Once this DataSet is modified, the DataGrid-View displays the new row, because the DataGridView and the BindingNavigator are bound to the same BindingSource object (and thus the same DataSet).

Examining the Autogenerated Code for FrmDisplayTable

Figure 20.34 presents the code for FrmDisplayTable. You do not need to write any of this code—the IDE generates it when you drag and drop the Authors table from the **Data Sources** window onto the Form. We modified the autogenerated code to add comments and split long lines for display purposes. The IDE also generates a considerable amount of additional code, such as the code that defines classes BooksDataSet and AuthorsTable-Adapter, as well as the designer code that declares the autogenerated objects in the component tray. The additional IDE-generated code resides in files visible in the **Solution**

```vb
 1   ' Fig. 20.34: FrmDisplayTable.vb
 2   ' Displays data from a database table in a DataGridView.
 3   Public Class FrmDisplayTable
 4      ' Click event handler for the Save Button in the
 5      ' BindingNavigator saves the changes made to the data
 6      Private Sub AuthorsBindingNavigatorSaveItem_Click( _
 7         ByVal sender As System.Object, ByVal e As System.EventArgs) _
 8         Handles AuthorsBindingNavigatorSaveItem.Click
 9
10         Me.Validate()
11         Me.AuthorsBindingSource.EndEdit()
12         Me.AuthorsTableAdapter.Update(Me.BooksDataSet.Authors)
13      End Sub ' AuthorsBindingNavigatorSaveItem_Click
14
15      ' loads data into the BooksDataSet.Authors table,
16      ' which is then displayed in the DataGridView
17      Private Sub FrmDisplayTable_Load(ByVal sender As System.Object, _
18         ByVal e As System.EventArgs) Handles MyBase.Load
19         ' TODO: This line of code loads data into the 'BooksDataSet.Authors'
20         ' table. You can move, or remove it, as needed.
21         Me.AuthorsTableAdapter.Fill(Me.BooksDataSet.Authors)
22      End Sub ' FrmDisplayTable_Load
23   End Class ' FrmDisplayTable
```

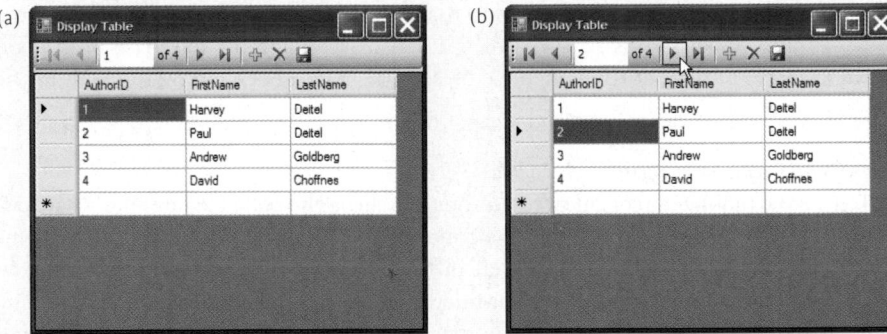

Fig. 20.34 | Auto-generated code for displaying data from a database table in a `DataGridView` control.

Explorer when you select **Show All Files**. We present only the code in `FrmDisplay-Table.vb`, because it is the only file you'll need to modify.

Lines 6–13 contain the `Click` event handler for the **Save** button in the `AuthorsBindingNavigator`. Recall that you click this button to save changes made to the data in the `DataGridView` in the underlying data source (i.e., the `Authors` table of the `Books` database). Saving the changes is a two-step process:

1. The `DataSet` associated with the `DataGridView` (indicated by its `BindingSource`) must be updated to include any changes made by the user.

2. The database on disk must be updated to match the new contents of the `DataSet`.

Before the event handler saves any changes, line 10 invokes `Me.Validate()` to validate the controls on the `Form`. If you implement `Validating` or `Validated` events for any of

Form's controls, these events enable you to validate user input and potentially indicate errors for invalid data. Line 11 invokes AuthorsBindingSource's `EndEdit` method to ensure that the object's associated data source (`BooksDataSet.Authors`) is updated with any changes made by the user to the currently selected row in the `DataGridView` (e.g., adding a row, changing a column value). Any changes to other rows were applied to the `DataSet` when you selected another row. Line 12 invokes AuthorsTableAdapter's `Update` method to write the modified version of the `Authors` table (in memory) to the SQL Server database on disk. The `Update` method executes the SQL statements (encapsulated in `Sql-Command` objects) necessary to make the data in the database's `Authors` table match the data in `BooksDataSet.Authors`.

The `FrmDisplayTable_Load` event handler (lines 17–22) executes when the program loads. This event handler fills the in-memory `DataSet` with data from the SQL Server database on disk. Once the `DataSet` is filled, the GUI control bound to it can display its data. Line 21 calls AuthorsTableAdapter's `Fill` method to retrieve information from the database, placing this information in the `DataSet` object provided as an argument. Recall that the IDE generated AuthorsTableAdapter to execute SqlCommands over the connection we created within the **Data Source Configuration Wizard**. Thus, the `Fill` method executes a SELECT statement to retrieve all the rows of the `Authors` table of the Books database, then places the result of this query in `BooksDataSet.Authors`. Recall that AuthorsData-GridView's DataSource property is set to AuthorsBindingSource (which references `BooksDataSet.Authors`). Thus, after this data source is loaded, the AuthorsDataGridView automatically displays the data retrieved from the database.

20.7 Querying the Books Database

Now that you have seen how to display an entire database table in a `DataGridView`, we demonstrate how to execute specific SQL SELECT queries on a database and display the results. Although this example only queries the data, the application could be modified easily to execute other SQL statements. Perform the following steps to build the example application, which executes custom queries against the `Titles` table of the Books database.

Step 1: Creating the Project
First, create a new Windows Application named `DisplayQueryResult`. Rename the Form `FrmDisplayQueryResult` and name its source file `FrmDisplayQueryResult.vb`, then set the Form's **Text** property to `Display Query Result`.

Step 2: Adding a Data Source to the Project
Perform the steps in Section 20.6.1 to include the Books database as a data source in the project and to create the BooksDataSet.

Step 3: Creating a `DataGridView` to Display the `Titles` Table
Drag the `Titles` node from the **Data Sources** window onto the Form to create a DataGrid-View that will display the entire contents of the `Titles` table.

Step 4: Adding Custom Queries to the `TitlesTableAdapter`
Recall that invoking a `TableAdapter`'s `Fill` method populates the `DataSet` passed as an argument with the entire contents of the database table that corresponds to that `Table-`

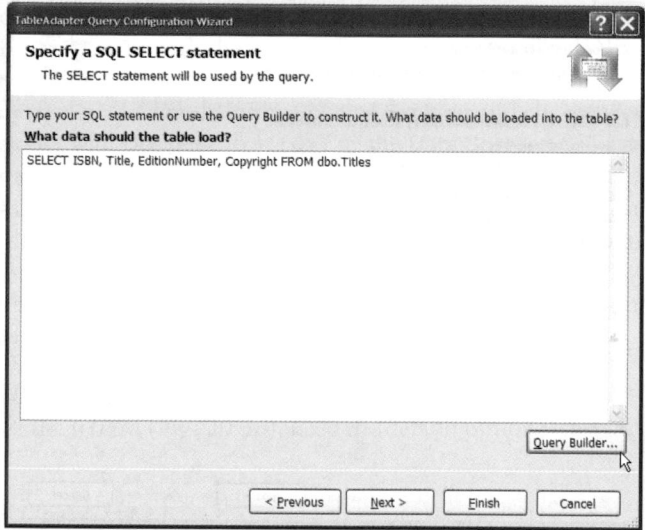

Fig. 20.38 | Specifying a SELECT statement for the query.

Step 8: Building a Query with *Query Builder*

Click the **Query Builder...** button to open the **Query Builder** (Fig. 20.39). The top portion of the **Query Builder** window contains a box listing the columns of the Titles table. By default, each column is checked (Fig. 20.39(a)), indicating that each column should be

(a)

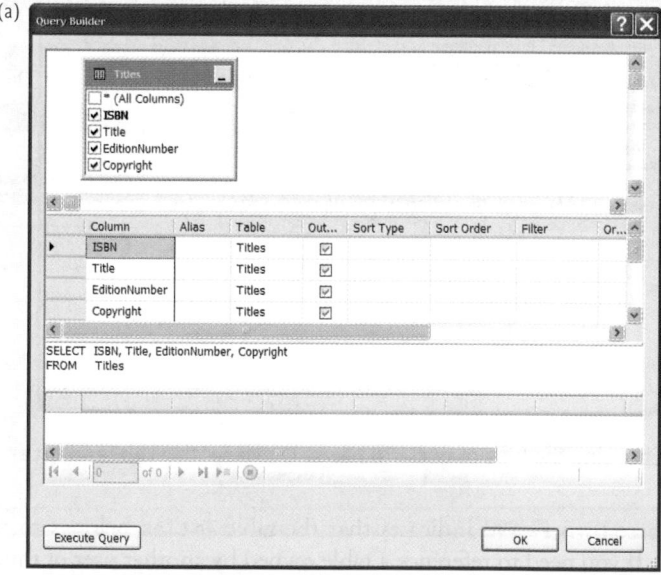

Fig. 20.39 | **Query Builder** after adding a WHERE clause by entering a value in the **Filter** column. (Part 1 of 2.)

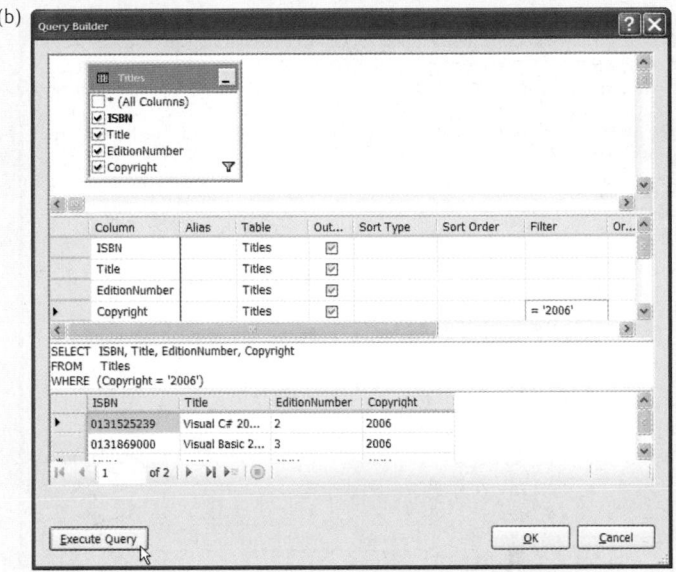

Fig. 20.39 | **Query Builder** after adding a WHERE clause by entering a value in the **Filter** column. (Part 2 of 2.)

returned by the query. The middle portion of the window contains a table in which each row corresponds to a column in the Titles table. To the right of the column names are columns in which you can enter values or make selections that modify the query. For example, to create a query that selects only books that are copyright 2006, type 2006 in the **Filter** column of the Copyright row then press *Enter*. Note that the **Query Builder** modifies your input to be "= '2006'" and adds an appropriate WHERE clause to the SELECT statement displayed in the middle of Fig. 20.39(b). Click the **Execute Query** button to test the query and display the results in the bottom portion of the **Query Builder** window. For more **Query Builder** information, see msdn2.microsoft.com/library/ms172013.aspx.

Step 9: Closing the Query Builder
Click **OK** to close the **Query Builder** and return to the **TableAdapter Query Configuration Wizard** (Fig. 20.40), which now displays the SQL query created in the preceding step. Click **Next** to continue.

Step 10: Setting the Names of the Autogenerated Methods That Perform the Query
After you specify the SQL query, you must name the methods that the IDE will generate to perform the query (Fig. 20.41). Two methods are generated by default—a "Fill method" that fills a DataTable parameter with the query result and a "Get method" that returns a new DataTable filled with the query result. The text boxes to enter names for these methods are prepopulated with FillBy and GetDataBy, respectively. Modify these names to FillWithCopyright2006 and GetDataWithCopyright2006, as shown in Fig. 20.41. Finally, click **Finish** to complete the wizard and return to the **Dataset Designer** (Fig. 20.42). Note that these methods are now listed in the TitlesTableAdapter section of the box representing the Titles table.

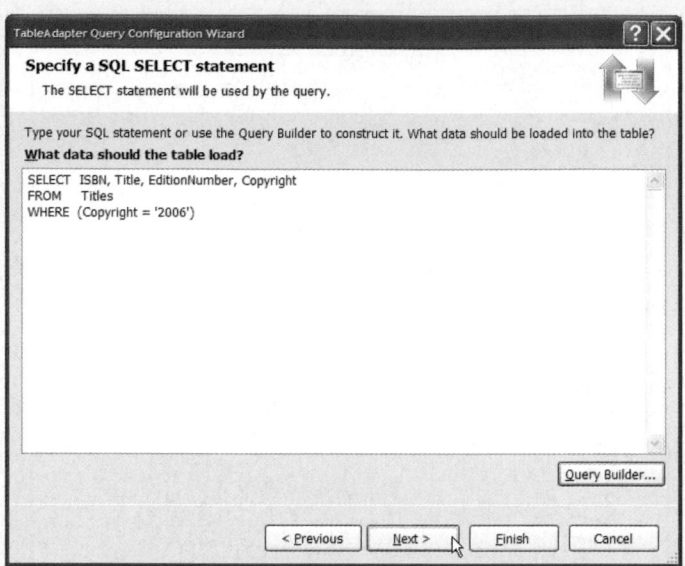

Fig. 20.40 | The SELECT statement created by the **Query Builder**.

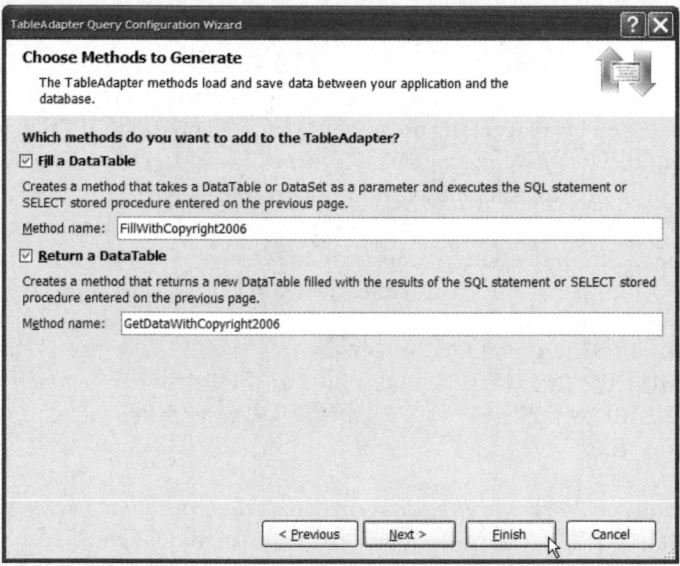

Fig. 20.41 | Specifying names for the methods to be added to the `TitlesTableAdapter`.

Step 11: Adding an Additional Query

Repeat *Steps 4–10* to add another query that selects all books whose titles end with the text "How to Program" and sorts the results by title in ascending order (see Section 20.4.3). In the **Query Builder**, enter `LIKE '%How to Program'` in the `Title` row's **Filter** column. To specify the sort order, select **Ascending** in the **Sort Type** column of the `Title` row. In the

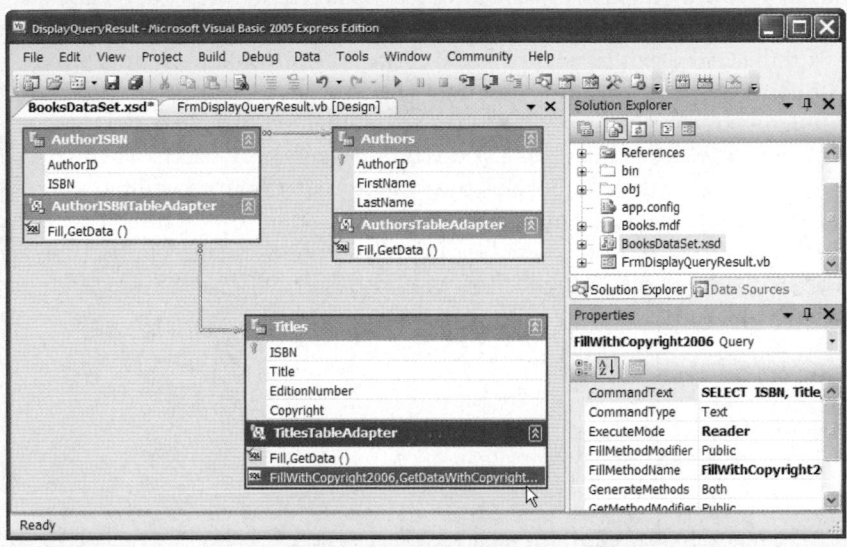

Fig. 20.42 | **Dataset Designer** after adding Fill and Get methods to the TitlesTableAdapter.

final step of the **TableAdapter Query Configuration Wizard**, name the Fill and Get methods FillWithHowToProgramBooks and GetDataForHowToProgramBooks, respectively.

Step 12: Adding a *ComboBox* to the *Form*

Return to the Form's **Design** view and add a ComboBox named cboQueries below the Data-GridView on the Form. Users will use this control to choose a SELECT query to execute. The results will be displayed in the DataGridView. Add three items to cboQueries—one to match each of the three queries that the TitlesTableAdapter can now perform:

```
SELECT ISBN, Title, EditionNumber, Copyright FROM Titles

SELECT ISBN, Title, EditionNumber, Copyright FROM Titles
WHERE (Copyright = '2006')

SELECT ISBN, Title, EditionNumber, Copyright FROM Titles
WHERE (Title LIKE '%How to Program') ORDER BY Title
```

Step 13: Customizing the *Form's* **Load** Event Handler

Add a line of code to the autogenerated FrmDisplayQueryResult_Load event handler, which sets the initial SelectedIndex of the cboQueries to 0. Recall that the Load event handler calls the Fill method by default, which executes the first query (the item in index 0). Thus, setting the SelectedIndex to 0 causes the ComboBox to display the query that is initially performed when FrmDisplayQueryResult first loads.

Step 14: Programming an Event Handler for the *ComboBox*

Next you must write code that will execute the appropriate query each time the user chooses a different item from cboQueries. Double click cboQueries in **Design** view to generate a cboQueries_SelectedIndexChanged event handler (lines 30–43) in the FrmDisplay-

QueryResult.vb file (Fig. 20.43). In the event handler, add a Select Case statement (lines 34–42) to invoke the method of TitlesTableAdapter that executes the query associated with the ComboBox's current selection. Recall that method Fill (line 36) executes a SELECT query that selects all rows, method FillWithCopyright2006 (line 38) executes a SELECT query that selects all rows in which the copyright year is 2006 and method Fill-WithHowToProgramBooks (lines 40–41) executes a query that selects all rows that have "How to Program" at the end of their titles and sorts them in ascending order by title. Each method fills BooksDataSet.Titles with only those rows returned by the corresponding query. Thanks to the data binding relationships created by the IDE, refilling BooksDataSet.Titles causes the TitlesDataGridView to display the selected query's result with no additional code.

```
1   ' Fig. 20.43: FrmDisplayQueryResult.vb
2   ' Displays the result of a user-selected query in a DataGridView.
3   Public Class FrmDisplayQueryResult
4      ' Click event handler for the Save Button in the
5      ' BindingNavigator saves the changes made to the data
6      Private Sub TitlesBindingNavigatorSaveItem_Click( _
7         ByVal sender As System.Object, ByVal e As System.EventArgs) _
8         Handles TitlesBindingNavigatorSaveItem.Click
9
10        Me.Validate()
11        Me.TitlesBindingSource.EndEdit()
12        Me.TitlesTableAdapter.Update(Me.BooksDataSet.Titles)
13     End Sub ' TitlesBindingNavigatorSaveItem_Click
14
15     ' loads data into the BooksDataSet.Titles table,
16     ' which is then displayed in the DataGridView
17     Private Sub FrmDisplayQueryResult_Load(ByVal sender As System.Object, _
18        ByVal e As System.EventArgs) Handles MyBase.Load
19        ' TODO: This line of code loads data into the 'BooksDataSet.Titles'
20        ' table. You can move, or remove it, as needed.
21        Me.TitlesTableAdapter.Fill(Me.BooksDataSet.Titles)
22
23        ' set the ComboBox to show the default query that
24        ' selects all books from the Titles table
25        cboQueries.SelectedIndex = 0
26     End Sub ' FrmDisplayQueryResult_Load
27
28     ' loads data into the BooksDataSet.Titles table based on
29     ' user-selected query
30     Private Sub cboQueries_SelectedIndexChanged( _
31        ByVal sender As System.Object, ByVal e As System.EventArgs) _
32        Handles cboQueries.SelectedIndexChanged
33        ' fill the Titles DataTable with the result of the selected query
34        Select Case cboQueries.SelectedIndex
35           Case 0
36              TitlesTableAdapter.Fill(BooksDataSet.Titles)
37           Case 1 ' books with copyright year 2006
38              TitlesTableAdapter.FillWithCopyright2006(BooksDataSet.Titles)
```

Fig. 20.43 | Displaying the result of a user-selected query in a DataGridView. (Part 1 of 2.)

```
39              Case 2 ' How to Program books, sorted by Title
40                 TitlesTableAdapter.FillWithHowToProgramBooks( _
41                    BooksDataSet.Titles)
42           End Select
43        End Sub ' cboQueries_SelectedIndexChanged
44     End Class ' FrmDisplayQueryResult
```

(a)
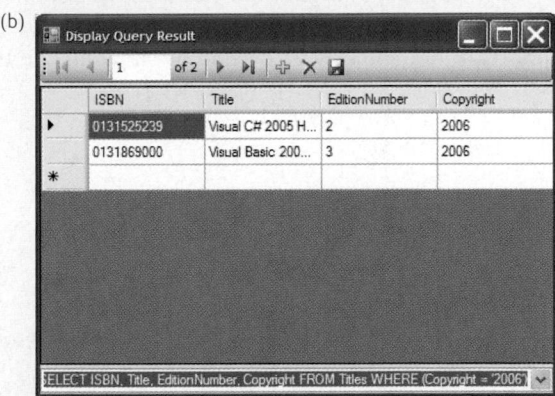

(b)

(c)
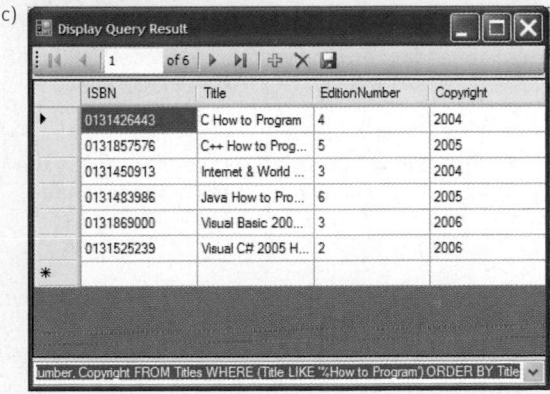

Fig. 20.43 | Displaying the result of a user-selected query in a DataGridView. (Part 2 of 2.)

Figure 20.43 also displays the output for `FrmDisplayQueryResult`. Figure 20.43(a) depicts the result of retrieving all rows from the `Titles` table. Figure 20.43(b) demonstrates the second query, which retrieves only rows for books with a 2006 copyright. Finally, Fig. 20.43(c) demonstrates the third query, which selects rows for How to Program books and sorts them in ascending order by title.

20.8 Programming with ADO.NET: Address Book Case Study

Our next example implements a simple address book application that enables users to insert rows into, locate rows from and update the SQL Server database `AddressBook.mdf`, which is included in the directory with this chapter's examples.

The `AddressBook` application (Fig. 20.44) provides a GUI through which users can execute SQL statements on the database. However, rather than displaying a database table in a `DataGridView`, this example presents data from a table one row at a time, using several `TextBox`es that display the values of each of the row's columns. A `BindingNavigator` allows you to control which row of the table is currently in view at any given time. The `BindingNavigator` also allows you to add new rows, delete rows, and save changes to the data. Note that lines 6–22 in Fig. 20.44 are similar to the corresponding lines of code in Figs. 20.34 and 20.43. We discuss the application's additional functionality and the code in lines 26–41 that supports it momentarily. We begin by showing you the steps to create this application.

```
 1   ' Fig. 20.44: FrmAddressBook.vb
 2   ' Allows users to manipulate an address book.
 3   Public Class FrmAddressBook
 4      ' Click event handler for the Save Button in the
 5      ' BindingNavigator saves the changes made to the data
 6      Private Sub AddressesBindingNavigatorSaveItem_Click( _
 7         ByVal sender As System.Object, ByVal e As System.EventArgs) _
 8         Handles AddressesBindingNavigatorSaveItem.Click
 9
10         Me.Validate()
11         Me.AddressesBindingSource.EndEdit()
12         Me.AddressesTableAdapter.Update(Me.AddressBookDataSet.Addresses)
13      End Sub ' AddressesBindingNavigatorSaveItem_Click
14
15      ' loads data into the AddressBookDataSet.Addresses table
16      Private Sub FrmAddressBook_Load(ByVal sender As System.Object, _
17         ByVal e As System.EventArgs) Handles MyBase.Load
18         ' TODO: This line of code loads data into the
19         ' 'AddressBookDataSet.Addresses' table. You can move, or remove
20         ' it, as needed.
21         Me.AddressesTableAdapter.Fill(Me.AddressBookDataSet.Addresses)
22      End Sub ' FrmAddressBook_Load
23
```

Fig. 20.44 | `AddressBook` application that allows you to manipulate entries in an address book database. (Part 1 of 2.)

```
24      ' loads data for the rows with the specified last name
25      ' into the AddressBookDataSet.Addresses table
26      Private Sub btnFind_Click(ByVal sender As System.Object, _
27         ByVal e As System.EventArgs) Handles btnFind.Click
28         ' fill the DataSet's DataTable with only rows
29         ' containing the user-specified last name
30         AddressesTableAdapter.FillByLastName( _
31            AddressBookDataSet.Addresses, txtFind.Text)
32      End Sub ' btnFind_Click
33
34      ' reloads AddressBookDataSet.Addresses with all rows
35      Private Sub btnBrowseAll_Click(ByVal sender As System.Object, _
36         ByVal e As System.EventArgs) Handles btnBrowseAll.Click
37         ' fill the DataSet's DataTable with all rows in the database
38         AddressesTableAdapter.Fill(AddressBookDataSet.Addresses)
39
40         txtFind.Text = "" ' clear Find TextBox
41      End Sub ' btnBrowseAll_Click
42   End Class ' FrmAddressBook
```

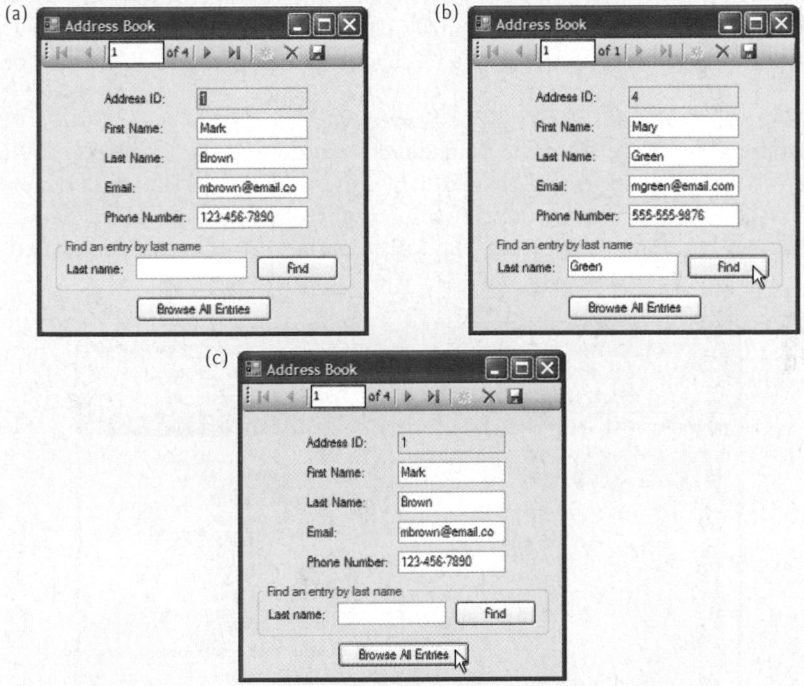

Fig. 20.44 | AddressBook application that allows you to manipulate entries in an address book database. (Part 2 of 2.)

Step 1: Creating the Project

Create a new Windows Application named AddressBook. Rename the Form FrmAddress-Book and name its source file FrmAddressBook.vb, then set the Form's **Text** property to Address Book.

Step 2: Adding the Database to the Project

As in Section 20.6.1, you must begin by adding the database to the project. After adding the `AddressBook.mdf` as a data source, the **Data Sources** window will list `AddressBook-DataSet`, which contains a table named `Addresses`.

Step 3: Indicating that the IDE Should Create a Set of *Labels* and *TextBoxes* to Display Each Row of Data

In the earlier sections, you dragged a node from the **Data Sources** window to the `Form` to create a `DataGridView` bound to the data source member represented by that node. The IDE allows you to specify the type of control(s) that it creates when you drag and drop a data source member onto a `Form`. In **Design** view, click the `Addresses` node in the **Data Sources** window (Fig. 20.45). Note that this node becomes a drop-down list when you select it. Click the down arrow to view the items in the list. The icon to the left of **Data-GridView** will initially be highlighted in blue, because the default control to be bound to a table is a `DataGridView` (as you saw in the earlier examples). Select the **Details** option in the drop-down list to indicate that the IDE should create a set of `Label`–`TextBox` pairs for each column name–column value pair when you drag and drop the `Addresses` table onto the `Form`. (You will see what this looks like in Fig. 20.46.) The drop-down list contains suggestions for controls to display the table's data, but you can also choose the **Customize...** option to select other controls that are capable of being bound to a table's data.

Step 4: Dragging the *Addresses* Data Source Node to the *Form*

Drag the `Addresses` node from the **Data Sources** window to the `Form` (Fig. 20.46). The IDE creates a series of `Label`s and `TextBox`es because you selected **Details** in the preceding step. As in the earlier examples, the IDE also creates a `BindingNavigator` and the other components in the component tray. The IDE sets the text of each `Label` based on the

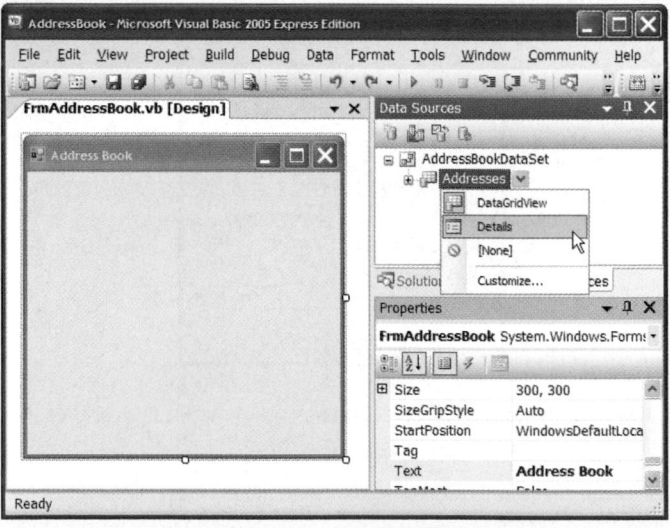

Fig. 20.45 | Selecting the control(s) to be created when dragging and dropping a data source member onto the `Form`.

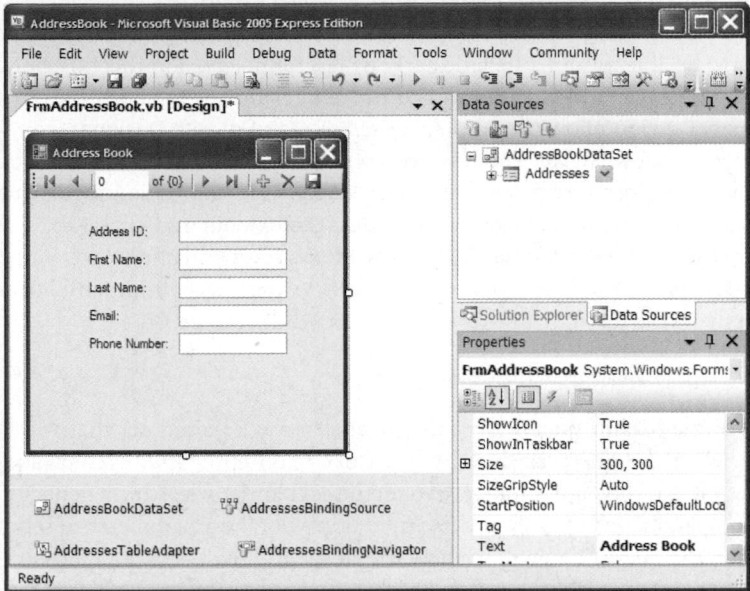

Fig. 20.46 | Displaying a table on a Form using a series of Labels and TextBoxes.

corresponding column name in the database table, and uses regular expressions to insert spaces into multiword column names to make the Labels more readable.

Step 5: Making the *AddressID TextBox ReadOnly*
The AddressID column of the Addresses table is an auto-incremented identity column, so users should not be allowed to edit the values in this column. Select the TextBox for the AddressID and set its ReadOnly property to True using the **Properties** window. Note that you may need to click in an empty part of the Form to deselect the other Labels and Text-Boxes before selecting the AddressID TextBox.

Step 6: Running the Application
Run the application and experiment with the controls in the BindingNavigator at the top of the window. Like the previous examples, this example fills a DataSet object (specifically an AddressBookDataSet object) with all the rows of a database table (i.e., Addresses). However, only a single row of the DataSet appears at any given time. The CD- or DVD-like buttons of the BindingNavigator allow you to change the currently displayed row (i.e., change the values in each of the TextBoxes). The buttons to add a row, delete a row and save changes also perform their designated tasks. Adding a row clears the TextBoxes and makes a new auto-incremented ID appear in the TextBox to the right of **Address ID**. After entering several address-book entries, click the **Save** button to record the new rows in the database. When you close and restart the application, your should be able to use the BindingNavigator controls to browse your entries. Recall from Section 20.6 that to allow changes to the database during changes, you must select the database in the **Solution Explorer**, then change its **Copy to Output Directory** property to **Copy if newer** in the **Properties** window.

*Step 7: Adding a Query to the **AddressesTableAdapter***

While the `BindingNavigator` allows you to browse the address book, it would be more convenient to be able to find a specific entry by last name. To add this functionality to the application, you must add a new query to the `AddressesTableAdapter` using the **Table-Adapter Query Configuration Wizard**. Click the **Edit DataSet with Designer** icon (🔣) in the **Data Sources** window. Select the box representing the `AddressesTableAdapter`. Right click the `TableAdapter`'s name and select **Add Query...**. In the **TableAdapter Query Configuration Wizard**, keep the default option **Use SQL Statements** and click **Next**. On the next screen, keep the default option **SELECT which returns rows** and click **Next**. Rather than use the **Query Builder** to form your query (as we did in the preceding example), modify the query directly in the text box in the wizard. Append the clause

```
WHERE LastName = @lastName
```

to the end of the default query. Note that `@lastName` is a parameter that will be replaced by a value when the query executes. Click **Next**, then enter `FillByLastName` and `Get-DataByLastName` as the names for the two methods that the wizard will generate. The query contains a parameter, so each of these methods will take a parameter to set the value of `@lastName` in the query. You will see how to call the `FillByLastName` method and specify a value for `@lastName` shortly. Click **Finish** to complete the wizard and return to the **Dataset Designer** (Fig. 20.47). Note that the new `Fill` and `Get` methods appear under the `AddressesTableAdapter` and that parameter `@lastName` is listed to the right of the method names.

Step 8: Adding Controls to Allow Users to Specify a Last Name to Locate

Now that you have created a query to locate rows with a specific last name, add controls to allow users to enter a last name and execute this query. Go to **Design** view (Fig. 20.48) and add to the Form a `Label` named `lblFind`, a `TextBox` named `txtFind` and a `Button` named `btnFind`. Place these controls in a `GroupBox` named `grpFind`, then set its **Text**

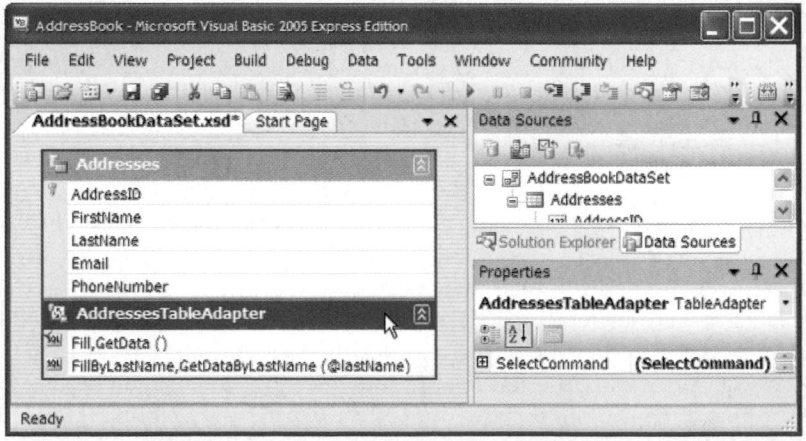

Fig. 20.47 | **Dataset Designer** for the `AddressBookDataSet` after adding a query to `AddressesTableAdapter`.

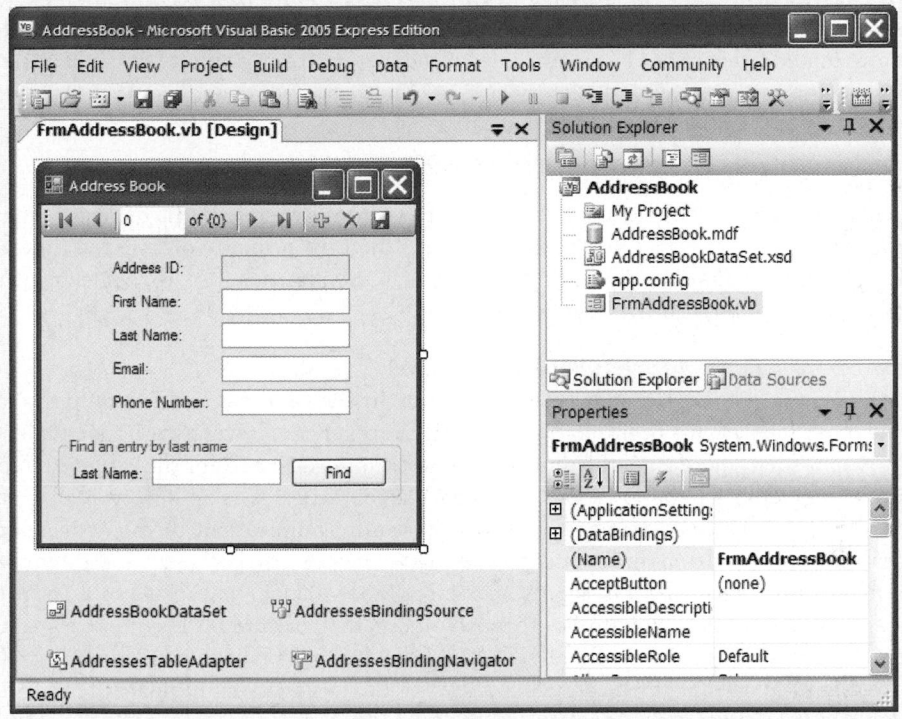

Fig. 20.48 | **Design** view after adding controls to locate a last name in the address book.

property to Find an entry by last name. Set the Text properties of the Label and Button as shown in Fig. 20.48.

Step 9: Programming an Event Handler That Locates the User-Specified Last Name
Double click btnFind to add a Click event handler for this Button. In the event handler, write the following lines of code (lines 30–31 of Fig. 20.44):

```
AddressesTableAdapter.FillByLastName( _
    AddressBookDataSet.Addresses, txtFind.Text)
```

The FillByLastName method replaces the current data in AddressBookDataSet.Addresses with data for only those rows with the last name entered in txtFind. Note that when invoking FillByLastName, you must pass the DataTable to be filled, as well as an argument specifying the last name to find. This argument becomes the value of the @lastName parameter in the SELECT statement created in *Step 7*. Start the application to test the new functionality. When you search for a specific entry (i.e., enter a last name and click Find), the BindingNavigator allows the user to browse only the rows containing the specified last name. This is because the data source bound to the Form's controls (i.e., AddressBookDataSet.Addresses) has changed and now contains only a limited number of rows. The database in this example is initially empty, so you'll need to add several records before testing the find capability.

Step 10: Allowing the User to Return to Browsing All Rows in the Database

To allow users to return to browsing all the rows after searching for specific rows, add a Button named btnBrowseAll below the grpFind. Set the Text property of btnBrowseAll to **Browse All Entries**. Double click btnBrowseAll in **Design** view to add a Click event handler to the code. Add a line of code that calls

```
AddressesTableAdapter.Fill(AddressBookDataSet.Addresses)
```

to refill the Addresses DataTable with all the rows from the table in the database (line 38 of Fig. 20.44). Also, add a line of code that clears the Text property of txtFind (line 40). Start the application. Find a specific last name as in the previous step, then click the btnBrowseAll button to test the new functionality.

Data Binding in the **AddressBook** Application

Dragging and dropping the Addresses node from the **Data Sources** window onto the Form FrmAddressBook in this example caused the IDE to generate several components in the component tray. These serve the same purposes as those generated for the earlier examples that use the Books database. In this case, AddressBookDataSet is an object of a strongly typed DataSet, AddressBookDataSet, whose structure mimics that of the AddressBook database. AddressesBindingSource is a BindingSource object that refers to the Addresses table of the AddressBookDataSet. AddressesTableAdapter encapsulates a SqlDataAdapter object configured with SqlCommand objects that execute SQL statements against the AddressBook database. Finally, AddressesBindingNavigator is bound to the AddressesBindingSource object, which allows you to indirectly manipulate the Addresses table of the AddressBookDataSet.

In each of the earlier examples using a DataGridView to display all the rows of a database table, the DataGridView's BindingSource property was set to the corresponding BindingSource object. In this example, you selected **Details** from the drop-down list for the Addresses table in the **Data Sources** window, so the values from a single row of the table appear on the Form in a set of TextBoxes. In this example, the IDE binds each TextBox to a specific column of the Addresses DataTable in the AddressBookDataSet. To do this, the IDE sets the TextBox's **DataBindings.Text** property. You can view this property by clicking the plus sign next to **(DataBindings)** in the **Properties** window (Fig. 20.49). Clicking the drop-down list for this property allows you to choose a BindingSource object and a property (i.e., column) within the associated data source to bind to the TextBox.

Consider the TextBox that displays the FirstName value—named FirstNameTextBox by the IDE. This control's DataBindings.Text property is set to the FirstName property of the AddressesBindingSource (which refers to AddressBookDataSet.Addresses). Thus, FirstNameTextBox always displays the value of the FirstName column in the currently selected row of AddressBookDataSet.Addresses. Each IDE-created TextBox on the Form is configured in a similar manner. Browsing the address book with the AddressesBindingNavigator changes the current position in AddressBookDataSet.Addresses, and thus changes the values displayed in each TextBox. Regardless of changes to the contents of AddressBookDataSet.Addresses, the TextBoxes remain bound to the same properties of the DataTable and always display the appropriate data. The TextBoxes do not display any values if the cached version of Addresses is empty (i.e., if the DataTable is empty because the query that filled the DataTable returned no rows).

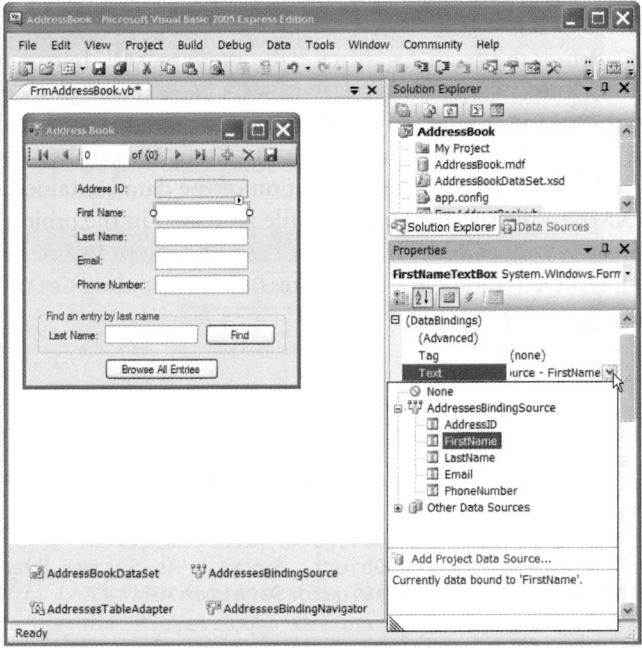

Fig. 20.49 | Viewing the `DataBindings.Text` property of a `TextBox` in the **Properties** window.

20.9 Using a DataSet to Read and Write XML

A powerful feature of ADO.NET is its ability to convert data stored in a data source to XML for exchanging data between applications in a portable format. Class `DataSet` of namespace `System.Data` provides methods `WriteXml`, `ReadXml` and `GetXml`, which enable developers to create XML documents from data sources and to convert data from XML into data sources.

Writing Data from a Data Source to an XML Document

The application of Fig. 20.50 populates a `DataSet` with statistics about baseball players, then writes the data to an XML document and displays the XML in a `TextBox`.

We created this GUI by adding the `Baseball.mdf` database (located in the chapter's examples directory) as a data source, then dragging the `Players` node from the **Data Sources** window to the `Form`. This action created the `BindingNavigator` and `DataGrid-View` seen in the output of Fig. 20.50. We then added the `Button btnWrite` and the `TextBox txtOutput`. The XML representation of the `Players` table should not be edited and will span more lines than the `TextBox` can display at once, so we set `txtOutput`'s `Read-Only` and `MultiLine` properties to `True` and its `ScrollBars` property to `Vertical`. Create the event handler for `btnWrite` by double clicking it in **Design** view.

The autogenerated `FrmXMLWriter_Load` event handler (lines 16–22) calls method `Fill` of class `PlayersTableAdapter` to populate `BaseballDataSet` with data from the `Players` table in the `Baseball` database. Note that the IDE binds the `DataGridView` to

20.10 Wrap-Up

This chapter introduced relational databases, SQL, ADO.NET and the IDE's visual programming tools for working with databases. You examined the contents of a simple Books database and learned about the relationships among the tables in the database. You then learned basic SQL to retrieve data from, add new data to, and update data in a database.

We discussed the classes of namespaces System.Data and System.Data.SqlClient that allow programs to connect to a database, then access and manipulate its data. We also explained ADO.NET's disconnected model, which enables a program to store data from a database temporarily in local memory as a DataSet.

The second part of the chapter focused on using the IDE's tools and wizards to access and manipulate data sources like a database in GUI applications. You learned how to add data sources to projects and how to use the IDE's drag-and-drop capabilities to display database tables in applications. We discussed how the IDE hides from you the SQL used to interact with the database. You also learned how to add custom queries to GUI applications so that you can display only those rows of data that meet specific criteria. Finally, you learned how to write data from a data source to an XML file.

In the next chapter, we demonstrate how to build Web applications using Microsoft's ASP.NET technology. We also introduce the concept of a three-tier application, in which an application is divided into three pieces that can reside on the same computer or can be distributed among separate computers across a network such as the Internet. One of these tiers—the information tier—typically stores data in an RDBMS like SQL Server.

20.11 Web Resources

msdn.microsoft.com/sql/
The SQL Server Developer Center provides up-to-date product information, downloads, articles and community forums.

msdn.microsoft.com/vstudio/express/sql/default.aspx
The home page for SQL Server 2005 Express provides how-to articles, blogs, newsgroups and other valuable resources.

msdn2.microsoft.com/library/system.data.aspx
Microsoft's documentation for the System.Data namespace.

msdn.microsoft.com/SQL/sqlreldata/TSQL/default.aspx
Microsoft's SQL language reference guide.

msdn2.microsoft.com/library/ms172013.aspx
Microsoft's documentation for the **Query Builder** and other visual database tools.

www.w3schools.com/sql/default.asp
The W3C's SQL tutorial presents basic and advanced SQL features with examples.

www.sql.org
This SQL portal provides links to many resources, including SQL syntax, tips, tutorials, books, magazines, discussion groups, companies with SQL services, SQL consultants and free software.

www.oracle.com/database/index.html
The home page for Oracle's database management systems.

www.sybase.com
The home page for the Sybase database management system.

www-306.ibm.com/software/data/db2/
The home page for IBM's DB2 database management system.

www.postgresql.org

The home page for the PostgreSQL database management system.

www.mysql.com

The home page for the MySQL database server.

Summary

Section 20.1 Introduction

- A database is an organized collection of data. A database management system (DBMS) provides mechanisms for storing, organizing, retrieving and modifying data for many users.

- Today's most popular database management systems are relational database management systems (RDBMS).

- SQL is the international standard language used almost universally with relational database systems to perform queries and manipulate data.

- Programs connect to, and interact with, relational databases via an interface—software that facilitates communications between a database management system and a program.

- Visual Basic programs communicate with databases and manipulate their data through ADO.NET.

Section 20.2 Relational Databases

- A relational database stores data in tables. Tables are composed of rows and columns in which values are stored.

- A primary key provides a unique value that cannot be duplicated in other rows of the same table. The primary key uniquely identifies each row.

- Each row of a table represents a record.

- Each column of a table represents a different attribute.

- The primary key can be composed of more than one column.

Section 20.3 Relational Database Overview: **Books** Database

- A foreign key is a column (or columns) in a table that matches the primary key column in another table.

- The foreign key helps maintain the Rule of Referential Integrity: Every foreign key value must appear as another table's primary key value. Foreign keys enable information from multiple tables to be joined together. There is a one-to-many relationship between a primary key and its corresponding foreign key.

- Every column in a primary key must have a value, and the value of the primary key must be unique. This is known as the Rule of Entity Integrity.

- A one-to-many relationship between tables indicates that a row in one table can have many related rows in a separate table.

Section 20.4 SQL

- SQL provides a rich set of language constructs that enable you to define complex queries to retrieve data from a database.

21

ASP.NET 2.0, Web Forms and Web Controls

OBJECTIVES

In this chapter you will learn:

- Web application development using Active Server Pages .NET (ASP.NET).

- To create Web Forms.

- To create ASP.NET applications consisting of multiple Web Forms.

- To maintain state information about a user with session tracking and cookies.

- To use the **Web Site Administration Tool** to modify Web application configuration settings.

- To control user access to Web applications using forms authentication and ASP.NET login controls.

- To use databases in ASP.NET applications.

- To design a master page and content pages to create a uniform look-and-feel for a Web site.

21.1 Introduction

In previous chapters, we used Windows Forms and controls to develop Windows applications. In this chapter, we introduce Web application development with Microsoft's Active Server Pages .NET (ASP.NET) 2.0 technology. Web-based applications create Web content for Web browser clients. This Web content includes Extensible HyperText Markup Language (XHTML), client-side scripting, images and binary data. Readers not familiar with XHTML should first read Appendix F, Introduction to XHTML: Part 1, and Appendix G, Introduction to XHTML: Part 2, before studying this chapter.

We present several examples that demonstrate Web application development using Web Forms, Web controls (also called ASP.NET server controls) and Visual Basic programming. Web Form files have the filename extension .aspx and contain the Web page's GUI. You customize Web Forms by adding Web controls including labels, text boxes, images, buttons and other GUI components. The Web Form file represents the Web page that is sent to the client browser. From this point onward, we refer to Web Form files as ASPX files.

An ASPX file created in Visual Studio typically has a corresponding class written in a .NET language, such as Visual Basic. This class contains event handlers, initialization code, utility methods and other supporting code. The file that contains this class is called the code-behind file and provides the ASPX file's programmatic implementation.

To develop the code and GUIs in this chapter, we used Microsoft Visual Web Developer 2005 Express—an IDE designed for developing ASP.NET Web applications. Visual Web Developer and Visual Basic 2005 Express share many common features and visual programming tools that simplify building complex applications, such as those that access a database (presented in Sections 21.7 and 21.8). The full version of Visual Studio 2005 includes the functionality of Visual Web Developer, so the instructions we present for Visual Web Developer also apply to Visual Studio 2005. Note that you must install either Visual Web Developer 2005 Express (available from msdn.microsoft.com/vstudio/ express/vwd/default.aspx) or a complete version of Visual Studio 2005 to implement the programs in this chapter and Chapter 22, Web Services.

21.2 Simple HTTP Transactions

Web application development requires a basic understanding of networking and the World Wide Web. In this section, we discuss the Hypertext Transfer Protocol (HTTP) and what occurs behind the scenes when a browser displays a Web page. HTTP specifies a set of methods and headers that allow clients and servers to interact and exchange information in a uniform and predictable manner.

In its simplest form, a Web page is nothing more than an XHTML document—a plain text file containing markup (i.e., tags) that indicate to a Web browser how to display and format the document's information. For example, the XHTML markup

```
<title>My Web Page</title>
```

indicates that the browser should display the text between the `<title>` start tag and the `</title>` end tag in the browser's title bar. XHTML documents also can contain hypertext data (usually called hyperlinks), which links to different pages or to other parts of the same page. When the user activates a hyperlink (usually by clicking it with the mouse), the requested Web page loads into the user's browser window.

Any XHTML document available for viewing over the Web has a corresponding Uniform Resource Locator (URL). A URL is an address indicating the location of an Internet resource, such as an XHTML document. The URL contains information that directs a browser to the resource that the user wishes to access. Computers that run Web server software make such resources available. When requesting ASP.NET Web applications, the Web server is usually Microsoft Internet Information Services (IIS). As we discuss shortly, it is also possible to test ASP.NET applications using the ASP.NET Development Server built into Visual Web Developer.

Let us examine the components of the URL

```
http://www.deitel.com/books/downloads.html
```

The http:// indicates that the resource is to be obtained using the HTTP protocol. The middle portion, www.deitel.com, is the server's fully qualified hostname—the name of the computer on which the resource resides. This computer usually is referred to as the host, because it houses and maintains resources. The hostname www.deitel.com is translated into an IP address (68.236.123.125), which identifies the server in a manner similar to how a telephone number uniquely defines a particular phone line. The hostname is translated into an IP address by a domain name system (DNS) server—a computer that maintains a database of hostnames and their corresponding IP addresses. This translation operation is called a DNS lookup.

The remainder of the URL (i.e., /books/downloads.html) specifies both the name of the requested resource (the XHTML document downloads.html) and its path, or location (/books), on the Web server. The path could specify the location of an actual directory on the Web server's file system. However, for security reasons, the path often specifies the location of a virtual directory. In such systems, the server translates the virtual directory into a real location on the server (or on another computer on the server's network), thus hiding the true location of the resource. Some resources are created dynamically and do not reside anywhere on the server computer. The hostname in the URL for such a resource specifies the correct server, and the path and resource information identify the location of the resource with which to respond to the client's request.

When given a URL, a Web browser performs a simple HTTP transaction to retrieve and display the Web page found at that address. Figure 21.1 illustrates the transaction in detail. This transaction consists of interaction between the Web browser (the client side) and the Web server application (the server side).

In Fig. 21.1, the Web browser sends an HTTP request to the server. The request (in its simplest form) is

    GET /books/downloads.html HTTP/1.1

The word GET is an HTTP method indicating that the client wishes to obtain a resource from the server. The remainder of the request provides the path name of the resource (an XHTML document) and the protocol's name and version number (HTTP/1.1).

Any server that understands HTTP version 1.1 can translate this request and respond appropriately. Figure 21.2 depicts the results of a successful request. The server first responds by sending a line of text that indicates the HTTP version, followed by a numeric code and a phrase describing the status of the transaction. For example,

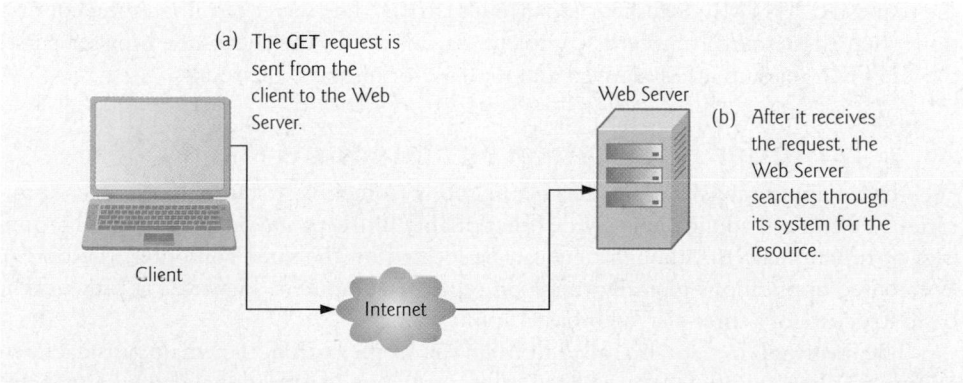

(a) The GET request is sent from the client to the Web Server.

Web Server

(b) After it receives the request, the Web Server searches through its system for the resource.

Client

Internet

Fig. 21.1 | Client interacting with Web server. *Step 1:* The GET request.

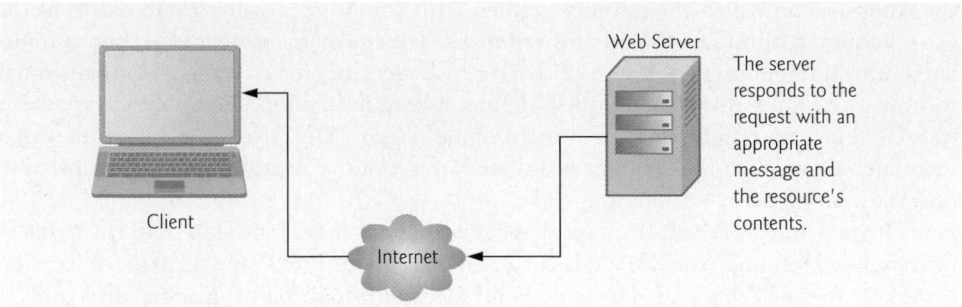

Fig. 21.2 | Client interacting with Web server. *Step 2:* The HTTP response.

> HTTP/1.1 200 OK

indicates success, whereas

> HTTP/1.1 404 Not found

informs the client that the Web server could not locate the requested resource.

The server then sends one or more **HTTP headers,** which provide additional information about the data that will be sent. In this case, the server is sending an XHTML text document, so the HTTP header for this example reads:

> Content-type: text/html

The information provided in this header specifies the **Multipurpose Internet Mail Extensions (MIME)** type of the content that the server is transmitting to the browser. MIME is an Internet standard that specifies data formats so that programs can interpret data correctly. For example, the MIME type text/plain indicates that the sent information is text that can be displayed directly, without any interpretation of the content as XHTML markup. Similarly, the MIME type image/jpeg indicates that the content is a JPEG image. When the browser receives this MIME type, it attempts to display the image.

The header or set of headers is followed by a blank line, which indicates to the client that the server is finished sending HTTP headers. The server then sends the contents of the requested XHTML document (downloads.html). The server terminates the connection when the resource transfer is complete. At this point, the client-side browser parses the XHTML markup it has received and **renders** (or displays) the results.

21.3 Multitier Application Architecture

Web-based applications are **multitier applications** (sometimes referred to as *n*-tier applications). Multitier applications divide functionality into separate **tiers** (i.e., logical groupings of functionality). Although tiers can be located on the same computer, the tiers of Web-based applications typically reside on separate computers. Figure 21.3 presents the basic structure of a three-tier Web-based application.

The **information tier** (also called the **data tier** or the **bottom tier**) maintains data pertaining to the application. This tier typically stores data in a relational database management system (RDBMS). We discussed RDBMSs in Chapter 20. For example, a retail store

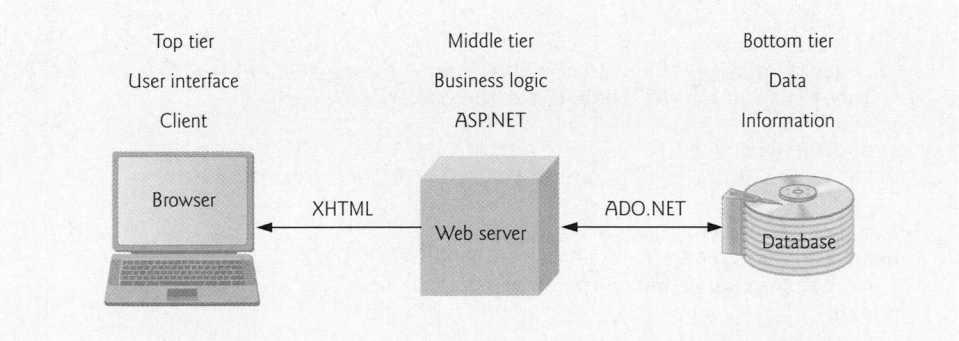

Fig. 21.3 | Three-tier architecture.

might have a database for storing product information, such as descriptions, prices and quantities in stock. The same database also might contain customer information, such as user names, billing addresses and credit card numbers. This tier can contain multiple databases, which together comprise the data needed for our application.

The **middle tier** implements **business logic**, **controller logic** and **presentation logic** to control interactions between the application's clients and the application's data. The middle tier acts as an intermediary between data in the information tier and the application's clients. The middle-tier controller logic processes client requests (such as requests to view a product catalog) and retrieves data from the database. The middle-tier presentation logic then processes data from the information tier and presents the content to the client. Web applications typically present data to clients as XHTML documents.

Business logic in the middle tier enforces **business rules** and ensures that data is reliable before the server application updates the database or presents the data to users. Business rules dictate how clients can and cannot access application data, and how applications process data. For example, a business rule in the middle tier of a retail store's Web-based application might ensure that all product quantities remain positive. A client request to set a negative quantity in the bottom tier's product information database would be rejected by the middle tier's business logic.

The **client tier**, or **top tier**, is the application's user interface, which gathers input and displays output. Users interact directly with the application through the user interface (typically viewed in a Web browser), keyboard and mouse. In response to user actions (e.g., clicking a hyperlink), the client tier interacts with the middle tier to make requests and to retrieve data from the information tier. The client tier then displays the data retrieved from the middle tier to the user. The client tier never directly interacts with the information tier.

21.4 Creating and Running a Simple Web-Form Example

Our first example displays the Web server's time of day in a browser window. When run, this program displays the text A Simple Web Form Example, followed by the Web server's time. As mentioned previously, the program consists of two related files—an ASPX file (Fig. 21.4) and a Visual Basic code-behind file (Fig. 21.5). We first display the markup, code and output, then we carefully guide you through the step-by-step process of creating this program. [*Note:* The markup in Fig. 21.4 and other ASPX file listings in this chapter

```
 1   <%-- Fig. 21.4: WebTime.aspx --%>
 2   <%-- A page that displays the current time in a Label. --%>
 3   <%@ Page Language="VB" AutoEventWireup="false" CodeFile="WebTime.aspx.vb"
 4      Inherits="WebTime" EnableSessionState="False" %>
 5
 6   <!DOCTYPE html PUBLIC "-//W3C//DTD XHTML 1.0 Transitional//EN"
 7      "http://www.w3.org/TR/xhtml1/DTD/xhtml1-transitional.dtd">
 8
 9   <html xmlns="http://www.w3.org/1999/xhtml" >
10   <head runat="server">
11      <title>A Simple Web Form Example</title>
12   </head>
13   <body>
14      <form id="form1" runat="server">
15      <div>
16         <h2>
17         Current time on the Web server:</h2>
18         <p>
19            <asp:Label ID="timeLabel" runat="server" BackColor="Black"
20               EnableViewState="False" Font-Size="XX-Large"
21               ForeColor="Yellow"></asp:Label>
22         </p>
23      </div>
24      </form>
25   </body>
26   </html>
```

Fig. 21.4 | ASPX file that displays the Web server's time.

is the same as the markup that appears in Visual Web Developer, but we have reformatted the markup for presentation purposes to make the code more readable.]

Visual Web Developer generates all the markup shown in Fig. 21.4 when you set the Web page's title, type text in the Web Form, drag a Label onto the Web Form and set the properties of the page's text and the Label. We discuss these steps in Section 21.4.6.

21.4.1 Examining an ASPX File

The ASPX file contains other information in addition to XHTML. Lines 1–2 are ASP.NET comments that indicate the figure number, the file name and the purpose of the file. ASP.NET comments begin with <%-- and terminate with --%>. We added these comments to the file. Lines 3–4 use a **Page** directive (in an ASPX file a directive is delimited by <%@ and %>) to specify information needed by ASP.NET to process this file. The **Language** attribute of the Page directive specifies the language of the code-behind file as Visual Basic ("VB"); the code-behind file (i.e., the **CodeFile**) is WebTime.aspx.vb. A code-behind file name usually consists of the full ASPX file name (e.g., WebTime.aspx) followed by the .vb extension.

The **AutoEventWireup** attribute (line 3) determines how Web Form events are handled. When AutoEventWireup is set to true, ASP.NET determines which methods in the class are called in response to an event generated by the Page. For example, ASP.NET will call methods Page_Init and Page_Load in the code-behind file to handle the Page's Init and Load events, respectively. (We discuss these events later in the chapter.)

The `Inherits` attribute (line 4) specifies the page's class name—in this case, `WebTime`. We say more about `Inherits` momentarily. [*Note:* We explicitly set the `EnableSession-State` attribute (line 4) to `False`. We explain the significance of this attribute later in the chapter. The IDE sometimes generates attribute values (e.g., `true` and `false`) and control names (as you will see later in the chapter) that do not adhere to our standard code capitalization conventions (i.e., `True` and `False`). Like Visual Basic, ASP.NET markup is not case-sensitive, so using a different case is not problematic. To remain consistent with the code generated by the IDE, we do not modify these values in our code listings or in our accompanying discussions.]

For this first ASPX file, we provide a brief discussion of the XHTML markup. We do not discuss the majority of the XHTML contained in subsequent ASPX files. Lines 6–7 contain the document type declaration, which specifies the document element name (HTML) and the PUBLIC Uniform Resource Identifier (URI) for the DTD that defines the XHTML vocabulary.

Lines 9–10 contain the `<html>` and `<head>` start tags, respectively. XHTML documents have the root element `html` and mark up information about the document in the `head` element. Also note that the `html` element specifies the XML namespace of the document using the `xmlns` attribute (see Section 19.4).

Notice the **runat** attribute in line 10, which is set to **"server"**. This attribute indicates that when a client requests this ASPX file, ASP.NET processes the `head` element and its nested elements on the server and generates the corresponding XHTML, which is then sent to the client. In this case, the XHTML sent to the client will be identical to the markup in the ASPX file. However, as you will see, ASP.NET can generate complex XHTML markup from simple elements in an ASPX file.

Line 11 sets the title of this Web page. We demonstrate how to set the title through a property in the IDE shortly. Line 13 contains the `<body>` start tag, which begins the body of the XHTML document; the body contains the main content that the browser displays. The `form` that contains our XHTML text and controls is defined in lines 14–24. Again, the `runat` attribute in the `form` element indicates that this element executes on the server, which generates equivalent XHTML and sends it to the client. Lines 15–23 contain a `div` element that groups the elements of the form in a block of markup.

Lines 16–17 are an XHTML `h2` heading element that contains text indicating the purpose of the Web page. As we demonstrate shortly, the IDE generates this element in response to typing text directly in the Web Form and selecting the text as a second-level heading.

Lines 18–22 contain a `p` element to mark up a paragraph of content in the browser. Lines 19–21 mark up a label Web control. The properties that we set in the **Properties** window, such as `Font-Size` and `BackColor` (i.e., background color), are attributes here. The `ID` attribute (line 19) assigns a name to the control so that it can be manipulated programmatically in the code-behind file. We set the control's `EnableViewState` attribute (line 20) to `False`. We explain the significance of this attribute later in the chapter.

The **asp:** tag prefix in the declaration of the `Label` tag (line 19) indicates that the label is an ASP.NET Web control, not an XHTML element. Each Web control maps to a corresponding XHTML element (or group of elements)—when processing a Web control on the server, ASP.NET generates XHTML markup that will be sent to the client to represent that control in a Web browser.

Portability Tip 21.1

The same Web control can map to different XHTML elements, depending on the client browser and the Web control's property settings.

In this example, the asp:Label control maps to the XHTML **span** element (i.e., ASP.NET creates a **span** element to represent this control in the client's Web browser). A span element contains text that is displayed in a Web page. This particular element is used because span elements allow formatting styles to be applied to text. Several of the property values that were applied to our label are represented as part of the **style** attribute of the span element. You will soon see what the generated span element's markup looks like.

The Web control in this example contains the runat="server" attribute–value pair (line 19), because this control must be processed on the server so that the server can translate the control into XHTML that can be rendered in the client browser. If this attribute pair is not present, the asp:Label element is written as text to the client (i.e., the control is not converted into a span element and does not render properly).

21.4.2 Examining a Code-Behind File

Figure 21.5 presents the code-behind file. Recall that the ASPX file in Fig. 21.4 references this file in line 3.

Line 3 begins the declaration of class WebTime. Recall from Section 9.6 that a class declaration can span multiple source-code files and that the separate portions of the class declaration in each file are known as partial classes. The Partial modifier in line 3 indicates that the code-behind file is a partial class. We discuss the remainder of this class shortly.

```vb
1  ' Fig. 21.5: WebTime.aspx.vb
2  ' Code-behind file for a page that displays the current time.
3  Partial Class WebTime
4     Inherits System.Web.UI.Page
5
6     ' initializes the contents of the page
7     Protected Sub Page_Init(ByVal sender As Object, _
8        ByVal e As System.EventArgs) Handles Me.Init
9        ' display the server's current time in timeLabel
10       timeLabel.Text = DateTime.Now.ToString("hh:mm:ss")
11    End Sub ' Page_Init
12 End Class ' WebTime
```

Fig. 21.5 | Code-behind file for a page that displays the Web server's time.

Line 4 indicates that `WebTime` inherits from class `Page` in namespace `System.Web.UI`. This namespace contains classes and controls that assist in building Web-based applications. Class `Page` provides event handlers and objects necessary for creating Web-based applications. In addition to class `Page` (from which all Web applications directly or indirectly inherit), `System.Web.UI` also includes class `Control`—the base class that provides common functionality for all Web controls.

Lines 7–11 define method `Page_Init`, which handles the page's `Init` event. This event indicates that the page is ready to be initialized. The only initialization required for this page is setting `timeLabel`'s `Text` property to the time on the server (i.e., the computer on which this code executes). The statement in line 10 retrieves the current time and formats it as *hh*:*mm*:*ss*. For example, 9 AM is formatted as 09:00:00, and 2:30 PM is formatted as 14:30:00. Notice that the code-behind file can access `timeLabel` (the `ID` of the `Label` in the ASPX file) programmatically, even though the file does not contain a declaration for a variable named `timeLabel`. You will learn why momentarily.

21.4.3 Relationship Between an ASPX File and a Code-Behind File

How are the ASPX and code-behind files used to create the Web page that is sent to the client? First, recall that class `WebTime` is the base class specified in line 4 of the ASPX file (Fig. 21.4). This class (partially declared in the code-behind file) inherits from `Page`, which defines general Web page functionality. Partial class `WebTime` inherits this functionality and defines some of its own (i.e., displaying the current time). The code in the code-behind file displays the time, whereas the code in the ASPX file defines the GUI.

When a client requests an ASPX file, ASP.NET creates two partial classes behind the scenes. The code-behind file contains one partial class named `WebTime` and ASP.NET generate another partial class containing the remainder of class `WebTime`, based on the markup in the ASPX file. For example, `WebTime.aspx` contains a `Label` Web control with `ID` `timeLabel`, so the generated partial class would contain a declaration for a variable named `timeLabel` of type `System.Web.UI.WebControls.Label`. Class `Label` represents a Web control defined in namespace `System.Web.UI.WebControls`, which contains various Web controls for designing a page's user interface. Web controls in this namespace derive from class `WebControl`. When compiled, the partial class that declares `timeLabel` combines with the code-behind file's partial class declaration to form the complete `WebTime` class. This explains why line 10 in Fig. 21.5 can access `timeLabel`, which is created in lines 19–21 of `WebTime.aspx` (Fig. 21.4)—method `Page_Init` and control `timeLabel` are actually members of the same class, but defined in separate partial classes.

The partial class generated by ASP.NET is based on the ASPX file that defines the page's visual representation. This partial class is combined with the one in Fig. 21.5, which defines the page's logic. The first time the Web page is requested, this class is compiled and an instance is created. This instance represents the page and creates the XHTML that is sent to the client. The assembly created from the compiled partial classes is placed in a subdirectory of

```
C:\WINDOWS\Microsoft.NET\Framework\VersionNumber\
    Temporary ASP.NET Files\WebTime
```

where *VersionNumber* is the version number of the .NET Framework (e.g., `v2.0.50727`) installed on your computer.

Once an instance of the Web page has been created, multiple clients can use it to access the page—no recompilation is necessary. The project will be recompiled only when you modify the application; changes are detected by the runtime environment, and the application is recompiled to reflect the altered content.

21.4.4 How the Code in an ASP.NET Web Page Executes

Let's look briefly at how the code for our Web page executes. When an instance of the page is created, the `PreInit` event occurs first, invoking method `Page_PreInit`. Method `Page_PreInit` can be used to set a page's theme and look-and-feel (and perform other tasks that are beyond this chapter's scope). The `Init` event occurs next, invoking method `Page_Init`. Method `Page_Init` is used to initialize objects and other aspects of the page. After `Page_Init` executes, the `Load` event occurs, and the `Page_Load` event handler executes. Although not present in this example, the `PreInit` and `Load` events are inherited from class `Page`. You will see examples of the `Page_Load` event handler later in the chapter. After the `Load` event handler finishes executing, the page processes events that are generated by the page's controls, such as user interactions with the GUI. When the Web Form object is ready for garbage collection, an `Unload` event occurs, which calls the `Page_Unload` event handler. This event, too, is inherited from class `Page`. `Page_Unload` typically contains code that releases resources used by the page. Other events occur as well, but are typically used only by ASP.NET controls to render themselves. You can learn more about a Page's event lifecycle at `msdn2.microsoft.com/en-US/library/ms178472.aspx`.

21.4.5 Examining the XHTML Generated by an ASP.NET Application

Figure 21.6 shows the XHTML generated by ASP.NET when a client browser requests `WebTime.aspx` (Fig. 21.4). To view this code, select **View > Source** in Internet Explorer. We added the comments in lines 1–2 and reformatted the XHTML for readability.

The markup in this page is similar to the ASPX file. Lines 7–9 define a document header comparable to that in Fig. 21.4. Lines 10–25 define the document's body. Line 11 begins the form, a mechanism for collecting user information and sending it to the Web server. In this particular program, the user does not submit data to the Web server for processing; however, processing user data is a crucial part of many applications that is facilitated by forms. We demonstrate how to submit form data to the server in later examples.

XHTML forms can contain visual and nonvisual components. Visual components include buttons and other GUI components with which users interact. Nonvisual components, called hidden inputs, store data, such as e-mail addresses, that the document author specifies. A hidden input is defined in lines 13–14. We discuss the precise meaning of this hidden input later in the chapter. Attribute `method` of the `form` element (line 11) specifies the method by which the Web browser submits the form to the server. The `action` attribute identifies the name and location of the resource that will be requested when this form is submitted—in this case, `WebTime.aspx`. Recall that the ASPX file's `form` element contained the `runat="server"` attribute–value pair (line 14 of Fig. 21.4). When the `form` is processed on the server, the `runat` attribute is removed. The `method` and `action` attributes are added, and the resulting XHTML `form` is sent to the client browser.

In the ASPX file, the form's `Label` (i.e., `timeLabel`) is a Web control. Here, we are viewing the XHTML created by our application, so the form contains a `span` element (lines 20–21 of Fig. 21.6) to represent the text in the label. In this particular case,

```
 1  <!-- Fig. 21.6: WebTime.html -->
 2  <!-- The XHTML generated when WebTime.aspx is loaded. -->
 3  <!DOCTYPE html PUBLIC "-//W3C//DTD XHTML 1.1//EN"
 4      "http://www.w3.org/TR/xhtml11/DTD/xhtml11.dtd">
 5
 6  <html xmlns="http://www.w3.org/1999/xhtml" >
 7  <head>
 8      <title>A Simple Web Form Example</title>
 9  </head>
10  <body>
11      <form name="form1" method="post" action="WebTime.aspx" id="form1">
12          <div>
13              <input type="hidden" name="__VIEWSTATE" id="__VIEWSTATE" value=
14                  "/wEPDwUJODExMDE5NzY5ZGSzVbs789nqEeoNueQCnCJQEUgykw==" />
15          </div>
16
17          <div>
18              <h2>Current time on the Web server:</h2>
19              <p>
20                  <span id="timeLabel" style="color:Yellow;
21                      background-color:Black;font-size:XX-Large;">13:51:12</span>
22              </p>
23          </div>
24      </form>
25  </body>
26  </html>
```

Fig. 21.6 | XHTML response when the browser requests `WebTime.aspx`.

ASP.NET maps the `Label` Web control to an XHTML `span` element. The formatting options that were specified as properties of `timeLabel`, such as the font size and color of the text in the `Label`, are now specified in the `style` attribute of the `span` element.

Notice that only those elements in the ASPX file marked with the `runat="server"` attribute–value pair or specified as Web controls are modified or replaced when the file is processed by the server. The pure XHTML elements, such as the `h2` in line 18, are sent to the browser as they appear in the ASPX file.

21.4.6 Building an ASP.NET Web Application

Now that we have presented the ASPX file, the code-behind file and the resulting Web page sent to the Web browser, we show the steps we used to create this application in Visual Web Developer.

Step 1: Creating the Web Application Project

Select **File > New Web Site...** to display the **New Web Site** dialog (Fig. 21.7). In this dialog, select **ASP.NET Web Site** in the **Templates** pane. Below this pane, there are two fields in which you can specify the type and location of the Web application you are creating. If it is not already selected, select **HTTP** from the drop-down list closest to **Location**. This indicates that the Web application should be configured to run as an IIS application using HTTP (either on your computer or on a remote computer). We want our project to be located in `http://localhost`, which is the URL for IIS's root directory (this URL nor-

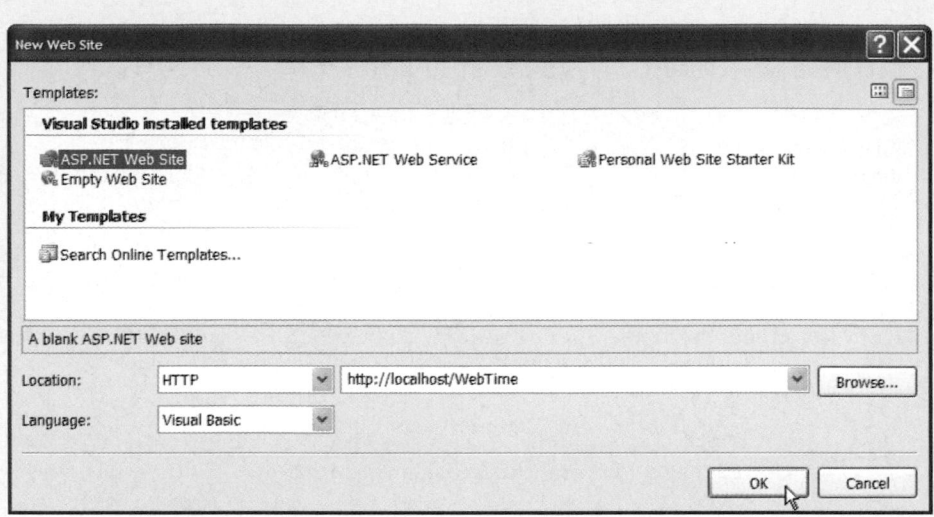

Fig. 21.7 | Creating an **ASP.NET Web Site** in Visual Web Developer.

mally corresponds to the C:\InetPub\wwwroot directory on your machine). The name lo-calhost indicates that the server resides on local computer. If the Web server were located on a different computer, localhost would be replaced with the appropriate IP address or hostname. By default, Visual Web Developer sets the location where the Web site will be created to http://localhost/WebSite, which we change to http://localhost/WebTime.

If you do not have IIS on your computer or do not have permission to access it, you can select **File System** from the drop-down list next to **Location** to create the Web application in a folder on your computer. You will be able to test the application using Visual Web Developer's internal ASP.NET Development Server, but you will not be able to access the application remotely over the Internet.

The **Language** drop-down list in the **New Web Site** dialog allows you to specify the language (i.e., Visual Basic, Visual C# or Visual J#) in which you will write the code-behind file(s) for the Web application. Change the setting to Visual Basic. Click **OK** to create the Web application project. This creates the directory C:\Inetpub\wwwroot\WebTime (in IIS) and makes it accessible through the URL http://localhost/WebTime. This action also creates a WebTime directory in the directory My Documents\Visual Studio 2005\Projects in which the project's solution files (e.g., WebTime.sln) are stored.

Step 2: Examining the Solution Explorer of the Newly Created Project
The next several figures describe the new project's content, beginning with the **Solution Explorer** shown in Fig. 21.8. Like Visual Basic 2005 Express, Visual Web Developer creates several files when you create a new project. It creates an ASPX file (i.e., Web Form) named Default.aspx for each new **ASP.NET Web Site** project. This file is open by default in the Web Forms Designer in **Source** mode when the project first loads (we discuss this momentarily). As mentioned previously, a code-behind file is included as part of the project. Visual Web Developer creates a code-behind file named Default.aspx.vb. To open the ASPX file's code-behind file, right click the ASPX file and select **View Code** or click the **View Code**

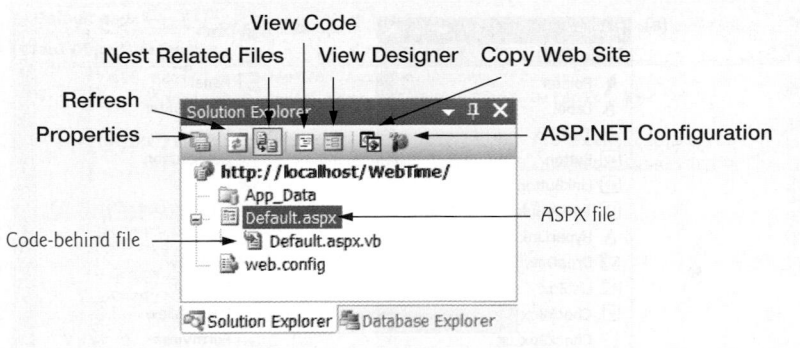

Fig. 21.8 | **Solution Explorer** window for project WebTime.

button (⊞) at the top of the **Solution Explorer**. Alternatively, you can expand the node for the ASPX file to reveal the node for the code-behind file (see Fig. 21.8). You can also choose to list all the files in the project individually (instead of nested) by clicking the **Nest Related Files** button—this option is turned on by default, so clicking the button toggles the option off.

The **Properties** and **Refresh** buttons in Visual Web Developer's **Solution Explorer** behave like those in Visual Basic 2005 Express. Visual Web Developer's **Solution Explorer** also contains the buttons **View Designer**, **Copy Web Site** and **ASP.NET Configuration**. The **View Designer** button allows you to open the Web Form in **Design** mode, which we discuss shortly. The **Copy Web Site** button opens a dialog that allows you to move the files in this project to another location, such as a remote Web server. This is useful if you are developing the application on your local computer, but want to make it available to the public from a different location. Finally, the **ASP.NET Configuration** button takes you to a Web page called the **Web Site Administration Tool**, where you can manipulate various settings and security options for your application. We discuss this tool in greater detail in Section 21.8.

Step 3: Examining the Toolbox in Visual Web Developer
Figure 21.9 shows the **Toolbox** displayed in the IDE when the project loads. Figure 21.9(a) displays the beginning of the **Standard** list of Web controls, and Fig. 21.9(b) displays the remaining Web controls, and the list of **Data** controls used in ASP.NET. We discuss specific controls in Fig. 21.9 as they are used throughout the chapter. Notice that some controls in the **Toolbox** are similar to the Windows controls presented earlier in the book.

Step 4: Examining the Web Forms Designer
Figure 21.10 shows the Web Forms Designer in **Source** mode, which appears in the center of the IDE. When the project loads for the first time, the Web Forms Designer displays the auto-generated ASPX file (i.e., Default.aspx) in **Source** mode, which allows you to view and edit the markup that comprises the Web page. The markup listed in Fig. 21.10 was created by the IDE and serves as a template that we will modify shortly. Clicking the **Design** button in the lower-left corner of the Web Forms Designer switches to **Design** mode (Fig. 21.11), which allows you to drag and drop controls from the **Toolbox** on the

appears as in line 4 of Fig. 21.4. The value of the Inherits attribute and the class name in the code-behind file must be identical; otherwise, you'll get errors when you build the Web application.

Step 8: Changing the Title of the Page

Before designing the content of the Web Form, we change its title from the default Untitled Page (line 9 of Fig. 21.10) to A Simple Web Form Example. To do so, open the ASPX file in **Source** mode and modify the text in the title element—i.e., the text between the tags <title> and </title>). Alternatively, you can open the ASPX file in **Design** mode and modify the Web Form's **Title** property in the **Properties** window. To view the Web Form's properties, select DOCUMENT from the drop-down list in the **Properties** window; DOCUMENT represents the Web Form in the **Properties** window.

Step 9: Designing the Page

Designing a Web Form is as simple as designing a Windows Form. To add controls to the page, drag-and-drop them from the **Toolbox** onto the Web Form in **Design** mode. Like the Web Form itself, each control is an object that has properties, methods and events. You can set these properties and events visually using the **Properties** window or programmatically in the code-behind file. However, unlike working with a Windows Form, you can type text directly on a Web Form at the cursor location or insert XHTML elements using menu commands.

Controls and other elements are placed sequentially on a Web Form, much like how text and images are placed in a document using word processing software like Microsoft Word. Controls are placed one after another in the order in which you drag-and-drop them onto the Web Form. The cursor indicates the point at which text and XHTML elements will be inserted. If you want to position a control between existing text or controls, you can drop the control at a specific position within the existing elements. You can also rearrange existing controls using drag-and-drop actions. The positions of controls and other elements are relative to the Web Form's upper-left corner. This type of layout is known as relative positioning.

An alternate type of layout is known as absolute positioning, in which controls are located exactly where they are dropped on the Web Form. You can enable absolute positioning in **Design** mode by selecting **Layout > Position > Auto-position Options....**, then clicking the first checkbox in the **Positioning options** pane of the **Options** dialog that appears.

Portability Tip 21.2

Absolute positioning is discouraged, because pages designed in this manner may not render correctly on computers with different screen resolutions and font sizes. This could cause absolutely positioned elements to overlap each other or display off-screen, requiring the client to scroll to see the full page content.

In this example, we use one piece of text and one Label. To add the text to the Web Form, click the blank Web Form in **Design** mode and type Current time on the Web server:. Visual Web Developer is a WYSIWYG (What You See Is What You Get) editor—whenever you make a change to a Web Form in **Design** mode, the IDE creates the markup (visible in **Source** mode) necessary to achieve the desired visual effects seen in Design mode. After adding the text to the Web Form, switch to **Source** mode. You should see that the IDE added this text to the div element that appears in the ASPX file by default. Back in **Design** mode, highlight the text you added. From the **Block Format** drop-down list (see Fig. 21.13), choose **Heading 2** to format this text as a heading that will appear bold in a font slightly larger than the default. This action encloses the text in an h2 element. Finally, click to the right of the text and press the *Enter* key to start a new paragraph. This action generates a p (paragraph) element in the ASPX file's markup. The IDE should now look like Fig. 21.13.

You can place a Label on a Web Form either by dragging-and-dropping or by double clicking the **Toolbox**'s **Label** control. Ensure that the cursor is in the new paragraph, then add a Label that will be used to display the time. Using the **Properties** window, set the (ID) property of the Label to timeLabel. Delete timeLabel's text, because this text will be set programmatically in the code-behind file. When a Label does not contain text, its name is displayed in square brackets in the Web Forms Designer (Fig. 21.14) as a placeholder for design and layout purposes. This text is not displayed at execution time. We set timeLabel's BackColor, ForeColor and Font-Size properties to Black, Yellow and XX-Large, respectively. To change the Label's font properties, select the Label, expand the Font node in the **Properties** window and change each relevant property. As the Label's properties are set, Visual Web Developer updates the ASPX file's contents. Figure 21.14 shows the IDE after setting these properties.

Next, set the Label's EnableViewState property to False. Finally, select DOCUMENT from the drop-down list in the **Properties** window and set the Web Form's EnableSessionState property to False. We discuss both of these properties later in the chapter.

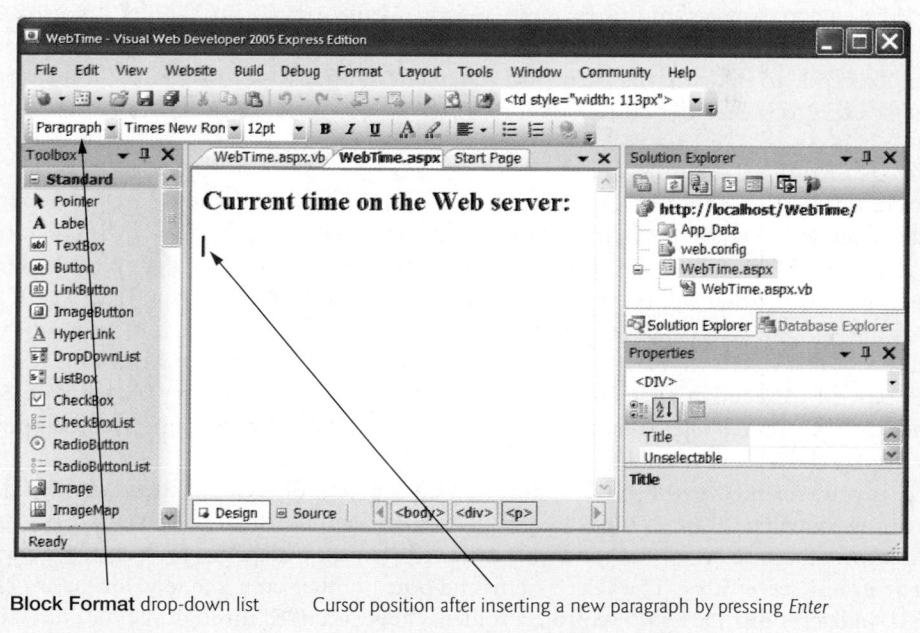

Block Format drop-down list   Cursor position after inserting a new paragraph by pressing *Enter*

Fig. 21.13 | WebTime.aspx after inserting text and a new paragraph.

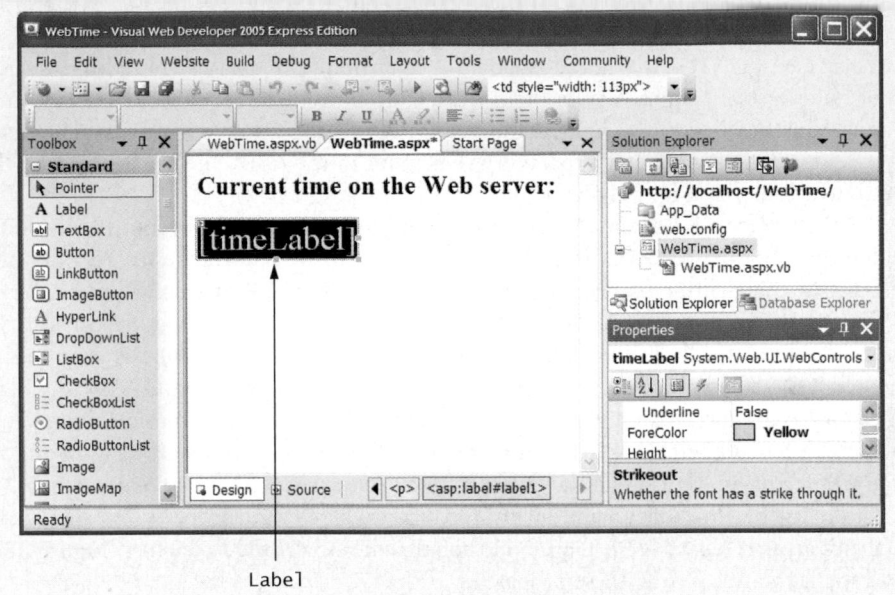

Fig. 21.14 | `WebTime.aspx` after adding a `Label` and setting its properties.

Step 10: Adding Page Logic

Now that you've designed the user interface, you'll add Visual Basic code to the code-behind file to obtain the server's time. Open `WebTime.aspx.vb` by double clicking its node in the **Solution Explorer**. In this example, we add a `Page_Init` event handler (lines 16–21 of Fig. 21.5) to the code-behind file. Recall that `Page_Init` handles the `Init` event and contains code to initialize the page. The statement in lines 10–11 of Fig. 21.5 sets `time-Label`'s text to the server's current time.

Step 11: Running the Program

After creating the Web Form, you can view it several ways. First, you can select **Debug > Start Without Debugging**, which runs the application by opening it in a browser window. If you created the application on your local IIS server (as we did in this example), the URL shown in the browser will be `http://localhost/WebTime/WebTime.aspx` (Fig. 21.5), indicating that the Web page (the ASPX file) is located within the virtual directory `WebTime` on the local IIS Web server. IIS must be running to test the Web site in a browser. IIS can be started by executing `inetmgr.exe` from **Start > Run...**, right clicking **Default Web Site** and selecting **Start**. [*Note:* You might need to expand the node representing your computer to display the **Default Web Site**.]

If you created the ASP.NET application on the local file system, the URL shown in the browser will be `http://localhost:`*PortNumber*`/WebTime/WebTime.aspx`, where *Port-Number* is the number of the randomly assigned port on which Visual Web Developer's built-in test server runs. The IDE assigns the port number on a per solution basis. This URL indicates that the `WebTime` project folder is being accessed through the root directory of the test server running at `localhost:`*PortNumber*. When you select **Debug > Start Without Debugging**, a tray icon appears near the bottom-right of your screen next to the computer's date and time to show that the **ASP.NET Development Server** is running. The test server stops when you exit Visual Web Developer.

To debug your application, you can select **Debug > Start Debugging** to view the Web page in a Web browser with debugging enabled. You cannot debug a Web application unless debugging is explicitly enabled by the `Web.config` file—a file that stores configuration settings for an ASP.NET Web application. You will rarely need to manually create or modify `Web.config`. The first time you select **Debug > Start Debugging** in a project, a dialog appears and asks whether you want the IDE to modify the `Web.config` file to enable debugging. After you click **OK**, the IDE enters **Running** mode. You can exit **Running** mode by selecting **Debug > Stop Debugging** in Visual Web Developer or by closing the browser window in which the ASPX file is displayed.

To view a specific ASPX file, you can right click either the Web Forms Designer or the ASPX file name (in the **Solution Explorer**) and select **View In Browser** to load the page in a Web browser. Right clicking the ASPX file in the **Solution Explorer** and selecting **Browse With...** also opens the page in a browser, but first allows you to specify the Web browser that should display the page and its screen resolution.

Finally, you can run your application by opening a browser window and typing the Web page's URL in the **Address** field. When testing an ASP.NET application on the same computer running IIS, type `http://localhost/`*ProjectFolder*`/`*PageName*`.aspx`, where *ProjectFolder* is the folder in which the page resides (usually the name of the project), and *PageName* is the name of the ASP.NET page. If your application resides on the local file system, you must first start the **ASP.NET Development Server** by running the application using one of the methods described above. Then you can type the URL (including the *PortNumber* found in the test server's tray icon) in the browser to execute the application.

Note that all of these methods of running the application compile the project for you. In fact, ASP.NET compiles your Web page whenever it changes between HTTP requests. For example, suppose you browse the page, then modify the ASPX file or add code to the code-behind file. When you reload the page, ASP.NET recompiles the page on the server before returning the HTTP response to the browser. This important new behavior of ASP.NET 2.0 ensures that clients always see the latest version of the page. You can manually compile a Web page or an entire Web site by selecting **Build Page** or **Build Site**, respectively, from the **Build** menu in Visual Web Developer.

Windows Firewall Settings

If you would like to test your Web application over a network, you may need to change your Windows Firewall settings. For security reasons, Windows Firewall does not allow remote access to a Web server on your local computer by default. To change this, open the Windows Firewall utility in the Windows Control Panel. Click the **Advanced** tab and select your network connection from the **Network Connection Settings** list, then click **Settings....** On the **Services** tab of the **Advanced Settings** dialog, ensure that **Web Server (HTTP)** is checked.

21.5 **Web Controls**

This section introduces some of the Web controls located in the **Standard** section of the **Toolbox** (Fig. 21.9). Figure 21.15 summarizes some of the Web controls used in the chapter examples.

Web Control	Description
Label	Displays text that the user cannot edit.
TextBox	Gathers user input and displays text.
Button	Triggers an event when clicked.
HyperLink	Displays a hyperlink.
DropDownList	Displays a drop-down list of choices from which a user can select an item.
RadioButtonList	Groups radio buttons.
Image	Displays images (e.g., GIF and JPG).

Fig. 21.15 | Commonly used Web controls.

21.5.1 Text and Graphics Controls

Figure 21.16 depicts a simple form for gathering user input. This example uses all the controls listed in Fig. 21.15, except Label, which you used in Section 21.4. The code in Fig. 21.16 was generated by Visual Web Developer in response to dragging controls onto the page in **Design** mode. To begin, create an ASP.NET Web Site named WebControls. [*Note:* This example does not contain any functionality—i.e., no action occurs when the user clicks **Register**. We ask you to provide the functionality as an exercise. In subsequent examples, we demonstrate how to add functionality to many of these Web controls.]

Before discussing the Web controls used in this ASPX file, we explain the XHTML that creates the layout seen in Fig. 21.16. The page contains an h3 heading element (line 16), followed by a series of additional XHTML blocks. We place most of the Web controls inside p elements (i.e., paragraphs), but we use an XHTML table element (lines 25–55) to organize the Image and TextBox controls in the user information section of the page. In the preceding section, we described how to add heading elements and paragraphs visually without manipulating any XHTML in the ASPX file directly. Visual Web Developer allows you to add a table in a similar manner.

Adding an XHTML Table to a Web Form

To create a table with two rows and two columns in **Design** mode, select the **Insert Table** command from the **Layout** menu. In the **Insert Table** dialog that appears, select the **Custom** radio button. In the **Layout** group box, change the values of **Rows** and **Columns** to 2. By default, the contents of a table cell are aligned vertically in the middle of the cell. We changed the vertical alignment of all cells in the table by clicking the **Cell Properties...** button, then selecting **top** from the **Vertical align** combo box in the resulting dialog. This causes the content of each table cell to align with the top of the cell. Click **OK** to close the **Cell Properties** dialog, then click **OK** to close the **Insert Table** dialog and create the table. Once a table is created, controls and text can be added to particular cells to create a neatly organized layout.

```
1    <%-- Fig. 21.16: WebControls.aspx --%>
2    <%-- Registration form that demonstrates Web controls. --%>
3    <%@ Page Language="VB" AutoEventWireup="false"
4       CodeFile="WebControls.aspx.vb" Inherits="WebControls" %>
5
6    <!DOCTYPE html PUBLIC "-//W3C//DTD XHTML 1.0 Transitional//EN"
7       "http://www.w3.org/TR/xhtml1/DTD/xhtml1-transitional.dtd">
8
9    <html xmlns="http://www.w3.org/1999/xhtml">
10   <head runat="server">
11      <title>Web Controls Demonstration</title>
12   </head>
13   <body>
14      <form id="form1" runat="server">
15      <div>
16         <h3>This is a sample registration form.</h3>
17         <p>
18            <em>Please fill in all fields and click Register.</em></p>
19         <p>
20            <asp:Image ID="userInformationImage" runat="server"
21               EnableViewState="False" ImageUrl="~/Images/user.png" />  
22            <span style="color: teal">
23               Please fill out the fields below.</span>
24         </p>
25         <table id="TABLE1">
26            <tr>
27               <td style="width: 230px; height: 21px" valign="top">
28                  <asp:Image ID="firstNameImage" runat="server"
29                     EnableViewState="False" ImageUrl="~/Images/fname.png" />
30                  <asp:TextBox ID="firstNameTextBox" runat="server"
31                     EnableViewState="False"></asp:TextBox>
32               </td>
33               <td style="width: 231px; height: 21px" valign="top">
34                  <asp:Image ID="lastNameImage" runat="server"
35                     EnableViewState="False" ImageUrl="~/Images/lname.png" />
36                  <asp:TextBox ID="lastNameTextBox" runat="server"
37                     EnableViewState="False"></asp:TextBox>
38               </td>
39            </tr>
40            <tr>
41               <td style="width: 230px" valign="top">
42                  <asp:Image ID="emailImage" runat="server"
43                     EnableViewState="False" ImageUrl="~/Images/email.png" />
44                  <asp:TextBox ID="emailTextBox" runat="server"
45                     EnableViewState="False"></asp:TextBox>
46               </td>
47               <td style="width: 231px" valign="top">
48                  <asp:Image ID="phoneImage" runat="server"
49                     EnableViewState="False" ImageUrl="~/Images/phone.png" />
50                  <asp:TextBox ID="phoneTextBox" runat="server"
51                     EnableViewState="False"></asp:TextBox>
52                  Must be in the form (555) 555-5555.
```

Fig. 21.16 | Web Form that demonstrates Web controls. (Part 1 of 3.)

```
53                    </td>
54                </tr>
55            </table>
56            <p>
57                <asp:Image ID="publicationsImage" runat="server"
58                    EnableViewState="False"
59                    ImageUrl="~/Images/publications.png" />  
60                <span style="color: teal">
61                    Which book would you like information about?</span>
62            </p>
63            <p>
64                <asp:DropDownList ID="booksDropDownList" runat="server"
65                    EnableViewState="False">
66                    <asp:ListItem>Visual Basic 2005 How to Program 3e
67                        </asp:ListItem>
68                    <asp:ListItem>Visual C# 2005 How to Program 2e
69                        </asp:ListItem>
70                    <asp:ListItem>Java How to Program 6e</asp:ListItem>
71                    <asp:ListItem>C++ How to Program 5e</asp:ListItem>
72                    <asp:ListItem>XML How to Program 1e</asp:ListItem>
73                </asp:DropDownList>
74            </p>
75            <p>
76                <asp:HyperLink ID="booksHyperLink" runat="server"
77                    EnableViewState="False" NavigateUrl="http://www.deitel.com"
78                    Target="_blank">
79                    Click here to view more information about our books
80                </asp:HyperLink>
81            </p>
82            <p>
83                <asp:Image ID="osImage" runat="server" EnableViewState="False"
84                    ImageUrl="~/Images/os.png" />  
85                <span style="color: teal">
86                    Which operating system are you using?</span>
87            </p>
88            <p>
89                <asp:RadioButtonList ID="operatingSystemRadioButtonList"
90                    runat="server" EnableViewState="False">
91                    <asp:ListItem>Windows XP</asp:ListItem>
92                    <asp:ListItem>Windows 2000</asp:ListItem>
93                    <asp:ListItem>Windows NT</asp:ListItem>
94                    <asp:ListItem>Linux</asp:ListItem>
95                    <asp:ListItem>Other</asp:ListItem>
96                </asp:RadioButtonList>
97            </p>
98            <p>
99                <asp:Button ID="registerButton" runat="server"
100                   EnableViewState="False" Text="Register" />
101           </p>
102        </div>
103        </form>
104 </body>
105 </html>
```

Fig. 21.16 | Web Form that demonstrates Web controls. (Part 2 of 3.)

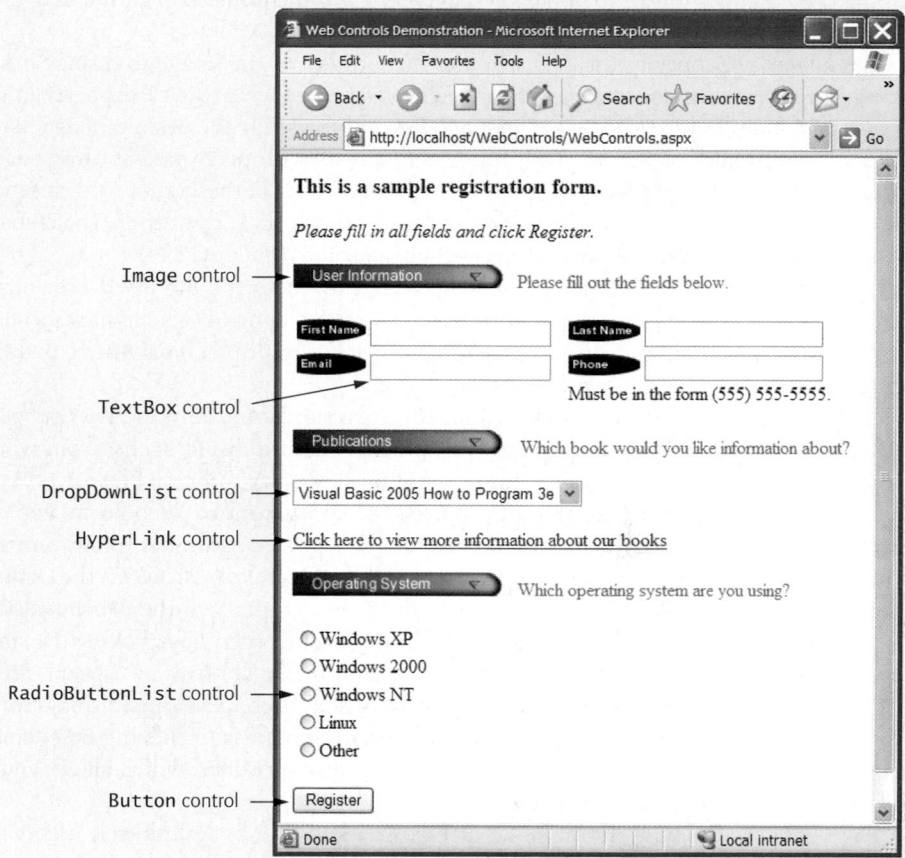

Image control —▶

TextBox control —▶

DropDownList control —▶

HyperLink control —▶

RadioButtonList control —▶

Button control —▶

Fig. 21.16 | Web Form that demonstrates Web controls. (Part 3 of 3.)

Setting the Color of Text on a Web Form

Notice that some of the instructions to the user on the form appear in a teal color. To set the color of a specific piece of text, highlight the text and select **Format > Foreground color...**. In the **Color Picker** dialog, click the **Named Colors** tab and choose a color. Click **OK** to apply the color. Note that the IDE places the colored text in an XHTML span element (e.g., lines 22–23) and applies the color using the span's style attribute.

Examining Web Controls on a Sample Registration Form

Lines 20–21 of Fig. 21.16 define an Image control, which inserts an image into a Web page. The images used in this example are located in the chapter's examples directory. You can download the examples from www.deitel.com/books/vbhtp3. Before an image can be displayed on a Web page using an Image Web control, the image must first be added to the project. We added an Images folder to this project (and to each example project in the chapter that uses images) by right clicking the location of the project in the **Solution Explorer**, selecting **New Folder** and entering the folder name Images. We then added each of the images used in the example to this folder by right clicking the folder, selecting **Add Existing Item...** and browsing for the files to add. You can also drag a folder full of images onto the project's location in the **Solution Explorer** to add the folder and all the images to the project.

The `ImageUrl` property (line 21) specifies the location of the image to display in the `Image` control. To select an image, click the ellipsis next to the `ImageUrl` property in the **Properties** window and use the **Select Image** dialog to browse for the desired image in the project's `Images` folder. When the IDE fills in the `ImageUrl` property based on your selection, it includes a tilde and forward slash (`~/`) at the beginning of the `ImageUrl`—this indicates that the `Images` folder is in the root directory of the project (i.e., `http://localhost/WebControls`, whose physical path is `C:\Inetpub\wwwroot\WebControls`).

Lines 25–55 contain the `table` element created by the steps discussed previously. Each `td` element contains an `Image` control and a `TextBox` control, which allows you to obtain text from the user and display text to the user. For example, lines 30–31 define a `TextBox` control used to collect the user's first name.

Lines 64–73 define a `DropDownList`. This control is similar to the Windows `ComboBox` control. When a user clicks the drop-down list, it expands and displays a list from which the user can make a selection. Each item in the drop-down list is defined by a `ListItem` element (lines 66–72). After dragging a `DropDownList` control onto a Web Form, you can add items to it using the **ListItem Collection Editor**. This process is similar to customizing a `ListBox` in a Windows application. In Visual Web Developer, you can access the **ListItem Collection Editor** by clicking the ellipsis next to the `Items` property of the `DropDownList`, or by using the **DropDownList Tasks** menu. You can open this menu by clicking the small arrowhead that appears in the upper-right corner of the control in **Design** mode (Fig. 21.17). This menu is called a smart tag menu. Visual Web Developer displays smart tag menus for many ASP.NET controls to facilitate common tasks. Clicking **Edit Items...** in the **DropDownList Tasks** menu opens the **ListItem Collection Editor**, which allows you to add `ListItem` elements to the `DropDownList`.

The `HyperLink` control (lines 76–80 of Fig. 21.16) adds a hyperlink to a Web page. The `NavigateUrl` property (line 77) of this control specifies the resource (i.e., `http://www.deitel.com`) that is requested when a user clicks the hyperlink. Setting the `Target` property to `_blank` specifies that the requested Web page should open in a new browser window. By default, `HyperLink` controls cause pages to open in the same browser window.

Lines 89–96 define a `RadioButtonList` control, which provides a series of radio buttons from which the user can select only one. Like options in a `DropDownList`, individual radio buttons are defined by `ListItem` elements. Note that, like the **DropDownList Tasks** smart tag menu, the **RadioButtonList Tasks** smart tag menu also provides an **Edit Items...** link to open the **ListItem Collection Editor**.

The final Web control in Fig. 21.16 is a `Button` (lines 99–100). A `Button` Web control represents a button that triggers an action when clicked. This control typically maps

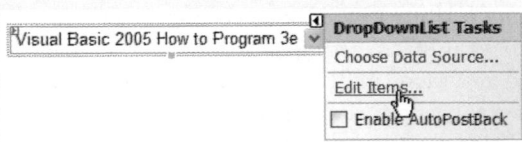

Fig. 21.17 | **DropDownList Tasks** smart tag menu.

to an XHTML input element with attribute type set to "button". As stated earlier, clicking the **Register** button in this example does not do anything.

21.5.2 AdRotator Control

Web pages often contain product or service advertisements, which usually consist of images. Although Web site authors want to include as many sponsors as possible, Web pages can display only a limited number of advertisements. To address this problem, ASP.NET provides the AdRotator Web control for displaying advertisements. Using advertisement data located in an XML file, an AdRotator randomly selects an image to display and generates a hyperlink to the Web page associated with that image. Browsers that do not support images display alternate text that is specified in the XML document. If a user clicks the image or substituted text, the browser loads the Web page associated with that image.

*Demonstrating the **AdRotator** Web Control*
Figure 21.18 demonstrates the AdRotator Web control. In this example, the "advertisements" that we rotate are the flags of 10 countries. When a user clicks the displayed flag image, the browser is redirected to a Web page containing information about the country that the flag represents. If a user refreshes the browser or requests the page again, one of the eleven flags is again chosen at random and displayed.

The ASPX file in Fig. 21.18 is similar to that in Fig. 21.4. However, instead of XHTML text and a Label, this page contains XHTML text (the h3 element in line 17) and an AdRotator control named countryRotator (lines 18–19). This page also contains an XmlDataSource control (lines 20–22), which supplies the data to the AdRotator control. The background attribute of the page's body element (line 13) is set to the image background.png, located in the project's Images folder. To specify this file, click the ellipsis provided next to the Background property of DOCUMENT in the **Properties** window and use the resulting dialog to select background.png from the Images folder. The images and XML file used in this example are both located in the chapter's examples directory.

```
1   <%-- Fig. 21.18: FlagRotator.aspx --%>
2   <%-- A Web Form that displays flags using an AdRotator control. --%>
3   <%@ Page Language="VB" AutoEventWireup="false"
4      CodeFile="FlagRotator.aspx.vb" Inherits="FlagRotator" %>
5
6   <!DOCTYPE html PUBLIC "-//W3C//DTD XHTML 1.0 Transitional//EN"
7      "http://www.w3.org/TR/xhtml1/DTD/xhtml1-transitional.dtd">
8
9   <html xmlns="http://www.w3.org/1999/xhtml" >
10  <head runat="server">
11     <title>Flag Rotator</title>
12  </head>
13  <body background="Images/background.png">
14     <form id="form1" runat="server">
15     <div>
16        <h3>AdRotator Example</h3>
17        <p>
```

Fig. 21.18 | Web Form that demonstrates the AdRotator Web control. (Part 1 of 2.)

```
18              <asp:AdRotator ID="countryRotator" runat="server"
19                 DataSourceID="adXmlDataSource" />
20              <asp:XmlDataSource ID="adXmlDataSource" runat="server"
21                 DataFile="~/App_Data/AdRotatorInformation.xml">
22              </asp:XmlDataSource>
23           </p>
24       </div>
25       </form>
26    </body>
27    </html>
```

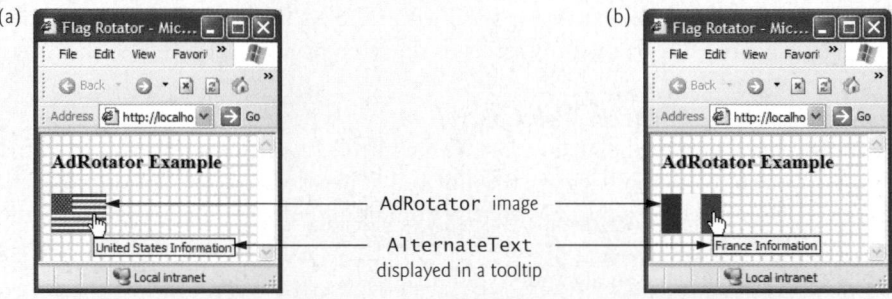

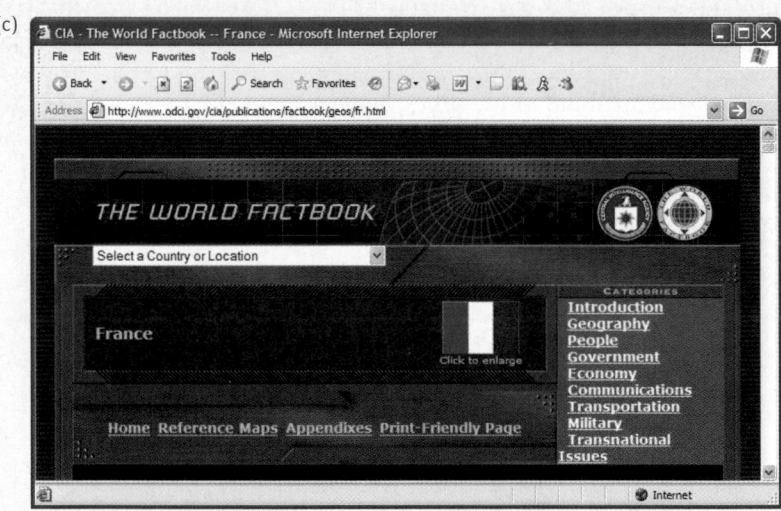

Fig. 21.18 | Web Form that demonstrates the `AdRotator` Web control. (Part 2 of 2.)

You do not need to add any code to the code-behind file, because the `AdRotator` control "does all the work." The output depicts two different requests. Figure 21.18(a) shows the first time the page is requested, when the American flag is shown. In the second request, as shown in Fig. 21.18(b), the French flag is displayed. Figure 21.18(c) depicts the Web page that loads when the French flag is clicked.

*Connecting Data to an **AdRotator** Control*

An AdRotator control accesses an XML file (presented shortly) to determine what advertisement (i.e., flag) image, hyperlink URL and alternate text to display and include in the page. To connect the AdRotator control to the XML file, we create an **XmlDataSource** control—one of several ASP.NET data controls (found in the **Data** section of the **Toolbox**) that encapsulate data sources and make such data available for Web controls. An XmlData-Source references an XML file containing data that will be used in an ASP.NET application. Later in the chapter, you will learn more about data-bound Web controls, as well as the SqlDataSource control, which retrieves data from a SQL Server database, and the ObjectDataSource control, which encapsulates an object that makes data available.

To build this example, we first add the XML file AdRotatorInformation.xml to the project. Each project created in Visual Web Developer contains an App_Data folder, which is intended to store all the data used by the project. Right click this folder in the **Solution Explorer** and select **Add Existing Item...**, then browse for AdRotatorInformation.xml on your computer. We provide this file in the chapter's examples directory in the subdirectory named exampleXMLFiles.

After adding the XML file to the project, drag an AdRotator control from the **Toolbox** to the Web Form. The **AdRotator Tasks** smart tag menu will open automatically. From this menu, select **<New Data Source...>** from the **Choose Data Source** drop-down list to start the **Data Source Configuration Wizard**. Select **XML File** as the data-source type. This causes the wizard to create an XmlDataSource with the ID specified in the bottom half of the wizard dialog. We set the ID of the control to adXmlDataSource. Click **OK** in the **Data Source Configuration Wizard** dialog. The **Configure Data Source - adXmlDataSource** dialog appears next. In this dialog's **Data File** section, click **Browse...** and, in the **Select XML File** dialog, locate and select the XML file you added to the App_Data folder. Click **OK** to exit this dialog, then click **OK** to exit the **Configure Data Source - adXmlDataSource** dialog. After completing these steps, the AdRotator is configured to use the XML file to determine which advertisements to display.

Examining an XML File Containing Advertisement Information

XML document AdRotatorInformation.xml (Fig. 21.19)—or any XML document used with an AdRotator control—must contain one **Advertisements** root element (lines 4–94). Within that element can be several **Ad** elements (e.g., lines 5–12), each of which provides information about a different advertisement. Element **ImageUrl** (line 6) specifies the path (location) of the advertisement's image, and element **NavigateUrl** (lines 7–9) specifies the URL for the Web page that loads when a user clicks the advertisement. Note that we reformatted this file for presentation purposes. The actual XML file cannot contain any whitespace before or after the URL in the NavigateUrl element, or the whitespace will be considered part of the URL, and the page will not load properly.

The **AlternateText** element (line 10) nested in each Ad element contains text that displays in place of the image when the browser cannot locate or render the image for some reason (i.e., the file is missing, or the browser is not capable of displaying it), or to assist the visually impaired. The AlternateText element's text is also a tooltip that Internet Explorer displays when a user places the mouse pointer over the image (Fig. 21.18). The **Impressions** element (line 56) specifies how often a particular image appears, relative to the other images. An advertisement that has a higher Impressions value displays more frequently than an advertisement with a lower value. In our example, the advertisements display with equal probability, because the value of each Impressions element is set to 1.

```xml
 1   <?xml version="1.0" encoding="utf-8"?>
 2   <!-- Fig. 21.19: AdRotatorInformation.xml -->
 3   <!-- XML file containing advertisement information. -->
 4   <Advertisements>
 5      <Ad>
 6         <ImageUrl>Images/france.png</ImageUrl>
 7         <NavigateUrl>
 8            http://www.odci.gov/cia/publications/factbook/geos/fr.html
 9         </NavigateUrl>
10         <AlternateText>France Information</AlternateText>
11         <Impressions>1</Impressions>
12      </Ad>
13
14      <Ad>
15         <ImageUrl>Images/germany.png</ImageUrl>
16         <NavigateUrl>
17            http://www.odci.gov/cia/publications/factbook/geos/gm.html
18         </NavigateUrl>
19         <AlternateText>Germany Information</AlternateText>
20         <Impressions>1</Impressions>
21      </Ad>
22
23      <Ad>
24         <ImageUrl>Images/italy.png</ImageUrl>
25         <NavigateUrl>
26            http://www.odci.gov/cia/publications/factbook/geos/it.html
27         </NavigateUrl>
28         <AlternateText>Italy Information</AlternateText>
29         <Impressions>1</Impressions>
30      </Ad>
31
32      <Ad>
33         <ImageUrl>Images/spain.png</ImageUrl>
34         <NavigateUrl>
35            http://www.odci.gov/cia/publications/factbook/geos/sp.html
36         </NavigateUrl>
37         <AlternateText>Spain Information</AlternateText>
38         <Impressions>1</Impressions>
39      </Ad>
40
41      <Ad>
42         <ImageUrl>Images/latvia.png</ImageUrl>
43         <NavigateUrl>
44            http://www.odci.gov/cia/publications/factbook/geos/lg.html
45         </NavigateUrl>
46         <AlternateText>Latvia Information</AlternateText>
47         <Impressions>1</Impressions>
48      </Ad>
```

Fig. 21.19 | XML file containing advertisement information used in AdRotator example. (Part 1 of 2.)

```
49
50      <Ad>
51          <ImageUrl>Images/peru.png</ImageUrl>
52          <NavigateUrl>
53              http://www.odci.gov/cia/publications/factbook/geos/pe.html
54          </NavigateUrl>
55          <AlternateText>Peru Information</AlternateText>
56          <Impressions>1</Impressions>
57      </Ad>
58
59      <Ad>
60          <ImageUrl>Images/senegal.png</ImageUrl>
61          <NavigateUrl>
62              http://www.odci.gov/cia/publications/factbook/geos/sg.html
63          </NavigateUrl>
64          <AlternateText>Senegal Information</AlternateText>
65          <Impressions>1</Impressions>
66      </Ad>
67
68      <Ad>
69          <ImageUrl>Images/sweden.png</ImageUrl>
70          <NavigateUrl>
71              http://www.odci.gov/cia/publications/factbook/geos/sw.html
72          </NavigateUrl>
73          <AlternateText>Sweden Information</AlternateText>
74          <Impressions>1</Impressions>
75      </Ad>
76
77      <Ad>
78          <ImageUrl>Images/thailand.png</ImageUrl>
79          <NavigateUrl>
80              http://www.odci.gov/cia/publications/factbook/geos/th.html
81          </NavigateUrl>
82          <AlternateText>Thailand Information</AlternateText>
83          <Impressions>1</Impressions>
84      </Ad>
85
86      <Ad>
87          <ImageUrl>Images/unitedstates.png</ImageUrl>
88          <NavigateUrl>
89              http://www.odci.gov/cia/publications/factbook/geos/us.html
90          </NavigateUrl>
91          <AlternateText>United States Information</AlternateText>
92          <Impressions>1</Impressions>
93      </Ad>
94  </Advertisements>
```

Fig. 21.19 | XML file containing advertisement information used in `AdRotator` example. (Part 2 of 2.)

21.5.3 Validation Controls

This section introduces a different type of Web control, called a **validation control** (or **validator**), which determines whether the data in another Web control is in the proper format. For example, validators could determine whether a user has provided information in a required field or whether a ZIP-code field contains exactly five digits. Validators provide a mechanism for validating user input on the client. When the XHTML for our page is created, the validator is converted into ECMAScript[1] that performs the validation. ECMAScript is a scripting language that enhances the functionality and appearance of Web pages and is typically executed on the client. However, some clients do not support scripting or disable scripting. So, for security reasons, validation is always performed on the server—whether or not scripting is enabled on the client.

Validating Input in a Web Form

The example in this section prompts the user to enter a name, e-mail address and phone number. A Web site could use a form like this to collect contact information from site visitors. After the user enters any data, but before the data is sent to the Web server, validators ensure that the user entered a value in each field and that the e-mail address and phone number values are in an acceptable format. In this example, (555) 123-4567, 555-123-4567 and 123-4567 are all considered valid phone numbers. Once the data is submitted, the Web server responds by displaying an appropriate message and an XHTML table repeating the submitted information. Note that a real business application would typically store the submitted data in a database or in a file on the server. We simply send the data back to the form to demonstrate that the server received the data.

Figure 21.20 presents the ASPX file. Like the Web Form in Fig. 21.16, this Web Form uses a `table` to organize the page's contents. Lines 24–25, 36–37 and 58–59 define TextBoxes for retrieving the user's name, e-mail address and phone number, respectively, and line 78 defines a **Submit** button. Lines 80–82 create a `Label` named `outputLabel` that displays the response from the server when the user successfully submits the form. Notice that `outputLabel`'s `Visible` property is initially set to `False` (line 81), so the `Label` does not appear in the client's browser when the page loads for the first time.

Using **RequiredFieldValidator** Controls

In this example, we use three `RequiredFieldValidator` controls (found in the **Validation** section of the **Toolbox**) to ensure that the name, e-mail address and phone number TextBoxes are not empty when the form is submitted. A `RequiredFieldValidator` makes an input control a required field. If such a field is empty, validation fails. For example, lines 26–30 define `RequiredFieldValidator` `nameInputValidator`, which confirms that `nameTextBox` is not empty. Line 28 associates `nameTextBox` with `nameInputValidator` by setting the validator's `ControlToValidate` property to `nameTextBox`. This indicates that `nameInputValidator` verifies the `nameTextBox`'s contents. We set the value of this property (and the validator's other properties) by selecting the validator in **Design** mode and using the **Properties** window to specify property values. Property `ErrorMessage`'s text (line 29) is displayed on the Web Form if the validation fails. If the user does not input any data in `nameTextBox` and attempts to submit the form, the `ErrorMessage` text is displayed in

---

1. ECMAScript (commonly known as JavaScript) is a scripting standard developed by ECMA International. Both Netscape's JavaScript and Microsoft's JScript implement the ECMAScript standard, but each provides additional features beyond the specification. For information on the current ECMAScript standard, visit www.ecma-international.org/publications/standards/Ecma-262.htm. See www.mozilla.org/js for information on JavaScript and msdn.microsoft.com/library/en-us/script56/html/js56jsoriJScript.asp for information on JScript.

red. Because we set the validator's `Display` property to `Dynamic` (line 28), the validator is displayed on the Web Form only when validation fails. Space is allocated dynamically when validation fails, causing the controls below the validator to shift downward to accommodate the `ErrorMessage`, as seen in Fig. 21.20(a)–(c).

Using RegularExpressionValidator Controls

This example also uses `RegularExpressionValidator` controls to match the e-mail address and phone number entered by the user against regular expressions. (Regular expressions are introduced in Chapter 16.) These controls determine whether the e-mail address and phone number were each entered in a valid format. For example, lines 44–51 create a `RegularExpressionValidator` named `emailFormatValidator`. Line 46 sets property `ControlToValidate` to `emailTextBox` to indicate that `emailFormatValidator` verifies the `emailTextBox`'s contents.

```
 1    <%-- Fig. 21.20: Validation.aspx --%>
 2    <%-- Form that demonstrates using validators to validate user input. --%>
 3    <%@ Page Language="VB" AutoEventWireup="false"
 4       CodeFile="Validation.aspx.vb" Inherits="Validation" %>
 5
 6    <!DOCTYPE html PUBLIC "-//W3C//DTD XHTML 1.0 Transitional//EN"
 7       "http://www.w3.org/TR/xhtml1/DTD/xhtml1-transitional.dtd">
 8
 9    <html xmlns="http://www.w3.org/1999/xhtml" >
10    <head runat="server">
11       <title>Demonstrating Validation Controls</title>
12    </head>
13    <body>
14       <form id="form1" runat="server">
15       <div>
16          Please fill out the following form.<br /><em>All fields are
17          required and must contain valid information.</em><br />
18          <br />
19          <table>
20             <tr>
21                <td style="width: 100px" valign="top">
22                   Name:</td>
23                <td style="width: 450px" valign="top">
24                   <asp:TextBox ID="nameTextBox" runat="server">
25                   </asp:TextBox><br />
26                   <asp:RequiredFieldValidator
27                      ID="nameInputValidator" runat="server"
28                      ControlToValidate="nameTextBox" Display="Dynamic"
29                      ErrorMessage="Please enter your name.">
30                   </asp:RequiredFieldValidator>
31                </td>
32             </tr>
33             <tr>
34                <td style-"width: 100px" valign="top">E-mail address:</td>
35                <td style="width: 450px" valign="top">
```

Fig. 21.20 | Validators used in a Web Form that retrieves user's contact information. (Part 1 of 4.)

```
36                  <asp:TextBox ID="emailTextBox" runat="server">
37                  </asp:TextBox>
38                   e.g., user@domain.com<br />
39                  <asp:RequiredFieldValidator
40                      ID="emailInputValidator" runat="server"
41                      ControlToValidate="emailTextBox" Display="Dynamic"
42                      ErrorMessage="Please enter your e-mail address.">
43                  </asp:RequiredFieldValidator>
44                  <asp:RegularExpressionValidator
45                      ID="emailFormatValidator" runat="server"
46                      ControlToValidate="emailTextBox" Display="Dynamic"
47                      ErrorMessage=
48                          "Please enter an e-mail address in a valid format."
49                      ValidationExpression=
50                          "\w+([-+.']\w+)*@\w+([-.]\w+)*\.\w+([-.]\w+)*">
51                  </asp:RegularExpressionValidator>
52              </td>
53          </tr>
54          <tr>
55              <td style="width: 100px; height: 21px" valign="top">
56              Phone number:</td>
57              <td style="width: 450px; height: 21px" valign="top">
58                  <asp:TextBox ID="phoneTextBox" runat="server">
59                  </asp:TextBox>
60                   e.g., (555) 555-1234<br />
61                  <asp:RequiredFieldValidator
62                      ID="phoneInputValidator" runat="server"
63                      ControlToValidate="phoneTextBox" Display="Dynamic"
64                      ErrorMessage="Please enter your phone number.">
65                  </asp:RequiredFieldValidator>
66                  <asp:RegularExpressionValidator
67                      ID="phoneFormatValidator" runat="server"
68                      ControlToValidate="phoneTextBox" Display="Dynamic"
69                      ErrorMessage=
70                          "Please enter a phone number in a valid format."
71                      ValidationExpression=
72                          "((\(\d{3}\) ?)|(\d{3}-))?\d{3}-\d{4}">
73                  </asp:RegularExpressionValidator>
74              </td>
75          </tr>
76      </table>
77      <br />
78      <asp:Button ID="submitButton" runat="server" Text="Submit" /><br />
79      <br />
80      <asp:Label ID="outputLabel" runat="server"
81          Text="Thank you for your submission." Visible="False">
82      </asp:Label>
83  </div>
84  </form>
85 </body>
86 </html>
```

Fig. 21.20 | Validators used in a Web Form that retrieves user's contact information. (Part 2 of 4.)

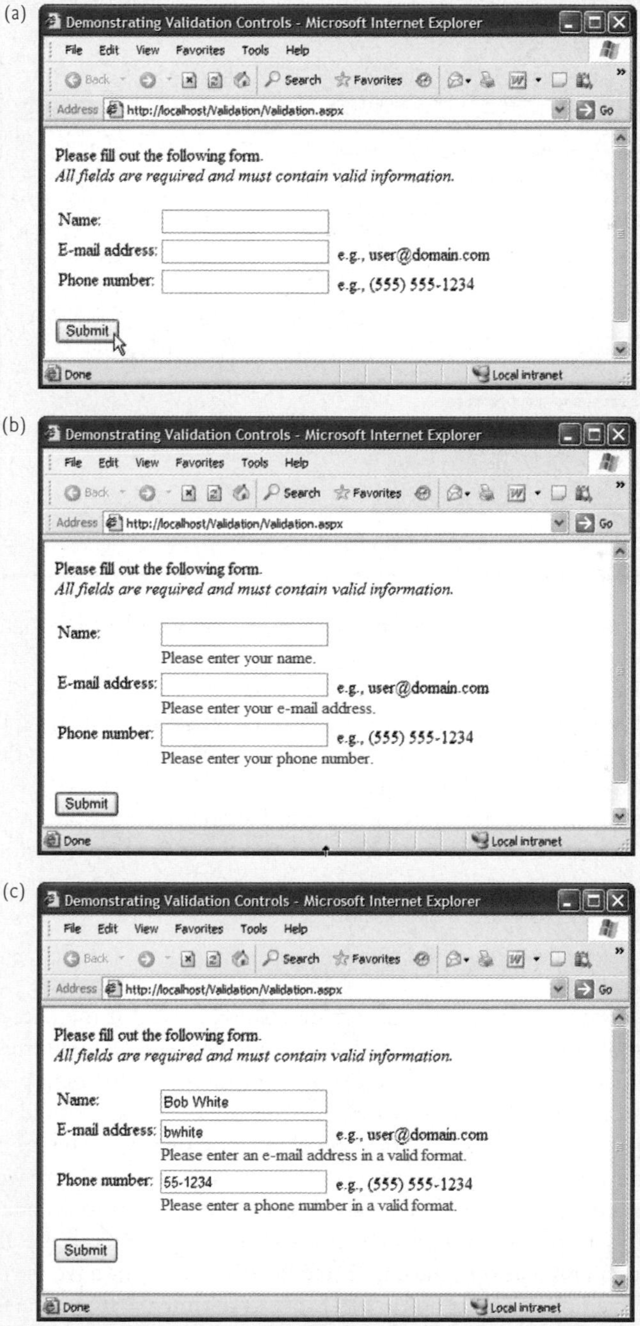

(a)

(b)

(c)

Fig. 21.20 | Validators used in a Web Form that retrieves user's contact information. (Part 3 of 4.)

(d)

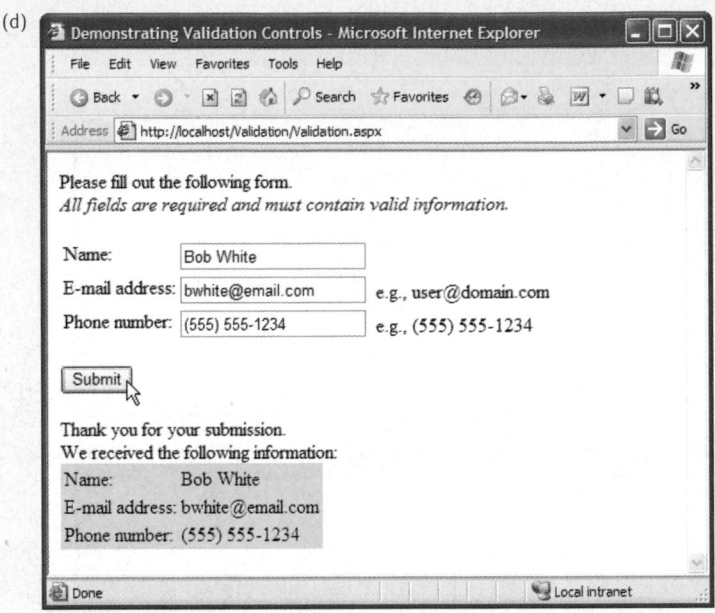

Fig. 21.20 | Validators used in a Web Form that retrieves user's contact information. (Part 4 of 4.)

A RegularExpressionValidator's ValidationExpression property specifies the regular expression that validates the ControlToValidate's contents. Clicking the ellipsis next to property ValidationExpression in the **Properties** window displays the **Regular Expression Editor** dialog, which contains a list of **Standard expressions** for phone numbers, ZIP codes and other formatted information. You can also write your own custom expression. For the emailFormatValidator, we selected the standard expression **Internet e-mail address**, which uses the validation expression

\w+([-+.']\w+)*@\w+([-.]\w+)*\.\w+([-.]\w+)*

This regular expression indicates that an e-mail address is valid if the part of the address before the @ symbol contains one or more word characters (i.e., alphanumeric characters or underscores), followed by zero or more strings comprised of a hyphen, plus sign, period or apostrophe and additional word characters. After the @ symbol, a valid e-mail address must contain one or more groups of word characters potentially separated by hyphens or periods, followed by a required period and another group of one or more word characters potentially separated by hyphens or periods. For example, bob.white@email.com, bob-white@my-email.com and bob's-personal.email@white.email.com are all valid e-mail addresses. If the user enters text in the emailTextBox that does not have the correct format and either clicks in a different text box or attempts to submit the form, the ErrorMessage text is displayed in red.

We also use RegularExpressionValidator phoneFormatValidator (lines 66–73) to ensure that the phoneTextBox contains a valid phone number before the form is submitted. In the **Regular Expression Editor** dialog, we select **U.S. phone number**, which assigns

$$((\backslash(\backslash d\{3\}\backslash) \ ?)|(\backslash d\{3\}-))?\backslash d\{3\}-\backslash d\{4\}$$

to the `ValidationExpression` property. This expression indicates that a phone number can contain a three-digit area code either in parentheses and followed by an optional space or without parentheses and followed by required hyphen. After an optional area code, a phone number must contain three digits, a hyphen and another four digits. For example, (555) 123-4567, 555-123-4567 and 123-4567 are all valid phone numbers.

If all five validators are successful (i.e., each `TextBox` is filled in, and the e-mail address and phone number provided are valid), clicking the **Submit** button sends the form's data to the server. As shown in Fig. 21.20(d), the server then responds by displaying the submitted data in the `outputLabel` (lines 80–82).

Examining the Code-Behind File for a Web Form That Receives User Input

Figure 21.21 depicts the code-behind file for the ASPX file in Fig. 21.20. Notice that this code-behind file does not contain any implementation related to the validators. We say more about this soon.

Web programmers using ASP.NET often design their Web pages so that the current page reloads when the user submits the form; this enables the program to receive input, process it as necessary and display the results in the same page when it is loaded the second time. These pages usually contain a form that when submitted, sends the values of all the controls to the server and causes the current page to be requested again. This event is

```vb
1   ' Fig. 21.21: Validation.aspx.vb
2   ' Code-behind file for the form demonstrating validation controls.
3   Partial Class Validation
4      Inherits System.Web.UI.Page
5
6      ' Page_Load event handler executes when the page is loaded
7      Protected Sub Page_Load(ByVal sender As Object, _
8         ByVal e As System.EventArgs) Handles Me.Load
9         ' if this is not the first time the page is loading
10        ' (i.e., the user has already submitted form data)
11        If IsPostBack Then
12           ' retrieve the values submitted by the user
13           Dim name As String = Request.Form("nameTextBox")
14           Dim email As String = Request.Form("emailTextBox")
15           Dim phone As String = Request.Form("phoneTextBox")
16
17           ' create a table indicating the submitted values
18           outputLabel.Text &= _
19              "<br />We received the following information:" & _
20              "<table style=""background-color: yellow"">" & _
21              "<tr><td>Name: </td><td>" & name & "</td></tr>" & _
22              "<tr><td>E-mail address: </td><td>" & email & "</td></tr>" & _
23              "<tr><td>Phone number: </td><td>" & phone & "</td></tr>" & _
24              "<table>"
25           outputLabel.Visible = True ' display the output message
26        End If
27     End Sub ' Page_Load
28  End Class ' Validation
```

Fig. 21.21 | Code-behind file for a Web Form that obtains a user's contact information.

known as a *postback*. Line 11 uses the **IsPostBack** property of class `Page` to determine whether the page is being loaded due to a postback. The first time that the Web page is requested, `IsPostBack` is `False`, and the page displays only the form for user input. When the postback occurs (from the user clicking **Submit**), `IsPostBack` is `True`.

Lines 13–15 use the **Request** object to retrieve the values of `nameTextBox`, `email-TextBox` and `phoneTextBox` from the `NameValueCollection` **Form**. When data is posted to the Web server, the XHTML form's data is accessible to the Web application through the `Request` object's `Form` array. Lines 18–24 append to `outputLabel`'s `Text` a line break, an additional message and an XHTML table containing the submitted data so the user knows that the server received the data correctly. In a real business application, the data would be stored in a database or file at this point in the application. Line 25 sets the `outputLabel`'s `Visible` property to `True`, so the user can see the thank you message and submitted data.

Examining the Client-Side XHTML for a Web Form with Validation
Figure 21.22 shows the XHTML and ECMAScript sent to the client browser when Val-idation.aspx loads after the postback. (We added the comments in lines 1–2.) To view this code, select **View > Source** in Internet Explorer. Lines 27–55, lines 126–190 and lines 196–212 contain the ECMAScript that provides the implementation for the validation controls and for performing the postback. ASP.NET generates this ECMAScript. You do not need to be able to create or even understand ECMAScript—the functionality defined for the controls in our application is converted to working ECMAScript for us.

```
1   <!-- Fig. 21.22 -->
2   <!-- The XHTML and ECMAScript generated for Validation.aspx -->
3   <!DOCTYPE html PUBLIC "-//W3C//DTD XHTML 1.0 Transitional//EN"
4       "http://www.w3.org/TR/xhtml1/DTD/xhtml1-transitional.dtd">
5   <html xmlns="http://www.w3.org/1999/xhtml" >
6   <head>
7   <title>Demonstrating Validation Controls</title>
8   </head>
9   <body>
10  <form name="form1" method="post" action="Validation.aspx"
11      onsubmit="javascript:return WebForm_OnSubmit();" id="form1">
12      <div>
13          <input type="hidden" name="__EVENTTARGET" id="__EVENTTARGET"
14              value="" />
15          <input type="hidden" name="__EVENTARGUMENT" id="__EVENTARGUMENT"
16              value="" />
17          <input type="hidden" name="__VIEWSTATE" id="__VIEWSTATE"
18              value="/wEPDwUJMzg4NDI1NzgzD2QWAgIDD2QWAgITDw8WBB4EVGV4dAWVA1RoY
19              W5rIH1vdSBmb3IgeW91ciBzdWJtaXNzaW9uLjxiciAvPld1IHJlY2VpdmVkIHRoZ
20              SBmb2xsb3dpbmcgaW5mb3JtYXRpb246PHRhYmxlIHN0eWxlPSJiYWNrZ3JvdW5kL
21              WNvbG9yOiB5ZWxsb3ciPjx0cj48dGQ+TmFtZTogPC90ZD48dGQ+Qm9iIFdoaXRlP
22              C90ZD48L3RyPjx0cj48dGQ+RS1tYW1sIGFkZHJlc3M6IDwvdGQ+PHRkPmJ3aGl0
23              ZUB1bWFpbC5jb208L3RkPjwvdHI+PHRyPjx0ZD5QaG9uZSBudW1iZXI6IDwvdGQ+
24              PHRkPig1NTUpIDU1NS0xMjM0PC90ZD48L3RyPjx0YWJsZT4eB1Zpc21ibGVnZGRk
25              qbjgKg1/lLZfogqihtkd1C7nmSk=" />
26      </div>
```

Fig. 21.22 | XHTML and ECMAScript generated by ASP.NET and sent to the browser when `Validation.aspx` is requested. (Part 1 of 5.)

```
27    <script type="text/javascript">
28    <!--
29    var theForm = document.forms['form1'];
30    if (!theForm) {
31       theForm = document.form1;
32    }
33    function __doPostBack(eventTarget, eventArgument) {
34       if (!theForm.onsubmit || (theForm.onsubmit() != false)) {
35          theForm.__EVENTTARGET.value = eventTarget;
36          theForm.__EVENTARGUMENT.value = eventArgument;
37          theForm.submit();
38       }
39    }
40    // -->
41    </script>
42    <script src="/Validation/WebResource.axd?d=g4BXOwpt2-0jwFwNi7BCNQ2
43       &amp;t=632670465355304640" type="text/javascript"></script>
44    <script src="/Validation/WebResource.axd?d=ZlFGPYdcOpaOPqraRf9s2PN8QeuH
45       PzQxnkR5mPVtAVc1&amp;t=632670465355304640"
46       type="text/javascript"></script>
47    <script type="text/javascript">
48    <!--
49    function WebForm_OnSubmit() {
50       if (typeof(ValidatorOnSubmit) == "function" &&
51          ValidatorOnSubmit() == false) return false;
52       return true;
53    }
54    // -->
55    </script>
56    <div>
57       Please fill out the following form.<br />
58       <em>All fields are required and must contain valid information.
59       </em><br />
60       <br />
61       <table>
62          <tr>
63             <td style="width: 100px" valign="top"> Name:</td>
64             <td style="width: 450px" valign="top">
65                <input name="nameTextBox" type="text" value="Bob White"
66                   id="nameTextBox" />
67                <br />
68                <span id="nameInputValidator"
69                   style="color:Red;display:none;">
70                   Please enter your name.</span> </td>
71          </tr>
72          <tr>
73             <td style="width: 100px" valign="top">E-mail address:</td>
74             <td style="width: 450px" valign="top">
75                <input name="emailTextBox" type="text"
76                   value="bwhite@email.com" id="emailTextBox" />
77                 e.g., user@domain.com<br />
```

Fig. 21.22 | XHTML and ECMAScript generated by ASP.NET and sent to the browser when Validation.aspx is requested. (Part 2 of 5.)

```
78              <span id="emailInputValidator"
79                  style="color:Red;display:none;">
80                  Please enter your e-mail address.</span>
81              <span id="emailFormatValidator"
82                  style="color:Red;display:none;">Please enter an e-mail
83                  address in a valid format.</span> </td>
84          </tr>
85          <tr>
86              <td style="width: 100px; height: 21px" valign="top">
87                  Phone number:</td>
88              <td style="width: 450px; height: 21px" valign="top">
89                  <input name="phoneTextBox" type="text"
90                      value="(555) 555-1234" id="phoneTextBox" />
91                   e.g., (555) 555-1234<br />
92                  <span id="phoneInputValidator"
93                      style="color:Red;display:none;">
94                      Please enter your phone number.</span>
95                  <span id="phoneFormatValidator"
96                      style="color:Red;display:none;">Please enter a phone
97                      number in a valid format.</span> </td>
98          </tr>
99      </table>
100     <br />
101     <input type="submit" name="submitButton" value="Submit"
102         onclick="javascript:WebForm_DoPostBackWithOptions(
103             new WebForm_PostBackOptions(&quot;submitButton&quot;,
104                 &quot;&quot;, true, &quot;&quot;, &quot;&quot;, false,
105                 false))" id="submitButton" />
106     <br />
107     <br />
108     <span id="outputLabel">Thank you for your submission.<br />
109         We received the following information:
110         <table style="background-color: yellow">
111             <tr>
112                 <td>Name: </td>
113                 <td>Bob White</td>
114             </tr>
115             <tr>
116                 <td>E-mail address: </td>
117                 <td>bwhite@email.com</td>
118             </tr>
119             <tr>
120                 <td>Phone number: </td>
121                 <td>(555) 555-1234</td>
122             </tr>
123         <table>
124     </span>
125 </div>
126 <script type="text/javascript">
127 <!--
```

Fig. 21.22 | XHTML and ECMAScript generated by ASP.NET and sent to the browser when Validation.aspx is requested. (Part 3 of 5.)

```
128         var Page_Validators = new Array(
129             document.getElementById("nameInputValidator"),
130             document.getElementById("emailInputValidator"),
131             document.getElementById("emailFormatValidator"),
132             document.getElementById("phoneInputValidator"),
133             document.getElementById("phoneFormatValidator"));
134     // -->
135     </script>
136     <script type="text/javascript">
137     <!--
138         var nameInputValidator = document.all ?
139             document.all["nameInputValidator"] :
140             document.getElementById("nameInputValidator");
141     nameInputValidator.controltovalidate = "nameTextBox";
142     nameInputValidator.errormessage = "Please enter your name.";
143     nameInputValidator.display = "Dynamic";
144     nameInputValidator.evaluationfunction =
145         "RequiredFieldValidatorEvaluateIsValid";
146     nameInputValidator.initialvalue = "";
147         var emailInputValidator = document.all ?
148             document.all["emailInputValidator"] :
149             document.getElementById("emailInputValidator");
150     emailInputValidator.controltovalidate = "emailTextBox";
151     emailInputValidator.errormessage =
152         "Please enter your e-mail address.";
153     emailInputValidator.display = "Dynamic";
154     emailInputValidator.evaluationfunction =
155         "RequiredFieldValidatorEvaluateIsValid";
156     emailInputValidator.initialvalue = "";
157         var emailFormatValidator = document.all ?
158             document.all["emailFormatValidator"] :
159             document.getElementById("emailFormatValidator");
160     emailFormatValidator.controltovalidate = "emailTextBox";
161     emailFormatValidator.errormessage =
162         "Please enter an e-mail address in a valid format.";
163     emailFormatValidator.display = "Dynamic";
164     emailFormatValidator.evaluationfunction =
165         "RegularExpressionValidatorEvaluateIsValid";
166     emailFormatValidator.validationexpression =
167         "\\w+([-+.\']\\w+)*@\\w+([-.]\\w+)*\\.\\w+([-.]\\w+)*";
168         var phoneInputValidator = document.all ?
169             document.all["phoneInputValidator"] :
170             document.getElementById("phoneInputValidator");
171     phoneInputValidator.controltovalidate = "phoneTextBox";
172     phoneInputValidator.errormessage =
173         "Please enter your phone number.";
174     phoneInputValidator.display = "Dynamic";
175     phoneInputValidator.evaluationfunction =
176         "RequiredFieldValidatorEvaluateIsValid";
177     phoneInputValidator.initialvalue = "";
```

Fig. 21.22 | XHTML and ECMAScript generated by ASP.NET and sent to the browser when
`Validation.aspx` is requested. (Part 4 of 5.)

```
178        var phoneFormatValidator = document.all ?
179           document.all["phoneFormatValidator"] :
180           document.getElementById("phoneFormatValidator");
181        phoneFormatValidator.controltovalidate = "phoneTextBox";
182        phoneFormatValidator.errormessage =
183           "Please enter a phone number in a valid format.";
184        phoneFormatValidator.display = "Dynamic";
185        phoneFormatValidator.evaluationfunction =
186           "RegularExpressionValidatorEvaluateIsValid";
187        phoneFormatValidator.validationexpression =
188           "((\\(\\d{3}\\) ?)|(\\d{3}-))?\\d{3}-\\d{4}";
189     // -->
190     </script>
191     <div>
192        <input type="hidden" name="__EVENTVALIDATION" id="__EVENTVALIDATION"
193           value="/wEWBQL6jZCbCAKLsYSOBwKCkfPgDAKE8IO1CQKSuuDUCOeNO37OTaQqZQ
194              OWPApDOKktGC5N" />
195     </div>
196     <script type="text/javascript">
197     <!--
198        var Page_ValidationActive = false;
199        if (typeof(ValidatorOnLoad) == "function") {
200           ValidatorOnLoad();
201        }
202
203        function ValidatorOnSubmit() {
204           if (Page_ValidationActive) {
205              return ValidatorCommonOnSubmit();
206           }
207           else {
208              return true;
209           }
210        }
211     // -->
212     </script>
213  </form>
214  </body>
215  </html>
```

Fig. 21.22 | XHTML and ECMAScript generated by ASP.NET and sent to the browser when `Validation.aspx` is requested. (Part 5 of 5.)

The `EnableViewState` attribute determines whether a Web control's value is retained when a postback occurs. Previously, we explicitly set this attribute to `False`. The default value, `True`, indicates that the control's value is retained. In Fig. 21.20(d), notice that the user input is retained after the postback occurs. A `hidden` input in the XHTML document (lines 17–25 of Fig. 21.22) contains the data of the controls on this page. This element is always named `__VIEWSTATE` and stores the controls' data as an encoded string.

Performance Tip 21.1

Setting `EnableViewState` *to* False *reduces the amount of data passed to the Web server with each request.*

21.6 Session Tracking

Originally, critics accused the Internet and e-business of failing to provide the kind of customized service typically experienced in "brick-and-mortar" stores. To address this problem, e-businesses began to establish mechanisms by which they could personalize users' browsing experiences, tailoring content to individual users while enabling them to bypass irrelevant information. Businesses achieve this level of service by tracking each customer's movement through the Internet and combining the collected data with information provided by the consumer, including billing information, personal preferences, interests and hobbies.

Personalization

Personalization makes it possible for e-businesses to communicate effectively with their customers and also improves users' ability to locate desired products and services. Companies that provide content of particular interest to users can establish relationships with customers and build on those relationships over time. Furthermore, by targeting consumers with personal offers, recommendations, advertisements, promotions and services, e-businesses create customer loyalty. Web sites can use sophisticated technology to allow visitors to customize home pages to suit their individual needs and preferences. Similarly, online shopping sites often store personal information for customers, tailoring notifications and special offers to their interests. Such services encourage customers to visit sites more frequently and make purchases more regularly.

Privacy

A trade-off exists, however, between personalized e-business service and protection of privacy. Some consumers embrace the idea of tailored content, but others fear the possible adverse consequences if the info they provide to e-businesses is released or collected by tracking technologies. Consumers and privacy advocates ask: What if the e-business to which we give personal data sells or gives that information to another organization without our knowledge? What if we do not want our actions on the Internet—a supposedly anonymous medium—to be tracked and recorded by unknown parties? What if unauthorized parties gain access to sensitive private data, such as credit-card numbers or medical history? All of these are questions that must be debated and addressed by programmers, consumers, e-businesses and lawmakers alike.

Recognizing Clients

To provide personalized services to consumers, e-businesses must be able to recognize clients when they request information from a site. As we have discussed, the request/response system on which the Web operates is facilitated by HTTP. Unfortunately, HTTP is a stateless protocol—it does not support persistent connections that would enable Web servers to maintain state information regarding particular clients. This means that Web servers cannot determine whether a request comes from a particular client or whether the same or different clients generate a series of requests. To circumvent this problem, sites can provide mechanisms by which they identify individual clients. A session represents a unique client on a Web site. If the client leaves a site and then returns later, the client will still be recognized as the same user. To help the server distinguish among clients, each client must identify itself to the server. Tracking individual clients, known as session tracking, can be achieved in a number of ways. One popular technique uses cookies (Section 21.6.1); another uses ASP.NET's HttpSessionState object (Section 21.6.2). Additional session-tracking techniques include the use of input form elements of type "hidden" and URL rewriting. Using "hidden" form elements, a Web Form can write session-tracking data into a form in the Web page that it returns to the client in response to a prior request. When the user submits the form in the new Web page, all the form data, including the "hidden" fields, is sent to the form handler on the Web server. When a Web site performs URL rewriting, the Web Form embeds session-tracking information directly in the URLs of hyperlinks that the user clicks to send subsequent requests to the Web server.

Note that our previous examples set the Web Form's EnableSessionState property to False. However, because we wish to use session tracking in the following examples, we keep this property's default setting—True.

21.6.1 Cookies

Cookies provide Web developers with a tool for personalizing Web pages. A cookie is a piece of data stored in a small text file on the user's computer. A cookie maintains information about the client during and between browser sessions. The first time a user visits the Web site, the user's computer might receive a cookie; this cookie is then reactivated each time the user revisits that site. The collected information is intended to be an anonymous record containing data that is used to personalize the user's future visits to the site. For example, cookies in a shopping application might store unique identifiers for users. When a user adds items to an online shopping cart or performs another task resulting in a request to the Web server, the server receives a cookie containing the user's unique identifier. The server then uses the unique identifier to locate the shopping cart and perform any necessary processing.

In addition to identifying users, cookies also can indicate users' shopping preferences. When a Web Form receives a request from a client, the Web Form can examine the cookie(s) it sent to the client during previous communications, identify the users's preferences and immediately display products of interest to the client.

Every HTTP-based interaction between a client and a server includes a header containing information either about the request (when the communication is from the client to the server) or about the response (when the communication is from the server to the client). When a Web Form receives a request, the header includes information such as the request type (e.g., Get) and any cookies that have been sent previously from the server to be stored on the client machine. When the server formulates its response, the header information contains any cookies the server wants to store on the client computer and other information, such as the MIME type of the response.

The expiration date of a cookie determines how long the cookie remains on the client's computer. If you do not set an expiration date for a cookie, the Web browser maintains the cookie for the duration of the browsing session. Otherwise, the Web browser maintains the cookie until the expiration date occurs. When the browser requests a resource from a Web server, cookies previously sent to the client by that Web server are returned to the Web server as part of the request formulated by the browser. Cookies are deleted when they expire.

Portability Tip 21.3

Users may disable cookies in their Web browsers to ensure that their privacy is protected. Such users will experience difficulty using Web applications that depend on cookies to maintain state information.

Using Cookies to Provide Book Recommendations

The next Web application demonstrates the use of cookies. The example contains two pages. In the first page (Figs. 21.23–21.24), users select a favorite programming language from a group of radio buttons and submit the XHTML form to the Web server for processing. The Web server responds by creating a cookie that stores a record of the chosen language, as well as the ISBN number for a book on that topic. The server then returns an XHTML document to the browser, allowing the user either to select another favorite programming language or to view the second page in our application (Figs. 21.25 and 21.26), which lists recommended books pertaining to the programming language that the user selected previously. When the user clicks the hyperlink, the cookies previously stored on the client are read and used to form the list of book recommendations.

The ASPX file in Fig. 21.23 contains five radio buttons (lines 20–26) with the values **Visual Basic 2005**, **Visual C# 2005**, **C**, **C++**, and **Java**. Recall that you can set the values of radio buttons via the **ListItem Collection Editor**, which you open either by clicking the RadioButtonList's Items property in the **Properties** window or by clicking the **Edit Items...** link in the **RadioButtonList Tasks** smart tag menu. The user selects a programming language by clicking one of the radio buttons. When the user clicks **Submit**, we'll create a cookie containing the selected language. Then, we'll add this cookie to the HTTP response header, so the cookie will be stored on the user's computer. Each time the user chooses a language and clicks **Submit**, a cookie is written to the client. Each time the client requests information from our Web application, the cookies are sent back to the server.

```
 1   <%-- Fig. 21.23: Options.aspx --%>
 2   <%-- Allows client to select programming languages and access --%>
 3   <%-- book recommendations. --%>
 4   <%@ Page Language="VB" AutoEventWireup="false"
 5      CodeFile="Options.aspx.vb" Inherits="Options" %>
 6
 7   <!DOCTYPE html PUBLIC "-//W3C//DTD XHTML 1.0 Transitional//EN"
 8      "http://www.w3.org/TR/xhtml1/DTD/xhtml1-transitional.dtd">
 9
10   <html xmlns="http://www.w3.org/1999/xhtml" >
11   <head runat="server">
12      <title>Cookies</title>
13   </head>
14   <body>
15      <form id="form1" runat="server">
16      <div>
17         <asp:Label ID="promptLabel" runat="server" Font-Bold="True"
18            Font-Size="Large" Text="Select a programming language:">
19         </asp:Label>
20         <asp:RadioButtonList ID="languageList" runat="server">
21            <asp:ListItem>Visual Basic 2005</asp:ListItem>
```

Fig. 21.23 | ASPX file that presents a list of programming languages. (Part 1 of 2.)

```
22              <asp:ListItem>Visual C# 2005</asp:ListItem>
23              <asp:ListItem>C</asp:ListItem>
24              <asp:ListItem>C++</asp:ListItem>
25              <asp:ListItem>Java</asp:ListItem>
26          </asp:RadioButtonList>
27          <asp:Button ID="submitButton" runat="server" Text="Submit" />
28          <asp:Label ID="responseLabel" runat="server" Font-Bold="True"
29              Font-Size="Large" Text="Welcome to cookies!" Visible="False">
30          </asp:Label><br />
31          <br />
32          <asp:HyperLink ID="languageLink" runat="server"
33              NavigateUrl="~/Options.aspx" Visible="False">
34              Click here to choose another language
35          </asp:HyperLink><br />
36          <br />
37          <asp:HyperLink ID="recommendationsLink" runat="server"
38              NavigateUrl="~/Recommendations.aspx" Visible="False">
39              Click here to get book recommendations
40          </asp:HyperLink>
41      </div>
42      </form>
43  </body>
44  </html>
```

(a)

(b)

(c)

(d)

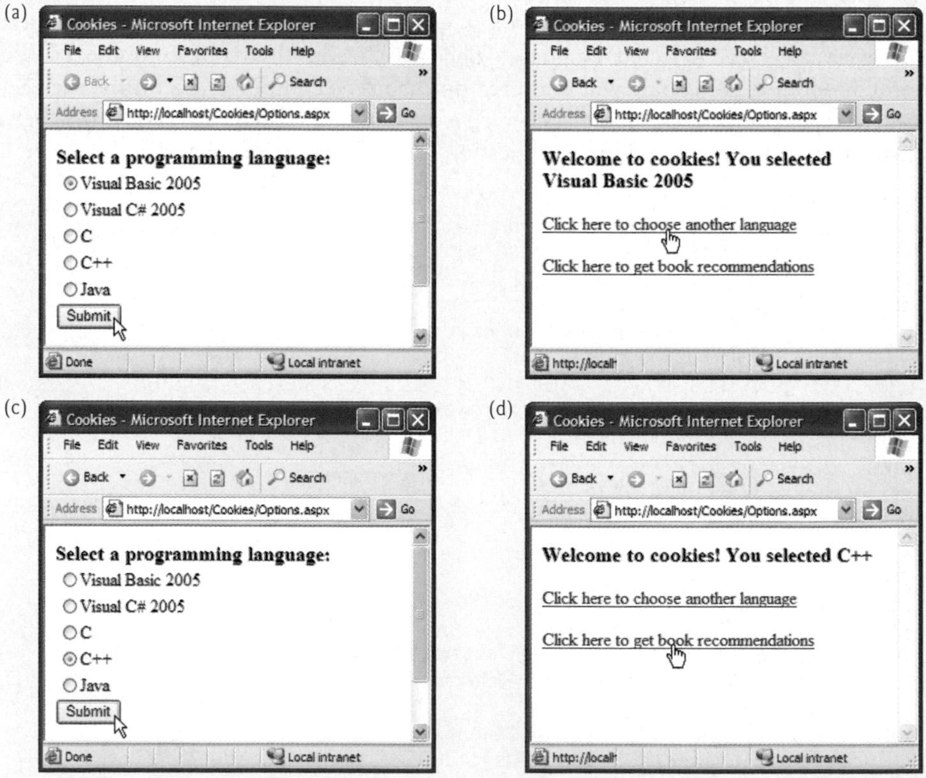

Fig. 21.23 | ASPX file that presents a list of programming languages. (Part 2 of 2.)

When the postback occurs, certain controls are hidden and others are displayed. The Label, RadioButtonList and Button used to select a language are hidden. Toward the bottom of the page, a Label and two HyperLinks are displayed. One link requests this page (lines 32–35), and the other requests Recommendations.aspx (lines 37–40). Clicking the first hyperlink (the one that requests the current page) does not cause a postback to occur. The file Options.aspx is specified in the NavigateUrl property of the hyperlink. When the hyperlink is clicked, a new request for this page occurs. Recall that earlier in the chapter, we set NavigateUrl to a remote Web site (http://www.deitel.com). To set this property to a page within the same ASP.NET application, click the ellipsis button next to the NavigateUrl property in the **Properties** window to open the **Select URL** dialog. Use this dialog to select a page within your project as the destination for the HyperLink.

Adding and Linking to a New Web Form

Setting the NavigateUrl property to a page in the current application requires that the destination page exist already. Thus, to set the NavigateUrl property of the second link (the one that requests the page with book recommendations) to Recommendations.aspx, you must first create this file by right clicking the project location in the **Solution Explorer** and selecting **Add New Item...** from the menu that appears. In the **Add New Item** dialog, select **Web Form** from the **Templates** pane and change the name of the file to Recommendations.aspx. Finally, check the box labeled **Place code in separate file** to indicate that the IDE should create a code-behind file for this ASPX file. Click **Add** to create the file. (We discuss the contents of this ASPX file and code-behind file shortly.) Once the Recommendations.aspx file exists, you can select it as the NavigateUrl value for a HyperLink in the **Select URL** dialog.

Writing Cookies in a Code-Behind File

Figure 21.24 presents the code-behind file for Options.aspx (Fig. 21.23). This file contains the code that writes a cookie to the client machine when the user selects a programming language. The code-behind file also modifies the appearance of the page in response to a postback.

```vb
 1   ' Fig. 21.24: Options.aspx.vb
 2   ' Processes user's selection of a programming language
 3   ' by displaying links and writing a cookie to the user's machine.
 4   Partial Class Options
 5       Inherits System.Web.UI.Page
 6       ' stores values to represent books as cookies
 7       Private books As New System.Collections.Hashtable()
 8
 9       ' initializes the Hashtable of values to be stored as cookies
10       Protected Sub Page_Init(ByVal sender As Object, _
11           ByVal e As System.EventArgs) Handles Me.Init
12           books.Add("Visual Basic 2005", "0-13-186900-0")
13           books.Add("Visual C# 2005", "0-13-152523-9")
14           books.Add("C", "0-13-142644-3")
15           books.Add("C++", "0-13-185757-6")
```

Fig. 21.24 | Code-behind file that writes a cookie to the client. (Part 1 of 2.)

Step 6: Modifying the Columns of the Data Source Displayed in the **GridView**

It is not necessary for site visitors to see the MessageID column when viewing past guest-book entries—this column is merely a unique primary key required by the Messages table within the database. Thus, we modify the GridView so that this column does not display on the Web Form. In the **GridView Tasks** smart tag menu, click **Edit Columns**. In the resulting **Fields** dialog (Fig. 21.38), select **MessageID** in the **Selected fields** pane, then click the **X**. This removes the MessageID column from the GridView. Click **OK** to return to the main IDE window. The GridView should now appear as in Fig. 21.33.

Step 7: Modifying the Way the **SqlDataSource** *Control Inserts Data*

When you create a SqlDataSource in the manner described here, it is configured to permit INSERT SQL operations against the database table from which it gathers data. You must specify the values to insert either programmatically or through other controls on the Web Form. In this example, we wish to insert the data entered by the user in the nameTextBox, emailTextBox and messageTextBox controls. We also want to insert the current date—we will specify the date to insert programmatically in the code-behind file, which we present shortly.

To configure the SqlDataSource to allow such an insertion, select the messagesSql-DataSource control then click the ellipsis button next to the control's **InsertQuery** property of the messagesSqlDataSource control in the **Properties** window. The **Command and Parameter Editor** (Fig. 21.39) that appears displays the INSERT command used by the Sql-DataSource control. This command contains parameters @Date, @Name, @Email and @Message. You must provide values for these parameters before they are inserted into the database. Each parameter is listed in the **Parameters** section of the **Command and Parameter Editor**. Because we will set the **Date** parameter programmatically, we do not modify it here. For each of the remaining three parameters, select the parameter, then select **Control**

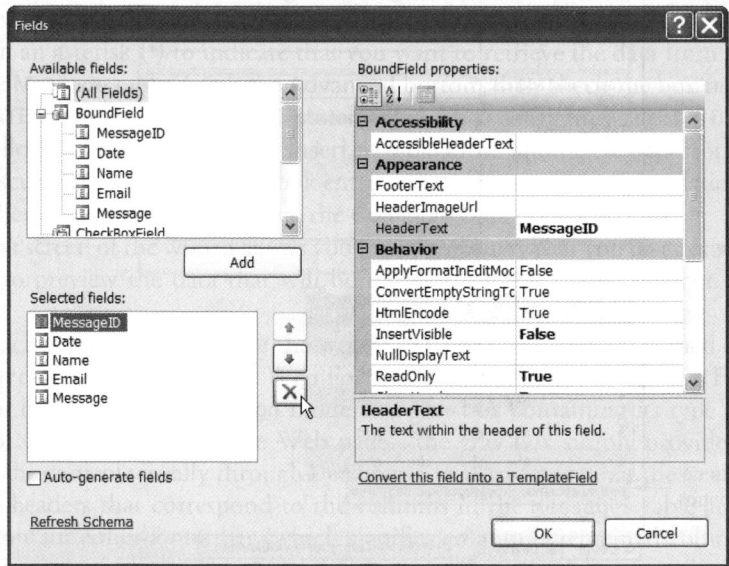

Fig. 21.38 | Removing the MessageID column from the GridView.

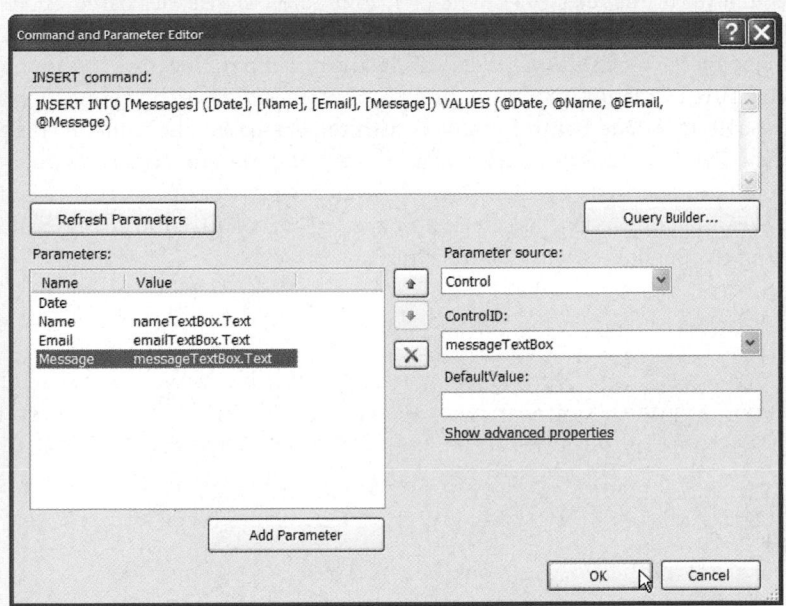

Fig. 21.39 | Setting up INSERT parameters based on control values.

from the **Parameter source** drop-down list. This indicates that the value of the parameter should be taken from a control. The **ControlID** drop-down list contains all the controls on the Web Form. Select the appropriate control for each parameter, then click **OK**. Now the SqlDataSource is configured to insert the user's name, e-mail address and message in the Messages table of the Guestbook database. We show how to set the date parameter and initiate the insert operation when the user clicks **Submit** shortly.

ASPX File for a Web Form That Interacts with a Database
The ASPX file generated by the guestbook GUI (and messagesSqlDataSource control) is shown in Fig. 21.40. This file contains a large amount of generated markup. We discuss only those parts that are new or noteworthy for the current example. Lines 19–58 contain the XHTML and ASP.NET elements that comprise the form that gathers user input. The GridView control appears in lines 60–85. The <asp:GridView> start tag (lines 60–63) contains properties that set various aspects of the GridView's appearance and behavior, such as whether grid lines should be displayed between rows and columns. The DataSourceID property identifies the data source that is used to fill the GridView with data at runtime.

Lines 66–75 define the Columns that appear in the GridView. Each column is represented as a **BoundField**, because the values in the columns are bound to values retrieved from the data source (i.e., the Messages table of the Guestbook database). The DataField property of each BoundField identifies the column in the data source to which the column in the GridView is bound. The HeaderText property indicates the text that appears as the column header. By default, this is the name of the column in the data source, but you can change this property as desired. Lines 76–84 contain nested elements that define the styles used to format the GridView's rows. The IDE configured these styles based on your selection of the **Simple** style in the **Auto Format** dialog for the GridView.

The messagesSqlDataSource is defined by the markup in lines 86–115 in Fig. 21.40. Line 87 contains a **ConnectionString** property, which indicates the connection through which the SqlDataSource control interacts with the database. The value of this property uses an **ASP.NET expression**, delimited by **<%$** and **%>**, to access the Guestbook-ConnectionString stored in the ConnectionStrings section of the application's Web.config configuration file. Recall that we created this connection string earlier in this section using the **Configure Data Source** wizard.

```
1   <%-- Fig. 21.40: Guestbook.aspx --%>
2   <%-- Guestbook Web application with a form for users to submit --%>
3   <%-- guestbook entires and a GridView to view existing entries. --%>
4   <%@ Page Language="VB" AutoEventWireup="false"
5      CodeFile="Guestbook.aspx.vb" Inherits="Guestbook" %>
6
7   <!DOCTYPE html PUBLIC "-//W3C//DTD XHTML 1.0 Transitional//EN"
8      "http://www.w3.org/TR/xhtml1/DTD/xhtml1-transitional.dtd">
9
10  <html xmlns="http://www.w3.org/1999/xhtml" >
11  <head runat="server">
12     <title>Guestbook</title>
13  </head>
14  <body>
15     <form id="form1" runat="server">
16     <div>
17        <h2>
18           Please leave a message in our guestbook:</h2>
19        <table>
20           <tr>
21              <td style="width: 130px; height: 21px" valign="top">
22                 Your name:<br />
23              </td>
24              <td style="width: 300px; height: 21px" valign="top">
25                 <asp:TextBox ID="nameTextBox" runat="server"
26                    Width="300px"></asp:TextBox>
27              </td>
28           </tr>
29           <tr>
30              <td style="width: 130px" valign="top">
31                 Your e-mail address:<br />
32              </td>
33              <td style="width: 300px" valign="top">
34                 <asp:TextBox ID="emailTextBox" runat="server"
35                    Width="300px"></asp:TextBox>
36              </td>
37           </tr>
38           <tr>
39              <td style="width: 130px" valign="top">
40                 Tell the world:<br />
41              </td>
```

Fig. 21.40 | ASPX file for the guestbook application. (Part 1 of 4.)

```
42              <td style="width: 300px" valign="top">
43                 <asp:TextBox ID="messageTextBox" runat="server"
44                    Height="100px" Rows="8" Width="300px">
45                    </asp:TextBox>
46              </td>
47           </tr>
48           <tr>
49              <td style="width: 130px" valign="top">
50              </td>
51              <td style="width: 300px" valign="top">
52                 <asp:Button ID="submitButton" runat="server"
53                    Text="Submit" />
54                 <asp:Button ID="clearButton" runat="server"
55                    Text="Clear" />
56              </td>
57           </tr>
58        </table>
59        <br />
60        <asp:GridView ID="messagesGridView" runat="server"
61           AutoGenerateColumns="False" CellPadding="4"
62           DataKeyNames="MessageID" DataSourceID="messagesSqlDataSource"
63           ForeColor="#333333" GridLines="None" Width="600px">
64           <FooterStyle BackColor="#1C5E55" Font-Bold="True"
65              ForeColor="White" />
66           <Columns>
67              <asp:BoundField DataField="Date" HeaderText="Date"
68                 SortExpression="Date" />
69              <asp:BoundField DataField="Name" HeaderText="Name"
70                 SortExpression="Name" />
71              <asp:BoundField DataField="Email" HeaderText="Email"
72                 SortExpression="Email" />
73              <asp:BoundField DataField="Message" HeaderText="Message"
74                 SortExpression="Message" />
75           </Columns>
76           <RowStyle BackColor="#E3EAEB" />
77           <EditRowStyle BackColor="#7C6F57" />
78           <SelectedRowStyle BackColor="#C5BBAF" Font-Bold="True"
79              ForeColor="#333333" />
80           <PagerStyle BackColor="#666666" ForeColor="White"
81              HorizontalAlign="Center" />
82           <HeaderStyle BackColor="#1C5E55" Font-Bold="True"
83              ForeColor="White" />
84           <AlternatingRowStyle BackColor="White" />
85        </asp:GridView>
86        <asp:SqlDataSource ID="messagesSqlDataSource" runat="server"
87           ConnectionString="<%$ ConnectionStrings:ConnectionString %>"
88           DeleteCommand="DELETE FROM [Messages] WHERE [MessageID] =
89              @MessageID" InsertCommand="INSERT INTO [Messages]
90              ([Date], [Name], [Email], [Message])
91              VALUES (@Date, @Name, @Email, @Message)"
92           SelectCommand="SELECT * FROM [Messages]" UpdateCommand=
93              "UPDATE [Messages] SET [Date] = @Date, [Name] = @Name,
```

Fig. 21.40 | ASPX file for the guestbook application. (Part 2 of 4.)

```
 94                  [Email] = @Email, [Message] = @Message
 95              WHERE [MessageID] = @MessageID">
 96          <DeleteParameters>
 97             <asp:Parameter Name="MessageID" Type="Int32" />
 98          </DeleteParameters>
 99          <UpdateParameters>
100             <asp:Parameter Name="Date" Type="String" />
101             <asp:Parameter Name="Name" Type="String" />
102             <asp:Parameter Name="Email" Type="String" />
103             <asp:Parameter Name="Message" Type="String" />
104             <asp:Parameter Name="MessageID" Type="Int32" />
105          </UpdateParameters>
106          <InsertParameters>
107             <asp:Parameter Name="Date" Type="String" />
108             <asp:ControlParameter ControlID="nameTextBox" Name="Name"
109                PropertyName="Text" Type="String" />
110             <asp:ControlParameter ControlID="emailTextBox" Name="Email"
111                PropertyName="Text" Type="String" />
112             <asp:ControlParameter ControlID="messageTextBox"
113                Name="Message" PropertyName="Text" Type="String" />
114          </InsertParameters>
115       </asp:SqlDataSource>
116    </div>
117    </form>
118 </body>
119 </html>
```

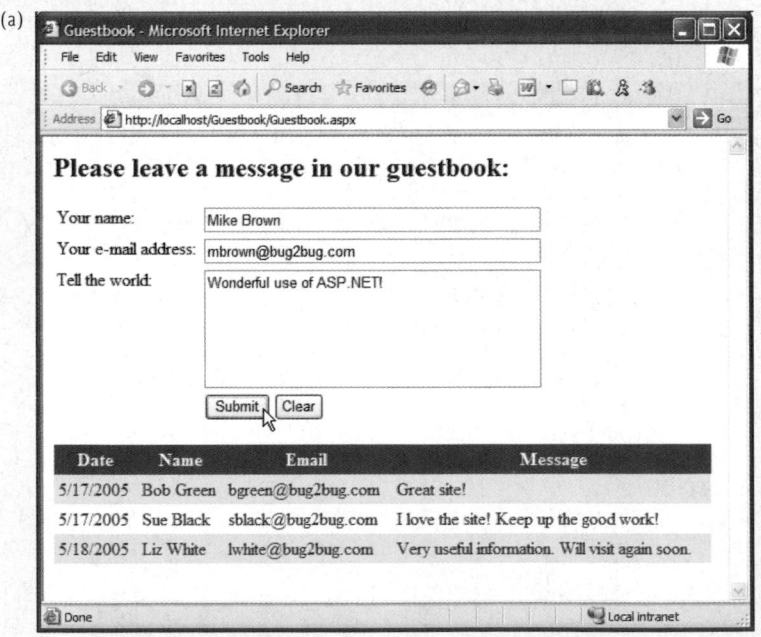

Fig. 21.40 | ASPX file for the guestbook application. (Part 3 of 4.)

(b)

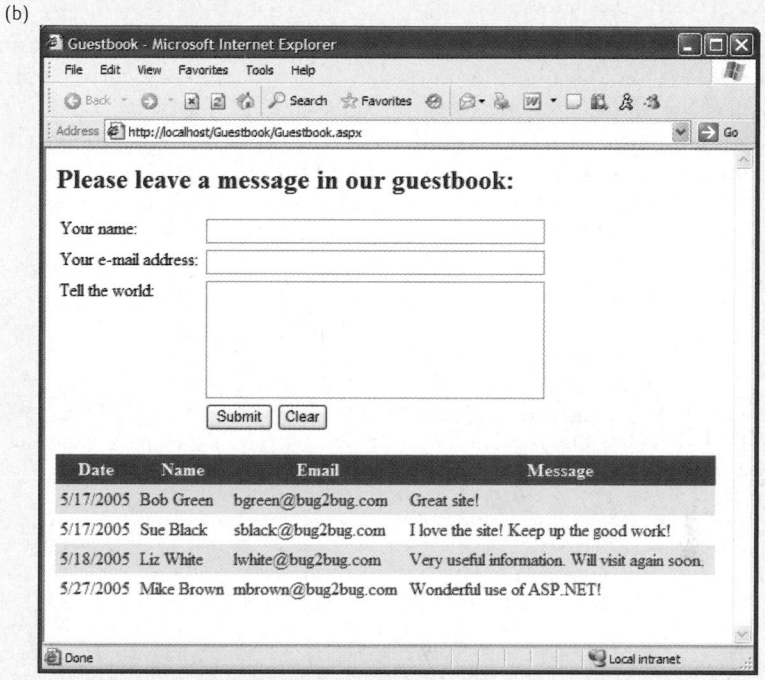

Fig. 21.40 | ASPX file for the guestbook application. (Part 4 of 4.)

As determined by our actions in the **Configure Data Source** wizard, this statement retrieves the data in all the columns in all the rows of the Messages table. Lines 88–95 define the `DeleteCommand`, `InsertCommand`, `SelectCommand` and `UpdateCommand` properties, which contain the DELETE, INSERT, SELECT and UPDATE SQL statements, respectively. These were generated by the **Configure Data Source** wizard. In this example, we use only the `InsertCommand`. We discuss invoking this command shortly.

Notice that the SQL commands used by the `SqlDataSource` contain several parameters (prefixed with @). Lines 96–114 contain elements that define the name, the type and, for some parameters, the source of the parameter. Parameters that are set programmatically are defined by `Parameter` elements containing Name and Type properties. For example, line 107 defines the Date parameter of Type String. This corresponds to the @Date parameter in the `InsertCommand` (line 91). Parameters that obtain their values from controls are defined by `ControlParameter` elements. Lines 108–113 contain markup that sets up the relationships between the INSERT parameters and the Web Form's TextBoxes. We established these relationships in the **Command and Parameter Editor** (Fig. 21.39). Each `ControlParameter` contains a `ControlID` property indicating the control from which the parameter gets its value. The `PropertyName` specifies the property that contains the actual value to be used as the parameter value. The IDE sets the `PropertyName` based on the type of control specified by the `ControlID` (indirectly via the **Command and Parameter Editor**). In this case, we use only TextBoxes, so the `PropertyName` of each `ControlParameter` is Text (e.g., the value of parameter @Name comes from nameTextBox.Text). However, if we were using a `DropDownList`, for example, the `PropertyName` would be `SelectedValue`.

21.7.2 Modifying the Code-Behind File for the Guestbook Application

After building the Web Form and configuring the data controls used in this example, double click the **Submit** and **Clear** buttons in **Design** view to create their corresponding Click event handlers in the Guestbook.aspx.vb code-behind file (Fig. 21.41). The IDE generates empty event handlers, so we must add the appropriate code to make these buttons work properly. The event handler for clearButton (lines 33–38) clears each TextBox by setting its Text property to an empty string. This resets the form for a new guestbook submission.

Lines 8–30 contain the event-handling code for submitButton, which adds the user's information to the Messages table of the Guestbook database. Recall that we configured

```vb
1   ' Fig. 21.41: Guestbook.aspx.vb
2   ' Code-behind file that defines event handlers for the guestbook.
3   Partial Class Guestbook
4      Inherits System.Web.UI.Page
5
6      ' Submit Button adds a new guestbook entry to the database,
7      ' clears the form and displays the updated list of guestbook entries
8      Protected Sub submitButton_Click(ByVal sender As Object, _
9         ByVal e As System.EventArgs) Handles submitButton.Click
10        ' create a date parameter to store the current date
11        Dim currentDate As New System.Web.UI.WebControls.Parameter( _
12           "Date", TypeCode.String, DateTime.Now.ToShortDateString())
13
14        ' set the @Date parameter to the date parameter
15        messagesSqlDataSource.InsertParameters.RemoveAt(0)
16        messagesSqlDataSource.InsertParameters.Add(currentDate)
17
18        ' execute an INSERT SQL statement to add a new row to the
19        ' Messages table in the Guestbook database that contains the
20        ' current date and the user's name, e-mail address and message
21        messagesSqlDataSource.Insert()
22
23        ' clear the TextBoxes
24        nameTextBox.Text = ""
25        emailTextBox.Text = ""
26        messageTextBox.Text = ""
27
28        ' update the GridView with the new database table contents
29        messagesGridView.DataBind()
30     End Sub ' submitButton_Click
31
32     ' Clear Button clears the Web Form's TextBoxes
33     Protected Sub clearButton_Click(ByVal sender As Object, _
34        ByVal e As System.EventArgs) Handles clearButton.Click
35        nameTextBox.Text = ""
36        emailTextBox.Text = ""
37        messageTextBox.Text = ""
38     End Sub ' clearButton_Click
39  End Class ' Guestbook
```

Fig. 21.41 | Code-behind file for the guestbook application.

messagesSqlDataSource's INSERT command to use the values of the TextBoxes on the Web Form as the parameter values inserted into the database. We have not yet specified the date value to be inserted, though. Lines 11–12 assign a String representation of the current date (e.g., "3/27/06") to a new object of type Parameter. This Parameter object is identified as "Date" and is given the current date as a default value. The SqlData-Source's InsertParameters collection contains an item named Date, which we Remove in line 15 and replace in line 16 by Adding our currentDate parameter. Invoking SqlData-Source method Insert in line 21 executes the INSERT command against the database, thus adding a row to the Messages table. After the data is inserted into the database, lines 24–26 clear the TextBoxes, and line 29 invokes messagesGridView's DataBind method to refresh the data that the GridView displays. This causes messagesSqlDataSource (the data source of the GridView) to execute its SELECT command to obtain the Messages table's newly updated data.

21.8 Case Study: Secure Books Database Application

This case study presents a Web application in which a user logs into a secure Web site to view a list of publications by an author of the user's choosing. The application consists of several ASPX files. Section 21.8.1 presents the application and explains the purpose of each of its Web pages. Section 21.8.2 provides step-by-step instructions to guide you through building the application and presents the markup in the ASPX files.

21.8.1 Examining the Completed Secure Books Database Application

This example uses a technique known as forms authentication to protect a page so that only users known to the Web site can access it. Such users are known as the site's members. Authentication is a crucial tool for sites that allow only members to enter the site or a portion of the site. In this application, Web site visitors must log in before they are allowed to view the publications in the Books database. The first page that a user would typically request is Login.aspx (Fig. 21.42). You will soon learn to create this page using a Login

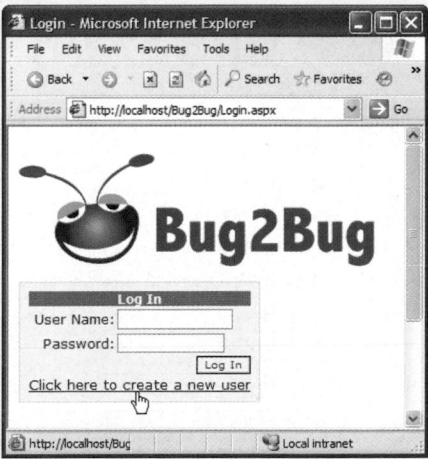

Fig. 21.42 | Login.aspx page of the secure books database application.

control, one of several **ASP.NET login controls** that help create secure applications using authentication. These controls are found in the **Login** section of the **Toolbox**.

The Login.aspx page allows a site visitor to enter an existing user name and password to log into the Web site. A first-time visitor must click the link below the **Log In** button to create a new user before logging in. Doing so redirects the visitor to CreateNewUser.aspx (Fig. 21.43), which contains a CreateUserWizard control that presents the visitor with a user registration form. We discuss the CreateUserWizard control in detail in Section 21.8.2. In Fig. 21.43, we use the password pa$$word for testing purposes—as you will learn, the CreateUserWizard requires that the password contain special characters for security purposes. Clicking **Create User** establishes a new user account. After creating the account, the user is automatically logged in and shown a success message (Fig. 21.44).

Clicking the **Continue** button on the confirmation page sends the user to Books.aspx (Fig. 21.45), which provides a drop-down list of authors and a table containing the ISBNs, titles, edition numbers and copyright years of books in the database. By default, all the books by Harvey Deitel are displayed. Links appear at the bottom of the table that allow you to access additional pages of data. When the user chooses an author, a postback occurs, and the page is updated to display information about books written by the selected author (Fig. 21.46).

Note that once the user creates an account and is logged in, Books.aspx displays a welcome message customized for the particular logged-in user. As you will soon see, a LoginName control provides this functionality. After you add this control to the page, ASP.NET handles the details of determining the user name.

Fig. 21.43 | CreateNewUser.aspx page of the secure book database application.

Fig. 21.44 | Message displayed to indicate that a user account was created successfully.

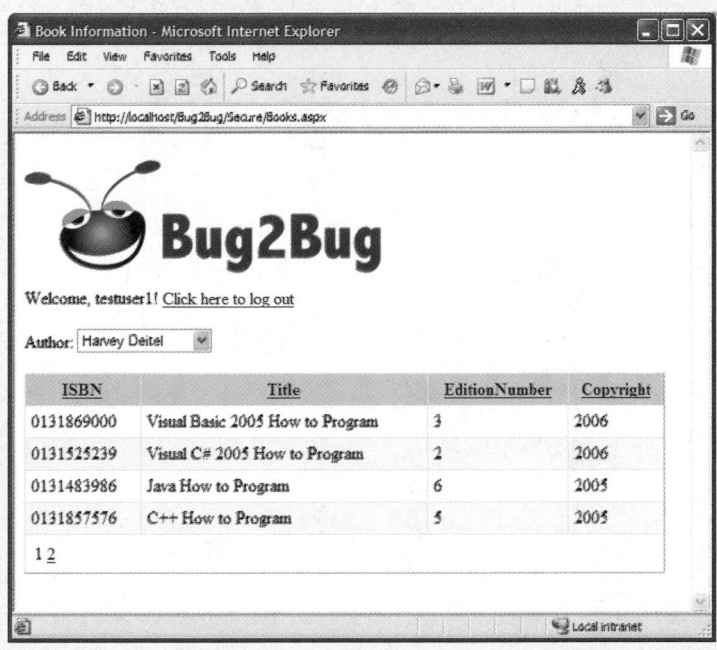

Fig. 21.45 | Books.aspx displaying books by Harvey Deitel (by default).

Clicking the **Click here to log out** link logs the user out, then sends the user back to Login.aspx (Fig. 21.47). This link is created by a LoginStatus control, which handles the log out details. After logging out, the user would need to log in through Login.aspx to view the book listing again. The Login control on this page receives the user name and password entered by a visitor. ASP.NET compares these values with user names and passwords stored in a database on the server. If there is a match, the visitor is **authenticated** (i.e., the user's identity is confirmed). We explain the authentication process in detail in

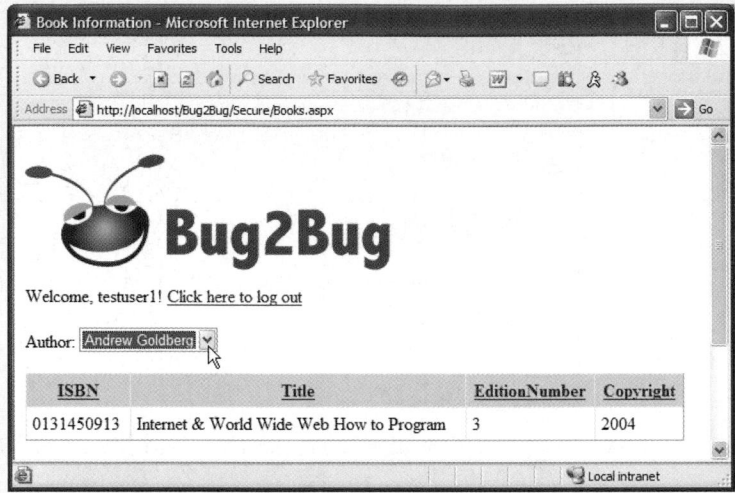

Fig. 21.46 | `Books.aspx` displaying books by Andrew Goldberg.

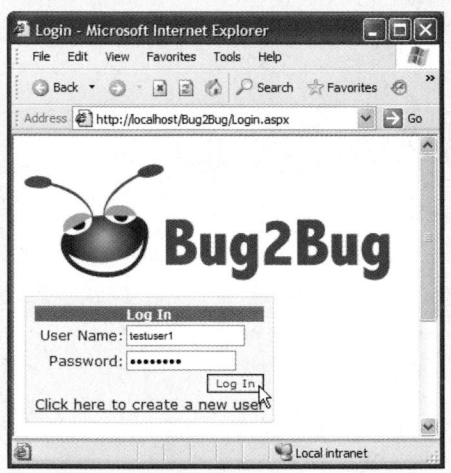

Fig. 21.47 | Logging in using the `Login` control.

Section 21.8.2. When an existing user is successfully authenticated, `Login.aspx` redirects the user to `Books.aspx` (Fig. 21.45). If the user's login attempt fails, an appropriate error message is displayed (Fig. 21.48).

Notice that `Login.aspx`, `CreateNewUser.aspx` and `Books.aspx` share the same page header containing the logo image from the fictional company Bug2Bug. Instead of placing this image at the top of each page, we use a **master page** to achieve this. As we demonstrate shortly, a master page defines common GUI elements that are inherited by each page in a set of **content pages**. Just as Visual Basic classes can inherit instance variables and methods from existing classes, content pages inherit elements from master pages—this is known as **visual inheritance**.

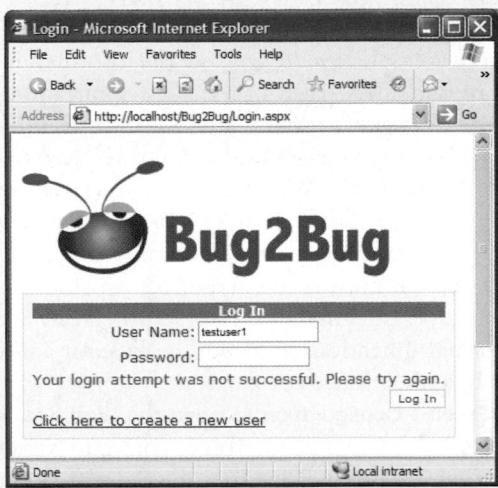

Fig. 21.48 | Error message displayed for an unsuccessful login attempt using the `Login` control.

21.8.2 Creating the Secure Books Database Application

Now that you are familiar with how this application behaves, you'll learn how to create it from scratch. Thanks to the rich set of login and data controls provided by ASP.NET, you will not have to write *any* code to create this application. In fact, the application does not contain any code-behind files. All of the functionality is specified through properties of controls, many of which are set through wizards and other visual programming tools. ASP.NET hides the details of authenticating users against a database of user names and passwords, displaying appropriate success or error messages and redirecting the user to the correct page based on the authentication results. We now discuss the steps you must perform to create the secure books database application.

Step 1: Creating the Web Site

Create a new **ASP.NET Web Site** at `http://localhost/Bug2Bug` as described previously. We will explicitly create each of the ASPX files that we need in this application, so delete the IDE-generated `Default.aspx` file (and its corresponding code-behind file) by selecting `Default.aspx` in the **Solution Explorer** and pressing the *Delete* key. Click **OK** in the confirmation dialog to delete these files.

Step 2: Setting Up the Web Site's Folders

Before building any of the pages in the Web site, we create folders to organize its contents. First, create an `Images` folder by right clicking the location of the Web site in the **Solution Explorer** and selecting **New Folder**, then add the `bug2bug.png` file to it. This image can be found in the examples directory for this chapter. Next, add the `Books.mdf` database file (located in the `exampleDatabases` subdirectory examples directory) to the project's `App_Data` folder. We show how to retrieve data from this database later in the section.

Step 3: Configuring the Application's Security Settings

In this application, we want to ensure that only authenticated users are allowed to access Books.aspx (created in *Step 9* and *Step 10*) to view the information in the database. Previously, we created all of our ASPX pages in the Web application's root directory (e.g., http://localhost/*ProjectName*). By default, any Web site visitor (regardless of whether the visitor is authenticated) can view pages in the root directory. ASP.NET allows you to restrict access to particular folders of a Web site. We do not want to restrict access to the root of the Web site, however, because all users must be able to view Login.aspx and CreateNewUser.aspx to log in and create user accounts, respectively. Thus, if we want to restrict access to Books.aspx, it must reside in a directory other than the root directory. Create a folder named Secure. Later in the section, we will create Books.aspx in this folder. First, let's enable forms authentication in our application and configure the Secure folder to restrict access to authenticated users only.

Select **Website > ASP.NET Configuration** to open the **Web Site Administration Tool** in a Web browser (Fig. 21.49). This tool allows you to configure various options that determine how your application behaves. Click either the **Security** link or the **Security** tab to open a Web page in which you can set security options (Fig. 21.50), such as the type of authentication the application should use. In the **Users** column, click **Select authentication type**. On the resulting page (Fig. 21.51), select the radio button next to **From the internet** to indicate that users will log in via a form on the Web site in which the user can enter a username and password (i.e., the application will use forms authentication). The default setting—**From a local network**—relies on users' Windows user names and passwords for authentication purposes. Click the **Done** button to save this change.

Fig. 21.49 | **Web Site Administration Tool** for configuring a Web application.

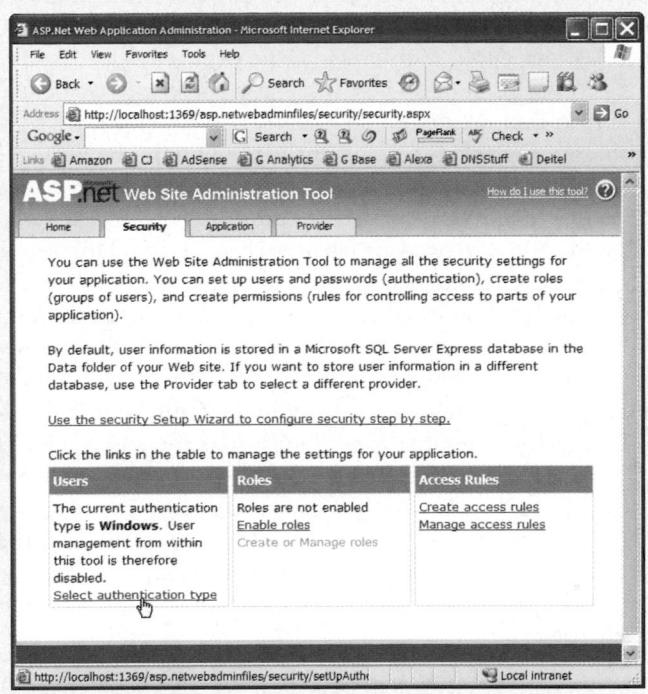

Fig. 21.50 | **Security** page of the **Web Site Administration Tool**.

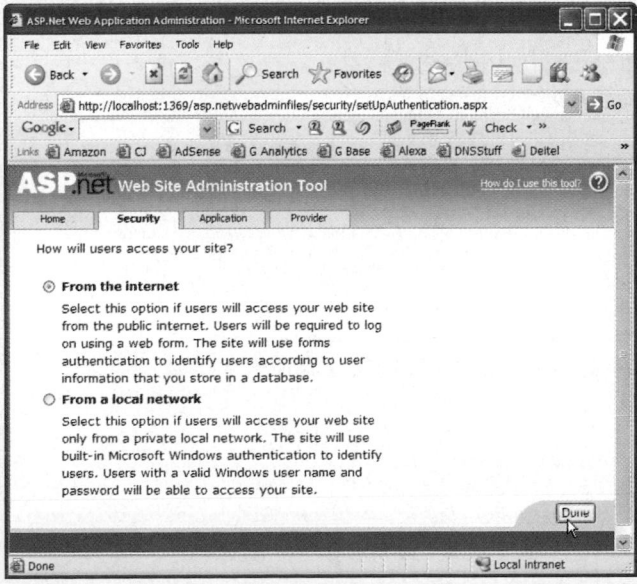

Fig. 21.51 | Choosing the type of authentication used by an ASP.NET Web application.

Now that forms authentication is enabled, the **Users** column on the main page of the **Web Site Administration Tool** (Fig. 21.52) provides links to create and manage users. As you saw in Section 21.8.1, our application provides the `CreateNewUser.aspx` page in which users can create their own accounts. Thus, while it is possible to create users through the **Web Site Administration Tool**, we do not do so here.

Even though no users exist at the moment, we configure the `Secure` folder to grant access only to authenticated users (i.e., deny access to all unauthenticated users). Click the **Create access rules** link in the **Access Rules** column of the **Web Site Administration Tool** (Fig. 21.52) to view the **Add New Access Rule** page (Fig. 21.53). This page is used to create an **access rule**—a rule that grants or denies access to a particular Web application directory for a specific user or group of users. Click the `Secure` directory in the left column of the page to identify the directory to which our access rule applies. In the middle column, select the radio button marked **Anonymous users** to specify that the rule applies to users who have not been authenticated. Finally, select **Deny** in the right column, labeled **Permission**, then click **OK**. This rule indicates that **anonymous users** (i.e., users who have not identified themselves by logging in) should be denied access to any pages in the `Secure` directory (e.g., `Books.aspx`). By default, anonymous users who attempt to load a page in the `Secure` directory are redirected to the `Login.aspx` page so that they can identify themselves. Note that because we did not set up any access rules for the `Bug2Bug` root directory, anonymous users may still access pages there (e.g., `Login.aspx`, `CreateNewUser.aspx`). We create these pages momentarily.

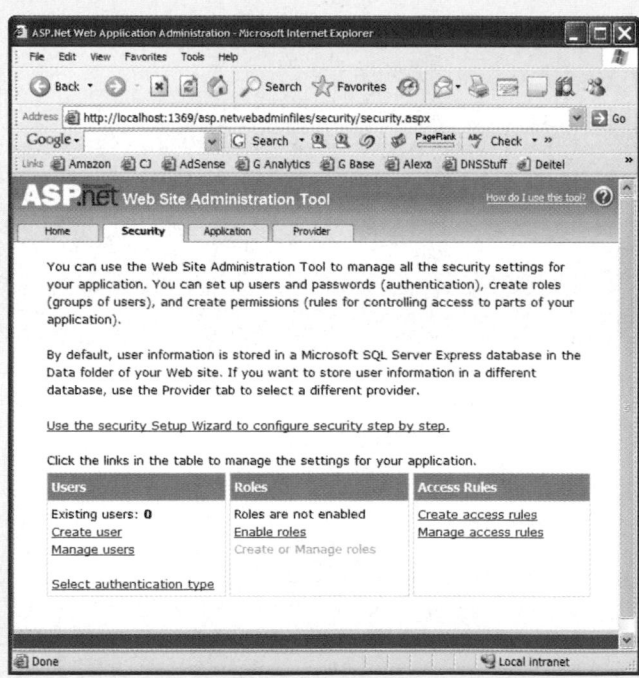

Fig. 21.52 | Main page of the **Web Site Administration Tool** after enabling forms authentication.

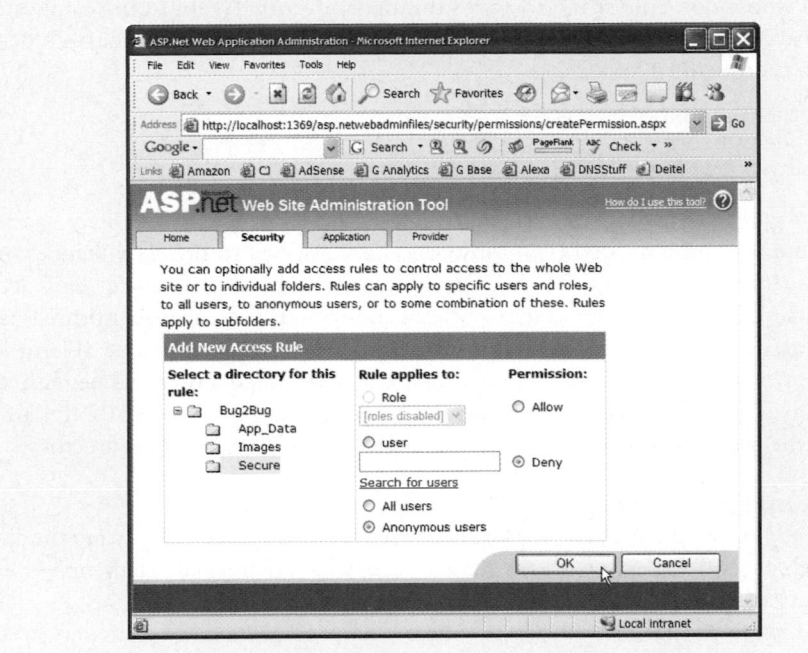

Fig. 21.53 | **Add New Access Rule** page used to configure directory access.

Step 4: Examining the Auto-Generated `Web.config` Files

We have now configured the application to use forms authentication and created an access rule to ensure that only authenticated users can access the `Secure` folder. Before creating the Web site's content, we examine how the changes made through the **Web Site Administration Tool** appear in the IDE. Recall that `Web.config` is an XML file used for application configuration, such as enabling debugging or storing database connection strings. Visual Web Developer generates two `Web.config` files in response to our actions using the **Web Site Administration Tool**—one in the application's root directory and one in the `Secure` folder. [*Note:* You may need to click the **Refresh** button in the **Solution Explorer** to see these files.] In an ASP.NET application, a page's configuration settings are determined by the current directory's `Web.config` file. The settings in this file take precedence over the settings in the root directory's `Web.config` file.

After setting the authentication type for the Web application, the IDE generates a `Web.config` file at `http://localhost/Bug2Bug/Web.config`, which contains an **authentication** element

```
<authentication mode="Forms" />
```

This element appears in the root directory's `Web.config` file, so the setting applies to the entire Web site. The value `"Forms"` of the mode attribute specifies that we want to use forms authentication. Had we left the authentication type set to **From a local network** in the **Web Site Administration Tool**, the mode attribute would be set to `"Windows"`.

After creating the access rule for the `Secure` folder, the IDE generates a second `Web.config` file in that folder. This file contains an **authorization** element that indicates who is, and who is not, authorized to access this folder over the Web. In this application, we want to allow only authenticated users to access the contents of the Secure folder, so the authorization element appears as

```
<authorization>
    <deny users="?" />
</authorization>
```

Rather than grant permission to each individual authenticated user, we deny access to those who are not authenticated (i.e., those who have not logged in). The **deny** element inside the authorization element specifies the users to whom we wish to deny access. When the users attribute's value is set to "?", all anonymous (i.e., unauthenticated) users are denied access to the folder. Thus, an unauthenticated user will not be able to load http://localhost/Bug2Bug/Secure/Books.aspx. Instead, such a user will be redirected to the Login.aspx page—when a user is denied access to a part of a site, ASP.NET by default sends the user to a page named Login.aspx in the application's root directory.

Step 5: Creating a Master Page

Now that you have established the application's security settings, you can create the application's Web pages. We begin with the master page, which defines the elements we want to appear on each page. A master page is like a base class in a visual inheritance hierarchy, and content pages are like derived classes. The master page contains placeholders for custom content created in each content page. The content pages visually inherit the master page's content, then add content in place of the master page's placeholders.

For example, you might want to include a navigation bar (i.e., a series of buttons for navigating a Web site) on every page of a site. If the site encompasses a large number of pages, adding markup to create the navigation bar for each page can be time consuming. Moreover, if you subsequently modify the navigation bar, every page on the site that uses it must be updated. By creating a master page, you can specify the navigation bar markup in one file and have it appear on all the content pages, with only a few lines of markup. If the navigation bar changes, only the master page changes—any content pages that use it are updated the next time the page is requested.

In this example, we want the Bug2Bug logo to appear as a header at the top of every page, so we will place an Image control in the master page. Each subsequent page we create will be a content page based on this master page and thus will include the header. To create a master page, right click the location of the Web site in the **Solution Explorer** and select **Add New Item....** In the **Add New Item** dialog, select **Master Page** from the template list and specify Bug2Bug.master as the filename. Master pages have the filename extension .master and, like Web Forms, can optionally use a code-behind file to define additional functionality. In this example, we do not need to specify any code for the master page, so leave the box labeled **Place code in a separate file** unchecked. Click **Add** to create the page.

The IDE opens the master page in **Source** mode (Fig. 21.54) when the file is first created. [*Note:* We added a line break in the DOCTYPE element for presentation purposes.] The markup for a master page is almost identical to that of a Web Form. One difference is that a master page contains a **Master** directive (line 1 in Fig. 21.54), which specifies that this file defines a master page using the indicated Language for any code. Because we chose not to use a code-behind file, the master page also contains a **script** element (lines 6–8). Code that would usually be placed in a code-behind file can be placed in a script element.

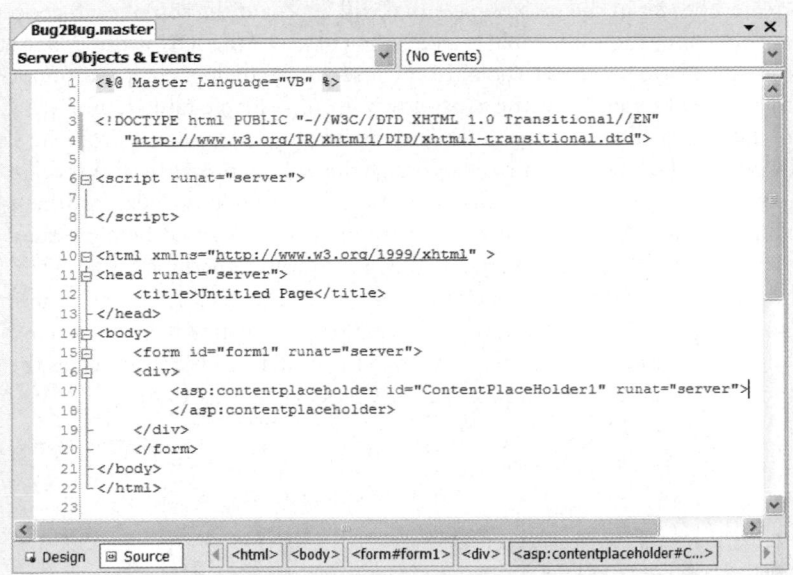

Fig. 21.54 | Master page in **Source** mode.

However, we remove the script element from this page, because we do not need to write any additional code. After deleting this block of markup, set the title of the page to Bug2Bug. Finally, notice that the master page contains a **ContentPlaceHolder** control (lines 17–18 of Fig. 21.54). This control serves as a placeholder for content that will be defined by a content page. You will see how to define content to replace the **Content-PlaceHolder** shortly.

At this point, you can edit the master page in **Design** mode (Fig. 21.55) as if it were an ASPX file. Notice that the ContentPlaceHolder control appears as a large rectangle with a gray bar indicating the control's type and ID. Using the **Properties** window, change the ID of this control to bodyContent.

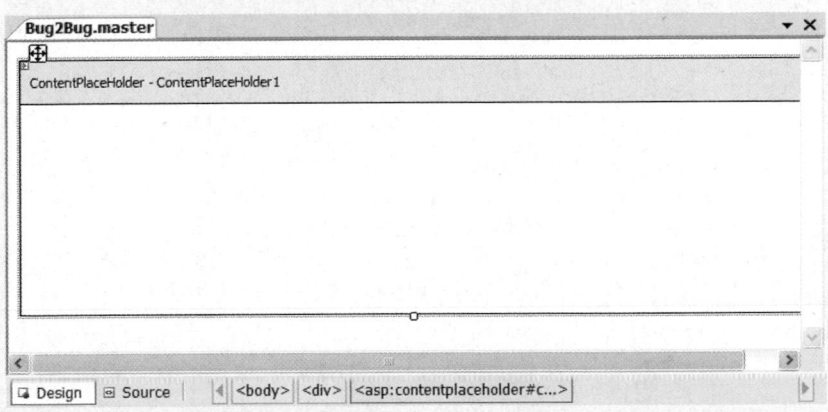

Fig. 21.55 | Master page in **Design** mode.

To create a header in the master page that will appear at the top of each content page, we insert a table into the master page. Place the cursor to the left of the ContentPlace-Holder and select **Layout > Insert Table**. In the **Insert Table** dialog, click the **Template** radio button, then select **Header** from the drop-down list of available table templates. Click **OK** to create a table that fills the page and contains two rows. Drag and drop the Content-PlaceHolder into the bottom table cell. Change the valign property of this cell to top, so the ContentPlaceHolder vertically aligns with the top of the cell. Next, set the Height of the top table cell to 130. Add to this cell an Image control named headerImage with its ImageUrl property set to the bug2bug.png file in the project's Images folder. (You can also simply drag the image from the **Solution Explorer** into the top cell.) Figure 21.56 shows the markup and **Design** view of the completed master page. As you will see in *Step 6*, a content page based on this master page displays the logo image defined here, as well as the content designed for that specific page (in place of the ContentPlaceHolder).

```
 1   <%-- Fig. 21.56: Bug2bug.master --%>
 2   <%-- Master page that defines common features of all pages in the --%>
 3   <%-- secure book database application. --%>
 4   <%@ Master Language="VB" %>
 5
 6   <!DOCTYPE html PUBLIC "-//W3C//DTD XHTML 1.0 Transitional//EN"
 7      "http://www.w3.org/TR/xhtml1/DTD/xhtml1-transitional.dtd">
 8
 9   <html xmlns="http://www.w3.org/1999/xhtml" >
10   <head runat="server">
11      <title>Bug2Bug</title>
12   </head>
13   <body>
14      <form id="form1" runat="server">
15      <div>
16        <table border="0" cellpadding="0" cellspacing="0"
17          style="width: 100%; height: 100%">
18          <tr>
19            <td height="130" style="width: 887px">
20              <asp:Image ID="headerImage" runat="server"
21                ImageUrl="~/Images/bug2bug.png" />
22            </td>
23          </tr>
24          <tr>
25            <td style="width: 887px" valign="top">
26              <asp:contentplaceholder id="bodyContent" runat="server">
27              </asp:contentplaceholder>
28            </td>
29          </tr>
30        </table>
31         
32      </div>
33      </form>
34   </body>
35   </html>
```

Fig. 21.56 | Bug2Bug.master page that defines a logo image header for all pages in the secure book database application. (Part 1 of 2.)

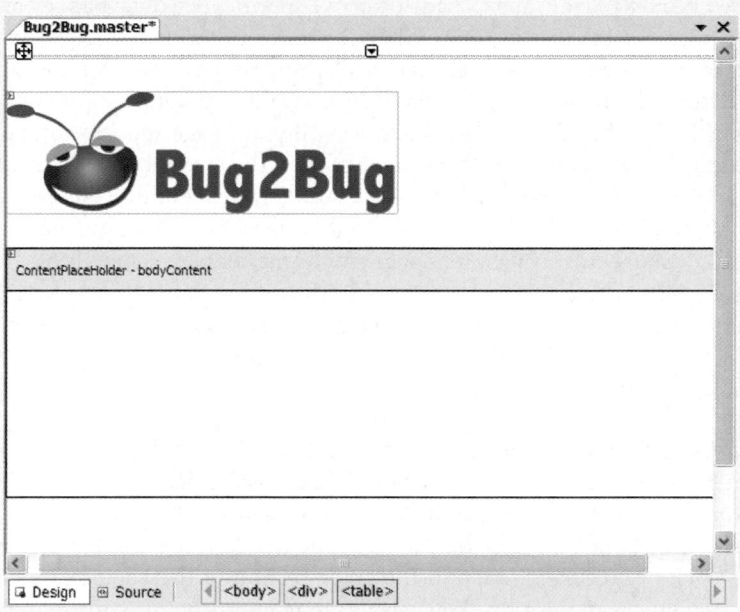

Fig. 21.56 | `Bug2Bug.master` page that defines a logo image header for all pages in the secure book database application. (Part 2 of 2.)

Step 6: Creating a Content Page

We now create a content page based on `Bug2Bug.master`. We begin by building `Create-NewUser.aspx`. To create this file, right click the master page in the **Solution Explorer** and select **Add Content Page**. This action causes a `Default.aspx` file, configured to use the master page, to be added to the project. Rename this file `CreateNewUser.aspx`, then open it in **Source** mode (Fig. 21.57). Note that this file contains a `Page` directive with a `Language` property, a `MasterPageFile` property and a `Title` property. The `Page` directive indicates the `MasterPageFile` that is used as a starting point for this new page's design. In this case, the `MasterPageFile` property is set to `"~/Bug2Bug.master"` to indicate that the current file is based on the master page we just created. The `Title` property specifies the title that will be displayed in the Web browser's title bar when the content page is loaded. This value, which we set to `Create a New User`, replaces the value (i.e., `Bug2Bug`) set in the `title` element of the master page.

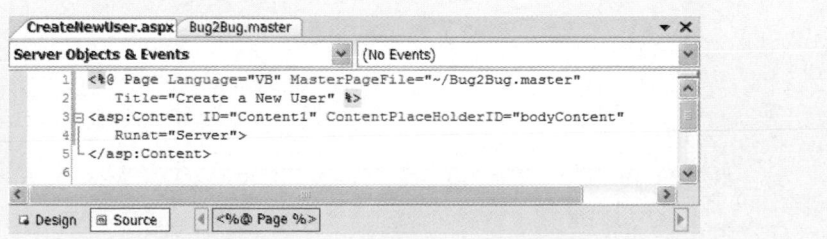

Fig. 21.57 | Content page `CreateNewUser.aspx` in **Source** mode.

Because CreateNewUser.aspx's Page directive specifies Bug2Bug.master as the page's MasterPageFile, the content page implicitly contains the contents of the master page, such as the DOCTYPE, html and body elements. The content page file does not duplicate the XHTML elements found in the master page. Instead, the content page contains a **Content** control (lines 3–5 in Fig. 21.57), in which we will place page-specific content that will replace the master page's ContentPlaceHolder when the content page is requested. The ContentPlaceHolderID property of the Content control identifies the ContentPlace-Holder in the master page that the control should replace—in this case, bodyContent.

The relationship between a content page and its master page is more evident in **Design** mode (Fig. 21.58). The gray shaded region contains the contents of the master page Bug2Bug.master as they will appear in CreateNewUser.aspx when rendered in a Web browser. The only editable part of this page is the Content control, which appears in place of the master page's ContentPlaceHolder.

Step 7: Adding a *CreateUserWizard* Control to a Content Page
Recall from Section 21.8.1 that CreateNewUser.aspx is the page in our Web site that allows first-time visitors to create user accounts. To provide this functionality, we use a CreateUserWizard control. Place the cursor inside the Content control in **Design** mode and double click CreateUserWizard in the **Login** section of the **Toolbox** to add it to the page at the current cursor position. You can also drag-and-drop the control onto the page. To change the CreateUserWizard's appearance, open the **CreateUserWizard Tasks** smart tag menu, and click **Auto Format**. Select the **Professional** color scheme.

As discussed previously, a CreateUserWizard provides a registration form that site visitors can use to create a user account. ASP.NET creates a SQL Server database (named ASPNETDB.MDF and located in the App_Data folder) to store the user names, passwords and other account information of the application's users. ASP.NET also enforces a default set of requirements for filling out the form. Each field on the form is required, the password must contain at least seven characters (including at least one non-alphanumeric character)

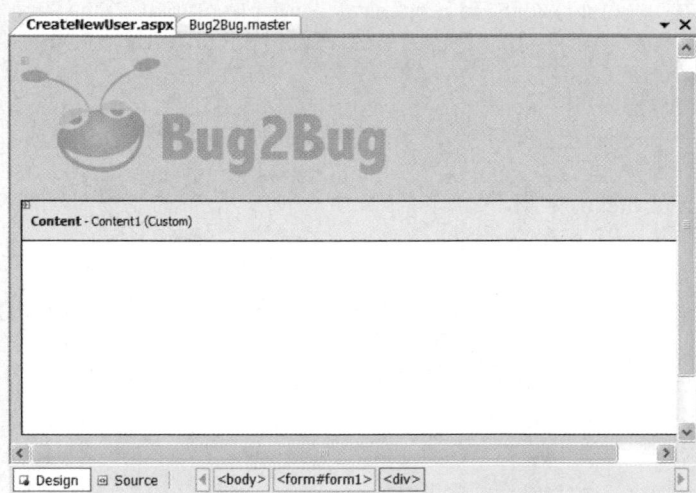

Fig. 21.58 | Content page CreateNewUser.aspx in **Design** mode.

and the two passwords entered must match. The form also asks for a security question and answer that can be used to identify a user in case the user needs to reset or recover the account's password.

After the user fills in the form's fields and clicks the **Create User** button to submit the account information, ASP.NET verifies that all the form's requirements were fulfilled and attempts to create the user account. If an error occurs (e.g., the user name already exists), the CreateUserWizard displays a message below the form. If the account is created successfully, the form is replaced by a confirmation message and a button that allows the user to continue. You can view this confirmation message in **Design** mode by selecting **Complete** from the **Step** drop-down list in the **CreateUserWizard Tasks** smart tag menu.

When a user account is created, ASP.NET automatically logs the user into the site (we say more about the login process shortly). At this point, the user is authenticated and allowed to access the Secure folder. After we create Books.aspx later in this section, we set the CreateUserWizard's ContinueDestinationPageUrl property to ~/Secure/ Books.aspx to indicate that the user should be redirected to Books.aspx after clicking the **Continue** button on the confirmation page.

Figure 21.59 presents the completed CreateNewUser.aspx file (reformatted for readability). Inside the Content control, the CreateUserWizard control is defined by the markup in lines 7–36. The start tag (lines 7–10) contains several properties that specify formatting styles for the control, as well as the ContinueDestinationPageUrl property, which you will set later in the chapter. Lines 11–16 specify the wizard's two steps— CreateUserWizardStep and CompleteWizardStep—in a WizardSteps element. Create-UserWizardStep and CompleteWizardStep are classes that encapsulate the details of creating a user and issuing a confirmation message. Finally, lines 17–35 contain elements that define additional styles used to format specific parts of the control.

The sample outputs in Fig. 21.59(a) and Fig. 21.59(b) demonstrate successfully creating a user account with CreateNewUser.aspx. We use the password pa$$word for testing purposes. This password satisfies the minimum length and special character requirement imposed by ASP.NET, but in a real application, you should use a password that is more difficult for someone to guess. Figure 21.59(c) illustrates the error message that appears when you attempt to create a second user account with the same user name—ASP.NET requires that each user name be unique.

```
1    <%-- Fig. 21.59: CreateNewUser.aspx --%>
2    <%-- Content page using a CreateUserWizard control to register users. --%>
3    <%@ Page Language="VB" MasterPageFile="~/Bug2Bug.master"
4       Title="Create a New User" %>
5    <asp:Content ID="Content1" ContentPlaceHolderID="bodyContent"
6       Runat="Server">
7       <asp:CreateUserWizard ID="CreateUserWizard1" runat="server"
8          BackColor="#F7F6F3" BorderColor="#E6E2D8" BorderStyle="Solid"
9          BorderWidth="1px" Font-Names="Verdana" Font-Size="0.8em"
10         ContinueDestinationPageUrl="~/Secure/Books.aspx">
11         <WizardSteps>
12            <asp:CreateUserWizardStep runat="server">
```

Fig. 21.59 | CreateNewUser.aspx content page that provides a user registration form. (Part 1 of 3.)

```
13              </asp:CreateUserWizardStep>
14              <asp:CompleteWizardStep runat="server">
15              </asp:CompleteWizardStep>
16          </WizardSteps>
17          <SideBarStyle BackColor="#5D7B9D" BorderWidth="0px"
18              Font-Size="0.9em" VerticalAlign="Top" />
19          <TitleTextStyle BackColor="#5D7B9D" Font-Bold="True"
20              ForeColor="White" />
21          <SideBarButtonStyle BorderWidth="0px" Font-Names="Verdana"
22              ForeColor="White" />
23          <NavigationButtonStyle BackColor="#FFFBFF" BorderColor="#CCCCCC"
24              BorderStyle="Solid" BorderWidth="1px" Font-Names="Verdana"
25              ForeColor="#284775" />
26          <HeaderStyle BackColor="#5D7B9D" BorderStyle="Solid"
27              Font-Bold="True" Font-Size="0.9em"
28              ForeColor="White" HorizontalAlign="Center" />
29          <CreateUserButtonStyle BackColor="#FFFBFF" BorderColor="#CCCCCC"
30              BorderStyle="Solid" BorderWidth="1px" Font-Names="Verdana"
31              ForeColor="#284775" />
32          <ContinueButtonStyle BackColor="#FFFBFF" BorderColor="#CCCCCC"
33              BorderStyle="Solid" BorderWidth="1px" Font-Names="Verdana"
34              ForeColor="#284775" />
35          <StepStyle BorderWidth="0px" />
36      </asp:CreateUserWizard>
37  </asp:Content>
```

(a)

(b)

Fig. 21.59 | `CreateNewUser.aspx` content page that provides a user registration form. (Part 2 of 3.)

Fig. 21.59 | `CreateNewUser.aspx` content page that provides a user registration form. (Part 3 of 3.)

Step 8: Creating a Login Page

Recall from Section 21.8.1 that `Login.aspx` is the page in our Web site that allows returning visitors to log into their user accounts. To create this functionality, add another content page named `Login.aspx` and set its title to `Login`. In **Design** mode, drag a `Login` control (located in the **Login** section of the **Toolbox**) to the page's **Content** control. Open the **Auto Format** dialog from the **Login Tasks** smart tag menu and set the control's color scheme to **Professional**.

Next, configure the `Login` control to display a link to the page for creating new users. Set the `Login` control's `CreateUserUrl` property to `CreateNewUser.aspx` by clicking the ellipsis button to the right of this property in the **Properties** window and selecting the `CreateNewUser.aspx` file in the resulting dialog. Then set the `CreateUserText` property to `Click here to create a new user`. These property values cause a link to appear in the `Login` control.

Finally, change the value of the `Login` control's `DisplayRememberMe` property to `False`. By default, the control displays a checkbox and the text `Remember me next time`. This can be used to allow a user to remain authenticated beyond a single browser session on the user's current computer. However, we want to require that users log in each time they visit the site, so we disable this option.

The `Login` control encapsulates the details of logging a user into a Web application (i.e., authenticating a user). When a user enters a user name and password, then clicks the **Log In** button, ASP.NET determines whether the information provided match those of an account in the membership database (i.e., `ASPNETDB.MDF` created by ASP.NET). If they match, the user is authenticated (i.e., the user's identity is confirmed), and the browser is redirected to the page specified by the `Login` control's `DestinationPageUrl` property. We set this property to the `Books.aspx` page after creating it in the next section. If the user's identity cannot be confirmed (i.e., the user is not authenticated), the `Login` control displays an error message (see Fig. 21.60), and the user can attempt to log in again.

Figure 21.60 presents the completed `Login.aspx` file. Note that, as in `CreateNewUser.aspx`, the `Page` directive indicates that this content page inherits content from `Bug2Bug.master`. In the `Content` control that replaces the master page's `ContentPlaceHolder` with `ID` bodyContent, lines 6–18 create a `Login` control. Note the `CreateUserText` and `CreateUserUrl` properties (lines 8–9) that we set using the **Properties** window. Line 11 in the start tag for the `Login` control contains the `DestinationPageUrl` (you will

```
1   <%-- Fig. 21.60: Login.aspx --%>
2   <%-- Content page using a Login control that authenticates users. --%>
3   <%@ Page Language="VB" MasterPageFile="~/Bug2Bug.master" Title="Login" %>
4   <asp:Content ID="Content1" ContentPlaceHolderID="bodyContent"
5      Runat="Server">
6      <asp:Login ID="Login1" runat="server" BackColor="#F7F6F3"
7         BorderColor="#E6E2D8" BorderPadding="4" BorderStyle="Solid"
8         BorderWidth="1px" CreateUserText="Click here to create a new user"
9         CreateUserUrl="~/CreateNewUser.aspx" DisplayRememberMe="False"
10        Font-Names="Verdana" Font-Size="0.8em" ForeColor="#333333"
11        DestinationPageUrl="~/Secure/Books.aspx">
12        <TitleTextStyle BackColor="#5D7B9D" Font-Bold="True"
13           Font-Size="0.9em" ForeColor="White" />
14        <InstructionTextStyle Font-Italic="True" ForeColor="Black" />
15        <TextBoxStyle Font-Size="0.8em" />
16        <LoginButtonStyle BackColor="#FFFBFF" BorderColor="#CCCCCC"
17           BorderStyle="Solid" BorderWidth="1px" Font-Names="Verdana"
18           Font-Size="0.8em" ForeColor="#284775" />
19     </asp:Login>
20   </asp:Content>
```

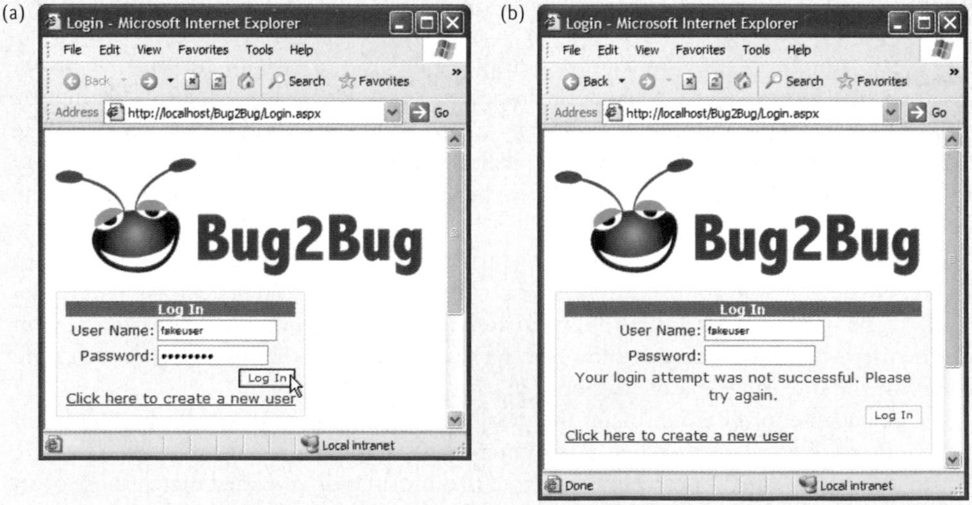

Fig. 21.60 | `Login.aspx` content page using a `login` control.

set this property in the next step). The elements in lines 12–18 define various formatting styles applied to parts of the control. Note that all of the functionality related to actually logging the user in or displaying error messages is completely hidden from you.

When a user enters the user name and password of an existing user account, ASP.NET authenticates the user and writes to the client an encrypted cookie containing information about the authenticated user. Encrypted data is data translated into a code that only the sender and receiver can understand—thereby keeping it private. The encrypted cookie contains a String user name and a Boolean value that specifies whether this cookie should persist (i.e., remain on the client's computer) beyond the current session. Our application authenticates the user only for the current session.

Step 9: Creating a Content Page That Only Authenticated Users Can Access

A user who has been authenticated will be redirected to Books.aspx. We now create the Books.aspx file in the Secure folder—the folder for which we set an access rule denying access to anonymous users. If an unauthenticated user requests this file, the user will be redirected to Login.aspx. From there, the user can either log in or a create a new account, both of which will authenticate the user, thus allowing the user to return to Books.aspx.

To create Books.aspx, right click the Secure folder in the **Solution Explorer** and select **Add New Item....** In the resulting dialog, select **Web Form** and specify the file name Books.aspx. Check the box **Select Master Page** to indicate that this Web Form should be created as a content page that references a master page, then click **Add**. In the **Select a Master Page** dialog, select Bug2Bug.master and click **OK**. The IDE creates the file and opens it in **Source** mode. Change the Title property of the Page directive to Book Information.

Step 10: Customizing the Secure Page

To customize the Books.aspx page for a particular user, we add a welcome message containing a LoginName control, which displays the current authenticated user name. Open Books.aspx in **Design** mode. In the Content control, type Welcome followed by a comma and a space. Then drag a LoginName control from the **Toolbox** onto the page. When this page executes on the server, the text [UserName] that appears in this control in **Design** mode will be replaced by the current user name. In **Source** mode, type an exclamation point (!) directly after the LoginName control (with no spaces in between). [*Note:* If you add the exclamation point in **Design** mode, the IDE may insert extra spaces or a line break between this character and the preceding control. Entering the ! in **Source** mode ensures that it appears adjacent to the user's name.]

Next, add a LoginStatus control, which will allow the user to log out of the Web site when finished viewing the listing of books in the database. A LoginStatus control renders on a Web page in one of two ways—by default, if the user is not authenticated, the control displays a hyperlink with the text Login; if the user is authenticated, the control displays a hyperlink with the text Logout. Each link performs the stated action. Add a LoginStatus control to the page by dragging it from the **Toolbox** onto the page. In this example, any user who reaches this page must already be authenticated, so the control will always render as a Logout link. The **LoginStatus Tasks** smart tag menu allows you switch between the control's **Views**. Select the **Logged In** view to see the Logout link. To change the actual text of this link, modify the control's LogoutText property to Click here to log out. Next, set the LogoutAction property to RedirectToLoginPage.

*Step 11: Connecting the **CreateUserWizard** and **Login** Controls to the Secure Page*
Now that we have created `Books.aspx`, we can specify that this is the page to which the `CreateUserWizard` and `Login` controls redirect users after they are authenticated. Open `CreateNewUser.aspx` in **Design** mode and set the `CreateUserWizard` control's `Continue-DestinationPageUrl` property to `Books.aspx`. Next, open `Login.aspx` and select `Books.aspx` as the `DestinationPageUrl` of the `Login` control.

At this point, you can run the Web application by selecting **Debug > Start Without Debugging**. First, create a user account on `CreateNewUser.aspx`, then notice how the `LoginName` and `LoginStatus` controls appear on `Books.aspx`. Next, log out of the site and log back in using `Login.aspx`.

*Step 12: Generating a **DataSet** Based on the **Books.mdf** Database*
Now, let's add the content (i.e., book information) to the secure page `Books.aspx`. This page will provide a `DropDownList` containing authors' names and a `GridView` displaying information about books written by the author selected in the `DropDownList`. A user will select an author from the `DropDownList` to cause the `GridView` to display information about only the books written by the selected author. As you will see, we create this functionality entirely in **Design** mode without writing any code.

To work with the `Books` database, we use an approach slightly different than in the preceding case study in which we accessed the `Guestbook` database using a `SqlDataSource` control. Here we use an **ObjectDataSource** control, which encapsulates an object that provides access to a data source. Recall that in Chapter 20, we accessed the `Books` database in a Windows application using `TableAdapters` configured to communicate with the database file. These `TableAdapters` placed a cached copy of the database's data in a `DataSet`, which the application then accessed. We use a similar approach in this example. An `ObjectDataSource` can encapsulate a `TableAdapter` and use its methods to access the data in the database. This helps separate the data-access logic from the presentation logic. As you will see shortly, the SQL statements used to retrieve data do not appear in the ASPX page when using an `ObjectDataSource`.

The first step in accessing data using an `ObjectDataSource` is to create a `DataSet` that contains the data from the `Books` database required by the application. In Visual Basic 2005 Express, this occurs automatically when you add a data source to a project. In Visual Web Developer, however, you must explicitly generate the `DataSet`. Right click the project's location in the **Solution Explorer** and select **Add New Item....** In the resulting dialog, select **DataSet** and specify `BooksDataSet.xsd` as the file name, then click **Add**. A dialog will appear that asks you whether the `DataSet` should be placed in an `App_Code` folder—a folder whose contents are compiled and made available to all parts of the project. Click **Yes** for the IDE to create this folder to store `BooksDataSet.xsd`.

*Step 13: Creating and Configuring an **AuthorsTableAdapter***
Once the `DataSet` is added, the **Dataset Designer** will appear, and the **TableAdapter Configuration Wizard** will open. Recall from Chapter 20 that this wizard allows you to configure a `TableAdapter` for filling a `DataTable` in a `DataSet` with data from a database. The `Books.aspx` page requires two sets of data—a list of authors that will be displayed in the page's `DropDownList` (created shortly) and a list of books written by a specific author. We focus on the first set of data here—the authors. Thus, we use the **TableAdapter Configura-**

tion Wizard first to configure an `AuthorsTableAdapter`. In the next step, we will configure a `TitlesTableAdapter`.

In the **TableAdapter Configuration Wizard**, select `Books.mdf` from the drop-down list. Then click **Next >** twice to save the connection string in the application's `Web.config` file and move to the **Choose a Command Type** screen.

In the wizard's **Choose a Command Type** screen, select **Use SQL statements** and click **Next >**. The next screen allows you to enter a `SELECT` statement for retrieving data from the database, which will then be placed in an `Authors DataTable` within the `Books-DataSet`. Enter the SQL statement

```
SELECT AuthorID, FirstName + ' ' + LastName AS Name FROM Authors
```

in the text box on the **Enter a SQL Statement** screen. This query selects the `AuthorID` of each row. This query's result will also contain a column named `Name` that is created by concatenating each row's `FirstName` and `LastName`, separated by a space. The **AS** SQL keyword allows you to generate a column in a query result—called an *alias*—that contains the result of a SQL expression (e.g., `FirstName + ' ' + LastName`). You will soon see how we use the result of this query to populate the `DropDownList` with items containing the authors' full names.

After entering the SQL statement, click the **Advanced Options...** button and uncheck **Generate Insert, Update and Delete statements**, since this application does not need to modify the database's contents. Click **OK** to close the **Advanced Options** dialog. Click **Next >** to advance to the **Choose Methods to Generate** screen. Leave the default names and click **Finish**. Notice that the **DataSet Designer** (Fig. 21.61) now displays a `DataTable` named `Authors` with `AuthorID` and `Name` members, and `Fill` and `GetData` methods.

Step 14: Creating and Configuring a *TitlesTableAdapter*

`Books.aspx` needs to access a list of books by a specific author and a list of authors. Thus we must create a `TitlesTableAdapter` that will retrieve the desired information from the database's `Titles` table. Right click the **Dataset Designer** and from the menu that appears, select **Add > TableAdapter...** to launch the **TableAdapter Configuration Wizard**. Make sure the `BooksConnectionString` is selected as the connection in the wizard's first screen, then click **Next >**. Choose **Use SQL statements** and click **Next >**.

In the **Enter a SQL Statement** screen, open the **Advanced Options** dialog and uncheck **Generate Insert, Update and Delete statements**, then click **OK**. Our application allows users to filter the books displayed by the author's name, so we need to build a query that takes an `AuthorID` as a parameter and returns the rows in the `Titles` table for books written by that author. To build this complex query, click the **Query Builder...** button.

Fig. 21.61 | Authors `DataTable` in the **Dataset Designer**.

In the **Add Table** dialog that appears, select **AuthorISBN** and click **Add**. Then **Add** the **Titles** table, too. Our query will require access to data in both of these tables. Click **Close** to exit the **Add Table** dialog. In the top pane of the **Query Builder** window (Fig. 21.62), check the box marked *** (All Columns)** in the **Titles** table. Next, in the middle pane, add a row with **Column** set to `AuthorISBN.AuthorID`. Uncheck the **Output** box, because we do not want the **AuthorID** to appear in our query result. Add an `@authorID` parameter in this row's **Filter** column. The SQL statement generated by these actions retrieves information about all books written by the author specified by parameter `@authorID`. The statement first merges the data from the `AuthorISBN` and `Titles` tables. The `INNER JOIN` clause specifies that the `ISBN` columns of each table are compared to determine which rows are merged. The `INNER JOIN` results in a temporary table containing the columns of both tables. The `WHERE` clause of the SQL statement restricts the book information from this temporary table to a specific author (i.e., all rows in which the `AuthorID` column is equal to `@authorID`).

Click **OK** to exit the **Query Builder**, then in the **TableAdapter Configuration Wizard**, click **Next >**. On the **Choose Methods to Generate** screen, enter `FillByAuthorID` and `GetDataByAuthorID` as the names of the two methods to be generated for the `TitlesTableAdapter`. Click **Finish** to exit the wizard. You should now see a `Titles DataTable` in the **Dataset Designer** (Fig. 21.63).

Step 15: Adding a *DropDownList* Containing Authors' First and Last Names

Now that we have created a `BooksDataSet` and configured the necessary `TableAdapters`, we add controls to `Books.aspx` that will display the data on the Web page. We first add

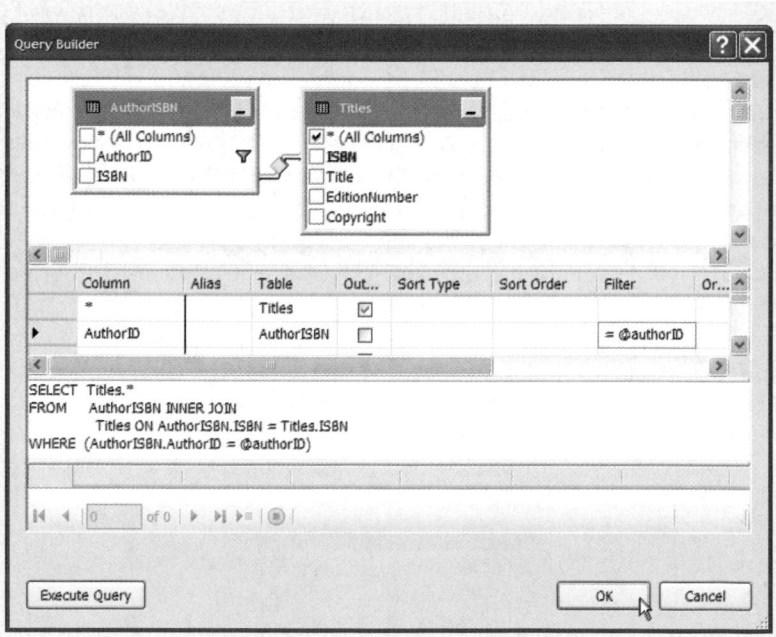

Fig. 21.62 | **Query Builder** for designing a query that selects books written by a particular author.

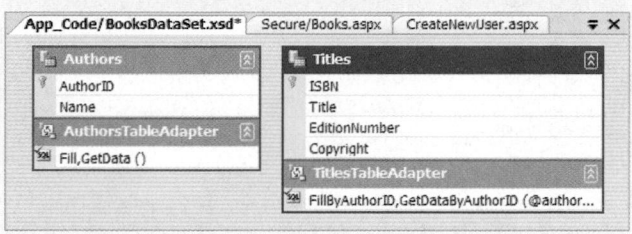

Fig. 21.63 | **Dataset Designer** after adding the `TitlesTableAdapter`.

the `DropDownList` from which users can select an author. Open `Books.aspx` in **Design** mode, then add the text `Author:` and a `DropDownList` control named `authorsDropDownList` in the page's `Content` control, below the existing content. The `DropDownList` initially displays the text `[Unbound]`. We now bind the list to a data source, so the list displays the author information placed in the `BooksDataSet` by the `AuthorsTableAdapter`. In the **DropDownList Tasks** smart tag menu, click **Choose Data Source...** to start the **Data Source Configuration Wizard**. Select **<New data source...>** from the **Select a data source** drop-down list in the first screen of the wizard. Doing so opens the **Choose a Data Source Type** screen. Select **Object** and set the ID to `authorsObjectDataSource`, then click **OK**.

An `ObjectDataSource` accesses data through another object, often called a **business object**. Recall from Section 21.3 that the middle tier of a three-tier application contains business logic that controls the way an application's top tier user interface (in this case, `Books.aspx`) accesses the bottom tier's data (in this case, the `Books.mdf` database file). Thus, a business object represents the middle tier of an application and mediates interactions between the other two tiers. In an ASP.NET Web application, a `TableAdapter` typically serves as the business object that retrieves the data from the bottom-tier database and makes it available to the top-tier user interface through a `DataSet`. In the **Choose a Business Object** screen of the **Configure Data Source** wizard (Fig. 21.64), select `BooksDataSet-TableAdapters.AuthorsTableAdapter`. [*Note:* You may need to save the project to see the `AuthorsTableAdapter`.] `BooksDataSetTableAdapters` is a namespace declared by the IDE when you create `BooksDataSet`. Click **Next >** to continue.

The **Define Data Methods** screen (Fig. 21.65) allows you to specify which method of the business object (in this case, `AuthorsTableAdapter`) should be used to obtain the data accessed through the `ObjectDataSource`. You can choose only methods that return data, so the only choice provided is the `GetData` method, which returns an `AuthorsDataTable`. Click **Finish** to close the **Configure Data Source** wizard and return to the **Data Source Configuration Wizard** for the `DropDownList` (Fig. 21.66). The newly created data source (i.e., `authorsObjectDataSource`) should be selected in the top drop-down list. The other two drop-down lists on this screen allow you to configure how the `DropDownList` control uses the data from the data source. Set `Name` as the data field to display and `AuthorID` as the data field to use as the value. Thus, when `authorsDropDownList` is rendered in a Web browser, the list items will display the names of the authors, but the underlying values associated with each item will be the `AuthorID`s of the authors. Finally, click **OK** to bind the `DropDownList` to the specified data.

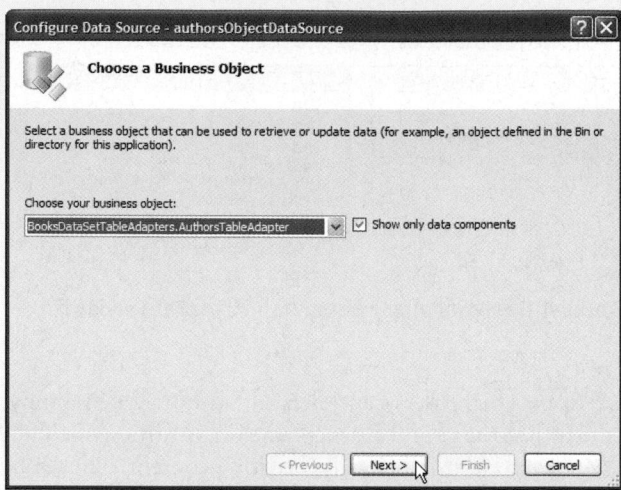

Fig. 21.64 | Choosing a business object for an `ObjectDataSource`.

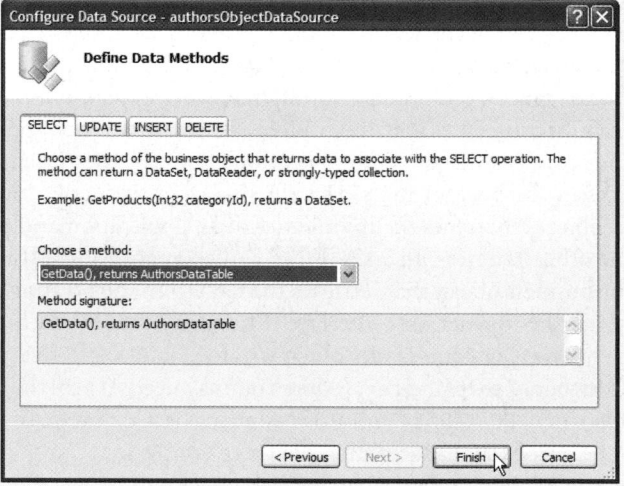

Fig. 21.65 | Choosing a data method of a business object for use with an `ObjectDataSource`.

The last step in configuring the `DropDownList` on `Books.aspx` is to set the control's `AutoPostBack` property to `True`. This property indicates that a postback occurs each time the user selects an item in the `DropDownList`. As you will see shortly, this causes the page's `GridView` (created in the next step) to display new data.

Step 16: Creating a `GridView` to Display the Selected Author's Books
We now add a `GridView` to `Books.aspx` for displaying the book information by the author selected in the `authorsDropDownList`. Add a `GridView` named `titlesGridView` below the other controls in the page's `Content` control.

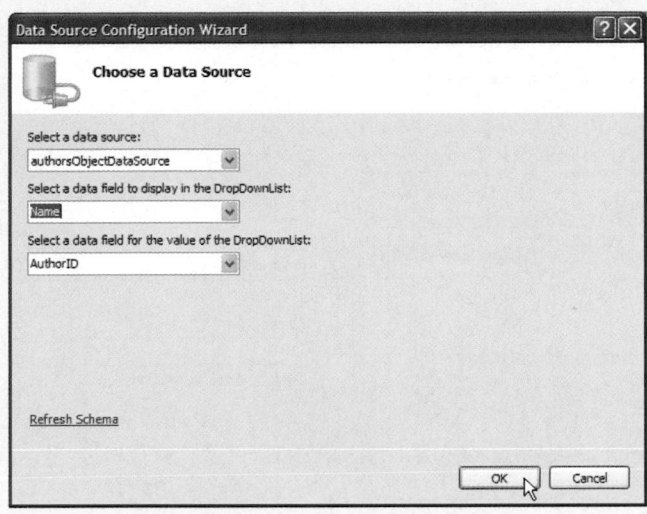

Fig. 21.66 | Choosing a data source for a DropDownList.

To bind the GridView to data from the Books database, select **<New data source...>** from the **Choose Data Source** drop-down list in the **GridView Tasks** smart tag menu. When the **Data Source Configuration Wizard** opens, select **Object** and set the ID of the data source to titlesObjectDataSource, then click **OK**. In the **Choose a Business Object** screen, select the BooksDataSetTableAdapters.TitlesTableAdapter from the drop-down list to indicate the object that will be used to access the data. Click **Next >**. In the **Define Data Methods** screen, leave the default selection of GetDataByAuthorID as the method that will be invoked to obtain the data for display in the GridView. Click **Next >**.

Recall that TitlesTableAdapter method GetDataByAuthorID requires a parameter to indicate the AuthorID for which data should be retrieved. The **Define Parameters** screen (Fig. 21.67) allows you to specify where to obtain the value of the @authorID parameter in the SQL statement executed by GetDataByAuthorID. Select **Control** from the **Parameter source** drop-down list. Select authorsDropDownList as the **ControlID** (i.e., the ID of the parameter source control). Next, enter 1 as the **DefaultValue**, so books by Harvey Deitel (who has AuthorID 1 in the database) display when the page first loads (i.e., before the user has made any selections using the authorsDropDownList). Finally, click **Finish** to exit the wizard. The GridView is now configured to display the data retrieved by TitlesTableAdapter.GetDataByAuthorID, using the value of the current selection in authorsDropDownList as the parameter. Thus, when the user selects a new author and a postback occurs, the GridView displays a new set of data.

Now that the GridView is tied to a data source, we modify several of the control's properties to adjust its appearance and behavior. Set the GridView's CellPadding property to 5, set the BackColor of the AlternatingRowStyle to LightYellow, and set the Back-Color of the HeaderStyle to LightGreen. Change the Width of the control to 600px to accommodate long data values.

Next, in the **GridView Tasks** smart tag menu, check **Enable Sorting**. This causes the column headings in the GridView to turn into hyperlinks that allow users to sort the data

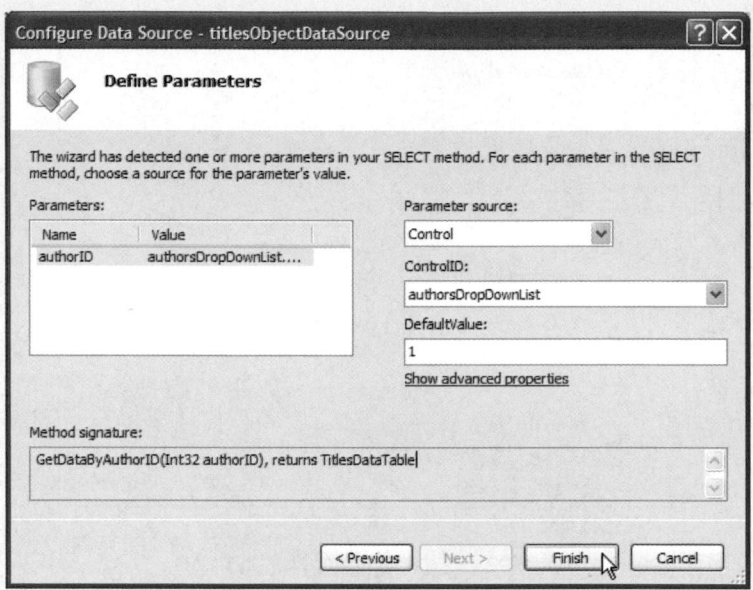

Fig. 21.67 | Choosing the data source for a parameter in a business object's data method.

in the GridView. For example, clicking the Titles heading in the Web browser will cause the displayed data to appear sorted in alphabetical order. Clicking this heading a second time will cause the data to be sorted in reverse alphabetical order. ASP.NET hides the details required to achieve this functionality.

Finally, in the **GridView Tasks** smart tag menu, check **Enable Paging**. This causes the GridView to split across multiple pages. The user can click the numbered links at the bottom of the GridView control to display a different page of data. GridView's **PageSize** property determines the number of entries per page. Set the PageSize property to 4 using the **Properties** window so that the GridView displays only four books per page. This technique for displaying data makes the site more readable and enables pages to load more quickly (because less data is displayed at one time). Note that, as with sorting data in a GridView, you do not need to add any code to achieve paging functionality. Fig. 21.68 displays the completed Books.aspx file in **Design** mode.

Step 17: Examining the Markup in Books.aspx
Figure 21.69 presents the markup in Books.aspx (reformatted for readability). Aside from the exclamation point in line 8, which we added manually in **Source** mode, all the remaining markup was generated by the IDE in response to the actions we performed in **Design** mode. The Content control (lines 5–53) defines page-specific content that will replace the ContentPlaceHolder named bodyContent. Recall that this control is located in the master page specified in line 3. Line 8 creates the LoginName control, which displays the authenticated user's name when the page is requested and viewed in a browser. Lines 9–11 create the LoginStatus control. Recall that this control is configured to redirect the user to the login page after logging out (i.e., clicking the hyperlink with the LogoutText).

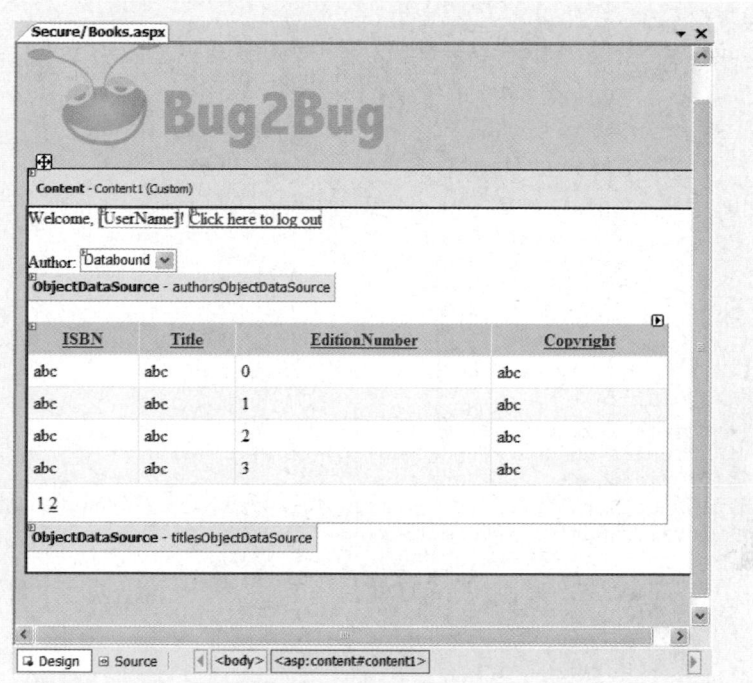

Fig. 21.68 | Completed `Books.aspx` in **Design** mode.

```
 1  <%-- Fig. 21.69: Books.aspx --%>
 2  <%-- Displays information from the Books database. --%>
 3  <%@ Page Language="VB" MasterPageFile="~/Bug2Bug.master"
 4     Title="Book Information" %>
 5  <asp:Content ID="Content1" ContentPlaceHolderID="bodyContent"
 6     Runat="Server">
 7     Welcome,
 8     <asp:LoginName ID="LoginName1" runat="server" />!
 9     <asp:LoginStatus ID="LoginStatus1" runat="server"
10        LogoutAction="RedirectToLoginPage"
11        LogoutText="Click here to log out" />
12     <br />
13     <br />
14     Author:
15     <asp:DropDownList ID="authorsDropDownList" runat="server"
16        AutoPostBack="True" DataSourceID="authorsObjectDataSource"
17        DataTextField="Name" DataValueField="AuthorID">
18     </asp:DropDownList>
19     <asp:ObjectDataSource ID="authorsObjectDataSource"
20        runat="server" OldValuesParameterFormatString="original_{0}"
21        SelectMethod="GetData"
22        TypeName="BooksDataSetTableAdapters.AuthorsTableAdapter">
23     </asp:ObjectDataSource>
24     <br />
```

Fig. 21.69 | Markup for the completed `Books.aspx` file. (Part 1 of 3.)

```
25      <br />
26      <asp:GridView ID="titlesGridView" runat="server" AllowPaging="True"
27          AllowSorting="True" AutoGenerateColumns="False" CellPadding="5"
28          DataKeyNames="ISBN" DataSourceID="titlesObjectDataSource"
29          PageSize="4" Width="600px">
30          <Columns>
31              <asp:BoundField DataField="ISBN" HeaderText="ISBN"
32                  ReadOnly="True" SortExpression="ISBN" />
33              <asp:BoundField DataField="Title" HeaderText="Title"
34                  SortExpression="Title" />
35              <asp:BoundField DataField="EditionNumber"
36                  HeaderText="EditionNumber" SortExpression="EditionNumber" />
37              <asp:BoundField DataField="Copyright" HeaderText="Copyright"
38                  SortExpression="Copyright" />
39          </Columns>
40          <HeaderStyle BackColor="LightGreen" />
41          <AlternatingRowStyle BackColor="LightYellow" />
42      </asp:GridView>
43      <asp:ObjectDataSource ID="titlesObjectDataSource" runat="server"
44          OldValuesParameterFormatString="original_{0}"
45          SelectMethod="GetDataByAuthorID"
46          TypeName="BooksDataSetTableAdapters.TitlesTableAdapter">
47          <SelectParameters>
48              <asp:ControlParameter ControlID="authorsDropDownList"
49                  DefaultValue="1" Name="authorID"
50                  PropertyName="SelectedValue" Type="Int32" />
51          </SelectParameters>
52      </asp:ObjectDataSource>
53  </asp:Content>
```

Fig. 21.69 | Markup for the completed Books.aspx file. (Part 2 of 3.)

(b)

(c)

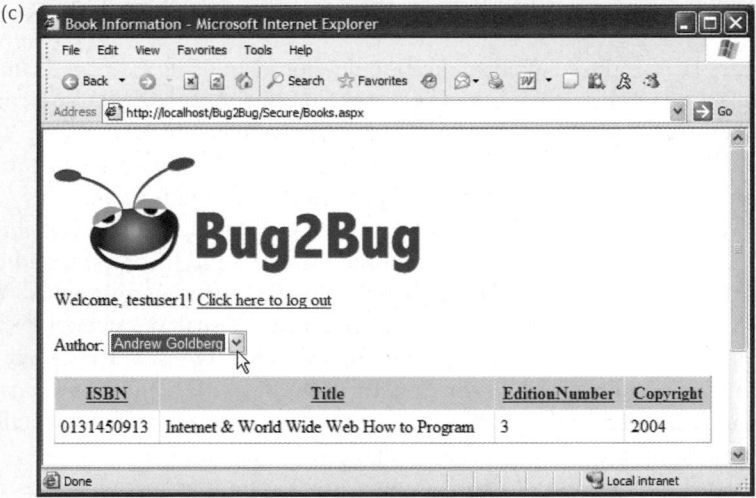

Fig. 21.69 | Markup for the completed `Books.aspx` file. (Part 3 of 3.)

Lines 15–18 define the `DropDownList` that displays the names of the authors in the `Books` database. Line 16 contains the control's `AutoPostBack` property, which indicates that changing the selected item in the list causes a postback to occur. The `DataSourceID` property in line 16 specifies that the `DropDownList`'s items are created based on the data obtained through the `authorsObjectDataSource` (defined in lines 19–23). Line 21 specifies that this `ObjectDataSource` accesses the `Books` database by calling method `GetData` of the `BooksDataSet`'s `AuthorsTableAdapter` (line 22).

Lines 26–42 create the `GridView` that displays information about the books written by the selected author. The start tag (lines 26–29) indicates that paging (with a page size of 4) and sorting are enabled in the `GridView`. The `AutoGenerateColumns` property indicates whether the columns in the `GridView` are generated at runtime based on the fields in the data source. This property is set to `False`, because the IDE-generated `Columns` element (lines 30–39) already specifies the columns for the `GridView` using `BoundFields`. Lines 43–52 define the `ObjectDataSource` used to fill the `GridView` with data. Recall that we configured `titlesObjectDataSource` to use method `GetDataByAuthorID` of the `Books-DataSet`'s `TitlesTableAdapter` for this purpose. The `ControlParameter` in lines 48–50 specifies that the value of method `GetDataByAuthorID`'s parameter comes from the `SelectedValue` property of the `authorsDropDownList`.

Figure 21.69(a) depicts the default appearance of `Books.aspx` in a Web browser. Because the `DefaultValue` property (line 49) of the `ControlParameter` for the `titles-ObjectDataSource` is set to 1, books by the author with `AuthorID` 1 (i.e., Harvey Deitel) are displayed when the page first loads. Note that the `GridView` displays paging links below the data, because the number of rows of data returned by `GetDataByAuthorID` is greater than the page size. Figure 21.69(b) shows the `GridView` after clicking the 2 link to view the second page of data. Figure 21.69(c) presents `Books.aspx` after the user selects a different author from the `authorsDropDownList`. The data fits on one page, so the `GridView` does not display paging links.

21.9 Wrap-Up

In this chapter, we introduced Web application development using ASP.NET and Visual Web Developer 2005 Express. We began by discussing the simple HTTP transactions that take place when you request and receive a Web page through a Web browser. You then learned about the three tiers (i.e., the client or top tier, the business logic or middle tier and the information or bottom tier) that comprise most Web applications.

Next, we explained the role of ASPX files (i.e., Web Form files) and code-behind files, and the relationship between them. We discussed how ASP.NET compiles and executes Web applications so that they can be displayed as XHTML in a Web browser. You also learned how to build an ASP.NET Web application using Visual Web Developer.

The chapter demonstrated several common ASP.NET Web controls used for displaying text and images on a Web Form. You learned how to use an `AdRotator` control to display randomly selected images. We also discussed validation controls, which allow you to ensure that user input on a Web page satisfies certain requirements.

We discussed the benefits of maintaining a user's state information across multiple pages of a Web site. We then demonstrated how you can include such functionality in a Web application using either cookies or session tracking with `HttpSessionState` objects.

Finally, we presented two case studies on building ASP.NET applications that interact with databases. First, we showed how to build a guestbook application that allows users to submit comments about a Web site. You learned how to save the user input in a SQL Server database and how to display past submissions on the Web page.

The second case study presented a secure Web application that requires users to log in before accessing information from the `Books` database (discussed in Chapter 20). You used the **Web Site Administration Tool** to configure the application to use forms authentication and prevent anonymous users from accessing the book information. This case study explained how to use the new ASP.NET 2.0 `Login`, `CreateUserWizard`, `LoginName` and `LoginStatus` controls to simplify user authentication. You also learned to create a uniform look-and-feel for a Web site using a master page and several content pages.

In the next chapter, we continue our coverage of ASP.NET technology with an introduction to Web services, which allow methods on one machine to call methods on other machines via common data formats and protocols, such as XML and HTTP. You will learn how Web services promote software reusability and interoperability across multiple computers on a network such as the Internet.

21.10 Web Resources

`asp.net`
This official Microsoft site overviews ASP.NET and provides a link for downloading Visual Web Developer. This site includes ASP.NET articles, links to useful ASP.NET resources and lists of books on Web development with ASP.NET.

`asp.net/QuickStartv20/aspnet/`
The ASP.NET QuickStart Tutorial from Microsoft provides code samples and discussion of fundamental ASP.NET topics.

`asp.net/guidedtour2/`
This guided tour of Visual Web Developer 2005 Express introduces key features in the IDE used to develop ASP.NET Web applications.

`www.15seconds.com`
This site offers ASP.NET news, articles, code samples, FAQs and links to valuable community resources, such as an ASP.NET message board and a mailing list.

`aspalliance.com`
This community site contains ASP.NET articles, tutorials and examples.

`aspadvice.com`
This site provides access to many e-mail lists where anyone can ask and respond to questions about ASP.NET and related technologies.

`www.asp101.com/aspdotnet/`
This site overviews ASP.NET and includes articles, code examples, a discussion board and links to ASP.NET resources. The code samples build on many of the techniques presented in the chapter, such as session tracking and connecting to a database.

`www.411asp.net`
This resource site provides programmers with ASP.NET tutorials and code samples. The community pages allow programmers to ask questions, answer questions and post messages.

`www.123aspx.com`
This site offers a directory of links to ASP.NET resources. The site also includes daily and weekly newsletters.

Summary

Section 21.1 Introduction
- Microsoft's ASP.NET technology is used for Web application development.
- Web-based applications create Web content for Web browser clients. This Web content includes XHTML, client-side scripting, images and binary data.

- A Web Form file represents a Web page that is sent to the client browser. Web Form files have the filename extension .aspx and contain a Web page's GUI. You customize Web Forms by adding Web controls.

- Every ASPX file created in Visual Studio has a corresponding class written in a .NET language. The file that contains this class is called the code-behind file and provides the ASPX file's programmatic implementation.

Section 21.2 Simple HTTP Transactions
- HTTP specifies a set of methods and headers that allow clients and servers to interact and exchange information in a uniform and predictable way.

- In its simplest form, a Web page is nothing more than an XHTML document. This document is a plain text file containing markup that describes to a Web browser how to display and format the document's information.

- Any XHTML document available for viewing over the Web has a corresponding URL.

- Computers that run Web server software make Internet resources such as Web pages available.

- The hostname is the name of the computer on which the resource resides. This computer usually is referred to as the host, because it houses and maintains resources.

- An IP address identifies a server in a manner similar to how a telephone number uniquely defines a particular phone line.

- MIME is an Internet standard that specifies the way in which certain types of data must be formatted so that programs can interpret the data correctly. Popular MIME types include text/plain and image/jpeg.

Section 21.3 Multitier Application Architecture
- Web applications are multitier applications (sometimes referred to as *n*-tier applications). Multitier applications divide functionality into separate tiers (i.e., logical groupings of functionality).

- The information tier, or bottom tier, maintains data pertaining to the application.

- The middle tier implements business logic, controller logic and presentation logic to control interactions between the application's clients and the application's data.

- The client (or top) tier is the application's user interface (typically viewed in a Web browser).

Section 21.4 Creating and Running a Simple Web-Form Example
- An ASP.NET Web Form typically consists of an ASPX file and a Visual Basic code-behind file.

- Visual Web Developer generates markup when you change a Web Form's properties and when you add text or controls to a Web Form.

Section 21.4.1 Examining an ASPX File
- ASP.NET comments begin with <%-- and terminate with --%>.

- A Page directive (delimited by <%@ and %>) specifies information needed by ASP.NET to process an ASPX file. The CodeFile attribute of the Page directive indicates the name of the corresponding code-behind file. The Language attribute specifies the .NET language used in this file.

- When a control's runat attribute is set to "server", the control is processed by ASP.NET on the server, generating an XHTML equivalent.

- The asp: tag prefix in a control declaration indicates that a control is an ASP.NET Web control.

- Each Web control maps to a corresponding XHTML element (or group of elements)—when processing a Web control on the server, ASP.NET generates XHTML markup that will be sent to the client to represent that control in a Web browser.

Section 21.4.2 Examining a Code-Behind File
- The code-behind file is a partial class.
- Namespace System.Web.UI contains classes for the creation of Web applications and controls.
- Class Page defines a standard Web page, providing event handlers and objects necessary for creating Web-based applications. All Web applications directly or indirectly inherit from class Page.
- Class Control is the base class that provides common functionality for all Web controls.
- Method Page_Init handles the Init event, which indicates that a page is ready to be initialized.

Section 21.4.3 Relationship Between an ASPX File and a Code-Behind File
- When a client requests an ASPX file, ASP.NET combines two partial classes—the one defined in the code-behind file and the one that ASP.NET generates based on the markup in the ASPX file that defines the page's GUI.
- ASP.NET compiles the combined partial classes and creates an instance that represents the page. This instance creates the XHTML that is sent to the client.
- Namespace System.Web.UI.WebControls contains Web controls (derived from class WebControl) for designing a page's user interface.

Section 21.4.4 How the Code in an ASP.NET Web Page Executes
- When an instance of a page is created, the PreInit event occurs first, invoking method Page_PreInit. The Init event occurs next, invoking method Page_Init. Then the Load event occurs, invoking method Page_Load.
- After Page_Load finishes executing, the page processes any events raised by the page's controls.
- When a Web Form object is ready for garbage collection, an Unload event occurs. Event handler Page_Unload is inherited from class Page and contains any code that releases resources.

Section 21.4.5 Examining the XHTML Generated by an ASP.NET Application
- A form is a mechanism for collecting user information and sending it to the Web server.
- XHTML forms can contain visual and nonvisual components.
- Nonvisual components in an XHTML form, called hidden inputs, store any data that the document author specifies.

Section 21.4.6 Building an ASP.NET Web Application
- The name localhost indicates that the server resides on the local computer. If the Web server were located on a different computer, localhost would be replaced with the appropriate IP address or hostname.
- DOCUMENT is the name used to represent a Web Form in the **Properties** window.
- The Web Forms Designer's **Source** mode allows you to view the markup that represents the user interface of a page. The **Design** mode allows you to view the page as it will look and modify it by dragging and dropping controls from the **Toolbox** onto the Web Form.
- Controls and other elements are placed sequentially on a Web Form, much like how text and images are placed in a document using word processing software like Microsoft Word. The positions of controls and other elements are relative to the Web Form's upper-left corner, so this type of layout is known as relative positioning.
- An alternate type of layout is known as absolute positioning, in which controls are located exactly where they are dropped on the Web Form.

- Visual Web Developer is a WYSIWYG (What You See Is What You Get) editor—whenever you make a change to a Web Form in **Design** mode, the IDE creates the markup (visible in **Source** mode) necessary to achieve the desired visual effects seen in **Design** mode.
- Web.config is a file that stores configuration settings for an ASP.NET Web application.

Section 21.5 Web Controls
- The **Standard** section of the **Toolbox** in Visual Web Developer contains several Web controls.

Section 21.5.1 Text and Graphics Controls
- The **Insert Table** command from the **Layout** menu in **Design** mode allows you to add an XHTML table to a Web Form.
- An Image control inserts an image into a Web page. The ImageUrl property specifies the file location of the image to display.
- A TextBox control allows the you to obtain text from the user and display text to the user.
- A DropDownList control provides a list of options to the user. Each item in the drop-down list is defined by a ListItem element.
- Visual Web Developer displays smart tag menus for many ASP.NET controls to facilitate performing common tasks. A smart tag menu is opened by clicking the small arrowhead that appears in the upper-right corner of the control in **Design** mode.
- A HyperLink control adds a hyperlink to a Web page. The NavigateUrl property of this control specifies the resource that is requested when a user clicks the hyperlink.
- A RadioButtonList control provides a series of radio buttons for the user.

Section 21.5.2 AdRotator Control
- ASP.NET provides the AdRotator Web control for displaying advertisements (or any other images). Using data from an XML file, the AdRotator control randomly selects an image to display and generates a hyperlink to the Web page associated with that image.
- An XmlDataSource references an XML file containing data that will be used in an ASP.NET application. The **AdRotator Tasks** smart tag menu allows you to create a new XmlDataSource that retrieves advertisement data from an XML file.
- The advertisement file used for an AdRotator control contains Ad elements, each of which provides information about a different advertisement.
- Element ImageUrl in an advertisement file specifies the path (location) of the advertisement's image, and element NavigateUrl specifies the URL that loads when a user clicks the advertisement.
- The AlternateText element contains text that displays in place of the image when the browser cannot locate or render the image for some reason, or to assist the visually impaired.
- Element Impressions specifies how often an image appears, relative to the other images.

Section 21.5.3 Validation Controls
- A validation control (or validator) determines whether the data in another Web control is in the proper format. Validators provide a mechanism for validating user input on the client.
- When the XHTML for a page is created, a validator is converted into ECMAScript. ECMAScript is a scripting language that enhances the functionality and appearance of Web pages.
- The Visible property of a control indicates whether the control appears in the client's browser.
- A RequiredFieldValidator ensures that a control receives user input before a form is submitted.
- A validator's ControlToValidate property indicates which control will be validated.

- A validator's `ErrorMessage` property contains text to be displayed if the validation fails.

- A `RegularExpressionValidator` matches a Web control's content against a regular expression. The regular expression that validates the input is assigned to property `ValidationExpression`.

- Web programmers using ASP.NET often design their Web pages so that the current page reloads when the user submits the form. This event is known as a postback.

- A `Page`'s `IsPostBack` property determines whether the page is being loaded due to a postback.

- When data is posted to the Web server, the XHTML form's data is accessible to the Web application through the `Request` object's `Form` array.

- The `EnableViewState` attribute determines whether a Web control's state persists (i.e., is retained) when a postback occurs.

Section 21.6 Session Tracking

- Personalization makes it possible for e-businesses to communicate effectively with their customers and also improves users' ability to locate desired products and services.

- To provide personalized services to consumers, e-businesses must be able to recognize clients when they request information from a site.

- The request/response system on which the Web operates is facilitated by HTTP. Unfortunately, HTTP is a stateless protocol—it does not support persistent connections that would enable Web servers to maintain state information regarding particular clients.

- A session represents a unique client on a Web site. If the client leaves a site and then returns later, the client will still be recognized as the same user. To help the server distinguish among clients, each client must identify itself to the server.

- Tracking individual clients is known as session tracking.

Section 21.6.1 Cookies

- A cookie is a piece of data stored in a small text file on the user's computer. A cookie maintains information about the client during and between browser sessions.

- A cookie object is of type `HttpCookie`. Properties `Name` and `Value` of class `HttpCookie` can be used to retrieve the key and value in a key–value pair (both strings) in a cookie.

- Cookies are sent and received as a collection of type `HttpCookieCollection`. An application on a server can write cookies to a client using the `Response` object's `Cookies` property. Cookies can be accessed programmatically using the `Request` object's `Cookies` property. Cookies can be read by an application only if they were created in the domain in which the application is running.

- When a Web Form receives a request, the header includes information such as the request type and any cookies that have been sent previously from the server to be stored on the client machine.

- When the server formulates its response, the header information includes any cookies the server wants to store on the client computer.

- The expiration date of a cookie determines how long the cookie remains on the client's computer. If you do not set an expiration date for a cookie, the Web browser maintains the cookie for the duration of the browsing session.

- Clients can disable cookies in their browsers. If they do this, they may not be able to use certain Web applications.

Section 21.6.2 Session Tracking with **HttpSessionState**

- Session-tracking capabilities are provided by FCL class `HttpSessionState`. Every Web Form includes an `HttpSessionState` object, which is accessible through property `Session` of class `Page`.

- When the Web page is requested, an `HttpSessionState` object is created and assigned to the Page's `Session` property. Also, a unique session ID is created for that client and a temporary cookie is written to the client so the server can identify the client on subsequent requests. Recall that clients may disable cookies in their Web browsers to ensure that their privacy is protected. Such clients will experience difficulty using Web applications that depend on `HttpSessionState` objects to maintain state information.

- The Page's `Session` property is often referred to as the `Session` object.

- The `Session` object's key–value pairs are often referred to as session items.

- Session items are placed into an `HttpSessionState` object by calling method `Add`.

- `HttpSessionState` objects can store any type of object (not just `strings`) as attribute values. This provides increased flexibility in maintaining client state information.

- Property `SessionID` contains the unique session ID. The first time a client connects to the Web server, a unique session ID is created for that client. When the client makes additional requests, the client's session ID is compared with the session IDs stored in the Web server's memory to retrieve the `HttpSessionState` object for that client.

- Property `Timeout` specifies the maximum amount of time that an `HttpSessionState` object can be inactive before it is discarded.

- Property `Count` provides the number of session items contained in a `Session` object.

- Indexing the `Session` object with a key name retrieves the corresponding value.

- Property `Keys` of class `HttpSessionState` returns a collection containing all the session's keys.

Section 21.7 Case Study: Connecting to a Database in ASP.NET

- A `GridView` ASP.NET data control displays data on a Web Form in a tabular format.

Section 21.7.1 Building a Web Form That Displays Data from a Database

- A `GridView`'s colors can be set using the **Auto Format...** link in the **GridView Tasks** smart tag menu.

- A SQL Server 2005 Express database used by an ASP.NET Web site should be located in the project's `App_Data` folder.

- A `SqlDataSource` control allows a Web application to interact with a database.

- When a `SqlDataSource` is configured to perform `INSERT` SQL operations against the database table from which it gathers data, you must specify the values to insert either programmatically or through other controls on the Web Form.

- The **Command and Parameter Editor**, accessed by clicking the ellipsis next to a `SqlDataSource`'s `InsertQuery` property, allows you to specify that parameter values come from controls.

- Each column in a `GridView` is represented as a `BoundField`.

- `SqlDataSource` property `ConnectionString` indicates the connection through which the `SqlDataSource` control interacts with the database.

- An ASP.NET expression, delimited by `<%$` and `%>`, can be used to access a connection string stored in an application's `Web.config` configuration file.

Section 21.7.2 Modifying the Code-Behind File for the Guestbook Application

- A `SqlDataSource`'s `InsertParameters` collection contains an item corresponding to each parameter in the `SqlDataSource`'s `INSERT` command. Setting the `DefaultValue` of this `Item` allows you to set the value to be inserted.

- `SqlDataSource` method `Insert` executes the control's `INSERT` command against the database.

- `GridView` method `DataBind` refreshes the information displayed in the `GridView`.

Section 21.8.1 Examining the Completed Secure Books Database Application

- Forms authentication is a technique that protects a page so that only users known to the Web site can access it. Such users are known as the site's members.

- ASP.NET login controls help create secure applications using authentication. These controls are found in the **Login** section of the **Toolbox**.

- When a user's identity is confirmed, the user is said to have been authenticated.

- A master page defines common GUI elements that are inherited by each page in a set of content pages. Just as Visual Basic classes can inherit instance variables and methods from existing classes, content pages inherit elements from master pages—this is known as visual inheritance.

Section 21.8.2 Creating the Secure Books Database Application

- ASP.NET hides the details of authenticating users, displaying appropriate success or error messages and redirecting the user to the correct page based on the authentication results.

- The **Web Site Administration Tool** allows you to configure an application's security settings, add site users and create access rules that determine who is allowed to access the site.

- By default, anonymous users who attempt to load a page in a directory to which they are denied access are redirected to a page named Login.aspx so that they can identify themselves.

- In an ASP.NET application, a page's configuration settings are determined by the current directory's Web.config file. The settings in this file take precedence over the settings in the root directory's Web.config file.

- A master page contains placeholders for custom content created in a content page, which visually inherits the master page's content, then adds content in place of the placeholders.

- Master pages have the filename extension .master and, like Web Forms, can optionally use a code-behind file to define additional functionality.

- A Master directive in an ASPX file specifies that the file defines a master page.

- A ContentPlaceHolder control serves as a placeholder for page-specific content defined by a content page using a Content control. The Content control will appear in place of the master page's ContentPlaceHolder when the content page is requested.

- A CreateUserWizard control provides a registration form that site visitors can use to create a user account. ASP.NET handles the details of creating a SQL Server database to store the user names, passwords and other account information of the application's users.

- A Login control encapsulates the details of logging a user into a Web application (i.e., authenticating a user by comparing the provided user name and password with those of an account in the ASP.NET-created membership database). If the user is authenticated, the browser is redirected to the page specified by the Login control's DestinationPageUrl property. If the user is not authenticated, the Login control displays an error message.

- ASP.NET writes to the client an encrypted cookie containing data about an authenticated user.

- Encrypted data is data translated into a code that only the sender and receiver can understand.

- A LoginName control displays the current authenticated user name on a Web Form.

- A LoginStatus control renders on a Web page in one of two ways—by default, if the user is not authenticated (the **Logged Out** view), the control displays a hyperlink with the text Login; if the user is authenticated (the **Logged In** view), the control displays a hyperlink with the text Logout. The LogoutText determines the text of the link in the **Logged In** view.

- An ObjectDataSource control encapsulates a business object that provides access to a data source. A business object (e.g., a TableAdapter) represents the middle tier of an application and mediates interactions between the bottom tier and the top tier.

- The AS SQL keyword allows you to generate a column in a query result—called an alias—that contains the result of a SQL expression.

- A DropDownList's AutoPostBack property indicates whether a postback occurs each time the user selects an item.

- When you **Enable Sorting** for a GridView, the column headings in the GridView turn into hyperlinks that allow users to sort the data it displays.

- When you **Enable Paging** for a GridView, the GridView divides its data among multiple pages. The user can click the numbered links at the bottom of the GridView control to display a different page of data. GridView's PageSize property determines the number of entries per page.

Terminology

<%-- --%> ASP.NET comment delimiters
<%$ %> ASP.NET expression delimiters
<%@ %> ASP.NET directive delimiters
absolute positioning
access rule in ASP.NET
action attribute of XHTML element form
Ad XML element in an AdRotator
    advertisement file
Add method of class Hashtable
Add method of class HttpSessionState
AdRotator ASP.NET Web control
Advertisements XML element in an AdRotator
    advertisement file
alias in SQL
AlternateText element in an AdRotator
    advertisement file
anonymous user
AS SQL keyword
asp: tag prefix
ASP.NET 20
ASP.NET comment
ASP.NET expression
ASP.NET login control
ASP.NET server control
ASP.NET Web Site in Visual Web Developer
ASPX file
.aspx filename extension
authenticating a user
authentication element in Web.config
authorization element in Web.config
AutoEventWireup attribute of ASP.NET page
AutoPostBack property of a DropDownList
bottom tier
BoundField ASP.NET element
Build Page command in Visual Web Developer
Build Site command in Visual Web Developer
business logic
business object

business rule
Button ASP.NET Web control
client tier
code-behind file
CodeFile attribute in a Page directive
ConnectionString property of a SqlDataSource
Content ASP.NET control
content page in ASP.NET
ContentPlaceHolder ASP.NET control
Control class
controller logic
ControlParameter ASP.NET element
ControlToValidate property of a
    validation control
cookie
Cookies collection of the Response object
Cookies property of class Request
Count property of class HttpSessionState
CreateUserWizard ASP.NET login control
data tier
DataSourceID property of a GridView
DeleteCommand property of a SqlDataSource
deny element in Web.config
Design mode in Visual Web Developer
directive in ASP.NET
Display property of a validation control
DNS (domain name system) server
DNS lookup
DOCUMENT property of a Web Form
domain name system (DNS) server
DropDownList ASP.NET Web control
ECMAScript
Enable Paging setting for a GridView
Enable Sorting setting for a GridView
EnableSessionState property of a Web Form
EnableViewState property of a Web control
encrypted data
ErrorMessage property of a validation control

tier in a multitier application
Timeout property of class HttpSessionState
Title property of a Page directive
Title property of a Web Form
title XHTML element
top tier
unique session ID of an ASP.NET client
Unload event of an ASP.NET page
UpdateCommand property of a SqlDataSource
validation control
ValidationExpression property of a
    RegularExpressionValidator control
validator
Value property of class HttpCookie
View In Browser command in Visual Web
    Developer

__VIEWSTATE hidden input
virtual directory
Visible property of an ASP.NET Web control
visual inheritance
Web application development
Web control
Web Form
Web server
Web Site Administration Tool
Web.config ASP.NET configuration file
WebControl class
WYSIWYG (What You See Is What You Get)
    editor
XHTML markup
XHTML tag
XmlDataSource ASP.NET data control

Self-Review Exercises

21.1   State whether each of the following is *true* or *false*. If *false*, explain why.
    a) Web Form file names end in .aspx.
    b) App.config is a file that stores configuration settings for an ASP.NET Web application.
    c) A maximum of one validation control can be placed on a Web Form.
    d) If no expiration date is set for a cookie, that cookie will be destroyed at the end of the browser session.
    e) A LoginStatus control displays the current authenticated user name on a Web Form.
    f) ASP.NET directives are delimited by <%@ and %>.
    g) An AdRotator control always displays all ads with equal frequency.
    h) Each Web control maps to exactly one corresponding XHTML element.
    i) A SqlDataSource control allows a Web application to interact with a database.

21.2   Fill in the blanks in each of the following statements:
    a) Web applications contain three basic tiers: _____, _____, and _____.
    b) The _____ Web control is similar to the ComboBox Windows control.
    c) A control which ensures that the data in another control is in the correct format is called a(n) _____.
    d) A(n) _____ occurs when a page requests itself.
    e) Every ASP.NET page inherits from class _____.
    f) When a page loads, the _____ event occurs first, followed by the _____ event.
    g) The _____ file contains the functionality for an ASP.NET page.
    h) A(n) _____ control provides a registration form that site visitors can use to create a user account.
    i) A(n) _____ defines common GUI elements that are inherited by each page in a set of _____.
    j) In a multitier application, the _____ tier controls interactions between the application's clients and the application's data.

Answers to Self-Review Exercises

21.1   a) True. b) False. Web.config is the file that stores configuration settings for an ASP.NET Web application. c) False. An unlimited number of validation controls can be placed on a Web

Form. d) True. e) False. A LoginName control displays the current authenticated user name on a Web Form. A LoginStatus control displays a link to either log in or log out, depending on whether the user is currently authenticated. f) True. g) False. The frequency with which the AdRotator displays ads is specified in the AdvertisementFile. h) False. A Web control can map to a group of XHTML elements—ASP.NET can generate complex XHTML markup from simple elements in an ASPX file. i) True.

21.2   a) bottom (information), middle (business logic), top (client). b) DropDownList. c) validator. d) postback. e) Page. f) PreInit, Init. g) code-behind. h) CreateUserWizard. i) master page, content pages. j) middle.

Exercises

21.3   (WebTime *Modification*) Modify the WebTime example to contain drop-down lists that allow the user to modify such Label properties as BackColor, ForeColor and Font-Size. Configure these drop-down lists so that a postback occurs whenever the user makes a selection. When the page reloads, it should reflect the specified changes to the properties of the Label displaying the time.

21.4   *(Page Hit Counter)* Create an ASP.NET page that uses a persistent cookie (i.e., a cookie with a distant expiration date) to keep track of how many times the client computer has visited the page. Set the HttpCookie object's Expires property to DateTime.Now.AddMonths(1) to cause the cookie to remain on the client's computer for one month. Display the number of page hits (i.e., the cookie's value) every time the page loads.

21.5   (WebControls *Modification*) Provide the following functionality for the example in Section 21.5.1: When users click **Register**, store their information in the Users table of the Registration.mdf database (provided in the chapter's examples directory). On postback, thank the user for providing the information.

21.6   *(Guestbook Application Modification)* Add validation to the guestbook application in Section 21.7. Use validation controls to ensure that the user provides a name, a valid e-mail address and a message.

22

Web Services

OBJECTIVES

In this chapter you will learn:

- What a Web service is.

- How to create Web services.

- The important part that XML and the XML-based Simple Object Access Protocol play in enabling Web services.

- The elements that comprise Web services, such as service descriptions.

- How to create a client that uses a Web service.

- How to use Web services with Windows applications and Web applications.

- How to use session tracking in Web services to maintain state information for the client.

- How to pass user-defined types to a Web service.

A client is to me a mere unit, a factor in a problem.
—Sir Arthur Conan Doyle

...if the simplest things of nature have a message that you understand, rejoice, for your soul is alive.
—Eleonora Duse

Protocol is everything.
—Francoise Giuliani

They also serve who only stand and wait.
—John Milton

Outline

22.1 Introduction

This chapter introduces Web services, which promote software reusability in distributed systems where applications execute across multiple computers on a network. A Web service is a class that allows its methods to be called by methods on other machines via common data formats and protocols, such as XML (see Chapter 19) and HTTP. In .NET, the over-the-network method calls are commonly implemented through the Simple Object Access Protocol (SOAP), an XML-based protocol describing how to mark up requests and responses so that they can be transferred via protocols such as HTTP. Using SOAP, applications represent and transmit data in a standardized XML-based format.

Microsoft is encouraging software vendors and e-businesses to deploy Web services. As increasing numbers of organizations worldwide have connected to the Internet, the concept of applications that call methods across a network has become more practical. Web services represent the next step in object-oriented programming—rather than developing software from a small number of class libraries provided at one location, programmers can access Web service class libraries distributed worldwide.

Web services facilitate collaboration and allow businesses to grow. By purchasing Web services and using extensive free Web services that are relevant to their businesses, companies can spend less time developing new applications. E-businesses can use Web services to provide their customers with enhanced shopping experiences. Consider an online music store. The store's Web site provides links to information about various CDs, enabling users to purchase the CDs or to learn about the artists. Another company that sells concert tickets provides a Web service that displays upcoming concert dates for various artists, then allows users to buy tickets. By consuming the concert-ticket Web service on its site, the online music store can provide an additional service to its customers and increase its site traffic. The company that sells concert tickets also benefits from the business relationship by selling more tickets and possibly by receiving revenue from the online music store for the use of its Web service. Many Web services are provided at no charge. For example, Amazon and Google offer free Web services that you can use in your own applications to access the information they provide.

Visual Web Developer and the .NET Framework provide a simple, user-friendly way to create Web services. In this chapter, we show how to use these tools to create, deploy and use Web services. For each example, we provide the code for the Web service, then present an application that uses the Web service. Our first examples analyze Web services and how they work in Visual Web Developer. Then we demonstrate Web services that use more sophisticated features, such as session tracking (discussed in Chapter 21), database access and manipulating objects of user-defined types.

We distinguish between Visual Basic 2005 Express and Visual Web Developer 2005 Express in this chapter. We create Web services in Visual Web Developer 2005 Express, and we create client applications that use these Web services using both Visual Basic 2005 Express and Visual Web Developer 2005 Express. The full version of Visual Studio 2005 includes the functionality of both Express editions.

22.2 .NET Web Services Basics

A Web service is a software component stored on one machine that can be accessed by an application (or other software component) on another machine over a network. The machine on which the Web service resides is referred to as a **remote machine**. The application (i.e., the client) that accesses the Web service sends a method call over a network to the remote machine, which processes the call and returns a response over the network to the application. This kind of distributed computing benefits various systems. For example, an application without direct access to certain data on another system might be able to retrieve this data via a Web service. Similarly, an application lacking the processing power necessary to perform specific computations could use a Web service to take advantage of another system's superior resources.

A Web service is implemented as a class. In previous chapters, we included each class in a project either by defining the class in the project or by adding a reference to a DLL containing the compiled class. All the pieces of an application resided on one machine. When a client uses a Web service, the class (and its compiled DLL) is stored on a remote machine—a compiled version of the Web service class is not placed in the current application's directory. We discuss what happens shortly.

Requests to and responses from Web services created with Visual Web Developer are typically transmitted via Simple Object Access Protocol (SOAP). So any client capable of generating and processing SOAP messages can interact with a Web service, regardless of the language in which the Web service is written. We say more about SOAP in Section 22.3.

It is possible for Web services to limit access to authorized clients. See the Web Resources at the end of the chapter for links to information on standard mechanisms and protocols that address Web service security concerns.

Web services have important implications for **business-to-business (B2B) transactions**. They enable businesses to conduct transactions via standardized, widely available Web services rather than relying on proprietary applications. Web services and SOAP are platform and language independent, so companies can collaborate via Web services without worrying about the compatibility of their hardware, software and communications technologies. Companies such as Amazon, Google, eBay and many others are using Web services to their advantage. To read case studies of Web services used in business, visit msdn.microsoft.com/webservices/understanding/casestudies/default.aspx.

22.2.1 Creating a Web Service in Visual Web Developer

To create a Web service in Visual Web Developer, you first create a project of type **ASP.NET Web Service**. Visual Web Developer then generates files to contain the code that implements the Web service and an ASMX file (which provides access to the Web service). Figure 22.1 displays the files that comprise a Web service.

Visual Web Developer generates code files for the Web service class and any other code that is part of the Web service implementation. In the Web service class, you define the methods that your Web service makes available to client applications. Like ASP.NET Web applications, ASP.NET Web services can be tested using Visual Web Developer's built-in test server. However, to make an ASP.NET Web service publicly accessible to clients outside Visual Web Developer, you must deploy the Web service to a Web server such as an Internet Information Services (IIS) Web server.

Methods in a Web service are invoked through a **Remote Procedure Call (RPC)**. These methods, which are marked with the `WebMethod` attribute, are often referred to as **Web service methods** or simply **Web methods**—we refer to them as Web methods from this point forward. Declaring a method with attribute `WebMethod` makes the method acces-

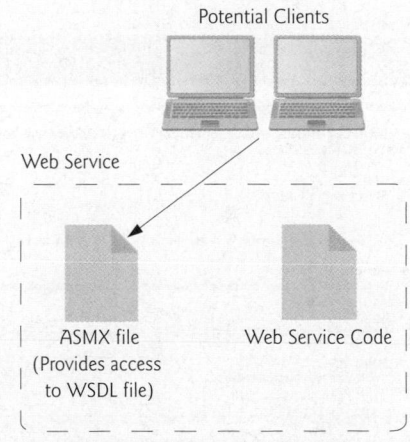

Potential Clients

Web Service

ASMX file
(Provides access
to WSDL file)

Web Service Code

Fig. 22.1 | Web service components.

sible to other classes through RPCs and is known as *exposing* a Web method. We discuss the details of exposing Web methods in Section 22.4.

22.2.2 Determining a Web Service's Functionality

Once you select a Web service to use, you must determine the Web service's functionality and how to use it. For this purpose, Web services normally contain a *service description*. This is an XML document that conforms to the *Web Service Description Language (WSDL)*—an XML vocabulary that defines the methods a Web service makes available and how clients interact with them. The WSDL document also specifies lower-level information that clients might need, such as the required formats for requests and responses.

WSDL documents are not meant to be read by developers; rather, WSDL documents are meant to be read by applications, so they know how to interact with the Web services described in the documents. Visual Web Developer generates an ASMX file when a Web service is constructed. Files with the `.asmx` filename extension are ASP.NET Web service files and are executed by ASP.NET on a Web server (e.g., IIS). When viewed in a Web browser, an ASMX file presents Web method descriptions and links to test pages that allow users to execute sample calls to these methods. We explain these test pages in greater detail later in this section. The ASMX file also specifies the Web service's implementation class, and optionally the code-behind file in which the Web service is defined and the assemblies referenced by the Web service. When the Web server receives a request for the Web service, it accesses the ASMX file, which, in turn, invokes the Web service implementation. To view more technical information about the Web service, developers can access the WSDL file (which is generated by ASP.NET). We show how to do this shortly.

The ASMX page in Fig. 22.2 displays information about the `HugeInteger` Web service that we create in Section 22.4. This Web service is designed to perform calculations with integers that contain a maximum of 100 digits. Most programming languages cannot

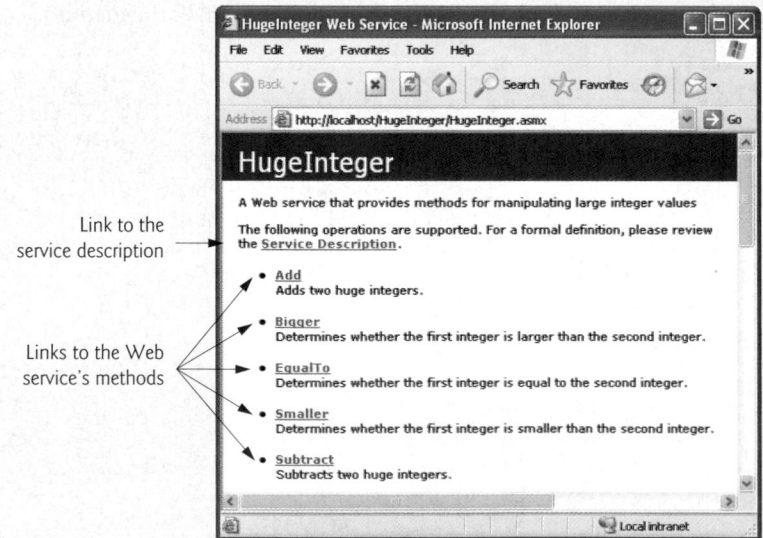

Fig. 22.2 | ASMX file rendered in a Web browser.

easily perform calculations using integers this large. The Web service provides client applications with methods that take two "huge integers" and determine their sum, their difference, which one is larger or smaller and whether the two numbers are equal. Note that the top of the page provides a link to the Web service's **Service Description**. ASP.NET generates the WSDL service description from the code you write to define the Web service. Client programs use a Web service's service description to validate Web method calls when the client programs are compiled.

ASP.NET generates WSDL information dynamically rather than creating an actual WSDL file. If a client requests the Web service's WSDL description (either by appending **?WSDL** to the ASMX file's URL or by clicking the **Service Description** link), ASP.NET generates the WSDL description, then returns it to the client for display in the Web browser. Generating the WSDL description dynamically ensures that clients receive the most current information about the Web service. It is common for an XML document (such as a WSDL description) to be created dynamically and not saved to disk.

When a user clicks the **Service Description** link at the top of the ASMX page in Fig. 22.2, the browser displays the generated WSDL document containing the service description for our `HugeInteger` Web service (Fig. 22.3).

22.2.3 Testing a Web Service's Methods

Below the **Service Description** link, the ASMX page shown in Fig. 22.2 lists the methods that the Web service offers. Clicking any method name requests a test page that describes the method (Fig. 22.4) and allows users to test the method by entering parameter values and clicking the **Invoke** button. (We discuss the process of testing a Web method shortly.)

Fig. 22.3 | Service description for our `HugeInteger` Web service.

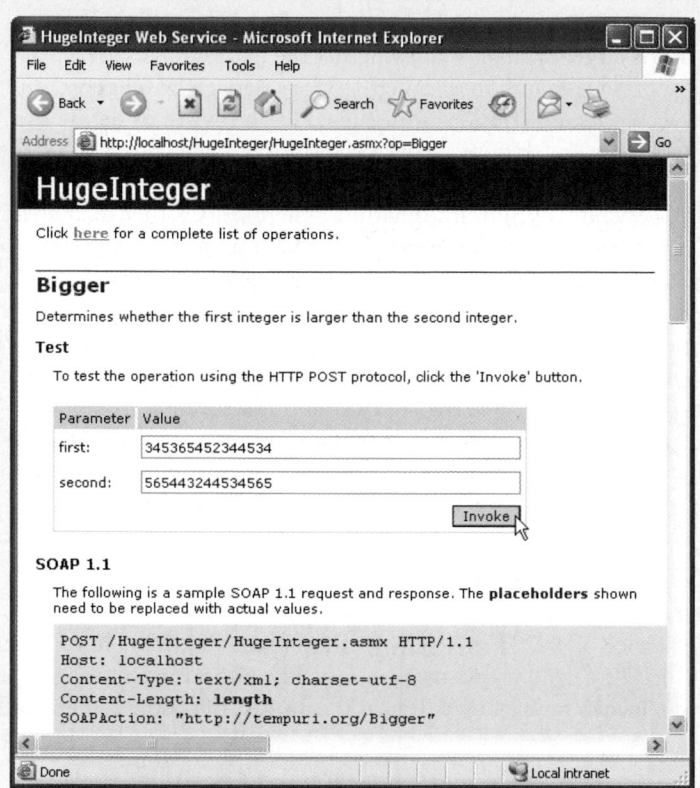

Fig. 22.4 | Invoking a Web method from a Web browser.

Below the **Invoke** button, the page displays sample request-and-response messages using SOAP and HTTP POST. These protocols are two options for sending and receiving messages in Web services. The protocol that transmits request-and-response messages is also known as the Web service's **wire format** or **wire protocol**, because it defines how information is sent "along the wire." SOAP is the more commonly used wire format, because SOAP messages can be sent using several transport protocols, whereas HTTP POST must use HTTP. When you test a Web service via an ASMX page (as in Fig. 22.4), the ASMX page uses HTTP POST to test the Web service methods. Later in this chapter, when we use Web services in our Visual Basic programs, we employ SOAP—the default protocol for .NET Web services.

Figure 22.4 depicts the test page for the HugeInteger Web method Bigger. From this page, users can test the method by entering values in the **first:** and **second:** fields, then clicking **Invoke**. The method executes, and a new Web browser window opens, displaying an XML document that contains the result (Fig. 22.5).

 Error-Prevention Tip 22.1

Using the ASMX page of a Web service to test and debug methods can help you make the Web service more reliable and robust.

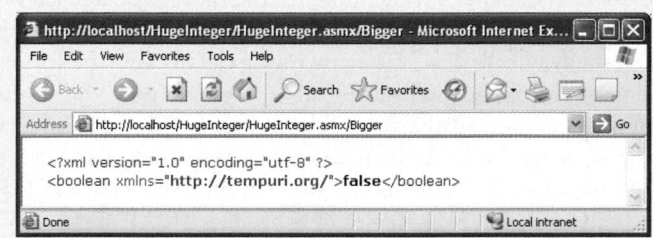

Fig. 22.5 | Results of invoking a Web method from a Web browser.

22.2.4 Building a Client to Use a Web Service

Now that we have discussed the different files that comprise a .NET Web service, let's examine the parts of a .NET Web service client (Fig. 22.6). A .NET client can be any type of .NET application, such as a Windows application, a console application or a Web application. You can enable a client application to consume a Web service by adding a Web reference to the client. This process adds files to the client application that allow the client to access the Web service. This section discusses Visual Basic 2005 Express, but the discussion also applies to Visual Web Developer 2005 Express.

To add a Web reference, right click the project name in the **Solution Explorer** and select **Add Web Reference…**. In the resulting dialog, specify the Web service to consume. The IDE then adds an appropriate Web reference to the client application. We demonstrate adding Web references in more detail in Section 22.4.

When you specify the Web service you want to consume, the IDE accesses the Web service's WSDL information and copies it into a WSDL file that is stored in the client project's `Web References` folder. This file is visible when you instruct Visual Basic 2005 to **Show All Files**. [*Note:* A copy of the WSDL file provides the client application with local access to the Web service's description. To ensure that the WSDL file is up-to-date, Visual Basic 2005 provides an **Update Web Reference** option (available by right clicking the Web

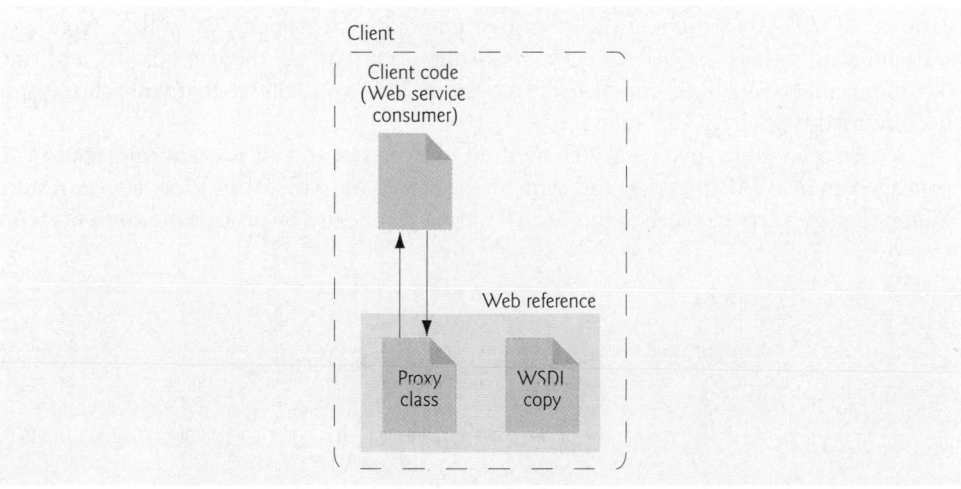

Fig. 22.6 | .NET Web service client after a Web reference has been added.

reference in the **Solution Explorer**), which updates the files in the Web References folder.] The WSDL information is used to create a proxy class, which handles all the "plumbing" required for Web method calls (i.e., the networking details and the formation of SOAP messages). Whenever the client application calls a Web method, the application actually calls a corresponding method in the proxy class. This method has the same name and parameters as the Web method that is being called, but formats the call to be sent as a request in a SOAP message. The Web service receives this request as a SOAP message, executes the method call and sends back the result as another SOAP message. When the client application receives the SOAP message containing the response, the proxy class deserializes it and returns the results as the return value of the Web method that was called. Figure 22.7 depicts the interactions among the client code, proxy class and Web service.

The .NET environment hides most of these details from you. Many aspects of Web service creation and consumption—such as generating WSDL files and proxy classes—are handled by Visual Web Developer, Visual Basic 2005 and ASP.NET. Although developers are relieved of the tedious process of creating these files, they can still modify the files if necessary. This is required only when developing advanced Web services—none of our examples require modifications to these files.

22.3 Simple Object Access Protocol (SOAP)

The Simple Object Access Protocol (SOAP) is a platform-independent protocol that uses XML to make remote procedure calls, typically over HTTP. Each request and response is packaged in a SOAP message—an XML message containing the information that a Web service requires to process the message. SOAP messages are written in XML so that they are human readable and platform independent. Most firewalls—security barriers that restrict communication among networks—do not restrict HTTP traffic. Thus, XML and HTTP enable computers on different platforms to send and receive SOAP messages with few limitations.

Web services also use SOAP for the extensive set of types it supports. The wire format used to transmit requests and responses must support all types passed between the applications. SOAP types include the primitive types (e.g., Integer), as well as DateTime, XmlNode and others. SOAP can also transmit arrays of all these types. In addition, DataSets can be serialized into SOAP. In Section 22.7, you will see that you can transmit user-defined types in SOAP messages.

When a program invokes a Web method, the request and all relevant information are packaged in a SOAP message and sent to the server on which the Web service resides. When the Web service receives this SOAP message, it begins to process the contents (con-

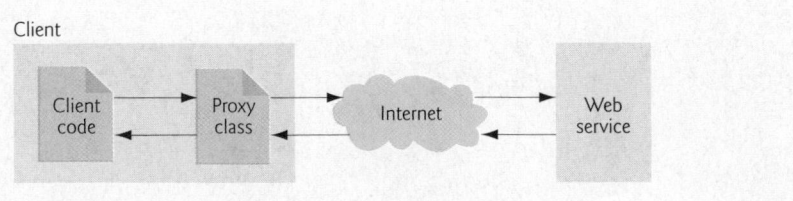

Fig. 22.7 | Interaction between a Web service client and a Web service.

tained in a SOAP envelope), which specify the method that the client wishes to execute and any arguments the client is passing to that method. This process of interpreting a SOAP message's contents is known as parsing a SOAP message. After the Web service receives and parses a request, the proper method is called with the specified arguments (if there are any), and the response is sent back to the client in another SOAP message. The client parses the response to retrieve the result of the method call.

The SOAP request in Fig. 22.8 was taken from the test page for the HugeInteger Web service's Bigger method (Fig. 22.4). Visual Basic 2005 creates such a message when a client wishes to execute the HugeInteger Web service's Bigger method. If the client is a Web application, Visual Web Developer creates the SOAP message. The message in Fig. 22.8 contains placeholders (length in line 4 and string in lines 16–17) representing values specific to a particular call to Bigger. If this were a real SOAP request, elements first and second (lines 16–17) would each contain an actual value passed from the client to the Web service, rather than the placeholder string. For example, if this envelope were transmitting the request from Fig. 22.4, element first and element second would contain the numbers displayed in the figure, and placeholder length (line 4) would contain the length of the SOAP message. Most programmers do not manipulate SOAP messages directly, but instead allow the .NET framework to handle the transmission details.

22.4 Publishing and Consuming Web Services

This section presents several examples of creating (also known as publishing) and using (also known as consuming) Web services. Recall that an application that consumes a Web service actually consists of two parts—a proxy class representing the Web service and a client application that accesses the Web service via an instance of the proxy class. The instance of the proxy class passes a Web method's arguments from the client application to

```
1   POST /HugeInteger/HugeInteger.asmx HTTP/1.1
2   Host: localhost
3   Content-Type: text/xml; charset=utf-8
4   Content-Length: length
5   SOAPAction: "http://www.deitel.com/Bigger"
6
7   <?xml version="1.0" encoding="utf-8"?>
8
9   <soap:Envelope
10     xmlns:xsi="http://www.w3.org/2001/XMLSchema-instance"
11     xmlns:xsd="http://www.w3.org/2001/XMLSchema"
12     xmlns:soap="http://schemas.xmlsoap.org/soap/envelope/">
13
14    <soap:Body>
15      <Bigger xmlns="http://www.deitel.com">
16        <first>string</first>
17        <second>string</second>
18      </Bigger>
19    </soap:Body>
20  </soap:Envelope>
```

Fig. 22.8 | SOAP request message for the HugeInteger Web service.

the Web service. When the Web method completes its task, the instance of the proxy class receives the result and parses it for the client application. Visual Basic 2005 and Visual Web Developer create these proxy classes for you. We demonstrate this momentarily.

22.4.1 Defining the HugeInteger Web Service

Figure 22.9 presents the code-behind file for the HugeInteger Web service that you will build in Section 22.4.2. When creating Web services in Visual Web Developer, you work almost exclusively in the code-behind file. As we mentioned earlier, this Web service is designed to perform calculations with integers that have a maximum of 100 digits. Long variables cannot handle integers of this size (i.e., an overflow occurs). The Web service provides methods that take two "huge integers" (represented as Strings) and determine their sum, their difference, which one is larger or smaller and whether the two numbers are equal. You can think of these methods as *services* available to programmers of other applications via the *Web* (hence the term Web services). Any programmer can access this Web service, use the methods and thus avoid writing 170 lines of code.

```vb
1   ' Fig. 22.9: HugeInteger.vb
2   ' HugeInteger Web service performs operations on large integers.
3   Imports System.Web
4   Imports System.Web.Services
5   Imports System.Web.Services.Protocols
6
7   <WebService(Namespace:="http://www.deitel.com/", _
8      Description:="A Web service that provides methods for" & _
9      " manipulating large integer values")> _
10  <WebServiceBinding(ConformsTo:=WsiProfiles.BasicProfile1_1)> _
11  <Global.Microsoft.VisualBasic.CompilerServices.DesignerGenerated()> _
12  Public Class HugeInteger
13     Inherits System.Web.Services.WebService
14
15     Private Const MAXIMUM As Integer = 100 ' maximum number of digits
16     Public number As Integer() ' array representing the huge integer
17
18     ' default constructor
19     Public Sub New()
20        number = New Integer(MAXIMUM - 1) {}
21     End Sub ' New
22
23     ' property that accepts an integer parameter
24     Public Property Digit(ByVal index As Integer) As Integer
25        Get
26           Return number(index)
27        End Get
28
29        Set(ByVal Value As Integer)
30           number(index) = Value
31        End Set
32     End Property ' Digit
33
```

Fig. 22.9 | HugeInteger Web service. (Part 1 of 4.)

```
34        ' returns String representation of HugeInteger
35        Public Overrides Function ToString() As String
36           Dim returnString As String = ""
37
38           For Each digit As Integer In number
39              returnString = digit & returnString
40           Next
41
42           Return returnString
43        End Function ' ToString
44
45        ' creates HugeInteger based on argument
46        Public Shared Function FromString(ByVal value As String) As HugeInteger
47           ' create temporary HugeInteger to be returned by the method
48           Dim parsedInteger As New HugeInteger()
49
50           For i As Integer = 0 To value.Length - 1
51              parsedInteger.Digit(i) = Int32.Parse( _
52                 value.Chars(value.Length - i - 1).ToString())
53           Next
54
55           Return parsedInteger
56        End Function ' FromString
57
58        ' WebMethod that adds integers represented by the String arguments
59        <WebMethod(Description:="Adds two huge integers.")> _
60        Public Function Add(ByVal first As String, ByVal second As String) _
61           As String
62
63           Dim carry As Integer = 0
64           Dim operand1 As HugeInteger = HugeInteger.FromString(first)
65           Dim operand2 As HugeInteger = HugeInteger.FromString(second)
66           Dim result As New HugeInteger() ' stores result of addition
67
68           ' perform addition algorithm for each digit
69           For i As Integer = 0 To MAXIMUM - 1
70              ' add two digits in same column
71              ' result is their sum, plus carry from
72              ' previous operation modulo 10
73              result.Digit(i) = _
74                 (operand1.Digit(i) + operand2.Digit(i) + carry) Mod 10
75
76              ' set carry to remainder of dividing sums of two digits by 10
77              carry = (operand1.Digit(i) + operand2.Digit(i) + carry) \ 10
78           Next
79
80           Return result.ToString()
81        End Function ' Add
82
83        ' WebMethod that subtracts integers represented by the String arguments
84        <WebMethod(Description:="Subtracts two huge integers.")> _
85        Public Function Subtract(ByVal first As String, _
86           ByVal second As String) As String
```

Fig. 22.9 | HugeInteger Web service. (Part 2 of 4.)

```
87
88        Dim operand1 As HugeInteger = HugeInteger.FromString(first)
89        Dim operand2 As HugeInteger = HugeInteger.FromString(second)
90        Dim result As New HugeInteger()
91
92        ' subtract bottom digit from top digit
93        For i As Integer = 0 To MAXIMUM - 1
94           ' if top digit is smaller than bottom digit we need to borrow
95           If operand1.Digit(i) < operand2.Digit(i) Then
96              Borrow(operand1, i)
97           End If
98
99           ' subtract bottom from top
100          result.Digit(i) = operand1.Digit(i) - operand2.Digit(i)
101       Next
102
103       Return result.ToString()
104    End Function ' Subtract
105
106    ' borrow 1 from next digit
107    Private Sub Borrow(ByVal hugeInteger As HugeInteger, _
108       ByVal place As Integer)
109
110       ' if no place to borrow from, signal problem
111       If place >= MAXIMUM - 1 Then
112          Throw New ArgumentException()
113
114          ' otherwise if next digit is zero, borrow from column to left
115       ElseIf hugeInteger.Digit(place + 1) = 0 Then
116          Borrow(hugeInteger, place + 1)
117       End If
118
119       ' add ten to current place because we borrowed and subtract one from
120       ' previous digit--this is the digit we borrowed from
121       hugeInteger.Digit(place) += 10
122       hugeInteger.Digit(place + 1) -= 1
123    End Sub ' Borrow
124
125    ' WebMethod that returns true if first integer is bigger than second
126    <WebMethod(Description:="Determines whether the first integer is " & _
127       "larger than the second integer.")> _
128    Public Function Bigger(ByVal first As String, _
129       ByVal second As String) As Boolean
130
131       Dim zeros() As Char = {"0"}
132
133       Try
134          ' if elimination of all zeros from result
135          ' of subtraction is an empty string,
136          ' numbers are equal, so return false, otherwise return true
137          If Subtract(first, second).Trim(zeros) = "" Then
138             Return False
```

Fig. 22.9 | HugeInteger Web service. (Part 3 of 4.)

```
139            Else
140                Return True
141            End If
142        Catch exception As ArgumentException
143            Return False ' first number was smaller, so return False
144        End Try
145    End Function ' Bigger
146
147    ' WebMethod returns True if first integer is smaller than second
148    <WebMethod(Description:="Determines whether the first integer " & _
149        "is smaller than the second integer.")> _
150    Public Function Smaller(ByVal first As String, _
151        ByVal second As String) As Boolean
152        ' if second is bigger than first, then first is smaller than second
153        Return Bigger(second, first)
154    End Function ' Smaller
155
156    ' WebMethod that returns true if two integers are equal
157    <WebMethod(Description:="Determines whether the first integer " & _
158        "is equal to the second integer.")> _
159    Public Function EqualTo(ByVal first As String, _
160        ByVal second As String) As Boolean
161
162        ' if either first is bigger than second, or first is
163        ' smaller than second, they are not equal
164        If Bigger(first, second) OrElse Smaller(first, second) Then
165            Return False
166        Else
167            Return True
168        End If
169    End Function ' EqualTo
170 End Class ' HugeInteger
```

Fig. 22.9 | HugeInteger Web service. (Part 4 of 4.)

Lines 7–9 contain a `WebService` attribute. Attaching this attribute to a Web service class declaration allows you to specify the Web service's namespace and description. Like an XML namespace (see Section 19.4), a Web service's namespace is used by client applications to differentiate that Web service from others available on the Web. Line 7 assigns http://www.deitel.com as the Web service's namespace using the `WebService` attribute's `Namespace` property. Lines 8–9 use the `WebService` attribute's `Description` property to describe the Web service's purpose—this appears in the ASMX page (Fig. 22.2).

Visual Web Developer places line 10 in all newly created Web services. This line indicates that the Web service conforms to the Basic Profile 1.1 (BP 1.1) developed by the Web Services Interoperability Organization (WS-I), a group dedicated to promoting interoperability among Web services developed on different platforms with different programming languages. BP 1.1 is a document that defines best practices for various aspects of Web service creation and consumption (www.WS-I.org). As we discussed in Section 22.2, the .NET environment hides many of these details from you. Setting the `WebServiceBinding` attribute's `ConformsTo` property to `WsiProfiles.BasicProfile1_1` instructs Visual Web Developer to perform its "behind-the-scenes" work, such as generating WSDL and ASMX files, in conformance with the guidelines laid out in BP 1.1. For more information on Web services interoperabilty and the Basic Profile 1.1, visit the WS-I Web site at www.ws-i.org.

By default, each new Web service class created in Visual Web Developer inherits from class System.Web.Services.WebService (line 13). Although a Web service need not derive from class WebService, this class provides members that are useful in determining information about the client and the Web service itself. Several methods in class Huge-Integer are tagged with the WebMethod attribute (lines 59, 84, 126, 148 and 157), which exposes a method so that it can be called remotely. When this attribute is absent, the method is not accessible to clients that consume the Web service. Note that this attribute, like the WebService attribute, contains a Description property that allows the ASMX page to display information about the method (see these descriptions shown in Fig. 22.2).

Common Programming Error 22.1

Failing to expose a method as a Web method by declaring it with the WebMethod attribute prevents clients of the Web service from accessing the method.

Portability Tip 22.1

Specify a namespace for each Web service so that it can be uniquely identified by clients. In general, you should use your company's domain name as the Web service's namespace, since company domain names are guaranteed to be unique.

Portability Tip 22.2

Specify descriptions for a Web service and its Web methods so that the Web service's clients can view information about the service in the service's ASMX page.

Common Programming Error 22.2

No method with the WebMethod attribute can be declared Shared—for a client to access a Web method, an instance of that Web service must exist.

Lines 24–32 define a Digit property, which provides access to any digit in a Huge-Integer. Lines 59–81 and 84–104 define Web methods Add and Subtract, which perform addition and subtraction, respectively. Method Borrow (lines 107–123) handles the case in which the digit that we are currently examining in the left operand is smaller than the corresponding digit in the right operand. For instance, when we subtract 19 from 32, we usually examine the numbers in the operands digit-by-digit, starting from the right. The number 2 is smaller than 9, so we add 10 to 2 (resulting in 12). After borrowing, we can subtract 9 from 12, resulting in 3 for the rightmost digit in the solution. We then subtract 1 from the 3 in 32—the next digit to the left (i.e., the digit we borrowed from). This leaves a 2 in the tens place. The corresponding digit in the other operand is now the 1 in 19. Subtracting 1 from 2 yields 1, making the corresponding digit in the result 1. The final result, when the digits are put together, is 13. Method Borrow is the method that adds 10 to the appropriate digits and subtracts 1 from the digits to the left. This is a utility method that is not intended to be called remotely, so it is not qualified with attribute WebMethod.

Recall that Fig. 22.2 presented a screen capture of the ASMX page HugeInteger.asmx for which the code-behind file HugeInteger.vb (Fig. 22.9) defines Web methods. A client application can invoke only the five methods listed in the screen capture in Fig. 22.2 (i.e., the methods qualified with the WebMethod attribute in Fig. 22.9).

22.4.2 Building a Web Service in Visual Web Developer

We now show you how to create the HugeInteger Web service. In the following steps, you will create an **ASP.NET Web Service** project that executes on your computer's local IIS Web server. To create the HugeInteger Web service in Visual Web Developer, perform the following steps:

Step 1: Creating the Project
To begin, you must create a project of type **ASP.NET Web Service**. Select **File > New Web Site...** to display the **New Web Site** dialog (Fig. 22.10). Select **ASP.NET Web Service** in the **Templates** pane. Select **HTTP** from the **Location** drop-down list to indicate that the files should be placed on a Web server. By default, Visual Web Developer indicates that it will place the files on the local machine's IIS Web server in a virtual directory named WebSite (http://localhost/WebSite). Replace the name WebSite with HugeInteger for this example. Next, select **Visual Basic** from the **Language** drop-down list to indicate that you will use Visual Basic to build this Web service. Visual Web Developer places the Web service project's solution file (.sln) in the My Documents\Visual Studio 2005\Projects folder. If you do not have access to an IIS Web server to build and test the examples in this chapter, you can select **File System** from the **Location** drop-down list. In this case, Visual Web Developer will place your Web service's files on your local hard disk. You will then be able to test the Web service using Visual Web Developer's built-in Web server.

Step 2: Examining the Newly Created Project
After you create the project, the code-behind file Service.vb, which contains code for a simple Web service (Fig. 22.11), is displayed by default. If the code-behind file is not

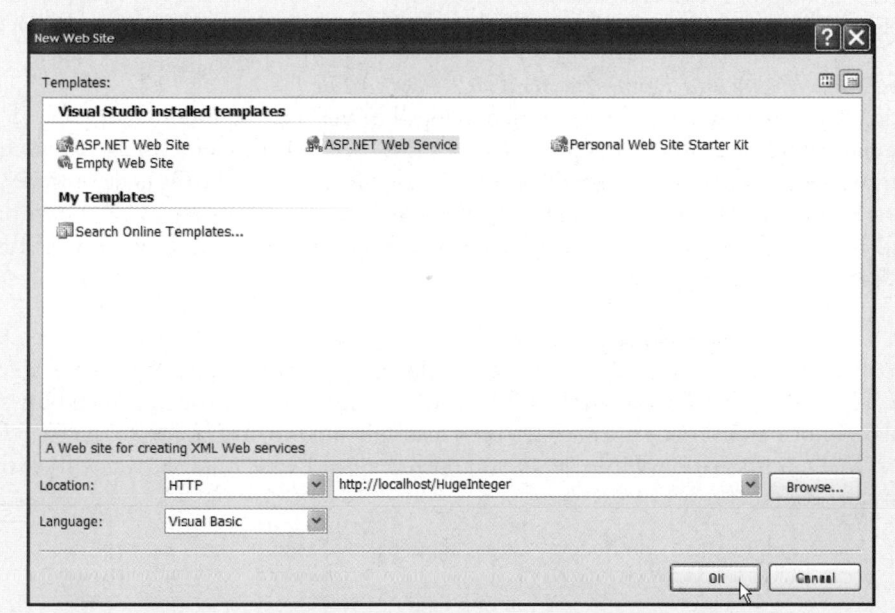

Fig. 22.10 | Creating an **ASP.NET Web Service** in Visual Web Developer.

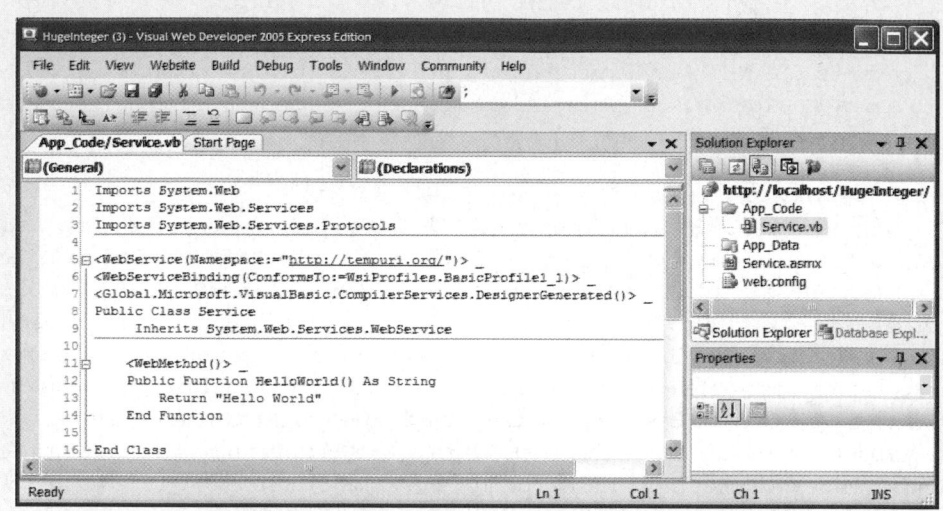

Fig. 22.11 | Code view of a Web service.

open, it can be opened by double clicking the file in the **App_Code** directory listed in the **Solution Explorer**. Visual Web Developer includes three `Imports` statements that are helpful for developing Web services (lines 1–3). By default, a new code-behind file defines a class named `Service` that is marked with the `WebService` and `WebServiceBinding` attributes (lines 5–6). The class contains a sample Web method named `HelloWorld` (lines 11–14). This method is a placeholder that you will replace with your own method(s).

Step 3: Modifying and Renaming the Code-Behind File

To create the `HugeInteger` Web service developed in this section, modify `Service.vb` by replacing all of the sample code provided by Visual Web Developer with all of the code from the `HugeInteger` code-behind file (Fig. 22.9). Then rename the file `HugeInteger.vb` (by right clicking the file in the **Solution Explorer** and choosing **Rename**). This code is provided in the examples directory for this chapter. You can download the examples from `www.deitel.com/books/vbhtp3/`.

Step 4: Examining the ASMX File

The **Solution Explorer** lists a `Service.asmx` file in addition to the code-behind file. Recall from Fig. 22.2 that a Web service's ASMX page, when accessed through a Web browser, displays information about the Web service's methods and provides access to the Web service's WSDL information. However, if you open the ASMX file on disk, you will see that it actually contains only

```
<%@ WebService Language="vb" CodeBehind="~/App_Code/Service.vb"
    Class="Service" %>
```

to indicate the programming language in which the Web service's code-behind file is written, the code-behind file's location and the class that defines the Web service. When you request the ASMX page through IIS, ASP.NET uses this information to generate the content displayed in the Web browser (i.e., the list of Web methods and their descriptions).

Step 5: Modifying the ASMX File
Whenever you change the name of the code-behind file or the name of the class that defines the Web service, you must modify the ASMX file accordingly. Thus, after defining class HugeInteger in the code-behind file HugeInteger.vb, modify the ASMX file to contain the lines

```
<%@ WebService Language="vb" CodeBehind="~/App_Code/HugeInteger.vb"
    Class="HugeInteger" %>
```

Error-Prevention Tip 22.2

Update the Web service's ASMX file appropriately whenever the name of a Web service's code-behind file or the class name changes. Visual Web Developer creates the ASMX file, but does not automatically update it when you make changes to other files in the project.

Step 6: Renaming the ASMX File
The final step in creating the HugeInteger Web service is to rename the ASMX file HugeInteger.asmx.

22.4.3 Deploying the HugeInteger Web Service

The Web service is already deployed because we created the HugeInteger Web service directly on our computer's local IIS server. You can choose **Build Web Site** from the **Build** menu to ensure that the Web service compiles without errors. You can also test the Web service directly from Visual Web Developer by selecting **Start Without Debugging** from the **Debug** menu. This opens a browser window that contains the ASMX page shown in Fig. 22.2. Clicking the link for a particular HugeInteger Web service method displays a Web page like the one in Fig. 22.4 that allows you to test the method. Note that you can also access the Web service's ASMX page from your computer by typing the following URL in a Web browser

```
http://localhost/HugeInteger/HugeInteger.asmx
```

Accessing the *HugeInteger* Web Service's ASMX Page from Another Computer
Eventually, you will want other clients to be able to access and use your Web service. If you deploy the Web service on an IIS Web server, a client can connect to that server to access the Web service with a URL of the form

```
http://host/HugeInteger/HugeInteger.asmx
```

where *host* is the hostname or IP address of the Web server. To access the Web service from another computer in your company's or school's local area network, you can replace *host* with the actual name of the computer on which IIS is running.

If you have the Windows XP Service Pack 2 operating system on the computer running IIS, that computer may not allow requests from other computers by default. If you wish to allow other computers to connect to your computer's Web server, perform the following steps:

1. Select **Start > Control Panel** to open your system's **Control Panel** window, then double click **Windows Firewall** to view the **Windows Firewall** settings dialog.

2. In the **Windows Firewall** settings dialog, click the **Advanced** tab, select **Local Area Connection** (or your network connection's name, if it is different) in the **Network Connection Settings** list box and click the **Settings...** button to display the **Advanced Settings** dialog.

3. In the **Advanced Settings** dialog, ensure that the checkbox for **Web Server (HTTP)** is checked to allow clients on other computers to submit requests to your computer's Web server.

4. Click **OK** in the **Advanced Settings** dialog, then click **OK** in the **Windows Firewall** settings dialog.

Accessing the HugeInteger Web Service's ASMX Page When the Web Service Executes in Visual Web Developer's Built-in Web Server

Recall from *Step 1* of Section 22.4.2 that if you do not have access to an IIS server to deploy and test your Web service, you can create the Web service on your computer's hard disk and use Visual Web Developer's built-in Web server to test the Web service. In this case, when you select **Start Without Debugging** from the **Debug** menu, Visual Web Developer executes its built-in Web server, then opens a Web browser containing the Web service's ASMX page so that you can test the Web service.

Web servers typically receive requests on port 80. To ensure that Visual Web Developer's built-in Web server does not conflict with another Web server running on your local computer, Visual Web Developer's Web server receives requests on a randomly selected port number. When a Web server receives requests on a port number other than port 80, the port number must be specified as part of the request. In this case, the URL to access the HugeInteger Web service's ASMX page would be of the form

```
http://host:portNumber/HugeInteger/HugeInteger.asmx
```

where *host* is the hostname or IP address of the computer on which Visual Web Developer's built-in Web server is running and *portNumber* is the specific port on which the Web server receives requests. You can see this port number in your Web browser's **Address** field when you test the Web service from Visual Web Developer. Unfortunately, Web services executed using Visual Web Developer's built-in server cannot be accessed over a network.

22.4.4 Creating a Client to Consume the HugeInteger Web Service

Now that you have defined and deployed the Web service, let's see how to consume it from a client application. In this section, you'll create a Windows application as the client using Visual Basic 2005. After creating the client application, you'll add a proxy class to the project that allows the client to access the Web service. Recall that the proxy class (or proxy) is generated from the Web service's WSDL file and enables the client to call Web methods over the Internet. The proxy class handles all the details of communicating with the Web service. The proxy class is hidden from you by default—you can view it in the **Solution Explorer** by clicking the **Show All Files** button. The proxy class's purpose is to make clients think that they are calling the Web methods directly.

This example demonstrates how to create a Web service client and generate a proxy class that allows the client to access the HugeInteger Web service. You will begin by creating a project and adding a Web reference to it. When you add the Web reference, the IDE will generate the appropriate proxy class. You will then create an instance of the proxy class and use it to call the Web service's methods. First, create a Windows application named UsingHugeIntegerWebService in Visual Basic 2005, then perform the following steps:

Step 1: Opening the Add Web Reference *Dialog*
Right click the project name in the **Solution Explorer** and select **Add Web Reference...** (Fig. 22.12).

Step 2: Locating Web Services on Your Computer
In the **Add Web Reference** dialog that appears (Fig. 22.13), click **Web services on the local machine** to locate Web references stored on the IIS Web server on your local computer (http://localhost). This server's files are located at C:\Inetpub\wwwroot by default. Note that the **Add Web Reference** dialog allows you to search for Web services in several different locations. Many companies that provide Web services simply distribute the exact URLs at which their Web services can be accessed. For this reason, the **Add Web Reference** dialog also allows you to enter the specific URL of a Web service in the **URL** field.

Step 3: Choosing the Web Service to Reference
Select the HugeInteger Web service from the list of available Web services (Fig. 22.14).

Step 4: Adding the Web Reference
Add the Web reference by clicking the **Add Reference** button (Fig. 22.15).

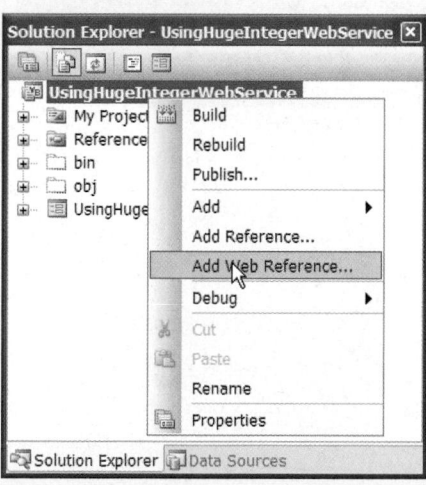

Fig. 22.12 | Adding a Web service reference to a project.

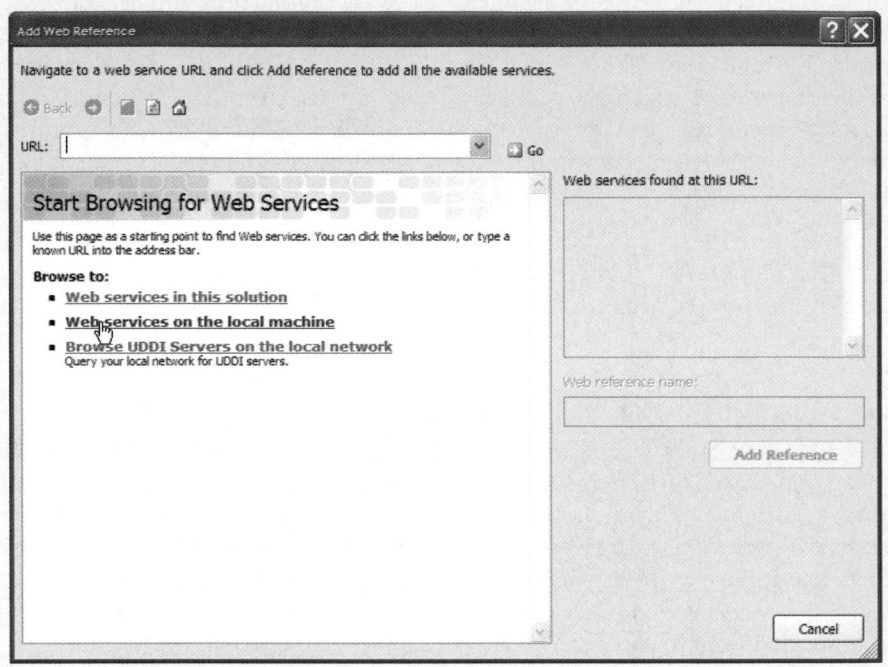

Fig. 22.13 | **Add Web Reference** dialog.

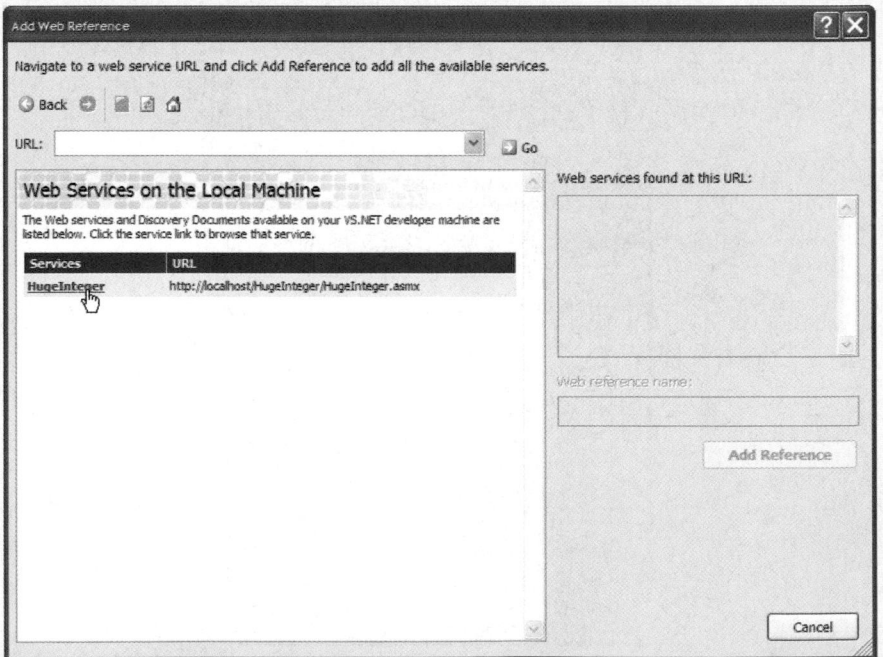

Fig. 22.14 | Web services located on `localhost`.

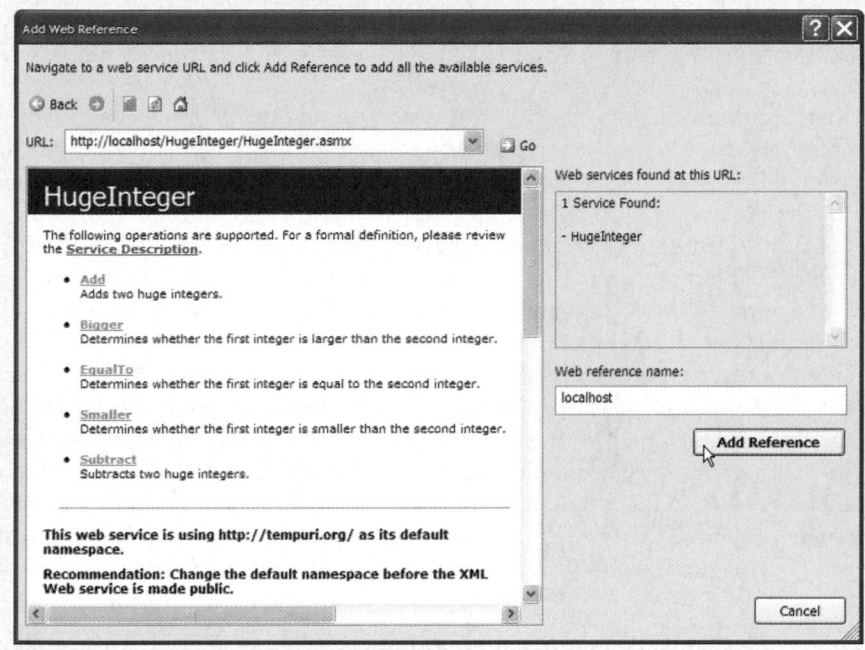

Fig. 22.15 | Web reference selection and description.

Step 5: Viewing the Web Reference in the Solution Explorer

The **Solution Explorer** (Fig. 22.16) should now contain a **Web References** folder with a node named after the domain name where the Web service is located. In this case, the name is `localhost` because we are using the local Web server. When we reference class `HugeInteger` in the client application, we will do so through the `localhost` namespace.

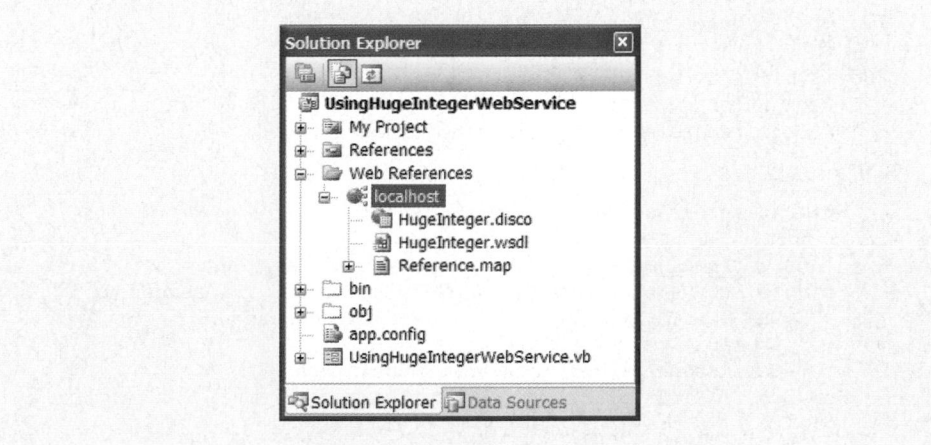

Fig. 22.16 | **Solution Explorer** after adding a Web reference to a project.

Notes on Creating a Client to Consume a Web Service

The steps we just presented also apply to adding Web references to Web applications created in Visual Web Developer. We present a Web application that consumes a Web service in Section 22.6.

When creating a client to consume a Web service, add the Web reference first so that Visual Basic 2005 (or Visual Web Developer) can recognize the Web service's class name. Once you add the Web reference to the client, it can access the Web service through an object of the proxy class. The proxy class (named `HugeInteger`) is located in namespace `localhost`, so you must use `localhost.HugeInteger` to reference this class. Although you must create an object of the proxy class to access the Web service, you do not need access to the proxy class's code. As we show in Section 22.4.5, you can invoke the proxy object's methods as if it were an object of the Web service class.

The steps that we just described work well if you know the appropriate Web service reference. However, what if you are trying to locate a new Web service? A technology to facilitate this process is **Universal Description, Discovery and Integration (UDDI)**. UDDI is an ongoing project to develop a set of specifications that define how Web services should be published so that programmers searching for Web services can find them. You can learn more about UDDI by visiting www.uddi.org and uddi.microsoft.com. You can also visit Web services directory sites like www.xmethods.net, which list many available Web services.

22.4.5 Consuming the HugeInteger Web Service

The Windows Form in Fig. 22.17 uses the `HugeInteger` Web service to perform computations with positive integers up to 100 digits long. You are already familiar with Visual Basic applications that use `Labels`, `TextBoxes` and `Buttons`, so we focus our discussions on the Web services concepts in this chapter's applications.

```vb
1   ' Fig. 22.17: UsingHugeIntegerWebService.vb
2   ' Using the HugeInteger Web Service.
3   Imports System.Web.Services.Protocols
4
5   Public Class UsingHugeIntegerWebService
6      ' declare a reference to Web service
7      Private remoteInteger As localhost.HugeInteger
8
9      ' character to trim from strings
10     Private zeros As Char() = New Char() {"0"c}
11
12     ' instantiates object to interact with Web service
13     Private Sub UsingHugeIntegerWebService_Load(ByVal sender As Object, _
14        ByVal e As System.EventArgs) Handles Me.Load
15        ' instantiate remoteInteger
16        remoteInteger = New localhost.HugeInteger()
17     End Sub ' UsingHugeIntegerWebService_Load
```

Fig. 22.17 | Using the `HugeInteger` Web service. (Part 1 of 5.)

```
18
19      ' adds two numbers input by user
20      Private Sub btnAdd_Click(ByVal sender As System.Object, _
21         ByVal e As System.EventArgs) Handles btnAdd.Click
22         ' make sure numbers do not exceed 100 digits and that both
23         ' are not 100 digits long, which would result in overflow
24         If txtFirst.Text.Length > 100 Or txtSecond.Text.Length > 100 _
25            Or (txtFirst.Text.Length = 100 And _
26               txtSecond.Text.Length = 100) Then
27            MessageBox.Show( _
28               "HugeIntegers must not be more than 100 digits" & _
29               vbCrLf & "Both integers cannot be of length 100: " & _
30               " this causes an overflow", "Error", _
31               MessageBoxButtons.OK, MessageBoxIcon.Information)
32         Else
33            ' perform addition
34            lblResult.Text = remoteInteger.Add( _
35               txtFirst.Text, txtSecond.Text).TrimStart(zeros)
36         End If
37      End Sub ' btnAdd_Click
38
39      ' subtracts two numbers input by user
40      Private Sub btnSubtract_Click(ByVal sender As System.Object, _
41         ByVal e As System.EventArgs) Handles btnSubtract.Click
42         ' ensure that HugeIntegers do not exceed 100 digits
43         If Not NumbersTooBig(txtFirst.Text, txtSecond.Text) Then
44            ' perform subtraction
45            Try
46               Dim result As String = remoteInteger.Subtract( _
47                  txtFirst.Text, txtSecond.Text).TrimStart(zeros)
48
49               If result = "" Then
50                  lblResult.Text = "0"
51               Else
52                  lblResult.Text = result
53               End If
54            Catch exception As SoapException
55               ' if WebMethod throws an exception,
56               ' then first argument was smaller than second
57               MessageBox.Show( _
58                  "First argument was smaller than the second")
59            End Try
60         End If
61      End Sub ' btnSubtract_Click
62
63      ' determines whether first number input is larger than the second
64      Private Sub btnLarger_Click(ByVal sender As System.Object, _
65         ByVal e As System.EventArgs) Handles btnLarger.Click
66         ' ensure that HugeIntegers do not exceed 100 digits
67         If Not NumbersTooBig(txtFirst.Text, txtSecond.Text) Then
68            ' call Web-service method to determine whether
69            ' first integer is larger than the second
```

Fig. 22.17 | Using the HugeInteger Web service. (Part 2 of 5.)

```
70          If remoteInteger.Bigger(txtFirst.Text, txtSecond.Text) Then
71              lblResult.Text = txtFirst.Text.TrimStart(zeros) & _
72                  " is larger than " & txtSecond.Text.TrimStart(zeros)
73          Else
74              lblResult.Text = txtFirst.Text.TrimStart(zeros) & _
75                  " is not larger than " + txtSecond.Text.TrimStart(zeros)
76          End If
77      End If
78  End Sub ' btnLarger_Click
79
80  ' determines whether first number input is smaller than the second
81  Private Sub btnSmaller_Click(ByVal sender As System.Object, _
82      ByVal e As System.EventArgs) Handles btnSmaller.Click
83      ' make sure HugeIntegers do not exceed 100 digits
84      If Not NumbersTooBig(txtFirst.Text, txtSecond.Text) Then
85          ' call Web-service method to determine if
86          ' first integer is smaller than second
87          If remoteInteger.Smaller(txtFirst.Text, txtSecond.Text) Then
88              lblResult.Text = txtFirst.Text.TrimStart(zeros) & _
89                  " is smaller than " + txtSecond.Text.TrimStart(zeros)
90          Else
91              lblResult.Text = txtFirst.Text.TrimStart(zeros) & _
92                  " is not smaller than " & txtSecond.Text.TrimStart(zeros)
93          End If
94      End If
95  End Sub ' btnSmaller_Click
96
97  ' determines whether the two numbers input are equal
98  Private Sub btnEqual_Click(ByVal sender As System.Object, _
99      ByVal e As System.EventArgs) Handles btnEqual.Click
100     ' ensure that HugeIntegers do not exceed 100 digits
101     If Not NumbersTooBig(txtFirst.Text, txtSecond.Text) Then
102         ' call Web-service method to determine if integers are equal
103         If remoteInteger.EqualTo(txtFirst.Text, txtSecond.Text) Then
104             lblResult.Text = txtFirst.Text.TrimStart(zeros) & _
105                 " is equal to " & txtSecond.Text.TrimStart(zeros)
106         Else
107             lblResult.Text = txtFirst.Text.TrimStart(zeros) & _
108                 " is not equal to " & txtSecond.Text.TrimStart(zeros)
109         End If
110     End If
111 End Sub ' btnEqual_Click
112
113 ' determines whether numbers input by user are too big
114 Private Function NumbersTooBig(ByVal first As String, _
115     ByVal second As String) As Boolean
116     ' display an error message if either number has too many digits
117     If (first.Length > 100) Or (second.Length > 100) Then
118         MessageBox.Show("HugeIntegers must be less than 100 digits", _
119             "Error", MessageBoxButtons.OK, MessageBoxIcon.Information)
120         Return True
121     End If
```

Fig. 22.17 | Using the HugeInteger Web service. (Part 3 of 5.)

```
122
123        Return False
124     End Function ' SizeCheck
125  End Class ' UsingHugeIntegerWebService
```

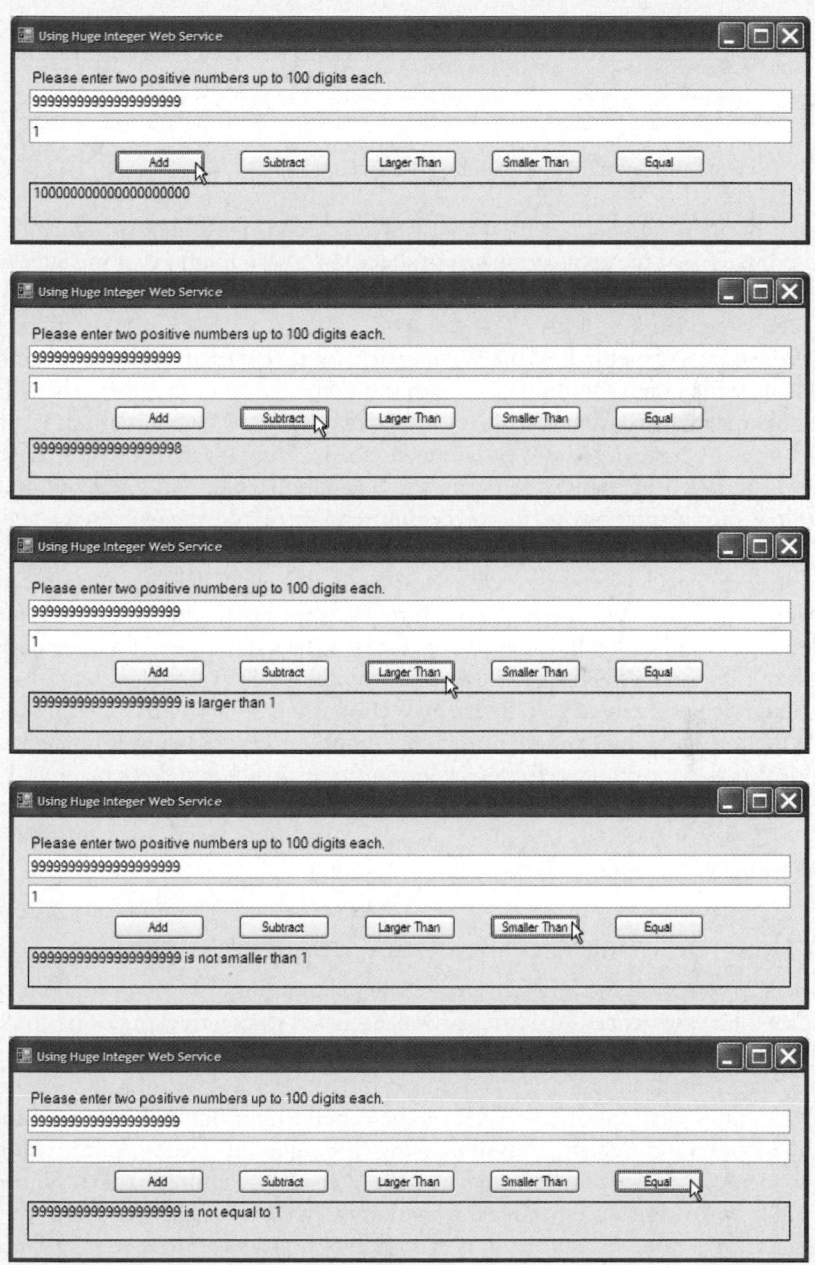

Fig. 22.17 | Using the HugeInteger Web service. (Part 4 of 5.)

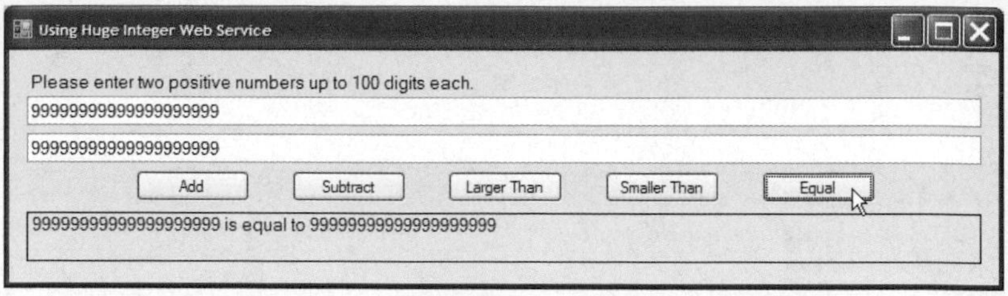

Fig. 22.17 | Using the `HugeInteger` Web service. (Part 5 of 5.)

Line 7 declares variable `remoteInteger` of type `localhost.HugeInteger`. This variable is used in each of the application's event handlers to call methods of the `HugeInteger` Web service. The proxy object is created and assigned to this variable at line 16 in the Form's `Load` event handler. Lines 34–35, 46–47, 70, 87 and 103 in the various button event handlers invoke methods of the Web service. Note that each call is made on the local proxy object, which then communicates with the Web service on the client's behalf. If you downloaded the example from www.deitel.com/books/vbhtp3, you might need to regenerate the proxy by removing the Web reference, then adding it again. To do so, right click **localhost** in the **Web References** folder in the **Solution Explorer** and select option **Delete**. Then follow the instructions in the preceding section to add the Web reference to the project.

The user inputs two integers, each up to 100 digits long. Clicking a button causes the application to invoke a Web method to perform the appropriate task and return the result. Note that client application `UsingHugeIntegerService` cannot perform operations using 100-digit numbers directly. Instead the application creates `String` representations of these numbers and passes them as arguments to Web methods that handle such tasks for the client. It then uses the return value of each operation to display an appropriate message.

Note that the application eliminates leading zeros in the numbers before displaying them by calling `String` method `TrimStart`. Like `String` method `Trim` (discussed in Chapter 16), `TrimStart` removes all occurrences of characters specified by a `Char` array (line 24) from the beginning of a `String`.

22.5 Session Tracking in Web Services

In Chapter 21, we described the advantages of maintaining information about users to personalize their experiences. In particular, we discussed session tracking using cookies and `HttpSessionState` objects. We will now incorporate session tracking into a Web service. Suppose a client application needs to call several methods from the same Web service, possibly several times each. In such a case, it can be beneficial for the Web service to maintain state information for the client. Session tracking eliminates the need for information about the client to be passed between the client and the Web service multiple times. For example, a Web service providing access to local restaurant reviews would benefit from storing the client user's street address. Once the user's address is stored in a session variable, Web methods can return personalized, localized results without requiring that the address be passed in each method call. This not only improves performance, but also requires less effort on the part of the programmer—less information is passed in each method call.

22.5.1 Creating a Blackjack Web Service

Storing session information can provide client programmers with a more intuitive Web service. Our next example is a Web service that assists programmers in developing a blackjack card game (Fig. 22.18). The Web service provides Web methods to deal a card and to evaluate a hand of cards. After presenting the Web service, we use it to serve as the dealer for a game of blackjack (Fig. 22.19). The blackjack Web service uses a session variable to maintain a unique deck of cards for each client application. Several clients can use the service at the same time, but Web method calls made by a specific client use only the deck stored in that client's session. Our example uses a simple subset of casino blackjack rules:

> Two cards each are dealt to the dealer and the player. The player's cards are dealt face up. Only the first of the dealer's cards is dealt face up. Each card has a value. A card numbered 2 through 10 is worth its face value. Jacks, queens and kings each count as 10. Aces can count as 1 or 11—whichever value is more beneficial to the player (as we will soon see). If the sum of the player's two initial cards is 21 (i.e., the player was dealt a card valued at 10 and an ace, which counts as 11 in this situation), the player has "blackjack" and immediately wins the game. Otherwise, the player can begin taking additional cards one at a time. These cards are dealt face up, and the player decides when to stop taking cards. If the player "busts" (i.e., the sum of the player's cards exceeds 21), the game is over, and the player loses. When the player is satisfied with the current set of cards, the player "stays" (i.e., stops taking cards), and the dealer's hidden card is revealed. If the dealer's total is 16 or less, the dealer must take another card; otherwise, the dealer must stay. The dealer must continue to take cards until the sum of the dealer's cards is greater than or equal to 17. If the dealer exceeds 21, the player wins. Otherwise, the hand with the higher point total wins. If the dealer and the player have the same point total, the game is a "push" (i.e., a tie), and no one wins.

The Web service (Fig. 22.18) provides methods to deal a card and to determine the point value of a hand. We represent each card as a `String` consisting of a digit (e.g., 1–13) representing the card's face (e.g., ace through king), followed by a space and a digit (e.g., 0–3) representing the card's suit (e.g., clubs, diamonds, hearts or spades). For example, the jack of hearts is represented as `"11 2"`, and the two of clubs is represented as `"2 0"`. After deploying the Web service, we create a Windows application that uses the `BlackjackWebService`'s Web methods to implement a game of blackjack. To create and deploy this Web service follow the steps presented in Sections 22.4.2–22.4.3 for the `HugeInteger` service.

Lines 15–16 define method `DealCard` as a Web method. Setting property `EnableSession` to `True` indicates that session information should be maintained and should be accessible to this method. This is required only for methods that must access the session information. Doing so allows the Web service to use an `HttpSessionState` object (named `Session` by ASP.NET) to maintain the deck of cards for each client application that uses this Web service (line 22). We can use `Session` to store objects for a specific client between method calls. We discussed session state in detail in Chapter 21.

Method `DealCard` removes a card from the deck and sends it to the client. Without using a session variable, the deck of cards would need to be passed back and forth with each method call. Using session state makes the method easy to call (it requires no arguments), and avoids the overhead of sending the deck over the network multiple times.

At this point, our Web service contains methods that use session variables. However, the Web service still cannot determine which session variables belong to which user. If two clients successfully call the `DealCard` method, the same deck would be manipulated. To

```
132              Case 2 ' hearts
133                 suitLetter = "h"c
134              Case Else ' spades
135                 suitLetter = "s"c
136           End Select
137
138           ' set displayBox to display appropriate image
139           displayBox.Image = Image.FromFile( _
140              "blackjack_images/" & face & suitLetter & ".png")
141        End Sub ' DisplayCard
142
143        ' displays all player cards and shows
144        ' appropriate game status message
145        Public Sub GameOver(ByVal winner As GameStatus)
146           ' display appropriate status image
147           If winner = GameStatus.PUSH Then ' push
148              statusPictureBox.Image = _
149                 Image.FromFile("blackjack_images/tie.png")
150           ElseIf winner = GameStatus.LOSE Then ' player loses
151              statusPictureBox.Image = _
152                 Image.FromFile("blackjack_images/lose.png")
153           ElseIf winner = GameStatus.BLACKJACK Then
154              ' player has blackjack
155              statusPictureBox.Image = _
156                 Image.FromFile("blackjack_images/blackjack.png")
157           Else ' player wins
158              statusPictureBox.Image = _
159                 Image.FromFile("blackjack_images/win.png")
160           End If
161
162           ' display final totals for dealer and player
163           lblDealerTotal.Text = _
164              "Dealer: " & dealer.GetHandValue(dealersCards)
165           lblPlayerTotal.Text = _
166              "Player: " & dealer.GetHandValue(playersCards)
167
168           ' reset controls for new game
169           btnStay.Enabled = False
170           btnHit.Enabled = False
171           btnDeal.Enabled = True
172        End Sub ' GameOver
173
174        ' deal two cards each to dealer and player
175        Private Sub btnDeal_Click(ByVal sender As System.Object, _
176           ByVal e As System.EventArgs) Handles btnDeal.Click
177           Dim card As String ' stores a card temporarily until added to a hand
178
179           ' clear card images
180           For Each cardImage As PictureBox In cardBoxes
181              cardImage.Image = Nothing
182           Next
183
```

Fig. 22.19 | Blackjack game that uses the Blackjack Web service. (Part 4 of 8.)

```
184          statusPictureBox.Image = Nothing ' clear status image
185          lblDealerTotal.Text = "" ' clear final total for dealer
186          lblPlayerTotal.Text = "" ' clear final total for player
187
188          ' create a new, shuffled deck on the remote machine
189          dealer.Shuffle()
190
191          ' deal two cards to player
192          playersCards = dealer.DealCard() ' deal a card to player's hand
193
194          ' update GUI to display new card
195          DisplayCard(11, playersCards)
196          card = dealer.DealCard() ' deal a second card
197          DisplayCard(12, card) ' update GUI to display new card
198          playersCards &= vbTab & card ' add second card to player's hand
199
200          ' deal two cards to dealer, only display face of first card
201          dealersCards = dealer.DealCard() ' deal a card to dealer's hand
202          DisplayCard(0, dealersCards) ' update GUI to display new card
203          card = dealer.DealCard() ' deal a second card
204          DisplayCard(1, "") ' update GUI to show face-down card
205          dealersCards &= vbTab & card ' add second card to dealer's hand
206
207          btnStay.Enabled = True ' allow player to stay
208          btnHit.Enabled = True ' allow player to hit
209          btnDeal.Enabled = False ' disable Deal Button
210
211          ' determine the value of the two hands
212          Dim dealerTotal As Integer = dealer.GetHandValue(dealersCards)
213          Dim playerTotal As Integer = dealer.GetHandValue(playersCards)
214
215          ' if hands equal 21, it is a push
216          If dealerTotal = playerTotal And dealerTotal = 21 Then
217             GameOver(GameStatus.PUSH)
218          ElseIf dealerTotal = 21 Then ' if dealer has 21, dealer wins
219             GameOver(GameStatus.LOSE)
220          ElseIf playerTotal = 21 Then ' player has blackjack
221             GameOver(GameStatus.BLACKJACK)
222          End If
223
224          currentDealerCard = 2 ' next dealer card has index 2 in cardBoxes
225          currentPlayerCard = 13 ' next player card has index 13 in cardBoxes
226       End Sub ' btnDeal_Click
227
228       ' deal another card to player
229       Private Sub btnHit_Click(ByVal sender As System.Object, _
230          ByVal e As System.EventArgs) Handles btnHit.Click
231          ' get player another card
232          Dim card As String = dealer.DealCard() ' deal new card
233          playersCards &= vbTab & card ' add new card to player's hand
234
235          ' update GUI to show new card
236          DisplayCard(currentPlayerCard, card)
```

Fig. 22.19 | Blackjack game that uses the Blackjack Web service. (Part 5 of 8.)

```
237        currentPlayerCard += 1
238
239     ' determine the value of the player's hand
240     Dim total As Integer = dealer.GetHandValue(playersCards)
241
242     ' if player exceeds 21, house wins
243     If total > 21 Then
244         GameOver(GameStatus.LOSE)
245     End If
246
247     ' if player has 21,
248     ' they cannot take more cards, and dealer plays
249     If total = 21 Then
250         btnHit.Enabled = False
251         DealerPlay()
252     End If
253   End Sub ' btnHit_Click
254
255 ' play the dealer's hand after the play chooses to stay
256 Private Sub btnStay_Click(ByVal sender As System.Object, _
257     ByVal e As System.EventArgs) Handles btnStay.Click
258     btnStay.Enabled = False ' disable Stay Button
259     btnHit.Enabled = False ' display Hit Button
260     btnDeal.Enabled = True ' re-enable Deal Button
261     DealerPlay() ' player chose to stay, so play the dealer's hand
262   End Sub ' btnStay_Click
263 End Class ' FrmBlackjack
```

a) Initial cards dealt to the player and the dealer when the user pressed the **Deal** button.

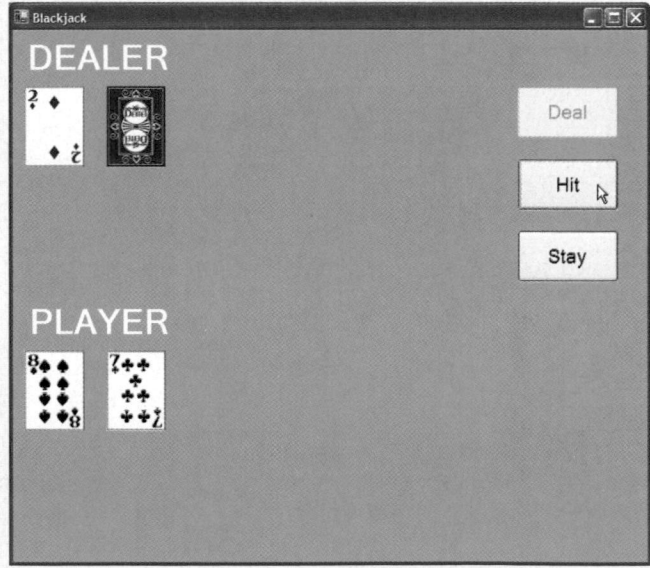

Fig. 22.19 | Blackjack game that uses the Blackjack Web service. (Part 6 of 8.)

b) Cards after the player pressed the **Hit** button twice, then the **Stay** button. In this case, the player won the game with a higher total than the dealer.

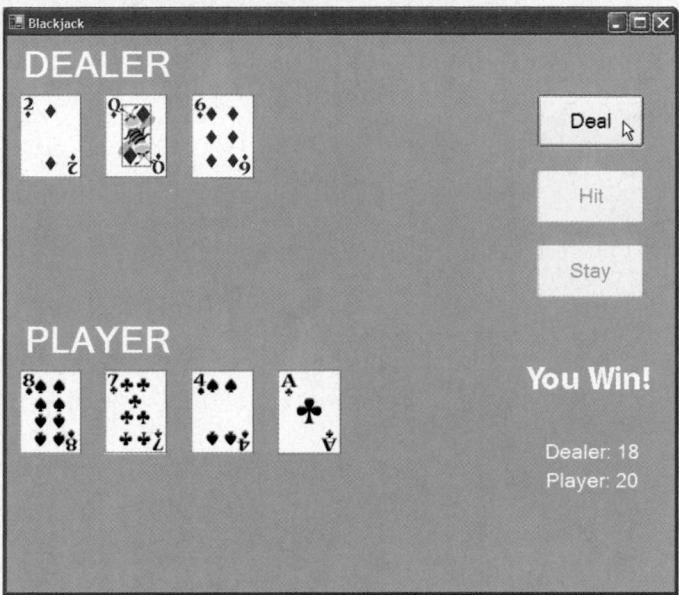

c) Cards after the player pressed the **Hit** button once, then the **Stay** button. In this case, the player busted (exceeded 21) and the dealer won the game.

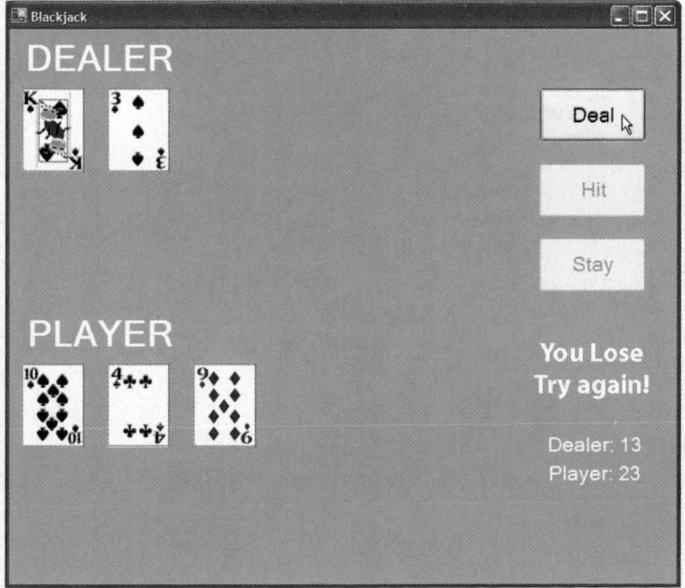

Fig. 22.19 | Blackjack game that uses the **Blackjack** Web service. (Part 7 of 8.)

d) Cards after the player pressed the **Deal** button. In this case, the player won with Blackjack because the first two cards were an ace and a card with a value of 10 (a jack in this case).

e) Cards after the player pressed the **Stay** button. In this case, the player and dealer push—they have the same card total.

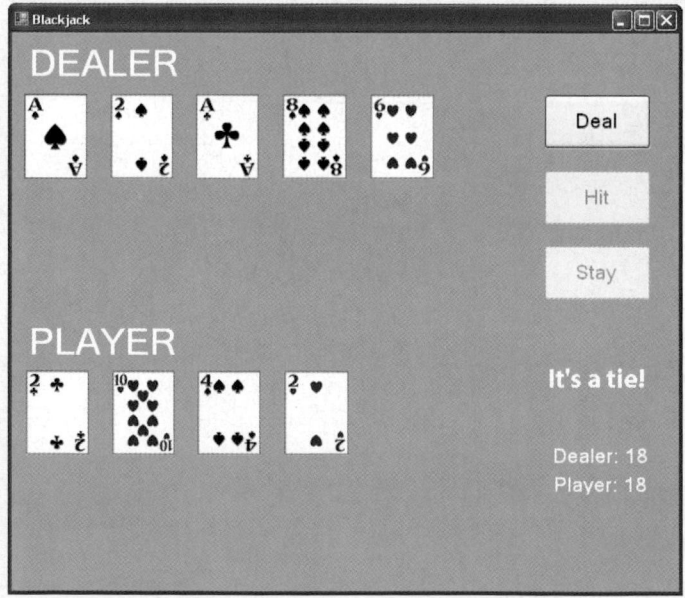

Fig. 22.19 | Blackjack game that uses the `Blackjack` Web service. (Part 8 of 8.)

If `dealButton_Click` does not call `GameOver`, the player can take more cards by clicking the **Hit** button. The event handler for this button is in lines 229–253. Each time a player clicks **Hit**, the program deals the player one more card (line 232) and displays it in the GUI. Line 240 evaluates the player's hand. If the player exceeds 21, the game is over, and the player loses. If the player has exactly 21, the player is not allowed to take any more cards, and method `DealerPlay` (lines 63–100) is called, causing the dealer to keep taking cards until the dealer's hand has a value of 17 or more (lines 73–81). If the dealer exceeds 21, the player wins (line 88); otherwise, the values of the hands are compared, and `GameOver` is called with the appropriate argument (lines 92–98).

Clicking the **Stay** button indicates that a player does not want to be dealt another card. The event handler for this button (lines 256–262) disables the **Hit** and **Stay** buttons, then calls method `DealerPlay`.

Method `DisplayCard` (lines 103–141) updates the GUI to display a newly dealt card. The method takes as arguments an integer representing the index of the `PictureBox` in the `ArrayList` that must have its image set, and a `String` representing the card. An empty `String` indicates that we wish to display the card face down. If method `DisplayCard` receives a `String` that's not empty, the program extracts the face and suit from the `String` and uses this information to find the correct image. The `Select Case` statement (lines 127–136) converts the number representing the suit to an integer and assigns the appropriate character to `suitLetter` (c for clubs, d for diamonds, h for hearts and s for spades). The character in `suitLetter` is used to complete the image's file name (lines 139–140).

22.6 Using Web Forms and Web Services

Our prior examples accessed Web services from Windows applications. You can just as easily use Web services in Web applications. In fact, because Web-based businesses are becoming increasingly prevalent, it is common for Web applications to consume Web services. Figure 22.20 presents an airline reservation Web service that receives information regarding the type of seat a customer wishes to reserve and makes a reservation if such a seat is available. Later in this section, we present a Web application that allows a customer to specify a reservation request, then uses the airline reservation Web service to attempt to execute the request. The code and database used in this example are provided with the chapter's examples, which can be downloaded from www.deitel.com/books/vbhtp3.

```
1   ' Fig. 22.20: ReservationWebService.vb
2   ' Airline reservation Web Service.Imports System.Web
3   Imports System.Web.Services
4   Imports System.Web.Services.Protocols
5
6   <WebService(Namespace:="http://www.deitel.com/")> _
7   <WebServiceBinding(ConformsTo:=WsiProfiles.BasicProfile1_1)> _
8   <Global.Microsoft.VisualBasic.CompilerServices.DesignerGenerated()> _
9   Public Class ReservationWebService
10      Inherits System.Web.Services.WebService
11      ' create TicketsDataSet object for caching data
12      ' from the Tickets database
13      Private ticketsDataSet As New TicketsDataSet()
```

Fig. 22.20 | Airline reservation Web service. (Part 1 of 2.)

```
14
15     ' create SeatsTableAdapter for interacting with the database
16     Private seatsTableAdapter As _
17       New TicketsDataSetTableAdapters.SeatsTableAdapter()
18
19     ' checks database to determine whether matching seat is available
20     <WebMethod(Description:="Method to reserve a seat.")> _
21     Public Function Reserve(ByVal seatType As String, _
22       ByVal classType As String) As Boolean
23       ' fill TicketsDataSet.Seats with rows that represent untaken
24       ' seats that match the specified seatType and classType
25       seatsTableAdapter.FillByTypeAndClass( _
26         ticketsDataSet.Seats, seatType, classType)
27
28       ' if the number of seats returned is nonzero,
29       ' obtain the first matching seat number and mark it as taken
30       If ticketsDataSet.Seats.Count <> 0 Then
31         Dim seatNumber As String = ticketsDataSet.Seats(0).Number
32
33         seatsTableAdapter.UpdateSeatAsTaken(seatNumber)
34         Return True ' seat was reserved
35       End If
36
37       Return False ' no seat was reserved
38     End Function ' Reserve
39   End Class ' ReservationWebService
```

Fig. 22.20 | Airline reservation Web service. (Part 2 of 2.)

The airline reservation Web service has a single Web method—Reserve (lines 20–38)—which searches a seat database (Tickets.mdf) to locate a seat matching a user's request. If it finds an appropriate seat, Reserve updates the database, makes the reservation and returns True; otherwise, no reservation is made, and the method returns False. Note that the statements at lines 25–26 and line 33, which query and update the database, use objects of classes TicketsDataSet and TicketsDataSetTableAdapters.SeatsTable-Adapter. Recall from Chapter 20 that DataSet and TableAdapter classes are created for you when you use the **DataSet Designer** to add a DataSet to a project. We discuss the steps for adding the TicketsDataSet in Section 22.6.1.

Reserve receives two parameters—a String representing the desired seat type (i.e., Window, Middle or Aisle) and a String representing the desired class type (i.e., Economy or First). Our database contains four columns—the seat number (i.e., 1–10), the seat type (i.e., Window, Middle or Aisle), the class type (i.e., Economy or First) and a column containing either 1 (true) or 0 (false) to indicate whether the seat is taken. Lines 25–26 retrieve the seat numbers of any available seats matching the requested seat and class type. This statement fills the Seats table in ticketsDataSet with the results of the query

```
SELECT Number
FROM Seats
WHERE (Taken = 0) AND (Type = @type) AND (Class = @class)
```

The parameters @type and @class in the query are replaced with values of the seatType and classType arguments to SeatsTableAdapter method FillByTypeAndClass. In line

30, if the number of rows in the Seats table (ticketsDataSet.Seats.Count) is not zero, there was at least one seat that matched the user's request. In this case, the Web service reserves the first matching seat number. We obtain the seat number in line 31 by accessing the Seats table's first element (i.e., Seats(0)—the first row in the table), then obtaining the value of that row's Number column. Line 33 invokes the SeatsTableAdapter method UpdateSeatAsTaken and passes to it seatNumber—the seat to reserve. The method uses the UPDATE statement

```
UPDATE Seats
SET Taken = 1
WHERE (Number = @number)
```

to mark the seat as taken in the database by replacing parameter @number with the value of seatNumber. Method Reserve returns True (line 34) to indicate that the reservation was successful. If there are no matching seats (line 30), Reserve returns False (line 37) to indicate that no seats matched the user's request.

22.6.1 Adding Data Components to a Web Service

Next, you'll use Visual Web Developer's tools to configure a DataSet that allows our Web service to interact with the Tickets.mdf SQL Server database file. You'll add a new DataSet to the project, then configure the DataSet's TableAdapter using the **TableAdapter Configuration Wizard**. The wizard allows you to select the data source (Tickets.mdf) and to create the SQL statements necessary to support the database operations discussed in Fig. 22.20's description. The following steps for configuring the DataSet and its corresponding TableAdapter are similar to those you saw in Chapters 20 and 21.

Step 1: Create *ReservationWebService* and Add a *DataSet* to the Project

Begin by creating an ASP.NET Web Service project named ReservationWebService. Rename the file Service.vb as ReservationWebService.vb and replace its code with the code in Fig. 22.20. Next, add a DataSet named TicketsDataSet to the project. Right click the **App_Code** folder in the **Solution Explorer** and select **Add New Item...** from the pop-up menu. In the **Add New Item** dialog, select **DataSet**, specify TicketsDataSet.xsd in the **Name** field and click **Add**. This displays the TicketsDataSet in design view and opens the **TableAdapter Configuration Wizard**. When you add a DataSet to a project, the IDE creates appropriate TableAdapter classes for interacting with the database tables.

Step 2: Select the Data Source and Create a Connection

You'll use the **TableAdapter Configuration Wizard** in the next several steps to configure a TableAdapter for manipulating the Seats table in the Tickets.mdf database. Now, you must select the database. In the **TableAdapter Configuration Wizard**, click the **New Connection...** button to display the **Add Connection** dialog. In this dialog, specify **Microsoft SQL Server Database File** as the **Data source**, then click the **Browse...** button to display the **Select SQL Server Database File** dialog. Locate Tickets.mdf on your computer, select it and click the **Open** button to return to the **Add Connection** dialog. Click the **Test Connection** button to test the database connection, then click **OK** to return to the **TableAdapter Configuration Wizard**. Click **Next >**, then click **Yes** when you are asked whether you would like to add the file to your project and modify the connection. Click **Next >** to save the connection string in the application configuration file.

Step 3: Open the Query Builder and Add the **Seats** Table from `Tickets.mdf`

You must specify how the `TableAdapter` will access the database. In this example, you'll use SQL statements, so choose **Use SQL Statements**, then click **Next >**. Click **Query Builder...** to display the **Query Builder** and **Add Table** dialogs. Before building a SQL query, you must specify the table(s) to use in the query. The `Tickets.mdf` database contains only one table, named `Seats`. Select this table from the **Tables** tab and click **Add**. Click **Close** to close the **Add Table** dialog.

Step 4: Configure a **SELECT** Query to Obtain Available Seats

Now let's create a query which selects seats that are not already reserved and that match a particular type and class. Select **Number** from the **Seats** table at the top of the **Query Builder** dialog. Next, specify the criteria for selecting seats. In the middle of the **Query Builder** dialog, click the cell below **Number** in the **Column** column and select **Taken**. In the **Filter** column of this row, type 0 (i.e., false) to indicate that we should select only seat numbers that are not taken. In the next row, select **Type** in the **Column** column and specify `@type` as the **Filter** to indicate that the filter value will be specified as an argument to the method that implements this query. In the next row, select **Class** in the **Column** column and specify `@class` as the **Filter** to indicate that this filter value also will be specified as a method argument. Uncheck the checkboxes in the **Output** column for the **Taken**, **Type** and **Class** rows. The **Query Builder** dialog should now appear as shown in Fig. 22.21. Click **OK** to close the **Query Builder** dialog. Click **Next >** to choose the methods to generate. Name the `Fill` and `Get` methods `FillByTypeAndClass` and `GetDataByTypeAndClass`, respectively. Click the **Finish** button to generate these methods.

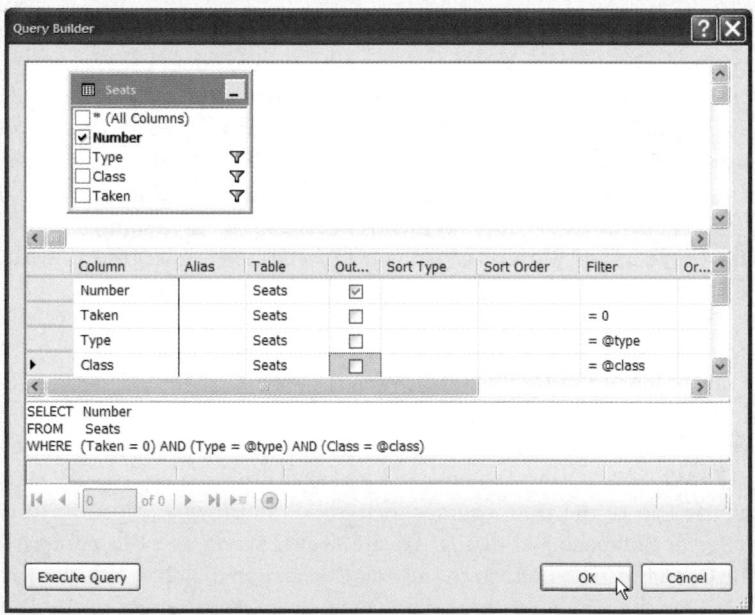

Fig. 22.21 | **QueryBuilder** dialog specifying a SELECT query that selects seats that are not already reserved and that match a particular type and class.

Step 5: Add Another Query to the SeatsTableAdapter for the TicketsDataSet
Now, you'll create an UPDATE query that reserves a seat. In the design area for the Tick-etsDataSet, click **SeatsTableAdapter** to select it, then right click it and select **Add Query...** to display the **TableAdapter Query Configuration Wizard**. Select **Use SQL Statements** and click **Next >**. Select **Update** as the query type and click **Next >**. Delete the existing UPDATE query. Click **Query Builder...** to display the **Query Builder** and **Add Table** dialogs. Then add the Seats table as you did in *Step 3* and click **Close** to return to the **Query Builder** dialog.

Step 6: Configure an UPDATE Statement to Reserve a Seat
In the **Query Builder** dialog, select the **Taken** column from the **Seats** table at the top of the dialog. In the middle of the dialog, place the value 1 (i.e., true) in the **New Value** column for the **Taken** row. In the row below **Taken**, select **Number**, uncheck the checkbox in the **Set** column and specify @number as the **Filter** value to indicate that the seat number will be specified as an argument to the method that implements this query. The **Query Builder** dialog should now appear as shown in Fig. 22.22. Click **OK** to return to the **TableAdapter Query Configuration Wizard**. Then click **Next >** to choose the name of the update method. Name the method UpdateSeatAsTaken, then click **Finish** to close the **TableAdapter Query Configuration Wizard**. At this point, you can use the ReservationWebService.asmx page to test the Web service's Reserve method. To do so, select **Start Without Debugging** from the **Debug** menu. In Section 22.6.2, we build a Web form to consume this Web service.

22.6.2 Creating a Web Form to Interact with the Airline Reservation Web Service

Figure 22.23 presents the code for a Web Form through which users can select seat types. This page allows users to reserve a seat on the basis of its class (Economy or First) and location (Aisle, Middle or Window) in a row of seats. The page then uses the airline reserva-

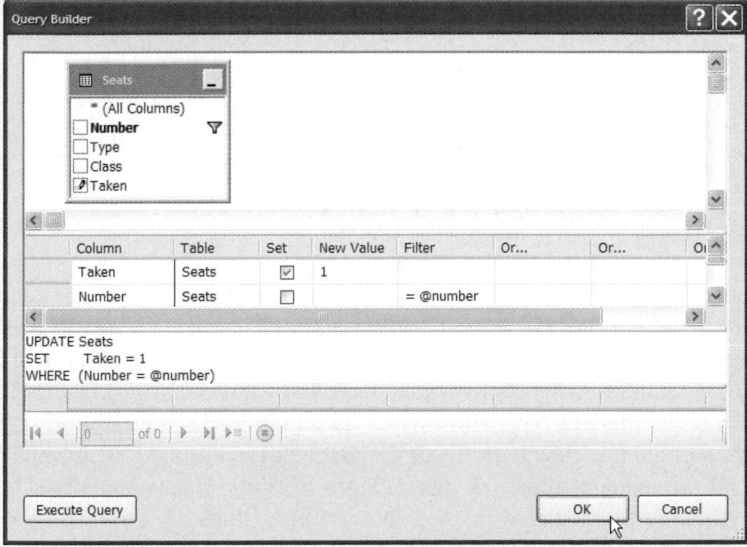

Fig. 22.22 | **QueryBuilder** dialog specifying an UPDATE statement that reserves a seat.

```
1    <%-- Fig. 22.23: ReservationClient.aspx                    --%>
2    <%-- Web Form that allows users to reserve seats on a plane. --%>
3    <%@ Page Language="VB" AutoEventWireup="false"
4       CodeFile="ReservationClient.aspx.vb" Inherits="ReservationClient" %>
5
6    <!DOCTYPE html PUBLIC "-//W3C//DTD XHTML 1.0 Transitional//EN"
7       "http://www.w3.org/TR/xhtml1/DTD/xhtml11-transitional.dtd">
8
9    <html xmlns="http://www.w3.org/1999/xhtml" >
10   <head runat="server">
11      <title>Ticket Reservation</title>
12   </head>
13   <body>
14      <form id="form1" runat="server">
15      <div>
16         <asp:Label ID="instructionsLabel" runat="server"
17            Text="Please select the seat type and class to reserve:">
18         </asp:Label>
19         <br /><br />
20         <asp:DropDownList ID="seatList" runat="server"
21            Height="22px" Width="100px">
22            <asp:ListItem>Aisle</asp:ListItem>
23            <asp:ListItem>Middle</asp:ListItem>
24            <asp:ListItem>Window</asp:ListItem>
25         </asp:DropDownList>
26             
27         <asp:DropDownList ID="classList" runat="server" Width="100px">
28            <asp:ListItem>Economy</asp:ListItem>
29            <asp:ListItem>First</asp:ListItem>
30         </asp:DropDownList>
31             
32         <asp:Button ID="reserveButton" runat="server" Text="Reserve"
33            Width="102px" />
34         <br /><br />
35         <asp:Label ID="errorLabel" runat="server" ForeColor="#C00000"
36            Height="19px" Width="343px"></asp:Label>
37      </div>
38      </form>
39   </body>
40   </html>
```

Fig. 22.23 | ASPX file that takes reservation information.

tion Web service to carry out users' requests. If the database request is not successful, the user is instructed to modify the request and try again. When you create this ASP.NET application, remember to add a Web reference to the ReservationWebService of Fig. 22.20

This page defines two DropDownList objects and a Button. One DropDownList (lines 20–25) displays all the seat types from which users can select. The second (lines 27–30) provides choices for the class type. Users click the Button named reserveButton (lines 32–33) to submit requests after making selections from the DropDownLists. The page also defines an initially blank Label named errorLabel (lines 35–36), which displays an appropriate message if no seat matching the user's selection is available. Line 9 of the code-behind file (Fig. 22.24) attaches an event handler to reserveButton.

Line 6 of Fig. 22.24 creates a ReservationWebService object. When the user clicks **Reserve** (Fig. 22.25), the reserveButton_Click event handler (lines 8–26 of Fig. 22.24) executes, and the page reloads. The event handler calls the Web service's Reserve method and passes to it the selected seat and class type as arguments (lines 10–11). If Reserve returns True, the application hides the GUI controls and displays a message thanking the user for making a reservation (line 20); otherwise, the application notifies the user that the type of seat requested is not available and instructs the user to try again (lines 23–24). You can use the techniques presented in Chapter 21 to build this ASP.NET Web Form. Figure 22.25 shows several user interactions with this Web application.

```vb
1   ' Fig. 22.24: ReservationClient.aspx.vb
2   ' ReservationClient code behind file.
3   Partial Class ReservationClient
4      Inherits System.Web.UI.Page
5      ' object of proxy type used to connect to Reservation Web service
6      Private ticketAgent As New localhost.ReservationWebService()
7
8      Protected Sub reserveButton_Click(ByVal sender As Object, _
9         ByVal e As System.EventArgs) Handles reserveButton.Click
10        If ticketAgent.Reserve(seatList.SelectedItem.Text, _
11           classList.SelectedItem.Text.ToString()) Then
12           ' hide other controls
13           instructionsLabel.Visible = False
14           seatList.Visible = False
15           classList.Visible = False
16           reserveButton.Visible = False
17           errorLabel.Visible = False
18
19           ' display message indicating success
20           Response.Write("Your reservation has been made. Thank you.")
21        Else ' WebMethod returned false, so signal failure
22           ' display message in the initially blank errorLabel
23           errorLabel.Text = "This type of seat is not available. " & _
24              "Please modify your request and try again."
25        End If
26     End Sub ' reserveButton_Click
27  End Class ' ReservationClient
```

Fig. 22.24 | Code-behind file for the reservation page.

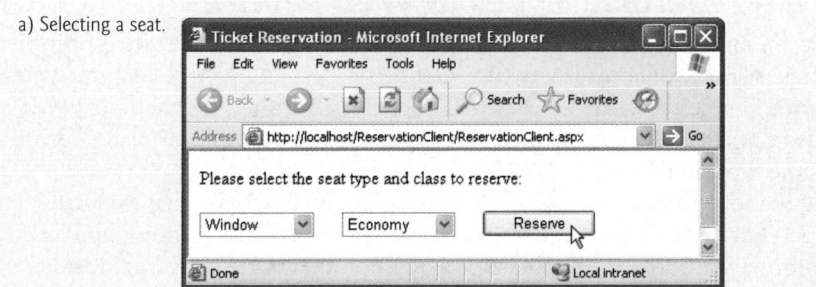

Fig. 22.25 | Ticket reservation Web Form sample execution. (Part 1 of 2.)

b) Seat reserved successfully.

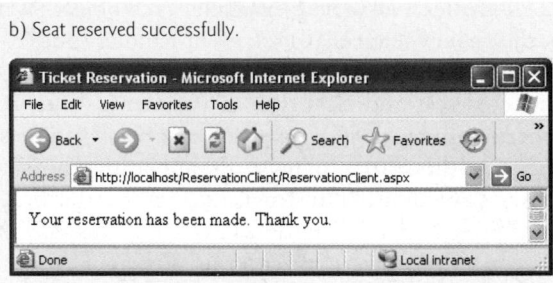

c) Attempting to reserve another seat.

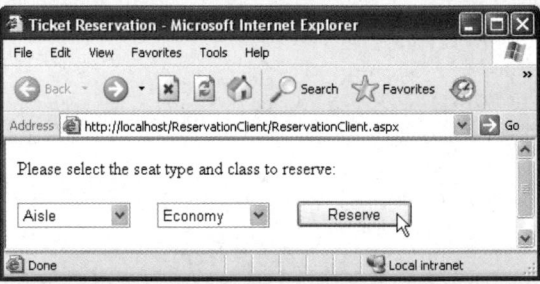

d) No seats match the requested type and class.

Fig. 22.25 | Ticket reservation Web Form sample execution. (Part 2 of 2.)

22.7 User-Defined Types in Web Services

The Web methods we have demonstrated so far all received and returned primitive-type values. It is also possible to process user-defined types—known as custom types—in a Web service. These types can be passed to or returned from Web methods. Web service clients also can use these user-defined types, because the proxy class created for the client contains the type definitions.

This section presents an EquationGenerator Web service that generates random arithmetic equations of type Equation. The client is a math-tutoring application that inputs information about the mathematical question that the user wishes to attempt (addition, subtraction or multiplication) and the skill level of the user (1 specifies equations using numbers from 1 to 10, 2 specifies equations involving numbers from 10 to 100, and

3 specifies equations containing numbers from 100 to 1000). The Web service then generates an equation consisting of random numbers in the proper range. The client application receives the `Equation` and displays the sample question to the user in a Windows Form.

Serialization of User-Defined Types

We mentioned earlier that all types passed to and from Web services must be supported by SOAP. How, then, can SOAP support a type that is not even created yet? Custom types that are sent to or from a Web service are serialized, enabling them to be passed in XML format. This process is referred to as XML serialization.

Requirements for User-Defined Types Used with Web Methods

Classes that are used to specify return types and parameter types for Web methods must meet several requirements:

1. They must provide a `Public` default or parameterless constructor. When a Web service or Web service consumer receives an XML serialized object, the .NET Framework must be able to call this constructor as part of the process of deserializing the object (i.e., converting it back to a Visual Basic object).

2. Properties and instance variables that should be serialized in XML format must be declared `Public`. (Note that the `Public` properties can be used to provide access to `Private` instance variables.)

3. Properties that should be serialized must provide both `Get` and `Set` accessors (even if they have empty bodies). Read-only properties are not serialized.

Any data that is not serialized simply receives its default value (or the value provided by the default or parameterless constructor) when an object of the class is deserialized.

Common Programming Error 22.3

Failure to define a default or parameterless `Public` constructor for a type being passed to or returned from a Web method is a runtime error.

Common Programming Error 22.4

Defining only the `Get` or `Set` accessor of a property for a user-defined type being passed to or returned from a Web method results in a property that is inaccessible to the client.

Software Engineering Observation 22.1

Clients of a Web service can access only the service's `Public` members. The programmer can provide `Public` properties to allow access to `Private` data.

Defining Class `Equation`

We define class `Equation` in Fig. 22.26. Lines 15–29 define a constructor that takes three arguments—two `Integer`s representing the left and right operands and a `String` that represents the arithmetic operation to perform. The constructor sets the `leftOperand`, `rightOperand` and `operationType` instance variables, then calculates the appropriate result. The parameterless constructor (lines 10–12) calls the three-argument constructor (lines 15–29) and passes some default values. We do not use the parameterless constructor explicitly, but the XML serialization mechanism uses it when objects of this class are deserialized. Because we provide a constructor with parameters, we must explicitly define the parameterless constructor in this class so that objects of the class can be passed to or returned from Web methods.

```vb
 1   ' Fig. 22.26: Equation.vb
 2   ' Class Equation that contains information about an equation.
 3   Public Class Equation
 4      Private leftOperand As Integer ' number to the left of the operator
 5      Private rightOperand As Integer ' number to the right of the operator
 6      Private resultValue As Integer ' result of the operation
 7      Private operationType As String ' type of the operation
 8
 9      ' required default constructor
10      Public Sub New()
11         MyClass.New(0, 0, "+")
12      End Sub ' parameterless New
13
14      ' three-argument constructor for class Equation
15      Public Sub New(ByVal leftValue As Integer, _
16         ByVal rightValue As Integer, ByVal type As String)
17         leftOperand = leftValue
18         rightOperand = rightValue
19         operationType = type
20
21         Select Case operationType ' perform appropriate operation
22            Case "+" ' addition
23               resultValue = leftOperand + rightOperand
24            Case "-" ' subtraction
25               resultValue = leftOperand - rightOperand
26            Case "*" ' multiplication
27               resultValue = leftOperand * rightOperand
28         End Select
29      End Sub ' three-parameter New
30
31      ' return string representation of the Equation object
32      Public Overrides Function ToString() As String
33         Return leftOperand.ToString() & " " & operationType & " " & _
34            rightOperand.ToString() & " = " & resultValue.ToString()
35      End Function ' ToString
36
37      ' property that returns a string representing left-hand side
38      Public Property LeftHandSide() As String
39         Get
40            Return leftOperand.ToString() & " " & operationType & " " & _
41               rightOperand.ToString()
42         End Get
43
44         Set(ByVal value As String) ' required set accessor
45            ' empty body
46         End Set
47      End Property ' LeftHandSide
```

Fig. 22.26 | Class that stores equation information. (Part 1 of 3.)

```
48
49       ' property that returns a string representing right-hand side
50       Public Property RightHandSide() As String
51          Get
52             Return resultValue.ToString()
53          End Get
54
55          Set(ByVal value As String) ' required set accessor
56             ' empty body
57          End Set
58       End Property ' RightHandSide
59
60       ' property to access the left operand
61       Public Property Left() As Integer
62          Get
63             Return leftOperand
64          End Get
65
66          Set(ByVal value As Integer)
67             leftOperand = value
68          End Set
69       End Property ' Left
70
71       ' property to access the right operand
72       Public Property Right() As Integer
73          Get
74             Return rightOperand
75          End Get
76
77          Set(ByVal value As Integer)
78             rightOperand = value
79          End Set
80       End Property ' Right
81
82       ' property to access the result of applying
83       ' an operation to the left and right operands
84       Public Property Result() As Integer
85          Get
86             Return resultValue
87          End Get
88
89          Set(ByVal value As Integer)
90             resultValue = value
91          End Set
92       End Property ' Result
93
94       ' property to access the operation
95       Public Property Operation() As String
96          Get
97             Return operationType
98          End Get
99
```

Fig. 22.26 | Class that stores equation information. (Part 2 of 3.)

```
100          Set(ByVal value As String)
101             operationType = value
102          End Set
103       End Property ' Operation
104    End Class ' Equation
```

Fig. 22.26 | Class that stores equation information. (Part 3 of 3.)

    Class Equation defines properties LeftHandSide (lines 38–47), RightHandSide (lines 50–58), Left (lines 61–69), Right (lines 72–80), Result (lines 84–92) and Operation (lines 95–103). The client of the Web service does not need to modify the values of properties LeftHandSide and RightHandSide. However, recall that a property can be serialized only if it has both a Get and a Set accessor—this is true even if the Set accessor has an empty body. LeftHandSide (lines 38–47) returns a String representing everything to the left of the equals (=) sign in the equation, and RightHandSide (lines 50–58) returns a String representing everything to the right of the equals (=) sign. Left (lines 61–69) returns the Integer to the left of the operator (known as the left operand), and Right (lines 72–80) returns the Integer to the right of the operator (known as the right operand). Result (lines 84–92) returns the solution to the equation, and Operation (lines 95–103) returns the operator in the equation. The client in this case study does not use the RightHandSide property, but we included it in case future clients choose to use it. Method ToString (lines 32–35) returns a String representation of the equation.

Creating the *EquationGenerator* Web Service

Figure 22.27 presents the EquationGenerator Web service, which creates random, customized Equations. This Web service contains only method GenerateEquation (lines 16–32), which takes two parameters—a String representing the mathematical operation (addition, subtraction or multiplication) and an Integer representing the difficulty level.

```
1    ' Fig. 22.27: EquationGeneratorWebService.vb
2    ' Web Service to generate random equations based on a specified
3    ' operation and difficulty level.
4    Imports System.Web
5    Imports System.Web.Services
6    Imports System.Web.Services.Protocols
7
8    <WebService(Namespace:="http://www.deitel.com/")> _
9    <WebServiceBinding(ConformsTo:=WsiProfiles.BasicProfile1_1)> _
10   <Global.Microsoft.VisualBasic.CompilerServices.DesignerGenerated()> _
11   Public Class EquationGeneratorWebService
12      Inherits System.Web.Services.WebService
13      ' Method to generate a math equation
14      <WebMethod(Description:="Method to generate a math equation.")> _
15      Public Function GenerateEquation(ByVal operation As String, _
16         ByVal level As Integer) As Equation
17         ' calculate maximum and minimum number to be used
18         Dim maximum As Integer = Convert.ToInt32(Math.Pow(10, level))
19         Dim minimum As Integer = Convert.ToInt32(Math.Pow(10, level - 1))
```

Fig. 22.27 | Web service that generates random equations. (Part 1 of 2.)

```
20
21        Dim randomObject As New Random() ' used to generate random numbers
22
23        ' create Equation consisting of two random
24        ' numbers in the range minimum to maximum
25        Dim newEquation As New Equation( _
26           randomObject.Next(minimum, maximum), _
27           randomObject.Next(minimum, maximum), operation)
28
29        Return newEquation
30     End Function ' GenerateEquation
31  End Class ' EquationGeneratorWebService
```

Fig. 22.27 | Web service that generates random equations. (Part 2 of 2.)

Testing the *EquationGenerator* Web Service

Figure 22.28 shows the result of testing the EquationGenerator Web service. Note that the return value from our Web method is XML-encoded. However, this example differs from previous ones in that the XML specifies the values for all Public properties and data of the object that is being returned. The return object has been serialized in XML. The client's object class takes this XML and deserializes it into an object of class Equation, that can be used by the client.

Note that an Equation object is *not* being passed between the Web service and the client. Rather, the information in the object is being sent as XML-encoded data. Clients created using .NET will take the information and create a new Equation object. Clients created on other platforms, however, may use the information differently. Readers creating clients on other platforms should check the Web services documentation for the specific platform they are using, to see how their clients may process custom types.

a) Invoking the GenerateEquation method to create a subtraction equation with numbers in the range 10–100.

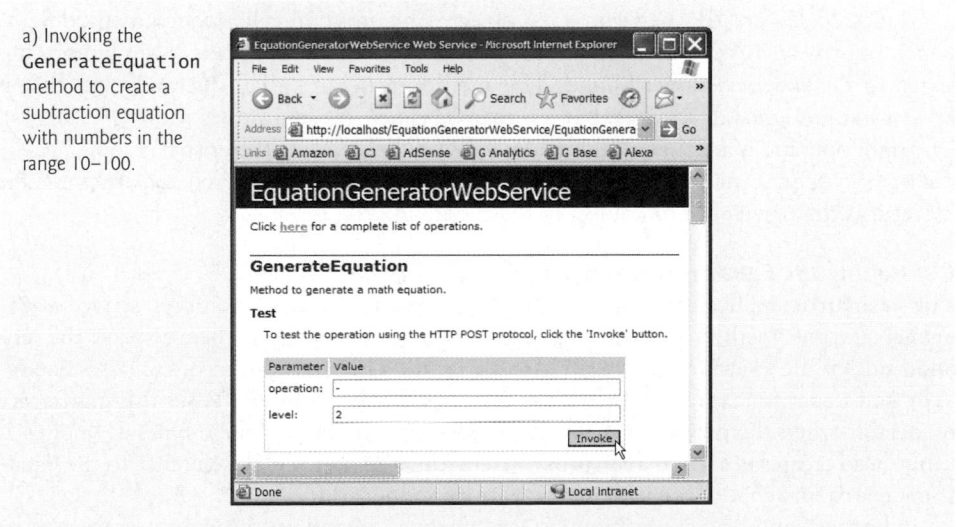

Fig. 22.28 | Returning an XML serialized object from a Web method. (Part 1 of 2.)

b) XML encoded results of invoking the `GenerateEquation` method to create a subtraction equation with numbers in the range 10–100.

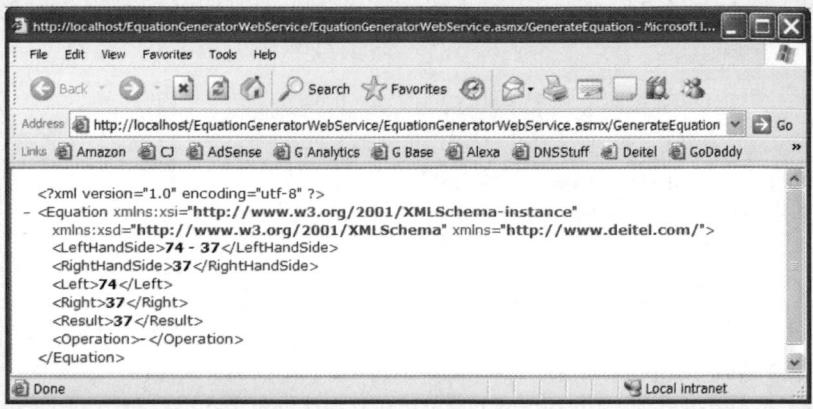

Fig. 22.28 | Returning an XML serialized object from a Web method. (Part 2 of 2.)

Let's examine Web method `GenerateEquation` more closely. Lines 18–19 of Fig. 22.27 define the upper and lower bounds for the random numbers that the method uses to generate an `Equation`. To set these limits, the program first calls `Shared` method `Pow` of class `Math`—this method raises its first argument to the power of its second argument. To calculate the value of `maximum` (the upper bound for any randomly generated numbers used to form an `Equation`), the program raises 10 to the power of the specified `level` argument (line 18). If `level` is 1, `maximum` is 10; if `level` is 2, `maximum` is 100; and if `level` is 3, `maximum` is 1000. Variable `minimum`'s value is determined by raising 10 to a power one less than `level` (line 19). This calculates the smallest number with `level` digits. If `level` is 1, `minimum` is 1; if `level` is 2, `minimum` is 10; and if `level` is 3, `minimum` is 100.

Lines 25–27 create a new `Equation` object. The program calls `Random` method `Next`, which returns an `Integer` that is greater than or equal to the specified lower bound, but less than the specified upper bound. This method generates a left operand value that is greater than or equal to `minimum` but less than `maximum` (i.e., a number with `level` digits). The right operand is another random number with the same characteristics. Line 27 passes the `String` operation received by `GenerateEquation` to the `Equation` constructor. Line 29 returns the new `Equation` object to the client.

*Consuming the **EquationGenerator** Web Service*
The `MathTutor` application (Fig. 22.29) calls the `EquationGenerator` Web service's `GenerateEquation` method to create an `Equation` object. The tutor then displays the left-hand side of the `Equation` and waits for user input. This example accesses classes `Generator` and `Equation` from the `localhost` namespace—both are placed in this namespace by default when the proxy is generated. We declare variables of these types at lines 6–7. Line 7 also creates the `Generator` proxy. (Remember to add a Web reference to the `EquationGeneratorWebService` when you create this application.

The math-tutoring application displays an equation and waits for the user to enter an answer. The default setting for the difficulty level is **1**, but the user can change this by choosing a level from the RadioButtons in the GroupBox labeled **Difficulty**. Clicking any of the levels invokes the corresponding RadioButton's CheckedChanged event handler (lines 69–87), which sets integer level to the level selected by the user. Although the default setting for the question type is **Addition**, the user also can change this by selecting one of the RadioButtons in the GroupBox labeled **Operation**. Doing so invokes the corresponding operation's event handlers in lines 45–66, which assigns to String operation the symbol corresponding to the user's selection. Each event handler also updates the Text property of the **Generate** button to match the newly selected operation.

Event handler btnGenerate_Click (lines 10–20) invokes EquationGenerator method GenerateEquation (line 13). After receiving an Equation object from the Web service, the handler displays the left-hand side of the equation in lblQuestion (line 16) and enables btnOK so that the user can enter an answer. When the user clicks **OK**, btnOK_Click (lines 23–42) checks whether the user provided the correct answer.

```vb
1   ' Fig. 22.29: FrmMathTutor.vb
2   ' Math tutoring program using Web service to generate random equations.
3   Public Class FrmMathTutor
4      Private operation As String = "+"
5      Private level As Integer = 1
6      Private currentEquation As localhost.Equation
7      Private generator As New localhost.EquationGeneratorWebService()
8
9      ' generates a new equation when user clicks button
10     Private Sub btnGenerate_Click(ByVal sender As System.Object, _
11        ByVal e As System.EventArgs) Handles btnGenerate.Click
12        ' generate equation using current operation and level
13        currentEquation = generator.GenerateEquation(operation, level)
14
15        ' display left-hand side of equation
16        lblQuestion.Text = currentEquation.LeftHandSide
17
18        btnOK.Enabled = True
19        txtAnswer.Enabled = True
20     End Sub ' btnGenerate_Click
21
22     ' check user's answer
23     Private Sub btnOK_Click(ByVal sender As System.Object, _
24        ByVal e As System.EventArgs) Handles btnOK.Click
25        ' determine correct result from Equation object
26        Dim answer As Integer = currentEquation.Result
27
28        If txtAnswer.Text <> "" Then
29           ' get user's answer
30           Dim userAnswer As Integer = Int32.Parse(txtAnswer.Text)
31
32           ' determine whether user's answer is correct
33           If answer = userAnswer Then
34              lblQuestion.Text = "" ' clear question
35              txtAnswer.Text = "" ' clear answer
```

Fig. 22.29 | Math-tutoring application. (Part 1 of 3.)

```
36              btnOK.Enabled = False ' disable OK button
37              MessageBox.Show("Correct! Good job!")
38          Else
39              MessageBox.Show("Incorrect. Try again.")
40          End If
41      End If
42   End Sub ' btnOK_Click
43
44   ' set the operation to addition
45   Private Sub radAddition_CheckedChanged( _
46      ByVal sender As System.Object, ByVal e As System.EventArgs) _
47      Handles radAddition.CheckedChanged
48      operation = "+"
49      btnGenerate.Text = "Generate " & radAddition.Text & " Example"
50   End Sub ' radAddition_CheckedChanged
51
52   ' set the operation to subtraction
53   Private Sub radSubtraction_CheckedChanged( _
54      ByVal sender As System.Object, ByVal e As System.EventArgs) _
55      Handles radSubtraction.CheckedChanged
56      operation = "-"
57      btnGenerate.Text = "Generate " & radSubtraction.Text & " Example"
58   End Sub ' radSubtraction_CheckedChanged
59
60   ' set the operation to multiplication
61   Private Sub radMultiplication_CheckedChanged( _
62      ByVal sender As System.Object, ByVal e As System.EventArgs) _
63      Handles radMultiplication.CheckedChanged
64      operation = "*"
65      btnGenerate.Text = "Generate " & radMultiplication.Text & " Example"
66   End Sub ' radMultiplication_CheckedChanged
67
68   ' set difficulty level to 1
69   Private Sub radLevelOne_CheckedChanged( _
70      ByVal sender As System.Object, ByVal e As System.EventArgs) _
71      Handles radLevelOne.CheckedChanged
72      level = 1
73   End Sub ' radLevelOne_CheckedChanged
74
75   ' set difficulty level to 2
76   Private Sub radLevelTwo_CheckedChanged( _
77      ByVal sender As System.Object, ByVal e As System.EventArgs) _
78      Handles radLevelTwo.CheckedChanged
79      level = 2
80   End Sub ' radLevelTwo_CheckedChanged
81
82   ' set difficulty level to 3
83   Private Sub radLevelThree_CheckedChanged( _
84      ByVal sender As System.Object, ByVal e As System.EventArgs) _
85      Handles radLevelThree.CheckedChanged
86      level = 3
87   End Sub ' radLevelThree_CheckedChanged
88 End Class ' FrmMathTutor
```

Fig. 22.29 | Math-tutoring application. (Part 2 of 3.)

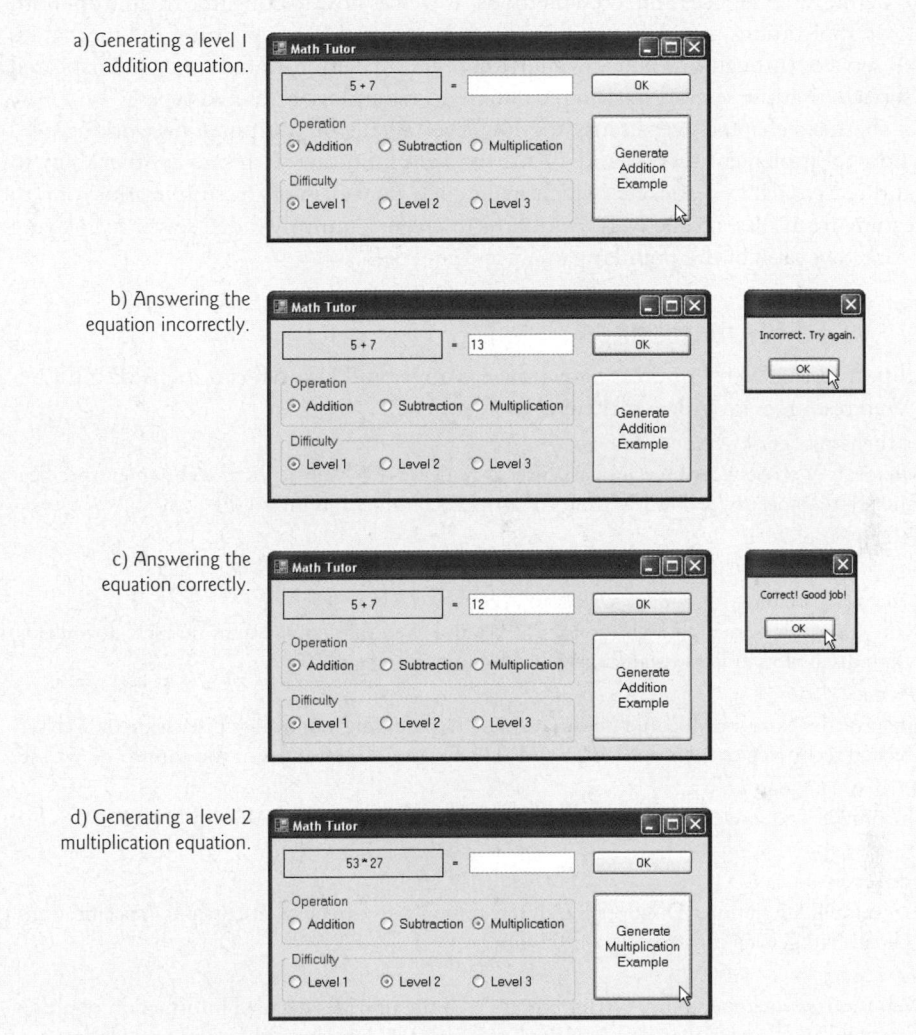

a) Generating a level 1 addition equation.

b) Answering the equation incorrectly.

c) Answering the equation correctly.

d) Generating a level 2 multiplication equation.

Fig. 22.29 | Math-tutoring application. (Part 3 of 3.)

22.8 Wrap-Up

This chapter introduced ASP.NET Web services—a technology that enables users to request and receive data via the Internet and promotes software reusability in distributed systems. You learned that a Web service is a class that allows client software to call the Web service's methods remotely via common data formats and protocols, such as XML, HTTP and SOAP. We discussed several benefits of this kind of distributed computing—e.g., clients can access certain data on remote machines, and clients lacking the processing power necessary to perform specific computations can leverage remote machines' resources.

We explained how Visual Basic 2005 Express, Visual Web Developer 2005 Express and the .NET Framework facilitate creating and consuming Web services. You learned how to define Web services and Web methods, as well as how to consume them from both Windows applications and ASP.NET Web applications. After explaining the mechanics of Web services through our `HugeInteger` example, we demonstrated more sophisticated Web services that use session tracking, database access and user-defined types.

In the next chapter, we discuss the low-level details of computer networking. We show how to implement servers and clients that communicate with one another, how to send and receive data via sockets (which make such transmissions as simple as writing to and reading from files, respectively), and how to create a multithreaded server for playing a networked version of the popular game Tic-Tac-Toe.

22.9 Web Resources

In addition to the Web resources shown here, you should also refer to the ASP.NET-related Web resources provided at the end of Chapter 21.

`msdn.microsoft.com/webservices`
The Microsoft Web Services Developer Center includes .NET Web services technology specifications and white papers as well as XML/SOAP articles, columns and links.

`www.webservices.org`
This site provides industry-related news, articles, resources and links on Web services.

`www-130.ibm.com/developerworks/webservices`
IBM's site for service-oriented architecture (SOA) and Web services includes articles, downloads, demos and discussion forums regarding Web services technology.

`www.w3.org/TR/wsdl`
This site provides extensive documentation on WSDL, including a thorough discussion of Web services–related technologies such as XML, SOAP, HTTP and MIME types in the context of WSDL.

`www.w3.org/TR/soap`
This site provides extensive documentation on SOAP messages, using SOAP with HTTP and SOAP security issues.

`www.uddi.com`
The Universal Description, Discovery and Integration site provides discussions, specifications, white papers and general information on UDDI.

`www.ws-i.org`
The Web Services Interoperability Organization's Web site provides detailed information regarding efforts to build Web services based on standards that promote interoperability and true platform independence.

`webservices.xml.com/security`
This site contains articles about Web services security issues and standard security protocols.

Summary

Section 22.1 Introduction

- Web services promote software reusability in distributed systems where applications execute across multiple computers on a network.
- Simple Object Access Protocol (SOAP) is an XML-based protocol that describes how to mark up requests and responses so that they can be transferred via protocols such as HTTP.
- Web services represent the next step in object-oriented programming. Programmers can develop applications using Web service class libraries distributed worldwide.

Section 22.2 .NET Web Services Basics
- A Web service is a software component stored on one machine that can be accessed by an application or software component on another machine over a network via standard Internet protocols.
- The machine on which a Web service resides is referred to as a remote machine.
- A client that accesses a Web service sends a method call over a network to the remote machine, which processes the call and returns a response over the network to the client.
- Requests to and responses from Web services created with Visual Web Developer are typically transmitted via SOAP. Any client capable of generating and processing SOAP messages can interact with a Web service, regardless of the language in which the Web service is written.
- Web services and SOAP are platform and language independent, so companies can collaborate via Web services without worrying about the compatibility of their hardware, software and communications technologies.

Section 22.2.1 Creating a Web Service in Visual Web Developer
- To create a Web service in Visual Web Developer, you first create a project of type **ASP.NET Web Service**. Visual Web Developer then generates files to contain the Web service code and an ASMX file (which provides access to the Web service).
- A Web service class defines the methods that the Web service makes available to clients.
- ASP.NET Web services can be tested using Visual Web Developer's built-in test server. However, to make an ASP.NET Web service publicly accessible to clients on other computers, you must deploy the Web service to a Web server such as Internet Information Services (IIS).
- Methods marked with the `WebMethod` attribute are invoked through Remote Procedure Calls (RPCs). These methods are often referred to as Web service methods or simply Web methods.

Section 22.2.2 Determining a Web Service's Functionality
- Web services normally contain a service description—an XML document that conforms to the Web Service Description Language (WSDL). WSDL is an XML vocabulary that defines the methods that a Web service makes available and how clients can interact with them.
- WSDL documents are meant to be read by applications, so they know how to interact with the Web services described in the documents.
- Visual Web Developer generates an ASMX file when a Web service is constructed, to offer a more human-understandable description of the Web service. Files with the `.asmx` filename extension are ASP.NET Web service files and are executed by ASP.NET on a Web server (e.g., IIS).
- When viewed in a Web browser, an ASMX file presents descriptions of Web methods and links to test pages that allow users to execute sample calls to these methods.
- If a client requests the Web service's WSDL description (either by appending `?WSDL` to the ASMX file's URL or by clicking the **Service Description** link in an ASMX page), ASP.NET generates the WSDL description, then returns it to the client for display in the Web browser.

Section 22.2.3 Testing a Web Service's Methods
- The protocol that transmits request and response messages is known as the Web service's wire format or wire protocol because it defines how information is sent "along the wire."
- SOAP is a popular wire format, because SOAP messages can be sent via several transport protocols.

Section 22.2.4 Building a Client to Use a Web Service
- For a client application to consume a Web service, you must add to the client application a Web reference that refers to the Web service.

- To add a Web reference in Visual Basic 2005 Express, right click the project name in the **Solution Explorer** and select **Add Web Reference….** Then, specify the Web service to consume.

- When you specify the Web service you want to consume, the IDE accesses the Web service's WSDL information and copies it to a WSDL file that is stored in the client project's Web References folder. This file is visible when you select **Show All Files** in the **Solution Explorer**.

- To ensure that the WSDL file is up-to-date, right click the Web reference in the **Solution Explorer** and select **Update Web Reference** to update the files in the **Web References** folder.

- The WSDL information is used to create a proxy class, which handles all the "plumbing" required for Web method calls (i.e., the networking details and the formation of SOAP messages).

- When a client calls a Web method, the client actually calls a corresponding method in the proxy class that has the same name and parameters as the Web method. The proxy formats the call to be sent as a request in a SOAP message. The Web service receives this request as a SOAP message, executes the method call and sends back the result as another SOAP message. When the client application receives the SOAP message containing the response, the proxy class decodes it and returns the results as the return value of the Web method that was called.

Section 22.3 Simple Object Access Protocol (SOAP)

- The Simple Object Access Protocol (SOAP) is a platform-independent protocol that uses XML to make remote procedure calls.

- Each request and response is packaged in a SOAP message containing the information that a Web service requires to process the message.

- SOAP supports an extensive set of types—the primitive types, DataSet, DateTime, XmlNode and others. SOAP can also transmit arrays of these types and objects of user-defined types.

- When a program invokes a Web method, the request and all relevant information are packaged in a SOAP message and sent to the server on which the Web service resides.

- A Web service receives a SOAP message and parses its contents (contained in a SOAP envelope) to determine the method that the client wishes to execute and the method's arguments.

- After a Web service parses a SOAP message, the proper method is called and the response is sent back to the client in another SOAP message. The client parses the response to retrieve the result.

Section 22.4 Publishing and Consuming Web Services

- Creating a Web service is also known as publishing the Web service.

- Using a Web service is also known as consuming the Web service.

- An application that consumes a Web service consists of a proxy class representing the Web service and a client application that accesses the Web service via an instance of the proxy class.

- The proxy passes a Web method's arguments from the client to the Web service. When the Web method completes its task, the proxy receives the result and parses it for the client application.

Section 22.4.1 Defining the **HugeInteger** Web Service

- The WebService attribute specifies a Web service class's namespace and description. Namespaces help clients differentiate between Web services. The WebService attribute's Namespace property specifies the namespace—usually a company's domain name, since all domain names are guaranteed to be unique. The Description property describes the Web service's purpose.

- By default, Visual Web Developer sets the WebServiceBinding attribute to indicate that the Web service conforms to the Basic Profile 1.1 (BP 1.1) developed by the Web Services Interoperability Organization (WS-I), a group dedicated to promoting interoperability among Web services developed on different platforms with different programming languages. BP 1.1 defines best practices for various aspects of creating and consuming Web services. Setting the WebServiceBinding attribute's ConformsTo property to WsiProfiles.BasicProfile1_1 instructs ASP.NET to generate WSDL and ASMX files, in conformance with BP 1.1 guidelines.

- Web service classes created in Visual Web Developer inherit from System.Web.Services.WebService, which provides members that are useful in determining information about the client and the Web service itself.

- The WebMethod attribute exposes a Web method so that it can be called remotely. When this attribute is absent, the method is not accessible to clients that consume the Web service.

- The WebMethod attribute's Description property allows the ASMX page to display information about the method.

Section 22.4.2 Building a Web Service in Visual Web Developer

- To create an **ASP.NET Web Service** project, first select **File > New Web Site...** to display the **New Web Site** dialog. In this dialog, select **ASP.NET Web Service** in the **Templates** pane. Select **HTTP** from the **Location** drop-down list to indicate that the files should be placed on a Web server. By default, Visual Web Developer places the files on the local machine's IIS Web server in a virtual directory named WebSite1 (http://localhost/WebSite1). Replace the name WebSite1 with your Web service's name. Next, select **Visual Basic** from the **Language** drop-down list to build the Web service with Visual Basic. The Web service project's solution file (.sln) is placed in the folder My Documents\Visual Studio 2005\Projects.

- If you do not have access to an IIS Web server to build and test your Web services, you can select **File System** from the **Location** drop-down list to place your Web service's files on your local hard disk. You can test the Web service using Visual Web Developer's built-in Web server.

- When an **ASP.NET Web Service** project is created, the code-behind file Service.vb contains code for a simple Web service named Service that contains a sample Web method named HelloWorld. This method is a placeholder that you will replace with your own method(s).

- The ASMX file displayed in the **Solution Explorer** indicates the programming language in which the Web service's code-behind file is written, the location of the code-behind file and the class that defines the Web service. When you request the ASMX page through IIS, ASP.NET uses this information to generate the list of Web methods and their descriptions.

- If you change the name of the code-behind file or the name of the class that defines the Web service, you must modify the ASMX file accordingly.

Section 22.4.3 Deploying the HugeInteger Web Service

- When you create a Web service directly on IIS, the Web service is already deployed.

- Choose **Build Web Site** from the **Build** menu to ensure that a Web service compiles without errors.

- You can test a Web service from Visual Web Developer by selecting **Start Without Debugging** from the **Debug** menu. This opens a browser window that contains the Web service's ASMX page. Click the link for a Web method to display a Web page that allows you to test the method.

- If you deploy a Web service on IIS, a client can connect to that server to access the Web service with a URL of the form http://*host*/*WebServiceName*/*WebServiceName*.asmx where *host* is the hostname or IP address of the server.

- If you have the Windows XP Service Pack 2 operating system on the computer running IIS, that computer may not allow requests from other computers by default. To allow other computers to connect to your computer's Web server, select **Start > Control Panel** to open your system's **Control Panel** window, then double click **Windows Firewall** to view the **Windows Firewall** settings dialog. In the **Windows Firewall** settings dialog, click the **Advanced** tab, select **Local Area Connection** (or your network connection's name if it is different) in the **Network Connection Settings** list box and click the **Settings...** button to display the **Advanced Settings** dialog. In the **Advanced Settings** dialog, ensure that the checkbox for **Web Server (HTTP)** is checked to allow clients on other computers to submit requests to your computer's Web server. Click **OK** in the **Advanced Settings** dialog, then click **OK** in the **Windows Firewall** settings dialog.

- To access a Web service that is running in Visual Web Developer's built-in Web server, you must specify the randomly generated port number chosen by Visual Web Developer, as in

    http://*host*:*portNumber*/*WebServiceName*/*WebServiceName*.asmx

where *host* is the hostname or IP address of the computer on which Visual Web Developer's built-in Web server is running and *portNumber* is the specific port on which the Web server receives requests. You can see this port number in your Web browser's **Address** field when you test the Web service from Visual Web Developer.

Section 22.4.4 Creating a Client to Consume the **HugeInteger** Web Service

- A client uses a proxy class to communicate with a Web service. The proxy class's purpose is to make clients think they are calling the Web methods directly.

- When you add a Web reference, the IDE generates an appropriate proxy class. You create an instance of the proxy class and use it to call the Web service's methods.

- To add a Web reference, right click the project name in the **Solution Explorer** and select **Add Web Reference....** In the **Add Web Reference** dialog that appears, click **Web services on the local machine** to locate Web references stored on IIS Web server on your local computer (http://localhost). Select the Web service from the list of available Web services, then click the **Add Reference** button. The **Solution Explorer** should now contain a **Web References** folder with a node named after the domain name where the Web service is located (localhost when using the local Web server).

- When creating a client to consume a Web service, add the Web reference first so that Visual Basic 2005 (or Visual Web Developer) can recognize an object of the Web service proxy class.

- Universal Description, Discovery and Integration (UDDI) is used to locate Web services.

Section 22.5 Session Tracking in Web Services

- Using session tracking eliminates the need for information about the client to be passed between the client and the Web service multiple times.

Section 22.5.1 Creating a Blackjack Web Service

- Storing session information can provide client programmers with a more intuitive Web service.

- Setting a WebMethod attribute's EnableSession property to True indicates that session information should be maintained in an HttpSessionState object (named Session by ASP.NET).

- A Web service with session tracking creates cookies to identify each client uniquely. A non-browser client application that wishes to use such a Web service must create a CookieContainer object to store cookies. A client Web browser with cookie handling enabled stores cookies automatically.

- An ArrayList is a dynamic array—its size can change at execution time. ArrayList method Add places an object in the ArrayList, and ArrayList method RemoveAt removes the element in the ArrayList at the index specified by its argument, thus reducing the size of the ArrayList by one.

Section 22.5.2 Consuming the Blackjack Web Service

- An object of class CookieContainer (namespace System.Net) stores the information from a cookie (created by a Web service that uses session tracking) in a Cookie object in the CookieContainer.

- A Cookie contains a unique identifier that a Web service can use to recognize the client when the client makes future requests. The cookie is sent back to the server with each request.

- If a client does not create a `CookieContainer` object when consuming a Web service that uses session tracking, the Web service creates a new `Session` object for each request, and the user's state information does not persist across requests.

Section 22.6 Using Web Forms and Web Services

- It is common for Web applications to consume Web services.

- You can use the **TableAdapter Configuration Wizard** to select a data source and to create the SQL statements necessary to support the database operations of your Web service.

- To add a `DataSet` to your Web service, right click the **App_Code** folder in the **Solution Explorer** and select **Add New Item...** from the pop-up menu. In the **Add New Item** dialog, select **DataSet**, specify the name of your `DataSet` in the **Name** field and click **Add**. This displays the `DataSet` in design view and opens the **TableAdapter Configuration Wizard**.

Section 22.7 User-Defined Types in Web Services

- It is possible to process user-defined types (also known as custom types) in a Web service. These types can be passed to or returned from Web methods. Web service clients also can use these user-defined types, because the proxy class created for the client contains these type definitions.

- Custom types that are sent to or from a Web service are serialized, enabling them to be passed in XML format. This process is referred to as XML serialization.

- Classes that are used to specify Web method return types and parameter types must provide a `public` default or parameterless constructor. Properties and instance variables that should be serialized in XML format must be declared `public`. Properties that should be serialized must provide both `Get` and `Set` accessors. Read-only properties are not serialized. Data that is not serialized simply receives its default value when an object of the class is deserialized.

Terminology

Add Web Reference dialog
`.asmx` filename extension
ASMX page
ASP.NET Web Service project
business-to-business (B2B) transactions
`ConformsTo` property of a
    `WebServiceBinding` attribute
consume a Web service
`CookieContainer` class
custom type
`Description` property of a `WebMethod` attribute
`Description` property of a `WebService` attribute
`EnableSession` property of a
    `WebMethod` attribute
expose a Web method
firewall
`.map` file
`Namespace` property of a `WebService` attribute
parse a SOAP message
proxy class for a Web service
publish a Web service
remote machine
Remote Procedure Call (RPC)

`RemoveAt` method of class `ArrayList`
request a Web service's WSDL description
service description for a Web service
session tracking in Web services
Simple Object Access Protocol (SOAP)
SOAP envelope
SOAP message
`System.Net` namespace
TableAdapter Configuration Wizard
Universal Description, Discovery and
    Integration (UDDI)
user-defined types in Web services
Web method
Web references
Web service
Web Service Description Language (WSDL)
Web service method
Web Services Interoperability
    Organization (WS-I)
`WebMethod` attribute
`WebService` attribute
`WebService` class
`WebServiceBinding` attribute

wire format   WS-I Basic Profile 1.1 (BP 1.1)
wire protocol   XML serialization

Self-Review Exercises

22.1   State whether each of the following is *true* or *false*. If *false*, explain why.

   a) The purpose of a Web service is to create objects of a class located on a remote machine. This class then can be instantiated and used on the local machine.

   b) You must explicitly create the proxy class after you add a Web reference to a client application.

   c) A proxy class communicating with a Web service normally uses SOAP to send and receive messages.

   d) A client application can invoke only those methods of a Web service that are tagged with the `WebMethod` attribute.

   e) To enable session tracking in a Web method, no action is required other than setting the `EnableSession` property to `True` in the `WebMethod` attribute.

   f) Web methods cannot be declared `Shared`.

   g) A user-defined type used in a Web service must define both `Get` and `Set` accessors for any property that will be serialized.

22.2   Fill in the blanks for each of the following statements:

   a) A message sent between an application and a Web service is placed in a(n) _____.

   b) A Web service can derive from class _____ to inherit members that determine information about the user, the application and other topics relevant to the Web service.

   c) The class that defines a Web service is located in the Web service's _____ file.

   d) Web service requests are typically transported over the Internet via the _____ protocol.

   e) To add a description for a Web method in an ASMX page, the _____ property of the `WebMethod` attribute is used.

   f) _____ transforms an object into a format that can be sent between a Web service and a client.

   g) By default, a proxy class is defined in a namespace whose name is that of the _____ in which the Web service is defined.

Answers to Self-Review Exercises

22.1   a) False. Web services are used to execute methods on remote machines. The Web service receives the arguments it needs to execute a particular method, executes the method and returns the result to the caller. b) False. The proxy is created by Visual Basic or Visual Web Developer when you add a Web reference to your project. The proxy class itself is hidden from you. c) True. d) True. e) False. A `CookieContainer` also must be created on the client side if the client is not a Web browser. f) True. g) True.

22.2   a) SOAP message or SOAP envelope. b) `System.Web.Services.WebService`. c) code-behind. d) HTTP. e) `Description`. f) XML serialization. g) domain.

Exercises

22.3   *(Phone Book Web Service)* Create a Web service that stores phone book entries in a database (`PhoneBook.mdf`, which is provided in the examples directory for this chapter) and a client application that consumes this service. Give the client user the capability to enter a new contact (Web method `AddEntry`) and to find contacts by last name (Web method `GetEntries`). Pass only primitive types as arguments to the Web service. Add a `DataSet` to the Web service project to enable the Web service to interact with the database. The GetEntries Web method should return an array of Strings that contains the matching phone book entries. Each String in the array should consist of the last name, first name and phone number for one phone book entry. When configuring the PhoneBookDataSetTableAdapters.PhoneBookTableAdapter that provides access to the Phone-Book.mdf database, first set up the SELECT query that will be used by the GetEntries Web method. Then, when you add the INSERT statement to the TableAdapter, the **TableAdapter Configuration Wizard** will preconfigure the INSERT statement for you. You will simply need to name the PhoneBook-DataSetTableAdapters.PhoneBookTableAdapter method that will perform the INSERT operation. The SELECT query that will find a phone book entry by last name should be:

```
SELECT LastName, FirstName, PhoneNumber
FROM PhoneBook
WHERE (LastName = @lastName)
```

The INSERT statement that inserts a new entry into the PhoneBook.mdf database should be:

```
INSERT INTO [PhoneBook] ([LastName], [FirstName], [PhoneNumber])
VALUES (@LastName, @FirstName, @PhoneNumber)
```

[*Note:* The **TableAdapter Configuration Wizard** adds the square brackets around each table name and column name by default when it configures the INSERT statement.]

22.4 *(Phone Book Web Service Modification)* Modify Exercise 22.3 so that it uses a class named PhoneBookEntry to represent a row in the database. The client application should provide objects of type PhoneBookEntry to the Web service when adding contacts and should receive objects of type PhoneBookEntry when searching for contacts.

22.5 *(Blackjack Web Service Modification)* Modify the blackjack Web service example in Section 22.5 to include class Card. Change Web method DealCard so that it returns an object of type Card. Also modify the client application to keep track of what cards have been dealt by using Card objects. Your Card class should include properties to determine the face and suit of the card.

22.6 *(Airline Reservation Web Service Modification)* Modify the airline reservation Web service in Section 22.6 so that it contains two separate Web methods—one that allows users to view all available seats, and another that allows users to reserve a particular seat that is currently available. Use an object of type Ticket to pass information to and from the Web service. The Web service must be able to handle cases in which two users view available seats, one reserves a seat and the second user tries to reserve the same seat, not knowing that it is now taken. To obtain the list of available seats, configure the SeatsTableAdapter with the SELECT query:

```
SELECT  Number, Type, Class
FROM    Seats
WHERE   (Taken = 0)
```

The names of the methods that execute this query should be FillWithAvailableSeats and GetAvailableSeats. To determine whether a specific seat is available, add the following SELECT query to the SeatsTableAdapter:

```
SELECT  Number
FROM    Seats
WHERE   (Number = @number) AND (Taken = 0)
```

The names of the methods that execute this query should be FillWithSpecificSeat and GetSpecificSeat. Finally, to reserve a specific seat, add the following UPDATE to the SeatsTableAdapter:

```
UPDATE Seats
SET    Taken = 1
WHERE  (Number = @number) AND (Taken = 0)
```

The name of the method that executes this UPDATE should be UpdateSeatAsTaken.

23

Networking: Streams-Based Sockets and Datagrams

OBJECTIVES

In this chapter you will learn:

- To implement networking applications that use sockets and datagrams.

- To implement clients and servers that communicate with one another.

- To implement network-based collaborative applications.

- To construct a multithreaded server.

- To use the `WebBrowser` class to add Web browsing capabilities to any application.

- To use .NET remoting to enable an application executing on one computer to invoke methods from an application executing on a different computer.

If the presence of electricity can be made visible in any part of a circuit, I see no reason why intelligence may not be transmitted instantaneously by electricity.
—Samuel F. B. Morse

What networks of railroads, highways and canals were in another age, the networks of telecommunications, information and computerization … are today.
—Bruno Kreisky

The port is near, the bells I hear, the people all exulting.
—Walt Whitman

Protocol is everything.
—Francois Giuliani

23.1 **Introduction**

There is much excitement about the Internet and the Web. The Internet ties the information world together. The Web makes the Internet easy to use and gives it the flair and sizzle of multimedia. Organizations see the Internet and the Web as crucial to their information-systems strategies. The .NET FCL provides a number of built-in networking capabilities that make it easy to develop Internet- and Web-based applications. Programs can search the world for information and collaborate with programs running on other computers internationally, nationally or just within an organization.

In Chapter 21, ASP.NET 2.0, Web Forms and Web Controls, and Chapter 22, Web Services, we began our presentation of .NET's networking and distributed-computing capabilities. We discussed ASP.NET, Web Forms and Web services—high-level networking technologies that enable programmers to develop distributed applications. In this chapter, we focus on the underlying networking technologies that support .NET's ASP.NET and Web services capabilities.

The chapter begins with an overview of the communication techniques and technologies used to transmit data over the Internet. Next, we present the basic concepts of establishing a connection between two applications using streams of data that are similar to file I/O. This connection-oriented approach enables programs to communicate with one another as easily as writing to, and reading from, files on disk. Then we present a simple chat application that uses these techniques to send messages between a client and a server. The chapter continues with a presentation and an example of connectionless techniques for transmitting data between applications—this approach is less reliable than establishing a connection between the applications, but much more efficient. Such techniques are typically used in applications such as streaming audio and video over the Internet. Next we present an example of a client-server Tic-Tac-Toe game that demonstrates how to create a simple multithreaded server. Then we demonstrate the new `WebBrowser` class for adding Web browsing capabilities to any application. The chapter concludes with a brief introduction to .NET remoting, which, like Web services (Chapter 22), enables distributed computing over networks.

23.2 Connection-Oriented vs. Connectionless Communication

There are two primary approaches to communicating between applications—connection oriented and connectionless. Connection-oriented communications are similar to the telephone system, in which a connection is established and held for the length of the session. Connectionless services are similar to the postal service, in which two letters mailed at the same time from the same place and to the same destination may actually take two dramatically different paths through the system and even arrive at different times, or not at all.

In a connection-oriented approach, computers send each other control information—through a technique called handshaking—to initiate an end-to-end connection. The Internet is an unreliable network, which means that data sent across the Internet may be damaged or lost. Data is sent in packets that contain pieces of the data along with information that helps the Internet route the packets to the proper destination. The Internet does not guarantee anything about the packets sent; they could arrive corrupted or out of order, as duplicates or not at all. The Internet makes only a "best effort" to deliver packets. A connection-oriented approach ensures reliable communications on unreliable networks, guaranteeing that sent packets will arrive at the intended recipient undamaged and be reassembled in the correct sequence.

In a connectionless approach, the two computers do not handshake before transmission, and reliability is not guaranteed—data sent may never reach the intended recipient. A connectionless approach, however, avoids the overhead associated with handshaking and enforcing reliability—less information often needs to be passed between the hosts.

23.3 Protocols for Transporting Data

There are many protocols for communicating between applications. Protocols are sets of rules that govern how two entities interact. In this chapter, we focus on the Transmission Control Protocol (TCP) and the User Datagram Protocol (UDP). .NET's TCP and UDP networking capabilities are defined in the System.Net.Sockets namespace.

The Transmission Control Protocol (TCP) is a connection-oriented communication protocol which guarantees that sent packets will arrive at the intended recipient undamaged and in the correct sequence. TCP allows protocols like HTTP (Chapter 21) to send information across a network as simply and reliably as writing to a file on a local computer. If packets of information don't arrive at the recipient, TCP ensures that the packets are sent again. If the packets arrive out of order, TCP reassembles them in the correct order transparently to the receiving application. If duplicate packets arrive, TCP discards them.

Applications that don't require TCP's reliable end-to-end transmission guaranty typically use the connectionless User Datagram Protocol (UDP). UDP incurs the minimum overhead necessary to communicate between applications. UDP makes no guarantees that packets, called datagrams, will reach their destination or arrive in their original order.

There are benefits to using UDP over TCP. UDP has little overhead because UDP datagrams do not need to carry the information that TCP packets carry to ensure reliability. UDP also reduces network traffic relative to TCP due to the absence of handshaking and retransmissions.

Unreliable communication is acceptable in many situations. First, reliability is not necessary for some applications, so the overhead imposed by a protocol that guarantees reliability can be avoided. Second, some applications, such as streaming audio and video, can tolerate occasional datagram loss. This usually results in a small pause (or "hiccup") in the audio or video being played. If the same application were run over TCP, a lost segment could cause a significant pause, since the protocol would wait until the lost segment was retransmitted and delivered correctly before continuing. Finally, applications that need to implement their own reliability mechanisms different from those provided by TCP can build such mechanisms over UDP.

23.4 Establishing a Simple TCP Server Using Stream Sockets

Typically, with TCP, a server "listens" (i.e., waits) for a connection request from a client. Often, the server program contains a control statement or block of code that executes continuously until the server receives a request. On receiving a request, the server establishes a connection to the client. The server then uses this connection—managed by a Socket object—to handle future requests from that client and to send data to the client. Since programs that communicate via TCP process the data they send and receive as streams of bytes, programmers sometimes refer to Sockets used with TCP as "stream Sockets."

Establishing a simple server with TCP and stream sockets requires five steps. First, create an object of class **TcpListener** of namespace System.Net.Sockets. This class represents a TCP stream socket through which a server can listen for requests. Creating a new TcpListener, as in

```
Dim server As New TcpListener(ipAddress, portNumber)
```

binds (assigns) the server application to the specified *portNumber*. A port number is a numeric identifier that an application uses to identify itself at a given network address, also known as an Internet Protocol Address (IP Address). IP addresses identify computers on the Internet. In fact, Web-site names, such as www.deitel.com, are aliases for IP addresses. An IP address is represented by an object of class **IPAddress** of namespace **System.Net**. Any application that performs networking identifies itself via an *IP address/port number pair*—no two applications can have the same port number at a given IP address. In fact, a socket combines an IP address and a port number to uniquely identify a service. Explicitly binding a socket to a connection port (using method **Bind** of class Socket) is usually unnecessary, because class TcpListener and other classes discussed in this chapter do it automatically, along with other socket-initialization operations.

> **Software Engineering Observation 23.1**
>
> *Port numbers can have values between 0 and 65535. Many operating systems reserve port numbers below 1024 for system services (such as e-mail and Web servers). Applications must be granted special privileges to use the reserved port numbers.*

To receive requests, a TcpListener first must listen for them. The second step in the connection process is to call TcpListener's **Start** method, which causes the TcpListener object to begin listening for connection requests. The server listens indefinitely for a request—that is, the server-side application waits until a client attempts to connect with it. The server creates a connection to the client when it receives a connection request. An object of class Socket (namespace **System.Net.Sockets**) manages a connection to a client.

Method `AcceptSocket` of class `TcpListener` accepts a connection request. This method returns a `Socket` object upon connection, as in the statement

```
Dim connection As Socket = server.AcceptSocket()
```

When the server receives a request, `AcceptSocket` calls method `Accept` of the `TcpListener`'s underlying `Socket` to make the connection. This is an example of how networking complexity is hidden from the programmer. You simply place the preceding statement in a server-side program—the classes of namespace `System.Net.Sockets` handle the details of accepting requests and establishing connections.

The third step establishes the streams used for communication with the client. In this step, we create a `NetworkStream` object that uses the connection's `Socket` object to send and receive data. In our forthcoming example, we use this `NetworkStream` object to create a `BinaryWriter` and a `BinaryReader` that will be used to send information to and receive information from the client, respectively.

Step 4 is the processing phase, in which the server and client communicate using the connection established in step three. In this step, the client uses `BinaryWriter` method `Write` and `BinaryReader` method `ReadString` to communicate.

The fifth step is the connection-termination phase. When the client and server finish communicating, the server calls method `Close` of the `BinaryReader`, `BinaryWriter`, `NetworkStream` and `Socket` to terminate the connection. The server can then return to step two to wait for the next connection request. Note that the `Socket` class's documentation (msdn2.microsoft.com/en-us/library/system.net.sockets.socket.aspx) recommends that you call method `Shutdown` before method `Close` to ensure that all data is sent and received before the `Socket` closes.

One problem associated with the server scheme described in this section is that step four **blocks** other requests while processing the connected client's request, and thus no other client can connect with the server while the code that defines the processing phase is executing. The most common technique for addressing this problem is to use multithreaded servers (multithreading was discussed in Chapter 15), which place the processing-phase code in a separate thread. For each connection request the server receives, it creates a `Thread` to process the connection, leaving its `TcpListener` (or `Socket`) free to receive other connections. We demonstrate a multithreaded server in Section 23.8.

Software Engineering Observation 23.2

Multithreaded servers can efficiently manage simultaneous connections with multiple clients. This architecture is precisely what popular Linux and Windows network servers use.

Software Engineering Observation 23.3

You can implement a multithreaded server to create a thread that manages network I/O across a Socket object returned by method `AcceptSocket`. You can also implement a multithreaded server to maintain a pool of threads that manage network I/O across newly created Sockets.

Performance Tip 23.1

In high-performance systems with abundant memory, a multithreaded server can be implemented to create a pool of threads. These threads can be assigned quickly to handle network I/O across multiple Sockets. Thus, when a connection is received, the server does not incur the overhead of thread creation.

23.5 Establishing a Simple TCP Client Using Stream Sockets

There are four steps to creating a simple TCP client. First, we create an object of class `Tcp-Client` (namespace `System.Net.Sockets`) to connect to the server. The connection is established by calling `TcpClient` method **Connect**. One overloaded version of this method takes two arguments—the server's IP address and its port number—as in:

```
Dim client As New TcpClient()
client.Connect(serverAddress, serverPortNumber)
```

The *serverPortNumber* is an `Integer` that represents the port number to which the server application is bound to listen for connection requests. The *serverAddress* can be either an `IPAddress` instance that encapsulates the server's IP address or a `String` that specifies the server's hostname or IP address. Method `Connect` also has an overloaded version to which you can pass an **IPEndPoint** object that represents an IP address/port number pair. `Tcp-Client` method `Connect` calls `Socket` method `Connect` to establish the connection. If the connection is successful, `TcpClient` method `Connect` returns a positive integer; otherwise, it returns 0.

In Step 2, the `TcpClient` uses its **GetStream** method to get a `NetworkStream` so that it can write to and read from the server. We then use the `NetworkStream` object to create a `BinaryWriter` and a `BinaryReader` that will be used to send information to and receive information from the server, respectively.

The third step is the processing phase, in which the client and the server communicate. In this phase of our example, the client uses `BinaryWriter` method `Write` and `BinaryReader` method `ReadString` to perform the appropriate communications. Using a process similar to that used by servers, a client can employ threads to prevent blocking of communication with other servers while processing data from one connection.

After the transmission is complete, Step 4 requires the client to close the connection by calling method `Close` on each of `BinaryReader`, `BinaryWriter`, `NetworkStream` and `TcpClient`. This closes each of the streams and the `TcpClient`'s `Socket` to terminate the connection with the server. At this point, a new connection can be established through method `Connect`, as we have described.

23.6 Client/Server Interaction with Stream-Socket Connections

Figures 23.1 and 23.2 use the classes and techniques discussed in the previous two sections to construct a simple client/server chat application. The server waits for a client's request to make a connection. When a client application connects to the server, the server application sends a `String` to the client, indicating that the connection was successful. The client then displays a message notifying the user that a connection has been established.

The client and server applications both contain `TextBox`es that enable users to type messages and send them to the other application. When either the client or the server sends the message "TERMINATE," the connection between the client and the server terminates. The server then waits for another client to request a connection. Figure 23.1 and Fig. 23.2 provide the code for classes `FrmChatServer` and `FrmChatClient`, respectively. Figure 23.2 also contains screen captures displaying the execution between the client and the server.

FrmChatServer Class

In class FrmChatServer (Fig. 23.1), FrmChatServer_Load (lines 17–22) creates a Thread that will accept connections from clients (line 20). The ThreadStart delegate object that is passed as the Thread constructor's argument specifies which method the Thread executes. Line 21 starts the Thread, which uses the ThreadStart delegate to invoke method RunServer (lines 93–159). This method initializes the server to receive connection requests and process connections. Line 102 instantiates a TcpListener object to listen for a connection request from a client at port 50000 (Step 1). Line 105 then calls TcpListener method Start, which causes the TcpListener to begin waiting for requests (Step 2).

```vb
 1  ' Fig. 23.1: FrmChatServer.vb
 2  ' Set up a server that will receive a connection from a client, send a
 3  ' string to the client, chat with the client and close the connection.
 4  Imports System.Threading
 5  Imports System.Net
 6  Imports System.Net.Sockets
 7  Imports System.IO
 8
 9  Public Class FrmChatServer
10     Private connection As Socket ' Socket for accepting a connection
11     Private readThread As Thread ' Thread for processing incoming messages
12     Private socketStream As NetworkStream ' network data stream
13     Private writer As BinaryWriter ' facilitates writing to the stream
14     Private reader As BinaryReader ' facilitates reading from the stream
15
16     ' initialize thread for reading
17     Private Sub FrmChatServer_Load(ByVal sender As System.Object, _
18        ByVal e As System.EventArgs) Handles MyBase.Load
19
20        readThread = New Thread(New ThreadStart(AddressOf RunServer))
21        readThread.Start()
22     End Sub ' FrmChatServer_Load
23
24     ' close all threads associated with this application
25     Private Sub FrmChatServer_FormClosing(ByVal sender As System.Object, _
26        ByVal e As System.Windows.Forms.FormClosingEventArgs) _
27        Handles MyBase.FormClosing
28
29        System.Environment.Exit(System.Environment.ExitCode)
30     End Sub ' FrmChatServer_FormClosing
31
32     ' Delegate that allows method DisplayMessage to be called
33     ' in the thread that creates and maintains the GUI
34     Private Delegate Sub DisplayDelegate(ByVal message As String)
35
36     ' method DisplayMessage sets txtDisplay's Text property
37     ' in a thread-safe manner
38     Private Sub DisplayMessage(ByVal message As String)
39        ' if modifying txtDisplay is not thread safe
40        If txtDisplay.InvokeRequired Then
```

Fig. 23.1 | Server portion of a client/server stream-socket connection. (Part 1 of 4.)

```vbnet
41              ' use inherited method Invoke to execute DisplayMessage
42              ' via a Delegate
43              Invoke(New DisplayDelegate(AddressOf DisplayMessage), _
44                 New Object() {message})
45           ' OK to modify txtDisplay in current thread
46           Else
47              txtDisplay.Text &= message
48           End If
49        End Sub ' DisplayMessage
50
51        ' Delegate that allows method DisableInput to be called
52        ' in the thread that creates and maintains the GUI
53        Private Delegate Sub DisableInputDelegate(ByVal value As Boolean)
54
55        ' method DisableInput sets txtInput's ReadOnly property
56        ' in a thread-safe manner
57        Private Sub DisableInput(ByVal value As Boolean)
58           ' if modifying txtInput is not thread safe
59           If txtInput.InvokeRequired Then
60              ' use inherited method Invoke to execute DisableInput
61              ' via a Delegate
62              Invoke(New DisableInputDelegate(AddressOf DisableInput), _
63                 New Object() {value})
64           ' OK to modify txtInput in current thread
65           Else
66              txtInput.ReadOnly = value
67           End If
68        End Sub ' DisableInput
69
70        ' send the text typed at the server to the client
71        Private Sub txtInput_KeyDown(ByVal sender As System.Object, _
72           ByVal e As System.Windows.Forms.KeyEventArgs) _
73           Handles txtInput.KeyDown
74           ' send the text to the client
75           Try
76              If e.KeyCode = Keys.Enter And txtInput.ReadOnly = False Then
77                 writer.Write("SERVER>>> " & txtInput.Text)
78                 txtDisplay.Text &= vbCrLf & "SERVER>>> " & txtInput.Text
79
80                 ' if the user at the server signaled termination
81                 ' sever the connection to the client
82                 If txtInput.Text = "TERMINATE" Then
83                    connection.Close()
84                 End If
85                 txtInput.Clear() ' clear the user's input
86              End If
87           Catch ex As SocketException
88              txtDisplay.Text &= vbCrLf & "Error writing object"
89           End Try
90        End Sub ' txtInput_KeyDown
91
```

Fig. 23.1 | Server portion of a client/server stream-socket connection. (Part 2 of 4.)

```
 92        ' allows a client to connect; displays text the client sends
 93        Public Sub RunServer()
 94           Dim listener As TcpListener
 95           Dim counter As Integer = 1
 96
 97           ' wait for a client connection and display the text
 98           ' that the client sends
 99           Try
100              ' Step 1: create TcpListener
101              Dim local As IPAddress = IPAddress.Parse("localhost")
102              listener = New TcpListener(local, 50000)
103
104              ' Step 2: TcpListener waits for connection request
105              listener.Start()
106
107              ' Step 3: establish connection upon client request
108              While True
109                 DisplayMessage("Waiting for connection" & vbCrLf)
110
111                 ' accept an incoming connection
112                 connection = listener.AcceptSocket()
113
114                 ' create NetworkStream object associated with socket
115                 socketStream = New NetworkStream(connection)
116
117                 ' create objects for transferring data across stream
118                 writer = New BinaryWriter(socketStream)
119                 reader = New BinaryReader(socketStream)
120
121                 DisplayMessage( _
122                    "Connection " & counter & " received." & vbCrLf)
123
124                 ' inform client that connection was successfull
125                 writer.Write("SERVER>>> Connection successful")
126
127                 DisableInput(False) ' enable txtInput
128                 Dim theReply As String = ""
129
130                 ' Step 4: read string data sent from client
131                 Do
132                    Try
133                       ' read the string sent to the server
134                       theReply = reader.ReadString()
135
136                       ' display the message
137                       DisplayMessage(vbCrLf & theReply)
138                    Catch ex As Exception
139                       ' handle exception if error reading data
140                       Exit Do
141                    End Try
142                 Loop While theReply <> "CLIENT>>> TERMINATE" And _
143                    connection.Connected
```

Fig. 23.1 | Server portion of a client/server stream-socket connection. (Part 3 of 4.)

```
144
145                DisplayMessage(vbCrLf & "User terminated connection" & vbCrLf)
146
147                ' Step 5: close connection
148                writer.Close()
149                reader.Close()
150                socketStream.Close()
151                connection.Close()
152
153                DisableInput(True) ' disable txtInput
154                counter += 1
155            End While
156        Catch ex As Exception
157            MessageBox.Show(ex.ToString())
158        End Try
159    End Sub ' RunServer
160 End Class ' FrmChatServer_Load
```

Fig. 23.1 | Server portion of a client/server stream-socket connection. (Part 4 of 4.)

Accepting the Connection and Establishing the Streams

Lines 108–155 are an infinite loop that begins by establishing the connection requested by the client (Step 3). Line 112 calls method AcceptSocket of the TcpListener object, which returns a Socket upon successful connection. The thread in which method Accept-Socket is called blocks (i.e., stops executing) until a connection is established. The returned Socket object manages the connection. Line 115 passes this Socket object as an argument to the constructor of a NetworkStream object, which provides access to streams across a network. In this example, the NetworkStream object uses the streams of the specified Socket. Lines 118–119 create instances of the **BinaryWriter** and **BinaryReader** classes for writing and reading data. We pass the NetworkStream object as an argument to each constructor—BinaryWriter can write bytes to the NetworkStream, and BinaryReader can read bytes from NetworkStream. Line 121 calls DisplayMessage, indicating that a connection was received. Next, we send a message to the client indicating that the connection was received. BinaryWriter method Write has many overloaded versions that write data of various types to a stream. Line 125 uses method Write to send the client a String notifying the user of a successful connection. This completes Step 3.

Receiving Messages from the Client

We now begin the processing phase (Step 4). Lines 131–143 loop until the server receives the message CLIENT>>> TERMINATE, which indicates that the connection should be terminated. Line 134 uses BinaryReader method ReadString to read a String from the stream. Method ReadString blocks until a String is read. This is why we execute method Run-Server in a separate Thread (created in lines 20–21, when the Form loads). This Thread ensures that the application's user can continue to interact with the GUI to send messages to the client, even when this thread is blocked while awaiting a message from the client.

Modifying GUI Controls from Separate Threads

Windows Form controls are not thread safe—a control that is modified from multiple threads is not guaranteed to be modified correctly. The Visual Studio 2005 Documentation recommends that only the thread which created the GUI should modify the controls.[1] Class Control provides method Invoke to help ensure this. Invoke takes two arguments—a Delegate representing a method that will modify the GUI and an array of Objects representing the parameters of the method. (Delegates were introduced in Section 13.3.3.) At some point after Invoke is called, the thread that originally created the GUI will (when not executing any other code) execute the method represented by the Delegate, passing the contents of the Object array as the method's arguments.

Line 34 declares a Delegate type named DisplayDelegate, which represents methods that take a String argument and do not return a value. Method DisplayMessage (lines 38–49) meets these requirements—it receives a String parameter named message and does not return a value. The If statement in line 40 tests txtDisplay's Invoke-Required property (inherited from class Control), which returns True if the current thread is not allowed to modify this control directly and returns False otherwise. If the current thread executing method DisplayMessage is not the thread that created the GUI, the If condition evaluates to True and lines 43–44 call method Invoke, passing it a new DisplayDelegate representing the method DisplayMessage *itself* and a new Object array consisting of the String argument message. This causes the thread that created the GUI to call method DisplayMessage again at a later time with the same String argument as the original call. When that call occurs from the thread that created the GUI, the method *is* allowed to modify txtDisplay directly, so the Else body (line 47) executes and appends message to txtDisplay's Text property.

Lines 53–68 define the Delegate, DisableInputDelegate, and a method, DisableInput, to allow any thread to modify the ReadOnly property of txtInput using the same techniques. A thread calls DisableInput with a Boolean argument (True to disable; False to enable). If DisableInput is not allowed to modify the control from the current thread, DisableInput calls method Invoke. This causes the thread that created the GUI to call DisableInput at a later time to set txtInput.ReadOnly's value to the Boolean argument.

Terminating the Connection with the Client
When the chat is complete, lines 148–151 close the BinaryWriter, BinaryReader, NetworkStream and Socket (Step 5) by invoking their respective Close methods. The server then waits for another client connection request by returning to the beginning of the loop (line 108).

Sending Messages to the Client
When the server application's user enters a String in the TextBox and presses the *Enter* key, event handler txtInput_KeyDown (lines 71–90) reads the String and sends it via method Write of class BinaryWriter. If a user terminates the server application, line 83 calls method Close of the Socket object to close the connection.

Terminating the Server Application
Lines 25–30 define event handler FrmChatServer_FormClosing for the FormClosing event. The event closes the application and calls method Exit of class Environment with parameter ExitCode. Method Exit terminates all threads associated with the application.

---

1. The MSDN article "How to: Make Thread-Safe Calls to Windows Forms Controls" can be found at msdn2.microsoft.com/en-us/library/ms171728.aspx.

FrmChatClient *Class*

Figure 23.2 lists the code for class FrmChatClient. Like the FrmChatServer object, the FrmChatClient object creates a Thread (lines 19–20) in its constructor to handle all incoming messages. FrmChatClient method RunClient (lines 86–133) connects to the FrmChatServer, receives data from the FrmChatServer and sends data to the FrmChatServer. Lines 94–95 instantiate a TcpClient object, then call its Connect method to establish a connection (Step 1). The first argument to method Connect is the name of the server—in our case, the server's name is "localhost", meaning that the server is located on the local computer. The localhost is also known as the loopback IP address and is equivalent to the IP address 127.0.0.1. This value sends the data transmission back to the sender's IP address. The second argument to method Connect is the server port number. This number must match the port number at which the server waits for connections. [*Note*: The host name localhost is commonly used to test networking applications on one computer. This is particularly useful if you don't have separate computers on which to execute the client and server. Normally, localhost would be replaced with the hostname or IP address of another computer.]

The FrmChatClient uses a NetworkStream to send data to and receive data from the server. The client obtains the NetworkStream in line 98 through a call to TcpClient method GetStream (Step 2). Lines 108–118 loop until the client receives the connection-termination message (SERVER>>> TERMINATE). Line 112 uses BinaryReader method ReadString to obtain the next message from the server (Step 3). Line 113 displays the message, and lines 121–124 close the BinaryWriter, BinaryReader, NetworkStream and TcpClient objects (Step 4).

Lines 33–67 declare DisplayDelegate, DisplayMessage, DisableInputDelegate and DisableInput just as in lines 34–68 of Fig. 23.1. These once again are used to ensure that the GUI is modified only by the thread that created the GUI controls.

When the user of the client application enters a String in the TextBox and presses the *Enter* key, event handler txtInput_KeyDown (lines 70–83) reads the String from the TextBox and sends it to the server via BinaryWriter method Write.

In this client/server chat program, the FrmChatServer receives a connection, processes it, closes it and waits for the next one. In a real-world application, a server would likely receive a connection, set up the connection to be processed as a separate thread of execution and wait for new connections. The separate threads that process existing connections could then continue to execute while the server concentrates on new connection requests.

```vb
1   ' Fig. 23.2: FrmChatClient.vb
2   ' Set up a client that will send information to and
3   ' read information from a server.
4   Imports System.Threading
5   Imports System.Net.Sockets
6   Imports System.IO
7
8   Public Class FrmChatClient
9      Private output As NetworkStream ' stream for receiving data
10     Private writer As BinaryWriter ' facilitates writing to the stream
```

Fig. 23.2 | Client portion of a client/server stream-socket connection. (Part 1 of 5.)

```vbnet
11    Private reader As BinaryReader ' facilitates reading from the stream
12    Private readThread As Thread ' Thread for processing incoming messages
13    Private message As String = ""
14
15    ' initialize thread for reading
16    Private Sub FrmChatClient_Load(ByVal sender As System.Object, _
17       ByVal e As System.EventArgs) Handles MyBase.Load
18
19       readThread = New Thread(New ThreadStart(AddressOf RunClient))
20       readThread.Start()
21    End Sub ' FrmChatClient_Load
22
23    ' close all threads associated with this application
24    Private Sub FrmChatClient_FormClosing(ByVal sender As System.Object, _
25       ByVal e As System.Windows.Forms.FormClosingEventArgs) _
26       Handles MyBase.FormClosing
27
28       System.Environment.Exit(System.Environment.ExitCode)
29    End Sub ' FrmChatClient_FormClosing
30
31    ' Delegate that allows method DisplayMessage to be called
32    ' in the thread that creates and maintains the GUI
33    Private Delegate Sub DisplayDelegate(ByVal message As String)
34
35    ' method DisplayMessage sets txtDisplay's Text property
36    ' in a thread-safe manner
37    Private Sub DisplayMessage(ByVal message As String)
38       ' if modifying txtDisplay is not thread safe
39       If txtDisplay.InvokeRequired Then
40          ' use inherited method Invoke to execute DisplayMessage
41          ' via a Delegate
42          Invoke(New DisplayDelegate(AddressOf DisplayMessage), _
43             New Object() {message})
44       ' OK to modify txtDisplay in current thread
45       Else
46          txtDisplay.Text &= message
47       End If
48    End Sub ' DisplayMessage
49
50    ' Delegate that allows method DisableInput to be called
51    ' in the thread that creates and maintains the GUI
52    Private Delegate Sub DisableInputDelegate(ByVal value As Boolean)
53
54    ' method DisableInput sets txtInput's ReadOnly property
55    ' in a thread-safe manner
56    Private Sub DisableInput(ByVal value As Boolean)
57       ' if modifying txtInput is not thread safe
58       If txtInput.InvokeRequired Then
59          ' use inherited method Invoke to execute DisableInput
60          ' via a Delegate
61          Invoke(New DisableInputDelegate(AddressOf DisableInput), _
62             New Object() {value})
```

Fig. 23.2 | Client portion of a client/server stream-socket connection. (Part 2 of 5.)

```
63                 ' OK to modify txtInput in current thread
64             Else
65                 txtInput.ReadOnly = value
66             End If
67         End Sub ' DisableInput
68
69         ' sends text the user typed to server
70         Private Sub txtInput_KeyDown(ByVal sender As System.Object, _
71             ByVal e As System.Windows.Forms.KeyEventArgs) _
72             Handles txtInput.KeyDown
73
74             Try
75                 If e.KeyCode = Keys.Enter And txtInput.ReadOnly = False Then
76                     writer.Write("CLIENT>>> " & txtInput.Text)
77                     txtDisplay.Text &= vbCrLf & "CLIENT>>> " & txtInput.Text
78                     txtInput.Clear()
79                 End If
80             Catch ex As SocketException
81                 txtDisplay.Text &= vbCrLf & "Error writing object"
82             End Try
83         End Sub ' txtInput_KeyDown
84
85         ' connect to server and display server-generated text
86         Public Sub RunClient()
87             Dim client As TcpClient
88
89             ' instantiate TcpClient for sending data to server
90             Try
91                 DisplayMessage("Attempting connection" & vbCrLf)
92
93                 ' Step 1: create TcpClient and connect to server
94                 client = New TcpClient()
95                 client.Connect("localhost", 50000)
96
97                 ' Step 2: get NetworkStream associated with TcpClient
98                 output = client.GetStream()
99
100                ' create objects for writing and reading across stream
101                writer = New BinaryWriter(output)
102                reader = New BinaryReader(output)
103
104                DisplayMessage(vbCrLf & "Got I/O streams" & vbCrLf)
105                DisableInput(False) ' enable txtInput
106
107                ' loop until server signals termination
108                Do
109                    ' Step 3: processing phase
110                    Try
111                        ' read message from server
112                        message = reader.ReadString()
113                        DisplayMessage(vbCrLf & message)
114                    Catch ex As Exception
```

Fig. 23.2 | Client portion of a client/server stream-socket connection. (Part 3 of 5.)

```
238                ' signal that the move is invalid
239             Else
240                writer.Write("Invalid move, try again.")
241             End If
242
243                ' if game is over, set done to True to exit while loop
244             If server.GameOver() Then
245                done = True
246             End If
247          End While
248
249          ' close the socket connection
250          writer.Close()
251          reader.Close()
252          socketStream.Close()
253          connection.Close()
254       End Sub  ' Run
255    End Class ' Player
```

Fig. 23.5 | Server side of client/server Tic-Tac-Toe program. (Part 6 of 6.)

Lines 44–59 define DisplayDelegate and DisplayMessage, allowing any thread to modify txtDisplay's Text property. This time, the DisplayMessage method is declared as Friend, so it can be called inside a method of class Player through a FrmTicTac-ToeServer reference. Classes in the same project can access each other's Friend members.

Thread getPlayers executes method SetUp (lines 62–86), which creates a TcpLis-tener object to listen for requests on port 50000 (lines 66–67). This object then listens for connection requests from the first and second players. Lines 70 and 76 instantiate Player objects representing the players, and lines 71–73 and 77–79 create two Threads that execute the Run methods of each Player object.

The Player constructor (Fig. 23.5, lines 153–172) receives as arguments a reference to the Socket object (i.e., the connection to the client), a reference to the FrmTicTac-ToeServer object and an Integer indicating the player number (from which the constructor infers the mark "X" or "O" used by that player). FrmTicTacToeServer calls method Run (lines 183–254) after instantiating a Player object. Lines 187–194 notify the server of a successful connection and send the client the Char that the client will place on the board when making a move. If Run is executing for Player "X", lines 205–217 execute, causing Player "X" to wait for a second player to connect. Lines 211–213 suspend the Player "X" Thread until the server signals that Player "O" has connected. The server notifies the Player of the connection by setting the Player's threadSuspended variable to False (line 83). When threadSuspended becomes False, Player exits the loop in lines 211–213.

Lines 220–247 in method Run enable the user to play the game. Each iteration of this statement waits for the client to send an Integer specifying where on the board to place the "X" or "O"—the Player then places the mark on the board if the specified mark location is valid (i.e., if that location does not already contain a mark). Note that the loop continues execution only if Boolean variable done is False. This variable is set to True by event handler FrmTicTacToeServer_FormClosing of class FrmTicTacToeServer, which is invoked when the server closes the connection.

Line 222 of Fig. 23.5 begins a loop that iterates until Socket property Available indicates that there is information to receive from the Socket (or until the server disconnects from the client). If there is none, the Thread sleeps for one second. On awakening, the Thread uses property Disconnected to check whether server variable disconnected is True (line 225). If so, the Thread exits the method (thus terminating the Thread); otherwise, the Thread loops again. However, if property Available indicates that there is data to receive, the loop in lines 222–228 terminates, enabling the information to be processed.

This information contains an Integer representing the location in which the client wants to place a mark. Line 231 calls method ReadInt32 of the BinaryReader object (which reads from the NetworkStream created with the Socket) to read this Integer. Line 235 then passes the Integer to FrmTicTacToeServer method ValidMove. If this method validates the move, the Player places the mark in the desired location.

Method ValidMove (lines 89–120) sends the client a message indicating whether the move was valid. Locations on the board correspond to numbers from 0 to 8 (0–2 for the top row, 3–5 for the middle and 6–8 for the bottom). All the statements in the method are enclosed in a SyncLock statement so that only one move can be attempted at a time. This prevents two players from modifying the game's state information simultaneously. If the Player attempting to validate a move is not the current player (i.e., the one allowed to make a move), that Player is placed in a *Wait* state until its turn. If the user attempts to place a mark on a location that already contains a mark, method ValidMove returns False. However, if the user has selected an unoccupied location (line 99), lines 101–105 place the mark on the local representation of the board. Line 111 notifies the other Player that a move has been made, and line 114 invokes the Pulse method so that the waiting Player can validate a move. The method then returns True to indicate that the move is valid.

When FrmTicTacToeClient (Fig. 23.6) executes, it creates a TextBox to display messages from the server and the Tic-Tac-Toe board representation. The board is created out of nine Square objects (Fig. 23.7) that contain Panels on which the user can click, indicating the position on the board in which to place a mark. FrmTicTacToeClient's Load event handler (lines 22–51) opens a connection to the server (line 43) and obtains a reference to the connection's associated NetworkStream object from TcpClient (line 44). Lines 49–50 start a thread to read messages sent from the server to the client. The server passes messages (e.g., whether each move is valid) to method ProcessMessage (lines 174–207). If the message indicates that a move is valid (line 178), the client sets its Mark to the current square (the square that the user clicked) and repaints the board. If the message indicates that a move is invalid (line 182), the client notifies the user to click a different square. If the message indicates that the opponent made a move (line 187), line 189 reads an Integer from the server specifying where on the board the client should place the opponent's Mark. FrmTicTacToeClient includes a Delegate/method pair for allowing threads to modify lblId's Text property (lines 92–107), as well as DisplayDelegate and DisplayMesage for modifying txtDisplay's Text property (lines 73–88).

```
1   ' Fig. 23.6: FrmTicTacToeClient.vb
2   ' Client for the TicTacToe program.
3   Imports System.Drawing
```

Fig. 23.6 | Client side of client/server Tic-Tac-Toe program. (Part 1 of 7.)

```vb
4   Imports System.Net.Sockets
5   Imports System.Threading
6   Imports System.IO
7
8   Public Class FrmTicTacToeClient
9      Private board(,) As Square ' local representation of the game board
10     Private currentSquareValue As Square ' Square that this player chose
11     Private outputThread As Thread ' Thread for receiving data from server
12     Private connection As TcpClient ' client to establish connection
13     Private stream As NetworkStream ' network data stream
14     Private writer As BinaryWriter ' facilitates writing to the stream
15     Private reader As BinaryReader ' facilitates reading from the stream
16     Private myMark As Char ' player's mark on the board
17     Private myTurn As Boolean ' is it this player's turn?
18     Private brush As SolidBrush ' brush for drawing X's and O's
19     Private done As Boolean = False ' True when game is over
20
21     ' initialize variables and thread for connecting to server
22     Private Sub FrmTicTacToeClient_Load(ByVal sender As System.Object, _
23        ByVal e As System.EventArgs) Handles MyBase.Load
24
25        board = New Square(3, 3) {}
26
27        ' create 9 Square objects and place them on the board
28        board(0, 0) = New Square(pnlBoard0, " "c, 0)
29        board(0, 1) = New Square(pnlBoard1, " "c, 1)
30        board(0, 2) = New Square(pnlBoard2, " "c, 2)
31        board(1, 0) = New Square(pnlBoard3, " "c, 3)
32        board(1, 1) = New Square(pnlBoard4, " "c, 4)
33        board(1, 2) = New Square(pnlBoard5, " "c, 5)
34        board(2, 0) = New Square(pnlBoard6, " "c, 6)
35        board(2, 1) = New Square(pnlBoard7, " "c, 7)
36        board(2, 2) = New Square(pnlBoard8, " "c, 8)
37
38        ' create a SolidBrush for writing on the Squares
39        brush = New SolidBrush(Color.Black)
40
41        ' make connection to server and get the associated
42        ' network stream
43        connection = New TcpClient("localhost", 50000)
44        stream = connection.GetStream()
45        writer = New BinaryWriter(stream)
46        reader = New BinaryReader(stream)
47
48        ' start a new thread for sending and receiving messages
49        outputThread = New Thread(New ThreadStart(AddressOf Run))
50        outputThread.Start()
51     End Sub ' FrmTicTacToeClient_Load
52
53     ' repaint the Squares
54     Private Sub FrmTicTacToeClient_Paint(ByVal sender As System.Object, _
55        ByVal e As System.Windows.Forms.PaintEventArgs) _
56        Handles MyBase.Paint
```

Fig. 23.6 | Client side of client/server Tic-Tac-Toe program. (Part 2 of 7.)

```vb
57
58          PaintSquares()
59      End Sub ' FrmTicTacToeClient_Paint
60
61      ' game is over
62      Private Sub FrmTicTacToeClient_FormClosing( _
63          ByVal sender As System.Object, _
64          ByVal e As System.Windows.Forms.FormClosingEventArgs) _
65          Handles MyBase.FormClosing
66
67          done = True
68          System.Environment.Exit(System.Environment.ExitCode)
69      End Sub ' FrmTicTacToeClient_FormClosing
70
71      ' Delegate that allows method DisplayMessage to be called
72      ' in the thread that creates and maintains the GUI
73      Private Delegate Sub DisplayDelegate(ByVal message As String)
74
75      ' method DisplayMessage sets txtDisplay's Text property
76      ' in a thread-safe manner
77      Private Sub DisplayMessage(ByVal message As String)
78          ' if modifying txtDisplay is not thread safe
79          If txtDisplay.InvokeRequired Then
80              ' use inherited method Invoke to execute DisplayMessage
81              ' via a Delegate
82              Invoke(New DisplayDelegate(AddressOf DisplayMessage), _
83                  New Object() {message})
84          ' OK to modify txtDisplay in current thread
85          Else
86              txtDisplay.Text &= message
87          End If
88      End Sub ' DisplayMessage
89
90      ' Delegate that allows method ChangeIdLabel to be called
91      ' in the thread that creates and maintains the GUI
92      Private Delegate Sub ChangeIdLabelDelegate(ByVal message As String)
93
94      ' method ChangeIdLabel sets txtDisplay's Text property
95      ' in a thread-safe manner
96      Private Sub ChangeIdLabel(ByVal label As String)
97          ' if modifying lblId is not thread safe
98          If lblId.InvokeRequired Then
99              ' use inherited method Invoke to execute ChangeIdLabel
100             ' via a Delegate
101             Invoke(New ChangeIdLabelDelegate(AddressOf ChangeIdLabel), _
102                 New Object() {label})
103         ' OK to modify lblId in current thread
104         Else
105             lblId.Text = label
106         End If
107     End Sub ' ChangeIdLabel
108
```

Fig. 23.6 | Client side of client/server Tic-Tac-Toe program. (Part 3 of 7.)

```vbnet
109      ' draws the mark of each square
110      Public Sub PaintSquares()
111         Dim g As Graphics
112
113         ' draw the appropriate mark on each panel
114         For row As Integer = 0 To 2
115
116            For column As Integer = 0 To 2
117               ' get the Graphics for each Panel
118               g = board(row, column).SquarePanel.CreateGraphics()
119
120               ' draw the appropriate letter on the panel
121               g.DrawString(board(row, column).Mark.ToString(), _
122                  pnlBoard0.Font, brush, 10, 8)
123            Next column
124
125         Next row
126      End Sub ' PaintSquares
127
128      ' send location of the clicked square to server
129      Private Sub square_MouseUp(ByVal sender As System.Object, _
130         ByVal e As System.Windows.Forms.MouseEventArgs) _
131         Handles pnlBoard0.MouseUp, pnlBoard5.MouseUp, pnlBoard4.MouseUp, _
132         pnlBoard3.MouseUp, pnlBoard2.MouseUp, pnlBoard1.MouseUp, _
133         pnlBoard8.MouseUp, pnlBoard7.MouseUp, pnlBoard6.MouseUp
134
135         ' for each square check if that square was clicked
136         For row As Integer = 0 To 2
137
138            For column As Integer = 0 To 2
139               If board(row, column).SquarePanel.Equals(sender) Then
140                  currentSquareValue = board(row, column)
141
142                  ' send the move to the server
143                  SendClickedSquare(board(row, column).Location)
144               End If
145            Next column
146         Next row
147      End Sub ' square_MouseUp
148
149      ' control thread that allows continuous update of the
150      ' TextBox display
151      Public Sub Run()
152         myMark = reader.ReadChar() ' first get players's mark (X or 0)
153         ChangeIdLabel("You are player """ & myMark & """")
154
155         If myMark = "X"c Then
156            myTurn = True
157         Else
158            myTurn = False
159         End If
160
```

Fig. 23.6 | Client side of client/server Tic-Tac-Toe program. (Part 4 of 7.)

```
161          ' process incom ing messages
162          Try
163              ' receive messages sent to client
164              While Not done
165                  ProcessMessage(reader.ReadString())
166              End While
167          Catch ex As IOException
168              MessageBox.Show("Server is down, game over", "Error", _
169                  MessageBoxButtons.OK, MessageBoxIcon.Error)
170          End Try
171      End Sub ' Run
172
173      ' process messages sent to client
174      Public Sub ProcessMessage(ByVal message As String)
175          ' if the move the player sent to the server is valid
176          ' update the display, set that square's mark to be
177          ' the mark of the current player and repaint the board
178          If message = "Valid move." Then
179              DisplayMessage("Valid move, please wait." & vbCrLf)
180              currentSquareValue.Mark = myMark
181              PaintSquares()
182          ElseIf message = "Invalid move, try again." Then
183              ' if the move is invalid, display that and it is now
184              ' this player's turn again
185              DisplayMessage(message & vbCrLf)
186              myTurn = True
187          ElseIf message = "Opponent moved." Then
188              ' if opponent moved, find location of their move
189              Dim location As Integer = reader.ReadInt32()
190
191              ' set that square to have the opponents mark and
192              ' repaint the board
193              If myMark = "X"c Then
194                  board(location \ 3, location Mod 3).Mark = "O"c
195              Else
196                  board(location \ 3, location Mod 3).Mark = "X"c
197              End If
198              PaintSquares()
199
200              DisplayMessage("Opponent moved.  Your turn." & vbCrLf)
201
202              ' it is now this player's turn
203              myTurn = True
204          Else
205              DisplayMessage(message & vbCrLf) ' display message
206          End If
207      End Sub ' ProcessMessage
208
209      ' sends the server the number of the clicked square
210      Public Sub SendClickedSquare(ByVal location As Integer)
211          ' if it is the current player's move right now
212          If myTurn Then
```

Fig. 23.6 | Client side of client/server Tic-Tac-Toe program. (Part 5 of 7.)

```
213              ' send the location of the move to the server
214              writer.Write(location)
215
216              ' it is now the other player's turn
217              myTurn = False
218         End If
219      End Sub ' SendClickedSquare
220
221      ' write-only property for the current square
222      Public WriteOnly Property CurrentSquare() As Square
223         Set(ByVal value As Square)
224            currentSquareValue = value
225         End Set
226      End Property ' CurrentSquare
227   End Class ' FrmTicTacToeClient
```

At the start of the game.

(a)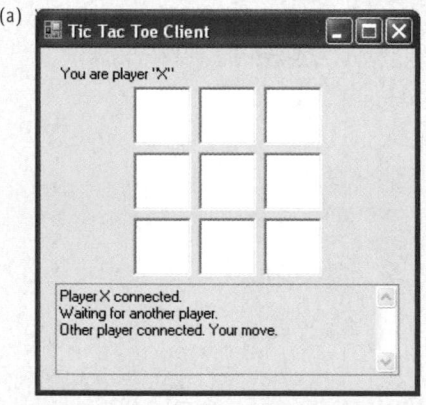

(b)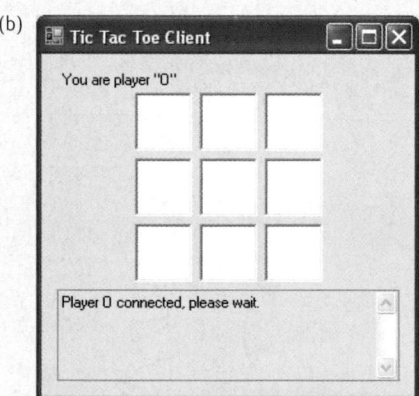

After Player X makes the first move.

(c)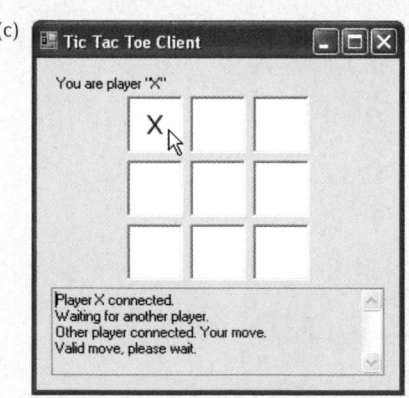

(d)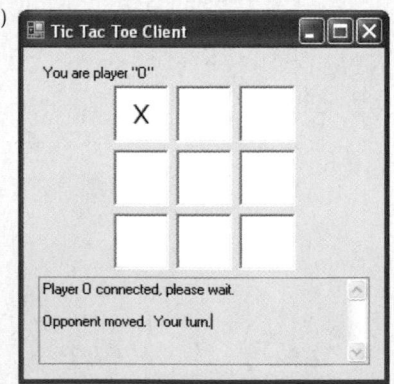

Fig. 23.6 | Client side of client/server Tic-Tac-Toe program. (Part 6 of 7.)

After Player O makes the second move.

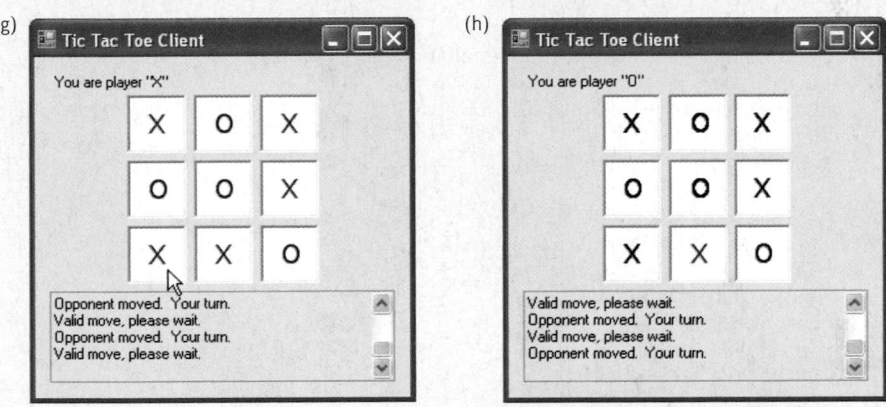

After Player X makes the final move.

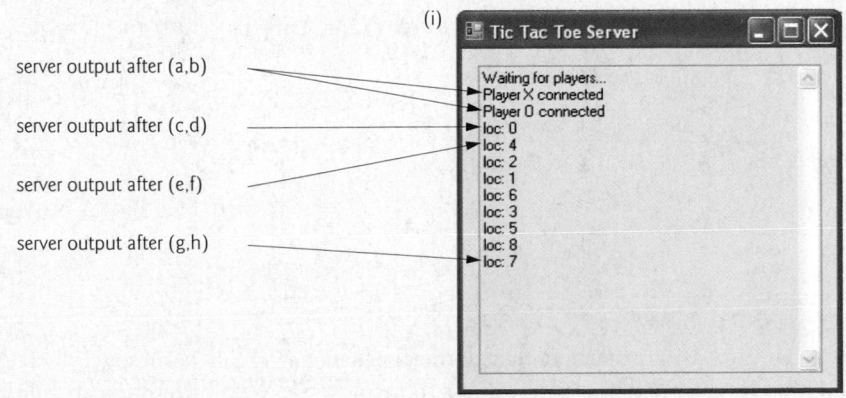

The Tie Tac Toe Server's output from the client interactions.

(i)

server output after (a,b)

server output after (c,d)

server output after (e,f)

server output after (g,h)

Fig. 23.6 | Client side of client/server Tic-Tac-Toe program. (Part 7 of 7.)

```vb
1   ' Fig. 23.7: Square.vb
2   ' A Square on the TicTacToe board.
3
4   ' the representation of a square in a tic-tac-toe grid
5   Public Class Square
6      Private panel As Panel ' GUI Panel that represents this Square
7      Private markValue As Char ' player's markValue on this Square (if any)
8
9      ' locationValue on the board of this Square
10     Private locationValue As Integer
11
12     ' constructor
13     Public Sub New(ByVal newPanel As Panel, ByVal newMark As Char, _
14        ByVal newLocation As Integer)
15
16        panel = newPanel
17        markValue = newMark
18        locationValue = newLocation
19     End Sub ' New
20
21     ' property SquarePanel; the panel which the square represents
22     Public ReadOnly Property SquarePanel() As Panel
23        Get
24           Return panel
25        End Get
26     End Property ' SquarePanel
27
28     ' property Mark; the markValue on the square
29     Public Property Mark() As Char
30        Get
31           Return markValue
32        End Get
33        Set(ByVal value As Char)
34           markValue = value
35        End Set
36     End Property ' Mark
37
38     ' property Location; the square's locationValue on the board
39     Public ReadOnly Property Location() As Integer
40        Get
41           Return locationValue
42        End Get
43     End Property ' Location
44  End Class ' Square
```

Fig. 23.7 | Class Square.

23.9 WebBrowser Class

With FCL 2.0, Microsoft introduced the WebBrowser class (namespace System.Windows.Forms), which enables applications to incorporate Web browsing capabilities. The control provides methods for navigating Web pages and maintains its own history of Web sites visited. It also generates events as the user interacts with the content displayed in the control so that your application can respond to events such as the user clicking the links displayed in the content.

Figure 23.8 demonstrates the WebBrowser class's capabilities. Class FrmBrowser provides the basic functionality of a Web browser, allowing the user to navigate to a URL, move backward and forward through the history of visited sites, and reload the current Web page.

```vb
 1  ' Fig. 23.8: FrmBrowser.vb
 2  ' WebBrowser class example.
 3
 4  Public Class FrmBrowser
 5     ' navigate back one page
 6     Private Sub btnBack_Click(ByVal sender As System.Object, _
 7        ByVal e As System.EventArgs) Handles btnBack.Click
 8
 9        webBrowser.GoBack()
10     End Sub ' btnBack_Click
11
12     ' navigate forward one page
13     Private Sub btnForward_Click(ByVal sender As System.Object, _
14        ByVal e As System.EventArgs) Handles btnForward.Click
15
16        webBrowser.GoForward()
17     End Sub ' btnForward_Click
18
19     ' stop loading the current page
20     Private Sub btnStop_Click(ByVal sender As System.Object, _
21        ByVal e As System.EventArgs) Handles btnStop.Click
22
23        webBrowser.Stop()
24     End Sub ' btnStop_Click
25
26     ' reload the current page
27     Private Sub btnReload_Click(ByVal sender As System.Object, _
28        ByVal e As System.EventArgs) Handles btnReload.Click
29
30        webBrowser.Refresh()
31     End Sub ' btnReload_Click
32
33     ' navigate to the user's home page
34     Private Sub btnHome_Click(ByVal sender As System.Object, _
35        ByVal e As System.EventArgs) Handles btnHome.Click
36
37        webBrowser.GoHome()
38     End Sub ' btnHome_Click
39
40     ' if the user pressed enter, navigate to the specified URL
41     Private Sub txtNavigation_KeyDown(ByVal sender As System.Object, _
42        ByVal e As System.Windows.Forms.KeyEventArgs) _
43        Handles txtNavigation.KeyDown
44
```

Fig. 23.8 | WebBrowser class example. (Part 1 of 3.)

```vbnet
45          If e.KeyCode = Keys.Enter Then
46             webBrowser.Navigate(txtNavigation.Text)
47          End If
48       End Sub ' txtNavigation_KeyDown
49
50       ' enable btnStop while the current page is loading
51       Private Sub webBrowser_Navigating(ByVal sender As System.Object, _
52          ByVal e As System.Windows.Forms.WebBrowserNavigatingEventArgs) _
53          Handles webBrowser.Navigating
54
55          btnStop.Enabled = True
56       End Sub ' webBrowser_Navigating
57
58       ' update the status text
59       Private Sub webBrowser_StatusTextChanged( _
60          ByVal sender As System.Object, ByVal e As System.EventArgs) _
61          Handles webBrowser.StatusTextChanged
62
63          txtStatus.Text = webBrowser.StatusText
64       End Sub ' webBrowser_StatusTextChanged
65
66       ' update the ProgressBar for how much of the page has been loaded
67       Private Sub webBrowser_ProgressChanged( _
68          ByVal sender As System.Object, ByVal e As _
69          System.Windows.Forms.WebBrowserProgressChangedEventArgs) _
70          Handles webBrowser.ProgressChanged
71          ' Check if e.MaximumProgress is 0 or
72          ' if e.MaximumProgress is less than e.CurrentProgress
73          If e.MaximumProgress <> 0 And _
74             e.MaximumProgress >= e.CurrentProgress Then
75
76             prgPage.Value = Convert.ToInt32( _
77                100 * e.CurrentProgress / e.MaximumProgress)
78          End If
79       End Sub ' webBrowser_ProgressChanged
80
81       ' update the web browser's controls appropriately
82       Private Sub webBrowser_DocumentCompleted( _
83          ByVal sender As System.Object, ByVal e As _
84          System.Windows.Forms.WebBrowserDocumentCompletedEventArgs) _
85          Handles webBrowser.DocumentCompleted
86          ' set the text in txtNavigation to the current page's URL
87          txtNavigation.Text = webBrowser.Url.ToString()
88
89          ' enable or disable btnBack and btnForward
90          btnBack.Enabled = webBrowser.CanGoBack
91          btnForward.Enabled = webBrowser.CanGoForward
92
93          ' disable btnStop
94          btnStop.Enabled = False
95
```

Fig. 23.8 | WebBrowser class example. (Part 2 of 3.)

```
96          ' clear the prgPage
97          prgPage.Value = 0
98      End Sub ' webBrowser_DocumentCompleted
99
100         ' update the title of the Browser
101     Private Sub webBrowser_DocumentTitleChanged( _
102         ByVal sender As System.Object, ByVal e As System.EventArgs) _
103         Handles webBrowser.DocumentTitleChanged
104
105         Me.Text = webBrowser.DocumentTitle & " - Browser"
106     End Sub ' webBrowser_DocumentTitleChanged
107 End Class ' FrmBrowser
```

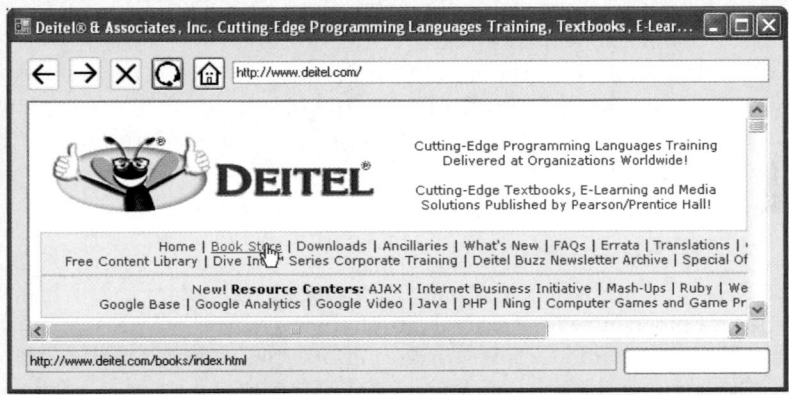

Fig. 23.8 | WebBrowser class example. (Part 3 of 3.)

Lines 6–38 define five Click event handlers, one for each of the five navigation Buttons that appear at the top of the Form. Each event handler calls a corresponding Web-Browser method. WebBrowser method **GoBack** (line 9) navigates back to the previous page in the navigation history. Method **GoForward** (line 16) navigates forward to the next page in the navigation history. Method **Stop** (line 23) stops loading the current page. Method **Refresh** (line 30) reloads the current page. Method **GoHome** (line 37) navigates to the user's home page, as defined under Internet Explorer's settings (under **Tools > Internet Options...** in the **Home page** section).

The TextBox to the right of the navigation buttons allows the user to enter the URL of a Web site to browse. When the user types each keystroke in the TextBox, the event handler in lines 41–48 executes. If the key pressed was *Enter*, line 46 calls WebBrowser method **Navigate** to retrieve the document at the specified URL.

A WebBrowser object generates a **Navigating** event when it starts loading a new page. When this occurs, the event handler in lines 51–56 executes, and line 55 enables btnStop so that the user can cancel the loading of the Web page.

Typically, a user can see the status of a loading Web page at the bottom of the browser window. For this reason, we include a TextBox control (named txtStatus) and a Pro-gressBar control (named prgPage) at the bottom of our Form. A WebBrowser object generates a **StatusTextChanged** event when its **StatusText** property changes. The event handler for this event (lines 59–64) assigns the new contents of the WebBrowser's Status-

Text property to txtStatus's Text property (line 63) so that the user can monitor the WebBrowser's status messages. A WebBrowser object generates a **ProgressChanged** event when its page-loading progress is updated. The ProgressChanged event handler (lines 67–79) updates prgPage's Value (lines 76–77) to reflect how much of the current document has been loaded.

When the WebBrowser finishes loading a document, it generates a **DocumentCompleted** event. This executes the event handler in lines 82–98. Line 87 updates the contents of txtNavigation so that it shows the URL of the currently loaded page (WebBrowser property Url). This is particularly important if the user browses to another Web page by clicking a link in the existing page. Lines 90–91 use properties **CanGoBack** and **CanGoForward** to determine whether the back and forward buttons should be enabled or disabled. Since the document is now loaded, line 94 disables btnStop. Line 97 sets prgPage's Value to 0 to indicate that no content is currently being loaded.

Lines 101–106 define an event handler for the **DocumentTitleChanged** event, which occurs when a new document is loaded in the WebBrowser. Line 105 sets FrmBrowser's Text property (which is displayed in the Form's title bar) to the WebBrowser's current **DocumentTitle**.

23.10 .NET Remoting

The .NET framework provides a distributed computing technology called .NET remoting that allows a program to invoke methods of objects located on other computers over a network, rather than communicate with streams of bytes (as demonstrated earlier in this chapter). .NET remoting is similar in concept to RMI (remote method invocation) in Java and RPC (remote procedure call) in procedural programming languages. .NET remoting is also similar to Web services (Chapter 22) with a few key differences. With Web services, a client application communicates with a Web service that is hosted by a Web server. The client and the Web service can be written in any language, as long as they can transmit messages in SOAP. With .NET remoting, a client application communicates with a server application, both of which must be written in .NET languages. Using .NET remoting, a client and a server can communicate via method calls, and objects can be transmitted between applications—a process known as marshaling the objects.

Channels

The client and the server are able to communicate with one another through channels. Channels typically use either the HTTP protocol or the TCP protocol to transmit messages. The advantage of an HTTP channel is that firewalls usually permit HTTP connections by default, while they normally block unfamiliar TCP connections. The advantage of a TCP channel is better performance than an HTTP channel. In a .NET remoting application, the client and the server each create a channel, and both channels must use the same protocol to communicate with one another. In our example, we use HTTP channels.

Marshaling

There are two ways to marshal an object—by value and by reference. Marshal-by-value requires that the object be serializable—that is, capable of being represented as a formatted message that can be sent between applications through a channel. The receiving end of the channel deserializes the object to obtain a copy of the original object. To enable an object to be serialized and deserialized, its class must be declared with the `<Serializable()>` attribute or must implement interface `ISerializable`.

Marshal-by-reference requires that the object's class extend class `MarshalByRefObject` of namespace `System`. An object that is marshaled by reference is referred to as a *remote object*, and its class is referred to as a *remote class*. When an object is marshaled by reference, the object itself is not transmitted. Instead, two *proxy* objects are created—a *transparent proxy* and a *real proxy*. The transparent proxy provides all the `Public` services of a remote object. Typically, a client calls the methods and properties of the transparent proxy as if it were the remote object. The transparent proxy then calls the `Invoke` method of the real proxy. This sends the appropriate message from the client channel to the server channel. The server receives this message and performs the specified method call or accesses the specified property on the actual object, which resides on the server. In our example, we marshal a remote object by reference.

Weather Information Application Using .NET Remoting

We now present a .NET remoting example that downloads the *Traveler's Forecast* weather information from the National Weather Service Web site:

```
http://iwin.nws.noaa.gov/iwin/us/traveler.html
```

[*Note:* As we developed this example, the National Weather Service indicated that the information provided on the *Traveler's Forecast* Web page would be provided via Web services in the near future. The information we use in this example depends directly on the format of the *Traveler's Forecast* Web page. If you have trouble running this example, please refer to the FAQ page for this book, which is accessible via `www.deitel.com/faq.html`. This potential problem demonstrates a benefit of using Web services or .NET remoting to implement distributed computing applications that may change in the future. Separating the server part of the application, which depends on the format of an outside data source, from the client part of the application allows the server implementation to be updated without requiring any changes to the client.]

Our .NET remoting application consists of five components:

1. Serializable class `CityWeather`, which represents the weather report for one city.

2. Interface `Report`, which declares a property `Reports` that a client application accesses via the marshaled object to obtain a collection of `CityWeather` objects.

3. Remote class `ReportInfo`, which extends class `MarshalByRefObject`, implements interface `Report` and will be instantiated only on the server.

4. A `WeatherServer` application that sets up a server channel and makes the `ReportInfo` class available at a particular URI (uniform resource identifier).

5. A `WeatherClient` application that sets up a client channel and requests a `ReportInfo` object from the `WeatherServer` to retrieve the day's weather report.

Class `CityWeather`

Class `CityWeather` (Fig. 23.9) contains weather information for one city. Class `CityWeather` will be published in the `Weather.dll` class library file that both the server application and the client application must reference. For this reason, you should place this class (and interface `Report` from Fig. 23.10) in a class library project. Class `CityWeather` is declared with attribute `Serializable` (line 4), which indicates that an object of class `CityWeather` can be marshaled by value. This is necessary because `CityWeather` objects will be returned by the `ReportInfo` object's `Reports` property, and the return values of the methods and properties declared by a remote class must themselves be marshaled by value from the server to the client. (The argument values in method calls will also be marshaled by value from the client to the server.) Thus when the client calls a `Get` accessor that returns `CityWeather` objects, the server channel will serialize the `CityWeather` objects in a message that the client channel can deserialize to create copies of the original `CityWeather` objects. Class `CityWeather` also implements interface `IComparable` (line 5) so that an `ArrayList` of `CityWeather` objects can be sorted alphabetically.

```vb
1    ' Fig. 23.9: CityWeather.vb
2    ' Class representing the weather information for one city.
3
4    <Serializable()> _
5    Public Class CityWeather : Implements IComparable
6       Private cityNameValue As String
7       Private descriptionValue As String
8       Private temperatureValue As String
9
10      Public Sub New(ByVal city As String, ByVal information As String, _
11         ByVal degrees As String)
12
13         cityNameValue = city
14         descriptionValue = information
15         temperatureValue = degrees
16      End Sub ' New
17
18      ' read-only property that gets city's name
19      Public ReadOnly Property CityName() As String
20         Get
21            Return cityNameValue
22         End Get
23      End Property ' CityName
24
25      ' read-only property that gets city's weather description
26      Public ReadOnly Property Description() As String
27         Get
28            Return descriptionValue
29         End Get
30      End Property ' Description
31
32      ' read-only property that gets city's temperature
33      Public ReadOnly Property Temperature() As String
34         Get
35            Return temperatureValue
36         End Get
37      End Property ' Temperature
```

Fig. 23.9 | Class `CityWeather`. (Part 1 of 2.)

```
38
39        ' implementation of CompareTo method for alphabetizing
40        Public Function CompareTo(ByVal obj As Object) _
41           As Integer Implements System.IComparable.CompareTo
42
43           Return String.Compare(CityName, CType(obj, CityWeather).CityName)
44        End Function ' CompareTo
45
46        ' return string representation of this CityWeather object
47        ' (used to display the weather report on the server console)
48        Public Overrides Function ToString() As String
49           Return CityName & " | " & Temperature & " | " & Description
50        End Function ' ToString
51     End Class ' CityWeather
```

Fig. 23.9 | Class CityWeather. (Part 2 of 2.)

CityWeather contains three instance variables (lines 6–8) for storing the city's name (cityNameValue), the high/low temperature information (temperatureValue) and the description of the weather condition (descriptionValue). The CityWeather constructor (lines 10–16) initializes the three instance variables. Lines 19–37 declare three read-only properties that allow the values of the three instance variables to be retrieved. CityWeather implements IComparable, so it must declare a method called CompareTo that takes an Object reference and returns an Integer (lines 40–44). Also, we want to alphabetize CityWeather objects by their cityNames, so CompareTo calls String method Compare with the cityNames of the two CityWeather objects (line 43). Class CityWeather also overrides the ToString method to display information for this city (lines 48–50). Method ToString is used by the server application to display the weather information retrieved from the *Traveler's Forecast* Web page in the console.

Interface **Report**

Figure 23.10 shows the code for interface Report. Interface Report also will be included with class CityWeather in the Weather.dll class library file, so it can be used in both the client and server applications. Report declares a read-only property (line 7) that returns an ArrayList of CityWeather objects (ArrayList was introduced in the example in Section 17.8). The client application will use this property to retrieve the information in the weather report—each city's name, high/low temperature and weather condition.

```
1     ' Fig. 23.10: Report.vb
2     ' Interface that defines a property for getting
3     ' the information in a weather report.
4     Imports System.Collections
5
6     Public Interface Report
7        ReadOnly Property Reports() As ArrayList
8     End Interface ' Report
```

Fig. 23.10 | Interface Report in namespace Weather.

Class **ReportInfo**

Remote class ReportInfo (Fig. 23.11) implements interface Report (line 9) of namespace Weather (specified by the Imports statement in line 7). ReportInfo also extends base class

```vb
1    ' Fig. 23.11: ReportInfo.vb
2    ' Class that implements interface Report, retrieves
3    ' and returns data on weather
4    Imports System.Collections
5    Imports System.IO
6    Imports System.Net
7    Imports Weather
8
9    Public Class ReportInfo : Inherits MarshalByRefObject : Implements Report
10       Private cityList As ArrayList ' cities, temperatures, descriptions
11
12       Public Sub New()
13          cityList = New ArrayList()
14
15          ' create WebClient to get access to Web page
16          Dim myClient As New WebClient()
17
18          ' get StreamReader for response so we can read page
19          Dim input As New StreamReader(myClient.OpenRead( _
20             "http://iwin.nws.noaa.gov/iwin/us/traveler.html"))
21
22          ' indicates first batch of cities
23          Dim separator1 As String = "TAV12"
24          ' indicates second batch of cities
25          Dim separator2 As String = "TAV13"
26
27          ' locate separator1 in Web page
28          While Not input.ReadLine().StartsWith(separator1) ' do nothing
29          End While
30          ReadCities(input) ' read the first batch of cities
31
32          ' locate separator2 in Web page
33          While Not input.ReadLine().StartsWith(separator2) ' do nothing
34          End While
35          ReadCities(input) ' read the second batch of cities
36
37          cityList.Sort() ' sort list of cities by alphabetical order
38          input.Close() ' close StreamReader to NWS server
39
40          ' display the data on the server side
41          Console.WriteLine("Data from NWS Web site:")
42
43          For Each city As CityWeather In cityList
44             Console.WriteLine(city)
45          Next city ' end foreach
46       End Sub ' New
47
```

Fig. 23.11 | Class ReportInfo, which implements interface Report, is marshaled by reference. (Part 1 of 2.)

```
48      ' utility method that reads a batch of cities
49      Private Sub ReadCities(ByVal input As StreamReader)
50         ' day format and night format
51         Dim dayFormat As String = _
52            "CITY              WEA      HI/LO    WEA      HI/LO"
53         Dim nightFormat As String = _
54            "CITY              WEA      LO/HI    WEA      LO/HI"
55         Dim inputLine As String = ""
56
57         ' locate header that begins weather information
58         Do
59            inputLine = input.ReadLine()
60         Loop While Not inputLine.Equals(dayFormat) And Not _
61            inputLine.Equals(nightFormat)
62
63         inputLine = input.ReadLine() ' get first city's data
64
65         ' while there are more cities to read
66         While inputLine.Length > 28
67            ' create CityWeather object for city
68            Dim weather As New CityWeather(inputLine.Substring(0, 16), _
69               inputLine.Substring(16, 7), inputLine.Substring(23, 7))
70
71            cityList.Add(weather) ' add to ArrayList
72            inputLine = input.ReadLine() ' get next city's data
73         End While ' end while
74      End Sub ' ReadCities
75
76      ' property for getting the cities' weather reports
77      Public ReadOnly Property Reports() As _
78         System.Collections.ArrayList Implements Weather.Report.Reports
79
80         Get
81            Return cityList
82         End Get
83      End Property ' Reports
84   End Class ' ReportInfo
```

Fig. 23.11 | Class ReportInfo, which implements interface Report, is marshaled by reference. (Part 2 of 2.)

MarshalByRefObject. Class ReportInfo is part of the remote WeatherServer application and will not be directly available to the client application.

Lines 12–46 declare the ReportInfo constructor. Line 16 creates a WebClient (namespace System.Net) object to interact with a data source that is specified by a URL—in this case, the URL for the NWS *Traveler's Forecast* page (http://iwin.nws.noaa.gov/iwin/us/traveler.html). Lines 19–20 call WebClient method OpenRead, which returns a Stream that the program can use to read data containing the weather information from the specified URL. This Stream is used to create a StreamReader object so that the program can read the Web page's HTML markup line-by-line.

The section of the Web page in which we are interested consists of two batches of cities—Albany through Reno, and Salt Lake City through Washington, D.C. The first batch occurs in a section that starts with the string "TAV12" while the second batch occurs in a section that starts with the string "TAV13". We declare variables separator1 and separator2 to store these strings. Lines 28–29 read the HTML markup one line at a time until "TAV12" is encountered. Then the program calls utility method ReadCities to read a batch of cities into ArrayList cityList. Next, lines 33–34 read the HTML markup one line at a time until "TAV13" is encountered, and line 35 makes another call to method ReadCities to read the second batch of cities. Line 37 calls method **Sort** of class Array-List to sort the CityWeather objects into alphabetical order by city name. Line 38 closes the StreamReader connection to the Web site. Lines 43–45 output the weather information for each city to the server application's console display.

Lines 49–74 declare utility method ReadCities, which takes a StreamReader object and reads the information for each city, creates a CityWeather object for it and places the CityWeather object in cityList. The loop in lines 58–61 continues to read the page one line at a time until it finds the header line that begins the weather forecast table. This line starts with either dayFormat (lines 51–52), indicating the header for the daytime information, or nightFormat (lines 53–54), indicating the header for the nighttime information. Because the line could be in either format based on the time of day, the loop-continuation condition checks for both (lines 60–61). Line 59 reads the next line from the Web page, which is the first line containing temperature information.

The loop in lines 66–73 creates a new CityWeather object to represent the current city. It parses the string containing the current weather data, separating the city name, the weather condition and the temperature. The CityWeather object is added to cityList. Then the next line from the page is read and stored in inputLine for the next iteration. This process continues while the length of the string read from the Web page is greater than 28 (the lines containing weather data are all longer than 28 characters). The first line shorter than this signals the end of that forecast section in the Web page.

Read-only property Reports (lines 77–83) implements the Report interface's Reports property to return cityList. The client application will remotely call this property to retrieve the day's weather report.

Class *WeatherServer*

Figure 23.12 contains the server code. The Imports statements in lines 4–6 specify .NET remoting namespaces System.Runtime.Remoting, System.Runtime.Remoting.Channels and System.Runtime.Remoting.Channels.Http. The first two namespaces are required for .NET remoting, and the third is required for HTTP channels. Namespace System.Runtime.Remoting.Channels.Http requires the project to reference the System.Runtime.Remoting assembly, which can be found under the **.NET** tab in the **Add References** menu. The Imports statement at line 7 specifies namespace Weather, which contains interface Report. Remember to add a reference to Weather.dll in this project.

```
1   ' Fig. 23.12: WeatherServer.cs
2   ' Server application that uses .NET remoting to send
3   ' weather report information to a client
4   Imports System.Runtime.Remoting
5   Imports System.Runtime.Remoting.Channels
```

Fig. 23.12 | Class WeatherServer exposes remote class ReportInfo. (Part 1 of 2.)

```
 6   Imports System.Runtime.Remoting.Channels.Http
 7   Imports Weather
 8
 9   Module WeatherServer
10      Sub Main()
11         ' establish HTTP channel
12         Dim channel As New HttpChannel(50000)
13         ChannelServices.RegisterChannel(channel, False)
14
15         ' register ReportInfo class
16         RemotingConfiguration.RegisterWellKnownServiceType( _
17            GetType(ReportInfo), "Report", WellKnownObjectMode.Singleton)
18
19         Console.WriteLine("Press Enter to terminate server.")
20         Console.ReadLine()
21      End Sub ' Main
22   End Module ' WeatherServer
```

Fig. 23.12 | Class `WeatherServer` exposes remote class `ReportInfo`. (Part 2 of 2.)

Lines 12–13 in `Main` register an HTTP channel on the current machine at port 50000—the port number that clients will use to connect to the `WeatherServer` remotely. The argument `False` in line 13 indicates that we do not wish to enable security, which is beyond the scope of this introduction. Lines 16–17 register the `ReportInfo` class type at the "Report" URI as a `Singleton` remote class. If a remote class is registered as **`Singleton`**, only one remote object will be created when the first client requests that remote class, and that remote object will service all clients. The alternative mode is **`SingleCall`**, where one remote object is created for each individual remote method call to the remote class. [*Note:* A `Singleton` remote object will be garbage collected after being idle for 5 minutes. A new `Singleton` remote object will be created by the server if another client requests one later. The article `msdn.microsoft.com/msdnmag/issues/03/12/LeaseManager/default.aspx` provides more information on the lifetime of remote objects.] The `ReportInfo` remote class is now available to clients at the URI "`http://`*IPAddress*`:50000/Report`" where *IPAddress* is the IP address of the computer on which the server is running. The channel remains open as long as the server application continues running, so line 20 waits for the user running the server application to press **Enter** before terminating the application.

Class *FrmWeatherClient*

`FrmWeatherClient` (Fig. 23.13) is a Windows application that uses .NET remoting to retrieve weather information from the `WeatherServer` and displays the information in a graphical, easy-to-read manner. The GUI contains 43 `Label`s—each displays the weather information for one city in the *Traveler's Forecast*. The `Label`s are placed in a `Panel` with a vertical scroll bar. Lines 5–7 are `Imports` statements for the namespaces that are required to perform .NET remoting. For this project, you must add references to the assembly `System.Runtime.Remoting` and the `Weather.dll` file we created earlier.

Method `FrmWeatherClient_Load` (lines 12–85) retrieves the weather information when this Windows application loads. Line 15 creates an HTTP channel without specifying a port number. This causes the `HttpChannel` constructor to choose any available port number on the client computer. A specific port number is not necessary because this

```vb
1    ' Fig. 23.13: WeatherClient.vb
2    ' Client that uses .NET remoting to retrieve a weather report.
3    Imports System.Collections
4    Imports System.Drawing
5    Imports System.Runtime.Remoting
6    Imports System.Runtime.Remoting.Channels
7    Imports System.Runtime.Remoting.Channels.Http
8    Imports Weather
9
10   Public Class FrmWeatherClient
11      ' retrieve weather data
12      Private Sub FrmWeatherClient_Load(ByVal sender As System.Object, _
13         ByVal e As System.EventArgs) Handles MyBase.Load
14         ' setup HTTP channel, does not need to provide a port number
15         Dim channel As New HttpChannel()
16         ChannelServices.RegisterChannel(channel, False)
17
18         ' obtain a proxy for an object that implements interface Report
19         Dim info As Report = CType(RemotingServices.Connect( _
20            GetType(Report), "http://localhost:50000/Report"), Report)
21
22         ' retrieve an ArrayList of CityWeather objects
23         Dim cities As ArrayList = info.Reports
24
25         ' create array and populate it with every Label
26         Dim cityLabels(43) As Label
27         Dim labelCounter As Integer = 0
28
29         Dim control As Control
30         For Each control In pnlDisplay.Controls
31            If TypeOf control Is Label Then
32               cityLabels(labelCounter) = CType(control, Label)
33               labelCounter += 1 ' increment Label counter
34            End If
35         Next control
36
37         ' create Hashtable and populate with all weather conditions
38         Dim weather As New Hashtable()
39         weather.Add("SUNNY", "sunny")
40         weather.Add("PTCLDY", "pcloudy")
41         weather.Add("CLOUDY", "mcloudy")
42         weather.Add("MOCLDY", "mcloudy")
43         weather.Add("VRYCLD", "mcloudy")
44         weather.Add("TSTRMS", "rain")
45         weather.Add("RAIN", "rain")
46         weather.Add("FZRAIN", "rain")
47         weather.Add("SNOW", "snow")
48         weather.Add("VRYHOT", "vryhot")
49         weather.Add("FAIR", "fair")
50         weather.Add("RNSNOW", "rnsnow")
51         weather.Add("SHWRS", "showers")
```

Fig. 23.13 | Class `WeatherClient` accesses a `ReportInfo` object remotely and displays the weather report. (Part 1 of 2.)

```
52        weather.Add("WINDY", "windy")
53        weather.Add("NOINFO", "noinfo")
54        weather.Add("MISG", "noinfo")
55        weather.Add("DRZL", "rain")
56        weather.Add("HAZE", "noinfo")
57        weather.Add("SMOKE", "mcloudy")
58        weather.Add("SNOSHW", "snow")
59        weather.Add("FLRRYS", "snow")
60        weather.Add("FOG", "noinfo")
61
62        ' create the font for the text output
63        Dim font As New Font("Courier New", 8, FontStyle.Bold)
64
65        ' for every city
66        For i As Integer = 0 To cities.Count - 1
67           ' use array cityLabels to find the next Label
68           Dim currentCity As Label = cityLabels(i)
69
70           ' use ArrayList cities to find the next CityWeather object
71           Dim city As CityWeather = CType(cities(i), CityWeather)
72
73           ' set current Label's image to image
74           ' corresponding to the city's weather condition -
75           ' find correct image name in Hashtable weather
76           currentCity.Image = New Bitmap("images\" & _
77              weather(city.Description.Trim()).ToString() & ".png")
78           currentCity.Font = font ' set font of Label
79           currentCity.ForeColor = Color.White ' set text color of Label
80
81           ' set Label's text to city name and temperature
82           currentCity.Text = _
83              vbCrLf & " " & city.CityName & city.Temperature
84        Next
85     End Sub ' FrmWeatherClient_Load
86  End Class ' FrmWeatherClient
```

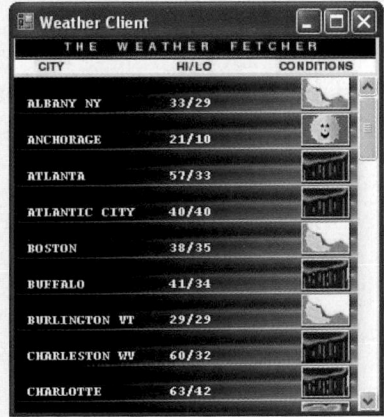 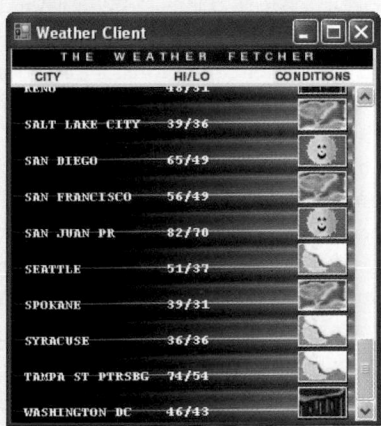

Fig. 23.13 | Class `WeatherClient` accesses a `ReportInfo` object remotely and displays the weather report. (Part 2 of 2.)

application does not have its own clients that need to know the port number in advance. Line 16 registers the channel on the client computer. This will allow the server to send information back to the client. Lines 19–20 declare a Report variable and assign to it a proxy for a Report object instantiated by the server. This proxy allows the client to remotely call ReportInfo's properties by redirecting method calls to the server. Remoting-Services method Connect connects to the server and returns a reference to the proxy for the Report object. For testing purposes, we execute the client and the server on the same computer, so we use localhost in the URL that represents the server application. To connect to a WeatherServer on a different computer, you must replace localhost with the name or IP address of the server computer. Line 23 retrieves the ArrayList of City-Weather objects generated by the ReportInfo constructor (lines 12–46 of Fig. 23.11). Variable cities now refers to an ArrayList of CityWeather objects that contains the information taken from the *Traveler's Forecast* Web page.

Because the application presents weather data for so many cities, we must establish a way to organize the information in the Labels and to ensure that each weather description is accompanied by an appropriate image. The program uses an array to store all the Labels, and a Hashtable (discussed further in Chapter 27, Collections) to store weather descriptions and the names of their corresponding images. A Hashtable stores key–value pairs, in which both the key and the value can be any type of object. Method Add adds key–value pairs to a Hashtable. The class also provides an indexer to return the values for particular keys in the Hashtable. Line 26 creates an array of Label references, and lines 30–35 place the Labels we created in the IDE's Form designer in the array so that they can be accessed programmatically to display weather information for individual cities. Line 38 creates Hashtable object weather to store pairs of weather conditions and the names for images associated with those conditions. Note that a given weather-description name does not necessarily correspond to the name of the PNG file containing the correct image. For example, both "TSTRMS" and "RAIN" weather conditions use the rain.png image file.

Lines 66–84 set each Label so that it contains a city name, the current temperature in the city and an image corresponding to the weather conditions for that city. Line 68 retrieves the Label that will display the weather information for the next city. Line 71 uses ArrayList cities to retrieve the CityWeather object that contains the weather information for the city. Lines 76–77 set the Label's image to the PNG image that corresponds to the city's weather conditions. This is done by eliminating any spaces in the description string by calling String method Trim and retrieving the name of the PNG image from the weather Hashtable. Lines 78–79 set Label's Font property to the Font object created at line 63, and the ForeColor property to white for readability against the black and blue background image on the Label. Lines 82–83 set the Text property to display the city's name and high/low temperatures. [*Note:* To preserve the layout of the client application's window, we set the MaximumSize and MinimumSize properties of the Windows Form to the same value so that the user cannot resize the window.]

Web Resources for .NET Remoting

This section provided a basic introduction to .NET remoting. There is much more to this powerful .NET framework capability. The following Web sites provide additional information. Searching for ".NET remoting" with most search engines yields many additional resources.

msdn.microsoft.com/library/en-us/cpguide/html/cpconaccessingobjectsinotherap-
plicationdomainsusingnetremoting.asp

The *.NET Framework Developer's Guide* on the MSDN Web site provides detailed information on
.NET remoting, including articles that include choosing between ASP.NET and .NET remoting,
an overview of .NET remoting, advanced .NET remoting techniques and .NET remoting examples.

msdn.microsoft.com/library/en-us/dndotnet/html/introremoting.asp

Offers a general overview of .NET remoting capabilties.

search.microsoft.com/search/results.aspx?qu=.net+remoting

Provides links to many .NET remoting articles and resources.

23.11 Wrap-Up

In this chapter, we presented both connection-oriented and connectionless networking
techniques. You learned that the Internet is an "unreliable" network that simply transmits
packets of data. We discussed two protocols for transmitting packets over the Internet—
the Transmission Control Protocol (TCP) and the User Datagram Protocol (UDP). You
learned that TCP is a connection-oriented communication protocol that guarantees sent
packets will arrive at the intended receiver undamaged and in the correct sequence. You
also learned that UDP is typically used in certain types of performance-oriented applications because it incurs minimum overhead for communicating between applications. We
presented some of .NET's capabilities for implementing communications with TCP and
UDP. We showed how to create a simple client/server chat application using stream sockets. We then showed how to send datagrams between a client and a server. You also saw a
multithreaded Tic-Tac-Toe server that allows two clients to connect simultaneously to the
server and play Tic-Tac-Toe against one another. We presented the new WebBrowser class,
which allows you to add Web browsing capabilities to your Windows applications. Finally, we demonstrated .NET remoting, a technology that allows a client application to remotely access the properties and methods of an object instantiated by a server application.
In Chapter 24, Data Structures, you will learn about dynamic data structures that can
grow or shrink at execution time.

Summary

Section 23.1 Introduction

- The Internet ties the information world together.
- The Web makes the Internet easy to use and gives it the flair and sizzle of multimedia.

Section 23.2 Connection-Oriented vs. Connectionless Communication

- There are two primary approaches to communicating between applications—connection oriented and connectionless.
- Connection-oriented communications are similar to the telephone system, in which a connection is established and held for the length of the session.
- Connectionless services are similar to the postal service, in which two letters mailed at the same
  time from one place to the same destination may actually take two dramatically different paths
  through the system and even arrive at different times, or not at all.
- Data is sent by TCP in packets that contain pieces of the data along with information that helps
  the Internet route the packets to the proper destination.

- The Internet does not guarantee anything about the packets sent; they could arrive corrupted or out of order, as duplicates or not at all. The Internet makes only a "best effort" to deliver packets.

- A connection-oriented approach guarantees that sent packets will arrive at the intended recipient undamaged and be reassembled into the correct sequence.

- In a connectionless approach, data sent may never reach the intended recipient. A connectionless approach, however, avoids the overhead associated with handshaking and enforcing reliability—less information often needs to be passed between the hosts.

Section 23.3 Protocols for Transporting Data

- Protocols are sets of rules that govern how two entities interact.

- .NET's Transmission Control Protocol (TCP) and User Datagram Protocol (UDP) networking capabilities are defined by classes of the System.Net.Sockets namespace.

- The Transmission Control Protocol (TCP) is a connection-oriented communication protocol that guarantees that sent packets will arrive at the intended recipient undamaged and in the correct sequence.

- If packets of information don't arrive at the recipient, TCP ensures that the packets are sent again. If packets arrive out of order, TCP reassembles them into the correct order, transparently to the application receiving the data. If duplicate packets arrive, TCP discards the duplicates.

- Applications that do not require reliable end-to-end transmission typically use the connectionless User Datagram Protocol (UDP).

- UDP makes no guarantees that packets, called datagrams, will reach their destination or arrive in their original order.

- UDP has little overhead because UDP datagrams do not need to carry the information that TCP packets carry to ensure reliability. This makes UDP desirable for streaming audio and video applications that can tolerate occasional datagram loss.

Section 23.4 Establishing a Simple TCP Server Using Stream Sockets

- Class IPAddress represents an Internet Protocol (IP) address.

- Establishing a simple server with TCP and stream sockets in .NET requires several steps. Step 1 is to create a TcpListener object. This class represents a TCP stream socket that a server can use to receive connections. To receive connections, the TcpListener must be listening for them. For the TcpListener to listen for client connections, its Start method must be called (Step 2). Tcp-Listener method AcceptSocket blocks indefinitely until a connection is established, at which point it returns a Socket (Step 3). Step 4 is the processing phase, in which the server and the client communicate via streams maintained by a NetworkStream object. When the client and server have finished communicating, the server closes the connection (Step 5). The server can then wait for another client's connection.

- A port number is an Integer ID number that an application uses to identify itself at a given network address.

- An individual application running on a computer is identified by an IP address/port number pair. Thus, no two processes can have the same port number at a given IP address.

Section 23.5 Establishing a Simple TCP Client Using Stream Sockets

- Class IPEndPoint represents an endpoint on a network.

- Establishing a simple client requires four steps. Step 1 is to create a TcpClient to connect to the server. This connection is established by calling TcpClient method Connect with two arguments—the server's IP address and the port number. In Step 2, the TcpClient uses method Get-

Stream to get a NetworkStream to write to and read from the server. Step 3 is the processing phase, in which the client and the server communicate. In Step 4, the client closes the connection.

Section 23.7 Connectionless Client/Server Interaction with Datagrams
- Class UdpClient is provided for connectionless transmission of data.
- Class UdpClient methods Send and Receive are used to transmit data.

Section 23.8 Client/Server Tic-Tac-Toe Using a Multithreaded Server
- Multithreaded servers can manage many simultaneous connections with multiple clients.

Section 23.9 WebBrowser Class
- Class WebBrowser provides Web browsing functionality and maintains its own navigation history.
- WebBrowser methods GoBack, GoForward, GoHome and Navigate are used for Web navigation. Method Stop cancels loading of the current page, and method Refresh reloads the current page.
- Many WebBrowser events, including StatusTextChanged, ProgressChanged and Document-TitleChanged, indicate changes in WebBrowser properties. The Navigating event occurs when the WebBrowser starts loading a page, and the DocumentCompleted event occurs when the page is finished loading.

Section 23.10 .NET Remoting
- .NET remoting is a distributed computing technology that allows a program to access objects on another machine over a network.
- .NET remoting is similar in concept to RMI (remote method invocation) in Java and RPC (remote procedure calls) in procedural programming languages.
- Marshal-by-value requires that the object be serializable—capable of being represented as a formatted message which the server can send through a channel to the client. To enable an object to be serialized and deserialized, its class must either be declared with the attribute <Serializable()> or must implement interface ISerializable.
- Marshal-by-reference requires that the object's class extend MarshalByRefObject. An object that is marshaled by reference is known as a remote object, and its class is referred to as a remote class.
- When an object is marshaled by reference, the client creates two proxy objects, a transparent proxy and a real proxy. The client application calls the methods and properties of the transparent proxy as if it were the remote object itself. The transparent proxy calls the real proxy to send a message to the server to perform the appropriate actions on the actual object.
- The parameters and return values of the methods and properties declared by a remote class will themselves be marshaled by value.
- Namespaces System.Runtime.Remoting and System.Runtime.Remoting.Channels are required for .NET remoting. Namespace System.Runtime.Remoting.Channels.Http is required for HTTP channels and is found in reference System.Runtime.Remoting.
- Class HttpChannel represents an HTTP channel. Its constructor takes an Integer port number. Shared method RegisterChannel of class ChannelServices takes an object of a class that implements interface IChannel, such as HttpChannel, and registers it on the local machine.
- Shared method RegisterWellKnownServiceType of class RemotingConfiguration takes a Type, a URI extension and a mode, Singleton or SingleCall, as arguments and makes the class type available to respond to clients that access the class at that URI.
- A Singleton remote class instantiates one remote object to service all clients. A SingleCall remote class instantiates one remote object for each individual method call.

- Shared method `Connect` of class `RemotingServices` takes a `Type` and a `URI` as arguments and returns a reference to the transparent proxy that enables method calls to the remote object.

- A `Hashtable` stores key–value pairs, in which both the key and the value can be any type of object. Method `Add` adds key–value pairs to a `Hashtable`. The indexer returns the value with which a particular key was placed in the `Hashtable`.

Terminology

127.0.0.1
`AcceptSocket` method of class `TcpListener`
`Add` method of class `Hashtable`
`BinaryReader` class
`BinaryWriter` class
`Bind` method of class `Socket`
binding a server to a port
blocking until connection received
`CanGoBack` property of class `WebBrowser`
`CanGoForward` property of class `WebBrowser`
channel
client
client/server chat application
client/server relationship
`Close` method of class `Socket`
`Close` method of class `TcpClient`
collaborative applications
`Connect` method of class `RemotingService`
`Connect` method of class `TcpClient`
connection attempt
connection between applications
connection between client and server terminates
connection port
connection to a client
connectionless communication
connectionless transmission via datagrams
connection-oriented communication
datagram
deserialize an object
`DocumentCompleted` event of class `WebBrowser`
`DocumentTitle` property of class `WebBrowser`
`DocumentTitleChanged` event of class
    `WebBrowser`
echo a packet
`Exit` method of class `Environment`
`ExitCode` property of class `Environment`
`GetStream` method of class `Socket`
`GoBack` method of class `WebBrowser`
`GoForward` method of class `WebBrowser`
`GoHome` method of class `WebBrowser`
handshaking
`HashTable` class

HTTP channel
IP (Internet Protocol) address
`IPAddress` class
`IPEndPoint` class
`Invoke` method
`InvokeRequired` property
`ISerializable` interface
localhost
`Loopback` Shared member of class `IPAddress`
marshal-by-reference
marshal-by-value
`MarshalByRefObject` class Marshaling
`Navigate` method of class `WebBrowser`
`Navigating` event of class `WebBrowser`
.NET remoting
network address
`NetworkStream` class
packet
port number
`ProgressChanged` event of class `WebBrowser`
protocol
proxy
`ReadString` method of class `BinaryReader`
real proxy
receive a request for connection
`Receive` method of class `UdpClient`
`ReceiveFrom` method of class `Socket`
`Refresh` method of class `WebBrowser`
remote class
`RemotingService` class
`Send` method of class `UdpClient`
`SendTo` method of class `Socket`
`Serializable` attribute
serialize an object
server
`SingleCall`
`Singleton`
socket
`Socket` class
`Sort` method of class `ArrayList`
`Start` method of class `TcpListener`
`StatusText` property of class `WebBrowser`

StatusTextChanged event of class WebBrowser
Stop method of class WebBrowser
stream socket
streams-based transmission
System.Net namespace
System.Net.Sockets namespace
System.Runtime.Remoting namespace
System.Runtime.Remoting.Channels
   namespace
System.RuntimeRemoting.Channels.HTTP
   namespace

TCP channel
TcpClient class
TcpListener class
Transmission Control Protocol (TCP)
transparent proxy
UdpClient class
Uniform Resource Identifier (URI)
User Datagram Protocol (UDP)
WebBrowser class
WebClient class
Write method of class BinaryWriter

Self-Review Exercises

23.1 State whether each of the following is *true* or *false*. If *false*, explain why.
a) UDP is a connection-oriented protocol.
b) Packet transmission over a network is reliable—packets are guaranteed to arrive in sequence.
c) TCP is preferred over UDP when applications require reliable packet transmission.
d) Each TcpListener can accept only one connection.
e) A TcpListener can listen for connections at more than one port at a time.
f) A UdpClient can send information only to one particular port.
g) Clients must know the port number at which the server is waiting for connections in order to connect to the server.
h) When an object is marshaled by reference, a copy of that object is created and sent to the client.
i) A Singleton remote class instantiates one remote object for each client.

23.2 Fill in the blanks in each of the following statements:
a) Many of .NET's networking classes are contained in namespaces _____ and _____.
b) Class _____ is used for unreliable but fast datagram transmission.
c) An object of class _____ represents an Internet Protocol (IP) address.
d) The two socket types discussed in this chapter are _____ and _____ sockets.
e) The acronym TCP stands for _____.
f) Class _____ listens for connections from clients.
g) Class _____ connects to TCP servers.
h) Class _____ provides access to stream data on a network.
i) Method _____ causes a WebBrowser to go to a particular URL.
j) A serializable class must either be declared with attribute _____ or extend class _____.
k) The _____ provides all the Public services of the remote object being marshaled by reference.

Answers to Self-Review Exercises

23.1 a) False. UDP is a connectionless protocol, and TCP is a connection-oriented protocol. b) False. Packets can be lost, arrive out of order or even be duplicated. c) True. d) False. TcpListener's AcceptSocket method may be called as often as necessary—each call will accept a new connection. e) False. A TcpListener can listen for connections at only one port at a time. f) False. A UdpClient can send information to any port represented by an IPEndPoint. g) True. h) False. When an object is marshaled by reference, the client application accesses the original remote object on the server, not a local copy. i) False. A `Singleton` remote class instantiates one remote object to service all clients.

23.2   a) `System.Net`, `System.Net.Sockets`. b) `UdpClient`. c) `IPAddress`. d) stream, datagram. e) Transmission Control Protocol. f) `TcpListener`. g) `TcpClient`. h) `NetworkStream`. i) `Navigate`. j) `Serializable`, `ISerializable`. k) transparent proxy.

Exercises

23.3   Use a socket connection to allow a client to specify a text file's name and have the server send the contents of the file or indicate that the file does not exist.

23.4   Modify Exercise 23.3 to allow the client to modify the contents of the file and send the file back to the server for storage. The user can edit the file in a `TextBox`, then click an `Update file on server` button to send the file back to the server.

23.5   Multithreaded servers are quite popular today, especially because of the increasing use of multiprocessing servers. Modify the simple server application presented in Section 23.6 to be a multithreaded server. Then use several client applications and have each of them connect to the server simultaneously. Use a `HashTable` (namespace `System.Collections`) to store the client threads. `HashTable` provides several properties and methods of use in this exercise. Property `Keys` returns an `ICollection` of keys currently found in the `HashTable`. Each key can then be used in the `HashTable`'s indexer to retrieve the corresponding value. Method `Add` places its arguments—a key and a value—into the `HashTable`. Method `Remove` deletes its argument—the key—from the `HashTable`.

23.6   Create a client/server application for the game of Hangman, using socket connections. The server should randomly pick a word or phrase from a file. After connecting, the client should be allowed to begin guessing. If a client guesses incorrectly five times, the game is over. Display the original phrase or word on the server. Display dashes (for letters that have not been guessed yet) and the letters that have been guessed in the word or phrase on the client. Model your client and server applications after the following screen captures:

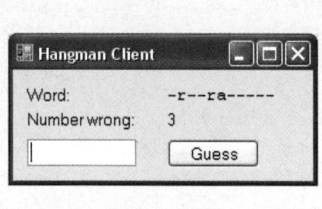

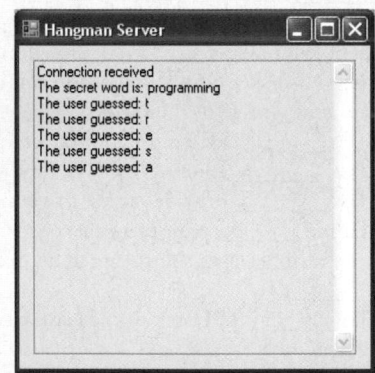

23.7   Modify the previous exercise to be a connectionless game using datagrams.

23.8   (*Checkers Game*) In the text, we presented a Tic-Tac-Toe program controlled by a multithreaded server. Develop a checkers program modeled after the Tic-Tac-Toe program. The two users should alternate making moves. Your program should mediate the players' moves, determining whose turn it is and allowing only valid moves. The players themselves will determine when the game is over. [*Caution:* This is a large project.]

23.9 *(Networked Morse Code)* Perhaps the most famous of all coding schemes is the Morse code, developed by Samuel Morse in the 1830s for use with the telegraph system. The Morse code assigns a series of dots and dashes to each letter of the alphabet, each digit and a few special characters (such as period, comma, colon and semicolon). In sound-oriented systems, the dot represents a short sound and the dash represents a long sound. Other representations of dots and dashes are used with light-oriented systems and signal-flag systems.

Separation between words is indicated by a space, or quite simply, the absence of a dot or dash. In a sound-oriented system, a space is indicated by a short period of time during which no sound is transmitted. The international version of the Morse code appears in Fig. 23.14.

Write a client/server application in which two clients can send Morse code messages to each other through a multithreaded server application. The client application should allow the user to type English-language phrases in a TextBox. When the user sends the message, the client application encodes the text in Morse code and sends the coded message through the server to the other client. Use one blank before and after each Morse-coded letter and three blanks before and after each Morse-coded word. When messages are received, they should be decoded and displayed as normal characters and as Morse code. The client should have one TextBox for typing and one TextBox for displaying the other client's messages.

Character	Code	Character	Code
A	.-	T	-
B	-...	U	..-
C	-.-.	V	...-
D	-..	W	.--
E	.	X	-..-
F	..-.	Y	-.--
G	--.	Z	--..
H	....		
I	..	Digits	
J	.---	0	-----
K	-.-	1	.----
L	.-..	2	..---
M	--	3	...--
N	-.	4	....-
O	---	5	.....
P	.--.	6	-....
Q	--.-	7	--...
R	.-.	8	---..
S	...	9	----.

Fig. 23.14 | English letters of the alphabet and decimal digits as expressed in international Morse code.

23.10   Write a bulletin board application that uses .NET remoting. Create a remote object that will allow the client application to list all available bulletins, retrieve the text of any bulletin and post a new bulletin. Each bulletin should be stored in a .txt file in the server's directory. Refer to Chapter 18, Files and Streams.

23.11   Write a quiz application that uses .NET remoting. Store one quiz question in a text file on the server machine. Allow the client to retrieve the question from the server and send an answer back to the server. You may wish to store records of who answered the quiz question correctly so the server can keep score.

24

Data Structures

OBJECTIVES

In this chapter you will learn:

- To form linked data structures using references, self-referential classes and recursion.

- How boxing and unboxing enable primitive-type values to be used where `Object`s are expected in a program.

- To create and manipulate dynamic data structures, such as linked lists, queues, stacks and binary trees.

- Various important applications of linked data structures.

- To create reusable data structures with classes, inheritance and composition.

24.1 **Introduction**

This chapter begins our three-chapter data structures treatment. The **data structures** that we've studied thus far have had fixed sizes, such as one- and two-dimensional arrays. Here we introduce **dynamic data structures** that can grow and shrink at execution time. Linked lists are collections of data items "lined up in a row"—users can make insertions and deletions anywhere in a linked list. Stacks are important in compilers and operating systems; insertions and deletions are made at only one end—the **top** of the stack. Queues represent waiting lines; insertions are only made at the back (also referred to as the **tail**) of a queue, and deletions are made only from the front (also referred to as the **head**) of a queue. Binary trees facilitate high-speed searching and sorting of data, efficient elimination of duplicate data items, representation of file system directories and compilation of expressions into machine language. All these data structures have many other interesting applications as well.

    We will discuss each of these data structures and implement programs that create and manipulate them. We use classes, inheritance and composition to create and package these data structures for reusability and maintainability. In Chapter 25, Generics, we introduce generics, which allow you to declare data structures that can be easily adapted to contain data of any type. In Chapter 26, Collections, we discuss the FCL's predefined classes that implement various data structures.

    The chapter examples are practical programs that will be useful in more advanced courses and in industrial applications. The programs focus on reference manipulation. The exercises offer a rich collection of useful applications.

24.2 **Primitive-Type Structures; Boxing and Unboxing**

The data structures we discuss in this chapter store `Object` references. As you'll soon see, these data structures can store both primitive- and reference-type values. This section discusses the mechanisms that enable primitive-type values to be manipulated as objects.

Primitive-Type Structures

Each primitive type (Appendix L, Primitive Types) has a corresponding `Structure` in namespace `System` that declares the primitive type. These `Structures` are called `Boolean`, `Byte`, `SByte`, `Char`, `Decimal`, `Double`, `Single`, `Int16`, `UInt16`, `Int32`, `UInt32`, `Int64` and `UInt64`. Types declared with keyword `Structure` are implicitly value types.

Primitive types are actually aliases for their corresponding Structures, so a variable of a primitive type can be declared using the primitive type's keyword or the Structure name—e.g., Integer and Int32 are interchangeable. The methods related to a primitive type are located in the corresponding Structure (e.g., method Parse, which converts a String to an Integer value, is located in Structure Int32). Refer to the online documentation for each Structure type to see the methods for manipulating values of that type.

Boxing and Unboxing Conversions

All primitive-type Structures inherit from class **ValueType** (namespace System). Class ValueType inherits from class Object. Thus, any primitive-type value can be assigned to an Object variable; this is referred to as **boxing**. With boxing, a primitive-type value is copied into an object so that the primitive-type value can be manipulated as an Object. Boxing can be performed either explicitly or implicitly, as shown in the following statements:

```
Dim i As Integer = 5 ' create an Integer value
Dim object1 As Object = _
   CType(i, Object) ' explicitly box the Integer value
Dim object2 As Object = i ' implicitly box the Integer value
```

After executing the preceding code, both object1 and object2 refer to two different objects that contain a copy of the integer value in Integer variable i.

Unboxing can be used to explicitly convert an Object reference to a primitive value, as shown in the following statement:

```
' explicitly unbox the Integer value
Dim int1 As Integer = CType(object1, Integer)
```

Explicitly attempting to unbox an Object reference that does not refer to the correct primitive value type causes an **InvalidCastException**.

In Chapters 25 and 26, we discuss Visual Basic's generics and .NET's generic collections. As you will see, generics eliminate the overhead of boxing and unboxing by enabling us to create and use collections of specific value types.

24.3 Self-Referential Classes

A self-referential class contains a reference member that refers to an object of the same class type. For example, the class declaration in Fig. 24.1 defines the shell of a self-referential class named Node. This type has two Private instance variables—Integer dataValue and Node reference nextNodeReference. Member nextNodeReference references an object of type Node, an object of the same type as the one being declared here—thus the term "self-referential class." Member nextNodeReference is referred to as a link (i.e., nextNodeReference can be used to "tie" an object of type Node to another object of the same type). Class Node also has two properties—one for instance variable dataValue (named Data) and another for instance variable nextNodeReference (named NextNode).

Self-referential objects can be linked together to form useful data structures, such as lists, queues, stacks and trees. Figure 24.2 illustrates two self-referential objects linked together to form a linked list. A backslash (representing a Nothing reference) is placed in the link member of the second self-referential object to indicate that the link does not refer to another object. A Nothing reference normally indicates the end of a data structure.

```
 1    ' Fig. 24.01: Node.vb
 2    ' Self-referential Node class.
 3    Class Node
 4       Private dataValue As Integer
 5       Private nextNodeReference As Node
 6
 7       Public Sub New(ByVal value As Integer)
 8          ' constructor body
 9       End Sub ' New
10
11       ' Property Data
12       Public Property Data() As Integer
13          Get
14             ' get body
15          End Get
16          Set(ByVal value As Integer)
17             ' set body
18          End Set
19       End Property ' Data
20
21       ' Property NextNode
22       Public Property NextNode As Node
23          Get
24             ' get next node
25          End Get
26          Set(ByVal nodeReference As Node)
27             ' set next node
28          End Set
29       End Property ' NextNode
30    End Class 'Node
```

Fig. 24.1 | Self-referential **Node** class declaration skeleton.

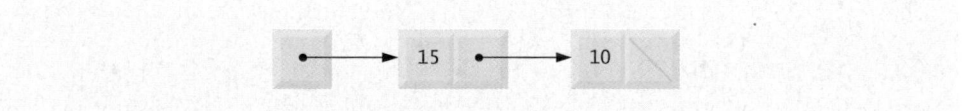

Fig. 24.2 | Self-referential class objects linked together.

Creating and maintaining dynamic data structures requires dynamic memory allocation—a program's ability to obtain more memory space at execution time to hold new nodes and to release space no longer needed. As you learned in Section 9.9, Visual Basic programs do not explicitly release dynamically allocated memory—rather, Visual Basic performs automatic garbage collection.

The New operator is essential to dynamic memory allocation. New takes as an operand the type of the object being dynamically allocated and returns a reference to an object of that type. For example, the statement

```
Dim nodeToAdd As New Node(10)
```

allocates the appropriate amount of memory to store a `Node` and stores a reference to this object in `nodeToAdd`. If no memory is available, `New` throws an `OutOfMemoryException`. The constructor argument `10` specifies the `Node` object's data.

The following sections discuss lists, stacks, queues and trees. These data structures are created and maintained with dynamic memory allocation and self-referential classes.

24.4 **Linked Lists**

A linked list is a linear collection (i.e., a sequence) of self-referential class objects called nodes, connected by reference links—thus the term "linked" list. A program accesses a linked list via a reference to the first node of the list. Each subsequent node is accessed via the link-reference member stored in the previous node. By convention, the link reference in the last node of a list is set to `Nothing` to mark the end of the list. Data is stored in a linked list dynamically—that is, each node is created as necessary. You can declare a node's class to store data of any type, including references to objects of other classes. Stacks and queues are also linear data structures—in fact, they are constrained versions of linked lists. Trees are non-linear data structures.

Lists of data can be stored in arrays, but linked lists provide several advantages. A linked list is appropriate when the number of data elements to be represented in the data structure is unpredictable. Unlike a linked list, the size of a conventional Visual Basic array cannot be altered, because the array size is fixed at creation time. Conventional arrays can become full, but linked lists become full only when the system has insufficient memory to satisfy dynamic memory allocation requests.

Performance Tip 24.1

An array can be declared to contain more elements than the number of items expected, possibly wasting memory. Linked lists provide better memory utilization in these situations, because they can grow and shrink at execution time.

Performance Tip 24.2

After locating the insertion point for a new item in a sorted linked list, inserting an element in the list is fast—only two references have to be modified. All existing nodes remain at their current locations in memory.

Programmers can maintain linked lists in sorted order simply by inserting each new element at the proper point in the list (locating the proper insertion point does take time). Existing list elements do not need to be moved.

Performance Tip 24.3

The elements of an array are stored contiguously in memory to allow immediate access to any array element—the address of any element can be calculated directly from its index. Linked lists do not afford such immediate access to their elements—an element can be accessed only by traversing the list from the front.

Performance Tip 24.4

Insertion and deletion in a sorted array can be time consuming—all the elements following the inserted or deleted element must be shifted appropriately.

Normally, linked-list nodes are not stored contiguously in memory. Rather, the nodes are said to be logically contiguous. Figure 24.3 illustrates a linked list with several nodes.

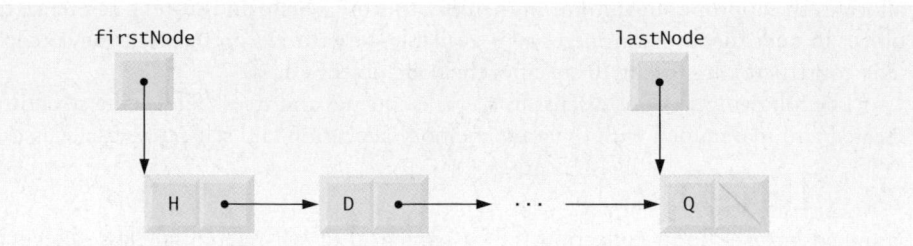

Fig. 24.3 | Linked list graphical representation.

Performance Tip 24.5

Using linked data structures and dynamic memory allocation (instead of arrays) for data structures that grow and shrink can save memory. Keep in mind, however, that reference links occupy space, and dynamic memory allocation incurs the overhead of method calls.

Linked List Implementation

The program in Figs. 24.4 and 24.5 uses an object of class List to manipulate a list of miscellaneous object types. The Main method of class ListTest (Fig. 24.5) creates a list of objects, inserts objects at the beginning of the list using List method InsertAtFront, inserts objects at the end of the list using List method InsertAtBack, deletes objects from the front of the list using List method RemoveFromFront and deletes objects from the end of the list using List method RemoveFromBack. After each insertion and deletion operation, the program invokes List method Print to display the current list contents. If an attempt is made to remove an item from an empty list, an EmptyListException is thrown. A detailed discussion of the program follows.

The program consists of four classes—ListNode (Fig. 24.4, lines 4–37), List (lines 40–153), EmptyListException (lines 156–160) and ListTest (Fig. 24.5). The classes in Fig. 24.4 create a linked-list library that can be reused throughout this chapter. You should place the code from Fig. 24.4 in its own class library project as described in Section 9.13. Name the project LinkedListLibrary.

Encapsulated in each List object is a linked list of ListNode objects. Class ListNode (Fig. 24.4, lines 4–37) contains instance variables dataValue and nextNodeReference. Member dataValue can refer to any object. [*Note:* Typically, a data structure will contain data of only one type, or data of any type derived from one base type.] In this example, we use data of various types derived from Object to demonstrate that our List class can store data of any type. Member nextNodeReference stores a reference to the next ListNode object in the linked list. The ListNode constructors (lines 10–12 and 16–19) enable us to initialize a ListNode that will be placed at the end of a List or before a specific ListNode in a List, respectively. A List accesses the ListNode member variables via properties NextNode (lines 22–29) and Data (lines 32–36), respectively.

```
1    ' Fig. 24.4: LinkedListLibrary.vb
2    ' Class ListNode and class List declarations.
3
```

Fig. 24.4 | ListNode, List and EmptyListException classes. (Part 1 of 4.)

```vbnet
4    Public Class ListNode
5       Private dataValue As Object ' stores data for this node
6       Private nextNodeReference As ListNode ' stores reference to next node
7
8       ' constructor to create a ListNode that contains data
9       ' and is the last node in the List
10      Public Sub New(ByVal data As Object)
11         MyClass.New(data, Nothing) ' invokes the other constructor
12      End Sub ' New
13
14      ' constructor to create a ListNode that contains data
15      ' and refers to the next ListNode in the List
16      Public Sub New(ByVal data As Object, ByVal nextNode As ListNode)
17         dataValue = data
18         nextNodeReference = nextNode
19      End Sub ' New
20
21      ' property NextNode
22      Public Property NextNode() As ListNode
23         Get
24            Return nextNodeReference
25         End Get
26         Set(ByVal value As ListNode)
27            nextNodeReference = value
28         End Set
29      End Property ' NextNode
30
31      ' property Data
32      Public ReadOnly Property Data() As Object
33         Get
34            Return dataValue
35         End Get
36      End Property ' Data
37   End Class ' ListNode
38
39   ' class List declaration
40   Public Class List
41      Private firstNode As ListNode
42      Private lastNode As ListNode
43      Private name As String ' string like "list" to display
44
45      ' construct empty List with "list" as its name
46      Public Sub New()
47         MyClass.New("list") ' invokes the other constructor
48      End Sub ' New
49
50      ' construct empty List with specified name
51      Public Sub New(ByVal listName As String)
52         name = listName
53         firstNode = Nothing
54         lastNode = Nothing
55      End Sub ' New
56
```

Fig. 24.4 | ListNode, List and EmptyListException classes. (Part 2 of 4.)

```vb
57      ' Insert object at front of List. If List is empty, firstNode and
58      ' lastNode will refer to same object. Otherwise, firstNode refers
59      ' to new node and the new node refers to the previous first node.
60      Public Sub InsertAtFront(ByVal insertItem As Object)
61          If IsEmpty() Then
62              lastNode = New ListNode(insertItem)
63              firstNode = lastNode
64          Else
65              firstNode = New ListNode(insertItem, firstNode)
66          End If
67      End Sub ' InsertAtFront
68
69      ' Insert object at end of List. If List is empty,
70      ' firstNode and lastNode will refer to same object.
71      ' Otherwise, lastNode's NextNode property refers to new node.
72      Public Sub InsertAtBack(ByVal insertItem As Object)
73          If IsEmpty() Then
74              lastNode = New ListNode(insertItem)
75              firstNode = lastNode
76          Else
77              lastNode.NextNode = New ListNode(insertItem)
78              lastNode = lastNode.NextNode
79          End If
80      End Sub ' InsertAtBack
81
82      ' remove first node from List
83      Public Function RemoveFromFront() As Object
84          If IsEmpty() Then
85              Throw New EmptyListException(name)
86          End If
87
88          Dim removeItem As Object = firstNode.Data ' retrieve data
89
90          ' reset firstNode and lastNode references
91          If firstNode.Equals(lastNode) Then
92              firstNode = Nothing
93              lastNode = Nothing
94          Else
95              firstNode = firstNode.NextNode
96          End If
97
98          Return removeItem ' return removed data
99      End Function ' RemoveFromFront
100
101     ' remove last node from List
102     Public Function RemoveFromBack() As Object
103         If IsEmpty() Then
104             Throw New EmptyListException(name)
105         End If
106
107         Dim removeItem As Object = lastNode.Data ' retrieve data
108
```

Fig. 24.4 | ListNode, List and EmptyListException classes. (Part 3 of 4.)

```vb
109          ' reset firstNode and lastNode references
110       If firstNode.Equals(lastNode) Then
111          firstNode = Nothing
112          lastNode = Nothing
113       Else
114          Dim current As ListNode = firstNode
115
116          ' loop while current node is not lastNode
117          While Not current.NextNode.Equals(lastNode)
118             current = current.NextNode ' move to next node
119          End While
120
121          ' current is new lastNode
122          lastNode = current
123          current.NextNode = Nothing
124       End If
125
126       Return removeItem ' return removed data
127    End Function ' RemoveFromBack
128
129    ' return True if List is empty
130    Public Function IsEmpty() As Boolean
131       Return firstNode Is Nothing
132    End Function ' IsEmpty
133
134    ' output List contents
135    Public Sub Print()
136       If IsEmpty() Then
137          Console.WriteLine("Empty " & name)
138          Return
139       End If
140
141       Console.Write("The " & name & " is: ")
142
143       Dim current As ListNode = firstNode
144
145       ' output current node data while not at end of list
146       While Not (current Is Nothing)
147          Console.Write(current.Data & " ")
148          current = current.NextNode
149       End While
150
151       Console.WriteLine(vbCrLF)
152    End Sub ' Print
153 End Class ' List
154
155 ' class EmptyListException declaration
156 Public Class EmptyListException : Inherits ApplicationException
157    Public Sub New(ByVal name As String)
158       MyBase.New("The " & name & " is empty")
159    End Sub ' New
160 End Class ' EmptyListException
```

Fig. 24.4 | ListNode, List and EmptyListException classes. (Part 4 of 4.)

Class `List` (lines 40–153) contains `Private` instance variables `firstNode` (a reference to the first `ListNode` in a `List`) and `lastNode` (a reference to the last `ListNode` in a `List`). The constructors (lines 46–48 and 51–55) initialize both references to `Nothing` and enable us to specify the `List`'s name for output purposes. `InsertAtFront` (lines 60–67), `Insert-AtBack` (lines 72–80), `RemoveFromFront` (lines 83–99) and `RemoveFromBack` (lines 102–127) are the primary methods of class `List`. Method `IsEmpty` (lines 130–132) is a **predicate method** that determines whether the list is empty (i.e., the reference to the first node of the list is `Nothing`). Predicate methods typically test a condition and do not modify the object on which they are called. If the list is empty, method `IsEmpty` returns `True`; otherwise, it returns `False`. Method `Print` (lines 135–153) displays the list's contents.

Class `EmptyListException` (lines 156–160) defines an exception class that we use to indicate illegal operations on an empty `List`.

Class `ListTest` (Fig. 24.5) uses the linked-list library to create and manipulate a linked list. [*Note:* In the project containing Fig. 24.5, you must add a reference to the class library containing the classes in Fig. 24.4. If you use our existing example, you may need to update this reference.] Line 8 creates a new `List` object and assigns it to variable `list`.

```vb
1   ' Fig. 24.5: ListTest.vb
2   ' Testing class List.
3   Imports LinkedListLibrary
4
5   ' class to test List class functionality
6   Module LinkTest
7      Sub Main()
8         Dim list As New List() ' create List container
9
10           ' create data to store in List
11           Dim aBoolean As Boolean = True
12           Dim aCharacter As Char = "$"c
13           Dim anInteger As Integer = 34567
14           Dim aString As String = "hello"
15
16           ' use List insert methods
17           list.InsertAtFront(aBoolean)
18           list.Print()
19           list.InsertAtFront(aCharacter)
20           list.Print()
21           list.InsertAtBack(anInteger)
22           list.Print()
23           list.InsertAtBack(aString)
24           list.Print()
25
26           ' use List remove methods
27           Dim removedObject As Object
28
29           ' remove data from list and print after each removal
30           Try
31              removedObject = list.RemoveFromFront()
32              Console.WriteLine(removedObject & " removed")
```

Fig. 24.5 | Linked list demonstration. (Part I of 2.)

```
33                list.Print()
34
35                removedObject = list.RemoveFromFront()
36                Console.WriteLine(removedObject & " removed")
37                list.Print()
38
39                removedObject = list.RemoveFromBack()
40                Console.WriteLine(removedObject & " removed")
41                list.Print()
42
43                removedObject = list.RemoveFromBack()
44                Console.WriteLine(removedObject & " removed")
45                list.Print()
46         Catch exception As EmptyListException
47             Console.Error.WriteLine( _
48                 vbCrLf & exception.ToString())
49         End Try
50      End Sub ' Main
51   End Module ' LinkTest
```

```
The list is: True

The list is: $ True

The list is: $ True 34567

The list is: $ True 34567 hello

$ removed
The list is: True 34567 hello

True removed
The list is: 34567 hello

hello removed
The list is: 34567

34567 removed
Empty list
```

Fig. 24.5 | Linked list demonstration. (Part 2 of 2.)

Lines 11–14 create data of various types to add to the list. Lines 17–24 use the List insertion methods to insert these values and use List method Print to output the contents of the list object after each insertion. Note that the values of the primitive-type variables are implicitly boxed in lines 17, 19 and 21 where Object references are expected. The code inside the Try block (lines 30–45) removes objects via List deletion methods, outputs each removed object and displays the list after every deletion. If there is an attempt to remove an object from an empty list, the Catch at lines 46–48 catches the EmptyListException and displays an error message.

Method *InsertAtFront*

Over the next several pages, we discuss each of the methods of class List in detail. Method InsertAtFront (Fig. 24.4, lines 60–67) places a new node at the front of the list. The method consists of three steps:

1. Call `IsEmpty` to determine whether the list is empty (line 61).

2. If the list is empty, set both `firstNode` and `lastNode` to refer to a new `ListNode` initialized with `insertItem` (lines 62–63). The `ListNode` constructor in lines 10–12 of Fig. 24.4 calls the `ListNode` constructor in lines 16–19, which sets instance variable `dataValue` to refer to the `Object` passed as the first argument and sets `nextNodeReference` to `Nothing`.

3. If the list is not empty, the new node is "linked" into the list by setting `firstNode` to refer to a new `ListNode` object initialized with `insertItem` and `firstNode` (line 65). The `ListNode` constructor (lines 16–19) sets instance variable `dataValue` to refer to the `Object` passed as the first argument, and performs the insertion by setting `nextNodeReference` to the `ListNode` passed as the second argument.

In Fig. 24.6, part (a) shows a list and a new node during the `InsertAtFront` operation and before the new node is linked into the list. The dashed lines and arrows in part (b) illustrate *Step 3* of the `InsertAtFront` operation, which enables the node containing 12 to become the new list front.

Method *InsertAtBack*

Method `InsertAtBack` (Fig. 24.4, lines 72–80) places a new node at the back of the list. The method consists of three steps:

1. Call `IsEmpty` to determine whether the list is empty (line 73).

2. If the list is empty, set both `firstNode` and `lastNode` to refer to a new `ListNode` initialized with `insertItem` (lines 74–75). The `ListNode` constructor in lines 10–12 calls the `ListNode` constructor in lines 16–19, which sets instance variable `dataValue` to refer to the `Object` passed as the first argument and sets `nextNode-Reference` to `Nothing`.

3. If the list is not empty, link the new node into the list by setting `lastNode` and `lastNode.NextNode` to refer to a new `ListNode` object initialized with `insertItem` (line 77). The `ListNode` constructor (lines 10–12) calls the constructor in lines 16–19, which sets instance variable `dataValue` to refer to the `Object` passed as an argument and sets the `nextNodeReference` reference to `Nothing`.

In Fig. 24.7, part (a) shows a list and a new node during the `InsertAtBack` operation and before the new node has been linked into the list. The dashed lines and arrows in part (b) illustrate *Step 3* of method `InsertAtBack`, which enables a new node to be added to the end of a list that is not empty.

Method *RemoveFromFront*

Method `RemoveFromFront` (Fig. 24.4, lines 83–99) removes the front node of the list and returns a reference to the removed data. The method throws an `EmptyListException` (line 85) if an attempt is made to remove a node from an empty list. Otherwise, the method returns a reference to the removed data. After determining that a `List` is not empty, the method consists of four steps to remove the first node:

1. Assign `firstNode.Data` (the data being removed from the list) to variable `removeItem` (line 88).

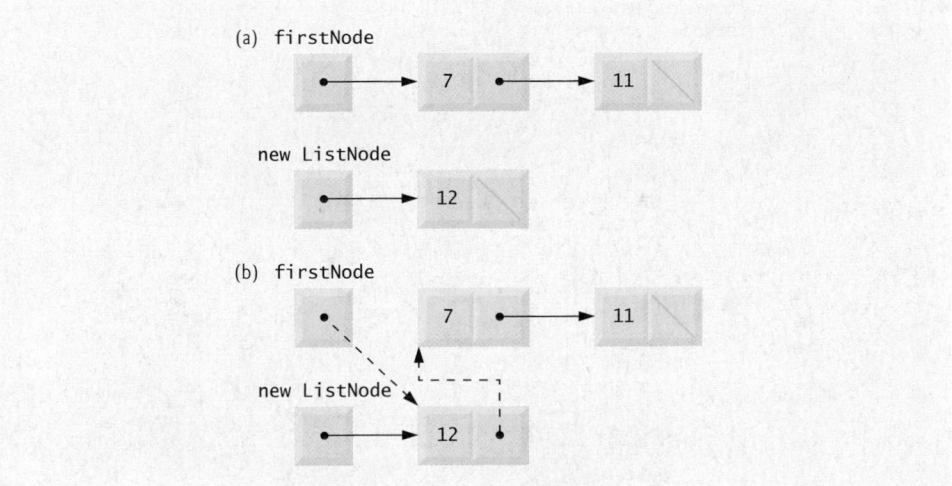

Fig. 24.6 | InsertAtFront operation.

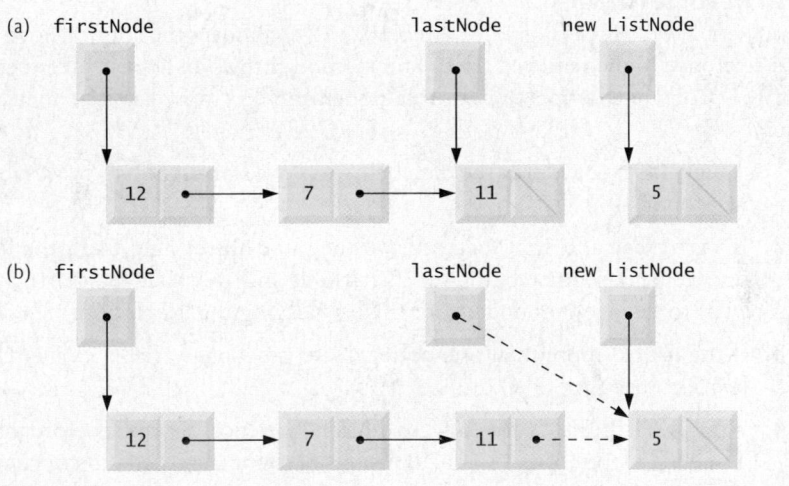

Fig. 24.7 | InsertAtBack operation.

2. If the objects to which firstNode and lastNode refer are the same object, the list has only one element, so the method sets firstNode and lastNode to Nothing (lines 92–93) to remove the node from the list (leaving the list empty).

3. If the list has more than one node, the method leaves reference lastNode as is and assigns firstNode.NextNode to firstNode (line 95). Thus, firstNode references the node that was previously the second node in the List.

4. Return the removeItem reference (line 98).

In Fig. 24.8, part (a) illustrates a list before a removal operation. The dashed lines and arrows in part (b) show the reference manipulations.

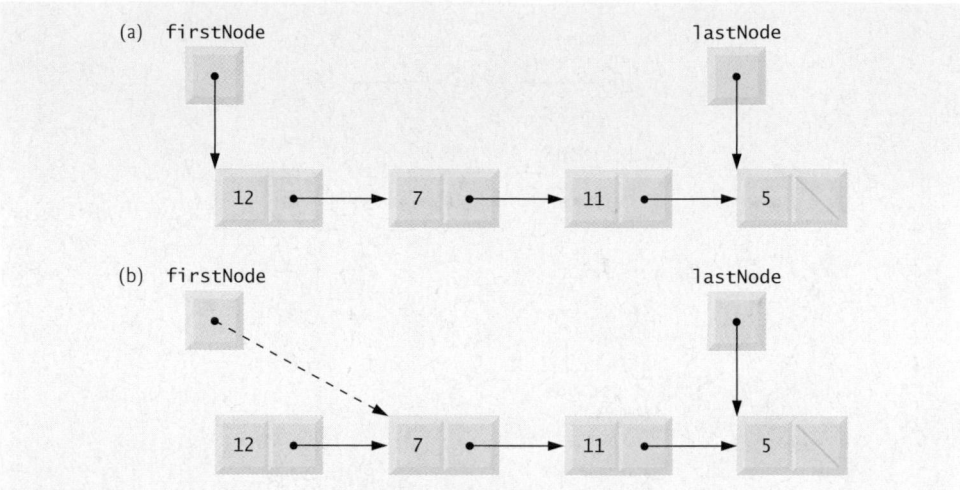

Fig. 24.8 | RemoveFromFront operation.

Method RemoveFromBack

Method RemoveFromBack (Fig. 24.4, lines 102–127) removes the last node of a list and returns a reference to the removed data. The method throws an EmptyListException (line 104) if the program attempts to remove a node from an empty list. The method consists of several steps:

1. Assign lastNode.Data (the data being removed from the list) to variable removeItem (line 107).

2. If firstNode and lastNode refer to the same object (line 110), the list has only one element, so the method sets firstNode and lastNode to Nothing (lines 111–112) to remove that node from the list (leaving the list empty).

3. If the list has more than one node, create ListNode variable current and assign it firstNode (line 114).

4. Now "walk the list" with current until it references the node before the last node. The While loop (lines 117–119) assigns current.NextNode to current as long as current.NextNode is not equal to lastNode.

5. After locating the second-to-last node, assign current to lastNode (line 122) to update which node is last in the list.

6. Set current.NextNode to Nothing (line 123) to remove the last node from the list and terminate the list at the current node.

7. Return the removeItem reference (line 126).

In Fig. 24.9, part (a) illustrates a list before a removal operation. The dashed lines and arrows in part (b) show the reference manipulations.

Method Print

Method Print (Fig. 24.4, lines 135–152) first determines whether the list is empty (line 136). If so, Print displays a String consisting of "Empty " and the list's name, then termi-

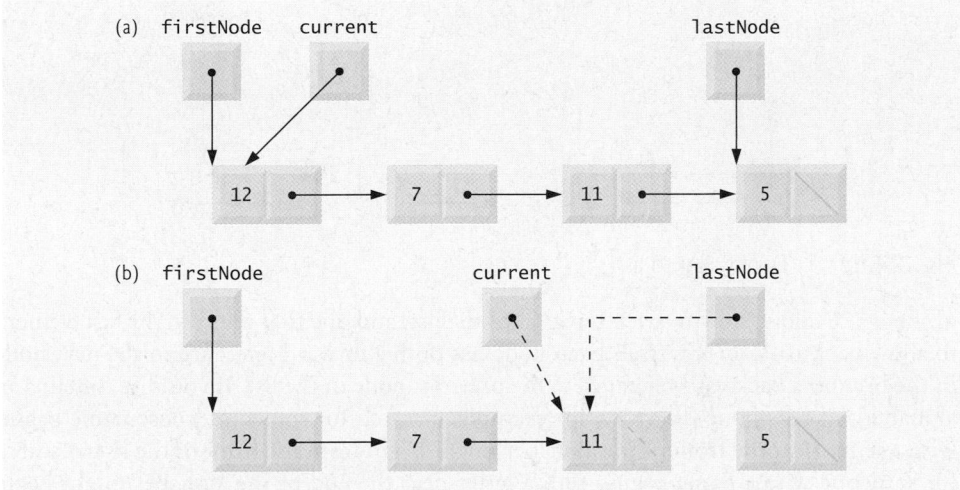

Fig. 24.9 | RemoveFromBack operation.

nates. Otherwise, Print outputs the data in the list. The method prints a String consisting of "The ", the list's name and " is: ". Then line 143 creates ListNode variable current and initializes it with firstNode. While current is not Nothing, there are more items in the list. Therefore, the method displays current.Data (line 147), then assigns current.NextNode to current (line 148) to move to the next node in the list.

Linear and Circular Singly Linked and Doubly Linked Lists

The kind of linked list we have been discussing is a **singly linked list**—the list begins with a reference to the first node, and each node contains a reference to the next node "in sequence." This list terminates with a node whose reference member has the value Nothing. A singly linked list may be traversed in only one direction.

A **circular, singly linked list** (Fig. 24.10) begins with a reference to the first node, and each node contains a reference to the next node. The "last node" does not contain a Nothing reference. Instead the reference in the last node points back to the first node, thus closing the "circle."

A **doubly linked list** (Fig. 24.11) allows traversals both forward and backward. Such a list is often implemented with two "start references"—one that refers to the first element

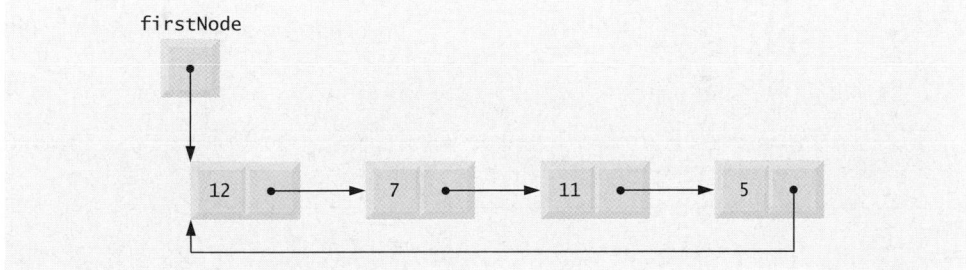

Fig. 24.10 | Circular, singly linked list.

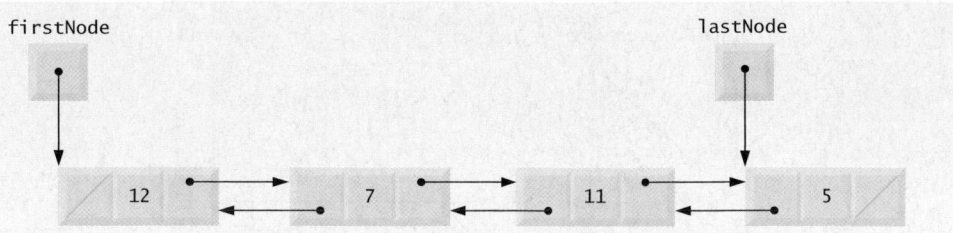

Fig. 24.11 | Doubly linked list.

of the list to allow front-to-back traversal of the list, and one that refers to the last element to allow back-to-front traversal. Each node has both a forward reference to the next node in the list and a backward reference to the previous node in the list. If your list contains an alphabetized telephone directory, for example, a search for someone whose name begins with a letter near the front of the alphabet might begin from the front of the list. A search for someone whose name begins with a letter near the end of the alphabet might begin from the back of the list.

In a **circular, doubly linked list** (Fig. 24.12), the forward reference of the last node refers to the first node, and the backward reference of the first node refers to the last node, thus closing the "circle."

24.5 Stacks

A **stack** is a constrained version of a linked list—a stack receives new nodes and releases nodes only at the top. For this reason, a stack is referred to as a **last-in, first-out** (LIFO) data structure.

The primary operations to manipulate a stack are **push** and **pop**. Operation push adds a new node to the top of the stack. Operation pop removes a node from the top of the stack and returns the data item from the popped node.

Stacks have many interesting applications. For example, when a program calls a method, the called method must know how to return to its caller, so the return address is pushed onto the method call stack. If a series of method calls occurs, the successive return values are pushed onto the stack in last-in, first-out order so that each method can return to its caller. Stacks support recursive method calls in the same manner that they do conventional non-recursive method calls.

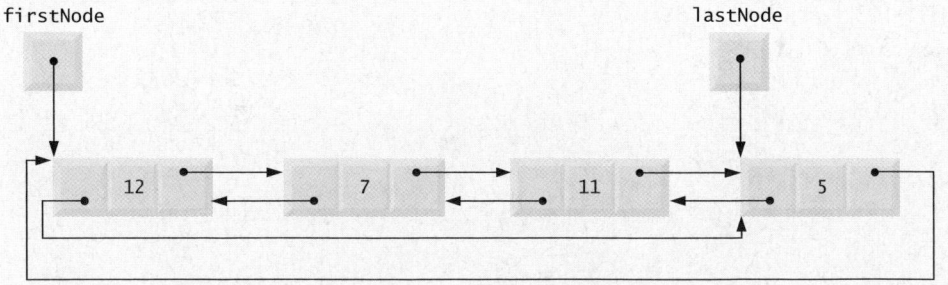

Fig. 24.12 | Circular, doubly linked list.

The System.Collections namespace contains class Stack for implementing and manipulating stacks that can grow and shrink during program execution. Chapters 25 and 26 both discuss class Stack.

In our next example, we take advantage of the close relationship between lists and stacks to implement a stack class by reusing a list class. We demonstrate two different forms of reusability. First, we implement the stack class by inheriting from class List of Fig. 24.4. Then we implement an identically performing stack class through composition by including a reference to a List object as a Private member of a stack class.

Stack Class That Inherits from List

The program of Figs. 24.13 and 24.14 creates a stack class by inheriting from class List of Fig. 24.4 (line 9). We want the stack to have methods Push, Pop, IsEmpty and Print. Essentially, these are the methods InsertAtFront, RemoveFromFront, IsEmpty and Print of class List. Of course, class List contains other methods (such as InsertAtBack and RemoveFromBack) that we would rather not make accessible through the Public interface of the stack. Remember that all methods in the Public interface of class List are inherited as Public methods of the derived class StackInheritance (Fig. 24.13).

The implementation of each StackInheritance method calls the appropriate List method—method Push calls InsertAtFront, method Pop calls RemoveFromFront. Class StackInheritance does not define methods IsEmpty and Print, because it inherits them from class List into StackInheritance's Public interface. Note that class StackInheritance uses namespace LinkedListLibrary (which is the name of the project you created in Fig. 24.4); thus, the class library that defines StackInheritance must have a reference to the LinkedListLibrary class library.

```vb
1   ' Fig. 24.13: StackInheritanceLibrary.vb
2   ' Implementing a stack by inheriting from class List.
3   Imports LinkedListLibrary
4
5   ' class StackInheritance inherits class List's capabilities
6   Public Class StackInheritance : Inherits List
7      ' pass name "stack" to List constructor
8      Public Sub New()
9         MyBase.New("stack")
10     End Sub ' New
11
12     ' place dataValue at top of stack by inserting
13     ' dataValue at front of linked list
14     Public Sub Push(ByVal dataValue As Object)
15        InsertAtFront(dataValue)
16     End Sub ' Push
17
18     ' remove item from top of stack by removing
19     ' item at front of linked list
20     Public Function Pop() As Object
21        Return RemoveFromFront()
22     End Function ' Pop
23  End Class ' StackInheritance
```

Fig. 24.13 | StackInheritance extends class List.

StackInheritanceTest's Main method (Fig. 24.14) uses class StackInheritance to create a stack of Objects called stack (line 8). Lines 11–14 define four values of various types to push onto and pop off the stack. The program pushes onto the stack (lines 17, 19, 21 and 23) a Boolean (True), a Char ('$'), an Integer (34567) and a String ("hello"). An infinite loop (lines 28–32) pops the elements from the stack. When the stack is empty, Pop throws an EmptyListException, and the program displays the exception's stack trace, which shows the program-execution stack at the time the exception occurred. The program uses method Print (inherited by StackInheritance from class List) to output the stack contents after each operation. Class StackInheritanceTest uses namespace LinkedListLibrary (Fig. 24.4) and namespace StackInheritanceLibrary (Fig. 24.13); thus, the solution for class StackInheritanceTest must have references to both class libraries.

```vb
 1   ' Fig. 24.14: StackInheritanceTest.vb
 2   ' Testing class StackInheritance.
 3   Imports StackInheritanceLibrary
 4   Imports LinkedListLibrary
 5
 6   Module StackInheritanceTest
 7      Sub Main()
 8         Dim stack As New StackInheritance()
 9
10         ' create objects to store in the stack
11         Dim aBoolean As Boolean = True
12         Dim aCharacter As Char = "$"c
13         Dim anInteger As Integer = 34567
14         Dim aString As String = "hello"
15
16         ' use method Push to add items to stack
17         stack.Push(aBoolean)
18         stack.Print()
19         stack.Push(aCharacter)
20         stack.Print()
21         stack.Push(anInteger)
22         stack.Print()
23         stack.Push(aString)
24         stack.Print()
25
26         ' remove items from stack
27         Try
28            While True
29               Dim removedObject As Object = stack.Pop()
30               Console.WriteLine(removedObject & " popped")
31               stack.Print()
32            End While
33         Catch exception As EmptyListException
34            ' if exception occurs, print stack trace
35            Console.Error.WriteLine(exception.StackTrace)
36         End Try
37      End Sub ' Main
38   End Module ' StackInheritanceTest
```

Fig. 24.14 | Using class StackInheritance. (Part 1 of 2.)

```
The stack is: True

The stack is: $ True

The stack is: 34567 $ True

The stack is: hello 34567 $ True

hello popped
The stack is: 34567 $ True

34567 popped
The stack is: $ True

$ popped
The stack is: True

True popped
Empty stack
   at LinkedListLibrary.List.RemoveFromFront()
   at StackInheritanceLibrary.StackInheritance.Pop()
   at StackInheritanceTest.StackInheritanceTest.Main(String[] args)
      in C:\examples\ch25\Fig25_14\StackInheritanceTest\
      StackInheritanceTest.cs:line 35
```

Fig. 24.14 | Using class `StackInheritance`. (Part 2 of 2.)

Stack Class That Contains a Reference to a List

Another way to implement a stack class is by reusing a list class through composition. The class in Fig. 24.15 uses a `Private` object of class `List` (line 6) in the declaration of class `StackComposition`. Composition enables us to hide the methods of class `List` that should not be in our stack's `Public` interface by providing `Public` interface methods only to the required `List` methods. This class implements each stack method by delegating its work to an appropriate `List` method. `StackComposition`'s methods call `List` methods `Insert-AtFront`, `RemoveFromFront`, `IsEmpty` and `Print`. In this example, we do not show class `StackCompositionTest`, because the only difference (from `StackInheritanceTest`) in this example is that we change the name of the stack class from `StackInheritance` to `StackComposition`. If you download and execute the application, you will see that the output is identical.

```vb
1   ' Fig. 24.15: StackCompositionLibrary.vb
2   ' StackComposition declaration with composed List object.
3   Imports LinkedListLibrary
4
5   Public Class StackComposition
6      Private stack As List
7
8      ' construct empty stack
9      Public Sub New()
10        stack = New List("stack")
11     End Sub ' New
```

Fig. 24.15 | `StackComposition` class encapsulates functionality of class `List`. (Part 1 of 2.)

```
12
13        ' add object to stack
14        Public Sub Push(ByVal dataValue As Object)
15           stack.InsertAtFront(dataValue)
16        End Sub ' Push
17
18        ' remove object from stack
19        Public Function Pop() As Object
20           Return stack.RemoveFromFront()
21        End Function ' Pop
22
23        ' determine whether stack is empty
24        Public Function IsEmpty() As Boolean
25           Return stack.IsEmpty()
26        End Function ' IsEmpty
27
28        ' output stack contents
29        Public Sub Print()
30           stack.Print()
31        End Sub ' Print
32     End Class ' StackComposition
```

Fig. 24.15 | `StackComposition` class encapsulates functionality of class `List`. (Part 2 of 2.)

24.6 Queues

Another commonly used data structure is the queue. A queue is similar to a checkout line in a supermarket—the cashier services the person at the beginning of the line first. Other customers enter the line only at the end and wait for service. Queue nodes are removed only from the head (or front) of the queue and are inserted only at the tail (or end). For this reason, a queue is a **first-in, first-out** (FIFO) data structure. The insert and remove operations are known as **enqueue** and **dequeue**.

Queues have many uses in computer systems. Most computers have only a single processor, so only one application at a time can be serviced. The operating system places each application requiring processor time in a queue. The application at the front of the queue is the next to receive service. Each application gradually advances to the front as the applications before it receive service.

Queues are also used to support **print spooling**. For example, a single printer might be shared by all the users in a network. Many users can send print jobs to the printer, even when the printer is busy. The operating system places these print jobs in a queue until the printer becomes available. A program called a **spooler** manages the queue to ensure that as each print job completes, the next print job is sent to the printer.

Information packets also wait in queues in computer networks. Each time a packet arrives at a network node, it must be routed to the next node along the path to the packet's final destination. The routing node routes one packet at a time, so additional packets are enqueued until the router can route them.

A file server in a computer network handles file-access requests from many clients throughout the network. Servers have a limited capacity to service requests from clients. When that capacity is exceeded, client requests wait in queues.

Queue Class That Inherits from List

The program of Figs. 24.16 and 24.17 creates a queue class by inheriting from a list class. We want the QueueInheritance class (Fig. 24.16) to have methods Enqueue, Dequeue, IsEmpty and Print. Essentially, these are the methods InsertAtBack, RemoveFromFront, IsEmpty and Print of class List. Of course, the list class contains other methods (such as InsertAtFront and RemoveFromBack) that we would rather not make accessible through the Public interface to the queue class. Remember that all methods in the Public interface of the List class are also Public methods of the derived class QueueInheritance.

The implementation of each QueueInheritance method calls the appropriate List method—method Enqueue calls InsertAtBack (line 14), and method Dequeue calls RemoveFromFront (line 20). Calls to IsEmpty and Print invoke the base-class versions that were inherited from class List into QueueInheritance's Public interface. Note that class QueueInheritance uses namespace LinkedListLibrary (Fig. 24.4); thus, the class library for QueueInheritance must have a reference to the LinkedListLibrary class library.

Class QueueInheritanceTest's Main method (Fig. 24.17) creates a QueueInheritance object called queue (line 9). Lines 12–15 define four values that will be enqueued and dequeued. The program enqueues (lines 18, 20, 22 and 24) a Boolean containing True, a Char containing '$', an Integer containing 34567 and a String containing "hello". Note that class QueueInheritanceTest uses namespace LinkedListLibrary and namespace QueueInheritanceLibrary; thus, the solution for class StackInheritanceTest must have references to both class libraries.

An infinite While loop (lines 32–36) dequeues the elements from the queue in FIFO order. When there are no objects left to dequeue, method Dequeue throws an EmptyListException, and the program displays the exception's stack trace, which shows the program execution stack at the time the exception occurred. The program uses method Print (inherited from class List) to output the contents of the queue after each operation. Note that class QueueInheritanceTest uses namespace LinkedListLibrary (Fig. 24.4) and namespace QueueInheritanceLibrary (Fig. 24.16); thus, the solution for class QueueInheritanceTest must have references to both class libraries.

```
1    ' Fig. 24.16: QueueInheritanceLibrary.vb
2    ' Implementing a queue by inheriting from class List.
3    Imports LinkedListLibrary
4
5    Public Class QueueInheritance : Inherits List
6       ' pass name "queue" to List constructor
7       Public Sub New()
8          MyBase.New("queue")
9       End Sub ' New
10
11      ' place dataValue at end of queue by inserting
12      ' dataValue at end of linked list
13      Public Sub Enqueue(ByVal dataValue As Object)
14         InsertAtBack(dataValue)
15      End Sub ' Enqueue
16
```

Fig. 24.16 | QueueInheritance extends class List. (Part 1 of 2.)

```
17          ' remove item from front of queue by removing
18          ' item at front of linked list
19          Public Function Dequeue() As Object
20             Return RemoveFromFront()
21          End Function ' Dequeue
22       End Class ' QueueInheritance
```

Fig. 24.16 | QueueInheritance extends class List. (Part 2 of 2.)

```
1    ' Fig. 24.17: QueueTest.vb
2    ' Testing class QueueInheritance.
3    Imports QueueInheritanceLibrary
4    Imports LinkedListLibrary
5
6    ' demonstrate functionality of class QueueInheritance
7    Module QueueTest
8       Sub Main()
9          Dim queue As New QueueInheritance()
10
11         ' create objects to store in the stack
12         Dim aBoolean As Boolean = True
13         Dim aCharacter As Char = "$"c
14         Dim anInteger As Integer = 34567
15         Dim aString As String = "hello"
16
17         ' use method Enqueue to add items to queue
18         queue.Enqueue(aBoolean)
19         queue.Print()
20         queue.Enqueue(aCharacter)
21         queue.Print()
22         queue.Enqueue(anInteger)
23         queue.Print()
24         queue.Enqueue(aString)
25         queue.Print()
26
27         ' use method Dequeue to remove items from queue
28         Dim removedObject As Object = Nothing
29
30         ' remove items from queue
31         Try
32            While True
33               removedObject = queue.Dequeue()
34               Console.WriteLine(removedObject & " dequeued")
35               queue.Print()
36            End While
37         Catch exception As EmptyListException
38            ' if exception occurs, print stack trace
39            Console.Error.WriteLine(exception.StackTrace)
40         End Try
41      End Sub ' Main
42   End Module ' QueueTest
```

Fig. 24.17 | Queue created by inheritance. (Part 1 of 2.)

```
The queue is: True

The queue is: True $

The queue is: True $ 34567

The queue is: True $ 34567 hello

True dequeued
The queue is: $ 34567 hello

$ dequeued
The queue is: 34567 hello

34567 dequeued
The queue is: hello

hello dequeued
Empty queue
   at LinkedListLibrary.List.RemoveFromFront()
   at QueueInheritanceLibrary.QueueInheritance.Dequeue()
   at QueueTest.QueueTest.Main(String[] args)
      in C:\examples\ch25\Fig25_17\QueueTest.cs:line 38
```

Fig. 24.17 | Queue created by inheritance. (Part 2 of 2.)

24.7 Trees

Linked lists, stacks and queues are **linear data structures** (i.e., **sequences**). A **tree** is a non-linear, two-dimensional data structure with special properties. Tree nodes contain two or more links.

Basic Terminology

We now discuss **binary trees** (Fig. 24.18)—trees whose nodes all contain two links (none, one or both of which may be Nothing). The **root node** is the first node in a tree. Each link

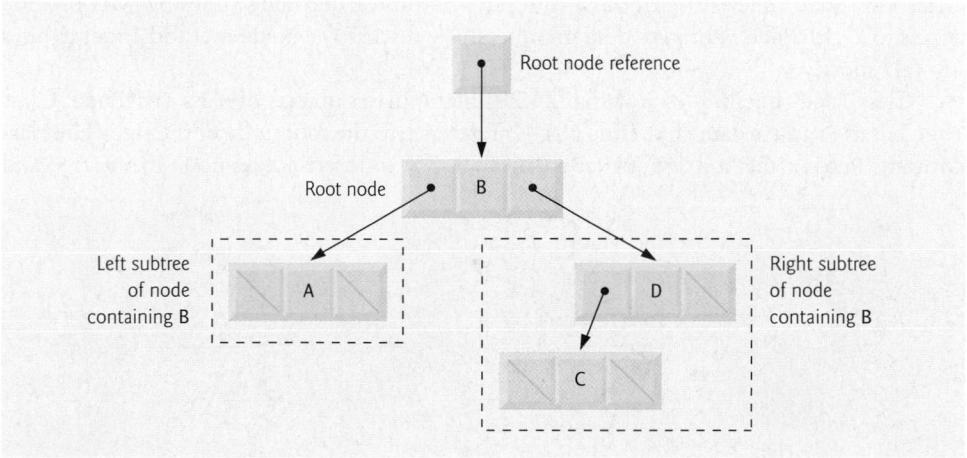

Fig. 24.18 | Binary tree graphical representation.

in the root node refers to a child. The left child is the first node in the left subtree, and the right child is the first node in the right subtree. The children of a specific node are called siblings. A node with no children is called a leaf node. Computer scientists normally draw trees from the root node down—exactly the opposite of the way most trees grow in nature.

Binary Search Trees

In our binary tree example, we create a special binary tree called a binary search tree. A binary search tree (with no duplicate node values) has the characteristic that the values in any left subtree are less than the value in the subtree's parent node, and the values in any right subtree are greater than the value in the subtree's parent node. Figure 24.19 illustrates a binary search tree with nine integer values. Note that the shape of the binary search tree that corresponds to a set of data can depend on the order in which the values are inserted into the tree.

24.7.1 Binary Search Tree of Integer Values

The application of Figs. 24.20 and 24.21 creates a binary search tree of integers and traverses it (i.e., walks through all its nodes) in three ways—using recursive inorder, preorder and postorder traversals. The program generates 10 random numbers and inserts each into the tree. Figure 24.20 defines class Tree in namespace BinaryTreeLibrary for reuse purposes (the name of the project is automatically used as the library's namespace). Figure 24.21 defines class TreeTest to demonstrate class Tree's functionality. Method Main of class TreeTest instantiates an empty Tree object, then randomly generates 10 integers and inserts each value in the binary tree by calling Tree method InsertNode. The program then performs preorder, inorder and postorder traversals of the tree. We discuss these traversals shortly.

Class TreeNode (lines 4–65 of Fig. 24.20) is a self-referential class containing three Private data members—leftNodeReference and rightNodeReference of type TreeNode and dataValue of type Integer. Initially, every TreeNode is a leaf node, so the constructor (lines 10–14) initializes leftNodeReference and rightNodeReference to Nothing. Properties LeftNode (lines 17–24), Data (lines 27–34) and RightNode (lines 37–44) provide access to a ListNode's Private data members. We discuss TreeNode method Insert (lines 48–64) shortly.

Class Tree (lines 68–149 of Fig. 24.20) manipulates objects of class TreeNode. Class Tree has as Private data root (line 69)—a reference to the root node of the tree. The class contains Public method InsertNode (lines 79–85) to insert a new node in the tree and

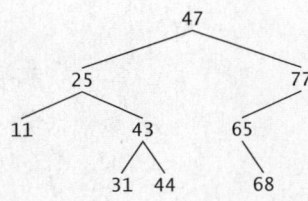

Fig. 24.19 | Binary search tree containing nine values.

Public methods PreorderTraversal (lines 88–90), InorderTraversal (lines 109–111) and PostorderTraversal (lines 130–132) to begin traversals of the tree. Each of these methods calls a separate recursive utility method to perform the traversal operations on the internal representation of the tree. The Tree constructor (lines 72–74) initializes root to Nothing to indicate that the tree initially is empty.

```vb
1   ' Fig. 24.20: BinaryTreeLibrary.vb
2   ' Declaration of class TreeNode and class Tree.
3
4   Public Class TreeNode
5      Private leftNodeReference As TreeNode ' link to left child
6      Private dataValue As Integer ' dataValue stored in node
7      Private rightNodeReference As TreeNode ' link to right child
8
9      ' initialize dataValue and make this a leaf node
10     Public Sub New(ByVal nodeData As Integer)
11        dataValue = nodeData
12        leftNodeReference = Nothing
13        rightNodeReference = Nothing
14     End Sub ' New
15
16     ' LeftNode property
17     Public Property LeftNode() As TreeNode
18        Get
19           Return leftNodeReference
20        End Get
21        Set(ByVal value As TreeNode)
22           leftNodeReference = value
23        End Set
24     End Property ' LeftNode
25
26     ' Data property
27     Public Property Data() As Integer
28        Get
29           Return dataValue
30        End Get
31        Set(ByVal value As Integer)
32           dataValue = value
33        End Set
34     End Property ' Data
35
36     ' RightNode property
37     Public Property RightNode() As TreeNode
38        Get
39           Return rightNodeReference
40        End Get
41        Set(ByVal value As TreeNode)
42           rightNodeReference = value
43        End Set
44     End Property ' RightNode
45
```

Fig. 24.20 | TreeNode and Tree classes for a binary search tree. (Part 1 of 3.)

```
46      ' recursively insert TreeNode into Tree that contains nodes;
47      ' ignore duplicate values
48      Public Sub Insert(ByVal insertValue As Integer)
49         If insertValue < data Then ' insert in left subtree
50            ' insert new TreeNode
51            If LeftNode Is Nothing Then
52               LeftNode = New TreeNode(insertValue)
53            Else ' continue traversing left subtree
54               LeftNode.Insert(insertValue)
55            End If
56         ElseIf insertValue > data Then ' insert in right subtree
57            ' insert new TreeNode
58            If RightNode Is Nothing Then
59               RightNode = New TreeNode(insertValue)
60            Else ' continue traversing right subtree
61               RightNode.Insert(insertValue)
62            End If
63         End If
64      End Sub ' Insert
65   End Class ' TreeNode
66
67   ' class Tree declaration
68   Public Class Tree
69      Private root As TreeNode ' reference to root node of tree
70
71      ' construct an empty Tree of integers
72      Public Sub New()
73         root = Nothing
74      End Sub ' New
75
76      ' Insert a new node in the binary search tree.
77      ' If the root node is Nothing, create the root node here.
78      ' Otherwise, call the insert method of class TreeNode.
79      Public Sub InsertNode(ByVal insertValue As Integer)
80         If root Is Nothing Then
81            root = New TreeNode(insertValue)
82         Else
83            root.Insert(insertValue)
84         End If
85      End Sub ' InsertNode
86
87      ' begin preorder traversal
88      Public Sub PreorderTraversal()
89         PreorderHelper(root)
90      End Sub ' PreorderTraversal
91
92      ' recursive method to perform preorder traversal
93      Private Sub PreorderHelper(ByVal node As TreeNode)
94         If node Is Nothing Then
95            Return
96         End If
97
```

Fig. 24.20 | TreeNode and Tree classes for a binary search tree. (Part 2 of 3.)

```vbnet
 98          ' output node data
 99          Console.Write(node.Data & " ")
100
101          ' traverse left subtree
102          PreorderHelper(node.LeftNode)
103
104          ' traverse right subtree
105          PreorderHelper(node.RightNode)
106      End Sub ' PreorderHelper
107
108      ' begin inorder traversal
109      Public Sub InorderTraversal()
110          InorderHelper(root)
111      End Sub ' InorderTraversal
112
113      ' recursive method to perform inorder traversal
114      Private Sub InorderHelper(ByVal node As TreeNode)
115          If node Is Nothing Then
116              Return
117          End If
118
119          ' traverse left subtree
120          InorderHelper(node.LeftNode)
121
122          ' output node data
123          Console.Write(node.Data & " ")
124
125          ' traverse right subtree
126          InorderHelper(node.RightNode)
127      End Sub ' InorderHelper
128
129      ' begin postorder traversal
130      Public Sub PostorderTraversal()
131          PostorderHelper(root)
132      End Sub ' PostorderTraversal
133
134      ' recursive method to perform postorder traversal
135      Private Sub PostorderHelper(ByVal node As TreeNode)
136          If node Is Nothing Then
137              Return
138          End If
139
140          ' traverse left subtree
141          PostorderHelper(node.LeftNode)
142
143          ' traverse right subtree
144          PostorderHelper(node.RightNode)
145
146          ' output node data
147          Console.Write(node.Data & " ")
148      End Sub ' PostorderHelper
149  End Class ' Tree
```

Fig. 24.20 | TreeNode and Tree classes for a binary search tree. (Part 3 of 3.)

```vb
1   ' Fig. 24.21: TreeTest.vb
2   ' This program tests class Tree.
3   Imports BinaryTreeLibrary
4
5   ' class TreeTest declaration
6   Module TreeTest
7      ' test class Tree
8      Sub Main()
9         Dim tree As New Tree()
10        Dim insertValue As Integer
11
12        Console.WriteLine("Inserting values: ")
13        Dim random As New Random()
14
15        ' insert 10 random integers from 0-99 in tree
16        Dim i As Integer
17        For i = 1 To 10
18           insertValue = random.Next(100)
19           Console.Write(insertValue & " ")
20
21           tree.InsertNode(insertValue)
22        Next i
23
24        ' perform preorder traversal of tree
25        Console.WriteLine(vbCrLf & vbCrLf & _
26           "Preorder traversal")
27        tree.PreorderTraversal()
28
29        ' perform inorder traversal of tree
30        Console.WriteLine(vbCrLf & vbCrLf & _
31           "Inorder traversal")
32        tree.InorderTraversal()
33
34        ' perform postorder traversal of tree
35        Console.WriteLine(vbCrLf & vbCrLf & _
36           "Postorder traversal")
37        tree.PostorderTraversal()
38     End Sub ' Main
39  End Module ' TreeTest
```

```
Inserting values:
39 69 94 47 50 72 55 41 97 73

Preorder traversal
39 69 47 41 50 55 94 72 73 97

Inorder traversal
39 41 47 50 55 69 72 73 94 97

Postorder traversal
41 55 50 47 73 72 97 94 69 39
```

Fig. 24.21 | Creating and traversing a binary tree.

Tree method InsertNode (lines 79–85) first determines whether the tree is empty. If so, line 81 allocates a new TreeNode, initializes the node with the integer being inserted in the tree and assigns the new node to root. If the tree is not empty, InsertNode calls TreeNode method Insert (lines 48–64), which recursively determines the location for the new node in the tree and inserts the node at that location. A node can be inserted only as a leaf node in a binary search tree.

TreeNode method Insert compares the value to insert with the data value in the root node. If the insert value is less than the root-node data, the program determines whether the left subtree is empty (line 51). If so, line 52 allocates a new TreeNode, initializes it with the integer being inserted and assigns the new node to reference leftNode. Otherwise, line 54 recursively calls Insert for the left subtree to insert the value into the left subtree. If the insert value is greater than the root-node data, the program determines whether the right subtree is empty (line 58). If so, line 59 allocates a new TreeNode, initializes it with the integer being inserted and assigns the new node to reference rightNode. Otherwise, line 61 recursively calls Insert for the right subtree to insert the value in the right subtree.

Methods InorderTraversal, PreorderTraversal and PostorderTraversal call the recursive helper methods InorderHelper (lines 114–127), PreorderHelper (lines 93–106) and PostorderHelper (lines 135–148), respectively, to traverse the tree and print the node values. The purpose of these helper methods in class Tree is to allow the programmer to start a traversal without needing to obtain a reference to the root node first, then call the recursive method with that reference. Methods InorderTraversal, PreorderTraversal and PostorderTraversal simply take Private variable root and pass it to the appropriate helper method to initiate a traversal of the tree. For the following discussion, we use the binary search tree shown in Fig. 24.22.

Inorder Traversal Algorithm

Method InorderHelper (lines 114–127) defines the steps for an inorder traversal. The steps are as follows:

1. If the argument is Nothing, return immediately.
2. Traverse the left subtree with a call to InorderHelper (line 120).
3. Process the value in the node (line 123).
4. Traverse the right subtree with a call to InorderHelper (line 126).

The inorder traversal does not process the value in a node until the values in the node's left subtree are processed. The inorder traversal of the tree in Fig. 24.22 is

    6 13 17 27 33 42 48

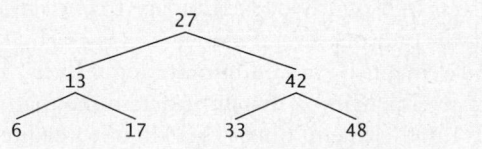

Fig. 24.22 | Binary search tree.

Note that the inorder traversal of a binary search tree prints the node values in ascending order. The process of creating a binary search tree actually sorts the data (when coupled with an inorder traversal)—thus, this process is called the **binary tree sort**.

Preorder Traversal Algorithm

Method `PreorderHelper` (lines 93–106) defines the steps for a preorder traversal. The steps are as follows:

1. If the argument is `Nothing`, return immediately.
2. Process the value in the node (line 99).
3. Traverse the left subtree with a call to `PreorderHelper` (line 102).
4. Traverse the right subtree with a call to `PreorderHelper` (line 105).

The preorder traversal processes the value in each node as the node is visited. After processing the value in a given node, the preorder traversal processes the values in the left subtree, then the values in the right subtree. The preorder traversal of the tree in Fig. 24.22 is

```
27 13 6 17 42 33 48
```

Postorder Traversal Algorithm

Method `PostorderHelper` (lines 135–148) defines the steps for a postorder traversal. The steps are as follows:

1. If the argument is `Nothing`, return immediately.
2. Traverse the left subtree with a call to `PostorderHelper` (line 141).
3. Traverse the right subtree with a call to `PostorderHelper` (line 144).
4. Process the value in the node (line 147).

The postorder traversal processes the value in each node after the values of all the node's children are processed. The postorder traversal of the tree in Fig. 24.22 is

```
6 17 13 33 48 42 27
```

Duplicate Elimination

The binary search tree facilitates **duplicate elimination.** While building a tree, the insertion operation recognizes attempts to insert a duplicate value, because a duplicate follows the same "go left" or "go right" decisions on each comparison as the original value did. Thus the insertion operation eventually compares the duplicate with a node containing the same value. At this point, the insertion operation might simply discard the duplicate value.

Searching a binary tree for a value that matches a key value is fast, especially for **tightly packed** binary trees. In a tightly packed binary tree, each level contains about twice as many elements as the previous level. Figure 24.22 is a tightly packed binary tree. A binary search tree with n elements has a minimum of $\log_2 n$ levels. Thus, at most $\log_2 n$ comparisons are required to either find a match or determine that no match exists. Searching a (tightly packed) 1,000-element binary search tree requires at most 10 comparisons, because $2^{10} > 1000$. Searching a (tightly packed) 1,000,000-element binary search tree requires at most 20 comparisons, because $2^{20} > 1,000,000$.

Overview of the Level-Order Traversal Binary Tree Exercise
Exercise 24.8 presents the algorithm for a level-order traversal of a binary tree. The level-order traversal visits the nodes of the tree row by row, starting at the root-node level. On each level of the tree, a level-order traversal visits the nodes from left to right.

24.7.2 Binary Search Tree of IComparable Objects

The binary tree example in Section 24.7.1 works nicely when all the data is of type Integer. Suppose that you want to manipulate a binary tree of Double values. You could rewrite the TreeNode and Tree classes with different names and customize the classes to manipulate Double values. Similarly, for each data type you could create customized versions of classes TreeNode and Tree. This results in a proliferation of code, which can become difficult to manage and maintain.

Ideally, we would like to define the functionality of a binary tree once and reuse that functionality for many data types. Languages like Visual Basic, C# and Java provide polymorphic capabilities that enable all objects to be manipulated in a uniform manner. Using such capabilities enables us to design a more flexible data structure. The new version of Visual Basic provides these capabilities with generics (Chapter 25).

In our next example, we take advantage of Visual Basic's polymorphic capabilities by implementing TreeNode and Tree classes that manipulate objects of any type that implements interface IComparable (namespace System). It is imperative to compare objects stored in a binary search if we are to determine the path to the insertion point of a new node. Classes that implement IComparable define method CompareTo, which compares the object that invokes the method with the object that the method receives as an argument. The method returns an Integer value less than zero if the calling object is less than the argument object, zero if the objects are equal and a positive value if the calling object is greater than the argument object. Also, the invoking and argument objects must be of the same data type; otherwise, the method throws an ArgumentException.

The program of Figs. 24.23 and 24.24 enhances the program from Section 24.7.1 to manipulate IComparable objects. One restriction on the new versions TreeNode and Tree in Fig. 24.23 is that each Tree object can contain objects of only one data type (e.g., all Strings or all Doubles). If a program attempts to insert multiple data types in the same Tree object, ArgumentExceptions will occur. We modified only seven lines of code in class TreeNode (lines 7, 11, 28, 32, 49, 50 and 57) and one line of code in class Tree (line 80) to enable processing of IComparable objects. With the exception of lines 50 and 57, all the other changes simply replaced the type Integer with the type IComparable. Lines 50 and 57 previously used the < and > operators to compare the value being inserted with the value in a given node. These lines now compare IComparable objects via the interface's CompareTo method, then test the method's return value to determine whether it is less than zero (the invoking object is less than the argument object) or greater than zero (the invoking object is greater than the argument object), respectively. [*Note:* If this class were written using generics, the type of data, Integer or IComparable could be replaced at compile time by any other type that implements the necessary operators and methods.]

Class TreeTest (Fig. 24.24) creates three Tree objects to store Integer, Double and String values, all of which the .NET Framework defines as IComparable types. The program populates the trees with the values in arrays integerArray (line 9), doubleArray (lines 10–11) and stringArray (lines 12–13), respectively.

```vb
1    ' Fig. 24.23: BinaryTreeLibrary2.vb
2    ' Declaration of class TreeNode and class Tree for IComparable
3    ' objects.
4
5    Public Class TreeNode
6       Private leftNodeValue As TreeNode ' link to left child
7       Private dataValue As IComparable ' dataValue stored in node
8       Private rightNodeValue As TreeNode ' link to right subtree
9
10      ' initialize dataValue and make this a leaf node
11      Public Sub New(ByVal nodeData As IComparable)
12         dataValue = nodeData
13         leftNodeValue = Nothing
14         rightNodeValue = Nothing
15      End Sub ' New
16
17      ' LeftNode property
18      Public Property LeftNode() As TreeNode
19         Get
20            Return leftNodeValue
21         End Get
22         Set(ByVal value As TreeNode)
23            leftNodeValue = value
24         End Set
25      End Property ' LeftNode
26
27      ' Data property
28      Public Property Data() As IComparable
29         Get
30            Return dataValue
31         End Get
32         Set(ByVal value As IComparable)
33            dataValue = value
34         End Set
35      End Property ' Data
36
37      ' RightNode property
38      Public Property RightNode() As TreeNode
39         Get
40            Return rightNodeValue
41         End Get
42         Set(ByVal value As TreeNode)
43            rightNodeValue = value
44         End Set
45      End Property ' RightNode
46
47      ' insert TreeNode into Tree that contains nodes;
48      ' ignore duplicate values
49      Public Sub Insert(ByVal insertValue As IComparable)
50         If insertValue.CompareTo(data) < 0 Then
51            ' insert in left subtree
52            If LeftNode Is Nothing Then
53               LeftNode = New TreeNode(insertValue)
```

Fig. 24.23 | TreeNode and Tree classes for manipulating IComparable objects. (Part 1 of 3.)

```vbnet
54            Else ' continue traversing left subtree
55               LeftNode.Insert(insertValue)
56            End If
57         ElseIf insertValue.CompareTo(data) > 0 Then
58            ' insert in right subtree
59            If RightNode Is Nothing Then
60               RightNode = New TreeNode(insertValue)
61            Else ' continue traversing right subtree
62               RightNode.Insert(insertValue)
63            End If
64         End If
65      End Sub ' Insert
66   End Class ' TreeNode
67
68   ' class Tree declaration
69   Public Class Tree
70      Private root As TreeNode
71
72      ' construct an empty Tree of integers
73      Public Sub New()
74         root = Nothing
75      End Sub ' New
76
77      ' Insert a new node in the binary search tree.
78      ' If the root node is Nothing, create the root node here.
79      ' Otherwise, call the insert method of class TreeNode.
80      Public Sub InsertNode(ByVal insertValue As IComparable)
81         If root Is Nothing Then
82            root = New TreeNode(insertValue)
83         Else
84            root.Insert(insertValue)
85         End If
86      End Sub ' InsertNode
87
88      ' begin preorder traversal
89      Public Sub PreorderTraversal()
90         PreorderHelper(root)
91      End Sub ' PreorderTraversal
92
93      ' recursive method to perform preorder traversal
94      Private Sub PreorderHelper(ByVal node As TreeNode)
95         If node Is Nothing Then
96            Return
97         End If
98         ' output node data
99         Console.Write(Convert.ToString(node.Data) & " ")
100
101         ' traverse left subtree
102         PreorderHelper(node.LeftNode)
103
104         ' traverse right subtree
105         PreorderHelper(node.RightNode)
106      End Sub ' PreorderHelper
```

Fig. 24.23 | TreeNode and Tree classes for manipulating IComparable objects. (Part 2 of 3.)

```
107
108      ' begin inorder traversal
109      Public Sub InorderTraversal()
110          InorderHelper(root)
111      End Sub ' InorderTraversal
112
113      ' recursive method to perform inorder traversal
114      Private Sub InorderHelper(ByVal node As TreeNode)
115          If node Is Nothing Then
116              Return
117          End If
118          ' traverse left subtree
119          InorderHelper(node.LeftNode)
120
121          ' output node data
122          Console.Write(Convert.ToString(node.Data) & " ")
123
124          ' traverse right subtree
125          InorderHelper(node.RightNode)
126      End Sub ' InorderHelper
127
128      ' begin postorder traversal
129      Public Sub PostorderTraversal()
130          PostorderHelper(root)
131      End Sub ' PostorderTraversal
132
133      ' recursive method to perform postorder traversal
134      Private Sub PostorderHelper(ByVal node As TreeNode)
135          If node Is Nothing Then
136              Return
137          End If
138          ' traverse left subtree
139          PostorderHelper(node.LeftNode)
140
141          ' traverse right subtree
142          PostorderHelper(node.RightNode)
143
144          ' output node data
145          Console.Write(Convert.ToString(node.Data) & " ")
146      End Sub ' PostorderHelper
147  End Class ' Tree
```

Fig. 24.23 | TreeNode and Tree classes for manipulating IComparable objects. (Part 3 of 3.)

```
1    ' Fig. 24.24: TreeTest.vb
2    ' This program tests class Tree.
3    Imports BinaryTreeLibrary2
4
5    ' class TreeTest declaration
6    Module TreeTest
7        ' test class Tree
8        Sub Main()
```

Fig. 24.24 | Demonstrating class Tree with IComparable objects. (Part 1 of 3.)

```vbnet
 9          Dim integerArray As Integer() = {8, 2, 4, 3, 1, 7, 5, 6}
10          Dim doubleArray As Double() = _
11             {8.8, 2.2, 4.4, 3.3, 1.1, 7.7, 5.5, 6.6}
12          Dim stringArray As String() = _
13             {"eight", "two", "four", "three", "one", "seven", "five", "six"}
14
15          ' create Integer Tree
16          Dim integerTree As New Tree()
17          populateTree(integerArray, integerTree, "integerTree")
18          traverseTree(integerTree, "integerTree")
19
20          ' create Double Tree
21          Dim doubleTree As New Tree()
22          populateTree(doubleArray, doubleTree, "doubleTree")
23          traverseTree(doubleTree, "doubleTree")
24
25          ' create String Tree
26          Dim stringTree As New Tree()
27          populateTree(stringArray, stringTree, "stringTree")
28          traverseTree(stringTree, "stringTree")
29       End Sub ' Main
30
31       ' populate Tree with array elements
32       Sub populateTree(ByVal array As Array, _
33          ByVal tree As Tree, ByVal name As String)
34
35          Console.WriteLine(vbCrLf & vbCrLf & _
36             vbCrLf & "Inserting into " & name & ":")
37
38          For Each data As IComparable In array
39             Console.Write(Convert.ToString(data) & " ")
40             tree.InsertNode(data)
41          Next data
42       End Sub ' populateTree
43
44       ' insert perform traversals
45       Sub traverseTree(ByVal tree As Tree, ByVal treeType As String)
46          ' perform preorder traveral of tree
47          Console.WriteLine(vbCrLf & vbCrLf & _
48             "Preorder traversal of " & treeType)
49          tree.PreorderTraversal()
50
51          ' perform inorder traveral of tree
52          Console.WriteLine(vbCrLf & vbCrLf & _
53             "Inorder traversal of " & treeType)
54          tree.InorderTraversal()
55
56          ' perform postorder traveral of tree
57          Console.WriteLine(vbCrLf & vbCrLf & _
58             "Postorder traversal of " & treeType)
59          tree.PostorderTraversal()
60       End Sub ' traverseTree
61    End Module ' TreeTest
```

Fig. 24.24 | Demonstrating class Tree with IComparable objects. (Part 2 of 3.)

```
Inserting into intTree:
8 2 4 3 1 7 5 6

Preorder traversal of intTree
8 2 1 4 3 7 5 6

Inorder traversal of intTree
1 2 3 4 5 6 7 8

Postorder traversal of intTree
1 3 6 5 7 4 2 8


Inserting into doubleTree:
8.8 2.2 4.4 3.3 1.1 7.7 5.5 6.6

Preorder traversal of doubleTree
8.8 2.2 1.1 4.4 3.3 7.7 5.5 6.6

Inorder traversal of doubleTree
1.1 2.2 3.3 4.4 5.5 6.6 7.7 8.8

Postorder traversal of doubleTree
1.1 3.3 6.6 5.5 7.7 4.4 2.2 8.8


Inserting into stringTree:
eight two four three one seven five six

Preorder traversal of stringTree
eight two four five three one seven six

Inorder traversal of stringTree
eight five four one seven six three two

Postorder traversal of stringTree
five six seven one three four two eight
```

Fig. 24.24 | Demonstrating class `Tree` with IComparable objects. (Part 3 of 3.)

Method `PopulateTree` (lines 32–42) receives as arguments an `Array` containing the initializer values for the `Tree`, a `Tree` in which the array elements will be placed and a `String` representing the `Tree` name, then inserts each `Array` element into the `Tree`. Method `TraverseTree` (lines 45–60) receives as arguments a `Tree` and a `String` representing the `Tree` name, then outputs the preorder, inorder and postorder traversals of the `Tree`. Note that the inorder traversal of each `Tree` outputs the data in sorted order regardless of the data type stored in the `Tree`. Our polymorphic implementation of class Tree invokes the appropriate data type's `CompareTo` method to determine the path to each value's insertion point by using the standard binary search tree insertion rules. Also note that the `Tree` of `String`s appears in alphabetical order.

24.8 Wrap-Up

In this chapter, you learned that primitive types are value-type `Structure`s, but can still be used anywhere `Object`s are expected in a program due to boxing and unboxing conversions. You learned that linked lists are collections of data items that are "linked together in a chain" and that a program can perform insertions and deletions anywhere in a linked list (though our implementation only performed insertions and deletions at the ends of the list). We demonstrated that the stack and queue data structures can be implemented as constrained versions of lists. For stacks, you saw that insertions and deletions are made only at the top—so stacks are known as last-in, first-out (LIFO) data structures. For queues, which represent waiting lines, you saw that insertions are made at the tail and deletions are made from the head—so queues are known as first-in, first-out (FIFO) data structures. We also presented the binary tree data structure. You saw a binary search tree that facilitated high-speed searching and sorting of data and efficient duplicate elimination. Finally, we presented a version of the binary tree data structure that processes IComparable objects and uses the CompareTo method to help determine where the object should be placed in the binary tree. In the next chapter, we introduce generics, a capability which allows you to declare a family of classes and methods that implement the same functionality on any type.

Summary

Section 24.1 Introduction
- Dynamic data structures can grow and shrink at execution time.

Section 24.2 Primitive-Type **Structure**s; Boxing and Unboxing
- All primitive-type names are aliases for corresponding Structures in namespace System. Each primitive type Structure has methods that manipulate the corresponding primitive-type values.
- Structures that represent primitive types inherit from class ValueType in namespace System.
- A boxing conversion creates an object that contains a copy of a primitive-type value.
- An unboxing conversion retrieves a primitive-type value from an object.

Section 24.3 Self-Referential Classes
- A self-referential class contains a data member that refers to an object of the same class type. Self-referential objects can be linked to form data structures, such as lists, queues, stacks and trees.
- Creating and maintaining dynamic data structures requires dynamic memory allocation—a program's ability to obtain more memory at execution time (to hold new nodes) and to release memory no longer needed.
- Operator New takes as an operand the type of the object being dynamically allocated, calls the appropriate constructor to initialize the object and returns a reference to the new object. If no memory is available, New throws an OutOfMemoryException.

Section 24.4 Linked Lists
- A linked list is a linear collection (i.e., a sequence) of self-referential class objects called nodes, connected by reference links.
- A node can contain instance variables of any type, including references to objects of other classes.
- A linked list is accessed via a reference to the first node of the list. Each subsequent node is accessed via the link-reference member stored in the previous node.
- By convention, the last node's link reference is set to Nothing to mark the end of the list.

Section 24.5 Stacks

- Stacks are important in compilers and operating systems.

- A stack is a constrained version of a linked list—new nodes can be added to and removed from a stack only at the top. A stack is referred to as a last-in, first-out (LIFO) data structure.

- The primary stack operations are push and pop. Operation push adds a new node to the top of the stack. Operation pop removes a node from the top of the stack and returns the data object from the popped node.

Section 24.6 Queues

- Queues represent waiting lines. Insertions occur at the back (also referred to as the tail) of a queue, and deletions occur from the front (also referred to as the head) of a queue.

- A queue is similar to a checkout line in a supermarket: The first person in line is served first; other customers enter the line at the end and wait to be served.

- Queue nodes are removed only from the head of the queue and are inserted only at the tail of the queue. For this reason, a queue is referred to as a first-in, first-out (FIFO) data structure.

- The insert and remove operations for a queue are known as enqueue and dequeue.

Section 24.7 Trees

- Binary trees facilitate high-speed searching and sorting of data.

- Tree nodes contain two or more links.

- A binary tree is a tree whose nodes all contain two links. The root node is the first node in a tree.

- Each link in the root node refers to a child. The left child is the root node of the left subtree, and the right child is the root node of the right subtree.

- The children of a node are called siblings. A node with no children is called a leaf node.

- A binary search tree (with no duplicate node values) has the characteristic that the values in any left subtree are less than the value in the subtree's parent node, and the values in any right subtree are greater than the value in the subtree's parent node.

- A node can be inserted only as a leaf node in a binary search tree.

- An inorder traversal of a binary search tree processes the node values in ascending order.

- The process of creating a binary search tree actually sorts the data (when coupled with an inorder traversal)—thus, the term "binary tree sort."

- In a preorder traversal, the value in each node is processed as the node is visited. After the value in a given node is processed, the values in the left subtree are processed, then the values in the right subtree are processed.

- In a postorder traversal, the value in each node is processed after the node's left and right subtrees are processed.

- A binary search tree facilitates duplicate elimination. As the tree is created, attempts to insert a duplicate value are recognized because a duplicate follows the same "go left" or "go right" decision on each comparison as the original value did. Thus, the duplicate eventually is compared with a node containing the same value, and can then be discarded.

Terminology

ArgumentException	boxing
binary search tree	child node
binary tree	circular, doubly linked list
binary tree sort	circular, singly linked list

collection
CompareTo method of interface IComparable
data structures
dequeue
doubly linked list
duplicate elimination
dynamic data structures
enqueue
first-in, first-out (FIFO) data structure
head of a queue
IComparable interface
inorder traversal of a binary tree
InvalidCastException
last-in, first-out (LIFO) data structure
leaf node
left child node
left subtree
level-order traversal of a binary tree
linear data structure
link
linked list
node
OutOfMemoryException
parent node

pop stack operation
postorder traversal of a binary tree
predicate method
preorder traversal of a binary tree
print spooling
push stack operation
queue
right child node
right subtree
root node
searching
self-referential class
sibling node
singly linked list
sorting
stack
Structure
tail of a queue
tightly packed binary tree
top of a stack
traverse a tree
tree
unboxing
ValueType class

Self-Review Exercises

24.1 State whether each of the following is *true* or *false*. If *false*, explain why.
   a) In a queue, the first item to be added is the last item to be removed.
   b) Trees can have no more than two child nodes per node.
   c) A tree node with no children is called a leaf node.
   d) Linked-list nodes are stored contiguously in memory.
   e) The primary operations of the stack data structure are enqueue and dequeue.
   f) Lists, stacks and queues are linear data structures.

24.2 Fill in the blanks in each of the following statements:
   a) A(n) _____ class is used to define nodes that form dynamic data structures, which can grow and shrink at execution time.
   b) Operator _____ allocates memory dynamically; this operator returns a reference to the allocated memory.
   c) A(n) _____ is a constrained version of a linked list in which nodes can be inserted and deleted only from the start of the list; this data structure returns node values in last-in, first-out order.
   d) A queue is a(n) _____ data structure, because the first nodes inserted are the first nodes removed.
   e) A(n) _____ is a constrained version of a linked list in which nodes can be inserted only at the end of the list and deleted only from the start of the list.
   f) A(n) _____ is a nonlinear, two-dimensional data structure that contains nodes with two or more links.
   g) The nodes of a(n) _____ tree contain two link members.
   h) The tree-traversal algorithm that processes the node and then processes all the nodes to its left followed by all the nodes to its right is called _____.

Answers to Self-Review Exercises

24.1 a) False. A queue is a first-in, first-out data structure—the first item added is the first item removed. b) False. In general, trees may have as many child nodes per node as necessary. Only binary trees are restricted to no more than two child nodes per node. c) True. d) False. Linked-list nodes are logically contiguous, but they need not be stored physically contiguously. e) False. They are the primary operations of a queue. The primary operations of a stack are push and pop. f) True.

24.2 a) self-referential. b) New. c) stack. d) first-in, first-out (FIFO). e) queue. f) tree. g) binary. h) preorder.

Exercises

24.3 Write a program that merges two ordered list objects of integers into a single ordered list object of integers. Method Merge of class ListMerge should receive references to each of the list objects to be merged and should return a reference to the merged list object.

24.4 Write a program that inputs a line of text and uses a stack object to print the line reversed.

24.5 Write a program that uses a stack to determine whether a string is a palindrome (i.e., the string is spelled identically backward and forward). The program should ignore capitalization, spaces and punctuation.

24.6 Stacks are used by compilers in the process of evaluating expressions and in generating machine-language code. In this and the next exercise, we investigate how compilers evaluate arithmetic expressions consisting only of constants, operators and parentheses.

Humans generally write expressions like 3 + 4 and 7 / 9, in which the operator (+ or / here) is written between its operands—this is called *infix notation*. Computers "prefer" *postfix notation*, in which the operator is written to the right of its two operands. The preceding infix expressions would appear in postfix notation as 3 4 + and 7 9 /, respectively.

To evaluate a complex infix expression, a compiler would first convert the expression to postfix notation, then evaluate the postfix version of the expression. Each of these algorithms requires only a single left-to-right pass of the expression. Each algorithm uses a stack object in support of its operation, and in each algorithm the stack is used for a different purpose.

In this exercise, you will write a Visual Basic version of the infix-to-postfix conversion algorithm. In the next exercise, you will write a Visual Basic version of the postfix expression evaluation algorithm.

Write class InfixToPostfixConverter to convert an ordinary infix arithmetic expression (assume that a valid expression is entered) with single-digit integers, such as (6 + 2) * 5 - 8 / 4, to a postfix expression. The postfix version of the preceding infix expression (note that no parentheses are needed) is 6 2 + 5 * 8 4 / -. The program should read the expression into StringBuilder infix, then use class StackInheritance (implemented in Fig. 24.13) to help create the postfix expression in StringBuilder postfix. The algorithm for creating a postfix expression is as follows:
   a) Push a left parenthesis '(' on the stack.
   b) Append a right parenthesis ')' to the end of infix.
   c) While the stack is not empty, read infix from left to right and do the following:
      If the current character in infix is a digit, append it to postfix.
      If the current character in infix is a left parenthesis, push it onto the stack.
      If the current character in infix is an operator:
         Pop operators (if there are any) at the top of the stack while they have equal or higher precedence than the current operator, and append the popped operators to postfix.
         Push the current character in infix onto the stack.

> If the current character in `infix` is a right parenthesis:
>> Pop operators from the top of the stack and append them to `postfix` until a left parenthesis is at the top of the stack.
>> Pop (and discard) the left parenthesis from the stack.

The following arithmetic operations are allowed in an expression:

+   addition
-   subtraction
*   multiplication
/   division
^   exponentiation
%   modulus

Some of the methods you may want to provide in your program follow:

a) Method `ConvertToPostfix`, which converts the infix expression to postfix notation.

b) Method `IsOperator`, which determines whether `c` is an operator.

c) Method `Precedence`, which determines whether the precedence of `operator1` (from the infix expression) is less than, equal to or greater than the precedence of `operator2` (from the stack). The method returns `True` if `operator1` has lower precedence than or equal precedence to `operator2`. Otherwise, `False` is returned.

24.7   Write class `PostfixEvaluator`, which evaluates a postfix expression such as

    6 2 + 5 * 8 4 / -

Assume the expression is valid. The program should read a postfix expression consisting of digits and operators into a `StringBuilder`. Using the stack class from Exercise 24.6, the program should scan the expression and evaluate it. The algorithm (for single-digit numbers) is as follows:

a) Append a right parenthesis (`')'`) to the end of the postfix expression. When the right-parenthesis character is encountered, no further processing is necessary.

b) When the right-parenthesis character has not been encountered, read the expression from left to right.

> If the current character is a digit, do the following:
>> Push its integer value on the stack (the integer value of a digit character is its value in the computer's character set minus the value of `'0'` in Unicode).

> Otherwise, if the current character is an *operator*:
>> Pop the two top elements of the stack into variables x and y.
>> Calculate y *operator* x.
>> Push the result of the calculation onto the stack.

c) When the right parenthesis is encountered in the expression, pop the top value of the stack. This is the result of the postfix expression.

[*Note:* In part (b) above (based on the sample expression at the beginning of this exercise), if the operator is `'/'`, the top of the stack is 4 and the next element in the stack is 8, then pop 4 into x, pop 8 into y, evaluate 8 / 4 and push the result, 2, back on the stack. This note also applies to operator `'-'`.] The arithmetic operations allowed in an expression are:

+   addition
-   subtraction
*   multiplication
/   division
^   exponentiation
%   modulus

You may want to provide the following methods:

a) Method `EvaluatePostfixExpression`, which evaluates the postfix expression.

b) Method `Calculate`, which evaluates the expression op1 *operator* op2.

24.8   (*Level-Order Binary Tree Traversal*) The program of Fig. 24.21 illustrated three recursive methods of traversing a binary tree—inorder, preorder, and postorder traversals. This exercise presents the *level-order traversal* of a binary tree, in which the node values are printed level by level, starting at the root-node level. The nodes on each level are printed from left to right. The level-order traversal is not a recursive algorithm. It uses a queue object to control the output of the nodes. The algorithm is as follows:

    a) Insert the root node in the queue.

    b) While there are nodes left in the queue, do the following:

            Get the next node in the queue.

            Print the node's value.

            If the reference to the left child of the node is not Nothing:

                Insert the left child node in the queue.

            If the reference to the right child of the node is not Nothing:

                Insert the right child node in the queue.

Write method LevelOrderTraversal to perform a level-order traversal of a binary tree object. Modify the program of Fig. 24.21 to use this method. [*Note:* You also will need to use the queue-processing methods of Fig. 24.16 in this program.]

25

Generics

OBJECTIVES

In this chapter you will learn:

- To create generic methods that perform identical tasks on arguments of different types.

- To create a generic **Stack** class that can be used to store objects of any class or interface type.

- To understand how to overload generic methods with non-generic methods or with other generic methods.

- To understand the **New** constraint of a type parameter.

- To apply multiple constraints to a type parameter.

- The relationship between generics and inheritance.

25.1 Introduction

In Chapter 24, we presented data structures that store and manipulate Object references. You could store any Object in these data structures. One inconvenient aspect of storing Object references occurs when retrieving them from a collection. An application normally needs to process specific types of objects. As a result, the Object references obtained from a collection typically need to be downcast to an appropriate type to allow the application to process the objects correctly. In addition, data of value types (e.g., Integer and Double) must be boxed to be manipulated with Object references, which increases the overhead of processing such data. Also, processing all data as type Object limits the Visual Basic compiler's ability to perform type checking.

Though we can easily create data structures that manipulate any type of data as Objects (as we did in Chapter 24), it would be nice if we could detect type mismatches at compile time—this is known as compile-time type safety. For example, if a Stack should store only Integer values, attempting to push a String onto that Stack should cause a compile-time error. Similarly, a Sort method should be able to compare elements that are all guaranteed to have the same type. If we create type-specific versions of class Stack and method Sort, the Visual Basic compiler would certainly be able to ensure compile-time type safety. However, this would require that we create many copies of the same basic code.

This chapter discusses one of Visual Basic's newest features—generics—which provides the means to create the general models mentioned above. Generic methods enable you to specify a set of related methods with a single method declaration. Generic classes enable you to specify a set of related classes with a single class declaration. Similarly, generic interfaces enable you to specify a set of related interfaces with a single interface declaration. Generics provide compile-time type safety. [*Note:* You can also implement generic Structures and Delegates. For more information, see the Visual Basic language specification version 8.0, available at www.microsoft.com/downloads/details.aspx?FamilyId=6D50D709-EAA4-44D7-8AF3-E14280403E6E&displaylang=en.]

We can write a generic method for sorting an array of objects, then invoke the generic method separately with an Integer array, a Double array, a String array and so on, to sort each different type of array. The compiler performs type checking to ensure that the array passed to the sorting method contains only elements of the same type. We can write a single generic Stack class that manipulates a stack of objects, then instantiate Stack objects for a stack of Integers, a stack of Doubles, a stack of Strings and so on. The compiler performs type checking to ensure that the Stack stores only elements of the same type.

This chapter presents examples of generic methods and generic classes. It also considers the relationships between generics and other Visual Basic features, such as overloading and inheritance. Chapter 26, Collections, discusses the .NET Framework's generic and non-generic collections classes. A collection is a data structure that maintains a group of related objects or values. The .NET Framework collection classes use generics to allow you to specify the exact types of object that a particular collection will store.

25.2 Motivation for Generic Methods

Overloaded methods are often used to perform similar operations on different types of data. To motivate the concepte of generic methods, let's begin with an example (Fig. 25.1) that contains three overloaded `PrintArray` methods (lines 19–25, 28–34 and 37–43). These methods display the elements of an `Integer` array, a `Double` array and a `Char` array, respectively. In Section 25.3, we reimplement this program more concisely and elegantly using a single generic method.

```vb
 1   ' Fig. 25.1: OverloadedMethods.vb
 2   ' Using overloaded methods to print arrays of different types.
 3   Module OverloadedMethods
 4      Sub Main()
 5         ' create arrays of Integer, Double and Char types
 6         Dim integerArray As Integer() = {1, 2, 3, 4, 5, 6}
 7         Dim doubleArray As Double() = {1.1, 2.2, 3.3, 4.4, 5.5, 6.6, 7.7}
 8         Dim charArray As Char() = {"H"c, "E"c, "L"c, "L"c, "O"c}
 9
10         Console.WriteLine("Array integerArray contains:")
11         PrintArray(integerArray) ' pass an Integer array argument
12         Console.WriteLine("Array doubleArray contains:")
13         PrintArray(doubleArray) ' pass a Double array argument
14         Console.WriteLine("Array charArray contains:")
15         PrintArray(charArray) ' pass a Char array
16      End Sub ' Main
17
18      ' output Integer array
19      Sub PrintArray(ByVal inputArray() As Integer)
20         For Each element As Integer In inputArray
21            Console.Write(element.ToString() & " ")
22         Next element
23
24         Console.WriteLine(vbCrLf)
25      End Sub ' PrintArray
26
27      ' output Double array
28      Sub PrintArray(ByVal inputArray() As Double)
29         For Each element As Double In inputArray
30            Console.Write(element.ToString() & " ")
31         Next element
32
33         Console.WriteLine(vbCrLf)
34      End Sub ' PrintArray
```

Fig. 25.1 | Displaying arrays of different types using overloaded methods. (Part 1 of 2.)

```
35
36          ' output Char array
37          Sub PrintArray(ByVal inputArray() As Char)
38              For Each element As Char In inputArray
39                  Console.Write(element.ToString() & " ")
40              Next element
41
42              Console.WriteLine(vbCrLf)
43          End Sub ' PrintArray
44      End Module ' OverloadedMethods
```

```
Array integerArray contains:
1 2 3 4 5 6

Array doubleArray contains:
1.1 2.2 3.3 4.4 5.5 6.6 7.7

Array charArray contains:
H E L L O
```

Fig. 25.1 | Displaying arrays of different types using overloaded methods. (Part 2 of 2.)

The program begins by declaring and initializing three arrays—six-element Integer array integerArray (line 6), seven-element Double array doubleArray (line 7) and five-element Char array charArray (line 8). Then lines 10–15 output the arrays.

When the compiler encounters a method call, it attempts to locate a method declaration that has the same method name and parameters that match the argument types in the method call. In this example, each PrintArray call exactly matches one of the PrintArray method declarations. For example, line 11 calls PrintArray with integerArray as its argument. At compile time, the compiler determines argument integerArray's type (i.e., Integer()), attempts to locate a method named PrintArray that specifies a single Integer() parameter (which it finds in lines 19–25) and sets up a call to that method. Similarly, when the compiler encounters the PrintArray call in line 13, it determines argument doubleArray's type (i.e., Double()), then attempts to locate a method named PrintArray that specifies a single Double() parameter (which it finds in lines 28–34) and sets up a call to that method. Finally, when the compiler encounters the PrintArray call in line 15, it determines argument charArray's type (i.e., Char()), then attempts to locate a method named PrintArray that specifies a single Char() parameter (which it finds in lines 37–43) and sets up a call to that method.

Study each PrintArray method. Note that the array element type (Integer, Double or Char) appears in two locations in each method—the method header (lines 19, 28 and 37) and the For Each statement header (lines 20, 29 and 38). If we replace the element type in each method with a generic name—we chose E to represent the "element" type—then all three methods would look like the one in Fig. 25.2. It appears that if we can replace the array element type in each of the three methods with a single "generic type parameter," then we should be able to declare one PrintArray method that can display the elements of *any* array. The method in Fig. 25.2 will not compile because its syntax is not correct—we declare a generic PrintArray method with the proper syntax in Fig. 25.3.

```
1    Public Sub PrintArray(ByVal inputArray() As E)
2       For Each element As E In inputArray
3          Console.Write(element.ToString() & " ")
4       Next element
5
6       Console.WriteLine(vbCrLf)
7    End Sub ' PrintArray
```

Fig. 25.2 | PrintArray method in which actual type names are replaced by convention with the generic name E (for "element"). [*Note:* This code will not compile.]

25.3 Generic Method Implementation

The overloaded methods of Fig. 25.1 can be more compactly and conveniently coded using a single generic method. You can write a single generic method declaration that can be called at different times with arguments of different types. Based on the types of the arguments passed to the generic method, the compiler handles each method call appropriately.

Figure 25.3 reimplements the application of Fig. 25.1 using a single generic Print-Array method (lines 19–25). Note that the PrintArray method calls in lines 11, 13 and 15 are identical to those in Fig. 25.1, the outputs of the two applications are identical and the code in Fig. 25.3 is 18 lines shorter than the code in Fig. 25.1. As illustrated in

```
1    ' Fig. 25.3: GenericMethod.vb
2    ' Using overloaded methods to print arrays of different types.
3    Module GenericMethod
4       Sub Main()
5          ' create arrays of integer, double and char
6          Dim integerArray As Integer() = {1, 2, 3, 4, 5, 6}
7          Dim doubleArray As Double() = {1.1, 2.2, 3.3, 4.4, 5.5, 6.6, 7.7}
8          Dim charArray As Char() = {"H"c, "E"c, "L"c, "L"c, "O"c}
9
10         Console.WriteLine("Array integerArray contains:")
11         PrintArray(integerArray) ' pass an integer array argument
12         Console.WriteLine("Array doubleArray contains:")
13         PrintArray(doubleArray) ' pass a double array argument
14         Console.WriteLine("Array charArray contains:")
15         PrintArray(charArray) ' pass a char array argument
16      End Sub ' Main
17
18      ' output array of all types
19      Public Sub PrintArray(Of E)(ByVal inputArray() As E)
20         For Each element As E In inputArray
21            Console.Write(element.ToString() & " ")
22         Next element
23
24         Console.WriteLine(vbCrLf)
25      End Sub ' PrintArray
26   End Module ' GenericMethod
```

Fig. 25.3 | Printing array elements using generic method PrintArray. (Part I of 2.)

```
Array integerArray contains:
1 2 3 4 5 6

Array doubleArray contains:
1.1 2.2 3.3 4.4 5.5 6.6 7.7

Array charArray contains:
H E L L O
```

Fig. 25.3 | Printing array elements using generic method `PrintArray`. (Part 2 of 2.)

Fig. 25.3, generics enable us to create and test our code once, then reuse the code for many different types of data. This demonstrates the expressive power of generics.

Line 19 begins method `PrintArray`'s declaration. All generic method declarations have a **type parameter list** delimited by parentheses—`(Of E)` in this example—that follows the method's name. Each type parameter list begins with the keyword `Of` and contains one or more **type parameters** separated by commas. A type parameter is an identifier that is used in place of actual type names. The type parameters can be used to declare the return type, the parameter types and the local variable types in a generic method declaration; the type parameters act as placeholders for the types of the arguments passed to the generic method. A generic method's body is declared like that of any other method. Note that the type parameter names throughout the method declaration must match those declared in the type parameter list. For example, line 20 declares `element` in the For Each statement as type `E`, which matches the type parameter (`E`) declared in line 19. Also, a type parameter can be declared only once in the type parameter list but can appear more than once in the method's parameter list. Type parameter names need not be unique among different generic methods.

Common Programming Error 25.1

If you forget to include the type parameter list when declaring a generic method, the compiler will not recognize the type parameter names when they are encountered in the method. This results in compilation errors.

Method `PrintArray`'s type parameter list (line 19) declares type parameter `E` as the placeholder for the array element type that `PrintArray` will output. Note that `E` appears in the method's parameter list as the array element type (line 19). The For Each statement header (line 20) also uses `E` as the `element` type. These are the same two locations where the overloaded `PrintArray` methods of Fig. 25.1 specified `Integer`, `Double` or `Char` as the array element type. The remainder of `PrintArray` is identical to the version in Fig. 25.1.

Good Programming Practice 25.1

According to msdn.microsoft.com/library/en-us/dndotnet/html/BestPractices.asp, it is recommended that type parameters be specified as individual capital letters. Typically, a type parameter that represents the type of an element in an array (or other collection) is named E for "element" or T for "type."

As in Fig. 25.1, the program in Fig. 25.3 begins by declaring and initializing six-element `Integer` array `integerArray` (line 6), seven-element `Double` array `doubleArray` (line 7) and five-element `Char` array `charArray` (line 8). Then each array is output by calling

PrintArray (lines 11, 13 and 15)—once with argument integerArray, once with argument doubleArray and once with argument charArray.

When the compiler encounters a method call, such as line 11, it analyzes the set of methods (both non-generic and generic) that might match the method call, looking for a method that matches the call exactly. If there are no exact matches, the compiler picks the best match. If there are no matching methods, or if there is more than one best match, the compiler generates an error. The complete details of method-call resolution can be found in Section 11.8.1 of the Visual Basic Language Specification version 8.0, which can be downloaded from:

> www.microsoft.com/downloads/details.aspx?
>   FamilyId=6D50D709-EAA4-44D7-8AF3-E14280403E6E&displaylang=en

For line 11, the compiler determines that an exact match occurs if the type parameter E in lines 19 and 20 of method PrintArray's declaration is replaced with the type of the elements in the method call's argument integerArray (i.e., Integer). Then the compiler sets up a call to PrintArray with Integer as the type argument for the type parameter E. This is known as the type inferencing process. The same process is repeated for the calls to method PrintArray in lines 13 and 15.

Common Programming Error 25.2

If the compiler cannot find a single non-generic or generic method declaration that is a best match for a method call, or if there are multiple best matches, a compilation error occurs.

You can also use **explicit type arguments** to indicate the exact type that should be used to call a generic function. For example, line 11 could be written as

```
PrintArray(Of Integer)(integerArray) ' call Integer version
```

In the preceding method call, the first set of parentheses contains the explicit type argument Integer that should be used to replace type parameter E in lines 19 and 20 of method PrintArray's declaration.

The compiler also determines whether the operations performed on the method's type parameters can be applied to elements of the type stored in the array argument. The only operation performed on the array elements in this example is to output the String representation of the elements. Line 21 calls ToString on the current array element being processed. Since all objects have a ToString method, the compiler is satisfied that line 21 performs a valid operation for any array element.

By declaring PrintArray as a generic method in Fig. 25.3, we eliminated the need for the overloaded methods of Fig. 25.1, saving 18 lines of code and creating a reusable method that can output the string representations of the elements of *any* array, not just arrays of Integer, Double or Char elements.

25.4 Type Constraints

In this section, we present a generic Maximum method that determines and returns the largest of its three arguments (all of the same type). The generic method in this example uses the type parameter to declare both the method's return type and its parameters. Normally, when comparing values to determine which one is greater, you would use the > operator.

However, this operator is not overloaded for use with every type that is built into the FCL or that might be defined by extending the FCL types. Generic code is restricted to performing operations that are guaranteed to work for every possible type. Thus, an expression like variable1 < variable2 is not allowed unless the compiler can ensure that the operator < is provided for every type that will ever be used in the generic code. Similarly, you cannot call a method on a generic-type variable unless the compiler can ensure that all types that will ever be used in the generic code support that method.

IComparable(Of T) Interface
It is possible to compare two objects of the same type if that type implements the generic interface IComparable(Of T) from namespace System. A benefit of implementing this interface is that IComparable(Of T) objects can be used with the sorting and searching methods of classes in the System.Collections.Generic namespace—we discuss these methods in Chapter 26, Collections. The structures in the FCL that correspond to the primitive types (such as Int32 for primitive type Integer) all implement this interface. Types that implement IComparable(Of T) must declare a CompareTo method for comparing objects. For example, if we have two Integers, integer1 and integer2, they can be compared with the expression:

```
integer1.CompareTo(integer2)
```

Method CompareTo must return 0 if the objects are equal, a negative integer if integer1 is less than integer2 or a positive integer if integer1 is greater than integer2. It is the responsibility of the programmer who declares a type that implements IComparable(Of T) to declare method CompareTo such that it compares the contents of two objects of that type and returns the appropriate result.

Specifying Type Constraints
Even though IComparable objects can be compared, they cannot be used with generic code by default, because not all types implement interface IComparable(Of T). We can, however, restrict the types that can be used with a generic method or class to ensure that they meet certain requirements. This feature—known as a **type constraint**—limits the type arguments that can be supplied to a particular type parameter. Figure 25.4 declares method Maximum (lines 16–31) with a type constraint that requires each of the method's arguments to be of type IComparable(Of T). This restriction is important because not all objects can be compared. However, all IComparable(Of T) objects are guaranteed to have a CompareTo method that can be used in method Maximum to determine the largest of its three arguments.

Generic method Maximum uses type parameter T as the return type of the method (line 17), as the type of method parameters x, y and z (line 17), and as the type of local variable max (line 18). Generic method Maximum specifies the type constraint for type parameter T in its type parameter list in line 16. In this case, the type parameter list (Of T As IComparable(Of T)) indicates that this method requires the type arguments to implement interface IComparable(Of T). If no type constraint is specified, the default type constraint is Object.

Visual Basic provides several kinds of type constraints. A **class constraint** indicates that the type argument must be an object of a specific base class or one of its subclasses. An **interface constraint** indicates that the type argument's class must implement a specific interface. The type constraint in line 16 is an example of an interface constraint, because

```
 1    ' Fig 25.4: MaximumTest.vb
 2    ' Generic method maximum returns the largest of three objects.
 3    Module MaximumTest
 4       Sub Main()
 5          Console.WriteLine("Maximum of {0}, {1} and {2} is {3}" & _
 6             vbCrLf, 3, 4, 5, Maximum(3, 4, 5))
 7          Console.WriteLine("Maximum of {0}, {1} and {2} is {3}" & _
 8             vbCrLf, 6.6, 8.8, 7.7, Maximum(6.6, 8.8, 7.7))
 9          Console.WriteLine("Maximum of {0}, {1} and {2} is {3}" & _
10             vbCrLf, "pear", "apple", "orange", _
11             Maximum("pear", "apple", "orange"))
12       End Sub ' Main
13
14       ' generic function determines the
15       ' largest of the IComparable objects
16       Public Function Maximum(Of T As IComparable(Of T)) _
17          (ByVal x As T, ByVal y As T, ByVal z As T) As T
18          Dim max As T = x ' assume x is initially the largest
19
20          ' compare y with max
21          If y.CompareTo(max) > 0 Then
22             max = y ' y is the largest so far
23          End If
24
25          ' compare z with max
26          If z.CompareTo(max) > 0 Then
27             max = z ' z is the largest
28          End If
29
30          Return max ' return largest object
31       End Function ' Maximum
32    End Module ' MaximumTest
```

```
Maximum of 3, 4 and 5 is 5

Maximum of 6.6, 8.8 and 7.7 is 8.8

Maximum of pear, apple and orange is pear
```

Fig. 25.4 | Generic method `Maximum` with a type constraint on its type parameter.

`IComparable(Of T)` is an interface. You can specify that the type argument must be a reference type or a value type by using the **reference type constraint** (`Class`) or the **value type constraint** (`Structure`), respectively. Finally, you can specify a **New constraint** to indicate that the generic code can use operator `New` to create new objects of the type represented by the type parameter. If a type parameter is specified with a `New` constraint, the type argument's class must be a concrete class. Also, the class must provide a `Public` parameterless or default constructor to ensure that objects of the class can be created without passing constructor arguments; otherwise, a compilation error occurs.

It is possible to apply **multiple constraints** to a type parameter. To do so, simply provide a comma-separated list of constraints in the type parameter list. If you have a class constraint, reference type constraint or value type constraint, it must be listed first—only one of these types of constraints can be used for each type parameter. Interface constraints (if any) are listed next. The `New` constraint is listed last (if there is one).

Analyzing the Code

Method `Maximum` assumes that its first argument (`x`) is the largest and assigns it to local variable `max` (line 18). Next, lines 21–23 determine whether `y` is greater than `max`. The condition invokes `y`'s `CompareTo` method to compare `y` to `max`. If `y` is greater than `max`, then `y` is assigned to variable `max` (line 22). Similarly, lines 26–28 determine whether `z` is greater than `max`. If so, line 27 assigns `z` to `max`. Then line 30 returns `max` to the caller.

In `Main` (lines 4–12), line 6 calls `Maximum` with the integers 3, 4 and 5. Generic method `Maximum` is a match for this call, but its arguments must implement interface `IComparable(Of T)` to ensure that they can be compared. Type `Integer` is a synonym for `Structure Int32`, which implements interface `IComparable(Of Integer)`. Thus, Integers (and other primitive types) are valid arguments to method `Maximum`.

Line 8 passes three `Double` arguments to `Maximum`. Again, this is allowed because primitive type `Double` is a synonym for the FCL's `Double Structure`, which implements `IComparable(Of Double)`. Line 11 passes `Maximum` three `Strings`, which are also `IComparable(Of String)` objects. Note that we intentionally placed the largest value in a different position in each method call (lines 6, 8 and 11) to show that the generic method always finds the maximum value, regardless of its position in the argument list and regardless of the inferred type argument.

25.5 Overloading Generic Methods

Generic methods can be overloaded. A class can provide two or more generic methods with the same name but different method parameters. For example, we could provide a second version of generic method `PrintArray` (Fig. 25.3) with the additional parameters `lowIndex` and `highIndex` that specify the portion of the array to output (see Exercise 25.8). A generic method can also be overloaded by another generic method with the same method name and a different number of type parameters, or by a generic method with different numbers of type parameters and method parameters.

A generic method can be overloaded by non-generic methods that have the same method name and number of parameters. When the compiler encounters a method call, it searches for the method declaration that most precisely matches the method name and the argument types specified in the call. For example, generic method `PrintArray` of Fig. 25.3 could be overloaded with a version specific to `Strings` that outputs the `Strings` in neat, tabular format (see Exercise 25.9). If the compiler cannot match a method call to either a non-generic method or a generic method, or if there is ambiguity due to multiple possible matches, the compiler generates an error. Generic methods can also be overloaded by non-generic methods that have the same method name but a different number of method parameters.

25.6 Generic Classes

The concept of a data structure (e.g., a stack) that contains data elements can be understood independently of the element type it manipulates. A generic class provides a means for describing a class's capabilities in a type-independent manner. You can then instantiate type-specific objects of the generic class. This capability is an opportunity for software re-usability.

Once you have a generic class, you can use a simple, concise notation to indicate the actual type(s) that should be used in place of the class's type parameter(s). At compilation time, the compiler ensures the type safety of your code, and the runtime system replaces type parameters with actual arguments to enable your client code to interact with the generic class.

One generic Stack class, for example, could be the basis for creating many Stack classes (e.g., "Stack of Double," "Stack of Integer," "Stack of Char," "Stack of Employee"). Figure 25.5 presents a generic Stack class declaration. A generic class declaration is similar to a non-generic class declaration, except that the class name is followed by a type parameter list (line 3). Type parameter E represents the element type the Stack will manipulate. As with generic methods, the type parameter list of a generic class can have one or more type parameters separated by commas. (You will create a generic class with two type parameters in Exercise 25.11.) Type parameter E is used throughout the Stack class declaration (Fig. 25.5) to represent the element type. Class Stack declares variable elements as an array of type E (line 5). This array (created at line 15 or 17) will store the Stack's elements. [*Note:* This example implements a Stack as an array. As you have seen in Chapter 24, Data Structures, Stacks also are commonly implemented as linked lists.]

```vb
 1    ' Fig. 25.5: Stack.vb
 2    ' Generic class Stack
 3    Public Class Stack(Of E)
 4       Private top As Integer ' location of the top element
 5       Private elements() As E ' array that stores Stack elements
 6
 7       ' parameterless constructor creates a Stack of the default size
 8       Public Sub New()
 9          MyClass.New(10) ' default stack size 10 elements
10       End Sub ' New
11
12       ' constructor creates a Stack of the specified number of elements
13       Public Sub New(ByVal stackSize As Integer)
14          If stackSize > 0 Then ' validate stackSize
15             elements = New E(stackSize - 1) {} ' create stackSize elements
16          Else
17             elements = New E(9) {} ' create 10 elements
18          End If
19
20          top = -1 ' Stack initially empty
21       End Sub ' New
22
23       ' push element onto the Stack; if successful, return true
24       ' otherwise, throw FullStackException
25       Public Sub Push(ByVal pushValue As E)
26          If top = elements.Length - 1 Then ' Stack is full
27             Throw New FullStackException(String.Format( _
28                "Stack is full, cannot push {0}", pushValue))
29          End If
```

Fig. 25.5 | Generic class Stack declaration. (Part 1 of 2.)

```
30
31            top += 1 ' increment top
32            elements(top) = pushValue ' place pushValue on Stack
33        End Sub ' Push
34
35        ' return the top element if not empty
36        ' else throw EmptyStackException
37        Public Function Pop() As E
38            If top = -1 Then ' Stack is empty
39                Throw New EmptyStackException("Stack is empty, cannot pop")
40            End If
41
42            top -= 1 ' decrement top
43            Return elements(top + 1) ' return top value
44        End Function ' Pop
45    End Class ' Stack
```

Fig. 25.5 | Generic class Stack declaration. (Part 2 of 2.)

Class Stack has two constructors. The parameterless constructor (lines 8–10) passes the default stack size (10) to the one-argument constructor (line 9) by invoking the constructor in lines 13–21. The one-argument constructor (lines 13–21) validates the stack-Size argument and creates an array of the specified stackSize if it is greater than 0 or an array of 10 elements otherwise.

Method Push (lines 25–33) first determines whether an attempt is being made to push an element onto a full Stack. If so, lines 27–28 throw a FullStackException (declared in Fig. 25.6). If the Stack is not full, line 31 increments the top counter to indicate the new top position, and line 32 places the argument in that location of array elements.

Method Pop (lines 37–44) first determines whether an attempt is being made to pop an element from an empty Stack. If so, line 39 throws an EmptyStackException (declared in Fig. 25.7). Otherwise, line 42 decrements the top counter to indicate the new top position, and line 43 returns the original top element of the Stack.

Classes FullStackException (Fig. 25.6) and EmptyStackException (Fig. 25.7) each provide a parameterless constructor and a one-argument constructor. The parameterless

```
1    ' Fig. 25.6: FullStackException.vb
2    ' Indicates a stack is full.
3    Public Class FullStackException : Inherits ApplicationException
4        ' parameterless constructor
5        Public Sub New()
6            MyBase.New("Stack is full")
7        End Sub ' New
8
9        ' one-parameter constructor
10       Public Sub New(ByVal exception As String)
11           MyBase.New(exception)
12       End Sub ' New
13   End Class ' FullStackException
```

Fig. 25.6 | FullStackException class declaration.

```
 1    ' Fig. 25.7: EmptyStackException.vb
 2    ' Indicates a stack is empty
 3    Public Class EmptyStackException : Inherits ApplicationException
 4       ' parameterless constructor
 5       Public Sub New()
 6          MyBase.New("Stack is empty")
 7       End Sub ' New
 8
 9       ' one-parameter constructor
10       Public Sub New(ByVal exception As String)
11          MyBase.New(exception)
12       End Sub ' New
13    End Class ' EmptyStackException
```

Fig. 25.7 | EmptyStackException class declaration.

constructor sets the default error message, and the one-argument constructor sets a custom error message.

As with generic methods, when a generic class is compiled, the compiler performs type checking on the class's type parameters to ensure that they can be used with the code in the generic class. The constraints determine the operations that can be performed on the type parameters. The runtime system replaces the type parameters with the actual types. For class Stack (Fig. 25.5), no type constraint is specified, so the default type constraint, Object, is used. The scope of a generic class's type parameter is the entire class.

Now let's consider an application (Fig. 25.8) that uses the Stack generic class. Lines 8–9 declare variables of type Stack(Of Double) (pronounced "Stack of Double") and Stack(Of Integer) (pronounced "Stack of Integer"). The types Double and Integer are the type arguments. The compiler replaces the type parameters in the generic class with the type arguments so that the compiler can perform type checking. Method Main instantiates objects doubleStack of size 5 (line 12) and integerStack of size 10 (line 13), then calls methods TestPushDouble (lines 22–38), TestPopDouble (lines 41–58), TestPushInteger (lines 61–77) and TestPopInteger (lines 80–97) to manipulate the two Stacks in this example.

Method TestPushDouble (lines 22–38) invokes method Push to place the Double values 1.1, 2.2, 3.3, 4.4 and 5.5 stored in array doubleElements onto doubleStack. The loop in lines 29–32 terminates when the test program attempts to Push a sixth value onto doubleStack (which is full, because doubleStack can store only five elements). In this case, the method throws a FullStackException (Fig. 25.6) to indicate that the Stack is full. Lines 33–36 catch this exception, and print the message and stack-trace information (see the output of Fig. 25.8). The stack trace indicates the exception that occurred and shows that Stack method Push generated the exception in line 27 of the file Stack.vb (Fig. 25.5). The trace also shows that method Push was called by StackTest method TestPushDouble in line 31 of StackTest.vb. This information enables you to determine the methods that were on the method call stack at the time that the exception occurred. The program catches the exception, so the Visual Basic runtime environment considers the exception to have been handled, and the program can continue executing.

Method TestPopDouble (lines 41–58) invokes Stack method Pop in an infinite loop to remove all the values from the stack. Note in the output that the values are popped in last-in, first-out (LIFO) order—this, of course, is the defining characteristic of stacks. The loop in lines 49–52 continues until the stack is empty. An EmptyStackException occurs when an attempt is made to pop from the empty stack. This causes the program to proceed to the Catch block (lines 53–56) and handle the exception, so that the program can continue executing. When the test program attempts to Pop a sixth value, the doubleStack is empty, so method Pop throws an EmptyStackException.

```vb
 1  ' Fig. 25.8: StackTest.vb
 2  ' Stack generic class test program.
 3  Module StackTest
 4     ' create arrays of doubles and integers
 5     Dim doubleElements() As Double = {1.1, 2.2, 3.3, 4.4, 5.5, 6.6}
 6     Dim integerElements() As Integer = {1, 2, 3, 4, 5, 6, 7, 8, 9, 10, 11}
 7
 8     Dim doubleStack As Stack(Of Double) ' stack stores double objects
 9     Dim integerStack As Stack(Of Integer) ' stack stores integer objects
10
11     Sub Main()
12        doubleStack = New Stack(Of Double)(5) ' Stack of doubles
13        integerStack = New Stack(Of Integer)(10) ' Stack of integers
14
15        TestPushDouble() ' push doubles onto doubleStack
16        TestPopDouble() ' pop doubles from doubleStack
17        TestPushInteger() ' push integers onto integerStack
18        TestPopInteger() ' pop integers from integerStack
19     End Sub ' Main
20
21     ' test Push method with doubleStack
22     Sub TestPushDouble()
23        ' push elements onto stack
24        Try
25           Console.WriteLine(vbCrLf & _
26              "Pushing elements onto doubleStack")
27
28           ' push elements onto stack
29           For Each element As Double In doubleElements
30              Console.Write("{0:F1} ", element)
31              doubleStack.Push(element) ' push onto doubleStack
32           Next element
33        Catch exception As FullStackException
34           Console.Error.WriteLine()
35           Console.Error.WriteLine("Message: " & exception.Message)
36           Console.Error.WriteLine(exception.StackTrace)
37        End Try
38     End Sub ' TestPushDouble
39
40     ' test Pop method with doubleStack
41     Sub TestPopDouble()
42        ' pop elements from stack
43        Try
44           Console.WriteLine(vbCrLf & _
45              "Popping elements from doubleStack")
```

Fig. 25.8 | Generic class Stack test program. (Part 1 of 3.)

```vb
46
47              Dim popValue As Double ' store element removed from stack
48              ' remove all elements from Stack
49              While True
50                 popValue = doubleStack.Pop() ' pop from doubleStack
51                 Console.Write("{0:F1} ", popValue)
52              End While
53           Catch exception As EmptyStackException
54              Console.Error.WriteLine()
55              Console.Error.WriteLine("Message: " & exception.Message)
56              Console.Error.WriteLine(exception.StackTrace)
57           End Try
58        End Sub ' TestPopDouble
59
60        ' test Push method with integerStack
61        Sub TestPushInteger()
62           ' push elements onto stack
63           Try
64              Console.WriteLine(vbCrLf & _
65                 "Pushing elements onto integerStack")
66
67              ' push elements onto stack
68              For Each element As Integer In integerElements
69                 Console.Write("{0} ", element)
70                 integerStack.Push(element) ' push onto integerStack
71              Next element
72           Catch exception As FullStackException
73              Console.Error.WriteLine()
74              Console.Error.WriteLine("Message: " & exception.Message)
75              Console.Error.WriteLine(exception.StackTrace)
76           End Try
77        End Sub ' TestPushInteger
78
79        ' test Pop method with integerStack
80        Sub TestPopInteger()
81           ' pop elements from stack
82           Try
83              Console.WriteLine(vbCrLf & _
84                 "Popping elements from integerStack")
85
86              Dim popValue As Integer ' store element removed from stack
87              ' remove all elements from Stack
88              While True
89                 popValue = integerStack.Pop() ' pop from integerStack
90                 Console.Write("{0} ", popValue)
91              End While
92           Catch exception As EmptyStackException
93              Console.Error.WriteLine()
94              Console.Error.WriteLine("Message: " & exception.Message)
95              Console.Error.WriteLine(exception.StackTrace)
96           End Try
97        End Sub ' TestPopInteger
98     End Module ' StackTest
```

Fig. 25.8 | Generic class Stack test program. (Part 2 of 3.)

```
Pushing elements onto doubleStack
1.1 2.2 3.3 4.4 5.5 6.6
Message: Stack is full, cannot push 6.6
   at Stack.Stack`1.Push(E pushValue) in
      C:\examples\ch25\Fig25_05-08\Stack\Stack.vb:line 27
   at Stack.StackTest.TestPushDouble() in
      C:\examples\ch25\Fig25_05-08\Stack\StackTest.vb:line 31

Popping elements from doubleStack
5.5 4.4 3.3 2.2 1.1
Message: Stack is empty, cannot pop
   at Stack.Stack`1.Pop() in
      C:\examples\ch25\Fig25_05-08\Stack\Stack.vb:line 39
   at Stack.StackTest.TestPopDouble() in
      C:\examples\ch25\Fig25_05-08\Stack\StackTest.vb:line 50

Pushing elements onto integerStack
1 2 3 4 5 6 7 8 9 10 11
Message: Stack is full, cannot push 11
   at Stack.Stack`1.Push(E pushValue) in
      C:\examples\ch25\Fig25_05-08\Stack\Stack.vb:line 27
   at Stack.StackTest.TestPushInteger() in
      C:\examples\ch25\Fig25_05-08\Stack\StackTest.vb:line 70

Popping elements from integerStack
10 9 8 7 6 5 4 3 2 1
Message: Stack is empty, cannot pop
   at Stack.Stack`1.Pop() in
      C:\examples\ch25\Fig25_05-08\Stack\Stack.vb:line 39
   at Stack.StackTest.TestPopInteger() in
      C:\examples\ch25\Fig25_05-08\Stack\StackTest.vb:line 89
```

Fig. 25.8 | Generic class Stack test program. (Part 3 of 3.)

Method TestPushInteger (lines 61–77) invokes Stack method Push to place values onto integerStack until it is full. Method TestPopInteger (lines 80–97) invokes Stack method Pop to remove values from integerStack until it is empty. Once again, note that the values pop off in last-in, first-out (LIFO) order.

Creating Generic Methods to Test Class Stack(Of E)

The code is almost identical in methods TestPushDouble and TestPushInteger for pushing values onto a Stack(Of Double) or a Stack(Of Integer), respectively. Similarly the code is almost identical in methods TestPopDouble and TestPopInteger for popping values from a Stack(Of Double) or a Stack(Of Integer), respectively. This presents another opportunity to use generic methods. Figure 25.9 declares generic method TestPush (lines 25–42) to perform the same tasks as TestPushDouble and TestPushInteger in Fig. 25.8—that is, Push values onto a Stack(Of E). Similarly, generic method TestPop (lines 44–62) performs the same tasks as TestPopDouble and TestPopInteger in Fig. 25.8—that is, Pop values off a Stack(Of E). Except for the slight differences in the stack traces, the output of Fig. 25.9 matches the output of Fig. 25.8.

Method Main (lines 11–23) creates the Stack(Of Double) and Stack(Of Integer) objects (lines 12–13) . Lines 16–22 invoke generic methods TestPush and TestPop to test the Stack objects.

```vb
 1    ' Fig 25.9: StackTest.vb
 2    ' Stack generic class test program.
 3    Module StackTest
 4       ' create arrays of doubles and integers
 5       Dim doubleElements() As Double = {1.1, 2.2, 3.3, 4.4, 5.5, 6.6}
 6       Dim integerElements() As Integer = {1, 2, 3, 4, 5, 6, 7, 8, 9, 10, 11}
 7
 8       Dim doubleStack As Stack(Of Double) ' stack stores double objects
 9       Dim integerStack As Stack(Of Integer) ' stack stores integer objects
10
11       Sub Main()
12          doubleStack = New Stack(Of Double)(5) ' Stack of doubles
13          integerStack = New Stack(Of Integer)(10) ' Stack of integers
14
15          ' push doubles onto doubleStack
16          TestPush("doubleStack", doubleStack, doubleElements)
17          ' pop doubles from doubleStack
18          TestPop("doubleStack", doubleStack)
19          ' push integers onto integerStack
20          TestPush("integerStack", integerStack, integerElements)
21          ' pop integers from integerStack
22          TestPop("integerStack", integerStack)
23       End Sub ' Main
24
25       Sub TestPush(Of E)(ByVal name As String, ByVal stack As Stack(Of E), _
26          ByVal elements() As E)
27          ' push elements onto stack
28          Try
29             Console.WriteLine(vbCrLf & _
30                "Pushing elements onto " & name)
31
32             ' push elements onto stack
33             For Each element As E In elements
34                Console.Write("{0} ", element)
35                stack.Push(element) ' push onto stack
36             Next element
37          Catch exception As FullStackException
38             Console.Error.WriteLine()
39             Console.Error.WriteLine("Message: " & exception.Message)
40             Console.Error.WriteLine(exception.StackTrace)
41          End Try
42       End Sub ' TestPush
43
44       Sub TestPop(Of E)(ByVal name As String, ByVal stack As Stack(Of E))
45          ' pop elements off stack
46          Try
47             Console.WriteLine(vbCrLf & _
48                "Popping elements from " & name)
49
50             Dim popValue As E ' store element removed from stack
51
```

Fig. 25.9 | Passing a generic type Stack to a generic method. (Part 1 of 2.)

```
52              ' remove all elements from Stack
53            While True
54                popValue = stack.Pop() ' pop from stack
55                Console.Write("{0} ", popValue)
56            End While
57          Catch exception As EmptyStackException
58              Console.Error.WriteLine()
59              Console.Error.WriteLine("Message: " & exception.Message)
60              Console.Error.WriteLine(exception.StackTrace)
61          End Try
62        End Sub ' TestPop
63    End Module ' StackTest
```

```
Pushing elements onto doubleStack
1.1 2.2 3.3 4.4 5.5 6.6
Message: Stack is full, cannot push 6.6
    at Stack.Stack`1.Push(E pushValue) in
      C:\examples\ch25\Fig25_09\Stack\Stack.vb:line 27
    at Stack.StackTest.TestPush[E](String name, Stack`1 stack,
      IEnumerable`1 elements)
      in C:\examples\ch25\Fig25_09\Stack\StackTest.vb:line 35

Popping elements from doubleStack
5.5 4.4 3.3 2.2 1.1
Message: Stack is empty, cannot pop
    at Stack.Stack`1.Pop()
      in C:\examples\ch25\Fig25_09\Stack\Stack.vb:line 39
    at Stack.StackTest.TestPop[E](String name, Stack`1 stack)
      in C:\examples\ch25\Fig25_09\Stack\StackTest.vb:line 54

Pushing elements onto integerStack
1 2 3 4 5 6 7 8 9 10 11
Message: Stack is full, cannot push 11
    at Stack.Stack`1.Push(E pushValue)
      in C:\examples\ch25\Fig25_09\Stack\Stack.vb:line 27
    at Stack.StackTest.TestPush[E](String name, Stack`1 stack,
      IEnumerable`1 elements)
      in C:\examples\ch25\Fig25_09\Stack\StackTest.vb:line 35

Popping elements from integerStack
10 9 8 7 6 5 4 3 2 1
Message: Stack is empty, cannot pop
    at Stack.Stack`1.Pop()
      in C:\examples\ch25\Fig25_09\Stack\Stack.vb:line 39
    at Stack.StackTest.TestPop[E](String name, Stack`1 stack)
      in C:\examples\ch25\Fig25_09\Stack\StackTest.vb:line 54
```

Fig. 25.9 | Passing a generic type Stack to a generic method. (Part 2 of 2.)

Generic method TestPush (lines 25–42) uses type parameter E (specified in line 25) to represent the type stored in the Stack. The generic method takes three arguments—a String that represents the name of the Stack object for output purposes, an object of type Stack(Of E) and an array of type E that contains the elements that will be Pushed onto Stack(Of E). Note that the compiler enforces consistency between the type of the Stack and the elements that will be pushed onto the Stack when Push is invoked, which is the type argument of the generic method call. Generic method `TestPop` (lines 44–62) takes two arguments—a `String` that represents the name of the `Stack` object for output purposes and an object of type `Stack(Of E)`.

25.7 **Notes on Generics and Inheritance**

Generics can be used with inheritance in several ways:

- A generic class can be derived from a non-generic class. For example, class `Object` (which is not a generic class) is a direct or indirect base class of every generic class.

- A generic class can be derived from another generic class. Recall that in Chapter 24, the non-generic `Stack` class (Fig. 24.13) inherits from the non-generic `List` class (Fig. 24.6). You could also create a generic `Stack` class by inheriting from a generic `List` class.

- A non-generic class can be derived from a generic class with a specific type argument. For example, you can implement a non-generic `AddressList` class which inherits from a generic `List` class that stores `Address` objects.

25.8 **Wrap-Up**

This chapter introduced generics—one of Visual Basic's newest capabilities. We discussed how generics ensure compile-time type safety by checking for type mismatches at compile time. You learned that the compiler will allow generic code to compile only if all the operations performed on the type parameters in the generic code are supported for all the types that could be used with the generic code. You also learned how to declare generic methods and classes using type parameters. We demonstrated how to use a type constraint to specify the requirements for a type parameter—a key component of compile-time type safety. We discussed several kinds of type constraints, including reference type constraints, value type constraints, class constraints, interface constraints and `New` constraints. You learned that a `New` constraint indicates that the type argument's class must be concrete and must provide a `Public` parameterless or default constructor so that objects of that type can be created with `New`. We also discussed how to implement multiple type constraints for a type parameter. We showed how generics improve code reuse. Finally, we mentioned several ways to use generics in inheritance. In the next chapter, we demonstrate the FCL's collection classes, interfaces and algorithms. Collection classes are pre-built data structures that you can reuse in your applications, saving you time. We present both generic collections and the older, non-generic collections.

Summary

Section 25.1 Introduction
- Generic methods enable you to specify a set of related methods with a single method declaration.
- Generic classes enable you to specify a set of related classes with a single class declaration.
- Generic interfaces enable you to specify a set of related interfaces with a single interface declaration.
- Generics provide compile-time type safety.

Section 25.2 Motivation for Generic Methods

- Overloaded methods are often used to perform similar operations on different types of data.

- When the compiler encounters a method call, it attempts to locate a method declaration that has the same method name and parameters that match the argument types in the method call.

Section 25.3 Generic Method Implementation

- If the same operations are performed by several overloaded methods, the overloaded methods can be more compactly and conveniently coded using a generic method.

- You can write a single generic method declaration that can be called at different times with arguments of different types. Based on the types of the arguments passed to the generic method, the compiler handles each method call appropriately.

- All generic methods have a type parameter list delimited by parentheses that follows the method's name. Each type parameter list contains one or more type parameters, separated by commas.

- A type parameter is used in place of actual type names. The type parameters can be used to declare the return type, parameter types and local variable types in a generic method declaration; the type parameters act as placeholders for the types of the arguments passed to the method.

- A generic method's body is declared like that of any other method. The type parameter names throughout the method declaration must match those declared in the type parameter list.

- A type parameter can be declared only once in the type parameter list but can appear more than once in the method's parameter list. Type parameter names need not be unique among different generic methods.

- When the compiler encounters a method call, it analyzes the set of methods (both non-generic and generic) that might match the method call, looking for a method that matches the call exactly. If there are no exact matches, the compiler picks the best match. If there are no matching methods, or if there is more than one best match, the compiler generates an error.

- You can use explicit type arguments to indicate the exact type that should be used to call a generic method.

Section 25.4 Type Constraints

- Generic code is restricted to performing operations that are guaranteed to work for every possible type. Thus, an expression like variable1 < variable2 is not allowed unless the compiler can ensure that the operator < is provided for every type that will ever be used in the generic code. Similarly, you cannot call a method on a variable of a generic type unless the compiler can ensure that all types that will ever be used for the variable support that method.

- It is possible to compare two objects of the same type if that type implements the generic interface IComparable(Of T) (of namespace System), which declares method CompareTo.

- IComparable(Of T) objects can be used with the sorting and searching methods of classes in the System.Collections.Generic namespace.

- The structures in the FCL that correspond to the primitive types all implement interface IComparable(Of T).

- If you declare a type that implements IComparable(Of T) you must define the method CompareTo such that it compares the contents of two objects of that type and returns the appropriate result.

- You can restrict the types that can be used with a generic method or class to ensure that they meet certain requirements. This feature—known as a type constraint—restricts the type of the argument supplied to a particular type parameter. For example, the type parameter list (Of T As IComparable(Of T)) indicates that the type arguments must implement interface IComparable(Of T). If no type constraint is specified, the default type constraint is Object.

- A class constraint indicates that the type argument must be an object of a specific base class or one of its subclasses.

- An interface constraint indicates that the type argument's class must implement that interface.

- You can specify that the type argument must be a reference type or a value type by using the reference type constraint (Class) or the value type constraint (Structure), respectively.

- You can specify a New constraint to indicate that the generic code can use operator New to create new objects of the type represented by the type parameter. If a type parameter is specified with a New constraint, the type argument's class must be concrete and must provide Public a parameterless or default constructor to ensure that objects of the class can be created without passing constructor arguments; otherwise, a compilation error occurs.

- It is possible to apply multiple constraints to a type parameter by providing a comma-separated list of constraints in the type parameter list.

- If you have a class constraint, reference type constraint or value type constraint, it must be listed first—only one of these types of constraints can be used for each type parameter. Interface constraints (if any) are listed next. The New constraint is listed last (if there is one).

Section 25.5 Overloading Generic Methods

- A generic method may be overloaded. A class can provide two or more generic methods with the same name but different method parameters.

- A generic method can also be overloaded by another generic method with the same method name and a different number of type parameters, or by a generic method with different numbers of type parameters and method parameters.

- A generic method can be overloaded by non-generic methods that have the same method name and number of parameters. When the compiler encounters a method call, it searches for the method declaration that matches the method name and the argument types specified in the call.

- Generic methods can also be overloaded by non-generic methods that have the same method name but a different number of method parameters.

Section 25.6 Generic Classes

- A generic class provides a means for describing a class's operations in a type-independent manner.

- Once you have a generic class, you can use a simple, concise notation to indicate the actual type(s) that should be used in place of the class's type parameter(s). At compilation time, the compiler ensures the type safety of your code, and the runtime system replaces type parameters with actual arguments to enable your client code to interact with the generic class.

- A generic class declaration is similar to a non-generic class declaration, except that the class name is followed by a type parameter list and possibly constraints on its type parameter.

- As with generic methods, the type parameter list of a generic class can have one or more type parameters separated by commas.

- When a generic class is compiled, the compiler performs type checking on the class's type parameters to ensure that they can be used with the code in the generic class. The constraints determine the operations that can be performed on the type parameters.

Section 25.7 Notes on Generics and Inheritance

- A generic class can be derived from a non-generic class.

- A generic class can be derived from another generic class.

- A non-generic class can be derived from a generic class.

Terminology

class constraint	multiple constraints
CompareTo method of interface IComparable(Of T)	New constraint
	Of keyword
compile-time type safety	overloading generic methods
default type constraint (Object) of a type parameter	reference type constraint (Class)
	scope of a type parameter
explicit type argument	type argument
generic class	type checking
generic interface	type constraint
generic method	type inference
generics	type parameter
IComparable(Of T) interface	type parameter list
interface constraint	value type constraint (Structure)

Self-Review Exercises

25.1 State whether each of the following is *true* or *false*. If *false*, explain why.
a) A generic method cannot have the same method name as a non-generic method.
b) All generic method declarations have a type parameter list that immediately precedes the method name.
c) A generic method can be overloaded by another generic method with the same method name but a different number of type parameters.
d) A type parameter can be declared only once in the type parameter list but can appear more than once in the method's parameter list.
e) Type parameter names among different generic methods must be unique.
f) The scope of a generic class's type parameter is the entire class.
g) A type parameter can have at most one interface constraint, but multiple class constraints.

25.2 Fill in the blanks in each of the following:
a) _____ enable you to specify, with a single method declaration, a set of related methods; _____ enable you to specify, with a single class declaration, a set of related classes.
b) A type parameter list is delimited by _____.
c) The _____ of a generic method can be used to specify the types of the arguments to the method, to specify the return type of the method and to declare variables within the method.
d) The statement "Dim objectStack as New Stack(Of Integer)();" indicates that objectStack stores _____.
e) In a generic class declaration, the class name is followed by a(n) _____.
f) The _____ constraint requires that the type argument must have a Public parameterless constructor.

Answers to Self-Review Exercises

25.1 a) False. A generic method can be overloaded by non-generic methods with the same or a different number of arguments. b) False. All generic method declarations have a type parameter list that immediately follows the method's name. c) True. d) True. e) False. Type parameter names among different generic methods need not be unique. f) True. g) False. A type parameter can have at most one class constraint, but multiple interface constraints.

25.2 a) Generic methods, Generic classes. b) parentheses. c) type parameters. d) `Integers`. e) type parameter list. f) `New`.

Exercises

25.3 Explain the use of the following notation in a Visual Basic program:

```
public Class Array(Of E)
```

25.4 How can generic methods be overloaded?

25.5 The compiler performs a matching process to determine which method to call when a method is invoked. Under what circumstances does an attempt to make a match result in a compile-time error?

25.6 Explain why a Visual Basic program might use the statement

```
Dim workerlist As New Array(Of Employee)();
```

25.7 Write a generic method, `Search`, that implements the linear search algorithm. Method `Search` should compare the search key with each element in the array until the search key is found or until the end of the array is reached. If the search key is found, return its location in the array; otherwise, return -1. Write a test application that inputs and searches an `Integer` array and a `Double` array. Provide buttons that the user can click to randomly generate `Integer` and `Double` values. Display the generated values in a `TextBox`, so that the user knows what values they can search for [*Hint:* The type parameter for method `Search` should be constrained with `IComparable(Of E)` so that you can use method `CompareTo` to compare the search key to the elements in the array.]

25.8 Overload generic method `PrintArray` of Fig. 25.3 so that it takes two additional `Integer` arguments: `lowIndex` and `highIndex`. A call to this method prints only the designated portion of the array. Validate `lowIndex` and `highIndex`. If either is out-of-range, or if `highIndex` is less than or equal to `lowIndex`, the overloaded `PrintArray` method should throw an `InvalidIndexException`; otherwise, `PrintArray` should return the number of elements printed. Then modify `Main` to exercise both versions of `PrintArray` on arrays `integerArray`, `doubleArray` and `charArray`. Test all capabilities of both versions of `PrintArray`.

25.9 Overload generic method `PrintArray` of Fig. 25.3 with a non-generic version that prints an array of strings in neat, tabular format, as shown in the sample output that follows:

```
Array stringArray contains:
one      two      three    four
five     six      seven    eight
```

25.10 Write a simple generic version of method `IsEqualTo` that compares its two arguments with the `Equals` method, and returns `True` if they are equal and `False` otherwise. Use this generic method in a program that calls `IsEqualTo` with a variety of primitive types, such as `Double` or `Integer`. What result do you get when you attempt to run this program?

25.11 Write a generic class `Pair` which has two type parameters, F and S, representing the types of the first and second element of the pair, respectively. Add properties (with `Get` and `Set` accessors) for the first and second elements of the pair. [*Hint:* The class header should be `Public Class Pair(Of F, S)`.]

25.12 Convert classes `TreeNode` and `Tree` from Figs. 24.20–24.21 into generic classes. To insert an object in a `Tree`, the object must be compared to the objects in existing `TreeNodes`. For this reason, classes `TreeNode` and `Tree` should specify `IComparable(Of E)` as the interface constraint of each class's type parameter. After modifying classes `TreeNode` and `Tree`, write a test application that creates three `Tree` objects—one that stores `Integers`, one that stores `Doubles` and one that stores `Strings`. Insert 10 values into each tree. Then output the preorder, inorder and postorder traversals for each `Tree`.

25.13 Modify your test program from Exercise 25.12 to use generic method `TestTree` to test the three `Tree` objects. The method should be called three times—once for each `Tree` object.

26

Collections

OBJECTIVES

In this chapter you will learn:

- The non-generic and generic collections that are provided by the .NET Framework.

- To use class **Array**'s **Shared** methods to manipulate arrays.

- To use enumerators to "walk through" a collection.

- To use the **For Each** statement with the .NET collections.

- To use non-generic collection classes **ArrayList**, **Stack** and **Hashtable**.

- To use generic collection classes **SortedDictionary** and **LinkedList**.

- To use synchronization wrappers to make collections safe in multithreaded applications.

26.1 Introduction

In Chapter 24, we discussed how to create and manipulate data structures. The discussion was "low level" in the sense that we painstakingly created each element of each data structure dynamically with New and modified the data structures by directly manipulating their elements and references to their elements. In this chapter, we consider the prepackaged data-structure classes provided by the .NET Framework. These classes are known as collection classes—they store collections of data. Each instance of one of these classes is a collection of items. Some examples of collections are the cards you hold in a card game, the songs stored in your computer, the real-estate records in your local registry of deeds (which map book numbers and page numbers to property owners), and the players on your favorite sports team.

Collection classes enable you to store sets of items by using existing data structures without concern for how they are implemented. This is a nice example of code reuse. You can code faster and expect excellent performance, maximizing execution speed and minimizing memory consumption. We discuss the collection interfaces that list the capabilities of each collection type, the implementation classes and the enumerators that "walk through" collections.

The .NET Framework provides three collections namespaces. The System.Collections namespace contains collections that store references to Objects. The System.Collections.Generic namespace (new to .NET 2.0) contains generic classes to store collections of specified types. (We introduced generic methods and classes in Chapter 25.) The System.Collections.Specialized namespace (also new to .NET 2.0) contains several collections that support specific types, such as Strings and bits. To learn more about the classes from this namespace, visit

msdn2.microsoft.com/en-us/library/system.collections.specialized.aspx

The collections in these namespaces provide standardized components that are written for broad reuse; you do not need to write your own collection classes.

26.2 **Collections Overview**

All the collection classes in the .NET Framework implement some combination of the collection interfaces. These interfaces declare the operations to be performed on various types of collections. Figure 26.1 lists some of the interfaces of the .NET Framework collections. All the interfaces in Fig. 26.1 are declared in namespace System.Collections and have generic analogues in namespace System.Collections.Generic. Implementations of these interfaces are provided within the framework. You may also create your own custom implementations.

Earlier versions of the .NET Framework provided the collection classes in the System.Collections and System.Collections.Specialized namespaces. These classes stored and manipulated Object references. You could store any Object in a collection. One inconvenient aspect of storing Object references occurs when retrieving them from a collection. An application normally needs to process specific types of objects, so the Object references obtained from a collection typically need to be downcast to an appropriate type.

The .NET Framework 2.0 now also includes the System.Collections.Generic namespace, which uses the generics capabilities we introduced in Chapter 25. Many of these new classes are simply generic counterparts of the classes in the System.Collections namespace. This means that you can specify the exact type that will be stored in a collection. You also receive the benefits of compile-time type checking—the compiler ensures that you are using appropriate types with your collection and, if not, issues compile-time error messages. Also, once you specify the type stored in a collection, any item you retrieve from the collection will have the correct type. This eliminates the need for explicit type casts that can

Interface	Description
ICollection	The root interface in the collections hierarchy from which interfaces IList and IDictionary inherit. Contains a Count property to determine the size of a collection and a CopyTo method for copying a collection's contents into a traditional array.
IList	An ordered collection that can be manipulated like an array. Provides an indexer for accessing elements with an Integer index. Also has methods for modifying and searching a collection, including Add, Remove, Contains and IndexOf.
IDictionary	A collection of values, indexed by an arbitrary "key" object. Provides an indexer for accessing elements with an Object index and methods for modifying the collection (e.g., Add, Remove). IDictionary property Keys contains the Objects used as indices, and property Values contains all the stored Objects.
IEnumerable	An object that can be enumerated. This interface contains exactly one method, GetEnumerator, which returns an IEnumerator object (discussed in Section 26.3). ICollection implements IEnumerable, so all collection classes implement IEnumerable directly or indirectly.

Fig. 26.1 | Some common collection interfaces.

throw InvalidCastExceptions at execution time if the referenced object is not of the appropriate type. This also eliminates the overhead of explicit casting, improving efficiency.

In this chapter, we demonstrate six collection classes—Array, ArrayList, Stack, Hashtable, generic SortedDictionary and generic LinkedList—plus built-in array capabilities. Namespace System.Collections provides several other data structures, including BitArray (a collection of true/false values), Queue and SortedList (a collection of key–value pairs that are sorted by key and can be accessed either by key or by index). Figure 26.2 summarizes many of the collection classes. We also discuss the IEnumerator interface. Collection classes can create enumerators that allow you to walk through the collections. Although these enumerators have different implementations, they all implement the IEnumerator interface so that they can be processed polymorphically. As we will soon see, the For Each statement is simply a convenient notation for using an enumerator. In the next section, we begin our discussion by examining enumerators and the collections capabilities for array manipulation.

Class	Implements	Description
System namespace:		
Array	IList	The base class of all conventional arrays. See Section 26.3.
System.Collections namespace:		
ArrayList	IList	Mimics a conventional array, but will grow or shrink as needed to accommodate the number of elements. See Section 26.4.1.
BitArray	ICollection	A memory-efficient array of Booleans.
Hashtable	IDictionary	An unordered collection of key–value pairs that can be accessed by key. See Section 26.4.3.
Queue	ICollection	A first-in, first-out (FIFO) collection. See Section 24.6.
SortedList	IDictionary	An ordered collection of key–value pairs that sorts data by keys and can be accessed either by key or by index.
Stack	ICollection	A last-in, first-out (LIFO) collection. See Section 26.4.2.
System.Collections.Generic namespace:		
Dictionary(Of K, E)	IDictionary(Of K, E)	A generic, unordered collection of key–value pairs that can be accessed by key.

Fig. 26.2 | Some collection classes of the .NET Framework. (Part 1 of 2.)

Class	Implements	Description
LinkedList(Of E)	ICollection(Of E)	A generic doubly linked list. See Section 26.5.2.
List(Of E)	IList(Of E)	A generic ArrayList.
Queue(Of E)	ICollection(Of E)	A generic Queue.
SortedDictionary _ (Of K, E)	IDictionary(Of K, E)	A generic Dictionary that sorts data by the keys in a binary tree. See Section 26.5.1.
SortedList(Of K, E)	IDictionary(Of K, E)	A generic SortedList.
Stack(Of E)	ICollection(Of E)	A generic Stack.

[*Note: All collection classes directly or indirectly implement ICollection and IEnumerable (or the equivalent generic interfaces ICollection(Of E) and IEnumerable(Of E)).*]

Fig. 26.2 | Some collection classes of the .NET Framework. (Part 2 of 2.)

26.3 Class Array and Enumerators

Chapter 8 presented basic array-processing capabilities. All arrays implicitly inherit from the MustInherit class Array (namespace System). Array property Length specifies the number of elements in the array. In addition, class Array provides Shared methods that provide algorithms for processing arrays. Typically, class Array overloads these methods—for example, Array method Reverse can reverse the order of the elements in an entire array or can reverse the elements in a specified range of elements in an array. For a complete list of class Array's Shared methods, visit:

msdn2.microsoft.com/en-us/library/system.array.aspx

Figure 26.3 demonstrates several Shared methods of class Array.

```
1   ' Fig. 26.3: UsingArray.vb
2   ' Array class Shared methods for common array manipulations.
3   Imports System.Collections
4
5   Module UsingArray
6      Private integerValues As Integer() = {1, 2, 3, 4, 5, 6}
7      Private doubleValues As Double() = {8.4, 9.3, 0.2, 7.9, 3.4}
8      Private integerValuesCopy As Integer()
9
10     Sub Main()
11        ' defaults to zeroes
12        integerValuesCopy = New Integer(integerValues.Length - 1) {}
13
14        Console.WriteLine("Initial array values:" & vbCrLf)
15        PrintArrays() ' output initial array contents
```

Fig. 26.3 | Array class used to perform common array manipulations. (Part 1 of 3.)

```
16
17          ' sort doubleValues
18          Array.Sort(doubleValues)
19
20          ' copy integerValues into integerValuesCopy
21          Array.Copy(integerValues, integerValuesCopy, integerValues.Length)
22
23          Console.WriteLine(vbCrLf & _
24             "Array values after Sort and Copy:" & vbCrLf)
25          PrintArrays() ' output array contents
26          Console.WriteLine()
27
28          ' search for 5 in integerValues
29          Dim result As Integer = Array.BinarySearch(integerValues, 5)
30
31          If (result >= 0) Then
32             Console.WriteLine("5 found at element {0} in integerValues", _
33                result)
34          Else
35             Console.WriteLine("5 not found in integerValues")
36          End If
37
38          ' search for 8763 in integerValues
39          result = Array.BinarySearch(integerValues, 8763)
40
41          If (result >= 0) Then
42             Console.WriteLine("8763 found at element {0} in integerValues", _
43                result)
44          Else
45             Console.WriteLine("8763 not found in integerValues")
46          End If
47       End Sub ' Main
48
49    ' output array content with enumerators
50    Private Sub PrintArrays()
51       Console.Write("doubleValues: ")
52
53       ' iterate through the Double array with an enumerator
54       Dim enumerator As IEnumerator = doubleValues.GetEnumerator()
55
56       While (enumerator.MoveNext())
57          Console.Write(enumerator.Current & " ")
58       End While
59
60       Console.Write(vbCrLf & "integerValues: ")
61
62       ' iterate through the integer array with an enumerator
63       enumerator = integerValues.GetEnumerator()
64
65       While (enumerator.MoveNext())
66          Console.Write(enumerator.Current & " ")
67       End While
68
```

Fig. 26.3 | Array class used to perform common array manipulations. (Part 2 of 3.)

```
69          Console.Write(vbCrLf & "integerValuesCopy: ")
70
71          ' iterate through the second integer array with a For Each statement
72          For Each element As Integer In integerValuesCopy
73             Console.Write(element & " ")
74          Next element
75
76          Console.WriteLine()
77       End Sub ' PrintArrays
78    End Module ' UsingArray
```

```
Initial array values:

doubleValues: 8.4 9.3 0.2 7.9 3.4
integerValues: 1 2 3 4 5 6
integerValuesCopy: 0 0 0 0 0 0

Array values after Sort and Copy:

doubleValues: 0.2 3.4 7.9 8.4 9.3
integerValues: 1 2 3 4 5 6
integerValuesCopy: 1 2 3 4 5 6

5 found at element 4 in integerValues
8763 not found in integerValues
```

Fig. 26.3 | Array class used to perform common array manipulations. (Part 3 of 3.)

The Imports statement in line 3 enables us to use the classes and interfaces of namespace System.Collections (such as interface IEnumerator, which we discuss shortly). A reference to the assembly for this namespace is implicitly included in every application, so we do not need to add any new references to the project file. Class Array is in namespace System, which is implicitly imported.

Our test class declares three array variables (lines 6–8). The first two lines initialize integerValues and doubleValues to an Integer and Double array, respectively. Variable integerValuesCopy is intended to demonstrate Array's Copy method, so it is declared, but does not yet refer to an array.

Line 12 initializes integerValuesCopy to an Integer array with the same length as array integerValues. Line 15 calls the PrintArrays method (lines 50–77) to output the initial contents of all three arrays. We discuss the PrintArrays method shortly. We can see from the output of Fig. 26.3 that each element of array integerValuesCopy is initialized to the default value 0.

Line 18 uses Shared Array method Sort to sort array doubleValues. When this method returns, the array contains its original elements sorted in ascending order.

Line 21 uses Shared Array method Copy to copy elements from array integerValues to array intValuesCopy. The first argument is the array to copy (integerValues), the second argument is the destination array (integerValuesCopy) and the third argument is an Integer representing the number of elements to copy (integerValues.Length specifies all elements).

Lines 29 and 39 invoke Shared Array method BinarySearch to perform binary searches on array integerValues. Method BinarySearch receives the *sorted* array to search and the key for which to search. The method returns the index in the array at which it finds the key (or a negative number otherwise). Note that `BinarySearch` assumes that it receives a sorted array.

Common Programming Error 26.1

Passing an unsorted array to `BinarySearch` is a logic error—the value returned is undefined.

The `PrintArrays` method (lines 50–77) uses class `Array`'s methods to loop though each array. Recall that `Array` implements the `IEnumerable` interface. All arrays inherit implicitly from `Array`, so both the `Integer()` and `Double()` array types implement `IEnumerable` interface method `GetEnumerator`, which returns an enumerator that can iterate over the collection. In line 54, the `GetEnumerator` method obtains an enumerator for array `doubleValues`. Interface `IEnumerator` (which all enumerators implement) defines methods `MoveNext` and `Reset` and property `Current`. `MoveNext` moves the enumerator to the next element in the collection. The first call to `MoveNext` positions the enumerator at the first element of the collection. `MoveNext` returns `True` if there is at least one more element in the collection; otherwise, the method returns `False`. Method `Reset` positions the enumerator before the first element of the collection. Methods `MoveNext` and `Reset` throw an `InvalidOperationException` if the contents of the collection are modified in any way after the enumerator is created. Property `Current` returns the object at the current location in the collection.

Common Programming Error 26.2

If a collection is modified after an enumerator is created for it, the enumerator immediately becomes invalid—a method called with the enumerator after this point throws an `Invalid-OperationException`. For this reason, enumerators are said to be "fail fast."

When an enumerator is returned by the `GetEnumerator` method in line 54, it is initially positioned *before* the first element in `Array` `doubleValues`. Then, when line 56 calls `MoveNext` in the first iteration of the loop, the enumerator advances to the first element in `doubleValues`. The loop in lines 56–58 iterates over the elements until the enumerator passes the end of `doubleValues` and `MoveNext` returns `False`. Each iteration of the loop uses the enumerator's `Current` property to obtain and output the current array element. Lines 63–67 iterate over array `integerValues`.

Note that `PrintArrays` is called twice (lines 15 and 25), so `GetEnumerator` is called twice on `doubleValues`. The `GetEnumerator` method (lines 54 and 63) always returns an enumerator positioned before the first element. Also note that the `IEnumerator` property `Current` is read only. Enumerators cannot be used to modify the contents of collections, only to obtain the contents.

The `For Each` statement in lines 72–74 iterates over the collection elements. The `For Each` statement implicitly obtains an enumerator via the `GetEnumerator` method of a collection and uses the enumerator's `MoveNext` method and `Current` property to traverse the collection, just as we did explicitly in lines 54–58 and lines 63–67. For this reason, we can use the `For Each` statement to iterate over *any* collection that implements the `IEnumerable` interface—not just arrays. We demonstrate this functionality in the next section when we discuss class `ArrayList`.

Other `Shared` `Array` methods include `Clear` (to set a range of elements to 0 or `Nothing`), `CreateInstance` (to create a new array of a specified type), `IndexOf` (to locate the first occurrence of an object in an array or portion of an array), `LastIndexOf` (to locate the last occurrence of an object in an array or portion of an array) and `Reverse` (to reverse the contents of an array or portion of an array).

26.4 **Non-Generic Collections**

The `System.Collections` namespace in the .NET Framework Class Library is the primary source for non-generic collections. These classes provide standard implementations of many of the data structures discussed in Chapter 24 with collections that store references of type `Object`. In this section, we demonstrate classes `ArrayList`, `Stack` and `Hashtable`.

26.4.1 Class `ArrayList`

In most programming languages, conventional arrays have a fixed size—they cannot grow or shrink dynamically to conform to an application's execution-time memory requirements. In some applications, this fixed-size limitation presents a problem for programmers. They must choose between using fixed-size arrays that are large enough to store the maximum number of elements the application may require, and dynamic data structures that can grow and shrink the amount of memory required to store data in response to an application's changing requirements at execution time.

The .NET Framework's `ArrayList` collection class mimics the functionality of conventional arrays and provides dynamic resizing of the collection through the class's methods. At any time, an `ArrayList` contains a certain number of elements less than or equal to its **capacity**—the number of elements currently reserved for the `ArrayList`. An application can manipulate the capacity with `ArrayList` property `Capacity`. If an `ArrayList` needs to grow, by default it doubles its `Capacity`.

Performance Tip 26.1

As with linked lists, inserting additional elements into an `ArrayList` whose current size is less than its capacity is a fast operation.

Performance Tip 26.2

It is a slow operation to insert an element into an `ArrayList` that needs to grow larger to accommodate a new element. An `ArrayList` that is at its capacity must have its memory reallocated and the existing values copied into it.

Performance Tip 26.3

If storage is at a premium, use method `TrimToSize` of class `ArrayList` to trim an `ArrayList` to its exact size. This will optimize the `ArrayList`'s memory use. Be careful—if the application needs to insert additional elements, the process will be slower because the `ArrayList` must grow dynamically (trimming leaves no room for growth).

Performance Tip 26.4

The default capacity increment, doubling the size of the `ArrayList`, may seem to waste storage, but doubling is an efficient way for an `ArrayList` to grow quickly to "about the right size." This is a much more efficient use of time than growing the `ArrayList` by one element at a time in response to insert operations.

ArrayLists store references to Objects. All classes derive from class Object, so an ArrayList can contain objects of any reference type and boxed primitive-type values. Figure 26.4 lists some useful methods and properties of class ArrayList.

Figure 26.5 demonstrates class ArrayList and several of its methods. Class Array-List belongs to the System.Collections namespace (line 3). Lines 6–8 declare two arrays of Strings (colors and removeColors) that we will use to fill two ArrayList objects. When the application begins execution, we create an ArrayList (named list) with an initial capacity of one element (line 11). The For Each statement in lines 15–17 adds the five elements of array colors to list via ArrayList's **Add** method, so list grows to accommodate these new elements. Line 21 uses ArrayList's overloaded constructor to create a new ArrayList (named removeList) initialized with the contents of array removeColors. This constructor can initialize the contents of an ArrayList with the elements of any ICollection passed to it. Many of the collection classes have such a constructor. Note that the constructor call in line 21 initializes ArrayList removeList in a manner similar to lines 15–17.

Method or property	Description
Add	Adds an Object to the ArrayList and returns an Integer specifying the index at which the Object was added.
Capacity	Property that gets and sets the number of elements for which space is currently reserved in the ArrayList.
Clear	Removes all the elements from the ArrayList.
Contains	Returns True if the specified Object is in the ArrayList; otherwise, returns False.
Count	Read-only property that gets the number of elements stored in the ArrayList.
IndexOf	Returns the index of the first occurrence of the specified Object in the ArrayList.
Insert	Inserts an Object at the specified index.
Remove	Removes the first occurrence of the specified Object.
RemoveAt	Removes an Object at the specified index.
RemoveRange	Removes a specified number of elements starting at a specified index in the ArrayList.
Sort	Sorts the ArrayList.
TrimToSize	Sets the Capacity of the ArrayList to the number of elements the ArrayList currently contains (Count).

Fig. 26.4 | Some methods and properties of class ArrayList.

```vbnet
1   ' Fig. 26.5: ArrayListTest.vb
2   ' Using class ArrayList.
3   Imports System.Collections
4
5   Module ArrayListTest
6      Private colors As String() = _
7         {"MAGENTA", "RED", "WHITE", "BLUE", "CYAN"}
8      Private removeColors As String() = {"RED", "WHITE", "BLUE"}
9
10     Sub Main()
11        Dim list As New ArrayList(1) ' initial capacity of 1
12
13        ' add the elements of the colors array
14        ' to the ArrayList list
15        For Each color As String In colors
16           list.Add(color) ' add color to the ArrayList list
17        Next color
18
19        ' add elements in the removeColors array to
20        ' the ArrayList removeList with the ArrayList constructor
21        Dim removeList As New ArrayList(removeColors)
22
23        Console.WriteLine("ArrayList: ")
24        DisplayInformation(list) ' output the list
25
26        ' remove from ArrayList list the colors in removeList
27        RemoveColorNames(list, removeList)
28
29        Console.WriteLine(vbCrLf & _
30           "ArrayList after calling RemoveColors: ")
31        DisplayInformation(list) ' output list contents
32     End Sub ' Main
33
34     ' displays information on the contents of an array list
35     Private Sub DisplayInformation(ByVal arrayList As ArrayList)
36        ' iterate through array list with a For Each statement
37        For Each element As Object In arrayList
38           Console.Write("{0} ", element) ' invokes ToString
39        Next element
40
41        ' display the size and capacity
42        Console.WriteLine(vbCrLf & "Size = {0}; Capacity = {1}", _
43           arrayList.Count, arrayList.Capacity)
44
45        Dim index As Integer = arrayList.IndexOf("BLUE")
46
47        If index <> -1 Then
48           Console.WriteLine("The array list contains BLUE at index {0}.", _
49              index)
50        Else
51           Console.WriteLine("The array list does not contain BLUE.")
52        End If
53     End Sub ' DisplayInformation
```

Fig. 26.5 | Using class ArrayList. (Part 1 of 2.)

```
54
55         ' remove colors specified in secondList from firstList
56     Private Sub RemoveColorNames(ByVal firstList As ArrayList, _
57         ByVal secondList As ArrayList)
58         ' iterate through second ArrayList like an array
59         For count As Integer = 0 To secondList.Count - 1
60             firstList.Remove(secondList(count))
61         Next count
62     End Sub ' RemoveColors
63   End Module ' ArrayListTest
```

```
ArrayList:
MAGENTA RED WHITE BLUE CYAN
Size = 5; Capacity = 8
The array list contains BLUE at index 3.

ArrayList after calling RemoveColors:
MAGENTA CYAN
Size = 2; Capacity = 8
The array list does not contain BLUE.
```

Fig. 26.5 | Using class ArrayList. (Part 2 of 2.)

Line 24 calls method DisplayInformation (lines 35–53) to output the contents of the list. This method uses a For Each statement to traverse the elements of an ArrayList. As we discussed in Section 26.3, the For Each statement is a convenient shorthand for calling ArrayList's GetEnumerator method and using an enumerator to traverse the elements of the collection. Also, we use an iteration variable of type Object because class ArrayList stores references to Objects.

We use properties **Count** and **Capacity** in lines 42–43 to display the current number of elements and the maximum number of elements that can be stored without allocating more memory to the ArrayList. The output of Fig. 26.5 indicates that the ArrayList has capacity 8—recall that an ArrayList doubles its capacity whenever it needs more space.

In line 45, we invoke method **IndexOf** to determine the position of the String "BLUE" in arrayList and store the result in local variable index. IndexOf returns -1 if the element is not found. Lines 47–52 determine whether arrayList contains "BLUE". If it does (i.e., index is not equal to -1), we output the index. ArrayList also provides method **Contains**, which simply returns True if an object is in the ArrayList, and False otherwise. Method Contains is preferred if we do not need the index of the element.

> **Performance Tip 26.5**
>
> *ArrayList methods IndexOf and Contains each perform a linear search, which is a costly operation for large ArrayLists. If the ArrayList is sorted, use ArrayList method BinarySearch to perform a more efficient search. Method BinarySearch returns the index of the element, or a negative number if the element is not found.*

After DisplayInformation returns, we call method RemoveColorNames (lines 56–62) with the two ArrayLists. Lines 59–61 iterate through secondList. Line 60 uses an indexer to access an ArrayList element by following the ArrayList reference name with parentheses (()) containing the desired element's index. An ArgumentOutOfRangeException occurs if the specified index is not both greater than 0 and less than the number of elements currently stored in the ArrayList (specified by the ArrayList's Count property).

We use the indexer to obtain each of secondList's elements, then remove each one from firstList with the **Remove** method. This method deletes a specified item from an ArrayList by performing a linear search and removing (only) the first occurrence of the specified object. All subsequent elements shift toward the beginning of the ArrayList to fill the emptied position.

After the call to RemoveColorNames, line 31 again outputs the contents of list, confirming that the elements of removeList were, indeed, removed.

26.4.2 Class Stack

The Stack class implements a stack data structure and provides much of the functionality that we defined in our own implementation in Section 24.5. Refer to that section for a discussion of stack concepts. We created a test application in Fig. 24.14 to demonstrate our StackInheritance data structure. We adapt Fig. 24.14 in Fig. 26.6 to demonstrate the .NET Framework collection class Stack.

```vb
1   ' Fig. 26.6: StackTest.vb
2   ' Demonstrating class Stack.
3   Imports System.Collections
4
5   Module StackTest
6      Sub Main()
7         Dim stack As New Stack() ' default Capacity of 10
8
9         ' create objects to store in the stack
10        Dim aBoolean As Boolean = True
11        Dim aCharacter As Char = "$"c
12        Dim anInteger As Integer = 34567
13        Dim aString As String = "hello"
14
15        ' use method Push to add items to (the top of) the stack
16        stack.Push(aBoolean)
17        PrintStack(stack)
18        stack.Push(aCharacter)
19        PrintStack(stack)
20        stack.Push(anInteger)
21        PrintStack(stack)
22        stack.Push(aString)
23        PrintStack(stack)
24
25        ' check the top element of the stack
26        Console.WriteLine("The top element of the stack is {0}" & _
27           vbCrLf, stack.Peek())
28
29        ' remove items from stack
30        Try
31           While True
32              Dim removedObject As Object = stack.Pop()
```

Fig. 26.6 | Demonstrating class Stack. (Part 1 of 2.)

```
33              Console.WriteLine(removedObject & " popped")
34              PrintStack(stack)
35           End While
36        Catch exception As InvalidOperationException
37           ' if exception occurs, print stack trace
38           Console.Error.WriteLine(exception)
39        End Try
40     End Sub ' Main
41
42     ' print the contents of a stack
43     Private Sub PrintStack(ByVal stack As Stack)
44        If stack.Count = 0 Then
45           ' the stack is empty
46           Console.WriteLine("stack is empty" & vbCrLf)
47        Else
48           Console.Write("The stack is: ")
49
50           ' iterate through the stack with a For Each statement
51           For Each element As Object In stack
52              Console.Write("{0} ", element) ' invokes ToString
53           Next element
54
55           Console.WriteLine(vbCrLf)
56        End If
57     End Sub ' PrintStack
58  End Module ' StackTest
```

```
The stack is: True

The stack is: $ True

The stack is: 34567 $ True

The stack is: hello 34567 $ True

The top element of the stack is hello

hello popped
The stack is: 34567 $ True

34567 popped
The stack is: $ True

$ popped
The stack is: True

True popped
stack is empty

System.InvalidOperationException: Stack empty.
   at System.Collections.Stack.Pop()
   at StackTest.StackTest.Main() in C:\examples\ch26\Fig26_06\StackTest\
      StackTest.vb:line 32
```

Fig. 26.6 | Demonstrating class Stack. (Part 2 of 2.)

Line 3 Imports class Stack. Line 7 creates a Stack with the default initial capacity (10 elements). Class Stack has methods Push and Pop to perform the basic stack operations.

Method Push takes an Object as an argument and inserts it at the top of the Stack. If the number of items on the Stack (the Count property) is equal to the capacity at the time of the Push operation, the Stack grows to accommodate more Objects. Lines 16, 18, 20 and 22 use method Push to add four elements (a Boolean, a Char, an Integer and a String) to the stack. After each Push, we invoke method PrintStack (lines 43–57) to output the contents of the stack. Note that this non-generic Stack class can store only references to Objects, so each of the value-type items—the Boolean, the Char and the Integer—are implicitly boxed before they are added to the Stack. (Namespace System.Collections.Generic provides a generic Stack class that has many of the same methods and properties used in Fig. 26.6.)

Method PrintStack (lines 43–57) uses Stack property Count to obtain the number of elements in Stack. If the stack is not empty (i.e., Count is not equal to 0), we use a For Each statement to iterate over the stack and output its contents by implicitly invoking the ToString method of each element. The For Each statement implicitly invokes Stack's GetEnumerator method, which we could have called explicitly to traverse the stack via an enumerator.

Method Peek returns the value of the top stack element, but does not remove the element from the Stack. We use Peek at line 27 to obtain the top object of the Stack, then output that object, implicitly invoking the object's ToString method. An InvalidOperationException occurs if the Stack is empty when the application calls Peek.

Method Pop takes no arguments—it removes and returns the object currently on top of the Stack. An infinite loop (lines 31–35) pops objects off the stack and outputs them until the stack is empty. When the application calls Pop on the empty stack, an InvalidOperationException is thrown. The Catch block (lines 36–38) outputs the exception, implicitly invoking the InvalidOperationException's ToString method to obtain its error message and stack trace.

Common Programming Error 26.3

Attempting to Peek or Pop an empty Stack (a Stack whose Count property is 0) causes an InvalidOperationException.

Although Fig. 26.6 does not demonstrate it, class Stack also has method Contains, which returns True if the Stack contains the specified object, and returns False otherwise.

26.4.3 Class Hashtable

When an application creates objects, it needs to manage those objects efficiently. This includes storing and retrieving objects. Storing and retrieving information with arrays is efficient if some aspect of your data directly matches the key value and if the keys are unique and tightly packed. If you have 100 employees with nine-digit Social Security numbers and you want to store and retrieve employee data by using the Social Security number as a key, it would nominally require an array with 999,999,999 elements, because there are 999,999,999 unique nine-digit numbers. If you have an array that large, you could get very high performance storing and retrieving employee records by simply using the Social Security number as the array index, but it would be a massive waste of memory.

Many applications have this problem—either the keys are of the wrong type (i.e., not non-negative integers), or they are of the right type, but they are sparsely spread over a large range.

What is needed is a high-speed scheme for converting keys such as Social Security numbers and inventory part numbers to unique array indices. Then, when an application needs to store something, the scheme could convert the application key rapidly to an index and the record of information could be stored at that location in the array. Retrieval occurs the same way—once the application has a key for which it wants to retrieve the data record, the application simply applies the conversion to the key, which produces the array subscript where the data resides in the array and retrieves the data.

The scheme we describe here is the basis of a technique called hashing, in which we store data in a data structure called a hash table. Why the name? Because, when we convert a key into an array subscript, we literally scramble the bits, making a "hash" of the number. The number actually has no real significance beyond its usefulness in storing and retrieving this particular data record.

A glitch in the scheme occurs when collisions occur (i.e., two different keys "hash into" the same cell, or element, in the array). Since we cannot store two different data records in the same space, we need to find an alternative home for all records beyond the first that hash to a particular array subscript. One scheme for doing this is to "hash again" (i.e., to reapply the hashing transformation to the key to provide a next candidate cell in the array). The hashing process is designed to be quite random, it is assumed is that an available cell will be found with just a few hashes.

Another scheme uses one hash to locate the first candidate cell. If the cell is occupied, successive cells are searched linearly until an available cell is found. Retrieval works the same way—the key is hashed once, and the resulting cell is checked to determine whether it contains the desired data. If it does, the search is complete. If it does not, successive cells are searched linearly until the desired data is found.

The most popular solution to hash-table collisions is to have each cell of the table be a hash "bucket"—typically, a linked list of all the key–value pairs that hash to that cell. This is the solution that the .NET Framework's `Hashtable` class implements.

The load factor affects the performance of hashing schemes. The load factor is the ratio of the number of objects stored in the hash table to the total number of cells of the hash table. As this ratio gets higher, the chance of collisions increases.

Performance Tip 26.6

The load factor in a hash table is a classic example of a space/time trade-off: By increasing the load factor, we get better memory utilization, but the application runs slower due to increased hashing collisions. By decreasing the load factor, we get better application speed because of reduced hashing collisions, but we get poorer memory utilization because a larger portion of the hash table remains empty.

The .NET Framework provides class `Hashtable` to enable you to easily employ hashing in applications. A hash function performs a calculation that determines where to place data in the hash table. The hash function is applied to the key in a key–value pair of objects. Class `Hashtable` can accept any `Object` as a key. For this reason, class `Object` defines method `GetHashCode`, which all classes inherit. Most classes that are candidates to be used as keys in a hash table override this method to provide one that performs efficient hash code calculations for a specific type. For example, a String has a hash code calculation that is based on the contents of the String. Figure 26.7 uses a Hashtable to count the number of occurrences of each word in a String.

Lines 4–5 contain Imports statements for the System.Text.RegularExpressions namespace (for class Regex, discussed in Chapter 16) and the System.Collections namespace (for class Hashtable). Class HashtableTest declares three methods. Method CollectWords (lines 17–40) inputs a String and returns a Hashtable in which each value stores the number of times that word appears in the String and the word is used as the key. Method DisplayHashtable (lines 43–54) displays in column format the Hashtable passed to it. The Main method (lines 8–14) invokes CollectWords (line 10), then passes the Hashtable returned by CollectWords to DisplayHashtable (line 13).

```vb
1   ' Fig. 26.7: HashtableTest.vb
2   ' Application counts the number of occurrences of each word in a String
3   ' and stores them in a hash table.
4   Imports System.Text.RegularExpressions
5   Imports System.Collections
6
7   Module HashtableTest
8      Sub Main()
9         ' create hash table based on user input
10        Dim table As Hashtable = CollectWords()
11
12        ' display hash table content
13        DisplayHashtable(table)
14     End Sub ' Main
15
16     ' create hash table from user input
17     Private Function CollectWords() As Hashtable
18        Dim table As New Hashtable() ' create a new hash table
19
20        Console.WriteLine("Enter a string: ") ' prompt for user input
21        Dim input As String = Console.ReadLine() ' get input
22
23        ' split input text into tokens
24        Dim words As String() = Regex.Split(input, "\s+")
25
26        ' processing input words
27        For Each word As String In words
28           Dim wordKey As String = word.ToLower() ' get word in lowercase
29
30           ' if the hash table contains the word
31           If table.ContainsKey(wordKey) Then
32              table(wordKey) = Convert.ToInt32(table(wordKey)) + 1
33           Else
34              ' add new word with a count of 1 to hash table
35              table.Add(wordKey, 1)
36           End If
37        Next
```

Fig. 26.7 | Application counts the number of occurrences of each word in a String and stores this information in a hash table. (Part 1 of 2.)

```
38
39          Return table
40      End Function ' CollectWords
41
42      ' display hash table content
43      Private Sub DisplayHashtable(ByVal table As Hashtable)
44          Console.WriteLine(vbCrLf & "Hashtable contains:" & _
45              vbCrLf & "{0,-12}{1,-12}", "Key:", "Value:")
46
47          ' generate output for each key in hash table
48          ' by iterating through the Keys property with a For Each statement
49          For Each key As Object In table.Keys
50              Console.WriteLine("{0,-12}{1,-12}", key, table(key))
51          Next
52
53          Console.WriteLine(vbCrLf & "size: {0}", table.Count)
54      End Sub ' DisplayHashtable
55  End Module ' HashtableTest
```

```
Enter a string:
As idle as a painted ship upon a painted ocean

Hashtable contains:
Key:        Value:
painted     2
a           2
upon        1
as          2
ship        1
idle        1
ocean       1

size: 7
```

Fig. 26.7 | Application counts the number of occurrences of each word in a `String` and stores this information in a hash table. (Part 2 of 2.)

Method `CollectWords` (lines 17–40) initializes local variable `table` with a new `Hashtable` (line 18) that has a default initial capacity of 0 elements and a default maximum load factor of 1.0. When the number of items in the `Hashtable` becomes greater than the number of cells times the load factor, the capacity is increased automatically. (This implementation detail is invisible to clients of the class.) Lines 20–21 prompt the user and input a `String`. We use `Shared` method `Split` of class `Regex` in line 24 to divide the `String` into words using whitespace characters as delimiters. This creates an array of "words," which we then store in local variable `words`.

The `For Each` statement in lines 27–37 iterates through the elements of array `words`. Each word is converted to lowercase with `String` method `ToLower`, then stored in variable `wordKey` (line 28). Line 31 calls `Hashtable` method `ContainsKey` to determine whether the word is in the hash table (and thus has occurred previously in the `String`). If the `Hashtable` does not contain an entry for the word, line 35 uses `Hashtable` method `Add` to create a new entry in the hash table, with the lowercase word as the key and an object containing

1 as the value. Note that autoboxing occurs when the application passes the Integer value 1 to method Add, because the hash table stores both the key and value as references to Objects.

Common Programming Error 26.4

Using the Add method to add a key that already exists in the hash table causes an ArgumentException.

If the word is already a key in the hash table, line 32 uses the Hashtable's indexer to obtain and set the key's associated value (the word count) in the hash table. We first downcast the value from an Object to an Integer. This unboxes the value so that we can increment it by 1. We then use the indexer to store the key's associated value. The incremented value is implicitly reboxed so that it can be stored in the hash table.

Invoking the Get accessor of a Hashtable indexer with a key that does not exist in the hash table returns a Nothing reference. Using the Set accessor with a key that does not exist in the hash table creates a new entry, as if you had used the Add method.

Line 39 returns the hash table to the Main method, which then passes it to method DisplayHashtable (lines 43–54), which displays all the entries. This method uses read-only property **Keys** (line 49) to get an ICollection that contains all the keys. Because ICollection extends IEnumerable, we can use this collection in the For Each statement in lines 49–51 to iterate over the keys of the hash table. This loop accesses and outputs each key and its value in a field width of -12. The negative field width indicates that the output should be left justified. Note that a hash table is not sorted, so the key–value pairs are not displayed in any particular order. Line 53 uses Hashtable property **Count** to get the number of key–value pairs in the Hashtable.

Lines 49–51 could also have used the For Each statement with the Hashtable object itself, rather than the Keys property. If you use a For Each statement with a Hashtable object, the iteration variable will be of type **DictionaryEntry**. The enumerator of a Hashtable (or any other class that implements **IDictionary**) uses the DictionaryEntry structure to store key–value pairs. This structure provides properties Key and Value for retrieving the key and value of the current element. If you do not need the key, class Hashtable also provides a read-only **Values** property that gets an ICollection of all the values stored in the Hashtable.

Problems with Non-Generic Collections

In the word-counting application in Fig. 26.7, our Hashtable stores its keys and data as Object references, even though we store only String keys and Integer values by convention. This results in some awkward code. For example, line 32 was forced to unbox and box the Integer data stored in the Hashtable every time it incremented the count for a particular key. This is inefficient. A similar problem occurs in lines 49 and 50—the iteration variable of the For Each statement is an Object reference. If we need to use any of its String-specific methods, we need an explicit downcast.

This can cause subtle bugs. Suppose we decide to improve the readability of Fig. 26.7 by using the indexer's Set accessor instead of the Add method to add a key–value pair in line 41, but accidentally type:

```
table(wordKey) = wordKey ' initialize to 1
```

This statement creates a new entry with a String key and String value instead of an Integer value of 1. Although the application will compile correctly, this is clearly incorrect. If a word appears twice, line 32 will try to downcast this String to an Integer, causing an InvalidCastException at execution time. The error that appears at execution time will indicate that the problem is in line 32, where the exception occurred, *not* in line 35. This makes the error more difficult to find and debug, especially in large software applications where the exception may occur in a different file—and even in a different assembly.

In Chapter 25, we introduced generics. In the next two sections, we demonstrate how to use generic collections, which can prevent the problem we just discussed.

26.5 Generic Collections

The System.Collections.Generic namespace in the FCL is a new addition for .NET 2.0. This namespace contains generic classes that allow us to create collections of specific types. As you saw in Fig. 26.2, many of the classes are simply generic versions of non-generic collections. A few classes implement new data structures. In this section, we demonstrate generic collections SortedDictionary and LinkedList.

26.5.1 Generic Class SortedDictionary

A dictionary is the general term for a collection of key–value pairs. A hash table is one way to implement a dictionary. The .NET Framework provides several implementations of dictionaries, both generic and non-generic (all of which implement the IDictionary interface in Fig. 26.1). The application in Fig. 26.8 is a modification of Fig. 26.7 that uses

```
 1    ' Fig. 26.8: SortedDictionaryTest.vb
 2    ' Application counts the number of occurrences of each word in a String
 3    ' and stores them in a generic sorted dictionary.
 4    Imports System.Text.RegularExpressions
 5    Imports System.Collections.Generic
 6
 7    Module StoredDictionaryTest
 8       Sub Main()
 9          ' create sorted dictionary based on user input
10          Dim dictionary As SortedDictionary(Of String, Integer) = _
11             CollectWords()
12
13          ' display sorted dictionary content
14          DisplayDictionary(dictionary)
15       End Sub ' Main
16
17       ' create sorted dictionary from user input
18       Private Function CollectWords() As SortedDictionary(Of String, Integer)
19          ' create a new sorted dictionary
20          Dim dictionary As New SortedDictionary(Of String, Integer)()
21
22          Console.WriteLine("Enter a string: ") ' prompt for user input
```

Fig. 26.8 | Application counts the number of occurrences of each word in a String and stores them in a generic sorted dictionary. (Part 1 of 2.)

```
23          Dim input As String = Console.ReadLine() ' get input
24
25          ' split input text into tokens
26          Dim words As String() = Regex.Split(input, "\s+")
27
28          ' processing input words
29          For Each word As String In words
30             Dim wordKey As String = word.ToLower() ' get word in lowercase
31
32             ' if the dictionary contains the word
33             If dictionary.ContainsKey(wordKey) Then
34                dictionary(wordKey) += 1
35             Else
36                ' add new word with a count of 1 to the dictionary
37                dictionary.Add(wordKey, 1)
38             End If
39          Next
40
41          Return dictionary
42       End Function ' CollectWords
43
44       ' display dictionary content
45       Private Sub DisplayDictionary(Of K, V)( _
46          ByVal dictionary As SortedDictionary(Of K, V))
47
48          Console.WriteLine(vbCrLf & "Sorted dictionary contains:" _
49             & vbCrLf & "{0,-12}{1,-12}", "Key:", "Value:")
50
51          ' generate output for each key in the sorted dictionary
52          ' by iterating through the Keys property with a For Each statement
53          For Each key As K In dictionary.Keys
54             Console.WriteLine("{0,-12}{1,-12}", key, dictionary(key))
55          Next
56
57          Console.WriteLine(vbCrLf & "size: {0}", dictionary.Count)
58       End Sub ' DisplayDictionary
59    End Module ' StoredDictionaryTest
```

```
Enter a string:
We few, we happy few, we band of brothers

Sorted dictionary contains:
Key:        Value:
band        1
brothers    1
few,        2
happy       1
of          1
we          3

size: 6
```

Fig. 26.8 | Application counts the number of occurrences of each word in a String and stores them in a generic sorted dictionary. (Part 2 of 2.)

the generic class `SortedDictionary`. Generic class `SortedDictionary` stores its key–value pairs in a binary search tree. We discuss binary trees in depth in Section 24.7. As the class name suggests, the entries in `SortedDictionary` are sorted in the tree by key. When the key implements generic interface `IComparable`, the `SortedDictionary` uses the results of `IComparable` method `CompareTo` to sort the keys. Note that despite these implementation details, we use the same `Public` methods, properties and indexers with classes `Hashtable` and `SortedDictionary` in the same ways. In fact, except for the generic-specific syntax, Fig. 26.8 looks remarkably similar to Fig. 26.7. That is the beauty of object-oriented programming.

Line 5 contains an `Imports` statement for the `System.Collections.Generic` namespace, which contains class `SortedDictionary`. The generic class `SortedDictionary` takes two type arguments—the first specifies the type of key (i.e., `String`), and the second specifies the type of value (i.e., `Integer`). We replaced the word `Hashtable` in lines 10, 18 and 20 with `SortedDictionary(Of String, Integer)` to create a dictionary of `Integer` values keyed with `Strings`. Now the compiler can check and notify us if we attempt to store an object of the wrong type in the dictionary. Also, because the compiler now knows that the data structure contains `Integer` values, there is no longer any need for the downcast in line 34. This allows line 34 to use the much more concise += notation.

Method `DisplayDictionary` (lines 45–58) has been modified to be completely generic. It takes type parameters `K` and `V`. These parameters are used in line 46 to indicate that `DisplayDictionary` takes a `SortedDictionary` with keys of type `K` and values of type `V`. We use type parameter `K` again in line 53 as the type of the iteration variable. This use of generics is a marvelous example of code reuse. If we decide to change the application to count the number of times each character appears in a `String`, method `DisplayDictionary` could receive an argument of type `SortedDictionary(Of Char, Integer)` without modification. This is precisely what you will do in Exercise 26.12.

Common Programming Error 26.5

Invoking the `Get` accessor of a `SortedDictionary` indexer with a key that does not exist in the collection causes a `KeyNotFoundException`. This behavior is different from that of the `Hashtable` indexer's `Get` accessor, which would return `Nothing`.

26.5.2 Generic Class `LinkedList`

Chapter 24 began our discussion of data structures with the concept of a linked list. We end our discussion with the .NET Framework's generic `LinkedList` class. The `LinkedList` class is a doubly-linked list—we can navigate the list both backwards and forwards with nodes of generic class `LinkedListNode`. Each node contains property `Value` and read-only properties `Previous` and `Next`. The `Value` property's type matches `LinkedList`'s single type parameter because it contains the data stored in the node. The `Previous` property gets a reference to the preceding node in the linked list (or `Nothing` if the node is the first in the list). Similarly, the `Next` property gets a reference to the subsequent reference in the linked list (or `Nothing` if the node is the last in the list). We demonstrate a few linked list manipulations in Fig. 26.9.

Line 3 `Imports` the `LinkedList` class. Lines 13–21 create `LinkedLists` list1 and list2 of `Strings` and fill them with the contents of arrays colors and colors2, respectively. Note that `LinkedList` is a generic class that has one type parameter for which we

```vb
 1    ' Fig. 26.9: LinkedListTest.vb
 2    ' Using LinkedLists.
 3    Imports System.Collections.Generic
 4
 5    Module LinkedListTest
 6       Private colors As String() = _
 7          {"black", "yellow", "green", "blue", "violet", "silver"}
 8       Private colors2 As String() = _
 9          {"gold", "white", "brown", "blue", "gray"}
10
11       ' set up and manipulate LinkedList objects
12       Sub Main()
13          Dim list1 As New LinkedList(Of String)()
14
15          ' add elements to first linked list
16          For Each color As String In colors
17             list1.AddLast(color)
18          Next
19
20          ' add elements to second linked list via constructor
21          Dim list2 As New LinkedList(Of String)(colors2)
22
23          Concatenate(list1, list2) ' concatenate list2 onto list1
24          PrintList(list1) ' print list1 elements
25
26          Console.WriteLine(vbCrLf & _
27             "Converting strings in list1 to uppercase" & vbCrLf)
28          ToUppercaseStrings(list1) ' convert to uppercase string
29          PrintList(list1) ' print list1 elements
30
31          Console.WriteLine(vbCrLf & _
32             "Deleting strings between BLACK and BROWN" & vbCrLf)
33          RemoveItemsBetween(list1, "BLACK", "BROWN")
34
35          PrintList(list1) ' print list1 elements
36          PrintReversedList(list1) ' print list in reverse order
37       End Sub ' Main
38
39       ' output list contents
40       Private Sub PrintList(Of E)(ByVal list As LinkedList(Of E))
41          Console.WriteLine("Linked list: ")
42
43          For Each value As E In list
44             Console.Write("{0} ", value)
45          Next value
46
47          Console.WriteLine()
48       End Sub ' PrintList
49
50       ' concatenate the second list on the end of the first list
51       Private Sub Concatenate(Of E)(ByVal list1 As LinkedList(Of E), _
52          ByVal list2 As LinkedList(Of E))
```

Fig. 26.9 | Using LinkedLists. (Part 1 of 3.)

```vbnet
53          ' concatenate lists by copying element values
54          ' in order from the second list to the first list
55          For Each value As E In list2
56             list1.AddLast(value) ' add new node
57          Next value
58       End Sub ' Concatenate
59
60       ' locate string objects and convert to uppercase
61       Private Sub ToUppercaseStrings(ByVal list As LinkedList(Of String))
62          ' iterate over the list by using the nodes
63          Dim currentNode As LinkedListNode(Of String) = list.First
64
65          While currentNode IsNot Nothing
66             currentNode.Value = _
67                currentNode.Value.ToUpper() ' convert to uppercase
68             currentNode = currentNode.Next ' get next node
69          End While
70       End Sub ' ToUppercaseStrings
71
72       ' delete list items between two given items
73       Private Sub RemoveItemsBetween(Of E)(ByVal list As LinkedList(Of E), _
74          ByVal startItem As E, ByVal endItem As E)
75          ' get the nodes corresponding to the start and end item
76          Dim currentNode As LinkedListNode(Of E) = list.Find(startItem)
77          Dim endNode As LinkedListNode(Of E) = list.Find(endItem)
78
79          ' remove items after the start item
80          ' until we find the last item or the end of the linked list
81          While currentNode.Next IsNot Nothing And _
82             Not currentNode.Next.Equals(endNode)
83             ' remove next node
84             list.Remove(currentNode.Next)
85          End While
86       End Sub ' RemoveItemsBetween
87
88       ' print reversed list
89       Private Sub PrintReversedList(Of E)(ByVal list As LinkedList(Of E))
90          Console.WriteLine("Reversed List:")
91
92          ' iterate over the list by using the nodes
93          Dim currentNode As LinkedListNode(Of E) = list.Last
94
95          While currentNode IsNot Nothing
96             Console.Write("{0} ", currentNode.Value)
97             currentNode = currentNode.Previous ' get previous node
98          End While
99
100          Console.WriteLine()
101       End Sub ' PrintReversedList
102    End Module ' LinkedListTest
```

Fig. 26.9 | Using LinkedLists. (Part 2 of 3.)

```
Linked list:
black yellow green blue violet silver gold white brown blue gray

Converting strings in list1 to uppercase

Linked list:
BLACK YELLOW GREEN BLUE VIOLET SILVER GOLD WHITE BROWN BLUE GRAY

Deleting strings between BLACK and BROWN

Linked list:
BLACK BROWN BLUE GRAY
Reversed List:
GRAY BLUE BROWN BLACK
```

Fig. 26.9 | Using LinkedLists. (Part 3 of 3.)

specify the type argument String in this example (lines 13 and 21). We demonstrate two ways to fill the lists. In lines 16–18, we use the For Each statement and method AddLast to fill list1. The AddLast method creates a new LinkedListNode and appends it to the end of the list. There is also an AddFirst method that inserts a node at the beginning of the list. Line 21 invokes the LinkedList constructor that takes a parameter of type IEnumerable(Of String). All arrays implicitly inherit from the generic interfaces IList and IEnumerable with the type of the array as the type argument, so the String array colors2 implements IEnumerable(Of String). The type parameter of this generic IEnumerable matches the type parameter of the generic LinkedList object. This constructor call (line 21) copies the contents of the array colors2 to list2.

Line 23 calls generic method Concatenate (lines 51–58) to append all elements of list2 to the end of list1. Line 24 calls method PrintList (lines 40–48) to output list1's contents. Line 28 calls method ToUppercaseStrings (lines 61–70) to convert each String element to uppercase, then line 29 calls PrintList again to display the modified Strings. Line 33 calls method RemoveItemsBetween (lines 73–86) to remove the elements between "BLACK" and "BROWN", but not including either. Line 35 outputs the list again, then line 36 invokes method PrintReversedList (lines 89–101) to print the list in reverse order.

Generic method Concatenate (lines 51–58) iterates over list2 with a For Each statement and calls method AddLast to append each value to the end of list1. The loop uses the LinkedList class's enumerator to obtain the values of the nodes. The loop creates a new node in list1 for each node in list2. One LinkedListNode cannot be a member of more than one LinkedList. Any attempt to add a node from one LinkedList to another generates an InvalidOperationException. If you want the same data to belong to more than one LinkedList, you must make a copy of the node for each list.

Generic method PrintList (lines 40–48) also uses a For Each statement to iterate over the values in a LinkedList and output them. Method ToUppercaseStrings (lines 61–70) takes a linked list of Strings and converts each String to uppercase. This method replaces the Strings stored in the list, so we cannot use an enumerator (via a For Each statement) as in the previous two methods. Recall that enumerators cannot be used to modify the values of elements in a collection. Instead, we obtain the first LinkedListNode via the First property (line 63), then loop through the list (lines 65–69). Each iteration of the loop obtains and updates the contents of currentNode via property Value, using

String method `ToUpper` to create an uppercase version of `color`. At the end of each iteration, we move the current node to the next node in the list by assigning to `currentNode` the node obtained by its own `Next` property (line 68). The `Next` property of the last node of the list returns `Nothing`, so when the loop iterates past the end of the list, the loop exits.

Note that it does not make sense to declare `ToUppercaseStrings` as a generic method, because it uses the `String`-specific methods of the values in the nodes. Methods `Print-List` (lines 40–48) and `Concatenate` (lines 51–58) do not need to use any `String`-specific methods, so they can be declared with generic type parameters to promote maximal code reuse.

Generic method `RemoveItemsBetween` (lines 73–86) removes a range of items between two nodes. Lines 76–77 obtain the two "boundary" nodes of the range by using method `Find`. This method performs a linear search, and returns the first node that contains a value equal to the passed argument. Method `Find` returns `Nothing` if the value is not found. We store the node preceding the range in local variable `currentNode` and the node following the range in `endNode`.

The loop in lines 81–85 removes all the elements between `currentNode` and `endNode`. On each iteration of the loop, we remove the node following `currentNode` by invoking method `Remove` (line 84). Method `Remove` takes a `LinkedListNode`, deletes that node from the `LinkedList` and fixes the references of the surrounding nodes. During the `Remove` call, `currentNode`'s `Next` property is assigned the node *following* the removed node, and that node's `Previous` property is assigned `currentNode`. The loop continues until there are no nodes left between `currentNode` and `endNode`, or until `currentNode` is the last node in the list. (There is also an overloaded version of method `Remove` that performs a linear search for the specified value and removes the first node in the list that contains it.)

Method `PrintReversedList` (lines 89–101) prints the list backwards by navigating the nodes manually. Line 93 obtains the last element of the list via the `Last` property and stores it in `currentNode`. The loop in lines 95–98 iterates through the list backwards by moving the `currentNode` reference to the previous node at the end of each iteration, then exits when it moves past the beginning of the list. Note how similar this code is to lines 65–69, which iterated through the list from the beginning to the end.

26.6 Synchronized Collections

In Chapter 15, we discussed multithreading. Most of the non-generic collections are unsynchronized by default, so they can operate efficiently when multithreading is not required. Because they are unsynchronized, however, concurrent access to a collection by multiple threads could cause logic errors in your programs. To prevent potential threading problems, synchronization wrappers are provided for many of the collections that might be accessed by multiple threads. A **wrapper** object receives method calls, adds thread synchronization (to prevent concurrent access to the collection) and passes the calls to the wrapped collection object. Most of the non-generic collection classes in the .NET Framework provide `Shared` method **Synchronized**, which returns a synchronized wrapper object for the specified object. For example, the following code creates a synchronized `ArrayList`:

```
Dim unsafeList As New ArrayList()
Dim threadSafeList As ArrayList = ArrayList.Synchronized(unsafeList)
```

The collections in the .NET Framework do not all provide wrappers for thread safety. Some do not guarantee any thread safety at all. Many of the generic collections are inherently thread-safe for reading, but not for writing. To determine whether a particular class supports thread-safe processing, check its documentation in the .NET Framework class library reference (msdn2.microsoft.com/en-us/library/ms306608.aspx).

Also recall that when a collection is modified, any enumerator returned previously by the GetEnumerator method becomes invalid and will throw an exception if its methods are invoked. Other threads may change the collection, so using an enumerator is not thread safe—thus, the For Each statement is not thread safe either. If you use an enumerator or a For Each statement in a multithreaded application, you should use the SyncLock statement to prevent other threads from using the collection or use a Try statement to catch the InvalidOperationException.

26.7 Wrap-Up

This chapter introduced the .NET Framework collection classes. You learned the hierarchy of interfaces that many of the collection classes implement. You saw how to use class Array to perform array manipulations. You learned that the System.Collections and System.Collections.Generic namespaces contain many non-generic and generic collection classes, respectively. We presented the non-generic classes ArrayList, Stack and Hashtable as well as the generic classes SortedDictionary and LinkedList. In doing so, we discussed data structures in greater depth. We discussed dynamically expanding collections, hashing schemes, and two implementations of a dictionary. You saw the advantages of generic collections over their non-generic counterparts.

You also learned how to use enumerators to traverse these data structures and obtain their contents. We demonstrated the For Each statement with many of the classes of the FCL, and explained that this works by using enumerators "behind the scenes" to traverse the collections. Finally, we discussed some of the issues that you should consider when using collections in multithreaded applications.

Summary

Section 26.1 Introduction
- The prepackaged data-structure classes provided by the .NET Framework are known as collection classes—they store collections of data.
- With collection classes, instead of creating data structures to store these sets of items, you simply use existing data structures, without concern for how they are implemented.

Section 26.2 Collections Overview
- The .NET Framework collections provide high-performance, high-quality implementations of common data structures and enable effective software reuse.
- Earlier versions of the .NET Framework provided the collection classes in the System.Collections namespace to store and manipulate Object references.
- The .NET Framework 2.0 now includes the System.Collections.Generic namespace, which contains classes that take advantage of .NET's generics capabilities.

Section 26.3 Class **Array** and Enumerators

- All arrays implicitly inherit from MustInherit class Array (namespace System).
- The Shared Array method Sort sorts an array.
- The Shared Array method Copy copies elements from one array to another.
- The Shared Array method BinarySearch performs binary searches on an array. This method assumes that it receives a sorted array.
- A collection's GetEnumerator method returns an enumerator that can iterate over the collection.
- All enumerators have methods MoveNext and Reset, and property Current.
- MoveNext moves the enumerator to the next element in the collection. MoveNext returns True if there is at least one more element in the collection; otherwise, the method returns False.
- Read-only property Current returns the object at the current location in the collection.
- If a collection is modified after an enumerator is created for it, the enumerator immediately becomes invalid.
- The For Each statement implicitly obtains an enumerator via the GetEnumerator method and uses the enumerator's MoveNext method and Current property to traverse the collection. This can be done with any collection that implements the IEnumerable interface—not just arrays.

Section 26.4.1 Class **ArrayList**

- In most programming languages, conventional arrays have a fixed size.
- The .NET Framework's ArrayList collection class mimics the functionality of conventional arrays and provides dynamic resizing of the collection.
- If an ArrayList needs to grow, it doubles its current Capacity by default.
- ArrayLists store references to Objects.
- ArrayList has a constructor that can initialize the contents of an ArrayList with the elements of any ICollection passed to it. Many of the collection classes have such a constructor.
- The Count and Capacity properties correspond respectively to the current number of elements in the ArrayList and the maximum number of elements that can be stored without allocating more memory to the ArrayList.
- Method IndexOf returns the position of a value in an ArrayList. IndexOf returns -1 if the element is not found.
- We can access an element of an ArrayList by following the ArrayList variable name with parentheses (()) containing the element's index.
- The Remove method removes the first occurrence of the specified object. All subsequent elements shift toward the beginning of the ArrayList to fill the emptied position.

Section 26.4.2 Class **Stack**

- Class Stack has methods Push and Pop to perform the basic stack operations.
- The non-generic Stack class can store only references to Objects, so value-type items are implicitly boxed before they are added to the Stack.
- Method Peek returns the value of, but does not remove, the top stack element.
- Attempting to Peek or Pop an empty Stack causes an InvalidOperationException.

Section 26.4.3 Class **Hashtable**

- Many applications need a high-speed scheme for converting keys to unique array indices. One such scheme is called hashing, in which we store data in a data structure called a hash table. The .NET Framework provides class Hashtable to enable you to employ hashing.

- Class `Hashtable` can accept any `Object` as a key.
- Method `ContainsKey` determines whether a key is in the hash table.
- `Hashtable` method `Add` creates a new entry in the hash table, with the first argument as the key and the second argument as the value.
- We can use the `Hashtable`'s indexer to obtain and set the key's associated value in the hash table.
- `Hashtable` property `Keys` returns an `ICollection` that contains all the keys.
- If you use a `For Each` statement with a `Hashtable`, the iteration variable is of type `Dictionary-Entry`, which has properties `Key` and `Value` for retrieving the key and value of the current element.

Section 26.5.1 Generic Class `SortedDictionary`

- A dictionary is the general term for a collection of key–value pairs. A hash table is one way to implement a dictionary.
- Generic class `SortedDictionary` stores its key–value pairs in a binary search tree.
- Generic class `SortedDictionary` takes two type arguments—the first specifies the type of key, and the second specifies the type of value.
- Invoking the `Get` accessor of a `SortedDictionary` indexer with a key that does not exist in the collection causes a `KeyNotFoundException`. This behavior is different from that of the `Hashtable` indexer's `Get` accessor, which would return `Nothing`.

Section 26.5.2 Generic Class `LinkedList`

- The `LinkedList` class implements a doubly-linked list.
- Each node contains property `Value` and read-only properties `Previous` and `Next`.
- The `LinkedList` class's enumerator is used to iterate over the values in the nodes, not the node objects themselves.
- One `LinkedListNode` cannot be a member of more than one `LinkedList`. Any attempt to add a node from one `LinkedList` to another generates an `InvalidOperationException`.
- Method `Find` performs a linear search on the list, and returns the first node that contains a value equal to the passed argument.
- Method `Remove` deletes a node from a `LinkedList`, then fixes the references of the surrounding nodes.

Section 26.6 Synchronized Collections

- Most of the non-generic collections are unsynchronized by default, so they can operate efficiently when multithreading is not required. Because they are unsynchronized, however, so concurrent access to a collection by multiple threads could cause errors.
- Many collection classes provide `Shared` method `Synchronized`, which returns a synchronized wrapper object for the specified object.
- Other threads may change a collection, so using an enumerator is not thread safe, and thus the `For Each` statement is not thread safe either. To ensure thread safety when iterating with an enumerator, wrap the loop in a `SyncLock` statement.

Terminology

Add method of class `ArrayList`	`Array` class
Add method of class `Hashtable`	`ArrayList` class
Addlist method of class `LinkedList`	`BinarySearch` method of class `ArrayList`
`ArgumentException`	capacity

Capacity property of class `ArrayList`
Clear method of class `Array`
Clear method of class `ArrayList`
collection
collection class
collision
Contains method of class `ArrayList`
Contains method of class `Stack`
ContainsKey method of class `Hashtable`
Copy method of interface `ICollection`
Count property of interface `ICollection`
CreateInstance method of class `Array`
Current property of interface `IEnumerator`
dictionary
DictionaryEntry variable of interface
    `IDictionary`
enumerator
Find method of class `LinkedList`
First property of class `LinkedList`
GetEnumerator method of interface
    `IEnumerable`
GetHashCode method of class `Object`
hash function
hash table
hashing
Hashtable class
ICollection interface
IDictionary interface
IEnumerable interface
IEnumerator interface
IList interface
IndexOf method of class `Array`
IndexOf method of class `ArrayList`
Integer indexer of class `ArrayList`

InvalidOperationException
KeyNotFoundException
Keys property of interface `IDictionary`
Last property of class `LinkedList`
LastIndexOf method of class `Array`
LinkedList generic class
LinkedListNode generic class
load factor
MoveNext method of interface `IEnumerator`
Next property of class `LinkedListNode`
Object indexer of class `Hashtable`
Peek method of class `Stack`
Pop method of class `Stack`
Previous property of class `LinkedListNode`
Push method of class `Stack`
Queue class
Remove method of class `ArrayList`
Remove method of class `LinkedList`
RemoveAt method of class `ArrayList`
RemoveRange method of class `ArrayList`
Reset method of interface `IEnumerator`
Sort method of class `Array`
Sort method of class `ArrayList`
SortedDictionary generic class
SortedList class
Stack class
Synchronized method
System.Collections namespace
System.Collections.Generic namespace
ToLower method of class `String`
ToUpper method of class `String`
TrimToSize method of class `ArrayList`
Value property of class `LinkedListNode`
Values property of interface `IDictionary`

Self-Review Exercises

26.1 Fill in the blanks in each of the following statements:

a) A(n) _____ is used to walk through a collection but cannot modify the collection during the iteration.

b) Class _____ provides the capabilities of an array-like data structure that can resize itself dynamically.

c) An element in an `ArrayList` can be accessed by using the `ArrayList`'s _____.

d) If you do not specify a capacity increment, an `ArrayList` will (by default) _____ its size each time additional capacity is needed.

e) Many collection classes offer a `Shared` method called _____ to create a thread-safe wrapper for use in multithreaded applications.

f) `IEnumerator` method _____ advances the enumerator to the next item.

g) If the collection it references has been altered since the enumerator's creation, calling method `Reset` will cause a(n) _____.

26.2 State whether each of the following is *true* or *false*. If *false*, explain why.
   a) Class Stack is in the System.Collections namespace.
   b) A class that implements interface IEnumerator defines only methods MoveNext and Reset.
   c) A hashtable stores key–value pairs.
   d) Values of primitive types may be stored directly in an ArrayList.
   e) An ArrayList can contain duplicate values.
   f) A Hashtable can contain duplicate keys.
   g) A LinkedList can contain duplicate values.
   h) Enumerators can change the values of elements, but cannot remove them.
   i) With hashing, as the load factor increases, the chance of collisions decreases.

Answers to Self-Review Exercises

26.1 a) enumerator (or For Each statement). b) ArrayList. c) indexer. d) double. e) Synchronized. f) MoveNext. g) InvalidOperationException.

26.2 a) True. b) False. Such a class also must implement property Current. c) True. d) False. An ArrayList stores only Objects. Autoboxing occurs when adding a value type to the ArrayList. You can prevent boxing by using generic class List with a value type. e) True. f) False. A Hashtable cannot contain duplicate keys. g) True. h) False. An enumerator cannot be used to change the values of elements. i) False. With hashing, as the load factor increases, there are fewer available slots relative to the total number of slots, so the chance of selecting an occupied slot (a collision) with a hashing operation increases.

Exercises

26.3 Define each of the following terms:
   a) ICollection
   b) Array
   c) IList
   d) load factor
   e) collision
   f) space–time trade-off in hashing
   g) Hashtable

26.4 Explain briefly the operation of each of the following methods of class ArrayList:
   a) Add
   b) Insert
   c) Remove
   d) Clear
   e) RemoveAt
   f) Contains
   g) IndexOf
   h) Count
   i) Capacity

26.5 Explain why inserting additional elements into an ArrayList object whose current size is less than its capacity is a relatively fast operation and why inserting additional elements into a full ArrayList is a relatively slow operation.

26.6 In our implementation of a stack in Fig. 24.13, we were able to quickly extend a linked list to create class StackInheritance. The .NET Framework designers chose not to use inheritance to create their Stack class. What are the negative aspects of inheritance, particularly for class Stack?

26.7 Briefly answer the following questions:

    a) What happens when you add a primitive type (e.g., Double) value to a non-generic collection?

    b) Can you print all the elements of a collection by using an IEnumerable object without explicitly calling its methods? If so, how?

26.8 Explain briefly the operation of each of the following enumerator-related methods:

    a) GetEnumerator

    b) Current

    c) MoveNext

26.9 Explain briefly the operation of each of the following methods and properties of class Hashtable:

    a) Add

    b) Keys

    c) Values

    d) ContainsKey

26.10 Determine whether each of the following statements is *true* or *false*. If *false*, explain why.

    a) Elements in an array must be sorted in ascending order before a BinarySearch can be performed.

    b) Method First gets the first node in a LinkedList.

    c) Class Array provides Shared method Sort for sorting array elements.

26.11 Write an application that reads in a series of first names and stores them in a LinkedList. Do not store duplicate names. Allow the user to search for a first name.

26.12 Modify the application in Fig. 26.8 to count the number of occurrences of each letter rather than of each word. For example, the string "HELLO THERE" contains two Hs, three Es, two Ls, one O, one T and one R. Display the results.

26.13 Use a SortedDictionary to create a reusable class for choosing from some of the predefined colors in class Color (in the System.Drawing namespace). The names of the colors should be used as keys, and the predefined Color objects should be used as values. Place this class in a class library that can be referenced from any Visual Basic application. Use your new class in a Windows application that allows the user to select a color and then changes the background color of the Form.

26.14 Write an application that determines and prints the number of duplicate words in a sentence. Treat uppercase and lowercase letters the same. Ignore punctuation.

26.15 Recall from Fig. 26.2 that class List is the generic equivalent of class ArrayList. Write an application that inserts 25 random integers from 0 to 100 in order into an object of class List. The application should calculate the sum of the elements and the floating-point average of the elements.

26.16 Write an application that creates a LinkedList object of 10 characters, then creates a second list object containing a copy of the first list, but in reverse order.

26.17 Write an application that takes a whole-number input from a user and determines whether it is prime. If the number is not prime, display the unique prime factors of the number. Remember that a prime number's factors are only 1 and the prime number itself. Every number that is not prime has a unique prime factorization. For example, consider the number 54. The prime factors of 54 are 2, 3, 3 and 3. When the values are multiplied together, the result is 54. For the number 54, the prime factors output should be 2 and 3. Use generic SortedDictionarys as part of your solution by recording the factors as the keys and using the Keys property to enumerate the factors.

Operator Precedence Chart

Operators are shown in decreasing order of precedence from top to bottom with each level of precedence separated by a horizontal line. Visual Basic operators associate from left to right.

Operator	Type
TypeOf	type comparison
^	exponentiation
+ –	unary plus unary minus
* /	multiplication division
\	integer division
Mod	modulus
+ –	addition subtraction
&	concatenation
<< >>	bitwise left shift bitwise right shift

Fig. A.1 | Operator precedence chart. (Part 1 of 2.)

Operator	Type
=	relational is equal to
<>	relational is not equal to
<	relational less than
<=	relational less than or equal to
>	relational greater than
>=	relational greater than or equal to
Like	pattern matching
Is	reference comparison
Not	logical negation
And	logical AND without short-circuit evaluation
AndAlso	logical AND with short-circuit evaluation
Or	logical inclusive OR without short-circuit evaluation
OrElse	logical inclusive OR with short-circuit evaluation
Xor	logical exclusive OR

Fig. A.1 | Operator precedence chart. (Part 2 of 2.)

B

Number Systems

OBJECTIVES

In this appendix you will learn:

- To understand basic number systems concepts, such as base, positional value and symbol value.

- To understand how to work with numbers represented in the binary, octal and hexadecimal number systems.

- To abbreviate binary numbers as octal numbers or hexadecimal numbers.

- To convert octal numbers and hexadecimal numbers to binary numbers.

- To convert back and forth between decimal numbers and their binary, octal and hexadecimal equivalents.

- To understand binary arithmetic and how negative binary numbers are represented using two's complement notation.

B.1 Introduction

In this appendix, we introduce the key number systems that programmers use, especially when they are working on software projects that require close interaction with machine-level hardware. Projects like this include operating systems, computer networking software, compilers, database systems and applications requiring high performance.

When we write an integer such as 227 or –63 in a program, the number is assumed to be in the decimal (base 10) number system. The digits in the decimal number system are 0, 1, 2, 3, 4, 5, 6, 7, 8 and 9. The lowest digit is 0 and the highest digit is 9—one less than the base of 10. Internally, computers use the binary (base 2) number system. The binary number system has only two digits, namely 0 and 1. Its lowest digit is 0 and its highest digit is 1—one less than the base of 2.

As you will see, binary numbers tend to be much longer than their decimal equivalents. Programmers who work in assembly languages and in high-level languages that enable programmers to reach down to the machine level, find it cumbersome to work with binary numbers. So two other number systems—the octal number system (base 8) and the hexadecimal number system (base 16)—are popular primarily because they make it convenient to abbreviate binary numbers.

In the octal number system, the digits range from 0 to 7. Because both the binary number system and the octal number system have fewer digits than the decimal number system, their digits are the same as the corresponding digits in decimal.

The hexadecimal number system poses a problem because it requires 16 digits—a lowest digit of 0 and a highest digit with a value equivalent to decimal 15 (one less than the base of 16). By convention, the letters A through F represent the hexadecimal digits corresponding to decimal values 10 through 15. Thus, in hexadecimal, you can have numbers like 876 consisting solely of decimal-like digits, numbers like 8A55F consisting of digits and letters and numbers like FFE consisting solely of letters. Occasionally, a hexadecimal number spells a common word such as FACE or FEED—this can appear strange to programmers accustomed to working with numbers. The digits of the binary, octal, decimal and hexadecimal number systems are summarized in Figs. B.1 and B.2.

Each of these number systems uses positional notation—each position in which a digit is written has a different positional value. For example, in the decimal number 937 (the 9, the 3 and the 7 are referred to as symbol values), we say that the 7 is written in the ones position, the 3 is written in the tens position and the 9 is written in the hundreds position. Note that each of these positions is a power of the base (base 10) and that these powers begin at 0 and increase by 1 as we move left in the number (Fig. B.3).

Binary digit	Octal digit	Decimal digit	Hexadecimal digit
0	0	0	0
1	1	1	1
	2	2	2
	3	3	3
	4	4	4
	5	5	5
	6	6	6
	7	7	7
		8	8
		9	9
			A (decimal value of 10)
			B (decimal value of 11)
			C (decimal value of 12)
			D (decimal value of 13)
			E (decimal value of 14)
			F (decimal value of 15)

Fig. B.I | Digits of the binary, octal, decimal and hexadecimal number systems.

Attribute	Binary	Octal	Decimal	Hexadecimal
Base	2	8	10	16
Lowest digit	0	0	0	0
Highest digit	1	7	9	F

Fig. B.2 | Comparing the binary, octal, decimal and hexadecimal number systems.

Positional values in the decimal number system			
Decimal digit	9	3	7
Position name	Hundreds	Tens	Ones
Positional value	100	10	1
Positional value as a power of the base (10)	10^2	10^1	10^0

Fig. B.3 | Positional values in the decimal number system.

For longer decimal numbers, the next positions to the left would be the thousands position (10 to the 3rd power), the ten-thousands position (10 to the 4th power), the hundred-thousands position (10 to the 5th power), the millions position (10 to the 6th power), the ten-millions position (10 to the 7th power) and so on.

In the binary number 101, the rightmost 1 is written in the ones position, the 0 is written in the twos position and the leftmost 1 is written in the fours position. Each position is a power of the base (base 2) and that these powers begin at 0 and increase by 1 as we move left in the number (Fig. B.4). So, $101 = 1 * 2^2 + 0 * 2^1 + 1 * 2^0 = 4 + 0 + 1 = 5$.

For longer binary numbers, the next positions to the left would be the eights position (2 to the 3rd power), the sixteens position (2 to the 4th power), the thirty-twos position (2 to the 5th power), the sixty-fours position (2 to the 6th power) and so on.

In the octal number 425, we say that the 5 is written in the ones position, the 2 is written in the eights position and the 4 is written in the sixty-fours position. Note that each of these positions is a power of the base (base 8) and that these powers begin at 0 and increase by 1 as we move left in the number (Fig. B.5).

For longer octal numbers, the next positions to the left would be the five-hundred-and-twelves position (8 to the 3rd power), the four-thousand-and-ninety-sixes position (8 to the 4th power), the thirty-two-thousand-seven-hundred-and-sixty-eights position (8 to the 5th power) and so on.

In the hexadecimal number 3DA, we say that the A is written in the ones position, the D is written in the sixteens position and the 3 is written in the two-hundred-and-fifty-sixes position. Note that each of these positions is a power of the base (base 16) and that these powers begin at 0 and increase by 1 as we move left in the number (Fig. B.6).

For longer hexadecimal numbers, the next positions to the left would be the four-thousand-and-ninety-sixes position (16 to the 3rd power), the sixty-five-thousand-five-hundred-and-thirty-sixes position (16 to the 4th power) and so on.

Positional values in the binary number system			
Binary digit	1	0	1
Position name	Fours	Twos	Ones
Positional value	4	2	1
Positional value as a power of the base (2)	2^2	2^1	2^0

Fig. B.4 | Positional values in the binary number system.

Positional values in the octal number system			
Decimal digit	4	2	5
Position name	Sixty-fours	Eights	Ones
Positional value	64	8	1
Positional value as a power of the base (8)	8^2	8^1	8^0

Fig. B.5 | Positional values in the octal number system.

Positional values in the hexadecimal number system			
Decimal digit	3	D	A
Position name	Two-hundred-and-fifty-sixes	Sixteens	Ones
Positional value	256	16	1
Positional value as a power of the base (16)	16^2	16^1	16^0

Fig. B.6 | Positional values in the hexadecimal number system.

B.2 Abbreviating Binary Numbers as Octal and Hexadecimal Numbers

The main use for octal and hexadecimal numbers in computing is for abbreviating lengthy binary representations. Figure B.7 highlights the fact that lengthy binary numbers can be expressed concisely in number systems with higher bases than the binary number system.

Decimal number	Binary representation	Octal representation	Hexadecimal representation
0	0	0	0
1	1	1	1
2	10	2	2
3	11	3	3
4	100	4	4
5	101	5	5
6	110	6	6
7	111	7	7
8	1000	10	8
9	1001	11	9
10	1010	12	A
11	1011	13	B
12	1100	14	C
13	1101	15	D
14	1110	16	E
15	1111	17	F
16	10000	20	10

Fig. B.7 | Decimal, binary, octal and hexadecimal equivalents.

A particularly important relationship that both the octal number system and the hexa-decimal number system have to the binary system is that the bases of octal and hexadec-imal (8 and 16 respectively) are powers of the base of the binary number system (base 2). Consider the following 12-digit binary number and its octal and hexadecimal equivalents. See if you can determine how this relationship makes it convenient to abbreviate binary numbers in octal or hexadecimal. The answer follows the numbers.

Binary number	Octal equivalent	Hexadecimal equivalent
100011010001	4321	8D1

To see how the binary number converts easily to octal, simply break the 12-digit binary number into groups of three consecutive bits each and write those groups over the corresponding digits of the octal number as follows:

100	011	010	001
4	3	2	1

Note that the octal digit you have written under each group of three bits corresponds precisely to the octal equivalent of that 3-digit binary number, as shown in Fig. B.7.

The same kind of relationship can be observed in converting from binary to hexadec-imal. Break the 12-digit binary number into groups of four consecutive bits each and write those groups over the corresponding digits of the hexadecimal number as follows:

1000	1101	0001
8	D	1

Notice that the hexadecimal digit you wrote under each group of four bits corre-sponds precisely to the hexadecimal equivalent of that 4-digit binary number as shown in Fig. B.7.

B.3 Converting Octal and Hexadecimal Numbers to Binary Numbers

In the previous section, you learned how to convert binary numbers to their octal and hexadecimal equivalents by forming groups of binary digits and simply rewriting them as their equivalent octal digit values or hexadecimal digit values. This process may be used in reverse to produce the binary equivalent of a given octal or hexadecimal number.

For example, the octal number 653 is converted to binary simply by writing the 6 as its 3-digit binary equivalent 110, the 5 as its 3-digit binary equivalent 101 and the 3 as its 3-digit binary equivalent 011 to form the 9-digit binary number 110101011.

The hexadecimal number FAD5 is converted to binary simply by writing the F as its 4-digit binary equivalent 1111, the A as its 4-digit binary equivalent 1010, the D as its 4-digit binary equivalent 1101 and the 5 as its 4-digit binary equivalent 0101 to form the 16-digit 1111101011010101.

B.4 Converting from Binary, Octal or Hexadecimal to Decimal

We are accustomed to working in decimal, and therefore it is often convenient to convert a binary, octal, or hexadecimal number to decimal to get a sense of what the number is "really" worth. Our diagrams in Section B.1 express the positional values in decimal. To convert a number to decimal from another base, multiply the decimal equivalent of each digit by its positional value and sum these products. For example, the binary number 110101 is converted to decimal 53, as shown in Fig. B.8.

To convert octal 7614 to decimal 3980, we use the same technique, this time using appropriate octal positional values, as shown in Fig. B.9.

To convert hexadecimal AD3B to decimal 44347, we use the same technique, this time using appropriate hexadecimal positional values, as shown in Fig. B.10.

B.5 Converting from Decimal to Binary, Octal or Hexadecimal

The conversions in Section B.4 follow naturally from the positional notation conventions. Converting from decimal to binary, octal, or hexadecimal also follows these conventions.

Converting a binary number to decimal					
Postional values:	32	16	8	4	2	1
Symbol values:	1	1	0	1	0	1
Products:	1*32=32	1*16=16	0*8=0	1*4=4	0*2=0	1*1=1
Sum:	= 32 + 16 + 0 + 4 + 0s + 1 = 53					

Fig. B.8 | Converting a binary number to decimal.

Converting an octal number to decimal			
Positional values:	512	64	8	1
Symbol values:	7	6	1	4
Products	7*512=3584	6*64=384	1*8=8	4*1=4
Sum:	= 3584 + 384 + 8 + 4 = 3980			

Fig. B.9 | Converting an octal number to decimal.

Converting a hexadecimal number to decimal			
Postional values:	4096	256	16	1
Symbol values:	A	D	3	B
Products	A*4096=40960	D*256=3328	3*16=48	B*1=11
Sum:	= 40960 + 3328 + 48 + 11 = 44347			

Fig. B.10 | Converting a hexadecimal number to decimal.

Suppose we wish to convert decimal 57 to binary. We write the positional values of the columns right to left until we reach a column whose positional value is greater than the decimal number. We don't need that column, so we discard it. Thus, we first write:

Positional values: 64   32   16   8   4   2   1

Then we discard the column with positional value 64, leaving:

Positional values: 32   16   8   4   2   1

Next we work from the leftmost column to the right. We divide 32 into 57 and observe that there is one 32 in 57 with a remainder of 25, so we write 1 in the 32 column. We divide 16 into 25 and observe that there is one 16 in 25 with a remainder of 9 and write 1 in the 16 column. We divide 8 into 9 and observe that there is one 8 in 9 with a remainder of 1. The next two columns each produce quotients of 0 when their positional values are divided into 1, so we write 0s in the 4 and 2 columns. Finally, 1 into 1 is 1, so we write 1 in the 1 column. This yields:

Positional values:	32	16	8	4	2	1
Symbol values:	1	1	1	0	0	1

and thus decimal 57 is equivalent to binary 111001.

To convert decimal 103 to octal, we write the positional values of the columns until we reach a column whose positional value is greater than the decimal number. We do not need that column, so we discard it. Thus, we first write:

Positional values: 512   64   8   1

Then we discard the column with positional value 512, yielding:

Positional values: 64   8   1

Next we work from the leftmost column to the right. We divide 64 into 103 and observe that there is one 64 in 103 with a remainder of 39, so we write 1 in the 64 column. We divide 8 into 39 and observe that there are four 8s in 39 with a remainder of 7 and write 4 in the 8 column. Finally, we divide 1 into 7 and observe that there are seven 1s in 7 with no remainder, so we write 7 in the 1 column. This yields:

Positional values:	64	8	1
Symbol values:	1	4	7

and thus decimal 103 is equivalent to octal 147.

To convert decimal 375 to hexadecimal, we write the positional values of the columns until we reach a column whose positional value is greater than the decimal number. We do not need that column, so we discard it. Thus, we first write:

Positional values: 4096   256   16   1

Then we discard the column with positional value 4096, yielding:

Positional values: 256   16   1

Next we work from the leftmost column to the right. We divide 256 into 375 and observe that there is one 256 in 375 with a remainder of 119, so we write 1 in the 256 column. We divide 16 into 119 and observe that there are seven 16s in 119 with a remainder of 7 and write 7 in the 16 column. Finally, we divide 1 into 7 and observe that there are seven 1s in 7 with no remainder, so we write 7 in the 1 column. This yields:

```
Positional values:   256     16      1
Symbol values:        1       7       7
```

and thus decimal 375 is equivalent to hexadecimal 177.

B.6 Negative Binary Numbers: Two's Complement Notation

The discussion so far in this appendix has focused on positive numbers. In this section, we explain how computers represent negative numbers using *two's complement notation*. First we explain how the two's complement of a binary number is formed, then we show why it represents the negative value of the given binary number.

Consider a machine with 32-bit integers. Suppose

```
Dim value As Integer = 13
```

The 32-bit representation of value is

```
00000000 00000000 00000000 00001101
```

To form the negative of value we first form its *one's complement* by combining value with &H7FFFFFFF using Visual Basic's Xor operator, as in:

```
onesComplement = value Xor &H7FFFFFFF
```

Internally, onesComplement is now value with each of its bits reversed—ones become zeros and zeros become ones, as follows:

```
value:
00000000 00000000 00000000 00001101

onesComplement
11111111 11111111 11111111 11110010
```

To form the two's complement of value, we simply add 1 to value's one's complement, which produces

```
Two's complement of value:
11111111 11111111 11111111 11110011
```

Now if this is in fact equal to −13, we should be able to add it to binary 13 and obtain a result of 0. Let us try this:

```
  00000000 00000000 00000000 00001101
+11111111 11111111 11111111 11110011
-------------------------------------
  00000000 00000000 00000000 00000000
```

The carry bit coming out of the leftmost column is discarded and we indeed get 0 as a result. If we add the one's complement of a number to the number, the result would be all 1s. The key to getting a result of all zeros is that the twos complement is one more than the one's complement. The addition of 1 causes each column to add to 0 with a carry of 1. The carry keeps moving leftward until it is discarded from the leftmost bit, and thus the resulting number is all zeros.

Computers actually perform a subtraction, such as

```
x = a - value;
```

by adding the two's complement of value to a, as follows:

```
x = a + (onesComplement + 1);
```

Suppose a is 27 and value is 13 as before. If the two's complement of value is actually the negative of value, then adding the two's complement of value to a should produce the result 14. Let us try this:

```
a  (i.e., 27)               00000000 00000000 00000000 00011011
+(onesComplement + 1)      +11111111 11111111 11111111 11110011
                           -------------------------------------
                            00000000 00000000 00000000 00001110
```

which is indeed equal to 14.

Summary

- An integer such as 19 or 227 or –63 in a program is assumed to be in the decimal (base 10) number system. The digits in the decimal number system are 0, 1, 2, 3, 4, 5, 6, 7, 8 and 9. The lowest digit is 0 and the highest digit is 9—one less than the base of 10.

- Internally, computers use the binary (base 2) number system. The binary number system has only two digits, namely 0 and 1. Its lowest digit is 0 and its highest digit is 1—one less than the base of 2.

- The octal number system (base 8) and the hexadecimal number system (base 16) are popular primarily because they make it convenient to abbreviate binary numbers.

- The digits of the octal number system range from 0 to 7.

- The hexadecimal number system poses a problem because it requires 16 digits—a lowest digit of 0 and a highest digit with a value equivalent to decimal 15 (one less than the base of 16). By convention, we use the letters A through F to represent the hexadecimal digits corresponding to decimal values 10 through 15.

- Each number system uses positional notation—each position in which a digit is written has a different positional value.

- A particularly important relationship of both the octal number system and the hexadecimal number system to the binary system is that the bases of octal and hexadecimal (8 and 16 respectively) are powers of the base of the binary number system (base 2).

- To convert an octal to a binary number, replace each octal digit with its three-digit binary equivalent.

- To convert a hexadecimal number to a binary number, simply replace each hexadecimal digit with its four-digit binary equivalent.

- Because we are accustomed to working in decimal, it is convenient to convert a binary, octal or hexadecimal number to decimal to get a sense of the number's "real" worth.

- To convert a number to decimal from another base, multiply the decimal equivalent of each digit by its positional value and sum the products.

- Computers represent negative numbers using two's complement notation.

- To form the negative of a value in binary, first form its one's complement by combining the value with &H7FFFFFFF using Visual Basic's Xor operator. This reverses the bits of the value. To form the two's complement of a value, simply add one to the value's one's complement.

Terminology

base	hexadecimal number system
base 2 number system	negative value
base 8 number system	octal number system
base 10 number system	one's complement notation
base 16 number system	positional notation
binary number system	positional value
conversions	symbol value
decimal number system	two's complement notation
digit	

Self-Review Exercises

B.1   Fill in the blanks in each of the following statements:

   a) The bases of the decimal, binary, octal and hexadecimal number systems are _____, _____, _____ and _____ respectively.

   b) The positional value of the rightmost digit of any number in either binary, octal, decimal or hexadecimal is always _____.

   c) The positional value of the digit to the left of the rightmost digit of any number in binary, octal, decimal or hexadecimal is always equal to _____.

B.2   State whether each of the following is *true* or *false*. If *false*, explain why.

   a) A popular reason for using the decimal number system is that it forms a convenient notation for abbreviating binary numbers simply by substituting one decimal digit per group of four binary bits.

   b) The highest digit in any base is one more than the base.

   c) The lowest digit in any base is one less than the base.

B.3   In general, the decimal, octal and hexadecimal representations of a given binary number contain (more/fewer) digits than the binary number contains.

B.4   The (octal / hexadecimal / decimal) representation of a large binary value is the most concise (of the given alternatives).

B.5   Fill in the missing values in this chart of positional values for the rightmost four positions in each of the indicated number systems:

decimal	1000	100	10	1
hexadecimal	...	256	...	...
binary	...	...	...	...
octal	512	...	8	...

B.6   Convert binary 110101011000 to octal and to hexadecimal.

B.7   Convert hexadecimal FACE to binary.

B.8   Convert octal 7316 to binary.

B.9   Convert hexadecimal 4FEC to octal. [*Hint:* First convert 4FEC to binary, then convert that binary number to octal.]

B.10   Convert binary 1101110 to decimal.

B.11   Convert octal 317 to decimal.

B.12   Convert hexadecimal EFD4 to decimal.

B.13   Convert decimal 177 to binary, to octal and to hexadecimal.

B.14   Show the binary representation of decimal 417. Then show the one's complement of 417 and the two's complement of 417.

B.15   What is the result when a number and its two's complement are added to each other?

Answers to Self-Review Exercises

B.1   a) 10, 2, 8, 16. b) 1 (the base raised to the zero power). c) The base of the number system.

B.2   a) False. Hexadecimal does this. b) False. The highest digit in any base is one less than the base. c) False. The lowest digit in any base is zero.

B.3   Fewer.

B.4   Hexadecimal.

B.5   Fill in the missing values in this chart of positional values for the rightmost four positions in each of the indicated number systems:

```
decimal        1000      100      10      1
hexadecimal    4096      256      16      1
binary            8        4       2      1
octal           512       64       8      1
```

B.6   Octal 6530; Hexadecimal D58.

B.7   Binary 1111 1010 1100 1110.

B.8   Binary 111 011 001 110.

B.9   Binary 0 100 111 111 101 100; Octal 47754.

B.10   Decimal 2+4+8+32+64=110.

B.11   Decimal 7+1*8+3*64=7+8+192=207.

B.12   Decimal 4+13*16+15*256+14*4096=61396.

B.13   Decimal 177
to binary:

```
256 128 64 32 16 8 4 2 1
128 64 32 16 8 4 2 1
(1*128)+(0*64)+(1*32)+(1*16)+(0*8)+(0*4)+(0*2)+(1*1)
10110001
```

to octal:

```
512 64 8 1
64 8 1
(2*64)+(6*8)+(1*1)
261
```

to hexadecimal:

```
256 16 1
16 1
(11*16)+(1*1)
(B*16)+(1*1)
B1
```

B.14   Binary:

```
512 256 128 64 32 16 8 4 2 1
256 128 64 32 16 8 4 2 1
(1*256)+(1*128)+(0*64)+(1*32)+(0*16)+(0*8)+(0*4)+(0*2)+(1*1)
110100001
```

One's complement: 001011110
Two's complement: 001011111
Check: Original binary number + its two's complement

```
110100001
001011111
---------
000000000
```

B.15 Zero.

Exercises

B.16 Some people argue that many of our calculations would be easier in the base 12 number system because 12 is divisible by so many more numbers than 10 (for base 10). What is the lowest digit in base 12? What would be the highest symbol for the digit in base 12? What are the positional values of the rightmost four positions of any number in the base 12 number system?

B.17 Complete the following chart of positional values for the rightmost four positions in each of the indicated number systems:

decimal	1000	100	10	1
base 6	...	...	6	...
base 13	...	169	...	...
base 3	27	...	...	...

B.18 Convert binary 100101111010 to octal and to hexadecimal.

B.19 Convert hexadecimal 3A7D to binary.

B.20 Convert hexadecimal 765F to octal. (*Hint:* First convert 765F to binary, then convert that binary number to octal.)

B.21 Convert binary 1011110 to decimal.

B.22 Convert octal 426 to decimal.

B.23 Convert hexadecimal FFFF to decimal.

B.24 Convert decimal 299 to binary, to octal and to hexadecimal.

B.25 Show the binary representation of decimal 779. Then show the one's complement of 779 and the two's complement of 779.

B.26 Show the two's complement of integer value −1 on a machine with 32-bit integers.

C

Using the Visual Studio 2005 Debugger

OBJECTIVES

In this appendix you will learn:

- To use the debugger to locate and correct logic errors in a program.

- To use breakpoints to pause program execution and allow you to examine the values of variables.

- To set, disable and remove breakpoints.

- To use the **Continue** command to continue execution from a breakpoint.

- To use the **Locals** window to view and modify variable values.

- To use the **Watch** window to evaluate expressions.

- To use the **Step Into**, **Step Out** and **Step Over** commands to execute a program line-by-line.

- To use the new Visual Studio 2005 debugging features Edit and Continue and Just My Code™ debugging.

C.1 Introduction

In Chapter 3, you learned that there are two types of errors—compilation errors and logic errors—and you learned how to eliminate compilation errors from your code. Logic errors, also called **bugs**, do not prevent a program from compiling successfully, but can cause a program to produce erroneous results, or terminate prematurely, when it runs. Most compiler vendors, like Microsoft, provide a tool called a **debugger**, which allows you to monitor the execution of your programs to locate and remove logic errors. A program must successfully compile before it can be used in the debugger—the debugger helps you analyze a program while it is running. The debugger allows you to suspend program execution, examine and set variable values and much more. In this appendix, we introduce the Visual Studio debugger, several of its debugging tools and new features added for Visual Studio 2005.

C.2 Breakpoints and the Continue Command

We begin by investigating **breakpoints**, which are markers that can be set at any executable line of code. When a running program reaches a breakpoint, execution pauses, allowing you to examine the values of variables to help determine whether logic errors exist. For example, you can examine the value of a variable that stores the result of a calculation to determine whether the calculation was performed correctly. You can also examine the value of an expression.

To illustrate the debugger features, we use the program in Figs. C.1 and C.2 that creates and manipulates an Account (Fig. C.1) object. This example is based on an exercise you created in Chapter 4 (Exercise 4.10), so it does not use features that are presented after Chapter 4. Execution begins in Main (lines 4–33 of Fig. C.2). Line 5 creates an Account object with an initial balance of $50.00. Account's constructor (lines 8–14 of Fig. C.1) accepts one argument, which specifies the Account's initial balance. Line 8 of Fig. C.2 outputs the initial account balance using Account property Balance. Lines 11–12 prompt the user for and input the withdrawalAmount. Lines 14–16 subtract the withdrawal amount from the Account's balanceValue using its Debit method. Lines 19–20 display the new balanceValue. Next, lines 23–32 perform similar steps to credit the account.

```vb
1   ' Fig. C.01: Account.vb
2   ' Account class with a constructor to initialize a customer's balance.
3   Public Class Account
4      ' instance variable that stores the balance
5      Private balanceValue As Integer
6
7      ' constructor
8      Public Sub New(ByVal initialBalance As Integer)
9         ' if initialBalance is not greater than 0,
10        ' balance is still initialized to 0 by default
11        If initialBalance > 0 Then
12           Balance = initialBalance
13        End If
14     End Sub ' New
15
16     ' credit (increases) the account by amount
17     Public Sub Credit(ByVal amount As Integer)
18        Balance = Balance + amount ' add amount to balance
19     End Sub ' Credit
20
21     ' debits (decreases) the account by amount
22     Public Sub Debit(ByVal amount As Integer)
23        If amount > Balance Then
24           Console.WriteLine("Debit amount exceeded account balance.")
25        End If
26
27        If amount <= Balance Then
28           Balance = Balance - amount ' subtract amount to balance
29        End If
30     End Sub ' Debit
31
32     ' property makes balanceValue available to clients;
33     ' no validation required
34     Public Property Balance() As Integer
35        Get ' returns the account balance
36           Return balanceValue
37        End Get
38
39        Set(ByVal value As Integer) ' sets the balance value
40           balanceValue = value
41        End Set
42     End Property ' Balance
43  End Class ' Account
```

Fig. C.1 | Account class with a constructor to initialize variable balance.

```vb
1   ' Fig. C.02 AccountTest.vb
2   ' Create and manipulate an Account object.
3   Module AccountTest
4      Sub Main() ' begins execution
5         Dim account1 As New Account(50) ' create Account object
```

Fig. C.2 | Creating and manipulating an Account object. (Part 1 of 2.)

```vb
6
7          ' display initial balance of each object
8          Console.WriteLine("account1 balance: " & account1.Balance)
9
10         ' obtain withdrawal input from Command Prompt
11         Console.Write("Enter withdrawal amount for account1: ")
12         Dim withdrawalAmount As Integer = Console.ReadLine()
13
14         Console.WriteLine(vbCrLf & "Subtracting " & withdrawalAmount & _
15            " from account1 balance")
16         account1.Debit(withdrawalAmount) ' subtract amount from account1
17
18         ' display balance
19         Console.WriteLine("account1 balance: " & account1.Balance)
20         Console.WriteLine()
21
22         ' obtain credit input from Command Prompt
23         Console.Write("Enter credit amount for account1: ")
24         Dim creditAmount As Integer = Console.ReadLine()
25
26         Console.WriteLine(vbCrLf & "Adding " & creditAmount & _
27            " to account1 balance")
28         account1.Credit(creditAmount) ' add amount to account1
29
30         ' display balance
31         Console.WriteLine("account1 balance: " & account1.Balance)
32         Console.WriteLine()
33      End Sub ' Main
34   End Module ' AccountTest
```

```
account1 balance: 50

Enter withdrawal amount for account1: 25

Subtracting 25 from account1 balance
account1 balance: 25

Enter credit amount for account1: 33

Adding 33 to account1 balance
account1 balance: 58
```

Fig. C.2 | Creating and manipulating an `Account` object. (Part 2 of 2.)

In the following steps, you will use breakpoints and various debugger commands to examine the value of the variable `withdrawalAmount` (declared in Fig. C.2) while the program executes.

1. *Inserting breakpoints in Visual Studio.* First, ensure that `AccountTest.vb` is open in the IDE's code editor. To insert a breakpoint, left click inside the **margin indicator bar** (the gray margin at the left of the code window in Fig. C.3) next to the line of code at which you wish to break, or right click that line of code and select **Breakpoint > Insert Breakpoint**. You can set as many breakpoints as you like.

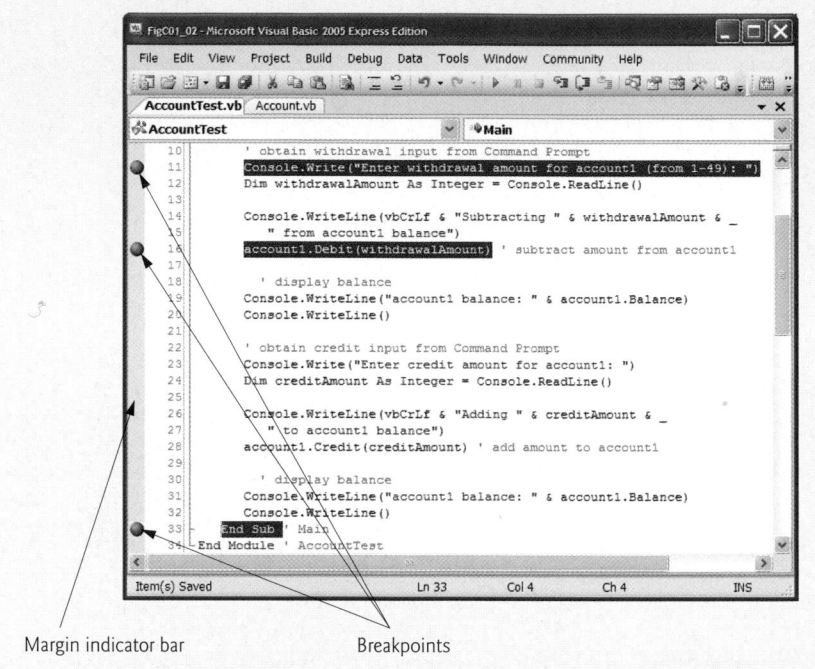

Fig. C.3 | Setting breakpoints.

Set breakpoints at lines 11, 16 and 33 of your code. A solid circle appears in the margin indicator bar where you clicked and the entire code statement is highlighted, indicating that breakpoints have been set (Fig. C.3). When the program runs, the debugger suspends execution at any line that contains a breakpoint. The program then enters **break mode**. Breakpoints can be set before running a program, in break mode and during execution.

2. *Beginning the debugging process.* After setting breakpoints in the code editor, select **Build > Build Account** to compile the program, then select **Debug > Start Debugging** (or press the *F5* key) to begin the debugging process. While debugging a console application, the Command Prompt window appears (Fig. C.4), allowing program interaction (input and output).

3. *Examining program execution.* Program execution pauses at the first breakpoint (line 11), and the IDE becomes the active window (Fig. C.5). The **yellow arrow** to the left of line 11 indicates that this line contains the next statement to execute. The IDE also highlights the line as well.

```
file:///C:/books/2005/vbhtp3/examples/AppC/FigC01_02/Account/bin/Debug/Account.EXE
account1 balance: 50
```

Fig. C.4 | **Account** program running.

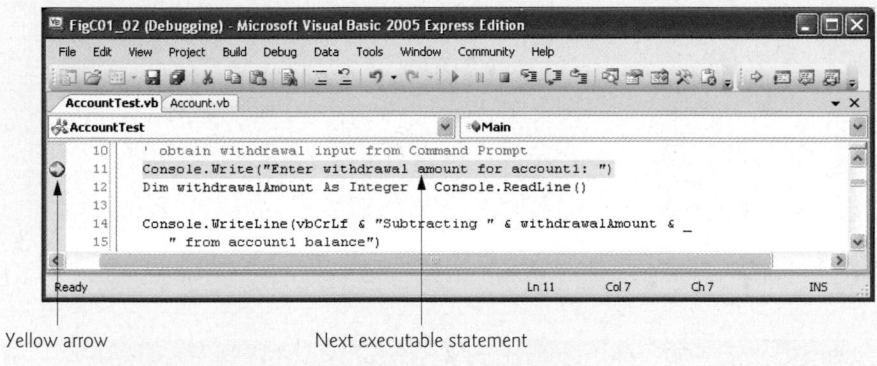

Yellow arrow   Next executable statement

Fig. C.5 | Program execution suspended at the first breakpoint.

4. ***Using the* Continue *command to resume execution.*** To resume execution, select **Debug > Continue** (or press the *F5* key). The **Continue command** will execute the statements from the current point in the program to the next breakpoint or the end of **Main**, whichever comes first. The program continues executing and pauses for input at line 12. Enter 25 in the Command Prompt window as the withdrawal amount. When you press *Enter*, the program executes until it stops at the next breakpoint (line 16). Notice that when you place the mouse pointer over the variable name **withdrawalAmount**, its value is displayed in a *Quick Info* box (Fig. C.6). As you'll see, this can help you spot logic errors in your programs.

5. ***Continuing program execution.*** Use the **Debug > Continue** command to execute line 16. The program then asks for you to input a credit (deposit) amount. Enter 33, then press *Enter*. The program displays the result of its calculation (Fig. C.7).

6. ***Disabling a breakpoint.*** To **disable a breakpoint**, right click a line of code in which the breakpoint has been set and select **Breakpoint > Disable Breakpoint**. The disabled breakpoint is indicated by a hollow circle (Fig. C.8)—the breakpoint can be re-enabled by right clicking the line marked by the hollow circle and selecting **Breakpoint > Enable Breakpoint**.

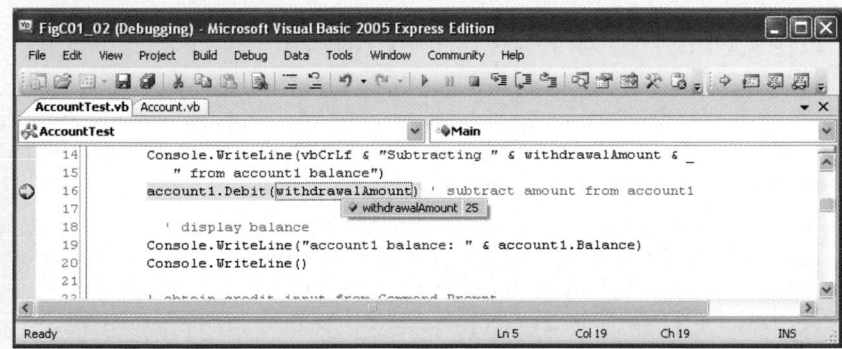

Fig. C.6 | *QuickInfo* box displays value of variable **depositAmount**.

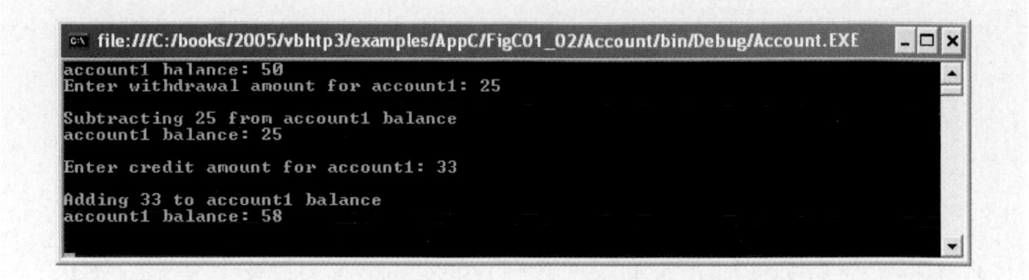

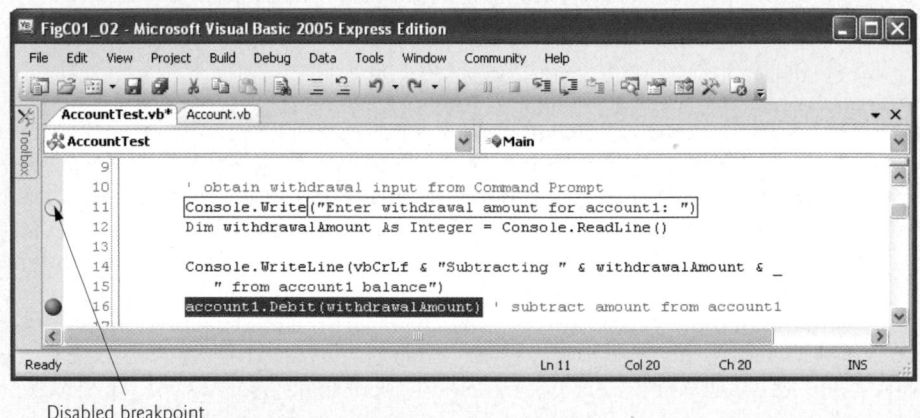

Fig. C.7 | Program output.

Fig. C.8 | Disabled breakpoint.

7. *Removing a breakpoint.* To remove a breakpoint that you no longer need, right click the line of code on which the breakpoint has been set and select **Breakpoint > Delete Breakpoint**. You also can remove a breakpoint by clicking the circle in the margin indicator bar.

8. *Finishing program execution.* Select **Debug > Continue** to execute the program to completion. Then delete all the breakpoints.

C.3 The Locals and Watch Windows

In the preceding section, you learned that the *Quick Info* feature allows you to examine the value of a variable. In this section, you will learn how to use the **Locals** window to assign new values to variables while your program is running. You will also use the **Watch** window to examine the values of expressions.

1. *Inserting breakpoints.* Set a breakpoint at line 16 (Fig. C.9) in the source code by left clicking in the margin indicator bar to the left of line 16. Use the same technique to set breakpoints at lines 19 and 20 as well.

2. *Starting debugging.* Select **Debug > Start Debugging**. Type 25 at the **Enter withdrawal amount for account1:** prompt (Fig. C.10) and press *Enter* so that the program reads the value you just entered. The program executes until the breakpoint at line 16.

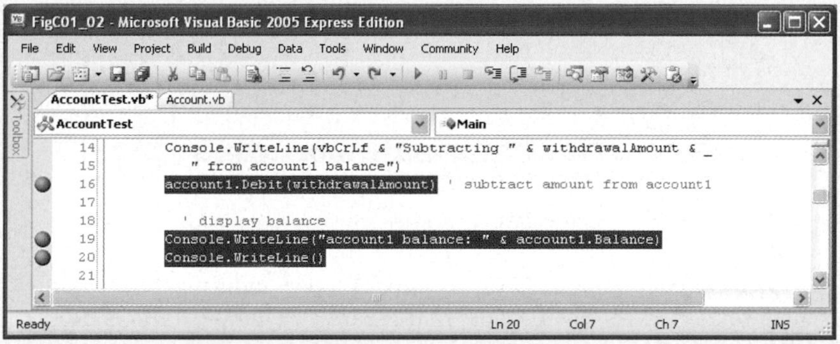

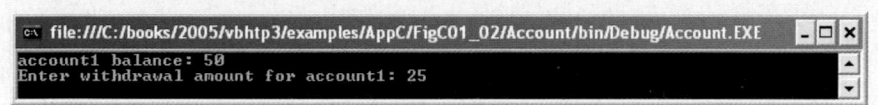

Fig. C.9 | Setting breakpoints at lines 16, 19 and 20.

Fig. C.10 | Entering the deposit amount before the breakpoint is reached.

3. *Suspending program execution.* When the program reaches line 16, Visual Studio suspends program execution and switches the program into break mode (Fig. C.11). At this point, the statement in line 12 (Fig. C.2) has input the with-drawalAmount that you entered (25), the statement in lines 14–15 has output that the program is subtracting that amount from the account1 balance and the statement in line 16 is the next statement that will execute.

4. *Examining data.* Once the program has entered break mode, you can explore the values of your local variables using the debugger's **Locals** window. To view the **Locals** window, select **Debug > Windows > Locals**. Click the plus box to the left of account1 in the **Name** column of the **Locals** window (Fig. C.12). This allows you

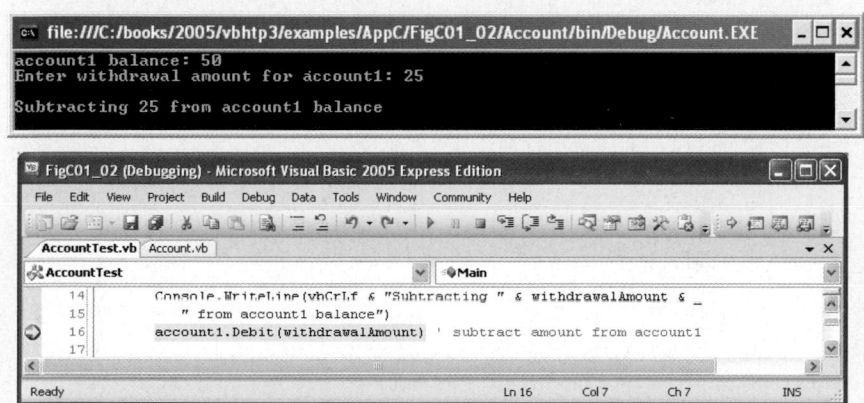

Fig. C.11 | Program execution pauses when debugger reaches the breakpoint at line 16.

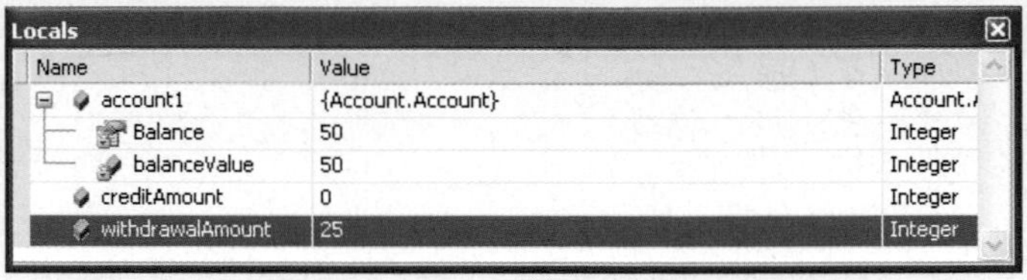

Fig. C.12 | Examining variable depositAmount.

to view each of account1's instance variable values individually, including the value for balanceValue (50). Note that the **Locals** window displays properties of a class as data, which is why you see both the Balance property and the balanceValue instance variable in the **Locals** window. In addition, the current value of local variable withdrawalAmount (25) is also displayed.

5. *Evaluating arithmetic and boolean expressions.* You can evaluate arithmetic and boolean expressions using the **Watch** window. Select **Debug > Windows > Watch** to display the window (Fig. C.13). In the first row of the **Name** column (which should be blank initially), type (withdrawalAmount + 10) * 5, then press *Enter*. The value 175 is displayed (Fig. C.13). In the next row of the **Name** column in the **Watch** window, type withdrawalAmount = 200, then press *Enter*. This expression determines whether the value contained in withdrawalAmount is 200. Expressions containing the = symbol are Boolean expressions. The value returned is False (Fig. C.13), because withdrawalAmount does not currently contain the value 200.

6. *Resuming execution.* Select **Debug > Continue** to resume execution. Line 16 executes, subtracting the account with the withdrawal amount, and the program enters break mode again at line 19. Select **Debug > Windows > Locals**. The updated balanceValue instance variable and Balance property value are now displayed (Fig. C.14).

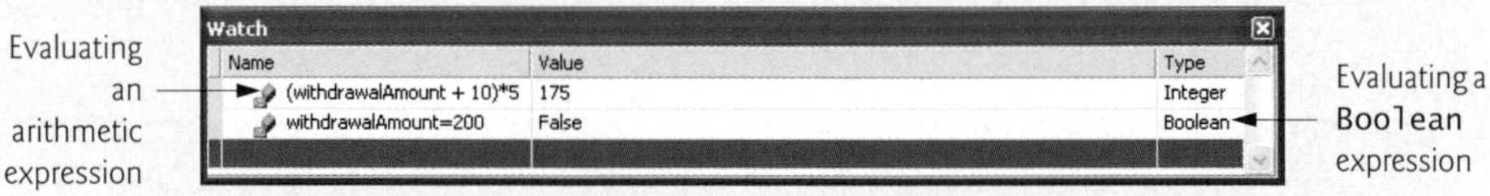

Evaluating an arithmetic expression

Evaluating a Boolean expression

Fig. C.13 | Examining the values of expressions.

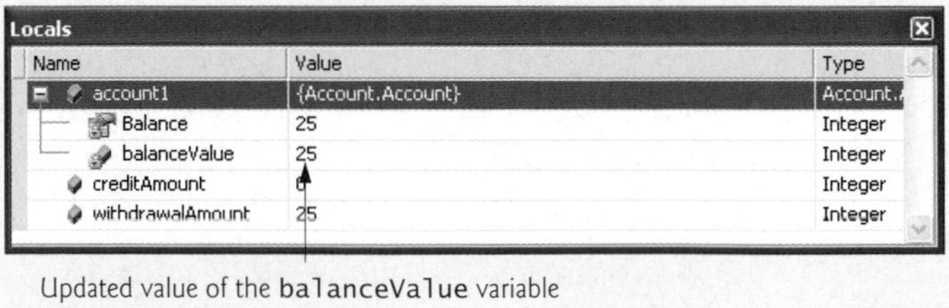

Updated value of the balanceValue variable

Fig. C.14 | Displaying the value of local variables.

7. *Modifying values.* Based on the value input by the user (25), the account balance output by the program should be 25. However, you can use the **Locals** window to change variable values during program execution. This can be valuable for experimenting with different values and for locating logic errors in programs. In the **Locals** window, click the **Value** field in the `balanceValue` row to select the value 25. Type 37, then press *Enter*. The debugger changes the value of `balanceValue` (and the `Balance` property as well), then displays its new value in red (Fig. C.15). Now select **Debug > Continue** to execute lines 19–20. Notice that the new value of `balanceValue` is displayed in the Command Prompt window.

8. *Stopping the debugging session.* Select **Debug > Stop Debugging**. Delete all breakpoints.

C.4 Controlling Execution Using the Step Into, Step Over, Step Out and Continue Commands

Sometimes you will need to execute a program line-by-line to find and fix logic errors. Stepping through a portion of your program this way can help you verify that a method's code executes correctly. The commands you learn in this section allow you to execute a method line-by-line, execute all the statements of a method or execute only the remaining statements of a method (if you have already executed some statements within the method).

1. *Setting a breakpoint.* Set a breakpoint at line 16 by left clicking in the margin indicator bar (Fig. C.16).

2. *Starting the debugger.* Select **Debug > Start Debugging**. Enter the value 25 at the **Enter withdrawal amount for account1:** prompt. Program execution halts when the program reaches the breakpoint at line 16.

3. *Using the Step Into command.* The **Step Into** command executes the next statement in the program (the yellow highlighted line of Fig. C.17) and immediately halts. If the statement to execute is a method call, control transfers to the called method. The **Step Into** command allows you to follow execution into a method and confirm its execution by individually executing each statement inside the method. Select **Debug > Step Into** (or press *F11*) to enter the `Debit` method (Fig. C.18).

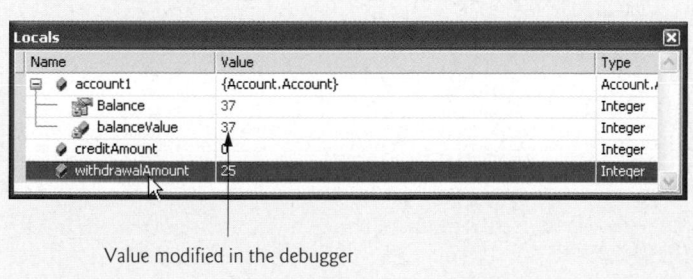

Value modified in the debugger

Fig. C.15 | Modifying the value of a variable.

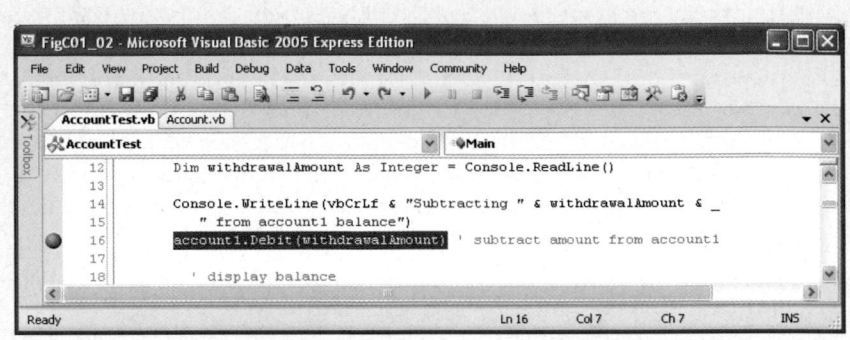

Fig. C.16 | Setting a breakpoint in the program.

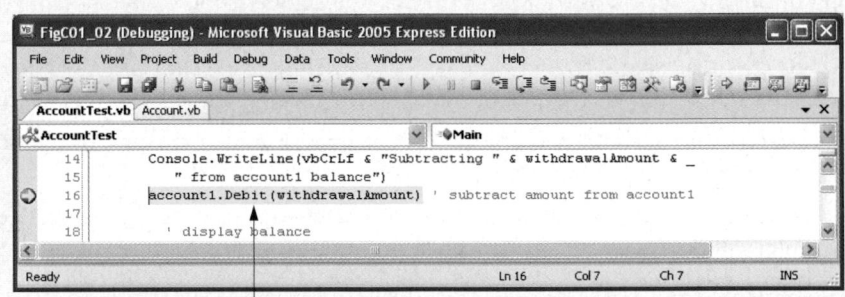

Next statement to execute is a method call

Fig. C.17 | The **Step Into** command will enter the Debit method.

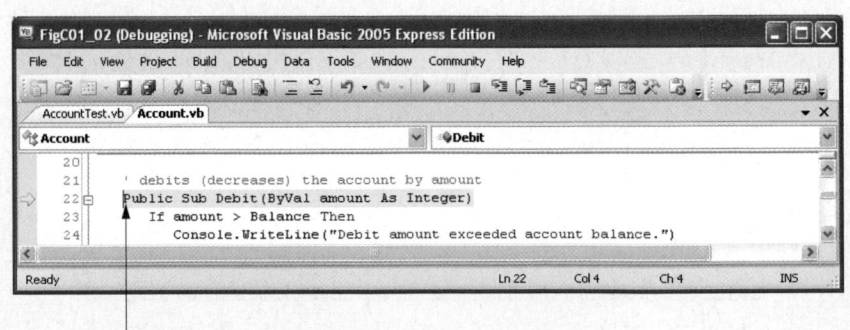

Next statement to execute

Fig. C.18 | Stepping into the Debit method.

4. *Using the* **Step Over** *command.* Select **Debug > Step Over** to enter the Debit method's body and transfer control to line 23 (Fig. C.19). The **Step Over** command behaves like the **Step Into** command when the next statement to execute does not contain a method call or access a property. You will see how the **Step Over** command differs from the **Step Into** command in *Step 10.*

5. *Using the* **Step Out** *command.* Select **Debug > Step Out** to execute the remaining statements in the method and return control to the calling method. Often, in lengthy methods, you will want to look at a few key lines of code, then continue debugging the caller's code. The **Step Out** command executes the remainder of a method and returns to the caller.

6. *Setting a breakpoint.* Set a breakpoint (Fig. C.20) at line 20 of Fig. C.2. You will make use of this breakpoint in the next step.

7. *Using the* **Continue** *command.* Select **Debug > Continue** to execute until the next breakpoint is reached at line 20. This feature saves time when you do not want to step line-by-line through many lines of code to reach the next breakpoint.

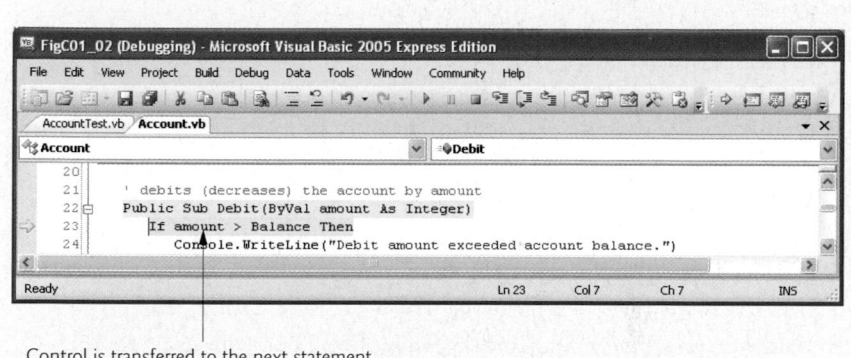

Control is transferred to the next statement

Fig. C.19 | Stepping over a statement in the `Credit` method.

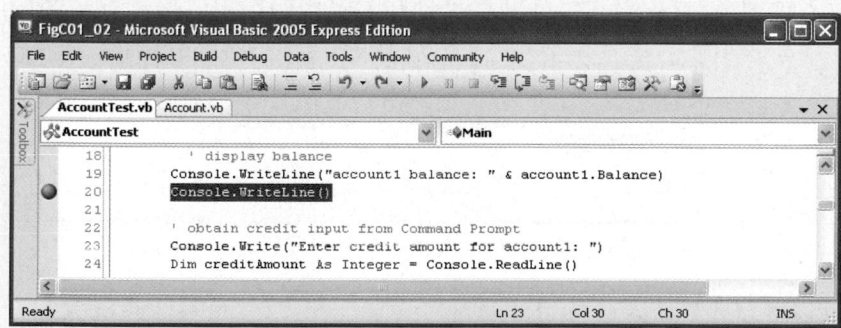

Fig. C.20 | Setting a second breakpoint in the program.

8. *Stopping the debugger.* Select **Debug > Stop Debugging** to end the debugging session.

9. *Starting the debugger.* Before we can demonstrate the next debugger feature, you must restart the debugger. Start it, as you did in *Step 2*, and enter the same value (25). The debugger pauses execution at line 16.

10. *Using the **Step Over** command.* Select **Debug > Step Over** (Fig. C.21). Recall that this command behaves like the **Step Into** command when the next statement to execute does not contain a method call. If the next statement to execute contains a method call, the called method executes in its entirety (without pausing execution at any statement inside the method—unless there is a breakpoint in the method), and the arrow advances to the next executable line (after the method call) in the current method. In this case, the debugger executes line 16 in Main (Fig. C.2), which calls the Debit method. Then, the debugger pauses execution at line 19, the next executable statement.

11. *Stopping the debugger.* Select **Debug > Stop Debugging**. Remove all remaining breakpoints.

C.5 Other Features

Visual Studio 2005 provides many new debugging features, that simplify the testing and debugging process. We discuss some of these features in this section.

C.5.1 Edit and Continue

The **Edit and Continue** feature allows you to make modifications or changes to your code in debug mode, then continue executing the program without having to recompile your code.

1. *Setting a breakpoint.* Set a breakpoint at line 11 in your example (Fig. C.22).

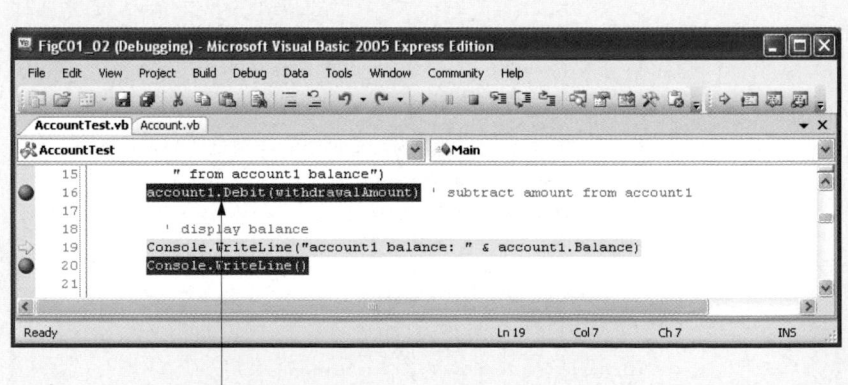

The Debit method executes without stepping into
it when you select the **Step Over** command

Fig. C.21 | Using the debugger's **Step Over** command.

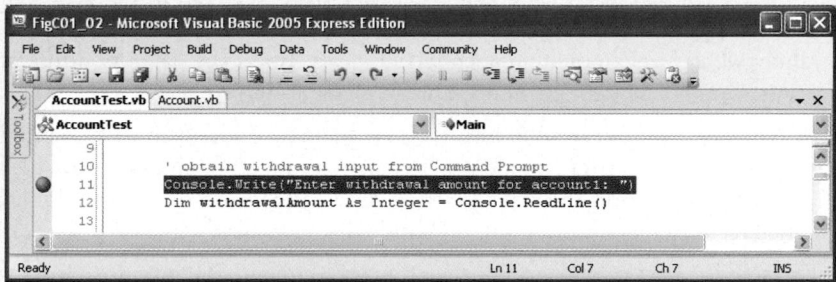

Fig. C.22 | Setting a breakpoint at line 11.

2. *Starting the debugger.* Select **Debug > Start Debugging**. When execution begins, the account1 balance is displayed. The debugger enters break mode when it reaches the breakpoint at line 11.

3. *Changing the input prompt text.* Suppose you wish to modify the input prompt text to provide the user with a range of values for variable withdrawalAmount. Rather than stopping the debugging process, add the text "(from 1-49):" to the end of "Enter withdrawal amount for account1" at line 11 in the code view window. Select **Debug > Continue**. The application prompts you for input using the updated text (Fig. C.23).

In this example, we wanted to make a change in the text for our input prompt before line 11 executes. However, if you want to make a change to a line that already executed, you must select a prior statement in your code from which to continue execution.

1. *Setting a breakpoint.* Set a breakpoint at line 14 (Fig. C.24).

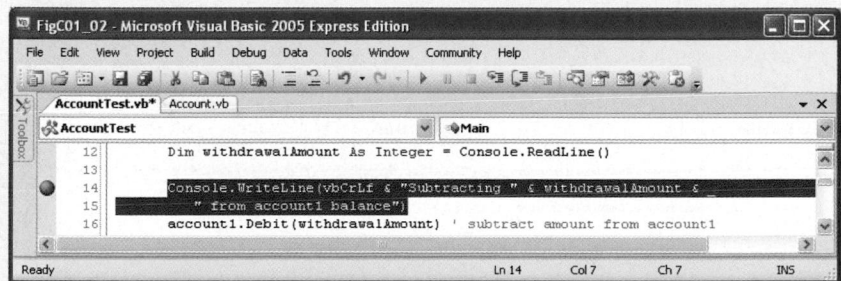

Fig. C.23 | Application prompt displaying the updated text.

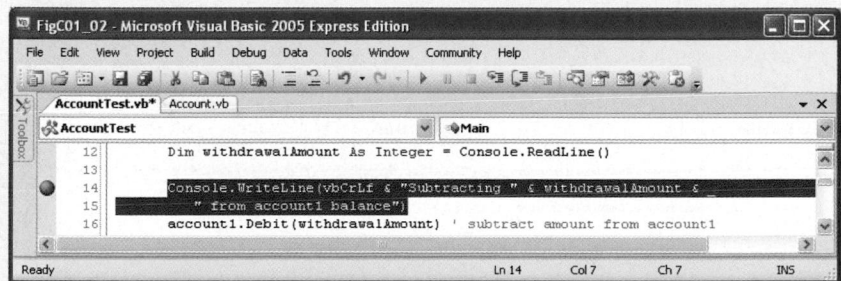

Fig. C.24 | Setting a breakpoint at line 14.

2. *Starting the debugger.* Delete the "(from 1-49)" text you just added in the previous steps. Select **Debug > Start Debugging**. When execution begins, the prompt **Enter withdrawal amount for account1:** appears. Enter the value 22 at the prompt (Fig. C.25). The debugger enters break mode at line 14 (Fig. C.25).

3. *Changing the input prompt text.* Let's say that you once again wish to modify the input prompt text to provide the user with a range of values for variable withdrawalAmount. Add the text "(from 1-49):" to the end of "Enter withdrawal amount for account1" in line 11 inside the code view window.

4. *Setting the next statement.* For the program to update the input prompt text correctly, you must set the execution point to a previous line of code. Right click in line 11 and select **Set Next Statement** from the menu that appears (Fig. C.26).

5. Select **Debug > Continue**. The application prompts you again for input using the updated text (Fig. C.27).

6. *Stopping the debugger.* Select **Debug > Stop Debugging**.

Certain types of change are not allowed with the Edit and Continue feature once the program begins execution. These include changing class names, adding or removing method parameters, adding public fields to a class and adding or removing methods. If a particular change that you make to your program is not allowed during the debugging process, Visual Studio displays a dialog box as shown in Fig. C.28.

C.5.2 Exception Assistant

Another new feature in Visual Studio 2005 is the Exception Assistant. You can run a program by selecting either **Debug > Start Debugging** or **Debug > Start Without Debugging**. If you select the option **Debug > Start Debugging** and the runtime environment detects uncaught exceptions, the application pauses, and a window called the **Exception Assistant** appears indicating where the exception occurred, the type of the exception and links to helpful information on handling the exception. We discuss the Exception Assistant in detail in Section 12.4.3.

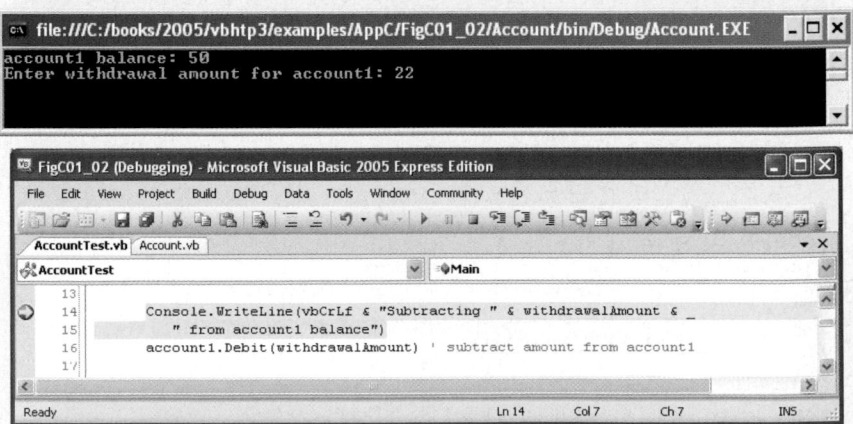

Fig. C.25 | Stopping execution at the breakpoint in line 14.

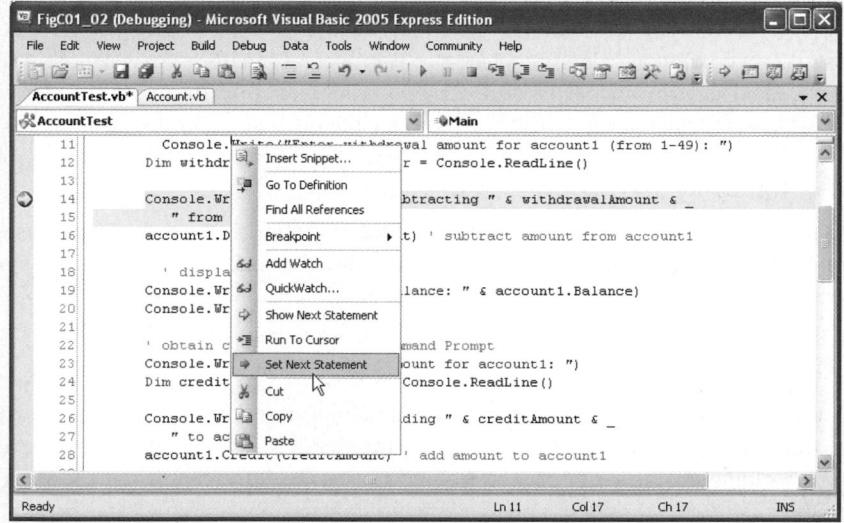

Fig. C.26 | Setting the next statement to execute.

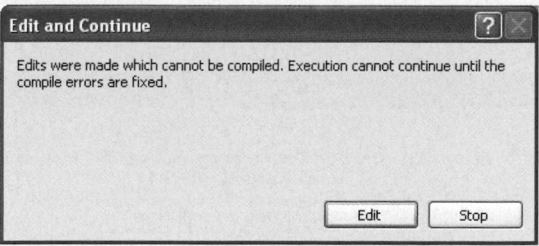

Fig. C.27 | Program execution continues with updated prompt text.

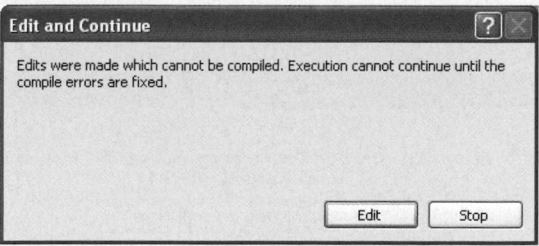

Fig. C.28 | Dialog box stating that certain program edits are not allowed during program execution.

C.5.3 Just My Code™ Debugging

Throughout this book, we produce increasingly substantial programs that often include a combination of code written by the programmer and code generated by Visual Studio. The IDE-generated code can be difficult for novices (and even experienced programmers) to understand—fortunately, you rarely need to look at this code. Visual Studio 2005 provides a new debugging feature called **Just My Code™**, that allows programmers to test and debug only the portion of the code they have written. When this option is enabled, the debugger will always step over method calls to methods of classes that you did not write.

This feature is not available in Visual Basic 2005 Express. If you have the complete Visual Studio 2005, you can change this setting in the debugger options. Select **Tools > Options...**. In the **Options** dialog, select the **Debugging** category to view the available debugging tools and options. Then click the checkbox that appears next to the **Enable Just My Code (Managed only)** option (Fig. C.29) to enable or disable this feature.

C.5.4 Other New Debugger Features

The Visual Studio 2005 debugger offers additional new features, such as visualizers, trace-points and more, which you can learn about at msdn.microsoft.com/vstudio/express/ vb/features/debug/default.aspx.

C.6 Wrap-Up

In this appendix, you learned how to enable the debugger and set breakpoints so that you can examine your code and results while a program executes. This capability enables you to locate and fix logic errors in your programs. You also learned how to continue execution after a program suspends execution at a breakpoint and how to disable and remove breakpoints.

We showed how to use the debugger's **Watch** and **Locals** windows to evaluate arithmetic and boolean expressions. We also demonstrated how to modify a variable's value during program execution so that you can see how changes in values affect your results.

You learned how to use the debugger's **Step Into** command to debug methods called during your program's execution. You saw how the **Step Over** command can be used to execute a method call without stopping the called method. You used the **Step Out** command to continue execution until the end of the current method. You also learned that the **Continue** command continues execution until another breakpoint is found or the program terminates.

Finally, we discussed new features of the Visual Studio 2005 debugger, including Edit and Continue, the Exception Assistant and Just My Code™ debugging.

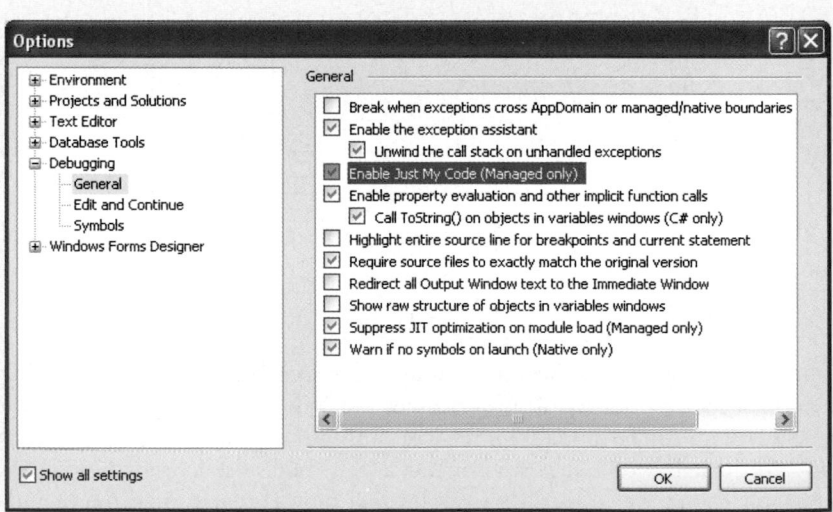

Fig. C.29 | Enabling the **Just My Code** debugging feature in Visual Studio.

Summary

Section C.1 Introduction
- Most compiler vendors, like Microsoft, provide software called a debugger, which allows you to monitor the execution of your programs to locate and remove logic errors.
- The debugger allows you to suspend program execution, examine and set variables, call methods without having to modify the program and much more.

Section C.2 Breakpoints and the Continue Command
- Breakpoints are markers that can be set at any executable line of code. When program execution reaches a breakpoint, execution pauses, allowing you to examine the values of variables to help you locate and correct logic errors.
- To insert a breakpoint in Visual Studio, left click inside the margin indicator bar next to the line of code at which you wish to break, or right click that line of code and select **Breakpoint > Insert Breakpoint**.
- A program is said to be in break mode when the debugger pauses the program's execution. Breakpoints can be set before running a program, in break mode or while a program is running.
- The **Continue** command will execute any statements between the next executable statement and the next breakpoint or the end of Main, whichever comes first.
- The value that the variable stores is displayed in a *Quick Info* box. In a sense, you are peeking inside the computer at the value of one of your variables.
- To disable a breakpoint, right click a line of code in which the breakpoint has been set and select **Breakpoint > Disable Breakpoint**.
- To remove a breakpoint that you no longer need, right click the line of code on which the breakpoint has been set and select **Breakpoint > Delete Breakpoint**. You also can remove a breakpoint by clicking the solid circle in the margin indicator bar.

Section C.3 The Locals and Watch Windows
- The **Locals** window enables you to assign new values to variables while your program is running.
- The **Watch** window allows you to examine the value of arithmetic and Boolean expressions.

Section C.4 Controlling Execution Using the Step Into, Step Over, Step Out and Continue Commands
- You can step through a portion of your program line-by-line to find and fix logic errors and verify that a method's code executes correctly.
- The **Step Into** command executes the next statement in the program and immediately halts. If the statement to be executed as a result of the **Step Into** command is a method call, control is transferred to the called method. The **Step Into** command allows you to enter a method and confirm its execution by individually executing each statement in the method.
- The **Step Over** command behaves like the **Step Into** command when the next statement to execute does not contain a method call or access a property.
- The **Step Out** command is used for situations where you do not want to continue stepping through the entire method line-by-line.

Section C.5 Other Features
- The Edit and Continue feature allows you to make modifications or changes to your code as the debugger is running.

- If you want to make a change to a particular line that has been executed, you must select a prior statement in your code from which to continue execution. The **Set Next Statement** will allow you to do this

- Certain types of change are not allowed with the Edit and Continue feature once the program begins execution. These include changing the name of a class, adding or removing method parameters, adding public fields to a class and adding or removing methods.

- The Exception Assistant indicates where the exception occurred, the type of the exception and links to helpful information on handling the exception.

- The Just My Code™ feature allows programmers to test and debug only the portion of code which they have written.

Terminology

break mode	logic error
breakpoint	margin indicator bar
bug	*Quick Info* box
Continue command	solid breakpoint circle
debugger	**Step Into** command
disable a breakpoint	**Step Out** command
Edit and Continue	**Step Over** command
Exception Assistant	suspend program execution
insert a breakpoint	Visual Studio debugger
Just My Code™ debugging	**Watch** window
Locals window	yellow arrow in break mode

Self-Review Exercises

C.1 Fill in the blanks in each of the following statements:
  a) When the debugger suspends program execution at a breakpoint, the program is said to be in _____ mode.
  b) The _____ feature in Visual Studio .NET allows you to "peek into the computer" and look at the value of a variable.
  c) You can examine the value of an expression by using the debugger's _____ window.
  d) The _____ command behaves like the **Step Into** command when the next statement to execute does not contain a method call or access a property.

C.2 State whether each of the following is *true* or *false*. If *false*, explain why.
  a) When program execution suspends at a breakpoint, the next statement to be executed is the statement after the breakpoint.
  b) When a variable's value is changed, the value changes to yellow in the **Locals** windows.
  c) During debugging, the **Step Out** command executes the remaining statements in the current method and returns program control to the place where the method was called.

Answers to Self-Review Exercises

C.1 a) break. b) *Quick Info* box. c) **Watch**. d) **Step Over**.

C.2 a) False. When program execution suspends at a breakpoint, the next statement to be executed is the statement at the breakpoint. b) False. A variable's value turns red when it is changed. c) True.

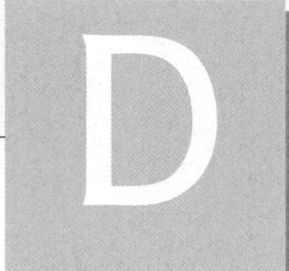

ASCII Character Set

	0	1	2	3	4	5	6	7	8	9
ASCII character set										
0	nul	soh	stx	etx	eot	enq	ack	bel	bs	ht
1	lf	vt	ff	cr	so	si	dle	dc1	dc2	dc3
2	dc4	nak	syn	etb	can	em	sub	esc	fs	gs
3	rs	us	sp	!	"	#	$	%	&	'
4	(	)	*	+	,	-	.	/	0	1
5	2	3	4	5	6	7	8	9	:	;
6	<	=	>	?	@	A	B	C	D	E
7	F	G	H	I	J	K	L	M	N	O
8	P	Q	R	S	T	U	V	W	X	Y
9	Z	[	\	]	^	_	`	a	b	c
10	d	e	f	g	h	i	j	k	l	m
11	n	o	p	q	r	s	t	u	v	w
12	x	y	z	{	|	}	~	del		

Fig. D.1 | ASCII character set.

The digits at the left of the table are the left digits of the decimal equivalent (0–127) of the character code, and the digits at the top of the table are the right digits of the character code. For example, the character code for "F" is 70, and the character code for "&" is 38.

Most users of this book are interested in the ASCII character set used to represent English characters on many computers. The ASCII character set is a subset of the Unicode character set used by Visual Basic to represent characters from most of the world's languages. For more information on the Unicode character set, see Appendix E.

Unicode®

OBJECTIVES

In this appendix you will learn:

- The mission of the Unicode Consortium.
- The design basis of Unicode.
- The three Unicode encoding forms: UTF-8, UTF-16 and UTF-32.
- Characters and glyphs.
- The advantages and disadvantages of using Unicode.
- A brief tour of the Unicode Consortium's Web site.

E.1 Introduction

The use of inconsistent character encodings (i.e., numeric values associated with characters) in the developing of global software products causes serious problems, because computers process information as numbers. For instance, the character "a" is converted to a numeric value so that a computer can manipulate that piece of data. Many countries and corporations have developed their own encoding systems that are incompatible with the encoding systems of other countries and corporations. For example, the Microsoft Windows operating system assigns the value 0xC0 to the character "A with a grave accent"; the Apple Macintosh operating system assigns that same value to an upside-down question mark. This results in the misrepresentation and possible corruption of data when data is not processed as intended.

In the absence of a widely-implemented universal character-encoding standard, global software developers had to localize their products extensively before distribution. Localization includes the language translation and cultural adaptation of content. The process of localization usually includes significant modifications to the source code (such as the conversion of numeric values and the underlying assumptions made by programmers), which results in increased costs and delays releasing the software. For example, some English-speaking programmers might design global software products assuming that a single character can be represented by one byte. However, when those products are localized for Asian markets, the programmer's assumptions are no longer valid; thus, the majority, if not the entirety, of the code needs to be rewritten. Localization is necessary with each release of a version. By the time a software product is localized for a particular market, a newer version, which needs to be localized as well, may be ready for distribution. As a result, it is cumbersome and costly to produce and distribute global software products in a market where there is no universal character-encoding standard.

In response to this situation, the Unicode Standard, an encoding standard that facilitates the production and distribution of software, was created. The Unicode Standard outlines a specification to produce consistent encoding of the world's characters and symbols. Software products that handle text encoded in the Unicode Standard need to be localized, but the localization process is simpler and more efficient because the numeric values need not be converted and the assumptions made by programmers about the character encoding are universal. The Unicode Standard is maintained by a nonprofit organization called the Unicode Consortium, whose members include Apple, IBM, Microsoft, Oracle, Sun Microsystems, Sybase and many others.

When the Consortium envisioned and developed the Unicode Standard, they wanted an encoding system that was universal, efficient, uniform and unambiguous. A universal encoding system encompasses all commonly used characters. An efficient encoding system allows text files to be parsed easily. A uniform encoding system assigns fixed values to all characters. An unambiguous encoding system represents a given character in a consistent manner. These four terms are referred to as the Unicode Standard design basis.

E.2 Unicode Transformation Formats

Although Unicode incorporates the limited ASCII character set (i.e., a collection of characters), it encompasses a more comprehensive character set. In ASCII each character is represented by a byte containing 0s and 1s. One byte is capable of storing the binary numbers from 0 to 255. Each character is assigned a number between 0 and 255; thus, ASCII-based systems can support only 256 characters, a tiny fraction of world's characters. Unicode extends the ASCII character set by encoding the vast majority of the world's characters. The Unicode Standard encodes all of those characters in a uniform numerical space from 0 to 10FFFF hexadecimal. An implementation will express these numbers in one of several transformation formats, choosing the one that best fits the particular application at hand.

Three such formats are in use, called UTF-8, UTF-16 and UTF-32, depending on the size of the units—in bits—being used. UTF-8, a variable-width encoding form, requires one to four bytes to express each Unicode character. UTF-8 data consists of 8-bit bytes (sequences of one, two, three or four bytes depending on the character being encoded) and is well suited for ASCII-based systems, where there is a predominance of one-byte characters (ASCII represents characters as one byte). Currently, UTF-8 is widely implemented in UNIX systems and in databases.

The variable-width UTF-16 encoding form expresses Unicode characters in units of 16 bits (i.e., as two adjacent bytes, or a short integer in many machines). Most characters of Unicode are expressed in a single 16-bit unit. However, characters with values above FFFF hexadecimal are expressed with an ordered pair of 16-bit units called surrogates. Surrogates are 16-bit integers in the range D800 through DFFF, which are used solely for the purpose of "escaping" into higher numbered characters. Approximately one million characters can be expressed in this manner. Although a surrogate pair requires 32 bits to represent characters, it is space-efficient to use these 16-bit units. Surrogates are rare characters in current implementations. Many string-handling implementations are written in terms of UTF-16. [*Note:* Details and sample code for UTF-16 handling are available on the Unicode Consortium Web site at www.unicode.org.]

Implementations that require significant use of rare characters or entire scripts encoded above FFFF hexadecimal should use UTF-32, a 32-bit, fixed-width encoding form that usually requires twice as much memory as UTF-16 encoded characters. The major advantage of the fixed-width UTF-32 encoding form is that it expresses all characters uniformly, so it is easy to handle in arrays.

There are few guidelines that state when to use a particular encoding form. The best encoding form to use depends on computer systems and business protocols, not on the data itself. Typically, the UTF-8 encoding form should be used where computer systems and business protocols require data to be handled in 8-bit units, particularly in legacy systems being upgraded, because it often simplifies changes to existing programs. For this reason, UTF-8 has become the encoding form of choice on the Internet. Likewise, UTF-

16 is the encoding form of choice on Microsoft Windows applications. UTF-32 is likely to become more widely used in the future as more characters are encoded with values above FFFF hexadecimal. Also, UTF-32 requires less sophisticated handling than UTF-16 in the presence of surrogate pairs. Figure E.1 shows the different ways in which the three encoding forms handle character encoding.

E.3 Characters and Glyphs

The Unicode Standard consists of characters, written components (i.e., alphabetic letters, numerals, punctuation marks, accent marks, etc.) that can be represented by numeric values. Examples of characters include: U+0041 LATIN CAPITAL LETTER A. In the first character representation, U+*yyyy* is a code value, in which U+ refers to Unicode code values, as opposed to other hexadecimal values. The *yyyy* represents a four-digit hexadecimal number of an encoded character. Code values are bit combinations that represent encoded characters. Characters are represented with glyphs, various shapes, fonts and sizes for displaying characters. There are no code values for glyphs in the Unicode Standard. Examples of glyphs are shown in Fig. E.2.

The Unicode Standard encompasses the alphabets, ideographs, syllabaries, punctuation marks, diacritics, mathematical operators and so on. that compose the written languages and scripts of the world. A diacritic is a special mark added to a character to distinguish it from another letter or to indicate an accent (e.g., in Spanish, the tilde "˜" above the character "n"). Currently, Unicode provides code values for 94,140 character representations, with more than 880,000 code values reserved for future expansion.

E.4 Advantages/Disadvantages of Unicode

The Unicode Standard has several significant advantages that promote its use. One is the impact it has on the performance of the international economy. Unicode standardizes the characters for the world's writing systems to a uniform model that promotes transferring

Character	UTF-8	UTF-16	UTF-32
Latin Capital Letter A	0x41	0x0041	0x00000041
Greek Capital Letter Alpha	0xCD 0x91	0x0391	0x00000391
CJK Unified Ideograph-4e95	0xE4 0xBA 0x95	0x4E95	0x00004E95
Old Italic Letter A	0xF0 0x80 0x83 0x80	0xDC00 0xDF00	0x00010300

Fig. E.1 | Correlation between the three encoding forms.

Fig. E.2 | Various glyphs of the character A.

and sharing data. Programs developed using such a schema maintain their accuracy because each character has a single definition (i.e., *a* is always U+0061, % is always U+0025). This enables corporations to manage the high demands of international markets by processing different writing systems at the same time. Also, all characters can be managed in an identical manner, thus avoiding any confusion caused by different character-code architectures. Moreover, managing data in a consistent manner eliminates data corruption, because data can be sorted, searched and manipulated via a consistent process.

Another advantage of the Unicode Standard is portability (i.e., the ability to execute software on disparate computers or with disparate operating systems). Most operating systems, databases, programming languages and Web browsers currently support, or are planning to support, Unicode. Additionally, Unicode includes more characters than any other character set in common use (although it does not yet include all of the world's characters).

A disadvantage of the Unicode Standard is the amount of memory required by UTF-16 and UTF-32. ASCII character sets are 8 bits in length, so they require less storage than the default 16-bit Unicode character set. However, the double-byte character set (DBCS) and the multi-byte character set (MBCS) that encode Asian characters (ideographs) require two to four bytes, respectively. In such instances, the UTF-16 or the UTF-32 encoding forms may be used with little hindrance on memory and performance.

E.5 Unicode Consortium's Web Site

If you would like to learn more about the Unicode Standard, visit www.unicode.org. This site provides a wealth of information about the Unicode Standard. Currently, the home page is organized into various sections: New to Unicode, General Information, The Consortium, The Unicode Standard, Work in Progress and For Members.

The New to Unicode section consists of four subsections: **What is Unicode?**, **How to Use this Site**, **FAQ** and **Glossary of Unicode Terms**. The first subsection provides a technical introduction to Unicode by describing design principles, character interpretations and assignments, text processing and Unicode conformance. This subsection is recommended reading for anyone new to Unicode. Also, this subsection provides a list of related links that provide the reader with additional information about Unicode. The **How to Use this Site** subsection contains information about using and navigating the site as well hyperlinks to additional resources.

The General Information section contains five subsections: **Where is my Character?**, **Display Problems?**, **Useful Resources**, **Unicode Enabled Products** and **Mail Lists**. The main areas covered in this section include a link to the Unicode code charts (a complete listing of code values) assembled by the Unicode Consortium as well as a detailed outline on how to locate an encoded character in the code chart. Also, the section contains advice on how to configure different operating systems and Web browsers so that the Unicode characters can be viewed properly. Moreover, from this section, the user can navigate to other sites that provide information on various topics, such as fonts, linguistics and such other standards as the Armenian Standards Page and the Chinese GB 18030 Encoding Standard.

The Consortium section consists of six subsections: **Who we are**, **Our Members**, **Job Postings**, **Press Info**, **Policies & Positions** and **Contact Us**. This section provides a list of the current Unicode Consortium members as well as information on how to become a member. Privileges for each member type—full, associate, specialist and individual—and the fees assessed to each member are listed here.

The For Members section consists of two subsections that are available only to consortium members: **Member Resources** and **Working Documents**.

The Unicode Standard section consists of five subsections: **Start Here**, **Latest Version**, **Code Charts**, **Unicode Character Database** and **Unihan Database**. This section describes the updates applied to the latest version of the Unicode Standard and categorizes all defined encoding. The user can learn how the latest version has been modified to encompass more features and capabilities. For instance, one enhancement of Version 3.1 is that it contains additional encoded characters.

The Key Specifications and Technical Publications sections provide all the Unicode technical documentation.

The Work in Progress section consists of seven subsections: **Calendar of Meetings**, **Proposals for Public Review**, **Unicode Technical Committee**, **UTC Meeting Minutes**, **Proposed Characters**, **Submitting Proposals** and **CLDR Technical Committee**. This section presents the user with a catalog of the recent characters included into the Unicode Standard scheme as well as those characters being considered for inclusion. If users determine that a character has been overlooked, then they can submit a written proposal for the inclusion of that character. The **Submitting Proposals** subsection contains strict guidelines that must be adhered to when submitting written proposals. In addition, this section provides information about upcoming and past technical committee meetings.

E.6 Using Unicode

Visual Studio uses Unicode UTF-16 encoding to represent all characters. Figure E.3 uses Visual Basic to display the text "Welcome to Unicode!" in eight different languages: English, French, German, Japanese, Portuguese, Russian, Spanish and Traditional Chinese.

```
 1   ' Fig. F.3: Unicode.vb
 2   ' Using Unicode encoding.
 3   Public Class FrmUnicodeDemo
 4      Private Sub FrmUnicodeDemo_Load(ByVal sender As System.Object, _
 5         ByVal e As System.EventArgs) Handles MyBase.Load
 6         'English
 7         lblEnglish.Text = ChrW(&H57) & ChrW(&H65) & ChrW(&H6C) & _
 8            ChrW(&H63) & ChrW(&H6F) & ChrW(&H6D) & ChrW(&H65) & _
 9            ChrW(&H20) & ChrW(&H74) & ChrW(&H6F) & ChrW(&H20) & _
10            "Unicode" & ChrW(&H21)
11
12         ' French
13         lblFrench.Text = ChrW(&H42) & ChrW(&H69) & ChrW(&H65) & _
14            ChrW(&H6E) & ChrW(&H76) & ChrW(&H65) & ChrW(&H6E) & _
15            ChrW(&H75) & ChrW(&H65) & ChrW(&H20) & ChrW(&H61) & _
16            ChrW(&H75) & ChrW(&H20) & "Unicode" & ChrW(&H21)
17
18         ' German
19         lblGerman.Text = ChrW(&H57) & ChrW(&H69) & ChrW(&H6C) & _
20            ChrW(&H6B) & ChrW(&H6F) & ChrW(&H6D) & ChrW(&H6D) & _
21            ChrW(&H65) & ChrW(&H6E) & ChrW(&H20) & ChrW(&H7A) & _
22            ChrW(&H75) & ChrW(&H20) & "Unicode" & ChrW(&H21)
```

Fig. E.3 | Windows application demonstrating Unicode encoding (Part 1 of 2).

```
23
24         ' Japanese
25         lblJapanese.Text = "Unicode " & ChrW(&H3078) & _
26            ChrW(&H3087) & ChrW(&H3045) & ChrW(&H3053) & _
27            ChrW(&H305D) & ChrW(&H21)
28
29         ' Portuguese
30         lblPortuguese.Text = ChrW(&H53) & ChrW(&HE9) & ChrW(&H6A) & _
31            ChrW(&H61) & ChrW(&H20) & ChrW(&H42) & _
32            ChrW(&H65) & ChrW(&H6D) & ChrW(&H76) & _
33            ChrW(&H69) & ChrW(&H6E) & ChrW(&H64) & _
34            ChrW(&H6F) & ChrW(&H20) & "Unicode" & ChrW(&H21)
35
36         ' Russian
37         lblRussian.Text = ChrW(&H414) & ChrW(&H43E) & ChrW(&H431) & _
38            ChrW(&H440) & ChrW(&H43E) & ChrW(&H20) & _
39            ChrW(&H43F) & ChrW(&H43E) & ChrW(&H436) & _
40            ChrW(&H430) & ChrW(&H43B) & ChrW(&H43E) & _
41            ChrW(&H432) & ChrW(&H430) & ChrW(&H442) & _
42            ChrW(&H44A) & ChrW(&H20) & ChrW(&H432) & _
43            ChrW(&H20) & "Unicode" & ChrW(&H21)
44
45         ' Spanish
46         lblSpanish.Text = ChrW(&H42) & ChrW(&H69) & ChrW(&H65) & _
47            ChrW(&H6E) & ChrW(&H76) & ChrW(&H65) & _
48            ChrW(&H6E) & ChrW(&H69) & ChrW(&H64) & _
49            ChrW(&H61) & ChrW(&H20) & ChrW(&H61) & _
50            ChrW(&H20) & "Unicode" & ChrW(&H21)
51
52         ' Traditional Chinese
53         lblChinese.Text = ChrW(&H6B22) & ChrW(&H8FCE) & _
54            ChrW(&H4F7F) & ChrW(&H7528) & ChrW(&H20) & _
55            "Unicode" & ChrW(&H21)
56      End Sub ' FrmUnicodeDemo_Load
57   End Class ' FrmUnicodeDemo
```

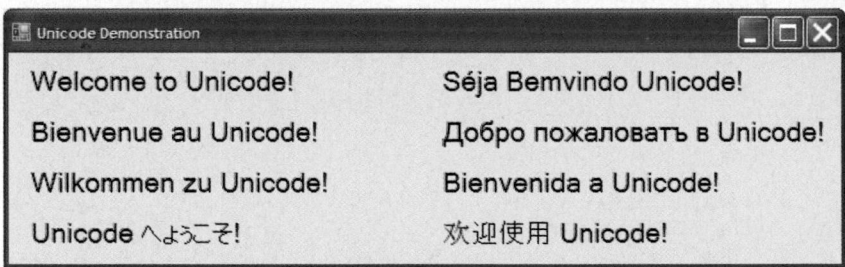

Fig. E.3 | Windows application demonstrating Unicode encoding (Part 2 of 2.).

The first welcome message (lines 13–16) contains the hexadecimal codes for the English text. The **Code Charts** page on the Unicode Consortium Web site contains a document that lists the code values for the **Basic Latin** block (or category), which includes the English alphabet. The hexadecimal codes in lines 13–14 equate to "Welcome." When using Unicode characters in Visual Basic, the format &H*yyyy* is used, where *yyyy* represents the hexadecimal Unicode encoding. For example, the letter "W" (in "Welcome") is denoted by &H57. [*Note:* The actual code for the letter "W" is &H0057, but Visual Studio removes the two zeros.] Line 15 contains the hexadecimal for the *space* character (&H20). The hexadecimal value for the word "to" is on line 15 and the word "Unicode" is on line 14. "Unicode" is not encoded because it is a registered trademark and has no equivalent translation in most languages. Line 16 also contains the &H21 notation for the exclamation mark (!).

The remaining welcome messages (lines 18–61) contain the hexadecimal codes for the other seven languages. The code values used for the French, German, Portuguese and Spanish text are located in the **Basic Latin** block, the code values used for the Traditional Chinese text are located in the **CJK Unified Ideographs** block, the code values used for the Russian text are located in the **Cyrillic** block and the code values used for the Japanese text are located in the **Hiragana** block.

[*Note:* To render the Asian characters in a Windows application, you would need to install the proper language files on your computer. To do this, open the **Regional Options** dialog from the **Control Panel** (**Start > Settings > Control Panel**). At the bottom of the **General** tab is a list of languages. Check the **Japanese** and the **Traditional Chinese** checkboxes and press **Apply**. Follow the directions of the install wizard to install the languages. For additional assistance, visit www.unicode.org/help/display_problems.html.]

E.7 **Character Ranges**

The Unicode Standard assigns code values, which range from 0000 (**Basic Latin**) to E007F (**Tags**), to the written characters of the world. Currently, there are code values for 94,140 characters. To simplify the search for a character and its associated code value, the Unicode Standard generally groups code values by script and function (i.e., Latin characters are grouped in a block, mathematical operators are grouped in another block, etc.). As a rule, a script is a single writing system that is used for multiple languages (e.g., the Latin script is used for English, French, Spanish, etc.). The **Code Charts** page on the Unicode Consortium Web site lists all the defined blocks and their respective code values. Figure E.4 lists some blocks (scripts) from the Web site and their range of code values.

Script	Range of Code Values
Arabic	U+0600–U+06FF
Basic Latin	U+0000–U+007F
Bengali (India)	U+0980–U+09FF
Cherokee (Native America)	U+13A0–U+13FF
CJK Unified Ideographs (East Asia)	U+4E00–U+9FAF
Cyrillic (Russia and Eastern Europe)	U+0400–U+04FF
Ethiopic	U+1200–U+137F

Fig. E.4 | Some character ranges. (Part 1 of 2.)

Script	Range of Code Values
Greek	U+0370–U+03FF
Hangul Jamo (Korea)	U+1100–U+11FF
Hebrew	U+0590–U+05FF
Hiragana (Japan)	U+3040–U+309F
Khmer (Cambodia)	U+1780–U+17FF
Lao (Laos)	U+0E80–U+0EFF
Mongolian	U+1800–U+18AF
Myanmar	U+1000–U+109F
Ogham (Ireland)	U+1680–U+169F
Runic (Germany and Scandinavia)	U+16A0–U+16FF
Sinhala (Sri Lanka)	U+0D80–U+0DFF
Telugu (India)	U+0C00–U+0C7F
Thai	U+0E00–U+0E7F

Fig. E.4 | Some character ranges. (Part 2 of 2.)

Summary

- Before Unicode, software developers were plagued by the use of inconsistent character encoding (i.e., numeric values for characters). Most countries and organizations had their own encoding systems, which were incompatible. A good example is the individual encoding systems on the Windows and Macintosh platforms.

- Computers process data by converting characters to numeric values. For instance, the character "a" is converted to a numeric value so that a computer can manipulate that piece of data.

- Without Unicode, localization of global software requires significant modifications to the source code, which results in increased cost and delays in releasing the product.

- Localization is necessary with each release of a version. By the time a software product is localized for a particular market, a newer version, which needs to be localized as well, is ready for distribution. As a result, it is cumbersome and costly to produce and distribute global software products in a market where there is no universal character-encoding standard.

- The Unicode Consortium developed the Unicode Standard in response to the serious problems created by multiple character encodings and the use of those encodings.

- The Unicode Standard facilitates the production and distribution of localized software. It outlines a specification for the consistent encoding of the world's characters and symbols.

- Software products that handle text encoded in the Unicode Standard need to be localized, but the localization process is simpler and more efficient because the numeric values need not be converted.

- The Unicode Standard is designed to be universal, efficient, uniform and unambiguous.

- A universal encoding system encompasses all commonly used characters; an efficient encoding system parses text files easily; a uniform encoding system assigns fixed values to all characters; and an unambiguous encoding system represents the same character for any given value.

- Unicode extends the limited ASCII character set to include all the major characters of the world.

- Unicode makes use of three Unicode Transformation Formats (UTF): UTF-8, UTF-16 and UTF-32, each of which may be appropriate for use in different contexts.

- UTF-8 data consists of 8-bit bytes (sequences of one, two, three or four bytes depending on the character being encoded) and is well suited for ASCII-based systems, where there is a predominance of one-byte characters (ASCII represents characters as one byte).

- UTF-8 is a variable-width encoding form that is more compact for text involving mostly Latin characters and ASCII punctuation.

- UTF-16 is the default encoding form of the Unicode Standard. It is a variable-width encoding form that uses 16-bit code units instead of bytes. Most characters are represented by a single unit, but some characters require surrogate pairs.

- Surrogates are 16-bit integers in the range D800 through DFFF, which are used solely for the purpose of "escaping" into higher numbered characters.

- Without surrogate pairs, the UTF-16 encoding form can only encompass 65,000 characters, but with the surrogate pairs, this is expanded to include over a million characters.

- UTF-32 is a 32-bit encoding form. The major advantage of the fixed-width encoding form is that it uniformly expresses all characters, so that they are easy to handle in arrays and so forth.

- The Unicode Standard consists of characters. A character is any written component that can be represented by a numeric value.

- Characters are represented with glyphs (various shapes, fonts and sizes for displaying characters).

- Code values are bit combinations that represent encoded characters. The Unicode notation for a code value is U+*yyyy*, in which U+ refers to the Unicode code values, as opposed to other hexadecimal values. The *yyyy* represents a four-digit hexadecimal number.

- Currently, the Unicode Standard provides code values for 94,140 character representations.

- An advantage of the Unicode Standard is its impact on the overall performance of the international economy. Applications that conform to an encoding standard can be processed easily by computers anywhere.

- Another advantage of the Unicode Standard is its portability. Applications written in Unicode can be easily transferred to different operating systems, databases, Web browsers and so on. Most companies currently support, or are planning to support, Unicode.

- To obtain more information about the Unicode Standard and the Unicode Consortium, visit `www.unicode.org`. It contains a link to the code charts, which contain the 16-bit code values for the currently encoded characters.

- The Unicode Standard has become the default encoding system for XML and any language derived from XML, such as XHTML.

- The Visual Basic IDE uses Unicode UTF-16 encoding to represent all characters.

- In the marking up of Visual Basic documents, the entity reference &H*yyyy* is used, where *yyyy* represents the hexadecimal code value.

Terminology

&H*yyyy* notation	portability
ASCII	script
block	surrogate
character	symbol
character set	unambiguous (Unicode design basis)
code value	Unicode Consortium
diacritic	Unicode design basis
double-byte character set (DBCS)	Unicode Standard
efficient (Unicode design basis)	Unicode Transformation Format (UTF)
encode	uniform (Unicode design basis)
entity reference	universal (Unicode design basis)
glyph	UTF-8
hexadecimal notation	UTF-16
localization	UTF-32
multi-byte character set (MBCS)	

Self-Review Exercises

E.1 Fill in the blanks in each of the following.
  a) Global software developers had to _____ their products to a specific market before distribution.
  b) The Unicode Standard is a(n) _____ standard that facilitates the uniform production and distribution of software products.
  c) The four design basis that constitute the Unicode Standard are: _____, _____, _____ and _____.
  d) A(n) _____ is the smallest written component the can be represented with a numeric value.
  e) Software that can execute on different operating systems is said to be _____.
  f) Of the three encoding forms, _____ is currently supported by Internet Explorer 5.5 and Netscape Communicator 6.

E.2 State whether each of the following is *true* or *false*. If *false*, explain why.
  a) The Unicode Standard encompasses all the world's characters.
  b) A Unicode code value is represented as U+*yyyy*, where *yyyy* represents a number in binary notation.
  c) A diacritic is a character with a special mark that emphasizes an accent.
  d) Unicode is portable.
  e) When designing Visual Basic programs, the entity reference is denoted by #U+*yyyy*.

Answers to Self-Review exercises

E.1 a) localize. b) encoding. c) universal, efficient, uniform, unambiguous. d) character. e) portable. f) UTF-8.

E.2 a) False. It encompasses the majority of the world's characters. b) False. The *yyyy* represents a hexadecimal number. c) False. A diacritic is a special mark added to a character to distinguish it from another letter or to indicate an accent. d) True. e) False. The entity reference is denoted by &H*yyyy*.

Exercises

E.3 Navigate to the Unicode Consortium Web site (`www.unicode.org`) and write the hexadecimal code values for the following characters. In which block are they located?
  a) Latin letter 'Z.'
  b) Latin letter 'n' with the 'tilde (~).'
  c) Greek letter 'delta.'
  d) Mathematical operator 'less than or equal to.'
  e) Punctuation symbol 'open quote (").'

E.4 Describe the Unicode Standard design basis.

E.5 Define the following terms:
  a) code value.
  b) surrogates.
  c) Unicode Standard.
  d) UTF-8.
  e) UTF-16.
  f) UTF-32.

E.6 Describe a scenario where it is optimal to store your data in UTF-16 format.

E.7 Using the Unicode Standard code values, create a program that prints your first and last name. If you know other writing systems, print your first and last name in those as well. Use a `Label` to display your name.

E.8 Write an ASP.NET program that prints "Welcome to Unicode!" in English, French, German, Japanese, Portuguese, Russian, Spanish and Traditional Chinese. Use the code values provided in Fig. E.3. In ASP.NET, a code value is represented the same way as in a Windows application (&H*yyyy*, where *yyyy* is a four-digit hexadecimal number).

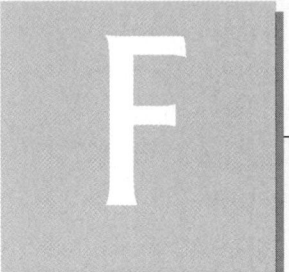

Introduction to XHTML: Part 1

OBJECTIVES

In this appendix, you will learn:

- To understand important components of XHTML documents.

- To use XHTML to create Web pages.

- To be able to add images to Web pages.

- To understand how to create and use hyperlinks to navigate Web pages.

- To be able to mark up lists of information.

F.1 Introduction

Welcome to the world of opportunity created by the World Wide Web. The Internet is now three decades old, but it was not until the Web became popular in the 1990s that the explosion of opportunity that we are still experiencing began. Exciting new developments occur almost daily—the pace of innovation is unprecedented by any other technology. In this appendix, you will develop your own Web pages.

This appendix begins unlocking the power of Web-based application development with XHTML—the Extensible HyperText Markup Language. The next appendix introduces more sophisticated XHTML techniques, such as tables, which are particularly useful for structuring information from databases (i.e., software that stores structured sets of data).

Unlike procedural programming languages such as C, Fortran, Cobol and Pascal, XHTML is a markup language that specifies the format of the text that is displayed in a Web browser such as Microsoft's Internet Explorer or Netscape.

One key issue when using XHTML is the separation of the presentation of a document (i.e., the document's appearance when rendered by a browser) from the structure of the document's information. XHTML is based on HTML (HyperText Markup Language)—a legacy technology of the World Wide Web Consortium (W3C). In HTML, it was common to specify the document's content, structure and formatting. Formatting might specify where the browser placed an element in a Web page or the fonts and colors used to display an element. XHTML 1.1 (W3C's latest version of W3C XHTML Recommendation at the time of publication) allows only a document's content and structure to appear in a valid XHTML document, and not its formatting. Normally, such formatting is specified with Cascading Style Sheets. All our examples in this appendix are based upon the XHTML 1.1 Recommendation.

F.2 Editing XHTML

In this appendix, we write XHTML in its source-code form. We create XHTML documents by typing them in a text editor (e.g., Notepad, Wordpad, vi, emacs) and saving them with either an `.html` or an `.htm` file-name extension.

Good Programming Practice F.1

Assign documents file names that describe their functionality. This practice can help you identify documents faster. It also helps people who want to link to a page, by giving them an easy-to-remember name. For example, if you are writing an XHTML document that contains product information, you might want to call it products.html.

Machines running specialized software called **Web servers** store XHTML documents. Clients (e.g., Web browsers) request specific **resources** such as the XHTML documents from the Web server. For example, typing www.deitel.com/books/downloads.html into a Web browser's address field requests downloads.html from the Web server running at www.deitel.com. This document is located on the server in a directory named books. For now, we simply place the XHTML documents on our machine and open them using Internet Explorer.

F.3 First XHTML Example

In this appendix and the next, we present XHTML markup and provide screen captures that show how Internet Explorer renders (i.e., displays) the XHTML.[1] Every XHTML document we show has line numbers for the reader's convenience. These line numbers are not part of the XHTML documents.

Our first example (Fig. F.1) is an XHTML document named main.html that displays the message "Welcome to XHTML!" in the browser.

The key line in the program is line 14, which tells the browser to display "Welcome to XHTML!" Now let us consider each line of the program.

Lines 1–3 are required in XHTML documents to conform with proper XHTML syntax. For now, copy and paste these lines into each XHTML document you create. The meaning of these lines is discussed in detail in Chapter 19, Extensible Markup Language (XML).

```
 1   <?xml version = "1.0"?>
 2   <!DOCTYPE html PUBLIC "-//W3C//DTD XHTML 1.1//EN"
 3      "http://www.w3.org/TR/xhtml11/DTD/xhtml11.dtd">
 4
 5   <!-- Fig. F.1: main.html -->
 6   <!-- Our first Web page  -->
 7
 8   <html xmlns = "http://www.w3.org/1999/xhtml">
 9      <head>
10         <title>Internet and WWW How to Program - Welcome</title>
11      </head>
12
13      <body>
14         <p>Welcome to XHTML!</p>
15      </body>
16   </html>
```

Fig. F.1 | First XHTML example. (Part 1 of 2.)

---

1. All the examples presented in this appendix are available at www.deitel.com/books/vbhtp3.

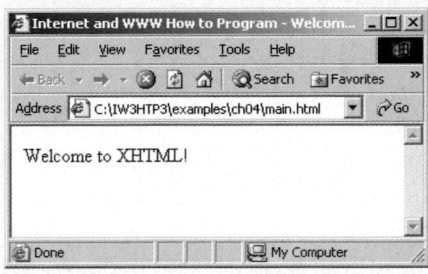

Fig. F.1 | First XHTML example. (Part 2 of 2.)

Lines 5–6 are XHTML comments. XHTML document creators insert comments to improve markup readability and describe the content of a document. Comments also help other people read and understand an XHTML document's markup and content. Comments do not cause the browser to perform any action when the user loads the XHTML document into the Web browser to view the document. XHTML comments always start with `<!--` and end with `-->`. Each of our XHTML examples includes comments that specify the figure number and file name, and provide a brief description of the example's purpose. Subsequent examples include comments in the markup, especially to highlight new features.

Good Programming Practice F.2

Place comments throughout your markup. Comments help other programmers understand the markup, assist in debugging and list useful information that you do not want the browser to render. Comments also help you understand your own markup when you revisit a document to modify or update it in the future.

XHTML markup contains text that represents the content of a document and elements that specify a document's structure. Some important elements of an XHTML document are the `html` element, the `head` element and the `body` element. The `html` element encloses the head section (represented by the `head` element) and the body section (represented by the `body` element). The head section contains information about the XHTML document, such as its title. The head section also can contain special document formatting instructions called style sheets and client-side programs called scripts for creating dynamic Web pages. The body section contains the page's content that the browser displays when the user visits the Web page.

XHTML documents delimit an element with start and end tags. A start tag consists of the element name in angle brackets (e.g., `<html>`). An end tag consists of the element name preceded by a / in angle brackets (e.g., `</html>`). In this example, lines 8 and 16 define the start and end of the `html` element. Note that the end tag in line 16 has the same name as the start tag, but is preceded by a / inside the angle brackets. Many start tags have attributes that provide additional information about an element. Browsers can use this additional information to determine how to process the element. Each attribute has a name and a value separated by an equals sign (=). Line 8 specifies a required attribute (`xmlns`) and value (`http://www.w3.org/1999/xhtml`) for the `html` element in an XHTML document. For now, simply copy and paste the `html` element start tag in line 8 into your XHTML documents. We discuss the details of the `html` element's `xmlns` attribute in Chapter 19, Extensible Markup Language (XML).

Common Programming Error F.1

Not enclosing attribute values in either single or double quotes is a syntax error. However, some Web browsers may still render the element correctly.

Common Programming Error F.2

Using uppercase letters in an XHTML element or attribute name is a syntax error. However, some Web browsers may still render the element correctly.

An XHTML document divides the `html` element into two sections—head and body. Lines 9–11 define the Web page's head section with a `head` element. Line 10 specifies a `title` element. This is called a **nested element** because it is enclosed in the `head` element's start and end tags. The `head` element is also a nested element because it is enclosed in the `html` element's start and end tags. The `title` element describes the Web page. Titles usually appear in the **title bar** at the top of the browser window and also as the text identifying a page when users add the page to their list of **Favorites** or **Bookmarks** that enables them to return to their favorite sites. Search engines (i.e., sites that allow users to search the Web) also use the `title` for cataloging purposes.

Good Programming Practice F.3

Indenting nested elements emphasizes a document's structure and promotes readability.

Common Programming Error F.3

XHTML does not permit tags to overlap—a nested element's end tag must appear in the document before the enclosing element's end tag. For example, the nested XHTML tags `<head><title>hello</head></title>` cause a syntax error, because the enclosing `head` element's ending `</head>` tag appears before the nested `title` element's ending `</title>` tag.

Good Programming Practice F.4

Use a consistent `title`-naming convention for all pages on a site. For example, if a site is named "Bailey's Web Site," then the `title` of the links page might be "Bailey's Web Site—Links." This practice can help users better understand the Web site's structure.

Line 13 opens the document's `body` element. The body section of an XHTML document specifies the document's content, which may include text and tags.

Some tags, such as the **paragraph tags** (`<p>` and `</p>`) in line 14, mark up text for display in a browser. All the text placed between the `<p>` and `</p>` tags forms one paragraph. When the browser renders a paragraph, a blank line usually precedes and follows paragraph text.

This document ends with two end tags (lines 15–16). These tags close the `body` and `html` elements, respectively. The `</html>` tag in an XHTML document informs the browser that the XHTML markup is complete.

To view this example in Internet Explorer, perform the following steps:

1. Download the examples from `www.deitel.com/books/vbhtp3`.

2. Launch Internet Explorer and select **Open...** from the **File** Menu. This displays the **Open** dialog.

3. Click the **Open** dialog's **Browse...** button to display the **Microsoft Internet Explorer** file dialog.

4. Navigate to the directory containing the examples for this appendix and select the file `main.html`, then click **Open**.

5. Click **OK** to have Internet Explorer render the document. Other examples are opened in a similar manner.

At this point your browser window should appear similar to the sample screen capture shown in Fig. F.1. (Note that we resized the browser window to save space in the book.)

F.4 **W3C XHTML Validation Service**

Programming Web-based applications can be complex, and XHTML documents must be written correctly to ensure that browsers process them properly. To promote correctly written documents, the World Wide Web Consortium (W3C) provides a validation service (`validator.w3.org`) for checking a document's syntax. Documents can be validated either from a URL that specifies the location of the file or by uploading a file to the site `validator.w3.org/file-upload.html`. Uploading a file copies the file from the user's computer to another computer on the Internet. Figure F.2 shows `main.html` (Fig. F.1) being uploaded for validation. The W3C's Web page indicates that the service name is **MarkUp Validation Service**, and the validation service is able to validate the syntax of XHTML documents. All the XHTML examples in this book have been validated successfully using `validator.w3.org`.

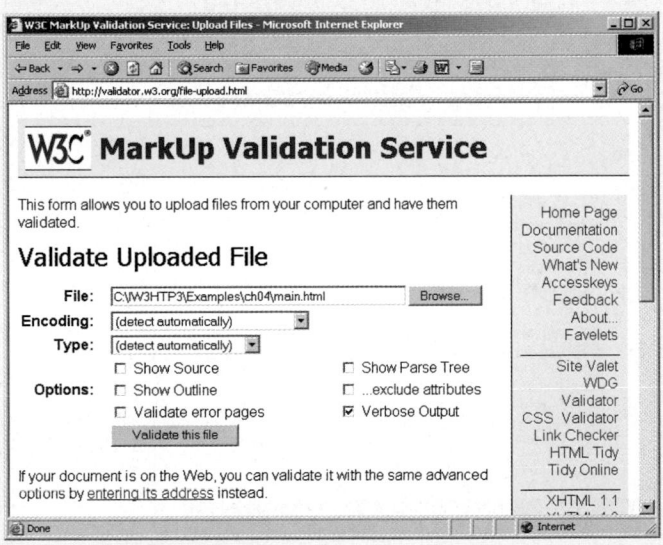

Fig. F.2 | Validating an XHTML document. (Courtesy of World Wide Web Consortium (W3C).)

By clicking **Browse…**, users can select files on their own computers for upload. After selecting a file, clicking the **Validate this file** button uploads and validates the file. Figure F.3 shows the results of validating `main.html`. This document does not contain any syntax errors. If a document does contain syntax errors, the validation service displays error messages describing the errors.

Error-Prevention Tip F.1

Most current browsers attempt to render XHTML documents even if they are invalid. This often leads to unexpected and possibly undesirable results. Use a validation service, such as the W3C MarkUp Validation Service, to confirm that an XHTML document is syntactically correct.

F.5 Headers

Some text in an XHTML document may be more important than other text. For example, the text in this section is considered more important than a footnote. XHTML provides six headers, called header elements, for specifying the relative importance of information. Figure F.4 demonstrates these elements (h1 through h6). Header element h1 (line 15) is considered the most significant header and is typically rendered in a larger font than the other five headers (lines 16–20). Each successive header element (i.e., h2, h3, etc.) is typically rendered in a progressively smaller font.

Portability Tip F.1

The text size used to display each header element can vary significantly between browsers.

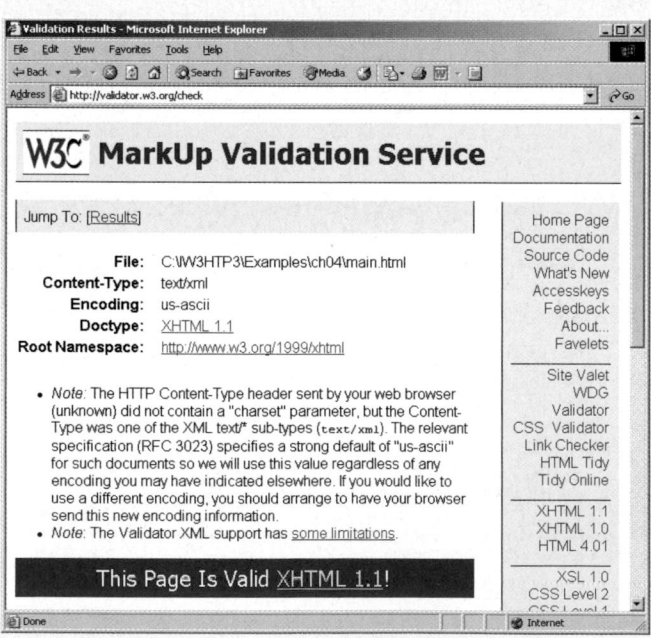

Fig. F.3 | XHTML validation results. (Courtesy of World Wide Web Consortium (W3C).)

```
 1    <?xml version = "1.0"?>
 2    <!DOCTYPE html PUBLIC "-//W3C//DTD XHTML 1.1//EN"
 3       "http://www.w3.org/TR/xhtml11/DTD/xhtml11.dtd">
 4
 5    <!-- Fig. F.4: header.html -->
 6    <!-- XHTML headers          -->
 7
 8    <html xmlns = "http://www.w3.org/1999/xhtml">
 9       <head>
10          <title>Internet and WWW How to Program - Headers</title>
11       </head>
12
13       <body>
14
15          <h1>Level 1 Header</h1>
16          <h2>Level 2 header</h2>
17          <h3>Level 3 header</h3>
18          <h4>Level 4 header</h4>
19          <h5>Level 5 header</h5>
20          <h6>Level 6 header</h6>
21
22       </body>
23    </html>
```

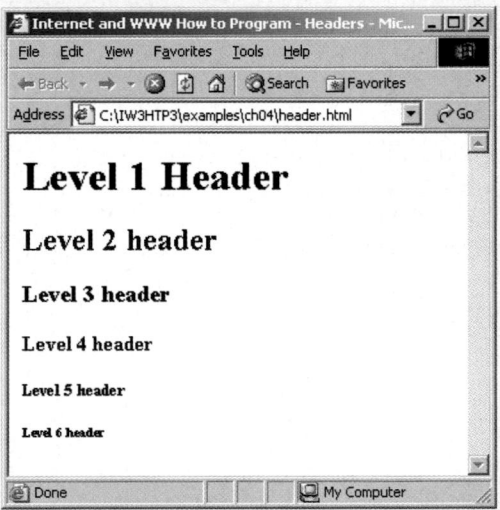

Fig. F.4 | Header elements h1 through h6.

 Look-and-Feel Observation F.1

Placing a header at the top of every XHTML page helps viewers understand the purpose of each page.

 Look-and-Feel Observation F.2

Use larger headers to emphasize more important sections of a Web page.

F.6 Linking

One of the most important XHTML features is the hyperlink, which references (or links to) other resources, such as XHTML documents and images. In XHTML, both text and images can act as hyperlinks. Web browsers typically underline text hyperlinks and color their text blue by default, so that users can distinguish hyperlinks from plain text. In Fig. F.5, we create text hyperlinks to four different Web sites.

Line 17 introduces the strong element. Browsers typically display such text in a bold font. Links are created using the a (anchor) element. Line 20 defines a hyperlink that links the text Deitel to the URL assigned to attribute href, which specifies the location of a linked resource, such as a Web page, a file or an e-mail address. This particular anchor element links to a Web page located at http://www.deitel.com. When a URL does not indicate a specific document on the Web site, the Web server returns a default Web page. This page is often called index.html; however, most Web servers can be configured to use any file as the default Web page for the site. (Open http://www.deitel.com in one browser window and http://www.deitel.com/index.html in a second browser window to confirm that they are identical.) If the Web server cannot locate a requested document, it returns an error indication to the Web browser, and the browser displays a Web page containing an error message to the user.

```
1    <?xml version = "1.0"?>
2    <!DOCTYPE html PUBLIC "-//W3C//DTD XHTML 1.1//EN"
3       "http://www.w3.org/TR/xhtml11/DTD/xhtml11.dtd">
4
5    <!-- Fig. F.5: links.html         -->
6    <!-- Introduction to hyperlinks -->
7
8    <html xmlns = "http://www.w3.org/1999/xhtml">
9       <head>
10          <title>Internet and WWW How to Program - Links</title>
11       </head>
12
13       <body>
14
15          <h1>Here are my favorite sites</h1>
16
17          <p><strong>Click a name to go to that page.</strong></p>
18
19          <!-- Create four text hyperlinks -->
20          <p><a href = "http://www.deitel.com">Deitel</a></p>
21
22          <p><a href = "http://www.prenhall.com">Prentice Hall</a></p>
23
24          <p><a href = "http://www.yahoo.com">Yahoo!</a></p>
25
26          <p><a href = "http://www.usatoday.com">USA Today</a></p>
27
28       </body>
29    </html>
```

Fig. F.5 | Linking to other Web pages. (Part I of 2.)

Fig. F.5 | Linking to other Web pages. (Part 2 of 2.)

Anchors can link to e-mail addresses using a `mailto:` URL. When someone clicks this type of anchored link, most browsers launch the default e-mail program (e.g., Outlook Express) to enable the user to write an e-mail message to the linked address. Figure F.6 demonstrates this type of anchor. Lines 17–19 contain an e-mail link. The form of an e-mail anchor is `<a href = "mailto:`*emailaddress*`">...</a>`. In this case, we link to the e-mail address `deitel@deitel.com`.

```
1   <?xml version = "1.0"?>
2   <!DOCTYPE html PUBLIC "-//W3C//DTD XHTML 1.1//EN"
3       "http://www.w3.org/TR/xhtml11/DTD/xhtml11.dtd">
4
5   <!-- Fig. F.6: contact.html  -->
6   <!-- Adding email hyperlinks -->
7
8   <html xmlns = "http://www.w3.org/1999/xhtml">
9       <head>
```

Fig. F.6 | Linking to an e-mail address. (Part 1 of 2.)

```
10          <title>Internet and WWW How to Program - Contact Page</title>
11      </head>
12
13      <body>
14
15          <p>
16              My e-mail address is
17              <a href = "mailto:deitel@deitel.com">
18                  deitel@deitel.com
19              </a>
20              . Click the address and your browser will
21              open an e-mail message and address it to me.
22          </p>
23      </body>
24  </html>
```

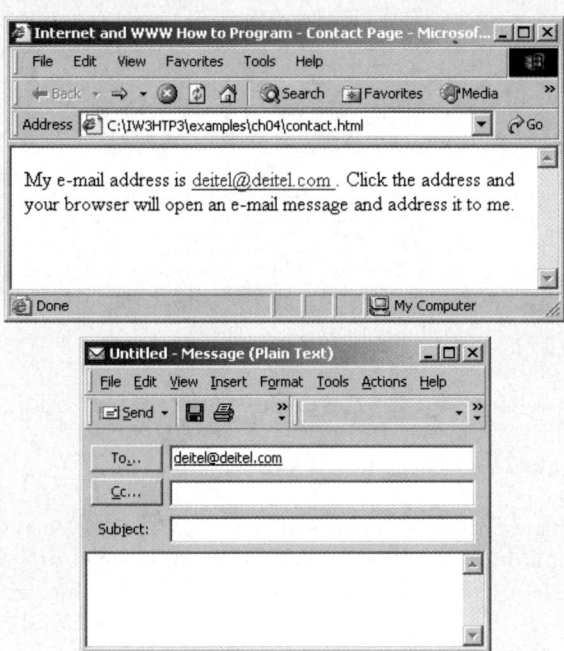

Fig. F.6 | Linking to an e-mail address. (Part 2 of 2.)

F.7 Images

The examples discussed so far demonstrate how to mark up documents that contain only text. However, most Web pages contain both text and images. In fact, images are an equal, if not essential, part of Web-page design. The three most popular image formats used by Web developers are Graphics Interchange Format (GIF), Joint Photographic Experts Group (JPEG) and Portable Network Graphics (PNG) images. Users can create images using specialized pieces of software, such as Adobe Photoshop Elements 2.0, Macromedia Fireworks (www.macromedia.com) and Jasc Paint Shop Pro (www.jasc.com). Images may also be acquired from various Web sites, such as the Yahoo! Picture Gallery (`gallery.ya-hoo.com`). Figure F.7 demonstrates how to incorporate images into Web pages.

Lines 16–17 use an *img* element to insert an image in the document. The image file's location is specified with the `img` element's `src` attribute. In this case, the image is located in the same directory as this XHTML document, so only the image's file name is required. Optional attributes `width` and `height` specify the image's width and height, respectively. The document author can scale an image by increasing or decreasing the values of the image `width` and `height` attributes. If these attributes are omitted, the browser uses the

```
1   <?xml version = "1.0"?>
2   <!DOCTYPE html PUBLIC "-//W3C//DTD XHTML 1.1//EN"
3       "http://www.w3.org/TR/xhtml11/DTD/xhtml11.dtd">
4
5   <!-- Fig. F.7: picture.html   -->
6   <!-- Adding images with XHTML -->
7
8   <html xmlns = "http://www.w3.org/1999/xhtml">
9      <head>
10         <title>Internet and WWW How to Program - Welcome</title>
11     </head>
12
13     <body>
14
15        <p>
16           <img src = "xmlhtp.jpg" height = "238" width = "183"
17              alt = "XML How to Program book cover" />
18           <img src = "jhtp.jpg" height = "238" width = "183"
19              alt = "Java How to Program book cover" />
20        </p>
21     </body>
22  </html>
```

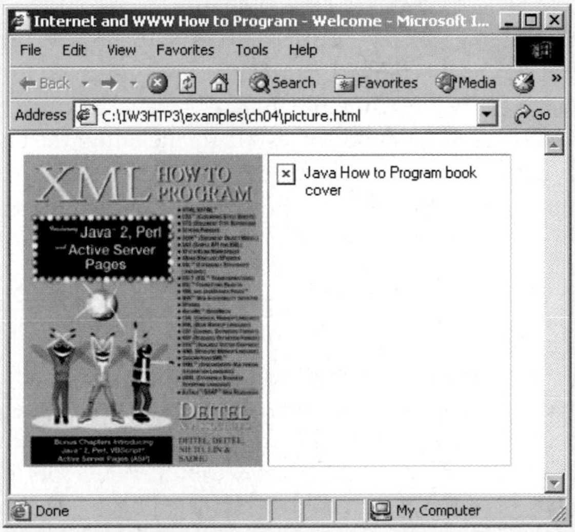

Fig. F.7 | Images in XHTML files.

image's actual width and height. Images are measured in pixels ("picture elements"), which represent dots of color on the screen. The image in Fig. F.7 is 183 pixels wide and 238 pixels high.

Good Programming Practice F.5

Always include the width and the height of an image inside the <img> tag. When the browser loads the XHTML file, it will know immediately from these attributes how much screen space to provide for the image and will lay out the page properly, even before it downloads the image.

Performance Tip F.1

Including the width and height attributes in an <img> tag can result in the browser loading and rendering pages faster.

Common Programming Error F.4

Entering new dimensions for an image that change its inherent width-to-height ratio distorts the appearance of the image. For example, if your image is 200 pixels wide and 100 pixels high, you should ensure that any new dimensions have a 2:1 width-to-height ratio.

Every img element in an XHTML document has an alt attribute. If a browser cannot render an image, the browser displays the alt attribute's value. A browser may not be able to render an image for several reasons. It may not support images—as is the case with a text-based browser (i.e., a browser that can display only text)—or the client may have disabled image viewing to reduce download time. Figure F.7 shows Internet Explorer 6 rendering the alt attribute's value when a document references a nonexistent image file (jhtp.jpg).

The alt attribute is important for creating accessible Web pages for users with disabilities, especially those with vision impairments who use text-based browsers. Specialized software called a speech synthesizer often is used by people with disabilities. This software application "speaks" the alt attribute's value so that the user knows what the browser is displaying.

Some XHTML elements (called empty elements) contain only attributes and do not mark up text (i.e., text is not placed between the start and end tags). Empty elements (e.g., img) must be terminated, either by using the forward slash character (/) inside the closing right angle bracket (>) of the start tag or by explicitly including the end tag. When using the forward slash character, we add a space before the forward slash to improve readability (as shown at the ends of lines 17 and 19). Rather than using the forward slash character, lines 18–19 could be written with a closing </img> tag as follows:

```
<img src = "jhtp.jpg" height = "238" width = "183"
    alt = "Java How to Program book cover"></img>
```

By using images as hyperlinks, Web developers can create graphical Web pages that link to other resources. In Fig. F.8, we create six different image hyperlinks.

Lines 17–20 create an image hyperlink by nesting an img element in an anchor (a) element. The value of the img element's src attribute value specifies that this image (links.jpg) resides in a directory named buttons. The buttons directory and the XHTML document are in the same directory. Images from other Web documents also can be referenced (after obtaining permission from the document's owner) by setting the src attribute to the name and location of the image. Clicking an image hyperlink takes a user to the Web page specified by the surrounding anchor element's `href` attribute.

```
1   <?xml version = "1.0"?>
2   <!DOCTYPE html PUBLIC "-//W3C//DTD XHTML 1.1//EN"
3      "http://www.w3.org/TR/xhtml11/DTD/xhtml11.dtd">
4
5   <!-- Fig. F.8: nav.html           -->
6   <!-- Using images as link anchors -->
7
8   <html xmlns = "http://www.w3.org/1999/xhtml">
9      <head>
10        <title>Internet and WWW How to Program - Navigation Bar
11        </title>
12     </head>
13
14     <body>
15
16        <p>
17           <a href = "links.html">
18              <img src = "buttons/links.jpg" width = "65"
19                 height = "50" alt = "Links Page" />
20           </a><br />
21
22           <a href = "list.html">
23              <img src = "buttons/list.jpg" width = "65"
24                 height = "50" alt = "List Example Page" />
25           </a><br />
26
27           <a href = "contact.html">
28              <img src = "buttons/contact.jpg" width = "65"
29                 height = "50" alt = "Contact Page" />
30           </a><br />
31
32           <a href = "header.html">
33              <img src = "buttons/header.jpg" width = "65"
34                 height = "50" alt = "Header Page" />
35           </a><br />
36
37           <a href = "table1.html">
38              <img src = "buttons/table.jpg" width = "65"
39                 height = "50" alt = "Table Page" />
40           </a><br />
41
42           <a href = "form.html">
43              <img src = "buttons/form.jpg" width = "65"
44                 height = "50" alt = "Feedback Form" />
45           </a><br />
46        </p>
47
48     </body>
49  </html>
```

Fig. F.8 | Images as link anchors. (Part 1 of 2.)

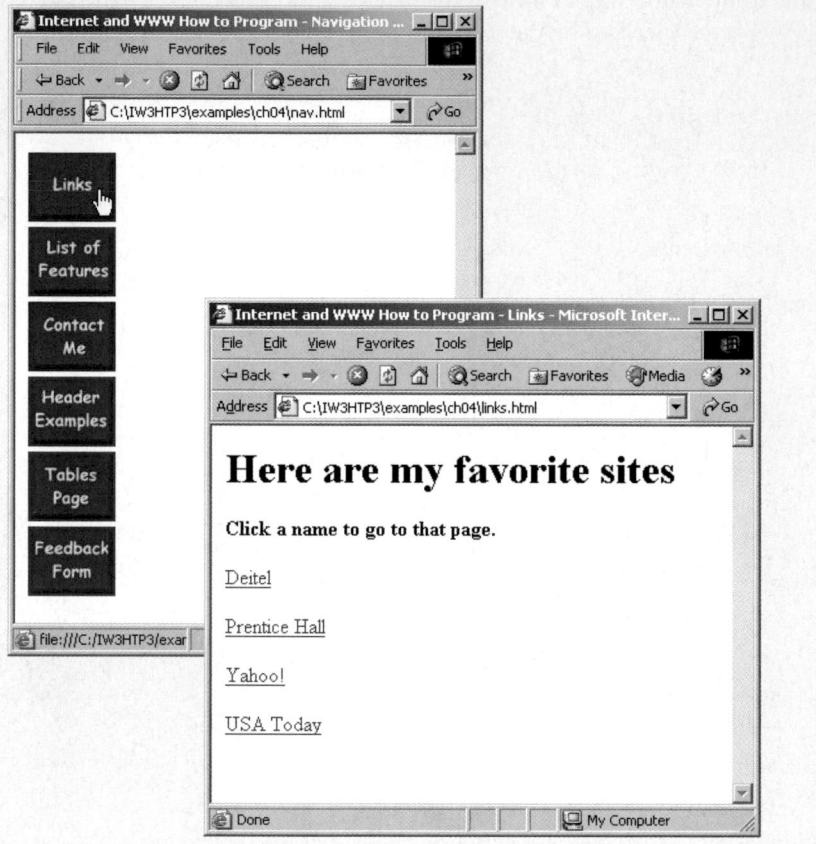

Fig. F.8 | Images as link anchors. (Part 2 of 2.)

In line 20, we introduce the **br element**, which most browsers render as a line break. Any markup or text following a br element is rendered on the next line. Like the img element, br is an example of an empty element terminated with a forward slash. We add a space before the forward slash to enhance readability. [*Note*: The last two image hyperlinks in Fig. F.8 link to XHTML documents (i.e., `table1.html` and `form.html`) presented as examples in Appendix G and included in the Appendix G examples directory. Clicking these links now will result in errors.]

F.8 Special Characters and More Line Breaks

When marking up text, certain characters or symbols (e.g., <) may be difficult to embed directly into an XHTML document. Some keyboards do not provide these symbols, or the presence of these symbols may cause syntax errors. For example, the markup

```
<p>if x < 10 then increment x by 1</p>
```

results in a syntax error because it uses the less-than character (<), which is reserved for start tags and end tags such as <p> and </p>. XHTML provides character entity references (in the form &*code*;) for representing special characters. We could correct the previous line by writing

```
<p>if x &lt; 10 then increment x by 1</p>
```

which uses the character entity reference < for the less-than symbol.

Figure F.9 demonstrates how to use special characters in an XHTML document. For a list of special characters, see Appendix H, XHTML Special Characters.

```
 1   <?xml version = "1.0"?>
 2   <!DOCTYPE html PUBLIC "-//W3C//DTD XHTML 1.1//EN"
 3      "http://www.w3.org/TR/xhtml11/DTD/xhtml11.dtd">
 4
 5   <!-- Fig. F.9: contact2.html       -->
 6   <!-- Inserting special characters -->
 7
 8   <html xmlns = "http://www.w3.org/1999/xhtml">
 9      <head>
10         <title>Internet and WWW How to Program - Contact Page
11         </title>
12      </head>
13
14      <body>
15
16         <!-- special characters are entered -->
17         <!-- using the form &code;          -->
18         <p>
19            Click
20            <a href = "mailto:deitel@deitel.com">here</a>
21            to open an e-mail message addressed to
22            deitel@deitel.com.
23         </p>
24
25         <hr /> <!-- inserts a horizontal rule -->
26
27         <p>All information on this site is <strong>&copy;</strong>
28            Deitel <strong>&amp;</strong> Associates, Inc. 2004.</p>
29
30         <!-- to strike through text use <del> tags   -->
31         <!-- to subscript text use <sub> tags         -->
32         <!-- to superscript text use <sup> tags       -->
33         <!-- these tags are nested inside other tags -->
34         <p><del>You may download 3.14 x 10<sup>2</sup>
35            characters worth of information from this site.</del>
36            Only <sub>one</sub> download per hour is permitted.</p>
37
38         <p>Note: <strong>&lt; &frac14;</strong> of the information
39            presented here is updated daily.</p>
40
41      </body>
42   </html>
```

Fig. F.9 | Special characters in XHTML. (Part 1 of 2.)

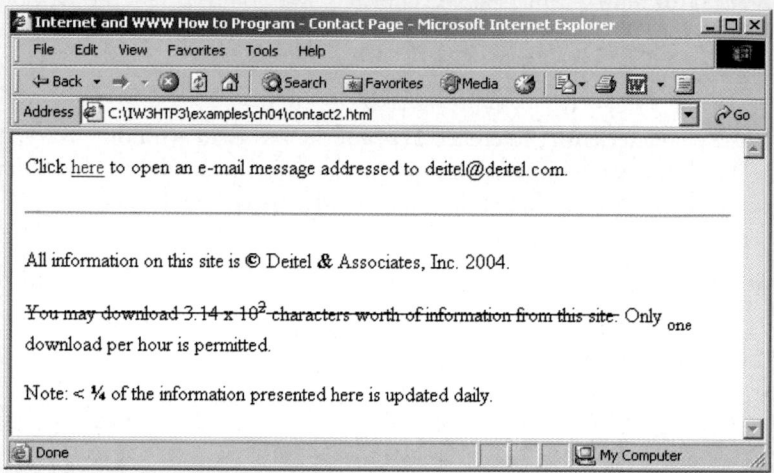

Fig. F.9 | Special characters in XHTML. (Part 2 of 2.)

Lines 27–28 contain other special characters, which can be expressed as either character entity references (i.e., word abbreviations such as amp for ampersand and copy for copyright) or numeric character references—decimal or hexadecimal (hex) values representing special characters. For example, the & character is represented in decimal and hexadecimal notation as & and &, respectively. Hexadecimal numbers are base 16 numbers—digits in a hexadecimal number have values from 0 to 15 (a total of 16 different values). The letters A–F represent the hexadecimal digits corresponding to decimal values 10–15. Thus in hexadecimal notation we can have numbers like 876 consisting solely of decimal-like digits, numbers like DA19F consisting of digits and letters and numbers like DCB consisting solely of letters. We discuss hexadecimal numbers in detail in Appendix B, Number Systems.

In lines 34–36, we introduce three new elements. Most browsers render the *del* element as strike-through text. With this format users can easily indicate document revisions. To superscript text (i.e., raise text on a line with a decreased font size) or subscript text (i.e., lower text on a line with a decreased font size), use the **sup** or **sub** element, respectively. We also use character entity reference < for a less-than sign and ¼ for the fraction 1/4 (line 38).

In addition to special characters, this document introduces a horizontal rule, indicated by the <hr /> tag in line 25. Most browsers render a horizontal rule as a horizontal line. The <hr /> tag also inserts a line break above and below the horizontal line.

F.9 Unordered Lists

Up to this point, we have presented basic XHTML elements and attributes for linking to resources, creating headers, using special characters and incorporating images. In this section, we discuss how to organize information on a Web page using lists. In Appendix G, we introduce another feature for organizing information, called a table. Figure F.10 displays text in an unordered list (i.e., a list that does not order its items by letter or number). The unordered list element **ul** creates a list in which each item begins with a bullet symbol

```
 1   <?xml version = "1.0"?>
 2   <!DOCTYPE html PUBLIC "-//W3C//DTD XHTML 1.1//EN"
 3      "http://www.w3.org/TR/xhtml11/DTD/xhtml11.dtd">
 4
 5   <!-- Fig. F.10: links2.html                -->
 6   <!-- Unordered list containing hyperlinks -->
 7
 8   <html xmlns = "http://www.w3.org/1999/xhtml">
 9      <head>
10         <title>Internet and WWW How to Program - Links</title>
11      </head>
12
13      <body>
14
15         <h1>Here are my favorite sites</h1>
16
17         <p><strong>Click on a name to go to that page.</strong></p>
18
19         <!-- create an unordered list -->
20         <ul>
21
22            <!-- add four list items -->
23            <li><a href = "http://www.deitel.com">Deitel</a></li>
24
25            <li><a href = "http://www.w3.org">W3C</a></li>
26
27            <li><a href = "http://www.yahoo.com">Yahoo!</a></li>
28
29            <li><a href = "http://www.cnn.com">CNN</a></li>
30         </ul>
31      </body>
32   </html>
```

Fig. F.10 | Unordered lists in XHTML.

(called a disc). Each entry in an unordered list (element ul in line 20) is an li (list item) element (lines 23, 25, 27 and 29). Most Web browsers render these elements with a line break and a bullet symbol indented from the beginning of the new line.

F.10 Nested and Ordered Lists

Lists may be nested to represent hierarchical relationships, as in an outline format. Figure F.11 demonstrates nested lists and ordered lists. The ordered list element ol creates a list in which each item begins with a number.

A Web browser indents each nested list to indicate a hierarchical relationship. The first ordered list begins at line 33. Items in an ordered list are enumerated one, two, three and so on. Nested ordered lists are enumerated in the same manner. The items in the outermost unordered list (line 18) are preceded by discs. List items nested inside the unordered list of line 18 are preceded by circles. Although not demonstrated in this example, subsequent nested list items are preceded by squares.

```
1   <?xml version = "1.0"?>
2   <!DOCTYPE html PUBLIC "-//W3C//DTD XHTML 1.1//EN"
3       "http://www.w3.org/TR/xhtml11/DTD/xhtml11.dtd">
4
5   <!-- Fig. F.11: list.html                    -->
6   <!-- Advanced Lists: nested and ordered -->
7
8   <html xmlns = "http://www.w3.org/1999/xhtml">
9       <head>
10          <title>Internet and WWW How to Program - Lists</title>
11      </head>
12
13      <body>
14
15          <h1>The Best Features of the Internet</h1>
16
17          <!-- create an unordered list -->
18          <ul>
19              <li>You can meet new people from countries around
20                  the world.</li>
21              <li>
22                  You have access to new media as it becomes public:
23
24                  <!-- this starts a nested list, which uses a -->
25                  <!-- modified bullet. The list ends when you -->
26                  <!-- close the <ul> tag.                      -->
27                  <ul>
28                      <li>New games</li>
29                      <li>
30                          New applications
31
32                          <!-- nested ordered list -->
33                          <ol>
34                              <li>For business</li>
```

Fig. F.11 | Nested and ordered lists in XHTML. (Part 1 of 2.)

```
35                          <li>For pleasure</li>
36                       </ol>
37                   </li>
38
39                   <li>Around the clock news</li>
40                   <li>Search engines</li>
41                   <li>Shopping</li>
42                   <li>
43                      Programming
44
45                      <!-- another nested ordered list -->
46                      <ol>
47                         <li>XML</li>
48                         <li>Java</li>
49                         <li>XHTML</li>
50                         <li>Scripts</li>
51                         <li>New languages</li>
52                      </ol>
53
54                   </li>
55
56              </ul> <!-- ends the nested list of line 27 -->
57          </li>
58
59          <li>Links</li>
60          <li>Keeping in touch with old friends</li>
61          <li>It is the technology of the future!</li>
62
63      </ul>     <!-- ends the unordered list of line 18 -->
64
65    </body>
66 </html>
```

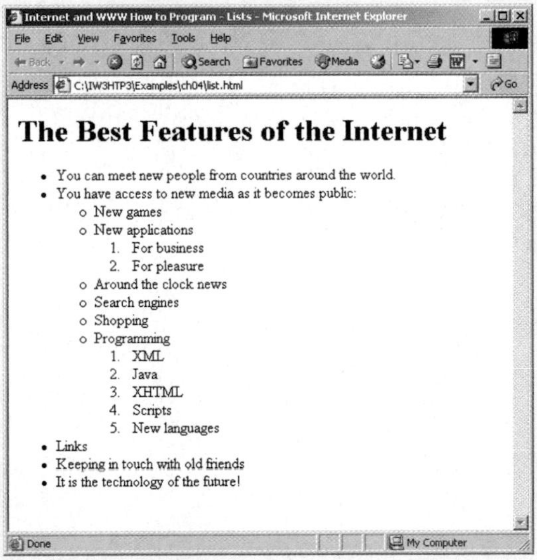

Fig. F.11 | Nested and ordered lists in XHTML. (Part 2 of 2.)

F.11 Web Resources

www.w3.org/TR/xhtml11

The *XHTML 1.1 Recommendation* contains XHTML 1.1 general information, compatibility issues, document type definition information, definitions, terminology and much more.

www.xhtml.org

XHTML.org provides XHTML development news and links to other XHTML resources, including books and articles.

www.w3schools.com/xhtml/default.asp

The *XHTML School* provides XHTML quizzes and references. This page also contains links to XHTML syntax, validation and document type definitions.

validator.w3.org

This is the W3C XHTML validation service site.

hotwired.lycos.com/webmonkey/00/50/index2a.html

This site provides an article about XHTML. Key sections of the article overview XHTML and discuss tags, attributes and anchors.

wdvl.com/Authoring/Languages/XML/XHTML

The *Web Developers Virtual Library* provides an introduction to XHTML. This site also contains articles, examples and links to other technologies.

www.w3.org/TR/2001/REC-xhtml11-20010531

The XHTML 1.1 DTD documentation site provides technical specifications of XHTML 1.1 syntax.

G

Introduction to XHTML: Part 2

Yea, from the table of my
memory
I'll wipe away all trivial
fond records.
—William Shakespeare

OBJECTIVES

In this appendix, you will learn:

- To be able to create tables with rows and columns of data.
- To be able to control table formatting.
- To be able to create and use forms.
- To be able to create and use image maps to aid in Web-page navigation.
- To be able to make Web pages accessible to search engines using `<meta>` tags.
- To be able to use the `frameset` element to display multiple Web pages in a single browser window.

G.1 Introduction

In the preceding appendix, we introduced XHTML. We built several complete Web pages featuring text, hyperlinks, images, horizontal rules and line breaks. In this appendix, we discuss more substantial XHTML features, including presentation of information in tables and incorporating forms for collecting information from a Web-page visitor. We also introduce internal linking and image maps for enhancing Web-page navigation, and frames for displaying multiple documents in the browser. By the end of this appendix, you will be familiar with the most commonly used XHTML features and will be able to create more complex Web documents.

G.2 Basic XHTML Tables

Tables are used to organize data in rows and columns. Our first example (Fig. G.1) creates a table with six rows and two columns to display price information for fruit.

Tables are defined with the **table** element (lines 16–66). Lines 16–18 specify the start tag for a **table** element that has several attributes. The **border** attribute specifies the table's border width in pixels. To create a table without a border, set border to "0". This example assigns attribute width the value "40%" to set the table's width to 40 percent of the browser's width. A developer can also set attribute width to a specified number of pixels. Try resizing the browser window to see how the width of the window affects the width of the table.

```
1   <?xml version = "1.0"?>
2   <!DOCTYPE html PUBLIC "-//W3C//DTD XHTML 1.1//EN"
3     "http://www.w3.org/TR/xhtml11/DTD/xhtml11.dtd">
4
5   <!-- Fig. G.1: table1.html  -->
6   <!-- Creating a basic table  -->
7
8   <html xmlns = "http://www.w3.org/1999/xhtml">
```

Fig. G.1 | XHTML table. (Part 1 of 3.)

```
 9    <head>
10       <title>A simple XHTML table</title>
11    </head>
12
13    <body>
14
15       <!-- the <table> tag opens a table -->
16       <table border = "1" width = "40%"
17          summary = "This table provides information about
18             the price of fruit">
19
20          <!-- the <caption> tag summarizes the table's   -->
21          <!-- contents (this helps the visually impaired) -->
22          <caption><strong>Price of Fruit</strong></caption>
23
24          <!-- the <thead> is the first section of a table -->
25          <!-- it formats the table header area            -->
26          <thead>
27             <tr>                    <!-- <tr> inserts a table row -->
28                <th>Fruit</th> <!-- insert a heading cell -->
29                <th>Price</th>
30             </tr>
31          </thead>
32
33          <!-- the <tfoot> is the last section of a table -->
34          <!-- it formats the table footer                -->
35          <tfoot>
36             <tr>
37                <th>Total</th>
38                <th>$3.75</th>
39             </tr>
40          </tfoot>
41
42          <!-- all table content is enclosed  -->
43          <!-- within the <tbody>             -->
44          <tbody>
45             <tr>
46                <td>Apple</td> <!-- insert a data cell -->
47                <td>$0.25</td>
48             </tr>
49
50             <tr>
51                <td>Orange</td>
52                <td>$0.50</td>
53             </tr>
54
55             <tr>
56                <td>Banana</td>
57                <td>$1.00</td>
58             </tr>
59
60             <tr>
61                <td>Pineapple</td>\
```

Fig. G.1 | XHTML table. (Part 2 of 3.)

```
62                      <td>$2.00</td>
63                  </tr>
64              </tbody>
65
66          </table>
67
68      </body>
69  </html>
```

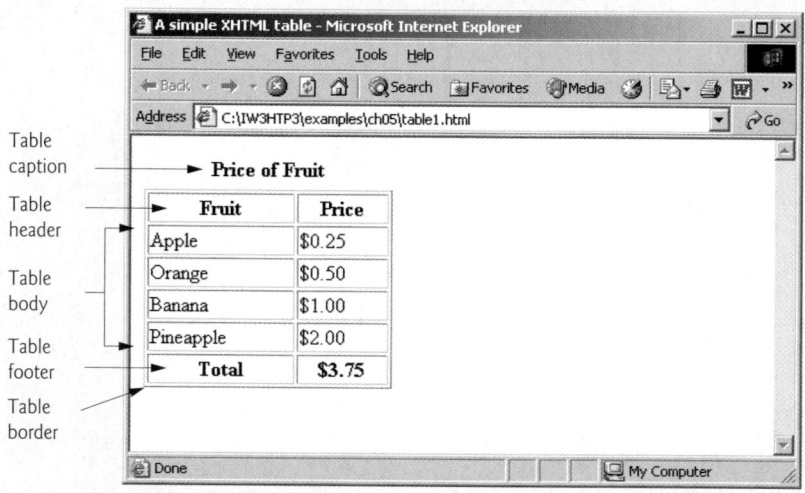

Table caption →
Table header →
Table body
Table footer →
Table border →

Fig. G.1 | XHTML table. (Part 3 of 3.)

As its name implies, attribute summary (lines 17–18) describes the table's contents. Speech devices use this attribute to make the table more accessible to users with visual impairments. The caption element (line 22) describes the table's content and helps text-based browsers interpret the table data. Text inside the <caption> tag is rendered above the table by most browsers. Attribute summary and element caption are two of the many XHTML features that make Web pages more accessible to users with disabilities.

A table has three distinct sections—head, body and foot. The head section (or header cell) is defined with a thead element (lines 26–31), which contains header information such as column names. Each tr element (lines 27–30) defines an individual table row. The columns in the head section are defined with th elements. Most browsers center text formatted by th (table header column) elements and display them in bold. Table header elements are nested inside table row elements.

The foot section (lines 35–40) is defined with a tfoot (table foot) element. The text placed in the footer commonly includes calculation results and footnotes. Like other sections, the foot section can contain table rows, and each row can contain columns.

The body section, or table body, contains the table's primary data. The table body (lines 44–64) is defined in a tbody element. In the body, each tr element specifies one row. Data cells contain individual pieces of data and are defined with td (table data) elements within each row.

G.3 Intermediate XHTML Tables and Formatting

In the preceding section, we explored the structure of a basic table. In Fig. G.2, we enhance our discussion of tables by introducing elements and attributes that allow the document author to build more complex tables.

The table begins in line 17. Element `colgroup` (lines 22–27) groups and formats columns. The *col* element (line 26) specifies two attributes in this example. The *align* attribute determines the alignment of text in the column. The `span` attribute determines how many columns the col element formats. In this case, we set `align`'s value to `"right"` and `span`'s value to `"1"` to right align text in the first column (the column containing the picture of the camel in the sample screen capture).

Table cells are sized to fit the data they contain. Document authors can create larger data cells by using the attributes `rowspan` and `colspan`. The values assigned to these attributes specify the number of rows or columns occupied by a cell. The th element at lines 36–39 uses the attribute rowspan = "2" to allow the cell containing the picture of the camel to use two vertically adjacent cells (thus the cell *spans* two rows). The th element in lines 42–45 uses the attribute colspan = "4" to widen the header cell (containing `Camelid comparison` and `Approximate as of 9/2002`) to span four cells.

Common Programming Error G.1

When using colspan *and* rowspan *to adjust the size of table data cells, keep in mind that the modified cells will occupy more than one column or row. Other rows or columns of the table must compensate for the extra rows or columns spanned by individual cells. If they do not, the formatting of your table will be distorted and you may inadvertently create more columns and rows than you originally intended.*

```
 1   <?xml version = "1.0"?>
 2   <!DOCTYPE html PUBLIC "-//W3C//DTD XHTML 1.1//EN"
 3      "http://www.w3.org/TR/xhtml11/DTD/xhtml11.dtd">
 4
 5   <!-- Fig. G.2: table2.html      -->
 6   <!-- Intermediate table design -->
 7
 8   <html xmlns = "http://www.w3.org/1999/xhtml">
 9      <head>
10         <title>Internet and WWW How to Program - Tables</title>
11      </head>
12
13      <body>
14
15         <h1>Table Example Page</h1>
16
17         <table border = "1">
18            <caption>Here is a more complex sample table.</caption>
19
20            <!-- <colgroup> and <col> tags are used to -->
21            <!-- format entire columns                 -->
22            <colgroup>
23
```

Fig. G.2 | Complex XHTML table. (Part 1 of 3.)

```
24          <!-- span attribute determines how many columns -->
25          <!-- the <col> tag affects                       -->
26          <col align = "right" span = "1" />
27      </colgroup>
28
29      <thead>
30
31          <!-- rowspans and colspans merge the specified    -->
32          <!-- number of cells vertically or horizontally   -->
33          <tr>
34
35              <!-- merge two rows -->
36              <th rowspan = "2">
37                  <img src = "camel.gif" width = "205"
38                      height = "167" alt = "Picture of a camel" />
39              </th>
40
41              <!-- merge four columns. -->
42              <th colspan = "4" valign = "top">
43                  <h1>Camelid comparison</h1><br />
44                  <p>Approximate as of 9/2002</p>
45              </th>
46          </tr>
47
48          <tr valign = "bottom">
49              <th># of Humps</th>
50              <th>Indigenous region</th>
51              <th>Spits?</th>
52              <th>Produces Wool?</th>
53          </tr>
54
55      </thead>
56
57      <tbody>
58
59          <tr>
60              <th>Camels (bactrian)</th>
61              <td>2</td>
62              <td>Africa/Asia</td>
63              <td>Yes</td>
64              <td>Yes</td>
65          </tr>
66
67          <tr>
68              <th>Llamas</th>
69              <td>1</td>
70              <td>Andes Mountains</td>
71              <td>Yes</td>
72              <td>Yes</td>
73          </tr>
74
75      </tbody>
76
```

Fig. G.2 | Complex XHTML table. (Part 2 of 3.)

```
77          </table>
78
79      </body>
80  </html>
```

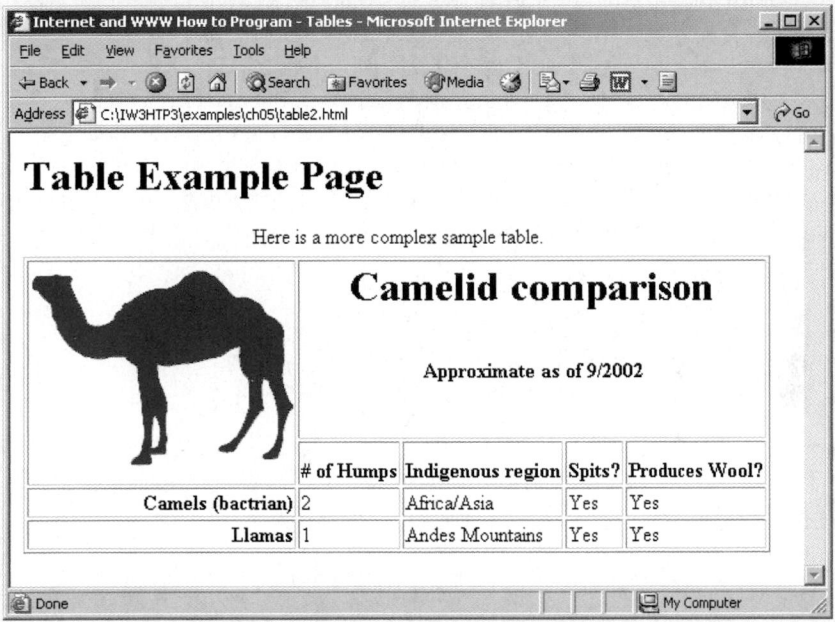

Fig. G.2 | Complex XHTML table. (Part 3 of 3.)

Line 42 introduces the attribute `valign`, which aligns data vertically and may be assigned one of four values—`"top"` aligns data with the top of the cell, `"middle"` vertically centers data (the default for all data and header cells), `"bottom"` aligns data with the bottom of the cell and `"baseline"` ignores the fonts used for the row data and sets the bottom of all text in the row on a common baseline (i.e., the horizontal line at which each character in a word is aligned).

G.4 Basic XHTML Forms

When browsing Web sites, users often need to provide such information as search keywords, e-mail addresses and zip codes. XHTML provides a mechanism, called a form, for collecting such data from a user.

Data that users enter on a Web page normally is sent to a Web server that provides access to a site's resources (e.g., XHTML documents, images). These resources are located either on the same machine as the Web server or on a machine that the Web server can access through the network. When a browser requests a Web page or file that is located on a server, the server processes the request and returns the requested resource. A request contains the name and path of the desired resource and the method of communication (called a protocol). XHTML documents use the Hypertext Transfer Protocol (HTTP).

Figure G.3 sends the form data to the Web server, which passes the form data to a CGI (**Common Gateway Interface**) script (i.e., a program) written in Perl, C or some other language. The script processes the data received from the Web server and typically returns information to the Web server. The Web server then sends the information as an XHTML document to the Web browser. [*Note:* This example demonstrates client-side functionality. If the form is submitted (by clicking **Submit Your Entries**) an error occurs because we have not yet configured the required server-side functionality.]

Forms can contain visual and nonvisual components. Visual components include clickable buttons and other graphical user interface components with which users interact. Nonvisual components, called **hidden inputs**, store any data that the document author specifies, such as e-mail addresses and XHTML document file names that act as links. The form is defined in lines 23–52 by a `form` element. Attribute `method` (line 23) specifies how the form's data is sent to the Web server.

```
1    <?xml version = "1.0"?>
2    <!DOCTYPE html PUBLIC "-//W3C//DTD XHTML 1.1//EN"
3       "http://www.w3.org/TR/xhtml11/DTD/xhtml11.dtd">
4
5    <!-- Fig. G.3: form.html   -->
6    <!-- Form Design Example 1 -->
7
8    <html xmlns = "http://www.w3.org/1999/xhtml">
9       <head>
10          <title>Internet and WWW How to Program - Forms</title>
11       </head>
12
13       <body>
14
15          <h1>Feedback Form</h1>
16
17          <p>Please fill out this form to help
18             us improve our site.</p>
19
20          <!-- this tag starts the form, gives the   -->
21          <!-- method of sending information and the -->
22          <!-- location of form scripts             -->
23          <form method = "post" action = "/cgi-bin/formmail">
24
25             <p>
26                <!-- hidden inputs contain non-visual -->
27                <!-- information                       -->
28                <input type = "hidden" name = "recipient"
29                   value = "deitel@deitel.com" />
30                <input type = "hidden" name = "subject"
31                   value = "Feedback Form" />
32                <input type = "hidden" name = "redirect"
33                   value = "main.html" />
34             </p>
35
```

Fig. G.3 | Form with hidden fields and a text box. (Part 1 of 2.)

```
36            <!-- <input type = "text"> inserts a text box -->
37            <p><label>Name:
38                <input name = "name" type = "text" size = "25"
39                    maxlength = "30" />
40            </label></p>
41
42            <p>
43                <!-- input types "submit" and "reset" insert  -->
44                <!-- buttons for submitting and clearing the  -->
45                <!-- form's contents                          -->
46                <input type = "submit" value =
47                    "Submit Your Entries" />
48                <input type = "reset" value =
49                    "Clear Your Entries" />
50            </p>
51
52        </form>
53
54    </body>
55 </html>
```

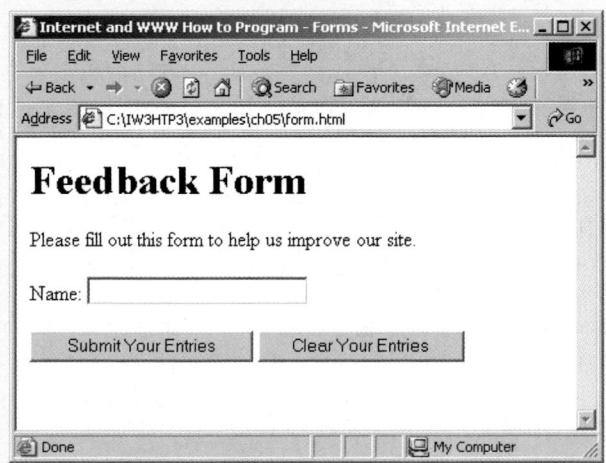

Fig. G.3 | Form with hidden fields and a text box. (Part 2 of 2.)

Using *method = "post"* appends form data to the browser request, which contains the protocol (i.e., HTTP) and the requested resource's URL. Scripts located on the Web server's computer (or on a computer accessible through the network) can access the form data sent as part of the request. For example, a script may take the form information and update an electronic mailing list. The other possible value, *method = "get"*, appends the form data directly to the end of the URL. For example, the URL /cgi-bin/formmail might have the form information name = bob appended to it.

The **action** attribute in the <form> tag specifies the URL of a script on the Web server; in this case, it specifies a script that e-mails form data to an address. Most Internet Service Providers (ISPs) have a script like this on their site; ask the Web site system administrator how to set up an XHTML document to use the script correctly.

Lines 28–33 define three **input** elements that specify data to provide to the script that processes the form (also called the **form handler**). These three **input** elements have the **type** attribute *"hidden"*, which allows the document author to send form data that is not input by a user.

The three hidden inputs are: an e-mail address to which the data will be sent, the e-mail's subject line and a URL where the browser will be redirected after submitting the form. Two other **input** attributes are *name*, which identifies the **input** element, and *value*, which provides the value that will be sent (or posted) to the Web server.

Good Programming Practice G.1

Place hidden input elements at the beginning of a form, immediately after the opening <form> tag. This placement allows document authors to locate hidden input elements quickly.

We introduce another **type** of **input** in lines 38–39. The *"text"* input inserts a text box into the form. Users can type data in text boxes. The **label** element (lines 37–40) provides users with information about the **input** element's purpose.

Look-and-Feel Observation G.1

Include a label element for each form element to help users determine the purpose of each form element.

The **input** element's **size** attribute specifies the number of characters visible in the text box. Optional attribute **maxlength** limits the number of characters input into the text box. In this case, the user is not permitted to type more than 30 characters into the text box.

There are two other types of **input** elements in lines 46–49. The *"submit"* input element is a button. When the user presses a "submit" button, the browser sends the data in the form to the Web server for processing. The **value** attribute sets the text displayed on the button (the default value is **Submit Query**). The *"reset"* input element allows a user to reset all **form** elements to their default values. The **value** attribute of the "reset" input element sets the text displayed on the button (the default value is **Reset**).

G.5 More Complex XHTML Forms

In the preceding section, we introduced basic forms. In this section, we introduce elements and attributes for creating more complex forms. Figure G.4 contains a form that solicits user feedback about a Web site.

```
1   <?xml version = "1.0"?>
2   <!DOCTYPE html PUBLIC "-//W3C//DTD XHTML 1.1//EN"
3       "http://www.w3.org/TR/xhtml11/DTD/xhtml11.dtd">
4
5   <!-- Fig. G.4: form2.html  -->
6   <!-- Form Design Example 2 -->
7
8   <html xmlns = "http://www.w3.org/1999/xhtml">
```

Fig. G.4 | Form with text areas, a password box and checkboxes. (Part 1 of 4.)

```
 9      <head>
10         <title>Internet and WWW How to Program - Forms</title>
11      </head>
12
13      <body>
14
15         <h1>Feedback Form</h1>
16
17         <p>Please fill out this form to help
18            us improve our site.</p>
19
20         <form method = "post" action = "/cgi-bin/formmail">
21
22            <p>
23               <input type = "hidden" name = "recipient"
24                  value = "deitel@deitel.com" />
25               <input type = "hidden" name = "subject"
26                  value = "Feedback Form" />
27               <input type = "hidden" name = "redirect"
28                  value = "main.html" />
29            </p>
30
31            <p><label>Name:
32               <input name = "name" type = "text" size = "25" />
33            </label></p>
34
35            <!-- <textarea> creates a multiline textbox -->
36            <p><label>Comments:<br />
37               <textarea name = "comments" rows = "4" cols = "36">
38   Enter your comments here.
39               </textarea>
40            </label></p>
41
42            <!-- <input type = "password"> inserts a    -->
43            <!-- textbox whose display is masked with   -->
44            <!-- asterisk characters                    -->
45            <p><label>E-mail Address:
46               <input name = "email" type = "password"
47                  size = "25" />
48            </label></p>
49
50            <p>
51               <strong>Things you liked:</strong><br />
52
53               <label>Site design
54               <input name = "thingsliked" type = "checkbox"
55                  value = "Design" /></label>
56
57               <label>Links
58               <input name = "thingsliked" type = "checkbox"
59                  value = "Links" /></label>
60
```

Fig. G.4 | Form with text areas, a password box and checkboxes. (Part 2 of 4.)

```
61              <label>Ease of use
62              <input name = "thingsliked" type = "checkbox"
63                  value = "Ease" /></label>
64
65              <label>Images
66              <input name = "thingsliked" type = "checkbox"
67                  value = "Images" /></label>
68
69              <label>Source code
70              <input name = "thingsliked" type = "checkbox"
71                  value = "Code" /></label>
72          </p>
73
74          <p>
75              <input type = "submit" value =
76                  "Submit Your Entries" />
77              <input type = "reset" value =
78                  "Clear Your Entries" />
79          </p>
80
81      </form>
82
83      </body>
84  </html>
```

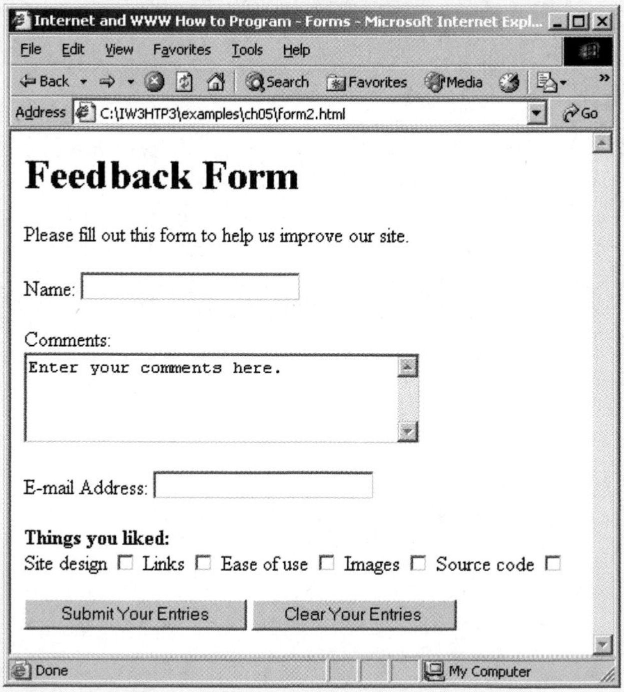

Fig. G.4 | Form with text areas, a password box and checkboxes. (Part 3 of 4.)

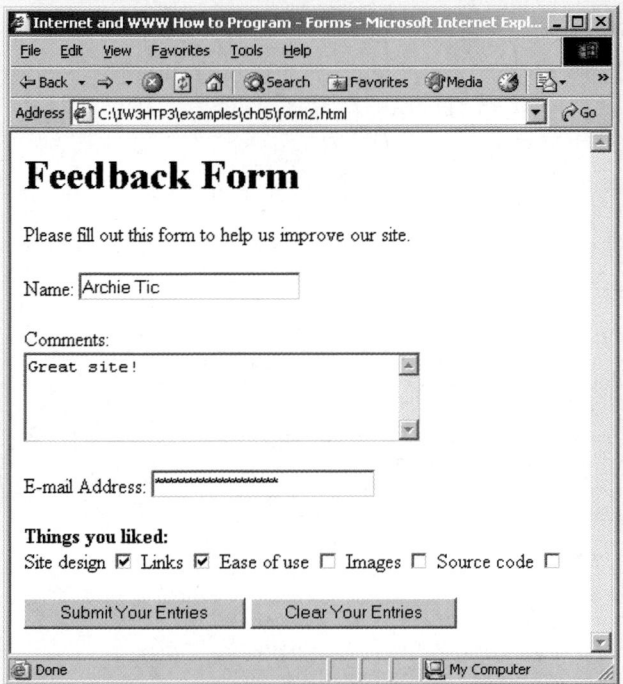

Fig. G.4 | Form with text areas, a password box and checkboxes. (Part 4 of 4.)

The `textarea` element (lines 37–39) inserts a multiline text box, called a text area, into the form. The number of rows is specified with the `rows` attribute, and the number of columns (i.e., characters) is specified with the `cols` attribute. In this example, the `textarea` is four rows high and 36 characters wide. To display default text in the text area, place the text between the `<textarea>` and `</textarea>` tags. Default text can be specified in other `input` types, such as text boxes, by using the `value` attribute

The *"password"* input in lines 46–47 inserts a password box with the specified `size`. A password box allows users to enter sensitive information, such as credit card numbers and passwords, by "masking" the information input with asterisks (*). The actual value input is sent to the Web server, not the characters that mask the input.

Lines 54–71 introduce the checkbox `form` element. Checkboxes enable users to select from a set of options. When a user selects a checkbox, a check mark appears in the check box. Otherwise, the checkbox remains empty. Each *"checkbox"* input creates a new checkbox. Checkboxes can be used individually or in groups. Checkboxes that belong to a group are assigned the same name (in this case, `"thingsliked"`).

Common Programming Error G.2

When your form has several checkboxes with the same name, you must make sure that they have different values, or the scripts running on the Web server will not be able to distinguish them.

We continue our discussion of forms by presenting a third example that introduces several additional form elements from which users can make selections (Fig. G.5). In this

```
 1   <?xml version = "1.0"?>
 2   <!DOCTYPE html PUBLIC "-//W3C//DTD XHTML 1.1//EN"
 3      "http://www.w3.org/TR/xhtml11/DTD/xhtml11.dtd">
 4
 5   <!-- Fig. G.5: form3.html  -->
 6   <!-- Form Design Example 3 -->
 7
 8   <html xmlns = "http://www.w3.org/1999/xhtml">
 9      <head>
10         <title>Internet and WWW How to Program - Forms</title>
11      </head>
12
13      <body>
14
15         <h1>Feedback Form</h1>
16
17         <p>Please fill out this form to help
18            us improve our site.</p>
19
20         <form method = "post" action = "/cgi-bin/formmail">
21
22            <p>
23               <input type = "hidden" name = "recipient"
24                  value = "deitel@deitel.com" />
25               <input type = "hidden" name = "subject"
26                  value = "Feedback Form" />
27               <input type = "hidden" name = "redirect"
28                  value = "main.html" />
29            </p>
30
31            <p><label>Name:
32               <input name = "name" type = "text" size = "25" />
33            </label></p>
34
35            <p><label>Comments:<br />
36               <textarea name = "comments" rows = "4"
37                  cols = "36"></textarea>
38            </label></p>
39
40            <p><label>E-mail Address:
41               <input name = "email" type = "password"
42                  size = "25" /></label></p>
43
44            <p>
45               <strong>Things you liked:</strong><br />
46
47               <label>Site design
48                  <input name = "thingsliked" type = "checkbox"
49                     value = "Design" /></label>
50
51               <label>Links
52                  <input name = "thingsliked" type = "checkbox"
53                     value = "Links" /></label>
```

Fig. G.5 | Form including radio buttons and a drop-down list. (Part 1 of 4.)

```
54
55            <label>Ease of use
56               <input name = "thingsliked" type = "checkbox"
57                  value = "Ease" /></label>
58
59            <label>Images
60               <input name = "thingsliked" type = "checkbox"
61                  value = "Images" /></label>
62
63            <label>Source code
64               <input name = "thingsliked" type = "checkbox"
65                  value = "Code" /></label>
66         </p>
67
68         <!-- <input type = "radio" /> creates a radio       -->
69         <!-- button. The difference between radio buttons -->
70         <!-- and checkboxes is that only one radio button -->
71         <!-- in a group can be selected.                    -->
72         <p>
73            <strong>How did you get to our site?:</strong><br />
74
75            <label>Search engine
76               <input name = "howtosite" type = "radio"
77                  value = "search engine" checked = "checked" />
78            </label>
79
80            <label>Links from another site
81               <input name = "howtosite" type = "radio"
82                  value = "link" /></label>
83
84            <label>Deitel.com Web site
85               <input name = "howtosite" type = "radio"
86                  value = "deitel.com" /></label>
87
88            <label>Reference in a book
89               <input name = "howtosite" type = "radio"
90                  value = "book" /></label>
91
92            <label>Other
93               <input name = "howtosite" type = "radio"
94                  value = "other" /></label>
95
96         </p>
97
98         <p>
99            <label>Rate our site:
100
101              <!-- the <select> tag presents a drop-down -->
102              <!-- list with choices indicated by the    -->
103              <!-- <option> tags                          -->
104              <select name = "rating">
105                 <option selected = "selected">Amazing</option>
106                 <option>10</option>
```

Fig. G.5 | Form including radio buttons and a drop-down list. (Part 2 of 4.)

```
107                         <option>9</option>
108                         <option>8</option>
109                         <option>7</option>
110                         <option>6</option>
111                         <option>5</option>
112                         <option>4</option>
113                         <option>3</option>
114                         <option>2</option>
115                         <option>1</option>
116                         <option>Awful</option>
117                     </select>
118
119                 </label>
120         </p>
121
122         <p>
123             <input type = "submit" value =
124                 "Submit Your Entries" />
125             <input type = "reset" value = "Clear Your Entries" />
126         </p>
127
128     </form>
129
130     </body>
131 </html>
```

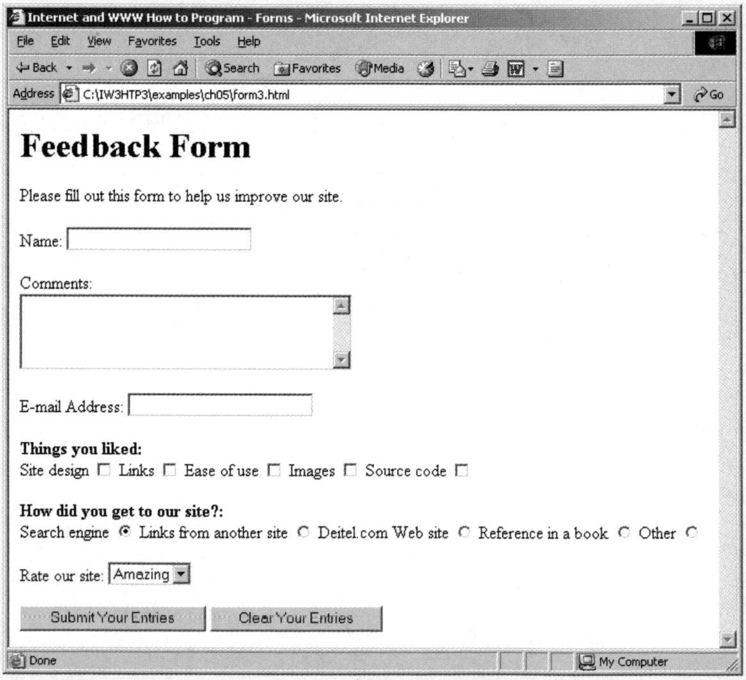

Fig. G.5 | Form including radio buttons and a drop-down list. (Part 3 of 4.)

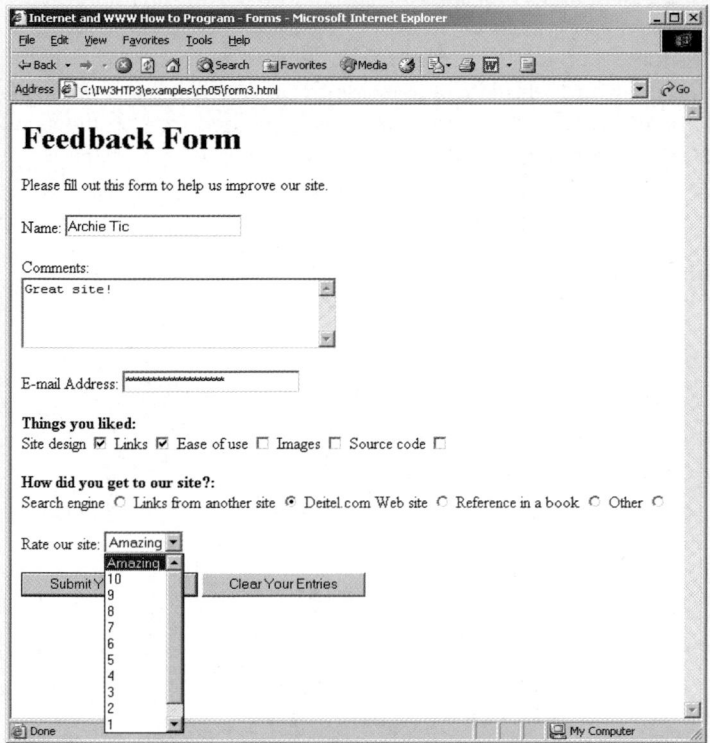

Fig. G.5 | Form including radio buttons and a drop-down list. (Part 4 of 4.)

example, we introduce two new `input` types. The first type is the radio button (lines 76–94) specified with type `"radio"`. Radio buttons are similar to checkboxes, except that only one radio button in a group of radio buttons may be selected at any time. The radio buttons in a group all have the same `name` attributes and are distinguished by their different `value` attributes. The attribute-value pair `checked = "checked"` (line 77) indicates which radio button, if any, is selected initially. The `checked` attribute also applies to checkboxes.

Common Programming Error G.3

Not setting the `name` attributes of the radio buttons in a form to the same name is a logic error because it lets the user select all of them at the same time.

The `select` element (lines 104–117) provides a drop-down list of items from which the user can select an item. The `name` attribute identifies the drop-down list. The `option` element (lines 105–116) adds items to the drop-down list. The `option` element's `selected` attribute specifies which item initially is displayed as the selected item.

G.6 Internal Linking

In Appendix F, we discussed how to hyperlink one Web page to another. Figure G.6 introduces internal linking—a mechanism that enables the user to jump between locations in the same document. Internal linking is useful for long documents that contain many sections. Clicking an internal link enables users to find a section without scrolling through the entire document.

Line 16 contains a tag with the *id* attribute (called `"features"`) for an internal hyperlink. To link to a tag with this attribute inside the same Web page, the `href` attribute of an anchor element includes the `id` attribute value preceded by a pound sign (as in `#features`). Lines 61–62 contain a hyperlink with the id `features` as its target. Selecting this hyperlink in a Web browser scrolls the browser window to the h1 tag in line 16.

```
 1   <?xml version = "1.0"?>
 2   <!DOCTYPE html PUBLIC "-//W3C//DTD XHTML 1.1//EN"
 3      "http://www.w3.org/TR/xhtml11/DTD/xhtml11.dtd">
 4
 5   <!-- Fig. G.6: links.html -->
 6   <!-- Internal Linking      -->
 7
 8   <html xmlns = "http://www.w3.org/1999/xhtml">
 9      <head>
10         <title>Internet and WWW How to Program - List</title>
11      </head>
12
13      <body>
14
15         <!-- id attribute creates an internal hyperlink destination -->
16         <h1 id = "features">The Best Features of the Internet</h1>
17
18         <!-- an internal link's address is "#id" -->
19         <p><a href = "#bugs">Go to <em>Favorite Bugs</em></a></p>
20
21         <ul>
22            <li>You can meet people from countries
23               around the world.</li>
24
25            <li>You have access to new media as it becomes public:
26               <ul>
27                  <li>New games</li>
28                  <li>New applications
29                     <ul>
30                        <li>For Business</li>
31                        <li>For Pleasure</li>
32                     </ul>
33                  </li>
34
35                  <li>Around the clock news</li>
36                  <li>Search Engines</li>
37                  <li>Shopping</li>
38                  <li>Programming
39                     <ul>
40                        <li>XHTML</li>
41                        <li>Java</li>
42                        <li>Dynamic HTML</li>
43                        <li>Scripts</li>
```

Fig. G.6 | Internal hyperlinks to make pages more navigable. (Part 1 of 3.)

```
44                          <li>New languages</li>
45                       </ul>
46                    </li>
47                 </ul>
48           </li>
49
50           <li>Links</li>
51           <li>Keeping in touch with old friends</li>
52           <li>It is the technology of the future!</li>
53        </ul>
54
55        <!-- id attribute creates an internal hyperlink destination -->
56        <h1 id = "bugs">My 3 Favorite Bugs</h1>
57
58        <p>
59
60           <!-- internal hyperlink to features -->
61           <a href = "#features">Go to <em>Favorite Features</em>
62           </a></p>
63
64        <ol>
65           <li>Fire Fly</li>
66           <li>Gal Ant</li>
67           <li>Roman Tic</li>
68        </ol>
69
70     </body>
71  </html>
```

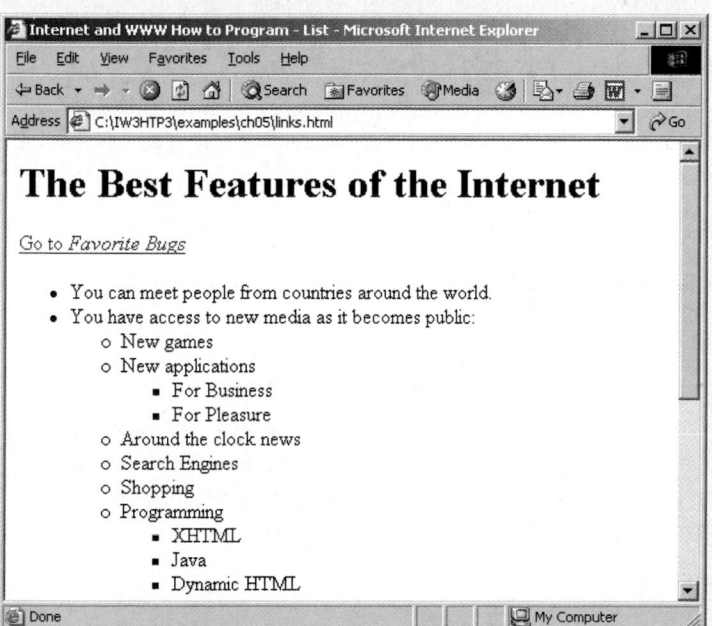

Fig. G.6 | Internal hyperlinks to make pages more navigable. (Part 2 of 3.)

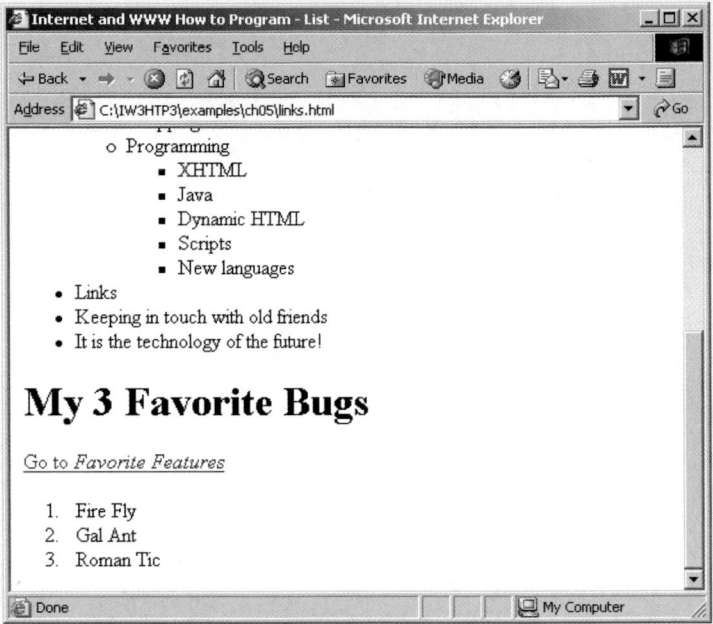

Fig. G.6 | Internal hyperlinks to make pages more navigable. (Part 3 of 3.)

Look-and-Feel Observation G.2

Internal hyperlinks are useful in XHTML documents that contain large amounts of information. Internal links to different parts of the page makes it easier for users to navigate the page. They do not have to scroll to find the section they want.

Although not demonstrated in this example, a hyperlink can specify an internal link in another document by specifying the document name followed by a pound sign and the id value, as in:

    href = "*filename*.html#*id*"

For example, to link to a tag with the id attribute called booklist in books.html, href is assigned "books.html#booklist".

G.7 Creating and Using Image Maps

In Appendix F, we demonstrated how images can be used as hyperlinks to link to other resources on the Internet. In this section, we introduce another technique for image linking called **image maps**, which designates certain areas of an image (called **hotspots**) as links.[1] Figure G.7 introduces image maps and hotspots.

---

1. Some Web browsers do not support XHTML 1.1 image maps. For this reason we use XHTML 1.0 Transitional, an earlier W3C version of XHTML. In order to validate the code in Figure G.7 as XHTML 1.1, remove the # from the usemap attribute of the img tag (line 53).

```
 1   <?xml version = "1.0" ?>
 2   <!DOCTYPE html PUBLIC "-//W3C//DTD XHTML 1.0 Transitional//EN"
 3      "http://www.w3.org/TR/xhtml1/DTD/xhtml1-transitional.dtd">
 4
 5   <!-- Fig. G.7: picture.html          -->
 6   <!-- Creating and Using Image Maps -->
 7
 8   <html xmlns = "http://www.w3.org/1999/xhtml">
 9      <head>
10         <title>
11            Internet and WWW How to Program - Image Map
12         </title>
13      </head>
14
15      <body>
16
17         <p>
18
19         <!-- the <map> tag defines an image map -->
20         <map id = "picture">
21
22            <!-- shape = "rect" indicates a rectangular     -->
23            <!-- area, with coordinates for the upper-left -->
24            <!-- and lower-right corners                    -->
25            <area href = "form.html" shape = "rect"
26               coords = "2,123,54,143"
27               alt = "Go to the feedback form" />
28            <area href = "contact.html" shape = "rect"
29               coords = "126,122,198,143"
30               alt = "Go to the contact page" />
31            <area href = "main.html" shape = "rect"
32               coords = "3,7,61,25" alt = "Go to the homepage" />
33            <area href = "links.html" shape = "rect"
34               coords = "168,5,197,25"
35               alt = "Go to the links page" />
36
37            <!-- value "poly" creates a hotspot in the shape -->
38            <!-- of a polygon, defined by coords             -->
39            <area shape = "poly" alt = "E-mail the Deitels"
40               coords = "162,25,154,39,158,54,169,51,183,39,161,26"
41               href = "mailto:deitel@deitel.com" />
42
43            <!-- shape = "circle" indicates a circular -->
44            <!-- area with the given center and radius -->
45            <area href = "mailto:deitel@deitel.com"
46               shape = "circle" coords = "100,36,33"
47               alt = "E-mail the Deitels" />
48         </map>
49
50         <!-- <img src =... usemap = "#id"> indicates that the -->
51         <!-- specified image map is used with this image       -->
52         <img src = "deitel.gif" width = "200" height = "144"
53            alt = "Deitel logo" usemap = "#picture" />
```

Fig. G.7 | Image with links anchored to an image map. (Part 1 of 2.)

```
54          </p>
55      </body>
56  </html>
```

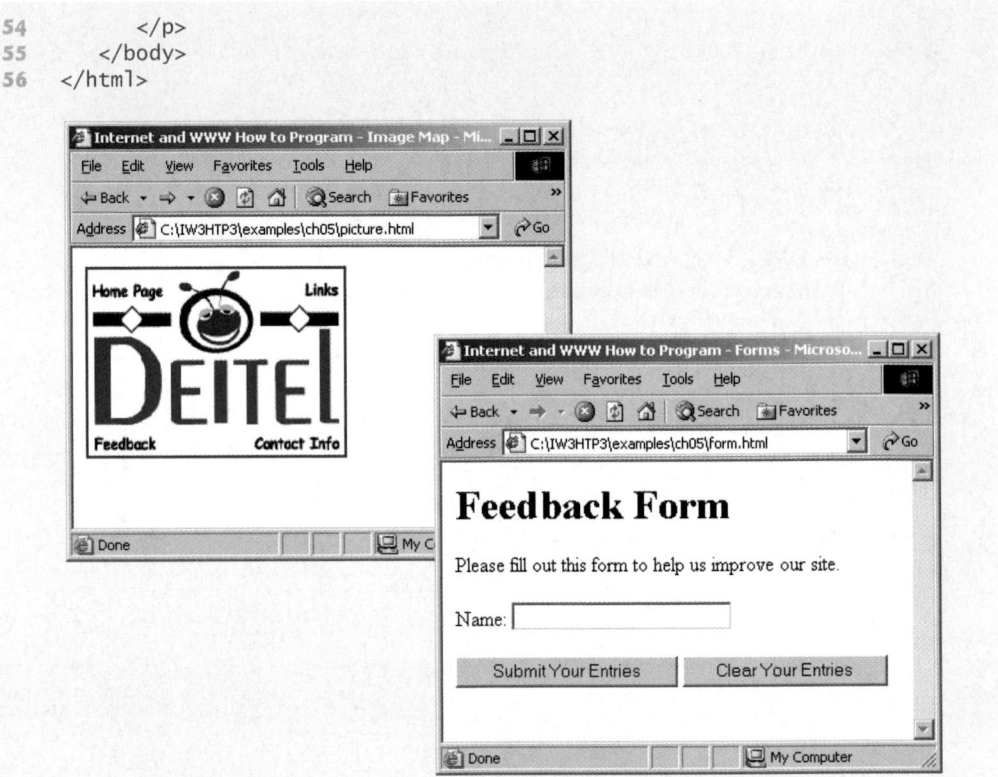

Fig. G.7 | Image with links anchored to an image map. (Part 2 of 2.)

Lines 20–48 define an image map by using a `map` element. Attribute *id* (line 20) identifies the image map. If `id` is omitted, the map cannot be referenced by an image (which we will see momentarily). Hotspots are defined with `area` elements (as shown in lines 25–27). Attribute `href` (line 25) specifies the link's target (i.e., the resource to which to link). Attributes `shape` (line 25) and `coords` (line 26) specify the hotspot's shape and coordinates, respectively. Attribute `alt` (line 27) provides alternative text for the link.

 Common Programming Error G.4

Not specifying an `id` attribute for a `map` element prevents an `img` element from using the `map`'s `area` elements to define hotspots.

The markup in lines 25–27 creates a rectangular hotspot (`shape = "rect"`) for the coordinates specified in the `coords` attribute. A coordinate pair consists of two numbers representing the locations of a point on the *x*-axis and the *y*-axis, respectively. The *x*-axis extends horizontally and the *y*-axis extends vertically from the upper-left corner of the image. Every point on an image has a unique *x*-*y*-coordinate. For rectangular hotspots, the required coordinates are those of the upper-left and lower-right corners of the rectangle. In this case, the upper-left corner of the rectangle is located at 2 on the *x*-axis and 123 on the *y*-axis, annotated as *(2, 123)*. The lower-right corner of the rectangle is at *(54, 143)*. Coordinates are measured in pixels.

> **Common Programming Error G.5**
>
> *Overlapping coordinates of an image map cause the browser to render the first hotspot it encounters for the area.*

The map area at lines 39–41 assigns the shape attribute *"poly"* to create a hotspot in the shape of a polygon using the coordinates in attribute coords. These coordinates represent each vertex, or corner, of the polygon. The browser connects these points with lines to form the hotspot's area.

The map area at lines 45–47 assigns the shape attribute *"circle"* to create a circular hotspot. In this case, the coords attribute specifies the circle's center coordinates and the circle's radius, in pixels.

To use an image map with an img element, you must assign the img element's usemap attribute to the id of a map. Lines 52–53 reference the image map "#picture". The image map is located within the same document, so internal linking is used.

G.8 meta Elements

Search engines are used to find Web sites. They usually catalog sites by following links from page to page (known as spidering or crawling) and saving identification and classification information for each page. One way that search engines catalog pages is by reading the content in each page's meta elements, which specify information about a document.

Two important attributes of the meta element are name, which identifies the type of meta element, and content, which provides the information search engines use to catalog pages. Figure G.8 introduces the meta element.

```
1   <?xml version = "1.0"?>
2   <!DOCTYPE html PUBLIC "-//W3C//DTD XHTML 1.1//EN"
3      "http://www.w3.org/TR/xhtml11/DTD/xhtml11.dtd">
4
5   <!-- Fig. G.8: main.html -->
6   <!-- <meta> tag            -->
7
8   <html xmlns = "http://www.w3.org/1999/xhtml">
9      <head>
10        <title>Internet and WWW How to Program - Welcome</title>
11
12        <!-- <meta> tags provide search engines with -->
13        <!-- information used to catalog a site       -->
14        <meta name = "keywords" content = "Web page, design,
15           XHTML, tutorial, personal, help, index, form,
16           contact, feedback, list, links, frame, deitel" />
17
18        <meta name = "description" content = "This Web site will
19           help you learn the basics of XHTML and Web page design
20           through the use of interactive examples and
21           instruction." />
22
23     </head>
```

Fig. G.8 | meta tags provide keywords and a description of a page. (Part 1 of 2.)

```
24
25      <body>
26
27         <h1>Welcome to Our Web Site!</h1>
28
29         <p>We have designed this site to teach about the wonders
30         of <strong><em>XHTML</em></strong>. <em>XHTML</em> is
31         better equipped than <em>HTML</em> to represent complex
32         data on the Internet. <em>XHTML</em> takes advantage of
33         XML's strict syntax to ensure well-formedness. Soon you
34         will know about many of the great new features of
35         <em>XHTML.</em></p>
36
37         <p>Have Fun With the Site!</p>
38
39      </body>
40   </html>
```

Fig. G.8 | meta tags provide keywords and a description of a page. (Part 2 of 2.)

Lines 14–16 demonstrate a *"keywords"* meta element. The content attribute of such a meta element provides search engines with a list of words that describe a page. These words are compared with words in search requests. Thus, including meta elements and their content information can draw more viewers to your site.

Lines 18–21 demonstrate a *"description"* meta element. The content attribute of such a meta element provides a three- to four-line description of a site, written in sentence form. Search engines also use this description to catalog your site and sometimes display this information as part of the search results.

Software Engineering Observation G.1

meta elements are not visible to users and must be placed inside the head section of your XHTML document. If meta elements are not placed in this section, they will not be read by search engines.

G.9 **frameset Element**

All of the Web pages we present in this book have the ability to link to other pages, but can display only one page at a time. Frames allow a Web developer to display more than one XHTML document in the browser simultaneously. Figure G.9 uses frames to display the documents in Fig. G.8 and Fig. G.10.

Most of our earlier examples adhere to the XHTML 1.1 document type, whereas these use the XHTML 1.0 document types.[2] These document types are specified in lines 2–3 and are required for documents that define framesets or use the `target` attribute to work with framesets.

A document that defines a frameset normally consists of an `html` element that contains a `head` element and a `frameset` element (lines 23–40). In Fig. G.9, the `<frameset>` tag (line 23) informs the browser that the page contains frames. Attribute `cols` specifies the frameset's column layout. The value of `cols` gives the width of each frame, either in pixels or as a percentage of the browser width. In this case, the attribute `cols = "110,*"` informs the browser that there are two vertical frames. The first frame extends 110 pixels from the left edge of the browser window, and the second frame fills the remainder of the browser width (as indicated by the asterisk). Similarly, `frameset` attribute *rows* can be used to specify the number of rows and the size of each row in a frameset.

```
1   <?xml version = "1.0"?>
2   <!DOCTYPE html PUBLIC "-//W3C//DTD XHTML 1.0 Frameset//EN"
3       "http://www.w3.org/TR/xhtml1/DTD/xhtml1-frameset.dtd">
4
5   <!-- Fig. G.9: index.html -->
6   <!-- XHTML Frames I        -->
7
8   <html xmlns = "http://www.w3.org/1999/xhtml">
9      <head>
10        <title>Internet and WWW How to Program - Main</title>
11        <meta name = "keywords" content = "Webpage, design,
12           XHTML, tutorial, personal, help, index, form,
13           contact, feedback, list, links, frame, deitel" />
14
15        <meta name = "description" content = "This Web site will
16           help you learn the basics of XHTML and Web page design
17           through the use of interactive examples
18           and instruction." />
19
20     </head>
21
22     <!-- the <frameset> tag sets the frame dimensions   -->
23     <frameset cols = "110,*">
```

Fig. G.9 | XHTML frames document with navigation and content. (Part 1 of 3.)

---

2. XHTML 1.1 no longer supports the use of frames. The W3C recommends using Cascading Style Sheets to achieve the same effect. Frames are still used by some Web sites and supported by most browsers, however. The `frameset` element and the `target` attribute are still supported in the XHTML 1.0 Frameset and the XHTML 1.0 Transitional document type definitions, respectively. Please refer to www.w3.org/TR/xhtml1/#dtds for more information.

```
24
25          <!-- frame elements specify which pages -->
26          <!-- are loaded into a given frame        -->
27          <frame name = "leftframe" src = "nav.html" />
28          <frame name = "main" src = "main.html" />
29
30          <noframes>
31             <body>
32                <p>This page uses frames, but your browser does not
33                support them.</p>
34
35                <p>Please, <a href = "nav.html">follow this link to
36                browse our site without frames</a>.</p>
37             </body>
38          </noframes>
39
40       </frameset>
41    </html>
```

Fig. G.9 | XHTML frames document with navigation and content. (Part 2 of 3.)

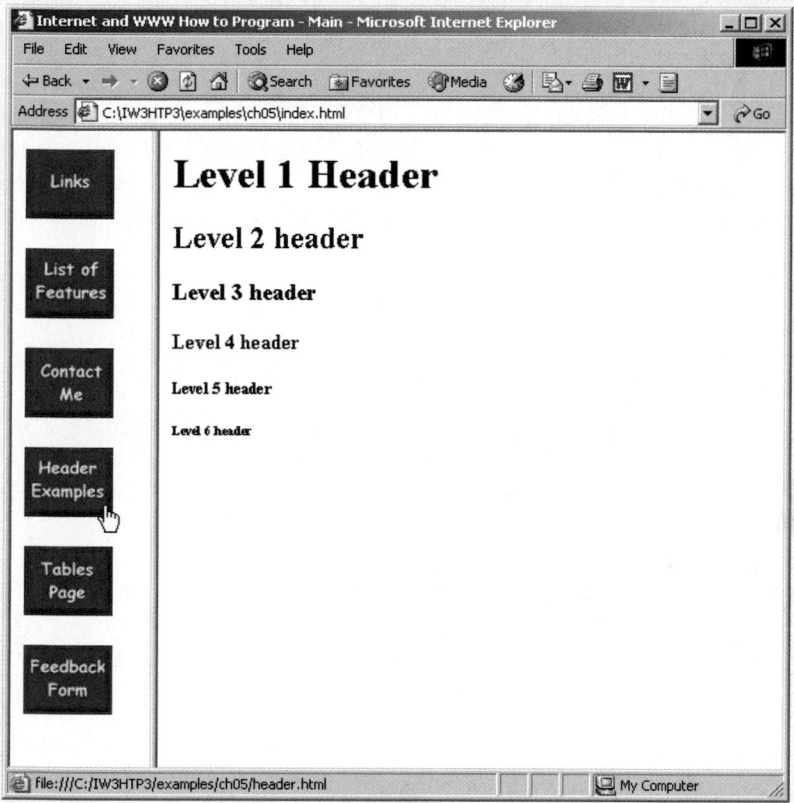

Fig. G.9 | XHTML frames document with navigation and content. (Part 3 of 3.)

The documents that will be loaded into the frameset are specified with frame elements (lines 27–28 in this example). Attribute src specifies the URL of the page to display in the frame. Each frame has name and src attributes. The first frame (which covers 110 pixels on the left side of the frameset), named leftframe, displays the page nav.html (Fig. G.10). The second frame, named main, displays the page main.html (Fig. G.8).

Attribute name identifies a frame, enabling hyperlinks in a frameset to specify the *target* frame in which a linked document should display when the user clicks the link. For example

```
<a href = "links.html" target = "main">
```

loads links.html in the frame whose name is "main".

Not all browsers support frames. XHTML provides the noframes element (lines 30–38) to enable XHTML document designers to specify alternative content for browsers that do not support frames.

Portability Tip G.1

Some browsers do not support frames. Use the noframes element inside a frameset to direct users to a nonframed version of your site.

Figure G.10 is the Web page displayed in the left frame of Fig. G.9. This XHTML document provides the navigation buttons that, when clicked, determine which document is displayed in the right frame.

Line 27 (Fig. G.9) displays the XHTML page in Fig. G.10. Anchor attribute `target` (line 18 in Fig. G.10) specifies that the linked documents are loaded in frame `main` (line 28 in Fig. G.9). A `target` can be set to a number of preset values: `"_blank"` loads the page into a new browser window, `"_self"` loads the page into the frame in which the anchor element appears and `"_top"` loads the page into the full browser window (i.e., removes the `frameset`).

```
 1   <?xml version = "1.0"?>
 2   <!DOCTYPE html PUBLIC "-//W3C//DTD XHTML 1.0 Transitional//EN"
 3      "http://www.w3.org/TR/xhtml1/DTD/xhtml1-transitional.dtd">
 4
 5   <!-- Fig. G.10: nav.html            -->
 6   <!-- Using images as link anchors -->
 7
 8   <html xmlns = "http://www.w3.org/1999/xhtml">
 9
10      <head>
11         <title>Internet and WWW How to Program - Navigation Bar
12         </title>
13      </head>
14
15      <body>
16
17         <p>
18            <a href = "links.html" target = "main">
19               <img src = "buttons/links.jpg" width = "65"
20                  height = "50" alt = "Links Page" />
21            </a><br />
22
23            <a href = "list.html" target = "main">
24               <img src = "buttons/list.jpg" width = "65"
25                  height = "50" alt = "List Example Page" />
26            </a><br />
27
28            <a href = "contact.html" target = "main">
29               <img src = "buttons/contact.jpg" width = "65"
30                  height = "50" alt = "Contact Page" />
31            </a><br />
32
33            <a href = "header.html" target = "main">
34               <img src = "buttons/header.jpg" width = "65"
35                  height = "50" alt = "Header Page" />
36            </a><br />
37
38            <a href = "table1.html" target = "main">
39               <img src = "buttons/table.jpg" width = "65"
40                  height = "50" alt = "Table Page" />
41            </a><br />
```

Fig. G.10 | XHTML document displayed in the left frame of Fig. G.9. (Part 1 of 2.)

```
42
43              <a href = "form.html" target = "main">
44                  <img src = "buttons/form.jpg" width = "65"
45                      height = "50" alt = "Feedback Form" />
46              </a><br />
47          </p>
48
49      </body>
50  </html>
```

Fig. G.10 | XHTML document displayed in the left frame of Fig. G.9. (Part 2 of 2.)

G.10 **Nested framesets**

You can use the frameset element to create more complex layouts in a Web page by nesting framesets, as in Fig. G.11. The nested frameset in this example displays the XHTML documents in Fig. G.7, Fig. G.8 and Fig. G.10.

```
1   <?xml version = "1.0"?>
2   <!DOCTYPE html PUBLIC "-//W3C//DTD XHTML 1.0 Frameset//EN"
3       "http://www.w3.org/TR/xhtml1/DTD/xhtml1-frameset.dtd">
4
5   <!-- Fig. G.11: index2.html -->
6   <!-- XHTML Frames II        -->
7
8   <html xmlns = "http://www.w3.org/1999/xhtml">
9       <head>
10          <title>Internet and WWW How to Program - Main</title>
11
12          <meta name = "keywords" content = "Webpage, design,
13              XHTML, tutorial, personal, help, index, form,
14              contact, feedback, list, links, frame, deitel" />
15
16          <meta name = "description" content = "This Web site will
17              help you learn the basics of XHTML and Web page design
18              through the use of interactive examples
19              and instruction." />
20
21      </head>
22
23  <frameset cols = "110,*">
24      <frame name = "leftframe" src = "nav.html" />
25
26      <!-- nested framesets are used to change the -->
27      <!-- formatting and layout of the frameset  -->
28      <frameset rows = "175,*">
29          <frame name = "picture" src = "picture.html" />
30          <frame name = "main" src = "main.html" />
31      </frameset>
32
```

Fig. G.11 | Framed Web site with a nested frameset. (Part 1 of 2.)

```
33        <noframes>
34          <body>
35            <p>This page uses frames, but your browser does not
36            support them.</p>
37
38            <p>Please, <a href = "nav.html">follow this link to
39            browse our site without frames</a>.</p>
40          </body>
41        </noframes>
42
43      </frameset>
44   </html>
```

Fig. G.11 | Framed Web site with a nested frameset. (Part 2 of 2.)

The outer `frameset` element (lines 23–43) defines two columns. The left frame extends over the first 110 pixels from the left edge of the browser, and the right frame occupies the rest of the window's width. The `frame` element in line 24 specifies that the document nav.html (Fig. G.10) will be displayed in the left column.

Lines 28–31 define a nested `frameset` element for the second column of the outer frameset. This `frameset` defines two rows. The first row extends 175 pixels from the top of the browser window, as indicated by rows = "175,*". The second row occupies the remainder of the browser window's height. The `frame` element at line 29 specifies that the first row of the nested `frameset` will display `picture.html` (Fig. G.7). The `frame` element in line 30 specifies that the second row of the nested `frameset` will display `main.html` (Fig. G.8).

Error-Prevention Tip G.1

When using nested `frameset` elements, indent every level of `<frame>` tag. This practice makes the page clearer and easier to debug.

G.11 Web Resources

www.vbxml.com/xhtml/articles/xhtml_tables

The *VBXML.com* Web site contains a tutorial on creating XHTML tables.

www.webreference.com/xml/reference/xhtml.html

This Web page contains a list of frequently used XHTML tags, such as header tags, table tags, frame tags and form tags. It also provides a description of each tag.

XHTML Special Characters

The table of Fig. H.1 shows many commonly used XHTML special characters—called **character entity references** by the World Wide Web Consortium. For a complete list of character entity references, see the site

www.w3.org/TR/REC-html40/sgml/entities.html

Character	XHTML encoding	Character	XHTML encoding
non-breaking space		ã	ã
§	§	å	å
©	©	ç	ç
®	®	è	è
π	¼	é	é
∫	½	ê	ê
Ω	¾	ì	ì
à	à	í	í
á	á	î	î
â	â	ñ	ñ

Fig. H.1 | XHTML special characters. (Part 1 of 2.)

Character	XHTML encoding	Character	XHTML encoding
ò	&#242;	ù	&#249;
ó	&#243;	ú	&#250;
ô	&#244;	û	&#251;
õ	&#245;	•	&#8226;
÷	&#247;	™	&#8482;

Fig. H.1 | XHTML special characters. (Part 2 of 2.)

XHTML Colors

Colors may be specified by using a standard name (such as aqua) or a hexadecimal RGB value (such as #00FFFF for aqua). Of the six hexadecimal digits in an RGB value, the first two represent the amount of red in the color, the middle two represent the amount of green in the color, and the last two represent the amount of blue in the color. For example, black is the absence of color and is defined by #000000, whereas white is the maximum amount of red, green and blue and is defined by #FFFFFF. Pure red is #FF0000, pure green (which is called lime) is #00FF00 and pure blue is #0000FF. Note that green in the standard is defined as #008000. Figure I.1 contains the XHTML standard color set. Figure I.2 contains the XHTML extended color set.

Color name	Value	Color name	Value
aqua	#00FFFF	navy	#000080
black	#000000	olive	#808000
blue	#0000FF	purple	#800080
fuchsia	#FF00FF	red	#FF0000
gray	#808080	silver	#C0C0C0
green	#008000	teal	#008080
lime	#00FF00	yellow	#FFFF00
maroon	#800000	white	#FFFFFF

Fig. I.1 | XHTML standard colors and hexadecimal RGB values.

Color name	Value	Color name	Value
aliceblue	#F0F8FF	darkslategray	#2F4F4F
antiquewhite	#FAEBD7	darkturquoise	#00CED1
aquamarine	#7FFFD4	darkviolet	#9400D3
azure	#F0FFFF	deeppink	#FF1493
beige	#F5F5DC	deepskyblue	#00BFFF
bisque	#FFE4C4	dimgray	#696969
blanchedalmond	#FFEBCD	dodgerblue	#1E90FF
blueviolet	#8A2BE2	firebrick	#B22222
brown	#A52A2A	floralwhite	#FFFAF0
burlywood	#DEB887	forestgreen	#228B22
cadetblue	#5F9EA0	gainsboro	#DCDCDC
chartreuse	#7FFF00	ghostwhite	#F8F8FF
chocolate	#D2691E	gold	#FFD700
coral	#FF7F50	goldenrod	#DAA520
cornflowerblue	#6495ED	greenyellow	#ADFF2F
cornsilk	#FFF8DC	honeydew	#F0FFF0
crimson	#DC1436	hotpink	#FF69B4
cyan	#00FFFF	indianred	#CD5C5C
darkblue	#00008B	indigo	#4B0082
darkcyan	#008B8B	ivory	#FFFFF0
darkgoldenrod	#B8860B	khaki	#F0E68C
darkgray	#A9A9A9	lavender	#E6E6FA
darkgreen	#006400	lavenderblush	#FFF0F5
darkkhaki	#BDB76B	lawngreen	#7CFC00
darkmagenta	#8B008B	lemonchiffon	#FFFACD
darkolivegreen	#556B2F	lightblue	#ADD8E6
darkorange	#FF8C00	lightcoral	#F08080
darkorchid	#9932CC	lightcyan	#E0FFFF
darkred	#8B0000	lightgoldenrodyellow	#FAFAD2
darksalmon	#E9967A	lightgreen	#90EE90
darkseagreen	#8FBC8F	lightgrey	#D3D3D3
darkslateblue	#483D8B	lightpink	#FFB6C1

Fig. I.2 | XHTML extended colors and hexadecimal RGB values (Part 1 of 2.).

Color name	Value	Color name	Value
lightsalmon	#FFA07A	palevioletred	#DB7093
lightseagreen	#20B2AA	papayawhip	#FFEFD5
lightskyblue	#87CEFA	peachpuff	#FFDAB9
lightslategray	#778899	peru	#CD853F
lightsteelblue	#B0C4DE	pink	#FFC0CB
lightyellow	#FFFFE0	plum	#DDA0DD
limegreen	#32CD32	powderblue	#B0E0E6
mediumaquamarine	#66CDAA	rosybrown	#BC8F8F
mediumblue	#0000CD	royalblue	#4169E1
mediumorchid	#BA55D3	saddlebrown	#8B4513
mediumpurple	#9370DB	salmon	#FA8072
mediumseagreen	#3CB371	sandybrown	#F4A460
mediumslateblue	#7B68EE	seagreen	#2E8B57
mediumspringgreen	#00FA9A	seashell	#FFF5EE
mediumturquoise	#48D1CC	sienna	#A0522D
mediumvioletred	#C71585	skyblue	#87CEEB
midnightblue	#191970	slateblue	#6A5ACD
mintcream	#F5FFFA	slategray	#708090
mistyrose	#FFE4E1	snow	#FFFAFA
moccasin	#FFE4B5	springgreen	#00FF7F
navajowhite	#FFDEAD	steelblue	#4682B4
oldlace	#FDF5E6	tan	#D2B48C
olivedrab	#6B8E23	thistle	#D8BFD8
orange	#FFA500	tomato	#FF6347
orangered	#FF4500	turquoise	#40E0D0
orchid	#DA70D6	violet	#EE82EE
palegoldenrod	#EEE8AA	wheat	#F5DEB3
palegreen	#98FB98	whitesmoke	#F5F5F5
paleturquoise	#AFEEEE	yellowgreen	#9ACD32

Fig. I.2 | XHTML extended colors and hexadecimal RGB values (Part 2 of 2.).

ATM Case Study Code

J.1 ATM Case Study Implementation

This appendix contains the complete working implementation of the ATM system that we designed in the nine Software Engineering Case Study sections in Chapters 1, 3–9 and 11. The implementation comprises 597 lines of Visual Basic code. We consider the 11 classes in the order in which we identified them in Section 4.9 (with the exception of `Transaction`, which was introduced in Chapter 11 as the base class of classes `Balance-Inquiry`, `Withdrawal` and `Deposit`):

- ATM
- Screen
- Keypad
- CashDispenser
- DepositSlot
- Account
- BankDatabase
- Transaction
- BalanceInquiry
- Withdrawal
- Deposit

We apply the guidelines discussed in Section 9.14 and Section 11.8 to code these classes based on how we modeled them in the UML class diagrams of Fig. 11.19 and Fig. 11.20. To develop the bodies of class methods, we refer to the activity diagrams presented in Section 6.11 and the communication and sequence diagrams presented in Section 7.20. Note that our ATM design does not specify all the program logic and may not specify all the attributes and operations required to complete the ATM implementation. This is a normal part of the object-oriented design process. As we implement the system, we complete the program logic and add attributes and behaviors as necessary to construct the ATM system specified by the requirements document in Section 3.10.

We conclude the discussion by presenting a Visual Basic application (ATMCaseStudy in Section J.13) that creates an object of class ATM and starts it by calling its run method. Recall that we are developing a first version of the ATM system that runs on a personal computer and uses the keyboard and monitor to approximate the ATM's keypad and screen. Also, we simulate the actions of the ATM's cash dispenser and deposit slot. We attempt to implement the system, however, so that real hardware versions of these devices could be integrated without significant code changes.

J.2 Class ATM

Class ATM (Fig. J.1) represents the ATM as a whole. Lines 4–10 implement the class's attributes. We determine all but one of these attributes from the UML class diagrams of Fig. 11.19 and Fig. 11.20. Line 4 declares the Boolean attribute userAuthenticated from Fig. 11.21. Line 5 declares an attribute not found in our UML design—an Integer attribute currentAccountNumber that keeps track of the account number of the current authenticated user. We will soon see how the class uses this attribute. Lines 6–10 declare reference-type attributes corresponding to the ATM class's associations modeled in the class diagram of Fig. 11.19. These attributes allow the ATM to access its parts (i.e., its Screen, Keypad, CashDispenser and DepositSlot) and interact with the bank's account information database (i.e., a BankDatabase object).

```vb
 1   ' ATM.vb
 2   ' Represents an automated teller machine.
 3   Public Class ATM
 4      Private userAuthenticated As Boolean ' whether user is authenticated
 5      Private currentAccountNumber As Integer ' user's account number
 6      Private screenHandle As Screen ' ATM's screen
 7      Private keypadHandle As Keypad ' ATM's keypad
 8      Private cashDispenserHandle As CashDispenser ' ATM's cash dispenser
 9      Private depositSlotHandle As DepositSlot ' ATM's deposit slot
10      Private bankDatabaseHandle As BankDatabase ' account database
11
12      ' enumeration constants represent main menu options
13      Private Enum MenuOption
14         BALANCE_INQUIRY = 1
15         WITHDRAWAL
16         DEPOSIT
17         EXIT_ATM
18      End Enum ' MenuOption
19
20      ' parameterless constructor initializes instance variables
21      Public Sub New()
22         userAuthenticated = False ' user is not authenticated to start
23         currentAccountNumber = 0 ' no current account number to start
24         screenHandle = New Screen() ' create screen
```

Fig. J.1 | Class ATM represents the ATM. (Part 1 of 3.)

```vbnet
25          keypadHandle = New Keypad() ' create keypad
26          cashDispenserHandle = New CashDispenser() ' create cash dispenser
27          depositSlotHandle = New DepositSlot() ' create deposit slot
28          bankDatabaseHandle = New BankDatabase() ' create database
29       End Sub ' New
30
31       ' start ATM
32       Public Sub Run()
33          ' welcome and authenticate users; perform transactions
34          While (True) ' infinite loop
35             ' loop while user is not yet authenticated
36             While (Not userAuthenticated)
37                screenHandle.DisplayMessageLine(vbCrLf & "Welcome!")
38                AuthenticateUser() ' authenticate user
39             End While
40
41             PerformTransactions() ' for authenticated user
42             userAuthenticated = False ' reset before next ATM session
43             currentAccountNumber = 0 ' reset before next ATM session
44             screenHandle.DisplayMessageLine(vbCrLf & "Thank you! Goodbye!")
45          End While
46       End Sub ' Run
47
48       ' attempt to authenticate user against database
49       Private Sub AuthenticateUser()
50          screenHandle.DisplayMessage(vbCrLf & _
51             "Please enter your account number: ")
52          Dim accountNumber As Integer = keypadHandle.GetInput()
53          screenHandle.DisplayMessage(vbCrLf & "Enter your PIN: ") ' prompt
54          Dim pin As Integer = keypadHandle.GetInput() ' get PIN
55
56          ' set userAuthenticated to Boolean value returned by database
57          userAuthenticated = _
58             bankDatabaseHandle.AuthenticateUser(accountNumber, pin)
59
60          ' check whether authentication succeeded
61          If userAuthenticated Then
62             currentAccountNumber = accountNumber ' save user's account #
63          Else
64             screenHandle.DisplayMessageLine( _
65                "Invalid account number or PIN. Please try again.")
66          End If
67       End Sub ' AuthenticateUser
68
69       ' display the main menu and perform transactions
70       Private Sub PerformTransactions()
71          Dim currentTransaction As Transaction ' transaction being processed
72          Dim userExited As Boolean = False ' user has not chosen to exit
73
74          ' loop while user has not chosen exit option
75          While (Not userExited)
76             ' show main menu and get user selection
77             Dim mainMenuSelection As Integer = DisplayMainMenu()
```

Fig. J.1 | Class ATM represents the ATM. (Part 2 of 3.)

```vb
78
79              ' decide how to proceed based on user's menu selection
80          Select Case (mainMenuSelection)
81              ' user chooses to perform one of three transaction types
82              Case MenuOption.BALANCE_INQUIRY, MenuOption.WITHDRAWAL, _
83                  MenuOption.DEPOSIT
84                  ' initialize as new object of chosen type
85                  currentTransaction = CreateTransaction(mainMenuSelection)
86                  currentTransaction.Execute() ' execute transaction
87              Case MenuOption.EXIT_ATM ' user chose to terminate session
88                  screenHandle.DisplayMessageLine( _
89                      vbCrLf & "Exiting the system...")
90                  userExited = True ' this ATM session should end
91              Case Else ' user did not enter an integer from 1-4
92                  screenHandle.DisplayMessageLine(vbCrLf & _
93                      "You did not enter a valid selection. Try again.")
94          End Select
95      End While
96  End Sub ' PerformTransactions
97
98  ' display the main menu and return an input selection
99  Private Function DisplayMainMenu() As Integer
100     screenHandle.DisplayMessageLine(vbCrLf & "Main menu:")
101     screenHandle.DisplayMessageLine("1 - View my balance")
102     screenHandle.DisplayMessageLine("2 - Withdraw cash")
103     screenHandle.DisplayMessageLine("3 - Deposit funds")
104     screenHandle.DisplayMessageLine("4 - Exit" & vbCrLf)
105     screenHandle.DisplayMessage("Enter a choice: ")
106     Return keypadHandle.GetInput() ' return user's selection
107 End Function ' DisplayMainMenu
108
109 ' return object of specified Transaction derived class
110 Private Function CreateTransaction(ByVal type As Integer) _
111     As Transaction
112     Dim temp As Transaction = Nothing ' temporary Transaction object
113
114     ' determine which type of Transaction to create
115     Select Case (type)
116         ' create new BalanceInquiry transaction
117         Case MenuOption.BALANCE_INQUIRY
118             temp = New BalanceInquiry( _
119                 currentAccountNumber, screenHandle, bankDatabaseHandle)
120         Case MenuOption.WITHDRAWAL ' create new Withdrawal transaction
121             temp = New Withdrawal(currentAccountNumber, screenHandle, _
122                 bankDatabaseHandle, keypadHandle, cashDispenserHandle)
123         Case MenuOption.DEPOSIT ' create new Deposit transaction
124             temp = New Deposit(currentAccountNumber, screenHandle, _
125                 bankDatabaseHandle, keypadHandle, depositSlotHandle)
126     End Select
127
128     Return temp
129 End Function ' CreateTransaction
130 End Class ' ATM
```

Fig. J.1 | Class ATM represents the ATM. (Part 3 of 3.)

Lines 13–18 declare an enumeration that corresponds to the four options in the ATM's main menu (i.e., balance inquiry, withdrawal, deposit and exit). Lines 21–29 declare class ATM's constructor, which initializes the class's attributes. When an ATM object is first created, no user is authenticated, so line 22 initializes userAuthenticated to False. Line 23 initializes currentAccountNumber to 0 because there is no current user yet. Lines 24–27 instantiate new objects to represent the parts of the ATM. Recall that class ATM has composition relationships with classes Screen, Keypad, CashDispenser and DepositSlot, so class ATM is responsible for their creation. Line 28 creates a new BankDatabase. As you will soon see, the BankDatabase creates two Account objects that can be used to test the ATM. [*Note:* If this were a real ATM system, the ATM class would receive a reference to an existing database object created by the bank. However, in this implementation we are only simulating the bank's database, so class ATM creates the BankDatabase object with which it interacts.]

Implementing the Operation

The class diagram of Fig. 11.20 does not list any operations for class ATM. We now implement one operation (i.e., Public method) in class ATM that allows an external client of the class (i.e., module ATMCaseStudy; Section J.13) to tell the ATM to run. ATM method Run (lines 32–46) uses an infinite loop (lines 34–45) to repeatedly welcome a user, attempt to authenticate the user and, if authentication succeeds, allow the user to perform transactions. After an authenticated user performs the desired transactions and chooses to exit, the ATM resets itself, displays a goodbye message to the user and restarts the process. We use an infinite loop here to simulate the fact that an ATM appears to run continuously until the bank turns it off (an action beyond the user's control). An ATM user has the option to exit the system, but does not have the ability to turn off the ATM completely.

Inside method Run's infinite loop, lines 36–39 cause the ATM to repeatedly welcome and attempt to authenticate the user as long as the user has not been authenticated (i.e., the condition Not userAuthenticated is True). Line 37 invokes method DisplayMessageLine of the ATM's screen to display a welcome message. Like Screen method DisplayMessage designed in the case study, method DisplayMessageLine (declared in lines 10–12 of Fig. J.2) displays a message to the user, but this method also outputs a newline after displaying the message. We add this method during implementation to give class Screen's clients more control over the placement of displayed messages. Line 38 invokes class ATM's Private utility method AuthenticateUser (declared in lines 49–67) to attempt to authenticate the user.

Authenticating the User

We refer to the requirements document to determine the steps necessary to authenticate the user before allowing transactions to occur. Lines 50–51 of method AuthenticateUser invoke method DisplayMessage of the ATM's screen to prompt the user to enter an account number. Line 52 invokes method GetInput of the ATM's keypad to obtain the user's input, then stores the integer value entered by the user in local variable accountNumber. Method AuthenticateUser next prompts the user to enter a PIN (line 53), and stores the PIN input by the user in local variable pin (line 54). Next, lines 57–58 attempt to authenticate the user by passing the accountNumber and pin entered by the user to the bank database's AuthenticateUser method. Class ATM sets its userAuthenticated attribute to the Boolean value returned by this method—userAuthenticated becomes True if authentication succeeds (i.e., accountNumber and pin match those of an existing Account in the bank database) and remains `False` otherwise. If `userAuthenticated` is `True`, line 62 saves the account number entered by the user (i.e., `accountNumber`) in the ATM attribute `current-AccountNumber`. The other methods of class `ATM` use this variable whenever an ATM session requires access to the user's account number. If `userAuthenticated` is `False`, lines 64–65 use the `screenHandle`'s `DisplayMessageLine` method to indicate that an invalid account number and/or PIN was entered, so the user must try again. Note that we set `current-AccountNumber` only after authenticating the user's account number and the associated PIN—if the database could not authenticate the user, `currentAccountNumber` remains 0.

After method `Run` attempts to authenticate the user (line 38), if `userAuthenticated` is still `False` (line 36), the `While` loop body (lines 37–38) executes again. If `userAuthenticated` is now `True`, the loop terminates and control continues with line 41, which calls class `ATM`'s `Private` utility method `PerformTransactions`.

Performing Transactions

Method `PerformTransactions` (lines 70–96) carries out an ATM session for an authenticated user. Line 71 declares local variable `Transaction` to which we assign a `Balance-Inquiry`, `Withdrawal` or `Deposit` object representing the ATM transaction currently being processed. Note that we use a `Transaction` variable here to allow us to take advantage of polymorphism. Also note that we name this variable after the role name included in the class diagram of Fig. 4.19—`currentTransaction`. Line 72 declares another local variable—a `Boolean` called `userExited` that keeps track of whether the user has chosen to exit. This variable controls a `While` loop (lines 75–95) that allows the user to execute an unlimited number of transactions before choosing to exit. Within this loop, line 77 displays the main menu and obtains the user's menu selection by calling `ATM` utility method `DisplayMainMenu` (declared in lines 99–107). This method displays the main menu by invoking methods of the `ATM`'s screen and returns a menu selection obtained from the user through the `ATM`'s keypad. Line 77 stores the user's selection returned by `DisplayMainMenu` in local variable `mainMenuSelection`.

After obtaining a main menu selection, method `PerformTransactions` uses a `Select Case` statement (lines 80–94) to respond to the selection appropriately. If `mainMenu-Selection` is equal to any of the three integer constants representing transaction types (i.e., if the user chose to perform a transaction), line 85 calls utility method `CreateTransaction` (declared in lines 110–129) to return a newly instantiated object of the type that corresponds to the selected transaction. Variable `currentTransaction` is assigned the reference returned by method `CreateTransaction`, then line 86 invokes method `Execute` of this transaction to execute it. We will discuss `Transaction` method `Execute` and the three `Transaction` derived classes shortly. Note that we assign to the `Transaction` variable `currentTransaction` an object of one of the three `Transaction` derived classes so that we can execute transactions polymorphically. For example, if the user chooses to perform a balance inquiry, `mainMenuSelection` equals `MenuOption.BALANCE_INQUIRY`, and `Create-Transaction` returns a `BalanceInquiry` object (line 85). Thus, `currentTransaction` refers to a `BalanceInquiry` and invoking `currentTransaction.Execute()` (line 86) results in `BalanceInquiry`'s version of `Execute` being called.

Creating Transactions

Method `CreateTransaction` (lines 110–129) uses a `Select Case` statement (lines 115–126) to instantiate a new `Transaction` derived class object of the type indicated by the parameter type. Recall that method `PerformTransactions` passes `mainMenuSelection` to method `CreateTransaction` only when `mainMenuSelection` contains a value corresponding to one of the three transaction types. So parameter `type` (line 110) receives one of the values `MenuOption.BALANCE_INQUIRY`, `MenuOption.WITHDRAWAL` or `MenuOption.DEPOSIT`. Each `Case` in the `Select Case` statement instantiates a new object by calling the appropriate `Transaction` derived class constructor. Note that each constructor has a unique parameter list, based on the specific data required to initialize the derived class object. A `BalanceInquiry` (lines 118–119) requires only the account number of the current user and the ATM's `screenHandle` and `bankDatabaseHandle`. In addition to these parameters, a `Withdrawal` (lines 121–122) requires the ATM's `keypadHandle` and `cashDispenserHandle`, and a `Deposit` (lines 124–125) requires the ATM's `keypadHandle` and `depositSlotHandle`. We discuss the transaction classes in more detail in Sections J.9–J.12.

After executing a transaction (line 86 in method `PerformTransactions`), `userExited` remains `False` and the `While` loop in lines 75–95 repeats, returning the user to the main menu. However, if a user does not perform a transaction and instead selects the main menu option to exit, line 90 sets `userExited` to `True` causing the condition in line 75 of the `While` loop (`Not userExited`) to become `False`. This `While` is the final statement of method `PerformTransactions`, so control returns to line 42 of the calling method `Run`. If the user enters an invalid main menu selection (i.e., not an integer in the range 1–4), lines 92–93 display an appropriate error message, `userExited` (as set in line 72) remains `False` and the user returns to the main menu to try again.

When method `PerformTransactions` returns control to method `Run`, the user has chosen to exit the system, so lines 42–43 reset the ATM's attributes `userAuthenticated` and `currentAccountNumber` to `False` and 0, respectively, to prepare for the next ATM user. Line 44 displays a goodbye message to the current user before the ATM welcomes the next user.

J.3 **Class Screen**

Class `Screen` (Fig. J.2) represents the screen of the ATM and encapsulates all aspects of displaying output to the user. Class `Screen` simulates a real ATM's screen with the computer monitor and outputs text messages using standard console output methods `Console.Write` and `Console.WriteLine`. In the design portion of this case study, we endowed class `Screen` with one operation—`DisplayMessage`. For greater flexibility in displaying messages to the `Screen`, we now declare three `Screen` methods—`DisplayMessage`, `DisplayMessageLine` and `DisplayDollarAmount`.

```vb
1  ' Screen.vb
2  ' Represents the screen of the ATM
3  Public Class Screen
4     ' displays a message without a terminating carriage return
5     Public Sub DisplayMessage(ByVal message As String)
6        Console.Write(message)
7     End Sub ' DisplayMessage
8
```

Fig. J.2 | Class `Screen` represents the screen of the ATM. (Part 1 of 2.)

```
 9      ' display a message with a terminating carriage return
10      Public Sub DisplayMessageLine(ByVal message As String)
11         Console.WriteLine(message)
12      End Sub ' DisplayMessageLine
13
14      ' display a dollar amount
15      Public Sub DisplayDollarAmount(ByVal amount As Decimal)
16         Console.Write("{0:C}", amount)
17      End Sub ' DisplayDollarAmount
18   End Class ' Screen
```

Fig. J.2 | Class Screen represents the screen of the ATM. (Part 2 of 2.)

Method DisplayMessage (lines 5–7) takes a String as an argument and prints it to the screen using Console.Write. The cursor stays on the same line, making this method appropriate for displaying prompts to the user. Method DisplayMessageLine (lines 10–12) does the same using Console.WriteLine, which outputs a newline to move the cursor to the next line. Finally, method DisplayDollarAmount (lines 15–17) outputs a properly formatted dollar amount (e.g., $1,234.56). Line 16 uses method Console.Write to output a Decimal value formatted as currency with two decimal places and commas to increase the readability of large dollar amounts.

J.4 Class Keypad

Class Keypad (Fig. J.3) represents the keypad of the ATM and is responsible for receiving all user input. Recall that we are simulating this hardware, so we use the computer's keyboard to approximate the keypad. We use method Console.ReadLine to obtain keyboard input from the user. A computer keyboard contains many keys not found on the ATM's keypad. We assume that the user presses only the keys on the computer keyboard that also appear on the keypad—the keys numbered 0–9 and the *Enter* key.

Method GetInput (lines 5–7) invokes Convert method ToInt32 to convert the input returned by Console.ReadLine (line 6) to an Integer value. [*Note:* Method ToInt32 can throw a FormatException if the user enters non-integer input. Because the real ATM's keypad permits only integer input, we simply assume that no exceptions will occur. See Chapter 12, Exception Handling, for information on catching and processing exceptions.] Recall that ReadLine obtains all the input used by the ATM. Class Keypad's GetInput method simply returns the integer input by the user. If a client of class Keypad requires

```
1   ' Keypad.vb
2   ' Represents the keypad of the ATM.
3   Public Class Keypad
4      ' return an integer value entered by user
5      Public Function GetInput() As Integer
6         Return Convert.ToInt32(Console.ReadLine())
7      End Function ' GetInput
8   End Class ' Keypad
```

Fig. J.3 | Class Keypad represents the ATM's keypad.

input that satisfies some particular criteria (i.e., a number corresponding to a valid menu option), the client must perform the appropriate error checking.

J.5 Class CashDispenser

Class CashDispenser (Fig. J.4) represents the cash dispenser of the ATM. Line 5 declares constant INITIAL_COUNT, which indicates the initial count of bills in the cash dispenser when the ATM starts (i.e., 500). Line 6 implements attribute billCount (modeled in Fig. 11.20), which keeps track of the number of bills remaining in the CashDispenser at any time. The constructor (lines 9–11) sets billCount to the initial count. [*Note:* We assume that the process of adding more bills to the CashDispenser and updating the billCount occur outside the ATM system.] Class CashDispenser has two Public methods—DispenseCash (lines 14–18) and IsSufficientCashAvailable (lines 21–31). The class trusts that a client (i.e., Withdrawal) calls method DispenseCash only after establishing that sufficient cash is available by calling method IsSufficientCashAvailable. Thus, DispenseCash simply simulates dispensing the requested amount without checking whether sufficient cash is available.

```vbnet
1    ' CashDispenser.vb
2    ' Represents the cash dispenser of the ATM
3    Public Class CashDispenser
4       ' the default initial number of bills in the case dispenser
5       Private Const INITIAL_COUNT As Integer = 500
6       Private billCount As Integer ' number of $20 bills remaining
7
8       ' parameterless constructor initializes billCount to INITIAL_COUNT
9       Public Sub New()
10          billCount = INITIAL_COUNT ' set billCount to INITIAL_COUNT
11       End Sub ' New
12
13       ' simulates dispensing of specified amount of cash
14       Public Sub DispenseCash(ByVal amount As Decimal)
15          ' number of $20 bills required
16          Dim billsRequired As Integer = (Convert.ToInt32(amount) \ 20)
17          billCount -= billsRequired
18       End Sub ' DispenseCash
19
20       ' indicates whether cash dispenser can dispense desired amount
21       Public Function IsSufficientCashAvailable(ByVal amount As Decimal) _
22          As Boolean
23          ' number of $20 bills required
24          Dim billsRequired As Integer = (Convert.ToInt32(amount) \ 20)
25
26          If (billCount >= billsRequired) Then
27             Return True ' enough bills available
28          Else
29             Return False ' not enough bills available
30          End If
31       End Function ' IsSufficientCashAvailable
32    End Class ' CashDispenser
```

Fig. J.4 | Class CashDispenser represents the ATM's cash dispenser.

Method IsSufficientCashAvailable (lines 21–31) has a parameter amount that specifies the amount of cash in question. Line 24 calculates the number of $20 bills required to dispense the specified amount. The ATM allows the user to choose only withdrawal amounts that are multiples of $20, so we convert amount to an integer value and divide it by 20 to obtain the number of billsRequired. Lines 26–30 return True if the CashDispenser's billCount is greater than or equal to billsRequired (i.e., enough bills are available) and False otherwise (i.e., not enough bills). For example, if a user wishes to withdraw $80 (i.e., billsRequired is 4), but only three bills remain (i.e., billCount is 3), the method returns False.

Method DispenseCash (lines 14–18) simulates cash dispensing. If our system were hooked up to a real hardware cash dispenser, this method would interact with the hardware device to physically dispense cash. Our simulated version of the method simply decreases the billCount of bills remaining by the number required to dispense the specified amount (line 17). Note that it is the responsibility of the client of the class (i.e., Withdrawal) to inform the user that cash has been dispensed—CashDispenser does not interact directly with Screen.

J.6 Class DepositSlot

Class DepositSlot (Fig. J.5) represents the deposit slot of the ATM. Like the version of class CashDispenser presented here, this version of class DepositSlot merely simulates the functionality of a real hardware deposit slot. DepositSlot has no attributes and only one method—IsDepositEnvelopeReceived (lines 6–8)—that indicates whether a deposit envelope was received.

Recall from the requirements document that the ATM allows the user up to two minutes to insert an envelope. The current version of method IsDepositEnvelopeReceived simply returns True immediately (line 7), because this is only a software simulation, and we assume that the user inserts an envelope within the required time frame. If an actual hardware deposit slot were connected to our system, method IsDepositEnvelopeReceived would be implemented to wait for a maximum of two minutes to receive a signal from the hardware deposit slot indicating that the user has indeed inserted a deposit envelope. If IsDepositEnvelopeReceived were to receive such a signal within two minutes, the method would return True. If two minutes were to elapse and the method still had not received a signal, then the method would return False.

```vb
1    ' DepositSlot.vb
2    ' Represents the deposit slot of the ATM
3    Public Class DepositSlot
4       ' indicates whether envelope was received (always returns true,
5       ' because this is only a software simulation of a real deposit slot)
6       Public Function IsDepositEnvelopeReceived() As Boolean
7          Return True ' deposit envelope was received
8       End Function ' IsDepositEnvelopeReceived
9    End Class ' DepositSlot
```

Fig. J.5 | Class DepositSlot represents the ATM's deposit slot.

J.7 Class Account

Class Account (Fig. J.6) represents a bank account. Each Account has four attributes (modeled in Fig. 11.20)—accountNumber, pin, availableBalance and totalBalance. Lines 4–7 implement these attributes as Private instance variables. Note that when we provide a property to access an instance variable, we create the instance variable name by appending Value to the end of the attribute name that was listed in the model. We provide a property with the same name as the attribute name (but starting with a capital letter) to access the instance variable. For example, property AccountNumber corresponds to the accountNumber attribute modeled in Fig. 11.20. Since clients of this class do not need to modify the accountNumberValue instance variable, AccountNumber is a ReadOnly property (i.e., it provides only a Get accessory).

```vb
1   ' Account.vb
2   ' Represents a bank account.
3   Public Class Account
4      Private accountNumberValue As Integer ' account number
5      Private pin As Integer ' PIN for authentication
6      Private availableBalanceValue As Decimal ' available withdrawal amount
7      Private totalBalanceValue As Decimal ' funds available+pending deposit
8
9      ' constructor initializes attributes
10     Public Sub New(ByVal theAccountNumber As Integer, _
11        ByVal thePIN As Integer, ByVal theAvailableBalance As Decimal, _
12        ByVal theTotalBalance As Decimal)
13        accountNumberValue = theAccountNumber
14        pin = thePIN
15        availableBalanceValue = theAvailableBalance
16        totalBalanceValue = theTotalBalance
17     End Sub ' New
18
19     ' property AccountNumber
20     Public ReadOnly Property AccountNumber() As Integer
21        Get
22           Return accountNumberValue
23        End Get
24     End Property ' AccountNumber
25
26     ' property AvailableBalance
27     Public ReadOnly Property AvailableBalance() As Decimal
28        Get
29           Return availableBalanceValue
30        End Get
31     End Property ' AvailableBalance
32
33     ' property TotalBalance
34     Public ReadOnly Property TotalBalance() As Decimal
35        Get
36           Return totalBalanceValue
37        End Get
38     End Property ' TotalBalance
```

Fig. J.6 | Class Account represents a bank account. (Part 1 of 2.)

```
39
40        ' determines whether a user-specified PIN matches PIN in Account
41        Public Function ValidatePIN(ByVal userPIN As Integer) As Boolean
42           If userPIN = pin Then
43              Return True
44           Else
45              Return False
46           End If
47        End Function ' ValidatePIN
48
49        ' credits the account (funds have not yet cleared)
50        Public Sub Credit(ByVal amount As Decimal)
51           totalBalanceValue += amount ' add to total balance
52        End Sub ' Credit
53
54        ' debits the account
55        Public Sub Debit(ByVal amount As Decimal)
56           availableBalanceValue -= amount ' subtract from available balance
57           totalBalanceValue -= amount ' subtract from total balance
58        End Sub ' Debit
59     End Class ' Account
```

Fig. J.6 | Class Account represents a bank account. (Part 2 of 2.)

Class Account has a constructor (lines 10–17) that takes an account number, the PIN established for the account, the initial available balance and the initial total balance as arguments. Lines 13–16 assign these values to the class's attributes (i.e., instance variables). Note that Account objects would normally be created externally to the ATM system. However, in this simulation, the Account objects are created in the BankDatabase class (Fig. J.7).

Public ReadOnly *Properties of Class* Account
ReadOnly property AccountNumber (lines 20–24) provides access to an Account's accountNumberValue. We include this property in our implementation so that a client of the class (e.g., BankDatabase) can identify a particular Account. For example, BankDatabase contains many Account objects, and it can access this property on each of its Account objects to locate the one with a specific account number.

ReadOnly properties AvailableBalance (lines 27–31) and TotalBalance (lines 34–38) allow clients to retrieve the values of Private Decimal instance variables available-BalanceValue and totalBalanceValue, respectively. Property AvailableBalance represents the amount of funds available for withdrawal. Property TotalBalance represents the amount of funds available, plus the amount of deposited funds still pending confirmation (of cash in deposit envelopes) or clearance (of checks in deposit envelopes).

Public *Methods of Class* Account
Method ValidatePIN (lines 41–47) determines whether a user-specified PIN (i.e., parameter userPIN) matches the PIN associated with the account (i.e., attribute pin). Recall that we modeled this method's parameter userPIN in the UML class diagram of Fig. 7.26. If the two PINs match, the method returns True (line 43); otherwise, it returns False (line 45).

Method `Credit` (lines 50–52) adds an amount of money (i.e., parameter `amount`) to an `Account` as part of a deposit transaction. Note that this method adds the `amount` only to instance variable `totalBalanceValue` (line 45). The money credited to an account during a deposit does not become available immediately, so we modify only the total balance. We assume that the bank updates the available balance appropriately at a later time when the amount of cash in the deposit envelope has been verified and when the checks in the deposit envelope have cleared. Our implementation of class `Account` includes only methods required for carrying out ATM transactions. Therefore, we omit the methods that some other bank system would invoke to add to instance variable `availableBalanceValue` (to confirm a deposit) or subtract from attribute `totalBalanceValue` (to reject a deposit).

Method `Debit` (lines 55–58) subtracts an amount of money (i.e., parameter `amount`) from an `Account` as part of a withdrawal transaction. This method subtracts the `amount` from both instance variable `availableBalanceValue` (line 56) and instance variable `totalBalanceValue` (line 57), because a withdrawal affects both measures of an account balance.

J.8 Class BankDatabase

Class `BankDatabase` (Fig. J.7) models the bank's database with which the ATM interacts to access and modify a user's account information. We determine one reference-type attribute for class `BankDatabase` based on its composition relationship with class `Account`. Recall from Fig. 11.19 that a `BankDatabase` is composed of zero or more objects of class `Account`. Line 4 implements attribute `accounts`—an array that will store `Account` objects—to implement this composition relationship. Class `BankDatabase` has a parameterless constructor (lines 7–13) that initializes `accounts` with new `Account` objects. We create two new `Account` objects with test data and place them in the array (lines 11–12). Note that the `Account` constructor has four parameters—the account number, the PIN assigned to the account, the initial available balance and the initial total balance.

Recall that class `BankDatabase` serves as an intermediary between class `ATM` and the actual `Account` objects that contain users' account information. Thus, methods of class `BankDatabase` invoke the corresponding methods and properties of the `Account` object belonging to the current ATM user.

Private *Utility Method* GetAccount

We include `Private` utility method `GetAccount` (lines 16–25) to allow the `BankDatabase` to obtain a reference to a particular `Account` within the `accounts` `ArrayList`. To locate the user's `Account`, the `BankDatabase` compares the value returned by property `AccountNumber` for each element of `accounts` to a specified account number until it finds a match. Lines 18–22 traverse the `accounts` `ArrayList`. If `currentAccount`'s account number equals the value of parameter `accountNumber`, the method returns `currentAccount`. If no account has the given account number, then line 24 returns `Nothing`.

Public *Methods*

Method `AuthenticateUser` (lines 29–40) proves or disproves the identity of an ATM user. This method takes a user-specified account number and a user-specified PIN as arguments and indicates whether they match the account number and PIN of an `Account` in

```vb
 1  ' BankDatabase.vb
 2  ' Represents the bank account information database
 3  Public Class BankDatabase
 4     Private accounts As Account() ' array of the bank's Accounts
 5
 6     ' parameterless BankDatabase constructor initializes accounts
 7     Public Sub New()
 8        ' create two Account objects for testing and
 9        ' place them in the accounts array
10        accounts = New Account(0 To 1) {} ' create accounts array
11        accounts(0) = New Account(12345, 54321, 1000, 1200)
12        accounts(1) = New Account(98765, 56789, 200, 200)
13     End Sub ' New
14
15     ' retrieve Account object containing specified account number
16     Private Function GetAccount(ByVal accountNumber As Integer) As Account
17        ' loop through accounts searching for matching account number
18        For Each currentAccount As Account In accounts
19           If currentAccount.AccountNumber = accountNumber Then
20              Return currentAccount
21           End If
22        Next
23
24        Return Nothing
25     End Function ' GetAccount
26
27     ' determine whether user-specified account number and PIN match
28     ' those of an account in the database
29     Public Function AuthenticateUser(ByVal userAccountNumber As Integer, _
30        ByVal userPIN As Integer) As Boolean
31        ' attempt to retrieve the account with the account number
32        Dim userAccount As Account = GetAccount(userAccountNumber)
33
34        ' if account exists, return result of Account function ValidatePIN
35        If (userAccount IsNot Nothing) Then
36           Return userAccount.ValidatePIN(userPIN)
37        Else
38           Return False ' account number not found, so return false
39        End If
40     End Function ' AuthenticateUser
41
42     ' return available balance of Account with specified account number
43     Public Function GetAvailableBalance( _
44        ByVal userAccountNumber As Integer) As Decimal
45        Dim userAccount As Account = GetAccount(userAccountNumber)
46        Return userAccount.AvailableBalance
47     End Function ' GetAvailableBalance
48
49     ' return total balance of Account with specified account number
50     Public Function GetTotalBalance( _
51        ByVal userAccountNumber As Integer) As Decimal
52        Dim userAccount As Account = GetAccount(userAccountNumber)
```

Fig. J.7 | Class BankDatabase represents the bank's account information database. (Part 1 of 2.)

```
53          Return userAccount.TotalBalance
54       End Function ' GetTotalBalance
55
56       ' credit the Account with specified account number
57       Public Sub Credit(ByVal userAccountNumber As Integer, _
58          ByVal amount As Decimal)
59          Dim userAccount As Account = GetAccount(userAccountNumber)
60          userAccount.Credit(amount)
61       End Sub ' Credit
62
63       ' debit the Account with specified account number
64       Public Sub Debit(ByVal userAccountNumber As Integer, _
65          ByVal amount As Decimal)
66          Dim userAccount As Account = GetAccount(userAccountNumber)
67          userAccount.Debit(amount)
68       End Sub ' Debit
69    End Class ' BankDatabase
```

Fig. J.7 | Class BankDatabase represents the bank's account information database. (Part 2 of 2.)

the database. Line 32 calls method GetAccount, which returns either an Account with userAccountNumber as its account number or Nothing to indicate that userAccountNumber is invalid. If GetAccount returns an Account object, line 36 returns the Boolean value returned by that object's ValidatePIN method. Note that BankDatabase's AuthenticateUser method does not perform the PIN comparison itself—rather, it forwards userPIN to the Account object's ValidatePIN method to do so. The value returned by Account method ValidatePIN (line 36) indicates whether the user-specified PIN matches the PIN of the user's Account, so method AuthenticateUser simply returns this value (line 36) to the client of the class (i.e., ATM).

BankDatabase trusts the ATM to invoke method AuthenticateUser and receive a return value of True before allowing the user to perform transactions. BankDatabase also trusts that each Transaction object created by the ATM contains the valid account number of the current authenticated user and that this is the account number passed to the remaining BankDatabase methods as argument userAccountNumber. Methods GetAvailableBalance (lines 43–47), GetTotalBalance (lines 50–54), Credit (lines 57–61) and Debit (lines 64–68) therefore simply retrieve the user's Account object with utility method GetAccount, then invoke the appropriate Account method on that object. We know that the calls to GetAccount within these methods will never return Nothing, because userAccountNumber must refer to an existing Account. Note that GetAvailableBalance and GetTotalBalance return the values returned by the corresponding Account properties. Also note that methods Credit and Debit simply redirect parameter amount to the Account methods they invoke.

J.9 Class Transaction

Class Transaction (Fig. J.8) is an abstract base class that represents the notion of an ATM transaction. It contains the common features of derived classes BalanceInquiry, Withdrawal and Deposit. This class expands upon the "skeleton" code first developed in Section 11.8. Line 3 declares this class to be MustInherit (the Visual Basic equivalent of

```vb
1    ' Transaction.vb
2    ' MustInherit base class Transaction represents an ATM transaction.
3    Public MustInherit Class Transaction
4       Private accountNumberValue As Integer ' indicates account involved
5       Private screenHandle As Screen ' ATM's screen
6       Private bankDatabaseHandle As BankDatabase ' account info database
7
8       ' constructor invoked by derived classes using MyBase.New
9       Public Sub New(ByVal userAccount As Integer, _
10         ByVal userScreen As Screen, ByVal database As BankDatabase)
11         accountNumberValue = userAccount
12         screenHandle = userScreen
13         bankDatabaseHandle = database
14      End Sub ' New
15
16      ' property AccountNumber
17      Public ReadOnly Property AccountNumber() As Integer
18         Get
19            Return accountNumberValue
20         End Get
21      End Property ' AccountNumber
22
23      ' property ScreenReference
24      Public ReadOnly Property ScreenReference() As Screen
25         Get
26            Return screenHandle
27         End Get
28      End Property ' ScreenReference
29
30      ' property BankDatabaseReference
31      Public ReadOnly Property BankDatabaseReference() As BankDatabase
32         Get
33            Return bankDatabaseHandle
34         End Get
35      End Property ' BankDatabaseReference
36
37      ' perform the transaction (overridden by each derived class)
38      Public MustOverride Sub Execute()
39   End Class ' Transaction
```

Fig. J.8 | MustInherit base class Transaction represents an ATM transaction.

an abstract class). Lines 4–6 declare the class's Private instance variables. Recall from the class diagram of Fig. 11.20 that class Transaction contains an property AccountNumber that indicates the account involved in the Transaction. Line 4 implements the instance variable accountNumberValue to maintain the AccountNumber property's data. We derive attributes screen (implemented as instance variable screenHandle in line 7) and bank-Database (implemented as instance variable bankDatabaseHandle in line 8) from class Transaction's associations modeled in Fig. 11.19. All transactions require access to the ATM's screen and the bank's database.

Class Transaction has a constructor (lines 9–14) that takes the current user's account number and references to the ATM's screen and the bank's database as arguments. Because

Transaction is a MustInherit class (line 3), this constructor will never be called directly to instantiate Transaction objects. Instead, this constructor will be invoked by the constructors of the Transaction derived classes via MyBase.New.

Class Transaction has three Public ReadOnly properties—AccountNumber (lines 17–21), ScreenReference (lines 24–28) and BankDatabaseReference (lines 31–35). Derived classes of Transaction inherit these properties and use them to gain access to class Transaction's Private instance variables. Note that we use the word "Reference" in the names of the ScreenReference and BankDatabaseReference properties for clarity—we wanted to avoid property names that are the same as the class names Screen and BankDatabase, which can be confusing.

Class Transaction also declares a MustOverride method Execute (line 38). It does not make sense to provide an implementation for this method in class Transaction, because a generic transaction cannot be executed. Thus, we declare this method to be MustOverride, forcing each Transaction derived class to provide its own concrete implementation that executes the particular type of transaction.

J.10 Class BalanceInquiry

Class BalanceInquiry (Fig. J.9) inherits from Transaction (line 4) and represents an ATM balance inquiry transaction. BalanceInquiry does not have any attributes of its own, but it inherits Transaction attributes accountNumber, screen and bankDatabase, which are accessible through Transaction's Public ReadOnly properties. The BalanceInquiry constructor (lines 7–10) takes arguments corresponding to these attributes and simply forwards them to Transaction's constructor using MyBase.New (line 9).

```vb
1   ' BalanceInquiry.vb
2   ' Represents a balance inquiry ATM transaction
3   Public Class BalanceInquiry
4      Inherits Transaction
5
6      ' BalanceInquiry constructor initializes base class variables
7      Public Sub New(ByVal userAccountNumber As Integer, _
8         ByVal atmScreen As Screen, ByVal atmBankDatabase As BankDatabase)
9         MyBase.New(userAccountNumber, atmScreen, atmBankDatabase)
10     End Sub ' New
11
12     ' performs transaction; overrides Transaction's MustOverride method
13     Public Overrides Sub Execute()
14        ' get the available balance for the current user's Account
15        Dim availableBalance As Decimal = _
16           BankDatabaseReference.GetAvailableBalance(AccountNumber)
17
18        ' get the total balance for the current user's Account
19        Dim totalBalance As Decimal = _
20           BankDatabaseReference.GetTotalBalance(AccountNumber)
21
22        ' display the balance information on the screen
23        ScreenReference.DisplayMessageLine(vbCrLf & "Balance Information:")
```

Fig. J.9 | Class BalanceInquiry represents a balance inquiry ATM transaction. (Part 1 of 2.)

```
24          ScreenReference.DisplayMessage(" - Available balance: ")
25          ScreenReference.DisplayDollarAmount(availableBalance)
26          ScreenReference.DisplayMessage(vbCrLf & " - Total balance: ")
27          ScreenReference.DisplayDollarAmount(totalBalance)
28          ScreenReference.DisplayMessageLine("")
29      End Sub ' Execute
30   End Class ' BalanceInquiry
```

Fig. J.9 | Class `BalanceInquiry` represents a balance inquiry ATM transaction. (Part 2 of 2.)

Class `BalanceInquiry` overrides `Transaction`'s `MustOverride` method `Execute` to provide a concrete implementation (lines 13–29) that performs the steps involved in a balance inquiry. Lines 15–16 obtain the specified `Account`'s available balance by invoking the inherited property `BankDatabaseReference`'s `GetAvailableBalance` method. Note that line 16 uses the inherited property `AccountNumber` is used to get the account number of the current user. Lines 19–24 retrieve the specified `Account`'s total balance. Lines 23–28 display the balance information on the ATM's screen using the inherited property `ScreenReference`. Recall that `DisplayDollarAmount` takes a `Decimal` argument and outputs it to the screen formatted as a dollar amount. For example, if a user's available balance is `1000.5`, line 25 outputs `$1,000.50`. Note that line 28 inserts a blank line of output to separate the balance information from subsequent output (i.e., the main menu repeated by class `ATM` after executing the `BalanceInquiry`).

J.11 Class `Withdrawal`

Class `Withdrawal` (Fig. J.10) extends `Transaction` and represents an ATM withdrawal transaction. This class expands upon the "skeleton" code for this class developed in Fig. 11.22. Recall from the class diagram of Fig. 11.19 that class `Withdrawal` has one attribute, `amount`, which line 6 implements as a `Decimal` instance variable. Fig. 11.19 models associations between class `Withdrawal` and classes `Keypad` and `CashDispenser`, for which lines 7–8 implement reference attributes `keypadHandle` and `dispenserHandle`, respectively. Line 11 declares a constant corresponding to the cancel menu option. We will soon discuss how the class uses this constant.

Class `Withdrawal`'s constructor (lines 14–23) has five parameters. It uses `MyBase.New` to pass parameters `userAccountNumber`, `atmScreen` and `atmBankDatabase` to base class `Transaction`'s constructor to set the attributes that `Withdrawal` inherits from `Transaction`. The constructor also takes references `atmKeypad` and `atmCashDispenser` as parameters and assigns them to variables `keypadHandle` and `dispenserHandle`.

Overriding *MustOverride* Method *Execute*
Class `Withdrawal` overrides `Transaction`'s `MustOverride` method `Execute` with a concrete implementation (lines 26–74) that performs the steps involved in a withdrawal. Line 27 declares and initializes a local `Boolean` variable `cashDispensed`. This variable indicates whether cash has been dispensed (i.e., whether the transaction has completed successfully) and is initially `False`. Line 30 declares and initializes to `False` a `Boolean` variable `transactionCanceled` to indicate that the transaction has not yet been canceled by the user.

```vb
 I    ' Withdrawal.vb
 2    ' Class Withdrawal represents an ATM withdrawal transaction.
 3    Public Class Withdrawal
 4       Inherits Transaction
 5
 6       Private amount As Decimal ' amount to withdraw
 7       Private keypadHandle As Keypad ' reference to Keypad
 8       Private dispenserHandle As CashDispenser ' reference to cash dispenser
 9
10       ' constant that corresponds to menu option to cancel
11       Private Const CANCELED As Integer = 6
12
13       ' Withdrawal constructor
14       Public Sub New(ByVal userAccountNumber As Integer, _
15          ByVal atmScreen As Screen, ByVal atmBankDatabase As BankDatabase, _
16          ByVal atmKeypad As Keypad, ByVal atmCashDispenser As CashDispenser)
17          ' initialize base class variables
18          MyBase.New(userAccountNumber, atmScreen, atmBankDatabase)
19
20          ' initialize references to keypad and cash dispenser
21          keypadHandle = atmKeypad
22          dispenserHandle = atmCashDispenser
23       End Sub ' New
24
25       ' perform transaction
26       Public Overrides Sub Execute()
27          Dim cashDispensed As Boolean = False ' cash was not dispensed yet
28
29          ' transaction was not canceled yet
30          Dim transactionCanceled As Boolean = False
31
32          ' loop until cash is dispensed or the user cancels
33          Do
34             ' obtain the chosen withdrawal amount from the user
35             Dim selection As Integer = DisplayMenuOfAmounts()
36
37             ' check whether user chose a withdrawal amount or canceled
38             If (selection <> CANCELED) Then
39                amount = selection ' set amount to the selected dollar amount
40
41                ' get available balance of account involved
42                Dim availableBalance As Decimal = _
43                   BankDatabaseReference.GetAvailableBalance(AccountNumber)
44
45                ' check whether the user has enough money in the account
46                If (amount <= availableBalance) Then
47                   ' check whether the cash dispenser has enough money
48                   If (dispenserHandle.IsSufficientCashAvailable(amount)) Then
49                      ' update the account involved to reflect withdrawal
50                      BankDatabaseReference.Debit(AccountNumber, amount)
51
52                      dispenserHandle.DispenseCash(amount) ' dispense cash
53                      cashDispensed = True ' cash was dispensed
```

Fig. J.10 | Class Withdrawal represents an ATM withdrawal transaction. (Part 1 of 3.)

```
54
55                        ' instruct user to take cash
56                    ScreenReference.DisplayMessageLine(vbCrLf & _
57                        "Please take your cash from the cash dispenser.")
58            Else ' cash dispenser does not have enough cash
59                    ScreenReference.DisplayMessageLine(vbCrLf & _
60                        "Insufficient cash available in the ATM." & _
61                        vbCrLf & vbCrLf & "Please choose a smaller amount.")
62                End If
63            Else ' not enough money available in user's account
64                ScreenReference.DisplayMessageLine(vbCrLf & _
65                    "Insufficient cash available in your account." & _
66                    vbCrLf & vbCrLf & "Please choose a smaller amount.")
67            End If
68        Else
69            ScreenReference.DisplayMessageLine( _
70                vbCrLf & "Canceling transaction...")
71            transactionCanceled = True ' user canceled the transaction
72        End If
73      Loop While ((Not cashDispensed) And (Not transactionCanceled))
74    End Sub ' Execute
75
76    ' display a menu of withdrawal amounts and the option to cancel;
77    ' return the chosen amount or 0 if the user chooses to cancel
78    Private Function DisplayMenuOfAmounts() As Integer
79        Dim userChoice As Integer = 0 ' variable to store return value
80
81        ' array of amounts to correspond to menu numbers
82        Dim amounts As Integer() = New Integer() { _
83            0, 20, 40, 60, 100, 200}
84
85        ' loop while no valid choice has been made
86        While (userChoice = 0)
87            ' display the menu
88            ScreenReference.DisplayMessageLine( _
89                vbCrLf & "Withdrawal options:")
90            ScreenReference.DisplayMessageLine("1 - $20")
91            ScreenReference.DisplayMessageLine("2 - $40")
92            ScreenReference.DisplayMessageLine("3 - $60")
93            ScreenReference.DisplayMessageLine("4 - $100")
94            ScreenReference.DisplayMessageLine("5 - $200")
95            ScreenReference.DisplayMessageLine("6 - Cancel transaction")
96            ScreenReference.DisplayMessage( _
97                vbCrLf & "Choose a withdrawal option (1-6): ")
98
99            ' get user input through keypad
100           Dim input As Integer = keypadHandle.GetInput()
101
102           ' determine how to proceed based on the input value
103           Select Case (input)
104               ' if the user chose a withdrawal amount (i.e., option
105               ' 1, 2, 3, 4, or 5), return the corresponding amount
106               ' from the amounts array
```

Fig. J.10 | Class Withdrawal represents an ATM withdrawal transaction. (Part 2 of 3.)

```
107                    Case 1 To 5
108                        userChoice = amounts(input) ' save user's choice
109                    Case CANCELED ' the user chose to cancel
110                        userChoice = CANCELED ' save user's choice
111                    Case Else
112                        ScreenReference.DisplayMessageLine( _
113                            vbCrLf & "Invalid selection. Try again.")
114                End Select
115            End While
116
117            Return userChoice
118        End Function ' DisplayMenuOfAmounts
119    End Class ' Withdrawal
```

Fig. J.10 | Class Withdrawal represents an ATM withdrawal transaction. (Part 3 of 3.)

Lines 33–73 contain a Do...Loop While statement that executes its body until cash is dispensed (i.e., until cashDispensed becomes True) or until the user chooses to cancel (i.e., until transactionCanceled becomes True). We use this loop to continuously return the user to the start of the transaction if an error occurs (i.e., the requested withdrawal amount is greater than the user's available balance or greater than the amount of cash in the cash dispenser). Line 35 displays a menu of withdrawal amounts and obtains a user selection by calling Private utility method DisplayMenuOfAmounts (declared in lines 78–118). This method displays the menu of amounts and returns either an Integer withdrawal amount or an Integer constant CANCELED to indicate that the user has chosen to cancel the transaction.

Displaying Options With Private Utility Method DisplayMenuOfAmounts
Method DisplayMenuOfAmounts (lines 81–121) first declares local variable userChoice (initially 0) to store the value that the method will return (line 82). Lines 82–83 declare an integer array of withdrawal amounts that correspond to the amounts displayed in the withdrawal menu. We ignore the first element in the array (index 0) because the menu has no option 0. The While statement at lines 86–115 repeats until userChoice takes on a value other than 0. We will see shortly that this occurs when the user makes a valid selection from the menu. Lines 88–97 display the withdrawal menu on the screen and prompt the user to enter a choice. Line 100 obtains integer input through the keypad. The Select Case statement at lines 103–114 determines how to proceed based on the user's input. If the user selects a number between 1 and 5, line 108 sets userChoice to the value of the element in the amounts array at index input. For example, if the user enters 3 to withdraw $60, line 108 sets userChoice to the value of amounts(3) (i.e., 60). Variable userChoice no longer equals 0, so the While at lines 86–115 terminates and line 117 returns user-Choice. If the user selects the cancel menu option, line 110 executes, setting userChoice to CANCELED and causing the method to return this value. If the user does not enter a valid menu selection, lines 112–113 display an error message and the user is returned to the withdrawal menu.

The If statement at line 38 in method Execute determines whether the user has selected a withdrawal amount or chosen to cancel. If the user cancels, lines 69–70 display an appropriate message to the user before returning control to the calling method (i.e., ATM method PerformTransactions). If the user has chosen a withdrawal amount, lines 39 assigns local variable selection to instance variable amount. Lines 42–43 retrieve the available balance of the current user's Account and store it in a local Decimal variable availableBalance. Next, the If statement at line 46 determines whether the selected amount is less than or equal to the user's available balance. If it is not, lines 64–66 display an error message. Control then continues to the end of the Do...Loop While, and the loop repeats because both cashDispensed and transactionCanceled are still False. If the user's balance is high enough, the If statement at line 48 determines whether the cash dispenser has enough money to satisfy the withdrawal request by invoking the cash dispenser's IsSufficientCashAvailable method. If this method returns False, lines 59–61 display an error message and the Do...Loop While repeats. If sufficient cash is available, then the requirements for the withdrawal are satisfied, and line 50 debits the user's account in the database by amount. Lines 52–53 then instruct the cash dispenser to dispense the cash to the user and set cashDispensed to True. Finally, lines 56–57 display a message to the user to take the dispensed cash. Because cashDispensed is now True, control continues after the Do...Loop While. No additional statements appear below the loop, so the method returns control to class ATM.

J.12 Class Deposit

Class Deposit (Fig. J.11) inherits from Transaction and represents an ATM deposit transaction. Recall from the class diagram of Fig. 11.20 that class Deposit has one attribute, amount, which line 6 implements as a Decimal instance variable. Lines 7–8 create reference attributes keypadHandle and depositSlotHandle that implement the associations between class Deposit and classes Keypad and DepositSlot modeled in Fig. 11.19. Line 11 declares a constant CANCELED that corresponds to the value a user enters to cancel. We will soon discuss how the class uses this constant.

```vb
 1   ' Deposit.vb
 2   ' Represents a deposit ATM transaction.
 3   Public Class Deposit
 4      Inherits Transaction
 5
 6      Private amount As Decimal ' amount to deposit
 7      Private keypadHandle As Keypad ' reference to Keypad
 8      Private depositSlotHandle As DepositSlot ' reference to deposit slot
 9
10      ' constant representing cancel option
11      Private Const CANCELED As Integer = 0
12
13      ' Deposit constructor initializes class's instance variables
14      Public Sub New(ByVal userAccountNumber As Integer, _
15         ByVal atmScreen As Screen, ByVal atmBankDatabase As BankDatabase, _
16         ByVal atmKeypad As Keypad, ByVal atmDepositSlot As DepositSlot)
17         ' initialize base class variables
18         MyBase.New(userAccountNumber, atmScreen, atmBankDatabase)
19
```

Fig. J.11 | Class Deposit represents an ATM deposit transaction. (Part 1 of 3.)

```vbnet
20          ' initialize references to keypad and deposit slot
21          keypadHandle = atmKeypad
22          depositSlotHandle = atmDepositSlot
23       End Sub ' New
24
25       ' perform transaction; overrides Transaction's MustOverride method
26       Public Overrides Sub Execute()
27          amount = PromptForDepositAmount() ' get deposit amount from user
28
29          ' check whether user entered a deposit amount or canceled
30          If (amount <> CANCELED) Then
31             ' request deposit envelope containing specified amount
32             ScreenReference.DisplayMessage(vbCrLf & _
33                "Please insert a deposit envelope containing ")
34             ScreenReference.DisplayDollarAmount(amount)
35             ScreenReference.DisplayMessageLine(" in the deposit slot.")
36
37             ' retrieve deposit envelope
38             Dim envelopeReceived As Boolean = _
39                depositSlotHandle.IsDepositEnvelopeReceived()
40
41             ' check whether deposit envelope was received
42             If envelopeReceived Then
43                ScreenReference.DisplayMessageLine(vbCrLf & _
44                   "Your envelope has been received." & vbCrLf & _
45                   "The money just deposited will not be available " & _
46                   "until we" & vbCrLf & "verify the amount of any " & _
47                   "enclosed cash, and any enclosed checks clear.")
48
49                ' credit account to reflect the deposit
50                BankDatabaseReference.Credit(AccountNumber, amount)
51             Else
52                ScreenReference.DisplayMessageLine(vbCrLf & _
53                   "You did not insert an envelope, so the ATM has " & _
54                   "canceled your transaction.")
55             End If
56          Else
57             ScreenReference.DisplayMessageLine( _
58                vbCrLf & "Canceling transaction...")
59          End If
60       End Sub ' Execute
61
62       ' prompt user to enter a deposit amount to credit
63       Private Function PromptForDepositAmount() As Decimal
64          ' display the prompt and receive input
65          ScreenReference.DisplayMessage(vbCrLf & _
66             "Please input a deposit amount in CENTS (or 0 to cancel): ")
67          Dim input As Integer = Convert.ToInt32(keypadHandle.GetInput())
68
69          ' check whether the user canceled or entered a valid amount
70          If (input = CANCELED) Then
71             Return CANCELED
```

Fig. J.11 | Class Deposit represents an ATM deposit transaction. (Part 2 of 3.)

```
72          Else
73             Return Convert.ToDecimal(input / 100)
74          End If
75       End Function ' PromptForDepositAmount
76    End Class ' Deposit
```

Fig. J.11 | Class `Deposit` represents an ATM deposit transaction. (Part 3 of 3.)

Like class `Withdrawal`, class `Deposit` contains a constructor (lines 14–23) that passes three parameters to base class `Transaction`'s constructor using `MyBase.New`. The constructor also has parameters `atmKeypad` and `atmDepositSlot`, which it assigns to corresponding reference attributes (lines 21–22).

Overriding *MustOverride Method Execute*

Method `Execute` (lines 26–60) overrides `MustOverride` method `Execute` in base class `Transaction` with a concrete implementation that performs the steps required in a deposit transaction. Line 27 prompts the user to enter a deposit amount by invoking `Private` utility method `PromptForDepositAmount` (declared in lines 63–75) and sets attribute `amount` to the value returned. Method `PromptForDepositAmount` asks the user to enter a deposit amount as an integer number of cents (because the ATM's keypad does not contain a decimal point; this is consistent with many real ATMs) and returns the `Decimal` value representing the dollar amount to be deposited.

Getting Deposit Amount With *Private Utility Method PromptForDepositAmount*

Lines 65–66 in method `PromptForDepositAmount` display a message on the screen asking the user to input a deposit amount as a number of cents or "0" to cancel the transaction. Line 67 receives the user's input from the keypad. The `If` statement at lines 70–74 determines whether the user has entered a real deposit amount or chosen to cancel. If the user chooses to cancel, line 71 returns the constant `CANCELED`. Otherwise, line 73 returns the deposit amount after converting from the number of cents to a dollar amount by dividing `input` by 100, then converting the result to a `Decimal`. For example, if the user enters 125 as the number of cents, line 73 returns 125 divided by 100, or `1.25`—125 cents is $1.25.

Lines 30–59 in method `Execute` determine whether the user chose to cancel the transaction rather than enter a deposit amount. If the user cancels, lines 57–58 display an appropriate message and the method returns. If the user enters a deposit amount, lines 32–35 instruct the user to insert a deposit envelope with the correct amount. Recall that `Screen` method `DisplayDollarAmount` outputs a `Decimal` value formatted as a dollar amount.

Lines 38–39 sets a local `Boolean` variable to the value returned by the deposit slot's `IsDepositEnvelopeReceived` method, indicating whether a deposit envelope has been received. Recall that we coded method `IsDepositEnvelopeReceived` (lines 6–8 of Fig. J.5) to always return `True`, because we are simulating the functionality of the deposit slot and assume that the user always inserts an envelope. However, we code method `Execute` of class `Deposit` to test for the possibility that the user does not insert an envelope—good software engineering demands that programs account for all possible return values. Thus, class `Deposit` is prepared for future versions of `IsDepositEnvelopeReceived` that could return `False`. Lines 43–50 execute if the deposit slot receives an envelope. Lines 43–47 display an appropriate message to the user. Line 50 credits the user's account in the database with the deposit amount. Lines 52–54 execute if the deposit slot does not receive a deposit envelope. In this case, we display a message to the user stating that the ATM has canceled the transaction. The method then returns without modifying the user's account.

J.13 Module ATMCaseStudy

Module ATMCaseStudy (Fig. J.12) simply allows us to start, or "turn on," the ATM and test the implementation of our ATM system model. Module ATMCaseStudy's Main method (lines 4–7) does nothing more than instantiate a new ATM object named theATM (line 5) and invoke its Run method (line 6) to start the ATM.

J.14 Wrap-Up

Now that we have presented the complete ATM implementation, you can see that many issues arose during implementation for which we did not provide detailed UML diagrams. This is not uncommon in an object-oriented design and implementation experience. For example, many attributes listed in the class diagrams were implemented as Visual Basic properties so that clients of the classes could gain controlled access to the underlying Private instance variables. We did not make these properties during our design process, because there was nothing in the requirements document or our design process to indicate that certain attributes would eventually need to be accessed outside of their classes.

We also encountered various issues with simulating hardware. A real world ATM is a hardware device that does not have a complete computer keyboard. One problem with using a computer keyboard to simulate the keypad is that the user can enter non-digits as input. We did not spend much time dealing with such issues, because this problem is not possible in a real ATM, which has only a numeric keypad. However, having to think about issues like this is a good thing. Quite typically, software designs for complete systems involve simulating hardware devices like the cash dispenser and keypad. Despite the fact that some aspects of our ATM may seem contrived, in real world systems, hardware design and implementation often occurs in parallel with software design and implementation. In such cases, the software cannot be implemented in final form because the hardware is not yet ready. So, software developers must simulate the hardware as we have done in this case study with the keypad, cash dispenser and deposit slot.

Congratulations on completing the entire software engineering ATM case study! We hope you found this experience to be valuable and that it reinforced many of the concepts that you learned in Chapters 1–11. We would sincerely appreciate your comments, criticisms and suggestions. You can reach us at deitel@deitel.com. We will respond promptly.

```vb
1    ' ATMCaseStudy.vb
2    ' Module for testing the ATM case study.
3    Module ATMCaseStudy
4       Sub Main()
5          Dim theATM As New ATM()
6          theATM.Run()
7       End Sub ' Main
8    End Module ' ATMCaseStudy
```

Fig. J.12 | ATMCaseStudy.vb starts the ATM.

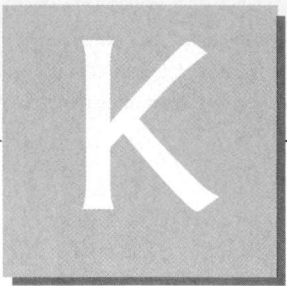

UML 2: Additional Diagram Types

K.1 Introduction

If you read the optional Software Engineering Case Study sections in Chapters 3–9 and 11, you should now have a comfortable grasp of the UML diagram types that we use to model our ATM system. The case study is intended for use in first- or second-semester courses, so we limit our discussion to a concise subset of the UML. The UML 2 provides 13 diagram types. The end of Section 3.10 summarizes the six diagram types that we use in the case study. This appendix lists and briefly defines the seven remaining diagram types.

K.2 Additional Diagram Types

The following are the seven diagram types that we have chosen not to use in our Software Engineering Case Study.

- **Object diagrams** model a "snapshot" of the system by modeling a system's objects and their relationships at a specific point in time. Each object represents an instance of a class from a class diagram, and several objects may be created from one class. For our ATM system, an object diagram could show several distinct Account objects side by side, illustrating that they are all part of the bank's account database.

- **Component diagrams** model the **artifacts** and **components**—resources (which include source files)—that make up the system.

- **Deployment diagrams** model the system's runtime requirements (such as the computer or computers on which the system will reside), memory requirements, or other devices the system requires during execution.

- **Package diagrams** model the hierarchical structure of **packages** (which are groups of classes) in the system at compile time and the relationships that exist between the packages.

- **Composite structure diagrams** model the internal structure of a complex object at runtime. New in UML 2, they allow system designers to hierarchically decompose a complex object into smaller parts. Composite structure diagrams are beyond the scope of our case study. They are more appropriate for larger industrial applications, which exhibit complex groupings of objects at execution time.

- **Interaction overview diagrams**, new in UML 2, provide a summary of control flow in the system by combining elements of several types of behavioral diagrams (e.g., activity diagrams, sequence diagrams).

- **Timing diagrams**, also new in UML 2, model the timing constraints imposed on stage changes and interactions between objects in a system.

To learn more about these diagrams and advanced UML topics, please visit www.uml.org and the Web resources listed at the ends of Section 1.17 and Section 3.10.

L

Primitive Types

Type	Size in bytes	Value range
SByte	1	−128 to 127, inclusive
Byte	1	0 to 255, inclusive
Boolean	2	True or False
Char	2	0 to 65,535, inclusive (representing the Unicode character set)
Short	2	−32,768 to 32,767, inclusive
UShort	2	0 to 65,535, inclusive
Integer	4	−2,147,483,648 to 2,147,483,647, inclusive
UInteger	4	0 to 4,294,967,295, inclusive
Single	4	negative range: −3.4028235E+38 to −1.401298E-45 positive range: 1.401298E−45 to 3.4028235E+38
Long	8	−9,223,372,036,854,775,808 to 9,223,372,036,854,775,807, inclusive
ULong	8	0 to 18,446,744,073,709,551,615, inclusive
Double	8	negative range: −1.79769313486231570E+308 to −4.94065645841246544E−324 positive range: 4.94065645841246544E−324 to 1.79769313486231570E+308
Date	8	0:00:00 on 1 January 0001 to 23:59:59 on 31 December 9999

Fig. L.1 | Primitive types. (Part 1 of 2.)

Type	Size in bytes	Value range
Decimal	16	Range with no decimal point: ±79,228,162,514,264,337,593,543,950,335 Range with 28 places to the right of the decimal point: ±7.9228162514264337593543950335 The smallest nonzero number is ±0.0000000000000000000000000001 (±1E–28)
String	Depends on platform	up to approximately 2 billion Unicode characters

Fig. L.I | Primitive types. (Part 2 of 2.)

Additional Primitive Type Information

This appendix is based on information from Section 7.3 of *The Microsoft Visual Basic Language Specification* (available at msdn2.microsoft.com/en-us/library/ms234437.aspx) and additional information provided at the site

msdn.microsoft.com/library/en-us/vblr7/html/vagrpDataType.asp

Index

G

The DEITEL® Suite of Products...

HOW TO PROGRAM BOOKS

Visual Basic® 2005 How to Program Third Edition

BOOK / CD-ROM

*©2006, 1500 pp., paper
(0-13-186900-0)*

The complete authoritative DEITEL® LIVE-CODE introduction to Visual Basic programming. *Visual Basic® 2005 How to Program, Third Edition* is up-to-date with Microsoft's Visual Basic 2005. The text includes comprehensive coverage of the fundamentals of object-oriented programming in Visual Basic including a new early classes and objects approach and a new optional automated teller machine (ATM) case study that teaches the fundamentals of software engineering and object-oriented design with the UML 2.0 in Chapters 1, 3–9 and 11. Additional integrated case studies appear throughout the text, including the **Time** class (Chapter 9), the **Employee** class (Chapters 10 and 11) and the **Gradebook** class (Chapters 4–9). This book also includes discussions of more advanced topics such as XML, ASP.NET, ADO.NET and Web services. New Visual Basic 2005 topics covered include partial classes, generics, the **My** namespace and Visual Studio's updated debugger features.

Visual C#® 2005 How to Program Second Edition

BOOK / CD-ROM

*©2006, 1589 pp., paper
(0-13-152523-9)*

The complete authoritative DEITEL® LIVE-CODE introduction to C# programming. *Visual C#® 2005 How to Program, Second Edition* is up-to-date with Microsoft's Visual C# 2005. The text includes comprehensive coverage of the fundamentals of object-oriented programming in C#, including a new early classes and objects approach and a new optional automated teller machine (ATM) case study that teaches the fundamentals of software engineering and object-oriented design with the UML 2.0 in Chapters 1, 3–9 and 11. Additional integrated case studies appear throughout the text, including the **Time** class (Chapter 9), the **Employee** class (Chapters 10 and 11) and the **Gradebook** class (Chapters 4–9). This book also includes discussions of more advanced topics such as XML, ASP.NET, ADO.NET and Web services. New Visual C# 2005 topics covered include partial classes, generics, the **My** namespace, .NET remoting and Visual Studio's updated debugger features.

Visual C++ .NET® How To Program

BOOK / CD-ROM

*©2004, 1400 pp., paper
(0-13-437377-4)*

Written by the authors of the world's best-selling introductory/intermediate C and C++ textbooks, this comprehensive book thoroughly examines Visual C++® .NET. *Visual C++® .NET How to Program* begins with a strong foundation in the introductory and intermediate programming principles students will need in industry, including fundamental topics such as arrays, functions and control statements. Readers learn the concepts of object-oriented programming, then the text explores such essential topics as networking, databases, XML and multimedia. Graphical user interfaces are also extensively covered, giving students the tools to build compelling and fully interactive programs using the "drag-and-drop" techniques provided by Visual Studio .NET 2003.

C How to Program Fourth Edition

BOOK / CD-ROM

*©2004, 1255 pp., paper
(0-13-142644-3)*

C How to Program, Fourth Edition—the world's best-selling C text—is designed for introductory through intermediate courses as well as programming languages survey courses. This comprehensive text is aimed at readers with little or no programming experience through intermediate audiences. Highly practical in approach, it introduces fundamental notions of structured programming and software engineering and gets up to speed quickly.

📖 A Student Solutions Manual is also available is for use with this text. Use ISBN 0-13-145245-2 to order the Student Solutions manual.

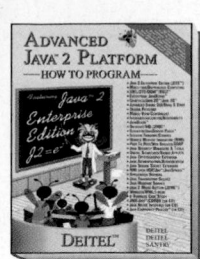

Advanced Java™ 2 Platform How to Program

BOOK / CD-ROM

©2002, 1811 pp., paper (0-13-089560-1)

Expanding on the world's best-selling Java textbook—*Java™ How to Program*—*Advanced Java™ 2 Platform How To Program* presents advanced Java topics for developing sophisticated, user-friendly GUIs; significant, scalable enterprise applications; wireless applications and distributed systems. Primarily based on Java 2 Enterprise Edition (J2EE), this textbook integrates technologies such as XML, JavaBeans, security, JDBC™, JavaServer Pages (JSP™), servlets, Remote Method Invocation (RMI), Enterprise JavaBeans™ (EJB), design patterns, Swing, J2ME™, Java 2D and 3D, XML, design patterns, CORBA, Jini™, JavaSpaces™, Jiro™, Java Management Extensions (JMX) and Peer-to-Peer networking with an introduction to JXTA.

Internet & World Wide Web How to Program Third Edition

BOOK / CD-ROM

©2004, 1250 pp., paper (0-13-145091-3)

This book introduces students with little or no programming experience to the exciting world of Web-based applications. This text provides in-depth coverage of introductory programming principles, various markup languages (XHTML, Dynamic HTML and XML), several scripting languages (JavaScript, JScript .NET, ColdFusion, Flash ActionScript, Perl, PHP, VBScript and Python), Web servers (IIS and Apache) and relational databases (MySQL)—all the skills and tools needed to create dynamic Web-based applications. The text contains a comprehensive introduction to ASP .NET and the Microsoft .NET Framework. A case study illustrating how to build an online message board using ASP .NET and XML is also included. New in this edition are chapters on Macromedia ColdFusion, Macromedia Dreamweaver and a much enhanced treatment of Flash, including a case study on building a video game in Flash. After mastering the material in this book, students will be well prepared to build real-world, industrial-strength, Web-based applications.

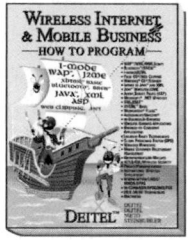

Wireless Internet & Mobile Business How to Program

©2002, 1292 pp., paper (0-13-062226-5)

This book offers a thorough treatment of both the management and technical aspects of this growing area, including coverage of current practices and future trends. The first half explores the business issues surrounding wireless technology and mobile business. The book then turns to programming for the wireless Internet, exploring topics such as WAP (including 2.0), WML, WMLScript, XML, XHTML™, wireless Java programming (J2ME™) and more. Other topics covered include career resources, wireless marketing, accessibility, Palm™, PocketPC, Windows CE, i-mode, Bluetooth, MIDP, MIDlets, ASP, Microsoft .NET Mobile Framework, BREW™, multimedia, Flash™ and VBScript.

Python How to Program

BOOK / CD-ROM

©2002, 1376 pp., paper (0-13-092361-3)

This exciting textbook provides a comprehensive introduction to Python—a powerful object-oriented programming language with clear syntax and the ability to bring together various technologies quickly and easily. This book covers introductory programming techniques and more advanced topics such as graphical user interfaces, databases, wireless Internet programming, networking, security, process management, multithreading, XHTML, CSS, PSP and multimedia. Readers will learn principles that are applicable to both systems development and Web programming.

XML How to Program

BOOK / CD-ROM

©2001, 934 pp., paper (0-13-028417-3)

This book is a comprehensive guide to programming in XML. It teaches how to use XML to create customized tags and includes chapters that address markup languages for science and technology, multimedia, commerce and many other fields. Concise introductions to Java, JavaServer Pages, VBScript, Active Server Pages and Perl/CGI provide readers with the essentials of these programming languages and server-side development technologies to enable them to work effectively with XML. The book also covers topics such as XSL, DOM™, SAX, a real-world e-commerce case study and a complete chapter on Web accessibility that addresses Voice XML. Other topics covered include XHTML, CSS, DTD, schema, parsers, XPath, XLink, namespaces, XBase, XInclude, XPointer, XSLT, XSL Formatting Objects, JavaServer Pages, XForms, topic maps, X3D, MathML, OpenMath, CML, BML, CDF, RDF, SVG, Cocoon, WML, XBRL and BizTalk™ and SOAP™ Web resources.

Perl How to Program

BOOK / CD-ROM

©2001, 1057 pp., paper (0-13-028418-1)

This comprehensive guide to Perl programming emphasizes the use of the Common Gateway Interface (CGI) with Perl to create powerful, dynamic multi-tier Web-based client/server applications. The book begins with a clear and careful introduction to programming concepts at a level suitable for beginners, and proceeds through advanced topics such as references and complex data structures. Key Perl topics such as regular expressions and string manipulation are covered in detail. The authors address important and topical issues such as object-oriented programming, the Perl database interface (DBI), graphics and security. Also included is a treatment of XML, a bonus chapter introducing the Python programming language, supplemental material on career resources and a complete chapter on Web accessibility.

e-Business & e-Commerce How to Program

BOOK / CD-ROM

©2001, 1254 pp., paper (0-13-028419-X)

This book explores programming technologies for developing Web-based e-business and e-commerce solutions, and covers e-business and e-commerce models and business issues. Readers learn a full range of options, from "build-your-own" to turnkey solutions. The book examines scores of the top e-businesses (examples include Amazon, eBay, Priceline, Travelocity, etc.), explaining the technical details of building successful e-business and e-commerce sites and their underlying business premises. Learn how to implement the dominant e-commerce models—shopping carts, auctions, name-your-own-price, comparison shopping and bots/intelligent agents—by using markup languages (HTML, Dynamic HTML and XML), scripting languages (JavaScript, VBScript and Perl), server-side technologies (Active Server Pages and Perl/CGI) and database (SQL and ADO), security and online payment technologies.

The SIMPLY SERIES!

The Deitels' *Simply Series* takes an engaging new approach to teaching programming languages from the ground up. The pedagogy of this series combines the DEITEL® signature *LIVE-CODE Approach* with an *APPLICATION-DRIVEN Tutorial Approach* to teach programming with outstanding pedagogical features that help students learn. We have merged the notion of a lab manual with that of a conventional textbook, creating a book in which readers build and execute complete applications from start to finish, while learning the fundamental concepts of programming!

Simply C++ An APPLICATION-DRIVEN Tutorial Approach

*©2005, 800 pp., paper
(0-13-142660-5)*

Simply C++ An APPLICATION-DRIVEN Tutorial Approach guides readers through building real-world applications that incorporate C++ programming fundamentals. Learn methods, functions, data types, control statements, procedures, arrays, object-oriented programming, strings and characters, pointers, references, templates, operator overloading and more in this comprehensive introduction to C++.

Simply Java™ Programming An APPLICATION-DRIVEN Tutorial Approach

*©2004, 950 pp., paper
(0-13-142648-6)*

Simply Java™ Programming An APPLICATION-DRIVEN Tutorial Approach guides readers through building real-world applications that incorporate Java programming fundamentals. Learn GUI design, components, methods, event-handling, types, control statements, arrays, object-oriented programming, exception-handling, strings and characters, sequential files and more in this comprehensive introduction to Java. We also include higher-end topics such as database programming, multimedia, graphics and Web applications development.

Simply C# An APPLICATION-DRIVEN Tutorial Approach

*©2004, 850 pp., paper
(0-13-142641-9)*

Simply C# An APPLICATION-DRIVEN Tutorial Approach guides readers through building real-world applications that incorporate C# programming fundamentals. Learn GUI design, controls, methods, functions, data types, control statements, procedures, arrays, object-oriented programming, strings and characters, sequential files and more in this comprehensive introduction to C#. We also include higher-end topics such as database programming, multimedia and graphics and Web applications development.

Simply Visual Basic® .NET An APPLICATION-DRIVEN Tutorial Approach

Visual Studio .NET 2002 Version:
*©2003, 830 pp., paper
(0-13-140553-5)*

Visual Studio .NET 2003 Version:
*©2004, 960 pp., paper
(0-13-142640-0)*

Simply Visual Basic® .NET An APPLICATION-DRIVEN Tutorial Approach guides readers through building real-world applications that incorporate Visual Basic .NET programming fundamentals. Learn GUI design, controls, methods, functions, data types, control statements, procedures, arrays, object-oriented programming, strings and characters, sequential files and more in this comprehensive introduction to Visual Basic .NET. We also include higher-end topics such as database programming, multimedia and graphics and Web applications development. If you're using Visual Studio® .NET 2002, choose *Simply Visual Basic .NET*; or, if you're using Visual Studio .NET 2003, you can use *Simply Visual Basic .NET 2003*, which includes updated screen captures and line numbers consistent with Visual Studio .NET 2003.

Premium content available with *Java™* and *Small Java™ How to Program, Sixth Edition* and *C++* and *Small C++ How to Program, Fifth Edition!*

Java and *Small Java How to Program, 6/e* and *C++* and *Small C++ How to Program, 5/e* are now available with six-month access to the Web-based *Multimedia Cyber Classroom* for students who purchase new copies of these books! The *Cyber Classroom* is an interactive, multimedia, tutorial version of DEITEL textbooks. *Cyber Classrooms* are a great value, giving students additional hands-on experience and study aids.

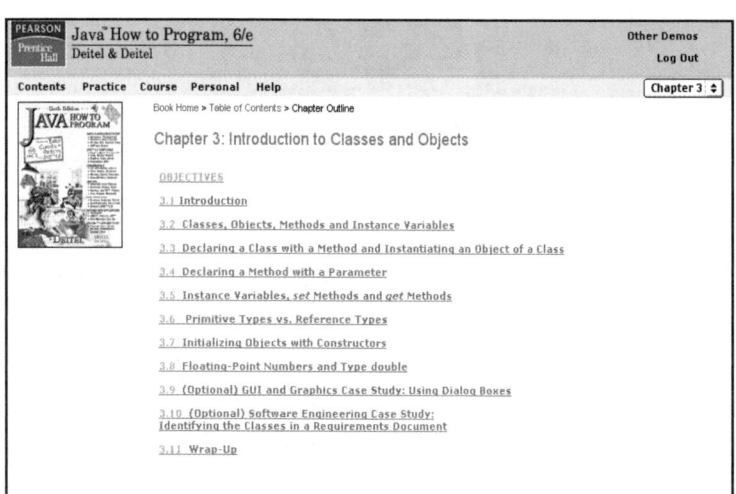

NOW AVAILABLE for Java and Small Java How to Program, 6/e and C++ and Small C++ How to Program, 5/e (with purchase of a new book)

DEITEL® Multimedia Cyber Classrooms *feature an e-book with the complete text of their corresponding* How to Program *titles.*

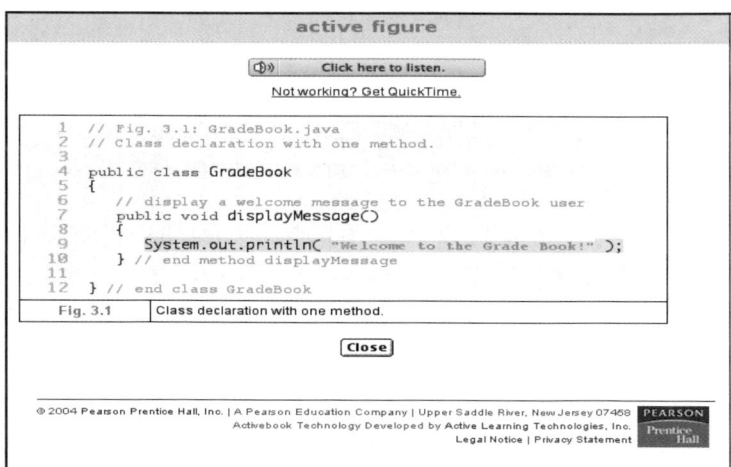

Unique audio "walkthroughs" of code examples reinforce key concepts.

MULTIMEDIA CYBER CLASSROOMS

DEITEL® *Multimedia Cyber Classrooms* include:

- The full text, illustrations and program listings of its corresponding *How to Program* book.

- Hours of detailed, expert audio descriptions of hundreds of lines of code that help to reinforce important concepts.

- An abundance of self-assessment material, including practice exams, hundreds of programming exercises and self-review questions and answers.

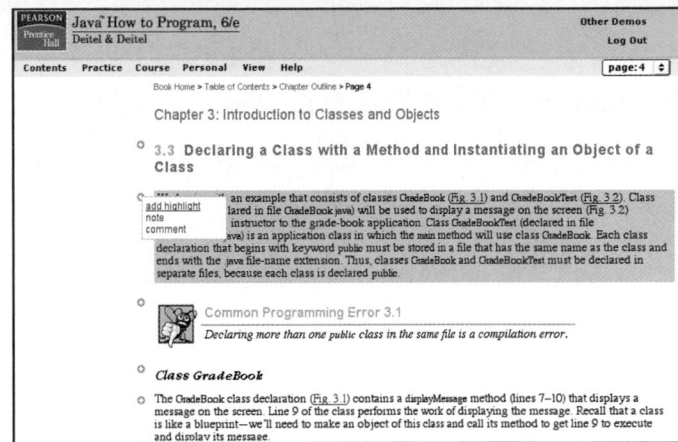

DEITEL® Multimedia Cyber Classrooms *offer a host of interactive features, such as highlighting of key sections of the text...*

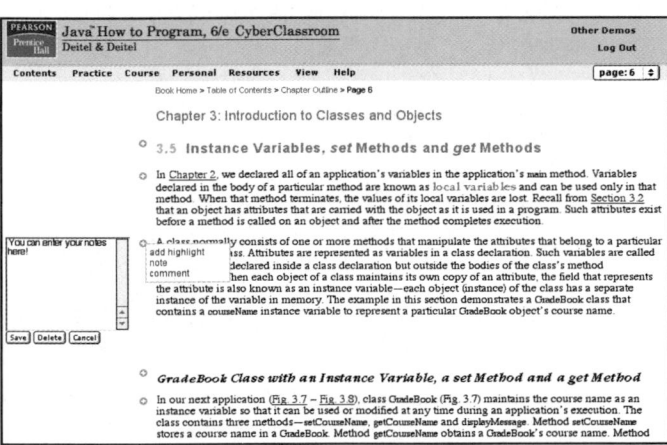

...*and the ability to write notes in the margin of a given page for future reference.*

- Intuitive browser-based interface designed to be easy and accessible.

- A Lab Manual featuring lab exercises as well as pre- and post-lab activities.

- Student Solutions to approximately one-half of the exercises in the textbook.

Students receive six-month access to a protected Web site via access code cards packaged with these new textbooks. (Simply tear the strip on the inside of the Cyber Classroom package to reveal access code.)

Note: For *Java How to Program, 6/e* and *Small Java How to Program, 6/e*, the instructor will need to "select" the Cyber Classroom card value pack.

> ## To redeem your access code or for more information, please visit:
> ### www·prenhall·com/deitel/ cyberclassroom

Deitel & Associates, Inc. provides intensive, lecture-and-laboratory courses to organizations worldwide. The programming courses use our signature *LIVE-CODE Approach*, presenting complete working programs.

Deitel & Associates, Inc. has trained over one million students and professionals worldwide through Dive Into® Series corporate training courses, public seminars, university teaching, *How to Program Series* textbooks, *DEITEL® Developer Series* books, *Simply Series* textbooks, *Cyber Classroom Series* multimedia packages, *Complete Training Course Series* textbook and multimedia packages, broadcast-satellite courses and Web-based training.

Educational Consulting

Deitel & Associates, Inc. offers complete educational consulting services for corporate training programs and professional schools including:

- Curriculum design and development
- Preparation of Instructor Guides
- Customized courses and course materials
- Design and implementation of professional training certificate programs
- Instructor certification
- Train-the-trainers programs
- Delivery of software-related corporate training programs

Visit our Web site for more information on our Dive Into® Series corporate training curriculum and to purchase our training products.

www.deitel.com/training

Would you like to review upcoming publications?

If you are a professor or senior industry professional interested in being a reviewer of our forthcoming publications, please contact us by email at `deitel@deitel.com`. Insert "Content Reviewer" in the subject heading.

Are you interested in a career in computer education, publishing and training?

We offer a limited number of full-time positions available for college graduates in computer science, information systems, information technology, management information systems and marketing. Please check our Web site for the latest job postings or contact us by email at `deitel@deitel.com`. Insert "Full-time Job" in the subject heading.

Are you a Boston-area college student looking for an internship?

We have a limited number of competitive summer positions and 20-hr./week school-year opportunities for computer science, IT/IS, MIS and marketing majors. Students work at our worldwide headquarters west of Boston. We also offer full-time internships for students taking a semester off from school. This is an excellent opportunity for students looking to gain industry experience and earn money to pay for school. Please contact us by email at `deitel@deitel.com`. Insert "Internship" in the subject heading.

Would you like to explore contract training opportunities with us?

Deitel & Associates, Inc. is looking for contract instructors to teach software-related topics at our clients' sites in the United States and worldwide. Applicants should be experienced professional trainers or college professors. For more information, please visit `www.deitel.com` and send your resume to Abbey Deitel at `abbey.deitel@deitel.com`.

Are you a training company in need of quality course materials?

Corporate training companies worldwide use our *How to Program Series* textbooks, *Complete Training Course Series* book and multimedia packages, *Simply Series* textbooks and our *DEITEL® Developer Series* books in their classes. We have extensive ancillary instructor materials for many of our products. For more details, please visit `www.deitel.com` or contact us by email at `deitel@deitel.com`.